The New Penguin Stereo Record and Cassette Guide

Edward Greenfield has been Record Critic of the *Guardian* since 1954 and from 1964 Music Critic too. At the end of 1960 he joined the reviewing panel of the *Gramophone*, specializing in operatic and orchestral issues. He is a regular broadcaster on music and records for the BBC, and has a weekly record programme on the BBC World Service. In 1958 he published a monograph on the operas of Puccini. More recently he has written studies on the recorded work of Joan Sutherland and André Previn. He has been a regular juror on International Record awards and has appeared with such artists as Elisabeth Schwarzkopf and Joan Sutherland in public interviews.

Robert Layton studied at Oxford with Edmund Rubbra for composition and with the late Egon Wellesz for the history of music. He spent two years in Sweden at the universities of Uppsala and Stockholm. He joined the BBC Music Division in 1959 and has been responsible for such programmes as *Interpretations on Record*. He has contributed 'A Quarterly Retrospect' to the *Gramophone* for a number of years, and he has written books on Berwald and Sibelius and has specialized in Scandinavian music. His recent publications include a monograph on the Dvořák symphonies and concertos for the BBC Music Guides, of which he is series General Editor, and the first volume of his translation of Erik Tawaststjerna's definitive study of Sibelius.

Ivan March is an ex-professional musician. He studied at Trinity College of Music, London, and later at the Royal Manchester College. After service in the RAF Central Band, he played the horn professionally for the BBC and has also travelled with the Carl Rosa and D'Oyly Carte opera companies. Now director of the Long Playing Record Library, the largest commercial lending library for classical music on LP and cassette tapes in the British Isles, he is a well-known lecturer, journalist, and personality in the world of recorded music. He is a regular contributor (reviewing both cassettes and records) to the *Gramophone*.

Edited by Ivan March

The New Penguin Stereo
Record and Cassette Guide

Edward Greenfield   Robert Layton   Ivan March

Penguin Books

Penguin Books Ltd, Harmondsworth, Middlesex, England
Penguin Books, 625 Madison Avenue, New York, New York 10022, U.S.A.
Penguin Books Australia Ltd, Ringwood, Victoria, Australia
Penguin Books Canada Ltd, 2801 John Street, Markham, Ontario, Canada L3R 1B4
Penguin Books (N.Z.) Ltd, 182–190 Wairau Road, Auckland 10, New Zealand

First published 1982

Made and printed in Great Britain by
Richard Clay (The Chaucer Press) Ltd, Bungay, Suffolk
Set in Monophoto Times

789. 9132

Contents

The Penguin Cassette Guide

*by Edward Greenfield, Robert Layton
and Ivan March*

edited by IVAN MARCH

is still available

This book provides background reviews of the key classical
recordings issued until 1979 on both cassette and disc (a
comment about the basic recording is usually followed by a
comparative assessment of the equivalent cassette). Collectors
will find this an admirable basic guide to which the new
1982 edition is supplementary.

*'Between them Messrs Greenfield, Layton and March reliably
cover as wide a musical spectrum as we could hope for. Every
aspect of the pre-recorded cassette is crammed into 838 pages of
entertaining, informative and superbly readable prose.* **The
Penguin Cassette Guide** *includes additional sections discussing
concerts of orchestral, choral, brass, and military band music,
instrumental and vocal recitals, with an appendix considering
cassettes for the car and background listening, plus a select list
of talking books and plays. Only Dolby tapes are included.'*

Gramophone (R.H.)

Prices: United Kingdom £4.95
       Australia $15.95 (recommended)
       Canada $10.95
       USA $12.50

Preface

The assumption by the gramophone of a role as fundamental as that of the printed score has gained even greater credence in the early 1980s. The international catalogue continues to expand at a remarkable pace to uncover forgotten music and offer the ordinary music-lover repertoire which hitherto has been the sole province of the musical scholar. The constant renewal of established masterpieces of the concert hall produces almost an embarrassment of riches, while in the opera house a revival and a new recording often go hand in hand.

Records inevitably focus the listener's attention on the character of the performance itself, heard against a background historical perspective which now extends over more than half a century of electric recording. Comparisons readily show that the current dedicated pursuit of authenticity of style and timbre, particularly in baroque repertoire, was usually less zealously observed by the previous generations of performers. While it is undoubtedly valuable to have an educated opinion of what the music sounded like in the composer's own time, sometimes considerations of scholarship can inhibit the music-making. There is also a sense of paradox in the modern revival of primitive older instruments which musicians of earlier periods had to strive to make sound adequate. Moreover, it seems reasonable to assume that a composer's vision is not confined by the inadequacies of performances and instruments available to him in his own lifetime. It is difficult to believe that Beethoven, for instance, would have preferred the effect of his later piano sonatas when heard on an early pianoforte, as compared with the modern Steinway with its richer dynamic shading and fuller sonority. Similarly, while the vitality of a Mozart symphony may be enhanced by vibrato-less string playing and astringent baroque timbres, the music's balancing elegance, warmth and humanity are not submerged when modern instruments are used, allowing their players greater flexibility of execution.

The collector can make up his own mind about these matters, for the gramophone already offers more than one generation of 'authenticity', with further fresh views undoubtedly still to come. Indeed this quest for new ways of approaching old music seems to be one method of filling the vacuum left by the contemporary music scene. An increasingly experienced and educated musical public continues to find very little late twentieth-century music with which it can identify. Much of it the gramophone documents faithfully, while concentrating on keeping the past alive. The dawning of the digital age seems likely to produce yet another recording renaissance, although the finest recordings of the analogue era are unlikely to be eclipsed artistically or sonically in the immediate foreseeable future. Undoubtedly the musical riches currently available in terms of stereo sound remain one of the great blessings of civilized society in the early eighties.

The Musicassette and the Compact Digital Disc

From the earliest days of Edison's cylinder phonograph, it was obvious to all listeners that the recorded sound offered only an approximation of the real thing. Some of the original distortions of a mechanical recording system, together with others added at the adoption of electronic techniques, have persisted to a diminishing extent right up to the present day. Unwanted background noises, compression of dynamic and frequency ranges, slight fluctuations in constancy of pitch, and clouding of detail (which experts call non-linear distortion) are all features of the reproduction chain with which readers will be familiar. Moreover, the vast improvement in the quality of the modern hi-fi reproducer itself has, in certain respects, been a mixed blessing. During the early gramophone era, the record groove contained much more information than primitive play-back machines could truthfully transmit. Today's super-sensitive modern pick-ups can reproduce virtually everything on the disc, but they cannot distinguish between the musical wave forms and groove debris, and they also faithfully transmit pressing imperfections to produce clicks and pops that can wreck the listener's concentration.

Undoubtedly, the record manufacturers have achieved considerable success in improving the standard of their pressing operation to meet modern requirements, especially where the hi-fi enthusiast is willing to pay extra for a 'custom' pressing. Yet a long-playing record which on first hearing is silent-surfaced can too easily develop background disturbances when it has been played a few times, and stored under normal domestic conditions. It is this which has caused collectors over the last few years to turn in increasing numbers to the musicassette as a partial or complete replacement of the LP disc for their source of recorded music. The case for the tape cassette has been argued fully in *The Penguin Cassette Guide*, and it is sufficient to say here that since that book was published in 1979 the quality and reliability of musicassettes produced by the major companies have become impressively consistent. While disc reproduction continues to offer a marginally greater range of sound and a more subtle inner transparency of detail than the equivalent tape, often the degree of difference is minimal and of comparatively little musical consequence. To balance this advantage the cassette offers a complete and permanent freedom from extraneous background noises (any hiss not removed by the Dolby noise reduction circuitry is constant, and much easier for the ear to tolerate). Also there is little or no appreciable deterioration of the quality over hundreds of playings, and the convenience, portability and lack of ritual in use which distinguish the tape medium make impressive bonus points. All the evidence suggests that the musicassette's share of the market will continue to expand in the immediate future at the expense of long-playing records, even while the recording world takes its exciting leap into the future with the advent of the compact digital disc, which appears to solve at a single stroke virtually all the problems of the present recording system.

Digital recording finally became practical towards the end of the 1970s. The idea of storing sound wave forms by numerical equivalents within a computer's memory bank for recording purposes had been feasible for more than a decade, but the technological problems of editing took some time to solve. Indeed, some of the earliest digital records were made in a single take to get over this difficulty. The so-called digital LPs now on sale in the shops were certainly recorded digitally, which brings clearer, often sharply clean detail, and lower distortion. But as these discs are pressed in the normal way they are still prone to the usual background noises. It is significant that the equivalent cassettes, normally transferred on chrome tape, mirror many of the improved features, notably the extra clarity of detail. Neither in their tape nor in their LP forms do these issues demonstrate the full potential of the digital method, but the finest of them offer a sound quality which is very impressive indeed, and which augurs well for the future.

The true digital disc is a wholly new conception. Philips and Sony are principally responsible for its technology. It is compact in size, measuring 12 cm (4¾ inches) in diameter, yet each side offers up to eighty minutes' playing time, long enough to contain Beethoven's *Choral symphony*. It is thought that initially these discs – reflecting the very earliest days of the gramophone – will be single-sided. The recorded information is cut into a single spiral track in the form of pits instead of wave forms, and this information is read by a laser beam. The speed at which the disc rotates is very fast, and the recorded information is read at a constant velocity. Thus the disc revolves more quickly as the pick-up nears its centre. There is no wear or deterioration in use and, given reasonable handling care, the lifetime of a compact digital disc has now no foreseeable limit. The main features of digital reproduction using this system give the following advantages:

a silent background for the music;
a breadth of dynamic range to equal that experienced at a live concert;

a frequency range covering the complete audio spectrum discernible by the human ear;
an absence of non-linear and other distortions;
absolute pitch security;
no loss of quality in the mastering or pressing process.

It all sounds elysian, but of course microphones are still needed to pick up the sound, and, as readers will know, this in itself is a source of many problems of balance. Human fallibility is not cancelled out by the digital process. To enjoy the benefits of these revolutionary new records, the collector will require a new playing deck, but not (hopefully) a new amplifier. Older LPs (and 78 r.p.m. discs) will in no way be compatible with the new system, so one's older record-player must be retained for a pre-digital collection. Record collectors are used to starting afresh; yet one more question-mark hangs over the universality of the new system. A paper presented at the 71st Convention of the Audio Engineering Society in Montreux, in March 1982, sets out the principles for a digital reproducing method, based on a standard audio musicassette, achieved with a thin film multi-track recording head with a recording potential of thirty-seven tracks! It is claimed that this new system can match the quality and playing time of the compact digital disc, and that by further advancement of the current technology it should be possible for the areal recording density to be doubled by using the tape in both directions.

Introduction

The object of *The Penguin Stereo and Cassette Guide* is to provide the serious collector with a comprehensive guide to the finest stereo records and cassettes of permanent music available in the United Kingdom. This edition includes concert and recital collections, and we have taken the opportunity of adding a few really outstanding reissues from the mono era. Our survey centres on records and tapes issued between 1977 and 1982. We have concentrated on newer issues because their availability is more certain, but older recordings are referred to in the text where they are still competitive. If an earlier version remains a prime recommendation for a given work, a comment on its character is included and the catalogue information relisted. The current economic uncertainty has had a profound effect on the stability of the world recording industry, with the result that many attractive earlier records are in uncertain supply. While the major manufacturers continue to keep their key current recordings in stock an older issue may not be re-pressed unless there is firm evidence of a continuing steady demand. With computerized stock control well established, policy decisions in this area can sometimes seem unimaginative and arbitrary. A listing in the *Gramophone Classical Catalogue* or the American *Schwann Record and Tape Guide* is not a certain proof of availability.

However, if the major labels no longer guarantee the continuation of recordings which are not in the 'bestseller' category, this vacuum has been more than filled by the specialist importers. During the preparation of this book an important group of small companies has become established in this field. They have undertaken to make available on a continuing basis a great deal of repertoire from the most important European catalogues, plus some American digital material. Conifer Records – perhaps the most enterprising and efficient of these organizations – has taken over distribution of EMI's whole European catalogue (i.e. those recordings not already available here on HMV and on Angel in the USA) and the World Records reissue series, alongside other important labels such as Arion, Barclay, Bluebell, Caprice, Erato, Jecklin, plus the English Lyrita catalogue. Harmonia Mundi has established its own UK distribution base and also handles Acanta and Calliope, while issues from Eastern Europe on Hungaroton and (especially) Supraphon are much easier to obtain than previously. So for the first time in this volume it has been possible to include and discuss major recordings from all these European sources, which can sometimes be easier to find in England than records listed in the British domestic catalogues. Moreover if they are not carried in stock, they are usually obtainable to special order. (Turnabout records, however, and other American Vox material are no longer distributed in the UK by Decca, and British collectors may find older issues particularly elusive.)

The other attractive feature of today's market-place is the flood of reissues in the middle and lower price-ranges, on which – with the premium-price arena now increasingly dominated by intermediate digital recordings – some of the finest earlier analogue repertoire is now reappearing. Apart from the continuation of the established mid priced labels (for example Decca Jubilee, DG Privilege and the newer Accolade, EMI Concert Classics and Greensleeve – Seraphim in the USA – and RCA Gold Seal) there are some valuable newcomers. CBS are currently re-combing their early stereo lists for material worthy to be included under a *Great Performances* logo; also from America stems the re-emergence of the Mercury Living Presence label with a carefully selected group of *Golden Imports*, handsomely sleeved and immaculately pressed in Holland.

Decca have introduced the Viva label for popular classical repertoire and Serenata to cover the baroque era; Philips also have a new baroque label, plus a beautifully presented Musica da Camera series. All these are in the mid-priced group. In the bargain range RCA have resuscitated their Victrola catalogue, with cassette equivalents transferred on chrome tape; their quality is every bit the equal of the discs, which they sometimes surpass in range and fidelity. The principal UK bargain label, Classics for Pleasure (now distributed by the Brilly Corporation in the USA), which continues to offer discs and cassettes of the highest quality, has now been joined by a rejuvenated Pickwick Contour series in the same price-range, drawing on Decca, DG and Philips for its source material.

Readers will find, therefore, that the scope of this volume is wider than ever before and it contains many treasures. As usual, pressure of space has forced us to be selective, and in dealing with imports we have concentrated on repertoire which is unique to the country of origin. In response to requests from readers we have taken the opportunity to expand our coverage in the fields of operetta, and of film background music which can stand up away from the visual images. Even allowing for omissions – for instance, the Ariola Eurodisc catalogue began to appear in Britain only as we were closing for press – we believe our survey is more comprehensive than ever, and readers who have difficulty in obtaining any listed recordings locally are offered below a reliable source of supply by mail order.

The sheer number of available records of artistic merit causes considerable problems in any assessment of overall and individual excellence. While in the case of a single popular repertoire work it might be ideal for the discussion to be conducted by a single reviewer, it was not always possible for one person to have access to every version, and division of reviewing responsibility inevitably leads to some clashes of opinion. Also there are certain works and certain recorded performances for which one or another of our team has a special affinity. Such a personal identification can often carry with it a special perception too. We feel that it is a strength of our basic style to let such conveyed pleasure or admiration for the merits of an individual recording come over directly to the reader, even if this produces a certain ambivalence in the matter of choice between competing recordings. Where disagreement is profound (and this has rarely happened), then readers will find an indication of this difference of opinion in the text.

We have considered and rejected the use of initials against individual reviews, since this is essentially a team project. The occasions for disagreement generally concern matters of aesthetics, for instance in the manner of recording balance, where a contrived effect may trouble some ears more than others, or in the matter of style, where the difference between robustness and refinement of approach produces controversy, rather than any question of artistic integrity.

EVALUATION

Unlike the early LPs, nearly all records issued now by the major companies are of a high technical standard, and most offer performances of a quality at least as high as is heard in the average concert hall. In deciding to adopt a starring system for the evaluation of records we have felt it necessary to use a wider margin than has sometimes been practised in the past, making use of from one to three stars.

The symbols (M) and (B) indicate whether a record is issued in the UK at medium or bargain price. Where no bracketed initial precedes the starring it can be taken that the issue is on a premium-priced label (currently ranging from about £5 to £6.50, although some imported digital LPs can cost as much as £8).

The key to our indications is as follows:
(M) Medium-priced label: in the price-range between £2.75 and £4.
(B) Bargain-priced label: £2.50 or below.

It is possible that, in current inflationary times, prices may rise during the life of this book, so that the above limitations become unrealistic, but the major manufacturers usually maintain the price ratios between labels when an overall increase is made.

Dig. This indicates that the master recording was digitally encoded.

*** An outstanding performance and recording in every way.

** A good performance and recording of today's normal high standard.

* A fair performance, reasonably well or well recorded.

Brackets round one or more of the stars indicate some reservations about its inclusion and readers are advised to refer to the text.

Our evaluation is normally applied to the record as a whole, unless there are two main works, or groups of works, on each side of the disc, and by different composers. In this case each is dealt with separately in its appropriate place. In the case of a collection of shorter works we feel there is little point in giving a different starring to each item, even if their merits are uneven, since the record can only be purchased as a complete programme.

ROSETTES

To a very few records we have awarded a rosette: ✿.

Unlike our general evaluation, where we have tried to be consistent, a rosette is a quite arbitrary compliment by a member of the reviewing team to a recorded performance which he finds shows special illumination, a magic, or spiritual quality

that places it in a very special class. The choice is essentially a personal one (although often it represents a shared view), and in some cases it is applied to an issue where certain reservations must also be mentioned in the text of the review. The rosette symbol is placed immediately before the normal evaluation and record number. It is quite small – we do not mean to imply an 'Academy award' but a personal token of appreciation for something uniquely valuable. We hope that once the reader has discovered and perhaps acquired a 'rosette' record, its special qualities will soon become apparent.

LAYOUT OF TEXT

We have aimed to make our style as simple as possible. All records are 12-inch LPs which play at 33¼ r.p.m. Immediately after the evaluation and before the catalogue numbers the record make and label are given, usually in abbreviated form (a key to the abbreviations is provided below). The catalogue number for the LP is given first, then (where available) the cassette equivalent in *italics*. Often the catalogue digits are the same for both, and the alphabetical prefixes indicate disc or cassette: e.g. Decca SXL/*KSXC* 6952.

Sometimes the cassette uses the full record number with an added prefix: e.g. HMV ASD/*TC-ASD* 3482, or CBS 76634/*40-*.

Where the catalogue number is

entirely in digits, often not all of them change to indicate the cassette: e.g. DG Priv. 2535/*3335* 176.

The numbers which follow in square brackets are US catalogue numbers; here a similar differentiation is made between disc and cassette issues.

ABBREVIATIONS

To save space we have adopted a number of standard abbreviations in listing orchestras and performing groups (a list is provided below), and the titles of works are often shortened, especially where they are listed several times. Artists' christian names are omitted where they are not absolutely necessary for identification purposes. We have also usually omitted details of the contents of operatic highlights collections. These can be found in the *Gramophone Classical Catalogue*, published quarterly by *Gramophone* magazine.

We have followed common practice in the use of the original language for titles where it seems sensible. In most cases English is used for orchestral and instrumental music and the original language for vocal music and opera. There are exceptions, however; for instance, the Johann Strauss discography uses the German language in the interests of consistency.

ORDER OF MUSIC

The order of music under each composer's name broadly follows that

adopted by the *Gramophone Classical Catalogue*: orchestral music, including concertos and symphonies; chamber music; solo instrumental music (in some cases with keyboard and organ music separated); vocal and choral music; opera; vocal collections; miscellaneous collections.

The *Gramophone Classical Catalogue* now usually elects to include stage works alongside opera; we have not generally followed this practice, preferring to list, for instance, ballet music and incidental music (where no vocal items are involved) in the general orchestral group. Within each group our listing follows an alphabetic sequence, and couplings within a single composer's output are *usually* discussed together instead of separately with cross-references. Occasionally and inevitably because of this alphabetical approach, different recordings of a given work can become separated when a record is listed and discussed under the first work of its alphabetical sequence. A cross-reference is then usually given (either within the listing or in the review) to any important alternative versions. The editor feels that alphabetical consistency is essential if the reader is to learn to find his way about.

CONCERTS AND RECITALS

Most collections of music intended to be regarded as concerts or recitals involve many composers and it is quite impractical to deal with them within the alphabetical composer index. They are grouped separately, at the end of the book, in three sections. In each section, recordings are usually arranged in alphabetical order of the performers' names: concerts of orchestral and concertante music under the name of the orchestra, ensemble or, if more important, conductor or soloist; instrumental recitals under the name of the instrumentalist; operatic and vocal recitals under the principal singer or vocal group as seems appropriate.

In certain cases where the compilation features many different performers it is listed alphabetically under its collective title, or the key word in that title (so *Favourite opera duets* is listed under 'Opera duets'). Sometimes for complicated collections only brief details of contents and performers are given; fuller information can usually be found in the *Gramophone Classical Catalogue*.

RECORD NUMBERS

Enormous care has gone into the checking of record and cassette numbers and contents to ensure that all details are correct, but the editor and publishers cannot be held responsible for any mistakes that may have crept in despite all our zealous checking. When ordering records or cassettes, readers are urged to provide their record-dealer with full details of the music and performers as well as the catalogue number.

DELETIONS

During the whole time we have been working on this book, the deletions axe has been falling all round us. Inevitably more records and cassettes will have been withdrawn in the period before we appear in print, and many others are likely to disappear during the lifetime of the book. Sometimes copies may still be found in specialist shops, and there remains the compensation that most really important and desirable recordings are eventually reissued, often on a less expensive label.

ACKNOWLEDGEMENTS

The editor and authors express herewith their gratitude to Mrs Judith Wardman for her help in the preparation of this volume, and also to E. T. Bryant, M.A., F.L.A., for his assistance with the task of proof-correcting. The editor also wishes to thank Raymond Cooke, the Managing Director of KEF Electronics, for his help with the preparation of the information about the compact digital disc and the possibility of a cassette alternative.

For American Readers

American catalogue numbers are included throughout this survey where they are known at the time of going to press. In each case the American domestic listing is given in square brackets immediately after the British catalogue number. The abbreviation [id.] indicates that the American and British numbers are identical. The addition of (d) immediately before the American number indicates some difference in the contents of the American issue; and sometimes a recording available on a single disc in the UK is only issued within an album collection in the USA or vice versa. We have taken care to check catalogue information as far as possible, but as all the editorial work has been done in England there is always the possibility of error and American readers are invited, when ordering records locally, to take the precaution of giving their dealer the fullest information about the music and recordings they want.

The indications (M) and (B) immediately before the starring of a disc refer only to the British record, as pricing systems are not always identical both sides of the Atlantic.

Where no American catalogue number is given this does not necessarily mean that a record is not available in the USA; the transatlantic issue may not have been made at the time of the publication of this *Guide*. Readers are advised to check the current *Schwann* catalogue and consult their local record store. Most important classical recordings are made today for international circulation, but certain works are better represented in Europe than in the USA. This particularly applies to the 'bargain' and medium-priced area. Where a required recording is not readily available locally it will probably be obtainable direct from England. Readers are invited to write to Squires Gate Music Centre, Blackpool, Lancashire, England. It is important to remember, however, that it is seldom safe or economic to have a single LP sent through the post and it is sensible to compile an order of reasonable size, so that the discs are self-protective against warping in transit. Tape cassettes offer few problems, especially when sent by air mail.

The three authors of *The Penguin Stereo Record and Cassette Guide* are all contributors to the authoritative British monthly periodical, *Gramophone*, which has an international circulation. The areas of music covered by the *Penguin Guide* also receive the fullest possible consideration in *Gramophone* and readers interested in keeping up to date with new issues on both disc and tape may wish to have regular access to this publication. It is stocked by certain stores in North America, and your local dealer may respond to pressure to carry it. If not it is possible to receive a regular monthly copy direct from England by annual subscription. The *Gramophone*'s publishers are proud of their airspeeded subscription service to North America. This involves air freighting of copies to New York and second-class postage thereafter. Normally within seventy-two hours of copies leaving the magazine's printers in southern England they are in the North American second-class mail system in New York. Readers can decide for themselves the likely date of arrival of their own copy. Please write direct to:

Subscription Department,
Gramophone,
177–179 Kenton Road,
Harrow,
Middlesex,
HA3 0HA,
England.

One of the more significant roles played by the international recording industry is to provide recordings of contemporary scores, and in this way the gramophone record becomes fundamental in establishing the reputation of music written in our own time. However, for understandable commercial reasons, the greater part of this output is permanently accessible only in its country of origin. Those recordings that are exported seldom remain available abroad for long periods (although there are honourable exceptions). A great deal of important twentieth-century American music is not readily obtainable in recorded form in Great Britain, whilst modern British and European composers are much more generously favoured. The reflection of this imbalance within these pages is obviously not the choice of the authors.

An International Mail-order Source for Recordings

Readers are urged to support a local dealer if he is prepared and able to give a proper service, and to remember that many records and cassettes involve a great deal of perseverance to obtain. If, however, difficulty is experienced in ordering recordings, we suggest the following mail-order alternative, which operates world-wide:

Squires Gate Music Centre,
Squires Gate Station Approach,
Blackpool,
Lancashire,
England.

Scrupulous care is taken in the visual inspection of records exported by this organization (which is operated under the direction of the Editor of *The Penguin Stereo Record and Cassette Guide*), and a full guarantee is made of safe delivery of any order undertaken. Please write for more details, enclosing a stamped addressed envelope if within the UK.

Abbreviations

Ac.	Academy
AcAM	Academy of Ancient Music
Acc.	Accolade
Ace	Ace of Diamonds
Amb. S.	Ambrosian Singers
Ang.	Angel
Arc.	Archive
Ar. Eur.	Ariola Eurodisc
ASMF	Academy of St Martin-in-the-Fields
ASV	Academy Sound and Vision
B	(see p. xiv)
Bar.	Baroque
Bav.	Bavarian
Bay.	Bayreuth
Blue.	Bluebell
Cal.	Calliope
Cam. Ac.	Camerata Academica
Camb.	Cambridge
Cap.	Caprice
Cath.	Cathedral
CBSO	City of Birmingham Symphony Orchestra
CfP	Classics for Pleasure
Ch.	Choir; Choral; Chorus
Chan.	Chandos
CO	Chamber Orchestra
Col.	Cologne
Coll.	Collegium
Coll. Aur.	Collegium Aureum
Coll. Mus.	Collegium Musicum
Con.	Contour
Concg. O.	Concertgebouw Orchestra of Amsterdam
Cons.	Consort
DG	Deutsche Grammophon
Dig.	digital recording
E.	English

ECO	English Chamber Orchestra
Ens.	Ensemble
Fest.	Festivo
Fr.	French
GO	Gewandhaus Orchestra
Gold	Gold Label
Gr. Écurie	La Grande Écurie et la Chambre du Roy
Green.	Greensleeve
HM	Harmonia Mundi
HMV	His Master's Voice
Hung.	Hungaroton
Hyp.	Hyperion
Jub.	Jubilee
L.	London
LACO	Los Angeles Chamber Orchestra
LAPO	Los Angeles Philharmonic Orchestra
Liszt CO	Ferenc Liszt Chamber Orchestra
Liv.	Liverpool
LOP	Lamoureux Orchestra of Paris
LPO	London Philharmonic Orchestra
LSO	London Symphony Orchestra
Lux.	Luxembourg
Lyr.	Lyrita
M	(see p. xiv)
Mer.	Meridian
Moz.	Mozart
Mun.	Munich
Mus. Ant.	Musica Antiqua
N.	North
Nat.	National
Neth.	Netherlands
None.	Nonesuch
NY	New York
O.	Orchestra
O-L	Oiseau-Lyre
Op.	Opera
Ph.	Philips
Phd.	Philadelphia
Philh.	Philharmonia
Philomus.	Philomusica
Pick.	Pickwick
PO	Philharmonic Orchestra

Priv.	Privilege
R.	Radio
ROHCG	Royal Opera House, Covent Garden
RSO	Radio Symphony Orchestra
S.	South
Salz.	Salzburg
SCO	Stuttgart Chamber Orchestra
Seq.	Sequenza
Ser.	Serenata
Sinf.	Sinfonietta
SNO	Scottish National Orchestra
SO	Symphony Orchestra
Soc.	Society
Sol. Ven.	I Solisti Veneti
SRO	Suisse Romande Orchestra
Sup.	Supraphon
Symph.	Symphonica
Tel.	Telefunken
Th.	Theatre
Turn.	Turnabout
Uni.	Unicorn-Kanchana
V.	Vienna
VCM	Vienna Concentus Musicus
VPO	Vienna Philharmonic Orchestra
VSO	Vienna Symphony Orchestra
W.	West
World	World Records

Abraham, Paul (1892–1960)

(i) *Die Blume von Hawaii*: highlights;
(ii) *Viktoria und ihr Husar*: highlights.
**(*) Tel. AF 6.21247. Lins, Staal, Operetta Ch. and O., with (i) Hoppe, Knittel, (ii) Schöner, Bartos, Friedauer; Grobe.

Paul Abraham achieved temporary fame with *Viktoria und ihr Husar* in 1930 and followed it with *Die Blume von Hawaii* in 1931. In the mid-thirties he moved to the USA, but by then his star was fading; the kind of music in which he excelled was no longer fashionable, and he died in obscurity. *Viktoria* is an attractive score in traditional operetta vein, with an obvious hit in the *Good night* duet, which Sonja Schöner and Donald Grobe sing splendidly. *Die Blume von Hawaii* is a fascinating amalgam of styles; the engaging title song (with its Hawaiian lilt) is matched by *Bin nur ein Jonny*, in which Heinz-Maria Lins evokes the spirit of Al Jolson. The closing number then reverts to operetta march tempo. The performances – presented potpourri-style – are thoroughly idiomatic and there is no lack of sparkle. The music is uneven and already incredibly dated, but fascinating in its nostalgic evocation of a long-past era. Bright, lively recording with plenty of atmosphere.

Albéniz, Isaac (1860–1909)

Cantos de España: Córdoba, Op. 232/4; Mallorca (Barcarolla), Op. 202; Piezas caracteristicas: Zambra Granadina; Torre bermeja, Op. 92/7, 12; Suite española: Granada; Sevilla; Cádiz; Asturias, Op. 47/1, 3–5.
*** CBS Dig. 36679/41- [Col. M/HMT 36679]. Williams (guitar).

Some of Albéniz's more colourful miniatures are here, and John Williams plays them most evocatively. His mood is slightly introvert, and the underlying technical skill is hidden in his concern for atmosphere. A most beguiling recital, recorded with great faithfulness and not over-projected. The chrome cassette is every bit the equal of the disc.

Albinoni, Tommaso (1671–1750)

Adagio in G min. (arr. Giazotto). *Oboe concertos: Op. 9/3* (for 2 oboes); *Op. 9/8. Violin concertos: Op. 9/1; Op. 10/8.*
(M) ** Ph. Seq. 6527/7311 107. I Musici.

Philips have, for no discernible reason, deleted their entire Universo medium-priced catalogue and are reissuing the repertoire on the Sequenza and Festivo labels (although, perversely, not every recording is available outside Europe). This collection remains attractive and still sounds well (it offers strikingly fresh quality in the cassette version). With Heinz Holliger the principal oboe soloist, the playing is distinguished (although the two oboes remain too forwardly balanced in the *Double concerto*). The *Adagio* sounds rather thin-textured: those seeking this particular piece might do better with one of the many recordings available which do not seek to permeate Giazotto's arrangement with a baroque sensibility.

Concerti a cinque, Op. 9: Nos. 2 in D min.; 5 in C; 8 in G min.; 11 in B flat.
(M) *** Ph. 9502/7313 012. Holliger, I Musici.

This issue offers all the solo oboe concertos in Albinoni's Op. 9. They are played with characteristic finesse and style and are sympathetically accompanied. The recording is excellent for its period (the late 1960s), and the cassette transfer is admirably fresh and clean.

Oboe concertos, Op. 7, Nos. 2 (for 2 oboes); *3; 5* (for 2 oboes); *6; 8* (for 2 oboes); *9; 11* (for 2 oboes); *12.*
*** DG Arc. 2533 409 [id.]. Holliger, Elhorst, Camerata Bern.

This record contains eight of the twelve concertos comprising Albinoni's Op. 7, which were published in Amsterdam in 1715. Four of them are oboe concertos, four others are for two oboes, and the remainder are for strings. Though not to be played all at one sitting, this is definitely a record to acquire. The music itself is fresh, inventive and original; it is far removed from the general-purpose baroquerie all too often exhumed for the gramophone. The ideas are memorable and there is a touching charm about many of the slow movements. The playing of Heinz Holliger, Hans Elhorst and the Camerata Bern is refined, persuasive and vital, and the recording could hardly be more truthful or better detailed. This is a most distinguished issue.

Trumpet concerto in B flat, Op. 7/3.
*** CBS 76862/40- [Col. M/*MT* 35856].
Bernard, ECO, Malcolm − HERTEL and HUMMEL: *Concertos.****

André Bernard's performance of this

concerto is so splendidly stylish that one forgets it was conceived for oboe. The recording is excellent, and the cassette has only marginally less upper range than the disc. With its excellent couplings this is worth investigating.

Alfvén, Hugo (1872–1960)

Symphony No. 4 in C min. (Från Havsbandet), Op. 39.
**(*) Blue. BELL 107. Söderström, Winbergh, Stockholm PO, Westerberg.

Alfvén is best known for his *Midsummer Vigil* and a handful of other lighter pieces. This long and somewhat self-indulgent symphony dates from 1919 and its subtitle is probably best translated as 'from the outermost skerries of the archipelago'. It evokes the otherworldly atmosphere of the beautiful archipelago that stretches out from Stockholm into the Baltic. There is a highly romantic programme which plots the emotions of two lovers, and which rather shocked contemporary opinion in Sweden as being excessively sensual. The musical language stems from Strauss and Wagner, and there is a considerable orchestral apparatus, quadruple woodwind, eight horns, two harps, celesta and piano etc. It is more successful in its evocation of nature than in its expression of feeling: the vocalise has distinctly Wagnerian overtones. The tenor is rather hard and unpleasing, and Söderström's vibrato is wide, but though the music is sometimes derivative, there is much that is colourful and atmospheric, and the recording is in the demonstration class, with marvellously detailed sound and great presence. The orchestral playing is altogether excellent, too, and though the work outstays its welcome it is difficult to imagine a more committed performance.

Alkan, Charles (1813–88)

Barcarolle, Op. 65/6; 12 Studies in all minor keys, Op. 39, Nos. 4–6, 7 (Symphonie) and 12 (Le Festin d'Ésope); Grande sonate, Op. 33: 2nd movt (Quasi Faust) only.
(M) ** RCA Gold GL/GK 42689. Lewenthal.

In keeping with a uniquely bizarre career as pianist and composer, Alkan's death was thought to have occurred while he was reaching for a volume of the *Talmud*. As a friend and rival of Chopin and Liszt, he sought to outdo those masters with his wildly impractical virtuoso pieces. For a century or more they were considered impossibly difficult, except by such a virtuoso pianist-composer as Busoni. Raymond Lewenthal, a dramatic young American, was one of the first to come to Alkan's aid, first editing, then performing and recording some of the more impressive pieces. One finds that, though the manner is often very grand, the actual matter is thin – as for example, in the twenty-five decorative variations on a simple theme (all of them illustrating different animals) that make up *Le Festin d'Ésope*. But Alkan has a distinctive flavour in his music, and with passionately dedicated playing by so ardent an advocate as Lewenthal, the result is well worth hearing on either disc or tape (which is cleanly transferred). The recording is good.

Barcarolle; Gigue, Op. 24; March, Op. 37; Nocturne No. 2; Saltarelle, Op. 23; Scherzo diabolico; Sonatine, Op. 61.
(M) *** HM HM 927. Ringeissen.

Bernard Ringeissen is slightly less flamboyant than either Lewenthal or Smith (see below), both of whom have nailed their colours to Alkan's mast, but he is fully equal to the cruel demands of this music. The *Sonatine*, incidentally, an extended, big-boned piece, is the only item on this record that duplicates Ronald Smith's discography. All this music is of interest, though none of it rewards repeated hearing. The recording is more than just acceptable; it has splendid presence and body. Though none of this is great music in the true sense of the word, it has strong personality and a vein of genuine poetry that makes one regret its neglect in the concert hall.

3 Petites Fantaisies, Op. 41; 12 Studies in all minor keys, Op. 39; 12 Studies in all major keys, Op. 35: No. 5, Allegro barbaro (only); 25 Preludes, Op. 31: No. 8, La Chanson de la folle au bord de la mer (only).
*** HMV SLS 5100 (3). Ronald Smith.

The *Twelve Studies in all the minor keys* include the *Symphony for piano* (Studies 4–7), the *Concerto for piano* (Studies 8–10) and *Le Festin d'Ésope* (No. 12); only the very first, *Comme le vent* (*Like the wind . . .*), could be reasonably described as a study in the normal sense of the word. These twelve pieces occupy five sides; the *Trois Petites Fantaisies* and two shorter pieces (the *Song of the Mad Woman on the Sea Shore* and the *Allegro barbaro*) complete the sixth. Some of this music is quite astonishing; much of it is prophetic, remarkably so when one recalls that the *Song of the Mad Woman* dates from 1847, and the Op. 41 fantasies even appear to presage Prokofiev. Ronald Smith plays it all with consummate ease. As in his earlier Alkan recordings the virtuosity is remarkable, and his understanding of this repertoire is beyond question. The recording too is appropriately vivid and realistic.

Allegri, Gregorio (1582–1652)

Miserere.
⊛ (B) *** CfP CFP/*TC-CFP* 40339.
Tallis Scholars, Phillips – MUNDY: *Vox Patris caelestis* ***; PALESTRINA: *Missa Papae Marcelli.***(*)

Allegri's motet makes an indelible effect on the listener by the repetition of a short but ravishing sequence, dominated by a soaring treble line. It was a liturgical 'pop' of its day, and its success persuaded the Vatican authorities to guard the manuscript and thus restrict performances solely to the Sistine Chapel. However, the piece made such an impression on Mozart that he wrote it out from memory so that it could be performed elsewhere. On record it has long been famous in a King's performance on Argo (SPA/*KCSP* 245), with an arresting account of the treble line from Roy Goodman. In this new CfP version the treble solo is taken by a girl, Alison Stamp (the Tallis Scholars are a mixed choir). Her performance is no less outstanding, and the effect of her memorable contribution is enhanced by the recording itself, which is superb. Peter Phillips emphasizes his use of a double choir by placing the solo group in the echoing distance of Merton College Chapel, Oxford, and the main choir directly in front of the listener. The contrasts are dramatic and hugely effective, the ethereal quality of the distanced singers clearly focused by the soaring treble line. This is music ideally suited to cassette (with its freedom from intrusive background noises) and the tape quality is superb, every bit the equal of the disc.

Alwyn, William (born 1905)

Autumn Legend; Concerto grosso No. 2 in G; (i) *Lyra Angelica* (concerto for harp).
*** Lyr. SRCS 108. LPO, composer, (i) with Ellis.

Alwyn's music is avowedly and unashamedly romantic, yet though the idiom is accessible the music is far from wanting in substance. The *Concerto grosso,* like the Elgar *Introduction and allegro,* is for string quartet contrasted with full strings, and, though traditional in outlook, it is nonetheless distinctive in utterance. 'Originality does not come by rejection of one's heritage; individuality is founded on the past.' The *Autumn Legend* pays homage to Bax though it is envisaged as 'a very personal tribute to Rossetti'; the *Lyra Angelica* is inspired by a less well-known poet, Giles Fletcher. It is a reflective piece, ideal for late-night listening, eloquently played by Osian Ellis and the LPO under the composer's authoritative direction, and recorded with splendid clarity and range.

Derby Day: overture.
*** Lyr. SRCS 95. LPO, composer – Concert (*Overtures*).***

This lively performance is part of an attractive anthology discussed in the Concerts section below.

Arensky, Anton (1861–1906)

Violin çoncerto in A min., Op. 54.
(M) *** Turn. TVS 34629 [id./*CT 2133*]. Rosand, R. Lux. O., Froment – RIMSKY-KORSAKOV: *Concert fantasy*; WIENIAWSKI: *Concert polonaise.***

This concerto, which is new to the catalogue, is a much later work than Arensky's *Symphony* and his *Suite,* Op. 7. It is a winning piece, with a particularly endearing second group theme, a tune which can only be exorcized with repeated hearing. No great claims should be made for it, but it is a refreshing change from the Bruch or Glazounov concertos. It is superbly played by the much underrated Aaron Rosand, who is well supported by the Radio Luxembourg Orchestra and capably recorded. This issue will give pleasure, even though the couplings are of limited interest.

era, and they have a certain interest in that Arne was well placed historically to look backward as well as forward in the matter of style. The music is amiable and lively if not especially memorable; here the organ concerto projects more readily than the harpsichord concerto, because of the balance. The recordings come from the mid-sixties and still sound vivid; the cassette transfer is admirably done..

Arnaud, Leo (born 1904)

3 Fanfares.
*** Telarc Dig. DG 10050 [id.]. Cleveland Symphonic Winds, Fennell – GRAINGER: *Lincolnshire Posy* etc.; VAUGHAN WILLIAMS: *Folksongs suite* etc.***

Arnaud, a pupil of Ravel and d'Indy, now lives in the USA. His *Three Fanfares* (*Olympic theme*, *La Chasse* and *Olympiad*) are admirably succinct, with a total playing time just over three minutes. They use traditional material and are brilliantly scored, the use of antiphonal horns and trumpets a striking feature. The playing here is marvellous and the recording spectacularly demonstration-worthy, crisp and clear, yet with the brass realistically recessed.

Arne, Thomas (1710–78)

6 Favourite concertos: Nos. 4 in B flat (for organ); *5 in G min.* (for harpsichord).
(M) ** DG Arc. Priv. 2547/3347 054. Salter, Lucerne Festival Strings, Baumgartner – BOYCE: *Symphonies.* ***

These Arne concertos, written for the composer's son Michael (who was a prodigy), date from the end of the baroque

Arnold, Malcolm (born 1921)

Beckus the Dandipratt: overture (see also below).
*** Lyr. SRCS 95. LSO, Braithwaite – Concert (*Overtures*).***

One of the colourful descriptive miniatures which established Malcolm Arnold's reputation for skilful manipulation of the orchestral palette. This brilliant performance, splendidly recorded, is part of a useful collection discussed in the Concerts section below.

(i) *Flute concertos Nos. 1, Op. 45; 2, Op. 11. Sinfoniettas Nos. 1, Op. 48; 2, Op. 65.*
*** HMV ASD 3487. Philh. O., Dilkes, (i) with Solum.

Malcolm Arnold does not always manage to keep his high spirits and exuberance from overstepping the mark, but there is little trace of vulgarity in any of these works and a great deal of charm and invention. The *First Sinfonietta* is distinguished by some excellent ideas, and the *Flute concertos* are both charming and resourceful. There is no doubt that Arnold's mastery of the orchestra is of a high order. John Solum plays excellently and receives good support from the Philharmonia under Neville Dilkes. The recorded sound has admirable freshness and a good sense of space. The flute is (only marginally) larger than life and the orchestra is both vivid and detailed.

Guitar concerto, Op. 67.
(M) *** RCA Gold GL/*GK* 13883 [AGL 1/*AGK 1* 3883]. Bream, Melos Ens., composer – GIULIANI: *Concerto.****
*** CBS 76715/40-. Williams, L. Sinf., Howarth – BROUWER: *Concerto.****

It was Julian Bream who pioneered Malcolm Arnold's *Guitar concerto* in the recording studio, and his performance has the freshness of new discovery. This version dates from 1961, although it was not released in stereo until 1970. The medium-price reissue wears its years lightly and the balance is good. With the composer directing, authenticity in matters of tempo is assured. The cassette transfer is admirably fresh and clean.

The CBS issue makes a splendid alternative. The recording is analytical and finely detailed, though John Williams is a shade larger than life, albeit not unacceptably so. Slightly more ambience might have given the orchestral timbre a shade more freshness, but in any event this is a first-class recording with great immediacy and presence. Julian Bream gives the more romantic, dreamier performance, but John Williams has concentration and eloquence. A finely characterized reading with good support from Elgar Howarth and the London Sinfonietta. The cassette transfer is faithful, though it has not quite the range of the disc.

Harmonica concerto.
(M) *** RCA Gold GL/*GK* 42747. Adler, RPO, Gould – *Concert.****
*** Argo ZRG 905. Reilly, L. Sinf., Atherton – BENJAMIN and VILLA-LOBOS: *Concertos.****

Malcolm Arnold wrote this concerto for Larry Adler, who gives a charismatic performance on RCA. He is forwardly balanced, but Morton Gould sees that most of the orchestral detail comes through. Tommy Reilly's is also a fine performance. He has the advantage of a much more natural balance, and he plays the music with understanding and warmth. The superb Argo recording and the fine accompaniment under David Atherton yield their own pleasures, but Adler's account of the finale has an unforgettable rhythmic élan and the RCA version is obstinately more memorable, in spite of the many virtues of the Argo disc. The RCA cassette is not very successful, with a poorly focused upper range.

4 Cornish dances, Op. 91; 8 English dances; 4 Scottish dances, Op. 59.
*** Lyr. SRCS 109. LPO, composer.

Starting with his first set of *English dances*, Malcolm Arnold has developed the most attractive genre in these sharply memorable pieces, all of them strong in character with immediate tuneful appeal. Arnold himself is his own best advocate (he was once an orchestral player in this very orchestra) and he presents swaggeringly effective performances, brilliantly recorded.

Serenade for guitar and string orchestra.
(*) CBS 76634/40- [Col. M35172]. Williams, ECO, Groves – CASTELNUOVO-TEDESCO: *Concerto*; DODGSON: *Concerto No. 2.*(*)

This is a short, beguiling piece, beautifully laid out for guitar and strings, and played with great poetry and charm by John Williams and the ECO. The sound is warm and pleasing even if the balance favours the distinguished soloist unduly. The cassette is well managed, though not especially extended in range.

*Symphony No. 1; Beckus the Dandi-
pratt: overture; Solitaire* (ballet):
Sarabande and Polka.
*** HMV ASD 3823. Bournemouth SO,
composer.

Arnold in his late twenties, already
successful as a film composer and about
to write some of the most approachable
and colourful pieces since the Second
World War, here made his first symphonic statement, one of total bitterness. But even here the idiom is direct
and immediately understandable, with
motifs sharply recognizable. This is a
strong performance under the composer
himself. The three pieces used as fill-
up make an excellent contrast, the rumbustious overture *Beckus the Dandipratt* (rather more measured than usual)
and the two pieces which Arnold added
to his *English dances* to form the ballet
Solitaire. These are demonstration items
of a recording which is superb throughout.

Symphony for brass, Op. 123.
**(*) Argo ZRG/*KZRC* 906 [id.]. Jones
Brass Ens. – PREMRU: *Music* ***;
SALZEDO: *Capriccio.***

A longish piece, lasting some twenty-
six minutes, and, as one would expect
from a former trumpeter, expertly scored
for his unusual forces (horn, tuba, four
trumpets and four trombones). Ultimately, the ideas remain a shade facile
and the invention wanting the last ounce
of distinction, but there are powerful
sonorities here. The Philip Jones group
plays with stunning ensemble and
precision, and is superbly recorded. For
those who respond to Arnold's muse, this
will be a three-star issue. The cassette is
impressive, but not quite so rich and free
as the disc. There is a sense of spectacle
and brilliance but a touch of harshness
too.

Auber, Daniel (1782–1871)

*Overtures: The Black Domino;
Crown Diamonds; Fra Diavolo;
Marco Spada; Masaniello (La
Muette de Portici); La Part du
diable.*
(M) (*) HMV Green. ESD/*TC-ESD*
7096. Monte Carlo Op. O., Cambre-
ling.

A new collection of Auber overtures is
sorely needed, as Wolff's excellent early
stereo disc (Decca Eclipse ECS 695) is
muddy in the bass. But this will not do.
Although Sylvain Cambreling shows
both warmth and understanding and
tries hard to produce stylish performances, the coarse playing of the Monte
Carlo orchestra, with poor ensemble and
suspect intonation, gives scant enjoyment. The reverberant recording, with its
wide dynamic, seems to throw a glare on
all the faults.

Manon Lescaut (complete).
**(*) EMI 2C 167 14056/8. Mesplé,
Orliac, Runge, Bisson, Greger, Ch.
and O. Lyrique of R. France, Marty.

Ending, like Puccini's setting of the
same story in 'a desert in Louisiana',
Auber's opera, written in the 1850s when
he was already seventy-four, bears little
relationship to that example of high
romanticism. Born ten years before Rossini, Auber died two years after Berlioz.
Here he demonstrated that the liveliness
that we know from his overtures persisted to the end. Scribe's libretto is a free
and often clumsy adaptation of the Pré-
vost novel, but the sequence of arias and
ensembles, conventional in their way,
restores some of the original poetry.
Manon herself is a coloratura soprano
(here the tweety but agile Mady Mesplé)
and Des Grieux a lyric tenor (here
the lightweight Jean-Claude Orliac). A

recording as lively as this with first-rate sound is very welcome.

Auric, Georges (born 1899)

Imaginées 1–6.
** EMI 2C 069 16287. Debost, Desurmont, Command, Lodeon, Parrenin Qt, Cazauran, Collard, Ens., Myrat.

Georges Auric's music has never gained the public following that Honegger, Milhaud and Poulenc command. *Imaginées* is a series of six works, begun in 1968, for various combinations: the first is for flute, the second for cello, the third for clarinet, all with piano; the fourth and sixth include a singer and are separated by a solo piano piece. The music is well crafted and intelligently resourceful, as one would expect, but no strong distinctive personality emerges; indeed some of the pieces are moderately tedious. However, these are accomplished performances and are well recorded.

Avison, Charles (1709–70)

Concertos, Op. 2/1, 3, 9, and 10; Op. 6/8 and 12.
*** HMV ASD/*TC-ASD* 3482. Bournemouth Sinf., Thomas.

Charles Avison, contemporary of Arne and Boyce, was one of the liveliest musical British composers of his period. He studied with Geminiani, but stayed for the whole of his working career in his home town of Newcastle upon Tyne. He wrote some fifty concertos for strings, of which these represent a splendid cross-section. Individualist that he was, Avison

refused to bow to current fashion (his forms were generally conservative for his time) but regularly introduced sharply original ideas, as in the strange chromatic fugue of No. 9 in D. Ronald Thomas directs the Bournemouth Sinfonietta in fresh, lively performances, richly recorded. On cassette the balance leans towards the middle and bass, with the upper range less bright than usual from HMV.

12 Concerti grossi after Scarlatti.
*** Ph. 6769 018 (3) [id.] ASMF, Marriner.

A handful of Avison's original concertos have become known on record, but it was a brilliant idea of Neville Marriner to delve into these endlessly refreshing concertos which Avison based on Scarlatti harpsichord sonatas. His transcriptions for strings were attractively free (borrowing was always acceptable for composers in the eighteenth century) and he varied the Scarlatti-based movements with original ones of his own. The playing is both refined and resilient under Marriner, and the recording is beautifully balanced.

Bach, Carl Philipp Emanuel (1714–88)

Cello concerto in A, Wq. 172.
*** HMV ASD/*TC-ASD* 3899 [Ang. SZ 37738]. Harrell, ECO, Zukerman – COUPERIN: *Pièces* *(*); VIVALDI: *Concertos.****

This is a splendid work with an intensely expressive Largo, whose poignancy Harrell brings out with great beauty. There is spirited playing in the outer movements, and though the coupling has its shortcomings it makes a good baroque collection, well recorded. The tape transfer is lively and made at a high level, although the resonant acoustic brings some lack of focus to the upper orchestral range.

Flute concerto in D min., Wq. 22.
(M) ** Decca Ser. SA/KSC 8. Nicolet, Stuttgart CO, Münchinger – CIMAROSA: *Double flute concerto.***

Flute concertos: in D min., Wq. 22; in G, Wq. 169.
(M) *** DG Arc. Priv. 2547/3347 021. Linde, Lucerne Festival Strings, Baumgartner.

A pair of most engaging works, nimbly and imaginatively played by Hans-Martin Linde with a stylishly conceived accompaniment under Rudolf Baumgartner. The string playing is both spirited and makes sensitive use of light and shade. The disc wears its years lightly and the sound on tape is first-class, quite its equal in every way.

On Decca Serenata a beautifully recorded and elegant performance of the *D minor Concerto*, Wq. 22, with its gracious slow movement and brilliant finale, marked *Allegro di molto.* Aurèle Nicolet is fully equal to both its musical and its technical demands, and Münchinger accompanies attentively. Devotees of 'authentic timbres', however, may feel that the sound here (equally rich and spacious on disc and cassette) is rather too ample and lacking in any kind of spikiness.

Flute concertos: in A min.; in B flat; in A; in G, Wq. 166/9.
(M) ** Ph. 6747 444 (2). Nicolet, Neth. CO, Zinman.

Flute concertos: in A min.; in B flat, Wq. 166/7.

**(*) DG Arc. 2533 455. Preston, E. Concert, Pinnock.

Aurèle Nicolet's set has the advantage of being complete. All four concertos derive from the 1750s and, as a glance at the Wotquenne numbers will show, they exist in alternative versions for cello and keyboard. The present arrangement was probably made at the behest of Frederick the Great. Nicolet uses a modern instrument, and his approach is less scholarly than that of Preston. Both soloist and orchestra play extremely well, but with rather lively tempi these performances make less of the music than the rival Archive disc. The Philips recording is well balanced and clean.

Stephen Preston plays a period instrument, which is inevitably less strong in the bottom octave than the modern flute. He gives performances of considerable accomplishment and virtuosity; he makes much of the introspection of the slow movement of the *A minor* and tosses off the finales with enormous facility. He receives excellent support from the English Concert under Trevor Pinnock, and the recording quality is very good too. However, some ears may find this record, with its slightly abrasive upper string sound, a little lacking in charm.

Organ concertos: in G, Wq. 34; in E flat, Wq. 35; Fantasia and fugue in C min., Wq. 119/7.
**(*) Erato STU 71115. Alain, Paillard CO, Paillard.

The G major concerto, which also exists in a version for the flute, dates from the mid-1750s, and its companion was composed four years later. The slow movement of the latter is particularly powerful and expressive, but all the music here is representative of C. P. E. Bach at something like his very best. Marie-Claire Alain plays with excellent style, and the orchestra produces a rich and well-focused sound even if ensemble is not always impeccable. One or two minor disturbances of pitch may worry some listeners, but, generally speaking, this is a welcome issue.

Double harpsichord concerto in F, Wq. 46.
*(*) HM 1C 065 99785. Leonhardt, Curtis, Coll. Aur. – J. S. BACH: *Harpsichord concerto No. 1.*(*) ·

This concerto is earlier and a good deal less interesting than the more celebrated concerto in E flat for fortepiano and harpsichord. It dates from 1740 and is scored for strings, horns and continuo. The most memorable of the three movements is the middle one, which has some characteristically introspective writing. Otherwise the thematic material and its working out are relatively uninteresting. Good playing from the distinguished soloists and the Collegium Aureum and acceptable but not outstanding recording, which dates from the mid-1960s.

Sinfonias: in C, Wq. 174; in D, Wq. 176; 6 Sinfonias, Wq. 182/1–6.
*** O-L DSLO 557/8 [id.]/*KDSLC2 7064.* AcAM, Hogwood.

6 Sinfonias, Wq. 182/1–6.
*** DG Arc. 2533 449 [id./*3310 449*]. E. Concert, Pinnock.
**(*) HM 1C 065 99691 (Nos. 2–5 only). Coll. Aur.

The sharp originality of C. P. E. Bach was never more apparent than in these symphonies. The six for strings, Wq. 182, written after he had left the employ of the Emperor of Prussia and could at last please himself in adventurous writing, are particularly striking in their unexpected twists of imagination, with wild, head-reeling modulations and sudden pauses which suggest the twentieth century rather than the eighteenth. The abrasiveness of such music comes out sharply

in an authentic performance like that of the Academy of Ancient Music, and though the angularity may not make it relaxing listening, Hogwood continually has one responding as to new music, not least in the dark, bare slow movements. The two symphonies with wind (on side four) are marginally less original; but, with superb recording, it is a remarkable and refreshing set. On tape the sound is clear but rather dry and when the brass enters the ear is conscious of some lack of amplitude.

The performing style of the English Concert is less abrasive than that of its rival and has more concern for eighteenth-century point and elegance without losing any degree of authenticity. This issue also has the advantage of fitting the six symphonies Wq. 182 on two sides instead of three. Excellent recording.

The Collegium Aureum disc (originally issued in the UK on BASF) was the début recording of these works on 'original instruments'. The playing has grip and impulse, and the resilient yet slightly grainy sound has virility and bite, and a strikingly fresh beauty too. The acoustic is both resonant and clean, and the continuo comes through in perfect overall balance. But, fine though this LP is, it has the irredeemable disadvantage of offering only four of the six symphonies.

4 Sinfonias, Wq. 183/1–4.
(M) *** Ph. 9502 013. ECO, Leppard.

This record is devoted to four symphonies published in Hamburg in 1780. The music is not merely historically interesting but is often characterized by an emotional insistence that is disturbing and a capacity to surprise that is quite remarkable. The playing is splendid, lively and vital, and the recording is exemplary, both in quality of sound and in balance.

Fantasy in C; Quartets for flute, viola, cello and piano in A min., D, and G, Wq. 93/5.
*** O-L DSLO 520. McGegan, Mackintosh, Pleeth, Hogwood.

The three quartets come from the last year of Bach's life and are all beautifully fashioned, civilized pieces with many of the expressive devices familiar from this composer. There is a highly chromatic slow movement for the D major work, and some of the outer movements are unpredictable and inventive. The *Fantasy* dates from the mid-1780s and is roughly contemporary with Mozart's *C minor Fantasy*. All the performances are first-rate: Christopher Hogwood uses a fortepiano rather than the specified harpsichord and secures a wide dynamic range and clean intelligent articulation. The recorded sound could hardly be bettered.

Trio sonatas: in C min., Wq. 161a; in B, Wq. 161b; in E, Wq. 162.
(M) **(*) Sup. 1111 1675. Ars Rediviva, Munclinger.

All these pieces date from the mid-century; the two numbered by Wotquenne as 161 appeared at Nürnberg in 1751, and the companion was composed in Potsdam in 1749. The *C minor Sonata* is of special interest in that it is an early instance of programmatic writing; it represents a dialogue between the sanguine and melancholic temperament, one which is resolved in favour of the former! It is an interesting piece, well played and recorded by Milan Munclinger, who is an elegant flautist. The *B major Sonata* is less remarkable, but Wq. 162, in which Munclinger is joined by the flautist Jiri Válek, is an appealing work, well worth hearing (see also below). For those who worry about these matters, the pitch is decidedly sharp.

Trio sonata in E, Wq. 162.
*** O-L DSLO 518 [id.]. Preston, McGegan, Ryan, Pleeth, Hogwood – J. S. BACH: *Trio sonata* ***; W. F. BACH: *Duo* etc.**

Stephen Preston and Nicholas McGegan play on period instruments and show why the flute was so cultivated at Potsdam as the instrument of sensibility. This sonata is an original and eloquent piece, well crafted and structured, with an expressive, inward-looking slow movement. It is persuasively played and truthfully recorded. The J. S. Bach coupling is an added attraction, though the fill-ups by W. F. Bach are less interesting.

Flute sonata in A min.
*** RCA RL/RK 25315 [ARL 1/ARK 1 3858]. Galway – STAMITZ: *Flute concertos.***(*)

This sonata for unaccompanied flute is an inspired and characteristically original piece, and James Galway gives it a marvellous performance, as striking for its insight as for its spontaneity. He is well recorded on both disc and cassette, but the couplings offer more conventional music.

Essay on the True Art of Playing Keyboard Instruments: 6 Sonatas, Wq. 63/1–6; 6 Sonatine nuove, Wq. 63/7–12.
*** O-L DSLO 589. Hogwood.

This record contains the twelve keyboard sonatas that C. P. E. Bach published with the first part of his *Essay on the True Art of Playing Keyboard Instruments* in 1753. These were to wield enormous influence for the remainder of the century on composers such as Haydn, Mozart and Beethoven. Despite their didactic intention, they are pieces of great expressive power and are played by Christopher Hogwood not only with virtuosity but with a rare vein of poetic feeling. He uses a 1761 Haas clavichord of

11

great beauty and is recorded excellently, though the disc should be played at low level.

6 Württemberg Sonatas, Wq. 49.
*** Tel. EK 6.35378 (2) [id.]. Van Asperen.

The six *Württemberg Sonatas* are not otherwise available and they contain musical invention of striking quality and originality. Composed in the early 1740s and dedicated to the Duke of Württemberg, these sonatas are at once more daring and powerfully expressive than their immediate predecessors, the so-called 'Prussian' set. They are arguably more suited to the clavichord than the harpsichord (they are too early for the fortepiano), and one small criticism of Bob van Asperen's performances concerns the range of dynamic contrast he achieves: this could ideally be wider. He uses a fine reproduction of a Dulcken harpsichord, and his approach has a welcome rhythmic freedom, a fine sense of line and an appropriate intensity of feeling when required. He is well recorded, and this pair of discs can be recommended.

Organ music: *Adagio in D min., Wq. n.v. 66; Fantasia and fugue in C min., Wq. 119/7; Fugues; in D min.; E flat, Wq. 119/6; Prelude in D, Wq. 70/7; Sonatas Nos. 1–6, Wq. 70/1–6.*
** Tel. EX 6.35453 (2) [id.]. Tachezi.

C. P. E. Bach's organ music was supposedly sponsored by Princess Anna Amalia, daughter of Frederick the Great, which meant that it was not too ambitious, technically, and needed also to be tailored to the organ she used. Herbert Tachezi here uses a restored eighteenth-century instrument at Castle Matzen, in the Austrian Tyrol, which is reputed to have some affinity with the original. The six *Sonatas* offer lively and expressive invention, the composer seemingly rising to the occasion, for the music almost never sounds simplistic, and it has moments of characteristic originality. The *Fantasia and fugue* is strong and expansive, and the *Adagio* is an engaging piece. The playing is good throughout; Tachezi is sometimes a trifle mannered but he is generally true to the spirit of the music. The recording is excellent.

Magnificat, Wq. 215.
*** Argo ZRG/*KZRC* 853 [id.]. Palmer, Watts, Tear, Roberts, King's College Ch., ASMF, Ledger.
** HM 1C 065 99624. Ameling, Lehane, Altmeyer, Hermann, Tölz Ch., Coll. Aur., Kurt Thomas.

One would have thought that the example of father Johann Sebastian in setting the *Magnificat* would be daunting to his son; but just before old Bach died, C.P.E. produced a setting which in terms of the *galant* style conveyed startling involvement. The magnificent opening chorus (repeated later in the setting of the *Gloria*) presents King's College Choir at its most exhilarating. This irresistible movement, here taken challengingly fast, leads to a whole series of sharply characterized numbers, including a sparkling tenor aria on *Quia fecit*. The whole is rounded off in a choral fugue as energetic as Handel's best, with barely a nod in father's direction. With vividly atmospheric recording the performance under Philip Ledger comes electrically to life, with choir, soloists and orchestra all in splendid form. The cassette transfer is extremely vivid too: only at the very end is there a suspicion that the level of modulation is fractionally high.

The Harmonia Mundi version is enjoyable, and Elly Ameling is outstanding among the soloists. But the performance overall has not the vitality of the Argo version, and although the splendour of the closing *Sicut erat* comes over impressively the resonant recording does not provide much inner detail.

Bach, Johann Christian
(1735–82)

Fortepiano concertos, Op. 1, Nos. 1–6; Op. 7, Nos. 1–6; Op. 13, Nos. 1–6.
(M) *** Ph. 6768 001 (5). Haebler, V. Capella Academica, Melkus.

J. C. Bach composed three sets of six clavier concertos, all attractive, well-wrought compositions. It would be difficult to find a more suitable or persuasive advocate than Ingrid Haebler, who is excellently accompanied and most truthfully recorded. J. C. Bach is at his freshest and most beguiling in some of these concerto movements, and this boxed set, which conveniently gathers them all together, cannot be too strongly recommended.

Six 'favourite' overtures: Nos. 1–3 in D; 4 in C; 5–6 in G.
*** O-L DSLO/DSLC 525. AcAM, Hogwood.

J. C. Bach's *Six 'favourite' overtures* were published as a set in London in 1763 for use in the concert hall, although their original derivation was theatrical. They are all short and succinct Italian-style pieces in three movements (fast–slow–fast), and they show great variety of invention and imaginative scoring (using double wind: oboes, sometimes flutes, horns and strings). The performances here are characteristically alert and vivid and there are many features to stay in the mind: the trio for wind instruments in the finale of No. 1; the attractively robust outer movements of No. 3; the Vivaldi-like figuration of the finale of No. 4; the tripping strings in the *Andante* of No. 5. This is not an issue to play all at once, but when dipped into it offers delightful music played in a refreshingly spirited (and authentic) way. The recording is excellent on disc, and the tape transfer is very good indeed, if fractionally mellower on side one than side two.

(i) *Sinfonia concertante in A, for violin, cello and orchestra. Sinfonia in E flat for double orchestra, Op. 18/1.*
*(*) HM 1C 065 99827. Coll. Aur., (i) with Maier, May.

This record offers poor value: the two-movement *Sinfonia concertante* is an agreeable work, with an attractively inventive rondo finale, but it lasts only 15'36". Its soloists are balanced very closely, which makes their period instruments sound unnecessarily pithy and minimizes the expressive effect of their playing. The *Sinfonia* on side two is a splendid piece. It has a fine central *Andante*, with a strong Mozartian flavour. The performance is lively and sympathetic, but the reverberant acoustic does not fully exploit the work's antiphonal possibilities. Side two plays for just 12'21".

6 Sinfonias, Op. 3 (ed. Erik Smith).
(M) *** Ph. 9502/7313 001. ASMF, Marriner.

These Op. 3 symphonies are recorded here for the first time. They were first played in 1765 'at Mrs Cornelys's' in Carlisle House, Soho Square, and are scored for strings with oboes and horns in subsidiary roles. Erik Smith, who has edited them, describes them as 'in essence Italian overtures, though with an unusual wealth of singing melody'. They are beguilingly played by the Academy of St Martin-in-the-Fields under Neville Marriner and beautifully recorded. None of this can be called great music but it has an easy-going and fluent charm. The tape transfer is of excellent quality, fresh and transparent.

Sinfonias, Op. 6/1–6; Op. 8/2–4; Op. 9/1–3. Overture: La Calamità de cuori.

(M) *** Ph. 6747 439 (2). Neth. CO, Zinman.

Sinfonias, Op. 6/3; Op. 9/2; Op. 18/2 and 4.
*** HMV ASD/*TC-ASD* 3544. Bournemouth Sinf., Montgomery.

Sinfonias, Op. 6/6; Op. 18/4 and 6.
** HM 1C 065/*265* 99759. Coll. Aur.

This highly attractive music calls for the most polished and elegant presentation, which it certainly receives from the Netherlands group under David Zinman. Indeed a case could be made for giving some of these pieces less elegance and greater weight, in the manner of the equally valid Bournemouth performances. Yet everything is most musically done on the Philips discs, not least the sound engineering, which achieves a realistic perspective between the various instruments as well as truthful tone quality. This modestly priced and delightful set would form an admirable starting-point for any collector about to embark on this composer.

Very good playing and excellent sound also make the Bournemouth set, directed by Kenneth Montgomery, an attractive proposition. Everything is very fresh, and the playing has both commitment and warmth. The two Op. 18 pieces are the most substantial. There are some odd touches (why the *notes inégales* in the first movement of Op. 9/2?) but these should not detract from the enjoyment this playing gives. The tape transfer is of excellent quality; the resonance brings some lack of transparency to the string tuttis, but the sound is full, with plenty of warmth and bloom.

The Collegium Aureum are less successful with the music of J. C. Bach than in their disc of sinfonias by Carl Philipp. But they are not helped by the recording, which, though full and pleasing, lacks brilliance. The playing itself is elegant but rather unsmiling. The slow movement of the G minor symphony, Op. 6/6, which is the longest work, with a side to itself,

has more emotional depth than is revealed here.

Bach, Johann Sebastian
(1685–1750)

The Art of Fugue; Brandenburg concertos Nos. 1–6; The Musical Offering; Orchestral suites Nos. 1–4.
(M) **(*) Ph. 6768 232 (6). ASMF, Marriner.

Marriner and the St Martin's Academy are refined interpreters of Bach, but the two major offerings here – the idiosyncratic earlier set of the *Brandenburgs*, using Thurston Dart's idea of the original text, and the self-conscious readings of the *Suites* – are less sympathetic than most of their records. Consistently good recording.

Brandenburg concertos Nos. 1–6, BWV 1046/51; Orchestral suites Nos. 1–4, BWV 1066/9.
(M) ** HM 1C 97 5300–30 (4). Coll. Aur.

The Collegium Aureum helped to pioneer the return to authentic textures with 'original instruments', but they sugared the pill a little by the use of a widely reverberant acoustic, which added a mellowing effect to the instrumental timbres, especially in the *Suites*. Here their recordings of Bach's major orchestral works are gathered together in a box at medium price. The performances are considered in more detail below; the sound quality itself is warmly beautiful.

Brandenburg concertos Nos. 1–6.
*** Ph. 6769/*7654* 058 (2) [id.]. ASMF, Marriner.
*** HMV SLS/*TC-SLS* 5155 (2) [Ang. SZ 3873]. Polish CO, Maksymiuk.
(M) *** HMV SXDW/*TC-SXDW* 3054

(2) [Ang. S/*4X2S* 3787]. Bath Festival O., Menuhin.
(M) **(*) ASV ACM 2038/9. Northern Sinfonia, Malcolm.
(M) **(*) Ph. 9502 014/5 [id.]. ASMF, Marriner.
(B) **(*) Decca DPA 577/8. Philomusica, Dart.
(M) ** Decca Jub. JB/*KJBC* 61/2 [Lon. 2301]. SCO, Münchinger.
** DG 2707 112 (2)/*3370 030* [id.]; also 2531/*3301* 332 (Nos. 1–3); 2531/*3301* 333 (Nos. 4–6) [id.]. Berlin PO, Karajan.
(B) ** Con. CC/*CCT* 7535 and 7541. Stuttgart Chamber Soloists, Couraud.
** HM 151/*283* 99643/4. Coll. Aur.
(M) *(*) Tel. Ref. AQ6/*CQ4* 41191/2 [2635/*2435* 043]. VCM, Harnoncourt.
(M) *(*) DG Priv. 2535/*3335* 142/3 [id.]. Lucerne Festival O., Baumgartner.
**(*) CBS 79227/40-. Carlos (synthesizer).

Brandenburg concerto No. 5.
(*) DG Arc. 2533/*3310* 440 [id.]. E. Concert, Pinnock – *Suite No. 4.*(*)

The newest ASMF recording of the *Brandenburgs* readily communicates warmth and enjoyment. In three of the concertos Marriner introduces such distinguished soloists as Henryk Szeryng, Jean-Pierre Rampal and Michala Petri, adding individuality without breaking the consistency of beautifully sprung performances. George Malcolm is an ideal continuo player. With superb playing, well-chosen speeds and refined recording, this is now on balance the best recommendation. The sound is equally natural on both disc and tape.

The Polish set of *Brandenburgs* (recorded when the orchestra was on tour in England in 1977) is surely the fastest on record. Some will undoubtedly resist, especially in No. 3, yet the crisp articulation and the buoyancy of the playing are exhilarating, here and elsewhere. The orchestra is augmented with English recorder soloists, who obviously enjoy themselves, as does the trumpeter, who is called to even greater flights of virtuosity than usual in No. 2. In No. 3 a slow movement from a G major violin sonata is interpolated between the two regular movements. No. 5 has a first-class contribution from the solo harpsichord player, Wladyslaw Klosiewicz. The balance throughout is excellent and the recording is admirably full and clear, with the splendidly transferred cassettes matching the discs in bloom and presence.

The reissue of Menuhin's 1959 set (in a folding double-sleeve) on HMV's mid-priced Concert Classics label is most welcome. The recording has been slightly freshened, but has not lost its bloom. The hint of overloading from the horns in No. 1 is perhaps slightly more noticeable (especially on the cassettes, which have less upper range than the discs) but otherwise the sound is well-balanced and clean. Rarely have the *Brandenburg* rhythms been sprung more joyfully, and tempi are uncontroversially apt. The soloists are outstanding, and there is a spontaneity here that is consistently satisfying.

George Malcolm's own set offers highly enjoyable, amiable performances, undoubtedly competitive in the medium price-range. They are very well recorded, although it might be felt that the balance in No. 4 makes the harpsichord too dominant. Malcolm's direction ensures rhythmic resilience throughout, and, more clearly than in many more brilliant performances, the players here convey the joy of Bach's inspiration. Much of the solo playing – for instance the oboe – is most sensitive, but by the highest international standards there is sometimes a shortfall in polish and precision.

On 9502 014/5 Marriner used an edition prepared by Thurston Dart which aims at re-creating the first version of these works, long before Bach thought of sending them to the Margrave of Brandenburg. So No. 1, for example, has only three movements; there is a horn instead of a trumpet in No. 2, and maddeningly squeaky sopranino recorders in No. 4. Often the sounds are delightful, but this is not the definitive set, and Marriner's newest recording is much more successful.

Dart himself recorded the concertos with the Philomusica orchestra in the early days of stereo. This bargain-priced Decca set offers fresh and electrifying performances marked by brisk tempi and clear textures. All the performances are enhanced by Dart's own harpsichord continuo, often provocatively elaborate but always rhythmically exhilarating. Like Maksymiuk, Dart interpolates a movement from a Bach violin sonata between the two regular movements of No. 3, which works well, but controversially he opts for trumpets instead of horns in No. 1. The result will not please everyone, but the extra brightness of the trumpets playing an octave higher than usual is certainly refreshing. The recording is a little wiry by today's standards but very acceptable when the two records are offered for the cost of one premium-priced LP.

Münchinger's recording is of Decca's best, and this Jubilee set also offers fresh and clean cassette transfers, as sophisticated as any available. The performances are stylish and have plenty of vitality, if not the detailed imagination of some of the finest rival versions.

Over the years Karajan's approach to Bach has been modified, at least in such relatively intimate works. These are not the inflated, over-smooth performances one might expect. The playing is highly polished, the rhythms resilient and, whatever the authenticists may say, the viola melody of the slow movement of No. 6 is a joy to the ear when played as sweetly as this. There are fresher performances than these, but they show Karajan in attractively lively mood, and the recording is full and vivid. The cassette box has a curious layout, with Nos. 1 and 5 coupled together on the first tape, and 2 and 4 backing 3 and 6 on the second.

The sound is of high quality, smooth and sleek rather than sharply detailed. The transfer level is modest, but there is no appreciable lack of range.

The Contour set is recorded very acceptably, with full, if rather resonant, sound. The horns are backwardly balanced in No. 1 and inner detail is blurred by the acoustic. The performances are variable; the rhythms of the first-movement allegros are generally well-sprung though not as irresistible as in some other versions. The trumpet soloist in No. 2 is excellent and so are the flutes in No. 4. Martin Galling's continuo is sensitive, and the recording allows his contribution to make its mark. The cassettes are less refined than the discs, but at bargain price this is worth considering.

Of the two recordings using original instruments, that by the Collegium Aureum (first issued here by BASF and now on Harmonia Mundi) is to be preferred to the Harnoncourt version. The use of older instruments can bring special rewards. Here the recorders create some engaging sounds, and No. 3 is buoyant and alert, with clean inner lines. No. 5 is strikingly fresh and clear, and although the bravura harpsichord contribution tends to dominate the texture too much the overall quality is beautiful. In No. 2 the balance does not unduly favour the trumpet, and the piquant timbres of the other instruments are freshly enjoyable.

Harnoncourt's Telefunken set, now reissued at medium price on the Reference label, was recorded in the Great Hall of the Schönburg Palace in Vienna. But to offset the resonance the close placing of the microphones has resulted in a consistently forward sound picture, with nothing like a real pianissimo at any time, even in slow movements. The interpretations are variable. Generally tempi are traditional, but here and there – as in the plodding speed for the first movement of No. 2 or the insensitively fast opening movement of No. 6 – the direction is less than convincing. The balance too has variable success. No. 1, for instance, suffers from a lack of internal clarity, while No. 5 gains from the crisp linear focus. The mixed brass, woodwind and strings in No. 2 integrate successfully, as does the sound of recorders and violin in No. 4. The cassettes are lively and clean to match the discs closely.

The Baumgartner performances are set in the traditional German mould, accurate but inclined to dullness in overall impression. Baumgartner seems for the most part content to go along with the score, contributing relatively little, although his soloists are often excellent. The 1961 recording sounds well enough and the cassettes are well managed, with the clarity of focus slipping occasionally (notably in Nos. 1 and 6).

Pinnock's coupling of No. 5 with the *Fourth Orchestral suite* seems perverse, but anyone who responds to the fresh, rather abrasive but nicely controlled style of performance will find this issue as enjoyable as the others, with excellent solo playing and recording.

The wit of Carlos in transcribing baroque music on the Moog synthesizer was never clearer than in his first essays on *Brandenburg concertos*. Over the years he completed a whole cycle (echoing the interpretative idiosyncrasies of other versions in different movements). There are diminishing returns on his wit, but there is no denying the liveliness.

Still recommended: Like Maksymiuk, Leppard adopts consistently fast tempi, but with sparkling and refined ECO playing his set remains very high on the list of current recommendations (Ph. 6747 166/7699 006 [id.]). Paillard's more traditional approach on Erato (STU 70801/2 [CRL 2 5801]) and Britten's spirited and imaginative Maltings recording (Decca SXL/KSXC 6774/5 [Lon. 2225]) should also still be considered.

Flute concertos in A min. (from BWV 1056; ed. Galway); E min.

(from BWV 1059 and BWV 35; ed. Radeke); Suite No. 2 in B min., BWV 1067.
*** RCA RL/RK 25119 [ARL 1/ARK 1 2907]. Galway, Zagreb Soloists, Ninic.

The two arranged concertos (one a reconstruction) prove an admirable vehicle for James Galway, and he plays the famous slow-movement cantilena of BWV 1056 (the *F minor Harpsichord concerto*) as beautifully as one would expect. He is balanced forwardly, and is in consequence slightly larger than life. In the *Suite in B minor* the orchestral textures are a little less transparent, but generally the sound is excellent on disc, and the transfer to tape is first-class in every way, with body as well as range and detail. The harpsichord continuo comes through without being insistent, which many listeners will like.

Triple concerto for flute, violin and harpsichord, BWV 1044; Oboe d'amore concerto in A, BWV 1055; Triple violin concerto in D, BWV 1064.
** DG Arc. 2533/3310 452 [id.]. Soloists, Mun. Bach O., Karl Richter.

In spite of the Archive label this is far from the current conception of authentic Bach performance. In the slow movement of the *Triple violin concerto* the effect is warmly romantic, partly because of the beguilingly rich recorded sound (equally effective on cassette and disc). Manfred Clement gives an attractive account of the *Oboe d'amore concerto*, and Aurèle Nicolet's flute playing in BWV 1044 is delightfully fresh. In the slow movement Richter provides a neat keyboard embroidery, but in the outer movements the harpsichord is much less attractively focused and rhythmically very insistent. However, the orchestral playing is of high quality.

Harpsichord concertos Nos. 1–7, BWV 1052/8; Double harpsichord concertos Nos. 1–3, BWV 1060/2; Triple harpsichord concertos Nos. 1 and 2, BWV 1063/4; Quadruple harpsichord concerto in A min., BWV 1065.
*** DG Arc. 2723 077 (4). Pinnock, Gilbert, Mortensen, Kraemer, E. Concert, Pinnock.

A useful and often distinguished set. Trevor Pinnock plays with real panache, his scholarship tempered by excellent musicianship. There are occasions when one feels his tempi are a little too fast and unrelenting, but for the most part there is little cause for complaint. On the contrary, the performances give much pleasure and the period instruments are better played than on most issues of this kind. Two of the records are digital and have the advantage of great clarity of texture, and all four discs sound excellent. Apart from the very quick tempi (particularly in the finale of BWV 1055) which strike an unsympathetic note – and baroque violins are not to every taste – this set is thoroughly recommendable.

Harpsichord concerto No. 1 in D min., BWV 1052.
*(*)HM 1C 065 99785. Leonhardt, Coll. Aur. – C. P. E. BACH: *Double concerto.* * (*)

Gustav Leonhardt's account of the *D minor Concerto* dates from the mid-1960s and shows the Dutch master at his least beguiling. Rhythms are metronomic and after a promisingly alert opening become rigid. While it would be an exaggeration to call this routine and uninspired, it gives a good deal less pleasure than many of its rivals, and for that matter Leonhardt's other records. The slow movement in particular is dull and the reading as a whole is disappointing.

Harpsichord concertos Nos. 1 in D min.; 2 in E; 4 in A, BWV 1052/3, and 1055.
(M) *** Ph. 9502/7313 002 [id.]. Leppard, ECO.

Harpsichord concertos Nos. 1 and 4; 5 in F min., BWV 1056.
(M) *** DG Arc. Priv. 2547/3347 010. Kirkpatrick, Lucerne Festival Strings, Baumgartner.

Taken from Leppard's deleted set of the concertos, this medium-price Philips issue makes an outstanding recommendation, generously filled with three concertos and including the greatest, the *D minor*. The recording is excellent. The DG Archive disc is also highly recommendable. Dating from 1959/60 these recordings were models of their period, with fresh, clean performances, beautifully scaled. The Lucerne players match the liveliness of Kirkpatrick, who hits an admirable balance between expressiveness and classical detachment. Fine sound, lacking only a little in range.

On cassette George Malcolm's coupling of the first two concertos (Decca Jub. JB/KJBC 9) remains technically first choice, the sound being of demonstration quality in its body and clarity. Münchinger, however, is a less imaginative accompanist than either Leppard or Baumgartner, and offers only two concertos. Both the Philips and DG tape transfers are of good quality: the Philips is fresh and transparent; the DG is especially vivid in the *D minor Concerto*, but with a lower level on side two, there is slightly less presence and detail in the other two works.

Clavier concertos Nos. 1, 4 and 5, BWV 1052, 1055/6.
*** Denon Dig. 7182 [id.]. Schiff (piano), ECO, Malcolm.

If Bach's keyboard concertos are to be given on the piano rather than the harpsichord – and there are many listeners for whom the substitution is an agreeable one – they could hardly be more persuasively presented than here. The recording is beautifully balanced, the sound absolutely truthful, fresh, vivid and clean. Andras Schiff never tries to pretend that he is not using a modern piano, and the lightness of his touch and his control of colour are a constant delight to the ear. Malcolm's accompaniments are both alert and resilient, and the actual sound of the strings is perfectly in scale. Outer movements have splendid vigour and transparency; slow movements are expressive and evocative in their control of atmosphere. Schiff's decoration in the *Larghetto* of the *A major* (No. 4) is admirable, as is his simple eloquence in the famous cantilena of the *F minor Concerto* (No. 5). This is highly recommended, and it is an example of digital recording at its most believable.

Clavier concerto No. 5 in F min., BWV 1056.
*** Decca SXL/*KSXC* 6952 [Lon. 7180/5-]. Larrocha (piano), I. Sinf., Zinman – HAYDN: *Concerto in D*; MOZART: *Concerto No. 12.***

David Zinman has recorded the *D minor Concerto* (BWV 1052) for Decca with Ashkenazy, like Alicia de Larrocha here, using a piano instead of a harpsichord. His robust accompaniments, rhythmically strong and alert, are matched by Miss de Larrocha with her clean, firm articulation, and their partnership is eminently satisfying, particularly in the famous and beautiful slow movement, which is shaped with a cool and moving simplicity. The Decca recording is first-class on disc and cassette alike, and as the generous couplings include a highly recommendable version of Mozart's K.414 and a lively performance of Haydn's most famous keyboard concerto the Bach might be regarded as a bonus.

Double harpsichord concertos Nos. 1 in C min.; 2 in C; 3 in C min., BWV 1060/2.
**(*) DG Arc. Dig. 2534/*3311* 002 [id.]. Pinnock, Gilbert, E. Concert.

Double harpsichord concertos Nos. 1 and 2; Harpsichord concerto No. 5 in F min., BWV 1056.
(M) *** Ph. 9502/*7313* 017. Leppard, Andrew Davis, ECO.

Both these issues derive from boxed sets (the Philips collection was issued in 1974 and is now withdrawn). The famous *F minor* solo concerto probably comes from a violin concerto; it and the *C minor Double concerto*, BWV 1060, based on a work envisaging two violins or a violin and oboe, occupy the first side of the Philips disc. On the reverse is the *C major Double concerto*, BWV 1061; it seems likely that this was conceived for two keyboards alone and that the strings were an afterthought in the outer movements. Leppard and Davis play with skill and flair, and the ECO shows plenty of life. It is less incisive than the English Concert under Pinnock but the performances overall have resilience and communicate such joy in the music that criticism is disarmed. The Philips balance is first-class, the harpsichords not too forward and the strings clear and fresh. The cassette – though not transferred at the highest level – is one of Philips' best, full and clean.

The character of the Pinnock performances is altogether more robust, with the balance forward and the performances very strongly projected. The combination of period instruments and playing of determined vigour certainly makes a bold impression, but the relatively unrelaxed approach to the slow movements will not appeal to all ears. The third of the double concertos, BWV 1062, is an alternative version of the *Concerto for two violins*, BWV 1043, and though the keyboard format has a certain fascination it is no match for the original, especially in the beautiful slow movement, with – as here – squeezed accompanying chords. The lively recording is equally effective on disc and cassette.

Triple harpsichord concertos Nos. 1 in D min.; 2 in C, BWV 1063/4; Quadruple harpsichord concerto in A min., BWV 1065.
**(*) DG Arc. Dig. 2534/*3311* 001 [id.]. Pinnock, Gilbert, Mortensen, Kraemer, E. Concert.

Like the *Double concertos* above, this is taken from Pinnock's integral boxed set, and again the music was originally conceived for other instruments. *The C major Concerto*, BWV 1064, was based on a triple violin concerto, and in the *Quadruple concerto* Bach drew on Vivaldi's Op. 3/10, originally for four violins. The slightly aggressive style of the music-making – everything alert, vigorously paced and forwardly projected – emphasizes the bravura of Bach's conceptions. The sound too has striking presence and clarity, yet is not without atmosphere. The cassette matches the disc very closely.

Violin concertos Nos. 1 in A min.; 2 in E, BWV 1041/2; (i) *Double violin concerto in D min., BWV 1043.*
(M) *** Ph. 9502/*7313* 016. Szeryng, Winterthur Coll. Mus., (i) with Rybar.
** Ph. 9500 226/*7300 537* [id.]. Szeryng, ASMF, Marriner, (i) with Hasson.
(M) *(*) Ph. Fest. 6570/*7310* 010. Goldberg, Neth. CO, (i) with Magyar.

The reissue of Szeryng's attractive performances with the Winterthur group, dating from the mid-sixties, can be cordially recommended at medium price. Szeryng plays the two solo concertos with dignity and classical feeling; the slow movements are particularly fine. Peter Rybar proves an excellent partner in the *Double concerto* (again the central movement is memorably poised and eloquently phrased). The accompaniments are sympathetic and lively, and the sound is fresh and full, the tape focus only fractionally less clean than the disc.

Szeryng's later record with the ASMF under Marriner has the advantage of a sumptuous, modern recording, which produces an excellent balance between the soloists and orchestra and a warm spread of sound. But in spontaneity the performances show no advance on the earlier versions and in depth of feeling and understanding they do not displace the finest of the rival accounts from Menuhin (HMV ASD 346 [Sera. S 60258]), Oistrakh (DG 138 820/*923 087* [id.]) or Perlman, where there are different couplings: HMV ASD 3076 [Ang. S 37076], which includes BWV 1060 for violin and oboe; and ASD/*TC-ASD* 2783 [Ang. S/*4XS* 36841]).

Szymon Goldberg is a player of the old school, and many collectors may find him just a little too romantic in the slow movements. However, he is an artist of stature and there is no want of personality here. Technically his playing has all the old assurance, and even if there are moments that sound a little rushed and unpolished (for instance, the finale of the *Double concerto*) there is far more to admire than to cavil at. The playing of the Netherlands Chamber Orchestra is very fine and they are well recorded. Were these performances lighter in touch they would rate a two-star recommendation. As it is, the fine CfP disc (CFP 40244) by Sillito and Bean, with the Virtuosi of England under Arthur Davison, remains far more recommendable in the medium and bargain range, and it includes one of the most beautiful accounts of the slow movement of the *Double concerto* on record.

Double violin concerto in D min., BWV 1043.
(M) ** DG Priv. 2535/*3335* 176. D. and I. Oistrakh, RPO, Eugene Goossens – BRUCH: *Concerto No. 1.***

The timbres of David and Igor Oistrakh are marginally different and provide a suitable contrast in their performance of the *Double concerto*; at the same time the musical partnership of father and son is both understanding and vibrant. Goossens's accompaniment is alert and although the recording is slightly dated – the orchestral upper range is not absolutely clean – the sound remains bright and lively. However, this seems short measure for a full LP side, and the coupling is not very apt. As sometimes happens with an older recording, the cassette has a smoother upper range than the disc and is generally preferable.

Double concerto in D min. for violin and oboe, BWV 1060.
(M) *** HMV SXLP/TC-SXLP 30294 [Ang. S 36103]. Menuhin, Goossens, Bath Festival CO – HANDEL and VIVALDI: *Concertos.****

This recording dates from 1962 but wears its years lightly, although the oboe is too backwardly balanced in the outer movements. But this is a vintage performance with both Menuhin and Leon Goossens on top form. The slow movement cantilena is most beautifully played. The couplings (especially the Handel) are highly recommendable, and the cassette transfer is immaculate, matching the disc closely.

Triple concerto in A min. for flute, violin and harpsichord, BWV 1044.
*** DG Arc. 2533 410 [id./3310 410]. Preston, Standage, Pinnock, E. Concert – *Suite No. 2.***(*)

Stephen Preston and Simon Standage both use baroque instruments and there is a suitable matching harpsichord timbre. All the artists play with genuine warmth and plenty of vitality too. Tempi are well judged and there is no want of style. This concerto is derived from

borrowed material (the A minor *Prelude and fugue*, BWV 894, and the *Trio sonata*, BWV 527, both for organ) but it could not sound more persuasive than it does here.

The Musical Offering, BWV 1079.
*** Ph. 9500 585/7300 708 [id.]. ASMF, Marriner.
*(*) DG Arc. 2533/3310 422 [id.]. Col. Mus. Ant., Goebel.

Neville Marriner uses his own edition and instrumentation: strings with three solo violins, solo viola and a solo cello; a flute and organ and harpsichord. He places the three-part *Ricercar* at the beginning (scored for organ) and the six-part *Ricercar* at the very end, scored for strings. As the centrepiece comes the *Trio sonata* (flute, violin and continuo) and on either side the canons. A snag is that this arrangement requires a turn-over in the middle of the *Trio sonata*. Thurston Dart advocated playing the three-part *Ricercar* on the fortepiano (as it was probably heard in Potsdam). The actual performance here is of high quality, though some of the playing is a trifle bland. It is, however, excellently recorded and generally must be numbered among the most successful accounts of the work. The cassette is transferred at an unadventurously modest level (for such a small-scale work), but the sound is natural and smooth, with no feeling that the upper range is restricted.

There are some good things on the Archive issue. The *Ricercars* open and close the work, but, unlike Marriner and Parikian, Reinhard Goebel places the canons together and follows them with the *Trio sonata*, in which there is no sideturn. The *Ricercars* are played on the harpsichord by Henk Boum, an impressive artist who is somewhat austere in making no registration changes, but has a strong grasp of the architecture. The six-part *Ricercar* is particularly fine, and the canons are also very successful. However, the centrepiece of the *Musical*

Offering is the *Trio sonata*, and this reading is simply too mannered and self-conscious (particularly in the slow movement) to be recommended.

Orchestral suites Nos. 1–4, BWV 1066/9.

(M) *** Ph. 6768 028/*7699 165* (2) [id.] ECO, Leppard.
**(*) DG Arc. 2723 072 (2)/*3310 175* [id.]. E. Concert, Pinnock.
**(*) Ph. 6769 012 (2)/*7699 087* [id.]. ASMF, Marriner.
**(*) HM 151 99618/9. Coll. Aur.
(M) ** Tel. Ref. AQ6/*CQ4* 41228/9. VCM, Harnoncourt.
(M) *(*) DG Arc. Priv. 2547/*3347* 008 and 023. Mun. Bach O., Richter.
(B) *(*) Decca DPA 589/90 [Lon. 2206]. SCO, Münchinger.
(M) (***) World mono SHB 68 (2). Busch Chamber Players.

Suites Nos. 1 and 3.

**(*) DG Arc. 2533/*3310* 411 [id.]. E. Concert, Pinnock.

Suite No. 2 (for flute and strings).

(*) DG Arc. 2533 410 [id./*3310 410*]. Preston, E. Concert, Pinnock – *Triple concerto.**
** HMV Dig. ASD 3948 [Ang. DS/*4XS* 37330]. Wilson, LACO, Schwarz – TELEMANN: *Suite in A min.***

Suites Nos. 2–3; Cantata No. 12: Sinfonia; Cantata No. 131: Sonata.

(M) ** Decca VIV/*KVIC* 8 [Lon. STS 15541/5-]. SRO, Ansermet.

Suite No. 4.

(*) DG Arc. 2533/*3310* 440 [id.]. E. Concert, Pinnock – *Brandenburg concerto No. 5.*(*)

Leppard's exhilarating performances have never been surpassed. In this mid-priced reissue, with first-rate sound, they cannot be bettered, sparklingly played and brilliantly recorded.

Trevor Pinnock boldly encourages a more abrasive style than most in the Bach *Suites*, with string tone which within its lights is beautifully controlled, but which to the unprepared listener could well sound disagreeable, with a bright edge to the squeezed vibrato-less timbre. Any epic feeling of baroque grandeur of the kind Marriner conveys in his Argo set is minimized here. Nevertheless, with a refreshingly alert approach to each movement in turn – not least to the slow introductions, which, as one would expect, are anything but ponderous – these are invigorating performances, beautifully sprung and splendidly recorded on disc. In the *B minor Suite*, although there could be more contrast in feeling, there is no sense that reverence for supposed authenticity is stifling musical spontaneity. When these performances first appeared the couplings seemed unnecessarily complicated, but now they have been reissued as a set, with a matching double-length tape which offers all four works at what is in effect half-price. Unfortunately the transfer is made at a very low level and the substance and range are diminished.

Fine as it is, Marriner's second recording of the *Suites* is no match for his first. The movements where he has changed his mind – for example, the famous *Air* from the *Suite No. 3*, which is here ponderously slow – are almost always less convincing, and that reflects an absence of the very qualities of urgency and spontaneity which made the earlier Argo version so enjoyable. The recording is refined, but in some ways less aptly balanced than the Argo. That set remains a good choice for those not insisting on period instruments. It uses an edition by Thurston Dart which successfully achieves a balance between scholarly authenticity and what is sensible in terms of modern recreative performances. The music-making is both expressive and exuberant and the recording is first-class on both disc and tape (ZRG/*KZRC* 687/8 [id.]). The Philips cassettes have less bite and detail, and there is a moment of congestion at the opening of the *Third Suite*.

In contrast to the Pinnock set, the approach of the Collegium Aureum, also using original instruments, is comparatively expressive; the famous *Air*, for example, is restrained but not without feeling. Tempi are often similar to modern practice, although the slow introductions are not as crisply dotted and the pulse is less measured. The woodwind instruments make some delightful baroque sounds, especially in Nos. 1 and 4. With the early trumpets, however, one has to accept moments of poor intonation in the upper register. But despite any reservations this set is enjoyable for stopping short of the ruthless authenticity of Pinnock and avoiding the heavy German rhythmic pulse of Richter and Münchinger.

Harnoncourt sounds altogether more academic. His approach is clean and literal, and the acoustic of the Telefunken recording is brighter and harder than that given to the Collegium Aureum. The result is not always sweet to the ear, and the prevailing *mezzo forte* becomes monotonous. But these are livelier, more compelling performances than those of the *Brandenburgs* on the same label. Slow introductions are taken fast in allemande-style, minuets are slow and – hardest point to accept – there is no concession to expressiveness in the *Air* from *Suite No. 3*. The *Sarabande* of No. 2 may sound a little disconcerting with its use of *notes inégales*, but the *Gigue* of No. 3, and for that matter all the fast movements and the fugues, are splendidly alert. With good Telefunken recording (on disc – the cassettes are rather insecure in texture) this is preferable to the DG Archive reissue of Richter's Munich performances, even though these are more sensibly coupled so that those wanting the two more popular suites, Nos. 2 and 3, can obtain them separately on 2547/3347 008.

The late Karl Richter's way with Bach was vigorous but lacking in finer rhythmic points (he did not observe the 'double-dotting' convention in the overtures) and without charm. These are strong, generally effective performances, certainly not wanting in structural weight. The recording, dating from the mid-sixties, still sounds well. Aurèle Nicolet is the excellent flute soloist in No. 2. On tape the high-level transfers produce robust yet lively sound, but there are moments of roughness when the trumpets are playing full out in No. 3 and some sense of strain when they enter again at the opening of No. 4.

The main advantage of the Münchinger set, recorded in 1962, is economy: both discs are offered in a double sleeve for slightly less than the cost of one premium-priced LP. The performances have a somewhat heavy tread, but Münchinger's comparatively stiff beat is mitigated by the discipline and alertness of the playing. The recording is brilliant in the Decca manner and does not sound too dated. Rampal's flute playing in the *Second Suite* is first-class.

The HMV digital version of the *Second Suite* is presented as a vehicle for the flautist Ransom Wilson, which is perhaps unfair since, for all his easy stylishness, he is not on this showing a specially individual artist. The playing of the Los Angeles Chamber Orchestra, crisp enough of ensemble, is often stodgy and square. Nor is the recording outstanding, well balanced as it is. This cannot match James Galway's charismatic version (see under *Flute concertos* above), which is also very well recorded.

Ansermet's Bach is warm-hearted, not for purists but not seriously unstylish. The performances do not lack freshness, although the full body of strings tends to swamp the continuo. There is some nimble and elegant solo flute playing from André Pepin in the *B minor Suite*. The bonuses are not memorable: Roger Reversy, the oboe soloist in the *Sinfonia* from *Cantata No. 12*, is accomplished but phrases rather stiffly. The sound remains good, and there is little to choose between disc and cassette. It is surprising that this obvious coupling is not more often used.

The Busch performances come from the mid-1930s and serve as a reminder that those 'inauthentic' years have something to teach us. For all the period limitations, string portamenti, sweet-toned vibrato, piano continuo and so on, these readings have a radiance and a joy in music-making that completely transcend their sonic shortcomings – which, it is worth noting, are remarkably few given the provenance. There is a naturalness of musical expression, a marvellous musicality from Marcel Moyse, the flautist in the *B minor Suite*, and a richness of feeling on the part of all concerned that make this a special document. One wonders whether future music-lovers coming to the standard versions in our present catalogue from the vantage-point of five decades on will discover as much joy and illumination in Marriner, Münchinger, Richter and others as we can in the Adolf Busch Chamber Players.

Still recommended: The recording by Marriner and the ASMF on Argo (see above) an excellent recommendation.

There is also available at bargain price (Contour CC/*CCT* 7504) an admirable performance of the *Second Suite*, nimbly played by Claude Monteux, with his father, Pierre, at the rostrum. It is coupled with Gluck's *Dance of the Blessed Spirits* and a stylish account of Mozart's *Second Flute concerto*. The recording is excellent if a little over-rich in texture. The cassette is muddy in the bass.

CHAMBER AND INSTRUMENTAL MUSIC

(Unaccompanied) *Cello suites Nos. 1-6, BWV 1007/12.*
(M) *** Ph. 6770 005 (3) [id. *7650 012*]. Gendron.
*(*) Ar. Eur. 25403 XDK (3). Mainardi.

No one artist holds all the secrets in this repertoire, but few succeed in producing such consistent beauty of tone as Maurice Gendron. He has, of course, the advantage of an excellent and truthful recording. His phrasing is unfailingly musical, and although Roger Fiske, writing in the *Gramophone*, spoke of the sobriety of these readings (save for No. 6, which he thought stunning), their restraint and fine judgement command admiration. They do not displace Tortelier (HMV SLS 798) or Fournier (DG 198186/8 [id.]) but can certainly be recommended alongside them, particularly as the recorded sound is so natural and vivid. The surfaces, too, are quite impeccable. No one has come near to the depth and imagination shown by Casals in his pre-war pioneering set, now transferred to mono LP and very much in a class of its own (HMV RLS 712).

Enrico Mainardi's set was made in Berlin in 1963-4, when the great cellist was in his late sixties. There is the refined well-spun tone and the aristocratic sense of line that give unfailing pleasure, and there is no want of musical depth. Unfortunately the problems of intonation that beset him in post-war years and the absence of a robust rhythmic drive in some of the faster movements diminish the success of this set, and the sound is not as vivid and realistic as one would expect in modern rivals.

Guitar transcriptions: *Prelude in C min., BWV 999; Prelude, fugue and allegro in E flat, BWV 998; Lute suite No. 1 in E min., BWV 996: Sarabande in E min. Unaccompanied violin sonata No. 1 in G min., BWV 1001: Fugue in A min. Partita No. 1 in B min., BWV 1002: Sarabande and Double. Partita No. 2 in D min., BWV 1004: Chaconne.*
(B) *** Con. CC/*CCT* 7519. Yepes.

Those who enjoy Bach on the guitar will find this a distinguished and enjoyable recital. Narciso Yepes is on top form and brings all the music to life compellingly, without romantic exaggeration. The programme includes the famous *Chaconne*, which is splendidly projected here. The sound is first-class, and the cassette transfer has only marginally less life at the top than the disc.

Lute suites Nos. 1 in E min., BWV 996; 2 in C min., BWV 997. Trio sonatas Nos. 1 in E flat, BWV 525; 5 in C, BWV 529 (ed. Bream). *Fugue in A* (trans. from BWV 1001); *Prelude in C min.* (trans. D min.), *BWV 999.*
**(*) RCA RL 42378 (2) [(d) LSC 2896]. Bream, Malcolm.

This compilation comes from records made in the late 1960s. The first record includes two of the *Lute suites*, played with great subtlety and mastery on the guitar; the second contains arrangements for lute and harpsichord of the *Trio sonatas in E flat* and *C* for organ. One may prefer the latter on the original instrument, but these transcriptions still give pleasure, for they are elegantly played and crisply recorded. Perhaps the harpsichord is a little less well defined in the bass register than is ideal.

Trio sonatas Nos. 1–4, BWV 1036/9.
*** DG Arc. 2533 448. Col. Mus. Ant.

Polished accounts of all four pieces. The *G major Sonata* is thought by some authorities to be a student work by Carl Philipp Emanuel Bach, and the *C major*, BWV 1037, is likewise variously attributed to Bach and to his pupil Johann Gottlieb Goldberg. However, the *G major*, BWV 1039, is indisputably by Bach, but the *D minor* is again probably by Wilhelm Friedemann or Carl Philipp Emanuel. In any event, these are lively and eminently well-recorded accounts that can be confidently recommended. No other disc currently on the market assembles all four together.

Trio sonatas Nos. 3 and 4 in G, BWV 1038/9; The Musical Offering, BWV 1079: Trio sonata in C.
*** RCA RL/RK 25280. Galway, Kyung-Wha Chung, Moll, Welsh.

With two such individual artists as Galway and Chung, both given to highly personal expressiveness, you might expect their Bach to be too wilful, but not so. These are refreshing performances of the two *Trio sonatas* with flute and of the comparable sonata from *The Musical Offering*, which some may even count slightly understated. The recording is fresh and clean on disc and cassette alike.

Trio sonata No. 4, BWV 1039.
*** O-L DSLO 518 [id.]. Preston, McGegan, Ryan, Pleeth, Hogwood – C. P. E. BACH: *Trio sonata ***; W. F. BACH: *Duo* etc.**

The *Trio sonata in G major* is probably better known in its alternative form for viola da gamba and continuo. Stephen Preston and Nicholas McGegan, playing period instruments, leave one in no doubt as to its expressive power, particularly in the chromatic lines of the slow movement. They are excellently recorded, and C. P. E. Bach's *E major Trio sonata* is a valuable coupling.

Viola da gamba sonatas Nos. 1–3, BWV 1027/9.
(M) *** HM HM 22225. Kuijken, Leonhardt.
(M) *(*) Ph. 9502 003 [id.]. Cervera, Puyana.

The three sonatas for viola da gamba and harpsichord come from Bach's Cöthen period, and the G minor is arguably the highest peak in this particular literature. Wieland Kuijken and Gustav Leonhardt are both sensitive and scholarly, their tempi well judged and their artistry in good evidence. Their phrasing is finely shaped and natural, and there is no sense of the relentless flow that can so often impair the faster movements. The slow movement of the G minor is very slow but the tempo obviously springs from musical conviction and as a result *feels* right. This is the best account of these sonatas to have appeared on the market for some years, and the recorded sound is faithful; it may be too immediate for some tastes, but adjustment of the controls gives a satisfactory result.

The performances by Marcel Cervera and Rafael Puyana are much less attractive. These works need cleaner, more stylish playing if they are not to sound muddy and dull. The recording in this mid-priced Philips reissue does not help.

Violin and harpsichord sonatas Nos. 1–6, BWV 1014/9.

*** HM 1C 151 99820/1. Kuijken, Leonhardt.

Sigiswald Kuijken uses a baroque violin, and both he and Gustav Leonhardt give us playing of rare eloquence. This issue is an admirable instance of the claims of authenticity and musical feeling pulling together rather than apart. The violinist does not shrink from an intelligent use of vibrato, and both artists demonstrate in every bar that scholarship is at their service and not an inhibiting task-master. As so often from this source, the harpsichord is extremely well recorded and the texture is lighter and cleaner than in many issues of this repertoire. This version is unlikely to be superseded for a very long time.

(Unaccompanied) *Violin sonatas Nos. 1–3, BWV 1001, 1003 and 1005; Violin partitas Nos. 1–3, BWV 1002, 1004 and 1006.*

*** Ph. 6703 076 (3). Accardo.
**(*) Ph. 6770 950 (2). Ayo.
* Ph. 6769/7654 053 (3). Kremer.

Salvatore Accardo gives us an impressive survey of this music, one which makes a useful alternative to those of other master violinists. In terms of both artistry and musicianship, he is hardly to be faulted, and he has, of course, an effortless virtuosity with which to realize his conception of each of these pieces. Phrasing is marvellously alive and sensitive, and there is no trace of mannerism or mere display. He is beautifully recorded by the Philips engineers. This version does not displace Milstein's set (see below), but can be recommended alongside it.

Like Accardo, Felix Ayo was closely associated with the famous I Musici and is also renowned for his purity of intonation and fine musicianship, both of which are in evidence here. He produces beautiful sound and playing of much feeling (the occasional ugliness in double stopping is the only blemish). Although the readings are unmannered, they are far from wanting in personality, and they have the advantage of very good sound. Perhaps they lack the stature of Milstein's readings but they have the merit of economy, being accommodated on two discs, as well as the inconvenience of side-turns in two of the pieces.

Gidon Kremer is an impressive player and there are no doubts about the sheer facility and accuracy of his readings, nor the technical excellence of the recordings. But he conveys little sense of musical enjoyment, dispatching the faster movements with an unfeeling and joyless brilliance. There is also an aggressive edge to his double-stopping and a general want of imagination in matters of phrasing. The discs are excellently produced and include a reproduction of the autograph MS. All the same, this set gives only limited pleasure. The layout on two cassettes, against three discs, is ill-conceived, as works are split between sides. The high-level transfer gives the violin presence, although there is a degree of fierceness on the first tape (especially on side two).

1

Reminder: Milstein's set is available on disc (DG 2709 047 [id.]) and in an immaculately transferred cassette box (*3371 030*).

Keyboard music

(All played on the harpsichord unless otherwise stated)

The Art of Fugue, BWV 1080.
*** HM 1C 165 99793/4. Leonhardt.

Versions of *The Art of Fugue* in instrumental transcriptions of various kinds as well as on the organ have not been rare, but harpsichord performances are few. Gustav Leonhardt argues most convincingly in the leaflet accompanying this set that a 'glance at the compass of the alto voice (down to B, second octave below middle C) in the first twelve fugues suffices to make sure that none of Bach's nevertheless richly varied ensemble groups can be used for the *Art of Fugue*'. The notation of polyphonic textures in full as opposed to short score was common in the seventeenth and eighteenth centuries (and even as early as 1580), and it has only been in the twentieth century that musicians have taken *The Art of Fugue* as 'ensemble music'. Leonhardt uses a copy by Martin Skowroneck of a Dulcken harpsichord of 1745, a responsive and beautiful instrument. Convincing though Leonhardt's scholarly essay is, it is his playing that clinches the truth of his musical argument. Every strand in the texture emerges with clarity and every phrase is allowed to speak for itself. In the 12th and 18th fugues Leonhardt is joined by Bob van Asperen. The great Dutch artist-scholar argues that from the 'unsustained instruments with keyboard range larger than four octaves, the harpsichord claims first place in *The Art of Fugue* (Bach left five harpsichords and no clavichord on his death), though organ and clavichord are not to be totally excluded, especially for certain pieces'.

Leonhardt does not include the unfinished fugue, but that will be the only reservation to cross the minds of most listeners. This is a very impressive and rewarding set, well recorded and produced.

Capriccio in B flat (on the departure of a beloved brother), BWV 992; Chromatic fantasia and fugue in D min., BWV 903; Fantasia in C min., BWV 906; Italian concerto in F, BWV 971; Toccata in G, BWV 916.
(M) ** DG Arc. 2547/3347 031. Kirkpatrick.

Ralph Kirkpatrick is a scholar of international repute and a fine musician, with a strong rhythmic grip and a highly developed sense of style. Here he plays a modern Neupert harpsichord and uses it to maximum effect in the *Chromatic fantasia*, with an impressive increase in tension at the climax of the fugue. The *Toccata* (from Bach's Weimar period) also brings well-realized opportunities for bravura. The *Capriccio*, BWV 992, is in essence a six-movement miniature suite with programmatic implications. It includes an engaging 'departure' section, with a posthorn motif implanted in the texture which Kirkpatrick plays with a nice rhythmic point. Elsewhere he sounds more pedantic, and the *Italian concerto* is frankly dull. The recordings date from the late 50s/early 60s and have considerable clarity and presence (the cassette transfer is bold and clear, matching the disc closely). Some ears might prefer a rather more recessed balance.

Chaconne (from *Violin partita No. 2*, BWV 1004, arr. Busoni).
*** RCA RL/*RK* 13342 [ARL/*A RK* 13342]. Rubinstein (piano) – FRANCK: *Prelude, chorale and fugue*; MOZART: *Rondo.****

Busoni's arrangement of the celebrated *Chaconne* for solo violin is a piece which has to be presented with flair as virtuoso piano music, and Rubinstein is an ideal choice of pianist. He recorded this performance in Rome in 1970, when he was already in his eighties, but the freshness and spirit are a delight. The recording is clangy but not unpleasantly so. The cassette reflects the disc in producing rather dry piano timbre but it has a wide dynamic range. With excellent couplings this is a highly recommendable issue.

Chorale prelude: Beloved Jesu, BWV 731; Chorale: Sanctify us (from Cantata No. 22), BWV 219 (both arr. Cohen).
*** Decca SXL/*KSXC* 6865 [Lon. 7085]. Larrocha (piano) – MOZART: *Piano sonatas.****

Alicia de Larrocha uses Bach as a prelude to her Mozart recital. The arrangements by Harriet Cohen are admirable, and they are played with fine sensibility and undemonstrative eloquence. The style is pianistic, far from rigid rhythmically, and the effect is wholly satisfying. The recording is first-class, and the transfer to tape loses little or nothing of the excellence of the disc.

Chromatic fantasia and fugue in D min., BWV 903; Fantasia in C min., BWV 906; Prelude and fugue in A min., BWV 894; Toccatas Nos. 1 in F sharp min., BWV 910; 3 in D, BWV 912.
** DG Arc. 2533 402 [id./*3310 402*]. Pinnock.

As in the companion record of *Toccatas*, Trevor Pinnock's sense of style is matched by his technical expertise. Sometimes his approach is rather literal, but at others he allows himself more expressive latitude. The playing is always rhythmically alive, but the close recording of the harpsichord and the high level combine to create a somewhat unrelentless dynamic, without a great deal of light and shade.

English suites Nos. 1–6, BWV 806/ 11; French suites Nos. 1–6, BWV 812/17.
*** Ph. 6709 500 (5). Leonhardt.

These performances are likely to remain unsurpassed for a long time. Gustav Leonhardt combines scholarship and artistry, and his learning never seems to inhibit his natural musical instincts. In the *English suites* he uses a Skowroneck harpsichord and in the *French* a Rubio based on Taskin; both are vividly captured on record, even if the discs are cut at a rather high level. This is an important issue, even though Leonhardt is not equally inspired in every movement. He is inconsistent in matters of repeats, sometimes observing them in both halves, sometimes only in one, sometimes not at all. He also shows an expansiveness and an expressive range which are refreshing.

English suites Nos. 1–6.
*** HM HM 1074/5. Gilbert.

Kenneth Gilbert uses a Couchet-Taskin of 1788 and is given a first-class recording. His playing has a fine sense of style, the rubato flowing naturally and never self-conscious, the ornamentation nicely judged. He is inconsistent in the matter of repeats, but this may be due to the desire to fit the six suites economically on to four sides. As the price is slightly lower than the premium range, this is excellent value, particularly as the recording itself is so realistic.

English suite No. 2 in A min., BWV 807; Partita No. 2 in C min., BWV 826; Toccata in C min., BWV 911.
*** DG 2531/*3301* 088 [id.]. Argerich (piano).

It is good to see Bach returning to the piano after more than two decades when pianists have tended to leave this repertoire to their harpsichord colleagues. One critic thought this style 'too dated for any but the most reactionary of Bach lovers'; so expectations of a genuine musical experience are naturally aroused. Martha Argerich does not disappoint: her playing is alive, keenly rhythmic but wonderfully flexible and rich in colour. There is none of the didacticism that marks Tureck, and her finger control is no less impressive. The textures are always varied and clean, and there is an intellectual and musical vitality here that is refreshing. Moreover Miss Argerich is beautifully recorded on both disc and cassette.

French suites Nos. 1–6, BWV 812/17.
(M) **(*) Decca Ser. SA/KSC 5. Dart (clavichord).

By cutting the repeats Thurston Dart managed to get all six suites on to a single medium-priced LP. The choice of the clavichord for works of this scale is questionable, as its tiny voice has a restricted range of timbre as well as dynamic. But Dart's playing is impeccable in style and has plenty of spontaneity. The balance tends to make the intimate clavichord image larger than life, but if the volume is cut well back a truthful image can be obtained. The admirable cassette transfer is ideal in this respect, as at the level necessary for faithful reproduction there is virtually no background noise.

French suite No. 5 in G, BWV 816;
Italian concerto in F, BWV 971;
Partita No. 7 in B min., BWV 831.
(M) *** Decca Ace SDD 564. Schiff (piano).

Andras Schiff belongs to the school of young Hungarian pianists that includes Zoltan Kocsis and Dezsö Ránki, and, judging from this Bach recital, he is fully

their equal. In addition to producing a wide range of keyboard colour, he is scrupulous in his observance of the correct conventions in the interpretation of Bach, and in this respect compares favourably with many harpsichordists. His playing is musically alive and imaginative: indeed, the *Italian concerto* is arguably the finest available on either harpsichord or piano, and the whole programme is an outstanding success. This was Schiff's first solo record on a UK label and will surely not be his last. The sound is very good indeed: the recording emanates from Japan.

Goldberg variations, BWV 988.
*** HM 1C 065 99710. Leonhardt.
*** DG Arc. 2533/3310 425 [id.]. Pinnock.
(M) **(*) DG Arc. Priv. 2547/3347 050 [198020]. Kirkpatrick.

Goldberg variations; Aria and variations in the Italian style, BWV 989.
*(*) CBS 79220 (2) [Col. M2 35900]. Tureck.

The great Dutch harpsichordist Gustav Leonhardt has recorded the *Goldberg* three times, and his last version, though the most beautifully recorded, will not necessarily enjoy universal appeal. This is an introvert and searching performance, at times very free rhythmically – indeed almost mannered. The *Black Pearl* variation is a case in point; but the reading is so thoughtful that no one can fail to find some illumination from it. His instrument is a Dowd copy of a Blanchet and tuned a semitone flat, as opposed to the Skowroneck copy of a Dulcken at our present-day pitch he used in his 1967 record (Tel. AW 6.41198). The sound is altogether mellower and more appealing, and though no repeats are observed, this version is fresher and more personal than his Das Alte Werk record.

Trevor Pinnock uses a Ruckers dating from 1646, modified over a century later by Taskin and restored most recently in 1968 by Hubert Bédard. He retains repeats in more than half the variations, which seems a good compromise in that variety is maintained yet there is no necessity for a third side. The playing is eminently vital and intelligent, with alert, finely articulated rhythm. If tempi are generally brisk, there are few with which listeners are likely to quarrel, and Pinnock shows himself flexible and imaginative in the inward-looking variations such as No. 25. The recording is very truthful and vivid, though it benefits from a slightly lower level setting than usual. In any event this can be recommended alongside Leonhardt's Harmonia Mundi version. Martin Galling's Turnabout record (TVS 34015) makes an excellent medium-priced recommendation.

Ralph Kirkpatrick's recording comes from the late 1950s and on its first appearance the *Stereo Record Guide* found it impressive: Kirkpatrick 'delights in light and subtle registration, and the music benefits both in clarity and colour ... the playing is lively where it should be, controlled and steady in the slow, stately, contrapuntal variations'. It also sounds extremely fresh in spite of the passage of time. Generally speaking, the account he gives sounds less pedantic than some of his other Bach records of this period. Kirkpatrick is a scholarly rather than an intuitive player and his thoughts are rarely without interest. Though not a first choice, this version is still worth considering, particularly as it has a price advantage over so many of its rivals. The cassette transfer is first-class, softer in treble outline than the LP, but wholly natural.

Rosalyn Tureck recorded the *Goldberg variations* on the piano in the 1950s in a fine mono set of two LPs. She is no stranger to the harpsichord and has been an exponent for the bulk of her concert career even though she is identified in the public mind with Bach on the piano. This issue offers admirably recorded sound

and undoubtedly repays study, but even though many of the variations have a natural lyrical flow and nearly all have some felicity, the reading is not free from self-consciousness and pedantry. Ultimately this is heavy going for all except the most dedicated of Tureck's admirers. A set that one would rather praise than play.

Italian concerto in F, BWV 571; Partita in B min., BWV 831.
(M) **(*) HMV SXLP/TC-SXLP 30416. Tureck (piano).
(M) *(*) HMV HQS 1392 [Ang. S 36096]. Kipnis.

Elegant and fastidious playing from Rosalyn Tureck that exhibits remarkable control of colour and masterly articulation. The recording was made in the early 1960s and is less fresh and vivid than recent piano records. The instrument has one or two tired notes in the *B minor Partita*, but these reservations should not seriously detract from the pleasure these immaculately played readings give. At times one feels Miss Tureck is drawing attention to her own remarkable pianism, and none of these performances is wholly free from traces of self-consciousness. The first movement of the *Italian concerto* is certainly on the slow side. But on the whole this is an impressive example of her art. The cassette transfer has been made at a high level and the sound is full and bold, if not especially crisp.

Igor Kipnis plays all the repeats in the *Partita*, so his performance spreads over to a second side. He decorates the repeats except in the *Sarabande*, which he regards as already decorated, playing it the first time round in a simplified form of his own. He does miss some points (the slurs over some phrases indicating in the eyes of most scholars equal notes) and is not always consistent in observing *notes inégales*. In both the *Partita* and the *Italian concerto* the instrument sounds very resonant. The playing has great vitality, but this would not be a first rec-ommendation in either work.

Partitas Nos. 1–6, BWV 825/30.
*** HM 1C 151 99840/2. Leonhardt.

This set was not conceived as an entity but recorded over a longish period (1964–71). The *Second Partita* is heard at today's pitch, the others are recorded a semitone lower, and there are some variations of quality in the recordings of different partitas. Nevertheless, these are searching and often profound readings. There are occasional exaggerations (the *Allemande* of the *First Suite*) and some of the dotted rhythms are over-emphatic – or stiff might be a better expression. Yet this still remains an impressive achievement, for the thoughts of this scholar-musician are always illuminating and his artistry compels admiration.

Toccatas Nos. 1 in F sharp min.; 3 in D; 4 in D min., BWV 910, 912/13.
*(*) CBS 76881 [Col. M/MT 35144]. Gould (piano).

Toccatas Nos. 2 in C min.; 4 in D min.; 5 in E min.; 6 in G min.; 7 in G, BWV 911, 913/16.
** DG Arc. 2533 403 [id.]. Pinnock.

Toccatas Nos. 2 and 5–7.
** CBS 76984/41- [Col. M/MT 35831]. Gould (piano). ·

Trevor Pinnock is a highly gifted artist and brings to this repertoire both scholarship and technical prowess. Rhythms are alive, and there are times when he almost seems relentless. Yet there are moments of great expressive freedom, and the rhapsodic quality of the slow sections in the *Toccatas* is vividly brought to life. Unfortunately pleasure is diminished by the rather close recorded sound, cut at too high a level and rather unrelieved in range.

Glenn Gould's first set combines the most fastidious and remarkable pianism with some impulsive, not to say wilful, touches. Though the playing is of the highest distinction, the actual piano tone is not, and the poor recorded sound plus the tiresome vocalise on which this artist seems to insist somewhat dampen one's enthusiasm for this release. In the second set there is some impressive playing, with contrapuntal strands being beautifully balanced and clarified. The recording is rather wanting in depth and colour (on disc and chrome cassette alike), but that is not unusual from this label.

The Well-tempered Clavier (48 Preludes and fugues), BMV 846/893.
** DG Arc. 2723 054 (5) [2714 004]. Walcha.
(M) ** HM HM 20309/13. Leonhardt.
(M) *(*) Saga mono 5132/6. Cole (piano).
(M) *(*) CBS 77427 (4). Gould (piano).

No single survey of *The Well-tempered Clavier* is likely to give universal satisfaction throughout all the *Forty-eight*. Walcha recorded them earlier on EMI's short-lived Baroque label (HQS 1042–7), but these are a good deal more satisfactory, even though traces of pedantry can still be found. This reading first appeared as part of the DG Archive Bach Edition in the mid-1970s: Book I is recorded on a restored Ruckers and Book II on a Hemsch. There is no question of the great German organist's keyboard mastery and his wonderful sense of control. He is at his best in those preludes and fugues that do not call for any vein of poetic feeling, for textures are unfolded with compelling clarity and impressive command of detail. There is an intellectual rigour that is undeniably imposing but he is at times somewhat inflexible (for example, in the *Prelude in B flat,* Book I) and rarely permits imagination and fantasy to take full wing in the more contemplative pieces. However, the overall picture is positive and he is excellently recorded.

Gustav Leonhardt also chooses the

harpsichord for the *Forty-eight*, playing a copy of a Taskin by David Rubio for Book I and an instrument of Martin Skowroneck for Book II. It must be said straight away that the attractions of this issue are much diminished by the quality of the recorded sound. Both instruments are closely balanced and even when the volume is reduced the perspective seems unnatural, as if one were leaning into the instrument itself. Tastes in matters of 'registration' are bound to differ, but there is little with which to quarrel and much to admire. This distinguished player and scholar possesses both the effortless technique and the musical insights that are required, and even if there are moments that seem a trifle pedantic – the *C sharp major Fugue* of Book II is rather 'spelt out' – this version offers more rewarding interpretative insights than most of the currently available rivals. Were the sound more sympathetic and appealing, this would be a first recommendation, for Leonhardt combines scholarship, technique and sensibility in no small measure.

Saga have reissued, at medium price, Maurice Cole's mono set from the early sixties. These thoughtful, musicianly accounts have served us well at the bargain end of the catalogue for many years. The surfaces are now impeccable and the sound quality appears to have been improved. At the same time it must be conceded that the acoustic is dry and the piano tone wanting a little in both freshness and timbre. This, alas, limits their appeal even though students will inevitably find much to learn from Maurice Cole's playing. For all its merits this reissue seems expensive when one remembers that on its first appearance the complete set (at ten shillings per disc) would have cost less than one record from the reissue at present-day prices.

Glenn Gould is highly eccentric but undoubtedly a master pianist. There is ample evidence of his finger dexterity and control of touch on these discs. Unfortunately the unappealing tone quality of the recording diminishes the value of this issue, and it must be recognized that Mr Gould's interpretations will not command undivided admiration.

The Well-tempered Clavier, Book I: Nos. 4, BWV 849; 9–13, BWV 854/ 8; Book II: Nos. 3, BWV 872; 6–7, BWV 875/6; 15, BWV 884; 24, BWV 893.
*** DG *2531/3301* 299 [id.]. Kempff (piano).

The great German pianist follows his earlier recital (DG *2530/3300* 807, still available) with another that is hardly less remarkable. The sleeve mentions that Kempff regards the preludes and fugues of the *Wohltemperierte Clavier* as poetic creations, no different in this respect from the piano sonatas of Beethoven', and that belief illumines every page of this anthology. Played like this, Bach is a joyful and compelling master, far removed from the relentless plod favoured by some harpsichordists. Though Kempff is well into his eighties, his intellectual vigour, technical command and musical feeling seem totally unimpaired. The sound is truthful and clear, and everyone who cares about Bach and piano playing should investigate this issue.

Organ music

Allabreve in D, BWV 589; Canzone in D min., BWV 588; Chorale preludes Nos. 1–45 (Orgelbüchlein), BWV 599/644; 6 Schübler chorale preludes, BWV 645/50; Chorales, BWV 690, 691, 706, 709, 711, 714, 731, 738; Chorale fughettas, BWV 696/9, 701, 703/4; Fugues: in C min., BWV 575; in G; in G min.; in B min., BWV 577/9; Pastorale in F, BWV 590; Preludes and fugues, BWV 536, 541, 543/8.

(M) ** HM HM 523 (6). Rogg (Silbermann organ, Arlesheim).

This is the least attractive of Lionel Rogg's three boxes of Bach's organ music recorded at Arlesheim. As in the other sets the recording is generally consistent in its body and clarity (though the *Preludes in C major and minor*, BWV 545/6, each have a hint of congestion at their openings). Rogg lays out the music with reliable clarity and structural control. His registration is apt if conventional; often one feels that he could have been more imaginative in this respect, especially in the *Orgelbüchlein*. There is the occasional exception: *In dulci jubilo* has striking colour and the *Pastorale* which opens the first disc is no less effective. But so often the playing seems too circumspect. Try the opening Schübler choral (*Wachet auf*), which is curiously stiff. During the *Preludes and fugues* the listener's concentration is tempted to falter, as the music is allowed to unfold with no attempt to increase or vary the basically low level of tension.

Allabreve in D, BWV 589; Canonic variations on Vom Himmel hoch, BWV 769; Chorale partita: Sei gegrüsset, Jesu gütig, BWV 768; Chorale preludes, BWV 726, 728/32, 735, 737; 6 Schübler chorale preludes, BWV 645/50; Concerto No. 6 in E flat, BWV 597; Fugue in B min., BWV 579; Preludes and fugues, BWV 544/5; Sonatas Nos. 1 in E flat, BWV 525; 3 in D min., BWV 527; Trio in D min., BWV 588.

⊕ (M) *** Argo D 150 D 3/*K 150 K 32* [id.]. Hurford (Wolff/Casavant organ, Our Lady of Sorrows, Toronto; Sharp organ of Knox Grammar School, Sydney, Australia; Grant, Degens and Bradbeer organ, New College, Oxford; Dutch organ, Eton College).

We award a symbolic rosette to this, the third (as released) of Peter Hurford's recital-styled collections in a projected complete recording of Bach's organ music for Argo. Hurford's approach is in its way as revolutionary in gramophone terms as Dorati's reappraisal of the Haydn *Symphonies* or the musical adventures of the Academy of Ancient Music in the baroque world (including the symphonies of Mozart). Hurford's playing has a comparable freshness. Rather than adhere to the German tradition, which favours sober registration and lets Bach's musical argument unfold in a controlled, sometimes tensionless manner to let the fugal detail register as clearly as the acoustic will allow, Hurford takes an almost orchestral approach, seeking to bring out all the music's colour and emotional resource. He uses several organs in each programme, grouping the pieces to match the character of each (often with uncanny aptness), and he receives consistent support from the Argo recording engineers. They provide superb sound, which has weight and where necessary a sense of spectacle and grandeur, yet always reveals inner detail with remarkable transparency. Moreover the cassettes match the discs closely and are a demonstration of the amazing breadth and range of recording possible when the boundaries of transferring technology are pressed to their limit.

This third box is exceptionally attractive; indeed it could well make a starting-point for a beginner in this repertoire. The choice of organs is characteristically imaginative and Hurford's registration gives endless pleasure. The *Sei gegrüsset* variations are a model of Bach exposition, cool yet never dull; the *Schübler chorales* are splendidly done, with the most remarkable variety of colour; and at the end of the recital the *Sonata in D minor*, BWV 527, with its deliciously dazzling finale, and the *E flat Concerto*, BWV 597, are no less engaging. The superb recording handles the closing section of the *Partita* (BWV 768) with impressive freedom and weight. On cassette, for some reason, the bass seems over-emphasized in the opening *Schübler chorale*, which is at the beginning of side three (there are two cassettes instead of three discs, which seems no great advantage); but elsewhere the sound balance, on tape and disc alike, is first-class.

Aria, BWV 587; Canzone in D min., BWV 588; Chorale variations: Ach, was soll ich Sünder machen; Allein Gott in der Höh' sei Ehr', BWV 770/71; Fantasias: in C min., BWV 562; in G, BWV 571; Fugue in C min. on a theme of Legrenzi, BWV 574; Fugues: in G, BWV 576; in G min., BWV 578; Passacaglia and fugue in C min., BWV 582; Pastorale in F, BWV 590; Pedal-Exercitium, BWV 598; Preludes: in A min., BWV 569; in C, BWV 567; Preludes and fugues: in C min.; in C, BWV 546/7; Trio in G, BWV 1027a.
(M) *** Argo D 177 D 3/*K 177 K 32* [id.]. Hurford.

In Volume 4 of his series Peter Hurford uses three organs, chosen with characteristic skill to show the music to its best advantage. The superb recording lets every detail register and gives each instrument an individual character so that the actual sound quality, whether on discs or cassettes (which are quite free from intermodulatory congestion), is consistently pleasing. The first collection uses the organ of Melk Abbey, Austria, and Hurford's registration in the serene *Pastorale*, BWV 590, is matched by the piquancy of colour he finds in the *Fantasia in G major*, with its effective use of light and shade. In the *Chorale variations* on *Ach, was soll*, BWV 770, Hurford keeps the melody firmly in front of the listener and at the same time achieves an almost orchestral variety in his characterization. The division between groups of pieces and the organs on which they are played is made using six sides on disc and (less attractively) four on tape.

Recital two was recorded in the cathedral of St Poulten (also in Austria), and its highlights include a splendid account of the *Fugue in G minor*, BWV 578, played with great spontaneity and clarity, and a powerful and strongly rhythmic *Canzone in D minor*. After the deliciously registered lightweight *Trio in G*, BWV 1027a, there is a massive contrast with the granite-hewn *Prelude and fugue in C minor*, BWV 546. The third section includes a major set of variations on the Trinity hymn *Allein Gott in der Höh'*, with a highly imaginative variety of treatments (Hurford omits Variations 3 and 8 as being unsuitable for organ, rather than keyboard), and closes with a masterly account of the famous *Passacaglia and fugue in C minor*, played with a tough cumulative force, yet with every detail clear. (On cassette this is one of the most impressive demonstrations of transferring technology in the entire series.) The third organ is a Canadian instrument in Toronto already used in Volume 3 (see above); heard alongside the Austrian instruments it proves to be every bit their equal in this repertoire. Overall this set contains many rarities which are often ignored, and many of them are very rewarding.

Canonic variations on Vom Himmel hoch, BWV 769; Chorale fantasias and variations, BWV 720, 727, 734, 736/7; 18 Leipzig chorale preludes, BWV 651/8; Chorale partitas, BWV 766/7; Fantasias: in C min., BWV 562; in G, BWV 572; Fugue on the Magnificat, BWV 722; Preludes and fugues; in C, BWV 531; in C min., BWV 549; in D, BWV 532; in D min., BWV 539; in E min., BWV 533; in F min., BWV 534; in G, BWV 550; in G min., BWV 535; Toccata and fugue in E, BWV 566; Trio in D min., BWV 583.
(M) **(*) HM HM 522 (6). Rogg (Silbermann organ, Arlesheim).

Rogg is at his very best in the Arnstadt *Preludes and fugues*, early works of great character which inspire performances of communicating vigour. In the chorales too his clear registration, with the theme kept unexaggeratedly to the fore, gives pleasure, but as so often with Rogg's performances the listener is inclined – in the Leipzig set in particular – to reflect that a more flamboyant approach would not be out of place. Some of the other large-scale works sound very pedantic, the approach measured and apparently uninvolved. Yet everything is beautifully clear and controlled, and those who do not seek conscious bravura and an extrovert style in this music should be well satisfied with the recorded sound, which is first-class. So are the pressings, but the accompanying booklet is in French.

Chorale partita: Christ, der du bist, BWV 766; Chorale preludes, BWV 715, 720, 722, 738; Concertos Nos. 3 in C, BWV 594; 5 in D min., BWV 596; Fantasias and fugues: in C, BWV 570 and 946; in C min., BWV 537; in G, BWV 577; Kleines harmonisches Labyrinth, BWV 591; 8 Short Preludes and fugues, BWV 553/60; Preludes and fugues: in D, BWV 532; in F min., BWV 534; Sonata No. 6 in G, BWV 530; Toccatas and fugues: in D min., BWV 538 (Dorian) and 565; Trio in G min., BWV 584.
(M) *** Argo D 207 D 3/K 207 K 33 [id.]. Hurford.

In Volume 5 Argo have sensibly reverted to a three-cassette layout, to match the discs. The recital opens with an arresting account of the powerful *Prelude and fugue in D*, which shows the spectacular range of the organ of Ratzeburg Cathedral in West Germany. This instrument is no less effective in the most famous of all Bach's organ works, the *Toccata and fugue in D minor*, BWV 565.

Opening with a superbly rhythmic flourish Hurford makes effective use of spatial and dynamic contrast, and the exhilaratingly paced fugue brings a suggestion of orchestral colour that recalls Stokowski's famous transcription in Disney's *Fantasia*. The *Sonata in G* shows a similar orchestral feeling; the attractive *Concerto*, BWV 596, after Vivaldi, and the fascinatingly titled *Kleines harmonisches Labyrinth* evoke an appropriately less extrovert style and again demonstrate Hurford's apt colouristic registration. These are both played on the Toronto organ, which was used to great effect in Volumes 3 and 4 of the series, and this instrument proves also a perfect choice for the *Eight Short Preludes and fugues*, BWV 553/60, presented with appealing simplicity, and the captivating *Fugue à la gigue*, BWV 577, which is irresistibly gay and buoyant. The way Hurford keeps all the music alive and constantly engages the ear with the sounds he creates (in the mellow *Fantasia in C*, for instance) continues to recommend this series above other Bach organ issues. The sound is first-class whether one chooses cassettes or discs. (There is just a hint of roughness at the opening of the *Prelude*, BWV 532, on the first tape, but it lasts for a few bars only and is of little consequence. Careless editing, however, has divided the booklet accompanying the cassettes into 'record' sides.)

Chorale partita: Sei gegrüsset, Jesu gütig, BWV 768; Chorale variations: Vom Himmel hoch, BWV 769; 6 Schübler chorale preludes, BWV 645/50.
** DG Arc. 2533 350. Walcha (organ of St-Pierre-le-Jeune, Strasbourg).

This recital is selected from Walcha's integral recording made at the beginning of the seventies. The playing is calm, assured and literal. Its control is never in doubt, but the *Schübler chorales* sound characteristically straitlaced and entirely lacking in charm. The recording is first-class. There is no doubt about the sense of authority conveyed by this record, but many listeners will find Walcha's approach rather stiff and unsmiling.

Chorale partita: Sei gegrüsset, Jesu gütig, BWV 768; Passacaglia in C min., BWV 582; Toccata and fugue in D min. (Dorian), BWV 538.
* DG Arc. 2533 441. Karl Richter (Silbermann organ, Freiburg Cath.).

This is not one of Karl Richter's more impressive organ records. The organ itself is not always very comfortably recorded: the upper range is grainy and some of the mixtures sound harsh. The overall sound is sometimes not entirely clean. The performances are competent but never inspiring: the tension in the *Passacaglia* seems to come and go, and the *Choral partita* (which is clumsily split between sides) lacks imaginative flair.

Choral preludes: Alle Menschen müssen sterben, BWV 643; Vater unser im Himmelreich, BWV 737; Fantasia and fugue in G min., BWV 542; Passacaglia and fugue in C min., BWV 582; Toccata in F, BWV 540.
**(*) Telarc Dig. DG 10049. Michael Murray (organ at Methuen Memorial Hall, Mass.).

The sound here is first-class, of course, though not more impressive and certainly not clearer than Peter Hurford's analogue Argo records. The acoustic is fairly reverberant, and this is an organ obviously intended by its builders to produce a wide panoply of sound rather than crystal-clear inner detail. It reproduces naturally and one feels the engineers have not sought spectacle for its own sake. The most impressive performance is of the *Passacaglia and fugue in C minor*, well paced and powerful. The two chorale preludes are effective, but

Michael Murray's approach to the *Fantasia and fugue* and *Toccata* is rather measured and pedantic. But he clearly understands the structure of all this music.

Chorale preludes, BWV 717, 725 (Te Deum), 739/41, 747, 755, 758, 765; Herr Christ, der einig Gottes-Sohn, Ahn. 55; Fugue in C min., BWV 575; Preludes and fugues: in A min., BWV 551; in C, BWV 531; in C min., BWV 549 and 575; in E min., BWV 548; in G, BWV 550; in G min., BWV 535; Sonata No. 2 in C min., BWV 526; Toccata, adagio and fugue in C, BWV 564; Trio in C min., BWV 585.
(M) *** Argo D 226 D 3/K 226 K 33 (3) [id.]. Hurford (organs of Ratzeburg Cath.; Our Lady of Sorrows, Toronto; Eton College).

Peter Hurford opens Volume 6 of his series with a massively unrelenting performance of the *Toccata and fugue in F* and then makes a suitable contrast with the lighter-textured *Sonata in C minor*. Highlights of this set include a splendid, dashing account of the *G major Prelude and fugue*, BWV 550, and a superb version of the *Toccata, adagio and fugue in C*, powerful yet relaxed. Elsewhere the playing is more deliberate than usual, notably so in the *A minor* and *G minor Preludes and fugues*, which come together on side five. The clear, unforced momentum reminds one of Lionel Rogg and in the spacious *Te Deum* setting (*Herr Gott, dich loben wir*) Hurford seems almost overawed by the religious implications of the music. The chorale preludes gathered together to close the recital are beautifully registered; every strand of texture is transparently clear. The recording of the three organs is up to the high standards of the series, on disc and tape alike. However, the otherwise admirable booklet with the tapes does not make it clear how the programme is divided among the instruments used. As in volume 5, the tape layout matches the discs.

Chorale preludes: Ach bleib' bei uns, BWV 649; Liebster Jesu, BWV 731; O Mensch, bewein, BWV 622; Wachet auf, BWV 645; Fantasia in G, BWV 572; Fugue in E flat (St Anne), BWV 552; Prelude and fugue in C, BWV 545; Toccata and fugue in D min., BWV 565.
(M) **(*) HMV Green. ESD/TC-ESD 7090. Rawsthorne (organ of Liverpool Cath.).

Those who like their Bach on a really big organ, with a distinctly non-baroque flavour, will find that Noel Rawsthorne's performances have plenty of vigour, and they are effectively registered too, especially the better-known chorale preludes. The two larger works have the right balance of momentum and controlled tension, and although the sound has a sense of spectacle, inner detail is seldom blurred. As sheer sound this is undoubtedly exciting. The tape transfer is impressive too and uncongested, except for slight closing cadential disturbances in BWV 545 and 565.

Chorale prelude: In dir ist Freude, BWV 615; Fantasia in G, BWV 572; Fugue in G min., BWV 578; Pedal-exercitium in G min., BWV 598; Prelude and fugue in B min., BWV 544; Toccata, adagio and fugue in C, BWV 564.
*** RCA RL/RK 25369. Curley (organ of Vangede Church, Copenhagen).

Carlo Curley is better-known for more flamboyant repertoire, but here, playing a magnificent Frobenius organ, he shows himself a first-class advocate of Bach's organ music. The performances throughout are tingling with life and colour. They have strength and character too – as the splendid *Toccato, adagio and fugue*

readily shows – but above all they communicate, and this is essentially a record for the non-organ specialist. There is even humour in the choice of registration for *In dir ist Freude* (a demonstration item), while the bravura at the opening and close of the *Fantasia in G major* is breathtaking. No less impressive is the control of detail and momentum of the *Fugue in G minor*. This is a very enjoyable and highly recommendable disc, and the cassette too is brilliantly transferred (indeed a slight tempering of the treble is useful on side two) and is clear and undistorted.

Chorale preludes: Kommst du nun, Jesu, BWV 650; Wachet auf, BWV 645; Fantasia and fugue in G min., BWV 542; Prelude and fugue in E flat, BWV 552; Toccata and fugue in D min., BWV 565.
(M) *** DG Priv. 2535/3335 611. Karl Richter (organ of Jaegersborg Church, Copenhagen).

This compilation, taken from recordings made in 1964 and 1967, represents Richter's Bach playing at its finest. The performance of the famous *Toccata and fugue in D minor* is outstanding, matching weight with vigour, and splendidly paced, while the other pieces are presented spontaneously and with a deceptive simplicity that disguises the underlying control. The *E flat Prelude and fugue*, which uses a very famous hymn for its fugal subject, is brought off especially well. The recording of the Danish organ is superb; it sounds slightly more reedy on disc than on tape, but both are of demonstration quality, with the pedal opening of BWV 542 caught without a ripple of distortion.

Chorale preludes and variations, BWV 690/713, 727, 734, 736; Concertos Nos. 1 in G; 2 in A min., BWV 592/3; Fantasia in G, BWV 572; Fantasia and fugue in G min., BWV 542; Preludes and fugues: in A, BWV

37

536; in E min., BWV 533; in G, BWV 541; Trio sonatas Nos. 4 in E min.; 5 in C, BWV 528/9.
(M) *** Argo D 120 D 3/K 120 K 33 [id.]. Hurford.

This was the first box to be issued in Peter Hurford's projected complete recording of Bach's organ music. It set the standards for the series by combining lively and engrossing performances – giving the listener the impression of hearing the music for the first time – and first-class recording. The layout (over either three discs or two cassettes) presents the various works intermixed, recital-style. Thus instead of (for instance) placing all the *Preludes and fugues* together they are separated by groups of chorales, and the *Trio sonatas* and transcribed solo *Concertos* are fitted within the overall scheme to enhance the stylistic contrast. It works well. Two different modern organs are used: for most of the programme Hurford plays on the Casavant instrument at the Church of Our Lady of Sorrows, Toronto, but in two of the *Preludes and fugues*, one of the *Concertos*, the *Trio sonatas* and certain of the *Chorales* he changes to the Ronald Sharp organ at Knox Grammar School, Sydney. Both instruments produce sound that is internally clear yet has admirable baroque colouring. Indeed the piquancy of the registration, often reedily robust in the *Chorales*, is a constant source of delight. The playing itself is fresh, vigorous and imaginative throughout, but the bigger set pieces have no want of breadth. Hurford's technical control is never in doubt, and a concern to bring the music to tingling life is the overriding feature of his interpretations. The recording is clean and sparkling, the sound never weighted down by puddingy bass, yet there is no lack of range at the bottom end. (On tape the resonance in the pedals may be very slightly reduced in the interest of preventing cross-modulation effects, but never enough to spoil the overall balance.)

Clavierübung, Part 3 (German organ Mass: Prelude and fugue in E flat, BWV 552; 9 Arrangements of the Kyrie and Gloria, BWV 669/77; 12 Arrangements of Catechism hymns, BWV 678/89); Chorale preludes, BWV 710/13, 718; Chorale variations, BWV 717 and 740; Fantasias and fugues; in C min., BWV 536; in G min., BWV 542; Passacaglia and fugue in C min., BWV 582; Toccatas and fugues: in D min., BWV 538 and 565; in F, BWV 540; Toccata, adagio and fugue in C, BWV 564; Trio sonatas Nos. 1–6, BWV 525/30.
(M) **(*) HM HM 521 (6). Rogg (Silbermann organ, Arlesheim).

Like the other two Harmonia Mundi albums in Lionel Rogg's second integral recording, this music is superbly recorded and the pressings are immaculate. The first disc opens with the *Passacaglia and fugue in C minor*, and Rogg's grave, indeed sombre mood immediately establishes his seriousness of purpose. The music is laid before the listener in the simplest manner; there is no conscious bravura, and the tension is held at a comparatively low level. In the so-called *German organ Mass*, where one might have expected a more expressive style, Rogg is content to let the music speak for itself. He does not seek to achieve a cumulative emotional force, even at the end of the fugues. The variety of the registration is impressive, but even in the chorales there is never any suggestion of using colour for its own sake. As in the companion issues, the accompanying booklet is in French.

Clavierübung, Part 3 (German organ Mass); Chorale preludes and variations, BWV 714, 716, 719, 721, 723/4; Fantasia in B min., BWV 563; Fugue on the Magnificat, BWV 733; Prelude and fugue in A min., BWV

543; Toccata and fugue in E (C), BWV 566.

(M) *** Argo D 138 D 3/*K 138 K 32* [id.]. Hurford (organs of New College Chapel, Oxford; Knox Grammar School, Sydney, Australia).

Peter Hurford's performance of the so-called *Organ Mass* is uncompromisingly sober. The music itself is essentially severe, with powerful contrasts made between weight and serenity. Hurford's account makes concessions only in the choice of registrations, which give colour to the expressive writing and lively detail to the more complex polyphony. The opening *Prelude* is massively presented and the *Fugue* is no less forceful, the two pieces making a kind of bracket to enclose the twenty-five diverse inner movements. The use of two different organs successfully adds variety of texture. We are then offered three major works to round off the recital; the closing *Prelude and fugue in A minor* is especially compelling. The sound is first-class; on tape one or two cadential climaxes have momentary hints of congestion, but never for more than a bar or two.

Fantasias and fugues: in C min., BWV 537; in G min., BWV 542; Passacaglia and fugue in C min., BWV 582; Toccata and fugue in D min., BWV 565.

(M) ** HM HM 771. Rogg (Silbermann organ, Arlesheim).

An excellent sampler of Rogg's literal way with Bach and of the fine recording of the Arlesheim organ. The playing is assured and strong, but rather pedantic; the two *Preludes and fugues* are very literal indeed.

Fantasia in G, BWV 572; Passacaglia in C min., BWV 582; Toccata, adagio and fugue in C, BWV 564; Trio sonata No. 1 in E flat, BWV 525.

(M) *** Argo ZK 10. Weir (organ of St Lawrence Church, Rotterdam).

By the side of Peter Hurford on the same label, Gillian Weir is less flamboyant, less ripe in her feeling for colour. Her registration in the slow movement of the *Trio sonata* is engagingly cool and in complete accord with the clear poised playing. The bravura in the *Fantasia in G* cannot escape the listener, yet there is no sense of the virtuosity being flaunted, and in consequence the closing pages are somewhat withdrawn in feeling. The remorseless tread of the *Passacaglia in C minor* is immensely compelling, and the companion *Toccata, adagio and fugue* is hardly less telling in its sense of controlled power. The recording of this characterful Dutch organ is marvellous, clear with a dry sparkle at the top, yet with a full resonant bass that never clouds the texture. An outstanding recital.

Fantasia in G, BWV 572; Pastorale in F, BWV 590; Trio sonatas Nos. 3 in D min., BWV 527; 6 in G, BWV 530.

(M) ** Tel. AQ6/CQ4 41142. Karl Richter (Schnitger organ of Ludgeri Church, Norden, E. Friesland).

The *Fantasia* sounds magnificent on the Ludgeri Church organ, and Richter creates a thrillingly registered sound. But in the two *Trio sonatas* he is unsmiling and conveys little charm. The *Pastorale* again impresses by the colouring Richter chooses; but it is a pity that the playing throughout this recital sounds so studied. The cassette transfer is first-class, bright and clean, yet with plenty of weight too.

Fantasia in G, BWV 572; Preludes and fugues: in C, BWV 545; in C min.; in G, BWV 549/50; in G min., BWV 535; Toccata and fugue in D min., BWV 565.

(M) *** Ph. Fest. 6570/7310 118. Rübsam (organ of Frauenfeld, Switzerland).

A splendid collection of early works, nearly all dating from Bach's Arnstadt and Weimar periods and full of exuberance of spirit. The *Fugue in G*, BWV 550, is especially memorable, but undoubtedly the highlight of the recital is the superb performance of the *Fantasia in G*. It opens with an exhilarating *Très vitement* and after a massive *Grave* middle section comes a brilliantly lightweight bravura finale. Wolfgang Rübsam's articulation is deliciously pointed. The recording of the Metzler organ has a fairly long reverberation period, and Rübsam anticipates this in his playing most successfully. The quality of the recorded sound is splendid, on tape as well as disc. Highly recommended.

Fantasia and fugue in G min., BWV 542; Passacaglia and fugue in C min., BWV 582; Toccata, adagio and fugue in C, BWV 564; Toccata and fugue in D min., BWV 565.
(M) *** HMV SXLP/TC-SXLP 30274. Germani (organ of the Royal Festival Hall, London).

This HMV reissue shows how well suited is the Festival Hall organ to stereo recording. Its 8,000 pipes are widely spread, and while there is only a suggestion here of point source in the sound, one can enjoy the impression of music originating from different sections of a broad area. •The acoustic too means that the quality of the sound itself is clear, yet full-blooded. The performances are first-class. The listener can hear every detail of the registration, and Fernando Germani's control of tension skilfully lets each fugue slowly build itself to an impressive climax. This especially applies to the *Passacaglia and fugue in C minor*, a riveting performance. The tape transfer is generally successful but has patches of congestion at cadential climaxes, notably at the culmination of BWV 564.

Fantasia and fugue in G min., BWV 542; Passacaglia and fugue in C min., BWV 582; Toccatas and fugues in D min., BWV 538 (Dorian) and 565.
(M) **(*) DG Arc. Priv. 2547/3347 011. Walcha (organ of St Laurenskerk, Alkmaar).

Lucid, well-controlled performances, beautifully laid out and effectively if soberly registered, but somewhat lacking in tension. The recording is first-class on disc, marginally less clean on tape, but fully acceptable.

(i) *18 Leipzig Chorale preludes, BWV 651/68. Chorale partita: O Gott, du frommer Gott; Chorale variations: Christ lag in Todesbanden, BWV 718; Concerto No. 4 in C, BWV 595; Fantasia and fugue in A min., BWV 561; Fugues: in G, BWV 580/1; in G min., BWV 131a; Prelude in G, BWV 568; Prelude and fugue in G min., BWV 539; Trio in G, BWV 586.*
(M) **(*) Argo D 227 D 3/K 227 K 33(3). Hurford, (i) with Alban Singers.

For two thirds of the content of Volume 7 of Peter Hurford's series, Argo have returned to his 1976 integral recording of the *Leipzig Chorale preludes*, where each of the organ performances is preceded by an admirably expressive (and often very beautiful) sung version of the chorale by the Alban Singers. The chorale preludes are played on the excellent Rieger organ of All Souls Unitarian Church, Washington, DC. The playing is impressive, but slightly less telling than the performances we have come to take for granted in this series. Tempi are sometimes relaxed, and the use of a tremolando stop with a rather wide beat will not appeal to all tastes. The alternation of voices and organ is highly effective, although the organ recording is not quite as crisp in focus as the later recordings.

This is readily demonstrated when for sides five and six Peter Hurford returns to the organs of Our Lady of Sorrows, Toronto, and Eton College, Windsor, where the sound is as crisp as the playing is buoyant. As usual the tape and disc quality is virtually identical.

6 *Schübler chorale preludes, BWV 645/50; Fantasia in C min., BWV 562; Fugue on the Magnificat, BWV 773; Passacaglia in C min., BWV 582.*
(M) ** Ph. Fest. 6570/7310 069. Rübsam (organ of Frauenfeld, Switzerland).

This collection opens with an exceptionally successful account of the *Passacaglia in C minor*, and the *Fantasia in C minor* and the *Fugue on the Magnificat* are strongly played too. However, in the *Schübler chorales* Wolfgang Rübsam is much more circumspect, and his registration is not nearly as imaginative as Simon Preston's (see above). The recording is of high quality and the cassette transfer first-class.

6 *Schübler chorale preludes, BWV 645/50; Pastorale in F, BWV 590; Prelude and fugue in B min., BWV 544.*
** Abbey LPB 760. Lumsden (organ of New College, Oxford).

A fine, musicianly account of the *Schübler chorales*, well contrasted in colour and expertly recorded. The tempi throughout are finely judged, though the registration in the *Pastorale*, BWV 590, could perhaps have been more varied. It is difficult to fault this playing, for David Lumsden is a distinguished musician; but at the same time it must be said that there are more compelling accounts of the *B minor Prelude and fugue* on the market. Good recording.

VOCAL AND CHORAL MUSIC

Cantatas

Sinfonias from Cantatas Nos. 29, 35, 49, 146, 169, 188.
** Erato STU 71116. Alain, Paillard CO, Paillard.

This interesting record is a programme of concerto movements for organ and orchestra culled from various cantatas. The sinfonia from Cantata No. 29 is a transcription of the *Prelude* from the *E major Partita for solo violin*; the one from Cantata No. 35 reconstructs the *D minor Concerto*, BWV 1059, with the organ instead of harpsichord as soloist. The second side is an organ version of the great *D minor Harpsichord concerto*, using the first two movements of Cantata No. 146 and the first of No. 188. The performances are generally of good quality (the organ is of the church of St-Donat in south-east France) and though greater polish would not come amiss from the orchestra, there is little to quarrel with. The recording is well-balanced and lively, and the programme amounts to more than a mere compilation of popular cantata movements.

Cantatas Nos. 5, 26, 38, 70, 80, 96, 115, 116, 130, 139, 140, 180.
*** DG Arc. 2722 030 (6). Mathis, Schmidt, Schreier, Fischer-Dieskau, Mun. Bach Ch. and O., Karl Richter.

This box collects cantatas that Bach composed for the last ten Sundays of Trinity, plus two others, a Reformation Festival piece (No. 80) and a cantata for St Michael's Day (No. 130). Most of these cantatas are chorale-based, and nearly all emerge with the dignity and majesty that one expects from these forces. Karl Richter's heavy tread seems over the years to have moderated into a more flexible and human gait, though a certain inflexibility and lack of imagination still surface occasionally. There are some odd touches: for example, the flute replaces the *flauto piccolo* in the opening of No. 96, thus diminishing the brilliance of the morning star apostrophized in the text. Richter also opted for the trumpets and drums in *Ein' feste Burg* (No. 80), which these days are thought to have been added by Wilhelm Friedemann Bach. Yet the attractions of this survey far outweigh any reservations. There is a vision and breadth to offset the Teutonic heaviness, and the solo singing is a welcome change from the boys who in the rival complete set try so manfully to cope with the cruelly demanding soprano parts. Fischer-Dieskau is perhaps too blustery at times but there are some splendid things from him too, and Edith Mathis is altogether excellent. The recordings are on the whole good, although, as in other issues in this series, the sound is often less than distinguished in tutti. On the whole, though, there is clarity and spaciousness enough to match this music, so much of which is little-known to the average listener.

Cantatas Nos. 9, 17, 27, 33, 100, 102, 105, 137, 148, 178–9, 187.
*** DG Arc. 2722 028 (6). Mathis, Hamari, Schreier, Fischer-Dieskau, Mun. Bach Ch. and O., Karl Richter.

This volume continues the 'unauthentic' series by Karl Richter and his Munich forces, and it forms a most welcome alternative to the Harnoncourt–Leonhardt cantata series on Telefunken. The chorus is probably larger than it should be, but the results are invariably musical, and Richter shows greater flexibility and imagination than has often been the case. The heavy Teutonic feeling has not entirely disappeared, but so much of this set is first-rate that reservations can be overruled. The soloists are thoroughly dependable, although Fischer-Dieskau is not on his best form. This issue

collects cantatas written for the middle Sundays after Trinity and includes half a dozen that are not otherwise available on record. Whatever one's feelings about 'authentic' Bach or one's reservations about Richter, these performances bring to life a great deal of inspired music that should enjoy the widest currency and the strongest appeal. Recordings are uniformly good, even though one would welcome a slightly more recessed balance.

Cantatas Nos. 11: Lobet Gott in seinen Reichen; 34: O ewiges Feuer.
**(*) HMV ASD/*TC-ASD* 4055. Marshall, Hodgson, Hill, Roberts, King's College Ch., ECO, Ledger.

Apart from boys' voices, the forces used here are traditional. In No. 11 (sometimes known as the *Ascension oratorio*) we encounter the theme Bach was to use later in the *Agnus Dei* of the *B minor Mass*. The solo singing is often impressive, though it could have been more prominently balanced (particularly Martyn Hill in *O ewiges Feuer*). Philip Ledger breaks up the phrases in the *Ach bleibe doch, mein Liebstes leben* in a way that draws attention to itself and inhibits the music's sweep and dignity. But there is some excellent singing and playing in the choruses, and though we have heard more compelling accounts of both cantatas this makes an attractive coupling, with a vivid cassette that matches the disc fairly closely.

Cantatas Nos. 11: Lobet Gott in seinen Reichen; 58: Ach Gott, wie manches Herzeleid; 78: Jesu, der du meine Seele; 198: Lass, Fürstin, lass noch einen Strahl (Funeral).
**(*) Erato STU 71099 (2). Girod, Elwes, Ihara, Huttenlocher, Lausanne Chamber Vocal Ens. and O., Corbóz.

The finest cantata here is the so-called Funeral cantata, *Lass, Fürstin*, written for the memorial service to the Princess Christiane Eberhardine, Electress of Saxony and Queen of Poland. Corbóz and his Swiss forces bring a fresh approach to bear, though their interpretation does not eclipse memories of the Jürgens account from the late 1960s, and the recording is not so transparent as the earlier Telefunken. There are some odd details, for instance discrepancies in note values (the choir singing in even notes while the accompaniment is dotted), and the contralto aria is wanting in real intensity. However, there are good things too. The performance of *Lobet Gott* is first-class, and the overall effect, in spite of the less than well-focused detail, is fresh and pleasing.

Cantata No. 30: Freue dich, erlöste Schar.
**(*) DG Arc. 2533 330 [id./3310 330].
Mathis, Reynolds, Schreier, Fischer-Dieskau, Mun. Bach Ch. and O., Karl Richter.

This cantata, written for the Feast of John the Baptist, is a larger-scale work of some forty minutes' duration. It is thought to be an expansion of the cantata *Angenehmes Widerau* (BWV 30a), composed in 1737 for the Feast of St John (24 June) the following year or perhaps a year or two later. The most impressive things here are the two arias of Fischer-Dieskau, but there is a great deal elsewhere that will give pleasure too. The trumpets and drums in the opening and closing chorus are inclined to be brash rather than noble (they are omitted in the Harnoncourt set), and the recording could be smoother. The choruses never approach distortion but the quality could with advantage be more transparent and clean. This is a splendid work and although Richter is a shade heavy-handed he conducts with sympathy. The cassette version is not available in the UK.

Cantatas Nos. 36: Schwingt freudig euch empor; 209: Non sa che sia dolore.
*** DG Arc. 2533 453 [id.]. Mathis, Schreier, Lorenz, Berlin Soloists, Berlin CO, Schreier.

Two secular cantatas in excellent performances. *Schwingt freudig euch empor* (BWV 36c) was written as a birthday cantata for a distinguished academician in Leipzig in 1725. Bach thought sufficiently highly of it to make no fewer than five versions of its material, two of them for church purposes and two other to celebrate birthdays or name-days. It is scored for chamber forces, and Peter Schreier secures light and clean playing. The companion cantata, *Non sa che sia dolore*, also written to celebrate a man of learning, is earlier than was previously thought: recent scholarship dates it from Weimar in 1714, and its Italianate character lends force to this view. It finds Edith Mathis in altogether excellent form throughout, and this version is to be preferred to Ewerhardt's or the Leonhardt set made in the early 1970s.

Cantatas Nos. 53: Schlage doch, gewünschte Stunde; 54: Widerstehe doch der Sünde; 169: Gott soll allein mein Herze haben.
* Erato STU 71161. Finnilä, Paillard CO, Paillard.

The best thing here is the performance of *Gott soll allein*, which finds Birgit Finnilä in good voice. Cantata No. 53 is not authentic, but it is a charming enough piece, if charm is the appropriate term for a funeral aria! Unfortunately the orchestral playing is not really distinguished, and string intonation in *Widerstehe doch der Sünde* is decidedly vulnerable. Here there is no organ continuo, though it is, of course, present in No. 169, whose sinfonia is familiar as the first movement of the *Harpsichord concerto in E*.

Cantatas Nos. (i) *65: Sie werden aus Saba alle kommen;* (ii) *66: Erfreut euch, ihr Herzen; 67: Halt' im Gedächtnis Jesum Christ;* (i) *68: Also hat Gott die Welt geliebt.*
*** Tel. EX 5. 35335 (2) [id.]. (i) Jelosits, Equiluz, Van der Meer, Tölz Ch., VCM, Harnoncourt; (ii) Esswood, Equiluz, Van Egmond, Hanover Boys' Ch., Ghent Coll. Vocale, Leonhardt Cons., Leonhardt.

This admirable enterprise, which got under way in the early 1970s during the life of the first *Penguin Stereo Record Guide*, continues to enrich the catalogue, and whatever qualifications one may make, it maintains a consistent and dedicated approach to the greatest repertory of its kind. Briefly, the series aims at the highest authenticity in terms of performance practice, observing the accepted conventions of the period and using authentic instruments or replicas. Boys replace women not only in the choruses but also as soloists, and the size of the musical forces is confined to what we know Bach himself would have expected. Naturally, the absence of famous soloists in the soprano roles will be regretted by many collectors; these can be found in alternative versions by Karl Richter and others. There are advantages in escaping from the sheer beauty of the glamorous celebrities in rival sets, for the imperfect yet other-worldly quality some of the boy soloists possess serves to focus interest on the music itself rather than on the voices. Less appealing perhaps is the quality of the violins, which eschew vibrato – and it would sometimes seem any kind of timbre! Each of the two-record volumes contains copious documentation: the texts of the cantatas in English and French translations, scholarly notes and copies of the scores either in the old Bach Gesellschaft editions or, where available, the Neue-BGG scores. It is probably true to say that the series has grown in strength over the past two or three years, and much of the self-conscious, slightly

inhibited flavour of the earliest sets has gone. Although in most cases we would not wish to see the Leonhardt and Harnoncourt versions as the only recordings in the field, they have so much to recommend them that nearly all the newcomers reviewed here should be investigated by everyone who has the means and inclinations to do so.

The best thing in this volume is Leonhardt's broad and spacious account of No. 66, which also offers some stunning playing on the natural trumpet. Harnoncourt's versions of Nos. 65 and 68 are a little wanting in charm and poetry (the dialogue between the voice of Christ and the chorus in No. 67 is also prosaic). But there is fine solo singing, and that and the instrumental playing outweigh other considerations. The recording too is well-focused and clean.

Cantatas Nos. 69 and 69a: Lobe den Herrn, meine Seele; 70: Wachet, betet; 71: Gott ist mein König; 72: Alles nur nach Gottes Willen.
*** Tel. EX 6.35340 (2) [id.]. Equiluz, Van der Meer, Visser, Tölz Ch., VCM, Harnoncourt.

Gott ist mein König, No. 71, is the earliest cantata of this set, dating from 1708 and written for the inauguration of the Mühlhausen town council. It is the only Bach cantata to have been printed during his lifetime and is an enchanting piece, full of invention and variety. This set also includes both versions of Cantata 69, *Lobe den Herrn, meine Seele*. Originally written for one of the town council election services in Bach's first year at Leipzig, it was adapted in 1730 and new material was added; only the numbers which differ or are new are re-recorded in this set. No. 72 employs more modest forces than the others and is an Epiphany cantata dating from 1726. Wilhelm Wiedl is the excellent treble throughout, and the other soloists and instrumentalists cannot be too highly praised. The choral singing is not above criticism but is still more than acceptable. Excellent recorded sound.

Cantatas Nos. 73: Herr, wie du willst; 74: Wer mich liebet; 75: Die Elenden sollen essen.
** Tel. EX 6.35341 (2) [id.]. Erler, Klein, Esswood, Equiluz, Kraus, Egmond, Hanover Boys' Ch., Ghent Coll. Vocale, Leonhardt Cons., Leonhardt.

All three of these cantatas come from the period 1723–5; Die Elenden sollen essen, No. 75, was the one Bach chose for his inaugural composition at St Nicholas's Church in Leipzig in 1723. No. 73 is an Epiphany piece written in the following year and has some strikingly original invention. No. 74 is a cantata for Whit Sunday, the second of two with this title. The merits of the Telefunken series are well enough established but some of its weaknesses emerge here: some sedate and really rather weak choral work and a reluctance to permit 'expressive' singing deprive the music of some of its cloquence, and the boy trebles, though possessed of musical and pleasing voices, are not fully equal to Bach's taxing writing. However, none of these cantatas is otherwise available, and the music really is worth getting to know.

Cantatas Nos. (i) 76: Die Himmel erzählen die Ehre Gottes; (ii) 77: Du sollst Gott, deinen Herrn, lieben; (i) 78: Jesu, der du meine Seele; (ii) 79: Gott, der Herr, ist Sonn' und Schild.
**(*) Tel. EX 6.35362 (2) [id.]. Esswood, (i) Wiedl, Equiluz, Van der Meer, Tölz Ch., VCM, Harnoncourt; (ii) Bratschke, Krauss, Van Egmond, Hanover Boys' Ch., Leonhardt Cons., Leonhardt.

Two of these cantatas are not otherwise available at present and all four are of outstanding interest. As always in authentic performances one is aware of constraints, and the ear longs for the bolder colours and greater power of modern instruments. However, there is too much good music here for such reservations to worry us for long. Two of the cantatas (77 and 79) are given by Gustav Leonhardt and sound excellent. There is some superb playing from Don Smithers in Du sollst Gott, deinen Herrn, lieben and some beautifully pure singing from the boy treble, Detlef Bratschke. The Harnoncourt performances are a little less satisfying and one feels the want of grandeur in the opening of No. 78 (Jesu, der du meine Seele), but again there are too many things to admire for small reservations to weigh too much in the balance. The quality of sound is very good indeed.

Cantatas Nos. 80: Ein' feste Burg; 81: Jesus schläft; 82: Ich habe genug; 83: Erfreute Zeit.
*(*) Tel. EX 6.35363 (2) [id.]. V. Boys' Ch. treble soloists, Esswood, Equiluz, Van Egmond, Huttenlocher, Van der Meer, Ch. Viennensis, Tölz Ch., VCM, Harnoncourt.

This is one of the less successful issues in the Telefunken series. Ich habe genug has been performed more impressively on other recordings, and Philippe Huttenlocher, though intelligent and thoughtful, is not always secure. Some of the choral singing elsewhere in this volume could do with more polish and incisiveness too. Ein' feste Burg is given minus the trumpets and drums thought to have been added by Wilhelm Friedemann, and here the gain in textural clarity is considerable. The singing of the treble is excellent in this cantata. No. 83 is an older recording, dating from the late 1960s; No. 81 is more impressive instrumentally than vocally. As all these cantatas are available in other versions, this set has less strong claims than its immediate neighbours in the series.

Those collecting the whole series will know what to expect.

Cantatas Nos. 80: Ein' feste Burg; 140: Wachet auf.
(M) ** DG Arc. Priv. 2547/*3347* 024 [198407/*924* 007]. Giebel, Töpper, Schreier, Adam, Leipzig Thomanerchor and GO, Mauersberger.

Serviceable rather than distinguished accounts of these two well-known cantatas. *Ein' feste Burg* is performed without the trumpets and drums of Wilhelm Friedemann, but with harpsichord rather than organ continuo. The recordings were made in the mid-1960s in Bach's own St Thomas's, Leipzig. Boys are used in the choruses; their intonation is not perfect. The solo singing is predictably good, and the recording has admirable clarity and definition. But Rudolf Mauersberger does not bring the highest sensitivity to bear on the phrasing, and some of the obbligati are routine. There is enough here to warrant a recommendation at medium price, but the qualifications should be noted. The tape transfer is fresh and clear, with good choral focus, although the level is rather low on side two (No. 140).

(i) *Cantata No. 80: Ein' feste Burg;* (ii) Motet: *Jesu, meine Freude.*
(M) Turn. TVS 37113. (i) Fahberg, Bence, Maier, Schaible, Ch., Württemberg CO, Rilling; (ii) Stuttgart Bach Ch. and Hymnuschorknaben, Gerhard.

These performances originally appeared in the early 1960s. Although Helmuth Rilling is a fine conductor with many admirable Bach cantata records to his credit, this version of *Ein' feste Burg* has little to recommend it; the tempi are slow. and the readings heavy-handed. Nor is *Jesu, meine Freude* much better, and there is some off-pitch singing to boot. Emphatically no stars.

Cantatas Nos. 82: Ich habe genug; 169: Gott soll allein mein Herze haben.
(M) *** HMV SXLP/*TC-SXLP* 30289 [Ang. S 36419]. Baker, Amb. S., Bath Festival O., Menuhin.

Ich habe genug is one of the best-known of Bach's cantatas, while No. 169 is a comparative rarity. The performances are expressive and intelligent, though Dame Janet Baker does not achieve quite the same heights of inspiration here as in her Oiseau-Lyre record of No. 159. Recording is admirably lifelike and reproduces smoothly. The tape transfer too is immaculate, clean and clear, with a natural bloom on the voice.

Cantatas Nos. (i) *84: Ich bin vergnügt; 85: Ich bin ein guter Hirt; 86: Wahrlich, wahrlich, ich sage euch; 87: Bisher habt ihr nichts gebeten in meinem Namen;* (ii) *88: Siehe, ich will viel Fischer aussenden; 89: Was soll ich aus dir machen; 90: Es reifet euch ein schrecklich Ende.*
** Tel. EX. 6.35364 (2) [id.]. Esswood, Equiluz, (i) Wiedl, Van der Meer, Tölz Ch., VCM, Harnoncourt; (ii) Klein, Van Egmond, Hanover Boys' Ch., Ghent Coll. Vocale, Leonhardt Cons., Leonhardt.

On the first record Harnoncourt directs polished but often uncommitted performances, though there is brave singing from the treble Wilhelm Wiedl in some cruelly demanding solo writing (*Ich bin vergnügt*). Leonhardt's performances are more effectively characterized, and there is some particularly fine obbligato trumpet playing from Don Smithers and eloquent singing from Max van Egmond. If the performances are of variable quality, the musical inspiration is not, and the set is worth acquiring for the sake of this neglected music, much of which is otherwise unobtainable.

Cantatas Nos. (i) *91: Gelobet seist du, Jesus Christ; 92: Ich hab' in Gottes Herz und Sinn;* (ii) *93: Wer nur den lieben Gott lässt walten; 94: Was frag' ich nach der Welt.*
*** Tel. EX 6.35441 (2) [id.]. Esswood, Equiluz, (i) Bratschke, Van Egmond, Hanover Boys' Ch., Ghent Coll. Vocale, Leonhardt Cons., Leonhardt; (ii) Wiedl, Van der Meer, Huttenlocher, Tölz Ch., VCM, Harnoncourt.

One of the most desirable of these Bach sets, with assured and confident playing from all concerned. Two of the cantatas (Nos. 91 and 94) are not otherwise available; the other two are included in Richter's surveys (see above). The cantatas, though not among Bach's greatest, include some marvellous and neglected music.

Cantatas Nos. (i) *95: Christus, der ist mein Leben; 96: Herr Christ, der ein'ge Gottessohn; 97: In allen meinen Taten;* (ii) *98: Was Gott tut.*
*** Tel. EX 6.35442 (2) [id.]. (i) Wiedl, Esswood, Equiluz, Huttenlocher, Van der Meer, Tölz Ch., VCM, Harnoncourt; (iv) Lengert, Equiluz, Esswood, Van Egmond, Hanover Boys' Ch., Ghent Coll. Vocale, Leonhardt Cons., Leonhardt.

Apart from No. 96, which is included in Richter's set of cantatas for the last ten Sundays after Trinity, these cantatas are not otherwise represented in the current catalogue. There are occasional weaknesses here (Philippe Huttenlocher is not altogether happy in No. 96), but the set is still well worth having. Harnoncourt is more stylistically assured and polished than Richter and the opening chorus is more imaginatively handled here. No. 95, on the theme of imminent death and the soul's departure from earth, is a wonderful piece, full of striking invention, and it fares excellently in these artists' hands.

Cantatas Nos. (i) *99: Was Gott tut;* (ii) *100: Was Gott tut;* (i) *101: Nimm von uns, Herr; 102: Herr, deine Augen sehen nach dem Glauben.*
** Tel. EX 6.35443 (2) [id.]. (i) Wiedl, Esswood, Equiluz, Huttenlocher, Tölz Ch., VCM, Harnoncourt; (ii) Bratschke, Esswood, Equiluz, Van Egmond, Hanover Boys' Ch., Ghent Coll. Vocale, Leonhardt Con., Leonhardt.

With this album Telefunken come to the twenty-fifth volume of the cantatas and pass the century! This is no mean achievement, and though inevitably there is unevenness in the series, it is still one of the triumphs of the recording industry. In this volume, Cantata No. 99 fares less well than the others, and the boy soloist, Wilhelm Wiedl, is not his usual self; nor is the Tölz choir at its most positive. Greater expressive intensity would not have come amiss in the chorus of No. 101, but it would be curmudgeonly to dwell on the shortcomings of this box – or of the series as a whole, for it serves to introduce collectors to unfamiliar works. Cantatas Nos. 100 and 102 are included in Richter's set; Nos. 99 and 101 are not available otherwise.

Cantatas Nos. (i; ii) *103. Ihr werdet weinen und heulen;* (iii; iv) *104: Du Hirte Israel, höre;* (v; vi) *105: Herr, gehe nicht ins Gericht;* (vi; ii) *106: Gottes Zeit (Actus tragicus).*
*** Tel. EX 6.35558 (2). (i) Esswood, Equiluz, Van Egmond; (ii) Hanover Boys' Ch., Coll. Vocale, Leonhardt Cons., Leonhardt; (iii) Esswood, Huttenlocher; (iv) Tölz Boys' Ch., VCM, Harnoncourt; (v) Wiedl, Equiluz, Van der Meer; (vi) Klein, Harten, Van Altena, Van Egmond.

Gustav Leonhardt directs Nos. 103 and 106, and Nikolaus Harnoncourt the other two. The best-known and most deeply moving is the 'Actus Tragicus'

(*Gottes Zeit ist die allerbeste Zeit*), which receives an exemplary performance that surpasses Leonhardt's account in the mid-1960s for Das Alte Werk, much praised by Alec Robertson. There is an excellent boy soloist and, as in the earlier disc, Frans Brüggen is one of the masterly recorder players. *Ihr werdet weinen und heulen* has rarely been put on disc and is a poignant and expressive piece that rewards attention. Both these performances are among the very finest to have reached us in this series. No. 105, *Herr, gehe nicht ins Gericht* is arguably one of the very deepest of all Bach cantatas, and since Ansermet's account was deleted, the only alternative version is by Richter. The Harnoncourt is perhaps wanting in expressive weight, but neither this fact nor the reservations one might feel about his account of No. 104, which is not otherwise available, diminishes the value of this excellent box, which comes with the usual notes and score.

Cantata No. 106: Gottes Zeit (*Actus tragicus*).

*** HM 1C 065/265 99751. Ameling, Lehane, Equiluz, McDaniel, Aachen Domchor, Coll. Aur., Pohl – TELE-MANN: *Funeral cantata.****

Cantatas Nos. 106; 140: Wachet auf.

** Mer. E 77016. Rödin, Hallin, Björkegren, Hagegård, Stockholm Bach Ch. and Bar. Ens., Ohrwall.

Gottes Zeit has been frequently recorded, but, except for Leonhardt's version in the Telefunken set (see above), no recent version has surpassed his earlier disc made in the mid-1960s. The Pohl recording dates from the late 1960s, and it can be recommended alongside the Telefunken version by Jürgen Jürgens, though the latter has a slightly more transparent and revealing sound. There is fine solo singing here, but the boys of the Aachen Cathedral Choir are not always as sure and firm as Jürgens's forces. The Collegium Aureum provide a

thoroughly musical support on their authentic instruments, and the warm acoustic flatters all concerned. The coupling is particularly attractive too; no need for hesitation here. The cassette matches the disc closely, although the choral focus on tape is slightly less clean.

The version from Stockholm has the merits of freshness and vitality, and there is excellent singing from Margot Rödin and Håkan Hagegård, as well as some musical and sensitive instrumental playing. *Wachet auf* is less impressive vocally (the often brilliant Margareta Hallin is not strongly cast in this repertoire), and the choral singing could perhaps be a little more strongly characterized. The good recording helps, but for both cantatas this is a useful alternative rather than a first choice.

Cantatas Nos. (i) 107: Was willst du dich betrüben; (ii) 108: Es ist euch gut; 109: Ich glaube, lieber Herr; 110: Unser Mund sei voll Lachens.

*** Tel. EX 6.35559 (2). (i) Klein, Equiluz, Van Egmond, Hanover Boys' Ch., Ghent Coll. Vocale, Leonhardt Cons., Leonhardt; (ii) Wiedl, Frangoulis, Stumpf, Lorenz, Esswood, Equiluz, Van der Meer, Tölz Ch., VCM, Harnoncourt.

Gustav Leonhardt gets splendid results in the expressive chorus which opens Cantata No. 107, and the singing throughout is of a high order. The cantatas all date from the period 1724–5; No. 110 borrows the overture from the *Suite No. 4 in D*, which is effectively used to accompany a four-part vocal texture. This is a festive cantata produced for Christmas Day in Leipzig in 1725 and again three years later, and is scored for relatively large forces. The high standards of this series are maintained throughout this volume, and that applies to performance, recording, pressings and presentation.

Cantata No. 118: O Jesu Christ mein's Lebens Licht.
(M) *(*) Uni. UNS 248. Soloists, L. Bach Soc. Ch., Steinitz Bach Players, Steinitz – *Magnificat.*(*)

See below under the coupling.

Cantatas Nos. 137: Lobe den Herren; 190: Singet dem Herrn.
**(*) HM 1C 065 99667. Wiedl, Kronwitter, Wand, Markus, Studer, Tölz Ch., Coll. Aur., Maier.

Cantata No. 137 was recorded twice by Richter (for Decca and later for Archive) but No. 190 is neglected. The latter is the more impressive of the two works; it does not survive complete but the first two sections were 'restored' in the 1940s by the scholar Walther Reinhardt. The performances are good rather than distinguished; the boy soloists sound nervous and the period instruments are not beyond reproach, but they give some idea of what this music must have sounded like during Bach's lifetime. The earlier cantata is chorale-based and in some ways less inspired than its companion; but the performances have such spirit and are so well recorded that collectors wanting this coupling need not hesitate.

Cantatas Nos. (i) 206: Schleicht, spielende Wellen; (ii) 208: Was mir behagt (Hunting cantata).
(M) *** Tel. DX 6.35370 (2). Jacobeit, Mathes, Spoorenberg, Brand, Villisech, Hamburg Monteverdi Ch., Amsterdam CO, cond. (i) Rieu, (ii) Jürgens.

These records originally appeared in the late 1960s and their attractions have not diminished over the years. *Schleicht, spielende Wellen* is particularly noteworthy for its fine opening chorus; the *Hunting cantata* is probably best-known for *Sheep may safely graze*, but the invention throughout is of a high order.

The performances are in every way satisfying and the recording is admirable.

Cantatas Nos. 207: Vereinigte Zwietracht der wechselnden Saiten; 214: Tönet, ihr Pauken!
*** DG Arc. 2533 401. Mathis, Hamari, Schreier, Lorenz, Adam, Berlin Soloists and CO, Schreier.

Vereinigte Zwietracht dates from 1726 and exists in two forms: six of the movements are identical in both (the differences affect the recitative), but the texts are completely different. Two of the movements will be familiar from Brandenburg No. 1, and the companion cantata, *Tönet, ihr Pauken!*, makes use of material that was to reappear in the *Christmas oratorio*. The performances are lively and sensitive, and the soloists are excellent. The choral singing could perhaps be more incisive, but in general this is a useful addition to the catalogue; neither cantata is otherwise available. Recording is well-balanced and the surfaces are impeccable.

Cantata No. 213: Herkules auf dem Scheidewege.
*** DG Arc. 2533 447 [id.]. Mathis, Watkinson, Schreier, Lorenz, Berlin Soloists and CO, Schreier.

Hercules at the Crossroads was composed in 1733 for the birthday celebrations of the young Prince Elector, Friedrich Christian of Saxony. Hercules is met at the crossroads by two women; one of them promises him a sensuous life of pleasure and the other virtue and fame, achieved by his own endeavours and hard work. His choice is clear (not surprisingly, given the occasion). Only a year later Bach was to incorporate no fewer than six of the thirteen movements of this cantata into the *Christmas oratorio*, to very different words. The dividing line between virtue and pleasure is sharper than between the secular and the sacred, it would seem! Schreier gets an extremely fresh response from his artists, and both vocally and instrumentally this can be warmly recommended.

Christmas oratorio, BWV 248.

*** HMV SLS/TC-SLS 5098 (3) [Ang. S 3840]. Ameling, Baker, Tear, Fischer-Dieskau, King's College Ch., ASMF, Ledger.

**(*) DG Arc. 2710 024 (3)/3376 012 [id.]. Hopfner, Hillebrand, Regensburg Ch. treble and alto soloists, Coll. St Emmeram, Schneidt.

With generally brisk tempi (controversially so in the alto's cradle song, *Schlafe mein Liebster*, in Part II) Philip Ledger directs an intensely refreshing performance which grows more winning the more one hears it. It was Ledger who played the harpsichord continuo in many of Benjamin Britten's performances of this work, and some of Britten's imagination comes through here, helped by four outstanding and stylish soloists. The King's acoustic gives a warm background to the nicely scaled performances of choir and orchestra; the timpani at the very start sound spectacularly impressive. However, the reverberant acoustic has obviously caused problems in the cassette transfer, and the recording on tape is not always well-focused in fortissimos and is generally without the edge of brilliance that this joyful work needs. Jochum's Bavarian recording on Philips makes the best buy on cassette, even though the layout on two tapes (against three discs) is much less convenient for access to separate sections of the work. The transfer is made at a low level, but the sound is natural and clear, and Jochum's dedication is matched by fine singing from an excellent team of soloists, Ameling, Fassbaender, Laubenthal and Prey (Philips 6703 037/7699 097).

On the Archive recording conducted by Hans-Martin Schneidt it may seem incongruous to hear the Virgin Mary's cradle song sung by a piping boy treble, but that is how Bach must have heard it, and here the easy authenticity makes for performance which, from the joyful fanfares of the opening sinfonia of the first cantata, is celebratory on an intimate scale. Ensemble is not always flawless, but the spirit is consistently compelling. Excellent recording; the tape transfer is generally smooth and pleasing, but lacks the last degree of range at the top, which seldom sparkles.

Christmas oratorio: choruses and arias.

(M) **(*) DG Priv. 2535/3335 369. Janowitz, Ludwig, Wunderlich, Crass, Mun. Bach Ch. and O., Karl Richter.

This is a good selection of items from a long work; they are taken mainly from the first, second and fourth cantatas of the six. Richter's direction has its prosaic moments, but the solo and choral singing is first-rate. The 1965 recording is good for its period, although on tape the choral sound lacks bite and sparkle (the solo voices are fully acceptable), and the selection is generous on choruses.

Christmas oratorio: highlights.

(M) ** Ph. Seq. 6527/7311 070. Ameling, Fassbaender, Laubenthal, Prey, Bav. R. Ch. and SO, Jochum.

This fairly generous sampler from Jochum's complete set tends rather to emphasize its stylistic shortcomings; its overall warmth and dedication are less striking when the music is presented piecemeal (although the selection is well balanced). The singing is excellent and the recording sounds very natural.

Magnificat in D, BWV 243.

(*) Argo ZRG/KZRC 854 [id. LP only]. Palmer, Watts, Tear, Roberts, King's College Ch., ASMF, Ledger – VIVALDI: *Magnificat*.(*)

** DG 2531/3301 048 [id.]. Tomowa-Sintow, Baltsa, Schreier, Luxon, German Op. Ch., Berlin PO, Karajan – STRAVINSKY: *Symphony of Psalms.***
** CBS 76884. Auger, Murray, Watts, Kraus, Huttenlocher, Schöne, Gächinger Kantorei, Stuttgart Bach Coll., Rilling.
(M) *(*) Uni. UNS 248. Molyneux, Esswood, Partridge, Noble, L. Bach Soc. Ch., Steinitz Bach Players, Steinitz – *Cantata No. 118.**(*)

Magnificat in E flat (original version), *BWV 243a.*
*** O-L DSLO/KDSLC 572. Nelson, Kirkby, C. Watkinson, Elliot, D. Watkinson, Christ Church Ch., AcAM, Preston – KUHNAU: *Der Gerechte kommt um.****

The original version of the *Magnificat* is textually different in detail (quite apart from being a semitone higher) and has four interpolations for the celebration of Christmas. Preston and the Academy of Ancient Music present a characteristically alert and fresh performance, and the Christ Church Choir is in excellent form. One might quibble at the use of women soloists instead of boys, but these three specialist singers have just the right incisive timbre and provide the insight of experience. The fill-up is a welcome rarity. Excellent recording and an outstandingly good tape transfer.

On Argo, Philip Ledger directs a lively and dramatic account. The warm acoustic of King's College Chapel creates problems of balance but surprisingly few of clarity, and with its apt and unusual coupling this is a most attractive version, highly recommendable if boys' voices are preferred in the chorus. The women soloists are outstanding, as is the St Martin's Academy. The four Christmas interpolations provide an additional attraction. However, the cassette is not one of Argo's best.

Karajan's reading of the *Magnificat* makes it an orchestral work with sub-sidiary chorus, and though the ingredients are polished and refined, the result is artificial. The soloists are excellent, but with its curious coupling this is not a competitive version.

Rilling's version includes the Christmas interpolations; there is some magnificent solo singing, and the contribution of the Gächinger Kantorei and the Stuttgart Bach Collegium is also to be admired. The recording lacks depth and perspective: the strings are too close in the *Et exultavit*, and both chorus and orchestra need to have more air round them.

Steinitz directs a characteristically energetic performance, also using the Christmas interpolations; but, apart from the contributions of the male soloists, it is not a sufficiently polished account to compete with the best. The *Funeral cantata*, No. 118, makes a good fill-up, and except for some odd balances the recording quality is good.

Mass in B min., BWV 232.
*** HMV Dig. SLS/TCC-SLS 5215 (3/2) [Ang. DS 3904]. Donath, Fasshaender, Ahnsjö, Holl, Bav. R. Ch. and SO, Jochum.
*** Ph. 6769 002/7699 076 [id.]. Marshall, Baker, Tear, Ramey, Ch. and ASMF, Marriner.

Jochum's memorably dedicated performance, marked by resilient rhythms, is the most completely satisfying version yet. The choral singing – by far the most important element in this work – is superb, and though the soloists are variably balanced, they make a clear-voiced team. Radiant recording both on disc and on the splendid chrome cassettes.

For Neville Marriner this was a larger recording project than he had undertaken before, and he rose superbly to the challenge. Predictably many of the tempi are daringly fast; *Et resurrexit*, for example, has the Academy chorus on its toes, but the rhythms are so resiliently sprung that the result is exhilarating, never hectic. An even more remarkable achievement is that in the great moments of contemplation such as *Et incarnatus* and *Crucifixus* Marriner finds a degree of inner intensity to match the gravity of Bach's inspiration, with tempi often slower than usual. That dedication is matched by the soloists, the superb soprano Margaret Marshall as much as the longer-established singers. This is a performance which finds the balance between small-scale authenticity and recognition of massive inspiration, neither too small nor too large, and with good atmospheric recording, not quite as defined as it might be on inner detail, this is fully recommendable. The cassette transfer, made at a modest level, lacks the last degree of upper range, but is naturally balanced.

Mass in B min.: highlights.
(M) **(*) Ph.Seq. 6527/*7311* 099 (from above set cond, Marriner).

This set of excerpts concentrates on the choral music from the *B minor Mass*; there are only three solo items. It provides a fair sampler of Marriner's style, rhythmically crisp in the fast passages yet with the fullest intensity when the music is contemplative. But this can only be seriously recommended for those whose budgets simply will not stretch to the complete work.

Masses in F, BWV 233; in A, BWV 234.
*** Argo ZRG/*KZRC* 873 [id.]. Eathorne, Esswood, Jenkins, Hickox Singers and O., Hickox.

Following the success of their earlier recording of the two Lutheran Masses BWV 235/6, Richard Hickox and his colleagues have now turned to the others. The performances are expressive but always in excellent style, and the soloists bring conviction and fine musicianship to

their parts. The *A major Mass*, which draws on Cantata No. 67 for its *Gloria*, is the more inspired of the two, but both offer many beauties. The relative neglect of these 'short' Masses is hard to understand when they are treated so persuasively, and they are finely recorded with a warm acoustic, well-balanced soloists and exemplary perspective. The tape transfer is vivid, with good presence for soloists and orchestra; but the choral climaxes are rather less refined than on disc.

Motets: *Fürchte dich nicht, BWV 228; Der Geist hilft, BWV 226; Jesu, meine Freude, BWV 227; Komm, Jesu, komm, BWV 229; Lobet den Herrn, BWV 230; Singet dem Herrn, BWV 225.*
*** Tel. Dig. EK 6.35470/*CZ4 42663* [id.]. Stockholm Bach Ch., VCM, Harnoncourt.

To Bach's motets, which include some of the greatest music he ever wrote for chorus, goes the honour of being the first of his vocal music to be issued digitally. The recording is very successful indeed, beautifully fresh and clear, the acoustic attractively resonant without clouding detail and the accompanying instrumental group giving discreet yet telling support. The vigour and joy of the singing come over splendidly in *Singet dem Herrn* (which opens the collection), while the expressive feeling of *Jesu, meine Freude* is matched by a sense of drama. The conductor's timing and use of pauses are finely judged, and the Stockholm Choir show stamina as well as sympathy; the spontaneity of their performances is impressive.

Motets: *Der Geist hilft, BWV 226; Jesu, meine Freude, BWV 227; Singet dem Herrn, BWV 225.*
(M) * DG Arc. Priv. 2547/*3347* 009. Leipzig Thomanerchor and GO, Kurt Thomas.

There is an attractive association here: these recordings were made in Leipzig by the choir from Bach's own church. A judicious orchestral backing is added, but even with this support the singing is not very sophisticated. The recording (which dates from the end of the fifties) is effective enough, and the tape transfer is of good quality, clear and bright, with good ambience. However, this cannot compare with the Telefunken set (see above) or the Argo recording in English of *Jesu, meine Freude* (see below).

Motet: *Jesus priceless treasure* (*Jesu, meine Freude*). Sacred part songs: *Die bitt're Leidenszeit; Brunnquell aller Güter; Es ist vollbracht; Gott lebet noch; Herr, nicht schicke deine Rache; Jesus ist das schönste Licht; O Jesuslein süss* (sung in English).
(M) *** Argo ZK/*KZKC* 67 [ZRG 5234]. King's College Ch., Willcocks.

There is a place in the catalogue for an English-language version of *Jesu, meine Freude*, and this performance surpasses any of the German-text recordings made on the continent which have been available at various times. The famous King's atmosphere is caught in a characteristic Argo manner, yet the words are clear, and the balance with the continuo of organ, cello and bass is admirable. David Willcocks and his choir have also recorded the work in German (HMV HQS 1254, coupled to other motets and the Cantata No. 147), and some may prefer that (unaccompanied) version. The items from the Schemelli hymn-book which are included on the Argo disc are, however, not otherwise available in recommendable versions. They are of fine musical quality and beautifully sung. The tape transfer is most successful, matching the disc in atmosphere and only fractionally less well-focused. Recommended.

St John Passion, BWV 245.
**(*) DG Arc. 2710 027 (3) [id.]. Hopfner, Baldin, Hillebrand, Ahrens, Regensburg Cath. Ch., Coll. St Emmeram, Schneidt.
**(*) Erato STU 71151 (3). Palmer, Finnilä, Equiluz, Van der Meer, Huttenlocher, Lausanne Vocal Ens. and CO, Corbóz.

The Archive set may not have quite the innocent exhilaration of Schneidt's recording of the *Christmas oratorio* (see above), but it too presents an unaggressively authentic performance on an attractively intimate scale. There is less bite in the drama than in many other versions of whatever degree of authenticity, but with the fresh tones of the Regensburg Domspatzen and the generally gentle tones of the instrumental ensemble, this version has a distinctive place. It is beautifully recorded.

Those who resist the idea of the new authenticity with its characteristic instrumental timbres will be well-pleased by Corbóz's middle-of-the-road reading with its fresh and lively choral singing and accomplished team of soloists. Corbóz is excellent in telling the Passion story, bringing out the drama of Bach's concept in a work more compact, less contemplative than the *St Matthew.* Kurt Equiluz with his distinctive high tenor makes an urgently effective Evangelist, always agile, and the recording is first-rate.

Still recommended: Britten's inspired recording followed a series of live performances at Aldeburgh and elsewhere. With excellent soloists and wonderfully vivid sound his Decca set remains a principal recommendation, a performance that makes you listen to the music afresh (SET 531/3 [Lon. 13104]).

St Matthew Passion, BWV 244 (sung in English).
**(*) Decca D 139 D 4/*K 139 K 44.* Tear, Shirley-Quirk, Loft, Hodgson,

Jenkins, Roberts, Bach Ch., St Paul's Cath. Ch. Boys, Thames CO, Willcocks.

St Matthew Passion (sung in German).
*** DG Arc. 2723 067/*3376 016* [id.].
Mathis, Baker, Schreier, Fischer-Dieskau, Salminen, Regensburg Cath. Ch., Mun. Bach Ch. and O., Karl Richter.

Richter used to be thought a somewhat dry, even prosaic interpreter of Bach, but this fine, expressive, but always stylish reading tells of warmth and affection. The new purists will object to Richter's rallentandos and the fluid approach to chorales, but in sum this has the feeling of a great spiritual experience flowing spontaneously, with outstanding contributions from soloists, choir and orchestra. If it seems odd that the performance appears on the Archive label, dedicated to scholarly authenticity, this only reflects developing standards; by the lights of a few years ago the scale and general approach are anything but romantic, only the expression. Peter Schreier makes a strong and intense Evangelist, Fischer-Dieskau is deeply committed as Jesus, with Matti Salminen darkly contrasted. Edith Mathis is sweet in tone if not always flawless of line, but best of all is Dame Janet Baker, whose rendering of *Erbarme dich* crowns what from first to last is an unusually impressive recording. The sound is spacious and generally well-balanced on disc, and the tape transfer is of excellent quality. The choral sound is less incisive than on LP (noticeably at the opening), but the wide dynamic range is encompassed without loss of amplitude, and the solo voices and orchestra are vividly and freshly projected. Klemperer's famous EMI set should not be forgotten, an act of devotion of such intensity that points of style and interpretation dwindle into insignificance (HMV SLS 827 [Ang. S 3599]); and

Münchinger's lively Decca recording has excellent soloists and first-class recording (SET 288/91 [Lon. 1431]); but Richter's new DG version is undoubtedly very satisfying.

It is a comment on current taste (of record companies if not perhaps the public) that the newest Decca set, conducted by Sir David Willcocks, was the first complete recording of the *St Matthew Passion* to be made in English for thirty years. The pity is that the performance fails to lift quite as it ought, remaining earthbound and conscientious where it should have the qualities of a spiritual experience. Willcocks, most experienced of choirmasters, draws light and rhythmic singing from his choirs in the choruses, and the chorales avoid heaviness. There is a good team of soloists, headed by Robert Tear, but Peter's denial – usually a supremely moving moment – is here prosaic. The recording is clean and well-balanced, and the cassette transfer is admirably fresh and clear; solo voices are well-projected and the choral textures are full and, if fractionally husky at times, for the most part very cleanly focused.

St Matthew Passion: excerpts.
** DG 2531/*3301* 137 (from above set cond. Richter).

This selection is framed by the opening and closing choruses, but it is otherwise a rather low-key recital, not attempting to capture the essence of the work, since many of the more dramatic moments are omitted. The singing itself is a favourable sampler for the complete set, and the recording is rich and spacious, the tape rather less sharply focused than the disc.

St Matthew Passion: arias and choruses.
(M) ** Ph. Fest. 6570/*7310* 011 [complete set 6770 018/*7650 018*]. Giebel, Höffgen, Haefliger, Berry, Ketelaars, Neth. R. Ch., St Willibrord Church Boys' Ch., Concg. O., Jochum.

An excellent and generous reminder of Jochum's recording. His is a romantic view of the work, spiritual and intense, but erring a little towards sentimentality. Nevertheless, as these excerpts readily show, the solo singing is strong and generally stylish, and the Netherlands Radio Chorus sings with great point and attack. The recording provides different perspectives of sound to distinguish contrasted forces, and the quality is very good, on disc and cassette alike. Jochum's warmth is fully conveyed, even though the actual selection is rather bitty.

Vocal collections

Mass in B minor: Agnus Dei; Qui sedes. St John Passion: All is fulfilled. St Matthew Passion: Grief for sin.
(M) *** Decca SPA/*KCSP* 531. Ferrier, LPO, Boult – HANDEL: *Arias.* ***

Decca have reissued this famous Kathleen Ferrier disc on their cheapest label. With a splendidly transferred cassette to match, it sounds remarkably vivid. Readers may remember that in the early days of stereo Sir Adrian Boult and the LPO re-recorded the accompaniments with such skill and devotion that the new orchestral sound completely masked the old. Even the voice seems to have the extra presence of the newer techniques.

St John Passion: (i) *All is fulfilled;* (ii) *Rest calm, O body pure and holy; The dear angel send.* (iii) *St Matthew Passion: Come, ye daughters; O sacred head; In tears of grief.*
(M) *** Decca SPA/*KCSP* 588. (i) Ferrier, LPO, Boult; (ii) King's College Ch., L. Philomus., Willcocks; (iii) Bach Ch., St Paul's Cath. Boys' Ch., Thames CO, Willcocks – HANDEL: *Messiah excerpts.* ***

An excellent and well-planned disc of Bach and Handel sung in English. Kathleen Ferrier's noble performance of *All is fulfilled* (with the famous added accompaniment in real stereo) is framed by freshly sung chorus and chorales taken from the Willcocks complete sets of the *Passions.* The sound is first-class, with no perceptible difference between tape and disc.

COLLECTION

Flute concerto in G min., BWV 1056; Oboe concerto in F, BWV 1053; Oboe d'amore concerto in A, BWV 1055; Double concerto for violin and oboe in D min., BWV 1060; Triple concerto for violin, oboe and flute in D min., BWV 1063; Triple violin concerto in D, BWV 1064; Suite No. 3 in D, BWV 1068. (i) *Cantata No. 170: Vergnügte Ruh'.*
(M) *** Argo D 241 D 3 (3)/*K 241 K 33.* Soloists, ASMF, Marriner, (i) with Baker.

The concertos included here (originally issued on Argo ZRG/*KZRC* 820–21) are conjectural reconstructions of Bach harpsichord concertos for alternative instruments that either did exist or might have existed in Bach's time. The purist may resist, but the sparkle and charm of these performances under Marriner, with soloists from among regular Academy members, tend to disarm criticism, for every concerto makes delightful listening. To make up this excellent medium-priced anthology Dame Janet Baker's distinguished performances of the cantata *Vergnügte Ruh'* and the Academy's outstanding version of the *Third Orchestral suite* are added. The recording is of Argo's highest quality on disc and cassette alike, although on tape there is a degree of roughness on top in the tuttis of the *Suite.*

ARRANGEMENTS

Suite No. 3 in D, BWV 1068: Air.
(Violin) *Partita No. 2 in D min.,*
BWV 1004: Chaconne; Partita No. 3
in E, BWV 1006: Preludio. Chorales:
Ein' feste Burg, BWV 720; Komm
süsser Tod (from BWV 229);
Wachet auf, BWV 645. Fugue in G
min., BWV 577; Cantata No. 165:
Arioso (all orch. Stokowski).
(M) *** RCA Gold GL/*GK* 42921 [ARL
1 0880]. LSO, Stokowski.

In his vintage days in Philadelphia
Stokowski made many records of his own
Bach transcriptions, inflated but flamboyantly convincing. This is a gloriously
enjoyable collection of some of the ripest,
recorded by the LSO under a nonagena-
rian Stokowski with opulent stereo
adding to the splendour. Not for the
purist, but highly enjoyable for everyone
else. With the medium-priced reissue on
Gold Seal has come a cassette, but,
though acceptable, it does not match the
LP in richness; the upper range is less
refined and there is an element of constriction at a couple of climaxes.

'Brandenburg Boogie' (arr. Holloway); *Brandenburg boogie; Jesu,*
joy of man's desiring; Groovy
gavottes 1–3; Fascinating fugue;
Sleepers awake; Aria; D minor
double; Minuet; Jig; Air on a G
string; Sicilienne; Funky flute.
**(*) EMI Dig. EMD/*TCC-ESD* 5536.
Duran, Grappelli, Holloway, Walley,
Ganley.

Unashamedly romantic phrasing here
from the flautist Elena Duran as well as
Stéphane Grappelli, making an uncompromisingly modern dress for some
very memorable tunes. It's all harmless
and often seductive, although Bach purists are warned to stay clear. The sound
is first-class, and the chrome cassette is

sparklingly clear, with excellent transients.

Bach, Wilhelm Friedemann
(1710–84)

Duo in F; Trio in A min.
** O-L DSLO 518 [id.]. Preston,
McGegan, Ryan, Pleeth, Hogwood –
C. P. E. BACH and J. S. BACH: *Trio sona-*
*tas.****

Wilhelm Friedemann is an interesting
figure, but the *Duo* for two flutes (a combination much favoured at the time) is
not particularly memorable or distinguished, though it is certainly well
played. So, too, is the single-movement
A minor Trio. But this is fill-up material
for two more substantial pieces.

Bainbridge, Simon
(born 1952)

Viola concerto.
*** Uni. Dig. RHD 400. Trampler,
Philh.O., Tilson Thomas – KNUSSEN:
*Symphony No. 3 etc.****

Simon Bainbridge is an exact contemporary of Oliver Knussen, with whose
Third Symphony and *Ophelia dances* this
concerto is coupled. Like Knussen he
studied with John Lambert and later with
Gunther Schuller. The *Viola concerto*
dates from 1976 and is an eloquent and
atmospheric piece. It is perhaps more
impressive in its inward, reflective sections than in the vigorous orchestral tutti,
and there is an appealing gentleness and
poetry in the slow movement. No praise
could be too high for the quality of the
performance and recording here; both

are outstanding. An issue well worth the attention of those who think they do not like contemporary music.

Baird, Tadeusz (1928–81)

Elegeia for orchestra.
(M) *** Sup. 1410 2734. Prague RSO, Kasprzyk – LUTOSLAWSKI: *Mi-Parti;* PENDERECKI: *Anaklasis* etc.***

A useful anthology of contemporary Polish music. Baird attracted attention in the early 1960s with his *Four Essays* for orchestra, highly evocative and inventive and well worth a place in the catalogue. Baird's style is expressionist, and the music arises from genuine feeling. This *Elegy*, which was composed in 1973, is perhaps less haunting than the *Essays*, but it too is atmospheric. It is well served by the recording engineers, and the Prague Radio Orchestra play with total commitment under Kasprzyk.

Balakirev, Mily (1837–1910)

Piano concerto No. 2 in A flat, Op. posth (completed by Liapunov).
(M) * Turn. TVS 34645. Ponti, Westphalian SO, Landau – LIAPUNOV: *Rhapsody.**

Balakirev was still in his teens when he wrote his *First Concerto,* only one movement of which survives. He began the *Second* in 1861, when he was in his mid-twenties, but could not be persuaded to write down the second and third movements until 1906. Even so he left the finale unfinished, and after his death Liapunov completed the work. The slow movement is the most poetic of the three, and in more persuasive hands it could be effective. Unfortunately the performance here is somewhat insensitive and the orchestral playing undistinguished. Moreover the recording is shallow, with lustreless strings, although the piano tone is clear.

Islamey; Overture on 3 Russian songs; Russia (symphonic poem).
*** HMV ASD/*TC-ASD* 3709. USSR SO, Svetlanov – GLINKA: *Ivan Susanin* etc.; SCRIABIN: *Day Dreams.***

Svetlanov conducts Liapunov's orchestral transcription of Balakirev's famous piano piece, rather than the customary orchestration of Casella. Liapounov's scoring is perhaps thicker and less effective, but it all comes off well in this assured and vivid performance. The recording is a little less detailed than one would like but has ample richness and body. The performances of the familiar *Russia* and the *Overture on three Russian songs* are committed and impassioned. The tape transfers are vivid and sparkling, the sound clear and slightly dry but with plenty of bloom on the woodwind; the engaging *Overture* approaches demonstration standard.

Symphony No. 1 in C.
(M) (***) HMV mono XLP/*TC-XLP* 60001. Philh. O., Karajan.

Issued originally in the days of 78, this 1950 recording presents one of Karajan's most inspired performances with the Philharmonia Orchestra in its first flush of success. The performance has a passion and intensity which match the sharp originality and ambitious scale of a work still underappreciated, one of the most colourful of Russian symphonies. The transfer is good, but the bass lacks weight. For those who need stereo, Beecham's version offers almost as many felicities on HMV SXLP 30171 [Sera. 60062] and has the advantage of

Borodin's *Prince Igor* dances as a bonus. But this is no longer available on cassette; the tape of the Karajan version has less glitter and edge than the disc, but gives rather more body and weight to the strings.

Thamar (symphonic poem).
*** HMV ASD 3660. USSR SO, Svetlanov – GLAZOUNOV: *Stenka Razin;* RACHMANINOV: *The Rock.****

Thamar has been rather neglected by the gramophone, though there have been fine performances by Beecham and Ansermet during the last two decades. Balakirev's colourful score benefits from opulent recording and Svetlanov produces playing of keen intensity from the USSR Symphony Orchestra. Only the somewhat raw brass disturb the texture in what is a compelling and atmospheric performance. It eclipses the Ansermet and is even to be preferred to Beecham's long-deleted mono account.

ful. Anyone who enjoys Delius, Strauss and Bax will feel at home in this discursive yet rewarding score, and the playing of the RPO (in particular Jack Brymer's important clarinet arabesques) could hardly be bettered. The cassette transfer is of excellent quality. As on disc, the tuttis show the recording's limitations; elsewhere the sound is warmly natural.

The Pierrot of the Minuet: overture.
(*) RCA RL/*RK* 25184. Bournemouth Sinf., Del Mar – BRIDGE: *Summer* etc.; BUTTERWORTH: *Banks of Green Willow.**

Bantock's comedy overture slightly outlasts its welcome, but in this lively reading it makes an attractive item in a highly enjoyable mixed bag of English pieces. First-rate performance and recording, though offering acceptable quality, has a less vivid dynamic range than the disc.

Bantock, Granville
(1868–1946)

Fifine at the Fair (tone poem).
(M) (***) HMV mono SXLP/*TC-SXLP* 30440. RPO, Beecham – DELIUS: *Songs of Sunset.****

Though the Delius coupling is in stereo, *Fifine at the Fair* is mono and dates from 1950. Such is the magic of Beecham's performance and the excellence of the HMV engineers that any sonic limitations are soon forgotten; indeed, readers need have no serious hesitations on that score. Bantock's piece dates from the first decade of the century and shows him at his strongest. Strauss is an obvious model yet there is a distinctive personality at work, and the orchestral textures are both opulent and resource-

Barber, Samuel (1910–81)

Adagio for strings, Op. 11.
(M) **(*) Ph. Fest. 6570/*7310* 181 [id.]. I Musici – BARTÓK: *Rumanian folk dances;* BRITTEN: *Simple symphony;* RESPIGHI: *Ancient airs.***(*)
(B) **(*) RCA VICS/*VK* 2001 [AGL 1/*AGK 1* 3790]. Boston SO, Munch – ELGAR: *Introduction and allegro;* TCHAIKOVSKY: *Serenade.***(*)

(i) *Adagio for strings, Op. 11; 2nd Essay for orchestra. Op. 17; Medea's Meditation and Dance of Vengeance, Op. 23a; The School for Scandal: overture.* (ii) *Dover Beach, Op. 3.*
(M) **(*) CBS 61898/40- [Odys.Y/*YT* 33230]. (i) NYPO, Schippers; (ii) Fischer-Dieskau, Juilliard Qt.

As Barber's famous *Adagio* was originally written for string quartet its performance on a small body of strings seems appropriate. The version by I Musici creates a gently elegiac mood and if the climax is less fiercely tense than some other performances, there is no want of poignancy. The recording is excellent on disc and cassette alike, and the imaginative couplings made this a thoroughly worthwhile medium-priced compilation.

Munch creates a spacious nobility at the climax of the *Adagio*, and his broad conception is fully convincing. The recording is full if slightly dated now, but the couplings make this issue well worth considering in the bargain price-range.

Drawn from earlier sources, the CBS mid-price collection made for the composer's seventieth birthday is a good anthology, including some of his most memorable works, not just the famous *Adagio* but the coolly atmospheric setting of Matthew Arnold (with Fischer-Dieskau immaculate in his English, treating the piece rightly like Lieder) and other short orchestral works. The recording quality is somewhat hard, but has transferred quite vividly to cassette, lacking only the last degree of upper range, and that not always disadvantageously. However, on tape the voice in *Dover Beach* lacks edge and presence.

Reminder: The finest recording of Barber's *Adagio* is by Marriner and the ASMF on Argo, imaginatively coupled to works by Copland, Cowell, Creston and Ives and superbly recorded on disc and tape alike (*ZRG/KZRC* 845 [id.]).

(i) *Violin concerto, Op. 14. Music for a scene from Shelley.* (ii) *Knoxville: Summer of 1915.*
(M) *** Uni. UNS 256. W. Australian SO, Measham, with (i) Thomas, (ii) McGurk.

Ronald Thomas captures the youthful innocence and rapture of Barber's heartwarming *Concerto*, and though the performance may lack the glamour and power of Stern and Bernstein, who recorded it in the mid-1960s, there is an unforced eloquence and naturalness that are deeply satisfying. The sound is well-balanced and completely truthful, and no one coming to this performance is likely to be unmoved. The concerto is coupled with *Knoxville* for soprano and orchestra, one of Barber's most evocative pieces, and an underrated early work, *Music for a scene from Shelley*, whose rich romantic textures are never overripe but seem to relate to genuinely felt experience. While the Stern/Bernstein version of the *Concerto* (CBS 61621 [Col. MS 6713]) is available, it must perhaps remain a first recommendation for its splendid panache and virtuosity, yet readers who enjoy purposeful, relaxed and committed music-making and excellent recorded sound should not overlook this fine Unicorn issue.

Ballade, Op. 46; 4 Excursions, Op. 20; Nocturne (Homage to John Field), Op. 33; Sonata, Op. 26.
**(*) Hyp. A 66016. Brownridge.

This record performs a useful function in the catalogue: it accommodates Barber's entire output for the piano on two sides, offering the only available versions of the *Ballade* (1972), the *Nocturne* and the endearing *Four Excursions*. These are not quite so crisp or characterful as in the old Andor Foldes mono record from the 1950s but in some details are more sensitive. Angela Brownridge gives a good account of herself in the dazzling *Sonata*; though she may not perhaps possess the transcendental virtuosity of a Horowitz (or of Van Cliburn, who also recorded it in the 1960s), she is nonetheless equal to its demands. The recording is not first-class; the resonant acoustic makes the piano sound slightly unfocused, yet the ear soon adjusts.

Barraqué, Jean (1928–73)

Piano sonata.
(M) *** Uni. UNS 236. Woodward.

This performance of Barraqué's *Sonata* by Roger Woodward, recorded in the early 1970s, earned the imprimatur of the composer himself. Barraqué's idiom is not readily accessible but there is a sense of creative urgency and purpose here. Some may find the language tortuous and convoluted but there can be no doubt that Woodward makes as good a case for it as anyone and he is assisted by excellent and well-focused recorded sound. This is highly specialized in its appeal but can be recommended to those interested in the avant-garde.

Barrios, Agustin (1885–1944)

Aconquija; Aire de Zamba; La catedral; Choro de suadade; Cueca; Estudio; Una limosna el amor de Dios; Madrigal (Gavota); Maxixa; Mazurka apassionata; Minuet; Preludio; Sueño en la floresta; Valse No. 3; Villancico de Navidad.
**(*) CBS 76662/40– [Col. M/MT 35145]. Williams.

Agustin Barrios is a little-known Paraguayan guitarist and composer who had the distinction of making (in 1909) the first known recording of a guitar. His music essentially belongs to the previous century. Its invention is fresh, if sometimes ingenuous, and the pieces here are well varied in style. In the expert hands of John Williams the collection provides a very entertaining recital, ideal for late-evening listening. Try the charming opening *La catedral* (sweet but not sugary) or the irresistible *Sueño en la floresta*, which ends the side in a breath-taking haze of fluttering figurations that remind one of Tarrega's *Recuerdos de la Alhambra*. The recording is excellent, both on disc and on cassette.

Bartók, Béla (1881–1945)

Concerto for orchestra.
(B) **(*) RCA VICS/*VK* 2005 [AGL 1 2909]. Chicago SO, Reiner.
** RCA Dig. RL 13421 [ARC 1/*ARK 1* 3421]. Phd. O., Ormandy.

Concerto for orchestra; Dance suite.
*** Dec. Dig. SXDL/*KSXDC* 7536 [Lon. LDR/*5-* 71036]. Chicago SO, Solti.

Concerto for orchestra; 2 Images, Op. 10.
**(*) DG 2531/*3301* 269 [id.]. Berlin PO, Maazel.

(i) *Concerto for orchestra;* (ii) *Rumanian folk dances.*
(M) *** Mercury SRI 75105. (i) LSO; (ii) Minneapolis SO; Dorati.

Fierce and biting on the one hand, joyful on the other, Sir Georg Solti's reading of Bartók's late display work comes as near being definitive as could be. With superlative playing from Solti's own Chicago orchestra and astonishingly vivid digital recording, it makes a clear first choice, and in addition provides a generous and apt coupling in the *Dance suite*, performed with a similar combination of sympathy and incisiveness. In the *Concerto* Solti has consulted original sources to suggest a faster speed than usual in the second movement, and this he makes entirely convincing. Otherwise these are marginally straighter readings than those in his 1966 coupling of the same works with the LSO, lacking just a little in wit and idiosyncrasy. The cassette transfer is strikingly brilliant: this is easily the finest

version of the *Concerto* available on
tape.

Dorati's Mercury version of the *Concerto* is one of his most exciting records.
He secures outstandingly brilliant and
committed playing from the LSO, who
open the work evocatively and combine
bite with a fiery ardour in the *Allegro*.
With the central movements strongly
characterized and an exhilarating finale
– the brass producing an electrifying
burst of excitement near the close – this
makes a strong recommendation at
medium price. The brilliantly lit recording has a tendency to shrillness, but it also
has a wide dynamic range and combines
atmosphere with vivid colouring. There
is a lower voltage in the *Rumanian dances*,
but Dorati is naturally understanding in
these folk-derived miniatures. The pressing is immaculate.

Maazel's reading of the *Concerto*,
exciting and very well played, has
warmth as well as bite, but lacks wit in
such a movement as the *Play of the
couples*. The recording is spectacular, full
and wide-ranging (far preferable to
Ormandy's digital version) but for some
reason the trumpet is balanced absurdly
far back. The unusual coupling further
recommends this issue, two early pieces
which in different ways anticipate much
later developments in Bartók's last, relatively mellow period. The cassette transfer is sophisticated, with good body and
detail, and it is a pity that the relatively
low transfer level has marginally reduced
the bite in the treble.

Reiner's performance was recorded in
the early days of stereo, but the sound is
remarkably good, spacious and vivid.
The performance is most satisfying, surprisingly straightforward from one
brought up in central Europe, but with
plenty of cutting edge. For those with
limited budgets this is well worth considering. The chrome tape is first-class.

In Ormandy's version, neither the performance nor even the digital recording
comes up to expectations. The one lacks
the committed urgency of his earlier CBS

version and is at times prosaic, and the
recording, though acceptable, gives little
idea of the extra inner clarity possible
with digital sound.

Piano concertos Nos. (i) *1 in A*; (ii) *2
in G*; (i) *3 in E*; (iii) *Sonata for 2
pianos and percussion.*
(M) *** Ph. 6768 053 (2). Bishop-
Kovacevich, with (i) LSO, (ii) BBC
SO, Colin Davis, (iii) Argerich,
Goudswaard, De Roo.

Piano concertos Nos. 1–2.
*** DG 2530/*3300* 901 [id.]. Pollini,
Chicago SO, Abbado.

Piano concertos Nos. 2–3.
⊛ *** Decca SXL/*KSXC* 6937 [Lon.
7167/5-]. Ashkenazy, LPO, Solti.

Piano concerto No. 3.
(M) **(*) HMV SXLP/*TC-SXLP*
30514. Ogdon, New Philh. O., Sargent
– SHOSTAKOVICH: *Piano concerto No.
2.****

Bartók's piano concertos are exceptionally well represented in the current
catalogue, with a wide permutation of
couplings; but the partnership of Ashkenazy and Solti, combined with superb
Decca sound, has set new standards in
this repertoire. Their first issue, coupling the *Second* and *Third Concertos*,
sparks off the energy and dash one
would expect only at a live performance.
With the Slavonic bite of the soloist
beautifully matching the Hungarian fire
of the conductor, the readings of both
works are wonderfully urgent and incisive. The tempi tend to be fast, but the
clarity of focus is superb, and the slow
movements bring a hushed inner concentration, beautifully captured in exceptionally refined recording. With red-
blooded Hungarian qualities underlined,
these two works from very different periods of Bartók's career, the later one
more mellow, seem far more closely akin
than usual. The cassette offers demonstration sound of quite extraordinary

vividness. If anything the *Third Concerto* is even more lively than the *Second*.

On Philips, Bishop-Kovacevich's readings of the three concertos, direct and incisive, are superbly matched by an electrifying account of the *Sonata for two pianos and percussion*, in which he is challenged by the more volatile artistry of Martha Argerich. It was originally coupled differently (see below), but this is both logical and satisfying. Most impressive of all is the pianist's handling of Bartók's often spare and always intense slow movements, here given concentrated power to compare with late Beethoven. Good clean Philips recording of mid-seventies vintage.

The newest DG issue forms a partnership between two of the most distinguished Italian musicians of the day, collaborating in performances of two formidable works which in their exuberance sweep away any idea that this might be forbidding music. Virtuosity goes with a sense of spontaneity. Rhythms in fast movements are freely and infectiously sprung to bring out bluff Bartókian humour rather than any brutality. The Chicago orchestra, vividly recorded, is in superb form. The cassette transfer offers bold, clear piano tone, and the atmosphere and detail of the slow movement are well caught. In the outer movements the reverberation loses some of the crispness of the orchestral focus, but there is good range.

Ogdon's performance of the *Third Concerto* was originally coupled to an impressive version of the *Sonata for two pianos and percussion*, in which he was joined by his wife, Brenda Lucas. Ogdon gives a fine performance of the *Concerto*, and although Sargent's accompaniment lacks the last degree of brilliance and intensity, this makes an enjoyable coupling for an outstanding version of Shostakovich's *Second Concerto*. The 1968 recording has come up well, especially on the bright, crisply transferred cassette.

Viola concerto.
*** DG 2531 249 [id.]. Benyamini, Orchestre de Paris, Barenboim – HINDEMITH: *Viola concerto.****

Bartók left his *Viola concerto* incomplete when he died in 1945 and it was fashioned into shape by the late Tibor Serly. It is a haunting, atmospheric piece with a quietly restrained vein of feeling that lends it strong appeal. It has been well served on record by Karlovský on Supraphon and Menuhin on HMV, but Daniel Benyamini eclipses all the competition and is admirably supported by Barenboim and the Orchestre de Paris. The problems of balancing viola and orchestra are numerous even when the scoring is so expertly judged as it is by Serly. The soloist is too forward and we seem to be hearing the orchestra in a more recessed acoustic. Tonally, however, the recording is thoroughly truthful and this reservation is not sufficient to inhibit the rewards of this fine recording.

Violin concertos Nos. 1 (1908); 2 in B min. (1938).
(M) *** HMV SXLP/*TC-SXLP* 30533. Menuhin, New Philh. O., Dorati.

Yehudi Menuhin was closely associated with Bartók in the last few years of the composer's life and made the pioneering commercial records of the 1938 concerto with Dorati and the Dallas Symphony Orchestra. This version, though not quite as fresh as that very first account, is thoroughly committed and beautifully recorded. It has a price advantage over both Itzhak Perlman and Kyung-Wha Chung (see below) and the additional attraction of including the early concerto that Bartók wrote for Stefi Geyer, which at the time of writing is not otherwise available. The cassette is every bit the equal of the disc, the quality full, yet strikingly clean and clearly detailed.

Violin concerto No. 2 in B min.
*** Decca SXL/*KSXC* 6802 [Lon. 7023/5-]. Kyung-Wha Chung, LPO, Solti.

**(*) CBS 76831/40- [Col. M/*MT*
35156]. Zukerman, LAPO, Mehta.

The combination of Chung and Solti
produces a fiery, diamond-bright performance in which the Hungarian inflections are sharply brought out. Where
the Perlman/Previn performance (HMV
ASD 3014 [Ang. S 37014]) is warm and
rich in confidence, treating this work
(validly enough) as a successor to the
great romantic concertos, Chung and
Solti interpret it less comfortably.
Though the angularity will not please
everyone, it is an equally characterful
reading. Bright Decca sound with forward violin, vivid on both disc and cassette alike.

There is a carefree quality in Zukerman's playing from the very start which
some will find appealing, but this performance lacks the full intensity of what is
among the most deeply felt of twentieth-
century concertos. It is a safe performance, lacking a little in poetry on the one
hand, excitement on the other. The recording is similarly safe but lacks inner
clarity. The cassette transfer is bright, but
thin, and lacking in bloom on top, although the bass remains resonant.

(i) *Dance suite; The Miraculous
Mandarin; The Wooden Prince;* (ii)
Bluebeard's Castle (all complete).
(M) *** CBS 79338 (3). (i) NYPO; (ii)
Troyanos, Nimsgern, BBC SO; all
cond. Boulez.
(M) ** Ph. 6768 600 (3) [Mer. 77012]. (i)
Philh. Hungarica, BBC SO or LSO;
(ii) Szönyi, Székely, LSO; all cond.
Dorati.

On CBS, Bartók's three works for the
stage bring out a warmly expressive side
of Boulez that at one time was hardly
suspected. With refined recording and
nice separation of voices and orchestra
(each in a slightly different acoustic),
Bluebeard's Castle is given a most compelling performance. The coupling of *The
Miraculous Mandarin* and the *Dance suite*

brings performances just as warm but a
degree less precise. What is lost in sheer
violence in the ballet is gained in emotional power. In the least convincing of
the three works Boulez is the most compelling of advocates, keeping his concentration through *The Wooden Prince*,
even though he insists on giving the score
absolutely uncut, which is rare. The recording is among CBS's best.

Dorati's recordings of Bartók's theatre
music were all made in the mid-sixties,
with varying success. *The Wooden Prince*
is given a freshly expressive reading, with
the Debussian textures brilliantly caught.
The Miraculous Mandarin, as contrasted
as could be in its brutality, finds Dorati
equally sympathetic, but in *Bluebeard's
Castle* he is less successful, and is not
helped by harsher recording and disappointing soloists (Olga Szönyi makes
an edgy and wobbly Judith). The *Dance
suite*, recorded much more recently, is
given a lively and colourful reading.

The Miraculous Mandarin (complete); *2 Portraits, Op. 5.*
**(*) Decca SXL 6882. VPO, Doh-
nányi.

Dohnányi's direction of *The Miraculous Mandarin*, which has long been
regarded as an unusually barbaric score,
is clean, precise and often beautiful. It is
far less violent and weighty than usual,
and not everyone will respond to what
one could almost describe as an unsuspected neoclassical element in the
score. Dohnányi's Bartók style is more
obviously suited to the *Two Portraits*, the
first of which is used also as the first
movement of the *Violin concerto No. 1.*
The playing of the Vienna Philharmonic
is radiantly beautiful, helped by spacious
recording. Erich Binder is a first-class
soloist in the *Portraits*.

*The Miraculous Mandarin: suite, Op.
19; Music for strings, percussion and
celesta.*
*** HMV ASD/*TC-ASD* 3655 [Ang.
SZ 37608]. Phd. O., Ormandy.

(M) *(*) DG Priv. 2535/*3335* 454 [2530 887]. Boston SO, Ozawa.

Music for strings, percussion and celesta.

(M) **(*) HMV SXLP/TC ÷ SXLP 30536 [Ang. S 35949]. Berlin PO, Karajan – HINDEMITH: *Mathis der Maler.*****

(M) **(*) DG Acc. 2542/*3342* 134 [2530 065]. Berlin PO, Karajan – STRAVINSKY: *Apollon Musagète.****

Ormandy and the Philadelphia Orchestra have recorded *The Miraculous Mandarin* before, but this new version does full justice to the opulence of the Philadelphia strings and the rich sonorities of their cellos and basses. The sheer magnificence of the orchestral sound is a joy in itself. *The Miraculous Mandarin* suite is dazzling and the only reservation to make concerns the *Music for strings, percussion and celesta*, where greater mystery is needed (at least in the first and third movements). There is no want of eloquence and passion, but the dynamic range at the pianissimo end of the spectrum leaves something to be desired. That apart, there is so much to enjoy and admire here that this issue can be strongly recommended: the orchestral playing as such and the recording too are of the very first order. The cassette transfer is admirably vivid and clean.

However, Solti's famous Decca coupling (SXL 6111 [Lon. 6783]) is by no means pushed into second place by the newer issue. Ormandy has the advantage of finer orchestral playing and an obviously more modern recording, but Solti shows a special feel for these scores, and the streak of ruthlessness in his make-up that sometimes mars performances of less barbaric music is given full rein in *The Miraculous Mandarin*, and creates a similar urgency in the *Music for strings, percussion and celesta.*

One would never recognize the Boston Symphony Orchestra from their DG record. The sound is aggressively close, with little sense of space round it, and the separate instrumental sections are so presented as to suggest multi-track technique with the sound mixed not at the time of recording but afterwards. It might be argued that aggressive sound is appropriate for Bartók, but the beauty of tone of the Boston players, above all the string sections, is only intermittently conveyed, with the violins in the *Music for strings* sounding thin and undernourished. The closeness exposes flaws in ensemble too, and the brilliant second and fourth movements sound relatively slack. *The Miraculous Mandarin* suite with its heavy orchestration is helped even less by the recording; there is little or no feeling of ambience. It is hard to believe that this was recorded in the opulent acoustic of Symphony Hall.

Karajan first recorded the *Music for strings, percussion and celesta* with the Philharmonia Orchestra in 1949 (Columbia LX 1371–74); the HMV version comes from 1960. Though not as well recorded as the 1969 remake for DG, this is a marvellously atmospheric and committed account, in some ways fresher and more spontaneous than the later version. The sound needs more body and colour in the middle and upper register but it is still perfectly acceptable and in view of the excellence of the performance (and the coupling) this should not deter readers from investing in it.

Karajan's Accolade version has the advantage of excellent sound and a luxuriant Stravinsky coupling that is no less attractive than the Hindemith on the HMV record. Karajan's view of the Bartók has remained essentially romantic. He avoids undue expressiveness in the opening slow fugue (except in a big rallentando at the end), but the third movement is given a performance in soft focus. Nevertheless the playing of the Berlin strings is a delight to the ear and at medium price this remains very worthwhile. There is a first-class cassette, clear and well detailed.

Rumanian folk dances (arr. Willner).

(M) **(*) Ph. Fest. 6570/7310 181 [id.]. I Musici – BARBER: *Adagio*; BRITTEN: *Simple symphony*; RESPIGHI: *Ancient airs*.**(*)

Bartók's suite of *Rumanian folk dances* sounds attractive in this transcription by Arthur Willner, and the performance by I Musici is spirited and warmly sympathetic. There may be a slight lack of bite, but there is a compensating touch of Italian sunshine. The recording is excellent on disc and tape alike.

Suite No. 1, Op. 3; 2 Pictures, Op. 10.
*** Decca SXL 6897 [Lon. 7120]. Detroit SO, Dorati.

The *Suite No. 1*, regarded as revolutionary at its first Viennese performance in 1905, now strikes the ear as conservative, but it is a warm and colourful work which demonstrates many of the strong and purposeful qualities that the mature Bartók developed, not just in the atmospheric memorability of much of the writing but in the structural control, with the five movements in arch form. Dorati's performance is strong and colourful to match, not quite as refined as it might be, but vigorous and brilliantly recorded, with an excellent and apt coupling in the much more advanced *Pictures* of 1910.

44 Duos.
*** HMV ASD 4011 [Ang. SZ 37540]. Perlman, Zukerman.

Though intended for educational use, and arranged in ascending order of difficulty, these miniatures emerge as little jewels of inspiration – the heart of Bartók revealed – when played with such warmth and intensity as here. Few will want to hear all forty-four at a single sitting, so it is a pity that the banding is not identified. The recording is warm and immediate to enhance the compelling performances.

Sonata for two pianos and percussion.
*** Ph. 9500 434/7300 644 [id.]. Argerich, Bishop-Kovacevich, Goudswaard, De Roo – DEBUSSY: *En blanc et noir*; MOZART: *Andante*.***

A strongly atmospheric and finely characterized performance (also available coupled to the *Piano concertos*: see above). This is most imaginative playing and is afforded a recording of exceptionally wide range and truthfulness. It would be difficult to imagine a more eloquent or better recorded account of this powerful work. The tape transfer, however, is made at a low level (the opening is recessed) and there is a lack of transient bite.

String quartets Nos. 1–6.
*** DG 2740 235 (3) [id.]. Tokyo Qt.
*** ASV Dig. DCAB 301 (3). Lindsay Qt.
*(**) RCA RL 02412 (3) [ARL 3 2412]. Guarneri Qt.

String quartets Nos. 1–2.
*** ASV Dig. DCA/ZCDCA 510. Lindsay Qt.
(M) **(*) Saga 5203. Fine Arts Qt.

String quartets Nos. 3–4.
*** ASV Dig. DCA/ZCDCA 509. Lindsay Qt.
(M) **(*) Saga 5204. Fine Arts Qt.

String quartets Nos. 5–6.
*** ASV Dig. DCA/ZCDCA 504. Lindsay Qt.
(M) **(*) Saga 5205. Fine Arts Qt.

It was the Tokyo Quartet's records of the *Second* and *Sixth* Bartók quartets (DG 2530 658 – now withdrawn in the UK) that alerted us to an exceptional group. These performances brought an almost ideal combination of fire and energy with detailed point and refinement. When, several years later, the group went on to record the rest of the cycle, the performances proved just as consistently satisfying, outshining direct rivals in almost every way. Though the polish is higher than in other versions – helped by splendid recording – the sense of commitment and seeming spontaneity is greater too. So the range of expression includes in the fullest measure not only the necessary Bartókian passion but the sparkle and wit, each interpretative problem closely considered and solved with finesse and assurance.

The Lindsay Quartet on ASV have the advantage of first-class digital sound, warmly atmospheric but nicely focused, and these are the only recordings available on cassette. The quality of the tape transfers is outstanding, combining presence with body and homogeneity of timbre, and giving excellent detail at *piano* and *pianissimo* levels. The discs are available separately or in a box with a modest price reduction. Searching and powerfully expressive, the Lindsay Quartet give strongly projected readings which can be recommended alongside though not in preference to the Tokyo set. Artistically the claims of both sets are very finely balanced, although the Lindsay readings, direct and committed, lack the last degree of pointed detail which makes those of the Tokyo players so compelling.

The Fine Arts recordings on the Saga mid-priced label are also available separately. They were made in the early sixties, and though the latest German pressings have improved the quality, the sound is obviously dated, with fairly high tape hiss. But at medium price the series is well worth considering for the sharply incisive and dramatic performances, so sharp in attack one might almost describe the approach as Stravinskian. Nonetheless there is nothing cold about this deeply committed playing.

The Guarneri players too give an impressive account of themselves in this challenging repertoire, and in terms of intonation, ensemble and tonal blend they are not to be faulted. Unfortunately they are let down by the recording, which is made in a rather dryish acoustic, so that the sound does not expand and open out. The unrelieved quality of the sound diminishes one's pleasure in what are highly accomplished readings. Good though these performances are, they do not represent a challenge to the Tokyo or Lindsay versions.

Piano music

Allegro barbaro; 4 Dirges, Op. 9a; 3 Hungarian folksongs from the Czik District; 15 Hungarian peasant songs; 8 Improvisations on Hungarian peasant songs, Op. 20; 7 Sketches, Op. 9b.
*** Ph. 9500/7300 876. Kocsis.

A marvellous recital, with playing of exceptional sensitivity and range. Zoltán Kocsis is always thoughtful, and his performance of the *Dirges* is penetrating and moving. He discovers a world of colour that leaves no doubt of the quality of his imagination and musicianship. Yet there is no want of drama and power when required. The *Songs from the Czik District* are exquisitely done, and so, for that matter, are all the pieces here. This is one of the finest Bartók recitals in the catalogue: it makes the old Andor Foldes set seem very monochrome indeed. The recording is stunningly lifelike; as piano sound, this is in the demonstration class. The cassette too is of Philips' best quality, full-bodied and clear.

For Children.
*** Tel. EK 6.35338 (2). Ránki.

For Children (revised versions). *10 Easy pieces; Sonatina.*
*** EMI 2C 167 16246/7. Béroff.

Bartók's pieces *For Children* are a collection of Hungarian (Book 1) and Slovak (Book 2) folksongs, which possess a beguiling simplicity and (when taken in small doses) unfailing musical interest.

The young Hungarian pianist Dezsö Ránki plays all eighty-five pieces with the utmost persuasion and with the art that conceals art, for the simplicity of some of these pieces is deceptive; darker currents lurk beneath their surface. He is given clean and well-focused recorded sound.

Choice between Michel Béroff and Dezsö Ránki is simplified by the fact that Béroff records the revised score while Ránki gives us the original edition of 1908–9. Béroff also finds space for some extra items, but in every other respect the honours are pretty evenly divided. Béroff's playing has an unaffected eloquence that is touching, and the recording is excellent.

sensibility and character, though in many pieces honours are evenly divided. The DG recording is very good indeed, and though Ránki remains first choice, this is still a strong contender for those wanting this repertoire in full.

Claude Helffer gives an intelligent account, though he tends to invest detail with greater expressive emphasis than this mostly simple music can bear. Greater simplicity would have yielded stronger artistic results, though this is not to deny that there is some fine playing during the course of the six sides. In the pieces requiring a second player Helffer is joined by Haakon Austbö (some artists such as Ránki play with the second part pre-recorded). The sound is realistic and fully acceptable.

Mikrokosmos (complete).
*** Tel. FK 6.35369 (3) [id.]. Ránki.
*** DG 2740 239 (3) [id.]. Francesch.
** HM HMU 968/70. Helffer (with Austbö).

Dezsö Ránki belongs to the younger generation of Hungarian pianists and has already made a name for himself as a brilliant virtuoso. The first books of *Mikrokosmos* are more for the delectation of the younger player – simple teaching pieces that are scarcely intended to be listened to – but the later pieces are richly inventive and make for rewarding listening. Ránki plays with an effortless eloquence and a welcome simplicity. He resists the temptation to make expressive points where none are required and plays with total dedication and command. He is very clearly recorded, with well-defined sound. Unfortunately this set has been withdrawn from the standard UK Telefunken catalogue and is available only as a special import.

Homero Francesch is an accomplished player too, and gives a thoroughly conscientious and faithful account of the 150-odd pieces in the *Mikrokosmos*. Ránki has the edge on him in terms of

Out of Doors (suite); *Piano sonata; Suite, Op. 14.*
*** CBS 76650. Perahia.

Murray Perahia brings to this repertoire a muscularity and fire that will exhilarate – and surprise – those who know only his Mozart concerto records. He attacks the keyboard with total yet disciplined abandon (if that is not a contradiction in terms) and gives us playing of exceptional imaginative vision. In *Out of Doors* there are delicate glints of light, scarcely perceptible rustling of foliage and insect chirrups, and Perahia does not pull his punches in the *Chase* or obscure the peasant earthiness of the *Musettes* movement. As in everything this artist gives us on record, there is total commitment; no phrase is ever given less than its full weight, yet there is no self-indulgent overstatement. Indeed these performances have so complete a ring of authenticity that one soon forgets to think of the player – in almost the same way as with Schnabel's Beethoven sonatas Op. 110 or Op. 111. The recording does not do full justice to Perahia's tone (judging from his Bartók performances in the concert hall): the acoustic is dry and the studio obviously smaller than the one used in Kocsis's much-admired Philips disc (see above). As a result the sound is a trifle metallic and wanting in bloom (though that is not entirely unsuited to this music). Were the recorded sound as good as for Kocsis, this would rate a rosette.

5 Songs, Op. 16.
*** Decca SXL 6964. Sass, Schiff – LISZT: *Lieder.****

Darkly beautiful, these settings of poems by Endre Ady come from the period leading up to Bartók's *Second Quartet*. The mood is tragic, the technique often adventurous, but the result seductive. Sylvia Sass and András Schiff, Hungarians both, give intense, persuasive performances, beautifully recorded.

Bluebeard's Castle (complete).
*** Decca SET/*KCET* 630 [Lon. 1174]. Sass, Kovats, LPO, Solti.
*(*) DG 2531 172 [id.]. Varady, Fischer-Dieskau, Bav. State Op. O., Sawallisch.

Solti directs a richly atmospheric reading of Bartók's ritualistic opera, not as searingly dramatic as one might have expected but with recording of spectacular range. The performance is introduced by the Hungarian verses which are printed in the score. The Hungarian soloists are tangily authentic, though their voices are not always perfectly steady, and Sylvia Sass is very appealing with her exquisite pianissimo singing. The recording – less analytical than is normal from Decca – produces a rich carpet of sound. The result is a more romantic effect than usual, and even reveals an affinity with Richard Strauss. Listeners who find the more vibrant approach of Boulez with Troyanos and Nimsgern (CBS 76518 [Col. M 34217]) or the brilliant earlier Decca account with Ludwig and Berry, conducted by Kertesz

(SET 311 [Lon. 1158]), too authentically uncompromising, may well respond to Sass's very appealing portrayal of Judith. Certainly Solti's approach is more positive than the badly balanced Sawallisch recording. The Decca cassette, moreover, offers demonstration sound, superbly rich and atmospheric. The two soloists on the DG version – in real life husband and wife – bring Lieder-like intensity to the almost ritualistic exchanges of Bluebeard and Judith. The pity is that their voices are recorded too close and the orchestral contribution lacks the bite and drama which are essential to this sharply structured piece.

Bax, Arnold (1883–1953)

Tintagel.
(M) *** HMV Green. ESD/*TC-ESD* 7092 [Ang. S 36415]. LSO, Barbirolli – DELIUS: *Collection;* IRELAND: *London overture.****

Barbirolli's performance of *Tintagel* was the first to be issued in stereo, and its reissue on HMV Greensleeve is most welcome. The sound is fresh and the splendid cassette matches the disc in its brightness and clarity. The performance is characteristically full-blooded. The sea vistas (with their musical reminders of Debussy as well as Wagner) are magnificently painted by players and recording engineers alike and Sir John sees that the memorable principal tune is given a fine romantic sweep. If the couplings are attractive this is highly recommendable.

Rhapsodic ballad (for unaccompanied cello).
*** Pearl SHE 547. Saram – L. BERKELEY and BRIDGE: *Trios.***

One does not associate Bax with so austere a medium as the unaccompanied cello. This dates from the beginning of the Second World War and is a passionately argued work, which uses as its point of departure the opening theme from Bax's 1929 *Overture, elegy and rondo*. It throws new light on the composer, who was not usually so concentrated in utterance. It is played with masterly command by Rohan de Saram, whose range of tone and colour does much to win over the most sceptical of critics. The recording is a shade close but fully acceptable, and the interest of this disc outweighs other considerations.

Beethoven, Ludwig van
(1770–1827)

Piano concertos Nos. 1–5; (i) *Choral fantasia, Op. 80.*
*** Ph. 6767 002 (5)/7699 061 [id.].
Brendel, LPO, Haitink, (i) with LPO Ch.
(M) *** HMV SLS/*TC-SLS* 5180 (4).
Barenboim, New Philh. O., Klemperer, (i) with John Alldis Ch.
(B) **(*) CfP CFP 78253 (4). Lill, SNO, Gibson, (i) with Ch.

(i) *Piano concertos Nos. 1–5. Für Elise, G.173; Rondo in C, Op. 51/1; Rondo a capriccioso, Op. 129; 32 Variations in C min., G.191.*
** HMV SLS/*TC-SLS* 5112 (4) [Ang. S/4X4S 3854]. Weissenberg, (i) with Berlin PO, Karajan.

(i) *Piano concertos Nos. 1–5. Andante favori; Für Elise; Polonaise in C, Op. 89; Variations in F, Op. 34.*
(M) (***) World mono SHB/*TC-SHB* 64 (4). Schnabel, (i) with LPO, Sargent.

Technically the Brendel recordings are superb and must be numbered among the best concerto recordings available in cassette or disc form. Given an artist of

Brendel's distinction, it would be surprising if this set were not in the first flight artistically, even though there are moments (for instance in the *Emperor*) when one's mind returns to his earlier Turnabout recordings, which sound less studied. Elsewhere there is no lack of spontaneity, and generally speaking the performances are as satisfying as the recording is rich. The perspective between soloist and orchestra is perfectly judged and the piano tone itself is remarkably lifelike, clean and well-focused throughout its register. There is general consent that these performances are among the very finest in the market, and as sound they certainly head the list.

Hardly less rewarding is the fascinating Barenboim/Klemperer set recorded at the end of the sixties and still sounding very well indeed, both on disc and in the bold, high-level cassette transfers. Indeed the tape box offers the ideal presentation of the music, with each of the concertos complete on one cassette side (the *Emperor* backed by the *Choral fantasia*). No more individual performances of the Beethoven concertos have ever been put on record. The combination of Barenboim and Klemperer is nothing if not inspired, and for every wilfulness of a measured Klemperer there is a youthful spark from the spontaneously combusting Barenboim. That may imply a lack of sympathy between conductor and soloist, but plainly this is not so. These recordings were made much more quickly than usual, with long takes allowing a sense of continuity rare on record. Some may not like an apparently spontaneous performance for repeated listening (in the *Emperor*, for example, Barenboim has some slight fluffs of finger) but the concentration is formidable and especially compelling in the slow movements, whether in the earliest concerto, No. 2 – here given an interpretation that is anything but Mozartian, and splendidly strong – or in the later concertos. No. 3 brings the most obviously wilful slow tempi, but, with fine rhythmic points from soloist and orchestra, the result is still vivid and compelling. No. 4 is anything but a delicate, feminine work, with basic tempi slow enough to avoid the need for much slowing when the lyrical counter-subjects emerge. The *Choral fantasia* too is given an inspired performance, with the weaknesses of Beethoven's writing wonderfully concealed when the music-making is so intense.

John Lill has never been more impressive on record than in his set of the Beethoven concertos; in each of the works he conveys a sense of spontaneity and a vein of poetry that in the studio have too often eluded him. Gibson and the Scottish National Orchestra provide strong, direct support, helped by good modern recording, and though there have been more strikingly individual readings than these, as a set they make a very impressive cycle. The records are issued in their original sleeves but within an attractively robust box, and the value for money is remarkable.

Alongside Brendel or Barenboim, Alexis Weissenberg's playing sounds rather run-of-the-mill, although there are individual felicities and Karajan and the Berlin Philharmonic Orchestra create a strong impression in the beautifully played accompaniments. Heard in isolation these performances, stylish and accurate, undoubtedly give pleasure, and the piano pieces acting as fillers are rewarding too. But the current competition is too strong for the set as a whole to be recommended. On tape, each concerto is complete on one side, with the miscellaneous piano pieces grouped together on side six. There are no complaints on sonic grounds in either medium.

Schnabel's performances fall into a special category. The concertos were recorded in 1932–3, save for the *B flat*, which dates from 1935; the solo pieces come from 1938 and some were unpublished. They are not to be confused with Schnabel's postwar cycle with Galliera and Dobrowen or his wartime accounts of Nos. 4 and 5, made in Chicago.

His playing has such enormous character that it transcends the limitations of sound that are inevitable at this period, the only possible exception being the *Emperor*. The orchestral playing is occasionally lacking the finesse that we take for granted nowadays, but Schnabel's impulsive, searching and poetic playing offers special rewards. Not everything is equally successful: there is some roughness in the first movement of No. 3, but there are some marvellously spirited touches. Schnabel may not be so illuminating in the concertos as he was in, say, the late *Piano sonatas*, but that is comparing one peak with another higher one. Among historic collections Solomon's has a surpassing claim on the collector, and Schnabel, though he often penetrates deeper, seldom attains the latter's poise. Nonetheless, these revealing performances are to be treasured, whether on disc or on the expertly transferred tapes, where the sound is consistently crisp and lively.

Piano concerto No. 1 in C, Op. 15.

(M) *** Ph. Fest. 6570/*7310* 134. Bishop-Kovacevich, BBC SO, Colin Davis.

*** Ph. 9500 252/*7300 563* [id.]. Brendel, LPO, Haitink.

(M) ** DG Priv. 2535/*3335* 273. Eschenbach, Berlin PO, Karajan.

*(*) DG 2531/*3301* 302 [id.]. Michelangeli, VSO, Giulini.

Piano concerto No. 1; Piano sonata No. 14 (Moonlight).

(M) **(*) Decca Jub. JB/*KJBC* 39 [in Lon. STS 15203/6]. Gulda, VPO, Stein.

The reissue of the Bishop-Kovacevich at medium price (albeit without its original sonata coupling) makes a highly attractive principal recommendation, even if one considers the undoubted attractions of Ashkenazy (Decca SXL/*KSXC* 6651 [Lon. 6853/5-]), Kempff (DG 138774/*3300 227*) and Brendel (see below). The combination of Bishop-

Kovacevich and Davis rarely fails to produce an exceptionally satisfying reading, and this performance, which combines clarity of articulation and deep thoughtfulness, is among the very finest versions of this concerto. Maybe Bishop-Kovacevich misses some of the exuberance of Kempff, but the unforced rightness of the interpretation may be judged from the fact that, though he keeps the pulse remarkably steady in the slow movement, the result still conveys spontaneity with no feeling of rigidity. An advantage over Kempff and Barenboim (among others) is that Bishop-Kovacevich uses the longest and most challenging of the cadenzas that Beethoven wrote for the first movement. The recording is beautifully refined in the Philips manner, and the cassette quality is splendid. (Unfortunately this issue may not continue to be available.)

There is a spontaneity about Brendel's playing in his Philips set of the Beethoven concertos that puts most of his performances rather in contrast with his concentrated but studied accounts of the *Piano sonatas* on the same label. Nowhere is this spontaneity more compelling than in the *First Concerto*, though in places neither the solo nor the orchestral playing is quite as tidy as one would expect of these performers. Good recording, with a matching cassette, rather over-ample in bass.

Gulda gives a strong, direct reading, just a little disappointing in the slow movement (extrovert, with eighteenth-century elements underlined) but otherwise very satisfying. The first movement also has Beethoven's third and longest cadenza, and the finale grows in crispness and point as it progresses, a delightful performance. Gulda's way of letting the music speak for itself also makes for a fresh and enjoyable reading of the *Moonlight sonata*. The recording is excellent, provided the unusual timbre of the piano, a little shallow on top, is acceptable. The tape transfer is of admirable quality, bright and vivid and generally well focused, though the acoustic is fairly resonant.

Eschenbach and Karajan choose a slow tempo for the first movement, and though the concentration holds the attention, the result here is closer to a chamber approach. A beautiful performance of the slow movement and a lightweight finale. The performance is attractive and interesting, but in its concentration on refinement (Karajan's doing?) it misses any sort of greatness. The recording is good.

Recorded at a live concert, the partnership of Michelangeli and Giulini is intensely disappointing, with Michelangeli strangely metrical – a fault accentuated by the forward balance and clangorous tone of the piano. Against such competition the contribution of Giulini and the orchestra is undistinguished.

Piano concertos Nos. 1–2.
*** Decca Dig. SXDL/*KSXDC* 7502 [Lon. LDR 10006]. Lupu, Israel PO, Mehta.

Lupu couples the two early concertos in an exceptionally generous digital disc. (Indeed such a coupling offers stiff competition, even to bargain-priced issues.) The readings find Lupu and Mehta favouring fast resilient speeds. The slow movements are treated with lightness too and throughout it is the pianist who dominates. Lupu's playing has both sparkle and sensitivity and its poetry is ever apparent. He never tries to invest detail with undue expressive intensity, nor does he view early Beethoven through the eyes of his maturity. These are marvellously articulated readings, and if the playing of the Israel Philharmonic is sometimes not very refined it is always sympathetic. The digital recording is outstandingly successful (both on disc and on the cassette, which is of demonstration standard). The balance is excellently judged and the sound combines comfort with great clarity. No attempt to be spectacular is made and the effect is consistently pleasing.

Piano concerto No. 2 in B flat, Op. 19.
*** Ph. 9500 471/*7300 628* [id.]. Brendel, LPO, Haitink – *Choral fantasia.****
(M) *** DG Acc. 2542/*3342* 136. [138775/ *3300 485*]. Kempff, Berlin PO, Leitner – *Concerto No. 4.****
(M) *** Ph. Fest. 6570/*7310* 059. Bishop-Kovacevich, BBC SO, Colin Davis – *Concerto No. 4.****
(M) **(*) HMV SXLP/*TC-SXLP* 30515. Gilels, Cleveland O., Szell – *Concerto No. 4.***(*)
(B) **(*) CfP CFP/*TC-CFP* 40271. Lill, SNO, Gibson – *Concerto No. 4.***(*)

Brendel and Haitink convey both the strength and the charm of the young Beethoven's first mature essay in piano concerto writing. The spontaneity of the playing is a delight, not least in the capriciousness of the finale, though the slow movement could be more gently treated – partly the fault of the recording's acoustic. The *Choral fantasia* makes an excellent coupling, with Brendel inspired in the opening cadenza. Vivid, immediate sound, with an excellent tape transfer of the *Concerto*, which is beautifully balanced. In the *Choral fantasia*, however, one might wish the level of transfer had been a little higher. Here, although the quality is refined, the choral detail lacks the last degree of crispness of focus.

There is intense competition in the medium price-range. Kempff's account of the *Second Concerto*, attractively coupled with the *Fourth*, has long been a favourite choice. Like No. 4 it is a less individual performance than on Kempff's earlier mono LP, but his playing is unmistakable in almost every bar and Leitner's conducting is both strong and sympathetic. The recording, from the early sixties, still sounds well and the tape

was one of the best of DG's early transfers, although it has not been remastered for the reissue.

For those who find Kempff's coupling too personal, Stephen Bishop-Kovacevich provides the ideal answer in a direct, thoughtful reading, with fine accompaniment from Sir Colin Davis and the BBC orchestra, and refined Philips recording, more modern than the DG, with clear, pellucid piano timbre. The sound is lighter in the bass than the other issues in this series, but that is the only indication of the length of the sides. The tape transfer is well managed too, clear and clean.

Gilels is an incomparable Beethoven player and we have long cherished his seraphic account of the *G major Concerto* with Leopold Ludwig. He is unfailingly illuminating and poetic, his playing consistently a matter for marvel. Szell is a less sympathetic accompanist. He keeps everything on a rather tight rein and rarely matches the humanity and vision of his soloist. The recording too is dry and clear rather than expansive. The cassette is of first-class quality, matching the disc closely.

In the bargain range John Lill's performance can be cordially welcomed. He plays with ease and imagination, and Gibson's accompaniment is well made if not showing any striking insights. With good modern recording this is excellent value. There is a first-class cassette too, with good body and range.

Piano concerto No. 3 in C minor, Op. 37.
(M) *** Ph. Fest. 6570/*7310* 135. Bishop-Kovacevich, BBC SO, Colin Davis.
(M) *** Ph. Seq. 6527/*7311* 090. Haskil, Lamoureux O., Markevitch.
**(*) DG 2531/*3301* 057 [id.]. Pollini, VPO, Boehm.
**(*) Ph. 9500 253 [id.]. Brendel, LPO, Haitink.
**(*) RCA RL/*RK* 11418 [ARL/*ARK* 11418]. Rubinstein, LPO, Barenboim.

(B) *(*) Con. CC/*CCT* 7509. Eschenbach, LSO, Henze.

*Piano concerto No. 3; 2 Rondos, Op.
51/1–2.*
**(*) Decca Dig. SXDL/*KSXDC* 7507
[Lon. LDR 10000]. Lupu, Israel PO,
Mehta.

Bishop-Kovacevich's performance has
stood the test of time and remains among
the most satisfying available accounts of
the *C minor Concerto.* The recording is
clear and refined, and the tape matches
the disc closely.

Haskil, in a clean, muscular style, gives
a most refreshing performance, one of
her relatively rare records made not long
before she died in 1960. Her first entry
establishes that feminine delicacy is not
her style. Intellectual concentration
married to sharp articulation (most remarkable in the left hand) characterize a
performance where even the delicate pianissimos at the end of the slow movement
convey strength rather than poetry. The
recording is excellent for its period. The
cassette transfer is admirable, well-
balanced, full and lively

The single-minded clarity of Pollini's
reading is no less refreshing. Boehm's
strong and sober accompaniment adds to
the purposefulness, though charm is
never present and warmth not often.
Nonetheless the concentration of playing, beautifully recorded (there is no
appreciable difference between tape and
disc), makes this a strong and individual
version.

In contrast Brendel and Haitink give
an easy, relaxed account of the first
movement, spontaneous-sounding, like
the rest of the set, with the timpani taps
of the coda even more measured and
mysterious than usual. If the other two
movements are less tense, with the finale
thrown off in a mercurial manner, this
adds up to a strong, persuasive performance, beautifully recorded.

Rubinstein in his eighties remained
among the freshest of Beethoven inter-

preters, and his partnership with Barenboim brings a most appealing performance, with an inspirationally eloquent
slow movement and joyously alert finale.
Unfortunately the recording balance
favours the piano to a marked degree,
and orchestral detail is masked (although
this is more striking on disc than on the
slightly drier tape). Even so this remains
very enjoyable, for the orchestral sound
has plenty of weight.

Radu Lupu has the benefit of digital
recording and very good it is too, on tape
and disc alike. His reading of the concerto is forthright and dramatic, yet attentive to every detail of colour and
dynamic nuance. He is unfailingly perceptive and musical, though unsmiling at
those moments where a gentle poetry
surfaces. In every sense a powerfully
conceived reading, somewhat let down by
the orchestral support: the first desks of
the Israel Philharmonic strings are not
heard to flattering effect and the wind
playing, though not insensitive, is far
from distinguished. Were the orchestral
response as impressive as either Lupu or
the Decca engineers, this would be a
strong front-runner, and Lupu offers
an immaculately played fill-up. However,
Bishop-Kovacevich, Pollini and Brendel,
among the more modern recordings,
remain preferable.

Eschenbach plays with imagination
and poetry; the opening of the slow movement is magical. But the performance is
hopelessly weighed down by the accompaniment under Hans Werner Henze,
who seems unable to produce more than
the most routine conducting in Beethoven. Despite the fine contribution of
the soloist and full recording (more
opaque on cassette than disc), this is not
a strong competitor, even at bargain
price, where John Lill (CfP CFP/*TC-
CFP* 40259) holds the field to himself.

Piano concerto No. 4 in G, Op. 58.
(M) *** DG Acc. 2542/*3342* 136 [138775/
3300 485]. Kempff, Berlin PO, Leitner
*Concerto No. 2.****

(M) *** Ph. Fest. 6570/*7310* 059. Bishop-Kovacevich, BBC SO, Colin Davis – *Concerto No. 2*.***

(M) **(*) HMV SXLP/*TC-SXLP* 30515 [(d) Ang. S 36030]. Gilels, Cleveland O., Szell – *Concerto No. 2*.**(*)

**(*) Ph. 9500 254/*7300 600* [id.]. Brendel, LPO, Haitink.

(B) **(*) CfP CFP/*TC-CFP* 40271. Lill, SNO, Gibson – *Concerto No. 2*.**(*)

*(*) Symph. SYM/*CSYM* 12 [Peters PLE 110]. Rosen, Symph. of L., Morris.

Piano concerto No. 4; Piano sonata No. 24.

(M) *** Decca Jub. JB/*KJBC* 41 [(d) in Lon. STS 15203/6]. Gulda, VPO, Stein.

Although Kempff's delicacy of fingerwork and his shading of tone colour are as effervescent as ever, this is not so personal a reading as his earlier mono version. There were moments in that of the purest magic, provided one was ready to accept some waywardness. The stereo version also allows some speed variation, but the increased sense of unity owes much, it is plain, to the fine control of the conductor, Leitner. The recording still sounds full and clear, though the cassette transfer is not quite so crisp in outline as in the coupling.

Bishop-Kovacevich's reading is intense and deeply thoughtful. He opens the concerto very gently, and the orchestral response matches his delicacy of feeling. Yet in seeking a balance between classicism and romanticism he leans further towards the former than Kempff. The slow movement matches poetic serenity with a firm orchestral contrast, and leads naturally to a swelling of pianistic fervour at the climax. The finale is joyfully alert, mercurial and lyrical, with bursts of sheer energy from the orchestra. The sound is satisfying, with excellent detail, the long side bringing a slightly reduced bass resonance compared with other issues in this fine series. The cassette transfer is clear and clean.

Gilels's Cleveland performance offers solo playing of the highest order. His slow movement is no less magical and searching than in his earlier account with Ludwig (HMV SXLP 30086, coupled to Mozart's *Third Violin concerto*) but in the outer movements Szell's rather hard-driven support and a somewhat dryish recording diminish the overall impact of this otherwise very distinguished issue. The cassette is of first-class quality, matching the disc closely.

On Decca Jubilee the freshness and poetry of Gulda's playing make for an exceptionally compelling reading, full of strong contrasts which have the excitement of the moment, never sounding forced. In the slow movement Gulda is deeply thoughtful without ever falling into sentimentality, and the finale is clean in its directness and strength. The piano sound is somewhat shallow on top, but the orchestral recording is excellent. The short *F sharp Sonata* is not a very generous coupling, and Gulda's tempi here are controversially fast; but this issue remains highly recommendable in the medium price-range. The tape transfer is first-class, well-balanced and vivid, although on side two the volume level rises dramatically. The piano image in the sonata is agreeable and full, if not so clean-cut as in the concerto.

Brendel gives a tough and strong reading, not as immaculate as one might expect on detail but presenting an almost impressionistic thrust of urgency in the first movement. With Brendel the slow movement is rapt in its simplicity and the finale is treated almost flippantly, with mercurial strokes of individuality which, with some slips of ensemble, suggest the immediacy of a live performance rather than the care of a studio recording. On tape the low-level transfer provides sound that is basically warm and natural, and the beauty of the recording is caught; nevertheless there is a lack of sparkle at the top, and inner detail is slightly masked, notably in the first movement. With no coupling this issue cannot be given a top recommendation either on tape or disc.

If John Lill can sometimes seem too uncompromising a pianist, the *Fourth Concerto* reveals that in this most poetic of Beethoven works he can relax with individual touches of imagination and a fine range of tone-colour. There is fire too in the first movement, though in all three Gibson is somewhat square in his accompaniment. With good modern recording this generous coupling makes a first-rate bargain, both on disc and on the excellent cassette.

The Rosen/Morris version, recorded after their account of the *Emperor*, avoids the worst faults of that emphatically unrecommendable record, but there is too little poetry in the reading for it to give complete pleasure. It is spacious and strong, with the soloist giving a characterful and positive view and underlining a massiveness which is sometimes forgotten. But the orchestral playing and recording are not ideally clean or well-balanced, and there are many more recommendable versions. Apart from those listed above, one must not forget the Ashkenazy/Solti performance, one of the finest of their complete series for Decca (SXL/*KSXC* 6654 [Lon. 6856/5-]). This is coupled with the *Leonora No. 3 Overture*, whereas Pollini's aristocratic account with Boehm, if no less distinguished, seems short measure at full price with no coupling (DG 2530/*3300* 791).

Piano concerto No. 5 in E flat (Emperor), Op. 73.

(M) *** Ph. Fest. 6570/*7310* 013 [id.]. Bishop-Kovacevich, LSO, Colin Davis.

(M) *** Ph. Seq. 6527/*7311* 055 [Fest. 6570/*7310* 086]. Arrau, Concg. O., Haitink.

*** Telarc Dig. DG 10065 [id.]. Serkin, Boston SO, Ozawa.

(M) *** DG Priv. 2535/*3335* 296 [2530 438/*3300 384*]. Eschenbach, Boston SO, Ozawa.

(B) **(*) Con. CC/*CCT* 7547 [Odys. 3216 0326]. Casadesus, Concg. O., Rosbaud.

**(*) DG 2531/*3301* [id.]. Pollini, VPO, Boehm.

**(*) Decca Dig. SXDL/*KSXDC* 7503 [Lon. LDR/5- 10005]. Lupu, Israel PO, Mehta.

**(*) Ph. 9500 243/*7300 542* [id.]. Brendel, LPO, Haitink.

(M) **(*) Decca Jub. JB/*KJBC* 18 [in Lon. STS 15203/6]. Gulda, VPO, Stein.

**(*) Decca SXL/*KSXC* 6899. Larrocha, LAPO, Mehta.

* Symph. SYM 10 [Peters PLE 024]. Symph. of L., Morris.

Piano concerto No. 5; Bagatelles, Op. 33/1, 3, 5 and 7.

(M) *(*) Mer. E 77001. Nakajima, Nuremberg SO, Tschupp.

Piano concerto No. 5; Overture: Egmont, Op. 84.

(M) *** Decca VIV/*KVIC* 14. Katchen, LSO, Gamba.

Bishop-Kovacevich's is one of the most deeply satisfying versions of this much-recorded concerto ever made. His is not a brash, extrovert way. With alert, sharp-edged accompaniment from Sir Colin Davis, he gives a clean dynamic performance of the outer movements, then in the central slow movement finds a depth of intensity that completely explodes any idea of this as a lighter central resting point. Even so he avoids weighing the simple plan down with unstylistic mannerisms: he relies simply on natural, unforced concentration in the most delicate, hushed tones. Fine recording, full-bodied, yet clear on both disc and tape (although the latter benefits from a bass cut), makes this Festivo reissue highly recommendable.

Those looking for a stronger, more commanding approach can safely turn to Arrau's magnificent version, used to launch Philips' mid-priced Sequenza label. It originally appeared as part of a complete cycle, and it is remarkable how much more spontaneous Arrau sounds here than in his previous account of the work, an early Columbia record (reissued on World Record Club). The slow movement in particular conveys the tension of a live performance – it sounds as though it might have been done in a single unedited take. Arrau is at his most commanding and authoritative in the outer movements, and the finale is most stylishly played. The recording is first-rate and, even without consideration of the reasonable price, this is one of the very finest available versions on any count. The tape is splendid, with boldly resonant piano tone.

With extraordinarily vivid recording Serkin's *Emperor* offers sound of spectacular realism. The great pianist is as commanding as ever, with fire and brilliance in plenty in the outer movements, yet there is also a degree of relaxation, of conscious enjoyment, that increases the degree of communication. The hushed expressive pianism that provides the lyrical contrast in the first movement is matched by the poised refinement of the *Adagio*; the finale is vigorously joyful. While this record is undoubtedly expensive (it costs more than twice as much as the admirable Arrau version), the sound could justify the price for those seeking to establish an exclusively digital collection. Ozawa's accompaniment is first-class.

Eschenbach too gives a highly satisfying interpretation, helped by the equally youthful urgency of his accompanist. With thoughtfulness and bravura combined, it stands among the finest versions, but the recording is reverberant even by Boston standards, which obscures a fair amount of inner detail. Even so, this remains a record that gives great satisfaction. The tape is transferred at quite a high level, but the upper range lacks the sparkle of the disc.

The 1964 Katchen/Gamba version has been reissued on Decca's new mid-priced label, Viva, and the sound remains impressively full and clear, although the cassette is less recommendable, with a narrower dynamic range. It is an excellent performance, full of characteristic animal energy. The first and last movements are taken at a spanking pace but not so fast that Katchen sounds at all rushed. Plainly he enjoyed himself all through, and with this pianist who had sometimes seemed too rigid in his recorded playing, it is good to find that here he seemed to be coaxing the orchestra to match his own delicacy. The slow movement is very relaxed, but with the tension admirably sustained, it contrasts well with the extreme bravura of the finale. The filler is a welcome and brightly played performance of the *Egmont overture*.

Casadesus and Rosbaud give a most beautiful interpretation, satisfyingly detailed and refined with a wonderfully serene *Adagio*. Though Arrau, with the same orchestra, is even more searching and better recorded, at bargain price this Contour issue is well worth considering. There is little to choose between disc and cassette; both are full and clear.

The clarity of Pollini's vision in his dedicated reading is never in doubt, and if at times his playing verges on the chilly, the strong and wise accompaniment of Boehm and the Vienna Philharmonic provides compensation. The slow movement is elegant, lacking the depth which the finest versions give it, and the finale is urgent and energetic rather than joyful. Excellent recording, with a first-class cassette transfer (one of the very best of the *Emperor*), combining fullness with brilliance.

Lupu gives a performance which, without lacking strength, brings thoughtfulness and poetry even to the magnificence of the first movement, with classical proportions made clear. The slow movement has delicacy and fantasy, the finale easy exhilaration, though neither conductor nor orchestra quite matches the soloist's distinction. Those who seek a digital *Emperor* will find the sound here wide-ranging and clean, although the cassette (unusually for Decca) is disappointing, with a lack of refinement in the orchestral tuttis of the first movement.

Brendel's *Emperor* is among the very best recordings as such at present on the market. The sound is vivid, full-bodied and beautifully balanced, with wide range and warmth. It goes without saying that there is much to admire from the artistic point of view too. The reading is spaciously conceived, and the phrasing has no lack of eloquence. But generally it is less spontaneous in feeling than Brendel's earlier Turnabout recording with Mehta, although that is not nearly so well recorded. Undoubtedly the new version will give satisfaction, but there is a studied quality about the music-making that keeps this performance from being at the top of the list. The tape transfer, made at rather a low level, is full and natural but lacks sparkle, particularly in the finale.

With its dramatically recorded opening (the tone of the Bösendorfer piano extremely vivid) Gulda's account of the first movement does not lack a robust quality, yet he plays less for excitement than for poetry. The passages in his reading of the *Emperor* that latch in the memory are the gentle ones, whether the half-tones of the second subject in the first movement or the serene phrases of the slow movement, here given with real *Innigkeit*. Although there are more individual performances available, this is not likely to disappoint. The tape matches the disc closely, apart from a slight slip of focus at the opening of the slow movement.

The easy command of Alicia de Larrocha makes for a strong and convincing account, lacking a little in refinement – not least in the slow movement, where she misses a genuine pianissimo – but natural and completely unpompous. The recording is excellent and the cassette transfer clear and clean, although there is a touch of dryness in the orchestral strings and

the upper range of the finale becomes slightly fierce.

Nakajima's imaginative and spontaneous-sounding version has won much admiration, and rightly so, but the sound by today's standards is poor and the orchestral playing inadequate.

The recording quality, boxy and unsympathetic with unreal balance between piano and orchestra, also puts the Rosen/Morris version out of serious contention. Rosen is a stylist Beethovenian, but he is given little chance to relax, and the orchestral playing is not ideally polished.

Still recommended: Even among the wealth of fine *Emperors* Kempff's version stands out as perhaps the most refreshing and imaginative of all, and it is splendidly recorded on both disc and cassette (DG 138777/*923 014*); and the versions by Gilels (HMV SXLP 30223) and Ashkenazy with Solti (Decca SXL 6655/*KSXC 16655* [Lon. 6857/5-]) are also of outstanding quality. At medium price Backhaus (Decca SPA/*KCSP* 452) has undoubted power and authority; John Lill offers a fully recommendable bargain version (CfP CFP/*TC-CFP* 40087).

Violin concerto in D, Op. 61.
*** HMV Dig. ASD/*TCC-ASD* 4059 [Ang. DS/*4ZS* 37471]. Perlman, Philh. O., Giulini.
*** DG 2530/*3300* 903 [id.]. Zukerman, Chicago SO, Barenboim.
*** CRD CRD 1053/*CRDC 4053*. Ronald Thomas, Bournemouth Sinf.
**(*) Decca Dig. SXDL/*KSXDC* 7508 [Lon. LDR/5- 10010]. Kyung-Wha Chung, VPO, Kondrashin.
**(*) DG 2531/*3301* 250 [id.]. Mutter, Berlin PO, Karajan.
**(*) Argo ZRG/*KZRC* 929. Iona Brown, ASMF, Marriner.
**(*) Ph. 9500 407/*7300 615* [id.]. Accardo, Leipzig GO, Masur.
(B) ** CfP CFP 40299. Campoli, LPO, Pritchard.

Violin concerto; Overture: Coriolan, Op. 62.

(B) *** CfP CFP/*TC-CFP* 40386 [Van. S 353]. Suk, New Philh. O., Boult.

(i) *Violin concerto;* (ii) *2 Romances, Opp. 40 and 50.*
(M) *** Ph. Fest. 6570/*7310* 051 [id.]. Grumiaux, with (i) New Philh. O., Galliera, (ii) Concg. O., Haitink.

Perlman's outstanding HMV digital recording of Beethoven's *Violin concerto* must be counted among the great recordings of this work alongside those of Kreisler (1926), Wolfgang Schneiderhan (1953 – a performance of profound beauty and unique classical serenity, recently available on DG Heliodor 2548/*3348* 299) and the famous 1976 record by Herman Krebbers, the concertmaster of the Concertgebouw Orchestra (just reissued on Philips Sequenza *6527/*7311* 126, an inspired account with a wonderful naturalness and totally unforced spontaneity).

Perlman's is the most commanding reading. The violin emerges in the first movement almost imperceptibly, rising gently from the orchestra, but there and throughout the performance the element of slight understatement, the refusal to adopt too romantically expressive a style makes for a compelling strength, perfectly matched by Giulini's thoughtful, direct accompaniment. Steadiness of pulse is a mark of this version, but there is never a feeling of rigidity, and the lyrical power of the music-making is a vital element. The beautiful slow movement has a quality of gentle rapture, almost matching Schneiderhan's sense of stillness and serenity, and the finale, joyfully, exuberantly fast, is charged with the fullest excitement. The digital recording is satisfyingly full and spacious, yet admirably clear, with an outstanding matching cassette which has a demonstration presence in the second and final movements.

Another outstanding version is the DG recording by Zukerman and Barenboim, who also take a spacious and persuasive view of the first movement, stretched to the limit but still held in complete concentration. If warmth and tonal richness are the qualities most wanted, then this is the ideal version, with the immaculate playing of the Chicago orchestra ripely recorded. However, on tape (which is transferred at a rather low level) the soloist is somewhat lacking in presence.

On a different scale but no less rewarding is the account recorded by CRD in Bournemouth. Ronald Thomas, directing from the violin, gives a thoughtful and direct reading which in its beauty and poise is most refreshing, particularly as the recorded sound is excellent and the playing of the Bournemouth Sinfonietta first-rate. Thomas may miss the finest flights of individual poetry, but the unity of the performance is totally compelling. The cassette transfer is clean and vivid; a little smoothing at the top is advantageous, but the solo violin has truthful timbre and presence.

The restoration of Grumiaux's earlier Philips recording to the catalogue on Festivo, coupled to appealing accounts of the two *Romances*, certainly makes a very competitive issue. The performance combines breadth and serenity. The balance of warmth and restraint in the slow movement is refreshing, especially in the beautiful second subject, and Grumiaux's variation on the main theme which follows has a graceful lightness of touch. Galliera accompanies eloquently and is in obvious rapport with his soloist. The recording is good and it has transferred well to cassette, although the ear readily perceives that the *Romances* are of a different recording vintage, the sound brighter and sharper.

Suk's version with the New Philharmonia under Boult – now re-issued on Classics for Pleasure – is extremely well recorded. As with Mutter and Karajan, the first movement is taken at an unusually slow tempo, and some may feel that there is not enough urgency and concentration to sustain the conception.

But Suk's playing is both noble and spacious. The performance is classical in style, although Suk, like Kreisler, pulls back at the G minor section in the development of the first movement. It is the breadth and grandeur of design that emerge. Sir Adrian observes the revisions in the score brought to light in Alan Tyson's edition. The eloquence of the slow movement and the lightness and sparkle of the finale are in no doubt. And though no one buys a record of the *Violin concerto* for the sake of the *Coriolan overture*, it would almost be worth it for Boult's impressively played account. The recording has striking body and excellent balance, and this makes a fine bargain in all respects.

Chung gives a measured and thoughtful reading which lacks the compulsion one would have predicted. That is largely due to the often prosaic conducting of Kondrashin. There is poetry in individual moments – the minor-key episode of the finale, for example, which alone justifies the unusually slow tempo – but with too little of the soloist's natural electricity conveyed and none of her volatile imagination, it must not be counted her final statement on a masterpiece. The digital recording is impressive on disc, but not outstanding; the cassette, however, is of demonstration quality, beautifully clear and with refined detail, the natural solo image heard against a luminous orchestral backcloth.

The slow basic tempi of Anne-Sophie Mutter's beautiful reading on DG were her own choice, she claims, and certainly not forced on her by her super-star conductor. The first two movements have rarely if ever on record been more expansively presented, but the purity of the solo playing and the concentration of the whole performance make the result intensely convincing. The finale is relaxed too but is well pointed, at a fair tempo, and presents the necessary contrast. Good atmospheric recording against the warm acoustic of the Philharmonie in Berlin. On cassette, however, while the first two movements sound vivid, the orchestral focus slips somewhat in the finale.

Iona Brown, a fine orchestral leader and director, gives an honest, clean-cut and always sympathetic account, never overfaced by the challenge, but with unusually analytic sound the chamber scale is not all gain here. Inevitably it seems a smaller work, in a way that it does not with Ronald Thomas. The recording is of the highest quality on disc and cassette alike.

Accardo is not only an artist of impeccable technique but a musician of genuine insight and spirituality. He gives a wholly dedicated and faithful account of the concerto, lacking only the last ounce of *Innigkeit*. Full justice is not done to his tone by the engineers, and it is necessary to tamper with the controls if a certain shrillness is to be removed. There is no doubt that, once this is done, the performance will give great pleasure, but it is not to be numbered among the greatest of the Beethoven concerto or of Accardo's records. Masur produces excellent results from the Leipzig orchestra, but the engineers have not secured the cleanest bass sound. The cassette has been transferred at a high level and also needs a degree of smoothing at the top.

Campoli first recorded the concerto in the early 1950s with Krips and the LSO. This version comes from 1962 and has the advantage of good though not distinguished recorded sound. Responding, perhaps, to criticism of his earlier account, Campoli takes a somewhat brisk view of the first movement (his tempo is close to that of Heifetz and Toscanini here) and relaxes more in the second, which makes a strong impression. Here his playing is lyrical and expressive, and has at times a seraphic elegance that is most moving. There are many musicianly touches in the outer movements, though his very first entry in the opening movement could be more beautiful. John Pritchard and the RPO give good support and the performance as a whole is enjoyable. All the same, in terms of sheer musical personality it does not compete with such outstanding medium-priced versions as those by Krebbers on Philips (see above) or David Oistrakh with Cluytens (HMV SXLP/*TC-SXLP* 30168 [Ang. S 35780]) where the cassette has been remastered to EMI's best quality.

Concerto movement in C, WoO. 5; Romance No. 1, Op. 40.
*** DG 2531 193 [id.]. Kremer (violin), LSO, Tchakarov – SCHUBERT: *Konzertstück* etc.***

The early *Concerto movement in C* reveals Beethoven at twenty writing on an ambitious scale but rarely if ever achieving the touches of individuality which mark his mature concertos. This first movement is performed in a completion by Wilfried Fischer, effective enough; and the mixed bag of trivial coupling items is certainly apt, all of them beautifully played by Kremer and splendidly recorded.

Triple concerto for violin, cello and piano in C, Op. 56.
*** Ph. 9500 382 [id./*7300 604*]. Beaux Arts Trio, LPO, Haitink.
*** DG 2531/*3301 262* [id.]. Mutter, Zeltser, Ma, Berlin PO, Karajan.
(M) **(*) HM HM 20335. Maier, Bijlsma, Badura-Skoda, Coll. Aur.
(M) ** Ph. Fest. 6570/*7310* 070 [id.]. Szeryng, Starker, Arrau, New Philh. O., Inbal.

The world's most distinguished regular piano trio is a natural choice when it comes to soloists for this great but wayward concerto. If the Beaux Arts cellist, Bernard Greenhouse, lacks the full vibrant character of a Rostropovich in his first entries on each theme, he is more clearly coordinated with his colleagues, and consistently the joy of this performance – with the soloists sharply focused

in front of the orchestra – is to relish the interplay between the instruments. The result adds up to a really satisfying structure instead of a series of separate and memorable passages. Haitink's splendid direction helps too, with powerful tuttis and fine rhythmic pointing in the polacca rhythms of the finale. The engineers as ever have found the problems of balance impossible to solve, with the orchestra damped down during solo passages, but the sound has the beauty and refinement of the best Philips offerings.

On DG, after an exceptionally positive account of the opening tutti, with Karajan building up a formidable crescendo, the soloists may seem rather small-scale, but there are benefits from the unity brought by the conductor when each of the young soloists has a positive contribution to make, no less effectively when the recording balance for once in this work does not unduly favour the solo instruments. Yo Yo Ma's playing is not immaculate, and he does not dominate each thematic statement as great cellists can, but the urgency, spontaneity and – in the slow movement – the depth of expressiveness make for an outstanding version, beautifully recorded on disc. On cassette the orchestral tuttis are rather opaque (this is most noticeable at the opening of the first movement) but the solo detail matches the disc closely.

The Harmonia Mundi issue seeks to re-establish the sound Beethoven might have expected to hear, and the tinny quality of the Broadwood grand of 1816 is initially disconcerting. Yet like other Beethoven interpretations by the Collegium Aureum this has individual points of revelation, not least in the way one can register the relationship of the work to the *concerto grosso*, then not long defunct. Recording is good, but not all detail is clear.

Arrau and his colleagues, adopting very unhurried tempi, run the risk of losing concentration, but this version, almost on a chamber scale, with fine rhythmic pointing, is still enjoyable at medium price and is helped by refined recording. Starker's dedicated and spacious reading of the great cello solo in the brief slow movement has rarely been matched. The level of the cassette transfer is only modest and the inner focus of the orchestra is somewhat blurred; the soloists are more clearly caught and the ear adjusts.

Still recommended: The HMV recording combining David Oistrakh, Rostropovich, and Sviatoslav Richter with the Berlin Philharmonic under Karajan still holds a special place in the catalogue. It is a strong, expansive account, somewhat larger than life but immensely compelling, even if the recording is over-reverberant. Moreover EMI have remastered the cassette (previously available only in non-Dolby form); it now matches the disc closely (ASD/TC-ASD 2582).

12 Contredanses, WoO. 14; 12 German dances, WoO. 8; 12 Minuets, WoO. 7.
*** Ph. 9500 567/7300 704 [id.]. ASMF, Marriner.

Even as a composer of light music Beethoven was a master, and this collection, beautifully played and superbly recorded, can be warmly recommended. The cassette, as so often with Philips, is pleasing but has an over-insistent bass, while the upper range lacks freshness.

Overtures: The Consecration of the House, Op. 124; Coriolan, Op. 62; The Creatures of Prometheus, Op. 43; Egmont, Op. 84; Fidelio, Op. 72c; King Stephen, Op. 117; Namensfeier, Op. 115; Leonora Nos. 1–3, Opp. 138; 72a; 72b, The Ruins of Athens, Op. 113.
*** DG Priv. 2726 079 (2) [2707 046]. Berlin PO, Karajan.

These two records come from the box

of three that DG issued during the Beethoven Year under the title Music for the stage. The Leonora No. 3 and Fidelio overtures come from the mid-sixties, however. There is a fastidiousness about some of the phrasing (for example in Leonora No. 2) and a smoothness of texture that sometimes seem out of character. Nonetheless one cannot but marvel at the superlative playing of the Berlin Philharmonic and the no less excellent recorded sound. There are impressive and exciting things about these performances and they have undoubted atmosphere. At Privilege price the set is excellent value.

Overtures: Coriolan, Op. 62; The Creatures of Prometheus, Op. 43; Egmont, Op. 84; Fidelio, Op. 72c; King Stephen, Op. 117; Leonora No. 3, Op. 72b.
*** DG 2531/3301 347 [id.]. VPO, Bernstein.

These lively, sympathetic performances were originally the fill-ups for Bernstein's set of the Beethoven symphonies. They are well recorded and make an excellent collection. The sound on cassette is first-class too; even though the level is not especially adventurous there is both body and brilliance.

Overtures: Coriolan, Op. 62; Egmont, Op. 84; Fidelio, Op. 72c; Leonora No. 3, Op. 72b; The Ruins of Athens, Op. 113.
(M) *** DG Acc. 2542/3342 141. Berlin PO, Karajan.

Impressive performances that can stand comparison with the finest now in the catalogue. Karajan's accounts of all these overtures show an imposing command of structure and detail as well as the customary virtuosity one expects from him and the Berlin Philharmonic. The only notable reservation is in Leo-

nora No. 3, where the tempo Karajan chooses in the coda strikes one as very brisk indeed. The recording is eminently acceptable even if it is not in the demonstration class. The cassette matches the disc very closely indeed.

Romances for violin and orchestra Nos. 1 in G, Op. 40; 2 in F, Op. 50.
*** CRD CRD 1069/*CRDC 4069*. Ronald Thomas, Bournemouth Sinf. – MENDELSSOHN: *Concerto;* SCHUBERT: *Konzertstück*.***

The purity of Ronald Thomas's intonation (particularly important in the double stopping at the start of Op. 40) makes for clean-cut, direct readings which with the Schubert make a good if unexpected coupling for his refreshing account of the Mendelssohn concerto. The recording is first-rate on disc and tape alike.

Symphonies Nos. 1–9. Overtures: Coriolan; The Creatures of Prometheus; Egmont; Fidelio.
**(*) HMV Dig. SLS/*TC–SLS* 5239 (8). Philh. O., Sanderling (with Armstrong, Finnie, Tear, Tomlinson, Philh. Ch.).

Symphonies Nos. 1–9. Overtures: Coriolan; Egmont; Fidelio; Leonora No. 3.
(M) *** HMV SLS 5178 (8) [*Ang. SZ* 3890]. LSO, Jochum (with Te Kanawa, Hamari, Burrows, Holl, LSO Ch.).
(M) *(**) CBS 79800 (8) [Col. M8X 35191]. Cleveland O., Maazel (with Popp, Obraztsova, Vickers, Talvela, Ch.).

Symphonies Nos. 1–9.
(M) *** DG 2740 216 (8)/*3378 090* [id.]. VPO, Bernstein (with Jones, Schwarz, Kollo, Moll, V. State Op. Ch.).
(B) **(*) Decca Jub. JBA 500/5. VPO, Schmidt-Isserstedt (with Sutherland, Horne, King, Talvela, V. State Op. Ch.).

(B) *(*) DG 2721 199 (8), RPO, Dorati (with Farley, Hodgson, Burrows, Bailey, Brighton Festival Ch.).

The mature wisdom of Eugen Jochum makes for an exceptionally satisfying cycle of Beethoven symphonies, one which reflects the central German tradition, not just textually – with the sort of minor revisions which used to be universal – but in its combination of weight and lyricism. Of each symphony Jochum takes a clear, positive view, full of characterful detail, bringing out the contrasts between each. So the *Eroica* is given a spacious reading, with the exposition repeat observed at a relatively slow tempo and the *Funeral march* dark and severe; the *Seventh* is full of rhythmic zest, with dotted rhythms sharply pointed, and the *Ninth* brings the finest performance, one full of dramatic tensions but relaxing in an almost Schubertian glow for the slow movement. The recording quality is warm and full.

Bernstein's cycle, dramatic, perceptive, rich in emotion but never sentimental, has a natural spontaneous quality that stems in part from his technique of recording. As in other recordings for DG Bernstein opted to have live performances recorded and then – with some tidying of detail – edited together. Those who remember the electrifying account of the first movement in the *Eroica* in his earlier New York cycle may be disappointed that the voltage here is lower, but with Bernstein's electricity matched against the traditional warmth of Viennese playing the results are consistently persuasive, culminating in a superb, triumphant account of the *Ninth* with a fast, tense first movement, a resilient scherzo, a hushed expansive reading of the *Adagio* and a dramatic account of the finale. Balances are not always perfect, with microphones placed in order to eliminate audience noise, but the results are generally undistracting. The cassette transfers are exceptionally successful, the sound fresh, open at the top and refined in detail. There is plenty of body too, and although the level is relatively modest, hiss is not a problem. The *Choral symphony* sounds unusually refined, with a good balance and the most natural, well-focused quality for chorus and soloists alike. The layout, with Nos. 1 and 2, 4 and 5, and 6 and 7 all back-to-back, is beyond criticism. With such enjoyable performances this could be a first recommendation for tape collectors.

The likenesses between Sanderling and Klemperer as Beethoven interpreters – both of them taking a rugged, unvarnished view – are underlined in the HMV cycle sponsored by the cigarette firm Du Maurier. Much of it is very fine, with the strong, forthright reading of the *Eroica*, the spaciously lilting account of the *Pastoral* and the direct and measured view of the *Ninth* the obvious high points. The first two symphonies are weighty in a very nineteenth-century way, and the *Fifth* – lacking a little in spontaneity – is on the heavy side. The disappointment is the *Seventh*, where slow speeds convey little of the work's dance-like qualities. The digital recording is clear but rather over-bright, with the violins of the Philharmonia often presented unflatteringly. The chrome tapes are of high quality, clean and clear, yet full, the brightness of the upper strings tempered just a little compared with the discs. Detail is excellent. The only disappointment is the *Ninth*, dry and light in the bass, with the choral focus far from sharp. The presentation has one eccentricity: No.2 is put at the beginning of the first cassette, with the turnover coming before the finale, and No. 1 then follows on.

Schmidt-Isserstedt's cycle, reissued at bargain price, presents a consistently musical view, not lacking strength, and without distracting idiosyncrasies. All the symphonies are beautifully played – the character of the VPO coming over strongly – and well recorded. Apart from the *Pastoral*, clean and classically straightforward but entirely lacking in charm, there is no outright disappoint-

ment here, and the series culminates in a splendid account of the *Ninth*, one which does not quite scale the heights but which, particularly in the slow movement and the finale (with outstanding soloists), conveys visionary strength. For some a reservation may be that the performances are not so strikingly individual as to compel repeated hearings, although the *Fourth* must be excepted from this general comment. It is a symphony well suited to Schmidt-Isserstedt's thoughtful, poetic style. The *Fifth* – not a symphony that regularly gets successful performances on record – also stands out, with a first movement that has both bite and breathing space, a nicely measured *Andante* and a gloriously triumphant finale. Only the scherzo invites controversy in its slow tempo. The *Seventh*, similarly, is compelling throughout. Tempi are generally judged with perfect regard for the often conflicting requirements of symphony and dance – not too ponderous and not too hectic. The first movement of the *Eighth* is slower than usual, and although the *Allegretto* is crisp and light, the minuet is rather heavily pointed, with a Brahmsian touch in the trio. These are all performances that one can live with, but their mood is essentially serious: only rarely do they spark one off with fresh joy in Beethoven. The first two symphonies (again with generally slow tempi), although the playing is nicely detailed, are seriously lacking in charm. The nine works are presented consecutively on twelve sides, which means that Nos. 4 and 6 are split over separate discs, but the quality of the sound is excellent.

Individually Maazel's readings bring consistently fine playing and a firm, direct style based on sharp rhythms and generally urgent tempi. As a set, however, the result is wearing because of its lack of light and shade; these are not in general performances that have one asking for more. The bright, rather close recording adds to the overall aggressiveness.

Dorati's Beethoven cycle generally

lacks just the quality which made his great Haydn series so consistently compelling, a sense of spontaneity and new discovery, a feeling of live performance. Speeds are generally well judged, the style rarely if ever controversial, yet from Dorati one expected greater vigour. It is typical of his approach that the *Ninth Symphony* conveys, even in the first movement, an atmosphere of easy optimism, with little mystery or stress. Like the rest this is a performance which is enjoyable on its own terms but misses much of the greatness of Beethoven. The recording is not ideally refined or perfectly balanced, but is bright and full-ranging.

Symphony No. 1 in C, Op. 21.
(M) **(*) DG Priv. 2726/*3372* 112 (2). LSO, Kubelik – *Symphony No. 9.***(*)

Kubelik's performance is, unusually, coupled to the *Choral symphony*. In No. 1 the LSO gives a strong performance in which Kubelik's relaxed manner helps to disguise the challenge of fast speeds. The recording is excellent on disc and cassette alike.

Symphonies Nos. 1–2.
(M) *** DG Acc. 2542/*3342* 102. Berlin PO, Karajan.
(M) *** Ph. Seq. 6572/*7311* 074. ASMF, Marriner.
**(*) DG 2531/*3301* 101 [id.]. Berlin PO, Karajan.
**(*) HMV Dig. ASD/*TCC–ASD* 4151. Philh. O., Sanderling.
**(*) CBS 76854/40-. Cleveland O., Maazel.
(M) ** DG Priv. 2535/*3335* 334. RPO, Dorati.

Refinement and strength are combined in Karajan's 1962 readings (now reissued on Accolade), which are consistently resilient and exciting. The fast tempi for the slow movements of both symphonies give an eighteenth-century quality, not in-

appropriate. The recording, finely balanced, hardly sounds its age, with no perceptible difference between tape and disc. Karajan's 1977 performances are just as exciting, polished and elegant as those of 1962, with firm lines giving the necessary strength. The manner is a degree weightier, with less controversial tempi for the slow movements. The recording, less well balanced, is weightier too, with close-up effects which are less believable. On the tape, which matches the disc closely, there is a feeling of slight recession of the orchestral image in *piano* and *pianissimo* passages.

Marriner presents the first two symphonies authentically with a Mozart-sized orchestra, and the result is lithe and fresh, with plenty of character but few if any quirks or mannerisms. Nor are the dramatic contrasts underplayed, for the chamber scale is most realistically captured in the excellent recording. The cassette too is first-class, lively and full-bodied. This is a most satisfying issue.

Sanderling presents the early symphonies with the weight of the nineteenth century already in them. Speeds in No. 1 are sprightlier than in No. 2, where Sanderling's spacious approach runs the risk – as Klemperer's did – of seeming too heavy. Clean but over-bright digital recording and an excellent cassette equivalent.

Maazel directs clean, efficient readings, beautifully played and unexceptionable in style, except that charm is missing and so is lightness of pointing. The recording is well-detailed and efficient to match but lacking in delicacy. The cassette transfers are of CBS's best, offering generally more enjoyable sound than the LP: the top is smoother without loss of bite. The exciting slow-movement climax of No. 2 has striking impact.

It is strange that Dorati, so consistently full of energy and sparkle in Haydn, sounds somewhat dull and unjoyful in the two Beethoven symphonies closest to Haydn. The recordings are good (the tape transfer better in No. 2 than in No.

1); but there are many finer versions
in the medium price-range, notably
Schmidt-Isserstedt on Decca Jubilee
(JB/*KJBC* 3).

Symphonies Nos. 1 and 4.
*** DG 2531/*3301* 308 [id.]. VPO,
Bernstein.

Except for Toscanini in mono, no
other conductor offers the coupling of
Nos. 1 and 4, and Bernstein's readings
are both strong and dramatic. Mock
pomposity in the introduction to No. 1
leads to a challengingly fast account of
the *Allegro*, obviously influenced by the
presence of an audience, though at other
times – as in the blaring brass of the finale
– that spur brings just a hint of vulgarity.
In No. 4 Bernstein's taut manner brings
out the compactness of argument. The
development is especially fine: in context
one registers it as the message of No. 1
retold in the language of the *Fifth*. The
live recording, not ideally balanced, is
very acceptable, on both tape and disc,
although the cassette transfer is made at
rather a low level.

Symphonies Nos. 1 and 5.
**(*) Ph. 9500 067 [id.] LPO, Haitink.

This is an unusual coupling. Haitink
directs a clean, unmannered reading of
No. 1 and a lithe and urgent one of the
Fifth, giving an illusion of live performance. The opening of the *Fifth* has the
pause between the two knocks of Fate
made shorter to present a unitary statement, a point typical of Haitink's
thoughtfulness. Good, well-balanced
recording. This is a satisfying if not
totally memorable pairing.

Symphonies Nos. 1 and 8.
(M) *(*) Ph. Fest. 6570/*7310* 131. Leipzig
GO, Masur.

Masur's coupling of Nos. 1 and 8 is
not a strong contender, though there are

many good things. The first movement
of No. 8 has breadth, but not the tautness
or concentration of, say, Bernstein. The
slow movement could do with slightly
more humour and sparkle. The *First
Symphony* is a little faceless, though it is
beautifully played. The Gewandhaus is
an orchestra of the highest culture, sensitivity and responsiveness, but pleasure
in its warmth and sonority is diminished
by a feeling that they are 'on automatic
pilot'. The performances are acceptable
enough but do not show these artists at
their very best. The recording is full and
resonant and it has transferred quite successfully to cassette.

*Symphony No. 2 in D, Op. 36; Over-
ture; The Creatures of Prometheus.*
**(*) DG 2531/*3301* 309 [id.]. VPO,
Bernstein.
**(*) Ph. 9500 257/*7300 545* [id.]. LPO,
Haitink.

*Symphony No. 2; Overtures: The
Consecration of the House; Leonora
No. 1.*
(M) *** Ph. Fest. 6570/*7310* 130. Leipzig
GO, Masur.

*Symphony No. 2; Overtures: Fidelio;
King Stephen.*
(M) *** Decca SPA/*KCSP* 584. LSO,
Monteux.

Masur's account of the *Second Symphony* is one of the best things in his cycle,
particularly the slow movement, which
has a natural eloquence and unforced
pace that is most appealing. It is a finely
proportioned account, well groomed and
neat, without ever losing either vitality or
fire. Masur observes the first-movement
repeat and hardly puts a foot wrong anywhere in the whole work (or the fill-ups),
and the sound is musically balanced, with
no trace of the overlit 'hi-fi' edge
favoured by some companies. With very
natural sound and a warm acoustic, this
can hold its own with the very best in the
catalogue.

One of the finest of Monteux's Beethoven series, the Decca reissue of his recording from the mid-sixties is excellent value in the lower-medium price-range. It is lighter in style than Masur's excellent Leipzig version, but the alertness of the LSO playing makes it strong and enjoyable. There is no first-movement exposition repeat, but Monteux structures the movement overall to take this into account. The overtures are well done too, although *Fidelio* is a little underpowered at the opening. The recording is full, lively and realistic on both disc and tape.

Bernstein's Vienna version at full price offers rather short measure for coupling, but the performance has touches that obviously stemmed from the inspiration of the moment, and the tension rises superbly at the end of the finale. Bernstein seems intent on emphasizing how much bigger a symphony this is than No. 1, and though the ensemble is not always flawless and the recording has a rather boomy bass, the liveness is captivating. The cassette transfer is sophisticated, but the level is too low for maximum bite at the top.

The merit of Haitink's Beethoven readings lies in their unobtrusive strength, and here, with tempi in the outer movements very close to Karajan's, he directs an eminently satisfying reading, not always perfectly polished in detail but full of dramatic light and shade conveying spontaneity. The tape transfer is of good quality, though side two seems marginally less fresh at the top than side one.

Symphonies Nos. 2 and 4.
(M) *** DG Priv. 2535/*3335* 441. Concg. O. or Israel PO, Kubelik.

This very apt coupling of the first two even-numbered symphonies is surprisingly rare, and Kubelik's beautiful readings, taken from his complete cycle for DG, make an excellent pair. The Concertgebouw Orchestra – sounding rather brighter than it usually has done on record – gives a performance of refinement and point, beautifully crisp of ensemble. The Israel orchestra in No. 4 plays with delicacy too, challenged to refinement by Kubelik's elegant conducting. The recordings are well matched and there are excellent cassette transfers, crisp and clean.

Symphony No. 3 in E flat (Eroica), Op. 55.
(M) *** DG Acc. 2542/*3342* 103. Berlin PO, Karajan.
*** ASV ALH/*ZCALH* 901. Hallé O., Loughran.
**(*) DG 2531/*3301* 310 [id.]. VPO, Bernstein.
**(*) DG 2531/*3301* 123 [id.]. LAPO, Giulini.
(M) **(*) DG Priv. 2535/*3335* 412. Berlin PO, Kubelik.
**(*) DG 2531/*3301* 103 [id.]. Berlin PO, Karajan.
(M) **(*) Ph. Fest. 6570/*7310* 204 (with slow-movement rehearsal sequence). Concg. O., Monteux.
** HM 1C 065 99629. Coll. Aur., Maier.
(M) ** DG Priv. 2535/*3335* 335. RPO, Dorati.
** Symph. SYM 5 [Peters PLE 020]. Symph. of L., Morris.
*(*) CBS Dig. 35883 [id.]. NYPO, Mehta.

Symphony No. 3; Overture: Coriolan.
*** Ph. Fest. 6570/*7310* 165. Leipzig GO, Masur.
*** Ph. 6500 986/*7300 459* [id.]. Concg. O., Haitink.

Symphony No. 3; Overture: Egmont.
*** HMV ASD/*TC-ASD* 3376 [Ang. S/ 4*XS* 37410]. LSO, Jochum.

Symphony No. 3; Overture: Fidelio.
(M) *** HMV SXLP/*TC-SXLP* 30310. Philh. O., Klemperer.
*** HMV Dig. ASD/*TCC–ASD* 4152. Philh. O., Sanderling.

A remarkable number of fine new recordings of the *Eroica* is balanced by the reissues. Indeed most readers will find Karajan's 1962 *Eroica*, now offered on Accolade, easier to live with than his more controversial 1977 version. But Karajan does not go unchallenged. Klemperer's famous Philharmonia recording is available again at medium price; Loughran's Hallé performance has also been reissued, and Bernstein, Haitink, Masur, Giulini and Kubelik all have something fresh to reveal in their newer versions. Perhaps most striking of all is Jochum's account, taken from his complete set. It is a magnificent reading, direct in outline and manner, but with keen refinement of detail. Tempi are all centrally convincing and though the exposition repeat is observed in the first movement, making the side extremely long, the sound is among the richest and best balanced ever given to this symphony. The glory of the performance lies above all in the dedicated account of the *Funeral March*, never overstated but darkly intense. Coupled with a fine version of the *Egmont overture* this is as recommendable on disc as it is on the tape, which matches it closely.

Karajan's Accolade *Eroica* is refreshing and urgent, without the hint of excessive tension which makes the first movement of his 1977 performance slightly controversial. The refinement of detail never gets in the way of the dramatic urgency, and this is an outstandingly safe, central recommendation, with the Berlin Philharmonic on top form. The cassette matches the disc closely, although side two is transferred at a slightly lower level and has marginally less bite. The tape, however, has the advantage of a bonus not included on the disc, a fine performance of the *Coriolan overture*.

Loughran began his projected cycle of Beethoven symphonies with an account of the *Eroica* which has all the rhythmic urgency and sense of spontaneity that make his Brahms cycle so compelling. This is a performance with minor flaws – the Hallé violins are not always sweet-

toned – but it is an exceptionally compelling one, with finely chosen tempi forthrightly maintained and a resilience of pulse in the first movement that is memorable. The recording quality is full and warm, but the closeness of balance in a relatively narrow stereo spectrum hardly does justice to the hushed playing in the *Funeral march*, and occasionally exposes individual instruments. An ingenious and original solution has been devised to get round the problem of including the first-movement exposition repeat and yet not making a break in the middle of the slow movement. This is achieved by having the first movement begin in mid-side. Then one turns over for movements two and three and back again for the finale. The cassette, of course, does not need to do this and plays straightforwardly. The transfer is clear, but the upper range is fierce, with a lack of bloom on the violins.

Kurt Masur's record of the *Eroica* is one of the unqualified successes of his Beethoven cycle with the Gewandhaus Orchestra. Although there is no exposition repeat, the first movement has a splendid sense of momentum. The *Funeral march* is finely paced and has a noble breadth, and the scherzo conveys the sense of cosmic energy held in magisterial control. The playing of the Gewandhaus Orchestra throughout is humane and civilized. The recording is naturally balanced, though the top could perhaps be more open; there is some bass resonance too. Totally straight, this finely proportioned account, though it may lack the tautness and concentration of Toscanini and Karajan, is among the best of its kind. Admirers of Weingartner will be drawn to it. The cassette transfer is full and lively, but seems to have only a modest expansion of volume and impact at climaxes.

Klemperer's second reading of the *Eroica* with the Philharmonia lacked something of the incandescence of his earlier mono performance, but the concentration was just as keen, with even slower tempo given natural unforced weight, most strikingly of all in the stoically intense account of the *Funeral march*. Only in the coda of the finale does the slow tempo bring some slackness. Well-balanced recording of early-sixties vintage and a vivid tape transfer. The overture, however, has a degree of congestion at its closing climax (on tape only).

Sanderling is at his finest in the *Eroica*. This more than anything sets the pattern for his complete cycle in its rugged honesty, marked by plain, unhurried speeds. There are more dramatic readings, more intense ones too, but with its inclusion of the exposition repeat, as well as bright, clean digital sound and a good fill-up it is a fair recommendation. The cassette and disc are closely matched.

Haitink's is a most satisfying and compelling reading, one which in its natural ebb and flow of tension rivets the attention from the start. Haitink's Beethoven style may seem to lack idiosyncrasy, but his concentration more than makes up for that, especially in the *Funeral march*, which is presented in seamless purity. Unfortunately the tape transfer falls short of the rich, clear sound which marks the disc, relatively lacking inner clarity.

Bernstein's 1966 recording (still available in the US on Columbia MS 6774 but withdrawn in the UK) was electrically intense, with a first movement almost as fast as Toscanini's – maintaining the tension over a fuller span by the inclusion of the exposition repeat – and a darkly tragic *Funeral march*. Compared with that, there is a degree of disappointment about his new Vienna version, with less incandescence in the first movement and a hard, clattering sound for the opening chords. The exposition repeat is still observed, however, and this is undoubtedly a strong, dramatic reading, with a superb, dedicated account of the *Funeral march*. This emerges as more clearly a march than before, yet very measured indeed, its intensity enhanced by the

presence of an audience. Both disc and tape offer a good sound.

With an extraordinarily measured view of the first movement Giulini's is an outstandingly refined and individual reading. If at first the performance seems lacking a little in tension, one comes to appreciate the long-breathed concentration which, without forcing, compels one to listen afresh. The playing is comparably refined and the recording undistracting, not at all recognizable as coming from this orchestra. The tape matches the disc fairly closely.

The glory of Kubelik's version is the wonderfully sombre and intense account of the *Funeral march*, very hushed at the start, with an exceptionally slow tempo superbly sustained. In the first movement Kubelik brings out lyricism as well as dramatic strength, with a fastish basic tempo persuasively variable. Excellent recording quality on both tape and disc, though the Berlin violins have sounded sweeter than this.

Not everyone will readily identify with the fiery intensity of fast tempi in the outer movements of Karajan's 1977 performance. Contrasts are heightened, with, if anything, an even more intense account of the *Funeral march* than in his earlier recordings. A point to consider is the absence of the exposition repeat in the first movement (until recent years rarely observed in recordings), but this is among the most polished as well as the most dramatic accounts available. The sound is full-blooded, though there are some intrusive close-up effects, and the cassette matches the disc closely.

Monteux seldom really disappoints in the recording studio, and his gift for bringing a score to life is readily demonstrated in the slow-movement rehearsal sequence of his Philips Concertgebouw recording from the early sixties. Perhaps the performance itself is rather too predictable and easy, although the conducting in the vigorous first movement – played without the exposition repeat but well structured – has considerable individuality. The scherzo and finale have plenty of spirit and are splendidly played; but more than anything it is the *Funeral march* which provides the ultimate test, and here Monteux gets away too easily. But this remains a satisfyingly central reading and the recording is well balanced, full and clean, although the low-level cassette transfer does not match the disc in range and sounds rather flabby at the top.

Maier in his search for authentic performing style might seem to have taken on too much of a challenge in this most massive of early-nineteenth-century symphonies. There is some lack of tension in the playing such as a regular conductor would have instilled, but the incisiveness of the clear textures makes amends, and the result has a freshness which is most compelling. The strings are not just reduced but use very little vibrato, while the horns in the trio of the scherzo have an attractive rasping quality. First-rate recording.

Dorati's view of the first movement is fast and emphatic, the result is a little rigid. He observes the exposition repeat. The *Funeral march*, crisp of detail, lacks inner tension. It is a good but not especially compelling version, well recorded, with a bright full-bodied tape transfer.

Wyn Morris gives a more compelling and often individual reading. His tempo for the first movement is as fast as Karajan's latest, yet there is no hint of haste as it regularly acquires a three-in-a-bar dance-like quality. The horn and woodwind playing is excellent, though ensemble is not always perfect, and until the closing bars, when Morris allows a marked slowing, the *Funeral march* lacks something in weight. The scherzo, like the first movement, is exceptionally fast but well sprung. However, the recording is not as clean on detail as it should be, with little brightness.

With CBS's digital sound heralded by fanfares of publicity, Mehta's version fails to live up to expectations. The

reading is sober rather than intense and is not helped by recording quality which by digital standards is muddy. Mehta, the extrovert, is much more successful in the scherzo and finale than in the first two movements.

Symphony No. 4 in B flat, Op. 60.
*** DG 2531/*3301* 104 [id.]. Berlin PO, Karajan.
(M) *** DG Acc. 2542/*3342* 104. Berlin PO, Karajan.

Symphony No. 4; Overture: Egmont.
⊛ (M) *** Ph. Fest. 6570/*7310* 132. Leipzig GO, Masur.
**(*) HMV Dig. ASD/*TCC–ASD* 4153. Philh. O., Sanderling.

Symphony No. 4; Overture: Leonora No. 3.
*** HMV ASD/*TC-ASD* 3627 [Ang. S/ *4XS* 37529]. LSO, Jochum.
*** Ph. 9500 258/*7300 661*. LPO, Haitink.

As can be seen above, the *Fourth* is exceptionally well served at both full and medium price, and many collectors will reflect that the Karajan versions, fine though they are, seem expensive on disc with no couplings (although, curiously, the Accolade tape includes the *Egmont overture*). But first choice rests with Masur or Jochum.

Masur's version is outstanding in every way, one of the finest in his complete Beethoven cycle. The recording is gloriously rich (with the cassette matching the disc fairly closely), yet the resonant sound does not cloud inner detail. Masur brings both imagination and poetry to his reading and he does not miss the work's essential dimension of humour. The measured sobriety of the slow introduction leads to a fizzing account of the *Allegro*, a little brusque in the second subject. Even that is a reflection of Masur's directness in Beethoven, and the Leipzig orchestra responds with marvellously alert and cultured playing; its rhythmic resilience and vitality are in themselves a source of pleasure. The accenting of the scherzo and the scurrying quavers of the finale are enunciated with exceptional clarity – a tribute too to the refinement of the recording – and there is a natural exuberance which is very satisfying. As if this was not enough, the Leipzig players then provide a magnificent account of *Egmont*.

Jochum's reading of the *Fourth* has been splendidly caught three times over, and the latest version with the LSO has even greater breadth, while bringing out the work's free, natural lyricism. The HMV recording is outstandingly full and rich, on disc and cassette alike, and the weighty account of the *Leonora No. 3 overture* makes a substantial coupling.

Haitink directs a sparkling account of the first movement, entirely natural and spontaneous-sounding, full of light and shade. There is lightness too in the *Adagio*, with nicely exaggerated dotted rhythms; this is a fresh, attractive reading, well played, well coupled and well recorded. The tape transfer has body and fair detail but lacks the last degree of range at the top.

Karajan's two versions are closely matched. The earlier 1962 reading is splendid, with the dynamic contrasts heavily underlined in the outer movements. In the slow movement there is a lyrical feel to the playing that suggests Schubert. The recording still sounds well, although the tape is less lively than the disc. In the later 1977 version the balance is even closer, exposing every flicker of *tremolando*. Yet the precision of the Berlin Philharmonic is a thing of wonder, and if anything Karajan conveys more weight and strength than before, with more emphasis on the *Adagio*. Only the extremely fast tempo for the finale marks a questionable development, but even there the brilliance and excitement are never in doubt. On tape the orchestral image is full-blooded and clear, but again the ear notices the tendency for the strings to recede in pianissimos.

Sanderling has specifically related the mood of the big slow introduction to a misty early morning in summer, and the weight and concentration are immediately impressive. The *Allegro*, characteristically measured, is less successful, relatively unsprung, but this is a powerful, undistracting reading, brightly recorded on disc and tape alike.

Symphonies Nos. 4 and 8.
** CBS 76855. Cleveland O., Maazel.

Maazel's coupling is generous, following a precedent set by Bernstein (whose record is still available in the US on Columbia MS 7412 but has been withdrawn in the UK). But whereas Bernstein's were performances of genuine stature, with great concentration and power, Maazel's versions are disappointing, lacking in charm and often too rigid. They are brilliantly played and sharply articulated, with matching close-up CBS sound, but other versions are more rewarding.

Symphony No. 5 in C min., Op. 67.
*** DG 2531/*3301* 105 [id.]. Berlin PO, Karajan.
(M) *** DG Acc. 2542/*3342* 105. Berlin PO, Karajan.
*** DG 2531/*3301* 311 [id.]. VPO, Bernstein.
(M) **(*) CBS 60106/*40*- [Col. MY 36719]. NYPO, Bernstein – SCHUBERT: *Symphony No. 8.***(*)
*(*) CBS 76672. Cleveland O., Maazel.

Symphony No. 5; Overture: Coriolan.
**(*) HMV Dig. ASD/*TCC-ASD* 4136. Philh. O., Sanderling.

Symphony No. 5; Overtures: Coriolan; Egmont.
*** ASV ALH/*ZCALH* 908. Hallé O., Loughran.

Symphony No. 5; Overture: Egmont.
(M) **(*) Decca SPA/*KCSP* 585. LSO, Monteux.

*(*) Telarc Dig. DG 10060. Boston SO, Ozawa.

Symphony No. 5; Overture: Fidelio.
(B) *** Con. CC/CCT 7526. Bav. RSO, Jochum.

Karajan's 1977 version is magnificent in every way, tough and urgently incisive, with fast tempi, bringing weight as well as excitement but no unwanted blatancy, even in the finale. The recording is satisfyingly wide-ranging in frequency and dynamic on both disc and tape.

Karajan's 1962 version with the same players is hardly less powerful and incisive than his later account and the recording is more naturally balanced. So heroic a reading makes an excellent recommendation at medium price. The cassette is not only well managed (only marginally less lively than the LP) but offers the *Leonora No. 3* and *Fidelio* overtures as a very considerable bonus; these come first, then the first movement of the symphony, with the remaining three movements on side two.

Loughran continues his Beethoven series with an exceptionally vibrant account of the *Fifth*. His first movement is leonine rather than massive, but by observing the repeats in both outer movements he underlines the scale of the symphony as well as its strength. After a direct yet lyrical *Andante* comes a fast scherzo, with nimble playing from the lower strings; and the release of exultant energy in the finale caps a performance which is notable above all for its vigour and forward impulse. The overtures too are splendidly played. The bright, vivid recording has transferred to tape with admirable presence and detail. It sounds best with a slight treble reduction.

Jochum's early DG recording makes a fine bargain in this Contour reissue. Although the opening bars are less dramatic than in some versions, Jochum launches into a finely vigorous reading, warmly lyrical in the slow movement, yet unmarred throughout by any romantic

exaggerations. He includes the first-movement exposition repeat, and the whole performance is gripping in a totally natural, unforced way. The recording hardly shows its age and the lively performance of the overture makes a fine bonus. As usual in this series the cassette has much less energy in the upper range than the disc, which reduces the dynamic contrast.

Monteux's Beethoven performances on record tended to be straight and direct, but here – in a previously unissued recording – the volatile Frenchman plays his part in a performance which has strength and drive as well as an element of waywardness. Unashamedly he presents the fate theme at the very start slower and more weightily than the very fast basic tempo of the movement, an effect which requires sleight of hand there and elsewhere. It is a personal reading but a compelling one in all four movements, with fine articulation from the LSO, though the brassiness of the finale is a little aggressive. *Egmont* has comparable urgency but less polish. The recording is excellent for its early-sixties vintage. The cassette is of demonstration quality, matching the disc very closely indeed.

Sanderling's reading of the *Fifth* is typical of his whole cycle, powerful and direct, lacking a little in rhythmic subtlety, almost too plain, but generally conveying a Klemperer-like ruggedness. A detailed point is that Sanderling at the start has – with fair justification – a shorter pause after the first knock of fate than after the second. The opening statement of the finale is massive rather than incisively dramatic. The digital sound is bold and clear, and the cassette is striking in its combination of body and a brilliant upper range.

Bernstein in his Vienna version rethought his reading of the *Fifth*, giving it resonance and spaciousness as well as drama. Some of the Toscanini-like tension of his earlier New York reading has evaporated from the first movement, but the warmth and conviction of the whole performance are most persuasive, ending with a blazing account of the finale. The recording, made at live concerts, is good though not ideal, and the cassette matches the disc closely, with plenty of body and impact.

Bernstein's New York version on CBS is a strong dramatic reading, not quite so distinguished as the *Eroica* he recorded at the same period, but concentrated and vital, with a balancing warmth in the slow movement. The recording is not distinguished, but although it lacks the widest dynamic range it has a fairly convincing ambient depth. Coupled with a dramatic and individual account of Schubert's *Unfinished* this lays fair claims to its place in this CBS 'Great performances' series.

Maazel in his Cleveland performance misses the spontaneous urgency that marked his Berlin recording of many years earlier. Even when tempi are fast the result has a tendency to squareness, and the slow movement is unduly heavy. The performance is not helped by the boxy, rather unresonant recording.

Ozawa's Telarc recording with the Boston Symphony Orchestra is well played and has impressively rich and well-balanced sound. But the reading, with fast outer movements and an uneventful *Andante*, seriously lacks electricity. Considering the wide dynamic range possible with digital techniques the opening of the finale is surprisingly wanting in drama. In a competitive field this expensive issue is a non-starter.

Still recommended: Carlos Kleiber's electrifying DG recording (2530 516/ *3300 472*) and Solti's fine Chicago version (Decca SXL/*KSXC* 6762 [Lon. 6930/*5*-]). Jochum's outstanding HMV version is available on cassette only (*TC–ASD 3484*).

Symphonies Nos. 5 and 8.
(M) **(*) DG Priv. 2535/*3335* 407. Boston SO or Cleveland O., Kubelik.

Kubelik's versions of Nos. 5 and 8 are both taken from the symphony cycle he recorded with nine different orchestras from different countries. No. 8 is for contractual reasons described on the sleeve as being played by 'members of the Cleveland Orchestra', and next to the resonant performance of the *Fifth*, in which the Boston players excel themselves, the string sound is somewhat thin; but both symphonies are given strong performances and the mid-seventies recordings, with the reservation noted, are first-rate. There is a lively tape (in spite of the rather low transfer level).

Symphonies Nos. (i) *5 and* (ii) *9.*
(B) *** Decca DPA 599/600. (i) LPO; (ii) Harper, Watts, Young, McIntyre, LSO Ch., LSO; both cond. Stokowski.

Decca's recoupling of Stokowski's recordings of the *Fifth* and *Ninth Symphonies* offers an excellent way to buy an outstanding version of the *Choral symphony* (see below) at about the cost of one premium-price LP yet with ample groove space and coupled with an almost equally compelling account of the *Fifth*, exceptionally strong in the outer movements and marred only by a sluggish tempo for the second-movement *Andante*.

Symphony No. 6 in F (Pastoral), Op. 68.
(M) *** CBS 60107/*40*- [Col. MY 36720]. Columbia SO, Walter.
*** HMV ASD/*TC-ASD* 3854 [Ang. S/ 4*ZS* 37639]. Phd. O., Muti.
*** ASV ALH/*ZCALH* 902. Hallé O., Loughran.
*** HMV Dig. ASD/*TCC–ASD* 4154. Philh. O., Sanderling.
*** CBS 76825/*40*- [Col. M/*MT* 35169]. ECO, Tilson Thomas.
*** Ph. 9500 256/*7300 544* [id.]. LPO, Haitink.
*** HMV ASD/*TC-ASD* 3583. LSO, Jochum.
(M) *** Ph. Seq. 6527/*7311* 045. Concg. O., Jochum.
**(*) DG 2531/*3301* 312 [id.]. VPO, Bernstein.

**(*) HMV ASD/*TC-ASD* 3456. LPO, Boult.
(B) **(*) Con. CC/*CCT* 7546 [Ph. 6500 463/*7300 361*]. BBC SO, Colin Davis.
**(*) DG 2531/*3301* 106 [id.]. Berlin PO, Karajan.
(M) ** DG Priv. 2535/*3335* 413. Orchestre de Paris, Kubelik.
(M) ** DG Priv. 2535/*3335* 219. RPO, Dorati.
** DG 2531/*3301* 266 [id.]. LAPO, Giulini.
(M) *(*) DG Acc. 2542/*3342* 106. Berlin PO, Karajan.

Symphony No. 6; Overtures: The Creatures of Prometheus: The Ruins of Athens.
(M) *** Ph. Fest. 6570/*7310* 133. Leipzig GO, Masur.

Symphony No. 6; Overture: Egmont.
(M) **(*) HMV SXLP/*TC-SXLP* 30313 [Ang. S 36684]. New Philh. O., Giulini.

Even in a highly competitive field Kurt Masur's performance with the Gewandhaus Orchestra claims a high place in the recommended listings. It is wholly unaffected and natural, one of the glories of the Gewandhaus cycle. There is no spurious eloquence at any point; the music unfolds in a beautifully natural fashion. Masur observes the first-movement exposition repeat and has a strong feeling for proportion. The recorded sound is open and spacious, the orchestra being well set back and sensibly balanced. There is also a bonus in the shape of two overtures that could tempt those who might otherwise be drawn towards the excellent bargain versions by Reiner and Cluytens (see below). The sound on tape is admirably lively and pleasingly rich and full-bodied, although the resonant bass produces an explosive effect at the climax of the *Storm.*

Bruno Walter was always famous for his interpretation of the *Pastoral symphony.* It was the only Beethoven symphony he recorded twice in the 78 era (although his second version with the Philadelphia Orchestra was disappointing). The present version dates from the beginning of the sixties and represents the peak of his Indian summer in the American recording studios. The whole performance glows, and the gentle warmth of phrasing is comparable with Klemperer's famous version. The slow movement is taken slightly fast, but there is no sense of hurry, and the tempo of the *Shepherd's merrymaking* is less controversial than Klemperer's. It is an affectionate and completely integrated performance from a master who thought and lived the work all his life. The sound is surprisingly full and hardly dates, making this a classic reissue, fully worthy of the 'Great performances' sobriquet that distinguishes this CBS medium-price series.

With the first two movements youthfully urgent, Muti's is an exhilarating performance, fresh and direct. It is a strong symphonic view, rather than a programmatic one. The recording is rich and wide-ranging, though high violins do not always live up to the 'Philadelphia sound'. The tape transfer is full, clear and clean.

Loughran's performance shows him at his most persuasive, conveying the joy of Beethoven's arrival in the countryside with seeming spontaneity, so that the whole performance carries forward in a single sweep. The slow movement is especially fine; in the scherzo the horns sing out exuberantly, so that after the storm the dewy radiance of the finale is the more refreshing. The Hallé is on peak form, and the recording is rich and bright. The cassette transfer is bold and clear, but in spite of a basic resonant warmth the upper strings lack bloom.

Sanderling's characteristically slow speeds give an easy geniality to the *Pastoral.* Like Jochum he omits the exposition repeat in the first movement, marring the balance of movements, but otherwise this is a warm, glowing account which rises in the *Shepherds' hymn* from rugged honesty to rapt dedication. Bright

93

digital recording, with very little difference between disc and chrome tape.

With the body of strings reduced to a size such as Beethoven would have expected, Tilson Thomas adopts generally fast tempi and makes them sound lithe and exhilarating, not at all hectic. It is a strong, attractive reading, but with close-up recording, many will not notice much difference from big-orchestra sound. The high-level tape transfer is bright to the point of fierceness, although it does not lack weight in the bass. But the *Storm* seems excessively brilliant, and side two generally is more aggressive-sounding than side one.

The lightness and freshness of Haitink's readings of the even-numbered Beethoven symphonies reappear in the *Pastoral*. The tempi are on the fast side, but never hectically so. In its unobtrusive way it is a consistently enjoyable reading, well recorded on disc. The cassette transfer is bass-heavy without a compensating range in the treble. The sound is rich and can be rebalanced to some extent, but there is a touch of congestion in the *Storm*.

Jochum's HMV version is among the most distinctive. His tempo for the first movement is exceptionally slow (slower than in his earlier recording for Philips), but the rhythms are so exquisitely sprung that the result has more the flavour of a country dance than usual, with a hint of rustic tone in some of the wind solos (presumably, with these LSO players, that is by intent). There is a dance element too in Jochum's *Scene by the brook*, with the lapping triplet rhythms pointed as delectably as by Klemperer. The scherzo is jaunty and sharp-hitting, the *Storm* is given classical strength, and the *Shepherds' merrymaking* is fresh and innocent, again with a persuasive lilt. This will not be everyone's first choice, but with full and finely balanced recording it is a most compelling reading. It has transferred smoothly to tape, the rich warm sound retaining its bloom and a good deal of detail.

Jochum's Philips recording of the *Pastoral* dates from the end of the sixties. It still sounds extremely well, resonantly full-bodied, vivid and clear. Like his newer HMV recording this is a leisurely reading, the countryside relaxing in the sunshine. In the first movement Jochum is essentially undramatic until the radiant final climax in the coda, which he links with the similar burst of energy in the finale. The slow movement has an Elysian stillness and repose; the *Storm* is not over-romanticized. With beautiful playing from the Concertgebouw Orchestra, the reading is sustained without a hint of lethargy and makes a splendid medium-priced alternative view of Beethoven's ever-fresh symphony. There is little appreciable difference in sound between the disc and the excellent cassette.

Joy and serenity are not qualities one would normally associate with any American conductor, even Bernstein, but here he draws those qualities from the Vienna Philharmonic in a warm, persuasive reading, not perfect of ensemble (this was made at live concerts) but very enjoyable. The balance seems slightly over-resonant in the bass on disc, but the high-level tape transfer produces vivid sound throughout.

One might compare Sir Adrian Boult's reading of the *Pastoral* with his classic view of Schubert's *Great C major Symphony*. In both by some sleight of hand he disguises every interpretative problem, making it all seem easy and fresh, poised and natural. It is an attractive formula, though some may find the very lack of idiosyncrasy less than completely satisfying, particularly in the slow movement, which has nothing like the magic of Klemperer's comparable reading. But with gloriously full recording, the *Storm* has rarely sounded so magisterial on record, or for that matter the culminating climax of the finale. The tape transfer is clear and full, marginally less refined in detail than the disc.

The bargain-priced Contour version by the BBC Symphony Orchestra under

Sir Colin Davis was recorded as recently as 1976 and has splendidly full and well-balanced sound, with disc and cassette very closely matched. The performance is broader and more expansive than Davis's earlier record with the LSO. The controversial point about the later account is the very measured reading of the fourth movement, the *Storm*. Though the playing is refined, inevitably it lacks something in excitement. Nonetheless it matches Davis's relaxed approach to the whole work.

Karajan's 1977 performance brought a more congenial reading than his earlier excessively tense 1962 recording with the same orchestra. It is fresh and alert, consistent with the rest of the cycle, a good dramatic version with polished playing and recording which is wide-ranging but suffers from the odd balances which mark the 1977 cycle. The tape transfer matches the disc but is marginally brighter on side two.

Giulini's New Philharmonia version, recorded in the mid-sixties, has better-balanced sound than his much later Los Angeles account. The warm, rounded quality (rather bland and bass heavy in the cassette transfer) suits the conductor's lyrical approach, which is supported by fine relaxed orchestral playing. However, the effect is a little sleepy, beautiful but uninvolving; Giulini's measured view makes a stronger and more convincing effect in his second recording in Los Angeles. But the DG engineers produce disappointing results and the balances and mixing make the sound unrealistic. (The cassette matches the disc closely).

With the Orchestre de Paris often slack in ensemble, Kubelik's DG version is the one disappointment of his Beethoven cycle with different orchestras, markedly less sharp and alert than the version he recorded earlier with the RPO. The sound is good but not as clean as in most of the rest of the series. The tape transfer is vivid, with plenty of range at the top.

Dorati takes the first movement disconcertingly fast in the most direct

manner, with few concessions to expressiveness. Provided one can adjust to that approach, the result is convincing, and the remaining movements are attractively fresh in a far less brutal way. The RPO strings are given an attractive bloom in the DG recording.

Karajan's 1962 version of the *Pastoral* was by far the least appealing of his first Berlin Beethoven cycle, with hectically fast tempi. The playing is very refined, but even at medium price there are far more persuasive versions.

Still recommended: Apart from the bargain versions by Cluytens (CfP CFP/TC-CFP 40017) and Reiner (RCA CCV/C4 5053 [LSC 2614/RK 1094]) mentioned above, Boehm's beautiful VPO recording still holds pride of place (DG 2530 142/3300 476).

Symphony No. 7 in A, Op. 92.
*** DG 2531/3301 313 [id.]. VPO, Bernstein.
(M) *** DG Priv. 2535/3335 252. Bav. RSO, Kubelik.
(M) *** DG Acc. 2542/3342 107. Berlin PO, Karajan.
*** ASV ALH/ZCALH 904. Hallé O., Loughran.
**(*) DG 2531/3301 107 [id.]. Berlin PO, Karajan.
(M) **(*) Decca SPA/KCSP 586. LSO, Monteux.
(M) **(*) DG Priv. 2535/3335 472. VPO, Kubelik.
**(*) HMV ASD/TC-ASD 3646 [Ang. S/4XS 37538]. Phd. O., Muti.
(B) * Con. CC/CCT 7502 [Lon. STS 15107]. VPO, Karajan.

Symphony No. 7; Overture: The Creatures of Prometheus.
*(*) HMV Dig. ASD/TCC-ASD 4155. Philh. O., Sanderling.

Symphony No. 7; Overture: Fidelio.
(M) *(*) Ph. Fest. 6570/7310 048. Leipzig GO, Masur.

95

As in the *Eroica* the Beethovenian tensions in Bernstein's Vienna performance of the *Seventh* are less marked than in his earlier New York recording, but that makes for extra spring and exhilaration in the lilting rhythms of the first movement, while the *Allegretto* is reposeful without falling into an ordinary *Andante* and the last two movements have the adrenalin flowing with a greater sense of occasion than in most of this Bernstein series. One almost regrets the lack of applause. The recording is among the best and brightest in the series, the cassette marginally less refined at the top than the disc (noticeable in the first tutti of the opening movement's *Allegro*) but well balanced and lively.

A lyrical Beethovenian, Kubelik directs a sparkling yet relaxed account of the *Seventh*, recorded in full and atmospheric sound. With his own Bavarian Radio Orchestra his reading is even warmer and more spontaneous-sounding than the Vienna recording he made for DG as part of his complete Beethoven cycle. On tape the sound is much drier than on disc, although clear. However, the disc has more bloom and is to be preferred.

Karajan is nothing if not consistent, and his 1962 and 1977 versions of the *Seventh* are remarkably similar. The 1962 version tingles with excitement. It is hard-driven in the Toscanini manner and never less than compelling, lacking only the last degree of resilience that slightly slower tempi might have allowed. There is not quite the lift to the dance rhythms that the Italian Toscanini managed to retain even when driving at his hardest. With excellent recording for its period it makes an attractive Accolade reissue, with a good equivalent tape, slightly less bright than the disc but with plenty of body and good detail.

Karajan's 1977 version is similarly tense, with the conductor emphasizing the work's dramatic rather than its dance-like qualities. The slow introduction, taken at a fastish tempo, is tough rather than monumental, and the main *Allegro* is fresh and bright and not very lilting in its 6/8 rhythm, though it is more sharply pointed here than in the earlier 1962 version. The *Allegretto* is this time a little weightier, but the consistency with the earlier reading is still a point to emphasize. With good, full recording, the tape as vivid as the disc, this can be recommended alongside the earlier account, which is, of course, less expensive.

Loughran's Beethoven is rugged and energetic. The energy shines through, even when – as in the outer movements – he chooses basic tempi a degree more relaxed than is common. Like his Brahms performances for CfP, this account of the *Seventh* conveys an immediate spontaneity, with light and shade fully contrasted. The playing of the Hallé is not always quite so refined as that on the finest rival versions, but this is a powerful contender, with full, atmospheric recording. All repeats are observed. The sound on cassette is full-bodied, but has slightly less range and refinement on top than the LP.

Monteux opens with a powerful slow introduction, followed by a hard-driven 6/8 *Allegro* but with the rhythms nicely pointed, and a fast *Allegretto*, to recall the famous early mono LP by Erich Kleiber. Then comes a wide speed change for the trio after the scherzo, and an absolute headlong finale, with the kind of excitement one usually finds only in a live performance. The effect is ultimately somewhat lightweight, although certainly charismatic. The recording is bright and quite full, but not as clean as the companion records of the *Second* and *Fifth* symphonies. The tape is first-class.

Kubelik's second medium-price reissue is from his cycle of Beethoven symphonies made with different orchestras. With the Vienna Philharmonic his reading of the *Seventh* rather lacks drama – the earlier recording with his own Bavarian orchestra has more bite – but in its understated way it is beautiful and refined, helped by excellent recording. The cassette transfer is full and lively, marginally cleaner on side two.

The vigour and drive of Muti's account of the *Seventh* are never in doubt, but, surprisingly, the ensemble of the Philadelphia Orchestra is less than immaculate. There is spontaneity, but it is paid for in lack of precision, which puts this below the very finest versions. It is a fair example of EMI's 'new Philadelphia sound'. The high-level cassette transfer brings a touch of roughness at the opening and close of the symphony and a degree of rawness to the upper string timbre. However, a cutback of treble improves matters considerably.

Sanderling's reading is disappointing, unsprung and heavy to the point of turgidity in the first movement and lacking intensity elsewhere, with generally slow speeds. The bright digital recording, with a corresponding chrome cassette, is well up to the standard of this series.

Masur gives us a well-shaped and finely played account of the symphony, very much in what Peter Stadlen once described as traditional 'lean-beef' Beethoven when referring to Weingartner. This is civilized and fine-grained, but somehow lacks the concentration and fire of Toscanini or the dramatic momentum of Colin Davis. Musical virtues are, as one would expect from these artists, not wanting, and the performance is not without insights, but ultimately it fails to storm the heavens – and surely every great performance of this symphony does just that. The cassette has plenty of weight and does not seriously lack brilliance, but the reverberation produces a degree of blurring in the loudest tuttis.

Karajan's 1960 recording of the *Seventh*, originally made for Decca, has been reissued at bargain price on Contour, the recording still sounding wide-ranging and full-bodied (on cassette it is bass-heavy, especially in the finale). It is interesting to compare it with the exciting Berlin version on Accolade, made only a year or so later. The effect in Vienna is

massive rather than incandescent; the performance refuses to catch fire and the result is heartless.

Reminder: Sir Colin Davis's two recordings remain high on the list of recommendations. The broader, more recent Philips recording (9500 219) has beautiful sound and the advantage of including all repeats; but the earlier mid-priced HMV version has a freshness to rival any performance ever recorded and the sound is excellent both on disc and on the newly remastered tape (SXLP/ TC-SXLP 20038 [Ang. S 37027]). Also outstanding are Solti's Chicago performance, immensely powerful and energetic (Decca SXL/*KSXC* 6764 [Lon. 6932/5-7053]), and, in the bargain range, Cluytens (CfP CFP 40018) and Reiner (RCA CCV/*C4* 5026 [LSC 1991/*RK 1150*]).

Symphony No. 8 in F, Op. 93.
(B) *** Con. CC/*CCT* 7503. VPO, Abbado – SCHUBERT: *Symphony No. 8.****

At bargain price Abbado's Contour reissue makes a splendid recommendation. The fresh, alert performance underlines the sun in this symphony. The tempi are all well chosen, the rhythms beautifully sprung and such key moments as the gentle pay-off to the first movement delicately pointed. Some of the abrasiveness of Beethoven is missing, but not the resilience. Coupled with an equally sunny account of Schubert's *Unfinished* and given first-rate recording, which in no way sounds dated, this is one of the highlights of the Contour catalogue. As is usual with this label, the cassette lacks the upper range of the disc, and the bass sounds muddy.

Symphonies Nos. 8; 9 in D min. (Choral), Op. 125.
*** DG 2707/*3370* 109 (2) [id.]. Tomowa-Sintow, Baltsa, Schreier,

97

Van Dam, V. Singverein, Berlin PO, Karajan.

(M) *** DG Acc. 2725/*3372* 101 (2). Janowitz, Rössl-Majdan, Kmentt, Berry, V. Singverein, Berlin PO, Karajan.

*** DG 2707 124/*3370 037* (2) [id.]. Jones, Schwarz, Kollo, Moll, V. State Op. Ch., VPO, Bernstein.

**(*) HMV Dig. SLS/*TCC–SLS* 5244 (2). Armstrong, Finnie, Tear, Tomlinson, Philh. Ch. and O., Sanderling.

**(*) Ph. 6747 390 (2) [id.]. Bode, Watts, Laubenthal, Luxon, LPO Ch., LPO, Haitink.

Symphony No. 9.
*** DG Dig. 2741/*3382* 009 (2) [id.]. Norman, Fassbaender, Domingo, Berry, Concert Singers of V. State Op., VPO, Boehm.

(M) *** Decca VIV/*KVIC* 1 [Lon. 21043/5-]. Harper, Watts, Young, McIntyre, LSO Ch., LSO, Stokowski.

**(*) ASV ALH/*ZCALH* 903. Buchanan, Hodgson, Mitchinson, Howell, Hallé Ch. and O., Loughran.

**(*) CBS 76999/*40-*. Popp, Obraztsova, Vickers, Talvela, Cleveland Ch. and O., Maazel.

(M) **(*) DG Priv. 2726/*3372* 112 (2). Donath, Berganza, Ochman, Stewart, Bav. R. Ch. and SO, Kubelik – *Symphony No. 1.***(*)

** Ph. Dig. 6769/*7654* 067 (2) [id.]. Janet Price, Finnila, Laubenthal, Rintzler, Concg. Ch. and O., Haitink.

(M) *(*) Ph. Fest. 6570/*7310* 012. Tomowa-Sintow, Burmeister, Schreier, Adam, Leipzig and Berlin Ch., Leipzig GO, Masur.

Symphony No. 9; Overtures: King Stephen; Leonora No. 3.
(M) **(*) HMV SXDW/*TC2 SXDW* 3051 (2) [Ang. S 3577]. Lövberg, Ludwig, Kmentt, Hotter, Philh. Ch. and O., Klemperer.

Fine as Karajan's earlier reading of the *Ninth* with the Berlin Philharmonic is, his 1977 performance reveals even greater insight, above all in the *Adagio*, where he conveys spiritual intensity at a slower tempo than before. In the finale the concluding eruption has an animal excitement rarely heard from this highly controlled conductor, and the soloists make an excellent team, with contralto, tenor and bass all finer than their predecessors. What is less satisfactory is the balance of the recording. The result may be wider in range but it is less atmospheric and less realistic than before, with the solo voices in the finale unnaturally close.

On the fourth side Karajan directs an electrically tense performance of the *Eighth*, missing some of the joy of Beethoven's 'little one', but justifying his brisk tempi in the brilliant playing of the orchestra. The cassette transfer of both works is of the highest quality: this is one of the very finest sounding recordings of the *Choral symphony* on tape.

The earlier Karajan version has been reissued at medium price on Accolade and remains excellent value. When recording his 1962 cycle Karajan, in a concentrated series of sessions, kept till the end the biggest challenge of all. The last two symphonies on the list were the *Eroica* and finally the *Ninth*. One senses that feeling of a challenge accepted in triumph throughout this incandescent reading of the symphony, one of the finest ever recorded. Though the great *Adagio* has received more intense readings, the hush of *pianissimo* has never been recorded with greater purity than here, and the electricity of the finale has all the tension of Karajan at his most inspired. The recording still sounds very well, spaced on three sides. Karajan's sharply dramatic reading of the *Eighth* makes an excellent fill-up. The tape transfer is clear and realistic, although the choral focus in the finale of No. 9 is somewhat grainy.

Boehm was one of the select handful of conductors who made records of the *Choral symphony* during the 78 era. Later he recorded it on mono LP for Philips and more recently as part of his 1972 complete set for DG. Just a few months before he died, he made his final statement on the work in this resplendent new digital set. With generally slow tempi his reading is spacious and powerful – the first movement even has a certain stoic quality – and in its broad concept it has much in common with Klemperer's famous version. Yet overall there is a transcending sense of a great occasion, and the concentration is unfailing, reaching its peak in the glorious finale, where ruggedness and strength well over into inspiration, and that in spite of a pacing nearly as individual as that of Stokowski, notably in the drum and fife march, which is much more serious in feeling than usual. But with an outburst of joy in the closing pages the listener is left in no doubt that this recording was the culmination of a long and distinguished career. With a fine, characterful team of soloists, and a freshly incisive chorus formed from singers of the Vienna State Opera this is strongly recommendable, and many will like the layout, with one movement complete on each side. The chrome cassettes match the discs very closely indeed (the choral focus and transients in the finale are very impressive); there is technically no finer *Choral symphony* on tape.

Bernstein's characterful account of the *Ninth* superbly crowns his Beethoven series, and in this two-disc set, coupled with a sympathetic account of the *Eighth*, it makes an excellent recommendation. The very start conveys immediate electricity, reflecting the presence of an audience, and the first movement is presented at white heat from first to last, with only a slight *rallentando* detracting from the thrust. The scherzo is resilient, the *Adagio* deeply convincing in its distinctive contrasting of inner meditation in a very slow first theme with lighter carefree interludes in a fast-flowing *Andante*. In the finale Gwyneth Jones's soprano is as well controlled as it ever has been on record, and otherwise this is a superb account,

sung and played with dedication if a fraction less intense than the earlier movements. The recording, unlike some others in the series, needs no apology: it is bright and immediate. The cassette transfer, however, has been made at rather a low level; the *Eighth Symphony* lacks upper range, and although No. 9 sounds more lively, the choral focus is not absolutely sharp, though the sound itself is bright.

Stokowski's version, reissued on Decca's newest budget label, Viva, makes an impressive first choice for the *Ninth* in the lower price-range. The recording – originally Phase Four – is excellent, only losing marginally in lower bass amplitude on three-sided versions, and remaining full and vivid. The cassette matches the disc closely. Unmistakably this is a great, compelling account of the *Ninth*. There is the sort of tension about this recorded performance which one expects from a great conductor in the concert hall, and that compulsion carries one over all of Stokowski's idiosyncrasies, including a fair amount of touching up in the orchestration. The first movement is strong and dramatic, taken at a Toscanini pace; the scherzo is light and pointed, with timpani cutting through; the slow movement has great depth and *Innigkeit*, and that perhaps more than anything con firms the greatness of the performance, for the finale, with some strangely slow tempi, is uneven, despite fine singing.

The weight and majesty of Beethoven's inspiration has rarely been so tellingly conveyed on record as in the historic early stereo recording of Klemperer. The angularity and lack of compromise are most compelling, though other versions may be more persuasive. In the finale it is sad that the glorious contribution of the chorus is not matched by the solo singing, with Hans Hotter unsteady and Aase Nordmo Lövberg at times raw-toned. Excellent recording for its period. The reissue is especially attractive in its cassette format, complete as it is on a single double-length tape. Side one contains the first three movements and side two the choral finale – sounding vivid and cleanly focused – and the overtures. Generally the orchestral quality is wide-ranging and clear, with plenty of weight.

Sanderling's recorded cycle with the Philharmonia developed out of a live series of concerts. The performances of the *Eighth* and *Ninth Symphonies* have a rugged directness – an unvarnished honesty, as one commentator put it – which makes special links here with the Philharmonia Klemperer versions. Like Klemperer, Sanderling prefers slowish tempi, maintained steadily. The *Ninth*, in clear digital sound, may lack mystery at the start, and the finale is dangerously slow; but the power of the work is splendidly caught. The soloists make an excellent team, but the Philharmonia Chorus is just below its best form, the singing of the sopranos not always well supported. The sound on tape matches the discs until the finale, where the choral focus is disappointing.

Loughran gives a direct and unaffected reading of the *Ninth* which may not scale the heights but which makes a fine culmination to his very recommendable series. The single-disc format means both that the turnover in the slow movement is at an uncomfortable point and that the recording lacks a little in immediacy. But with an interpretation which calls attention to the music rather than to any idiosyncrasy, no one will be disappointed who has ever responded to Loughran's Beethoven. All the repeats are observed in the scherzo. Soloists and choir in the finale are first-rate. The cassette transfer is full-bodied and clear, although in the finale soloists and chorus lack something in presence.

The monumental grandeur of the *Ninth* stands well to Maazel's urgent and often aggressive Beethoven style. His is a strong performance, but one which misses warmer, deeper feelings. The solo quartet is a fine one – Vickers characterful if miscast – and the choral singing is energetic. The recording matches the

reading in its clarity and forwardness, and the cassette transfer is one of CBS's best, vivid and lively with the finale clear and excitingly projected.

The peak of Haitink's Beethoven cycle is the *Eroica* in an outstandingly thoughtful and concentrated reading. By comparison the LPO version of the *Ninth*, warm and confident in the first movement, not cataclysmic, is, like the rest of the cycle, a shade lacking in weight. The slow movement too is easy and warm and the finale not quite the culmination required, though very exciting at the close. The recording is good if not ideally clean on detail.

Haitink's later digital recording was made at a live concert in the Concertgebouw, but one would not know that: there are few if any signs of an audience, and – disappointingly – the performance rather fails to convey the feeling of an occasion, lacking a little in tension even in comparison with Haitink's earlier studio version with the LPO. The reading, as before, is satisfyingly unidiosyncratic, direct and honest. But with this work one needs more. The chrome tapes are very disappointing: the low level brings a lack of impact and range, and in the finale the chorus is very poorly focused.

In his tour of international orchestras for his complete Beethoven cycle, Kubelik reserved for his own orchestra the most challenging, culminating task. With glowing tone from the players it is less a monumental reading than a warm, understanding one. There is a Mendelssohnian lightness in the scherzo, and the slow movement has sun as well as serenity in it, leading on consistently to the jollifications of the finale. Excellent recording, although the level of the cassette transfer is modest. The sound on tape remains full and clear but the discs have slightly more range.

In its original format Masur's version was spread over three sides. Its transfer to two involves a side-break in the slow movement, which will rule it out of court for some collectors. Masur gives a spacious, well-proportioned and noble account that is well worth hearing. But competition is stiff and in spite of the first-class Leipzig orchestral playing the Schmidt-Isserstedt version (Decca JB/KJBC 1 [Lon. 1159]) is more strongly characterized. Solti's splendid set is also still highly recommended. Spread out spaciously over four sides, with superb recording, it has a matching cassette transfer of the highest quality (Decca 6BB 121/2/KBB2 7041 [Lon. CSP/5- 8]).

CHAMBER MUSIC

Clarinet trio in B flat, Op. 11.
*** Ph. 9500 670/7300 826 [id.]. Pieterson, Pressler, Greenhouse – BRAHMS: *Clarinet trio.****
(M) *** Decca Ace SDD/KSDC 528. Schmidl, New V. Octet (members) – *Septet.****
**(*) CRD 1045 (with *Clarinet trio* by Archbishop Rudolph of Austria). Nash Ens.

This *Trio* comes from 1798 and its last movement consists of a set of variations on a theme from Weigl's opera *L'Amor marinaro.* Beethoven later thought sufficiently well of the work to consider writing another finale for it and letting the variations stand on their own as a separate entity. George Pieterson is the first clarinet of the Concertgebouw Orchestra, and his playing is distinguished by refined tone and sensitive phrasing; Menahem Pressler, the pianist of the Beaux Arts Trio, is no less vital and imaginative than he is in the sparkling set of Haydn *Trios*, and the Op. 11 *Trio* here sounds more persuasive than in any rival performance. This is a distinguished and enjoyable record, and the tape transfer is excellent too, warm and vivid.

The New Vienna Octet also make a better case for the Op. 11 *Trio* than most of their rivals. The playing is wonderfully alert and has both sparkle and warmth. In this repertoire couplings tend to deter-

mine choice, and in that respect this Decca Ace of Diamonds issue cannot be faulted; taken on artistic merit alone this is second to none. The sound is first-rate, with little difference between the disc and the admirable high-level tape.

The Nash Ensemble's account has a royal rarity as coupling; Archduke Rudolph was a son of an Austrian emperor. But his claim to fame is as a pupil and friend of Beethoven; he was a good enough pianist to take part in the *Triple concerto* and he subscribed to the fund that gave support to Beethoven after the onset of his deafness. His *Clarinet trio* is incomplete: of the closing rondo, only a fragment survives, and this performance ends with the slow movement, a set of variations on a theme by yet another prince, Louis Ferdinand of Prussia. The music may be no great shakes but it is more than just a curiosity, and its inclusion on this record is welcome. The playing is thoroughly persuasive, with some attractive pianism from the excellent Clifford Benson. Much the same goes for the performance of the Beethoven *Trio*, and though obviously not an indispensable issue, this is well worth investigating for interest.

Clarinet trio; Horn sonata in F, Op. 17, 7 Variations on Mozart's 'Bei Männern' from 'Die Zauberflöte', WoO. 46.
*** ASV ACA 1005. Music Group of L.

Well-recorded and finely played versions of some less important Beethoven pieces. This is natural, unaffected playing – thoroughly musical and unfailingly intelligent, and the sound quality is faithful. In Alan Civil's hands the *Horn sonata* holds its own against some distinguished rival versions, and the performance of the *Clarinet trio*, with Keith Puddy in excellent form, also has much to commend it.

Cor anglais sonata in F, Op. 17. Trio

in C, Op. 87; Variations on Mozart's 'Là ci darem', WoO. 28 (both for 2 oboes and cor anglais).
*** Ph. 9500 672/7300 767 [id.]. Holliger, Elhorst, Bourgue, Wyttenbach.

An enterprising issue. The *C major Trio*, Op. 87, occupies one side. Despite its late opus number, it is an early work dating from 1794, and its scale is larger than its neglect would lead one to expect. There are four movements, which show no mean degree of organic cohesion and an awareness of formal design. The *Là ci darem Variations* were performed in 1797 but not published until the present century. They are also ingeniously written and often diverting. The *Horn sonata*, Op. 17, which is somewhat later (1800), transposes to the cor anglais quite effectively. It goes without saying that these artists make the most of the possibilities here and are accorded excellent and well-balanced sound. None of this is major Beethoven but the catalogues are richer for its appearance. The cassette transfer matches the disc closely: it is strikingly fresh and clear.

Horn sonata in F, Op. 17; Trio for piano, flute and bassoon in G, WoO. 37.
*** DG 2531 293. Bloom, Barenboim, Debost, Sennedat.

Of the artists here, three are members of the Orchestre de Paris, and Daniel Barenboim is its conductor. Myron Bloom, who originally comes from Cleveland, is a horn player of distinction even if his view of the *Horn sonata* does not efface memories of the Tuckwell–Ashkenazy performance on Decca. The *Trio* is not an important work but it is far from unattractive, and Barenboim plays with sensitivity and imagination. The DG recording is well balanced.

Wind music: *March in B flat, WoO. 29; Octet in E flat, Op. 103; Quintet in E flat* (for oboe, 3 horns, bassoon); *Rondino in E flat for wind octet, G. 146; Sextet in E flat, Op. 71.*
*** Ph. 9500 087 [id.]. Neth. Wind Ens.

Crisp, clean and alert performances from the Netherlands Wind Ensemble, splendidly recorded. None of this music is important but it is all enjoyable. The same repertoire is available from the London Wind Soloists and Jack Brymer at medium price but the richer Philips recording gives this a slight edge over its rival.

Piano quartets Nos. 1 in E flat; 2 in D; 3 in C, WoO. 36/1–3; 4 in E flat, Op. 16.
(M) *** Sup. 1112 211/2. Martinu Piano Qt.

Three of these pieces were written in Bonn when Beethoven was a mere fifteen years of age; the other is an arrangement of the *Piano and wind quintet*, and is hardly superior to it. However, Beethoven thought well enough of the *C major* to draw on it for material in his Op. 2 *Sonatas*. The Martinu Piano Quartet gives perceptive and musical accounts of all four pieces, observing the first repeats even in the slow movements; and the piano, which has the most interesting material, is felicitously played by Emil Leichner. The sound is warm and well balanced.

Piano and wind quintet in E flat, Op. 16.
*** CRD CRD 1067/CRDC 4067. Nash Ens. – MOZART: *Quintet.****

The Nash Ensemble (with Ian Brown as pianist) gives a fresh and intelligent account of the *Quintet*, which makes an excellent alternative to the long-admired Ashkenazy set with the London Wind Soloists. This *Quintet* is no masterpiece and may need the greater projection that the Decca team brings to it, but this is natural and unforced playing that yields equally musical rewards. The recording balance is less forward than Decca's, and the overall result is more pleasing. The cassette is first-class too.

Piano trios: in B flat, Op. 11; No. 4 in D (Ghost), Op. 70/1; 10 Variations on 'Ich bin der Schneider Kakadu', Op. 121a.
(M) *** Ph. 6527/*7311* 077. Beaux Arts Trio.

Piano trio No. 4.
(M) ** HMV SXLP/*TC-SXLP* 30523. H. and Y. Menuhin, Gendron – SCHUBERT: *Trout quintet.***

Piano trios Nos. 4; 5 in E flat, Op. 70/1–2.
(M) **(*) DG Acc. 2542/*3342* 125. Kempff, Szeryng, Fournier.

Piano trio No. 6 in B flat (Archduke), Op. 97.
(M) **(*) DG Acc. 2542/*3342* 118 [2530 147]. Kempff, Szeryng, Fournier.
** Ph. 9500/*7300* 895 [id.]. Beaux Arts Trio.

The Beaux Arts version of the *Archduke* was designed as a twenty-fifth anniversary issue, but sadly it proved one of the least compelling recordings from that superb group. The first movement, at a very slow tempo, sounds self-conscious and mannered; the scherzo fails to maintain its spring and so does the finale. The slow variations have little sense of flow. The recording quality is excellent, and as ever the ensemble is immaculate. The cassette is of excellent quality, if without quite the sharpness of internal focus of the disc.

The other Beaux Arts issue is an economical and attractive rearrangement of performances that originally appeared in different couplings. The Op. 11 trio, which is split over two sides of the disc, is usually heard in its clarinet version. The

Beaux Arts players are on excellent form here, and they project the drama and intensity of the *Ghost trio* to brilliant effect. The *Kakadu variations* are played with characteristic elegance too. The recordings date from the mid-1960s (when Daniel Guilet was the violinist) but they still sound fresh and lifelike. Good value, particularly at medium price. The cassette transfer is natural and well balanced.

Kempff and his colleagues give a crystalline reading of the *Archduke*. It is the clarity and imagination of Kempff's playing which set the tone of the whole performance. He it is who grips the listener's attention with his individual touches of genius, so that by comparison Szeryng and Fournier sound less than inspired. An interesting but not a definitive version. In the coupling of the two Op. 70 *Trios* the performances are again comparatively restrained. As a whole these are sweet and lyrical rather than dramatic readings, but they are naturally recorded. Both issues are available in excellent cassette versions, with fresh, clean transfers.

On the HMV disc the *Ghost trio* makes a generous coupling for the *Trout quintet*. This performance dates from the mid-1960s, and on its first appearance we deplored the fact that the piano part was outweighed by the closer balance given to violin and cello; and we still feel that this diminishes the attractions of a good performance. The sound is also rather dry, and this is especially noticeable on the cassette, where the violin timbre lacks bloom.

Septet in E flat, Op. 20.
(M) *** Decca Ace SDD/*KSDC* 528. New V. Octet (members) – *Clarinet trio.****
**(*) Ph. 9500/*7300* 973 [id.]. ASMF Chamber Ens.
(M) ** DG Priv. 2535/*3335* 328. Berlin Octet (members) – MOZART: *Sonata for bassoon and cello.***

103

** HM 1C 065 99713. Coll. Aur.
(M) ** Ph. Seq. 6527/7311 066. Berlin
Philharmonic Octet (members).

The older Vienna Octet's recording
(also on Decca Ace of Diamonds) has
held sway in the catalogue for more than
two decades. It has great lightness of
touch and spontaneity and the *Penguin
Stereo Record Guide* forecast that it
would be 'a long time before [this] work
receives a better all-round performance'.
Like the earlier ensemble, the New
Vienna Octet consists of the first desks of
the VPO, though the membership is different from the 1977 Vienna Philharmonic Chamber Ensemble on DG. This
later version has all the elegance of the
earlier two but conveys a sparkle and a
sense of enjoyment that are thoroughly
exhilarating. In terms of spirit and
exuberance it is altogether special. The
recording is first-class and the Decca
cassette transfer is equally admirable.

The Academy players give a highly
accomplished and thoroughly musical
account of the *Septet* which has the merit
of excellent balance and truthful recording, the cassette only marginally less
clean and lively than the disc. It is completely enjoyable and thoroughly recommendable, and were competition not
quite so stiff it would rate an unqualified
three stars. But it does not have quite the
same sense of character or profile as its
rivals.

Made in the mid-1960s, the Berlin
Octet's Privilege version has much to
recommend it, not least the highly
accomplished wind playing. By comparison with its rivals, however, it seems
a shade self-aware and is not free from
expressive point-making. The recording
is excellent on disc and cassette alike.

The Collegium Aureum retains some
modern practices (a little vibrato and the
occasional expressive bulge) but plays
with plenty of life. The clarinet is less
smooth than in our day, and the horn
somewhat uneven (had it been even, there
would have been no need for the valve

horn). It seems a paradox that our age
should revive instruments that musicians
of the period found inadequate. The
playing is splendidly accomplished and
admirably recorded, and collectors wishing to sample the *Septet* on period
instruments need not hesitate. For the
non-specialist collector there are better
and cheaper records.

On the Philips Sequenza reissue the
Berlin players take a somewhat solemn
view. This is a refined performance,
beautifully recorded, but next to the
Decca version it lacks wit and sparkle.
The high-level tape transfer produces
excellent quality, and there is little to
choose between tape and disc.

Serenade for string trio, Op. 8.
**(*) CBS 76832 [Col. M/*MT* 35152].
Perlman, Zukerman, Harrell –
DOHNÁNYI: *Serenade.***(*)

Although the *Serenade* is not one of
Beethoven's greatest works in this
medium, it is well worth having, particularly in so masterly a performance.
Unfortunately, the recording is on the
dry side and calls for some tolerance on
this score. However, the quality of the
performance and the interest of the
coupling outweigh any other considerations.

String quartets Nos. 1–16 (com-
plete).
(B) * CBS GM 101 (10) [Col. M3 30084;
D3M 34094; M4 31740]. Juilliard Qt.

It is not possible to do full justice to a
ten-record set in a few lines, and it goes
without saying that there are some impressive things here, as one would expect
from such experienced and distinguished
players. As a whole, however, these
readings cannot be strongly recommended: the Juilliard players rarely give
themselves enough time to allow phrases
to expand naturally, and in slow movements, particularly in the later quartets,

there is far too little sense of inner repose. These are not performances that bring one closer to Beethoven, and they convey little or no sense of musical spontaneity. Moreover, the engineers have not succeeded in producing a sympathetic or particularly musical sound. This is a non-starter.

String quartets Nos. 1–6, Op. 18/1–6.
*** HMV SLS/*TC–SLS* 5217 (3). Alban Berg Qt.
*** Ph. 6703 081 (3) [id.]. Italian Qt.
** RCA RL 03486 [ARL 3 3486]. Cleveland Qt.
(M) ** Sup. 1111 2731/3. Smetana Qt.

Generally speaking, the Alban Berg set of the Op. 18 quartets is a strong front-runner. The affectation that we noted in this Quartet's set of the *Rasumovskys* (the tendency to exaggerate dynamic extremes) is less obtrusive here, and the overall sense of style is so sure, and the technical accomplishment so satisfying, that few readers are likely to be disappointed. Moreover, the quality of the recorded sound is altogether excellent, and in this respect, for some collectors the clarity and body may well tip the scales in the Berg Quartet's favour. It can certainly be recommended alongside the Italian Quartet issue, and this has the advantage of an excellent cassette alternative.

The Italian Quartet's performances are in superb style and are beautifully recorded. This box replaces the individual issues. The Cleveland offers a coherent and thoughtful account of the Op. 18 quartets, perhaps more impetuous than the Végh and the Italian performances and, in the long run, probably less satisfying. But the Cleveland players have obviously thought deeply about these quartets, and in the accompanying notes they argue coherently for the accuracy of Beethoven's metronome markings. They are unusual in that they repeat

the second halves of the first movements of the *A major* and *B flat Quartets* (the latter is taken at an enormous speed). The readings as a whole are not free from expressive point-making, and there are some pretty controversial interpretative decisions: the development of the first movement of the *C minor* is too symphonic in feeling and the introduction to the finale is rushed. Both the Italian and the Végh Quartets are more reposeful and humane: the Cleveland sometimes seem to try too hard to make detail come alive and they indulge in agogic exaggerations, albeit of a musical and legitimate nature. The playing is enormously accomplished; the recording is a little too hard in climaxes.

The Smetana Quartet has polish and finesse but does not give strongly individual or memorable accounts of these quartets. There are many things to admire, of course, and the performances are nothing if not accomplished; and the quality of the recorded sound remains perfectly acceptable. But the freshness and the personal insights that one recalls from many of this Quartet's earlier recordings are lacking, and these good, well-played readings fail to kindle enthusiasm. With such strong rivals on the market, this set is not competitive.

String quartets Nos. 7 in F; 8 in E min.; 9 in C (Rasumovsky Nos. 1–3), Op. 59/1–3; 10 in E flat (Harp), Op. 74; 11 in F min., Op. 95.
*** Valois CMB 32 (3). Végh Qt.
*** Cal. CAL 163436 (3). Talich Qt.
(M) **(*) HMV SLS/*TC-SLS* 5171 (3). Alban Berg Qt.
(M) ** RCA RL 03010 (4) [ARL 4 3010]. Cleveland Qt.

String quartets No. 7–9.
(M) *** Decca Ace D 214 D 2 (2). Gabrieli Qt.

String quartets Nos. 8 and 11.
*** Cal. CAL 1634. Talich Qt.

String quartets Nos. 10 and 11.
(M) *** Ph. 6570/*7310* 746. Italian Qt.
(M) **(*) Decca Ace SDD/*KSDC* 551.
Gabrieli Qt.
(M) *(*) Argo ZK 81. Allegri Qt.

The Végh performances were originally issued on the Telefunken label, but
have now reverted to an import label,
Valois, so may need some perseverance
to obtain. But on balance, the Végh
Quartet gives us by far the most searching
and thoughtful account of the middle-
period quartets, and for once it is possible
to speak of one set being the best. These
performances may not always have the
high technical finish that distinguishes
the Italians or other rivals, but they possess abundant humanity and insight.
Végh himself commands great beauty of
tone and range of colour; his phrases
breathe naturally and yet he constantly
surprises one by the imaginative way he
shapes a line or the sheer quality and
range of the *pianissimo* tone on which he
can draw. He is occasionally under the
note, but this is rarely disturbing. At no
point does one feel, either from him or
from his colleagues, that beauty of tone
is the first and overriding consideration.
Beauty is the by-product, as it were, of
the search for truth and never an end in
itself. All the way through, right from the
opening of Op. 59/1, one feels they offer
the *tempo giusto*, and throughout they
show the same alertness of articulation
and rhythmic grasp, yet with a flexibility
and subtlety that are masterly. Only in
the slow movement of Op. 59/1 does one
feel that the Italian Quartet is more
searching, though it is undoubtedly the
more perfect quartet in many ways.

The Talich Quartet was formed in the
1960s and takes its name from its violist,
Jan Talich, nephew of the great Czech
conductor. These performances have the
air of authority and the fine musical
judgement that distinguishes their versions of the late quartets. The recordings
are similar too, with a tendency to be a
little bottom-heavy (as, for that matter,

are those of the Végh Quartet). Tempi are
sensible throughout, and the phrasing is
unfailingly musical.

The Gabrieli Quartet gives an account
of the three *Rasumovskys* that can hold
its own with the very best of its rivals.
The layout of the two records differs
from its immediate rivals: the Hungarians have one record per quartet; coupling the *C major* with the *Harp*, and the
Italians accommodate Op. 59/1 and the
first movement of Op. 59/2 on the first
record, and the rest on the second. The
Gabrielis begin with the *E minor*, observing the exposition repeat in the first
movement, and then proceed to the first
movement of Op. 59/1. Although the
ensemble of the Italians is superior in one
or two places and their tonal blend is
more finely integrated, this playing is still
extremely impressive and often really
distinguished. The recording is warm and
vivid. In the absence of the Italians, this
can be recommended alongside (but not
in preference to) the Végh or Talich
Quartets.

The Alban Berg Quartet is an assured
and alert group with finely blended tone
and excellent attack. They have been
particularly successful in their Mozart
and Schubert issues and have an enviable
reputation – rightly so. Generally speaking, they favour rather brisk tempi in the
first movements, which they dispatch
with exemplary polish and accuracy of
intonation. Indeed, an almost unsmiling
momentum is maintained when they
reach the quaver theme in thirds in the
first movement of Op. 59/1, where almost
every other quartet relaxes just a little.
The slow movement of Op. 59/1 is free
from excessive point-making of the kind
that mars the Cleveland version, and
throughout this quartet and its companions there is much perceptive music-
making. Rhythms are marvellously
sprung and every phrase is vividly characterized. One generalization can be
made: there is a distinct tendency to exaggerate dynamic extremes. The introduction to Op. 59/3 suffers in this respect,

and the results sound self-conscious. In the first movements of Op. 59/2 and Op. 95 the brilliance of the attack almost draws attention to itself, and perhaps the recording quality, which is a little closely balanced, gives it a slightly more aggressive quality than it really has. As quartet playing, however, this is superlative and in some respects (such as ensemble and intonation) it would be difficult to fault. But this is not the whole picture, and while this remains the most accomplished and generally successful *Rasumovsky* set to appear since our last volume, it does not dislodge either the Végh or the Italians. The Végh are by no means as perfect in terms of ensemble and they are not as well recorded but both they and the excellently recorded Philips set of the Italians inhabit a world far more closely related to the deep humanity and vision of this music. The Alban Berg recordings of the *Rasumovskys* are alone in the tape catalogue; the cassette transfers are of admirable quality, rich and clear.

The Cleveland Quartet is an accomplished body with a well integrated approach to these scores, a splendid unanimity of ensemble and fine intonation. Dynamic nuances are faithfully observed and there is a wide range of colour as well as a distinctive surface polish. As a body, however, these players favour an overtly (and, perhaps, overly) expressive style that will not be to all tastes. The leader's tone is sweet but a little wanting in richness, though the lack of warmth in the overall sound quality may enhance this impression. At times the Cleveland's sonority is impressively big and symphonic, as if they were relating this music to Beethoven's middle-period orchestral output. There is a lot of expressive point-making, particularly in the slow movements of Op. 59/1 and 2, and again the first movement of Op. 95, where they pull back for the D flat theme, which is then sentimentalized. There is no doubting the virtuosity of the group (the finale of Op. 59/3 is played with tremendous attack and brilliance) but the humanity and

depth of these scores are better revealed elsewhere. The recordings, too, are a little wanting in warmth, though there is clarity and separation.

The Gabrielis offer well-shaped and sensibly conceived readings of Opp. 74 and 95 which fall short of the last ounce of polish when put alongside their major rivals. Their playing has no lack of vitality or fire and they throw themselves into the third movement of Op. 95 with genuine spirit. The recording is well balanced but is not quite as refined on cassette as on disc. Although this is arguably the best of the newer issues of this coupling it does not displace the Italian Quartet, who are as eloquent as they are unmannered, and provide beautifully shaped readings, splendidly recorded on both disc and tape.

There is some sensitive playing from the Allegri Quartet in the slow movements of the *Harp* and Op. 95 and no want of musical intelligence. But the playing can also be a little heavy-handed and wanting in refinement, though some of this impression may be due to a rather bottom-heavy recording.

String quartets Nos. 12 in E flat, Op. 127; 13 in B flat, Op. 130; 14 in C sharp min., Op. 131; 15 in A min., Op. 132; 16 in F, Op. 135; Grosse Fuge, Op. 133.
(M) *** Ph. 6768 341 (2) (without Nos. 14–15). Italian Qt.
*(*) DG 2740 168 [2711 018]. LaSalle Qt.
(M) * Argo D 155 D 4 [id.]. Aeolian Qt.

String quartets Nos. 12 and 16.
*** Cal. CAL 1640. Talich Qt.

String quartet No. 13: Grosse Fuge.
*** Cal. CAL 1637. Talich Qt.

String quartet No. 14.
*** Cal. CAL 1638. Talich Qt.

String quartet No. 15.
*** Cal. CAL 1639. Talich Qt.

Of all modern accounts of the late quartets, the Talich versions are the first that can match those of the Végh and Italian Quartets. One is immediately gripped by the purity of the sound these artists produce and the effortlessness of their phrasing. As a quartet their ensemble and intonation are impeccable, and they possess both depth of feeling and insight. Their reading of Op. 132 brings one close to the heart of this music, particularly in the *Heiliger Dankgesang*, where they show great inwardness. There is little to fault elsewhere; the readings unfold with a totally unforced naturalness; tempi have that feeling of rightness one recognizes in masterly performances, and the dynamic range is wide without being exaggerated. They can be recommended alongside the Italians, though the latter have the advantage of more transparent and vivid recording. As in the Végh Quartet's recordings, the sound here is just a shade bottom-heavy, but at the same time both ensembles bring a rich humanity to bear on these masterpieces.

If recorded sound were the sole criterion in this repertoire, the LaSalle Quartet would head the list of recommendations. The DG engineers have produced a recording of great splendour which has all the opulence and presence one could ask for. The players themselves are unfailingly impressive technically and they bring unanimity of ensemble and fine total blend to these awe-inspiring scores. But there is no sense of awe or mystery here, no feeling of inwardness or depth. They are light-years removed from the Végh, the Talich or the Italian Quartets, all of whom bring us much closer to this music.

The Aeolian players are artists of no mean accomplishment and fine musicianship, but their survey of the late quartets is something of a disappointment. It has the feeling of routine about it: nothing seems freshly experienced, and in spite of many thoughtful and perceptive touches, the performances rarely go very

deep. The Argo sound is somewhat reverberant, though detail registers reasonably well. There is little to attract the collector here or to reward repeated hearings.

String quartet No. 14 (arr. for string orch.).
(***) DG 2531 077 [id.]. VPO, Bernstein.

Bernstein is not the first to perform late Beethoven quartets in this fashion: Toscanini recorded two movements of Op. 135, and Mitropoulos conducted Op. 131 in the 1940s, a performance which Bernstein attended and now emulates. Obviously the added weight and the different colour that the full strings offer make for losses as well as gains; the intimacy of private feeling becomes transformed into the outpouring of public sentiment. There is no doubt as to the commitment and depth of feeling that Bernstein brings to this performance, dedicated to the memory of his wife; nor are there doubts as to the quality of the response he evokes from the Vienna Philharmonic strings. This is not a record about which we are in agreement: many collectors would never play it more than once. What one can agree about is that, if this is to be done at all, it could not be given more eloquent advocacy than it is here. The recording has excellent range and clarity.

String quintets in E flat, Op. 4; in C min., Op. 104.
(M) ** Sup. 1112 128. Suk Quintet.

These are both early works in spite of the high opus number for the *C minor*. The latter is a transcription of the Op. 1/3 *Piano trio* which Beethoven made in 1817; the *E flat Quintet*, Op. 4, is probably better known in its arrangement for wind octet, published many years later as Op. 103. There are differences: the scherzo was rewritten and an additional trio section added. The playing of the Suk Quintet is musicianly and persuasive, and the only reservation concerns the quality of the recorded sound, which could do with more body and presence.

String quintet in C, Op. 29.
*(*) RCA RL/*RK* 13354 [ARL 1/*ARK 1* 3354]. Guarneri Qt, Zukerman – MENDELSSOHN: *Quintet.**(*)

Recordings of the *C major String quintet* are not legion, so any newcomer deserves a welcome. The Guarneri Quartet and Pinchas Zukerman bring high voltage but less than perfect finish to the work, and, although there are impressive things here, these distinguished artists are not at their happiest: nor, for that matter, is the recording as rich and refined as RCA's best. The coupling is bold and enterprising, a neglected Mendelssohn rarity, but better versions of both works exist. This does not displace the Vienna version on Ace of Diamonds, coupled with the *Sextet in E flat*, Op. 81b, which is better recorded and also cheaper (Decca SDD 419).

Violin sonatas Nos. 1–10.
⊛ *** Decca D 92 D 5/*K 92 K 53* [Lon. 2501/5-]. Perlman, Ashkenazy.
(M) *** Ph. 6768 036 (4). D. Oistrakh, Oborin.
(M) **(*) RCA RL 42004 (5). Heifetz; Bay or Brooks Smith.

The Ashkenazy/Perlman set is unlikely to be surpassed on disc or cassette for many years to come. Perlman and Ashkenazy are for the 1970s what Kreisler and Rupp were for the 1930s and forties, Grumiaux and Haskil for the fifties, and Oistrakh and Oborin for the sixties. These performances offer a blend of classical purity and spontaneous vitality that is irresistible. Their musicianship and judgement are matched by a poise and elegance that give consistent

pleasure. It would be difficult to improve on the balance between the two instruments, both of which are recorded with vivid realism and truthfulness of timbre on disc and cassette alike.

The versions by David Oistrakh and Lev Oborin are also performances to treasure. There is a relaxed joy in music-making, an almost effortless lyricism and an infectious sparkle. At times the Grumiaux/Haskil (mono) set goes deeper, and there is none of the tension that marks (some would say disfigures) the Heifetz/Bay set. The recording is rather wider in separation than we favour nowadays, but it is a beautiful sound in every other respect.

From Heifetz and Emmanuel Bay (Brooks Smith is the pianist in the *Kreutzer* only) masterly and electrifying performances, full of tension and power even if the recordings are dryish and two-dimensional. Some listeners may feel they are overdriven; at times there is an almost demonic quality, and Heifetz's outsize personality dominates the proceedings even when he is performing an accompanimental role. He brings plenty of dramatic intensity to the *C minor*, Op. 30/2, and to the serene *G major* companion of that set. Not everyone will respond to these performances, any more than they do to Toscanini's Beethoven, but there is no doubt that this is a stunning set which no keen collector can ignore.

Violin sonatas Nos. 5 in F (Spring), Op. 24; 9 in A (Kreutzer), Op. 47.
*** Decca SXL/*KSXC* 6990. Perlman, Ashkenazy.

An obvious recoupling from the Perlman/Ashkenazy series. The manner has a youthful freshness, yet the style is classical. The dynamism is there but never becomes too extrovert, and the music unfolds naturally and spontaneously. The recording quality is outstanding on both disc and tape.

Violin sonatas Nos. 6 in A; 7 in C min., Op. 30/1–2.
*** Decca SXL/*KSXC* 6791 [Lon. 7014/ 5-]. Perlman, Ashkenazy.

This, the last of the Decca series to be issued separately, is well up to the standard of the others; discernment is matched by spontaneity, and the recording is immaculate on both disc and cassette.

Violin sonatas No. 8 in G, Op. 30/3; 9 in A (Kreutzer), Op. 47.
*** HMV ASD/*TC-ASD* 3675. Zukerman, Barenboim.

Sweeter and more lyrical in feeling than Perlman and Ashkenazy but no less characterful and satisfying. The playing has spontaneity as well as a strong grasp of structure, even though in the *Kreutzer* Barenboim is the more commanding personality. This is a useful alternative to the Perlman set and almost equally well recorded. The tape version reproduces admirably.

Piano sonatas

Piano sonatas Nos. 1–32.
*** Decca D 258 D 12 (12) (with *Andante favori*). Ashkenazy.
(B) *** DG mono 2740 228 (10). Kempff.

No need to say much about Ashkenazy's self-recommending set, which has occupied him over the best part of a decade or more. These are eminently sound, well-recorded performances that deserve to rank alongside the best. Crisply articulated, intelligently shaped, not always inspired but never less than musically satisfying – and with consistently lifelike recording to boot.

The Kempff cycle, the earlier of the two that he recorded for DG, is the more personal, the more individual, at times the more wilful; but for any listener who

responds to Kempff's visionary clarity and concentration it is a magical series of interpretations. No other set of the sonatas so clearly gives the impression of new discovery, of fresh inspiration in the composer as in the pianist.

In the early sonatas Kempff's clarity presents an ideal (though the very opening movement of the *First Sonata* is controversially slow); but he has sometimes been accused of being too light in the big sonatas of the middle period. What this set demonstrates is that sharpness of impact makes for a toughness to compensate for any lack of sheer volume, while the inspirational manner brings out the quirky turns of last-period invention with incisive inevitability.

Even the first movement of the *Hammerklavier* has one marvelling not just at the concentration and power but at the beauty of sound, while the fugal finale brings the most remarkable example of Kempff's clarity, a towering performance, no less powerful for not being thunderous. Such personal performances will not please everyone, but for those who respond the experience is unique. The mid-fifties mono sound has been beautifully transferred, with only a slight lightness of bass. It compares favourably with the later stereo set.

Piano sonatas Nos. 1–3, 5–8, 13–14, 16–17, 18–20, 23–4, 28.
**(*) ASV ACMB 601 (6). Lill.

Piano sonatas Nos. 4, 9–12, 15, 21–2, 25–7, 29–32.
**(*) ASV ACMB 602 (6). Lill.

John Lill's forthright, uncompromising way with Beethoven – almost entirely lacking in charm – will not be to all tastes, but his playing has both strength and spontaneity. The manner is always direct and determined, with extreme speeds in both directions. There are some parallels here with the solo playing of Backhaus; the tendency to brusqueness and the non-romantic response are offset by a sometimes elemental communication of the composer's fiery spirit. The recording is generally truthful in timbre and balance, though sometimes sounding very close.

Piano sonatas Nos. 1–7.
*** Nimbus D/C 901 (4). Roberts.
(M) **(*) O-L D 182 D 3 (3). Binns (fortepiano).
(M) (***) HMV mono RLS/*TC-RLS* 753 (3). Schnabel.

Bernard Roberts's integral recording of the Beethoven sonatas is a most remarkable achievement, for each sonata was recorded complete at a single sitting. The direct-cut recording technique meant that there was no possibility of pausing between movements, yet, so far from being inhibited, Roberts with his direct, clean-cut Beethoven style conveys a keener electricity the more he is challenged. The readings have a freshness and intensity which are most compelling. Roberts, an outstanding chamber music pianist, deliberately adopts a less idiosyncratic style here than do most of his rivals, and the result is intensely refreshing, helped by the vivid, amply reverberant recording.

Malcolm Binns is an underrated artist whose musicianship and intelligence have made a strong impression both in the concert hall and in the recording studio. It would be a pity if his interest in period instruments, as evidenced here and in the Hummel sonatas he has recorded, were to stand in the way of his recording early Beethoven on a modern Steinway. He plays the three Op. 2 sonatas on an instrument by Heilmann of Mainz, reputed to be the finest German piano-builder after Stein, and Opp. 7 and 10 on a Broadwood. The Heilmann is an instrument of the kind that Haydn, Mozart and Beethoven would have played. Its lighter action and colouring serve to clarify the texture of this familiar music, and the same must be said of the Broadwood, though its bass is richer. Malcolm Binns

shows himself equal both in artistry and in technical fluency to the special problems this repertoire poses, and the recording engineers have secured sound that is in every way truthful and clean. In recommending this, there is no point in denying that our preference for the richer dynamic range and fuller sonority of a modern Steinway remains unshaken, and it is to the impressive surveys of the sonatas by Brendel, Kempff, Gilels (alas, still incomplete) and other masters that the majority of collectors will turn.

At last the pioneering Beethoven Sonata Society records made by Artur Schnabel are back in circulation and in excellent transfers. Schnabel somehow penetrated deeper than any other pianist into the spirit of Beethoven, even though others offer greater beauty of sound. His technical limitations are well known but even they are turned to advantage here: these performances centre so much on things of the spirit that the occasional lack of finish seems in character, reflecting the impatience of the spirit with the flesh. The earlier sonatas are generally not so fine as the late: the *A major*, Op. 2/2, is ungainly at times, but particularly in the slow movements – there is scarcely anything not illuminated. The cassettes match the discs closely; the familiar brittle quality of the original 78s is immediately apparent, but often the sound has surprising body too, and the timbre in slow movements has plenty of colour and bloom.

Piano sonatas Nos. 1 in F min., Op. 2/1; 7 in D, Op. 10/3.
*** Decca SXL/*KSXC* 6960 [Lon. 7190/5-]. Ashkenazy.

Ashkenazy made an earlier recording of Op. 10/3 in 1973 (it was coupled to the *Appassionata* on SXL 6603); now he has had second thoughts, and this new performance has more unity without loss of spontaneity. In the *F minor Sonata* his way is mercurial yet thrusting and has fine lyric feeling when the music is in repose. The recording maintains the high standard of the series, and the cassette is full-bodied and clear.

Piano sonatas Nos. 1; 20 in G, Op. 49/2; 26 in E flat (Les Adieux), Op. 81a.
**(*) Ph. 9500 507/7300 667 [id.]. Brendel.

Brendel takes both repeats in the first movement of the *F minor*, Op. 2/1, and in his hands the whole sonata is made to sound the important work it is. This is worthy to stand alongside Sviatoslav Richter's reading. In *Les Adieux* Brendel is at times a shade self-conscious, but there are some wonderful details, such as the rapt pianissimo he achieves just before the finale. The recording, as always in this series, is clean and rounded; the cassette too offers admirable quality, well balanced and natural.

Piano sonatas Nos. 1; 24 in F sharp, Op. 78; 28 in A, Op. 101.
(M) **(*) ASV ACM/ZCACM 2028. Lill.

This first record of John Lill's series offers some of the finest (and most characteristic) performances in the cycle. Lill's deliberation at the opening of the Sonata No. 1 gives the first movement great character, and the slow movement too is eloquently played. The *Adagio* of No. 28 again shows the keen grip and intelligence of Lill's approach. The piano is recorded very close and has remarkable presence (on disc and cassette alike), and while the timbre has both body and colour the upper range is inclined to harden in fortissimos.

Piano sonatas Nos. 2 in A; 3 in C, Op. 2/2–3.
(M) ** ASV ACM/ZCACM 2023. Lill.

There is a directness of utterance about

John Lill's Beethoven which is undoubtedly compulsive, particularly as the recording has great presence and the tone is admirably secure and realistic, on disc and tape alike. Lill brings a formidable technique to both sonatas, and the first movement of Op. 2/2 is crisply articulated, though at times it could do with greater lightness of touch. The slow movement of Op. 2/3 makes a strong impression, though some will feel that the fortissimo outbursts are over-characterized. John Lill is not strong on charm, yet there is an integrity about his playing that the listener cannot fail to notice. These performances may seem quite attractive in their mid-priced reissue, but it would be idle to pretend that they compete with Ashkenazy, who offers the same coupling on Decca SXL/KSXC 6808 [Lon. 7028/5-].

Piano sonatas Nos. 2; 15 in D (Pastoral), Op. 28.
*** Ph. 9500 539/7300 680 [id.]. Brendel.

Two of the very finest performances in Alfred Brendel's cycle, very beautifully recorded too. The *A major* sparkles with vitality and intelligence, and the *Pastoral* has a magic that has rarely been equalled on disc. The cassette matches the disc closely; the *Pastoral* is strikingly clear and vivid.

Piano sonatas Nos. 3 in C, Op. 2/3; 11 in B flat, Op. 22.
*** Ph. 9500 540/7300 681 [id.]. Brendel.

A fresh, sparkling account of Op. 2/3, thoroughly exhilarating and totally satisfying, and the relatively neglected *B flat Sonata*, Op. 22, is given with no less elegance and vitality. No reservations here. The cassette too offers first-class quality, the piano timbre warmly natural, yet with excellent presence and detail.

Piano sonatas Nos. 4 in E flat, Op. 7; 5 in C min., Op. 10/1.

*** Ph. 9500 506 [id.]. Brendel.

The *E flat Sonata,* Op. 7, is still comparatively neglected (only the *B flat,* Op. 22, has fewer listings in the current catalogues). It finds Brendel at his most persuasive and is given with warmth and refinement matched by beautiful recorded sound. The fill-up, Op. 10/1, lasts less than twenty minutes; but Michelangeli took two sides over Op. 7 alone, so it would be curmudgeonly to complain of short measure here.

Piano sonatas Nos. 4; 9 in E; 10 in G, Op. 14/1–2.
*** Decca SXL/*KSXC* 6961 [Lon. 7191]. Ashkenazy.

A superb disc, one of the very finest in Ashkenazy's memorably poetic series. Warmth and intelligence are matched, and Ashkenazy is especially persuasive in the two Op. 14 sonatas, producing elegant, crisply articulated performances of striking character. The cassette is of demonstration quality, outstanding in its presence: the piano seems to be in the room.

Piano sonatas Nos. 4; 21 in C (Waldstein), Op. 53.
(M) **(*) ASV ACM/*ZCACM* 2018. Lill.

In these two large-scale sonatas Lill's clean-cut, incisive style makes for performances that are generally refreshing but lacking a little in gentler qualities; even the rather formal slow movement of Op. 7 is given an uncompromising quality. The articulation from fingers of steel is thrilling, but the rhythms too rarely spring. The recording is bright and clean to match the performances; the cassette transfer is first-class, full, bold and clear.

Piano sonatas Nos. 5 in C min.; 6 in F; 7 in D, Op. 10/1–3.
(M) ** ASV ACM/*ZCACM* 2031. Lill.

These are among the more disappointing of Lill's Beethoven sonata readings, rather square and charmless. The great D minor slow movement of Op. 10/3 is taken challengingly slowly, but there is little feeling of flow. Bright recording to match others in the series; the well-focused realism is equally striking on disc and cassette.

Piano sonatas Nos. 5–6; 15 in D (Pastoral), Op. 28.
*** Decca SXL/*KSXC* 6804 [Lon. 7024/5-]. Ashkenazy.

Ashkenazy gives characteristically thoughtful and alert performances of an attractive grouping of three early sonatas. At times the tempi are questionably fast (the finale of Op. 10/2) or slow (the first movement of Op. 28), but Ashkenazy's freshness of manner silences criticism; and like the others in the series this is an outstanding issue, particularly as the recording is again first-rate on both disc and cassette.

Piano sonatas Nos. 8–15.
**(*) Nimbus D/C 902 (4). Roberts.
(M) (***) HMV mono RLS/*TC-RLS* 754 (3). Schnabel.

Bernard Roberts's survey continues, maintaining the same high standards of the first two volumes, with recording that matches presence and realism with immaculate direct-cut pressings. The readings do not have the penetration of Schnabel's, but they have genuine breadth, and if the *Moonlight* and *Pathétique* (for instance) have received more memorable treatment in other hands, Roberts's playing is not without individuality; moreover his performances give genuine pleasure and satisfaction.

Schnabel's Beethoven (as we have said above) is unfailingly illuminating, and the second volume of transfers of his pre-war Sonata Society recordings equals the standards of the first. The slow movements in particular penetrate more deeply than with almost any other artist, and technical shortcomings such as rushed triplets and the odd unevenness are warts on the most lifelike Beethoven we have. In terms of artistic truth these are the performances by which others are measured, and the transfers have never sounded as good. The tapes are at a slightly lower level than in Volume 1 and the piano has slightly less presence, though the *Pathétique* sounds well and so do Opp. 22 and 26.

Piano sonatas Nos. 8; 14 in C sharp min. (Moonlight), Op. 27/2; 21 in C (Waldstein), Op. 53.
(M) ** Decca Jub. JB/*KJBC* 105 [Lon. 6806]. Lupu.
(B) ** Con. CC/*CCT* 7529. Firkusny.

Radu Lupu is an unfailingly sensitive artist, and he has the undoubted gift of creating spontaneity in the recording studio; but sometimes his playing can seem mannered, as in his rather deliberate approach to the famous slow movement of the *Pathétique* sonata, or at the opening of the *Moonlight*. But the playing carries conviction, and the performances of both these works are individual and enjoyable. Lupu is less successful in holding the concentration of the *Waldstein* finale, after having prepared the opening beautifully, and it is this that lets down an otherwise impressive issue. The Decca recording is first-rate in every way, sonorous and clear, a real piano sound; and the cassette too offers demonstration quality.

Rudolf Firkusny's Contour reissue has a Decca Phase Four source and the recording is characteristically close and immediate. It is truthfully balanced, however, the timbre full and natural, slightly warmer on cassette but with a sharper focus on disc, though there is not too much difference between them. The performances are eminently musical and well shaped, though lacking in drama.

The opening of the *Moonlight* and the slow movement of the *Pathétique* are appealing, but the account of the *Waldstein* is under-characterized.

Piano sonatas Nos. 8 in C min. (Pathétique), Op. 13; 12 in A flat, Op. 26; 14 in C sharp min. (Moonlight), Op. 27/2.
*(*) HMV ASD/*TC-ASD* 3695. Eschenbach.

Christoph Eschenbach achieves greater poetry and depth in the first movement of the *Moonlight* and the slow movement of Op. 26, where his pianistic refinement is heard to best advantage, but the first movement of Op. 26 is intolerably mannered and self-conscious: he pulls the second variation about mercilessly, and there are some very ugly touches in the minor variation too. The recording has warmth and clarity on both disc and tape, but the recital cannot be recommended except for the perceptive account of the *Moonlight*.

Piano sonatas Nos. 8; 13 in E flat; 14 (Moonlight), Op. 27/1–2.
*** DG Dig. 2532/*3302* 008 [id.]. Gilels.

Gilels is served by superb sound, and, as always, his performances leave the overriding impression of wisdom. Yet this disc, coupling the two Op. 27 sonatas together on one side and the *Pathétique* on the other, does not quite rank among his very best (such as the *Waldstein* and Op. 101). The opening movement of the *Moonlight* is wonderfully serene, and there are many felicities. But the first movement of the *E flat Sonata* is strangely reserved (the wonderful change to C major so subtly illuminated by Schnabel goes relatively unremarked here), as if Gilels feared the charge of self-indulgence or out-of-period sentiment. However, such are the strengths of this playing that few will quarrel with the magnificence of his conceptions of all three pieces. The digital recording is marvellously lifelike, and so is the chrome cassette: the piano has striking presence.

Piano sonatas Nos. 8; 14; 23 in F min. (Appassionata), Op. 57.
*** Ph. 9500/7300 899 [id.]. Brendel.
(M) ** CBS 61937/40- [Col. MY 37219]. Serkin.
** CBS 76892/40- [Col. M/MT 34509]. Horowitz.
(B) ** CfP CFP/TC-CFP 40352. Chorzempa.
(M) ** ASV ACM/ZCACM 2015. Lill.

Among the five additions to the records and cassettes combining the three most popular named sonatas, only Brendel's, offering undeniably impressive performances and excellent recording, could be advocated as an alternative to present recommendations, notably Kempff (DG 139300/3300 506) and Barenboim (HMV HQS/TC-HQS 1076 [Ang. S/ 4XS 36424]). Barenboim's coupling is now available on a first-class cassette.

Rudolf Serkin's readings date from the early 1960s and it is a pity that he is not better served by the engineers, but the sound is somewhat shallow and wanting in timbre on disc and cassette alike. The performances are impressive enough by any standards. Serkin repeats the slow introduction to the first movement of the *Pathétique* (the only other pianist who does this is Zimerman); indeed, he is not ungenerous with repeats. There are no agogic distortions and little attempt to beguile with pianistic charm. This is pure and unadulterated Beethoven, incisive and dramatic.

Vladimir Horowitz's account of the *Appassionata* was recorded in 1972 but the other two sonatas come from the early 1960s. There is much here that is powerfully conceived and finely executed, but there are strange touches as well; the first movement of the *Moonlight* is curiously earthbound. The recorded sound is a little shallow, though the *Appassionata* fares best. It is not perhaps as incandescent here as in Horowitz's earlier mono version, but it is nonetheless compelling and fascinating. Not the greatest Beethoven sonata record, nor the finest Horowitz record, perhaps, but one which admirers of the great pianist will want to investigate despite its sonic limitations. The sound on the cassette is dry and shallow, without much bloom or colour.

Daniel Chorzempa has the advantage not only of economy but also of first-class sound (with no perceptible difference between disc and the high-level tape). Chorzempa's reputation was made in the organ loft but here his technical command of the piano keyboard is never in doubt. The interpretations are rather studied, the readings of a serious young man taking great care in matters of both detail and structure. The clarity of the style is well projected but there is also a total absence of romantic charm.

John Lill plays the opening of the *Moonlight* more evocatively, and then makes a striking contrast in the finale, which is taken with furious bravura. The slow movement of the *Pathétique* is thoughtful but lacks something in poetic feeling. This is strong, intelligent playing, but at times one has the impression that the drama is overdone. The piano image has striking realism and forward projection – some will feel the balance is a shade too close – with a first-class tape transfer that matches the disc closely.

Piano sonatas Nos. 8; 14; 28 in A, Op. 101.
** Ph. 9500 319/7300 591 [id.]. Dichter.

Misha Dichter enters a strongly competitive field and is well served by the Philips engineers, who produce sound of great fidelity and naturalness. The best thing on the record is Op. 101, which is played freely and expressively. If it does not match the incomparable Gilels account, it has greater warmth than Pollini's masterly version without having its stature. There is no shortage of *Pathétiques* and *Moonlights* in the catalogue; Misha Dichter gives finely grained and well-prepared accounts of both. The tape is faithful in timbre; detail is slightly less sharply focused at pianissimo level.

Piano sonatas Nos. 8; 22 in F, Op. 54; 23 in F min. (Appassionata), Op. 57.
(M) *** DG Priv. 2535/3335 354. Kempff.

With Kempff's individual Beethoven style producing textures of rare transparency, this coupling of two favourite named sonatas with the little *F major* makes an excellent mid-price issue. The opening of the *Moonlight* is gently evocative, the contrast in the finale perfectly balanced; the *Appassionata* is characteristically clear-headed. The sound is fair, clear and rather dry. On tape, side two is transferred at a markedly higher level; the *Appassionata* is given considerable presence, but the timbre becomes brittle on top.

Piano sonatas Nos. 9 in E; 10 in G, Op. 14/1–2; 30 in E, Op. 109.
(M) ** ASV ACM/ZCACM 2026. Lill.

For the two small-scale early sonatas Lill scales down the aggressiveness in his approach to Beethoven. The results are clear and refreshing if lacking in charm. There is not much fun, for example, in the finale of the *G major*. Op. 109 is given a somewhat four-square performance, the structural freedom of the first movement underplayed and put in a strict sonata frame. Bright, clear recording, as in the rest of this series, and the tape transfer is admirable, firm and with good presence.

Piano sonatas Nos. 11 in B flat, Op. 22; 12 in A flat (Funeral march), Op. 26.

**(*) Decca SXL/*KSXC* 6929. Ashkenazy.

.Ashkenazy's account of Op. 22 is expert but less perceptive than Brendel's. The latter finds more wit and poetry, though Ashkenazy is handicapped by a less revealing recording. There are some fine things in the Op. 26 sonata, even though again he does not search out the subtleties of the opening variation movement as do Gilels, Richter and Brendel. Of course, the playing is still impressive, particularly in the scherzo and the finale, and this side is better recorded too. But generally speaking, this is one of the less successful of Ashkenazy's cycle. The cassette transfer is of very high quality, matching the disc closely.

Piano sonatas Nos. 12; 16 in G, Op. 31/1.
*** Ph. 9500 541/7300 682 [id.]. Brendel.

The Op. 26 sonata receives a surpassingly beautiful reading at Brendel's hands, and the *G major*, Op. 31/1, is no less perceptively played. As usual in this series, the recorded sound is of the highest quality, fresh in timbre and wide in range, doing full justice to the colour and refinement of Brendel's pianism. The tape matches the disc closely, only lacking the last degree of sharpness of focus at the top.

Piano sonatas Nos. 12; 22 in F, Op. 54; 25 in G, Op. 79; 31 in A flat, Op. 110.
(M) ** ASV ACM/ZCACM 2027. Lill.

Charm plays no part at all in John Lill's Beethoven; that is clear not just in the rugged account of the *Funeral march* of Op. 26 but in the first two movements as well, the lyrical variations and the sparkling scherzo. There is no compromise either in the two small sonatas; the first movement of Op. 79 is brutally fast. Even the lyrical first movement of

Op. 110, very slow and square, keeps to the pattern of ruggedness, though the intensity of Lill's playing is never in doubt, and the bright recording matches his readings. The cassette, like the disc, has striking presence.

Piano sonatas Nos. 12; 23 in F min. (Appassionata), Op. 57.
(M) **(*) RCA Gold GL/*GK* 42706 [VICS 1427]. Sviatoslav Richter.

Richter's coupling of Op. 26 and the *Appassionata* makes a welcome return to the catalogue. As always, Richter puts his personal stamp on the music. He observes Beethoven's markings scrupulously and in Op. 26, where others manipulate the tempo, he maintains his pace and the music's intensity. The *Funeral march* is seen as the work's focal point, and the finale is played rapidly, evoking associations with Chopin's *B flat minor Sonata*. The *Appassionata* has great power and drama. Richter uses the widest dynamic range, and the bravura, especially in the finale, is stunning. The recording sounds somewhat shallow now (on cassette it is almost unacceptably dry and lacking bloom) but the presence and spontaneity of the music-making are well projected.

Piano sonatas Nos. 13 in E flat; 14 in C sharp min. (Moonlight), Op. 27/1–2; 16 in G, Op. 31/1.
*** Decca SXL/*KSXC* 6889 [Lon. 7111/5-]. Ashkenazy.

There is a difference in acoustic between the two Op. 27 sonatas, which occupy the same side. Ashkenazy's account of Op. 31/1 is perhaps the strongest of the three performances, though there is much to admire throughout; his growing interest in the baton does not seem to have impaired his prowess at the keyboard. In the opening of Op. 27/1 he does

not find the depths that distinguished the old Schnabel set, but in every other respect this is formidable playing; the *G major* is thoughtful and compelling, though it does not quite achieve the stature of Gilels's classic DG account. The tape transfer is impressively wide in range but the fortissimos are inclined to harden under pressure; otherwise the sound is full and clear.

Piano sonatas Nos. 13; 17 in D min. (Tempest), Op. 31/2; 19 in G min., Op. 49/1.
(M) ** ASV ACM/*ZCACM* 2029. Lill.

Lill's account of Op. 27/1 is thoughtful, but not really imaginative enough, and memories of the marvellous range of colour that Schnabel produced in the first movement flood back. There is no want of fire in Op. 31/2, but it is in no sense a performance of real stature. The two-movement *G minor Sonata* is played with effective simplicity. The piano tone is firm and secure, somewhat hard on top, especially in the clear cassette version.

Piano sonatas Nos. 13; 17; 22 in F, Op. 54.
*** Ph. 9500 503 [Id.]. Brendel.

Except perhaps in the late sonatas, Brendel's is the most satisfying of all the Beethoven sonata cycles that appeared in the 1970s. These performances are among the very best: the *D minor* is dramatic without ever becoming too tempestuous, and Brendel makes the most of the dramatic contrasts in the *E flat*, Op. 27/1. Superbly truthful recording.

Piano sonatas Nos. 14 in C sharp min. (Moonlight), Op. 27/2; 17 in D min. (Tempest), Op. 31/2; 26 in E flat (Les Adieux), Op. 81a.
*** DG Priv. 2535/*3335* 316. Kempff.

Kempff's individuality in Beethoven is nowhere more clearly established than in this coupling; the understated clarity of his playing gives an otherworldly quality to the outer movements of the *Moonlight*, both the opening *Adagio* (more flowing than usual) and the rushing finale (more measured and clearer). The *D minor Sonata* and *Les Adieux* may be less weightily dramatic than in other readings, but the concentration is irresistible. The recording is clear and not lacking in colour; the tape transfers are well managed (although the level is modest): the sound in the *Tempest* is comparatively shallow, but there is no lack of bloom on Op. 27/2.

Piano sonatas Nos. 14; 18 in E flat, Op. 31/2; Für Elise, G. 173.
** Ph. 9500 665/7300 763. Davidovich.

First-class sound, as one would expect from this source, and impressive pianism too, as one would also expect from a former Warsaw Prize winner. Bella Davidovich is up against formidable opposition, however, and was perhaps unwise to choose this particular repertoire for one of her first records in the West. She is inclined to make expressive points, not leaving the music to speak for itself. There are many more poetic accounts of the *Moonlight* to be had than this.

Piano sonatas Nos. 15 in D (Pastoral), Op. 28; 26 in E flat (Les Adieux), Op. 81a; 27 in E min., Op. 90.
(M) **(*) ASV ACM/ZCACM 2014. Lill.

As sound this is undeniably impressive, and though the sound picture slightly favours the bass end of the instrument the treble has no lack of clarity. John Lill adopts very deliberate tempi in the *Pastoral sonata*, where one feels some want to flow, yet *Les Adieux* is a distinct suc-cess, though Brendel's performance has even more character, and at no time is Gilels challenged, either in *Les Adieux* or in the E minor work, even though Lill is obviously at home in this too, and all three sonatas here show his thoughtful musicianship at its most communicative. The cassette transfer is first-class, matching the disc closely.

Piano sonatas Nos. 16–25.
**(*) Nimbus D/C 903 (4). Roberts.

Bernard Roberts brings sound good sense to everything he does. He has become something of a vogue pianist: he is every bit as good as he was a few years ago when no one was putting him on disc or on the radio and he deserves much of his present exposure. These performances are recorded in one take and cut direct to disc, and the sound is both immediate and clean; in fact, it is very lifelike indeed. Generally speaking, the playing is robust, alive, sensitive, well proportioned and always intelligent though in such sonatas as the *Appassionata* and the *Waldstein* Roberts's insights and finesse are not superior to those of, say, Brendel, Kempff and Gilels.

Piano sonatas Nos. 16–22; 24.
(M) (***) HMV mono RLS/TC-RLS 755 (3). Schnabel.

Schnabel is in a special category and, for all his idiosyncrasies, he can no more be ignored in this repertoire than Weingartner, Toscanini or Furtwängler in the symphonies. Few artists are more searching in the slow movement of the *Waldstein* or as characterful in its first movement. Music-making of outsize personality which readers should hear no matter how many rival accounts they may have. Exemplary transfers from the original 78s; the cassettes too – made at the highest level – are the finest in the series so far, offering remarkable presence.

Piano sonatas Nos. 16 in G; 18 in E flat, Op. 31/1 and 3; 20 in G, Op. 49/2.
(M) ** ASV ACM/ZCACM 2022. Lill.

The first movement of Op. 31/1 is keenly alive and cleanly articulated here, if somewhat aggressive. The slow movement is characteristically direct and there are some sensitive touches. In the *E flat Sonata* there is much to admire and Op. 49/2 again shows Lill's strong yet emotionally reserved way with Beethoven, minimizing charm and indeed warmth. The recording has striking truthfulness and presence, especially on the cassette, which is of demonstration quality.

Piano sonatas Nos. 17 in D min. (Tempest); 18 in E flat, Op. 31/2–3.
*** Decca SXL/KSXC 6871 [Lon. 7088]. Ashkenazy.

These are among the best of Ashkenazy's Beethoven cycle. He brings concentration of mind together with a spontaneity of feeling that illumine both works. The command of keyboard colour is as always impressive, and both in terms of dramatic tension and the sense of architecture these are thoroughly satisfying performances. The recorded sound is also of high quality and the cassette is exceptionally vivid and clear, with bold transients and a natural underlying sonority.

Piano sonatas No. 17; 21 in C (Waldstein), Op. 53.
(M) *** Ph. 6570/7310 190 [id.]. Arrau.

The performance of the *D minor Sonata* is consistently on Arrau's highest plane, although one could ask for a tauter finale. Recoupled with the *Waldstein* it makes a splendid disc, showing the Chilean pianist at the height of his powers. Other versions may be more mercurial, but this has an epic vision, measured but with the overall structure marvellously in control. The technical mastery is in no doubt. While not as incandescent as the Gilels version this remains very satisfying. The recordings (from the mid-sixties) sound, if anything, better than they did on their original issue, and now there is a well-managed cassette equivalent.

Piano sonatas Nos. 21; 23 in F min. (Appassionata), Op. 57.
⊛ *** DG 2531/3301 143 [id.]. Gilels.

These sonatas have appeared in various couplings but this one is probably the strongest. The first edition of the *Penguin Stereo Record Guide* hailed this account of the *Appassionata* as among the finest ever made, and much the same must be said of Gilels's *Waldstein*. It has a technical perfection denied even to Schnabel, and though in the slow movement Schnabel finds special depths, Gilels is hardly less searching and profound. These are performances to relish, to study and to keep for special occasions. Excellent recording on both disc and cassette, although – as has been noticed before on Gilels's DG tapes – when he is playing *sotto voce*, in the middle register especially, the image tends to lose some of its presence.

Piano sonatas Nos. 22 in F, Op. 54; 24 in F sharp, Op. 78 (see also under Sonata No. 29); 25 in G, Op. 79; 27 in E min., Op. 90.
*** Decca SXL/KSXC 6962. Ashkenazy.

Another worthwhile addition to the catalogue. Ashkenazy is in top form, and his readings of these sonatas are as masterly and penetrating as anything he has given us. He is splendidly recorded, and the cassette transfer is of the highest quality, projecting a piano image that is natural and firm.

Piano sonatas Nos. 23 (Appassionata), 25, 26 (Les Adieux), 27–8, 29 (Hammerklavier), 30–32.

119

BEETHOVEN

⊛ (***) HMV mono RLS/*TC-RLS* 758
(4). Schnabel.

Of all the Schnabel sets this is the most
indispensable. No performance of the
later sonatas, Opp. 109–111, has surpassed these, not even Schnabel's own RCA
recordings of Opp. 109 and 111 made in
the 1940s. The *Arietta* of Op. 111, the first
movement of Op. 110 and . . . one could
go on – have a depth and authority that
remain unrivalled. If Schnabel's pianism
was not always immaculate (there are
plenty of wrong notes in the *Hammerklavier*), he brings one closer to the spirit
of this music than any other artist. No
self-respecting collector should be without this powerful and searching document. The sound is remarkably good,
and the cassette transfers are beautifully
clean and clear. On tape each sonata is
offered uninterrupted, with the nine
works spread over four sides. Sometimes,
as in the first movement of Op. 79 (at the
beginning of side three), there is a slightly
brittle quality, but the slow movements
of the late sonatas are strikingly full in
timbre, Schnabel's subtle control of
colour faithfully caught.

Piano sonatas Nos. 24–32.
(M) **(*) O-L D 185 D 3 (3). Binns.

This is a set to investigate, for it gives
us the late sonatas on instruments that
Beethoven himself knew (but could not,
of course, have heard). But those who
like their Beethoven on a modern Steinway and whose minds and ears are closed
to contemporary instruments should give
this box a miss. Binns uses a Graf for Op.
111 and a Haschka for the *Hammerklavier*, both Viennese instruments. He
chooses a Dulcken of about 1785 for the
earlier sonatas, Broadwoods for Opp.
109 and 110 (albeit of slightly different
periods – 1814 and 1819 respectively), a
Clementi for Op. 90, and an Erard for
Op. 101. There is an excellent booklet
describing each instrument in some
detail. The differences between them are

often quite striking, and space does not
permit discussion of them here; the
basic test is whether one would want
Binns playing Beethoven sonatas if the
added dimension of period instrumental colour were removed, or
whether this is merely a guided tour
around the Colt Collection using Beethoven sonatas by way of illustration.
Malcolm Binns satisfies the listener
musically as well as historically, although played on period instruments
the most searching of Beethoven's
thoughts (in Opp. 110 and 111) seem to
lose something of their depth and mystery. Yet the exercise is undoubtedly
illuminating and given the modest price –
and the excellent value (no other three-
record box offers all the sonatas from
Op. 78 onwards) – it can be confidently
recommended. It goes without saying that
few would consider it as their *only* version
of these great works, but as a supplement it
is revealing and thought-provoking.

Piano sonatas Nos. 26–32.
*** Nimbus D/C 904 (5). Roberts.

With their few idiosyncrasies Bernard
Roberts's readings of the late sonatas can
consistently be registered as the listener's
own inner vision from Beethoven turned
into sound. Roberts's achievement in
recording even the *Hammerklavier* and
Op. 111 direct-to-disc in single takes is
nothing less than astonishing, and
though some will positively demand
more personal, more idiosyncratic readings, there is none of the lack of concentration which afflicts other would-be
scalers of these peaks, nor even any feeling of cautiousness. With the exception
that Roberts, forthright in everything, is
reluctant to allow a gentle pianissimo, the
revelation here is consistently satisfying.
The sound is outstandingly fine.

Piano sonatas Nos. 27–32.
*** DG 2740 166/*3371 033* [id.]. Pollini.

Here is playing of the highest order of
mastery. Pollini's *Hammerklavier* (see

below) is among the best to have been recorded in recent years. Hardly less impressive is the eloquent account of Op. 111, which has a peerless authority and expressive power. Joan Chissell spoke of the 'noble purity' of these performances, and that telling phrase aptly sums them up. The slow movement of Op. 110 may be a trifle fast for some tastes, and in the A major work Gilels has the greater poetry and humanity. But, taken by and large, this series is a magnificent achievement and as sheer pianism it is quite stunning. The recording has excellent body and transparency and there is little to choose between the disc and cassette, so impressive is the latter. This set won the 1977 Gramophone Critics' Award for instrumental music, and rightly so.

Piano sonatas Nos. 28 in A, Op. 101; 30 in E, Op. 109.
*** Decca SXL/*KSXC* 6809 [Lon. 7029/5-]. Ashkenazy.

Distinguished performances of both sonatas, as one would expect, and an impressive sense of repose in the slow movement of Op. 109. Perhaps Gilels finds greater depth in Op. 101, but this is not to deny that Ashkenazy is searching and masterly too. The sound is of excellent quality, with exceptional dynamic range. The cassette transfer too is admirably clear and clean, with only a minor degree of hardening on fortissimos.

Piano sonatas Nos. 28; 32 in C min., Op. 111.
*** DG 2530/*3300* 870. Pollini.

Pollini's account of Op. 101 is finely shaped and no subtlety of phrasing or dynamic nuance goes unnoticed. He holds the first movement more tautly together than, say, Brendel, who sees this movement in a different light, though Pollini is by no means inflexible. He is equally impressive in the finale, which is

superbly fashioned and has an imposing sense of energy and power, yet is never overdriven. Gilels perhaps brings greater wisdom and humanity to the sonata, but Pollini's is an impressive account for all that. So, too, is his Op. 111, though on record he has stiff competition, and the broader tempi adopted by Bishop-Kovacevich or Schnabel in the *Arietta* pay greater dividends and enable them to find depths that ultimately elude Pollini in this movement. But this is by any standards a most searching and masterly account and the recording is of the same high standard as in the *Hammerklavier*. There is no difference to speak of in the disc and cassette versions. (NB. Although the above boxed set remains available, this individual issue has been withdrawn as we go to press.)

Piano sonata No. 29 in B flat (Hammerklavier), Op. 106.
*** DG 2530/*3300* 869 [id.]. Pollini.
(M) *** Ph. Fest. 6570/*7310* 055 (with Sonata No. 24). Arrau.
(M) ** ASV ACM/*ZCACM* 2032. Lill.
Piano sonatas Nos. 29; 30 in E, Op. 109.
(M) *** DG Priv. 2535/*3335* 329. Kempff.

Pollini's is among the finest *Hammerklaviers* of recent years, perhaps the most impressive to have appeared in stereo. Some details may be more tellingly illuminated by other masters such as Brendel or Arrau, but no other version currently before the public is more perfect: superb rhythmic grip, alert articulation and sensitivity to line as well as a masterly control of the long paragraph. No one quite matches Pollini's stunning finale; its strength and controlled power silence criticism. Moreover, the sound is most impressive, wide-ranging and realistic, and there is scarcely any difference between disc and cassette. (NB. As above, this individual issue has been withdrawn in the U.K.)

121

Arrau's reading of Beethoven's most challenging sonata was among the very finest achievements of his sonata cycle, and it is good to have it separately on a mid-price label. Arrau's studio waywardness is kept in check, and the slow movement in particular is superbly convincing, hushed and intense. With refined recording, and the brief Op. 78 sonata for fill-up, this makes an attractive offering. The cassette is generally full and clear.

Even in the *Hammerklavier* Kempff preserves his clarity, with speeds slower than usual in the fast movements and faster in the great *Adagio*. It is nonetheless a profound and concentrated reading, the compelling statement of a master, and it is good to have it in this medium-price reissue, generously coupled with an equally searching reading of Op. 109. Acceptable recording.

John Lill's speed in the great slow movement is so slow that ASV have resorted to the device of putting the finale at the beginning of side one, before the first movement, so that the slow movement can be contained on side two without a break. Unfortunately Lill does not convey the necessary concentration, and though the outer movements pack tremendous virtuoso punch, this does not compare with the finest versions. The recording is a little clangy. The cassette, which is laid out straightforwardly, faithfully matches the disc, clean but shallower than the best of this series.

Piano sonata No. 32 in C min., Op. 111.
**(*) DG Dig. 2532/3302 036 [id.].
Pogorelich – SCHUMANN: *Études symphoniques* etc.**(*)

Ivo Pogorelich produces consistent beauty of tone throughout the sonata, and his account of this masterpiece contains many felicities. It is imposing piano playing and impressive music-making. At times he seems to view Beethoven through Lisztian eyes, but there is much that is powerful here. Pogorelich

has a strong personality and will provoke equally strong reactions. There are self-indulgent touches here and there but also moments of illumination. The sound is truthful and well balanced on both disc and tape.

Miscellaneous piano music

7 Bagatelles, Op. 33.
*** Decca SXL/*KSXC* 6951 [Lon. 7179]. Larrocha – MOZART: *Sonatas Nos. 4 and 8.****

Alicia de Larrocha displays her usual finesse in the Op. 33 *Bagatelles*, and her articulation in the faster pieces is exhilaratingly crisp and clean. Her playing is consistently polished and sympathetic, and each of these miniatures is surely characterized. She is beautifully recorded (the cassette has every bit as much presence as the disc), and, with its fine Mozart coupling, this can be recommended.

33 Variations in C on a waltz by Diabelli, Op. 120.
*** Ph. 9500 381 [id.]. Brendel.
** Symph. SYM 9 [Peters PLE/*PCE* 042]. Rosen.

Recorded live, Alfred Brendel's later version of the *Diabelli variations* has an energy and urgency lacking in some of his other Philips recordings. The playing is understandably not flawless, but the tensions are superbly conveyed. The sound is first-rate, though not as delicate in dynamic range as in a studio recording.

Charles Rosen's view of this Everest of piano literature is purposeful and tough, hard to the point of being unrelenting. With clear, somewhat twangy recording to match, one misses the gentler half-tones (as for example in the great *Adagio* variation, No. 29, where Rosen ignores the *mezza-voce* marking at a trivially fast tempo), but there is much to satisfy in such a formidably intense reading.

VOCAL MUSIC

Ah! perfido, Op. 65. Egmont, Op. 84: Die Trommel gerühret; Freudvoll und Leidvoll. No, non turbati.
*** Ph. 9500 307 [id./7300 582]. Baker, ECO, Leppard – SCHUBERT: *Alfonso und Estrella* etc.⁺⁺⁺

Clärchen's two songs from *Egmont* – the first a rousing call to arms – make an excellent coupling for the more ambitious scena *Ah! perfido* and the Metastasio setting *No, non turbati.* All are given electrically intense performances, and Schubert orchestral songs make a good coupling. Excellent recording.

Choral fantasia in C, Op. 80.
*** Ph. 9500 471/7300 628 [id.]. Brendel (piano), LPO Ch., LPO, Haitink – *Piano concerto No. 2.****

This is discussed above under the coupling.

Christus am Ölberge, Op. 85.
(M) **(*) Turn. TVS 34458 [id./CT 2252]. Rebmann, Bartel, Messthaler, S. German Ch., Stuttgart PO, Bloser.

With Beethoven depicting Christ (a tenor) as another Florestan, this oratorio is a stronger and more interesting work than has often been thought. This is not a high-powered performance, but it is convincingly spontaneous and live, and very welcome on a mid-price label. The recording is a little dated but fully acceptable.

Egmont (incidental music), Op. 84. The Creatures of Prometheus overture, Op. 43.
(M) *** Decca Jub. JB/KJBC 119. Lorengar, Wussow, VPO, Szell.

The problems of performing Beethoven's incidental music for Goethe's *Egmont* in its original dramatic

context are partially solved here by drawing on a text by the Austrian poet Franz Grillparzer and using the *melodrama* of the final peroration from Goethe, vibrantly spoken by Klausjuergen Wussow. The snag is that, whereas the experience of listening to the music is eminently renewable, even German listeners find repetition of the text unrewarding. So for this reissue the narrative has been cut well back, though Goethe's *melodrama* remains. It is a fair compromise; Szell is a gripping advocate, and the songs are movingly sung by Pilar Lorengar. Abbado's performance of the *Prometheus overture* is an excellent makeweight. The cassette transfer is extremely vivid but has an element of fierceness in the upper range.

Folksong arrangements: Behold, my love; Come, fill, fill, my good fellow; Duncan Gray; The elfin fairies; Faithful Johnnie; He promised me at parting; Highlander's lament; Highland watch; The Miller of Dee; Music, love and wine; Oh, had my fate been joined with thine; Oh, sweet were the hours; The pulse of an Irishman; Put around the bright wine.
(M) *** DG Priv. 2535 241. Mathis, Young, Fischer-Dieskau, RIAS Chamber Ch.; Röhn (violin), Donderer (cello), Engel (piano).

This delightful disc comes from the bicentenary set of vocal music that DG issued in 1970. It need hardly be said that the singing is of the highest order, and for those who have not heard any of Beethoven's folksong arrangements it is a must. Beethoven obviously lavished much attention on them, and this issue is as successful as the delightful compilation Fischer-Dieskau made in the midsixties of folksong settings by Haydn, Beethoven and Weber, surely one of the greatest records of its kind. This deserves a strong and unqualified recommendation.

Folksong arrangements: *The British Light Dragoons; Cease your funning; Come draw we round; Cupid's kindness; Good night; The kiss, dear maid; O harp of Erin; O Mary at thy window be; On the Massacre of Glencoe; The pulse of an Irishman; The return to Ulster; Sally in our alley; The soldier; 'Tis sunshine at last; The Vale of Clwyd; When mortals all.*
*** RCA RL 13417. White; Kavafian (violin), Ma (cello), Sanders (piano).

The charm of the Irish-American singer Robert White exactly suits the still underrated folksong settings which Beethoven made on commission. White's positive and sympathetic singing makes each one striking and memorable. Most notable of all is *The British Light Dragoons*, with White relishing in each stanza the 'whack' from the soldiers' long swords. The accompaniments are nicely done by Ani Kavafian, Yo-Yo Ma and Samuel Sanders. A delightful collection, well recorded.

Mass in C, Op. 86.
*** Ph. 9500 636/*7300 741* [id.]. Eda-Pierre, Payne, Tear, Moll, LSO Ch., LSO, Colin Davis.
(M) *** HMV SXLP/*TC-SXLP* 30284. Vyvyan, Sinclair, Lewis, Nowakowski, Beecham Ch. Soc., RPO, Beecham.

The freshness of the choral singing and the clarity of the sound make Davis's an outstandingly dramatic version of the *Mass in C*. The cry *Passus* ('suffered') in the *Credo* has rarely if ever been so tellingly presented on record. The quartet of soloists is first-rate. The recording, well focused, spacious and atmospheric, is given a natural concert-hall balance and it sounds equally well on disc and cassette.

Beecham's is a vintage performance, passionately committed, and makes one appreciate how this strong and dramatic

work followed directly on from the late and great Haydn Masses, a commission from Prince Esterhazy. With a first-rate team of soloists and excellent choral singing, it is an outstanding mid-price recommendation. The 1958 stereo is very good for its period and the tape transfer is first-class, vivid and lively, with clear choral sound.

Missa solemnis in D, Op. 123.
*** DG 2707 110/*3370 029* (2) [id.]. Moser, Schwarz, Kollo, Moll, Netherlands Ch., Concg. O., Bernstein.
(M) **(*) HMV SLS/*TC-SLS* 5198 [Ang. S 3595]. Schwarzkopf, Ludwig, Gedda, Zaccaria, V. Singverein, Philh. O., Karajan.
*(*) Decca D 87 D 2/*K 87 K 22* [Lon. 12111/5-]. Popp, Minton, Walker, Howell, Chicago Ch. and SO, Solti.

Bernstein's DG version with the Concertgebouw was edited together from tapes of two live performances, and the result has a spiritual intensity matched by very few rivals. Edda Moser is not an ideal soprano soloist, but the others are outstanding, and the *Benedictus* is made angelically beautiful by the radiant playing of the Concertgebouw concertmaster, Hermann Krebbers. The recording is a little light in bass, but outstandingly clear as well as atmospheric. On cassette, although the balance is somewhat recessed, the transfer is impressively clear, full-bodied and free from distortion.

The glory of Karajan's first version of the *Missa solemnis*, recorded in 1958, lies above all in the singing of the soloists. The chorus may lack something in incisiveness (largely a question of recording), but the orchestra, then at its peak, plays superbly, sustaining even the most measured tempi in Karajan's warmly expansive reading. The stereo is good for its period, but hardly matches the sound of his two later versions, and the cassette transfer is disappointing, offering an unrefined choral focus.

Solti's view of the work is essentially dramatic, hardly at all spiritual. With full-ranging sound, brilliant and forward, the result might have been involving, like Solti's Chicago readings of the Beethoven symphonies, but there is a series of shortcomings which between them detract from the impact of the performance. In the first place the ensemble is far less crisp than one expects from this source, with some ragged playing in the orchestra and poor coordination with the chorus. The choral contribution is variably successful, with some entries sharply incisive (the tenors, for example, in *Glorificamus* in the *Gloria*) but others which are dim. The solo team is not well matched either, and the discrepancies are made the more glaring by unnatural forward positioning for the voices. In addition, the women overweigh the men, and the first entry for the tenor in the *Kyrie* is so feeble as to make one lose patience at the very start. He does not improve much, though Lucia Popp, Yvonne Minton and Gwynne Howell all have splendid moments. The tape transfer is impressively full and uncongested. However, the narrow dynamics of the recording (on disc as well as tape) minimize the element of contrast; the violin solos in the *Benedictus* are made to sound larger than life.

Reminder: Jochum's inspired reading, also recorded in Holland (and with Krebbers again playing in the *Benedictus*), remains a top recommendation (Ph. 6799 001); and Karajan's third HMV recording (SLS 979 [Ang. S 3821]) is notably more colourful and better recorded than his two earlier versions.

OPERA

Fidelio (complete).
(M) *** HMV SLS/TC-SLS 5231 [Ang. S 3773]. Dernesch, Vickers, Ridderbusch, Van Dam, Kelemen, German Op. Ch., Berlin PO, Karajan.
** Decca Dig. D 178 D 3/*K 178 K 32.*

Behrens, Hofmann, Sotin, Adam, Ghazarian, Kuebler, Howell, Chicago Ch. and SO, Solti.

Karajan's splendid 1971 recording has been reissued on two discs (or tapes), providing what amounts almost to a bargain-priced version to challenge the famous Klemperer set (HMV SLS/TC-SLS 5006 [Ang. S 3625]). The refurbished sound seems to have gained rather than lost in immediacy and fullness in the remastering. Comparison between Karajan's strong and heroic reading and Klemperer's version with its incandescent spiritual strength is fascinating. Both have very similar merits, underlining the symphonic character of the work with their weight of utterance. Both may miss some of the sparkle of the opening scenes; but it is better that seriousness should enter too early than too late. Since seriousness is the keynote it is rather surprising to find Karajan using bass and baritone soloists lighter than usual. Both the Rocco (Ridderbusch) and the Don Fernando (Van Dam) lack something in resonance in their lower range. Yet they sing dramatically and intelligently and there is the advantage that the Pizarro of Zoltan Kelemen sounds the more biting and powerful as a result – a fine performance. Jon Vickers as Florestan is if anything even finer than he was for Klemperer, and though Helga Dernesch as Leonore does not have quite the clear-focused mastery of Christa Ludwig in the Klemperer set, this is still a glorious, thrilling performance, far outshining lesser rivals than Ludwig. The orchestral playing is superb. The cassette quality is admirably bright, clear and vivid. Unlike the Klemperer tapes, the side divisions are not tailored to match the ends of acts, but the sharpness of focus of the sound is striking: the *Abscheulicher*, with its vibrant horns, and the following scene with the *Prisoners' chorus* have splendid presence and projection, yet there is no suspicion of peaking.

125

Solti's set was the first-ever digital recording of an opera. The sound is full, clean and vividly atmospheric, matched by the conductor's urgent and intense direction. With fine choral singing the ensembles are excellent, but the solo singing is too flawed for comfort. Hildegard Behrens seems ungainly in the great *Abscheulicher*, the voice sounding less beautiful than usual; and both Peter Hofmann as Florestan and Theo Adam as Pizarro too often produce harsh unattractive tone. The cassette transfer is extremely sophisticated, matching the clarity and excellence of the discs. The layout, with one act on each of the two cassettes, is superior and the libretto/booklet is well designed and clearly printed.

Fidelio: highlights.
(M) *** HMV SXLP/*TC-SXLP* 30307. Ludwig, Vickers, Frick, Berry, Crass, Philh. Ch. and O., Klemperer.
*** DG 2537/*3306* 048. Janowitz, Kollo, Jungwirth, Sotin, Fischer-Dieskau, V. State Op. Ch., VPO, Bernstein.
** Decca Dig. SXDL/*KSXDC* 7529 (from above set cond. Solti).

Klemperer's outstanding version of *Fidelio* deserves to be represented in every collection, and this well-chosen selection – lacking only Pizarro's aria and the very end of the opera to be ideal – is most welcome at medium price. The confrontation quartet in Act 2 has never been more dramatically presented on record. The cassette transfer too is first-class, vivid and clear.

An excellent and generous selection too from Bernstein's strong and dramatic performance. Recording balances are not always ideal, but the sound is vivid on disc and cassette alike.

Choosing highlights from Solti's flawed performance of *Fidelio* inevitably underlines the weaknesses, when Behrens lacks full control in the first part of the *Abscheulicher* and Theo Adam is so gritty a Pizzaro. But the selection is generous,

and it is good to have the end of the finale included. The digital recording is excellent, although on cassette the choral focus is not quite as sharp as on disc.

Bellini, Vincenzo (1801–35)

Oboe concerto in E flat.
(M) *** DG Priv. 2535/*3335* 417 [139152]. Holliger, Bamberg SO, Maag – CIMAROSA, DONIZETTI, SALIERI: *Concertos.****

Bellini's *Oboe concerto* seems too brief, so beautifully is it played here. It is part of an irresistible anthology, immaculately recorded on both disc and cassette. Highly recommended.

Norma (complete).
*** HMV SLS/*TC-SLS* 5186 (3) [Ang. S 3615]. Callas, Corelli, Zaccaria, Ludwig, Palma, Ch. and O. of La Scala, Milan, Serafin.
** CBS 79327 (3) [Col. M3X 35902]. Scotto, Giacomini, Troyanos, Plishka, Crook, Murray, Ambrosian Op. Ch., Nat. PO, Levine.

By the time Callas recorded her stereo version of *Norma* in the early sixties, the tendency to hardness and unsteadiness in the voice above the stave, always apparent, had grown more serious; but the interpretation was as sharply illuminating as ever, a unique assumption helped – as the earlier mono performance was not – by a strong cast. Christa Ludwig as Adalgisa brings not just rich firm tone but a real feeling for Italian style, and despite moments of coarseness Corelli sings heroically. Serafin as ever is the most persuasive of Bellini conductors, and the recording is good for its period, with an excellent cassette transfer. The layout is on two cassettes, with no attempt made to apportion acts to sides;

the reduction of the libretto gives very small print. (Callas's earlier 1954 mono set is also available (HMV SLS/*TC-SLS* 5115), offering a unique reminder of the diva at her vocal peak, but the rest of the cast is flawed.)

Renata Scotto as Norma has many beautiful moments, but above pianissimo in the upper register the voice too regularly acquires a heavy beat, and the sound becomes ugly. The close recording does not help, any more than it does with Tatiana Troyanos as Adalgisa, whose vibrato is exaggerated. Giuseppe Giacomini sings with fair style but little imagination, and Levine's conducting is far too brutal for such a piece, favouring aggressively fast tempi.

Reminder: The outstanding Bonynge set with Sutherland and Horne remains available on Decca SET 424/6/*K 21 K 32* [Lon. 1394/5-].

I Puritani (complete).
(M) **(*) HMV SLS/*TC-SLS* 5201 (3) [Ang. SX 3881]. Caballé, Kraus, Manuguerra, Hamari, Amb. Op. Ch., Philh. O., Muti.

In the HMV version of *I Puritani* Riccardo Muti's contribution is the most distinguished. As the very opening demonstrates, his attention to detail and pointing of rhythm make for refreshing results, and the warm but luminous recording is excellent. But both the principal soloists – Bellini stylists on their day – indulge in distracting mannerisms, hardly allowing even a single bar to be presented straight in the big numbers, pulling and tugging in each direction, rarely sounding spontaneous in such deliberate expressiveness. The big ensemble *A te, o cara*, in its fussiness at slow speed, loses the surge of exhilaration which the earlier Decca set with Sutherland and Pavarotti shows so strongly (SET 587/9/*K 25 K 32* [Lon. 13111/5-]). The HMV cassette transfer is very successful and is better laid out than the discs, with Act 1 complete on the first of

the two tapes and the remaining two acts allotted a side each.

La Sonnambula (complete).
*** Decca D 230 D 3/*K 230 K 33* (3). Sutherland, Pavarotti, Della Jones, Ghiaurov, L. Op. Ch., Nat. PO, Bonynge.
(M) ** HMV SLS/*TC-SLS* 5134 (2). Callas, Monti, Cossotto, Zaccaria, Ratti, Ch. and O. of La Scala, Milan, Votto.

Sutherland in her second complete recording sings with richness and ease in even the most spectacular coloratura, matched in the tenor role this time by an equal (if not always so stylish) star. Ensembles as well as display arias have an authentic Bellinian surge. Excellent recording, with matching chrome tapes.

Substantially cut, the Callas version was recorded in mono in 1957, yet it gives a vivid picture of the diva at the peak of her powers. By temperament she may not have related closely to Bellini's heroine, but the village girl's simple devotion through all trials is touchingly caught, most of all in the recitatives.

Benatzky, Ralph (1887–1957)

Im Weissen Rössl (*White Horse Inn;* complete).
**(*) HMV SLS/*TC-SLS* 5184 (2). [Ang. SZX 3897]. Rothenberger; Minich, Jüten, Schary, Orth, Kraus, Mun. Children's Ch., Bav. R. Ch., Mun. RO, Mattes.

British listeners will search in vain for what for them is the most famous chorus from *White Horse Inn, Goodbye*. It was written for London, and is omitted from this very German account. Much of it is highly enjoyable, and the presentation is certainly authentic, but a lighter, even more resilient style would have given the fizz that such a piece really needs. Even so it is good to have the regular operetta repertory augmented with pieces like this that with the gramophone are generally left on one side. Anneliese Rothenberger is not specially well suited to the role of Josepha, but Peter Minich is the ideal light tenor for Leopold. The recording is atmospheric in the German Electrola manner, and the cassette transfer offers admirable quality, vivid and ripely colourful, with good projection and clear choral sound.

Im Weissen Rössl (abridged).
(M) **(*) Tel. AF 6.21255. Marion Briner, Minich, Chryst, Mayer, Kremling, Reichel, Buhlan, Fritz, Sorel, Horbiger, Ch. and Operetta O., Breuer.

Many will feel that a single disc is ideal for *White Horse Inn*, and this Telefunken issue is one of an attractive operetta series recorded in authentic style. It features all the important numbers, presented in two continuous pot-pourris. The singing is spirited and there is some splendid yodelling from Helga Reichel. The direction is lively and the recording has both atmosphere and good projection. Though the presentation is slightly less sophisticated than the HMV complete set, that is not necessarily a disadvantage, and the excellent Peter Minich is common to both recordings. The cassette is non-Dolby.

Benda, Jiří Antonín
(1722–95)

Harpsichord concertos: in C; D; F; G; G min.; Divertimento in G.
(M) ** Sup. 1111 2761/2. Hála, Novák Quintet.

Jiří Antonín, the younger brother of

Franz (František) Benda, made his reputation as a composer of melodramas (music with spoken dialogue), the best-known of which are *Ariadne auf Naxos*, *Medea* and *Pygmalion*. These concertos reflect something of the influence of C. P. E. Bach, with whom Benda came into contact during his formative years at the Prussian court. Not all the pieces recorded here with single strings are of equal interest; intelligently laid out though they are, the melodic inspiration is not always distinctive enough to engage one's whole-hearted sympathy. The performances are alert and well recorded, though the first violin is rather too prominently placed.

Benjamin, Arthur (1893–1960)

Harmonica concerto.
*** Argo ZRG 905. Reilly, L. Sinf., Atherton – ARNOLD and VILLA-LOBOS: *Concertos.***
(M) *** RCA GL/GK 42747. Adler, Orch., Gould – *Concert.***

Choice is difficult here. The work was written for Larry Adler, and he gives the more charismatic performance. But he is very forwardly balanced, and although Morton Gould provides admirable support the orchestral recording is rather lacking in substance. The Argo sound is infinitely finer, and in the beautiful slow movement, which has a strong hint of Vaughan Williams (who prompted Benjamin to write the work), there is far more depth and atmosphere. Tommy Reilly plays with great sympathy and he is more naturally balanced with the orchestra. The RCA tape transfer lacks refinement in the upper range.

Bennett, Richard Rodney
(born 1936)

(i) *Aubade for orchestra;* (ii) *Spells.*
**(*) Argo ZRG 907. Philh. O., (i)
Atherton, (ii) Willcocks, with Man-
ning, Bach Ch.

Spells is an ambitious choral work, a
setting of verses by Kathleen Raine,
which skilfully gets an amateur choir
singing confidently in a serial idiom. Not
that the Bach Choir is as dramatic and
colourful as the music really demands,
and it is Jane Manning who, above all in
Love Spell, the longest of the six movements, conveys the work's magical flavour. *Aubade* is one of Bennett's most
attractive shorter orchestral works, here
well conducted by David Atherton. The
recording is good, though the choral
sound could be clearer.

Berg, Alban (1885–1935)

*Chamber concerto for piano, violin
and 13 wind.*
*** Argo ZRG 937. Crossley, Pauk,
L. Sinf., Atherton – STRAVINSKY:
*Agon.***
(i) *Chamber concerto.* (ii) *4 Pieces for
clarinet and piano, Op. 5. Piano sonata,
Op. 1.*
*** DG 2531 007 [id.]. Barenboim, with
(i) Zukerman, Ens. Intercontem-
porain, Boulez, (ii) Pay.

As a birthday tribute to his friend and
teacher Schoenberg, Berg wrote the
Chamber concerto, his most concentratedly formalized work, a piece that can
very easily seem cold and inexpressive.
Atherton rightly takes the opposite view
that for all its complexity it is romantic

at heart, so that one hears it as a melodic
work full of warmth and good humour,
and the waltz rhythms are given a
genuine Viennese flavour. Pauk and
Crossley are outstanding soloists, the
Sinfonietta plays with precision as well
as commitment, and the recording is excellent, with the difficult balance problems intelligently solved.

Boulez sets brisk tempi for the
Chamber concerto, seeking to give it classical incisiveness, but the strong expressive personalities of the pianist and
violinist tend towards a more romantic
view. The result is characterful and convincing, and it is aptly coupled with the
clarinet pieces (with Antony Pay an outstanding soloist) and the high-romantic
solo *Piano sonata* in one movement.
Good recording.

Chamber concerto: Adagio (trans.
for violin, clarinet, piano).
*** DG 2531 213 [id.]. Boston Chamber
Players – DEBUSSY: *Prélude;* SCHOEN-
BERG: *Chamber symphony.***

Berg's own transcription of the middle
movement of the *Chamber concerto*
makes an apt coupling for the other two
offbeat arrangements. Very well played
and recorded.

Violin concerto.
*** DG 2531/*3301* 110 [id.]. Perlman,
Boston SO, Ozawa – STRAVINSKY:
*Concerto.***

Perlman's performance of the Berg
Violin concerto is totally commanding. The effortless precision of the playing goes with great warmth of expression,
so that the usual impression of 'wrong-
note romanticism' gives way to total
purposefulness. The Boston orchestra
plays superbly, and though the balance favours the soloist, the recording
is excellent, with a faithful tape transfer.

Lyric suite.
**(*) CBS 76305/40- [Col. M 35166].
NYPO. Boulez – SCHOENBERG: *Ver-
klaerte Nacht.***(*)

*Lyric suite; 3 Pieces; 3 Pieces for
orchestra, Op. 6.*
*** DG 2531 144. Berlin PO, Karajan.

At once delicate of texture – arguably
too detailed, as the recording presents the
orchestra – and strongly purposeful,
Karajan's readings of these important
Berg pieces make an attractive coupling.
The dark romanticism behind the Op. 6
pieces in particular, linking back to
Mahler, is compellingly presented.
Refined recording.

Boulez offers the *Lyric suite* spread
over one side (short measure at only fifteen minutes). He is not as sumptuously
recorded as Karajan, nor is his reading
as subtle or refined, and the pianissimo
tone of the New Yorkers does not match
that of the Berlin Philharmonic. However, this is fine playing (dodecaphony
with a human face), and some will prefer
the greater urgency and emotional
strength of Boulez's approach. The CBS
recording is perfectly acceptable and the
cassette transfer is quite vivid.

Lulu (original version).
*** Decca D 48 D 3/*K 48 K 32* (3) [Lon.
13120/5-]. Silja, Fassbaender, Berry,
Hopferweiser, Moll, Krenn, VPO,
Dohnányi.

Lulu (with orchestration of Act 3
completed by Cerha).
*** DG 2740 213/*3378* 086 (3) [id.].
Stratas, Minton, Schwarz, Mazura,
Blankenheim, Riegel, Tear, Paris Op.
O., Boulez.

The full three-act structure of Berg's
Lulu, first unveiled by Boulez in his Paris
Opéra production and here treated to
studio recording, was a revelation with
few parallels. The third act, musically
even stronger than the first two and dra-

matically essential in making sense of the
stylized plan based on a palindrome,
transforms the opera. Although it ends
with a lurid portrayal of Jack the
Ripper's murder of Lulu – here recorded
with hair-raising vividness – the nastiness
of the subject is put in context, made
more acceptable artistically. The very end
of the opera, with Yvonne Minton singing the Countess Geschwitz's lament, is
most moving, though Lulu remains to the
last a repulsive heroine. Teresa Stratas's
bright, clear soprano is well recorded,
and there is hardly a weak link in the cast.
The recording is a little lacking in clarity
and atmosphere compared with the
Decca version of Acts 1 and 2. On tape,
although the transfer level is modest, the
naturalness and detail of the sound demonstrate DG's best standards, and the
climaxes are accommodated without
strain. The layout on four cassettes follows the discs, with side eight given to
commentaries on the work by Douglas
Jarman (in English), Friedrich Cerha (in
German) and Pierre Boulez (in French);
translations are provided in the booklet
libretto (easier to read in the disc than
the characteristic narrow DG tape
format). Altogether this is a historic
issue, presenting an intensely involving
performance of a work which in some
ways is more lyrically approachable than
Wozzeck.

Recordings earlier than the Decca set
on disc were made during live performances, so Dohnányi was the first to
achieve anything like precision. The pity
is that he was not able to record the completed Act 3, for which Boulez had first
recording rights. Instead Dohnányi follows traditional practice in using the two
movements of the *Lulu suite* as a replacement. Anja Silja is vividly in character,
attacking the stratospheric top notes with
ease, always singing with power and
rarely falling into her usual hardness.
Walter Berry too is exceptionally strong
as Dr Schön, aptly sinister, and even the
small roles are cast from strength. The
Vienna Philharmonic plays ravishingly,

underlining the opera's status – whatever the formal patterns behind the notes, and whatever the subject – as an offshoot of romanticism. The cassettes, like the discs, set new standards, with sound of amazing richness and depth.

(i) *Lulu: suite,* (ii) *Der Wein.*
**(*) CBS 76575 [Col. M/MT 35849].
NYPO, Boulez, with (i) Blegen, (ii) Norman.

Jessye Norman sings with apt sensuousness in *Der Wein,* one of the most closely argued but also one of the most deeply emotional of Berg's works, written at the same period as the opera *Lulu.* Boulez persuades his New Yorkers to play this difficult music with affection, and though the soloist in the *Lulu suite* is less convincing, more cautious, that too is given a very compelling reading, recorded not with ideal clarity but with warm impact.

Wozzeck (complete).
*** Decca Dig. D 231 D 2/K 231 K 22 (2). Waechter, Silja, Winkler, Laubenthal, Jahn, Malta, Sramek, VPO, Dohnányi.
(M) **(*) CBS 79251 (2) [Col. M2 30852]. Berry, Strauss, Weikenmeier, Uhl, Doench, Paris Op Ch and O., Boulez.

Dohnányi, with refined textures and superb playing from the Vienna Philharmonic, presents an account of *Wozzeck* that is not only more accurate than any other on record but also more beautiful. It may lack some of the bite of Pierre Boulez's CBS version and some of the romantic warmth of Karl Boehm's set (DG 2707 023, which is also beautiful and has a highly distinctive, almost noble Wozzeck in Fischer Dieskau); but with superb digital sound the Decca set stands as first choice. Unfortunately the beauty of the performance does not extend to Eberhard Waechter's vocal quality in the name part, but he gives a thoughtful,

sensitive performance. The edge of Anja Silja's voice and her natural vibrancy of character make her a memorable Marie, first cousin of Lulu. An excellent supporting cast too. As usual with Decca, the cassette transfer is of admirable quality, the sound richly atmospheric as well as clear and vivid.

Walter Berry's view of the hero's character includes a strong element of brutishness, and Boulez's uncompromising, thrustful view of the whole score matches this conception; he is less concerned with pure atmosphere than with emotional drive, and undoubtedly he provides a powerful experience. One is made to suffer. This reissue on two discs is generous, particularly as there is little or no loss of quality, though with such long sides there is no room for bands between scenes.

Berio, Luciano (born 1925)

Coro.
*** DG 2531 270 [id.]. Cologne R. Ch. and SO, composer.

Coro is one of the most ambitious of Berio's works, with each of forty singers paired with an instrumentalist and with folk verse on basic themes contrasted with poems of Pablo Neruda. The striking line *Come and see the blood in the streets* keeps recurring to hammer home the composer's political message, though *Coro* makes its impact musically, with overtones of the ritualistic elements in Stravinsky's *Les Noces.* Of his generation of leading avant-gardists Berio remains the most approachable, almost identifiably Italian in his acceptance of melody. The composer directs a committed performance here, helped by the impact of the forward sound.

Berkeley, Lennox
(born 1903)

Antiphon.
(M) **(*) Uni. UNS 260. Westminster
Cath. String O., Mawby – M.
BERKELEY: *Meditations*; IRELAND:
*Concertino pastorale.***(*)

Written for the St Martin's Academy
to play at the Cheltenham Festival in
1973, Sir Lennox Berkeley's *Antiphon*
presents a skilful set of variations on a
plainchant theme, not a strongly characterized piece but a satisfyingly
thoughtful one. The strings here could be
more polished, but the coupling is apt
and attractive.

(i) *Piano concerto in B flat, Op. 29;*
(ii) *Symphony No. 2, Op. 51.*
*** Lyr. SRCS 94. (i) Wilde, New Philh.
O.; (ii) LPO; both cond. Braithwaite.

Sir Lennox Berkeley's *Second Symphony* dates from 1957, though he made
some small revisions in 1976, not long
before this record was made. It is the
work of a sophisticated and cultured
musical mind; textures are clean and the
ideas are beautifully laid out. This is
civilized music and its originality is all the
more rewarding for the restrained expressive means. The *Piano concerto* is a
much earlier piece, written in the immediate wake of the war, and though it is
more traditional in layout, it is by no
means less rewarding. It is every bit as
well performed here as the symphony,
and the Lyrita recording has impeccable
clarity, depth and realism. A valuable
addition to the discography of English
music.

(i) *Piano and wind quintet, Op. 90. 6
Preludes, Op. 23; Scherzo, Op. 32/2.*
(ii) *Another Spring (3 songs), Op. 93.*

**(*) Mer. E 77017. Horsley, with (i)
Lord, Fell, Baker, Kerry Camden, (ii)
Loring.

Berkeley's *Quintet* is, as its opus number
suggests, a late piece, dating from 1974.
It was commissioned by the Chamber
Music Society of Lincoln Center. It is
fluent, inventive music, well laid out for
the medium, and is nicely played here by
Colin Horsley and his wind players.
There is a substantial first movement,
perhaps the best of the four, and a fine
set of variations as finale. The piano
Preludes come off attractively, and so do
the appealing Walter de la Mare settings
(Op. 93). Berkeley's meticulous craftsmanship is always in evidence, and the
recording, though not distinguished
(there is too much reverberance in the
piano pieces), is fully acceptable.

String trio, Op. 19.
** Pearl SHE 547. Georgiadis, Hawkins,
Cummings – BAX: *Rhapsodic bal-
lad* ***; BRIDGE: *Trio.***

Berkeley's *Trio* comes from 1944 and
is as expertly crafted and musically rewarding as one expects from this fastidious and sensitive master. Its elegance is
well conveyed by the three artists
recorded here, and though the piece may
not have the darker overtones of its companions, it is far from merely lightweight
in character. The recording is slightly
closer than is ideal, but the interest of this
disc outweighs any such reservations.

Berkeley, Michael
(born 1948)

Meditations.
(M) **(*) Uni. UNS 260. Westminster
Cath. String O., Mawby – L.
BERKELEY: *Antiphon;* IRELAND: *Con-
certino pastorale.***(*)

Michael Berkeley's *Meditations* won the Guinness Prize for Composition. It is a thoughtful, beautifully written piece, which, like his father's *Antiphon*, has links with plainchant. This performance could be more polished but is persuasive enough.

Berlioz, Hector (1803–69)

Harold in Italy, Op. 16.
*** HMV ASD 3389 [Ang. S/4XS 37413]. McInnes, Orchestre Nat. de France, Bernstein.
**(*) CBS 76593 [Col. M/MT 34541]. Zukerman, Orchestre de Paris, Barenboim.
(M) **(*) HMV SXLP/TC-SXLP 30314 [Ang. S 36123]. Menuhin, Philh. O., Colin Davis.
*(*) Decca SXL/KSXC 6783 [Lon. 7097/5-]. Vernon, Cleveland O., Maazel.
(B) *(*) RCA VICS/VK 2004 [AGL 1 1526]. Primrose, Boston SO, Munch.

With the understanding players of the Orchestre National, Bernstein gives a performance that is both exciting and introspective. His earlier account with his own New York Philharmonic was sharper-focused than this, thanks in part to the recording, and its tauter discipline made for a performance at once fiercer and more purposeful. But with French players Bernstein's slightly more relaxed manner is in some ways more authentic, so that the galloping rhythms of the first and third movements are more lilting if fractionally less precise. Donald McInnes is a violist with a superb rich and even tone, one who responds at all times to the conductor but who has plenty of individuality. The recording is not always ideally clean in detail but is opulent in its spread.

When Zukerman forsakes his violin for the viola he emerges as a master of the larger instrument. His solo work here is wonderfully rich and resonant, a powerful and characterful element in Barenboim's ripely romantic and highly dramatic reading. The recording is rather larger than life.

Both Bernstein and Barenboim prove more forceful conductors in this work than Sir Colin Davis, who may perhaps in this earlier HMV version have been overfaced by his viola soloist. The fact is that the Menuhin/Philharmonia recording openly treats the work as a concerto, with the soloist often dictating the rhythm which the orchestra has to follow. But this remains an enjoyable version, now more competitive in this medium-priced reissue. The sound is full and lively on disc, rather more bland on tape (although side two has more edge than side one and the finale springs readily to life).

A well-recorded and excellently played account from Robert Vernon and the Cleveland Orchestra under Maazel. In terms of imagination and insight, however, it does not displace the Bernstein set on HMV (or for that matter his earlier CBS account with William Lincer, which evokes memories of Koussevitzky's incandescent record with William Primrose).

Primrose's stereo recording with Munch does not match his earlier mono record (with Koussevitzky). Munch's direction of the outer movements is tense without creating real electricity, and the inner movements lack charm. The recording is rather brash, and even at bargain price this is not a real competitor.

Overtures: Béatrice et Bénédict; Benvenuto Cellini, Op. 23; Le Carnaval romain, Op. 9; Le Corsaire, Op. 21. Roméo et Juliette, Op. 17: Queen Mab scherzo. Les Troyens: Royal hunt and storm.
(M) *** RCA Gold GL/GK 42696. Boston SO, Munch.

This classic disc offers not only the

finest collection of Berlioz overtures available in stereo but also a superb performance of the *Queen Mab scherzo* (with gossamer string textures) and a riveting version of the *Royal hunt and storm*. Here there is wonderfully poetic horn playing at the magical opening and a gripping climax, where one hardly misses the chorus, so sharply focused is the orchestral brass tutti. The recording inevitably sounds dated (though it has been crisply remastered for the Gold Seal reissue), but Munch shows a very special feeling for this repertoire. A rosette is deserved for the performances, but not, perhaps, for the sound. The cassette has an unacceptably compressed dynamic range.

Overture: Le Carnaval romain, Op. 9.

(M) *** HMV SXLP/*TC-SXLP* 30450 [Ang. S 35613]. Philh. O., Karajan – LISZT: *Les Préludes*; RESPIGHI: *Pines*.***

A charismatic performance, splendidly played and with hardly dated recording, which acts as a bonus to superb accounts of *Les Préludes* and *The Pines of Rome*. The cassette transfer level is not as high as usual from EMI, and the sound on tape lacks the last degree of glitter.

Romance, rêverie et caprice, Op. 8
*** DG Dig. 2532/*3302* 011 [id.]. Perlman, Orchestre de Paris, Barenboim – LALO: *Symphonie espagnole*.***

Berlioz's short concertante work for violin and orchestra uses material originally intended for *Benvenuto Cellini*. Perlman's ripely romantic approach to the *Rêverie* brings out the individuality of the melody, and with a sympathetic accompaniment from Barenboim the work as a whole is given considerable substance. First-rate digital recording, with disc and cassette closely matched.

Symphonie fantastique, Op. 14.
(M) *** HMV SXLP/*TC-SXLP* 30295 [Ang. S/4XS 60165]. French Nat. RO, Beecham.

**(*) HMV ASD/*TC-ASD* 3946 [Ang. S/4XS 37485]. LSO, Previn.

**(*) Decca SXL/*KSXC* 6938 [Lon. 7168/5-]. VPO, Haitink.

** Decca Dig. SXDL/*KSXDC* 7512 [Lon. LDR 10013]. NYPO, Mehta.

(M) ** Ph. Seq. 6527/*7311* 081 [6570/*7310* 031]. LSO, Colin Davis.

** DG 2531/*3301* 092 [id.]. Orchestre de Paris, Barenboim.

(M) *(*) DG Priv. 2535/*3335* 256. [id.]. Berlin PO, Karajan.

(M) *(*) CBS 61910/*40*- [Col. M/*MT* 31843]. NYPO, Bernstein.

(B) *(*) CfP CFP 40281. Hallé O., Loughran.

Beecham's account still enjoys classic status, though it is now some twenty years old. The sound is amazingly fresh and vivid, while the performance has a demonic intensity that is immediately compelling. Gounod wrote that 'with Berlioz, all impressions, all sensations – whether joyful or sad – are expressed in extremes to the point of delirium', and Beecham brought to this score all the fire and temperament, all the magic and affection in his armoury. He drew from the French National Radio Orchestra playing of great rhythmic subtlety; the waltz has never sounded more elegant. This is an indispensable record, and the clear, bright tape transfer is admirable.

Helped by sound of superb quality, André Previn presents the *Symphonie fantastique* as above all a symphonic structure. Some may find him not atmospheric or colourful enough, but on its own direct terms it is a most compelling reading, one which completely avoids vulgarity. The tape transfer has bright detail and plenty of impact, though it is not so rich as the LP.

Haitink with the Vienna Philharmonic may sound a little unidiomatic in French music, but the freshness and refinement of the reading, helped by clean, atmospheric sound, will suit those who prefer a degree of detachment even in this high romantic symphony. The cassette transfer is not one of Decca's very best: it has not quite the upper range of the disc, and in the finale the bass drum offers minor problems.

Mehta's reading is fresh and direct but not specially illuminating. The disc's chief claim to attention lies in the digital recording (Decca's first with this orchestra), which is wide-ranging and atmospheric. The cassette too is extremely vivid, but it has a less spectacular dynamic range: the big climaxes fail to expand as dramatically as in some versions.

Sir Colin Davis's earlier recording has been reissued in an admirably fresh transfer on Philips's new medium-priced label. The quality is slightly dry and gives a less massive, less atmospheric sound picture than in Davis's re-recording with the Concertgebouw Orchestra. The first movement begins with a fine sense of anticipation, but the tension is not always maintained throughout the movement, and the *Adagio*, although beautifully played, is a little detached. The two final movements are very exciting. In the *March to the scaffold* Davis gives the rhythm exactly the right spring, and by doing the rarely heard repeat he adds to our pleasure. The finale is gripping to the last bar, with really taut orchestral playing and clear projection from the recording. The cassette is clear and clean, with vivid brass and string detail.

Barenboim's version is disappointing, with the first movement hectic and erratic. Only in the *March to the scaffold* and the finale does the performance suddenly acquire the necessary sharpness of focus. Warm recording.

Karajan's earlier recording, now on Privilege, was altogether too erratic to be entirely convincing, while Bernstein's New York version cannot compare with his later HMV (now deleted), either in

recording quality or in interpretation, which is here distractingly wilful. In the bargain range Loughran's account is also disappointing, heavy in places and rarely exciting, although there are touches which reveal this conductor's characteristic freshness of approach. However, in this price range Prêtre's RCA recording, dating from the earliest days of stereo, has recently been remastered and reissued on Camden (CCV 5048). The sound is astonishingly vivid and the performance remarkably successful, the interpretation far more exciting than many records costing more than twice as much. But first choice, regardless of price, rests with Martinon (HMV ASD/ TC-ASD 3263 [Ang. S/4XS 37138]), Karajan's newest Berlin recording (DG 2530 597/3300 498), and the Beecham listed above.

Symphonie fantastique, Op. 14 (arr. for piano by Liszt).
**(*) CBS 76861. Mezzena.

Liszt's transcription of the *Symphonie fantastique* is a work of art in its own right and an astonishing and exhilarating experience. Hallé recalled an occasion when Berlioz conducted the *March to the scaffold* and was immediately followed by Liszt playing his own piano transcription, with 'an effect even surpassing that of the full orchestra and creating an indescribable furore'. Even those who know the *Fantastique* inside out will learn something from Liszt's remarkable recreation. Bruno Mezzena plays with great sympathy, insight and brilliance, producing some highly sensitive colour. Unfortunately the recording was made in a rather smaller studio than is desirable, and although the engineers make the best of a bad job there is a lack of transparency at the top and of openness in climaxes that must be noted. Superb surfaces.

La Damnation de Faust, Op. 24.
*** Decca Dig. D 259 D 3/*K 259 K 33*
(3). Von Stade, Riegel, Van Dam,
King, Chicago Ch. and SO, Solti.
** DG 2709 087 (3) [id.]. Minton, Dom-
ingo, Fischer-Dieskau, Bastin, Ch.,
Orchestre de Paris, Barenboim.

Solti's performance, searingly dramatic, is given stunning digital sound (and
matching chrome tapes) to make the ride
to Hell supremely exciting. But, with Von
Stade singing tenderly, this is a warmly
expressive performance too; and the
Hungarian march has rarely had such
sparkle and swagger.

Barenboim's freely romantic reading is
orchestrally most persuasive, but the
variable singing of the choir and controversial casting of the soloists make it
less recommendable than it might be.
Much will depend on individual responses to Fischer-Dieskau in the role of
Mephistopheles, very forceful and detailed but hardly idiomatic, and Domingo is far more cavalier in tackling the
role of Faust than he usually is in French
music. He is not flatteringly recorded,
generally too close, and the balance does
not help Yvonne Minton either.

*La Damnation de Faust: Hungarian
march; Dance of the Sylphs; Minuet
of the Will-o'-the-Wisps. Les Troyens: Royal hunt and storm; Trojan
march.*
(M) **(*) HMV Green. ESD/*TC-ESD*
7097. Ch., CBSO, Frémaux –
IBERT: *Divertissement* **(*); SATIE:
Gymnopédies.***

First-class playing in the pieces from
The Damnation of Faust and superb recording: the *Hungarian march* is very
exciting. In the *Royal hunt and storm*,
however, the opening horn solo is played
lustily rather than poetically, as in the
Munch version, although later the use of
the chorus is effective at the climax.

*L'Enfance du Christ, Op. 25; Re-
quiem Mass, Op. 5; Te Deum, Op. 22.*
(M) *** Ph. 6768 002 (5). Baker, Tappy,
Langridge, Tagliavini, Herincx, Allen,
Rouleau, Bastin, John Alldis Ch.,
Wandsworth School Boys' Ch., LSO
Ch., LSO, Colin Davis.

Three of Sir Colin Davis's finest sets
are offered here at what amounts to
upper medium price. With fine recording
(though the *Te Deum* dates from 1969)
and immaculate pressings this can be
recommended.

L'Enfance du Christ, Op. 25.
*** Ph. 6700 106/*7699 058* (2) [id.].
Baker, Tappy, Langridge, Allen, Her-
incx, Rouleau, Bastin, John Alldis
Ch., LSO, Colin Davis.

Davis characteristically directs a fresh
and refined reading of one of Berlioz's
most directly appealing works. The
beautifully balanced recording intensifies
the colour and atmosphere of the writing,
so that for example the *Nocturnal march*
in the first part is wonderfully mysterious. There is a fine complement of
soloists, and though Eric Tappy's tone as
narrator is not always sweet, his sense of
style is immaculate. Others are not
always quite so idiomatic, but Janet
Baker and Thomas Allen, as ever, both
sing beautifully. Good cassette sound,
although the transfer level is very low. On
disc the contrast with Davis's earlier version on Oiseau-Lyre (now deleted) is not
as clear-cut as one might expect, for at
times the earlier performance was fresher
and more urgent; the recording remains
remarkably bright and clean for its early
sixties vintage, and Pears was a sweeter-
toned, more characterful narrator.

*Herminie; La Mort de Cléopâtre, Op.
18/1 (scènes lyriques).*
*** Ph. 9500 683/*7300 778* [id.]. Baker,
LSO, Colin Davis.

La Mort de Cléopâtre.
(M) **(*) CBS 61891/40-. Minton,
BBC SO, Boulez – ELGAR: *Sea
Pictures.***(*)

These two dramatic scenas make an
apt coupling: both were written as entries
for the Prix de Rome, early works which
yet give many hints of the mature Berlioz,
even presenting specific hints of material
later used in the *Symphonie fantastique*
(the idée fixe) and the *Roman Carnival
overture* (the melody of the introduction).
Janet Baker sings with passionate intensity, while Davis draws committed playing from the LSO. Excellent recording on
both disc and cassette.

Yvonne Minton's account of *La Mort
de Cléopâtre*, is dramatically incisive, less
varied of expression than Janet Baker's
but strongly committed too. The coupling on a mid-price reissue is sensible and
attractive. Close but vivid recording, and
a good cassette.

Les Nuits d'été (song cycle), *Op. 7.*
**(*) Ph. 9500 783/7300 857 [id.].
Norman, LSO, Colin Davis – RAVEL:
*Shéhérazade.***(*)
(M) ** RCA Gold GL/GK 13792 [AGL
1/AGK 1 3792]. Leontyne Price, Chi-
cago SO, Reiner – FALLA: *El amor
brujo.***(*)

Jessye Norman is in fine voice here but
does not get fully inside this most magical
of orchestral song cycles. There is no lack
of voluptuousness, but the word meanings are less subtly registered than in the
finest rival versions. Davis's tempi too
are sometimes over-deliberate. The recording is pleasing, atmospheric on both
disc and cassette.

Leontyne Price seems uncharacteristically cool and uninvolved amid the
subtleties of Berlioz's cycle, and Reiner is
less sympathetic here than in his fiery
account of the Falla on the reverse. Good
recording for its late-fifties vintage, with
a clear, clean cassette equivalent.

Still recommended: The collaboration of
Dame Janet Baker and Sir John Barbirolli produces ravishing results (HMV
ASD 2444 [Ang. S 36505]); this is an
outstandingly beautiful record. The
alternative version from Régine Crespin
and Ansermet (Decca JB/KJBC 15 [Lon.
25821/5-]) is also superb in a more direct
way, more operatic in feeling but a *tour
de force*, and the recording is both glowing and brilliant.

*Requiem Mass (Grande Messe des
morts), Op. 5.*
*** HMV Dig. SLS/TCC-SLS 5209 (2).
Tear, LPO Ch., LPO, Previn.
**(*) DG 2707 119 (2) [id.]. Domingo,
Ch. and Orchestre de Paris, Baren-
boim.
*(*) Decca D 137 D 2/K 137 K 22 (2)
[Lon. 12115/5-]. Riegel, Cleveland Ch.
and O., Maazel.

Previn's version of Berlioz's great
choral work is the most impressive so far
put on disc or tape. Spectacular digital
sound allows the registration of the
extremes of dynamic in this extraordinary work for massed forces. The gradations of pianissimo against total pianissimo are breathtakingly caught, making
the great outbursts all the more telling.
There is fine bloom on the voices, and
the separation of sound gives a feeling of
reality to the massed brass and multiple
timpani, even though current digital
techniques still fall short of conveying the
full expansive glory experienced in a big
cathedral. The double-length chrome
cassette matches the discs closely. It
catches the full amplitude of the climaxes
without problems; only in the pianissimo
passages (especially at the very opening
of the work) is the sharpness of focus
marginally less firm than with the LPs,
and even here the difference is marginal.
Previn's view is direct and incisive (like
that of Sir Colin Davis on his long-
established version), not underlining
expressiveness but concentrating on

rhythmic qualities. So the *Rex tremendae* is given superb buoyancy, even if Previn misses some of the animal excitement captured by other conductors, such as Bernstein (see below). Robert Tear is a sensitive soloist, though the voice is balanced rather close. The cassette is presented in a box (with booklet) like the discs.

With its distant sound, transferred at a lowish level, it is hard to obtain from the Barenboim version the sort of impact which marks out Previn's forward and direct reading in digital sound. This is an expressive reading, but unlike Bernstein, who similarly takes an expressive view, Barenboim tends to prefer measured tempi, with fewer stringendi. It is a performance which conveys the mystery and awe of the piece rather than its brazen drama, though it certainly has plenty of power, and the singing of the chorus (trained by Arthur Oldham) is outstandingly fine, with no raw tone from any section even under stress.

Maazel's version has clean Decca recording, but the result is strangely unatmospheric, with the choir set at a distance. The performance too is uninvolving and at times prosaic. The cassette transfer shows Decca's engineering at its most impressive; the *Tuba mirum* with its spectacular brass is especially effective.

However, the Bernstein (CBS 79205 [Col. M2 34202]) and Davis (6700 019) sets still take pride of place, with the Previn leading the field.

Roméo et Juliette, Op. 17.
*** DG 2707 115/*3370 036* [id.]. Minton, Araiza, Bastin, Ch. and Orchestre de Paris, Barenboim.
*(*) Erato STU 71083 (3). Denize, Corazza, Thau, Rhine Op. Ch., Strasbourg PO, Lombard.

Roméo et Juliette: Love scene.
(M) *** DG Priv. 2535/*3335* 422 [2530 308/*3300 284*]. San Francisco SO, Ozawa – PROKOFIEV and TCHAIKOVSKY: *Romeo and Juliet.****

Barenboim directs a warmly romantic reading of Berlioz's great dramatic symphony. He takes a very flexible view of such great set-pieces as the love scene, which here sounds very Wagnerian in a *Tristan*-like way. Though Barenboim's own magnetic purposefulness holds the work together, the playing of the Paris Orchestra has its lapses, for example in the *Queen Mab scherzo*, which misses something in mercurial lightness. With a first-rate team of soloists and warmly atmospheric recording on disc and tape alike, it makes a welcome alternative to the long-established Ozawa and Davis versions.

With rather dull recording and often poor ensemble, the Lombard version is hardly competitive, though individual soloists make distinguished contributions.

Ozawa's Privilege reissue attractively couples three very contrasted views of Shakespeare's lovers. The Berlioz has all the warmth and glow required in this vision of the great love scene and it is very well recorded on both disc and cassette (there is no appreciable difference).

OPERA

Béatrice et Bénédict (complete).
*** Ph. 6700 121 (2). Baker, Tear, Eda-Pierre, Allen, Lloyd, Van Allen, Watts, John Alldis Ch., LSO, Colin Davis.

Well produced for records, with a smattering of French dialogue between numbers, *Béatrice et Bénédict* here reveals itself as less an opera than a dramatic symphony, one of the important Berlioz works (like *Romeo and Juliet*) which refuse to fit in a conventional category. The score presents not just witty and brilliant music for the hero and heroine (Dame Janet Baker and Robert Tear at their most pointed) but sensuously beautiful passages such as the duet for Hero and Ursula at the end of Act 1 and the trio they later share with

Beatrice, both incidental to the drama but very important for the musical structure. First-rate solo and choral singing, brilliant playing and outstanding recording. Davis's earlier Oiseau-Lyre set, still sounding remarkably fresh and vigorous (SOL 256/7), is not entirely superseded, but the new Philips version takes pride of place.

Benvenuto Cellini: highlights.
(M) **(*) Ph. Fest. 6570/7310 094. Gedda, Eda-Pierre, Bastin, Massard, Blackwell, Berbié, Soyer, Lloyd, ROHCG Ch., BBC SO, Colin Davis.

This attractive selection from a vivid but wayward opera is recommended to all those Berliozians who resist the complete set. Unfortunately the most memorable passage of all, where the *Roman Carnival* material is used with choral additions, is omitted.

Les Troyens: highlights.
(M) *** Ph. Fest. 6570/7310 098. Vickers, Veasey, Lindholm, Glossop, ROHCG Ch. and O., Colin Davis.

Les Troyens: Trojan march; Royal hunt and storm.
(M) *** HMV SXLP/TC-SXLP 30260. Beecham Ch. Soc., RPO, Beecham –
BIZET: *Symphony*; DELIBES: *Le Roi s'amuse.****

The Philips issue gives an attractive and generous selection from Berlioz's masterpiece. The excerpts, chosen from Acts 1, 4 and 5, include the *Royal hunt and storm*, the *Trojan march* and the two dramatic Act 5 scenas, Aeneas's *Inutiles regrets!* and Dido's *Je vais mourir* followed by her *Adieu*. The recording emerges vividly throughout, on disc and cassette alike.

Beecham's version of the *Royal hunt and storm* has splendid panache and atmosphere, and the *Trojan march* is characteristically ebullient. The recordings are good – though the choral focus

in the former piece is not very clean – and have transferred to cassette successfully. A most attractive compilation.

COLLECTION

Harold in Italy: Finale. Symphonie fantastique: March to the scaffold. La Belle Voyageuse. L'Enfance du Christ: Shepherds' chorus. La Damnation de Faust: Hungarian march. Nuits d'été. Roméo et Juliette: Grand ball. Te Deum: excerpts. Benvenuto Cellini, Act 1: *Finale.*
(M) **(*) Ph. 6833 249/7431 123. Various artists, cond. Colin Davis.

This generous collection of snippets from Davis's Berlioz series put together as a sampler is well worth investigating at medium price, even though the selection is arbitrary. Side two is best, with the well-chosen excerpts from *Benvenuto Cellini* and *Romeo and Juliet* the most memorable items. The recording is consistently good on disc; the sound is more uneven on cassette.

Berners, Lord (Gerald)
(1883–1950)

Piano music: *Dispute entre le papillon et le crapaud; Fragments psychologiques; Le poisson d'or; Polka; Trois Petites Marches funèbres.* Piano duet: *Valses bourgeoises.* Vocal music: *Come on, Algernon; Dialogue between Tom Filuter and his man; 3 English songs; Lieder album: 3 Songs in the German manner; Red roses and red noses; 3 Sea songs; Trois chansons.*
*** Uni. RHS 355. Dickinson, Dickerson, Bradshaw, Bennett.

Berners was a vintage English eccentric, as a composer something of an English Satie. These pieces often have a comparably haunting quality, so that in the end the immediate joke matters less than the musical invention, limited as it is. The musicians here have all performed these pieces in concert, and the results can hardly be faulted, even if one would sometimes welcome a more sparkling manner. A valuable and enjoyable collection, well recorded.

Bernstein, Leonard

(born 1918)

(i) *Candide overture; Fancy Free; On the Town: 3 Dances.* (ii) *Prelude, fugue and riffs.*
(M) *** CBS 61816/40- [Col. MS 6677]).
(i) NYPO, composer; (ii) Benny Goodman, Columbia Jazz Combo.

This collection of some of Leonard Bernstein's most approachable works, most of them with jazz overtones and including both of the sailor-based dramatic pieces, makes an excellent mid-price issue. The overture to *Candide* is one of the most exhilarating of the century, an equivalent to Rossini. The recording is aptly hard and bright, and the performances irrepressible. The cassette is acceptable but has less range than the disc.

Dybbuk (ballet): *Suites Nos. 1 and 2.*
*** DG 2531 348 [id.]. Sperry, Fifer, NYPO, composer.

These two suites between them are no shorter than the original ballet (one of Bernstein's toughest works, on the sinister subject of a lost spirit), dividing the original score broadly between passages involving vocal elements and those purely instrumental. The first suite is the

longer and more dramatic, the second the more contemplative. Even the jazzy dance sequences typical of Bernstein (often in seven-in-a-bar rhythms) acquire a bitter quality. Bernstein directs strong, colourful performances, cleanly recorded, with excellent vocal contributions from Paul Sperry and Bruce Fifer.

Fancy Free (ballet); (i) *Serenade after Plato's Symposium* (for solo violin, string orch., harp and percussion).
⊛ *** DG 2531 196 [id.]. Israel PO, composer, (i) with Kremer.

There are earlier versions of both works, but this surpasses any of them. Perhaps Isaac Stern was a more extrovert protagonist in his pioneering mono recording of the *Serenade* (never available in the UK) but Gidon Kremer has all the nervous intensity and vibrant energy to do justice to this powerful and inventive score. The *Serenade* must rank among Bernstein's most resourceful and inspired creations, full of ideas, often thrilling and exciting, and equally often moving. *Fancy Free* is more familiar stuff, and though the Israel Philharmonic does not match the New York orchestra (see above) in its sheer virtuosity or its command of jazz rhythms, it still plays with tremendous spirit and also enjoys the merit of outstanding recording quality. Both performances have the spontaneity of a live occasion, and cannot be too strongly recommended.

Symphonies Nos. 1 (Jeremiah); 2 (The Age of Anxiety); 3 (Kaddish). Chichester Psalms.
*** DG 2709 077 (3) [id.]. Ludwig, Foss, Caballé; Wager (speaker), V. Boys' Ch., Israel PO, composer.

Bernstein's musical invention is always memorable if at times a little too facile to match the ambitiousness of his symphonic aim, but the compelling confidence of his writing speaks of a genius stretching himself to the limit. The *Jeremiah symphony* dates from Bernstein's early twenties and ends with a moving passage from *Lamentations* for the mezzo soloist. As its title suggests, the *Second Symphony* was inspired by the poem of W. H. Auden, with the various movements directly reflecting dramatic passages from it, though no words are set in this work for orchestra alone. The *Third Symphony*, written in memory of President Kennedy, is the most impressive of all, and is here recorded in a revised version which concentrates the original concept of a dialogue between man and God, a challenge from earth to heaven. The revision has a male speaker instead of female, and the result is less self-conscious. These performances with the Israel Philharmonic are not always quite as polished or forceful as those Bernstein recorded earlier in New York, but with excellent recording they never fail to reflect the warmth of Bernstein's writing.

Songfest (cycle of American poems for 6 singers and orch.).
*** DG 2531 044 [id.]. Dale, Elias, Williams, Rosenshein, Reardon, Gramm, Nat. SO of Washington, composer.

Songfest, one of Bernstein's most richly varied works, is a sequence of poems which ingeniously uses all six singers solo and in various combinations. Not only the plan but the writing too is ingenious, one song using strict serialism in the most approachable, idiomatically American way. Characteristically, Bernstein often chooses controversial words to set, and by his personal fervour welds a very disparate group of pieces together into a warmly satisfying whole, comparable with Britten's *Serenade*, *Nocturne* or *Spring symphony*. Outstanding performance and recording.

Berwald, Franz (1796–1868)

Symphonies Nos. 1 in G min. (Sérieuse); 2 in D (Capricieuse); 3 in C (Singulière); 4 in E flat. (i) Piano concerto in D. (ii) Violin concerto in C sharp min. Overtures: Estrella di Soria; The Queen of Golconda. Tone poems: Festival of the Bayadères; Play of the Elves; Racing; Reminiscences from the Norwegian Mountains; Serious and Joyful Fancies.
**(*) HMV SLS 5096 (4) [Ang. S 6113]. RPO, Björlin, with (i) Migdal, (ii) Tellefsen.

Piano concerto; Violin concerto; Play of the Elves; Serious and Joyful Fancies.
*** EMI 7C 061 35471 (from above set).

All Berwald's important orchestral music is here. The four symphonies come from the brief outburst of creative activity in the first half of the 1840s after his marriage, and most of the tone poems are of the same period. The *Violin concerto in C sharp minor* is much earlier, dating from 1820, when Berwald was still active as a violinist. It is a slight but pleasing work, by no means so individual as the *G minor Quartet* of 1818, but well worth hearing, particularly when it is as persuasively played as it is here by the Norwegian violinist Arve Tellefsen. It explores no great depths and its melodic invention is somewhat bland, but there is a good deal of charm to commend it. The *Piano concerto*, a late work dating from the mid-1850s, is a strange piece. The soloist plays throughout: there is not a bar's rest, and the score bears a note to the effect that the concerto can be performed without orchestra. Marian Migdal, a Polish-born pianist, plays it with poetry, sensitivity and panache; he is scrupulous in his observance of dynamic markings, and his command of keyboard colour is most impressive. So, too, is his handling of rubato, which is most musical and natural. Playing that is so affectionate and perceptive cannot fail to win friends for this concerto, which in spite of its Chopinesque gestures has a quiet and persuasive individuality.

Berwald's reputation rests largely on the symphonies, however, and they possess a refreshing vigour and an imaginative vitality that step well outside the comparatively pale atmosphere of the Scandinavian musical world of the 1840s. Their originality in matters of form is well known; what cannot be too often stressed is that all four have a sparkle and freshness of vision that deserve wider recognition and a more secure foothold in the international repertoire. The tone poems are wholly neglected, but their invention is often captivating. Both they and the two opera overtures are full of resourceful and finely drawn ideas, and their transparent and bright textures enhance their appeal.

Obviously this is a self-recommending set and it would be good to commend it without reservation, for the music deserves every support. However, Ulf Björlin does not fully succeed in drawing from the RPO playing of the highest order. There is a certain want of tension in shaping melodic lines and a certain limpness of direction. Ehrling and the LSO are more vital and alert in the *Singulière* and the E flat symphony, and much the same can be said of Dorati and the Stockholm Philharmonic on RCA in the *Capricieuse*. Nevertheless there is far too much to admire in the tone poems and the concertos to allow such considerations too great a weight. Moreover the EMI engineers have given the set a splendid recording, and in its way this is an indispensable issue. The separate EMI import issue containing the two concertos and two short orchestral works is the more welcome in view of these reservations, and it is to be hoped that the other tone poems will follow.

Grand septet in B flat.
*** CRD CRD 1044/*CRDC 4044*. Nash Ens. – HUMMEL: *Septet.****

Berwald's only *Septet* is a work of genuine quality and deserves a secure place in the repertory instead of on its periphery. It dates from 1828 and is for the same forces as the Beethoven and Kreutzer *Septets*; the invention is lively and the ideas have charm. It is eminently well played by the Nash Ensemble and finely recorded. The cassette (as is usual with CRD) is an altogether excellent transfer, matching the disc closely.

String quartet in G min.
*** CRD CRD 1061/*CRDC 4061*. Chilingirian Qt – WIKMANSON: *Quartet.****

Berwald composed four quartets: two in 1849 after the symphonies, and two in his mid-twenties. The *G minor Quartet*, and a companion in B flat which has not survived, date from 1818. This work did not appear in print until the 1940s, when the parts of the middle movements were discovered during stocktaking at the Royal Swedish Academy of Music. It is, as one would expect from an accomplished violinist, a remarkably assured piece, and the first movement is full of modulatory audacities. If the thematic substance has not the same quality of inspiration as in Arriaga's quartets, it is still both characterful and appealing. The trio of the scherzo has a touching charm that is almost Schubertian, though it is impossible that Berwald could have been aware of his great contemporary. This is a highly interesting and often bold quartet, and the Chilingirian players give a well-shaped and sensitive account of it. They are truthfully recorded, and the coupling – another Swedish quartet – enhances the attractions of this issue. The cassette transfer is outstandingly fresh and clear. Strongly recommended.

Biber, Heinrich (1644–1704)

Battalia in D; Fidicinium sacro-profanum: Sonata No. 8 in B flat; Country churchgoing sonata in B flat; Sonata in D min.
(M) **(*) DG Arc. Priv. 2547/3347 004. VCM, Harnoncourt – MUFFAT: *Exquisitioris harmoniae.***(*)

Heinrich Biber, a Bohemian musician who made his reputation in Vienna and Salzburg, was an acclaimed virtuoso on the violin as well as a composer. His *Country churchgoing sonata* is an engagingly 'descriptive' Sunday-morning village scene, while the more famous *Battle* simulation has attractively ingenious special effects. The *Sonata in D minor* includes a solo trombone within the basic group of strings and continuo. All this music is well played and effectively projected, using instruments of the period, and, although it is uneven, its best moments are undoubtedly lively and imaginative. Good recording and a fairly high-level cassette, not quite so refined as the disc.

Binchois, Gilles de
(*c.* 1400–1460)

Motets: *Agnus Dei; Asperges me; Gloria, laus et honor; Veni creator spiritus.*
(*) DG Arc. 2533 404 [id.]. L. Pro Cantione Antiqua, Turner – BUSNOIS: *Mass.***

Binchois flourished during the period of Philip the Good (1420–67) and is among the greatest of the Burgundians. These four motets vindicate his reputation as a composer of church music, and though his chansons have enjoyed eminence, this less well-known material is revealed as masterly and inspired. The performances could be more persuasive were they a shade more natural and relaxed, but for the most part they give great pleasure. Of greater concern is the quality of the recording, cut at far too high a level. However, this is an admirable introduction to this repertoire and to music of the Burgundian court.

Birtwistle, Harrison
(born 1934)

Punch and Judy (opera).
*** Decca HEAD 24/5 [id.]. Bryn-Julson, DeGaetani, Langridge, Roberts, Wilson-Johnson, Tomlinson, L. Sinf., Atherton.

Punch and Judy is a brutal ritualistic piece, 'the first modern English opera' as it was called when it first appeared at the Aldeburgh Festival in 1968. Characteristically, in setting the traditional puppet story Birtwistle has adopted a sharp, abrasive style, the more angular because Stephen Pruslin's libretto has a stylized patterning based on nursery rhymes and children's games. It may not make easy listening, but it is not easy to forget either, for behind the aggressiveness Birtwistle's writing has a way of touching an emotional chord, just as Stravinsky's so often does. Heard on record, Punch's war-cry and first murder (his wife Judy battered to death) have an impact that reminds one of the shower-bath murder in the film *Psycho*, itself intensified by music. Stephen Roberts is outstanding as Punch, and among the others there is not a single weak link. David Atherton, conductor from the first performances, excels himself with the Sinfonietta. Clear vivid recording.

Bizet, Georges (1838–75)

L'Arlésienne (incidental music): suites Nos. 1–2; *Carmen: suites Nos. 1–2.*
**(*) Ph. 9500 566/*7300 715* [id.]. ASMF, Marriner.
(M) **(*) Ph. Seq. 6527/*7311* 083. LOP, Markevitch.

L'Arlésienne: suites Nos. 1–2; Carmen: suite No. 1.
❀ (M) *** HMV SXLP/*TC-SXLP* 30276. RPO, Beecham.
*** DG 2531/*3301* 329 [id.]. LSO, Abbado.

L'Arlésienne: suites Nos. 1–2; Jeux d'enfants.
**(*) Decca SXL/*KSXC* 6903 [Lon. 7127]. Cleveland O., Maazel.
** CBS Dig. 36713. Toronto SO, Andrew Davis.

Carmen: suites Nos. 1–2.
(*) Telarc Dig. DG 10048 [id.]. St Louis SO, Slatkin – GRIEG: *Peer Gynt.*(*)

Among recent couplings of *L'Arlésienne* and *Carmen*, Abbado's DG recording with the LSO stands out. The orchestral playing is characteristically refined, the wind solos cultured and elegant, especially in *L'Arlésienne*, where the pacing of the music is nicely judged. A vibrant accelerando at the end of the *Farandole* only serves to emphasize the obvious spontaneity of the music-making. There is warmth too, of course, and in the opening *Prélude* of the *Carmen* suite plenty of spirit. With vivid, truthful recording, this is very attractive. The sound of the cassette is virtually identical with that of the disc, though there is a very slight loss of transient bite on side two.

Maazel's Cleveland coupling of *L'Arlésienne* and the delightful *Jeux d'enfants* is also outstanding. Maazel coaxes some

real pianissimo playing from the Cleveland Orchestra, who respond to this music with relish. They are especially good in *Jeux d'enfants*; its miniature qualities and colour are engagingly caught, and the closing *Galop* is delightfully vivacious. Maazel chooses fast tempi in *L'Arlésienne*, and the famous saxophone solo in the *Prélude* does not achieve the haunting quality famous in the Beecham version. But the Decca recording is extremely vivid, and the cassette is only marginally less crisp than the disc.

Andrew Davis's similar coupling is disappointing. It is all well played, and the digital recording – if a little artificial in balance – is impressively firm and brilliant. But there is a curious lack of vivacity, although *Jeux d'enfants* has more sparkle than *L'Arlésienne*.

Marriner's collection is generous, offering eleven items from *Carmen* and both *L'Arlésienne* suites, missing out only the *Intermezzo* from the second. The recording too is attractively rich and naturally balanced. But the musical characterization – in spite of fine LSO solo playing, notably from the flautist, Peter Lloyd – is sometimes lacking in flair and indeed *brio*. There are minor touches of eccentricity – Marriner's tempo suddenly quickens for the middle section of the *Minuet* from the *Second L'Arlésienne* suite, and although there is much to ravish the ear, the orchestrations of the vocal numbers from *Carmen* are not always convincing. The cassette transfer is good; there is some lack of glitter, and the inner focus of fortissimos is less sharp than on disc.

The Telarc digital recordings of the *Carmen* orchestral suites made in St Louis have a self-conscious glittering brilliance. But there is a natural perspective, and the orchestral colour is very telling, helped by good playing, if with no special sophistication. Audiophiles will undoubtedly respond to the range and vividness of the sound: the only snag is that the bass drum is over-recorded and muddies the texture at one or two climaxes. The pressing itself is immaculate.

In the medium price-range Markevitch's selection is well played and vividly characterized. The recording is rich and colourful, rather more reverberant in *Carmen* than in *L'Arlésienne*, which is brighter and more forwardly balanced on disc and cassette alike.

However, Beecham's performances have been successfully reissued on HMV and they have a very special place in the catalogue. Besides the beauty and unique character of the wind solos, Beecham's deliciously sprightly *Minuet* from *L'Arlésienne* and his gently affectionate way with the lovely *Adagietto* are irresistibly persuasive, as is the characteristic swagger in the opening *Carmen Prélude*, the cymbals marvellously telling. The recording sounds astonishingly full and vivid, and there is no appreciable difference between disc and cassette (the transients just marginally sharper on the former, the latter displaying slightly more fullness).

Symphony in C.
(M) *** HMV SXLP/*TC-SXLP* 30260 [(d) Ang S 60192], French Nat. RO, Beecham BERLIOZ: *Troyens; excerpts*; DELIBES: *Le Roi s'amuse.****
(M) **(*) CBS 60112/40- [Col. MY 36725], NYPO, Bernstein – PROKOFIEV: *Symphony No. 1 etc.***

Symphony in C; Jeux d'enfants.
*** Ph. 9500 443/7300 649 [id.]. Concg. O., Haitink.

Symphony in C; Jeux d'enfants: La Jolie Fille de Perth: suite.
(M) **(*) DG Priv. 2535/3335 238 [id.]. ORTF O., Martinon.

Marriner's Academy performance of Bizet's *Symphony*, beautifully played and recorded (Argo ZRG/*KZRC* 719), still holds its place at the top of the list, but Beecham's reissued version from the beginning of the sixties is no less attractive if the couplings are suitable. No one has ever quite matched Sir Thomas in the way he brought out the spring-like qualities in this youthful work. The playing of the French orchestra is not quite so polished as that of Marriner's group, but Beecham's panache more than makes amends, and the slow movement is delightful. The resonant recording still sounds well and it has been successfully transferred to cassette.

Haitink's version is also very fine, though the Philips coupling is not very generous. His reading obviously takes into account the reverberant Amsterdam acoustic, for it is essentially broad and spacious. The slow movement is particularly eloquent, with a beautiful oboe solo. *Jeux d'enfants* is also delectably played. First-rate Philips recording, slightly less crisp on tape than on disc.

Bernstein's CBS recording has been remastered, and though it is still rather brightly lit it can be made to yield a satisfactory balance. The performance is characteristically brilliant, and the high spirits of the orchestral response bring a sense of exhilaration which is especially attractive in the last two movements. The slow movement is affectionately done, with a fine oboe solo, the contrast in the middle section heightened by the precision of the playing. Originally this was coupled with *The Sorcerer's Apprentice* as well as the Prokofiev; now the measure is slightly shorter.

Although Martinon's performance has not quite the magic of the Marriner or Beecham accounts, it is still very good indeed, and the couplings make this a most attractive proposition. Although the recording is not quite as transparent as in Ansermet's Decca version of this coupling, available on disc but not as yet on cassette, the orchestral playing under Martinon has just that extra charm and sparkle that make all the difference.

Te Deum.

(M) ** Turn. TVS 37134 [Can. 31104].
Lovaas, Jerusalem, Philh. Vocal Ens.,
Stuttgart PO, Zanotelli – POULENC:
*Gloria.***

Bizet's *Te Deum* is a student work, not
at all typical of the mature composer, but
with excellent soloists (the tenor, Siegfried Jerusalem, then a striking newcomer making one of his first recordings)
and energetic conducting, it makes a
good coupling for the Poulenc *Gloria.*
The recording is lively and quite clear,
even if the balance leaves something to
be desired.

OPERA

Carmen (complete).

*** DG 2709 083/*3371 040* (3) [id.]. Berganza, Domingo, Cotrubas, Milnes,
Amb. S., LSO, Abbado.

Superbly disciplined, Abbado's performance nails its colours to the mast at
the very start in a breathtakingly fast
account of the opening prelude. Through
the four acts there are other examples of
idiosyncratic tempi, but the whole entertainment hangs together with keen compulsion, reflecting the fact that these
same performers – Sherrill Milnes as
Escamillo excepted – took part in the
Edinburgh Festival production directly
associated with this recording project.
Conductor and orchestra can take a large
share of credit for the performance's success, for though the singing is never less
than enjoyable, it is on the whole less
characterful than on some rival sets.
Teresa Berganza is a seductive if somewhat unsmiling Carmen – not without
sensuality, and producing consistently
beautiful tone, but lacking some of the
flair which makes for a three-dimensional
portrait. If you want a restrained and
thoughtful view, then Tatiana Troyanos
in Solti's set (see below), also opposite the
admirably consistent Placido Domingo,

is preferable. Ileana Cotrubas as Micaela
is not always as sweetly steady as she can
be; Milnes makes a heroic matador. The
spoken dialogue is excellently produced,
and the sound is vivid, betraying not at
all that the sessions took place in different
studios (in London as well as Edinburgh). The focus on cassette is less sharp
than on disc.

Still recommended: Solti's brilliant
Decca set with Troyanos, Domingo and
Van Dam holds its place at the top of the
list (Decca D 11 D 3/*K 11 K 33* [Lon.
13115/5-]). Beecham's set with Los
Angeles also has a special place in the
catalogue (HMV SLS/*TC-SLS* 5021
[Ang. S 3613]).

Carmen: highlights.

*** Decca SET/*KCET* 621. Troyanos,
Domingo, Van Dam, Te Kanawa,
John Alldis Ch., LPO, Solti.

(M) *** HMV Green. ESD/*TC-ESD*
7047. [Ang. S 35818]. Los Angeles,
Gedda, Micheau, Blanc, French R.
Ch. and O., Beecham.

*** DG 2537/*3306* 049 (from above set
cond. Abbado).

(M) ** Decca SPA/*KCSP* 539. Resnik,
Del Monaco, Sutherland, Krause,
Geneva Ch., SRO, Schippers.

Any collection of 'highlights' from
Carmen is bound to leave out favourite
items, but the selection from Solti's
sharply characterful set is generous and
the recording is superb on disc and cassette alike.

Beecham's compilation, on HMV's
Greensleeve label, has the advantage of
economy and is a delightful collection of
plums from Bizet's masterly score. The
sound is excellent, though the tape is
slightly less refined than the disc.

The DG selection is not as generous
as some but it makes a good sampler of
Abbado's forceful, sharply etched reading, with first-rate recording (although
the tape is less cleanly focused than the
disc).

On Decca's cheapest label the excerpts

from the Schippers version are worth considering for the contribution of Joan Sutherland as Micaela. Resnik is a characterful Carmen, but the microphone is not always kind to the voice, and Del Monaco is a coarse Don José.

Carmen: highlights (sung in English). Act 1: Prelude; Habañera; Duet; Seguidilla. Act 2: Toreador Song; Quintet; Duet Flower Song and Finale. Act 3: Card Trio; Micaela's Aria.
(M) **(*) HMV Green. ESD/TC-ESD 7081. Johnson, Smith, Herincx, Robson, Hunter, Greene, Stoddart, Moyle, Sadler's Wells O., Colin Davis.

This was one of the most successful of the Sadler's Wells discs, thanks both to the forceful conducting of Sir Colin Davis and to the rich-voiced, reliable singing of Patricia Johnson as Carmen. Nor is Johnson reliable and no more: time and again her phrasing is most imaginative and memorable. It is good that the microphone catches her voice so well. Donald Smith, the Don José, was criticized in his stage performances for stiff acting, but on record he provides a wonderfully attractive, ringing tone. The selection is well made, and the ensemble work has the authentic enthusiasm of a live performance. The recording is very lively, but on cassette there is some peakiness on the voices on the first side.

Les Pêcheurs de perles (complete).
** HMV SLS/TC-SLS 5113 [Ang. SX/4X2X 3856]. Cotrubas, Vanzo, Sarabia, Soyer, Paris Op. Ch. and O., Prêtre.

A modern version of this most atmospheric opera was certainly needed, but Prêtre's set is a mixed success. Ileana Cotrubas is superb as the high priestess, Leila, projecting character as well as singing beautifully. The tenor, Alain

Vanzo, is also most stylish, but after that the snags begin, not just with the singing (Sarabia a variably focused baritone) but with the conducting (Prêtre is generally fast, unlilting and unfeeling) and with the recording (not sufficiently atmospheric). In principle it may seem a positive gain to have the original 1863 score reinstated, but it is hard not to feel disappointed when the great duet for the pearlfishers culminates not in a rich reprise of the big melody but in a tinkly little waltz theme. The cassettes are well managed, smooth and detailed.

Les Pêcheurs de perles: highlights.
(M) *(*) HMV SXLP/TC-SXLP 30304. Micheau, Gedda, Blanc, Paris Opéra-Comique Ch. and O., Dervaux –
GOUNOD: Roméo: highlights *(*)

Gedda and Blanc are in ringing voice for the pearlfishers' duet, but it is not a subtle reading, and too many of these excerpts from a not very distinguished complete set are similarly disappointing. But as a medium-price selection, interestingly coupled, it may be worth considering. Early-sixties recording, fair for its period.

Blackford, Richard
(born 1954)

Sir Gawain and the Green Knight (opera).
*** Argo ZK 85. Huehns, Hitching, Spooner, Earle, Flowers, Handel Op. Ch., Ch. and O. of Royal College of Music Junior Dept, composer.

Commissioned for the villagers of Blewbury in Berkshire to perform, this simple adaptation of Arthurian romance has an immediate attraction, with freshly inventive music simple enough for amateurs to sing. Here, with some professional stiffening, the performance is more apt for record, and the sound is first-rate.

Blake, David (born 1936)

(i) *Violin concerto;* (ii) *In Praise of Krishna.*
*** Argo ZRG 922. (i) Iona Brown, Philh. O., Del Mar; (ii) Cahill, Northern Sinfonia, composer.

The lyricism of Blake's *Violin concerto* within a broadly serial framework, together with challenging bravura, reflect the qualities of the dedicatee, Iona Brown, who here gives a passionately committed performance. Each of the two movements is sharply divided into contrasted halves, slow–fast followed by fast–slow, with the art and landscape of Italy a direct inspiration. The cantata to Bengali words, *In Praise of Krishna*, is even more sensuous in its idiom, with Teresa Cahill a sweet-toned soloist.

Bliss, Arthur (1891–1975)

Adam Zero (ballet); *suite. Checkmate* (ballet): *suite.*
*** HMV ASD/*TC-ASD* 3687. Royal Liv. PO, Handley.

Checkmate: 5 Dances.
(*) Chan. ABR/*ABT* 1018. W. Australian SO, Schönzeler – RUBBRA: *Symphony No. 5.*(*)

Checkmate was Arthur Bliss's first ballet score and was composed for the Royal Ballet's first visit to Paris in 1937. The idea of a ballet based on chess, with all its opportunities for symbolism and heraldic splendour, appealed to Bliss,

and the score he produced remains one of his most inventive creations. The HMV issue, following the precedent the composer himself set in compiling an orchestral suite, omits the main body of the action preceding the final checkmate. The *Adam Zero* music is more extensively represented, spilling over to the second side; and much of its invention seems empty nowadays. Yet Vernon Handley makes out the strongest case for both scores and secures playing of great spirit from the Liverpool orchestra. The EMI engineers produce finely detailed and full-blooded sound. Admirers of Bliss's music need not hesitate here and though *Adam Zero* may not show his muse at its most fertile, there are still good things in it. Excellent tape transfers, vivid, full and clear.

The five dances on the Chandos issue are well played under Hans-Hubert Schönzeler, and otherwise not represented in the catalogue at present. (Nor, for that matter, is the coupling, Edmund Rubbra's *Fifth Symphony*.) If the performance is not in the very first flight, it is still well worth having. The cassette transfer of the Bliss is made at a low level and the sound is disappointing, with poor transients.

(i) *Piano concerto. March of Homage; Welcome the Queen.*
*** Uni. Kanchana Dig. DKP 9006. Royal Liv. PO, Atherton, (i) with Fowke.

The concerto was written for British Week at the New York World Fair in 1939, and Bliss attempted a bravura work on a very large scale. From the dashing double octaves at the start the pianistic style throughout has much of Rachmaninov and Liszt in it, though the idiom is very much Bliss's own, with some of his most memorable material. It is a work which needs a passionately committed soloist, and that is what it finds here in Philip Fowke, urgent and expressive, well matched by David Atherton and the Liverpool orchestra. The two occasional pieces are given lively performances and full-blooded sound. The digital recording is full and vivid, with the piano naturally balanced, less forward than is common. There is a tendency for the acoustic to be a shade over-resonant in the concerto (especially noticeable at the opening), which produces less internal clarity of focus than one expects with a digital master. But this is a first-class and rewarding issue.

A Colour symphony; Things to Come (incidental music for H. G. Wells film).
*** HMV ASD 3416. RPO, Groves.

Bliss's *Colour symphony* dates from 1922, and this is its first recording since the composer's own, made in the mid-1950s. Inspired by a chance encounter with a book on heraldry, Bliss conceived this series of mood pictures on the theme of the symbolic meanings associated with the primary colours. The work is too episodic to be truly symphonic but it is nonetheless highly effective and is expertly scored. It comes into its own in this sympathetic performance. *Things to Come* is given in an extended form admirably assembled by Christopher Palmer, who has also scored the opening *Prologue*, since the full score and parts do not survive. This work dates more than the *Symphony* and its style is at times somewhat eclectic. But its invention is always attractive, and the splendid *March* offers what is perhaps the single most memorable idea to come from the pen of its composer. Sir Charles Groves and the RPO are splendid advocates, and the HMV engineers lavish on it their richest and most natural sound. Admirers of Bliss need not hesitate.

Discourse for orchestra; Meditations

on a theme by John Blow; Overture Edinburgh.
*** HMV ASD 3878. CBSO, Handley.

Discourse was a commission from the Louisville Orchestra in 1957, which Bliss subsequently revised for larger orchestra in the mid-1960s. Like the *Edinburgh overture* (1956), it shows Bliss in extrovert but by no means unappealing mood: only the brash ending lets it down. By far the most substantial and worthwhile of these three works is *Meditations on a theme by John Blow*, which is given a persuasive and committed reading that even surpasses the earlier Lyrita version recorded by the same orchestra under Hugo Rignold. Admirers of the composer should not miss this issue and they can be assured of the technical excellence of the recording.

Morning Heroes.
(M) **(*) HMV Green. ESD/*TC-ESD* 7133. Westbrook (narrator), Royal Liv. PO and Ch., Groves.

Morning Heroes is an elegiac work, written as a tribute to the composer's brother and all who fell in the First World War. The sincerity of the writing is never in doubt, but there is less contrast here than in comparable war-inspired works by Vaughan Williams and Britten. One misses both the anger of those other composers and their passages of total simplicity, but it is good that one of Bliss's most ambitious works should be available in so strong a performance. Good recording and an excellent cassette, expansive like the disc, with an excellent choral focus.

Bloch, Ernest (1880–1959)

Concerto grosso for strings with piano obbligato.

*** HMV ASD 3732 [Ang. S 37577]. Grier, ASMF, Marriner – MARTIN: *Petite symphonie concertante.***

Bloch's *Concerto grosso* once enjoyed great popularity, and its neoclassicism still has strong appeal. The Academy of St Martin-in-the-Fields bring to it a splendidly alert ensemble, and Francis Grier is the excellent pianist; the recording strikes an admirable balance between strings and piano without any attempt to give the latter concerto-soloist status. This may not be one of Bloch's most deeply personal works but it is thoroughly enjoyable, and is not otherwise available.

(i) *Schelomo (Hebraic rhapsody for cello and orchestra);* (ii) *Suite for viola and orchestra.*
(M) ** Turn. TVS 34622 [id.]. (i) Varga, Westphalian SO, Landau; (ii) Katims, Seattle SO, Siegl.

The viola is forwardly balanced in the *Suite*, and at times the evocative orchestral score is masked; the orchestra itself is admirably balanced and the acoustic warm and open. The *Suite* dates from 1919 and was originally written for viola and piano. It is highly atmospheric and colourful, though at times just a little diffuse. This is its only recording at present, and the thirty minutes' duration involves a slightly lower-level cut than is ideal. *Schelomo*, which occupies the second side, runs into much stiffer competition. But Varga's playing is totally committed, and the more vivid recording brings the orchestra into better focus. Rostropovich brings greater fervour and personality to the score, and there is a wonderfully ecstatic quality there that makes his version (HMV ASD 3334 [Ang. S 37256]) well worth the extra outlay. Given that proviso, those wanting this particular coupling can rest assured that this is a good performance of no mean character.

Suite hébraïque for viola and orchestra.
(M) * Turn. TVS 34687 [id.]. Thompson, Boston MIT SO, Epstein – HINDEMITH: *Viola concerto;* MARTIN: *Sonata da chiesa.**

Bloch's work is not so generously represented that one can afford to overlook any addition to the catalogue. But this account of his *Suite hébraïque*, which dates from the 1950s, is so lacklustre as to do his cause scant justice. The sound is edgy and the soloist, though obviously musical, is not a strong enough personality to carry the day. A workmanlike but ultimately uninspired reading.

Sacred service.
** Chan. ABR/ABT 1001. Berkman, L. Chorale and Concord Singers, LSO, Simon.

Bloch's *Sacred Service* has been neglected by the gramophone since the composer's own pioneering record and Leonard Bernstein's version made in the 1960s (still available in the US [Col. MS 6221] but not in the UK). Its reappearance in the catalogue must be welcomed, particularly in such vivid sound. The singing is perhaps wanting in ardour and intensity, and there could be greater attention to dynamic nuances. However, it would be unfair to dwell on the shortcomings of this performance in the light of so much that is good, not least of which is the orchestral playing. The recording is spacious and well focused. The cassette too is a distinct success and well balanced, although its upper range is slightly restricted compared with the disc.

Blow, John (1649–1708)

Organ voluntary in A; Echo voluntary

in G; Evening service in G; Let thy
hand be strengthened; O pray for the
peace of Jerusalem; Salvator mundi.
** Mer. E 77013. Ely Cath. Ch., Wills
(organ) – PURCELL: Collection.**

As Purcell's mentor (both preceding
and succeeding him as organist at Westminster Abbey), Blow was a master of
English church music, overshadowed
though he was by his pupil. This single
side of anthems and voluntaries is a good
successor to the fine Blow record from
King's College Choir (Argo ZRG 767,
recently deleted), though it cannot match
it in polish or finesse. Good atmospheric
recording, but the organ balance is variable.

Boccherini, Luigi
(1743–1805)

Cello concerto in B flat (arr. Grütz-
macher; see also below).
(M) ** DG Arc. Priv. 2547/3347 046 [(d)
2535/3335 179]. Fournier, Lucerne
Festival Strings, Baumgartner – TAR-
TINI and VIVALDI: Concertos.**

Fournier plays splendidly; the slow
movement is beautifully done, and the
finale maintains the same level. He is
recorded, however, with a balance that
gives a nasal quality to the cello's upper
register and exaggerates the upper partials. A strong treble cut is needed. This
fault is much less insistent on the tape,
which otherwise has both life and
warmth: a clear case where the sound
on the cassette is preferable to the
disc.

Cello concerto No. 2 in D.
*** DG 2530/3300 974. [id.]. Ros-
tropovich, Zürich Coll. Mus., Sacher –
TARTINI and VIVALDI: Concertos.***

Cello concertos Nos. 2; 3 in G.
*** Erato STU 71369. Lodéon, Lausanne CO, Jordan.

Although essentially a performance in
the grand manner (with Rostropovich
providing his own cadenzas), the music-
making in the DG issue also has tremendous vitality, with extremely lively outer
movements to balance the eloquence of
the Adagio. The forceful nature of the
performance is short on charm and so
perhaps a little out of character for an
essentially elegant composer like Boccherini; but Rostropovich is so compelling that reservations are swept aside. He
is given an alert accompaniment by
Sacher, and the recording has fine body
and presence. The tape transfer too has
excellent range and detail.

Frédéric Lodéon is a young French
player, barely thirty years of age, and
obviously an artist of accomplishment.
His playing has genuine style and real
eloquence, and in the G major Concerto,
unearthed by Maurice Gendron, he is
wonderfully fresh and fervent. The Lausanne orchestra gives him excellent support, but the balance does tend to favour
the soloist. That apart, there is little to
fault in these performances of music that
has more to commend it than meets the
eye; the slow movement of the D major
concerto has genuine tenderness and
depth.

Cello concertos Nos. 9 in B flat (original version); 10 in D, Op. 34.
*** Erato STU 70997. Lodéon, Bournemouth Sinf., Guschlbauer.

Frédéric Lodéon gives us the original
version of the famous B flat Concerto, a
totally different work from the Grützmacher, which such artists as Fournier
(see above) and Jacqueline du Pré have
recorded. (Grützmacher totally redrafted
the outer movements, using material
from other Boccherini pieces; his middle
movement was drawn from yet another
source and is even less related to the

original.) Lodéon plays splendidly in both this and the *D major Concerto* on the reverse (which is not to be confused with the *D major Concerto* above). Thoroughly musical playing throughout from the Bournemouth Sinfonietta and well-balanced recorded sound; this is a most desirable issue.

Sinfonia in D min. (La Casa del Diavolo), Op. 12/4; Sinfonia in D min., Op. 41.
** Erato STU 70828. Sol. Ven., Scimone.

The *Sinfonia La Casa del Diavolo* includes material on which Gluck's *Don Juan* ballet draws, and whose *Sturm und Drang* credentials are not in doubt. Neither the quality of performance here nor the recording can be said to match that of Leppard's Philharmonia account (now deleted), for I Solisti Veneti have not their sonority and polish. The other symphony is an interesting piece, however, not otherwise available, and this issue retains a claim on collectors in this field.

Guitar quintets Nos. 1–7, G.446/51; 9, G.453.
*** Ph. 6768 268 (3). Pepe Romero, Iona Brown, Latchem, Shingles, Vigay.

Boccherini wrote or arranged twelve *Guitar quintets*, but only the present eight have survived, plus another version of G.448. Although some of the music is bland it is nearly all agreeably tuneful in an unostentatious way, and there are some highly imaginative touches, with attractive hints of melancholy and underlying passion. These performances by Pepe Romero (often willing to take a relatively minor role) and members of the ASMF Chamber Group are wholly admirable, and Philips are especially good at balancing textures of this kind in the most natural way, the guitar able to be assertive when required without over-balancing the ensemble. This is a delightfully undemanding set to dip into in the late evening.

Guitar quintets Nos. 1 in D min.; 2 in E, G. 445/6; 7 in E min., G. 451.
*** Ph. 9500/7300 985 [id.] (from above set).

All three quintets here were reworked by the composer from piano quintets. The guitar's role is for the most part a subsidiary one, although it often adds spice to the texture (as is apparent near the very beginning of No. 7, which opens the recital). There are touches of blandness, but there are attractive movements in all three works. G.446 has a *Polacca* for its finale, but the most consistently inventive piece is the *E minor Quintet*, G.451. The performances are unfailingly warm and sensitive, and the recording is first-class, with an immaculate cassette.

Guitar quintets Nos. 3 in B flat, G. 447; 9 in C (La Ritirata di Madrid), G. 453.
*** Ph. 9500 789/7300 861 [id.] (from above set).

Both works here are arrangements. No. 3 comes from the *Piano quintet*, Op. 57/2; the first three movements of No. 9 originate in the *Piano quintet*, Op. 56/3, and the finale which gives it its subtitle, *La Ritirata di Madrid*, is familiar from a string quintet, Op. 30/6. This picturesque evocation of Spanish life is created with a set of twelve short variations set in a long, slow crescendo, followed by a similarly graduated decrescendo, a kind of Spanish patrol with the 'night watch' disappearing into the distance at the close. Both works are melodically engaging in Boccherini's elegant rococo style, and they are beautifully played and recorded, the guitar balanced within the string group, yet able to dominate when required. The cassette needs a bass cut, then matches the disc fairly closely, although the sound is slightly less transparent.

Guitar quintets Nos. 4 in D (Fandango); 5 in D; 6 in G, G. 448/50.
*** Ph. 9500 621/7300 737 [id.] (from above set).

Guitar quintets Nos. 5-6, G. 449/50.
*** CBS Dig. 36671/41-. Williams, L. Qt
– GUASTAVINO: *Las Presencias.* ***

Two of the *Quintets* recorded here are new to the gramophone: the *D major*, and *G major*, Nos. 449–50 in the Gérard catalogue. Both are arrangements of other works made for the benefit of the Marquis of Benavent, and only in the *D major* does the guitar emerge into the foreground. Boccherini's music often reveals unsuspected depths and has a melancholy and pathos that colours its polite discourse in subtle but memorable ways. The three quintets on the Philips issue show him at his most bland, and though they make pleasant listening, they possess no darker undercurrents. The performances are thoroughly effective and are well recorded. The cassette, though smooth and well balanced, has some loss of range at the top (the transfer level is unadventurous, in spite of the modest instrumentation).

On CBS the two quintets G. 449/50 are impeccably played, though the recording favours a rather forward balance, with little acoustic ambience. The sound is most musically judged and reproduces a fully acceptable result, though the effect is more natural if reproduced at a lower level setting than normal, since the digital recording is cut at a high level. The high-level chrome tape transfer has plenty of range; although there is a slight over-emphasis at the bass end, the treble is fresh and bright. Good performances, though the rival Romero set offers the advantage of a third Boccherini quintet rather than the somewhat uninteresting Guastavino fill-up.

6 Oboe quintets, Op. 45.
(M) *** Argo ZK 93. Francis, Allegri Qt.
An attractive medium-price record. These quintets, written in 1797, were published as Op. 45 though Boccherini's own catalogue lists them as 55. They have a sunny grace that is altogether beguiling, and a gentle, wistful lyricism that is unfailing in its appeal. Excellent playing and recording.

String quartets: in D; in E flat, Op. 6/1 and 3; in E flat, Op. 58/2.
*** Ph. 9500 305 [id.]. Italian Qt.

The Italian Quartet recorded the *D major Quartet*, Op. 6/1, in the days of 78s, when they were still known as the 'New Italian Quartet', and were rightly hailed for their freshness and refinement of tone as well as their wide dynamic range. They include this and another from the same set – a remarkably beautiful piece it is, too – plus a much later quartet from the 1790s. Boccherini is all too readily dismissed as *la femme de Haydn*, but underneath the surface charm and elegance that one associates with him, there are deeper currents and an altogether special pathos to disturb the attentive listener. The Italian Quartet give excellently vital and sensitive performances and they are eminently well recorded, even if the sound image could with advantage be more recessed.

String quartets, Op. 32/1–6.
*** Tel. EK 6.35337 (2). Esterhazy Qt.

There are more than 130 Boccherini quintets, and his fecundity in the quartet medium is scarcely less. This set dates from 1780, about the same period as Haydn's Op. 33. They may, ultimately, lack the depth and vision of Haydn and Mozart, but to listen to this set is to be amazed that music of this quality has been so long neglected. Its originality and the quality of the inspiration, its freshness and grace, can scarcely be exaggerated, and these performances, on original period instruments, are both committed and authoritative, with no want of charm to boot. This is a thoroughly rewarding set and is beautifully recorded.

String quintets: in C min., Op. 31/4; in D, Op. 40/2; in G min., Op. 42/4.
*** Tel. AW 6.42353 [id.]. Esterhazy Qt, Van der Meer.

Generally speaking, Boccherini's quintets are winners; the invention is consistently inspired and the textures have warmth and variety of interest. These are mellifluous in sonority and could hardly be played with greater eloquence and charm. Boccherini often hides pathos beneath a surface of apparent blandness, and these artists seem fully aware of the undercurrents beneath the well-mannered surface. The quality of the recording is excellent, and the surfaces smooth.

String trios Nos. 1–6.
*** HM HM 2375. Ferraras, Molinaro, Pocaterra.

Boccherini was enormously prolific but these six trios were his very first work. He called them an *'opera piccola'*, and all six are short, three-movement pieces of characteristic charm and warmth, remarkably assured and finished in their layout, particularly given the composer's youth. They date from 1760, when he was seventeen, and were published in Paris seven years later as Op. 2. There are some hints of the Boccherini to come (minuets with the melancholy charm he was to make so much his own) as well as much invention that is beguiling and distinctive. The performances are highly accomplished and the recording lively and truthful.

Boellmann, Leon (1862–97)

Symphonic variations (for cello and orch.), *Op. 23.*
*** HMV ASD/*TC-ASD* 3728. Paul Tortelier, RPO, Yan-Pascal Tortelier – BRUCH: *Kol Nidrei* ***; SCHUMANN: *Concerto.***(*)

Boellmann's main interest as a composer lay in organ music, but this set of variations, when played so persuasively by his compatriot Tortelier, makes a most attractive unexpected item in a romantic concerto anthology. The cellist's son draws comparably sympathetic playing from the RPO, well recorded. The tape transfer is fresh and well balanced.

Boieldieu, François
(1775–1834)

Harp concerto in 3 tempi, in C.
*** Argo ZRG/*KZRC* 930. Robles, ASMF, Iona Brown – DITTERSDORF and HANDEL: *Concertos.****

Boieldieu's *Harp concerto* has been recorded before, but never more attractively. Iona Brown and the Academy set the scene with an alert, vigorous introduction and Miss Robles provides contrasting delicacy. Much play is made of the possibilities of light and shade, the harp providing gentle echo effects in repeated phrases; some might feel this is overdone but it is certainly engaging. The slow movement is delightful and the lilt of the finale irresistible. The recording is first-class, with a most convincing balance, and the cassette is of demonstration quality, one of Argo's finest.

Boito, Arrigo (1842 1918)

Sinfonia in A minor.
*** Erato STU 71040. Monte Carlo Op.
O., Scimone – PUCCINI: *Capriccio
sinfonico* etc.***

An interesting if unimportant novelty
included with a fascinating collection of
Puccini's orchestral music. Performance
and recording are excellent.

Mefistofele (opera): *Prologue.*
** DG 2707 100/*3370 022* (2) [id.].
Ghiaurov, V. State Op. Ch., VPO,
Bernstein – LISZT: *Faust symphony.****

Although there are two recordings of
the complete opera, the only other complete version of the *Prologue* to *Mefistofele* is Toscanini's classic account from
1954 (now long deleted). This recording
was made in Vienna and finds Ghiaurov
in excellent form. The sound is wide in
range but could generally be described as
acceptable rather than distinguished.
Moreover, unusually for DG, the level of
the cassette transfer has been miscalcul-
ated, so that the cataclysmic effects at the
opening offer severe distortion, though
the quality improves later.

Bolling, Claude (born 1930)

California suite (film incidental
music).
*** CBS 79331. Laws, Shank, composer,
Grierson, Demonico, Manne, Tede-
sco.

*California suite; Suite for flute and
jazz piano.*
*** RCA Dig. RL/*RK* 25348. Duran,
Holloway, Walley, Ganley, Kain.

Suite for flute and jazz piano.

*** CBS 73900 [Col. M/*MT* 35864].
Rampal, composer, Sabiani, Hédiguer.

Claude Bolling's *California suite* is a
collection of incidental music from Neil
Simon's film of the same name. Bolling's
own recording includes slightly more
music and runs for about twelve minutes
longer than the RCA selection. But in
this kind of composition, which implies
an improvisatory element from the performing musicians, the differences between the two versions are rather more
than that of quantity. Obviously the
composer's performance has extra
authority and Hubert Laws, his flautist,
makes a splendid partner. The CBS recording too is first-class.

However, for most collectors the sin-
gular advantage of the RCA record is its
inclusion of the engaging *Suite for flute
and jazz piano*, offering a full hour of
music in excellent digital sound (with a
fine cassette to match the disc closely).
Virtually all the important music from
the film score is included (*Hanna, Beverly
Hills* and *Love theme* are all nostalgically
memorable) and both here and in the
Suite Elena Duran proves an immensely
gifted soloist. Her playing is sprightly,
vivacious and beguilingly expressive in
feeling. Laurie Holloway, her pianist,
also makes an excellent contribution, not
always matching the composer, perhaps,
but always sympathetic and stylish. He is
especially good in his gentle arpeggios
accompanying the reprise of the *Love
theme*.

Bolling's own version of the *Suite for
flute and jazz piano* is greatly helped by
the splendid flute playing of Jean-Pierre
Rampal, whose phrasing of the two lyrical movements, *Sentimentale* and *Irlan-
daise*, is very persuasive. The rhythmic
background (Marcel Sabiani, drums, and
Max Hédiguer, string bass) acts as a
modern equivalent of the baroque continuo, and the two movements which
look back towards this period, *Baroque
and blue* and *Fugace*, are attractively cul-

tivated. The composer's own contribution is authoritative and the CBS sound excellent; but the more economical RCA version is very good too.

Concerto for classic guitar and jazz piano.
**(*) EMI Dig. EMD/*TC-EMD* 5535 [Ang. DS/*4ZS* 37327]. Romero, Shearing, Manne, Brown.

Bolling's concertante piece is in effect a suite in seven movements with titles like *Hispanic dance, Mexicaine, Serenade* and so on. Its invention is quite lively, with one catchy theme, although the work tends as a whole to outstay its welcome. It certainly has a jazzy flavour and is likely to appeal to those whose tastes find stimulation in that area and who enjoy the combination of guitar, piano (George Shearing in very good form), drums and string bass. The performance is undoubtedly spontaneous and the recording vivid, with an excellent cassette.

Suite for violin and jazz piano.
**(*) CBS 73833/40- [Col. M/*MT* 35128]. Zukerman, composer, Hédiguer, Sabiani.

Bolling's *Suite* displays characteristic facility and melodic fluency. Its style verges on pastiche, notably in the *Ragtime*, where the evocation of Scott Joplin is unmistakably accurate. There are eight movements altogether; the *Valse lente* (No. 7) is rather engaging in its evocatively old-fashioned way, like the opening *Romance* and the *Caprice* which follows. The writing moves easily from the manner of the pre-jazz-era salon to Grappelli-like syncopations. The lively closing *Hora* is especially effective. It is superbly played by Zukerman, who is given expert support and good recording with a forward balance.

Bononcini, Antonio
(1677–1726)

Stabat Mater.
*** Argo ZRG 850. Palmer, Langridge, Esswood, Keyte, St John's College Ch., Philomusica O., Guest – CALDARA: *Crucifixus*; LOTTI: *Crucifixus.****

Antonio Bononcini is not to be confused with Handel's rival, Giovanni (1670–1747), his older brother. He did compose, at the age of twenty-one, an opera *Il trionfo di Camilla, regina dei Volsci*, that became a great success not only in Italy but in London. His *Stabat Mater* appears to have been composed in Vienna before he returned to Modena in 1716. It is a work of genuine melodic distinction and an affecting tenderness; there are some striking harmonies and in general a nobility and expressiveness that leave a strong impression. The performance is wholly admirable and is well recorded. The work is quite long and the two fill-ups are each less than five minutes.

Bononcini, Giovanni
(1670–1747)

Cantate pastoral: Care luci del mio ben; Ecco, Dorinda, il giorno; Misero pastorello; Siedi Amarilli.
*** DG Arc. 2533 450 [id.]. Jacobs, Kuijken, Van Dael, Kuijken, Kohnen.

This record collects four cantatas of much interest and no mean quality. Bononcini is largely remembered as the rival that Handel roundly put to flight, but the great composer showed considerable interest in his music, and reminders of the Handelian style are in evidence here. The four cantatas come from a collection, *Cantate e Duetti*, which appeared in London in 1721, and are inventive and expressive pieces, given here with real elegance and finish. This disc should be investigated by anyone with a taste for Handel's solo cantatas – or for that matter Bach's. The counter-tenor René Jacobs's singing is vital and intelligent and is accorded an excellent balance from the engineers.

Bonporti, Francesco
(1672–1749)

Violin concertos, Op. 11/4, 6, 8–9.
(M) *** Ph. 9502 004 [id.]. Michelucci, I Musici.

Bonporti's Op. 11 concertos come from 1720 or thereabouts and show the influence of Corelli; they have dignity, vitality and imagination. These performances by Roberto Michelucci and I Musici date from 1970 and sound as immaculate now as they did then.

Borodin, Alexander
(1833–87)

In the Steppes of Central Asia. Prince Igor: Overture; Polovtsian dances; Polovtsian march.
(B) *(*) CfP CFP 40309. LPO, Susskind – MUSSORGSKY: *Night on the Bare Mountain.*(*)

In the Steppes of Central Asia opens poetically and atmospherically here, but the performance is let down by Susskind's lack of imagination in matters of tempi and rhythm (there is too little con-

trast between the work's two principal themes), although the orchestral playing is of a high standard. Similarly he shows a lack of flair in the music from *Prince Igor*, and the *Polovtsian dances* never really catch fire at the end. The recording is vivid and makes an excellent impact, so that in spite of the conductor's too studied approach the music does not fail to communicate.

Symphonies Nos. 1 in E flat; 2 in B min.; 3 in A min. (Unfinished); Prince Igor: Overture; (i) Polovtsian dances.
*** CBS 79214 (2) [Col. M2 34587]. Toronto SO, Andrew Davis, (i) with Mendelssohn Ch.

Symphonies Nos. 1 and 3.
**(*) RCA RL/*RK* 25322 [(d) in CRL 3 2790]. Nat. PO, Tjeknavorian.

Symphony No. 2.
(B) **(*) Con. CC/*CCT* 7533. SRO, Varviso – TCHAIKOVSKY: *Francesca da Rimini.***
(M) ** Ph. Fest. 6570/*7310* 105 [id.]. Monte Carlo Op. O., Benzi – RIMSKY-KORSAKOV: *Tsar Saltan.***(*)

Symphony No. 2; In the Steppes of Central Asia; Nocturne for strings (arr. Gerhardt); (i) *Prince Igor: Polovtsian dances.*
**(*) RCA RL/*RK* 25225 [(d) in CRL 3 2790]. Nat. PO, Tjeknavorian, (i) with John Alldis Ch.

Though the *Second* is the best-known of Borodin's symphonies, both its companions deserve popularity. The *First* is colourful and ebullient, with a particularly appealing scherzo, while the pastoral two-movement torso completed from sketches by Glazounov is a delight. Andrew Davis conducts characterful and vital accounts of all three, but the Toronto Symphony Orchestra is not flattered by the recording, which is lacking in natural ambience and bloom. Tjeknavorian's recordings were originally issued in a boxed set including some valuable rarities, notably the *Petite suite* and the contribution to *Mlada*, a composite ballet. The box is still available in the USA; in the UK the records are being reissued separately, with satisfactory tape equivalents. Tjeknavorian's performances, while lacking the last ounce of character, are polished and full of colour, and the orchestral response is on the whole lively. The RCA recordings are certainly vivid and well balanced, with wide range and a warm ambience. Andrew Davis is at times more vital and imaginative, but the quality of both the playing in Toronto and the CBS recording fall short of the ideal, so on balance Tjeknavorian is to be preferred.

Varviso's Contour reissue of the *Second* has the advantage of a vintage Decca recording from the late sixties which is first-class: vivid, rich and well detailed. The performance has plenty of life and colour (it is less individual in control of tempi than Benzi's or Tjeknavorian's) and the Suisse Romande Orchestra is in good form, providing a full romantic sweep when the big tune comes back at the end of the slow movement. The scherzo too has plenty of sparkle, and though the coupling is less spontaneous as a performance this is competitive at bargain price. The cassette is less recommendable, with a more limited range.

The playing of the Monte Carlo orchestra on Philips is less sophisticated. However the upper strings, if not polished, are undoubtedly eloquent and they produce an impressive surge of tone at the climax of the slow movement. The cellos lack body, and the wind playing is not impeccable either. Yet Benzi produces an exhilaratingly lively performance, full of spirit and character. He varies the tempo of the main tune of the first movement with great freedom, but the effect is of a live performance and the spontaneity is obvious. The exuberance of both scherzo and finale tends to disarm criticism, although some ears may

find the interpretation as a whole too wilful. The sound is bright and vivid on disc and cassette alike.

String quartets Nos. 1 in A; 2 in D.
*** Decca SXL 6983. Fitzwilliam Qt.

A useful and valuable coupling. Borodin's *First Quartet* has been neglected for many years, and this is its first UK stereo recording. It is full of good things and is played with warmth and commitment by the Fitzwilliam Quartet, who also give a fresh-eyed account of the more familiar *D major Quartet*. Good recording and balance make this a most attractive proposition.

Prince Igor: Overture; Polovtsian dances.
*** Telarc Dig. DG 10039 [id.]. Atlanta Ch. and SO, Shaw – STRAVINSKY: *Firebird suite.***(*)

Prince Igor: Prelude, Act 3 (March); Polovtsian dances.
(M) **(*) HMV *TC-IDL 505.* Philh. O., Matačic – RIMSKY-KORSAKOV: *Scheherazade.***(*)

Prince Igor: Polovtsian dances.
(M) *** HMV SXLP/*TC-SXLP* 30445. Philh. O., Karajan – MUSSORGSKY: *Pictures* etc.***

*** DG 2536/*3336* 379 [id.]. Chicago SO, Barenboim – MUSSORGSKY: *Night***; RIMSKY-KORSAKOV: *Capriccio* etc.**(*)

(M) **(*) Ph. Fest. 6570/*7310* 191 [id.]. Netherlands R. Ch., Concg. O., Markevitch – RIMSKY-KORSAKOV: *Russian Easter Festival overture*; TCHAIKOVSKY: *1812.***(*)

It would be churlish not to give the remarkable Telarc digital recording of the *Polovtsian dances* a full recommendation. The choral singing is less clearly focused in the lyrical sections of the score than at climaxes, but the singers undoubtedly rise to the occasion. The entry of the bass drum is riveting and the closing section very exciting. The vivid sound balance is equally impressive in the overture, and if the Atlanta orchestra does not possess the body of string timbre to make the very most of the sweeping second subject the playing has vitality and spontaneity in its favour. Robert Shaw's overall direction is thoroughly musical.

Karajan's version, with the Philharmonia on top form, is played with such virtuosity and élan that the ear hardly misses the chorus. The recording is from the early sixties and sounds well, although Barenboim's 1977 recording, made in Chicago, is also splendidly played and offers more sumptuous sound, with striking colour and detail, the cassette only marginally less brilliant than the disc.

Markevitch has the advantage both of economy and a very good chorus. The Netherlands group not only sings vigorously in the closing pages but is very good – full-toned and clearly focused – in the lyrical music too. It is obviously a finer body of singers than Robert Shaw has available in Atlanta, and Markevitch directs a full-blooded and exciting performance. The Philips sound is good too and the overall balance realistic (the cassette has slightly less range and brilliance than the disc but is effective enough). However, there is not the feeling of sheer spectacle afforded by the Telarc disc.

· Matačic's recording is offered on tape only, in an HMV medium-price series guaranteeing an hour of music. Again the Philharmonia is on top form and the playing is full of adrenalin. The high-level transfer *almost* oversteps the mark with the powerful drum-beats in the *Dances*, but the sound has a spectacular feel about it in consequence, with brilliance to match the playing.

Boulez, Pierre (born 1926)

Piano sonata No. 2.
*** DG 2530 803 [id.]. Pollini – WEBERN: *Variations for piano.****

Written early in Boulez's career, the *Second Piano sonata* is a virtuoso *tour de force*, requiring a performer who is more than a modern-music specialist if its qualities are to be fully realized. Pollini, with his depth of concentration, thinking through the notes (and pauses), as well as in his flawless technique, is an ideal interpreter, finding poetry where others can seem dry. Excellent recording.

Boyce, William (1710-79)

Concerti grossi: in B flat; in B min.; in E min.; Overture in F.
*** Chan. ABR/*ABT* 1005. Cantilena, Shepherd.

Though these *Concerti grossi* have not quite the consistent originality which makes the Boyce symphonies so refreshing, the energy of the writing – splendidly conveyed in these performances – is recognizably the same, with fugal passages that turn in unexpected directions. The overture which complements these three *Concerti grossi* (all that Boyce completed) was written for the New Year's Ode in 1762, a French overture with fugue. Good recording; the high-level cassette transfer is full and natural yet has not quite the range at the top of the disc, although side two is noticeably livelier than side one.

12 Overtures.
**(*) Chan. DBR/*DBT* 2002 (2). Cantilena, Shepherd.

The eight Boyce symphonies have been

recorded many times, but this collection, put together ten years later in 1770 though including at least one work from as early as 1745, has much of comparable vigour. Unfortunately the first overture is not one of the best, but each has its attractions, and those which bring out the brass are most exciting. In 1770 Boyce, already deaf, was regarded as old-fashioned and was never given a proper hearing with this music. Cantilena's performances are not always as crisp and vigorous as they might be, but they certainly convey enough of the freshness of Boyce's inspiration, and the recording, though oddly balanced, is convincingly atmospheric. On cassette the sound is much brighter (to the point of fierceness) on the first tape than on the second, which is better balanced without loss of vividness.

Symphonies Nos. 1–8.
*** CRD CRD 1056/*CRDC 4056.*
Bournemouth Sinf., Ronald Thomas.
*** Argo ZRG/*KZRC* 874 [id.].
ASMF, Marriner.

Even against such strong competition as the catalogue provides in these superb symphonies, Thomas and the Bournemouth Sinfonietta are outstanding, with buoyant playing set against a recording which captures the full bloom of the orchestra. The tempi are often rather brisker than those adopted by Marriner. This is an excellent set, highly recommendable, and the cassette is first-rate too, the sound vivid and rich, with little loss of inner clarity.

Marriner also treats these superb examples of English baroque to exhilarating performances, with the rhythmic subtleties both in fast music and slow guaranteed to enchant. The recording, ample and full in the acoustic of St John's, Smith Square, is of demonstration quality on disc, though the cassette is drier and needs a reduction of treble and an increase of bass to sound its best.

Symphonies Nos. 4 in F; 5 in D; 8 in D min.
(M) *** DG Arc. Priv. 2547/*3347* 054.
Lucerne Festival O., Baumgartner –
ARNE: *Concertos.***

Baumgartner offers three of the most attractive *Symphonies* coupled to a pair of Arne concertos. Arne and Boyce were contemporaries; on the evidence here, Boyce was the more interesting composer, although the comparison is well worth making. Performances are sound and have plenty of life, and the mid-sixties recording is fresh and vivid on disc and cassette.

Anthems: *I have surely built thee an house; O be joyful; O give thanks; Save me, O God; Turn thee unto me.*
** Abbey ABY 811. Soloists, Worcester Cath. Ch. and Academy, Hunt.

Though not as polished or as pure-toned as the great collegiate choirs, that of Worcester Cathedral has built up a strong reputation in English music such as these magnificent anthems of Boyce. Some of the solo contributions are slightly insecure, but with a naturally balanced recording, fresh and clear in detail, this can be recommended.

Brahms, Johannes
(1833–97)

Piano concertos Nos. 1–2.
(M) *** DG Priv. 2726 082 (2). Gilels, Berlin PO, Jochum.
(M) **(*) Ph. 6769 013 (2) [9500 410 and 414/*7300 618/9*]. Dichter, Leipzig GO, Masur.
** DG 2707 127/*3370 039* (2) [id.]. Pollini, VPO, Boehm or Abbado.
(M) ** Ph. 6770/*7650* 006 [id.]. Brendel, Concg. O., Schmidt-Isserstedt.

Those wanting the two Brahms *Piano concertos* linked together will find the Gilels performances very satisfying, although they are now, of course, also available separately at mid-price (see below).

No grumbles about Misha Dichter's Brahms, which is as expansive and sonorous as one could wish. The recording is far more satisfactory than Masur's set of the Brahms symphonies or his version of the *Double concerto* with Accardo and Schiff. Dichter's readings have both strength and (not inappropriately) poetry, and the playing of the Leipzig orchestra is a good deal more committed than in the symphony cycle. Readers could do worse than invest in this set; neither performance has quite the stature of Gilels, but for those for whom good, well-balanced sound is a prime consideration, this ranks high on the current lists.

Pollini's accounts of the two *Piano concertos* are unevenly matched; his version of the *First* under Boehm does not command the listener's response as his fine version of the *Second* with Abbado does (see below).

Brendel is a powerful, positive pianist and these were the last recordings made by Schmidt-Isserstedt, who provides very positive direction, especially in the *First Concerto* – no mere accompaniment but a forceful symphonic partnership with the soloist. This is the more successful of the two performances, for though the central slow movement could be more hushed and intense, the outer movements, with fair freedom of tempo, are impressively dramatic. The balance, however, is not ideal, with the piano unusually close for Philips. The *Second Concerto* is more realistic in this respect, but the performance falls a little below expectations. Brendel seems too judicious and adopts a deliberately restrained approach, so keen is he to eschew the grand manner. The results, though always commanding respect, are not wholly convincing. On cassette the sound

is full and natural (the transfers are made at quite a high level), but orchestral detail is less telling than on disc. The second tape, however, offers a bonus of two *Hungarian dances* (which are not mentioned in the accompanying notes).

Piano concerto No. 1 in D min., Op. 15.

(M) *** DG Acc. 2542/*3342* 126 [2530 258]. Gilels, Berlin PO, Jochum.

(M) *** Decca Jub. JB/*KJBC* 102 [Lon. 6329]. Curzon, LSO, Szell.

(M) *** HMV SXLP/*TC-SXLP* 30283. Barenboim, New Philh. O., Barbirolli.

*** RCA RL/*RK* 12044 [ARL 1/*ARK 1* 2044]. Rubinstein, Chicago SO, Reiner.

(B) *** CfP CFP 40343. Tirimo, LPO, Sanderling.

** Ph. 9500/*7300* 871. Bishop-Kovacevich, LSO, Colin Davis.

(M) ** Ph. Fest. 6570/*7310* 052 [6500 018/ *7300 051*]. Arrau, Concg. O., Haitink.

** HMV ASD/*TC-ASD* 3762 [Ang. SZ 37568]. Ohlsson, LPO, Tennstedt.

*(*) DG 2531/*3301* 294 [id.]. Pollini, VPO, Boehm.

*(*) CBS Dig. 35850 [Col. M/*HMT* 35950]. Berman, Chicago 50, Leinsdorf.

From Gilels a combination of magisterial strength and a warmth, humanity and depth that are altogether inspiring. Jochum is a superb accompanist, and the only reservation is the recording, which though warm does not focus the piano and orchestra in truthful proportion. For all that, however, this remains an outstanding performance artistically. On cassette the focus at the very opening is less than sharp, but the quality immediately settles down to give vivid orchestral sound and a firm, rich piano image.

Curzon has a leonine power that fully matches Brahms's keyboard style and penetrates both the reflective inner world of the slow movement and the abundantly vital and massive opening movement. Now available in a welcome Jubilee reissue this is among the very best versions available, though the recording gives evidence of close-microphone techniques, used within a reverberant acoustic. The strings have a tendency to fierceness, especially in the powerful opening tutti of the first movement, yet there is no doubt of the vivid projection this gives to the music-making, and the piano balance is satisfying. The cassette transfer is outstandingly vivid, wide in range, with the opening cleanly caught: this is every bit the equal of the disc.

Barenboim and Barbirolli are superbly recorded on disc, and their playing is heroic and marvellously spacious. Tempi are broad and measured, but the performance is sustained by its intensity of concentration. The recording has not transferred comfortably to tape; the piano timbre is convincing, but the orchestra lacks focus and warmth.

Recorded in April 1954, Rubinstein's Chicago version was one of RCA's first experiments in stereo. In that form the recording did not appear for twenty-six years, but when it did it easily outshone Rubinstein's subsequent Boston version, not just in the spontaneity and sparkle of the performance but in the recording, with a warmer acoustic and better balance. Ever a poetic and lyrical Brahmsian, Rubinstein is most persuasive in all three movements, and is helped by Reiner's imaginative accompaniment, more volatile than Leinsdorf's. Apart from a little huskiness in the opening tutti the cassette transfer is well managed and is quite the equal of the disc.

The stopwatch indicates how slow Tirimo's tempi are in all three movements, and the opening tutti initially suggests heaviness, but Sanderling and Tirimo amply justify their straight measured manner in the thoughtful concentration of the whole reading. One has no feeling of the performance dragging,

for crisp, lifted rhythms prevent that in the outer movements and the slow movement has a rapt quality to compare with that of Barenboim (HMV) or Arrau (Philips), holding one's attention as a live performance would. With good modern stereo it makes a first-rate bargain.

If recording quality is a secondary consideration, Stephen Bishop-Kovacevich's account of the concerto should figure high in the lists. He plays with great tenderness and lyrical feeling, and in the slow movement he achieves great inwardness of feeling and poetry. There is no attention-seeking expressive point-making and no attempt to either exaggerate or understate the combative, leonine side of the solo part. He is sympathetically supported by the LSO under Sir Colin Davis, though woodwind intonation is not above reproach. Unfortunately, the sound is opaque and bottom-heavy, and is not in the same league as the very best versions. The cassette is not especially well focused.

Arrau's reading has vision and power, and though there are some characteristic agogic distortions that will not convince all listeners, he is majestic and eloquent. There is never an ugly sonority even in moments of the greatest vehemence. By the side of Curzon he seems idiosyncratic, particularly in the slow movement, but given the excellence of the recorded sound and the warmth of Haitink's support, this is well worth considering in the medium-price range. The cassette needs a high-level playback for good results; then the balance is realistic and satisfying.

Garrick Ohlsson offers a finely controlled and spaciously conceived account, one that has the measure of the nobility of the work. This is a classical reading and Ohlsson is scrupulous in following Brahms's dynamic and expressive indications. There is much to admire and little to fault in this reading, though perhaps the last ounce of poetry and spontaneity are missing when one compares him with such rivals as Gilels, Rubinstein and Curzon. Tennstedt and the LPO give superb support, though the first movement may strike some readers as a little too measured in its approach. The recording is excellent on disc and tape. The small reservations one has do not detract from the overall satisfaction that this fleet-fingered, finely considered reading gives, but at the same time it does not displace any of the three-star recommendations either as a performance or recording.

With Pollini there is always much to admire, not least the masterly pianism. But he brings little spontaneity or tenderness to this concerto and this performance in no way matches his admired account of the *Second*. This is uncommitted and wanting in passion. Good recording.

Although CBS provide Lazar Berman and the Chicago Symphony Orchestra with clean and well-focused recorded sound, the overall impression left by the performance is disappointing. Details are not easily faulted, but both the distinguished pianist and the Chicago orchestra sound less committed and inspired than one would expect. Given the competition, this version cannot be given a strong recommendation.

Piano concerto No. 2 in B flat, Op. 83.

(M) *** DG Acc. 2542/*3342* 151 [2530 259]. Gilels, Berlin PO, Jochum.

*** Ph. 9500 682/*7300 777* [id] Bishop-Kovacevich, LSO, Colin Davis.

(M) *** RCA Gold GL/*GK* 11267 [AGL 1/*AGK 1* 1267]. Sviatoslav Richter, Chicago SO, Leinsdorf.

(M) **(*) Decca Jub. JB/*KJBC* 94. Backhaus, VPO, Boehm.

(B) **(*) CfP CFP 40344. Tirimo, LPO, Levi.

(M) ** Ph. Fest. 6570/*7310* 052 [6500 019]. Arrau, Concg. O., Haitink.

** ASV ALH/*ZCALH* 910. Lill, Hallé O., Loughran.

The reissue of the Gilels/Jochum recording on DG's mid-priced Accolade label makes a clear first recommendation for the *B flat major Concerto*. The partnership of Gilels and Jochum produces music-making of rare magic, and if the resonant recording has some want of sharpness of focus (and causes the occasional marginal slip of refinement in tutti on cassette), the spacious acoustic and rich piano timbre seem well suited to this massive concerto.

Stephen Bishop-Kovacevich is better served in his account of the *Second* than he was in No. 1. Indeed, his version must be numbered among the very finest now before the public. The performance combines poetic feeling and intellectual strength, and reflects an unforced, natural eloquence that compels admiration. The first movement simply unfolds without any false urgency; the second is sparkling and fresh, and in the slow movement there is a rapt, poetic quality that almost matches Gilels. The finale has wit and delicacy, and Sir Colin provides wholly sympathetic support throughout; the unnamed cellist in the slow movement plays with both tenderness and nobility. This is the best version we have had since the Gilels/Jochum and can be recommended alongside it. The recording is finely detailed and naturally balanced on disc, but the cassette has less range and is very much second-best.

This reissue of Richter's 1961 recording with Leinsdorf is most welcome. The performance has all the intensity of a live occasion and finds Richter in splendid form. It is a wayward account, mannered in places, but with impressive weight and authority; it is far more spontaneous and dashing than Richter's later recording with Maazel and the Orchestre de Paris (now deleted in the UK). This reading catches fire, and although the quality of the recorded sound calls for some tolerance (it dates from the early 1960s) it is not lacking in atmosphere. The cassette too is fully acceptable.

Backhaus was always a controversial artist, inspiring fervent allegiance from his admirers and indifference from others. His playing even before the war had an element of didacticism, and some of his performances in later years were literal and dry. He recorded the Brahms in his eighties and the rugged strength of his conception is matched by playing of remarkable power, even though there are moments of untidiness. His is a broad, magisterial account with, perhaps, too little poetry for some Brahms-lovers but much compensating strength. Tempi are inclined to be spacious but there is no loss of momentum or architectural grip. The recording wears its years remarkably well: it was made in the mid-1960s and sounds very fresh and finely detailed. The cassette offers a sound that is suitably rich and expansive but lacks the last degree of upper range.

With the young Israeli Yoel Levi conducting, Martino Tirimo – whose first major recording this was – gives a commanding if measured account of the first movement, not always quite tidy in its occasional impulsiveness. The second and fourth movements too have slow basic tempi, but the clarity of articulation gives a sharpness of focus to conceal that, and both are made exuberant and joyful. Though the recording starts with a hint of tape hiss, it has fine weight and range, giving an unusually truthful balance to the piano. An excellent bargain.

Arrau's account of the concerto is competitive at medium price. There are one or two idiosyncratic touches (bars 89–91 in the first movement) and some detail is underlined expressively in this artist's characteristic way; but the playing has a splendid combination of aristocratic finesse and warmth of feeling, and Haitink and the Concertgebouw Orchestra give excellent support. The engineers strike the right balance between the piano and orchestra, and the orchestral texture

is better focused and cleaner than in the earlier Arrau recording. Although this is probably not a first choice, it must figure high on the list and should not be missed by admirers of the great Chilean pianist.

John Lill first recorded the *Second Concerto* not long after winning the Moscow Tchaikovsky Competition. This newer version with the Hallé Orchestra under James Loughran is in many ways a strong account, well thought out, finely paced and without the slightest trace of self-indulgence. The opening has a powerful masculine ring, particularly the build-up just before the orchestral tutti, and it is the space and power of Brahms's conception that are given priority rather than his poetry. Not that the performance is wanting in feeling or imagination. There is a stronger sense of the philosopher musing rather than the poet dreaming. The recorded sound is eminently well balanced, though climaxes do not open out as much as they might. Recommendable though it is, it does not displace Gilels or Bishop-Kovacevich.

Violin concerto in D, Op. 77.
(M) *** Ph. Fest. 6570/*7310* 172 [id.]. Krebbers, Concg. O., Haitink.
(M) *** HMV SXLP/*TC-SXLP* 30186. Menuhin, Berlin PO, Kempe.
*** HMV ASD/*TC-ASD* 3385 [Ang. S/ *4XS* 37286]. Perlman, Chicago SO, Giulini.
(M) **(*) HMV SXLP/*TC-SXLP* 30264 [Ang. S 35836]. David Oistrakh, French Nat. RO, Klemperer.
**(*) Ph. 9500 624/*7300 729* [id.]. Accardo, Leipzig GO, Masur.
**(*) HMV Dig. ASD 3973 [Ang. DS 37798]. Hoelscher, N. German RO, Tennstedt.
(M) **(*) DG Acc. 2542/*3342* 117 [138930]. Ferras, Berlin PO, Karajan.
** DG 2531/*3301* 251 [id.]. Zukerman, Orchestre de Paris, Barenboim.
** RCA RL/*RK* 25231. Mordkovitch, Philh. O., Sanderling.

*(*) CBS 76836/40- [Col. M/*MT* 35146].
Stern, NYPO, Mehta.

Hermann Krebbers, concertmaster of
the Concertgebouw and a master violinist of the first order in his own right, gives
one of the most deeply satisfying readings of Brahms's *Violin concerto* ever
recorded, strong and urgent yet tenderly
poetic too, and always full of spontaneous imagination. The total commitment
behind the performance is the work not
only of the soloist but of his colleagues
and their conductor, who perform as at a
live concert. The recording, with the
violin slightly forward but not obtrusively so, is full and immediate. The new
Festivo tape transfer has been made at
a very high level, and the sound is extremely vivid and lively, although on our
copy there was a hint of strain in the
orchestral tuttis of the outer movements.

The recording made by Menuhin with
Kempe and the Berlin Philharmonic at
the end of the fifties was one of his
supreme achievements in the recording
studio. He was in superb form, producing
tone of resplendent richness, and the
reading is also memorable for its warmth
and nobility. He was splendidly accompanied by Kempe, and the Berlin Philharmonic was inspired to outstanding
playing – the oboe solo in the slow movement is particularly beautiful. The sound
is remarkably satisfying and well
balanced and it has transferred equally
well to cassette, the spacious qualities of
the recording well caught, the soloist
given presence without added edge.

A distinguished account of the solo
part from Perlman, finely supported by
Giulini and the Chicago Symphony
Orchestra, a reading of darker hue than
is customary, with a thoughtful, searching slow movement rather than the
autumnal rhapsody which it so often
becomes. Giulini could be tauter, perhaps, in the first movement but the songful playing of Perlman always holds the
listener. The recording places the soloist
rather too forward, and the orchestral

detail could be more transparent.
Admirers of Perlman, however, need
not hesitate; granted a certain want of
impetus in the first movement, this is
an impressive and convincing performance.

The conjunction of two such positive
artists as Oistrakh and Klemperer made
for a reading characterful to the point of
idiosyncrasy, monumental and strong
rather than sweetly lyrical; the opening
of the first movement has a feeling of
engulfing power. The slow movement is
particularly fine, and the French oboist
plays beautifully. Oistrakh sounds
superbly poised and confident, and in the
finale, if the tempo is a shade deliberate,
the total effect is one of clear gain. The
recording is excellent and the tape transfer full-bodied yet clear.

The precision of Accardo's playing in
even the most fearsome double-stopping
makes for a reading that is refreshing in
its solo work. The tempi are unusually
slow, with Accardo's poetry given room
to breathe without mannerism. The
accompaniment lacks dramatic bite and
some clarity of focus, but the playing of
the Leipzig orchestra is characteristically
refined. The recording too is comfortable
rather than clear.

Beautifully recorded in luminous digital sound, Ulf Hoelscher's reading is
somewhat undercharacterized. After a
powerful, rich-toned tutti the entry of the
soloist is disappointing, not helped by a
backward balance, which may reflect
sounds in a concert hall more accurately
than most recordings; the trouble is that
some of the woodwind then sound louder
than the violin.

Much depends on one's attitude to
Ferras's tone colour whether the Ferras/
Karajan version is a good recommendation or not. DG have placed him close,
so that the smallness of tone that in the
concert hall is disappointing is certainly
not evident here. Moreover there is a
jewelled accuracy about the playing that
is most appealing, and Karajan conducts
vividly. The recording is of good quality

and the high-level cassette transfer is of demonstration liveliness.

Zukerman is rightly famed for his sweetness of tone, and his general approach can often seem a little bland by comparison with the greatest artists. This is a well-conceived reading that has finish and facility yet ultimately leaves the listener untouched by any feeling that he is in contact with great music. Zukerman is exposed to a close balance, but this does not mask the Orchestre de Paris under Barenboim, who give excellent support and receive a well-detailed recording in spite of the unrealistic perspective. On cassette the balance for the soloist sounds much less forward; otherwise the quality for both soloist and orchestra is good, although there is a slight loss of focus in the tuttis of the finale.

Lydia Mordkovitch is an Israeli artist born and bred in Russia, where she studied for a time with Oistrakh. Her playing is spacious and often noble, and she never succumbs to self-indulgence. The first movement could perhaps be more tautly argued but in general this reading deserves praise. Sanderling secures playing of great eloquence from the Philharmonia Orchestra and the overall sound is good without being quite in the demonstration bracket. The main drawback is the somewhat forward placing of the soloist, though this does not seriously mask the Philharmonia. Detail comes across clearly and there is a good deal of warmth too, but the strings sound harder in climaxes (above the stave) than with Zukerman or Krebbers. Nonetheless this is well worth considering.

Isaac Stern recorded the Brahms with Ormandy and the Philadelphia Orchestra in 1960, and this remake has none of the freshness and spontaneity of that version. Needless to say, Stern has the measure of the work's lyricism and its rhetoric, and there are many thoughtful touches. But the orchestral playing under Mehta is not particularly distinguished: it is a little undercharacterized, and the recording is not in the first flight either.

Double concerto for violin and cello in A min., Op. 102.
*** HMV ASD/*TC-ASD* 3905 [Ang. S/ 4*XS* 36062]. Perlman, Rostropovich, Concg. O., Haitink.

Double concerto; Academic Festival overture, Op. 80.
**(*) CBS 74003 [Col. M/*HMT* 35894]. Zukerman, Harrell, NYPO, Mehta.

Double concerto; Variations on a theme of Haydn, Op. 56a.
** Ph. 9500 623/*7300 728* [id.]. Accardo, Schiff, Leipzig GO, Masur.

Perlman and Rostropovich present their solo roles in giant size. This is partly a result of the recording balance but is also due to their strong, positive playing, which yet is not over-romantic or wilful. Haitink is the stabilizing force that holds the reading together with generally steady tempi, and though the orchestra is placed rather at a distance, the EMI engineers, on their first visit to the Concertgebouw, have generally coped well with the notorious problems of the Amsterdam hall. The format on two full sides is extravagant, but the fullness of the tonal spectrum justifies it. The cassette transfer is admirably clear and clean, but without loss of amplitude: Rostropovich's tone is strikingly full and resonant.

There is much to admire in the performance by Pinchas Zukerman and Lynn Harrell, who are more truthfully balanced than are many others (namely Perlman and Rostropovich, or Schneiderhan and Starker). The soloists – especially Lynn Harrell – play with much beauty of tone and sensitivity, though there are moments when one feels that they almost make too much of dynamic contrasts and expressive detail at the expense of continuity of line. The orchestral support is less refined, though it is in no way inadequate and has plenty of spirit. In addition to the good balance between soloists and orchestra, the sound is finely judged and clean, though wanting the transparency and bloom of the finest rivals.

Salvatore Accardo and Heinrich Schiff bring warmth, lyricism and imagination to the *Double concerto*, and though this may not be the most exciting account of it on the market, it is surely among the most thoughtful and refined. There is nothing here that is not completely felt, but, unlike the Perlman/Rostropovich version, there is no hint of too much projection (the only reservation that one might in time feel about that superb account). Everything here seems unforced. The orchestral playing is admirably shaped and always responsive, but the balance is distinctly recessed. The soloists are forward, though not excessively so, but the orchestral detail is by no means as well defined as one would like. The texture should be better ventilated and the tuttis need firmer body. This does not displace Oistrakh and Rostropovich (HMV ASD 3312 [Ang. S 36032]) or the more recent Perlman/Rostropovich, but its claim on the allegiance of collectors is quite strong. The cassette transfer is strikingly successful in the *Concerto*, full yet with good detail; in the *Variations* the ear notices a slight lack of upper range.

Hungarian dances Nos. 1, 3, 5–6.
(M) **(*) DG Priv. 2535/3335 628. Berlin PO, Karajan – LISZT: *Hungarian rhapsodies* etc.***

Karajan's performances certainly have panache; but, with very brightly lit recording, their character is of extrovert brilliance rather than warmth. But the Liszt couplings (Fricsay's splendid version of *Les Préludes* as well as two *Hungarian rhapsodies*) are outstanding, and this is an attractive collection. The cassette tempers the upper range slightly, without losing the sparkle; many will find its sound balance preferable to the disc.

Hungarian dances Nos. 1, 5–7, 12–13, 19, 21.

(M) *** Decca VIV/*KVIC* 18 [Lon. STS 15009]. VPO, Reiner – DVOŘÁK: *Slavonic dances.****

This was a favourite record of the late John Culshaw, and the recording (from the beginning of the 1960s) wears its years lightly. Reiner indulges himself in rubato and effects of his own (witness No. 12); but the affection of the music-making is obvious, and the sound balances brilliance with ambient warmth. The cassette matches the disc closely. Those wanting an inexpensive coupling of the Dvořák and Brahms dances need look no further than this.

Serenade No. 1 in D, Op. 11.
(M) *** Decca Jub. JB/*KJBC* 86 [Lon. 6567]. LSO, Kertesz.
*** Ph. 9500 322 [id./*7300 584*]. Concg. O., Haitink.

The late Istvan Kertesz gives a beautifully relaxed and warm-hearted account of this marvellous score, whose comparative neglect is unaccountable. The playing is as fresh as is the recorded sound. The engineers provide an excellently balanced and vivid recording, and the Decca reissue has the advantage on price. The cassette transfer is of excellent quality, warm, yet fresh and clear.

A finely proportioned, relaxed yet vital account from Haitink and the Concertgebouw Orchestra. The wind-playing is particularly distinguished, and while the players obviously relish the many delights of this under-rated score, the architecture is firmly held together without the slightest trace of expressive indulgence. The balance places the listener fairly well back, but the perspective is true to life and the sound blends admirably.

Serenade No. 2 in A, Op. 16.
(M) *** Decca Jub. JB/*KJBC* 87. LSO, Kertesz – DVOŘÁK: *Serenade.****

'I was in a perfectly blissful mood. I have rarely written music with such delight', wrote Brahms to Joachim when arranging this delectable *Serenade* for piano duet. The work has surprisingly autumnal colourings, and one would not be surprised to learn that it was a late rather than an early work. It was in fact begun before Brahms had finished the *D major Serenade* and thus dates from his mid-twenties. Kertesz gives an alert yet at the same time relaxed account of it. Moreover this offers excellent value by including the Dvořák *Wind serenade* in an . altogether admirable reading. The cassette quality has an attractive warmth; indeed, a slight bass cut may improve the balance.

Symphonies Nos. 1–4; Academic Festival overture, Op. 80; Tragic overture, Op. 81; Variations on a theme of Haydn, Op. 56a.
*** Decca D 151 D 4/*K 151 K 44* (4) [Lon. 2406/5-] (without *Variations*). Chicago SO, Solti.
*** Decca D 39 D 4/*K 39 K 44* (4) [Lon. 2405/5-]. Cleveland O., Maazel.
(B) ** HMV SLS 5241 (4) (without *Academic Festival overture*). Philh. or New Philh. O., Giulini.
(*) Ph. 6769 009/*7699 109* (4) [id.]. Leipzig GO, Masur.

Symphonies Nos. 1–4; Tragic overture.
*** DG 2740 193/*3371 041* (4) [id.]. Berlin PO, Karajan.

Broadly, Karajan's 1978 cycle shows that his readings of the Brahms symphonies, with lyrical and dramatic elements finely balanced, have changed little over the years, though it is worth noting that his approach to No. 3 is now stronger and more direct, with less mannered phrasing in the third movement. The playing of the Berlin Philharmonic remains uniquely sweet, and the ensemble is finely polished. If the results

are not always as incisively alert or as warm in texture as Karajan's earlier Berlin performances, that is partly due to less flattering recorded sound. Balance and top response are not always kind to the exposed violins, though in this the cassette version is preferable to the discs.

Sir Georg Solti came to the Brahms symphonies after a quarter-century of experience in the recording studio, having purposely left them aside over the years. His study was intensely serious, and that is reflected in his often measured but always forceful renderings. Those who think of Solti as a conductor who always whips up excitement may be surprised at the sobriety of the approach, but in a way these performances are the counterparts of those he recorded of the Beethoven symphonies, important and thoughtful statements, lacking only a degree of the fantasy and idiosyncrasy which makes fine performances great. Superb playing and recording; on cassette the bass balance is slightly over-resonant at times, but generally the sound is massively rich and full-blooded, with characteristic Decca vividness and detail.

The clarity, fullness and brilliance of the Decca recording for Maazel are vividly impressive, bringing out the brazen qualities of the interpretations. Unfortunately they are not uniformly satisfying, often detached to the point of being chilly, lacking the sort of tensions one expects in live performances. But the playing, with one or two exceptions, is superlatively good, as one would expect from the Clevelanders. The fill-ups are more generous than in some rival sets, but Maazel does not observe exposition repeats in *Symphonies 1* and *2*.

Giulini's cycle dates from the early sixties but was issued complete only in the early eighties. It is a valuable and illuminating set, showing Giulini a typically thoughtful and direct Brahmsian. From the evidence of the records it was a project which started better than it went on. Nos. 1 and 2 are given strong and refined readings, never forced but naturally dramatic. Characteristically the finale of No. 1 is taken at a measured tempo. No. 3, after a superb, commanding opening, is then much less compelling, with some surprisingly ragged ensemble and a sour oboe, partly compensated by a superb horn in the third-movement solo. As a performance No. 4 is more successful, though the orchestra had by this time become the New Philharmonia. What is disappointing is the quality of sound, with little or no bloom on the strings and some constriction at climaxes. At bargain price with two valuable fill-ups, well played, the set is worth hearing, though Loughran and the Hallé are finer on every count.

Given the success of Masur's Beethoven cycle, his Brahms set is a great disappointment. The orchestral playing in itself is of a high order, but none of these performances is fully characterized. They sound routine and workaday, and rarely engage the listener's sympathies. The recording is well balanced but does not succeed in relieving the boredom which rapidly sets in. A non-starter. But as it happens the tape layout is ideal, with each symphony complete on one cassette side and the orchestral works together on the third cassette. The sound is excellent. **Still recommended:** Among boxed sets those by Boult (HMV SLS 5009) and Klemperer (HMV SLS 804) continue to hold pride of place. Both include the overtures, and Boult also offers the *Alto rhapsody*.

Symphony No. 1 in C min., Op. 68.
*** DG 2531/*3301* 131 [id.]. Berlin PO, Karajan.
(M) *** DG Acc. 2542/*3342* 166. Berlin PO, Karajan.
(M) *** RCA Gold GL/*GK* 25191. Dresden State O., Sanderling.
*** Decca SXL/*KSXC* 6924 [Lon. 7198]. Chicago SO, Solti.
**(*) Decca SXL/*KSXC* 6796 [Lon. 7017/5-]. VPO, Mehta.

(M) ** DG Acc. 2542/*3342* 138. VPO, Abbado.
(B) ** Con. CC/*CCT* 7514. Berlin PO, Boehm.
** DG 2530/*3300* 959 [id.]. VPO, Boehm.

When Karajan has performed the four Brahms symphonies as a cycle in concert, he has always put No. 1 last, a sign that it is the one with which he most completely identifies. So it is in this performance, his fifth on record, if anything even bigger in scale than his earlier Berlin version of 1964. He has grown more direct in his Brahmsian manner too, but the Berlin solo playing has never been more persuasive. Recording balance is somewhat close, giving edge to the high violins, but it remains an outstanding version. The tape transfer is full and clear. Yet the earlier performance is still highly recommendable, the sound amazingly good.

The magnificence of the Dresden orchestra is heard to good advantage in their account of the *First Symphony*. Sanderling's reading has such natural warmth and is so strongly characterized that it has the keenest claims on the collector. Everyone plays as if they meant every note and this sense of conviction gives the performance a rare eloquence. With excellent recording on disc (the tape is a bit fierce on side one; side two is admirable), this will be the preferred reading for many, despite some agogic distortions during its course.

With the Chicago orchestra's playing as refined as any on record, Solti here directs a performance both spacious and purposeful, with the first movement given modular consistency between sections by a single pulse preserved as far as possible. Some will want more relaxation, for the tension and electricity remain here even when tempi are expansive. The recording is both atmospheric and clear, and the cassette is outstandingly rich and full without loss of range at the top, although there is some excessive bass resonance to cut back.

Mehta more than most conductors responds in different ways to different orchestras, and he is never so sympathetic as when he is conducting the Vienna Philharmonic. This is a mellow reading of a dramatic symphony, with generally expansive tempi and beautiful playing, not as perceptive of detail as the best rivals but superbly recorded in both media.

Abbado's *First* opens impressively enough, with finely drawn lines and expressive, sensitive phrasing. But he pulls back at bar 103 and again during the course of the second group. The exposition repeat is observed but there is a ruinous go-slow beginning at bar 294 which may prove irksome on repetition. Abbado pays fastidious attention to dynamics and to beauty of phrasing, and the tonal balance could scarcely be improved upon. However, the agogic distortions in which he indulges are a distinct handicap and prevent an unqualified recommendation. The playing of the Vienna Philharmonic and the quality of the recording are both excellent. There is no appreciable difference in sound between tape and disc.

With its relatively slow tempi, the performance from Boehm's 1976 Vienna cycle has a certain massive quality. The interpretation is very much in the German tradition, and many will find the rhythmic pulse too robust and deliberate. The recording is quite well balanced but the violin sound (on disc and tape alike) is not as sweet as one normally expects from the Vienna orchestra. It is fascinating to compare this reading with Boehm's earlier Berlin version. In the sixties Boehm's preference for slow tempi was not so extreme, and the result – with polished playing from the Berliners – is more centrally recommendable, especially in this bargain-price Contour reissue. The recording is well balanced, although it begins to show its age. The cassette is more opaque than the disc, but remains acceptable.

Symphony No. 2 in D, Op. 73.
*** DG 2531/*3301* 132 [id.]. Berlin PO, Karajan.
(M) *** HMV SXLP/*TC-SXLP* 30513. Philh. O., Karajan – SCHUBERT: *Symphony No. 8.****
(M) *** DG Acc. 2542/*3342* 167. Berlin PO, Karajan.
**(*) DG Dig. 2532/*3302* 014 [id.]. LAPO, Giulini.
** CBS 76830/40- [Col. M/*MT* 35158]. NYPO, Mehta.

Symphony No. 2; Academic Festival overture.
(M) ** Ph. Fest. 6570/*7310* 108 [id.]. LSO, Monteux.

Symphony No. 2; Tragic overture.
**(*) Decca SXL/*KSXC* 6925 [Lon. 7199/5-]. Chicago SO, Solti.
(M) ** RCA Gold GL/*GK* 25266. Dresden State O., Sanderling.
*(*) Decca SXL/*KSXC* 6834 [Lon. 7094/5-]. Cleveland O., Maazel.

Symphony No. 2; (i) *Alto rhapsody, Op. 53.*
(M) *** HMV SXLP/*TC-SXLP* 30529 [Ang. S 37032]. LPO, Boult, (i) with Baker, John Alldis Ch.

For many readers Boult's version will occupy a special place of honour. It has warmth, dignity and nobility and offers playing of great expressive power and a striking sense of spontaneity. The 1971 recording was of HMV's highest quality, and as the fill-up is a memorable account of the *Alto rhapsody* from Dame Janet Baker, the claims of this medium-priced reissue are indeed strong. The cassette too has been remastered and is highly successful; the *Rhapsody* is notably clear and clean.

Karajan's commanding new Berlin Philharmonic version, fresh and generally direct, is helped by superb playing from the Berlin orchestra. In the third movement this latest reading from Karajan is less affectionate than before and the finale is now very fast, challenging even the Berlin players. The recording, in the latterday Karajan/Berlin manner, is balanced relatively close but with lively atmosphere. The cassette is first-class in every way.

However, the reissue on HMV of Karajan's 1957 account with the Philharmonia Orchestra, very generously coupled at medium price, must also be seriously considered. In this splendid earlier performance the symphony unfolds with an unforced naturalness that is warmly compelling. The first movement is marvellously spacious and the horn solo (bars 455–77) is hauntingly poetic, more so than in either of the later records Karajan has made. Yet for all the relaxed atmosphere the grip that both his Berlin accounts have shown is strongly evident here. The slight blemishes (intonation between wind and strings at the beginning of the development, and a tape join later on) will worry no one. The recording has slightly less range than the modern accounts (the cassette transfer is somewhat unrefined at both ends of the spectrum, and both the Boult and the Solti cassettes are technically superior), but it is rich and beautifully balanced. Despite its age this is one of the best disc versions of the Second on the market, and the substantial Schubert bonus is no less recommendable.

Karajan's 1964 account was among the sunniest and most lyrical readings of the Second Symphony, and its sound is fully competitive even now, although the cassette (as with the companion Accolade reissue of the First) is rather bass-heavy. It fully justifies its position high in our recommendations list, though the recording does not quite match the later Karajan in terms of range, and it is without the bonus provided by the 1957 HMV version. However, it remains in every way a satisfying reissue.

The restraint which made Giulini's recording of Beethoven's Eroica symphony with the same orchestra so individual yet so compelling is evident in Brahms too. The result is less im-

mediately magnetic, particularly in the first movement, and the recording is not one of DG's most vivid; but admirers of this conductor will find many points of fresh illumination. The chrome cassette is of matching quality, but again not one of DG's finest; the upper range is not quite as extended as some.

A powerful, weighty performance from Solti, its lyrical feeling passionately expressed in richly unholstered textures. The reading displays a broad nobility, but the charm and delicately gracious qualities of the music, which Abbado for one finds readily, are much less part of Solti's view. Yet the lyric power of the playing is hard to resist, especially when the recording is so full-blooded and brilliant. Solti includes the first-movement exposition repeat and offers a splendidly committed account of the Tragic overture as a bonus. The cassette is of comparable quality, full-bodied and bright, though there is some excessive bass resonance in the overture.

Monteux offers relaxed, idiomatic playing and an eminently sound reading, well recorded; but both he and Sanderling on RCA are below their best here. The latter's performance with the Dresden orchestra strikes one as a shade too mannered, although the playing is of the highest quality.

Mehta's is an unexceptionable reading; the easy lyricism of No. 2 suits his preference for not intruding on Brahms, though for many this will be a degree too anonymous still. Fair recording.

Starting with a horn solo decidedly on the flat side of the note, Maazel's account never really recovers, despite some beautiful playing from all sections. In the first movement the evenly stressed rhythm contradicts the expressive phrasing; the slow movement is big and rich but has little forward pulse, while the finale ends with blaring vulgarity. Rich Decca recording of good Cleveland vintage.

Symphony No. 3 in F, Op. 90. Academic Festival overture.
(M) *** HMV SXLP/*TC-SXLP* 30255. Philh. O., Klemperer.
*** Decca SXL/*KSXC* 6902 [Lon. 7200]. Chicago SO, Solti.

Symphony No. 3; Tragic overture.
*** DG 2531/*3301* 133 [id.]. Berlin PO, Karajan.

Symphony No. 3; Variations on a theme of Haydn.
(M) *** RCA Gold GL/*GK* 25216. Dresden State O., Sanderling.
(M) *(*) DG Acc. 2542/*3342* 121 [2535/*3335* 293]. Dresden State O., Abbado.

Karajan gives superb grandeur to the opening of No. 3, but then characteristically refuses to observe the exposition repeat, which in this of all Brahms's first movements is necessary as a balance with the others. Comparing this 1978 reading with Karajan's earlier 1964 version, one finds him a degree more direct, noticeably less mannered in his treatment of the third movement, but just as dynamic and compelling. The overture too is superbly done, and though one may criticize the recording balance, the result is powerful and immediate. The cassette matches the disc fairly closely (the texture is a little less clean at the opening). However, the level drops slightly on side two, with a corresponding marginal loss of immediacy.

Though given good rather than outstanding recorded sound, Sanderling's is a marvellously rich performance; his slow movement is particularly warm-hearted and generous in feeling. This is deeply experienced and yet spontaneous. The Dresden orchestra play with such eloquence that for some this will be the most rewarding version of all. The cassette transfer is good, but has not quite the refinement of the disc (especially at the opening). It responds to a slight treble filter or marginal cut without losing too much brightness.

Klemperer's account is even more individual than his other Brahms symphony performances. With slow speeds and all repeats taken his timing is much more extended than usual. But for all his expansiveness Klemperer does not make the music sound opulent. There is a severity about his approach which may at first seem unappealing, but which comes to underline the strength of the architecture. The recording is excellent for its period, and the cassette transfer has been remastered to produce clean, vivid textures with plenty of weight and breadth.

With dynamic contrasts heightened – helped by the gloriously resonant playing of the Chicago orchestra – and with unusually spacious tempi in the middle movements (the second is more an *adagio* than an *andante*), Solti takes a big-scale view of the *Third*, by far the shortest of the Brahms symphonies. The epically grand opening, Solti seems to say, demands an equivalent status for the rest; and the result, lacking a little in Brahmsian idiosyncrasy, is most compelling. Solti's Brahms should not be underestimated and with wonderfully rich sound this gives much satisfaction. The cassette transfer is wide in range and full, but there is some edginess on the upper strings and an excess of bass resonance.

Abbado with the Dresden orchestra must, alas, be ruled out on account of the mannered tempo changes in which he indulges. The playing is beautiful, as it is for Sanderling, but whereas his expressive changes seem organic Abbado's do not. The recording is excellent and the cassette transfer quite well managed, although it has not the sharpness of detail of Abbado's splendid version of the *Second Symphony*.

Symphony No. 4 in E min., Op. 98.
*** DG 2531/*3301* 134 [id.]. Berlin PO, Karajan.
(M) *** RCA Gold GL/*GK* 25279. Dresden State O., Sanderling.

(M) *** HMV SXLP/*TC-SXLP* 30503.
Philh. O., Karajan.
*** DG Dig. 2532/*3302* 003 [id.]. VPO,
Carlos Kleiber.
*** Decca SXL/*KSXC* 6890 [Lon.
7201]. Chicago SO, Solti.
(M) *** Decca Jub. JB/*KJBC* 85. VPO,
Kertesz.
* CBS 76949/*40*- [Col. M/*MT* 35837].
NYPO, Mehta.

*Symphony No. 4; Academic Festival
overture.*

(M) **(*) DG Acc. 2542/*3342* 120 [2535/
3335 360]. LSO or Berlin PO,
Abbado.
** Decca SXL/*KSXC* 6836 [Lon. 7096/
5-]. Cleveland O., Maazel.

Brahms's *Fourth Symphony* is now
extremely well represented. Indeed one
might say that there are interpretations
and recordings to suit every taste, and the
medium price-range is especially well
served, not only by Karajan but also by
Kertesz and, notably, Sanderling, whose
RCA Dresden version is striking for its
eloquence and richness of timbre.

In his newest DG recording Karajan
refuses to overstate the first movement,
starting with deceptive reticence. His
easily lyrical style, less moulded in this
1978 reading than in his 1964 (DG) account, is fresh and unaffected, and highly
persuasive. The scherzo, fierce and
strong, leads to a clean, weighty account
of the finale. The overall performance is
very satisfying. The recording is of a piece
with the others in the series, with balances
not quite natural. The cassette transfer is
of outstanding quality, in many ways
preferable to the disc; it is rich and clear,
with excellent detail and a fine body to
the string tone.

Sanderling's version balances fire with
lyrical feeling in satisfying proportions.
The sumptuous body of tone created by
the Dresden orchestra is splendidly
caught in a richly resonant recording (the
high-level cassette transfer matching the
disc closely). The symphony is beautifully

played and eloquently shaped, with some
of the classical strength that distinguished this orchestra's account of the
work under Karl Boehm in the days of
78s. It has a warmth and sense of enjoyment that make it an enormously rewarding performance.

Karajan's glowing HMV account
from the mid-1950s holds its own with
his mid-sixties Berlin version, and is in
many ways to be preferred to several
more recent issues. The keynote of the
performance is its complete naturalness;
the symphony unfolds at an unforced
pace and possesses a glowing eloquence
that is unfailingly impressive. The sound
is amazingly fine given that it is twenty-
eight years old: the strings have a more
natural timbre and sonority than they do
even in the Kleiber digital recording.
Naturally the range is not as wide as in a
modern record but the sound has refreshing warmth and the balance is excellently judged, though, compared with
the disc, the tape is a little thick-textured
and is less refined at both ends of the
spectrum. The Philharmonia play marvellously for Karajan, and both artistically
and technically this is to be preferred to
the Klemperer version made only a year
or two later.

Any record from Carlos Kleiber is an
event and his is a performance of real
stature. Everything is shaped with the
attention to detail one would expect from
this great conductor. Apart from one
moment of expressive emphasis at bar 44
in the first movement, his reading is
completely free from eccentricity. The
digital recording is impressive, but the
strings above the stave sound a little shrill
and glassy, while at the other end of the
spectrum one feels a want of opulence in
the bass. A gripping and compelling performance, though not more impressive
than Karajan's last Berlin version. The
cassette transfer (on chrome tape) is outstanding in its body and clarity, if anything a little kinder than the disc to the
upper string timbre.

After a full twenty-five years recording

for Decca, Solti at last came round to Brahms, and this account of No. 4 was the first result of that project. The most distinctive point about the reading, after a very direct, fast and steady first movement, is that the *Andante moderato* of the second movement is very slow indeed, more an *adagio*. It is not just that it starts slowly, as in some other versions; Solti characteristically maintains that speed with complete concentration. Not everyone will like the result, but it is unfailingly pure and strong, not only in the slow movement but throughout. The playing of the Chicago orchestra is magnificent – note the cellos in the second subject of the first movement, and the articulation of the anapaestic rhythms in the scherzo – and the recording is full and precise. The high-level cassette transfer matches the disc in its massive richness of texture, although the very resonant bass needs cutting back.

Kertesz too has the advantage of first-class modern Decca recording. This is a distinguished performance, the finest of his Brahms cycle. It is a serious, straight-faced reading, powerful yet resilient, with the slow movement emerging as an elegy – aptly enough, since this was one of the last records that Kertesz made before his tragic death. On the one hand there is dignity and grandeur, on the other delicacy and lyricism. At Jubilee price this remains competitive.

Abbado's warm lyricism is certainly appealing, partnered as it is by excellent recording (the cassette is glowingly rich, although the rather resonant bass needs cutting back). This reading is fresh and undistracting rather than dramatic or compelling. It comes from the series Abbado recorded with different orchestras in 1973; here the LSO is in excellent form. With a good fill-up and at medium price, this is worth considering, but many will want a version with more individuality and power.

Beautifully played, Maazel's Cleveland version, like the rest of his set, has an element of routine to it, a good studio performance rather than a live communication. Excellent recording and a brilliant cassette, not lacking depth but not especially rich in the middle area.

Mehta's is an intensely disappointing reading with a pedestrian interpretation and ill-focused recording.

Tragic overture, Op. 81; Variations on a theme of Haydn (St Anthony Chorale), Op. 56a; (i) *Alto rhapsody, Op. 53.*
**(*) Con.CC/CCT 7536 [DG 2536 396]. VPO, Boehm, (i) with Ludwig, V. Singverein.

The spacious account of the *Alto rhapsody* is the gem of Boehm's collection of shorter Brahms pieces. Christa Ludwig is wonderfully intense in her illumination of both words and music, producing glorious tone-colours despite the extra strain on breath-control from the slow tempi. The *Tragic overture* is given a strong traditional reading; but, with the violin section somewhat unflatteringly recorded, the *Variations* have their disappointments, very much in the heavyweight German tradition and with generally slow tempi made heavier by even stressing. Note too that no room was found for the *Academic Festival overture*. However, at bargain price this is well worth considering for the beautiful performance of the *Rhapsody*, and there are surprisingly few available versions of the *Variations* not coupled to one of the symphonies. The cassette transfer is perfectly acceptable although it lacks some of the bright upper range of the LP (not necessarily a disadvantage). The turnover comes, irritatingly, in the middle of the *Variations*, but the break is not clumsy.

CHAMBER MUSIC

Cello sonatas Nos. 1 in E min., Op. 38; 2 in F, Op. 99.

**(*) Decca SXL/*KSXC* 6979. Harrell, Ashkenazy.
** HMV ASD/*TC ASD* 3612. Tortelier, Pau.

Cello sonata No. 1.
*(*) Nimbus 2111. Fleming, Parsons –
SCHUBERT: *Arpeggione sonata.***

Harrell and Ashkenazy give almost ideal performances of the two Brahms *Cello sonatas*, strong and passionate as well as poetic. But although they are naturally recorded and well balanced, the acoustic is resonant and the imagery lacks the last degree of sharpness of focus. The cassette transfer is first-class but reflects the slightly hazy quality of the disc.

Paul Tortelier and Maria de la Pau give a less intensely emotional and more classical reading of the *Sonatas* than Du Pré and Barenboim (HMV ASD 2436 [Ang. S 36544]). Du Pré and Barenboim dwell intently on detail, often with telling effect; theirs is a more youthful, ardent and romantic view. In this respect the Torteliers are nearer to Piatigorsky and Rubinstein; unfortunately this latter RCA recording has been withdrawn in the UK, although still available in the USA [ARL 1/*ARK 1* 2085]. Piatigorsky and Rubinstein's readings bear the stamp of authority, with aristocratic bearing and profound sensitivity in every phrase; they are well recorded too. The Tortelier versions are not quite their equal, but they are satisfying nonetheless, and the sound is good (though the cassette is not as sharply focused as the disc).

Amaryllis Fleming and Geoffrey Parsons play with passionate commitment but without any excessive rubato or expressive indulgence. There is a good sense of forward movement and a keen awareness of the importance of phrasing. Geoffrey Parsons has enormous vitality yet never swamps his partner. Unfortunately the Nimbus recording is simply not expansive enough, though the quadrophonic encoding may in part account for this.

Clarinet quintet, Op. 115; Horn trio, Op. 40; Piano quartets Nos. 1 and 2, Opp. 25/6; Piano quintet, Op. 34; String quartets Nos. 1, Op. 51/1; 3, Op. 67; Violin sonatas Nos. 1, Op. 78; 3, Op. 108.
(M) (***) World mono SHB/*TC-SHB* 61 (7). Busch Qt with Serkin, Kell, Aubrey Brain etc.

After their success in transferring the Busch Quartet's records of Beethoven and Schubert, World Records have now assembled all their Brahms in one box. They have made a superb job of the transfers from 78s, and have restored some performances that are classics of the gramophone. Kell's account of the *Clarinet quintet* is little short of sublime, and the *F minor Piano quintet* with Serkin is enormously powerful, spacious and vital. Everything in these pre-war performances was as controlled and impassioned as one could possibly wish, and few are the performers who have come closer to this music since. The two postwar recordings (the *G minor Piano quartet* and the Op. 67 *String quartet*) are not quite in the same class, but everything else is very special indeed. Listeners used to stereo ambience will find the quality rather dry, and the string portamenti may worry some ears. But the marvellously spontaneous version of the *Horn trio* sounds particularly realistic, and elsewhere the ear quickly adjusts. The tape box is no less successful than the discs.

Clarinet quintet in B min., Op. 115.
*** Chan. ABR/*ABT* 1035. Hilton, Lindsay Qt.
(M) *** Decca Ace SDD 575. Schmidl, New V. Octet (members) – WEBER: *Introduction* etc.***
(M) **(*) Argo ZK/*KZKC* 62. Brymer, Allegri Qt – WAGNER: *Adagio.***(*)

The Decca version with Peter Schmidl and members of the New Vienna Octet has very strong attractions, but the performance by Janet Hilton and the Lindsay Quartet has an individuality that makes it even more memorable. At times Janet Hilton is bolder than Schmidl, especially in the Zigeuner interlude at the centre of the *Adagio*, where she provides an exciting burst of bravura. Her lilting syncopations in the third movement are delightful, and the theme and variations of the finale are full of character. The recording has striking presence, with a realistic overall balance, and the cassette transfer is of the highest quality; there is little appreciable difference between disc and tape, the former showing only a hint of extra range at the top.

But at medium price and with an engaging coupling the Decca version can also be recommended warmly. Schmidl gives an altogether stronger performance than Alfred Boskovsky's earlier Ace of Diamonds version (Decca SDD 249 [Lon. STS 15408]). The soaring opening clarinet theme establishes the passionate commitment of the playing, and the degree of contrast between the *Andantino* third movement and the finale is particularly successful. The *Adagio* is played tenderly and expressively; the element of nostalgia (which dominated Boskovsky's approach) is not missing here, although it is held in balance with the other emotional demands of the music. Schmidl has a warmly luminous tone which he colours with considerable subtlety, and the silkily serene Viennese string playing is equally sympathetic. The recording is splendid.

Jack Brymer gives a masterly and finely poised account which in terms of polish and finesse can hold its own with the very best. Apart from Brymer's well-characterized playing, the Allegri Quartet are also in excellent shape, and they are given the benefit of eminently truthful recording, with an admirable cassette transfer to match. But it must be conceded that something of the nostalgia and the melancholy of this score eludes

them, and the Hilton and Schmidl versions are more searching.

Clarinet sonatas Nos. 1 in F min.; 2 in E flat, Op. 120/1–2.
*** Chan. ABR/ABT 1020. Hilton, Frankl.

Janet Hilton and Peter Frankl give attractively straightforward accounts of the *Clarinet sonatas*. They seem at first sight less sophisticated and idiosyncratic than some of their rivals (notably Gervase de Peyer and Daniel Barenboim) but nonetheless they offer considerable artistic rewards. At times one feels that perhaps the pianist's phrasing could be more imaginative, but for the most part these performances have warmth and good musical sense, and the recording is natural, forward without being obtrusively close. The cassette is most successful too, with a high-level transfer giving presence to both artists and fine body of tone within an attractively warm acoustic.

Clarinet trio in A, Op. 114.
*** Ph. 9500 670/7300 826 [id.]. Pieterson, Pressler, Greenhouse – BEETHOVEN: *Clarinet trio.****

The *Clarinet trio* is not generously represented on record, but this issue by George Pieterson and members of the Beaux Arts Trio is unlikely to be surpassed either as a performance or recording for many years. Masterly playing from all three artists. The cassette transfer is enjoyably warm and natural.

Piano quartet No. 1 in G min., Op. 25.
(M) **(*) DG Acc. 2542/3342 140 [2530 133]. Gilels, Amadeus Qt.

As might be expected, Gilels's account of the *G minor Quartet* with members of the Amadeus has much to recommend it.

The great Soviet pianist is in impressive form and most listeners will respond to the withdrawn delicacy of the scherzo and the gipsy fire of the finale. The slow movement is perhaps somewhat wanting in ardour and the Amadeus do not sound as committed and fresh as their keyboard partner. At medium price, however, this version enjoys an additional advantage, and in any event rival versions are hardly thick on the ground. The DG recording is well balanced and clean, and admirers of these distinguished artists need not hesitate. The high-level cassette transfer is first-class, vivid, wide-ranging and well-balanced.

Piano quartet No. 1, Op. 25 (orch. Schoenberg).
*** DG 2531 198 [id.]. Junge Deutsche PO, Zender.
(M) *(*) CBS 61887 (with BACH: Prelude and fugue in E flat, BWV 552). Chicago SO, Craft.

The German Philharmonic Youth Orchestra is drawn from the various colleges of music in the Federal Republic and is not strictly speaking comparable with, say, the National Youth Orchestra in Britain. It is a large ensemble, numbering some 140 players, and is of excellent quality, though the very size of the strings tends to outbalance the wind. Schoenberg spoke of the G minor Piano quartet as 'another Brahms symphony' and apparently adored it. His scoring has been widely admired by many distinguished musicians, but it strikes the present writer as thick and overladen in texture, and the use of the xylophone is inelegant and bizarre. Those who admire this arrangement, however, can rest assured that the performance on DG is thoroughly committed, and though the woodwind is reticent, the balance is otherwise first-class. The overall sound picture has great naturalness and the strings have opulence. There is no fill-up but despite that and the fact that it is at full price, it is a strong frontrunner.

Robert Craft's version is uncompetitive even making allowances for its undoubted price advantage. The sound is not rich enough; climaxes need to expand more if the effect is to be really acceptable. As a performance it is far from inadequate, though it falls short of distinction. The coupling, a transcription of a Bach Prelude and fugue, does not greatly enhance the claims of this disc, for the performance lacks the agogic freedom that Schoenberg marks, and again the recording is not in the first flight.

Piano quintet in F min., Op. 34.
*** DG 2531/3301 197 [id.]. Pollini, Italian Qt.
(M) **(*) DG Priv. 2535/3335 418 [139397]. Eschenbach, Amadeus Qt.

There is some electrifying and commanding playing from Pollini, and the Italian Quartet is eloquent too. The balance, however, is very much in the pianist's favour; he dominates the texture rather more than is desirable, and occasionally masks the lower strings. There are minor agogic exaggerations but neither these nor the other reservations need necessarily put off prospective purchasers. The cassette offers admirable quality, cleanly focused and well balanced, to match the disc closely.

Christoph Eschenbach gives a powerful – sometimes overprojected – account of his part and the Amadeus provide impressive support. This version is by no means to be dismissed at medium price, for the recording is excellent. The high-level cassette transfer too is outstandingly successful, full-bodied and clear. But Richter's famous mono recording with the Borodin Quartet has been reissued on Saga (5448), and current pressings are of high quality; those willing to accept the rather dated sound will find that this memorable performance is in an altogether different class.

Piano trios Nos. 1 in B, Op. 8; 2 in C, Op. 87; 3 in C min., Op. 101; 4 in A, Op. posth.

(M) *** Ph. 6770/7650 007 (2) [id.]. Beaux Arts Trio.

(M) *(*) HMV SLS 5114 (2). Frankl, Pauk, Kirshbaum.

Piano trios Nos. 1 and 3.

(M) *** Decca Ace SDD 540. Katchen, Suk, Starker.

Piano trio No. 2; Cello sonata No. 2, Op. 99.

(M) *** Decca Ace SDD 541. Katchen, Suk, Starker.

The Beaux Arts set was originally issued on two separate full-priced discs at the beginning of 1968. Now they are together in a box with an excellent tape equivalent. The set includes the *A major Trio*, which may or may not be authentic, but is certainly rewarding. The performances are splendid, with strongly paced, dramatic allegros, consistently alert, and thoughtful, sensitive playing in slow movements. Characterization is positive (yet not over-forceful), and structural considerations are well judged: each reading has its own special individuality. The sound is first-class, and the cassettes offer demonstration quality, the resonance of Bernard Greenhouse's cello richly caught without any clouding of the focus.

Julius Katchen and his team judge the tempi admirably and resist the temptation to dwell too lovingly on detail. In addition they are given really excellent recording. SDD 541 represents the results of Katchen's last recording sessions before his untimely death. They were held at the Maltings, and the results have a warmth that did not always characterize Katchen's recording of Brahms. The coupling may be unconventional, but both the tough *C major Trio* and the epic, thrustful *Cello sonata* are given strong and characterful performances.

On HMV, workmanlike and expertly

played performances that give pleasure and satisfaction yet at the same time fall short of being memorable. All three players are unfailingly reliable musicians but Peter Frankl does not shed new light on these scores in the way that Menahem Pressler does in the Beaux Arts version. Were the sound quality fresher and more cleanly focused this would be a good two-star recommendation.

String quartets Nos. 1 in C min.; 2 in A min., Op. 51/1–2.

(M) ** Argo ZK 89. Allegri Qt.

* DG 2531/3301 255 [id.]. LaSalle Qt.

The Allegri players are warmer and more humane than the LaSalle Quartet and their accounts of these masterpieces are eminently well served by the engineers. Their playing falls short of the distinction or elegance that their finest rivals can command, but this is a serviceable and recommendable coupling.

The LaSalle Quartet give efficient, streamlined accounts of both quartets but convey little sense of feeling or tenderness. These are not performances that bring one closer to the music, though there is no question of the polish and expertise of these players, or the quality of the recording, which is equally impressive on both disc and tape. Our recommendation for this coupling, however, remains with the Weller Quartet (Decca Ace of Diamonds SDD 322 [Lon. STS 15245]).

String quartet No. 3 in B flat, Op. 67.

(M) *** Decca Ace SDD 510. Musikverein Qt – SCHUMANN: *Quartet No. 1.****

*(*) DG 2531/3301 343 [id.]. LaSalle Qt – SCHUMANN: *Piano quintet.*(*)*

There have been some fine accounts of this quartet in the catalogue, notably those by the Italian and Melos quartets. This version by the Musikverein Quartet (formerly known as the Küchl Quartet after its first violin) is arguably the finest of them all. The playing is effortlessly natural and has both warmth and finesse, and it is most truthfully recorded. These artists made a great impression with their finely poised Mozart quartets (K.575 and 590), and their excellence is here matched by a clean, bright recording which has no lack of-depth.

A high degree of technical finish marks the LaSalle account, and the first movement is broad and almost symphonic in their hands. But other players offer more in terms of humanity and spontaneity, and in spite of good recording on disc and cassette alike this is no match for its rivals, especially the Musikverein version, which is also cheaper.

String quintets Nos. 1 in F, Op. 36; 2 in G, Op. 11; String sextets Nos. 1 in B flat, Op. 18; 2 in G, Op. 36.
(M) ** DG Priv. 2733 011 [(d) 139430, 139353]. Augmented Amadeus Qt.

These performances were all discussed in earlier editions of the *Penguin Stereo Record Guide* when they were available separately or included in the fifteen-disc set of Brahms chamber music. The merits of this compilation in assembling four relatively little-played but inspired works are obvious, but the performances are a shade too perfumed to be ideal. Both the Amadeus and their two guests, Cecil Aronowitz and William Pleeth, display the utmost finish and accomplishment, but their suavity and elegance seem to be achieved at the expense of depth.

String sextets Nos. 1 in B flat, Op. 18; 2 in G, Op. 36.
(M) **(*) Ph. 6570/7310 570. Berlin Philharmonic Octet (members).

The Berlin performances of the two *String sextets* were originally issued on separate discs. Now they are coupled together for one of the first issues in Philips's new 'Musica da Camera' mid-

priced chamber-music series. The Berlin ensemble respond readily to the glories of the *Second Sextet*, playing with warmth and eloquence; the *First* is slightly less committed, but still shows a greater degree of feeling than either the Amadeus or the (deleted) Menuhin versions. The original recordings, spacious and well balanced, still sound tonally satisfactory, although the newer CRD versions (see below) are even finer.

String sextet No. 1 in B flat, Op. 18.
*** CRD CRD 1034/CRDC 4034. Augmented Alberni Qt – SCHUBERT: *String quartet No. 12 (Quartettsatz).* ***

Brahms-lovers who normally fight shy of his chamber music are urged to try this work (scored for two violins, two violas and two cellos) with its richly orchestral textures. The second-movement theme and variations is immediately attractive, while the *Ländler*-like trio of the scherzo will surely find a ready response in any lover of Viennese-style melody. In short this is a most rewarding piece, especially when it is played as eloquently as it is here, with a ripely blended recording to match the warmth of the playing. At times one might feel that a degree more fire would be welcome, but the performance does not lack spontaneity. The tape transfer is immaculate and beautifully balanced.

String sextet No. 2 in G, Op. 36.
*** CRD CRD 1046/CRDC 4046. Augmented Alberni Qt – BRUCKNER: *Intermezzo and trio.* ***

A splendid account of the *Second String sextet* to match the excellence of the *First* by this same group. Both works have proved elusive in the recording studio, but now we have thoroughly recommendable versions on disc and tape. The playing is splendidly alive and succeeds in matching expressive feeling with

vigour. The finale is especially spirited.
On tape the sound is full-blooded, with a
fresh, clean treble.

*Violin sonatas Nos. 1 in G, Op. 78; 2
in A, Op. 100; 3 in D min., Op. 108.*
(M) *** Decca Ace SDD/*KSDC* 542.
Suk, Katchen.

Violin sonatas Nos. 2–3.
** DG 2530 806. Zukerman, Barenboim.

Decca have squeezed all three sonatas
on a single disc with no loss in quality;
indeed the recording of the violin is
especially smooth and real and the piano
tone has both amplitude and clarity. The
balance is excellent. Suk's personal blend
of romanticism and the classical tradition
is warmly attractive but small in scale.
These are intimate performances, with
much less of the grand manner than
Szeryng and Rubinstein found in their
readings on RCA. But in their own way
they are most enjoyable, and in many
respects they are a first choice. The cassette offers superb quality: one of Decca's
demonstration tapes.

Highly polished performances from
Zukerman and Barenboim, generally
well recorded. Zukerman's approach
tends to be much the same in both works,
and some listeners may find him a shade
too suave and sweet. But there is much
more to admire than to cavil at, and
Barenboim is particularly strong and
thoughtful in this repertoire. Although
this would not displace the Suk/Katchen
set, which has all three sonatas, it is well
worth considering as an alternative.

PIANO MUSIC

4 Ballades, Op. 10.
*** DG Dig. 2532/*3302* 017 [id.]. Michelangeli – SCHUBERT: *Sonata No. 4.* **

*4 Ballades; 2 Rhapsodies, Op. 79;
Waltzes, Op. 39.*

(M) **(*) Decca Ace SDD 535 [Lon. STS
15527]. Katchen.

*4 Ballades; Variations and fugue on a
theme by Handel, Op. 24.*
**(*) Ph. 9500 446/*7300 652* [id.]. Arrau.

Fantasias, Op. 116; Pieces, Op. 76.
(M) ** Decca Ace SDD 533. Katchen.

Michelangeli plays an instrument
made in the 1910s which produces a
wonderfully blended tone and a fine
mellow sonority. The *Ballades* are given
a performance of the greatest distinction
and without the slightly aloof quality that
at times disturbs his readings. Gilels has
the greater insight and inwardness, perhaps, but there is no doubt that this is
very fine playing, and it is superbly
recorded, with the chrome cassette
matching the disc closely.

Arrau's record offers some masterly
piano playing and splendidly full sound.
As always, Arrau draws a marvellous
range of sonority from the keyboard and
there are moments of characteristic insight and penetration. But, generally
speaking, the *Ballades* need just a shade
more poetic feeling than he brings to
them. Here Gilels remains unchallenged.
The performance of the *Handel variations*
ranks among the finest on record, though
again some listeners may be troubled by
this or that detail to which Arrau lends
expressive significance. However, this is
playing of strong personality and tonal
finesse. The cassette is full in timbre
(especially in the *Ballades*), but the upper
range lacks the last degree of crispness of
focus.

Katchen's style in Brahms is distinctive. There is a hardness about it that
suits some works better than others. In
general the bigger, tougher pieces come
off better than the gentle *Intermezzi*,
which lack the sort of inner tension that
Curzon or Kempff can convey. But such
pieces as the two *Rhapsodies*, Op. 79, are
splendidly done, and so are the *Ballades*.
The *Waltzes*, brief trivial ideas but on the
whole extrovert, come somewhere in

between. Katchen misses some of the magic with his uncoaxing style, but the brightness is still attractive. The recording of the whole cycle can be recommended in Decca's bright, slightly percussive manner of the mid-sixties.

Hungarian dances Nos. 1–21 (for piano duet).
(M) **(*) Decca Ace SDD 536. Katchen, Marty.

Katchen and Marty are first-rate, offering playing with real sparkle, and the recording is suitably brilliant. But Katchen plays Book 1 in Brahms's later arrangement for piano solo, so this is an alternative choice.

3 Intermezzi, Op. 117; 6 Pieces, Op. 118; 4 Pieces, Op. 119.
(M) ** Decca Acc SDD 532. Katchen.

6 Pieces, Op. 118; 4 Pieces, Op. 119; Rhapsody in G min., Op. 79/2.
*** Decca SXL 6831 [Lon. 7051]. Lupu.

4 Pieces, Op. 119; Variations and fugue on a theme of Handel.
** CBS 76913/40- [Col. M/MT 35177]. Serkin.

Radu Lupu's late Brahms is quite outstanding in every way. He brings to this repertoire both concentration and depth of feeling. There is great intensity and inwardness when these qualities are required, and a keyboard mastery that is second to none. The quality of the recorded sound is wide in range and splendidly immediate, and his delicacy of colouring is most truthfully conveyed. This is undoubtedly one of the best Brahms recitals currently before the public, and no connoisseur of this repertoire should overlook it.

Katchen is at his best in the stronger, more intense pieces; in the gentler music he is sometimes less persuasive, though his playing is never devoid of sensitivity. He is clearly if not very luminously recorded.

There are perceptive touches from Serkin in the Op. 119 *Intermezzi*, though the *B minor* has some curiously heavy-handed accents. The account of the *Handel variations* is also a compound of penetration and some curiously ugly mannerisms. Serkin is always an artist who inspires some awe for his quality of mind, and students of the piano and of Brahms should seek this out. The sound quality, however, is rather shallow and clangorous (the tape matches the disc); the studio obviously poses problems; and on these grounds Radu Lupu is to be preferred in Op. 119 and Katchen in the *Variations*.

18 Liebeslieder waltzes, Op. 52; Variations on a theme by Robert Schumann, Op. 23; Waltzes, Op. 39 (for piano duet).
** HMV ASD 4079. Béroff, Collard.

The recording here is disappointingly clangorous, but the performances of Béroff and Collard are brilliant and persuasive. The rare *Variations* make a valuable makeweight to the two sets of waltzes.

Piano sonatas Nos. 1 in C, Op. 1; 2 in F sharp min., Op. 2.
*** DG 2531 252 [id.]. Zimerman.
(M) ** Decca Ace SDD 534. Katchen.

Piano sonata No. 3 in F min., Op. 5; Scherzo in E flat min., Op. 4.
(M) ** Decca Ace SDD 539. Katchen.

These early sonatas have been well served by Katchen, Arrau and others, but never better than by Krystian Zimerman. He brings to them qualities of mind and spirit that more than justify the plaudits which greeted his record on its first appearance. The perfection of his technique can be taken for granted, but there is also a surpassing artistry that leaves no doubt that one is in the presence of a master. At the same time, such is its quality that attention is exclusively concentrated on Brahms and not Zimerman. Those who have hitherto regarded the *C major Sonata*, with its echoes of the *Hammerklavier*, as an uninteresting piece should lose no time in hearing Zimerman's performance. The work emerges with an altogether fresh urgency and expressive power, and the young Polish pianist has the qualities of intellect and temperament to do it full justice. The recorded sound is very good indeed.

Katchen's playing of the first two sonatas hardly achieves the same compelling intensity as Zimerman, but the result is always exciting. These performances are brilliant and assured, and Katchen's account of Op. 5 is similarly commanding. The recording is excellent. But in the *F minor Sonata* Curzon, also on Ace of Diamonds (Decca SDD 498 [Lon. STS 15272]), has a more perceptive and humane approach, and one continues to prefer his greater intensity and freshness. Technically too this record is of the finest Decca vintage.

Double piano sonata in F min., Op. 34b; Variations on a theme by Haydn, Op. 56b.
* DG 2531/*3301* 100 [id.]. Kontarsky Duo.

This distinguished partnership sets great store by clarity of texture, and the result can sometimes seem a little clinical. The *Sonata* actually began as a string quintet before migrating to the keyboard, and then ending life as the *Piano quintet*. The Kontarskys make heavy weather of much of it, and are too prone to point-making and interrupting the rhythmic flow of the music to be wholly recommendable. The very opening theme is treated in an extremely mannered fashion, and, generally speaking, one feels the lack of a true inner tension. Much the same applies to the *Haydn vari-*

ations, which are not otherwise represented in the catalogue. The Eden and Tamir version of the Op. 34b *Sonata* remains first choice (Decca SXL 6303 [Lon. 6533]).

Variations on a Hungarian song, Op. 21/2; Variations on an original theme, Op. 21/1; Variations on a theme by Schumann, Op. 9.
(M) *** Decca Ace SDD 537. Katchen.

One of the most worthwhile of the complete Brahms cycle that Julius Katchen recorded. The *Schumann* is a neglected work and so are the others, and they are played with the utmost persuasiveness and artistry by Katchen, who is also given the benefit of a vivid recording. This is a most compelling issue.

Variations and fugue on a theme by Handel, Op. 24; Variations on a theme by Paganini, Op. 35.
(M) *(*) Decca Ace SDD 538 [Lon. STS 15150]. Katchen.

Brilliant though these performances are, they are not the finest of Katchen's impressive cycle. Oddly enough, for all their sheer pyrotechnical display, they remain curiously uncompelling. One admired the *Ballades* and the *Schumann variations* much more; these sound comparatively unspontaneous by their side.

VOCAL AND CHORAL MUSIC

Agnes; Die Botschaft; Dein blaues Auge; Der Frühling; Heimweh; Immer leiser; In den Beeren; Der Jäger; Komm bald; Des liebsten Schwur; Das Mädchen spricht; Spanisches Lied; Die Trauernde; Vergebliches Ständchen; Volkskinderlieder: Sandmännchen; Von ewiger Liebe; Von waldbekränzter Höhe; Wiegenlied.

**(*) Ph. 9500 398 [id./7300 796]. Amel-
ing, Baldwin.

Elly Ameling's fresh bright soprano is
well suited to most of these songs, but
inevitably in such a demanding setting as
Von ewiger Liebe she lacks weight and
depth of expression. Within its limits it is
a charming recital, well recorded.

Die Botschaft. (i) *2 Songs with viola,
Op. 91 (Gestillte Sehnsucht; Geist-
liches Wiegenlied). Immer leiser; Die
Mainacht; Meine Liebe ist grün; O
komme, holde Sommernacht; Ständ-
chen; Therese; Der Tod das ist die
kühle Nacht; Von ewiger Liebe; Wie
Melodien zieht es mir.*
**(*) Ph. 9500 785/7300 859. Norman,
Parsons, with (i) Von Wrochem.

The scale and tonal range of Jessye
Norman's voice are ideal for many of
these songs, but in some of them there is
a studied quality which makes the result
a little too static. That is particularly so
in the most ambitious of the songs, *Von
ewiger Liebe*, which mistakenly is put
first. Nonetheless, there is much distinguished singing and playing here, and it
is superbly recorded. The cassette has not
quite the refinement of the disc, the voice
losing something in presence at low level,
and becoming slightly fierce at fortissimo.

*A German requiem, Op. 45. Varia-
tions on a theme of Haydn, Op. 56a.*
**(*) Decca D 135 D 2/K 135 K 22 (2)
[Lon. 12114/5-]. Te Kanawa, Weikl,
Chicago Ch. and O., Solti.

(i) *A German requiem;* (ii) *Alto rhap-
sody, Op. 53.*
**(*) CBS 79211 (2) [Col. M/MT 34583].
New Philh. O., Maazel, with (i) Cot-
rubas, Prey, New Philh. Ch., (ii)
Minton, Amb. S.

*A German requiem; Schicksalslied,
Op. 54.*

**(*) Ph. 6769/7654 055 (2) [id.]. Jano-
witz, Krause, V. State Op. Ch., VPO,
Haitink.

Haitink (like Solti) chooses very slow
tempi in the *German requiem*. There is a
rapt quality in this glowing performance
that creates an atmosphere of simple
dedication; at slow speed *Denn alles
Fleisch (All flesh is grass)* is made the
more relentless when, with total concentration, textures are so sharply clarified.
The digital recording offers beautiful
sound on disc (the cassettes, transferred
at a low level, are disappointingly amor-
phous and bass-heavy), and with outstanding soloists – Gundula Janowitz
notably pure and poised – this is very
persuasive, even if Klemperer (see below)
shows even more grip. The fill-up is the
rarely recorded *Schicksalslied (Song of
Destiny)*, which is most welcome and is
admirably sung and played.

Even more strikingly than in his set of
the Brahms symphonies Solti here
favours very expansive tempi, smooth
lines and refined textures. There is much
that is beautiful, even if the result overall
is not as involving as it might be. Kiri Te
Kanawa sings radiantly, but Bernd Weikl
with his rather gritty baritone is not ideal.
Fine recording, glowing and clear, with
an excellent tape equivalent, full-blooded
and only fractionally less cleanly detailed
in the choral pianissimos.

Maazel directs a strong unaffected
performance, most impressive in the
great choral climaxes such as *Denn alles
Fleisch*. There is more sense of spontaneity here than in Maazel's Cleveland
records of the Brahms symphonies, and
the warm acoustic is apt for the music.
The soloists are both good, though Cotrubas's beautiful tone has a hint of unsteadiness, exaggerated by the recording.
The fill-up is welcome, though not
generous: Yvonne Minton sings with
gloriously full tone and expansive phrasing, but hardly needs such a close balance
of recording.

Still recommended: Measured and

monumental, but uniquely powerful, Klemperer's set (HMV SLS 821 [Ang. S 3624) has strong claims on the collector, and the recording still sounds well. In complete contrast with Klemperer's four-square account, there is Karajan's HMV recording (SLS 996 [Ang. S 3838]), more opulent in sound, the reading smooth and moulded.

Mädchenlieder; Zigeunerlieder, Op. 100.
*** Mer. E 77042. Walker, Vignoles –
DVOŘÁK: *Folksongs* etc.***

It was Brahms's own suggestion to put together four of his songs on maidenly themes. Sarah Walker sings them with fine characterful tone and rich insight. The *Zigeunerlieder* too are most satisfyingly done if with fewer magic touches than one might expect from this remarkable singer. Excellent accompaniment from Roger Vignoles and truthful recording.

4 Serious songs, Op. 121. (i) *2 Songs with viola, Op. 91.* Songs: *Auf dem Kirchhofe; Der Jäger; Regenlied; Sapphische Ode; Ständchen; Therese; Vergebliches Ständchen; Wie Melodien zieht es mir.*
*** HMV ASD/*TC-ASD* 3605. [Ang. S 37519]. Baker, Previn, (i) with Aronowitz.

The gravity and nobility of Dame Janet Baker's singing in the *Four Serious songs* underline the weight of the biblical words while presenting them with a far wider and more beautiful range of tone-colour than is common. André Previn's accompaniment is placed rather backwardly, but his rhythmic control provides fine support, and in the more varied songs on the reverse the partnership blossoms still further, best of all in the two *Viola songs*, which are ravishingly sung and played, with the late Cecil Aronowitz making his last appearance on record. The witty *Vergebliches Ständchen* is taken more slowly than usual, with pauses exaggerated, but like the other performances it emerges warm and compelling. Apart from the piano balance the recording is excellent. The tape transfer has plenty of presence, but the vocal projection is rather fierce in fortissimos.

Brian, Havergal (1876–1972)

Symphonies Nos. 8 in B flat minor; 9 in A minor.
*** HMV ASD 3486. Royal Liv. PO, Groves.

It is astonishing that Havergal Brian's music has been so shamefully neglected by the recording companies in favour of avant-garde scores of much more dubious merit. But following on Lyrita's recording of the *Sixth* and *Sixteenth Symphonies* this enterprising coupling from HMV undoubtedly deserves support. Groves gives a splendid account of the *Ninth*, a work of undoubted power and atmosphere. No. 8 is a rather more complex and enigmatic piece, and the performance is marginally less assured. But there is fine orchestral playing throughout and the coupling merits the strongest recommendation, for the music's harmonic language is not too 'difficult' for anyone who enjoys Mahler to come to terms with. The recording is first-class.

Symphonies Nos. (i) *10 in C min.;* (ii) *21 in E flat.*
(M) ** Uni. UNS 265. Leicestershire Schools SO, (i) Loughran, (ii) Pinkett.

It was left to a small company and an amateur orchestra to make this first recording of a Brian symphony. Both are works of his old age; No. 10, a powerfully-wrought and original one-movement work, dates from 1953–4 and is the more immediately appealing of the two. No. 21 was composed when he was in his late eighties and is in four movements. There need be no serious reservations about the recording, and the performances are astonishingly accomplished.

Bridge, Frank (1879–1941)

Dance poem; Dance rhapsody; Overture Rebus.
*** Lyr. SRCS 114. LPO, Braithwaite.

This anthology spans Frank Bridge's creative career: the *Dance rhapsody* dates from 1908 and is a virtuoso piece which bears witness to the influence of Ravel, though that is more pronounced in the *Dance poem* of 1909. These are valuable additions to Bridge's representation on record, though the most important work here is the *Overture Rebus*, his last piece, dating from 1940, much sparer and more original in its scoring – and, for that matter, in substance. It would be hard to imagine more responsive and idiomatic orchestral playing than the LPO's under Nicholas Braithwaite or more sumptuous and vivid recorded sound, which is particularly well defined in the bass.

Lament for string orchestra; Two Old English songs (1, Sally in our alley; 2, Cherry ripe); Rosemary (Entracte No. 1); Sir Roger de Coverley (Christmas dance); Suite for string orchestra.
*** Lyr. SRCS 73. LPO, Boult.

All these pieces are expertly crafted and, though light in character, they are far from insignificant. They are nicely played by the LPO under Sir Adrian and recorded with great clarity and presence. A useful though not essential part of the Frank Bridge discography.

(i) *Oration: Concerto elegiaco for cello and orchestra. Allegro moderato* (from unfinished *Symphony for strings); 2 Poems.*
*** Lyr. SRCS 104. LPO, Braithwaite, (i) with Lloyd Webber.

Oration is one of Bridge's most searching and ambitious works, a full-scale cello concerto in a single movement half an hour long. It was inspired by the tragedy of the First World War, in which some of Bridge's closest friends had been killed. Julian Lloyd Webber gives a passionately committed performance, and although Braithwaite does not hold the massive structure together with quite the consistent tension it needs (slow music outlasts fast by a substantial margin) the mastery of the piece is not in doubt. The couplings are excellent, guaranteed to fascinate and equally extending our appreciation of a highly individual and long-neglected composer. Excellent recording.

Suite for string orchestra; Summer; There Is a Willow Grows Aslant a Brook (impression for small orchestra).
*** RCA RL/RK 25184. Bournemouth Sinf., Del Mar – BANTOCK: *Pierrot* **(*); BUTTERWORTH: *Banks of Green Willow.****

Norman Del Mar draws glowing performances from the Sinfonietta of these Bridge pieces. Most valuable of all is the tone poem *Summer*, with its highly original evocative instrumentation. Glowing recording quality to match; the tape transfer is smooth and natural but slightly diffuse in character. The dynamic range is less strikingly wide than on the LP.

There Is a Willow Grows Aslant a Brook.

(M) *** HMV Green. ESD/TC-ESD 7100. E. Sinfonia, Dilkes – Concert (English music).***

Bridge's 'impression', beautifully played, is a highlight in an excellent concert of English music, warmly recorded on both disc and cassette (see the Concerts section below).

Cello sonata.
** Nimbus 2117. Hocks, Jones – KODÁLY: Sonata.*(*)

The young cellist Christian Hocks brings freshness and commitment to Frank Bridge's Sonata. He is forwardly placed by comparison with the pianist, who plays with great sensitivity and imagination, but the recording is acceptable, albeit not distinguished. But while the recording by Rostropovich and Benjamin Britten on Decca remains available it is a first choice both artistically and for recorded quality (SXL 6426 [Lon. 6449]).

Elegy for cello and piano.
*** ASV ACA/ZCACA 1001. Lloyd Webber, McCabe – BRITTEN: Suite ***; IRELAND: Sonata.**(*)

Though written as early as 1911, the Elegy, darkly poignant, points forward to the sparer, more austere style of later Bridge. It is good to have this important miniature included on this richly varied disc. The performance is deeply committed, though the recording balance strongly favours the cello. The cassette matches the disc closely.

Trio (Rhapsody).
** Pearl SHE 547. Georgiadis, Hawkins, Watson – BAX: Rhapsodic ballad ***; BERKELEY: Trio.**

The Trio is for the unusual combination of two violins and viola, and comes from 1928, the period of the Third Quartet

and the Second Piano trio. It is exploratory, questing and powerfully inventive, though not in every respect satisfying. It is played with conviction and some passion by these three players, and only the dryness of the recording lets things down.

Piano sonata; 4 Characteristic pieces (Water Nymphs; Fragrance; Bittersweet; Fireflies); 3 Lyrics (Heart's Ease; Dainty Rogue; The Hedgerow); 3 Poems (Solitude; Ecstasy; Sunset).
*** Uni. RHS 359. Parkin.

Bridge's Sonata is a powerful and dark work which reflects the emotional turbulence and sense of grief that the 1914–18 war inspired. Its eloquence and concentration of feeling will impress even those who do not readily respond to Bridge's art. Eric Parkin certainly brings gifts of eloquent persuasion and intellectual grip to this music, and succeeds in viewing it with the right blend of passion and objectivity. He also seems at home with the less ambitious piano works recorded on this disc and makes out an impressive case for the softer-centred pieces, such as Sunset, as well as the more exploratory ones (including the remarkable Solitude). He is accorded clear and well-focused sound, and the disc has the advantage of a particularly perceptive and helpful sleeve-note from Christopher Palmer.

Britten, Benjamin (1913–76)

Violin concerto in D min., Op. 15.
*** HMV ASD/TC-ASD 3483. Haendel, Bournemouth SO, Berglund – WALTON: Violin concerto.***

Ida Haendel's performance is a worthy challenger to Mark Lubotsky's account

coupled with Britten's *Piano concerto*
(Decca SXL/*KSXC* 6512 [Lon. 6723]).
Miss Haendel's ravishing playing places
the work firmly in the European tradition. She brings great panache and
brilliance to the music as well as a great
expressive warmth. This is a reading very
much in the grand manner, and it finds
Paavo Berglund in excellent form. His
support is sensitive in matters of detail
and full of atmosphere. The recording is
the richest and most successfully realistic
of all, with a beautifully spacious perspective and warm, velvety string tone
that is positively Mediterranean in feeling. The soloist is balanced a little close,
but generally the security of her technique can stand up to such a revealing
spotlight. The Lubotsky version has the
authority of the composer's direction,
but the Haendel has no less conviction
and spirit. The tape transfer must be accounted one of the most successful now
on the market: it is difficult to tell much
difference between it and the LP.

Simple symphony (for strings), *Op.
4.*
**(*) Abbey ABY 810. Scottish Bar.
Ens., Friedman – ELGAR: *Serenade* **;
WARLOCK: *Capriol suite*; WILLIAM-
SON: *English lyrics.* **(*)
(M) **(*) Ph. Fest. 6570/7310 181 [id.]. I
Musici – BARBER: *Adagio*; BARTÓK:
Rumanian folk dances; RESPIGHI:
*Ancient airs.***(*)

The Scottish Baroque Ensemble gives
an energetic, warm-hearted performance
of the youthful Britten inspiration, well
recorded but not as polished as most of
its rivals. The *Sentimental saraband* is
particularly successful, played with feeling yet with the right degree of restraint,
and the *Playful pizzicato* shows real high
spirits.
The playing of I Musici is distinguished
but the Italian group takes Britten's work
rather seriously. There is an earnest
quality to the *Playful pizzicato* here that

misses some of its nursery rhyme fun.
However, in all other respects the performance is excellent, and the *Saraband* is
played with an engaging quality of wistful tenderness. The sound is first-rate on
disc and cassette alike.

Sinfonia da Requiem, Op. 20.
(M) **(*) CBS 61167/40- [Odys. Y
31016]. St Louis SO, Previn – COP-
LAND: *Red Pony.***(*)

Neither in virtuosity, precision nor
vividness of sound can Previn's St Louis
performance of the *Sinfonia da Requiem*
quite match his later HMV version with
the LSO (ASD 3154 [Ang. S 37142]), but
this first of his serious orchestral recordings gives ample evidence of his energy,
with the urgency of the inspiration never
faltering for a moment. With its attractive Copland coupling it makes a good
medium-price issue. The tape transfer is
very successful (it benefits from a small
bass cut). The later HMV recording is
not available on cassette.

*Suite on English folksongs (A time
there was), Op. 30; Peter Grimes: 4
Sea interludes and Passacaglia.*
**(*) CBS 76640 [Col. M/*MT* 34529].
NYPO, Bernstein.

On the face of it Britten's *Suite on
English folksongs* with its title quoted
from Hardy is a relatively lightweight
work, but this performance, like the première at the Maltings in 1975, reveals a
darkness and weight of expression
behind the seemingly trivial plan. The
third movement, *Hankin Booby*, written
for the opening of the Queen Elizabeth
Hall in London, is an angular piece in
which woodwind squeals in imitation of
medieval manners. The other movements
are less abrasive. For violins alone, *Hunt
the squirrel* is brief, brilliant and witty;
the final movement, *Lord Melbourne*,
with its extended cor anglais solo, is
plainly music written in the shadow of
death. Bernstein's performance misses a

little of the wit, but is warmly sympathetic, and the dramatic account of the *Grimes Interludes* makes a fair coupling. Recording is good but not as full-ranging in the *Interludes* as, for example, the Previn HMV version.

Variations on a theme of Frank Bridge, Op. 10.

⊛ (M) *** HMV mono XLP/*TC-XLP* 60002. Philh. O., Karajan – VAUGHAN WILLIAMS: *Tallis fantasia.* ⊛ ***

If all stereo issues of the 1980s sounded like this mono recording of the mid-1950s, there would be no need for a *Penguin Stereo Record Guide*! The sound is astonishingly fresh and vivid, and the playing of the Philharmonia strings is of the highest order of distinction. They produce beautifully blended tone, rich and full-bodied yet marvellously delicate at the pianissimo end of the dynamic spectrum. Karajan's reading is unaffected yet impassioned, quite electrifying in the *Funeral march*. The quality on cassette is at the very least as impressive as the disc (at times even more so) and one can hardly believe this is not real stereo. Indeed the recording compares well with some of the finest digital stereo issues of the eighties. This is an issue that should never be out of the catalogue.

The Young Person's Guide to the Orchestra (Variations and fugue on a theme of Purcell), Op. 34.

(M) *** HMV Green. ESD/*TC-ESD* 7114. Royal Liv. PO, Groves – PROKOFIEV: *Peter*; SAINT-SAËNS: *Carnival.****

(B) **(*) Con. CC/*CCT* 7519. Connery, RPO, Dorati – PROKOFIEV: *Peter.****

** RCA RL/*RK* 12743 [ARL 1/*ARK 1* 2743] (without narration). Phd. O., Ormandy – PROKOFIEV: *Peter.***(*)

Groves's recording has been imaginatively and generously recoupled (at medium price) with excellent versions of *Peter and the Wolf* and the *Carnival of the Animals*, making a superb anthology for children of all ages. Groves's performance of the *Variations* is lively and genial; if it lacks the last degree of finesse, it has both high spirits and a fine sense of pace. The trumpet variation displays splendid bravura, and the flute and clarinet variations too are engagingly extrovert. The recording is first-class, vividly colourful and full-bodied, with an outstandingly brilliant cassette transfer to match the disc in clarity of focus.

The Sean Connery/Dorati version is obviously aimed at the listener whose knowledge of the orchestra is minimal. Connery's easy style is attractive and this version should go down well with young people, even if some of the points are made rather heavily. The orchestral playing is generally first-rate. This is perhaps not a version for everyone, but many will like it for its spontaneity, to which Connery contributes not a little. The recording was originally made using Decca's Phase Four techniques, which can – and do – bring forward solo instruments. But in this instance such a balance seems justifiable and the sound is clear, with instrumental timbres slightly exaggerated by the close microphones. As so often with Contour reissues, the cassette has a restricted range; here the transients are unacceptably blunted.

Ormandy's performance is straightforward and very well played. It has no special individuality, and the recording is brilliant rather than sumptuous, although not dry. There is some blurring on the cassette at the opening and close of the work.

Still recommended: Britten's own recording (Decca SXL/ *KSXC* 6450 [Lon. 6671]) and Previn's (HMV ASD/*TC-ASD* 2935 [Ang. S/ *4XS* 36962]) continue to head the recommendations.

Lachrymae (for viola and piano), *Op. 48.*

(M) *** Sup. 1111 2694. Kodousek, Novotná – CLARKE and ECCLES: *Sonatas.****

Britten's *Lachrymae* dates from 1950 and is a much underrated piece, inspired by Dowland (it is subtitled *Reflections on a Song by John Dowland*). Its dark-toned melancholy is finely conveyed by Josef Kodousek and his sensitive partner, Kveta Novotná, and the coupling is undoubtedly enterprising.

String quartet No. 1 in D, Op. 25.
**(*) CRD CRD 1051/*CRDC 4051.*
Alberni Qt – SHOSTAKOVICH: *Piano quintet.***(*)

String quartets Nos. 2 in C, Op. 36; 3, Op. 94.
*** Decca SXL 6893. Amadeus Qt.
*** CRD CRD 1095/*CRDC 4095.* Alberni Qt.

Those who do not wish to duplicate Britten's *Second Quartet* (if they possess either the Amadeus or the Allegri versions) will find the well-recorded and conscientiously played reading of the *First* on CRD an admirable choice. The Alberni Quartet have good ensemble and intonation, and the sound is well detailed. The cassette transfer is of CRD's usual outstanding quality, with a high-level transfer bringing wide range, body and detail.

The *Third String quartet*, written for the Amadeus Quartet at the very end of the composer's life, is a spare, seemingly wayward work that reveals its depth of feeling with the repetition possible on record. The brooding *Passacaglia* shows clearly enough that, despite Britten's serious illness during his final years, his individual inspiration still burned. That movement is here strikingly contrasted with the forceful *Chaconne* which ends the *Second Quartet*, written in 1945 to commemorate the 250th anniversary of Purcell's death. The Amadeus recording, made in 1963, is the perfect coupling for

their newly recorded version of the *Third.* The recorded sound is excellent in both.

The Alberni performances are a degree less refined than those by the Amadeus, but they have a thrusting, gutsy quality which many will prefer, and the CRD recording is richer and fuller. An excellent cassette version is also available.

Suite for unaccompanied cello No. 3, Op. 87.
*** ASV ACA/*ZCACA* 1001. Lloyd Webber – BRIDGE: *Elegy* ***; IRELAND: *Sonata.***(*)

The *Third Suite* which Britten wrote for Rostropovich may be less ambitious in plan than its predecessors, but in such a performance as Lloyd Webber's the very directness and lyrical approachability in the sharply characterized sequence of pieces – *Marcia, Canto, Barcarolla, Dialogo, Fuga* etc. – make for the extra emotional impact. With Lloyd Webber the climax of the extended final *Passacaglia* is extraordinarily powerful, and all through he brings out what might be described as the schizophrenic side of the work, the play between registers high and low. These sharp contrasts are used not just to imply full orchestral textures but to interweave opposing ideas as the movements merge. The recording is full and warm; the cassette balance is wholly natural (although the level could have been a little higher).

Collection: (i) *Prelude and fugue on a theme of Vittoria.* (ii) *Festival Te Deum; Hymn of St Columba.* (iii) *Hymn to St Cecilia.* (ii) *Hymn to St Peter; Hymn to the Virgin; Jubilate Deo; Missa brevis.*
(M) *** Argo ZK 19. (i) Preston (organ); (ii) St John's College Ch., Guest; Runnett (organ); (iii) LSO Ch., Malcolm.

A useful anthology of some of Britten's shorter choral works. The *Vittoria*

Prelude and fugue is Britten's only solo
organ piece and it is excellently played
and recorded here. The recordings of the
Festival Te Deum, *Hymn to the Virgin* and
Jubilate Deo were originally presented
within a highly praised collection of twentieth-century English church music, with
the St John's Choir in superb form. While
the *Hymn to the Virgin* was an early work,
written in 1930, the *Hymn to St Cecilia* is
a much more ambitious piece, written
just before the war, when Britten's technique was already prodigious. The setting exactly matches the imaginative,
capricious words of Auden. A highly recommendable and generous disc.

A Ceremony of Carols, Op. 28 (with
carols arr. Ellis: *Away in a manger;
Coventry carol; Deck the hall; Ding
dong merrily on high; I saw three
ships; Once in Royal David's city;
We've been awhile a-wandering*).
**(*) RCA RL/*RK* 30467 [ARL 1/*ARK
1* 3437]. V. Boys' Ch., Harrer; Ellis
(harp).

The Vienna Boys – for whom Britten
wrote his *Golden Vanity* – give a brisk and
fresh account of the *Ceremony of Carols*,
beautifully tuned and not marred by the
fruity tones which sometimes come from
this choir. The processionals at the beginning and end are not very atmospheric, but the recording is fresh to
match the voices. Osian Ellis, who
accompanies in the Britten work, then
provides some fancy arrangements of
British carols with harp accompaniment,
shouts and contrived dissonances.

(i) *Les Illuminations* (song cycle), *Op.
18*. (ii) *Serenade for tenor, horn and
strings, Op. 31*.
*** DG 2531/*3301* 199 [id.]. Tear, cond.
Giulini, with (i) Philh. O., (ii) Clevenger, Chicago SO.

Giulini has long been a persuasive

advocate of Britten's music, and the fact
that these two excellent performances
were recorded on opposite sides of the
Atlantic adds to the attractions, for the
Philharmonia produces playing of
warmth and resonance to match that of
the Chicago orchestra. Without apology
Giulini presents both cycles as full-scale
orchestra works, and though some detail
may be lost, the strength of Britten's
writing amply justifies it. Tear is at his
finest in both cycles, more open than in
his earlier recording of the *Serenade*.
Dale Clevenger is a superb horn-player,
and though in places some may find him
unidiomatic it is good to have a fresh
view in such music. Soloists are balanced
rather close, in an otherwise excellent
vivid recording. The cassette too is of
outstanding, demonstration quality.

Spring symphony, Op. 44.
*** HMV ASD/*TC-ASD* 3650 [Ang. S
37562]. Armstrong, Baker, Tear, St
Clement Dane's School Boys' Ch.,
LSO Ch., LSO, Previn.

Just as Colin Davis's interpretation of
Peter Grimes provides a strikingly new
view of a work of which the composer
seems the natural interpreter, so André
Previn's reading of the *Spring symphony*
is valuably distinctive. Like Britten,
Previn makes this above all a work of
exultation, a genuine celebration of
spring; but here more than in Britten's
recording the kernel of what the work has
to say comes out in the longest of the solo
settings, using Auden's poem *Out on the
lawn I lie in bed*. With Janet Baker as
soloist it rises above the lazily atmospheric mood of the opening to evoke the
threat of war and darkness. Perhaps
surprisingly, it is Britten who generally
adopts faster tempi and a sharper rhythmic style, whereas Previn is generally the
more atmospheric and mysterious, grad-
ing the climaxes and shading the tones
over longer spans. He also takes more
care over pointing Britten's pay-offs,

often with the help of Robert Tear's sense of timing, as at the very end on *I cease*. Rich, atmospheric recording with glorious bass resonances, and a good cassette, clear and full, if not quite as ample at the bottom end of the spectrum. The choral climaxes are well caught.

The Little Sweep (complete).
*** HMV ASD/*TC-ASD* 3608. Lloyd, Tear, Monck, Begg, Benson, Wells, Finchley Children's Music Group, Choral Scholars of King's College, Medici Qt, two pianos, percussion, Ledger.

The composer's own recording of *The Little Sweep* – the operatic second half of the entertainment *Let's Make an Opera* – was in mono only, and one principal gain in this recording directed by Britten's longtime collaborator at the Aldeburgh Festival is the vividness of atmosphere. The game of hide-and-seek sounds much more real, and though the words are not always ideally clear, there is a good illusion of having an audience and not a trained choir singing them. In the cast Sam Monck as the little sweep himself is delightfully fresh-toned and artless – less expressive than the star-to-be, David Hemmings, on Britten's record, but just as appealing – and among the others the outstanding contributor is Heather Begg as the dragon-like Miss Baggott, bringing out the occasional likenesses with Gilbert and Sullivan in some of the patter ensembles. Apart from the cast of grown-ups, the solos are taken by members of the Finchley Children's Music Group, and Ledger's direction follows very much in the tradition set by the composer himself without lacking impetus. On cassette (because of the resonance) the transients are slightly less crisp than on disc, but otherwise the transfer is successful.

Peter Grimes (complete).
*** Ph. 6769 014/*7699 089* (3) [id.].
Vickers, Harper, Summers, Bain-

bridge, Robinson, ROHCG, Ch. and O., Colin Davis.

Colin Davis takes a fundamentally darker, tougher view of *Peter Grimes* than the composer himself. In some ways the result is even more powerful if less varied and atmospheric, with the Borough turned into a dark place full of Strindbergian tensions and Grimes himself, powerful physically (no intellectual misplaced), turned into a Hardy-like figure. It was Jon Vickers's heroic interpretation in the Met. production in New York which first prompted Davis to press for a new recording, and the result sheds keen new illumination on what arguably remains the greatest of Britten's operas. In no way can it be said to supplant the composer's own unique recording on Decca; and Peter Pears's richly detailed and keenly sensitive performance in the name part remains unique too, even though Vickers is so plainly closer in frame and spirit to Crabbe's rough fisherman. Slow-spoken and weighty, Vickers is frighteningly intense. On the Davis set Heather Harper as Ellen Orford is far more moving than her opposite number on Decca, and generally the Philips cast is younger-voiced and fresher, with especially fine contributions from Jonathan Summers as Balstrode (a late choice) and Thomas Allen as Ned Keene. It is a pity the recording producer did not favour the sort of atmospheric effects which set the seal on the Decca version as a riveting experience, but this reinforces Davis's point about the actual notes needing no outside aid. The recording, made at All Saints, Tooting Graveney (not the ideal venue), is rich and vivid, with fine balancing. The Philips tape transfer is of excellent quality, warmly atmospheric and with natural vocal timbre. But the Decca set remains one of the great achievements of the stereo era. Few opera recordings have such claims to be definitive, and the superbly atmospheric recording is as effective on cassette as it is on disc (SXL 2150/2/K 71 K 33 [Lon. 1305]).

Peter Grimes: 4 Sea interludes.
(M) *** Ph. Seq. 6527/7311 112.
ROHCGO, Colin Davis – TIPPETT: *Midsummer Marriage: Dances.****

Davis recorded the *Four Sea interludes* as a dry run before his complete recording of Britten's opera. In many ways these performances are even more spontaneously convincing than the later ones, beautifully played. Well-coupled with the Tippett, they make an excellent medium-price issue. The cassette is of good quality but transferred at a rather low level.

Reminder: Previn's superbly atmospheric version of the *Four Sea interludes* also includes the *Passacaglia* and is coupled with an equally outstanding account of the *Sinfonia da requiem* (HMV ASD 3154 [Ang. S 37142]). With demonstration sound this disc was given a rosette in the second edition of the *Penguin Stereo Record Guide*.

Brouwer, Leo (born 1939)

Guitar concerto.
*** CBS 76715/40-. Williams, L. Sinf., Howarth – ARNOLD: *Concerto.****

Leo Brouwer is a Cuban composer with the kind of avant-garde credentials and fashionable advocacy that inspire vigilance. The intelligent sleeve-note speaks of his being inspired by Ives, Cage, Nono and Xenakis, as well as the ideals of the Cuban revolution! His *Guitar concerto* is strangely powerful and haunting, yet it is not easy to describe it in a way that conveys its character. Its atmosphere is redolent of a jungle-like landscape in which half-real and half-imagined whispers mingle with the cries of exotic birds and the crackle of a living, insect-infested undergrowth. Yet this makes it sound colourful and attractive like some wild Villa-Lobos piece. In fact there is something dark, sour and disturbing about this music. John Williams and the ensemble play as if they believed every note of it, and though it may have less substance than appears, it is undeniably thought-provoking and imaginative. The recording is of good quality; the cassette is less wide-ranging than the disc.

Bruch, Max (1838–1920)

Adagio appassionato; Violin concertos Nos. 1–3; In Memoriam; Konzertstück; Romanze; Scottish fantasia; Serenade.
*** Ph. 6768 065 (4). Accardo, Leipzig GO, Masur.

Although the *G minor Concerto* is the masterpiece here, Accardo's playing is so persuasive in its restrained eloquence that even the less inspired pieces give pleasure. Both the soloist and orchestra play superbly and it is difficult to imagine the set being surpassed for many years to come. The recording is of the highest quality too; the sound is natural, fresh and vivid.

Adagio appassionato, Op. 57; Violin concerto No. 3 in D min., Op. 58; Romanze, Op. 42.
*** Ph. 9500 589/7300 711 [id.]. Accardo, Leipzig GO, Masur.

No one could pretend that the *D minor Concerto* is as inventive or as concentrated as the famous *G minor*, and to be truthful there is much here that is unmemorable. Such is the quality of the playing, however, that the listener is beguiled into thinking it a better work than it is. The melodic invention in the

Adagio appassionato and the *Romanze* is not particularly distinguished either but Accardo and this fine orchestra make out an excellent case for them. The recording is superb. The cassette is slightly less refined in the upper range than the LP, with a tendency to fierceness; but it yields to the controls.

Violin concerto No. 1 in G min., Op. 26.

DG 2531/*3301* 304 [id.]. Mintz, Chicago SO, Abbado – MENDELS-SOHN: *Concerto.(*)

DG Dig. 2532/*3302* 016 [id.]. Mutter, Berlin PO, Karajan – MENDELSSOHN: *Concerto.*

(*) CBS 76726/40- [Col. M/*MT* 35132]. Zukerman, LAPO, Mehta – LALO: *Symphonie espagnole.**

(M) **(*) CBS 61933/40- [Col. MS 7003]. Stern, Phd. O., Ormandy – LALO: *Symphonie espagnole.***(*)

(M) ** DG Priv. 2535/*3335* 176. I. Oistrakh, RPO, D. Oistrakh – BACH: *Double concerto.***

** Erato STU 71164. Amoyal, RPO, Scimone – GLAZOUNOV: *Concerto.****

(B) ** CFP CFP/*TC-CFP* 40374. Milstein, Philh. O., Barzin – MENDELS-SOHN; *Concerto.***

(M) *(*) DG Priv. 2535/*3335* 294 [id.]. Yong Uck Kim, Bamberg SO, Kamu – MENDELSSOHN: *Concerto.***

Shlomo Mintz is a Russian-born player who studied in Israel and then at the Juilliard. This is his first commercial record and makes an exciting début; his account of the Bruch is exceptionally exciting and warm-blooded. No doubt some of the sheer size of his tone can be attributed to the flattering forward balance, which also means that dynamic shading is less evident than it might be. Mintz certainly makes the listener hang on to every phrase and his playing is undoubtedly compelling. The vibrato is wide (one notices it at the pianissimo opening of the *Adagio*) and for some ears

there may be an impression of over-projection and a lack of the kind of inner communion that Perlman (see below) conveys so effectively. Nevertheless this approach is so distinctive and interesting that few listeners will not be fired. The Chicago Symphony Orchestra plays with great brilliance and enthusiasm and Abbado's direction is sympathetic. Marvellously vivid recording (if one accepts the forward balance of the soloist), which has more presence than many digital discs. On cassette, however, the resonance brings a lack of refinement in the orchestral tuttis.

In Anne-Sophie Mutter's hands the concerto has an air of chaste sweetness, shedding much of its ripe, sensuous quality but retaining its romantic feeling. There is a delicacy and tenderness here which are very appealing, and, although the tuttis have plenty of fire, Karajan sensitively scales down his accompaniment in the lyrical passages to match his soloist. There is no doubt of the dedication and conviction of the solo playing or of its natural spontaneity. The digital recording provides a natural balance and a vivid orchestral texture. Though not as rich in timbre as Mintz's performance, this has a pervading freshness that gives much pleasure. The tape is first-class

Zukerman's is a passionately extrovert performance, tempered by a genuine tenderness in the slow movement. The brilliantly lit recording increases the sense of fiery energy in the outer sections; and with the excitement of the solo playing and the strongly committed accompaniment the larger-than-life effect is almost overwhelming. The cassette matches the disc closely, though it is marginally less refined in the extremely vivid tuttis.

Stern's version, dating from the end of the sixties, is even more unrealistically balanced, with the soloist displaying more opulence of tone than the orchestra, which itself is rather coarsely recorded. Nevertheless this is one of the great classic recordings of the work, warm-hearted and rich-toned, with a very moving account of the slow movement which sustains the greatest possible intensity. The finale too has wonderful fire and spirit. Ormandy's accompaniment is first-class and triumphs over the unrealistic balance. The cassette matches the disc fairly closely, but is rather less refined.

The Oistrakhs' DG Privilege version has been recoupled with the Bach *Double concerto*, a fine performance featuring the same partnership, but hardly an imaginative choice. The Bruch is passionately done, father and son combining to make the close of the *Adagio* swell up into a surge of feeling. The first movement is well shaped and the finale has splendid rhythmic verve. The snag is the recording, which is aggressively brilliant and slightly harsh, lacking opulence. The cassette has a smoother upper range (without loss of definition) and is preferable to the disc.

Pierre Amoyal is an eloquent player whose purity of tone and intonation and generosity of feeling make him a joy to listen to. In the Bruch he lacks something of the panache of Perlman or Stern; he is closer to Yong Uck Kim (whose playing is underrated), but he has a fine sense of line. The RPO under Scimone give good support and the recording has plenty of detail and body, even if the soloist is placed rather further forward than is ideal.

Milstein's aristocratic and lyrical playing undoubtedly gives pleasure and he is well supported. The recording is good, although it could be fresher and more expansive. However, at bargain price this is certainly excellent value.

Yong Uck Kim's performances of both the Bruch and the Mendelssohn impress by their purity of style and understated feeling. But such an approach is rather less successful in this ripely romantic work than in the coupling, which readily responds to such delicacy of feeling. Unfortunately the orchestral accompaniment does not match the solo playing in finesse, but the recording is good and well balanced; the tape is slightly less transparent than the disc.

Reminder: Perlman's and Menuhin's couplings of the Bruch and Mendelssohn *Concertos* both retain their places at the top of the list of recommendations. Perlman (HMV ASD/TC-ASD 2926 [Ang. S/4XS 36963] is splendidly recorded and the cassette has been remastered to have its full dynamic range restored (the tape orchestral focus is slightly less sharp than the disc). Menuhin (HMV ASD/TC-ASD 334 [Ang. S 36920]) also now has his performance available on a Dolbyized tape (which needs a treble cut to sound its best).

Violin concertos Nos. 1; 2 in D min., Op. 44.
(***) Ph. 9500 422/7300 460 [id.]. Accardo, Leipzig GO, Masur.

These performances are taken from Accardo's complete set (see above), but in this transfer the sound is shrill and fierce, with the disc cut at a very high level. The cassette has a similar quality, and neither can be recommended.

In Memoriam, Op. 65; Serenade, Op. 75.
*** Ph. 9500 590/7300 712 [id.]. Accardo, Leipzig GO, Masur.

The *Serenade*, a four-movement piece dating from the turn of the century, was originally intended to be a fourth violin concerto. It is an engaging if relatively insubstantial work. The *In Memoriam* is finer (Bruch himself thought highly of it); it has genuine depth and nobility. Performances here are excellent, and the sound is first-class on disc and cassette alike.

Kol Nidrei, Op. 47.
*** HMV ASD/TC-ASD 3728. Paul Tortelier, RPO, Yan-Pascal Tortelier — BOELLMANN: *Symphonic variations* ***; SCHUMANN: *Concerto.* **(*)

The withdrawn, prayerful Bruch piece makes a good contrast with the more ambitious works on this issue, all well played and recorded. The cassette transfer is quite well managed; the sound is clear and fairly wide-ranging.

Konzertstück, Op. 84; Scottish fantasia, Op. 46.
*** Ph. 9500 423/7300 641 [id.]. Accardo, Leipzig GO, Masur.

The *Konzertstück* dates from 1911 and is one of Bruch's last works. As in the case of the *Serenade*, Bruch had toyed with the idea of calling it a violin concerto, but he finally decided on *Konzertstück* as the piece has only two movements. This is its first complete recording, but the American violinist Maud Powell made a disc of part of the slow movement in Bruch's lifetime. The composer wrote in horror to a friend: 'She appears to have played the *Adagio*, shortened by half, into a machine. I really gave her a piece of my mind about this.' One wonders what he would have thought of the present version. Neither this nor the *Scottish fantasia*, written more than three decades earlier, is great music, but it is made the most of by Accardo and the Leipzig orchestra, and is superbly recorded. The cassette transfer is lively but the upper range lacks the refinement of the disc.

Bruckner, Anton (1824–96)

Symphonies Nos. 0; 1–9.
(M) **(*) DG 2740 253 (12). Chicago SO, Barenboim.
Symphonies Nos. 1–9.
*** DG 2740 264 (11) [id.]. Berlin PO, Karajan.

It is a pity that Karajan does not include the *Nullte* in his cycle, and No. 6 is

less concentrated than the rest. But with its spacious speeds, dramatic contrasts and refined playing the cycle overall sets new standards, even if the digital recording for Nos. 1–3 has the orchestral sound closer and less alluring than the rest.

Barenboim's cycle has many excellent things, not least the account of No. 8 (see below), an admirable *Sixth* and a more than serviceable version of the *Ninth*. Barenboim gives us the underrated *Nullte* (see below), though here he is less successful than Haitink. He brings keener and deeper responses in No. 3, and although these performances are not to be recommended in preference to Karajan and Jochum, at their best – as in the *Eighth* – they deserve to rank alongside them, which is no mean achievement. In Nos. 1–3 and 8 Barenboim has the advantage of excellent digital sound. No one investing in this set is likely to be greatly disappointed, though the Karajan cycle will give deeper satisfaction.

Symphony No. 0 in D min.
**(*) DG 2531 319. Chicago SO, Barenboim.

Bruckner's early *D minor Symphony* contains some inspired music; the opening of the finale is a particularly generous idea, and so too is the noble second theme of the first movement. It is a far from negligible work and is as worthy of inclusion in the canon as the *Symphony No. 1 in C minor*. Daniel Barenboim shows evident affection for it but is not content to let the music speak for itself. He gets a generally positive response from the Chicago Symphony. Haitink, however, shows a far stronger sense of the work's structure, and his performance (Ph. SAL 3602 [802 724]) has an unforced eloquence; his recording, too, is as good if not better than the Chicago version.

Symphony No. 1 in C min.
*** HMV ASD/TC-ASD 3825. Dresden State O., Jochum.

Here is a performance which has the measure of Bruckner's majesty and breadth, and which establishes a strong atmosphere from the very outset. There may be some details that came off better in Jochum's earlier set with the Berlin Philharmonic, but the Dresden orchestra plays with an unforced and natural eloquence that silences criticism. As in his earlier recording, Jochum follows the Nowak edition (the 1866 version, modified by some revisions made in the 1890s). The recorded sound is well balanced and spacious; the horn vibrato worries some listeners, but most will find it acceptable. This is arguably the finest account of this underrated symphony that has so far been put on record; it certainly surpasses current rivals, whether available separately or in boxes. The cassette too is one of EMI's very best, with a wide dynamic range and plenty of body and life; and big climaxes are accommodated without strain.

Symphony No. 3 in D min.
*** DG Dig. 2532/*3302* 007 [id.]. Berlin PO, Karajan.
(M) *** DG Priv. 2535/*3335* 265. Bav. RSO, Jochum.

Karajan, using the Nowak edition, directs a performance of enormous intensity and dramatic contrasts. It is not one of his most flawlessly polished readings of Bruckner, but the urgency and sense of spontaneity are ample compensation, and with well-balanced, wide-ranging digital sound it makes an excellent recommendation on disc and cassette alike; they are a very close match.

Jochum also uses the Nowak edition, based on Bruckner's 1888–9 revision rather than the earlier and more extended score of 1878 edited by Oeser. Readers wanting the 1878 edition will have to turn to the noble account given by Haitink. Apart from the textual question the Jochum DG version has wonderful

atmosphere and glorious playing to recommend it. The recording, made in the mid-1960s, still sounds remarkably fine, though not as clear as Karajan's digital version. The cassette too is excellent.

Symphony No. 4 in E flat (*Romantic*).
*** Decca Dig. SXDL/*KSXDC* 7538. Chicago SO, Solti.
(M) *** Decca Jub. JB/*KJBC* 120. VPO, Boehm.
(M) *** Ph. Seq. 6527/*7311* 101 [835385]. Concg. O., Haitink.
** HM 16 065 99738. Cologne RSO, Wand.

As a Brucknerian Solti can hardly be faulted, choosing admirable tempi, keeping concentration taut through the longest paragraphs, and presenting the architecture of the work in total clarity. Raptness is there too, and only the relative lack of Brucknerian idiosyncrasy will disappoint those who prefer a more loving, personal approach. Like Klemperer, Haitink and Boehm, Solti prefers the Nowak edition with the opening motif brought back on the horns at the end of the finale. The tape transfer is one of Decca's finest, with impressive clarity and amplitude and, like the digital disc, striking ambient warmth.

Boehm's very compelling version is beautifully shaped, finely played and splendidly recorded on disc and cassette alike. At medium price it deserves the strongest recommendation.

Haitink's performance has been reissued again on the mid-priced Sequenza label. It is noble and unmannered; the recording is excellent, and the orchestral playing eloquent. The tape is good. Excellent value.

Günter Wand's reading has been much acclaimed in some quarters. His tempi are inclined to be a little brisker than usual, which serves to hold the architecture together more tautly than is sometimes the case. The orchestral playing is good though not in the top drawer, and the recording is fully acceptable. This is a good, serviceable and often perceptive account, but it falls short of the highest distinction. Jochum (DG 2535 111 [id.]) and Karajan (2530/3300 674 [id.]) still hold important places at the top of the list of recommendations.

Symphony No. 5 in B flat.
*** DG 2707 101/3370 025 (2) [id.]. Berlin PO, Karajan.
**(*) Decca Dig. D 221 D 2/K 221 K 22 (2) [Lon. LDR 10031]. Chicago SO, Solti.
*(*) DG 2707 113 (2) [id.]. Chicago SO, Barenboim.
(M) * CBS 61818/40-. Phd. O., Ormandy.

Karajan's reading is not just poised and polished; it is superbly structured on every level, clear on detail as well as on overall architecture. Maybe the slow movement lacks some of the simple dedication which makes Jochum's reading with the same orchestra (currently out of the catalogue) so compelling, but here as in his other Bruckner performances for DG, Karajan takes a patrician view of this great and individual symphonist. The playing of the Berlin Philharmonic is magnificent and the recording rich and opulent to match, more spacious than some other recent offerings from this source. The cassette transfer is sophisticated and refined in detail (although, as usual in Karajan DG recordings, the perspective changes slightly in the pianissimos).

Even in Bruckner Solti's conducting tends to give off electric sparks, and the precise control of this performance underlines dramatic contrasts, helped by the clarity and brilliance of the digital recording. The slow movement finds the necessary warmth, with Solti in what for him might be counted Elgarian mood. Like the discs the outstanding cassette transfer offers sound which is sharply defined in its clarity of focus, and the biggest climaxes bring no hint of congestion.

Daniel Barenboim's account with the Chicago Symphony Orchestra falls short on many counts and offers no challenge to Karajan's masterly version. It is disfigured by some curiously self-conscious touches: why, for instance, the loss of momentum before the entry of the chorale in the finale? There is some good playing from the Chicago orchestra, but Barenboim does not seem to have the measure of the work's architecture or vision, strange in an artist whose Brucknerian credentials have been amply demonstrated elsewhere in this cycle.

Ormandy's version with the Philadelphia Orchestra lacks atmosphere and mystery, and in compressing three sides on to two there has been some loss in warmth and richness. Despite the apparent saving, Karajan and Haitink (Ph. 6700 055) are well worth the extra outlay.

Symphony No. 6 in A.
*** DG 2531 043 [id.]. Chicago SO, Barenboim.
(M) *** HMV SXLP/TC-SXLP 30448. New Philh. O., Klemperer.
(M) **(*) DG 2535/3335 415 Bav. RSO, Jochum.
**(*) DG 2531/3301 295 [id.]. Berlin PO, Karajan.
**(*) Decca SXL/KSXC 6946 [Lon. 7173/5-]. Chicago SO, Solti.

Having been unenthusiastic about other symphonies in Barenboim's Bruckner cycle, it is a pleasure to respond positively to his account of the *Sixth*, which is not only his finest Bruckner so far but one of his very finest discs as a conductor. He has grasped the right balance between tempi in all four movements, and does not succumb to the temptation to disturb the musical flow by unnecessary point-making. It is a performance of genuine sweep and strong atmosphere, and the playing of the Chicago Symphony Orchestra radiates genuine inner conviction and warmth. Moreover, the DG engineers have produced a glorious and sonorous recording which does justice to the artists.

Starting with a spacious account of the first movement, grandly majestic, sharply architectural, Klemperer directs a characteristically strong and direct reading. It is disarmingly simple rather than expressive in the slow movement (faster than usual) but is always concentrated and strong, with splendid playing from the orchestra and recording that hardly shows its early-sixties vintage. The cassette transfer too is admirable. Bruckner's massive climaxes are accommodated without strain – in spite of the high level – and the inner detail is excellent. The brass is very telling (particularly the horns) and the string tone is warm and clear.

At medium price Jochum's account (using the Nowak edition) is also highly competitive. He produces a finely paced reading with radiant textures and a marvellous sense of atmosphere. In terms of sound, this is not quite as richly detailed or refined in sonority as the new Barenboim issue, but those unwilling to face the extra outlay will find that Jochum is well served by the engineers too. The sound blends well, and though the upper strings are not quite as fresh as in the Barenboim or Karajan versions, few will quarrel with this record on technical grounds. The cassette transfer is made at a high level; the upper range is rather fierce and the bass is slightly dry. With rebalancing, a more than acceptable quality can be obtained, but the LP is preferable.

In this less expansive Bruckner symphony, posing a lesser challenge, Karajan is not so commanding as usual in his Bruckner recordings. It is still a compelling performance, tonally very beautiful and with a glowing account of the slow movement that keeps it in proportion – not quite the match of the sublime slow movements of Nos. 8 and 9. The cassette transfer is brilliant without being fierce; it is cleanly focused, slightly dry in the bass.

Solti offers a strong, rhetorical reading, powerfully convincing in the outer movements and helped by playing and recording of outstanding quality. Where he is less persuasive is in the slow movement, which fails to flow quite as it should; the expressiveness does not sound truly spontaneous. The cassette transfer is first-class, with fine body, transparency of detail and a complete absence of congestion.

Symphony No. 7 in E.
*** DG 2707 102/3370 023 (2) [id.]. Berlin PO, Karajan – WAGNER: *Siegfried idyll.****
*** Ph. 6769 028/7699 113 (2) [id.]. Concg. O., Haitink – WAGNER: *Siegfried idyll.****
*** HMV SLS 5194 (2). [Ang. 2ZB 3892]. Dresden State O., Jochum.
(M) ** Ph. 6833 253. Concg. O., Haitink.
*(*) Uni. RHS/UKC 356. Danish State RO, Sanderling.

Symphony No. 7; (i) *Helgoland;* (i; ii) *Psalm 150.*
** DG 2707 116 (2) [id.]. Chicago SO, Barenboim, with (i) Chicago S. Ch.; (ii) Welting.

Like Bruckner's *Fourth*, Karajan recorded the *Seventh* for HMV five years before his DG version. The earlier reading showed a superb feeling for the work's architecture, and the playing of the Berlin Philharmonic was gorgeous. Yet in the newer DG version Karajan draws even more compelling playing from them, and this version shows even greater power and nobility. It is undoubtedly a great performance and is splendidly served by the engineers, with a richly textured string quality matched by brass timbres of comparable bite and sonority. The cassette transfer too is very impressive, nearly matching the discs in refinement.

Haitink's later reading of the *Seventh* is more searching and spacious than the version he recorded in the 1960s. The first movement is considerably slower and gains in mystery and atmosphere, and the *Adagio* expands in vision too. Yet there is nothing studied here; both movements grow with an unforced naturalness that is deeply impressive, and there is an altogether richer world of feeling. The Concertgebouw Orchestra play with their accustomed opulence of tone and marvellously blended ensemble, and the recording is wider in range and has greater presence. This goes to the top of the list and can be recommended alongside the Karajan, which is similarly coupled. The tape transfer is comparably sophisticated; the great slow-movement climax, resplendently capped with its cymbal clash, is caught without strain. There is just a hint of roughness in the closing fortissimo of the finale, but not enough to spoil the listener's pleasure.

Jochum's Dresden reading is also extremely fine. With fuller, closer recording, it may miss the hushed intensity that so marked Jochum's Berlin recording for DG (2726 054), which remains one of the finest versions of all. But with his understanding of Bruckner developing towards a more direct, more monumental approach, the authority of this performance, matched by splendid playing from the Dresden orchestra, is never in doubt.

Barenboim's account of the *Seventh* must be numbered among his more successful ventures in this terrain. One point in its favour are the enterprising couplings, *Helgoland*, a short cantata of some merit, and the setting of *Psalm 150*, rather than the more usual *Siegfried idyll*. Barenboim also gives a noble account of the first movement and offers some thoughtful and perceptive moments elsewhere. However, the well-lit Chicago sound lacks the cultured sonorities of the Berlin and Amsterdam orchestras, and the performance as a whole has not the

quality of inspiration or the sheer atmosphere of the very finest. This is not a performance that stays in the mind afterwards as do Karajan's, Haitink's and Jochum's.

Haitink's one-disc version of the *Seventh* has the merits of directness and grasp of architecture. It is by no means as expansive, spacious – or for that matter expensive – as his two-record version made in 1979, and though this is well balanced and finely conceived, the later version has far greater sensitivity to atmosphere. At medium price Jochum's DG version (see above) still holds its own and does not need a turn-over in the slow movement.

In the absence of stiffer competition, Sanderling's record would be an attractive proposition, for he has a keen sympathy with Bruckner's sense of pace, and gives a finely shaped and well-proportioned account of the symphony. The Danish Radio Orchestra is not, however, in the very first rank these days, and though the playing is good and the recorded sound acceptable (with the cassette matching the disc closely), this version is not distinguished enough to offer a serious challenge to the first recommendations.

Symphony No. 8 in C min.
*** HMV SLS/*TC-SLS* 5147 (2) [Ang. S 3893]. Dresden State O., Jochum.

Symphony No. 8. (i) Te Deum.
*** DG Dig. 2741/*3382* 007 (2). Chicago SO, Barenboim, (i) with Norman, Minton, Rendall, Ramey, Ch.

Even in Bruckner's most expansive symphony there is a volatile element in Barenboim's reading. The passionate manner which expresses itself in flexible phrasing and urgent *stringendi* takes something from the ruggedness of the work. At times it is almost as though Bruckner were being given a neurotic streak, reviving the false old idea of a link with Mahler. But that may exaggerate the point, for, with superb playing and digital recording which, apart from some thinness on high violin tone, is excellent, this is a fine, concentrated version. The chrome tape offers demonstration quality. In the *Symphony* the bloom and clarity of the strings is matched by the resonance and bite of the brass; the *Te Deum* sounds remarkably fresh and incisive, yet full-bodied, losing little on the disc in the fullest choral climaxes.

With the benefit of superb wide-ranging modern recording, Jochum's Dresden version of this most searching and expansive of the Bruckner symphonies is a performance of incandescent warmth. In the great *Adagio* Jochum may not build the climaxes with such towering intensity as, for example, Karajan does, but his flexible, spontaneous-sounding style in Bruckner is here consistently persuasive from the mysterious opening of the first movement onwards. As in his earlier Berlin version for DG, Jochum opts for the Nowak edition rather than the Haas with its amplification of the finale (preferred by Karajan and Haitink). The transfer to tape is not wholly successful. The quality is vivid for much of the time but the climaxes of the first movement harshen, the big climax of the slow movement is not quite comfortable, and there is a degree of congestion at the opening of the finale too.

Reminder: Karajan's versions should not be forgotten. He has recorded the *Eighth* twice in stereo, and both performances are noble and searching. The 1958 version on HMV makes a remarkable bargain in its medium-priced reissue (HMV SXDW 3024), where the recording has splendid definition and depth as well as great warmth and presence. The newer DG recording of 1976 costs nearly twice as much, but has great richness and refinement and offers an outstanding cassette equivalent, one of DG's very best (2707 085/*3370 019*).

Symphony No. 9 in D min.

(M) *** DG Acc. 2542/*3342* 129. Berlin PO, Karajan.

(M) *** Decca Jub. JB/*KJBC* 108. VPO, Mehta.

*(*) HMV ASD/*TC-ASD* 3382 [Ang. S/ *4XS* 37287]. Chicago SO, Giulini.

The Accolade reissue offers a glorious performance of Bruckner's last, uncompleted symphony, moulded in a way that is characteristic of Karajan, with a simple, direct nobility that is sometimes missing in his work. Here he seems not to feel it necessary to underline, but with glowing playing from the Berlin Philharmonic and superb recording he gives the illusion of letting the music speak for itself. Yet no one has a clearer idea of Bruckner's architecture, and as one appreciates the subtle gradation of climax in the concluding slow movement, one knows how firmly Karajan's sights have been set on this goal all along. Even in a competitive field this stands out. The differences between this superlative version from the late sixties and Karajan's later one (DG 2530/*3300* 828), recorded with the same orchestra eight years later, are relatively small. The clue lies principally in the differences of recording quality, sharper and closer in the latter version to suggest that Karajan wanted to convey a tougher impression. Where the earlier version brings natural gravity and profound contemplation in greater measure, with manners a degree more affectionate, the newer one concentrates on strength and impact. As before, the playing of the Berlin Philharmonic is immaculate. The Accolade cassette is generally well managed. Although the transfer level is not really high, the recording's atmosphere and the detail are well captured, and the only real drawback is the splitting of the scherzo, which turns over for the reprise of the first section, so unnecessary on a cassette.

Mehta's reading has moments of considerable power and orchestral playing of great splendour. There is a touch of febrile, oversweet vibrato on the strings at the opening of the finale, which is somewhat tiresome on repetition, but this remains a satisfying version even if it does not match Karajan's Accolade version in overall cogency. Decca's recording is up to the high standards of the house; the cassette transfer is first-class too.

Giulini's version is a good deal less persuasive than its rivals. There is no lack of power or grandeur, and, predictably, Giulini expands enormous care over detail, fashioning each phrase with care and thought. Indeed, that may lie at the heart of the problem, for in some way the sheer mystery of this noble score seems to elude him, even though he uncovers much beauty of detail. The recording on both disc and tape has a fine, spacious sound. But something goes awry in the horn parts in the first movement (bars 551 onwards), and this issue cannot challenge Karajan's.

Intermezzo and trio for string quintet.
*** CRD CRD 1046/*CRDC 4046*. Augmented Alberni Qt – BRAHMS: *Sextet No. 2.* ***

Bruckner wrote this attractive *Intermezzo and trio* as an alternative move ment for the scherzo of his *Quintet in F major*, which was considered 'too difficult'. Following on after the vigorous finale of the Brahms *Sextet* the autumnal feeling of the Bruckner with its lighter (but still rich) textures makes a most pleasing encore. The recording is excellent and the tape transfer is freshly vivid, with fine range and detail.

Helgoland.
*** Symph. SYM/*CSYM* 11 [Peters PLE 043]. Amb. Male-Voice Ch., Symph. of L., Morris – WAGNER: *Das Liebesmahl der Apostel.***(*)

Helgoland was written during the long-delayed composition of Bruckner's *Ninth*

Symphony, and might be regarded as a secular counterpart to the *Te Deum*. It is as well to ignore the banal words of Dr August Silberstein about the North Sea island which in succession was under the crowns of Denmark and Great Britain before being ceded to Germany. Though latterly the work has been underprized, early responses were more enthusiastic than was common with Bruckner, and this recording, well conducted by Wyn Morris, helps to explain why. The sound is atmospheric and spacious, and although, as in the Wagner coupling, the chorus is backwardly balanced, the final climax has splendid breadth. The excellent tape transfer matches the disc closely.

Mass No. 2 in E min.; Te Deum.
*(*) Decca SXL/*KSXC* 6837 [Lon. 26506/5]. Blegen, Lilova, Ahnsjö, Meven, V. State Op. Ch., VPO, Mehta.

Both these works are well served on records, the *Mass* by Norrington and Barenboim, the *Te Deum* by Karajan, Barenboim and others. Even if they were not, this Mehta issue would still have few attractions, not because the recording is inadequate or lacking in realism, but because the performances are not really idiomatic. Mehta is a shade too expressive and his chorus a little too operatic in character as well as name. In cassette form Karajan's account of the *Te Deum* (DG 2530/*3300* 704) is not to be missed.

Bruhns, Nikolaus (c. 1665–97)

Preludes Nos. 1 in G; 2–3 in E min.; Variations on 'Nun komm, der heiden Heiland'.

⊛ (M) *** Argo ZK 65. Weir (organ of Clare College, Cambridge) – SCHEIDT: *Passamezzo variations.****

Bruhns died young and left only five organ works, of which four are recorded here. His individuality is striking, and so is the quirky originality of his musical style, which freely interchanges fugal passages and sections of fantasia using the most florid bravura. The *First Praeludium in G major* (which for some reason is placed second on side two) has the kind of immediate appeal which could make it famous if regularly heard; its memorable fugal subject reminds one a little of Bach's *Fugue à la gigue.* Gillian Weir has the full measure of this music, finding a perfect balance between the fantasy and the structural needs of each piece. She dazzles the ear not only with her vigour and virtuosity but also with some quite delicious registration on an organ that seems exactly right for the music. This repertoire is most rewarding and can be cordially recommended even to those who normally fight shy of pre-Bach organ composers. The recording is marvellous, a demonstration of clarity and sonority admirably combined.

Buller, John (20th century)

Proença (Provençal).
(M) *** Uni. Dig. UNS 266. Sarah and Timothy Walker, BBC SO, Elder.

Exuberance, energy and speed are not qualities one can often associate with new music, but they certainly apply to this masterly evocation of medieval Provence written in 1977, a work confidently large both in length and in the forces used. The sequence of settings of troubadour songs, often wild, often sensuous, brings out a surprising modernity in the attitudes of the original poets, relevant still after 700

years. So a love poem by a woman poet speaks with an absence of inhibition which even now sounds daring, and that is reflected in the music, with Sarah Walker a passionately committed soloist. Another layer is provided in the occasional contributions on electric guitar from Timothy Walker, adding a wild, amplified dimension to the sound. Mark Elder in his first recording superbly confirms the promise he has shown in the concert hall and opera house. The digital recording is aptly spectacular.

Busnois, Antoine (d. 1492)

Missa: L'Homme armé.
*** DG Arc. 2533 404 [id.]. L. Pro Cantione Antiqua, Turner – BINCHOIS: *Motets.***(*)

Busnois was at the court of Charles the Bold (1467–77) when this splendid Mass on *L'Homme armé* was composed. Together with the Dufay Mass *Se la face ay pale* recorded by the late David Munrow, this gives an invaluable glimpse of the period, though the textures here are richer and more sumptuous than in the Dufay work of fifteen or so years earlier. Bruno Turner and the London Pro Cantione Antiqua are eloquent in their advocacy of the score and are well recorded. Unfortunately the level is too high and listeners will have to adjust the controls accordingly; but this is an indispensable issue.

Busoni, Ferruccio (1866–1924)

(i) *Piano concerto, Op. 39. Elegy No. 4 (Turandots Frauengemach); Sonatina No. 6 (Chamber fantasy on Bizet's 'Carmen'); 9 Variations on a Chopin prelude, Op. 22.*

(M) *** HMV SXDW/*TC2-SXDW* 3053. Ogdon, (i) with John Alldis Ch., RPO, Revenaugh.

Busoni's *Piano concerto* is a strange and totally unconventional work, cast in five movements, the last of which incorporates a setting of lines from Oehlenschläger's *Aladdin*. Busoni composed it between 1902 and 1904 at a time when he had toyed with the idea of an opera based on *Aladdin*. The concerto runs to sixty-eight minutes and spreads over three sides. It is a commonplace to speak of Busoni bestriding two cultures, north and south of the Alps, but although there are Italian songs in the fourth movement, it is to Brahms that our thoughts turn in the Prologue, even if it is a Brahms suffused with Mediterranean light. This is not Busoni's greatest work but it has much striking and powerful invention, particularly in the first three movements. In Dent's words, it is more often the orchestra which 'seems possessed of the composer's prophetic inspiration', while Busoni sits at the piano, 'listens, comments, decorates and dreams'. John Ogdon has the measure of this extraordinary piece, and his magisterial and enthusiastic advocacy does much for it. The John Alldis Choir is first-rate in the final *Cantico*, and the orchestral support is thoroughly sympathetic. The recording dates from the late 1960s and is wonderfully clean and wide-ranging. No less impressive is the EMI transfer of part of Ogdon's début recital over twenty years ago, which brings three otherwise unobtainable Busoni rarities back into circulation. The playing is brilliant and exhilarating, and judging from the sound could have been recorded yesterday. On cassette the reverberant recording tends to lose some of its focus in the concerto's spaciously powerful tuttis, but the piano timbre is full and clear. At medium price this issue is an outstanding bargain, and though the concerto is certainly uneven it is well worth investigating.

Butterworth, George
(1885–1916)

The Banks of Green Willow (idyll).
*** RCA RL/*RK* 25184. Bournemouth Sinf., Del Mar – BRIDGE: *Summer* etc.***; BANTOCK: *Pierrot.***(*)

The Banks of Green Willow; A Shropshire Lad.
(M) *** HMV Green. ESD/*TC-ESD* 7100. E. Sinfonia, Dilkes – *Concert (English music).****

Butterworth's evocative tone poem *The Banks of Green Willow* is presented with glowing persuasiveness by Del Mar, an excellent item in a beautifully varied concert of English music very well recorded. The cassette offers atmospheric, slightly diffuse sound quality, with a somewhat restricted dynamic range. The performances by Dilkes and the English Sinfonia are also sensitive, and with fine, ripe recording on both disc and cassette this makes an excellent recommendation; the couplings include music by Bax, Frank Bridge and Harty (see the Concerts section below).

English idylls Nos. 1–2.
(M) *** HMV Green. ESD/*TC-ESD* 7101. E. Sinfonia, Dilkes – *Concert.****

Butterworth's delightful *Idylls* are beautifully played here. The HMV recording is perfectly judged, warm and spacious, and it sounds equally well on disc and on the excellent cassette. The collection includes Walter Leigh's *Harpsichord concerto*, a splendid performance of Warlock's *Capriol suite*, and music by E. J. Moeran and John Ireland.

Love Blows as the Wind (3 songs).
*** HMV ASD/*TC-ASD* 3896. Tear, CBSO, Handley – ELGAR: *Songs* ***; VAUGHAN WILLIAMS: *On Wenlock Edge.***(*)

These charming songs to words by W. E. Henley provide an excellent makeweight for a mixed bag of orchestral songs based on the first recording of Vaughan Williams's cycle in its orchestral form. The sound is enjoyably warm and atmospheric and the cassette retains the aural richness without losing focus.

Byrd, William (1543–1623)

My Ladye Nevells Booke: excerpts (*4th Pavan and galliards; Qui passe; The battell; Sellinger's round; Monsieur's alman; Hugh Ashton's ground; A galliard's gigge; The second ground; 5th Pavan and galliard; The Carman's Whistle; A voluntary*).
*** O-L DSLO 566. Hogwood (chamber organ, virginal or harpsichord).

This recital is a selection from Christopher Hogwood's impressive complete recording of *My Ladye Nevells Booke*, offering a dozen or so of its forty-two numbers. Compiled by John Baldwin of Windsor, a Gentleman of the Chapel Royal, *Ladye Nevells Booke* is probably the finest collection of keyboard music of the sixteenth century. Hogwood's expert and sensitive performances on a variety of period instruments earned the complete set a rosette in the second edition of the *Penguin Stereo Record Guide*, and this offering gives an excellent taste of his achievement.

Mass for three voices; Mass for four voices; Mass for five voices; Ave verum corpus; Great service; Magnificat; Nunc dimittis.
(M) *** Argo ZK 53/4. King's College Ch., Willcocks.

This set happily reissues at medium price two of the finest of the King's re-cords from the early sixties. In the *Mass for five voices, Ave verum* and *Great service*, which were recorded in 1960, the style is more reticent, less forceful than in the famous coupling of the *Masses for three* and *four voices*, made three years later. These beautiful settings are sustained with an inevitability of phrasing and a control of sonority and dynamic that completely capture the music's spirit and emotional feeling. The recording of all this music is wonderfully clean and atmospheric, the acoustic perfectly judged so that the music seems to float in space yet retain its substance and clarity of focus.

Mass for five voices. Motets: *Alleluia, cognoverunt discipuli; Ave Maria; Christe qui lux es et dies; Civitas sancti tui; Laetentur coeli; Miserere mei; Ne irascaris, Domine.*
(M) *** HM HM 213 [Van HM 7]. Deller Cons.

Whether or not it is historically correct for Byrd's five-part Mass to be sung by solo voices, the great merit of this performance is its clarity, exposing the miracle of Byrd's polyphony, even though the tonal matching is not always flawless. The motets on the reverse are well chosen to illustrate the range of Byrd's religious music. This is perhaps the finest of the Deller Consort's records made for Harmonia Mundi in the years before Alfred Deller's death. It is very cleanly recorded.

Motets: *Beata es; Beati mundo corde; Confirma hoc Deus; Gaudeamus omnes; Iustorum animae; Non vos relinquam; Salve, sancta parens; Senex puerum; Tribulationes civitatum; Visita, quaesumus Domine.*
(M) **(*) Ph. 9502 030 [id.]. William Byrd Ch., Gavin Turner.

With one exception all these pieces

come from the two books of the *Gradualia* (1602 and 1607). The Byrd Choir give well-blended performances that resist the temptation to linger expressively and are at times rather emphatically spirited. Gavin Turner moves the music along vigorously; there is room for a more relaxed, reposeful approach to many of these pieces. The recording is made in a sympathetic acoustic and is well balanced.

Caccini, Giulio (1550–1618)

Euridice (complete).
*** Arion ARN 238023 (2). Diestchy, Foronda, Dextre, Fuente, Mok, Santos, Encabo, Chapinal, Ch. and Instrumental Ens., Zayas.

Caccini's *Euridice* enjoys the distinction of being the first *published* opera, as opposed to the first to be staged, and has taken longer than almost any other to reach the gramophone: 380 years to be exact, though practical difficulties stood in its way for the best part of that time! This performance derives from three live occasions at Rennes in January 1980 and the cast is largely Spanish. So too is the conductor, Rodrigo de Zayas, who has also edited the score and plays the continuo part on the theorbo. His handling of the score is the soul of taste and he secures excellent singing from his cast, with the possible exception of Inigo Foronda, who betrays unsteadiness at times. Nonetheless, this is an enterprising and highly interesting venture, and extremely well recorded. Caccini's opera is not long (well under two hours) and it has moments of tender lyricism which make it well worth having and which more than compensate for its want of dramatic flair.

Caldara, Antonio (1670–1736)

Crucifixus.
*** Argo ZRG 850. St John's College Ch., Guest – A. BONONCINI: *Stabat Mater*; LOTTI: *Crucifixus*.***

Antonio Caldara settled in Vienna and established an enviable reputation as a master of opera – he composed nearly a hundred! The *Crucifixus* is an elaborate sixteen-part setting of great eloquence and is a welcome makeweight to Bononcini's beautiful piece. The treble lines have some moments of insecurity but otherwise the performance is impressive.

Campion, Thomas (1567–1620)

Ayres: *All looks be pale; The cypress curtain of the night; Fain would I wed; Fair, if you expect admiring; Fire, fire; Harden now thy tired heart; I care not for these ladies; It fell on a summer's day; Jack and Joan they think no ill; Never love unless you can; Never weather-beaten sail; So sweet is thy discourse; Sweet, exclude me not; What if a day* (2 versions). Masque music: *Come ashore, merry mates; Move now with measured sound; Now hath Flora rob'd her bowers; While dancing rests.*
(M) *** Mer. E 77009. L. Camerata, Simpson or Mason.

As poet as well as composer Thomas Campion was one of the most sensitive of the Elizabethans, and this charming disc of intensely refreshing performances gives a splendid cross-section of his vocal work, including several settings of his words by others hands, including Coper-

205

ario. It is a pity the texts are not provided; but Glenda Simpson with her bright boyish soprano is a most sympathetic interpreter, ably supported by the talented group she directs. The recording is first-rate.

Campra, André (1660–1744)

Requiem Mass.
*** Erato STU 71310. Nelson, Harris, Orliac, Evans, Roberts, Monteverdi Ch., E. Bar. Soloists, Gardiner.

The music of André Campra, who came from Provence and had Italian blood, often possesses a genial lyricism that seems essentially Mediterranean. Although he is best-known now for *L'Europe galante* and other *opéras-ballets*, he wrote a large quantity of sacred music, psalm settings and motets. This *Requiem* is a lovely work, with luminous textures and often beguiling harmonies, and its neglect is difficult to understand. John Eliot Gardiner and his team of fine singers and players have clearly lavished much affection on this performance, and they bring to it intelligence and sensitivity. Campra is one of the most delightful composers of this period and this admirably recorded disc should go some way towards gaining him a rightful place in the repertoire.

Carissimi, Giacomo
(1605–74)

Cantatas: *Amor mio, che cosa è questo?; Apritevi, inferni; Bel tempo per me se n'andò; Deh, memoria; In un mar di pensieri; No, no, mio core; Suonerà l'ultima tromba; V'intendo, v'intendo, occhi.*

**(*) O-L DSLO 547. Hill, Spencer, Jones, Hogwood.

Such works as *Jephte* and *Baltazar* have been well represented over the years, but Carissimi's cantatas, which number about 150, are relative rarities on disc. They have expressive power allied to musical purity (Carissimi has been called the Bernini of music), and the eight solo cantatas recorded here offer striking instances of word painting and dramatic harmonic colouring. There is no want of chromaticism when the images of the texts inspire such treatment. There are numerous vocal challenges to which Martyn Hill rises gallantly, though greater dramatic range and variety might have helped at times. This music needs projection, but no collector need feel that these excellently recorded cantatas are merely of historical interest. They are often very beautiful indeed, and the instrumental support is admirably restrained and expert.

Castelnuovo-Tedesco, Mario (1895–1968)

Guitar concerto in D, Op. 99.
(B) *** Con. CC/*CCT* 7510. Behrend, Berlin PO, Peters – RODRIGO: *Concierto de Aranjuez.****
(*) CBS 76634/40- [Col. M 35172]. Williams, ECO, Groves – ARNOLD: *Serenade*; DODGSON: *Concerto No. 2.*(*)

Behrend's is an exceptionally attractive performance, the finest available now that John Williams's earlier version with Ormandy has been withdrawn by CBS in favour of his later partnership with Groves. Behrend's playing is strong in personality, and with a bright recording (sounding nearly as well on cassette as on the excellent disc) this is highly enjoyable. Reinhard Peters, the conductor, lets the impetus fall off marginally in the finale but this is not serious, and elsewhere he accompanies very effectively, with first-rate playing from the Berlin Philharmonic. As the coupling is one of the best available versions of the Rodrigo, this is a real bargain.

Though the newer CBS version is more vividly recorded, John Williams's earlier account, with Ormandy and the Philadelphia Orchestra, was fresher and had more pace. He is placed far forward here, so that it is not always possible to locate him in relation to his colleagues. But if the sound is synthetic as far as perspective is concerned, it is by no means unpleasing. These artists make the most of the slow movement's poetry, and the concerto has no want of charm. The attractions of the collection are the two accompanying works, particularly Stephen Dodgson's *Second Concerto*. The cassette transfer is satisfactory but has rather less range than the disc.

Cavalli, Francesco (1602–76)

Ercole amante (complete).
*** Erato STU 71329 (3). Alliot-Lugaz, Hill-Smith, Palmer, Hardy, Crouzat, Cold, Tomlinson, Miller, Lewis, Cassinelli, Corbóz, E. Bach Festival Ch. and Bar. O., Corbóz.

Originally commissioned for the wedding celebrations of Louis XIV but finally performed (with little success) some two years late, *Ercole amante* is one of Cavalli's later and greatest operas. Its profundity, with moving laments and monumental choral passages, brings it closer to the operas of Monteverdi than the other Cavalli works so far recorded. The snag is the libretto, but on record that drawback is minimized. This fine performance under Michel Corbóz was a

direct result of the enterprise of Lina Lalandi and her English Bach Festival. Ulrik Cold, with his clean-cut bass, makes a fine Hercules, and the rest of the cast is excellent, with outstanding contributions from John Tomlinson in three roles and Patricia Miller as Dejanira. First-rate recording.

Certon, Pierre (d. 1572)

Mass: *Sur le pont d'Avignon.* Chansons: *Amour a tort; Ce n'est a vous; C'est grand pityé; De tout le mal; En espérant; Entre vous gentilz hommes; Heilas ne fringuerons nous; Je l'ay aymé; Je ne veulx poinct; Martin s'en alla; Plus ne suys; Que n'est-elle auprès de moy; Si ta beaulté; Ung jour que Madame dormait.*
(M) *** HM HM 1034. Boston Camerata, Cohen.

Pierre Certon is hardly a familiar name but this Mass and the accompanying secular songs give him strong claims to attention. He was active in Paris during the period 1530–70 and held the title of master of the choir at the Sainte-Chapelle in Paris. (He also gets a mention from Rabelais in the *Nouveau Prologue* to the second book of *Pantagruel*.) The Mass *Sur le pont d'Avignon* has genuine appeal, and the chansons with which it is coupled also exercise a real charm over the listener. The Mass is performed *a cappella*, and the chansons enjoy instrumental support. In both sacred and secular works the Boston Camerata bring musical accomplishment and stylistic understanding to bear, and they are well served by the engineers. Enterprising and interesting.

Chabrier, Emmanuel
(1841–94)

España (rhapsody).
*** HMV Dig. ASD/*TCC-ASD* 3902
[Ang. DS/*4ZS* 37742]. Phd. O., Muti
– FALLA: *Three-cornered Hat*; RAVEL:
*Rapsodie.****
** Decca SXL/*KSXC* 6956. LAPO,
Lopez-Cobós – FALLA: *Three-cornered
Hat* **(*); RIMSKY-KORSAKOV: *Cap-
riccio.***

Muti's manner is brisk but lilting in
Chabrier's dance rhythms, an apt makeweight for two other works inspired by
the Spanish sun. The digital recording is
one of the best from Philadelphia, with
the reverberation clouding detail only
slightly. The chrome cassette transfer
shows striking range and brilliance (the
brass has thrilling presence), balanced by
a clear, resonant bass.
An enjoyable, more relaxed performance from Lopez-Cobós, with no lack of
rhythmic resilience, and attractive in its
way. It is very well recorded on disc and
tape alike, but it lacks the excitement and
glitter of Muti's version.

Le Roi malgré lui: Fête polonaise.
(M) * Turn. TVS 34570 [id.]. R. Lux. O.,
Cao – LALO: *Rapsodie norvégienne* *;
MASSENET: *Scènes hongroises.*(*)

A lively but rhythmically unsubtle
performance. The recording is bright but
shallow.

Suite pastorale.
(M) *** Mercury SRI 75029. Detroit SO,
Paray – CHAUSSON: *Symphony.***

A wholly delightful account of Chabrier's engaging suite, given playing that
is at once warm and polished, neat and
perfectly in scale. The recording too is
first-class.

Trois Valses romantiques (for 2
pianos).
(M) ** Turn. TVS 34586 [id.]. Dosse,
Petit – SAINT-SAËNS: *Carnival*;
SÉVERAC: *Le Soldat de plomb.***

Tasteful performances. Some might
feel that the recording acoustic is slightly
too reverberant but it is not unpleasingly
so; and this collection is worthwhile for
Séverac's *Le Soldat de plomb.*

Chaminade, Cécile
(1857–1944)

*Concertino for flute and orchestra,
Op. 107.*
*** RCA RL/*RK* 25109 [ARL 1/*ARK 1*
3777]. Galway, RPO, Dutoit – FAURÉ:
Fantaisie; IBERT: *Concerto*; POULENC:
*Sonata.****

The Chaminade *Concertino* undoubtedly has great charm. The principal
theme of the first movement is of the kind
that insinuates itself irresistibly into the
subconscious, and the work has a delightful period atmosphere. It is splendidly played by James Galway, who is
given excellent support by the RPO
under Charles Dutoit. The recording is
admirably spacious and finely detailed,
and it has also transferred to cassette with
excellent presence and no lack of bloom.
Altogether this is a most desirable and
enjoyable anthology.

Charpentier, Marc-Antoine
(1634–1704)

Beatus vir; Le Jugement dernier
(oratorio).

*** Erato STU 71222. Vieira, Brunner, Ihara, Zaepffel, Ramirez, Huttenlocher, Lisbon Gulbenkian Foundation Ch. and O., Corbóz.

A welcome addition to the growing representation of Charpentier on record. Performances and recording are admirable, and *Le Jugement dernier*, which occupies the first side, is an imposing work. Charpentier's teacher, Carissimi, had set the same text, and the oratorio form, though he never used that name, occupied an important place in Charpentier's output: he produced no fewer than thirty-four. They are more diverse in character than Carissimi's; in fact, they are closer to French operatic recitative in the narrative sections than to the Italian style.

Caecilia, Virgo et Martyr; Filius prodigus (oratorios).
(M) *** HM HM 10 066. Grenat, Benet, Laplenie, Reinhard, Studer, Instrumental Ens., Christie.

As the sleeve-note puts it, these Latin oratorios or dramatic motets of Charpentier occupy 'an isolated, if elevated position in French seventeenth-century music'. The two works recorded here come from different periods of his life: *Caecilia, Virgo et Martyr* was composed for the Duchesse de Guise in 1675, when he wrote a number of works on the subject of St Cecilia; the second, on the theme of the Prodigal Son dates from the later period when Charpentier was *maître de chapelle* at St Louis-le-Grand (1684–98), and is richer in expressive harmonies and poignant dissonances. The music could scarcely find more eloquent advocates than these artists under William Christie; its stature and nobility is fully conveyed here. An altogether splendid coupling, beautifully recorded too.

Judith (oratorio).
** Erato STU 71282. Alliot-Lugaz, Russell, York-Skinner, Roden, Goldthorpe, Jackson, Tomlinson, E. Bach Festival Ch., and O.

As a pupil of Carissimi, Charpentier's interest in the oratorio, the short narrative choral pieces that when brought to France were known as *histoires sacrées*, was a natural development, and he was one of its most celebrated exponents. This work tells the story of Judith and Holofernes, and it inspires some characteristically individual music from Charpentier's pen. His harmonic style is richer and more resourceful than Lully and many other French baroque composers before Rameau, and here, in spite of a performance that is a little wanting in dramatic flair, readers will find no lack of musical rewards. The recording is well balanced, and if the performance had slightly more character, this would be a three-star recommendation. No conductor is named.

Leçons de ténèbres.
(M) *** HM HM/*HM40*- 1005/7. Jacobs, Nelson, Verkinderen, Kuijken, Christie, Junghänel.

Charpentier was an almost exact contemporary of Lully whom he outlived but whose shadow served to obscure him during his lifetime. These *Leçons de ténèbres* are eloquent and moving pieces, worthy of comparison with Purcell and more substantial musically than Couperin's later setting. Since the falsetto tradition was weak, it seems unlikely that any of the music was intended for male alto, a fact that the counter-tenor René Jacobs readily concedes in his notes. Yet his performance (like that of his colleagues) is so authentic in every respect that it is difficult to imagine it being surpassed. The pursuit of authenticity often produces inhibited phrasing and overcareful voice production, but here the results are a tribute both to musicianship and to scholarship. This music has depth and these artists reveal its stature to fine effect. The recording is as distinguished as the performances; the cassette transfer too is admirable (although it needs a bass cut), and the packaging is excellent, with bilingual notes, clearly printed.

Magnificat; Te Deum.
*** HMV ASD/TC-ASD 3482 [Ang. S 37470]. Lott, Harrhy, Brett, Partridge, Roberts, King's College Ch., ASMF, Ledger.

This is the best-known of Charpentier's *Te Deum* settings written for the Sainte-Chapelle. There is a mixture of choruses, solo numbers and concertante movements, for which Charpentier provides invention of no mean distinction. The *Magnificat* is in D minor, for double choir, and has a good deal of antiphonal writing. Although none of this music has the depth of Purcell, it has a *douceur* and a freshness that make it highly appealing. The performances have vitality and boldness, and the singing is stylish. The sound is excellent, well balanced and atmospheric; the cassette is rather less clearly defined than the disc.

Missa Assumpta est Maria. Dialogus inter Christum et peccatores.
**(*) Erato STU 71281. Nelson, Alliot-Lugaz, Russell, York-Skinner, Goldthorpe, Jackson, Rayner Cook, E. Bach Festival Ch. and Bar. O.

An unusually interesting record, even though it is flawed. The Mass is an expressive and beautiful work composed for the Sainte-Chapelle in Paris in 1699, not long before Charpentier's death. It is among the finest specimens of its kind in French music of this period, and its directness of utterance and depth of feeling give it a special claim on the collector's attention. It is for six-part choir and an orchestra of strings, flutes, continuo

and organ, and although this performance may be wanting in finish it reveals much sensitivity and an awareness of the beauties of the score. The fill-up on the second side, the *Dialogus inter Christum et peccatores*, is one of the *histoires sacrées* that blend elements of the French and Italian styles (notably that of Carissimi). The performance here is marred by the obtrusive vibrato of the two sopranos, but the record as a whole is rewarding and the sound quality is good. No conductor is named.

David et Jonathas (opera; complete).
*** Erato STU 71435 (3). Alliot-Lugaz, Huttenlocher, Soyer, David, Jacobs, Lyons Op. Ch., E. Bach Festival O., Corbóz.

David et Jonathas comes from 1688, the year after Lully's death had brought to an end his monopoly of the musical stage, and precedes Charpentier's only real opera, *Médée* (1693). Although the formula and the instrumental layout are thoroughly Lullian, Charpentier's music has greater imagination and musical substance than Lully's. The action follows the biblical narrative in broad outline, and much of the music (which is new to the gramophone) is fresh and inventive, remarkably free from period cliché. It confirms the impression made by many other Charpentier records during the last few years, that in him France has one of her most inspired baroque masters. This performance is marked by some good singing, though there are passages which would, one feels, benefit from greater finish. But Michel Corbóz gets excellent results from his artists generally and is well recorded. One or two sides are short (one is 16′ 40″ only) but no matter: this rarity is still worth the price.

Chausson, Ernest (1855–99)

Poème for violin and orchestra.
*** Decca SXL/*KSXC* 6851 [Lon. 7073/
5-]. Kyung-Wha Chung, RPO, Dutoit
– RAVEL: *Tzigane*; SAINT-SAËNS:
Havanaise etc. ***

This beautiful work is already well
represented in the catalogue, notably by
Perlman's splendid account (HMV ASD
3125 [Ang. S 37118]). Chung's performance is deeply emotional; some will prefer
a more restrained approach, but with
committed accompaniment from the
orchestra and excellent recording this
makes an admirable foil for the virtuoso
concertante pieces with which it is
coupled. The tape transfer is very successful; a slight treble reduction is useful,
but then the sound has pleasing bloom
and detail.

Symphony in B flat, Op. 20.
(M) ** Mercury SRI 75029. Detroit SO,
Paray – CHABRIER: *Suite pasto-
rale.****

Paray's passionate advocacy of the
Chausson symphony is undoubtedly
arresting, the pacing exhilarating without
the music being over-driven. The ardour
of the finale and its apotheosis is particularly convincing, and the score's
Franckian affinities are well brought out.
The performance is certainly distinctive,
and if the recording is less distinguished,
a slight attenuation at both ends of the
sound spectrum adjusts the overall balance satisfactorily.

*Concerto for violin, piano and string
quartet, Op. 21.*
*** Telarc Dig. DG 10046 [id.]. Maazel,
Margalit, Cleveland O. Qt.

Since the pioneering records by Thib-
aud and Cortot, versions of the Chausson

Concerto have hardly been thick on the
ground, and there is no current rival to
this superbly recorded version. Even if
there were, it would have to be very good
to surpass this. There is a wide range of
dynamics, and though there are times
when one would have welcomed more
emotional restraint, the performance
is both sensitive and accomplished.
Maazel's vibrato in the slow movement
may not be to all tastes but it would be
ungenerous to withhold a star, particularly in view of the spectacular clarity
and presence of the recording.

Poème de l'amour et de la mer.
⊛ *** HMV ASD/*TC-ASD* 3455
[Ang. S 37401]. Baker, LSO, Previn
– DUPARC: *Mélodies.* ⊛ ***
** Symph. SYM/*CSYM* 6 [Peters PLE/
PCE 021]. Caballé, Symph. of L.,
Morris – DEBUSSY: *La Damoiselle
élue.***

Dame Janet Baker, always at her most
inspired in French music, gives a glorious, heart-felt performance, both radiant
and searching, so that this picture of love
in two aspects, first emergent, then past,
has a sharpness of focus often denied it.
She is superbly supported by Previn and
the London Symphony Orchestra, with
clarity and warmth combined; the recording is of demonstration quality, and
the cassette transfer is glowingly atmospheric.

Montserrat Caballé, singing a role
often taken by a mezzo-soprano, gives a
warm and expressive reading, though
beside Janet Baker's it seems to lack a
specific understanding either of the
words or of the music. But anyone attracted by the rare Debussy on the reverse
need not hesitate. Warm, rather vague
recording to match the interpretation; the
cassette has a restricted dynamic range
and is not recommended.

Cherubini, Luigi (1760–1842)

Requiem in C min.
** Ph. 9500 715/*7300 805* [id.]. ORF Ch.
and SO, Gardelli.

Cherubini's *C minor Requiem* was
recorded by both Toscanini and Giulini in
the 1950s, but this version with Austrian
Radio forces is the first for many years.
Composed in 1816 for the anniversary of
the death of King Louis XVI, it is notable
for its dignity and nobility rather than
any strong melodic or harmonic appeal.
Given a performance of Toscanini's
dramatic intensity, the work makes a
very strong impact; but although Gardelli is well served by his forces and is well
recorded, the performance as a whole
lacks tautness and fervour. Those who
know the work will welcome this issue,
but those who do not will not be fully
persuaded of its stature.

Requiem in D min.
*** HMV ASD/*TC-ASD* 3073 [Ang. S
37096]. Amb. S., New Philh. O., Muti.
*** Decca Dig. SXDL 7518 [Lon. LDR
10034]. Ch. de Brassus, SRO and
Lausanne PA Choirs, SRO, Stein.

The darkness of tone in the use of male
voices in Cherubini's *D minor Requiem*
goes with much solemn minor-key music
(a little inflated by Beethovenian standards) and some striking anticipations of
Verdi. In this fine, committed performance under Muti, the listener forgets the
scarcity of really memorable melodies,
and relishes the drama and the distinctive
textures, particularly as the recording is
outstandingly fine. The high-level HMV
tape transfer is also very successful.
Stein's performance on Decca provides
an excellent alternative, and the digital
recording is if anything even more impressive, helping to bring out the dramatic side of the work, the scale that of a
cathedral rather than a church. The singing of the Brassus choir is less incisive
than that of the Ambrosian Singers on
the HMV version, though the balance is
more forward.

Chopin, Frédéric (1810–49)

*Piano concertos Nos. 1–2; Andante
spianato and Grande polonaise bril-
lante, Op. 22; Fantasy on Polish airs,
Op. 13; Krakowiak rondo, Op. 14;
Variations on 'Là ci darem', Op. 2.*
(M) *(*) Ph. 6747 003 (3). Arrau, LPO,
Inbal.

This set offers Chopin's output for
piano and orchestra in immaculately
aristocratic performances by Claudio
Arrau. His expressive hesitations do not
always grow naturally out of what has
gone before, and his rubato will inevitably convince some listeners less than
others. The recording balance gives the
distinguished soloist undue prominence,
but the overall sound is reasonably fresh
and truthful in timbre.

*Piano concerto No. 1 in E min., Op.
11.*
*** DG 2531/*3301* 125 [id.]. Zimerman,
LAPO, Giulini.
(M) **(*) CBS 61931/*40-* [Odys. Y/*YT*
32369]. Gilels, Phd. O., Ormandy.
*(**) CBS 76970/*40-* [Col. M/*MT*
35893]. Perahia, NYPO, Mehta.

*Piano concerto No. 1; Andante
spianato and Grande polonaise brillante, Op. 22.*
* Ph. 9500/*7300* 889 [id.]. Davidovich,
LSO, Marriner.

Krystian Zimerman's is arguably the
finest version of the *First Concerto* to
have appeared in the 1970s, and is worthy
to stand alongside Pollini's classic ac-

count and Gilels's famous recording from the mid-sixties. He is fresh, poetic and individual in his approach, and is afforded a cleanly detailed recording by the DG engineers. A sparkling, beautifully characterized reading which differs in many details from Zimerman's concert performances that we have heard broadcast, but which remains spontaneous and freshly elegant. The cassette transfer is first-class – of DG's best quality.

It is good to see the Gilels recording returning to circulation, even if the sound does not flatter either him or the Philadelphia Orchestra. This is one of the most poetic and thoughtful accounts of the concerto currently before the public. Gilels does not match the youthful fire of Pollini or Zimerman, but the lambent quality and sensitivity of his playing, with every phrase breathing naturally, make it one of the most desirable of records. Ormandy gives good support, but the engineers do not succeed in capturing the rich sonority of the Philadelphia strings. The cassette matches the disc closely, slightly more restricted in range.

Murray Perahia produces some wonderfully poetic playing, with an unforced naturalness and sense of grace that one expects from an artist of his quality. But there are inevitable hazards in partnering him with a conductor of Zubin Mehta's calibre, and even if there are moments of that special insight that illumines everything Perahia does, it would be idle to pretend that this is the success for which one had hoped. From Perahia one would expect a Chopin E minor Concerto of altogether rare delicacy and flair, of the kind he has given us in the concert hall, but the orchestral playing is so coarse-grained in tutti and shows such little real sensitivity elsewhere that it is neither worthy of nor inspiring for this soloist. Given better casting Perahia could give us an account of this concerto superior to any on record, but this is not it. The tape transfer is first-class, one of CBS's very best, vivid and clear and quite the equal of the disc.

Bella Davidovich won the Chopin Competition in 1955, thus preceding Pollini, Argerich and Zimerman. She has not, however, had the same exposure as they have, and until recently she was little known outside the Soviet Union. An earlier record of this concerto that she made with the Moscow Radio Orchestra under Yansons enjoyed brief currency on the Classics for Pleasure label; this newer version enjoys superior recording, but it must be said that neither soloist nor conductor brings special qualities to it. It lacks the distinction not only of such rivals as Zimerman, Gilels, Pollini, Argerich and Perahia but of many pianists one can hear in the concert hall who have not been given the chance of making a record.

For many, bearing in mind its price, Pollini's version (HMV SXLP/TC-SXLP 30160 [Sera. S/4XS 60066]) will remain first choice, and it is now available on cassette as well as disc. The tape transfer is first-class, beautifully balanced, indeed one of EMI's demonstration issues.

Piano concerto No. 2 in F min., Op. 21.

** DG 2531/*3301* 042 [id.]. Argerich, Nat. SO of Washington, Rostropovich – SCHUMANN: *Concerto.***

Piano concerto No. 2; Andante spianato and Grande polonaise brillante, Op. 22.

*** DG 2531/*3301* 126 [id.]. Zimerman, LAPO, Giulini.

(M) *** DG Priv. 2535/*3335* 221 [id.]. Vásáry, Berlin PO, Kulka.

Piano concerto No. 2; 3 Nouvelles Études, Op. posth.; Scherzo No. 2, Op. 31.

** RCA RL/*RK* 12868 [ARL 1 /*ARK 1 2868*]. Ax, Phd. O., Ormandy.

Krystian Zimerman's version of the *F minor Concerto* has won much acclaim and rightly so. It combines qualities of freshness and poetic sensibility with effortless pianism. Elegant, aristocratic, sparkling – all these adjectives spring to mind: this has youthful spontaneity and at the same time a magisterial authority. In discussing the *E minor Concerto* we spoke of the DG recording being 'cleanly detailed' without perhaps sufficiently stressing the fact that the balance favoured the soloist a little too much. In this respect the *F minor* is an improvement, though the piano is still marginally too close to do full justice to the magic this remarkable young artist achieves in the concert hall. Among recent versions this leads the field without question. The tape transfer is first-class in every way, though (like the *First Concerto*) it benefits from a slight bass cut.

At medium price Vásáry's disc is fully competitive. One must not forget Ashkenazy (whose poetic version is heard within an attractive recital of solo piano music: Decca SXL 6693) or Alicia de Larrocha (whose coupling is an outstanding version of Falla's *Nights in the Gardens of Spain*: Decca SXL 6528/ *KSXC 16528* [Lon. 6733/5-]), but Vásáry's performance is one of his finest Chopin recordings; moreover it is splendidly recorded. The balance is exceptionally convincing and the sound itself first-class, equally impressive on disc and tape. The slow movement is played most beautifully, and in the outer movements, the orchestral direction has striking character and vigour. The fillers are generous; the *Andante spianato* is especially beguiling.

A strong but not always very romantic performance from Argerich, with Rostropovich at times accompanying over-emphatically. The playing has undoubted fire, and the slow movement has an eloquent central climax, but its full poetry does not emerge until the closing pages and the finale, though energetic, is not really memorable. Excellent recording and a lively cassette transfer.

Emanuel Ax has a fine sense of style and a natural feeling for the shape of Chopin's phrases. His is a classical reading of great poise and delicacy, with subtle colouring and finely judged rubato. He does not possess the temperament of Argerich, who is brisker and more masculine. Ormandy is a supportive accompanist, but unfortunately the RCA recording, though well balanced, is somewhat lacking in transparency (on cassette it is bass-heavy too). By comparison with the Zimerman or Ashkenazy issues this is opaque. The perspective between soloist and orchestra is excellent, and were the sound better-detailed this would be a stronger recommendation.

A Month in the Country (ballet; arr. Lanchbery); *Barcarolle, Op. 60; Waltz in E major, Op. posth.*
(M) ** HMV Green. ESD/*TC-ESD* 7037. Gammon, ROHCGO, Lanchbery.

John Lanchbery's score for Sir Frederick Ashton's ballet based on Turgenev's *A Month in the Country* is constructed from concertante works that Chopin wrote in his late teens, the *Fantasy on Polish airs*, the *Grande polonaise brillante* (which the composer joined to the *Andante spianato* years later) and the *Là ci darem variations* (using Mozart's air from *Don Giovanni*). Lanchbery comments – not unfairly – that Chopin's scoring is 'slender and at times sketchy', and so he has added his own touching up (although it does not seem to make a great deal of difference). The result is a very lightweight score which needs a pianist like Rubinstein to bring it fully to life. Philip Gammon's playing is musical and accomplished, and the orchestral accompaniment is tasteful. The recording is good.

Cello sonata in G min., Op. 65; Introduction and Polonaise brillante in C, Op. 3.

*** DG 2531/3301 201 [id.]. Rostropovich, Argerich – SCHUMANN:
Adagio and allegro.***

With such characterful artists as Rostropovich and Argerich challenging each
other, this is a memorably warm and
convincing account of the Cello sonata,
Chopin's last published work, a piece
which clicks into focus in such a performance. The contrasts of character between expressive cello and brilliant piano
are also richly caught in the Introduction
and Polonaise, and the recording is warm
to match. The cassette transfer is faithful
and refined, although the modest level
means that the cello timbre has rather less
bite than on disc.

PIANO MUSIC

Collection: 4 Ballades; Études, Opp.
10 and 25; 4 Impromptus and Fan-
taisie-impromptu; 20 Nocturnes;
Polonaise No. 6 in A flat, Op. 53; 4
Scherzi; Piano sonatas Nos. 2–3;
Variations on a national air; Waltzes
1–17.
(M) **(*) DG 2740 163 (6). Vásáry.

This sizeable collection of Chopin's
most important piano music is well worth
the attention of collectors. Although
there are several works where one can do
better on other records, there are few
compilations so reliable both in terms of
technical brilliance and for poetic insight.
Tamás Vásáry is a fastidious artist and
there are few performances here that will
disappoint the most discriminating
listener.

Ballades Nos. 1 in G min., Op. 23; 2
in F, Op. 38; 3 in A flat, Op. 47; 4 in
F min., Op. 52.
* Nimbus 2110. Perlemuter.

Ballades Nos. 1–4; Allegro de con-
cert, Op. 46; Introduction and varia-
tions on 'Je vends des scapulaires' in
B flat, Op. 12.
*** CRD CRD 1060/CRDC 4060.
Milne.

Ballades Nos. 1–4; Fantasy in F min.,
Op. 49.
*** Ph. 9500 393/7300 605 [id.]. Arrau.

Ballades Nos. 1–4; Impromptus Nos.
1–3; Fantaisie impromptu.
(M) **(*) DG Priv. 2535/3335 284 [id.].
Vásáry.

Distinguished performances from
Arrau, as one would expect, beautifully
recorded by the Philips engineers. There
is scant evidence of Arrau's advancing
years, though in his youth there would
have been a more thrilling sense of exhilaration and virtuosity. But there is
breadth and perception in abundance
here all the same. This does not displace
Ashkenazy's set, but it will not disappoint Arrau's admirers. The rich colouring and weight of the recording are
equally impressive on disc and cassette.

Hamish Milne gives thoughtful and
individual performances of the Ballades.
They may initially sound understated,
but in their freshness and concentration
they prove poetic and compelling. Similarly he plays the two rarities with total
conviction, suggesting that the Allegro de
concert at least (originally a sketch for a
third piano concerto) is most unjustly
neglected. The recorded sound is first-
rate, and that with very long sides indeed.
The cassette transfer too is first-class;
there is minimal difference between tape
and disc.

From DG a generous and on the whole
attractive coupling. Vásáry is rather
matter-of-fact in the Impromptus, but the
Ballades are imaginatively played, and
the performances, although personal,
offer poetry as well as bravura. The G
minor is outstanding, with a fine romantic sweep, but Nos. 2, 3 and 4 are each

individual and rewarding. The recording is rather dry but faithful and clear on both LP and the equivalent tape.

Vlado Perlemuter's reputation as an interpreter of Chopin is legendary, and it is a pity that the Nimbus recording of the *Ballades*, made when the French pianist was in his seventies, offers only a glimpse of his stature. The range of colour and dynamic shading and the overall sense of mastery are not what they once were, at least on this evidence, and in any case the recording is too unfocused and unflattering to be competitive.

Barcarolle in F sharp, Op. 60; Berceuse in D flat, Op. 57; Fantasia in F min., Op. 49; Funeral march in C min., Op. 72/2; 3 Nouvelles Études, Op. posth.; Polonaise-fantaisie in A flat, Op. 61.
(M) **(*) CBS 61166/40-. Fou Ts'ong.

Fou Ts'ong is a pianist of intelligence and sensibility, and his admirers need not hesitate here. The recording (though not distinguished) is well balanced, and is certainly more than adequate. The cassette is admirably clear and full, one of CBS's best. Fou Ts'ong is at present an underrated artist.

Barcarolle, Op. 60; Impromptus Nos. 1–3; 4 (Fantaisie-impromptu); Waltzes Nos. 15–19, Op. posth.
*** Ph. 9500/7300 963 [id.]. Arrau.

Although Arrau's Chopin is seldom mercurial it is never inflexible and it has its own special insights. The *Fantaisie-impromptu*, with its nobly contoured central melody, is a highlight here. The richly coloured piano timbre, warm in the middle, resonant in the bass, contributes a good deal to the character of this record. The cassette transfer too is outstanding; there is little appreciable difference between disc and tape.

3 Ecossaises, Op. 72/3; Introduction and variations on a German air, 'Der Schweizerbub'; Polonaises Nos. 8 in D min., Op. 71/1; 11 in B flat min. (Adieu); 13 in G min.; 14 in B flat; 15 in A flat; 16 in G sharp min.; Rondo in F, Op. 5; Rondo in C min., Op 1.
*** Decca SXL/KSXC 6981. Ashkenazy.

The *Polonaise in G minor* is Chopin's earliest known composition, and this fifth volume of Ashkenazy's collected edition covers very early works, written between 1817 (when he was only seven) and 1826, the year of the *Variations* and the *B flat minor Polonaise*. Ashkenazy's performances are magical, fresh and direct but full of touches of insight. Superb recorded sound and a matching cassette, notably well focused at the top.

Études, Op. 10/1–12; Op. 25/1–12.
(M) **(*) DG Priv. 2535/3335 266 [id.]. Vásáry.
(M) ** CBS 61886/40-. Fou Ts'ong.
(M) *(*) Ph. 6570/7310 016. Magaloff.

Études, Opp. 10 and 25; Waltzes Nos. 1–19.
(M) **(*) DG Priv. 2721 208 (2). Vásáry.

Vásáry's performances have been in and out of the catalogue in various packages and formats and at many price levels. On each appearance their attractions seem stronger: Vásáry is a poetic artist and his keyboard prowess is second to none. There is elegance in the *Waltzes*, brilliance in the *Études* when required, and fine intelligence and taste throughout. The recording still sounds remarkably fresh, and admirers of this artist need not hesitate.

Fou Ts'ong is at his best here and gives an impressive demonstration of his fine musicianship and expressive powers. Indeed, many individual studies compare well with the very finest available on record, though no easy equation emerges from comparisons. His insights are no less penetrating than Vásáry's, and his powerful technique is not in question either. He is not as well recorded as Ashkenazy (and the cassette is rather clattery in the upper range). Moreover CBS have omitted to provide scrolls between each of the studies, surely a mistake in so competitive a market. Impressive pianism and no mean artistry, but not a performance that eclipses the Pollini (DG 2530 291/*3300 287*) or Ashkenazy (Decca SXL/*KSXC* 6710) sets.

Idiomatic readings from Nikita Magaloff, who is cleanly recorded. These are eminently serviceable accounts, with felicitous touches that compel admiration, but they fall short of the distinction and authority that both Pollini and Ashkenazy bring to this repertoire.

Impromptus Nos. 1 in A flat, Op. 29; 2 in F sharp, Op. 36; 3 in G flat, Op. 51; Fantaisie-impromptu, Op. 66; Scherzi Nos. 1–4.
*(*) DG 2536/*3336* 378. Szidon.

Roberto Szidon is a strong player but he is more convincing in the *Impromptus*, which are given an appropriate improvisatory quality, than in the *Scherzi*. Here his playing is distinguished by an impressive dexterity and attack, and its brilliance and power are never in doubt; yet, although there are sensitive touches, one would welcome greater poetic feeling in some of the more reflective moments. The DG recording is full and clear.

Nocturnes Nos. 1–21.
***DG Dig. 2741/*3382* 012 [id.]. Barenboim.
*** Ph 6747 485/*7699 088* [id.]. Arrau.
(M) **(*) CBS 61827/*40-* (Nos. 1–8; 19–21); 61828/*40-* (Nos. 9–18). Fou Ts'ong.

Barenboim's playing is of exceptional eloquence, and he is superbly recorded

(the chrome tapes outstanding alongside the discs). These are intense, poetic and thoughtful readings, the phrasing beautifully moulded, following rather in the mid-European tradition. In this Barenboim has something in common with Arrau, whose approach clearly reflects his boyhood training in Germany, creating tonal warmth coupled with inner tensions of the kind one expects in Beethoven. In the *Nocturnes* it can be apt to have an element of seriousness, and this too is a very compelling cycle, given rich, refined recording on both disc and cassette.

Fou Ts'ong sometimes reminds one of Solomon – and there can surely be no higher tribute. He is at his very best in the gentle poetic pieces; in the more robust *Nocturnes* his rubato is less subtle, the style not so relaxed. But this is undoubtedly distinguished, and with good recording (the cassettes too are among CBS's best transfers) it is competitive at medium price. But Rubinstein's RCA set of *Nocturnes 1–19* remains in a class of its own (SB 6731/2 [LSC 7050]).

Polonaises Nos. 1–7.
(M) ** DG Priv. 2535/*3335* 258. Cherkassky.
*(*) DG 2531/*3301* 094 (Nos. 1–6). Berman.
(M) *(*) Ph. Fest. 6570/*7310* 137. Magaloff.

Polonaises Nos. 3, 4 and 6.
*** DG 2531 099 [id.]. Gilels – *Sonata No. 3.****

Shura Cherkassky is sometimes an idiosyncratic artist, and his playing here has certain eccentricities of style and tempo. Compared with Pollini (DG 2530/*3300* 659), this sometimes sounds wilful, but it has a redeeming spontaneity. The recording is good though not distinguished.

Lazar Berman gives less character and colour to these *Polonaises* than do many of his rivals. These readings possess a certain magisterial command, and the recording is good, but Berman does not invest each phrase with the intensity of Pollini or the sheer poetry of Gilels. His record appeared within weeks of the latter's splendid version of three of the *Polonaises* (discussed below under their coupling), and they do not inhabit the same world.

Our general comments on Nikita Magaloff's other Chopin recordings apply here. These are well-played, well-recorded accounts, offering fine pianism and good musical intelligence, but with little of the flair and poetic intensity that the greatest of Magaloff's rivals command.

24 Preludes, Op. 28; Preludes Nos. 25 in C sharp min., Op. 45; 26 in A flat, Op. posth.
(B) *** Con. CC/*CCT* 7511 [DG 2530 231]. Eschenbach.
(M) **(*) CGS 61944/*40-*. Fou Ts'ong.
(M) **(*) Ph. Seq. 6527/*7311* 091 [6500 622/*7300 335*]. Arrau.

26 Preludes (as above); *3 Nouvelles Études, Op. posth.*
(M) ** Ph. Fest. 6750/*7310* 071. Magaloff.

24 Preludes, Op. 28.
** Ph. 9500 666. Davidovich.

24 Preludes; Ballade No. 2; Waltz in A flat, Op. 34.
*** Decca SXL/*KSXC* 6877 [Lon. 7101/*5-*]. Ashkenazy.

Ashkenazy's set of the *Preludes* forms part of his chronological surveys. All the music in this issue was published in 1838–9; the Op. 38 *Ballade* and the *Waltz*, which was written in 1835 but not published until three years later, precede the *Preludes*. Ashkenazy gives a dramatic and powerful reading that takes its place alongside those of Perahia (CBS 76422/*40-* [Col. M 33507]) and Pollini (DG 2530/*3300* 550).

Reissued at bargain price Eschenbach's set is very competitive. He is beautifully recorded; the tone is warm, clear and resonant, completely natural, and the cassette is successful too, slightly fuller if with a marginally restricted upper range. The performances are characteristically musical and perceptive, thoughtful, with the bravura (which is never in doubt) never aggressively extrovert. Occasionally there is a hint of undercharacterization, which brings a slightly unidiomatic quality, but as a set this gives much pleasure.

Fou Ts'ong indulges in some mannered rubato in the opening *Prelude*, and there are other attention-seeking touches (the sudden hushed tone in bar 5 of the second), against which must be offset some outstanding playing elsewhere. The sound is also good (better perhaps than Perahia's on the same label) and there is an excellent cassette. At medium price this is distinctly competitive.

The Arrau set is much admired, and he certainly receives an opulent, full-bodied recording, on disc and tape alike, which does justice to his subtle nuances of tone. Every prelude bears the imprint of a strong personality, to which not all listeners respond. Arrau can sometimes sound a shade calculated (his rubato seeming arbitrary and contrived), but there is little evidence of this here. His *Preludes* appear to spring from an inner conviction, even if the outward results will not be universally liked.

Magaloff, like Arrau and Fou Ts'ong, comes in the medium price-range, and like these artists he has his own special insights to offer. Magaloff's bonus of the three posthumous *Études* is considerable and he also has the advantage of good recorded sound on both disc and tape. The fact remains, however, that other versions are even more rewarding.

Bella Davidovich, a Warsaw prize-winner in the 1950s, is extremely well recorded by the Philips engineers. One feels as if a piano were in the room, with a perspective, not always fully realized by the engineers in piano recording, which rings true; the image seems totally believable. Miss Davidovich plays these much-recorded pieces with no mean degree of accomplishment and personality, though she is not always scrupulous about dynamic nuances. In terms of musical character she is not the equal of Ashkenazy or even (at medium price) Arrau or Fou Ts'ong, and her record offers distinctly short measure. Yet there is genuine insight here.

Scherzi Nos. 1 in B min., Op. 20; 2 in B flat min., Op. 31; 3 in C sharp min., Op. 39; 4 in E, Op. 54.
(M) *** HMV SXLP/TC–SXLP 30510. Sviatoslav Richter.
(M) ** DG 2535/3335 285. Vásáry.
(B) *(*) CfP CFP 40333. Petrov.

Electrifying playing from Richter. He is at his most imaginative in No. 3, but throughout there is characteristic flair. The recording is a little dry but not shallow, and the cassette transfer is excellent.

Vásáry's elegant performances come from the mid-1960s and have stood the test of time very well. His pianism is distinguished by good taste and exemplary technique, and though the recording is not as richly detailed as in some modern accounts, for example Richter's, it is fully acceptable.

Nicolai Petrov brings fine technique and accomplished musicianship to the *Scherzi*, though there are no special qualities of insight to commend. Good though this playing is in its way, it must yield in terms of both breadth and imagination to the finest of his rivals, among whom Ashkenazy (Decca SXL/KSXC 6334 [Lon. 6562/5-]) must take pride of place. The quality of the recording is acceptable rather than outstanding, and despite its modest price this is not very competitive.

Piano sonata No. 1 in C min., Op. 4;

Contredanse in G flat; Funeral march in C min., Op. 72/2; Mazurkas: in B flat; in G; in A min., Op. 68/2; Nocturne in E min., Op. 72/1; Polonaise in B flat, Op. 71/2; Rondo in C, Op. 73; Waltzes: in E flat; in A flat, Op. posth.
*** Decca SXL/KSXC 6911 [Lon. 7135]. Ashkenazy.

This record does not, as might at first sight be thought, depart from the chronological plan of Ashkenazy's series. Despite their late opus numbers these *Mazurkas* and other pieces all date from 1827–9, though many of them did not appear in print until after Chopin's death. The *C minor Sonata*, Op. 4, is the rarity here: it comes from 1827 and, apart from Magaloff's complete edition on Philips, this is its only available recording at present. It is not deeply characteristic and is of greater interest to students of Chopin's style and budding pianists than to the wider musical public. Ashkenazy makes out a more persuasive case than anyone who has recorded it so far, but the distance Chopin covered between this and the two concertos is really quite amazing. There are some marvellous pieces among the shorter works on the second side, notably the *A minor Mazurka*, Op. 68/2, and the *E minor Nocturne*, Op. 72/1.

Piano sonatas Nos. 2 in B flat (Funeral march), Op. 35; 3 in B min., Op. 58.
**(*) DG 2531/3301 289 [Id.]. Argerich.
(M) ** DG Priv. 2535/3335 230. Vásáry.
(M) ** CBS 61149/40-. Fou Ts'ong.
*(*) Nimbus 2109. Perlemuter.

Piano sonata No. 2; Études, Op. 10/8 in F; 10 in A flat; Op. 25/6 in G sharp min.; Nocturne in E flat, Op. 55/2; Scherzo No. 3, Op. 39.
*** DG 2531/3301 346 [id.]. Pogorelich.

Piano sonata No. 3.
*** DG 2531 099 [id.]. Gilels – *Polonaises.****

Piano sonata No. 3; Berceuse, Op. 57; Mazurkas, Op. 59/1–5; Nocturnes in F min.; in E flat, Op. 55/1–2.
*** Decca SXL/*KSXC* 6810 [Lon. 7030/5-]. Ashkenazy.

Piano sonata No. 3; 3 Mazurkas, Op. 59/1–3; Polonaise No. 6 in A flat, Op. 53; Polonaise fantaisie, Op. 61.
(M) **(*) DG Acc. 2542/*3342* 110 [139317]. Argerich.

Gilels's account of the *B minor Sonata* is thoughtful and ruminative, seen through a powerful mind and wholly individual fingers, and there are some highly personal touches, for example the gentle undulating accompaniment, like quietly tolling bells, caressing the second group of the first movement. There is a beautifully pensive and delicately coloured slow movement; the first movement is expansive and warmly lyrical, and there is not a bar that does not set one thinking anew about this music. An altogether haunting reading and an obligatory acquisition even if it does not prompt one to discard Lipatti, Perahia or Rubinstein. The three *Polonaises* are superb; they have majesty, grandeur and poetry. A rather special record altogether.

Ivo Pogorelich is the Yugoslav pianist who leapt to prominence during the 1980 Warsaw Chopin Competition. Martha Argerich was so incensed when he was eliminated before the final round that she resigned from the jury in protest. The attendant publicity has led to far greater exposure for Pogorelich than for the winner, Thai Son Dang from Vietnam. It is obvious that Pogorelich possesses an outsize personality and a keen awareness of colour. He is a commanding pianist of undoubted charisma, and his playing has temperament and fire in abundance.

There are many wilful touches here and some agogic mannerisms that will not have universal appeal. All the same, these are performances to be reckoned with. The balance is close and probably does not do full justice to the quality of his pianissimo tone – which, even as it is, sounds remarkable. The cassette transfer is first-class, well balanced and clear.

The Decca issue continues Ashkenazy's distinguished series with a memorable performance of the *B minor Sonata* (some might not like the accelerando treatment of the finale, but it is undoubtedly exciting), set within a beautifully arranged programme. The *Berceuse* is played gently, but the *Mazurkas* bring a splendid element of contrast. Ashkenazy's flexible, poetic phrasing is always a joy. The recording is well up to the high standard set by this series, on disc and tape alike.

Both sides of Martha Argerich's full-priced record are reissues: the *B flat minor Sonata* dates from 1975 and the *B minor* from 1968. Both are fiery, impetuous and brilliant performances, with no want of poetic vision to commend them. They hold their own with many in the catalogue, though both have a highly-strung quality that will not be to all tastes. The recordings are well balanced and sound fresh, although on tape the quality is rather dry and lacking in bloom. The *B minor Sonata* is also available on an attractive Accolade medium-priced reissue coupled with *Mazurkas* and *Polonaises*. The *Mazurkas* are beautifully wrought and nicely recorded, and those who respond to Miss Argerich's quixotic temperament in the sonata (recorded not long after her success in the Warsaw competition) need not hesitate. The tape transfer is successful; the sound is slightly shallow, but bold and not without resonance in the bass.

Both sonatas fare admirably in Vásáry's hands. The performances are unaffected, beautifully shaped and controlled with a masterly sense of rubato. Very natural and highly accomplished;

moreover they are given good recorded sound, on disc and cassette alike, which stands the passage of time extremely well (these accounts originally appeared in the mid-1960s). At the same time, Vásáry does not bring those very special qualities of individuality that mark the accounts of Argerich, Perahia and Rubinstein, though he gives great satisfaction nonetheless.

Though not a first choice for this coupling, Fou Ts'ong is perceptive and brilliant in both sonatas. His sensitivity is always in evidence, and there is poetry when required. The recorded quality is acceptable though not distinguished.

Despite Perlemuter's great reputation his coupling of the sonatas does not survive comparison with such poetic readings as Argerich's and Perahia's. The piano sound is not particularly satisfactory, with clangorous climaxes and unappealing colour, and the playing lacks the finish and command of more youthful rivals.

Waltzes Nos. 1–14.
*** DG 2530/*3300* 965 [id.]. Zimerman.
*** Ph. 9500 739/*7300 824* [id.]. Arrau.
(M) **(*) Ph. Fest. 6570/*7310* 050. Magaloff.
** Ar. Eur. 89754/*56363* RK. Anda.
(M) ** DG Priv. 2535/*3335* 267 [id.]. Vásáry.
(M) (***) World mono SH 383. Cortot.

Very distinguished playing from the Polish pianist Krystian Zimerman, who won the 1975 Warsaw competition at the age of eighteen. He is in the same line as Pollini and Argerich (who also record for DG), and his account of the *Waltzes* is uncommonly mature. The playing has a spontaneity and polish that have prompted comparison with Rubinstein and Lipatti – and rightly so. There is a sparkle and finesse that are established in the opening bars of the *E flat Waltz* and that inform everything on the record. Yet while there is every evidence of buo-

yant virtuosity and youthful brilliance, there is no want of perception and poetic insight. This is very fine indeed and is well recorded. This is arguably the finest version of the *Waltzes* to have appeared since Lipatti's, for the Rubinstein is let down by shallow recording. The cassette transfer is truthful but made at a low level. Detail is good, but there is some loss of presence.

Arrau produces his own specially rich, rounded tone colours and is accorded beautiful sound by the Philips engineers. These are performances of elegance and finesse, though there are, as always, moments when the great pianist invests detail with a heavier significance than some listeners may feel is justified. But these are readings of real personality, and however the individual collector may respond, they are searching and considered. The tape quality is bold and full but lacks a little sparkle at the top compared with the disc.

Magaloff too is beautifully recorded on disc and cassette alike, the piano tone rich, with no suggestion of plumminess, the treble bright yet never hard-edged. The performances too are most enjoyable, lacking the last degree of individuality, perhaps, but well characterized and communicative. The rubato is nicely judged, never wilful, and there are continual contrasts between intimacy and bravura (the *Grande valse brillante* is notably successful). Perhaps the most attractive feature about this set is the spontaneous onward flow, each waltz seen within the context of the complete cycle.

Anda's performances have something in common with those of Arrau, broad in feeling, warmly expressive but lacking something in glitter. Although they are not without insights, they are sometimes suave and do not always seem completely spontaneous. The sound is full (not quite so rich as the Philips quality for Arrau) and most truthful in balance. The cassette too is extremely faithful.

Vásáry's tempi are fast and his manner

sometimes seems unnecessarily brisk. He is more persuasive in the relaxed, lyrical pieces, and elsewhere there is the occasional flash of poetry, but for the most part the performances, although not lacking style, have less individuality, and they seldom charm the ear. The recording is crisp and clean, but the piano quality is rather dry.

Cortot's classic accounts of the *Waltzes* have been out of circulation for so long that newcomers to them will not fail to respond to their freshness and individuality, even if not everything Cortot does is to modern taste. He is extraordinarily vital and fiery, impulsive, poetic and totally compelling. Recorded in 1934, the performances have transferred well to LP, even if the sound is limited in range and colour. Sparkling playing of this order, highly personal and far from perfect, is in a special category; no Chopin lover should be without this set even if it involves duplication.

Miscellaneous recitals

Albumblatt in E, B. 151; Allegro de concert in A, Op. 46; Cantabile in B flat, B. 34; Contredanse in G flat, B. 17; Funeral march in C min., Op. 72/2; Largo in E flat, B. 109; Mazurka in D, B. 4; Nocturnes: in C min., B. 108; in E flat, Op. 9/2; Rondo in C, B. 26.

** Pearl SHE 544. Lear.

A sensibly planned recital of off-beat Chopin played with evident dedication and capably recorded. The *Allegro de concert* (1841) was a reworking of material Chopin had intended for his third concerto; most of the other pieces here waited for publication until after Chopin's death. If none of them is a masterpiece, all are worth having on record. Angela Lear is a gifted artist, though perhaps lacking the spontaneity and authority of more established Chopin interpreters.

'Favourites': (i) *Ballade No. 1;* (ii) *Études Nos. 5, Op. 10/6; 12 (Revolutionary), Op. 10/12; 13, Op. 25/1; 21, Op. 25/9;* (iii) *Fantaisie-impromptu, Op. 66;* (i) *Mazurkas Nos. 5, Op. 7/1; 23, Op. 33/2;* (iv) *Nocturnes Nos. 10, Op. 32/2; 15, Op. 56/1;* (iii) *Prelude No. 15 (Raindrop), Op. 28;* (i) *Polonaises Nos. 3 (Military); 6 (Heroic);* (i) *Waltzes Nos. 7, Op. 64/2; 11, Op. 70/1.*

(M) **(*) HMV *TC-IDL 509.* (i) Malcuzynski; (ii) Kersenbaum; (iii) Ogdon; (iv) Lympany.

A generally excellent anthology, issued on tape only, with a series of splendid performances from Malcuzynski at its heart. His contributions are polished and stylish and have great character. Moreover they show a feeling for the grand manner and have a strong romantic impulse. The opening *Ballade* illustrates this well, but the two most famous *Polonaises* are the highlight of the tape, and they are also superbly recorded, with bold, sparkling piano timbre, attractively resonant in the bass. The sound throughout is never less than excellent, and there are other fine performances here too, notably John Ogdon's account of the *Raindrop* prelude and Sylvia Kersenbaum's *Revolutionary study*, which follows on excitingly. The layout of the programme is managed admirably and in spite of the varying sources the listener is given the feeling of a recital, even though the degree of electricity in the playing may vary.

Ballade No. 2, Op. 38; Études: in A, F min., Op. 25/1–2; Impromptu No. 2, Op. 36; Mazurkas Nos. 44, Op. 67/3; 47, Op. 68/2; Nocturnes Nos. 15, Op. 55/1; 20, Op. posth.; Scherzo No. 2, Op. 31; Piano sonata No. 2, Op. 35: Funeral march (only); Waltz No. 1, Op. 18.

(M) *** DG Priv. 2535/3335 211. Vásáry.

Among arbitrarily arranged Chopin collections made from older recordings, this stands out for its balance and for the attractive arrangement of items, so that each sets off the character of the pieces before and after it. The recital opens with the two *Études*; then comes a splendidly brilliant account of the *Scherzo in B flat minor*, followed by the *Nocturne in C sharp minor*, the *Impromptu* and two diverse *Mazurkas*. Side two opens with the famous slow movement from the *Sonata*, Op. 35, moves on to the *Ballade in F major*, which is beautifully played, and the *Grande valse brillante*. The recital closes nostalgically with the *Nocturne in F minor*. Vásáry is on top form throughout, and the recording is excellent, varying a little in level between items, but always naturally balanced. A first-rate issue in every way, equally attractive on disc and cassette.

Ballade No. 3 in A flat, Op. 47; Barcarolle in F sharp, Op. 60; Berceuse in D flat, Op. 57; Fantaisie-impromptu, Op. 66; Impromptu No. 1 in A flat, Op. 29; Scherzo No. 3 in C sharp min., Op. 39; Piano sonata No. 2 in B flat min. (Funeral march), Op. 35.
(B) **(*) Con. CC/*CCT* 7543. Kempff

This exceedingly generous sampler of Kempff's individuality in Chopin makes a fine bargain. Kempff is not at his best in music that calls for striking bravura, like the *Scherzo*, or the finale of the *Sonata*, but his special quality of poetry infuses the overall performance of Op. 35 with great romantic warmth. Kempff's shading of phrases, even if the rubato is slightly mannered, also illuminates pieces like the *Barcarolle* and *Berceuse*, while the *Ballade* and *Fantaisie-impromptu* are full of personality. The recording is bold and clear, a little variable between items. On cassette the timbre is a little plummy, although this is less noticeable on side two.

Ballade No. 3; Fantaisie in F min., Op. 49; Mazurkas, Op. 50/1–3; Nocturnes, Op. 48, Nos. 1 in C min.; 2 in F sharp min.; Prelude in C sharp min., Op. 45; Tarantelle, Op. 43.
*** Decca SXL/*KSXC* 6922 [Lon. 7150/5-]. Ashkenazy.

Ashkenazy is recording the complete Chopin piano music, but instead of adopting the usual generic approach he is compiling a series of mixed programmes that have the benefit of musical contrast and show something of Chopin's development. Here he comes to the years 1840–41, which offer two of the very greatest works, the third *Ballade* and the *F minor Fantasy*. Both are played with exceptional warmth and sonority; incidentally, the former is a new performance and not a reissue of Ashkenazy's mid-sixties account, available in various formats and couplings ever since. The *Mazurkas* are beautifully done too, and each side is sensibly planned. The recording maintains the high standard of the series, and the cassette transfer is of outstanding quality, the piano timbre warm and full with excellent range at both ends of the spectrum.

'Favourites': (i) *Ballade No. 4, Op. 52;* (ii) *Barcarolle in F sharp major, Op. 60;* (iii) *Boléro in C major, Op. 19;* (i) *Étude in C min. (Revolutionary), Op. 10/12;* (iv) *Mazurkas Nos. 5, Op. 7/1; 47, Op. 68/2; Polonaise No. 6, Op. 53;* (v) *Preludes, Op. 28, Nos. 3 in G major; 5 in D major;* (vi) *Waltzes Nos. 1, Op. 18 (Grande valse brillante); 7, Op. 64/2.*
(B) **(*) Con. CC/*CCT* 7513. (i) Sviatoslav Richter; (ii) Argerich; (iii) von Karolyi; (iv) Vásáry; (v) Anda; (vi) Askenase.

The title 'Favourites' stretches the word a little, but with such a glittering array of talent this recital cannot fail to be rewarding. Even the least interesting player here, Julian von Karolyi, is at his best in the little-known *Boléro*, not one of Chopin's most revealing essays. But many of the others are favourites, and the excitement of Richter's impetuous *Revolutionary study* and the more controlled heroism of Vásáry's *Polonaise in A flat major* contrast well with the style of Askenase's *Waltzes* (bold playing this), and the effortless brilliance of Anda's *Études*. Richter's *Ballade No. 4* is a personal reading but always interesting; Vásáry's *Mazurkas* are in the best tradition of Chopin playing. All are well recorded, and the cassette matches the disc fairly closely.

Ballade No. 4; Berceuse; Études, Op. 10/12; Op. 25/2 and 7; Fantaisie-impromptu; Mazurkas: in A min., Op. 17/4; in F min., Op. 68/4; Nocturne in B, Op. 32/1.
(M) *(*) Argo ZK 59. Van Barthold.

This medium-price record is of unusual interest in that the piano is a Broadwood that Chopin himself used on his last visit to England in 1848; and the recital includes pieces that Chopin played during that period. The limitations of the instrument in terms of power and sonority, particularly at the top, are well known. Kenneth van Barthold gives serviceable rather than inspired accounts of the pieces; he chooses the shorter realization by Franchomme of the *Mazurka*, Op. 68/4, rather than the complete version. Unfortunately the success of this issue does not extend much beyond its value in enabling us to hear Chopin played on an instrument he is known to have used.

Barcarolle, Op. 60; Études, Op. 10, Nos. 5. (Black keys); 8 in F; 12 (Revolutionary); Op. 25, Nos. 1 in A flat; 6 in G sharp min. (Thirds); Impromptu No. 2, Op. 36; Polonaise

No. 6 (Heroic); Scherzo No. 2, Op. 31; Waltz No. 5, Op. 42.
*** RCA RL 37071. Fialkowska.

Janina Fialkowska · is a formidable player who takes all the technical challenges of this Chopin programme in her stride. Apart from her superb control, she has a wide dynamic range and a genuine feeling for subtlety of keyboard colour. Textures are always clean, and there is considerable poetic feeling too. This is a very good recital and it benefits from sound of clarity and presence.

Barcarolle, Op. 60; Mazurkas, Op. 63/1–3; Op. 67/2 and 4; Op. 68/4; Nocturnes, Op. 61/1–2; Polonaise fantaisie, Op. 61; Waltzes, Op. 64/1–3.
*** Decca SXL/*KSXC* 6801 [Lon. 7022/5-]. Ashkenazy.

Continuing his chronological survey of Chopin's output, Ashkenazy here brings us music from 1845–6 to the end of Chopin's life. The sound quality is impressively lifelike (with a first-class cassette equivalent) and has considerable depth in the bass. (The recording was made in All Saints' Church, Petersham.) The performances have strong personality and an aristocratic poise, even though one takes issue with the odd tempo: the *Waltzes* are a little fast.

'Favourite pieces': (i) *Étude in E, Op. 10/3; Fantaisie-impromptu, Op. 66;* (ii) *Mazurkas Nos. 5, Op. 27/1;* (iii) *23, Op. 33/2;* (iv) *Nocturnes, Op. 9/2;* (ii) *Op. 55/1; Polonaises Nos. 3, Op. 40/1;* (v) *6, Op. 53;* (iv) *Prelude in D flat, Op. 28/15;* (vi) *Waltzes Nos. 1, Op. 18; 6; 7, Op. 64/1–2; 11, Op. 70/1.*
(M) **(*) Decca Viva VIV/*KVIC* 13. (i) Davis; (ii) Vered; (iii) Magaloff; (iv) Cooper; (v) Katchen; (vi) Katin.

Although with so many sources the recording quality tends to vary somewhat between items, the performances are generally good and often excellent. Ilana Vered's opening *Polonaise* is arresting, as is Katchen's, which closes side one. Peter Katin's *Waltzes* are stylish, and Joseph Cooper plays the *Raindrop prelude*, Op. 28/15, and the *E flat Nocturne* memorably. The recital is well composed and the sound is always reliable, the cassette sometimes slightly less rounded in timbre than the disc, but never shallow.

Arrangements by Leopold Godowsky: *Études: Op. 10, Nos. 1, 3, 5* (2 versions), *6–7; Op. 25, No. 1; Trois Nouvelles Études: No. 1, Op. posth.; Waltzes, Op. 64/1 and 3; Op. 69/1; Op. 70/2–3; Op. 18* (concert paraphrase).
** O L DSLO 26. Bolet.

It seems remarkable today that anyone should want to try to 'improve' on Chopin, yet Leopold Godowsky (1870–1938) made transcriptions of a great deal of his music, elaborating the textures in such a way as to place the new versions beyond the reach of all but the bravest virtuosi. It must be said that these performances by Jorge Bolet show the most remarkable technical command of Godowsky's complexities, but what he fails to do is to convince the listener that the prodigious effort is really worth while. A degree more audacity of manner might have helped, but, brilliant as the playing is, one is not persuaded to enjoy oneself in spite of all preconceptions. The recording is of good quality.

Cilea, Francesco (1866–1950)

Adriana Lecouvreur (complete).
*** CBS 79310 (3) [Col. M3 34588].

Scotto, Domingo, Obraztsova, Milnes, Amb. Op. Ch., Philh. O., Levine.

This is a curious but attractive opera with one pervading Grand Tune that should alone ensure its survival. It is the story of a great actress caught up in international intrigue, and in the manner of the veristic school we are given a chance to observe her for a moment or two in her roles before she deals with her own life-drama. Renata Scotto gives a vibrant, volatile, dramatically strong account of the title role, not as electrifying as Maria Callas would have been (to judge by her recordings of the two big arias) but vividly convincing as a great actress. The tendency of her voice to spread on top is exaggerated by the closeness of balance of the voices, but her control of legato and a beautiful line amply compensate. Domingo, Milnes and Obraztsova make a strong supporting team, not always idiomatic but always relishing the melodrama, while Levine draws committed playing from the Philharmonia. The Decca set with Tebaldi (SET 221/3 [Lon. 1331]), which served its purpose for many years, is not quite superseded, for though Tebaldi's consistently rich and beautiful singing misses the delicacy as well as the flamboyance of Adriana's character, and Del Monaco sings coarsely, the recording is more atmospherically balanced.

Cimarosa, Domenico
(1749–1801)

Double flute concerto in G.
(M) ** Decca Ser. SA/*KSC* 8. Aurèle and Christiane Nicolet, Stuttgart CO, Münchinger – C. P. E. BACH: *Flute concerto.***

Although not momentous music, Cimarosa's concerto for two flutes has undeniable charm, and its gay final rondo is quite memorable. The only drawback is the composer's emphasis on florid writing with the two solo instruments playing consistently in thirds and sixths. The performance here is warmly gracious, with a good accompaniment and excellent sound on disc and cassette alike.

Oboe concerto (arr. Benjamin).
(M) *** DG Priv. 2535/*3335* 417 [139152]. Holliger, Bamberg SO, Maag – BELLINI, DONIZETTI, SALIERI: *Concertos.****

This enchanting concerto was arranged by Arthur Benjamin from four single-movement keyboard sonatas. It sounds in no way manufactured and is one of the finest concertante works available for the oboe. Holliger brings out its classical spirit and is wholly persuasive, though his approach is slightly less resilient than the famous version by Lady Barbirolli (Evelyn Rothwell) accompanied by her husband on Pye (now deleted). The DG recording is first-class (with an immaculate matching cassette), and the three couplings are equally desirable.

Requiem (rev. Negri).
(M) *** Ph. 9502/*7313* 005 [id.]. Ameling, Finnilä, Van Vrooman, Widmer, Montreux Festival Ch., Lausanne CO, Negri.

Cimarosa's *Requiem*, an impressive, even formidable work, puts an unexpected slant on the composer of the brilliant comic opera with which his name is most usually associated. The choral writing, whether in big contrapuntal numbers or in more homophonic passages with solo interpolations, is most assured, and it is a pity that the choral singing here is slightly blurred by rather

reverberant recording, and not more incisive in effect. Vittorio Negri secures excellent playing from the Lausanne orchestra, best-known for its contributions to Haydn opera recordings under Dorati. The tape transfer is exceptionally successful, one of Philips' very best cassettes, with the choral sound full and rich and almost better focused than on the disc.

Il Matrimonio segreto (complete).
*** DG 2740 171 (3) [2709 069]. Fischer-Dieskau, Varady, Auger, Hamari, Davies, Rinaldi, ECO, Barenboim.

Il Matrimonio segreto: highlights.
*** DG 2537 043 (from above set).

Barenboim directs a fizzing performance of Cimarosa's comic masterpiece. This operatic comedy of manners involving a rich old merchant and his two daughters may not have the finesse of the greatest Mozart, and in duller hands it can seem conventional, but not here when the singing is as sparkling as the playing. The joys are similar to Mozart, and some of the ensembles in particular, not least the Act 1 finale, relate directly to *Figaro*. Fischer-Dieskau relishes the chance to characterize the old man, Geronimo, but the three principal women singers are even more compelling, with Arleen Auger and Julia Varady singing superbly; their sisterly duets (especially the lively Act 1 example with its crisp triplets) are among the most captivating items in the whole work. Alberto Rinaldi as Count Robinson, promised to the elder daughter, Ryland Davies as Paolino, secretly married to the younger, along with Julia Hamari as Geronimo's sister make up an outstanding cast, and the recording, though sometimes over-resonant in the bass, is warmly atmospheric. The single disc of highlights makes a generous and attractive sampler.

Clarke, Rebecca (1886–1979)

Viola sonata.
(M) *** Sup. 1111 2694. Koďousek,
Novotná – BRITTEN: *Lachrymae*;
ECCLES: *Sonata.****

Most readers will be astonished on
examining the sleeve to learn that this
Sonata is 'one of the best works ever
written for the viola' – high praise indeed
for a musician who is hardly a household
name. In the early years of the century
Rebecca Clarke was a well-established
violist, a pupil of Stanford, and an obviously accomplished composer. In the
1940s she married the pianist James Fris-
kin, a Bach interpreter of real quality.
Her *Sonata*, written in 1919, occupies the
whole of the second side of the disc and
is a fine piece, fluent, well argued, finely
constructed and in idiom not unrelated to
the world of Bax, Bloch and Ireland.
Josef Koďousek and Kveta Novotná
deserve gratitude for rediscovering this
rewarding piece, which is new to the
gramophone and is superbly served
here.

Clementi, Muzio (1752–1832)

*Symphonies Nos. 1 in C; 2 in D; 3 in
G (Great National Symphony); 4 in
D.*
*** Erato STU 71174 (2). Philh. O.,
Scimone.

Clementi, publisher as well as composer, tragically failed to put most of his
symphonic output into print, and it has
been left to modern scholars to unearth
and in many cases reconstruct the works
which were being performed around
1800, some of them prompted by
Haydn's visits to London. All four works
here, made available thanks to the re-

searches of Pietro Spada, amply explain
Clementi's high reputation in his lifetime as a composer for the orchestra, not
just the piano. The most immediately
striking is the *Great National Symphony*,
with *God Save the King* ingeniously
worked into the third movement so that
its presence does not emerge until near
the end. Scimone's performances with
the Philharmonia are both lively and
sympathetic, and the recording is excellent.

*Sonata No. 1 in D for flute, cello and
piano, Op. 22.*
(M) ** Turn. TVS 34575. New York
Camerata – HAYDN: *Flute trio*;
HUMMEL: *Adagio.***

This is a work of considerable charm,
and it is played here with classical feeling,
its scale nicely judged; the mood of the
engaging *Allegretto innocente* is delightfully caught. The balance is forward, but
not unacceptably so, and the recording is
full.

Clérambault, Louis-Nicolas (1676–1749)

Harpsichord suites; in C; in C min.
(M) *** Argo ZK 64. Gilbert – LA
GUERRE: *Suite.****

The two suites recorded here represent
only a fraction of Clérambault's output
for the harpsichord, but this is all that
survives. Both suites were published
during his lifetime in 1702 or 1704. They
have splendidly improvisatory preludes
rather in the style of Louis Couperin, and
are notated without barlines. Although
not as distinctive or original as Clérambault's organ music, the suites have
a genuine vein of lyricism, not inappropriate in a composer of so much

vocal music, and they are most persuasively and authoritatively played by Kenneth Gilbert on a period instrument, a 1747 harpsichord of Sebastian Garnier.

Médée; Orphée (cantatas).
*** DG Arc. 2533 442 [id.]. Yakar, Geobel, Hazelzet, Medlam, Curtis.

Though best-known nowadays for keyboard music, Clérambault was famous during his lifetime for his cantatas. Both these pieces come from the first of his five books of cantatas and appeared in 1710. During his day *Orphée* was widely thought of as Clérambault's masterpiece; in the hands of these artists its attractions reside in its melodic freshness and variety of invention. Both *Orphée* and the more dramatic *Médée* make considerable demands on the soprano soloist, and Rachel Yakar rises to them with distinction. The instrumentalists use period instruments or copies and give her excellent support. Neither cantata overstays its welcome (*Orphée* lasts less than twenty minutes), and both are well recorded. An attractive and spirited introduction to a repertoire which, though short-lived (the cantata was virtually extinct by the middle of the eighteenth century in France), is well worth investigation.

Coates, Eric (1886–1958)

Dancing Nights (concert valse); *The Enchanted Garden* (ballet); *London Calling* (march); *The Selfish Giant* (phantasy for orchestra); *The Seven Seas* (march); *The Three Men* (suite).
(M) *** HMV Green. ESD 7062. Sydney SO, Lanchbery.

A welcome collection, even though only *The Three Men* could be called vintage Eric Coates. The last movement, in particular, is irresistible, with its affectionate interpolation of *Johnny Comes down to Hilo*, which wittily turns into *Three Blind Mice*. Neither *The Enchanted Garden* nor *The Selfish Giant* (inspired by Oscar Wilde's children's story) shows Coates's invention at its most memorable. Both are expertly constructed, however, and display the composer's characteristic orchestral flair, while the writing undoubtedly sounds spontaneous. The *Seven Seas* march (used as a TV theme) has a jolly main tune; the waltz *Dancing Nights* is agreeable and includes a surprisingly pointed allusion to Ravel's *La Valse*. The performances here are vigorous and spirited. They are very well played too (and Coates demands a good deal of instrumental virtuosity to sound as crisp in ensemble as this). The recording is spacious and lively; the acoustic is just right for the music.

Four Ways suite: Northwards; Eastwards. London suite. Three Elizabeths suite.
(M) **(*) Mercury SRI 75109. L. Pops O., Fennell.

Polished, spirited and sympathetic performances of two of Coates's best-known suites, including the most popular march of all, *Knightsbridge*. The novelty is the inclusion of the engaging excerpts from the *Four Ways suite*, played with great rhythmic character. Fennell's pacing throughout is well judged and he never pushes too hard. The slow movement of the *Three Elizabeths* is nicely expressive but suffers (as does the rest of the programme, to a greater or lesser extent) from the close, clear recording, which seeks brilliance and detail rather than warmth and atmosphere.

From Meadow to Mayfair suite: In the Country; Evening in Town; The Merrymakers overture; Summer Days suite; Three Bears (phantasy); Three Elizabeths suite: March.
*** Lyr. SRCS 107. New Philh. O., Boult.

Dame Ethel Smyth once described Eric Coates (then at the end of his career as orchestral violist and in his early days as a composer) as 'the man who writes tunes'. And so he did, a profusion of memorable ones. But his music had great craftsmanship too; and lightweight though it is, it lies firmly within the English tradition. Here Boult finds its affinities with Elgar in delicacy of scoring and hints of nostalgia. *Summer Days*, written during the summer of 1919, was the first work that Coates composed as an ex-orchestral player. It includes a justly famous waltz, *At the dance*, graciously elegant and with hardly any Viennese influence. It is a joy to hear this engaging music played with such finesse by a first-class orchestra obviously enjoying the experience, and the only reservation about Boult's approach is his slowing down for the central section of the famous march from *The Three Elizabeths*, which is out of character. The recording is splendid, matching Lyrita's predictable high standards.

Coperario, John
(*c*. 1575–1626)

Consort music: *Fantasia; Two Fantasias – Almonds – Ayrs; Fantasia à 3; Fantasia à 4; Fantasia à 5 chiu pue miravi.* (i) *Songs of Mourning: To the most sacred King James; To the most sacred Queen Anne; To the high and mighty Prince Charles; To the most princely and virtuous the Lady Elizabeth; To the most illustrious and mighty Frederick V, Count Palatine of the Rhine; To the most disconsolate Great Britain; To the world.*
*** O-L DSLO 511. Cons. of Musicke, Rooley, (i) with Hill, Rooley, Jones.

Coperario or Coprario revised his name after a visit to Italy in 1604 (he was born John Cooper). His influence on the English repertoire for viols has been compared to that of Thomas Morley on the English madrigal. His own pieces for viols are contrapuntal but purer and freer than so many of the *In nomines* of the Elizabethan period, and many of them are quite impassioned, particularly the five-part *Fantasia Chi puo miravi* included in this anthology. The first side brings us the *Songs of Mourning*, written on the death of James I's eldest son, Henry Prince of Wales, to poems by Campion, richly expressive pieces that are given superbly by Martyn Hill and colleagues, while the second side is given over to instrumental music. It is well worth investigating this often beautiful music, here eloquently played and truthfully recorded, much of it for the first time. This is well up to the high standards of the Florilegium label, not least in the elegance of its presentation. Strongly recommended.

Consort music: *Fantasias Nos. 1–3, 5, 8; 2 Almains; 2 Galliards. Funeral Teares* (cycle of 7 songs).
*** O-L DSLO 576. Kirkby, York Skinner, Cons. of Musicke, Rooley.

The *Funeral Teares* of 1606 can be thought of as the first English song cycle, and its tone of elegiac intensity makes it a quite affecting experience. The music is darkly passionate and sensitively performed here, as are the *Fantasias* and

other instrumental pieces. A valuable
addition to the growing representation of
this hitherto underrated master – and
excellently recorded into the bargain.

Copland, Aaron (born 1900)

Appalachian Spring (ballet): full
original version for small orch.
(M) *** CBS 61894/40- [Col. M/*MT*
32736]. Columbia CO, composer.

Appalachian Spring (complete
ballet); *Music for Movies* (suite).
*** Argo ZRG 935 [id.]. L. Sinf., How-
arth.

(i) *Appalachian Spring suite;* (ii) *Billy
the Kid: Celebration;* (i) *El Salón
Mexico;* (iii) *Fanfare for the Common Man;* (ii) *Rodeo: Hoe Down.*
(M) *** CBS 61431/40- [Col. MS 7521].
(i) NYPO, Bernstein; (ii) LSO, composer; (iii) Phd. O., Ormandy.

*Appalachian Spring suite; Fanfare
for the Common Man.*
(M) **(*) WEA PRIM 3. Wren O., Snell
– GERSHWIN: *American.***(*)

*Appalachian Spring suite; El Salón
Mexico; Rodeo.*
*** RCA RL/*RK* 12862 [ARL 1/*ARK 1*
2862]. Dallas SO, Mata.

*Appalachian Spring suite; The
Tender Land* (opera): *suite.*
(M) *** RCA Gold GL/*GK* 42705 [LSC
2401]. Boston SO, composer.

Copland turned his *Appalachian
Spring* ballet for Martha Graham into an
orchestral suite which rightly has become
one of his most popular works; but the
full original version, with its sparer, more
cutting instrumentation, has more bite.
This recording under the composer also
includes a passage omitted from the full
orchestral score, a substantial sequence

leading up to the final fortissimo appearance of the celebrated Shaker hymn
Simple gifts. Copland draws alert, refreshing performances from his chosen
players, and they are very well recorded,
making an outstanding mid-price issue.
The cassette – one of CBS's very best – is
remarkably full and vivid.

While the composer's recording occupies a very special place in the catalogue,
the Argo version by the London Sinfonietta under Elgar Howarth has the advantage of a splendid modern recording and
an attractively appropriate coupling.
The ballet (32′ 47″) is complete on one
side, yet the sound loses nothing in amplitude and has an almost digital clarity. The tingling rhythmic bite of the
strings is balanced by tenderly expressive
qualities in the score's lyrical pages.

The *Music for Movies* was drawn together by the composer from his film
scores for *The City, Of Mice and Men*
(both 1939) and *Our Town* (1940). The
evocative opening picture of the *New
England Countryside* occupies the same
musical world as the ballet, and the
jaunty third piece, *Sunday traffic*, has a
marked choreographic feeling. Again
fine playing and first-rate recording.

Eduardo Mata's coupling brings together three of Copland's most characteristic, colourful and approachable
scores in lively, sympathetic performances, brilliantly played and recorded. It
is a lesson to everyone that Dallas has
acquired an orchestra as accomplished as
this. This issue is highly recommendable,
one of the most attractive Copland records in the catalogue. The cassette
transfer is bright and vivid in *Appalachian Spring,* but the lower transfer
level for the other two works (on side
one) reduces the transient bite, although
the sound retains its warmth and colour.

Bernstein's recording of *Appalachian
Spring* is very brightly lit, but the excessive brilliance of the sound is tempered
in the excellent tape transfer. The ballet
suite is superbly played by the NYPO,
and the account of *El Salón Mexico* is

quite stunning for its rhythmic incisiveness and flair. In the original full-priced format these works were coupled with the *Dance* movement from *Music for the Theatre*; now this is replaced by the *Fanfare for the Common Man* (Ormandy) and movements from the composer's LSO recordings of *Billy the Kid* and *Rodeo*. At medium price this compilation (called 'The best of Copland') is certainly good value.

Copland's own Boston recording of *Appalachian Spring* brings out the humanity of the music more strikingly than Bernstein's version, and the recording does not sound excessively dated. However, the coupling of the orchestral suite from the opera *The Tender Land* will prove less attractive for many readers. We are given the love duet virtually complete, the party music from Act 2, and the quintet *The promise of living*, which forms the first-act finale.

Howard Snell's performance of *Appalachian Spring* with an orchestra well known through commercial radio lacks something in refinement compared with the best available, but it is beautifully recorded and well coupled. Snell, a brass player himself (long the principal trumpet of the LSO), draws outstanding performances from his players in the *Fanfare*.

Billy the Kid (ballet suite); *Rodeo: 4 Dance episodes.*
(M) *** CBS 60114/40- [Col. MY 36727].
NYPO, Bernstein.

Both these scores are right up Bernstein's street, and his performances are in no way inferior to the composer's own. With marvellous playing from the New York Philharmonic, rhymically pungent and immaculate in ensemble, everything glitters and glows spontaneously. Bernstein finds a depth of beauty too in the quiet lyrical music; he is clearly totally identified with every bar, and this readily communicates itself to the listener. The

recording is forward and brilliant, but does not lack ambient atmosphere. It has been remastered and sounds fuller than in the original premium-priced issue. The cassette is lively and full-bodied.

(i) *Clarinet concerto;* (ii) *Fanfare for the Common Man;* (iii) *Piano concerto.*
(M) *** CBS 61837 [(d) Col. MS 6497 and 6698]. (i) Goodman, Columbia SO, composer; (ii) LSO, composer; (iii) composer, NYPO, Bernstein. -

This mid-price collection recorded by the composer both as pianist and conductor makes a welcome addition to CBS's 'Meet the composer' series, designed to celebrate Copland's eightieth birthday. The recordings vary in quality, and Copland's playing in the *Piano concerto* lacks something in virtuoso flair, but few will be disappointed. It is good too to have Benny Goodman in a work he himself inspired.

Dance symphony; Short symphony (No. 2).
(M) *** CBS 61997/40- [Col. MS 7223].
LSO, composer.

Dance symphony.
(M) ** Turn. TVS 34670 [id.]. (Boston) MIT SO, Epstein - PISTON: *The Incredible Flutist.****

The *Dance symphony* dates from 1929 and its companion from only a few years later. Both are short, full of originality and energy and tautly constructed. They are rewarding scores, though the listener approaching them for the first time may feel that the influence of Stravinsky has not yet been fully assimilated. The composer's performances are extremely telling and the playing of the LSO could scarcely be bettered, even by an American orchestra. The CBS recording has warmth and brilliance as well as richness of detail and a more natural perspective than is often the case in records from this source. On a cassette the sound is bright and slightly astringent.

It would be idle to pretend that the orchestra of the Massachusetts Institute of Technology is a virtuoso body (there is some less than accurate intonation); nor is the Turnabout recording first-class. But what the playing here lacks in polish it makes up for in vitality, and the music is well projected. Moreover the coupling is valuable.

Fanfare for the Common Man.
(M) *** Decca SPA/KCSP 525. LAPO, Mehta – GERSHWIN: *American* etc.***

The use of Copland's *Fanfare* on television has made it specially popular, and the dramatic presentation here should satisfy all tastes. The opening on the drums is highly spectacular, and the brass has splendid sonority too in this vivid recording, equally effective on disc and tape. With its attractive couplings this is a highly recommendable issue on all counts.

An Outdoor overture; Our Town; 2 Pieces for string orchestra; Quiet City.
(M) *** CBS 61728/40- [Col. MS 7375]. LSO, composer.

Our Town is particularly evocative and affecting in its simplicity: the music comes from a score to Thornton Wilder's play of the same name. Written in 1940, it is one of Copland's most endearing shorter compositions and, like its companions here, shows his talents at their freshest. The *Two Pieces for strings* are much earlier, dating from the 1920s and originally designed for string quartet. Both are powerfully wrought, and *Quiet City*, which also originated in incidental music, is another rewarding piece. Its evocative tapestry features cor anglais and trumpet soloists, and the playing here is first-class. Although the balance is not always ideal the recording through-

out has genuine body and warmth of tone, and the performances under the composer's own baton are predictably expert. This is one of the finest of Copland's own records in the CBS series. The cassette transfer is wide-ranging and lively.

The Red Pony (film score): *suite.*
(*) CBS 61167/40- [Odys. Y 31016]. St Louis SO, Previn – BRITTEN: *Sinfonia da Requiem.*(*)

In this first of his serious orchestral recordings – made in 1963 – Previn immediately established his personal electricity as a conductor, underlining the expressiveness a degree more than he learnt to do later, but in giving consistent warmth and colour to a generous selection from Copland's characterful score for the film of Steinbeck's story. The recording is not of the most refined, but with the Britten coupling it makes a good mid-price issue. The cassette transfer is rather fierce in the treble but responds to taming.

El Salón Mexico.
(M) *** HMV Green. ESD/TC-ESD 7073 [Ang. S/4XS 37314]. Utah SO, Abravanel – GROFÉ: *Grand Canyon.****

Though this is short measure for a full LP side, Abravanel is given plenty of groove space and a rich and spacious recording to enhance Copland's 'picture postcard' image of a Mexican dance hall. There is characterful solo playing from the Utah orchestra and a lively rhythmic feeling, although this performance does not match Bernstein's with the NYPO for dynamism and precision. But coupled with Grofé's more lavish orchestral canvas this is an attractive issue. The cassette matches the disc closely, the focus only marginally less sharp.

Symphony No. 3.
⊛(M) *** CBS 61869/40- [Col. M 35113]. Philh. O., composer.

Copland and the LSO recorded his *Third Symphony* for Everest in the early days of stereo, and that record (Everest 3018) remains a fine bargain. The newer version has more *gravitas*, a fine recording of great breadth and atmosphere, and splendid Philharmonia playing, especially from the woodwind soloists. By the side of Bernstein's vibrant account with the NYPO (CBS 61681 [Col. MS 6954]) the composer's approach seems comparatively mellow, even gentle at times (as in the scherzo, with its almost oriental delicacy, where Bernstein draws links with Prokofiev and Shostakovich). But Copland's natural authority is commanding and the work's freshness of inspiration communicates anew, especially in the eloquent slow movement. Any listener who responds to the famous *Fanfare for the Common Man* will be delighted to find it in use here as a launching pad for the finale: the way it steals in is sheer magic. Apart from one or two explosive drum entries the cassette matches the disc closely, and the work is highly enjoyable in its tape format.

Piano music: *Down a Country Lane; In Evening Air; Midsummer nocturne; Night Thoughts (Homage to Ives); Passacaglia; 4 Piano blues; Piano fantasy; Piano sonata, Piano variations; Scherzo humoristique; The Cat and the Mouse; Sunday Afternoon music; The Young Pioneers.*
*** CBS 79234 (2) [Col. M2 35901]. Smit.

The sound quality here may not be ideal – the piano is recorded in a rather small acoustic – but this is nonetheless an important and valuable set. It contains all of Copland's piano music right from the earliest pre-Boulanger days down to his most recent work, *Night Thoughts*, composed in 1972 as a tribute to Ives. The two most important works, the *Sonata* (1941) and the *Fantasy* (1957),

occupy a side each, and neither is otherwise currently available in stereo: indeed none of the Copland piano music is! Leo Smit has been closely associated with Copland's music over the years (the first of the *Four Piano blues* and the *Midsummer nocturne* of 1947, which here receives its first recording, are both dedicated to him), and he recorded the *Sonata* in the days of 78s. It would be difficult to find anyone who is more inside the idiom and whose command of nervous energy so well matches the needs of this vital music. Authoritative, stimulating, vivid performances.

(i) *Old American songs, Sets 1 and 2.*
(ii) *12 Poems of Emily Dickinson.*
(M) **(*) CBS 61993/40- [(d) Col. MS 6497 and M 30375]. (i) Warfield, Columbia SO, composer; (ii) Addison, composer.

Sentimental, witty, and attractive after their many guises, the *Old American songs* rightly form one of the most popular groups in Copland's vocal output. William Warfield sings them with great warmth and affection, bringing genuine American style to support a vigorous voice and a real talent for this kind of repertoire. Needless to say, Copland's direction of the orchestra is a delight from start to finish. Anybody wishing to become painlessly acquainted with modern American vocal music could hardly find a better introduction. In the settings of Emily Dickinson it is good to hear Copland accompanying at the piano, but the recording is coarse and close and Adele Addison is a soprano who may bring out American folk associations but whose timbre is often shrill as recorded. This quality is slightly toned down in the cassette transfer, which remains admirably vivid in the *Old American songs*.

Corelli, Arcangelo
(1653–1713)

Concerti grossi, Op. 6/1–12.
*** HM 1C 065 99613 (Nos. 1–4); 99728 (Nos. 5–8); 99803 (Nos. 9–12). La Petite Bande, Kuijken.
** Chan. Dig. DBRD/*DBRT* 3002 (2). Cantilena, Shepherd.

Corelli is not as well served as Vivaldi, yet these concertos are no less substantial – indeed, if anything, more so – than the Venetian master's: La Petite Bande offers a useful alternative to the Academy of St Martin-in-the-Fields' recording on Argo (ZRG 773/5), and in some respects this may be regarded as superior. Authentic instruments are used, but to excellent effect; the textures are more transparent as a result, and the playing is always expressive and musical. The recordings are made in a highly sympathetic acoustic, that of the Cedernsaal at Schloss Kirchheim, and are splendidly lifelike. These performances convey more of the nobility and grandeur of Corelli than the Argo set.

Although digitally recorded, with an excellent cassette equivalent, the Cantilena performances are not as polished as those by the ASMF, nor do they have the authentic feeling and nobility of the playing by La Petite Bande. The approach is genial; slow movements are sometimes rather lazy-sounding, while the livelier music lacks the pointed rhythmic resilience of the Argo set.

Coste, Napoleon (1806–83)

(i) *March and Scherzo, Op. 33; Le Montagnard, Op. 34. Adagio and Minuet, Op. 50; Andante and Polonaise* (*Souvenirs de Jura*), *Op. 44;*

Rondo, Op. 40; La Source du Lyson, Op. 47.
*** Chan. ABR/*ABT* 1031. Wynberg (guitar), (i) with Anderson (oboe).

Napoleon Coste, who was the son of a French army officer – hence the christian name – made his career in Paris, where he studied under Sor. He was reputedly an admirer of Berlioz, but his own music, although attractive and often atmospheric in feeling, displays little of the quirky originality of that master. Of the solo guitar music, the fantasy *La Source du Lyson* is attractively picturesque, its second movement a pleasing *Andante* in pastoral style. The two works for oboe and guitar are even more engaging, ingenuous but effectively laid out. Here the creamy tone of the oboist, John Anderson, is persuasive, and Simon Wynberg makes the most of the solo pieces, recorded in a suitably warm acoustic. The recording is of high quality, with little to choose between disc and cassette.

Couperin, François
(1668–1733)

5 Pièces en concert (arr. Bazelaire).
*(*) HMV ASD/*TC-ASD* 3899 [Ang. SZ 37738]. Harrell, ECO, Zukerman – C. P. E. BACH and VIVALDI: *Concertos.****

These arrangements, very much out of period, are rather a blot on an otherwise attractive baroque record.

Harpsichord suites, Book 1, Ordres 1–5.
(M) *** HM HM 351/4. Gilbert.

Harpsichord suites, Book 2, Ordres 6–12; L'Art de toucher le clavecin, Preludes 1–8; Allemande.
(M) *** HM HM 355/8. Gilbert.

Harpsichord suites, Book 3, Ordres 13–19. (i) *3rd Concert Royal; 2nd Concert Royal: Echoes.*
(M) *** HM HM 359/62. Gilbert, (i) with Lyman-Silbiger.

Harpsichord suites, Book 4, Ordres 20–27.
(M) *** HM HM 363/6. Gilbert.

The Canadian scholar Kenneth Gilbert has edited the complete keyboard works of Couperin, and his recording of them is made on an exact copy of an instrument by Henry Hemsch (1750) made by Hubbard in Boston. It is slightly below modern pitch and tuned to unequal temperament, which Couperin is known to have preferred. Kenneth Gilbert's performances are scrupulous in matters of registration, following what is known of eighteenth-century practice in France. Changes of registration within a piece are rare, but it must not be thought that his playing is in any way cautious or austere. There is no want of expressive range throughout the series and Professor Gilbert plays with authority and taste – and, more to the point, artistry. He is also well served by the engineers. In the later records, Books 2, 3 and 4, a different recording venue is used: the first Book (Ordres 1–5) was recorded in Montreal and the others in the Abbey of St-Benoît-du-Lac, which produces a slightly richer sonority. Readers should note that the sound throughout the series is of excellent quality and altogether on a par with the performances. It is impossible to dwell on the individual felicities of each Ordre. As with the *48*, there is little to be gained in making recommendations to start with any particular disc; the important thing is to start somewhere. (Perhaps the *Huitième Ordre*, containing the famous *Pasacaille*, might make a good beginning, though Professor Gilbert does not play it with the panache of the late Thurston Dart.) Once started, the listener will want to explore this rewarding world more

fully, and there is no doubt that Kenneth Gilbert is an eminently authoritative guide.

Pièces de clavecin, Book 1: La Ténébreuse. Book 2: Les Moissonneurs; Les Baricades mistérieuses; Le Moucheron; Passacaille; L'Etincelante. Book 3: Le Rossignol en amour; Le Carillon de Cythère; L'Amour au berceau; Musète de Taverni; Les Petits Moulins à vent; Sœur Monique; Le Tic-toc-choc. Book 4: Les Tricoteuses.
*** Mer. E 77012. Woolley.

This is a useful introduction to Couperin's keyboard music, assembling some of his most popular and accessible pieces. Robert Woolley is a young and persuasive harpsichordist; he understands the period conventions thoroughly and also conveys a sense of pleasure in what he is doing. He is recorded at a rather high level but otherwise there is little to fault here, except the somewhat haphazard tonal sequence.

Trois Leçons de ténèbres.
(M) *** HM HM 210. Deller, Todd, Perulli, Chapuis.

Trois Leçons de ténèbres; Motet pour le jour de Pâques.
*** O-L DSLO 536 [id.]. Nelson, Kirkby, Ryan, Hogwood.

The *Trois Leçons de ténèbres* were written for performance on Good Friday and were the only ecclesiastical music Couperin published during his lifetime. Unlike Bach's cantatas, Couperin's settings had female voices in mind, and he could barely have hoped for more ethereal timbres than those of Judith Nelson and Emma Kirkby. Purity and restraint rather than warmth and humanity are the keynote of these performances, but few are likely to complain of the results. The recordings are admirably vivid, and the

Easter motet is an additional attraction.

Deller's account of the *Trois Leçons* is less authentic, since this music, written for a convent, did not envisage performance by male voices. In every other respect, however, it has a wonderful authenticity of feeling and a blend of scholarship and artistry that gives it a special claim on the attention of collectors. Though less pure than its Oiseau-Lyre rival, Deller's has greater insight and no less spirituality. Both approaches are very different; some may be swayed by the presence of a fill-up in Hogwood's recording, but, except for those who do not respond to Deller's art, this carries stronger persuasive powers.

Couperin, Louis (1626–61)

Harpsichord suites: in A min.; in C; in F; Pavane in F sharp min.
*** HM 1C 065 99871. Leonhardt.

Gustav Leonhardt duplicates some of the repertoire recorded by Alan Curtis (DG Arc. 2533 325) and pays his rival the compliment of using his edition. Whereas Curtis uses an undated instrument from the seventeenth century, probably French and recently restored to excellent condition, Leonhardt plays a copy by Skowroneck of a 1680 French instrument. The sound is altogether more vivid and appealing, and the quality of the recording is completely natural and lifelike. Louis Couperin's music is not always as rich in character or invention as that of his nephew, and it needs playing of this order to show it to best advantage. Leonhardt's playing has such subtlety and panache that he makes the most of the grandeur and refinement of this music, to whose sensibility he seems wholly attuned. This is the best introduction to Louis Couperin's music now before the public.

Dandrieu, Jean-François (1681–1738)

Premier Livre de pièces d'orgue: Pièces (in A. min. and G min.).
(m) *** Argo ZK 84. Weir (organs of St Leonhard, Basle, and St Maximin, Thionville).

Dandrieu was a younger contemporary of Couperin le Grand and, like him, came from a musical family. He spent most of his life as organist at Saint Merry in Paris and at the Royal Chapel. The *First Book of Organ Pieces*, published in 1739, a year after his death, contains a number of suites, two of which are recorded here, consisting of an offertory, several other short movements and a series of couplets which comprise the organ's contribution to the Magnificat. The music is more than just historically interesting; the invention is full of character and resource. Gillian Weir plays each suite on a different instrument, both of them recorded in a lively acoustic, and her interpretations are marked by authority and taste. The engineers provide first-class sound, and readers interested in this repertory (and even those who are not) should investigate this thoroughly satisfying issue.

Danyel, John (c. 1565–c. 1630)

Lute songs (1606): *Coy Daphne fled; Thou pretty bird; Me whose desires are still abroad; Like as the lute delights; Dost thou withdraw thy grace; Why canst thou not; Stay, cruel, stay; Time, cruel time; Grief keep within; Drop not, mine eyes; Have all our passions; Let not Cloris think; Can doleful notes; No, let*

chromatic tunes; Uncertain tunes; Eyes, look no more; If I could shut the gate, I die whenas I do not see; What delight can they enjoy; Now the earth, the skies, the air.
*** O-L DSLO 563. Cons. of Musicke, Rooley.

These unpretentious examples of the art of the Elizabethan lutenist John Danyel (virtually all of his songs that have survived) are performed with typical style and polish by the members of the Consort of Musicke. Specially fine is *Like as the lute delights*, with the words 'a wailing descant on the sweetest ground' ingeniously illustrated in music. The recording is first-rate.

by the standards of the 1860s in Russia a highly original piece. Its flowing conversational cantilena nowadays sounds a little too easy-going, but it is a compact work which satisfyingly culminates in a highly dramatic representation of the Stone Guest's appearance and the Don's disappearance. Mark Ermler directs Bolshoi forces in a vigorous performance with Vladimir Atlantov giving a positive if at times over-loud rendering as the tenor Don and Alexander Vedernikov bull-like in resonance. Impressive among the women is the mezzo-soprano Tamara Sinyavskaya in the role of the actress Laura. Full-bodied if sometimes coarse recording. No libretto is included. The arias on the fourth side are all valuable rarities.

Dargomizhsky, Alexander
(1813–69)

(i) *The Stone Guest* (complete). (ii) *Russalka: Miller's aria.* (with arias: (iii) VERTOVSKY: *Tomb of Ascold:* Stranger's aria and chorus. (iv) RUBINSTEIN: *The Demon:* Tamara's song. (v) RIMSKY-KORSAKOV: *Servilia:* Servilia's aria. (vi) NAPRAVNIK: *Dubrovsky:* Vladimir's romanza. (vii) SEROV: *Power of Evil:* Yeromka's song.)
*** HMV SLS 5196 (2). (i) Atlantov, Milashkina, Vedernikov, Vernigora, Filippov, Sinyavskaya, Bolshoi Theatre Ch. and O., Ermler; (ii) Vedernikov; (iii) Kondratyuk; (iv) Bieshu; (v) Khristich; (vi) Atlantov; (vii) Reshetin.

Dargomizhsky took the Don Juan story as recounted by Pushkin (with Donna Anna as the widow, not the daughter, of the murdered Commendatore), and with a side-long glance or two at Mozart he fashioned what was

Davis, Carl (born 1936)

Music for television: *suites from: The Commanding Sea; Fair Stood the Wind for France; The Old Curiosity Shop; Oppenheimer.*
*** EMI Dig. EMC/TC-EMC 3361. Orch., composer.

Carl Davis is the master of the special technique – essential for TV incidental music – of encapsulating atmospheric and musical feeling within short musical paragraphs. This is strikingly shown in the title music for *Fair Stood the Wind for France*, which has a haunting leitmotive to establish the mood of the H. E. Bates story set in occupied France during the Second World War. *The Commanding Sea* has some splendid orchestral seascapes, using wind and brass, strings and organ in a characteristically individual way; *Oppenheimer* and *The Old Curiosity Shop* offer a series of orchestral vignettes, skilfully and (especially in the latter case) wittily scored, the instrumentation both economical and telling. The music is all splendidly played by a select orchestral group of sessions musicians under the composer. The EMI digital recording is of demonstration standard, spectacular when required (in the sea music) and always clear and natural. There is remarkably little difference between disc and cassette.

Debussy, Claude (1862–1918)

(i) *Danses sacrée et profane. Images; Jeux; Marche écossaise; La Mer; Nocturnes; Prélude à l'après-midi d'un faune.* (ii) *Rhapsody for clarinet and orchestra.*
(M) *** Ph. 6768 284 (3). Concg. Ch. and O., Haitink, with (i) Badings, (ii) Pieterson.

Outstanding performances and recording. The *Images* and *Jeux* are about the best now available, and all the other performances on these three records are among the very finest now before the public. Immaculate surfaces and clean, revealing, well-balanced recording make this a most desirable set.

(i) *Fantasy for piano and orchestra;* (ii) *Rhapsody for clarinet and orchestra;* (iii) *Rhapsody for saxophone and orchestra.*
*** Erato STU 71400. Monte Carlo Op. O., Jordan, with (i) Queffélec, (ii) Morf, (iii) Delangle.

Not a well-filled but certainly a well-played and excellently recorded disc. The *Rhapsodies* for saxophone and clarinet respectively are underrated, though they have rarely been absent from the catalogue (even in pre-war days, when Piero Copolla recorded them). Here they receive eloquent performances, as also does the *Fantasy for piano and orchestra.* Not

a strong work this, but in Anne Queffélec's hands it makes a good impression. Those who missed Jean-Rodolphe Kars' excellent account on Decca can make amends with this newcomer.

Images; (i) *Danses sacrée et profane.*
*** Ph. 9500 509/7300 669 [id.]. Concg. O., Haitink, (i) with Badings.

Images; Prélude à l'après-midi d'un faune.
*** HMV Dig. ASD/TCC-ASD 3804 [Ang. DS/4ZS 37674]. LSO, Previn.
(M) *** DG Priv. 2535/3335 370 [2530 145]. Boston SO, Tilson Thomas.

Haitink's reading of *Images* is second to none in its firmness of grip and fidelity to the score. His *Gigues* is scrupulously prepared and beautifully played by the wonderful Dutch orchestra: the sonorities are delicate and the dynamic shadings sensitively observed, though there could be even more atmosphere both here and in *Les parfums de la nuit.* The superlative quality of the orchestral playing is matched by recording of a high order, scarcely less impressive in its range and body than the digital recording EMI have provided for Previn. The fill-up differs: Haitink gives us an attractive account of the beguiling *Danses sacrée et profane,* with elegant playing from the harpist Vera Badings, who is excellently balanced. An impressive, indeed distinguished record. The tape is more opaque than the disc in *Images* (though still impressive); the quality in the *Danses,* however, is admirably fresh.

Previn's account of *Images* was the first EMI digital record to appear, and technically it is a triumphant success. Detail emerges more clearly than in any of its rivals, yet there is no highlighting and no interference in the natural perspective one would expect to encounter in reality. Every colour and sonority, however subtle, registers, and so vivid is the picture that there seems no intermediary between the musicians and the listener. Such is the clarity that this factor outweighs such reservations as one might have (it won both the *Gramophone* awards for the best sound and the best orchestral record of 1979). There is much to admire in Previn's performance too. Dynamic nuances are carefully observed; there is much felicitous wind playing and no want of intelligent and musical phrasing. By the side of some of Previn's rivals there does seem to be a want of atmosphere in *Gigues*, which comes over much more magically in Tilson Thomas's record. Nor is that last ounce of concentration and electricity that is the hallmark of a great performance present in the other movements, particularly *Rondes de printemps*. Previn himself has given us more atmospheric accounts of the *Prélude à l'après-midi d'un faune* than this, though none is more vividly captured by the engineers. The chrome cassette is hardly less demonstration-worthy than the disc, with the widest range, a natural balance and vivid detail.

Michael Tilson Thomas offers the same coupling as Previn, though the technical success of the EMI record has somewhat overshadowed rival achievements. Tilson Thomas's record was made in the early 1970s and does not match the digital recording in terms of clarity, depth and range. It has two strong advantages, however. First, it is better played and far more atmospheric; it conveys the flavour of *Gigues* and the languor of the middle movement of *Ibéria* far more convincingly than most of its rivals, and the playing is fresher and more committed too. Secondly, this is a mid-price issue. Moreover, the recording, though it must yield to the EMI, or for that matter to the Philips, is very good indeed. It is truthfully balanced, there is plenty of presence and body, and no want of detail. This is in every way a splendid record, and the tape is also impressive. The transfer level is modest, but detail is good and the recording's atmosphere is well caught.

Images: Ibéria (only); *Jeux; Nocturnes* (*Nuages; Fêtes;* (i) *Sirènes*).
*(*) Decca SXL/KSXC 6904 [Lon. 7128/5-]. Cleveland O., Maazel, (i) with female ch.

A well-filled and spectacularly well-recorded issue which offers all three *Nocturnes* as well as both *Jeux* and *Ibéria* in superbly disciplined performances from Maazel and the Cleveland Orchestra. Alas, there is too little magic in any of these readings. The analytical balance does not always help: the wind are by no means distant enough at the opening of *Nuages*, and although Maazel is far from insensitive to matters of dynamic nuance, there are inconsistencies in the observance of some of the pianissimo or *ppp* markings. The viola tone at Fig. 6 in *Nuages* sounds over-nourished, and in the slow movement of *Ibéria* some expressive detail is overglamorized. The *Ibéria* is taut and on the whole much better played than Previn's, but it does not possess the character and sensitivity of the finest rivals. *Jeux* is much less atmospheric than almost any other performance on record, though it must be said that every detail comes over with clarity and presence in this well-lit recording. In neither the *Nocturnes* nor either of its companions would these be first recommendations. *Ibéria* is split over two sides.

Jeux; (i) *Nocturnes.*
*** Ph. 9500 674/7300 769 [id.]. Concg. O., Haitink, (i) with women's ch. of Coll. Mus.

Jeux. (i) *Nocturnes. Tarantelle styrienne.*
(M) ** Decca ECS 816. SRO, Ansermet, (i) with female ch.

However overstocked the catalogue may be, there must always be a place for performances and recording of the quality of the Philips issue. The playing of the Concertgebouw Orchestra is of the highest order, and Haitink's *Jeux* far surpasses any recent rivals. Indeed it even matches such historic accounts as those of Cluytens and the Paris Conservatoire Orchestra and de Sabata's pioneering set of 78s. His reading is wonderfully expansive and sensitive to atmosphere, and *Jeux* undoubtedly scores over Boulez's much (and rightly) admired version from the more measured tempo and pensive approach that Haitink chooses. Competition is even stiffer in the *Nocturnes*, but this great orchestra and conductor hold their own. The cruel vocal line in *Sirènes* taxes the women of the Collegium Musicum Amstelodamense, but few versions, even those of Abbado and Giulini, are quite so beguiling and seductive as Haitink's. Add to this an equally admirable recorded quality, with transparent textures, splendidly defined detail and truthful perspective – in short demonstration sound – and the result is very distinguished indeed. So is the handsome presentation, which reproduces Whistler's *Nocturne in Blue and Silver* to striking effect. The quality on cassette is richly atmospheric too, with only a slight loss of range at the top compared with the disc.

Ansermet's account of *Jeux* has plenty of atmosphere: it is in fact one of his finest Debussy records. The *Nocturnes*, though perfectly acceptable, is not the most distinguished account in the catalogue; *Sirènes* is a bit lack-lustre. However, at medium price this is well worth considering, and the recording is admirably clear and detailed in spite of its age (it comes from the late 50s–early 60s).

La Mer.
*** DG 2531/*3301* 264 [id.]. LAPO, Giulini – RAVEL: *Ma Mère l'Oye; Rapsodie.****
(*) Centaur Dig. CRC 1007 [id.]. LSO, Mackerras – RAVEL: *Daphnis.*(*)
*(*) Decca SXL/*KSXC* 6905 [Lon. 7129/5-]. Cleveland O., Maazel – SCRIABIN: *Poème de l'extase.**(*)

La Mer; Marche écossaise; Prélude à l'après-midi d'un faune; (i) *Rhapsody for clarinet and orchestra.*
*** Ph. 9500 359/*7300 586* [id.]. Concg. O., Haitink, (i) with Pieterson.

La Mer; Le Martyre de Saint Sébastien: incidental music.
(M) (***) World mono SH 374. Philh. O., Cantelli.

La Mer; (i) *Nocturnes.*
*** DG 2531/*3301* 056 [id.]. Orchestre de Paris, Barenboim, (i) with women's ch.
(M) *(*) Ph. Fest. 6570/*7310* 089 [id.]. Concg. O., Inbal, (i) with women of Neth. R. Ch.

La Mer; Prélude à l'après-midi d'un faune.
(M) *** DG Acc. 2542/*3342* 116 [(d) 138923]. Berlin PO, Karajan – RAVEL: *Boléro.****
** HMV ASD/*TC-ASD* 3431 [Ang. S/*4XS* 37438]. Berlin PO, Karajan – RAVEL: *Boléro.****
** Decca SXL/*KSXC* 6813 [Lon. 7033/5-]. Chicago SO, Solti – RAVEL: *Boléro.***

Even after a decade and a half Karajan's DG account of *La Mer* is very much in a class of its own. So strong is its evocative power that one almost feels one can see and smell the ocean. It enshrines the spirit of the work as effectively as it observes its letter, and the sumptuous playing of the Berlin orchestra, for all its virtuosity and beauty of sound, is totally self-effacing. The performance of the *Prélude à l'après-midi d'un faune* is no less outstanding, the cool perfection of the opening flute solo matched by ravishing string playing in the central section. These performances are now recoupled with *Boléro* instead of the magical version of the second suite from *Daphnis et Chloé*, no doubt to compete with the newer EMI remake. However, this would still lead the field even if it were at full price! The cassette transfer is of outstanding quality, matching the disc closely, although there is a degree of background hiss noticeable at pianissimo levels

Giulini's version of *La Mer* is also very fine. During his tenure at Los Angeles he has produced a sound from the orchestra that is infinitely more cultured; the string texture is both richer and finer-textured, and the wind blend is altogether more homogeneous. There is much excitement here as well as poetry. The way in which Giulini shapes the hushed D flat passage towards the end of *Dialogue du vent et de la mer* is quite magical, and a model of the sensitivity that does not draw attention to itself. The sound is fully acceptable, though perhaps not entirely natural. This does not displace the DG Karajan or banish memories of Giulini's own Philharmonia set, but it is highly competitive and those wanting this particular coupling on disc need not hesitate. The cassette is disappointing; the transfer level is low and pianissimo detail is not sharply focused, while the climaxes lack range at the top.

The Cantelli disc is another EMI recording from the mid-1950s which, in spite of its mono source, can compare remarkably well with many of today's issues. World Records have made no attempt to transcribe these performances into fake stereo, but the sound is all the better for that. Indeed it is remarkably good for its period. Having long been treasured in its short-lived original ALP 1228, its reappearance is doubly welcome. Cantelli secures a performance of *La Mer* that can stand alongside any of its day, including the celebrated Giulini account of the early 1960s; and his version of the four symphonic fragments from *Le Martyre de Saint Sébastien* has never been surpassed on disc. He is wholly attuned to its mysticism and powerful atmosphere, and the Philharmonia Orchestra plays with enormous feeling

Surprisingly with a digital issue it is the recording rather than the performance

that sets a limit on recommending the Mackerras version. The performance is urgent and strong rather than refined, and the sound good but not outstanding, with close-up balance of particular instruments.

Haitink's reading of *La Mer* is much closer to Karajan's tempo in his 1965 recording than in his more recent EMI version. Both conductors pay close attention to dynamic gradations and both secure playing of great sensitivity and virtuosity from their respective orchestras. *De l'aube à midi sur la mer* has real atmosphere in Haitink's hands. The *Jeux de vagues* is no less fresh; the *Dialogue du vent et de la mer* is both fast and exciting. An interesting point is that the brief fanfares that Debussy removed eight bars before Fig. 60 are restored (as they were by Ansermet), but Haitink gives them to horns. (Karajan, who omitted them in the DG version, restores them in his HMV record, but on trumpets.) The *Prélude à l'après-midi d'un faune* and the undervalued *Clarinet rhapsody* are atmospherically played too, though the former is more languorous in Karajan's hands. The Philips recording is truthful, natural, with beautiful perspective and realistic colour, a marvellously refined sound. The cassette is not quite so impressive; the upper range is less telling and refined.

Barenboim's coupling certainly offers first-rate recording, and the performances, although highly individual in their control of tempo, have great electricity. For some ears the effect (with the wind balanced rather forward) may lack the subtlety that distinguished the Karajan or Giulini versions, but there is a fervour that more than compensates: *Sirènes* develops a feeling of soaring ecstasy, and the closing pages with the chorus are very beautiful. Similarly Barenboim creates a superb climax in the *Jeux de vagues* of *La Mer*, and the finale is no less exciting. The recording has a wide dynamic range, and although the tape transfer is not made at a very high level, detail is good and the climaxes expand most impressively.

241

Karajan's 1978 re-recording of *La Mer* for HMV may not have the supreme refinement of his earlier version – partly a question of the warmer, vaguer recording – but it has a comparable concentration, with the structure persuasively and inevitably built. At the very opening of the work the extremes of dynamic and tempo may seem exaggerated, and at times there is a suggestion of the pursuit of beauty of sound for its own sake, but there is never any doubt about the brilliance and virtuosity of the Berlin orchestra. The *Prélude* has an appropriate languor and poetry, and there is a persuasive warmth about this performance, beautifully moulded; but again the earlier version distilled greater atmosphere and magic. The new recording is well engineered, although the cassette is not quite the equal of the disc.

Whether or not influenced by the character of the Ravel coupling, Solti treats the evocative Debussy works as virtuoso showpieces. That works very well in the two fast movements of *La Mer* (helped by brightly analytical recording), but much of the poetry is lost in the opening movement, not to mention *L'Après-midi*. Like the disc the cassette sound is brightly lit, verging on fierceness.

The Cleveland Orchestra plays magnificently enough for Maazel, but his *La Mer* is neither as atmospheric nor as imaginative as the best of its rivals. The analytical recording, though well-lit and finely detailed (the cassette as vivid as the disc), does not redeem matters.

Inbal's account does little to make the pulse beat faster. His tempi are brisk, but though the orchestral playing is of a high standard, both *La Mer* and the *Nocturnes* sound prosaic and rarely rise above the routine.

Celle sonata in D min.
*** ASV ALH/*ZCALH* 911. Lloyd Webber, Yitkin Seow – RACHMANINOV: *Cello sonata* etc.***

Like Debussy's other late chamber works, this is a concentrated piece, quirkily original, not least in the central *Serenade*, with its sharp pizzicatos imitating the guitar. Lloyd Webber and his fine partner are as persuasive in Debussy as in Rachmaninov, and they are beautifully recorded.

Cello sonata; Petite pièce for clarinet and piano; Première Rapsodie for clarinet and piano; Sonata for flute, viola and harp; Violin sonata; Syrinx for solo flute.
*** Chan. ABR/*ABT* 1036. Athena Ens.

This set scores over rival versions in being more generously filled. In addition to the three late sonatas and *Syrinx* we are given the two clarinet pieces (the *Rapsodie* is better-known in its orchestral form). The most ethereal of these pieces is the *Sonata for flute, viola and harp*, whose other-worldly quality is beautifully conveyed here; indeed this version can hold its own with the best in the catalogue. In the case of the other sonatas there are strong competitors (Kyung-Wha Chung and Oistrakh in the *Violin sonata*, Rostropovich with Britten in the *Cello sonata*). The works for wind are especially successful in the cassette version, which sounds admirably fresh; the string pieces are slightly less immediate.

Cello sonata; Sonata for flute, viola and harp; Violin sonata.
(M) *** DG Priv. 2535/*3335* 455 [2530 049]. Boston Symphony Chamber Players.

Debussy's three wartime sonatas make an excellent coupling, and these sensitive and well-recorded accounts are particularly attractive at medium price. Memories of the earlier Philips set with Grumiaux and Gendron are not entirely eclipsed, but the Bostonians, who include Joseph Silverstein as violinist and Michael Tilson Thomas as an elegant pianist, do not disappoint in any of these beautiful pieces. The cassette transfer is excellent, atmospheric, smooth, yet without loss of definition.

Prélude à l'après-midi d'un faune (trans. Eisler).
*** DG 2531 213 [id.]. Boston Chamber Players – BERG: *Chamber concerto: Adagio;* SCHOENBERG: *Chamber symphony.****

Hanns Eisler's transcription for chamber group of the *Prélude*, very fresh and skilful if hardly as atmospheric as the original, was found among Schoenberg's manuscripts, and has been attractively resurrected on this fascinating record. Superb playing and recording.

String quartet in G min.
⊛ *** DG 2531/*3301* 203 [id.]. Melos Qt – RAVEL: *Quartet.* ⊛ ***
(M) * Argo ZK/*KZKC* 46. Aeolian Qt – RAVEL: *Quartet.**

The Melos Quartet of Stuttgart is a much admired ensemble whose reputation can only be enhanced by this outstanding coupling. The playing of the quartet is distinguished by perfect intonation and ensemble, scrupulous accuracy in the observance of dynamic markings, a natural sense of flow and great tonal beauty. It would be difficult to imagine a finer account of the Debussy than this; and though the Italian Quartet recording on Philips has long been a yardstick against which newcomers are measured, the Melos have the advantage of excellent recorded sound, wider in range and sonority than the Philips; the balance is neither too forward nor too reticent, and is truthful in matters of perspective as well as of timbre. The cassette too is most successful, with only a hint of fierceness in the upper range at climaxes, which is easily smoothed.

Neither the Debussy nor the Ravel quartets receive the subtlety and polish that they require from the Aeolian Quartet. Given the strength of the opposition, this issue is a non-starter.

Violin sonata in G min.
⊛ *** Decca SXL/*KSXC* 6944 [Lon. 7171]. Kyung-Wha Chung, Lupu – FRANCK: *Sonata.* ⊛ ***
(M) *** Ph. Fest. 6570/*7310* 206 [id.]. D. Oistrakh, Bauer – PROKOFIEV: *5 Melodies;* RAVEL and YSAŸE: *Sonatas.****
** CBS 76813 [Col. M 35179]. Zukerman, Neikrug – FAURÉ: *Sonata No. 1* etc.**

Kyung-Wha Chung and Radu Lupu are superbly balanced and most truthfully recorded. This is arguably the best account of the Debussy *Sonata* since the late David Oistrakh's Philips record of the mid-1960s with Frida Bauer. The only snag, perhaps, is that this is a rather short side at a little over fourteen minutes: the Franck is accommodated on the other side, so there would have been room for another substantial piece. Kyung-Wha Chung plays with marvellous character and penetration, and her partnership with Radu Lupu could hardly be more fruitful. Nothing is pushed to extremes, and everything is in perfect perspective, as far as both the playing and the recording are concerned.

In some ways the Oistrakh is the most impressive version ever put on record. Oistrakh's tone is mellifluous yet other-worldly; he produces a rich yet fine-spun line and conveys all the poetry and atmosphere of this score. Tribute must also be paid to his fine partner, Frida Bauer, whose imaginative response is no less keen. Beautifully proportioned, both as a performance and in terms of sound. The couplings are no less appealing; the Prokofiev pieces are particularly attractive. The cassette transfer is naturally balanced to match the disc fairly closely.

Zukerman seems more at home in the Debussy than in the more elusive Fauré (not that his early *A major Sonata* is as problematic or as inaccessible as the *E minor*, which might have made the more logical coupling since it was composed in the same year as the Debussy). Zukerman plays with great sweetness of tone and without any expressive self-indulgence, and he is well supported by Marc Neikrug. Good recording.

PIANO MUSIC

2 Arabesques; Ballade; Children's Corner; Danse bohémienne; Hommage à Joseph Haydn; Mazurka; Nocturne; Le Petit Nègre; Tarantelle styrienne; Valse romantique.
(M) ** Saga 5480. Rev.

Children's Corner is the best-known item here and the most substantial. Livia Rev plays it well enough, though without quite the elegance we find in Pascal Rogé's more expensive record (see below). That is coupled with Book 1 of the *Préludes*, while Miss Rev has various odds and ends which the collector intent on having everything will want but which is not always essential Debussy.

2 Arabesques; Danse bohémienne; Estampes; Mazurka; Pour le piano; Rêverie; Suite bergamasque.
*** Decca SXL/*KSXC* 6855. Rogé.

An excellent performance of the *Suite bergamasque*, with crisp, well-articulated playing in the *Passepied* and genuine poetry in the famous *Clair de lune*. *Pour le piano* is no less effective, and only in *La soirée dans Grenade* does one feel that perhaps a shade more atmosphere would not be out of place. But this is a minor quibble, and there is much to admire here: Rogé is both vital and sensitive, and his intelligence and fine technique are always in evidence. The sound is superbly

well defined on both LP and cassette. The disc is a shade more open at the top (this is where the difference really shows) but otherwise there is very little to choose between them. The quality is eminently secure and firm and the bottom end of the piano reproduces in a most lifelike fashion. If this is not quite as distinguished as Michelangeli's Debussy (DG 2530/*3300* 226), it is nonetheless very beautiful playing.

Berceuse héroïque; D'un cahier d'esquisses; Études, Books 1 and 2; Morceau de concours No. 6.
(M) *** Saga 5475. Rev.

The *Études* are not so generously represented in the catalogue as the *Préludes* or the *Images*, and the only alternative on a single record is by Peter Frankl (Turn. TVS 37025) and dates from the 1960s. Livia Rev is more imaginative, and her playing has considerable poetic feeling as well as great technical accomplishment. This is a worthy successor to her earlier Debussy records, and at midprice it can be confidently recommended. By the time this book appears in print one can expect Pascal Rogé to have reached the *Études* in his complete survey, but Miss Lev's Saga record, which has excellent surfaces, will remain artistically satisfying and it has a distinct price advantage.

Children's Corner; Préludes, Book 1 (complete).
*** Decca SXL/*KSXC* 6928. Rogé.

Pascal Rogé brings genuine poetic feeling and refinement of keyboard colour to the first book of the *Préludes*. He communicates atmosphere and character in no small measure and has much greater warmth than Michelangeli. In addition to the good Decca recording, there is a fill-up, which neither Michelangeli nor Arrau offers. Rogé plays *Children's Corner* with neat elegance. A very impressive disc and arguably the best buy in this repertoire – at least among modern records. The cassette transfer, made at a high level, offers beautiful quality, like the disc, but the warm resonance of the sound sometimes softens the transients in the *Préludes*, although (as the *Golliwogg's cakewalk* readily shows) this is less noticeable in *Children's Corner*.

Danse; D'un cahier d'esquisses; Images, Sets 1 and 2; L'Isle joyeuse; Masques.
*** Decca SXL/*KSXC* 6957. Rogé.

Pascal Rogé produces consistently beautiful tone, and this recital gives great pleasure on that score. His playing is distinguished by keen intelligence and sympathy, as well as a subtle command of colour, and moreover he is supported by recording quality of real excellence. There are occasional moments when one feels the need for more dramatic projection (in the earlier part of *L'Isle joyeuse* he tends to understate a little) and the *Hommage à Rameau* movement calls for more concentration (one feels that it needs to be held together just a shade more tautly). But there is so much to enjoy here and such accomplished pianism and finesse that any individual qualifications are unlikely to disturb even the most discriminating listener. Strongly recommended. The cassette quality is first-class, although (perhaps because of the transfer level, modest for Decca) the treble has marginally less range than on the disc.

En blanc et noir.
*** Ph. 9500 434/*7300 644* [id.]. Argerich, Bishop-Kovacevich — BARTÓK: *Sonata*; MOZART: *Andante.****

An intensely vital and imaginative account of one of Debussy's most neglected yet rewarding scores. *En blanc et noir* comes from the last years of his life

and is full of unexpected touches. This is the finest account yet to have appeared on record and certainly the best recorded. On tape, however, the low transfer level has brought less sharp definition than on disc, although the quality is pleasing.

Estampes; Images, Sets 1 and 2.
*** Ph. 9500/*7300* 965 [id.]. Arrau.

Arrau has been consistently underrated as a Debussy interpreter, though some records he made for American Columbia in the 1950s should have alerted one to his stature. Good though his accounts of the two Books of *Préludes* are, this is arguably even finer. Indeed, it is one of his very best records and combines sensitivity and atmosphere with a warmth that somehow eludes Michelangeli in his much (and rightly) admired Debussy records. Arrau is superbly recorded too and cannot be too highly recommended. There is little appreciable difference in sound between the disc and the excellent cassette.

Estampes; Images, Sets 1 and 2; Préludes Books 1 and 2.
⊛ *** HMV mono RLS/*TC-RLS* 752 (2). Gieseking.

In his day Walter Gieseking was something of a legend as a Debussy interpreter, and these superb transfers testify to his magic. The performances derive from LPs that appeared in the mid-1950s and not his earlier coarse-groove 78s, some of which are even more inspired than the remakes. The later versions are fine enough in all conscience and possess the advantage of splendid sound, which in these impeccable transfers often conveys the illusion and richness of sonority of modern stereo. Gieseking penetrates the atmosphere of the *Préludes* more deeply than almost any other artist, though there are individual pieces where Michelangeli or Richter may be as successful in one detail

245

or another. In addition to the *Préludes*, this compilation offers the *Estampes* and both sets of *Images*; all in all, superb value! On cassette the sound is extraordinarily rich and full, a demonstration of EMI's transfer technology at its finest.

Élégie; Estampes; Images (1894); *Images* (*Sets 1 and 2*); *L'Isle joyeuse; Masques; Page d'album; La plus que lente; Pour le piano; Rêverie; Suite bergamasque.*
(M) *** Saga SAGD 5463 (2). Rev.

Livia Rev has long been an underrated pianist, and it is good to see the Debussy venture on which she is engaged receiving such wide and just acclaim. This compilation can hold its own with any in the catalogue and is cheaper than most competitors. Livia Rev has sensibility, a finely developed sense of colour, a keen awareness of atmosphere and fleet fingers. What more could one want in this repertoire? She is moreover decently recorded and the pressings are admirably smooth.

Préludes, Book 1 (see also under *Children's Corner*).
*** Ph. 9500 676/7300 771 [id.]. Arrau.
**(*) DG 2531/3301 200 [id.]. Michelangeli.

Préludes, Book 2.
*** Ph. 9500 747/7300 832 [id.]. Arrau.
(M) *** Saga 5442. Rev.

Arrau is an impressive Debussy interpreter and his account of Book 1 makes one regret that he has not recorded more of this composer. True, the *Danseuses de Delphes* are perhaps a little too stately; generally speaking, Arrau's tempi are unhurried, but that is no bad thing. There are some beautifully coloured details and a fine sense of atmosphere. This has not the glacial perfection of Michelangeli,

but it has more warmth of appeal. The recording is richly defined and has plenty of bloom; the quality in both disc and cassette formats is extremely impressive.

It goes without saying that Michelangeli's account reveals the highest pianistic distinction. It is in many ways a wholly compelling and masterful reading of these miniature tone poems, with hardly a note or dynamic out of place, and it can be confidently recommended. Yet it remains for the most part remote and cool; authoritative playing that is somehow wanting in mystery and humanity. Clean, detailed recording; the tape transfer is natural and secure in timbre.

Arrau's account of Book 2 is an invaluable record – to be treasured alongside the classic accounts of Gieseking and Casadesus. At first Arrau's approach in *Brouillards* and *Feuilles mortes* seems a bit too leisurely, but these pieces gain in atmosphere at this speed. It is difficult to imagine a more penetrating or revealing account of *Canopes*, whose other-worldly melancholy is fully conveyed. Not everything is equally successful: *Les fées sont d'exquises danseuses* and *Feux d'artifice* would have sounded a shade lighter and more effortlessly wrought a few years ago. The Philips recording is extremely impressive – really vivid and lifelike – and there is no appreciable difference between the disc and the cassette, which is strikingly rich in colour with a natural bass resonance yet no loss of range at the top.

Livia Rev is a highly sensitive and accomplished artist whose Debussy series must be accounted an uncommon success. Her account of Book 2 of the *Préludes* has stiff competition but holds its own against all comers in terms of sensibility and atmosphere. Her keyboard mastery is beyond question and she is a fine colourist. She receives a very good recording, with admirably smooth surfaces, and she has, of course, the advantage of being on a medium-priced label.

VOCAL MUSIC

Song cycles: *Ariettes oubliées; 3 Ballades de François Villon; 3 Chansons de Bilitis; 2 Chansons de France; 4 Chansons de jeunesse; Fêtes galantes 1 and 2; 5 Poèmes de Charles Baudelaire; 3 Poèmes de Stéphane Mallarmé; Le Promenoir des deux amants; 4 Proses lyriques.* Mélodies: *Aimons-nous et dormons; Les Angélus; Beau soir; La Belle au bois dormant; Les Cloches; Dans le jardin; En sourdine; L'Échelonnement des haies; Fleur des blés; Jane; Mandoline; La Mer est plus belle; Noël des enfants; Nuit d'étoiles; Paysage sentimental; Romance; Rondeau; Rondel chinois; Voici que le printemps; Zéphyr.*
**(*) EMI 2C 165 16371/4. Ameling, Command, Mesplé, Von Stade, Souzay; Baldwin.

This box collects Debussy's vocal output on to eight sides, and it is an obvious convenience to have all sixty songs in one place. Debussy's songs are probably less revealing than his piano music; were they his only music to survive, our picture of him would be less complete than if we had only his keyboard or his orchestral music. All the same, the greatest of these songs, such as the *Chansons de Bilitis* and the *Fêtes galantes*, are indeed inspired and are in no sense diminished by the less interesting earlier ones. It is inevitable in an enterprise of this scale that not all the performances are of equal accomplishment. The unifying factor throughout is Dalton Baldwin; he provides polished accompaniments, though there are, it is true, more poetic Debussians. Gérard Souzay's Villon songs are one of the triumphs of the set, as are the *Chansons de Bilitis* of Michèle Command. It must be said that Mady Mesplé is not the most persuasive advocate for the less in-spired earlier songs. But, though not an unqualified success, this is still a useful set in repertoire which is not over-represented at present, and it would be curmudgeonly not to give it a warm welcome.

(i) *3 Ballades de François Villon;* (ii) *La Damoiselle élue;* (iii) *Invocation;* (iv) *Salut printemps.*
**(*) DG 2531 263 [id.]. (i) Fischer-Dieskau; (ii) Hendricks, Taillon; (iii) Pezzino; (iv) Vallancien; Ch. and Orchestre de Paris, Barenboim.

Although this record gives shorter measure than we expect on a full-price label, it does at least offer some Debussy rarities. The *Villon Ballades* are seldom heard in their orchestral form, and the *Invocation* and *Salut printemps* are very early pieces, written when Debussy was twenty or so, and entered for the Prix de Rome. The fugue subject of the *Salut printemps* was provided by Gounod and Debussy's piece earned the disapproval of the jury. Neither this nor its successor, the *Invocation*, is first-class Debussy, but both are well worth having on record. Also welcome is *La Damoiselle élue*; Barbara Hendricks sings with great sensitivity and beauty, and Barenboim draws playing of genuine atmosphere from the Orchestre de Paris. There are problems of intonation with the chorus, but that apart, this is an intelligently planned and rewarding issue, well recorded too.

5 Poèmes de Baudelaire; 3 Poèmes de Stéphane Mallarmé. Mélodies: *Les Angélus; Dans le jardin; L'Échelonnement des haies; Fleur des blés; Mandoline; Nuit d'étoiles; L'Ombre des arbres; Romance; Le Son du cor s'afflige.*
**(*) Nimbus 2127. Cuénod, Isepp.

Debussy song recitals are not so thick on the ground that we can afford to neg-

247

lect any newcomer, and this issue is rather remarkable, since few singers these days record at the age of seventy-five. Older readers may recall that the tenor Hugues Cuénod took part in Nadia Boulanger's famous pre-war records of Monteverdi madrigals, and he has for long taken character parts in opera, such as the Astrologer in *Le Coq d'or*. Of course the voice has lost its bloom and there are vocal deficiencies; but these are few and the characterization of the songs could hardly be bettered, nor could the enunciation – or the piano playing. So, while allowances must perforce be made, there is much here to invite admiration, and the recording is fully acceptable too.

La Damoiselle élue.
** Symph. SYM/*CSYM* 6 [Peters PLE/ *PCE* 021]. Caballé, Coster, Amb. Ladies Ch., Symph. of L., Morris – CHAUSSON: *Poème de l'amour.* **

Debussy's early cantata *La Damoiselle élue* has been seriously neglected on record. It is a highly evocative setting of Rossetti in translation, using women's chorus and mezzo-soprano solo as well as a soprano for the central role of the Blessed Damozel. This rich and expressive performance is focused, predictably enough, on Caballé's radiant performance of the principal solo, with her timbre sometimes suggesting her compatriot Victoria de los Angeles. She produces ecstatic high pianissimos but at times allows scooping up to notes, and her French enunciation is idiosyncratic. Warm recording, which brings out some of the unexpected *Parsifal* echoes. The tape cannot be recommended; it is muffled with a restricted range.

Pelléas et Mélisande (complete).
⊛ *** HMV SLS/*TC-SLS* 5172 (3) [Ang. SZX 3885]. Stilwell, Von Stade, Van Dam, Raimondi, Ch. of German Op., Berlin, Berlin PO, Karajan.
*** Erato STU 71296 (3). Tappy, Yakar, Huttenlocher, Loup, Taillon, Monte Carlo Op. Ch. and O., Jordan.

Karajan promised that this would be his finest achievement on record, and he was not far wrong. It is a performance that sets Debussy's masterpiece as a natural successor to Wagner's *Tristan* rather than its antithesis. To that extent the interpretation is controversial, for this is essentially a rich and passionate performance with the orchestral tapestry at the centre and the singers providing a verbal obbligato. Debussy after all rests a high proportion of his argument on the many interludes between scenes; paradoxically the result of this approach is more not less dramatic, for Karajan's concentration carries one in total involvement through a story that can seem inconsequential. The playing of the Berlin Philharmonic is both polished and deeply committed, and the cast comes near the ideal, with Frederica von Stade a tenderly affecting heroine and Richard Stilwell a youthful, upstanding hero set against the dark incisive Golaud of Van Dam. The recording is outstandingly rich and atmospheric on disc and cassette alike.

Armin Jordan's sensitive and idiomatic version on Erato provides an excellent alternative for those who find Karajan's treatment too large-scale. At its centre is the finely focused Golaud of Huttenlocher, fresh and expressive, well contrasted with the tenor of Eric Tappy, a brighter-toned singer than is usual for Pelléas, a role generally taken by a *bariton marin*. Rachel Yakar's vocal acting as Mélisande is first-rate, and though neither the playing nor the recording matches that given to Karajan, the whole performance is most convincing.

Delalande, Michel-Richard
(1657–1726)

3 Leçons de ténèbres.
*** Erato STU 71147. Etcheverry, Charbonnier, Boulay.

A very different Lalande appears here from the one we know from the more celebrated *Sinfonies pour les soupers du roi*. These are for the relatively austere combination of voice and continuo favoured in France at this time and perhaps best-known from their use by Couperin and Charpentier. Lalande brings a distinctive personal stamp to his settings and is no less a master of the arioso style than his contemporaries; indeed in melodic richness some of this is even finer than the Couperin version. And the continuo realization was spontaneous and not prepared in every detail beforehand; it sounds fresh and immediate without having the fussiness that often marks continuo realizations. Micaëla Etcheverry is an excellent soloist, and the artists are eminently well balanced and recorded.

Delibes, Léo (1836–91)

Coppélia (complete).
** Ph. 6769 035/7699 126 (2) [id.]. Rotterdam PO, Zinman.

David Zinman's performance of *Coppélia* is beautifully played and smoothly recorded. It has no want of vigour or refinement, but it lacks the character of Jean-Baptiste Mari's outstanding set with the Paris Opera Orchestra (HMV SLS/TC-SLS 5091 [Ang. S/4XS2 3843]), to which we gave a rosette in the second edition of the *Penguin Stereo Record Guide*. The Philips tape transfer is made at a very low level, with a conse-

quent loss of immediacy and range compared with the discs. Fortunately the HMV tapes have been remastered and now make a satisfactory alternative to the LPs.

Coppélia: highlights; Sylvia: highlights.
**(*) Decca SXL 6776 [Lond. 6993]. SRO or New Philh. O., Bonynge.

Bonynge's selection from *Sylvia* is particularly enjoyable. He mixes a couple of unfamiliar items in with the usual suite and is served with most beautiful playing by the New Philharmonia. The *Coppélia* selection is less imaginative. Most of the music is taken from Act 1 and too little comes from the two succeeding acts. The absence of the *Automatons* number is regrettable (that was not omitted even in the very first extensive selection from this ballet on 78 r.p.m. discs, conducted by Constant Lambert). Also the orchestral playing in Geneva is not as polished as that in London, for all Bonynge's obvious care. But despite these reservations, this is still very enjoyable with its vivid Decca recording.

Le Roi s'amuse: ballet music.
(M) *** HMV SXLP/TC-SXLP 30260. RPO, Beecham – BIZET: Symphony; BERLIOZ: Troyens: excerpts.***

Delibes's ballet music for *Le Roi s'amuse* is not an independent work, but was written for a revival of Victor Hugo's play in 1882. The music has an element of pastiche and its grace and elegance are superbly realized under Beecham's baton. Indeed the orchestral playing is a constant source of delight. The recording is very good too, and it has transferred well to tape apart from a little thickness of texture in the broader tuttis. This is a delightful compilation

Sylvia (complete).
*** HMV SLS/TC-SLS 5126 (2) [Ang. S/4X2S 3860]. Paris Op., Mari.

The ballet *Sylvia* appeared five years after *Coppélia* and was first produced at the Paris Opera in 1875. While confirming the success of the earlier work, *Sylvia* has never displaced it in the affections of the public, and understandably so. It is an attractive score with some memorable tunes, but to be honest nearly all of these are contained in the suite, and in the full score we hear them more than once. But if the work is not as consistently inspired as *Coppélia*, it contains some delightful music and characteristically felicitous scoring. Jean-Baptiste Mari's natural sympathy and warmth make the very most of this, and he is supported throughout by beautiful orchestral playing and rich, glowing recording. The cassette transfer offers EMI's best quality, full yet clear, with bloom on woodwind and strings alike.

Delius, Frederick (1862–1934)

Air and dance; Fennimore and Gerda: Intermezzo; Hassan: Intermezzo and Serenade; Koanga: La Calinda; On Hearing the First Cuckoo in Spring; A Song before Sunrise; Summer Night on the River; A Village Romeo and Juliet: The Walk to the Paradise Garden.
*** Argo ZRG/*KZRC* 875. [id.]. ASMF, Marriner.

No grumbles here: these are lovely performances, warm, tender and eloquent. They are played superbly and recorded in a splendid acoustic. The recording is beautifully balanced – the distant cuckoo is highly evocative – though with a relatively small band of strings the sound inevitably has less body than with a full orchestral group. The cassette transfer is first-class. No collector need hesitate.

Air and dance; Koanga: La Calinda; 5 Little Pieces (Mazurka for a little girl; Waltz for a little girl; Waltz; Lullaby for a modern baby; Toccata); Sonata for string orchestra (all arr. Fenby).
*** HMV ASD/*TC-ASD* 3688. Duran, Bournemouth Sinf., Fenby.

Eric Fenby makes his conducting début here, and he arranged the entire programme. It is undeniably slight, but the playing is both polished and affectionate and the recorded sound has an enticing bloom and warmth, with an excellent cassette that matches the disc closely.

Brigg Fair; Eventyr; In a Summer Garden; A Song of Summer.
(B) *** CfP Dig. CFP/*TC-CFP* 40373. Hallé O., Handley.

Although the tempi are sometimes controversial, Handley is an understanding and exciting Delian, and these pieces are beautifully played. The digital recording is superb, matching clarity of definition with ambient lustre and rich colouring, on disc and cassette alike. A splendid bargain in every way.

Dance rhapsody No. 2; Florida suite; Over the Hills and Far Away.
(M) *** HMV SXLP/*TC-SXLP* 30415. [Ang. Sera. S 60212]. RPO, Beecham.

The *Florida suite*, Delius's first orchestral work, is lightweight, but strong in melodic appeal and orchestral colour. The tune we know as *La Calinda* appears in the first movement. Elsewhere the Negro influences absorbed by Delius even suggest a Dvořákian flavour. The writing is untypical of the mature Delius rather in the same way as the *Karelia* suite is of Sibelius. With the *Second Dance rhapsody* and the somewhat episodic *Over the Hills* this makes a fine medium-priced anthology, and the recording sounds astonishingly undated. The tape matches the disc closely; the quality is both vivid and transparent. An indispensable reissue,

Fennimore and Gerda: Intermezzo; Irmelin: Prelude; Koanga: La Calinda (arr. Fenby); *On Hearing the First Cuckoo in Spring; Sleigh Ride; A Song before Sunrise; Summer Night on the River; A Village Romeo and Juliet: The Walk to the Paradise Garden* (arr. Beecham).
(B) *** CfP CFP/*TC-CFP* 40304. LPO, Handley.

All Delius conductors are haunted by the ghost of Beecham, whose close identification with the composer has deterred challenging batons. While his readings are still an indispensable cornerstone for any library, it is good to welcome more up-to-date recordings. Here Vernon Handley covers much the same ground as Neville Marriner (see above), but he includes the *Irmelin Prelude* for good measure, and this issue has a considerable price advantage over the Argo. Some collectors may find Handley's *Walk to the Paradise Garden* a little overheated in sentiment; but, generally speaking, this is a successful anthology, with expansive and imaginative phrasing, and the LPO responds with some fine wind playing. The quality of the recorded sound is admirable; the acoustic is appropriately warm and open, while the engineers succeed in meeting the diverse claims of tonal homogeneity and clarity of texture. At times the wind seem a trifle too close, but there need be no serious reservation on technical grounds. The tape transfer is as successful as the disc, clear in detail with plenty of warmth and body.

Irmelin: Prelude; A Song of Summer; The Walk to the Paradise Garden (A Village Romeo and Juliet).

(M) *** HMV Green. ESD/*TC-ESD* 7092 [Ang. S 36415], I.SO, Barbirolli – BAX: *Tintagel*, IRELAND: *London overture*.***

These are richly romantic rather than delicately subtle performances: Sir John does not provide the limpid evanescent textures for which Beecham was famous. The music is most persuasive not when it is in repose but rather when Barbirolli can bring his almost Italianate romanticism to Delius's passionate arching string phrases. Lovely playing throughout, and first-rate sound. The tape transfer too is of outstanding quality, clear in detail, yet with plenty of warmth and bloom.

String quartet.
*** O-L DSLO 47. Fitzwilliam Qt
SIBELIUS: *Quartet.****

The Delius quartet is rarely heard either in the concert hall or on record (a Pye disc made by the Fidelio Quartet in the early 1970s did not survive very long). The Fitzwilliam Quartet make out a more convincing case for this score than any other we have had and they play with evident affection and commitment. Ensemble and intonation are excellent; phrases are carefully matched and rhythms vitally articulated. Undoubtedly the best (and best-known) movement is more familiar in Eric Fenby's arrangement for strings (*Late Swallows*) but it sounds eloquent in these young players' hands. The recording too is excellent.

Violin sonatas Nos. 1–3.
(M) *** Uni. UNS 258. Holmes, Fenby.
**(*) HMV ASD 3864. Menuhin, Fenby.

Eric Fenby with the help of Ralph Holmes has often given deeply illuminating as well as witty lectures on his years as Delius's amanuensis. These sonatas, particularly the last, which we owe entirely to Fenby's ability to transcribe the blind and paralysed composer's inspirations, form an important part of his theme. On the Unicorn disc we have a historic and moving set of all three sonatas – among the finest of all Delius's chamber works – which amply confirms the high claims made by Fenby for their cogency of argument. Though Fenby as pianist may not be a virtuoso, the persuasiveness of his playing and that of Ralph Holmes makes this one of the most treasurable of Delius records. Fenby himself contributes a spoken introduction. First-class recording.

Even Menuhin (with the help of the ever-perceptive Fenby as accompanist) cannot outshine the persuasive, idiomatic performances on Unicorn. Menuhin is helped by rich recording (the violin sound is more resonant), and his playing is always warm and sympathetic; but the detail of the other version, not to mention the bonus of Fenby's talk, makes it preferable.

VOCAL AND CHORAL MUSIC

(i) *Appalachia. Brigg Fair.*
(M) *** HMV Green. ESD/*TC-ESD* 7099. Hallé O., Barbirolli, (i) with Jenkins, Amb. S.

The reissue on HMV Greensleeve of Barbirolli's account of *Appalachia* is most welcome. Beecham's famous LP was marred by an unconvincing soloist but in every other respect was totally magical. Barbirolli dwells a little too lovingly on detail to suit all tastes, but for the most part he gives an admirably atmospheric reading that conveys, with the help of a richly detailed recording, the exotic and vivid colouring of Delius's score. The performance of *Brigg Fair* is no less evocative. The cassette transfer is clear, with good detail and choral focus, but the sound lacks something in bloom at the top, and the first climax of *Appalachia* has a touch of fierceness.

Appalachia; Sea Drift.
*** Argo ZRG/*KZRC* 934. Shirley-Quirk, LSO Ch., RPO, Hickox.

This exceptionally generous coupling brings fresh and dedicated performances under Richard Hickox, urgent in their expressiveness rather than lingering. John Shirley-Quirk sings with characteristic sensitivity, and the chorus – trained by Hickox – is outstanding. The long sides do not prevent the recording from being fresh and clean. The cassette transfer is vivid but the choral focus is less refined than on disc.

2 Aquarelles. (i) *Caprice and elegy. Fantastic dance; Irmelin: Prelude; Koanga: La Calinda; A Song of Summer.* (ii) *Cynara.* (ii; iii) *Idyll.* (iv) *A Late Lark.* (v) *Songs of Farewell.*
*** Uni. Dig. DKP 9008/9. RPO, Fenby, with (i) Julian Lloyd Webber; (ii) Allen; (iii) Lott; (iv) Rolfe Johnson; (v) Amb. S.

Eric Fenby, the musician without whom these works of Delius's last period would literally not exist, draws loving, dedicated performances from the RPO, and the digital recording is outstandingly fine. *A Song of Summer* is the finest of the works which Fenby took down from the dictation of the blind, paralysed and irascible composer, but the *Songs of Farewell* (to words of Whitman) and the love scene entitled *Idyll*, rescued from an abortive opera project, are most beautiful too, with Felicity Lott and Thomas Allen especially impressive in the *Idyll*. These major works, like such trifles as the *Fantastic dance* (dedicated to Fenby), were based on earlier sketches, while other items here were arranged by Fenby with the composer's approval. The *Irmelin Prelude*, for example, took material from the opera at a time when it seemed it would never receive a full performance. Christopher Palmer's notes on the pieces are deeply sympathetic as well as informative, making this two-disc issue essential for anyone interested in Delius.

Hassan (incidental music).
**(*) HMV ASD/*TC-ASD* 3777. Hill, Rayner Cook, Ch., Bournemouth Sinf., Handley.

Although the recording in its immediacy lacks atmosphere, Handley secures clean-cut, enjoyable performances of all the pieces Delius wrote for Flecker's play *Hassan* (including a choral version of the famous *Serenade*). Both playing and singing are first-rate, and though memories of Beecham's briefer selection from the incidental music are rarely if ever effaced, this is a most valuable issue for Delians. The tape transfer is smooth and well-balanced, with only marginally less range than the disc.

Songs of Sunset.
(M) *** HMV SXLP/*TC-SXLP* 30440. Cameron, Forrester, Beecham Ch. Soc., RPO, Beecham – BANTOCK: *Fifine.****

The *Songs of Sunset*, which were composed in the immediate wake of *Sea Drift* and *A Mass of Life*, are settings of poems by Dowson on the theme of the transience of life and of a love. They are among Delius's most deeply characteristic works, and this performance issued during the centenary year (1963) must count among the indispensable records in any Delius or Beecham collection. Beecham made another recording of it immediately after the war (that is included in the World Records compilation devoted to Beecham's Delius 1946–52), but this version has the advantage of better sound and greater atmosphere It now appears for the first time in stereo (the coupling is too early a recording for stereo, but the sound is remarkably good).

OPERA

The Magic Fountain.
*** BBC BBC 2001 (2). Mitchinson, Pring, Welsby, Anglas, Thomas, BBC Singers, BBC Concert O., Del Mar.

This BBC recording is taken direct from the world première performance given on Radio 3 in November 1977. In this passionately committed reading under Del Mar, *The Magic Fountain* emerges as arguably the most consistently inspired of the Delius operas. Writing in the 1890s, Delius was influenced in his plot by *Tristan*: the heroine's hatred of the hero – a Spanish nobleman searching for the Fountain of Eternal Youth – turns to passionate love. The pity is that Delius's dramatic sense let him down. There is much beautiful atmospheric writing – particularly for the chorus – and although none of these soloists is perfect and the sound effects are sometimes intrusive, this is a most valuable and enjoyable set, cleanly recorded.

Destouches, André
(1672–1749)

Première Suite des éléments (ballet music).
*** O-L DSLO 562 [id.]. AcAM, Hogwood – REBEL: *Les Éléments.****

A few years before Rebel composed his highly original ballet on *The Elements*, André Destouches, even better-connected as a court composer, wrote this ballet on the same theme. The result is less original but still well worth hearing, especially in this refreshing performance on original instruments.

Dittersdorf, Karl von
(1739–99)

Harp concerto in A (arr. Pilley).
*** Argo ZRG/*KZRC* 930. Robles,
ASMF, Iona Brown – BOIELDIEU and
HANDEL: *Concertos.****

Dittersdorf's *Harp concerto* is a transcription of an unfinished keyboard concerto with additional wind parts. It is an
elegant piece, not quite as memorable as
the Boieldieu coupling but very pleasing
when played with such style. The recording too is from Argo's topmost drawer.
There is no perceptible difference between disc and cassette; both are of demonstration quality.

Dodgson, Stephen
(born 1924)

(i) *Guitar concerto No. 1.* (i–ii) *Duo
concertante for harpsichord and
guitar. Partita No. 1 for guitar.*
(M) **(*) CBS 61841/40-. Williams, with
(i) ECO, Groves; (ii) Puyana.

Stephen Dodgson is a civilized composer whose invention is matched by
good taste and fine craftsmanship. John
Williams is an eloquent and authoritative
exponent and the *Concerto* could hardly
hope for a more persuasive performance.
Much the same goes for the companion
pieces; the rewarding and resourceful
Duo concertante is splendidly played. The
recording, while not in the very first
flight, is still very good indeed, and readers need not hesitate on this count. The
cassette transfers are of CBS's best
quality, losing comparatively little
compared with the disc. In the *Concerto*
the orchestra is given an attractive sense
of space.

Guitar concerto No. 2.
**(*) CBS 76634/40- [Col. M 35172].
Williams, ECO, Groves – ARNOLD:
Serenade; CASTELNUOVO-TEDESCO:
Concerto.**(*)

This concerto was written in 1972
expressly for John Williams, who has
consistently championed the music of
Stephen Dodgson. It is a work of both
charm and substance; the ideas hold the
listener, the textures are varied and imaginative, and the sound world is fresh
and luminous. This performance is expert
and although the sound picture is not
perfectly natural (the guitar is closely
observed and looms too large in the aural
canvas) few will object. The overall
timbre is faithful and orchestral detail is
vivid and in good perspective. More
bloom and expansiveness in the top
register, and it would rate three stars. But
this is a rewarding work and an authoritative performance.

Dohnányi, Ernst von
(1877–1960)

*Variations on a nursery tune for piano
and orchestra, Op. 25.*
** CBS 76910/40- [Col. M/*MT* 35832].
Entremont, Nat. PO, Kamu –
LITOLFF: *Scherzo*; R. STRAUSS: *Bur-
leske.* **

(i) *Variations on a nursery tune. Rur-
alia Hungarica* (suite), *Op. 32b.*
*** Hung. SLPX 12149. Budapest SO,
Lehel, (i) with Lantos.

Although recordings of the *Nursery
variations* are legion, the *Ruralia Hungarica* suite is something of a rarity. Much
of Dohnányi's music is often thought
of as Brahmsian, and it is true that he
is by no means as national in outlook
as either Bartók or Kodály. Yet *Ruralia*

Hungarica, though a cultivated score, still has an element of peasant earthiness. There is, too, in its five movements wide variety of mood and it rises to considerable eloquence. György Lehel and the Budapest orchestra successfully convey its exuberance and poetry, and the pianist in the *Variations*, István Lantos, is characterful as well as brilliant. The recorded sound is truthful and well balanced.

With the piano balanced close, the Entremont version of the *Variations* lacks delicacy and charm, but this issue might be considered for the Strauss coupling. The boldly resonant sound (some ears will find it overblown) has been transferred to tape successfully.

Reminder: Cristina Ortiz's superbly recorded account of the *Variations*, equally attractive on disc and tape, and awarded a rosette in the second edition of the *Penguin Stereo Record Guide*, is coupled on HMV to Rachmaninov's *Rhapsody on a theme of Paganini* (ASD/ TC-ASD 3197 [Ang. S 37178]); and Katchen's identical coupling with Boult and the LPO makes a highly distinguished mid-price recommendation (Decca Ace SDD 428 [Lon. STS/5-15406]).

Serenade in C, Op. 10.
**(*) CBS 76832 [Col. M/MT 35152].
Perlman, Zukerman, Harrell – BEETHOVEN: *Serenade*.**(*)

This is an expressive and inventive piece with a particularly beautiful slow movement. The present issue resembles its pioneering record by Heifetz, Primrose and Feuerman in two respects: the brilliance and mastery of the playing and the dryness of the recording! It is not otherwise available, however, and as a performance it is difficult to imagine it being bettered.

Donizetti, Gaetano
(1797–1848)

Cor anglais concerto in G.
(M) *** DG Priv. 2535/*3335* 417 [139152]. Holliger, Bamberg SO, Maag – BELLINI, CIMAROSA, SALIERI: *Concertos.****

Holliger changes from oboe to cor anglais for Donizetti's attractive concerto, yet plays as stylishly and nimbly as ever. This is an outstanding collection, equally desirable on disc and tape.

Ballet music from: *L'Assedio di Calais; Don Sébastien; La Favorita; Les Martyres.*
*** Ph. 9500 673/*7300 768*. Philh. O., Almeida.

Music from the baroque period has given us dozens of records which are validly used for aural wallpaper. This ballet music from four of the operas which were presented in Paris provides a nineteenth-century equivalent, sparkling, refreshing dances of no great originality, delivered here with great zest and resilience and excellently recorded. The cassette does not quite match the disc in sparkle, but the balance is good and the effect lively. If only Philips had used a bit more level this would have been an outstanding tape.

Overtures: Don Pasquale; Linda di Chamounix; Maria di Rohan; Marin Faliero; Les Martyres.
*** Erato STU 71211. Monte Carlo Op. O., Scimone.

These sprightly performances of overtures which in a generalized way could be fitted to almost any kind of opera make up an attractive and entertaining collection, lightness and energy presented without involvement. The recording is bright to match the performances.

String quartet No. 4 in D (arr. for string orch.).
(M) *** Argo ZK 26/7. ASMF, Marriner – ROSSINI: *Sonatas*.***

This delightful 'prentice work has sunny lyricism and a melodic freshness that speak of youthful genius. The composer's craftsmanship is obvious and the writing is such that (like Verdi's single *Quartet*) it lends itself readily to performance by a string orchestra, especially when the playing is as warm-hearted and polished as it is on this immaculately recorded Argo disc. This is now part of a medium-priced two-disc set coupled to the Rossini *String sonatas*, one of the treasures of the Argo catalogue.

String quartet No. 13 in A.
*** CRD CRD 1066/*CRDC 4066.*
Alberni Qt – PUCCINI: *Crisantemi*; VERDI: *Quartet*.***

This, the thirteenth of nearly twenty quartets which Donizetti wrote in his early twenties, is an endearing work with a scherzo echoing that in Beethoven's *Eroica* and with many twists of argument that are attractively unpredictable. It is well coupled here with other works for string quartet by Italian opera composers, all in strong, committed performances and well recorded. The cassette transfer has plenty of character with good body and detail, although the treble is brighter and has more edge than in the couplings.

Miserere in D min.
(M) **(*) Hung. SLPX 12147. Pászthy, Bende, Slovak Philharmonic Ch., and O., Maklári.

Written at the age of twenty-three when Donizetti had just completed his studies, this *Miserere* presents a setting of Psalm 51 (Vulgate 50) which happily and fluently keeps straying into a secular style more appropriate for opera, with

jollity always ready to take over from penitence. The soprano, for example, has an aria with sweet violin solo and pizzicato bass which asks for salvation from bloodshed; but at least in the outer movements the composer presents a properly grave face, with the finale sporting a fully-fledged fugue. It is an agreeable curiosity, here given a committed performance helped by well-balanced recording.

Requiem.
(M) ** Decca Ace SDD 566. Cortez, Pavarotti, Bruson, Washington, O. e Coro Ente Lirico Arena di Verona, Fackler.

There are passages in this *Requiem* which may well have influenced Verdi when he came to write his masterpiece. Generally Donizetti's inspiration is short-winded, and it is not helped here by limited performance and recording and generally indifferent singing and playing. Pavarotti is the obvious star, singing flamboyantly in his big solo, *Ingemisco*.

OPERA

L'Elisir d'amore (complete).
*** CBS 79210/40- (2) [Col. MZ 34585]. Cotrubas, Domingo, Evans, Wixell, Watson, ROHCG Ch. and O., Pritchard.

Geared to a successful Covent Garden production, this CBS issue presents a strong and enjoyable performance, well sung and well characterized. Delight centres very much on the delectable Adina of Ileana Cotrubas. Quite apart from the delicacy of her singing, she presents a sparkling, flirtatious character to underline the point of the whole story. Placido Domingo by contrast is more a conventional hero and less the world's fool that Nemorino should be. It is a large voice for the role, and *Una furtiva lagrima* is not pure enough in its legato; but otherwise his singing is stylish and vigorous. Sir Geraint Evans gives a vivid characterization as Dr Dulcamara, though the microphone sometimes brings out roughness of tone, and Ingvar Wixell is an upstanding Belcore. Bright, nicely balanced recording and effective stereo staging. Our review tape set was undistinguished, with poor focus and discoloration of the upper partials, but by the time we are in print this will almost certainly have been remastered.

Reminder: The Decca set should not be forgotten, with Sutherland in top form, Pavarotti an ideal Nemorino, vividly portraying the wounded innocent, and Spiro Malas a superb Dulcamara (SET 503/5/*K 154 K 32* [Lon. 13101]). The cassette transfer matches the recording excellence of the discs.

La Favorita (complete).

**(*) Decca D 96 D 3/*K 96 K 33* (3) [Lon. 13113/5-]. Pavarotti, Cossotto, Bacquier, Ghiaurov, Cotrubas, Ch. and O. of Teatro Comunale, Bologna, Bonynge.

No opera of Donizetti shows more clearly than *La Favorita* just how deeply he influenced the development of Verdi. Almost every scene brings anticipations not just of early Verdi but of the middle operas and even of such mature masterpieces as *Don Carlo* and *La Forza del destino*. *La Favorita* may not have so many headily memorable tunes as the finest Donizetti operas, but red-blooded drama provides ample compensation. Set in Spain in the early fourteenth century, the story revolves round the predicament of Fernando – strongly and imaginatively sung here by Pavarotti – torn between religious devotion and love for the beautiful Leonora, who (unknown to him) is the mistress of the king. This recording made in Bologna is not ideal – showing signs that the sessions were not easy – but the colour and vigour of the writing are never in doubt. The

mezzo role of the heroine is taken by Fiorenza Cossotto, formidably powerful if not quite at her finest, while Ileana Cotrubas comparably is imaginative as her confidant Ines, but not quite at her peak. Bacquier and Ghiaurov make up a team which should have been even better, but which will still give much satisfaction. Bright Decca recording, again not quite out of the top drawer. The cassette transfer is generally well managed.

Linda di Chamounix: Ah! tardai troppo ... O luce di quest' anima. Lucia di Lammermoor: Ancor non giunse! ... Regnava nel silenzio; Mad scene (complete).

⊛ (M) *** Decca Jub. JB/*KJBC* 97 [Lon. 25111/5-]. Sutherland, Paris Conservatoire O., Santi – VERDI: *Arias.***

No rave notice could really exaggerate the quality of this singing, and in many ways the first recording made by Joan Sutherland of the *Lucia* Mad scene has not been surpassed by either of her complete recordings of the opera (1961 and 1971). In fact this issue must be set on a pedestal as one of the finest and most dramatically thrilling displays of coloratura ever recorded. It is not just that Sutherland shows here a Tetrazzini-like perfection, but that she makes these stylized tunes and florid passages into something intensely moving. The youthful freshness of the voice is extremely appealing, and the tonal beauty is often quite magical. With its atmospheric stereo recording this remains one of the gramophone's great recital discs, and the newly transferred Jubilee cassette matches the disc very closely in vividness and range.

Lucia di Lammermoor (complete).

**(*) Ph. 6703 080/*7699 056* (3) [id.]. Caballé, Carreras, Sardinero, Ahnsjö, Ramey, Amb. S., New Philh. O., Lopez-Cobós.

DONIZETTI

(M) **(*) HMV SLS/TC-SLS 5166 (2) [Ang. S/4X2S 3601]. Callas, Tagliavini, Cappuccilli, Ladysz, Philh. Ch. and O., Serafin.
(M) (***) HMV mono SLS/TC-SLS 5056 (2). Callas, Di Stefano, Gobbi, Maggio Musicale Fiorentino, Serafin.

The idea behind the set with Caballé is fascinating, a return to what the conductor, Jesus Lopez-Cobós, believes is Donizetti's original concept, an opera for a dramatic soprano, not a light coloratura. Compared with the text we know, transpositions paradoxically are for the most part upwards (made possible when no stratospheric coloratura additions are needed); but Cobós's direction hardly compensates for the lack of brilliance, and, José Carreras apart, the singing, even that of Caballé, is not especially persuasive. Good, refined recording.

Maria Callas's flashing-eyed interpretation of the role of Lucia remains unique, though in her second recording (SLS/TC-SLS 5166) the voice has its edgy and unsteady moments to mar enjoyment. One instance is at the end of the Act 1 duet with Edgardo, where Callas on the final phrase moves sharpwards and Tagliavini – here past his best – flatwards. Serafin's conducting is a model of perception, and the stereo recording is fair for its period. The cassette transfer is admirable, with a fresh, lively overall sound balance and only the occasional peaking on the diva's fortissimo high notes. The score has the cuts which used to be conventional in the theatre.

The earlier mono set, which dates from 1954, is given an effective remastering, which brings out the solo voices well, although the acoustic is confined and the choral sound less well focused. It was Callas who, some years before Sutherland, emerged as the Lucia of our time and established this as a vividly dramatic role, not just an excuse for pretty coloratura. Here, needless to say, is not the portrait of a sweet girl, wronged and wilting, but a formidably tragic characterization. The diva is vocally better controlled than in her later stereo set (indeed some of the coloratura is excitingly brilliant in its own right) and there are memorable if not always perfectly stylish contributions from Di Stefano and Gobbi. As in the later set, the text has the usual stage cuts, but Callas's irresistible musical imagination, her ability to turn a well-known phrase with unforgettable inflection, supremely justifies the preservation of a historic recording. The cassettes are less successful than the discs in making the most of the restricted sound.

Still recommended: Sutherland's two Decca recordings keep their special place in the catalogue. The earlier 1961 set (Ace GOS 663/5) offers the voice of a younger singer and the coloratura virtuosity is breathtaking. The later version shows power as well as delicacy, and with the support of Pavarotti and Milnes and the performance enhanced by superb recording quality, on both disc and tape, this makes an obvious general recommendation (SET 528/30/K 2 L 22 [Lon. 13103/5-]).

Lucia di Lammermoor: highlights.
(M) ** Ph. Fest. 6570/7310 155 (from above set cond. Lopez-Cobós).

This selection from the Philips set is generous, but with limp starts to most items the sparkle of the piece is missing, and not just because of the conductor's insistence on eliminating the usual display element. Caballé as Lucia sounds undercharacterized, with an unexpected hard edge in the upper register, and it is disappointing to have the Mad scene cut off after *Alfin son tua*. Much the most enjoyable item is Carreras's account of the tenor's long final aria. At medium price this makes a fair sampler of a controversial edition.

There is also an excellent highlights selection from the later Sutherland set on both disc and cassette: Decca SET/KCET 559 [Lon. 26332].

Lucrezia Borgia (complete).
*** Decca D 93 D 3/*K 93 K 32* (3) [Lon. 13129/5-]. Sutherland, Aragall, Horne, Wixell, London Op. Voices, Nat. PO, Bonynge.

In preparation for her formidable appearances as Lucrezia at Covent Garden and elsewhere, Dame Joan Sutherland made this vivid and dramatic recording with a first-rate cast. In this opera Bonynge believes in underlining the contrasts, bringing out the anticipations of Verdi – as in the funeral chant and bell tolling in the last act, which provided something of a model for the *Miserere* in *Il Trovatore*.
Sutherland is in her element. In one or two places she falls into the old swooning style, but as in the theatre her singing is masterly not only in its technical assurance but in its power and conviction, which make the impossible story of poisoner-heroine moving and even sympathetic. Aragall sings stylishly too, and though Wixell's timbre is hardly Italianate he is a commanding Alfonso. Marilyn Horne in the breeches role of Orsini is impressive in the brilliant *Brindisi* of the last act, but earlier she has moments of unsteadiness. The recording is full and brilliant on disc and tape alike. The layout on tape is superior, with sides tailored to the ends of each act. Thanks to researches by Richard Bonynge the set also includes extra material for the tenor, including an aria newly discovered, *T'amo qual dama un angelo.*

Maria de Rudenz (complete).
*(**) CBS 79345 (3). Ricciarelli, Nucci, Cupido, Ch. and O. of Teatro La Fenice, Inbal.

William Ashbrook in his detailed study of Donizetti was dismissive of this opera: 'It is difficult to believe that *Maria di Rudenz* will ever see the stage again', he said. Undeterred, the Fenice Theatre in Venice put on a new production, and

CBS recorded it live. The sound is rough and the performance very variable, with a principal tenor who for all his heroic tone sings under the note. What matters is that number after number is proved to be Donizetti of the very highest quality, written two years after *Lucia di Lammermoor.* He may fill in with choruses of mourning that are absurdly jolly, but the material is far more memorable than many an opera of this vintage, and some of the arias vie with anything Donizetti ever wrote. There is also a magnificent ensemble at the end of Act 1, where the crazed heroine, believed dead, emerges at the wedding ceremony of her rival and puts an end to it. The absurdity of the story (a variation on *La Nonne sanglante,* cheerfully gruesome) is hardly a bar to enjoyment on record, and the performances of Katia Ricciarelli and Leo Nucci in the two principal roles (the baritone here more important than the tenor) provide the necessary focus. For all its imperfection (which includes loud contributions from prompter and audience alike), this recording of a long-lost melodrama is well worth investigating.

Maria Stuarda: highlights.
*** Decca SET/*KCET* 624. Sutherland, Pavarotti, Tourangeau, Ch. and O. of Teatro Comunale, Bologna, Bonynge.

Donizetti's slanted story of Mary Queen of Scots prompted a highly coloured reading from Richard Bonynge with his wife, Joan Sutherland, as the heroine. This disc presents a well-chosen selection of items from the complete set, with brilliant recording. (The admirable complete set is still available on Decca D 2 D 3/*K 2 A 33* [Lon. 13117/5-]).

Arias: *Don Sébastien: Deserto in terra. Il Duca d'Alba: Inosservato, penetrava . . . Angelo casto e bel. La Favorita: Spirto gentil. Lucia di Lammermoor: Tomba degli avi miei . . . Fra poco a me.*

*** Decca SXL/*KSXC* 6377 [Lon. 26087/5-]. Pavarotti, V. Op. O., Downes – VERDI: *Arias.* ***

This recital record was one of the first to alert the world to the emergence of a new star among tenors. The beauty and purity of the voice in every register are marvellously caught, and if at this early stage in his career Pavarotti seems at times just a little cautious, there are no distracting mannerisms or vulgarities to mar enjoyment. Recording very true and vivid on disc and cassette alike.

Arias: *L'Elisir d'amore: Prendi, per me sei libero. La Figlia del reggimento: Convien partir. Lucrezia Borgia: Tranquillo ei posa! . . . Com'è bello!*
** HMV ASD/*TC-ASD* 3984. Callas, Paris Conservatoire O., Rescigno – ROSSINI: *Arias.* *(*)

This is a fair example of the latter-day Callas (the recording dates from the midsixties), never very sweet-toned yet demonstrating the usual Callas fire. But the singing does not show her at her most imaginative, and there are few phrases that stick in the memory by their sheer individuality. Indeed there are patches approaching dullness, and that is not Donizetti's fault. Good, bright recording, and a vivid tape transfer with few hints of strain at peaks.

Dowland, John (1563–1626)

Consort music: *Alman a 2; Can she excuse galliard; Captain Piper's pavan and galliard; Dowland's first galliard; Fortune my foe; Frog galliard; Katherine Darcie's galliard; Lachrimae antiquae novae pavan and galliard; Lachrimae pavan; Lady, if*
you so spite me; La Mia Barbara pavan and galliard; Mistress Nichol's alman; Mistress Nichol's alman a 2; Mistress Nichol's alman a 5; M. John Langton's pavan and galliard; Pavan a 4; Round battell galliard; Susanna fair galliard; Tarleton's jigge; Volta a 4; Were every thought an eye.*
*** O-L DSLO/*KDSLC* 533 [id.]. Cons. of Musicke, Rooley.

It is by no means certain that all the music recorded here is authentic Dowland, but this anthology does serve to remind us how widely his music was admired and arranged during his lifetime. Three of the *Pavans* and *Galliards* come from Thomas Simpson's *Opusculum* (1610) and two of the *Pavans* are direct recompositions of Dowland's *Lachrimae*. Four of the settings are from Morley's *Consort Lessons*, and there are five pieces from the Cambridge MS. that are performed most attractively here. Marvellous playing comes in the pieces from Simpson's *Taffel-consort* (1621). The recording maintains the high standard of this Oiseau-Lyre series, although the forward balance brings a comparatively limited dynamic range. In all other respects the sound is first-class, and the tape transfer offers quality sophisticated in detail and timbre.

Consort music: *Captain Digorie Piper, his pavan and galliard; Fortune my foe; Lachrimae; Lady Hunsdon's almain; Lord Souch's galliard; Mistress Winter's jump; The shoemaker's wife (a toy); Sir George Whitehead's almain; Sir Henry Guildford's almain; Sir Henry Umpton's funeral; Sir John Smith's almain; Sir Thomas Collier's galliard; Suzanna.*
*** Hyp. Dig. A 66010. Extempore String Ens.

The Extempore Ensemble's technique of improvising and elaborating in Elizabethan consort music is aptly exploited here in an attractively varied selection of pieces by Dowland. Performers in turn are each allowed what the jazz musician would recognize as a 'break', and on record, as in concert, the result sounds the more spontaneous. Excellent recording.

'Miscellany': Come again; Earl of Essex galliard; Galliard; if my compaints; 2 Lachrimae; Lachrimae Doolande; Lady Rich galliard; Lord Chamberlayne his galliard; Lord Willoughbie's welcome home; Pavan Lachrymae; Pipers pavan; Solus cum sola pavan; Sorrow, stay.
*** O-L DSLO 556. Cons. of Musicke, Rooley.

This is an anthology of arrangements of Dowland's music, presented not as second-best (as we today think of arrangements) but as a genuine illumination, a heightening of the original inspiration. Particularly attractive are the items for two or more lutes. As ever, Rooley draws most stylish playing from the Consort, and the recording is exemplary.

Lachrimae.
*** H M 1C 065 99604. Scola Cantorum Basiliensis, Wenzinger.

Wenzinger's version of the *Lachrimae* is not of recent provenance (it dates from 1962) but the performances are wonderfully expressive and deeply musical. It is this profound musicianship that outweighs all other considerations and prompts one to prefer this issue, at long last available domestically, to any of its rivals. Anthony Rooley's version (O-L DSLO 517) has the merit of clarity and authenticity (not that Wenzinger's group is lacking in either), but this version has the benefit of superbly eloquent playing from first-class instrumentalists, and the recorded sound is warm and rich. To be recommended alongside the Rooley but in some ways to be preferred.

Complete lute music (divided into 5 separate recitals).
*** O-L D 187 D 5 (5). Bailes, Lindberg, North, Rooley, Wilson.

This impressive five-record survey of Dowland's lute music is entrusted to more than one player and contains a number of surprises. Though Dowland is best-known for his melancholy – *semper dolens* etc. – he has far greater range than the popular imagination would give him credit for. Of particular note are some of the fantasias on Jakob Lindberg's record; their chromatic boldness and fantasy place them among the greatest music for this instrument. Taken in large doses some of the dances and genre pieces do not make the best effect, but if they are heard in judicious musical context, their expressive power is without peer at this time. Both Christopher Wilson and Anthony Bailes play very freely and expressively (some may feel they could do with a tauter sense of rhythm), but they and their colleagues give performances that are dedicated and highly accomplished. The notes in this set are worth mentioning for they are authoritative and helpful. The only reservation concerns the balance of the recordings, which is slightly too close to avoid fingerboard noises and the odd sniff and grunt. With suitable adjustment of the controls this can be made fully acceptable, and such a tiny reservation should not deter readers from investigating a veritable treasure trove.

Lute music: *Almaine; Dowland's first galliard; Earl of Derby, His galliard; Earl of Essex galliard; Frog galliard; Lachrimae antiquae; Lachrimae verae; Lady Rich, Her galliard; Lord d'Lisle's galliard; Melancholie galliard; Mrs Vaux's gigge; My Lady Hunsdon's puffe; Semper Dowland, semper dolens; The shoemaker's wife (a toy); Sir Henry Gifford's almaine; Sir John Smith's almaine.*

*** RCA RL/*RK* 42760 [LSC 2987].
Bream.

This record dates from the late 1960s
but does not betray its age; on the contrary, it sounds as fresh as any modern
recording. Julian Bream captures the
melancholy and eloquence of these
beautiful miniatures, and produces an
astonishing range of colour from the lute.
Each phrase is shaped with care and
affection, and nothing is in the least routine. This is one of the most outstanding
Dowland records currently on the
market, for Bream projects these pieces
with wonderful character and sympathy.
The recording is cut at a rather higher
level than required, and should be played
back at a lower setting if a true impression of the instrument is to result. Noise-
less surfaces enhance this production.

Lute music: *Captain Digorie Piper's
galliard; 2 Fancies (Nos. 5 and 73);
Farewell; Forlorn hope fancy; Galliard to Lachrimae; Mr Langton's
galliard; My Lord Chamberlain, his
galliard; My Lord Willoughby's welcome home; Piper's pavan; Resolution; Sir John Souche's galliard.*
*** RCA RL/*RK* 11491 [ARL 1/*ARK* 1
1491]. Bream.

An impeccably played recital, as might
be expected from this fine artist. Bream
captures the dolorous colouring of Dowland's galliards with uncanny insight,
and the music is full of atmosphere. The
recording is well nigh perfect. It needs to
be reproduced at a relatively low level,
but then the illusion is complete. The tape
transfer is immaculate and the background is silent.

Keyboard transcriptions by Dowland of music by others: ANON.: *Can
shee; Can she excuse; Dowland's
almayne; Frog's galliard; Pavion
solus cum sola.* BYRD: *Pavana*

lachrymae. FARNABY: *Lachrimae
pavan.* MORLEY: *Pavana and Gal-
liard.* PEERSON and BULL: *Piper's
pavan and Galliard.* SIEFERT:
Paduana (La mia Barbara).
SCHILDT: *Paduana lachrymae.*
WILBYE: *The frogge.*
*** O-L DSLO 552 [id.]. Tilney.

This interesting anthology is less 'transcriptions for the keyboard of Dowland'
but rather pieces composed 'after' Dowland. The Byrd is closest to a transcription, while the Melchior Schildt is almost
a recomposition. In any event these performances are elegant and have plenty of
body, and the recording, if cut at a high
level, is faithful and vivid.

VOCAL MUSIC

Ayres and Lute-lessons: *Captain
Candish's galliard; Lady Laiton's
almain; Preludium and Lachrimae
pavan; Semper Dowland, Semper
dolens; Musical Banquet: Lady, if
you so spite me. A Pilgrim's Solace:
Shall I strive?; Tell me true love.* (i)
*First Booke of Songes: Awake, sweet
love; Can she excuse?; Come again!;
Go crystal tears. Second Booke of
Songes: Fine knacks for ladies; Shall
I sue?; Sorrow, stay. Third Booke of
Songes: Flow not so fast; Me, me and
none but me; What if I never speed?;
When Phoebus first did Daphne love.*
(M) *** Saga 5449. Spencer, (i) with J.
Bowman.

This record contains songs from all
three *Bookes* as well as some lute solos
played in exemplary fashion by Robert
Spencer. In many respects this makes an
admirable introduction to Dowland's
art, since it includes such justly popular
pieces as *Fine knacks for ladies, Come
again! sweet love doth now invite* and
Sorrow, stay. Moreover they are sung

with wonderful artistry by James Bowman, who brings sensitivity and intelligence to each song, and characterizes them far more powerfully than do his colleagues in the *Complete Works* project on the Oiseau-Lyre Florilegium label. There is no lack of contrast, and each phrase is floated with imagination. The recording is excellent too, and the price is very reasonable. By the side of this issue, many of the songs on the Florilegium set seem inhibited.

Henry Noell Lamentations: Lord, turn not away; Lord, in thy wrath; Lord, consider my distress; O Lord of whom I do depend; Where Righteousness doth say; Lord, to thee I make my moan; Lord, hear my prayer. Psalmes: All people that on earth do dwell (2 versions); *Behold and have regard; Lord, to thee I make my moan; My Soul praise the Lord; A prayer for the Queen's most excellent Majesty; Put me not to rebuke, O Lord. Sacred songs: An heart that's broken; I shame at my unworthiness; Sorrow, come.*
*** O-L DSLO 551 [id.]. Cons. of Musicke, Rooley.

In his comprehensive survey of Dowland's music for Oiseau-Lyre, Anthony Rooley here presents a superb collection of motets and sacred songs, an invaluable counterpart of the better-known secular works, instrumental and vocal. The recording, as ever from this source, is first-rate.

Second Booke of Songes (1600): *I saw my lady weep; Flow my tears; Sorrow, stay; Die not before thy day; Mourn, day is with darkness fled; Time's eldest son; Then sit thee down; When others say Venite; Praise blindness eyes; O sweet words; If floods of tears; Fine knacks for*

ladies; Now cease my wond'ring eyes; Come, ye heavy states of night; White as lilies was her face; Woeful heart; A shepherd in a shade; Faction that ever dwells; Shall I sue; Toss not my soul; Clear or cloudy; Humour say what mak'st thou here.
**(*) O-L DSLO 528/9 [id.]. Cons. of Musicke, Rooley.

The *Second Booke* contains many of Dowland's best-known songs, such as *Fine knacks for ladies, I saw my lady weep* and *Flow my tears.* Incidentally, the latter are performed on lute and two voices, the bass line being sung by David Thomas; this is quite authentic, though many listeners will retain an affection for its solo treatment. The solo songs are given with great restraint and good musical judgement, while the consort pieces receive expressive treatment. Emma Kirkby gives an excellent account of *Come, ye heavy states of night* and *Clear or cloudy.* Perhaps it is invidious to single her out, as the standard of performance throughout is distinguished. Refined intelligence is shown throughout by all taking part. This will inevitably be the most sought-after of the *Bookes of Songs* since it contains so many of Dowland's finest and most inspired pieces. The recording is of the highest quality.

Third Booke of Songes (1603); *Farewell too fair; Time stands still; Behold a wonder here; Daphne was not so chaste; Me, me and none but me; When Phoebus first did Daphne love; Say, Love, if ever thou didst find; Flow not so fast, ye fountains; What if I never speed; Love stood amazed; Lend your ears to my sorrow; By a fountain where I lay; O, what hath overwrought; Farewell unkind; Weep you no more, sad fountains; Fie on this feigning; I must complain; It was a time when silly bees; The lowest*

trees; What poor astronomers; Come when I call.
**(*) O-L DSLO 531/2 [id.]. Cons. of Musicke, Rooley.

Although there are certain details with which to quarrel – a general air of sobriety and an excessive restraint in colouring words – there is a great deal of pleasure to be derived from this project. The performers show dedication and accomplishment, and in all cases they are expertly served by the engineers. David Thomas gives an excellent account of himself in *What poor astronomers they are*, and Emma Kirkby's voice is a delight too. The whole set is well worth investigation and an impressive achievement; the instrumental support is of high quality, as is the presentation. Apart from a certain reluctance to characterize, this set commands admiration.

A Pilgrimes Solace (Fourth Booke of Songes): Disdain me still; Stay, sweet, awhile; To ask for all thy love; Love, those beams that breed; Shall I strive with words to move; Were every thought an eye; Stay, time, awhile thy flying; Tell me, true love; Go, nightly cares; From silent night; Lasso vita mia; In this trembling shadow; If that a sinner's sighs; Thou mighty God; When David's life; When the poor cripple; Where sin sore wounding; My heart and tongue were twins; Up, merry mates; Welcome, black night; Cease these false sports.
**(*) O-L DSLO 585/6 [id.]. Cons. of Musicke, Rooley.

A Pilgrimes Solace, Dowland's *Fourth Booke of Songes*, appeared when he was fifty. In its Preface he dwells on the decline of his fortunes in life and love, and of the remorseless advance of age. In a collection pervaded by melancholy, variety has been achieved here by using contrasts of texture: some of the songs are

performed in consort, others are given to different singers. Emma Kirkby sings with great purity and beauty of tone, though she is not always as warm or poignant as the verse and music would warrant. However, hers is a most beautiful voice, and the set also offers some perceptive singing from Martyn Hill. Anthony Rooley's playing is accomplished and so is his direction of the proceedings. The eloquence of this music comes over.

Dowland, Robert
(*c.* 1585–1641)

Collection: *'A musicall banquet'* (1610): HOLBORNE: *My heavy sprite.* MARTIN: *Change thy mind.* HALES: *O eyes, leave off your weeping.* ANON.: *Go, my flock; O dear life.* PASSAV: *Amor su arco desarmado; Sta notte mi sognava; Vuestros ojos tienen d'Amor; O bella più.* BATCHELAR: *To plead my faith.* TESSIER: *In a grove most rich of shade.* DOWLAND, John: *Far from triumphing court; Lady, if you spite me; In darkness let me dwell.* GUEDRON: *Si le parler; Ce penser qui; Vous que le bonheur rappelle.* MEGLI: *Si di farmi morire.* CACCINI: *Dovrò dunque morire; Amarilli mia bella.*
*(*) O-L DSLO 555. Cons. of Musicke, Rooley.

Robert Dowland, the great lutenist's son, compiled and published but did not compose this 'musicall banquet'. The composers range from his celebrated father to lesser-known masters such as Holborne and Tessier or more familiar ones such as Caccini. The anthology is dedicated to Sir Robert Sidney, and, as in many similar instances, is scarcely intended for continuous performance.

Indeed the songs do not possess a particularly wide emotional range, and readers tempted by this music will find it best to take three or four songs at a time rather than a whole side. Not all the performances are equally satisfying; problems of intonation arise in some of them and may well pose difficulties for listeners. The recordings are faithful enough and the music is not otherwise recorded (apart from Dowland's pieces); but the issue does not inspire great enthusiasm.

Dufay, Guillaume
(*c.* 1400–1474)

Complete secular music.
*** O-L D 237 D 6 (6). Medieval Ens. of L., dir. Peter and Timothy Davies; Kite (organ and clavichord).

The collector with special interests in this period will naturally acquire this handsomely produced and lovingly performed set, but the non-specialist might well be deterred by the sheer scale of the enterprise: ninety-six songs are quite a lot. There is no alternative collection and apart from the late David Munrow's records and those of the Munich Capella Antiqua, this repertoire is not generously served. What will surprise those who dip into these discs is the range, beauty and accessibility of this music. There is nothing really specialized about this art save for the conventions within which the sensibility works. The texts that Peter and Timothy Davies use are those established by Heinrich Bessler, and where the songs survive only with a fragmentary poem, they give the music in purely instrumental form. The documentation is thorough and the performances have great commitment and sympathy to commend them. The actual sound quality

is of the first order, and readers who investigate the contents of this collection will be rewarded with much delight.

Missa ecce ancilla Domini.
(M) **(*) HM HM 997. Clemenčic Cons., Clemenčic.

Missa ecce ancilla Domini. Chansons: *Anima mea liquefacta est; Je me complains; Navre je suy.* Motets: *Ave regina coelorum; Ecclesie militantis; Gloria resurrexit dominus.*
(M) *** None. H 71367 [id.]. Pomerium Musices, Blachly.

Dufay's *Missa ecce ancilla Domini* is one of his greatest works. Recent scholarship suggests that this Mass was conceived for the Cambrai Cathedral Choir and would have been performed without instrumental support. But René Clemenčic argues for its being written for a festive occasion and even adds instrumental parts of his own for trumpet and drums. The performance has obvious commitment, and there is a fine sense of flow here. The addition of instrumental support masks some of the lines, and though the greater variety and sense of colour this brings will appeal to some listeners, trumpets and drums in a Mass for the Virgin Mary are a little dubious at this period. The singing has much feeling to commend it and the recording is undoubtedly clean.

Alexander Blachly uses ten singers in his account of the Mass, which tallies with recent research. There is no instrumental support whatever and the version Blachly records has the advantage of greater textural accuracy. His edition returns to the manuscript sources (whereas the Clemenčic version draws on the complete edition). Much of the writing is austere (some of it only two-part), but its effect is of grave and compelling beauty. The Pomerium Musices sing with eloquence and are well served by the engineers. There is the additional attraction of a number of chansons and motets on the second side.

Dukas, Paul (1865–1935)

L'Apprenti sorcier (The Sorcerer's Apprentice).
(M) *** Chan. CBR/*CBT* 1003. SNO, Gibson – ROSSINI: *La Boutique fantasque*; SAINT-SAËNS: *Danse macabre.****
(M) *** Decca Jub. JB/*KJBC* 36 [Lon. 6367]. SRO, Ansermet – HONEGGER: *Pacific 231*; RAVEL: *Boléro* etc.***
(*) CBS 76909/40- [Col. M/*MT* 35843]. Orchestre Nat. de France, Maazel – OFFENBACH: *Gaîté Parisienne*(*); SAINT-SAËNS: *Danse macabre.****

Gibson is given the advantage of brilliant modern recording (although the cassette has marginally less sparkle than the disc). His basic tempo is convincing and he secures excellent playing from the Scottish National Orchestra. The performance is straightforward rather than imaginatively evocative, but there is fine momentum and zest. Moreover the couplings in this medium-priced reissue are attractive, especially the splendid account of *La Boutique fantasque.*

Ansermet's performance is more relaxed, yet it has a cumulative effect: one has a feeling of real calamity before the magician hurriedly returns to put right the mischief his apprentice has wrought. There is atmosphere here, but the recording (though equally impressive on disc or tape) has less brilliance than the Chandos version.

Maazel's performance is spirited and characterful, but he loses something by broadening the climax. The recording is good, though the cassette has not the range of the disc. If the couplings are suitable this will give pleasure.

L'Apprenti sorcier; La Péri (with Fanfare); Polyeucte: overture.
⊛ *** Ph. 9500 533/*7300 677* [id.]. Rotterdam PO, Zinman.

Those who cherish rosy memories of the pre-war set of *La Péri* by Philippe Gaubert and the Paris Conservatoire Orchestra will not be disappointed by this newcomer, which is every bit as haunting and atmospheric. In fact David Zinman and the Rotterdam Philharmonic give us what is arguably the finest account of Dukas's colourful score ever to have been put on record. Here is a conductor acutely sensitive to the most delicate colourings and the hushed atmosphere of this evocative score, and he captures its fairy-tale spirit better than any of his rivals. This account is better-played than Ansermet's from the late 1950s and more magical than the now deleted Boulez version, and it is certainly better recorded. The engineers have given us a natural balance with wide-ranging dynamics and a truthful perspective. *L'Apprenti sorcier* receives an effective performance, as does the less interesting *Polyeucte overture.* The cassette is one of Philips' best, although in *La Péri* textures are more refined in detail on the disc.

Duparc, Henri (1848–1933)

Mélodies: *Au pays où se fait la guerre; L'Invitation au voyage; Le Manoire de Rosemonde; Phidylé; La Vie antérieure.*
⊛ *** HMV ASD/*TC-ASD* 3455 [Ang. S 37401]. Baker, LSO, Previn – CHAUSSON: *Poème de l'amour.* ⊛ ***

Duparc, most sparing of composers, actually dared to orchestrate some of the handful of songs he wrote in his early career. Purist lovers of French mélodie will no doubt prefer the original piano accompaniments, but this record will triumphantly prove to non-specialists that the extra richness and colour of the orchestral versions add to the depth and intensity of these exceptionally sensitive word-settings, especially in the greatest of them all, *Phidylé*. But as Baker and Previn present them, each one of these songs is a jewelled miniature of breath-taking beauty, and the clear, ripe, beautifully balanced recording is fully worthy of the performances. The cassette is marginally less clear than the disc, but the sound remains gloriously atmospheric.

Duruflé, Maurice (born 1902)

Organ suite, Op. 5.
**(*) Abbey LPB 792. Cleobury –
FRANCK: *Grande pièce symphonique.***(*)

Now in his early eighties, Maurice Duruflé remains one of the least flamboyant and prolific of composers. He has published barely more than a dozen works in his lifetime, the best-known of which is his *Requiem*. The *Suite*, Op. 5, dates from the early 1930s and is a pleasing atmospheric piece, fastidious in its layout and always dignified. Stephen Cleobury gives a fine account of the work, and the organ of Westminster Abbey is musically recorded; the dynamic range is wide, and the resonance of the Abbey and the discreet balance militates a little against the greatest clarity in the final *Toccata*. Yet on good equipment this will yield more than acceptable results, and since recordings of this fine music have never been legion, this is worth investigation.

Messe cum jubilo, Op. 11.
*** Argo ZRG 938. Roberts, Richard Hickox Singers, Philip Jones Brass Ens., Hickox – LANGLAIS: *Mass.***(*)

Duruflé's *Mass* is a rather serene if pale work, full of subtle, muted colourings

and reflective in spirit. Not strongly distinctive but nonetheless rewarding, particularly in such capable hands as those of the Richard Hickox Singers and Alistair Ross (organ). Well-defined detail and good balance make this a more attractive proposition than the Langlais coupling.

Requiem, Op. 9; Danse lente, Op. 6/2.
*** CBS 76633 [Col. M 34547]. Te Kanawa, Nimsgern, Amb. S., Desborough School Ch., New Philh. O., Andrew Davis.
(i) *Requiem*. Motets on Gregorian chants: *Tantum ergo; Tu es Petrus.*
*** HMV Dig. ASD/TCC-ASD 4086. King's College Ch., Ledger, (i) with Baker, Roberts; Butt (organ).

Andrew Davis directs a warm and atmospheric reading of Duruflé's beautiful setting of the *Requiem*, using the full orchestral version with its richer colourings. Kiri Te Kanawa sings radiantly in the *Pie Jésu*, and the darkness of Siegmund Nimsgern's voice is well caught. In such a performance Duruflé establishes his claims for individuality even in the face of Fauré's comparable setting. The fill-up is welcome too, and the recording is excellent, nicely atmospheric.

Philip Ledger's version of the *Requiem* uses organ rather than orchestral accompaniment. (Duruflé made two orchestral versions of the score – Andrew Davis opts for the richer of the two.) Yet such is the clarity of the recording and the sense of atmosphere engendered by the performance (and enhanced by the acoustic) that one scarcely misses the additional dimension of colour that the orchestra provides. The singing is splendid, and the grave beauty and emotional restraint of Duruflé's music splendidly conveyed. Many will prefer this version to the Davis, the absence of the orchestra notwithstanding, as it is so beautifully recorded. The chrome cassette, however, transferred at only a modest level, has disappointingly poor definition, especially at the opening.

Dutilleux, Henri (born 1916)

Symphony No. 1.
*** Cal. CAL 1861. Lille PO, Jean-Claude Casadesus.

Henri Dutilleux is best-known in this country for his *Cello concerto* (*Tout un monde lointain*), which Rostropovich recorded (HMV ASD 3145 [Ang. S 37146]), and for a ballet, *Le Loup*. The first of his symphonies dates from 1951 and must be numbered among the most successful post-war French symphonies. It has fertility of invention, a marvellous feeling for colour and superb craftsmanship. Dutilleux is a master of the evocative texture, luminous and exotic, not unlike the tropical atmosphere one encounters in some Roussel. The work also holds together very well: there is an impressive *Passacaglia* to start with and a richly inventive scherzo. Martinon and the ORTF Orchestre National have recorded the work for Inédits, but this performance under Jean-Claude Casadesus is in no sense inferior and readers with inquiring minds will find this a rewarding investment (though the work is so short that there would have been room for a fill-up).

Dvořák, Antonin (1841–1904)

Overtures: Carnaval, Op. 92; In Nature's Realm, Op. 91; My Home, Op. 62; Othello, Op. 93.
(M) *** Sup. 4101 990. Prague RSO, Krombholc.

A welcome and competitive anthology, bringing the three overtures of 1891–2

together with the earlier *My Home* of 1882. The Prague Radio Symphony Orchestra is a fine body and (on the evidence of this record) cannot be greatly inferior to the Philharmonic. Krombholc is an impressive conductor who secures admirably vivid yet straightforward performances, with no touch of affectation. The sound is, as usual in records from this source, a little reverberant, and Kertesz's Decca recordings made in the mid-1960s (see below) offer more analytical detail as well as presence. But between the performances there is really very little to choose, and the competitive price makes this an attractive proposition, particularly in view of the spirit and excellence of the playing.

Carnaval overture, Op. 92; The Golden Spinning Wheel, Op. 109; Scherzo capriccioso, Op. 109.
(M) *** Decca Jub. JB/KJBC 109. LSO, Kertesz.

For their Jubilee reissue Decca have recoupled Kertesz's Dvořák series recorded with the LSO. This group, coupling *The Golden Spinning Wheel*, with its evocative horn calls, to outstanding versions of *Carnaval* and the *Scherzo capriccioso*, is most attractive. First-class LSO playing and vivid recording from a vintage Decca period.

Cello concerto in B min., Op. 104.
(B) *** CfP CFP/TC-CFP 40361. Robert Cohen, LPO, Macal – TCHAIKOVSKY: *Rococo variations.****
(B) *(**) RCA VICS/VK 2002 [AGL 1/AGK 1 3878]. Piatigorsky, Boston SO, Munch.
*(*) HMV ASD/TC-ASD 3452 [Ang. S/ 4XS 37457]. Rostropovich, LPO, Giulini – SAINT-SAËNS: *Concerto No. 1.***

Cello concerto; Rondo in G min., Op. 94; Silent Woods, Op. 68.

(M) *** Ph. Fest. 6570/7310 112 [id.].
Gendron, LPO, Haitink.
**(*) HMV ASD/TC-ASD 3652 (without *Rondo*). Tortelier, LSO, Previn.
** Ph. 6514/7337 071 (without *Rondo*).
Schiff, Concg. O., Colin Davis.
(M) * Turn. TVS 37099 [id.]. Nelsova, St Louis SO, Susskind.

Robert Cohen was only twenty when he recorded the Dvořák *Concerto*, but his is anything but an immature reading, strong and forthright, very secure technically, with poetry never impaired by his preference for keeping steady speeds. The result is most satisfying, helped by comparably incisive and understanding accompaniment from the Czech conductor Zdenek Macal. With first-rate modern recording and a generous coupling, it makes an excellent choice irrespective of price, and as a bargain issue it is outstanding. The cassette matches the disc very closely indeed; if anything the cassette gives the cello slightly more body.

Gendron's performance is also very attractive. Like Robert Cohen's, his image is a little less larger-than-life than those of Tortelier and Rostropovich, but his performance projects admirably. It is unidiosyncratic, marvellously fresh and lyrical, and has the advantage of impeccable orchestral support from the LPO under Haitink. There is a real spontaneity about this playing, and its warmth is splendidly captured by the Philips engineers, who produce magnificent sound. There are two engaging fill-ups. The cassette transfer is first-class, matching the disc closely.

The richness of Tortelier's reading has long been appreciated on record, and his 1978 recording with Previn has a satisfying centrality, not as passionately romantic as Rostropovich, not as urgent as Harrell on RCA, but with the tenderness as well as the power of the work held in perfect equilibrium. What is less perfect is the balance of the recording, favouring the cellist a little too much,

though the fullness, weight and warmth of the EMI sound are impressive, with the strongly rhythmic playing of the LSO well caught. The cassette transfer catches the reverberant recording admirably, with richly resonant tone for the soloist.

Heinrich Schiff, who made such a promising start to his recording career in the Saint-Saëns concerto (now deleted), is disappointing in the bigger challenge of the Dvořák. The confidence of his concert appearances is here muted and the result is wayward, with Sir Colin Davis less at ease than usual in Dvořák. *Silent Woods*, the coupling, is not memorable either. The recording is good on disk and tape alike.

Piatigorsky's performance has undoubted presence and fervour; he is at his finest here, and Munch provides a powerful and vivid accompaniment. But with a forward balance and a fierce recording – partly caused by the acoustic throwback of the Boston auditorium – this cannot be recommended very enthusiastically, even at bargain price.

Rostropovich has recorded the concerto three times before (with Talich, Boult and Karajan). The DG recording with Karajan offers as a bonus a marvellous performance of the Tchaikovsky *Rococo variations*, and that coupling is now available on Accolade (see the Concerts section, p. 916). The version recorded with Boult in the late 1950s still sounds amazingly fresh and vital; no one would guess its age. The balance is superbly judged, the texture is open and vivid and it has recently been made available on cassette – very well transferred – so that there can be no reservations in recommending this classic account at medium price (HMV SXLP/TC-SXLP 30176 [Ang. S/4XG 60136]). The newest HMV performance is Rostropovich's least successful on record. He makes heavy weather of most of the concerto, and his unrelieved emotional intensity is matched by Giulini, who focuses attention on beauty of detail rather than structural cohesion. But of course there are many beauties that compel admiration, and the engineering is impressive.

Zara Nelsova is an admirably eloquent soloist and her performance is a fine one; moreover she is well supported by the St Louis Orchestra under Walter Susskind. Unfortunately the recording is simply not refined enough to compete with the best of its rivals. Gendron offers exactly the same programme, and his performance has every bit as much warmth and is far more truthfully recorded.

Piano concerto in G min., Op. 33.
*** HMV ASD/*TC-ASD* 3371 [Ang. S 37329]. Sviatoslav Richter, Bav. State O., Carlos Kleiber.
(M) ** Sup. 1110 2373. Kvapil, Brno State PO, Jílek.

Dvořák's *Piano concerto* comes from a vintage period which also saw the completion of the *F major Symphony*. Richter plays the solo part in its original form (and not the more pianistically 'effective' revision), and his judgement is triumphantly vindicated. This is the most persuasive and masterly account of the concerto ever committed to disc; its ideas emerge with an engaging freshness and warmth, while the greater simplicity of Dvořák's own keyboard writing proves in Richter's hands to be the more telling and profound. Never has the slow movement sounded so moving as it does here. Carlos Kleiber secures excellent results from the Bavarian orchestra, and the recording, though not in the demonstration class, has clarity and good definition to commend it. A most impressive record, which one hopes will restore the work to greater public favour. The cassette was originally transferred at too high a level, with resulting coarseness and distortion. It is likely to have been remastered by the time we are in print.

Radoslav Kvapil is an admired interpreter of Dvořák and has recorded all his piano music. He lacks the poetic insight of Richter, and the orchestral playing under František Jílek is no match for

Kleiber's; nor is the recording so finely detailed. There are good things here, but it is very much a second choice.

Violin concerto in A min., Op. 53.
(B) *** CfP CFP/*TC-CFP* 40349. Krebbers, Amsterdam PO, Kersjes – TCHAIKOVSKY: *Concerto.****

Violin concerto; Romance in F min., Op. 11.
*** Ph. 9500 406/*7300 614* [id.]. Accardo, Concg. O., Colin Davis.
(M) *** Sup. 1410 2423. Suk, Czech PO, Neumann.

Accardo's is a noble performance and he is given splendid support by the Concertgebouw Orchestra under Sir Colin Davis. With such superb versions as Suk's and Perlman's on the market, any newcomer must have special claims. To begin with, the Philips recording is by far the most detailed and has greater body than its rivals. Secondly, the performance is finely characterized, with the distinguished soloist making the most but never too much of the rhetoric and poetry. Accardo is slightly too forward, perhaps, but this small reservation apart, his version deserves unqualified praise. The slow movement is inward and the finale has a splendid singing quality, even if the Suk version has slightly more sparkle and spring in this movement. There is beautiful playing from all concerned in the *Romance* too. The cassette offers pleasingly full sound, but the upper range does not match that of the disc.

Suk recorded the same coupling in 1961, but this newer Supraphon recording is an improvement on the earlier disc. It is fresher and clearer, and although the balance places the soloist well forward, orchestral detail comes through. As before, Suk's performance is lyrical in the simplest possible way, and its eloquent innocence is endearing. The *Romance* is also played with skill and affection. At medium price this Supraphon issue is fully competitive.

Krebbers offers a characteristically fresh and incisive reading, bringing out the Czech overtones in the first movement and giving a simple and reposeful account of the slow movement and an infectiously lilting one of the finale. He receives good support from the Amsterdam orchestra, and though the recording slightly overemphasizes the top it is clean and well-balanced. On tape the slightly edgy treble response is softened without loss of overall vividness. With a stylish performance of the Tchaikovsky *Concerto* this makes an excellent bargain coupling, a formidable rival for more expensive versions.

Czech suite, Op. 39; Nocturne for strings in B, Op. 40; Polka for Prague students in B flat, Op. 53a; Polonaise in E flat; Prague waltzes.
*** Decca Dig. SXDL/*KSXDC* 7522. Detroit SO, Dorati.

A collection of Dvořák rarities exhilaratingly performed and brilliantly recorded. The *Czech suite* can sometimes outstay its welcome, but certainly not here. The other items too have the brightness and freshness that mark out the Dvořák *Slavonic dances*, especially the *Polka* and *Polonaise*. The most charming piece of all is the set of *Waltzes* written for balls in Prague – Viennese music with a Czech accent – while the lovely *Nocturne* with its subtle drone bass makes an apt filler. The recording has an attractive warmth and bloom to balance its brightness, and this is as impressive on cassette as it is on disc, although on the tape there is a momentary excess of bass resonance in the *Polonaise*.

The Golden Spinning Wheel, Op. 109.
(M) ** Sup. 1101 889. Ostrava Janáček PO, Trhlík – JANÁČEK: *Taras Bulba.***

A good account of Dvořák's tone poem from the Ostrava forces under Otakar Trhlík coupled with *Taras Bulba.* The coupling is likely to sway the reader in this instance since although neither the Dvořák nor the Janáček is in any way unsatisfactory, in neither case would this record be a first choice. The Dvořák belongs to the last years of his life and is the third of the tone poems he wrote in 1896, immediately after the *Cello concerto.* Though not as consistently inspired as *The Wood Dove*, it is still a work of some beauty, and Trhlík's orchestra gives a well-shaped and far from insensitive performance. However, it does not displace Beecham's post-war set (available in the World Record box) or the versions by Kertesz (see above) and Kubelik, differently coupled. Well-balanced recording, albeit a little thin in the upper register.

Scherzo capriccioso, Op. 66.
(M) **(*) Ph. Fest. 6570/*7310* 176 [id.]. Concg. O., Haitink – MUSSORGSKY: *Pictures;* TCHAIKOVSKY: *Capriccio italien;* GLINKA: *Russlan overture.***(*)

Scherzo capriccioso; Slavonic rhapsody No. 3, Op. 45/3.
*** HMV SLS/*TC-SLS* 5151 (2) [Ang. S 3870]. Dresden State O., Berglund – SMETANA: *Má Vlast.****

Berglund's *Scherzo capriccioso* is warmly engaging, not the most brilliantly exciting version on record, but with plenty of impetus and a lilting second subject. The *Slavonic rhapsody* is superbly done, and the recording is first-class throughout. An excellent coupling for the finest available version of *Má Vlast*, and equally impressive on disc or tape.

Haitink's account has come up well in this reissue. It has an attractive lyrical character and is not without charm, yet there is no affectation. The recording is well-balanced, the woodwind detail telling as it should, and there is more sparkle than in the original issue. The cassette is well-balanced too.

Serenade for strings in E, Op. 22.
*** DG Dig. 2532/*3302* 012 [id.]. Berlin PO, Karajan – TCHAIKOVSKY: *Serenade.****
(*) ASV Dig. DCA/*ZCDCA* 505. Orch. of St John's, Lubbock – TCHAIKOVSKY: *Serenade.*(*)

Serenade for strings; Symphonic variations, Op. 78.
**(*) RCA RL/*RK* 25230. LSO, Tjeknavorian.
(B) ** CfP CFP 40345. LPO, Macal.

There are already two outstanding couplings of the Dvořák and Tchaikovsky *String serenades* (by Leppard on Philips and Marriner on Argo), but the Academy issue was the first to offer digital mastering. The strings are given striking presence and focus here, although the sound is very brightly lit in the treble (the cassette matches the disc closely in this respect), and the resonance of middle and bass frequencies is less telling than in (for instance) Leppard's analogue recording. Lubbock gives a strongly characterized performance, with an athletic scherzo and brilliant finale contrasting well with the work's lyrical elements. Those who enjoy crystal-clear sound may find this worth investigating; others will feel that the greater warmth of the Philips disc (9500 105) is more satisfying for repeated listening.

Hard on the heels of the ASV disc came Karajan's digital version, also very brilliantly recorded and superbly played. Karajan's phrasing in the opening movement is more indulgent than Lubbock's, and there is greater expressive weight, with the colouring darker. Karajan's warmth is obvious, and the DG sound has both brilliance and body (especially on the chrome cassette, which is slightly mellower than the disc). For those wanting the extra clarity of digital recording this will have considerable attractions,

but otherwise Leppard with his natural flow and fresh lyrical feeling remains first choice.

The coupling with the *Symphonic variations* is a good one, long dominated in the past by Colin Davis and the LSO on Philips. (That issue will presumably be made available again at medium price during the lifetime of this volume.) Tjeknavorian gives often leisurely but generally sympathetic readings of both works. In the *Serenade* there is a danger of self-indulgence, but his approach works well in the neglected *Symphonic variations*, where the highly original Variation No. 14 is given extra intensity at a very slow speed. With first-rate playing from the LSO and clean recording quality on both disc and cassette, it makes a very recommendable issue.

Zdenek Macal's record with the LPO has the advantage of economy and is well-recorded. Neither the playing nor Macal's reading has the freshness or distinction that this delightful music calls for, but it has the merit of straightforwardness. A serviceable rather than distinguished issue, whose second star is due to its modest price.

Serenade for wind in D min., Op. 44.
(M) *** Ph. Fest. 6570/*7310* 205. Neth. Wind Ens., De Waart – GOUNOD: *Petite symphonie*; SCHUBERT: *Octet, D.72* (excerpts).***
(M) *** Decca Jub. JB/*KJBC* 87. LSO members, Kertesz – BRAHMS: *Serenade No. 2.****

The playing of the Netherlands Wind Ensemble under Edo de Waart blends spontaneity and discipline in just the right proportions. It is not easy to imagine a more refreshing and delightful performance, and given such musically balanced and vividly recorded sound (as well as attractive couplings) the claims of this issue will be seen to be pressing, and even more so now that it has been reissued in the medium price-range. The sound on cassette matches the disc closely. (If the transfer had been given a fraction more level the difference would have been imperceptible.)

Kertesz too gives a delightful performance of the enchanting *Wind serenade*, which is accorded splendid treatment by the Decca engineers. The cassette transfer has a full, lively quality, although the resonance tends to spread the focus somewhat in the slow movement.

Slavonic dances Nos. 1–16, Opp. 46/ 1–8, 72/1–8.

(M) ** Sup. 1110 2981/2. Czech PO, Kosler.

Slavonic dances Nos. 1–16; My Home overture, Op. 62; Scherzo capriccioso, Op. 66.

(M) *** DG Priv. 2726 122 (2) [2530 466 and 593]. Bav. RSO, Kubelik.

Slavonic dances Nos. 1, 3, 8, 9–10.

(M) *** Decca VIV/K VIC 18 [Lon. STS 15009]. VPO, Reiner – BRAHMS: *Hungarian dances.****

Dvořák's sixteen *Slavonic dances* are not easy to fit on two LP sides (with dividing bands) without some loss of amplitude or range in the recording. DG have solved this problem (but relatively expensively) by using two full discs with fillers. For those who want the best regardless of cost, this pair of medium-priced LPs makes a first-class recommendation, for the complete set, with polished, sparkling orchestral playing splendidly recorded. The extra items are very well done too.

The Czech Philharmonic Orchestra have a special feeling for this repertoire, and provide touches of phrasing and colour that are not always found in other versions. However, the recording, though good, has not quite the brilliance and range of Kubelik's set, there are no fillers, and the discs do not enjoy a price advantage. Kosler's direction is alert and sympathetic, but Kubelik sparkles even more.

Reiner's way with Dvořák's dance music is indulgent but has plenty of sparkle, and the Vienna Philharmonic are clearly enjoying themselves. The sound of this reissue hardly dates at all, and any reservations about the conductor's idiosyncrasies are soon forgotten in the pleasure of listening to such colourful music so vivaciously presented. The cassette matches the disc closely.

Symphonies Nos. 1–9.

(M) **(*) Ph. 6770 045. LSO, Rowicki.

Rowicki's Dvořák cycle was rather overshadowed when it first appeared on separate records by the Kertesz series with the same orchestra. Heard as a whole in this mid-price box, Rowicki's readings present a consistent and satisfying view of Dvořák, slightly understating the expressiveness of slow movements and often in fast movements adding a touch of fierceness. The opening of No. 6, for example, with the syncopated accompaniment very cleanly defined, sounds unusually fresh and individual, even if one would not always want to hear it interpreted in that way. The recording is pleasantly refined, excellent for its mid-sixties vintage. One must remember, however, that the Kertesz Decca box of the symphonies, to which we awarded a rosette in the *Penguin Stereo Record Guide*, is still available (D 6 D 7), while the cassette box of the more popular symphonies (Nos. 5–9), also rosetted, offers a very sophisticated tape alternative (K 6/K 53).

Symphony No. 1 in C min. (The Bells of Zlonice), Op. 3.

(M) *** Decca Jub. JB/KJBC 110 [(d) in SVBX 5137]. LSO, Kertesz.

This symphony, written early in 1865, was lost for over half a century, and even when the score turned up in Germany in the possession of a namesake of the composer (no relation) it had to wait years for performance, and was not published until 1961. But Dvořák remembered it when on the fly-leaf of the score of the *New World* he made a complete list of his symphonies. Clearly, had he kept hold of the score he would have made revisions. Though the piece took him only five weeks to write, it is the longest of all his symphonies – over fifty-four minutes in this performance – and the fluency is not always matched by the memorability of the material. But it still has much attractive writing in it, and no one should miss it who has enjoyed the other early Dvořák symphonies. Zlonice was the place where Dvořák served his musical (and butcher's) apprenticeship, but the music is not intended to convey a programme. The LSO under Kertesz play excellently and give us the complete score without any of the cuts introduced into the earlier LP on Supraphon under Václav Neumann. The Decca recording has splendid detail and presence; the cassette transfer is admirably lively and vivid, with a striking upper range, although it is a little dry in the bass.

Symphony No. 2 in B flat, Op. 4.
(M) *** Decca Jub. JB/*KJBC* 111 [(d) in SVBX 5137]. LSO, Kertesz.

Dvořák wrote his *Second Symphony* in 1865 within months of his *First*, but then he left it on the shelf for a full fifteen years before submitting it to a thorough revision. The original 260 pages of score were contracted to 212, and though this left the finale in an oddly unbalanced state, it is surprising that Dvořák's publisher, Simrock, refused to take the work when it was submitted to him along with Symphonies Nos. 3 and 4. Admittedly the ideas are not so strongly Dvořákian as they might be, and some movements tend to outstay their welcome, but anyone who has ever been charmed by Dvořák's wide-eyed genius will find much to enjoy, notably in the highly engaging ideas of the first movement. One oddity – and weakness – is that each movement has a

slow introduction, a case of the composer 'clearing his throat' before launching out. As in his other Dvořák performances, Kertesz takes a crisp, fresh, straightforward approach to the music, and the recording is first-rate. Thus this symphony is admirably served in every way, and the scherzo has all the authentic, idiomatic flavour one could possibly want. The recording has the finest qualities of the Decca set.

Symphony No. 3 in E flat, Op. 10;
Symphonic variations, Op. 78.
(M) *** Decca Jub. JB/*KJBC* 112 [(d) in SVBX 5137]. LSO, Kertesz.

This was the first of Dvořák's symphonies to show the full exuberance of his genius. When he wrote it in 1873 – eight years after the first two – he was very much under the influence of Wagner, but nowhere do the Wagnerian ideas really conceal the essential Dvořák. Even the unashamed crib from *Lohengrin* in the middle section (D flat major) of the slow movement has a Dvořákian freshness, particularly here, as Kertesz adopts a fastish speed – faster than the score would strictly allow – and deliberately lightens the texture. This very long slow movement is in any case the weakest of the three, but the outer movements are both delightful and need no apology whatever. The very opening of the symphony with its 6/8 rhythm and rising-scale motifs can hardly miss, and the dotted rhythms of the second subject are equally engaging. For its Jubilee reissue the symphony has been generously recoupled with the *Symphonic variations*, a splendid work, with Brahmsian derivations but always showing the Czech composer's freshness of spirit, which Kertesz readily demonstrates. The playing of the LSO is consistently alert and polished, and the Decca recording is bright and vivid.

Symphony No. 4 in D min., Op. 13;
In Nature's Realm overture, Op. 91.

(M) *** Decca Jub. JB/*KJBC* 113. LSO, Kertesz.

Compared with the exuberant symphonies which flank it on either side in the Dvořák canon, this is a disappointment. The opening theme – a fanfare-like idea – is not so characterful as one expects, but then the second subject soars aloft in triple time. The slow movement begins with so close a crib from the *Pilgrims' Music* in *Tannhäuser* one wonders how Dvořák had the face to write it, but the variations which follow are attractive, and the scherzo has a delightful lolloping theme, which unfortunately gives way to a horribly blatant march trio with far too many cymbal crashes in it. The finale, despite rhythmic monotony, has at least one highly characteristic and attractive episode. And, whatever the shortcomings of the work, there is much that is memorable. Kertesz gives a good dramatic performance, and receives excellent recording quality. Compared with the disc the cassette has a slight loss of focus in tutti, caused by the resonance.

Symphony No. 5 in F (originally Op. 24 (1875); published as Op. 76); *Hussite overture, Op. 67.*
(M) *** Decca Jub. JB/*KJBC* 114 [(d) Lon. 6511]. LSO, Kertesz.

Even more than most Dvořák, the *Fifth Symphony* is a work to make one share, if only for a moment, in the happy emotions of a saint, and what could be more welcome in modern nerve-racked life? The feeling of joy is here expressed so intensely that it provokes tears rather than laughter, and it is hard to understand why this marvellous work has been neglected for so long. It used to be called the *Pastoral*, but although it shares Beethoven's key and uses the flute a great deal (a Dvořákian characteristic) the nickname is not specially apt. What initially strikes one are the echoes of Wagner – forest murmurs (Bohemian

ones) in the opening pages, a direct lift from *Siegfried's Rhine Journey* in the second theme and so on – but by the time he wrote the work, 1875, Dvořák's individuality as a musician was well established, and the composer's signature is in effect written on every bar. The slow movement is as beautiful as any in the symphonies, the scherzo is a gloriously bouncing piece with themes squandered generously, and the finale, though long, is intensely original in structure and argument. Kertesz's performance is straight and dramatic, with tempi very well chosen to allow for infectious rhythmic pointing. The new Jubilee coupling is the *Hussite overture*, patriotic in inspiration and including themes based on the Hussite hymn and St Wenceslas plainchant. Excellent Decca recording throughout.

Symphony No. 6 in D, Op. 60; My Home overture, Op. 62.
(M) *** Decca Jub. JB/*KJBC* 115. LSO, Kertesz.

If the three immediately preceding Dvořák symphonies reflect the influence of Wagner, this one just as clearly reflects that of Brahms, and particularly of the Brahms *Second Symphony*. Not only the shape of themes but the actual layout of the first movement have strong affinities with the Brahmsian model, but Kertesz's performance effectively underlines the individuality of the writing as well. This is a marvellous work that with the *Fifth* and *Seventh* forms the backbone of the Dvořák cycle, and that is hardly an idea we should have been likely to advance before Kertesz gave us fresh insight into these vividly inspired works. His reading is fresh, literal and dramatic in his characteristic Dvořák manner, and his tempi are eminently well-chosen. The *My Home overture* was written as an expression of patriotic Czech sentiment at a time when, under the thumb of the Austrians, the Czechs were turning to music as an important safety-valve. The themes are taken from Czech folk music (one of them will be recognized from the Czech national anthem). The excellent recording is well up to the high standard of the series.

Symphony No. 7 in D min., Op. 70.
*** Lodia Dig. LOD/*LOC* 782. Philharmonic SO, Paita.
*** HMV ASD 3869 [Ang. SZ/*4SZ* 39717]. LPO, Rostropovich.
**(*) RCA RL/*RK* 13555 [ARL 1/*ARK 1* 3555]. Phd. O., Ormandy.

Symphony No. 7; The Noonday Witch, Op. 108.
(M) *** Decca Jub. JB/*KJBC* 116 [(d) in SVBX 5139]. LSO, Kertesz.

Paita's splendid new digital recording is outstanding in every way, a performance of striking lyrical ardour, matching excitement with warmth, and bringing spontaneity and freshness to every bar. The admirably balanced sound is demonstrably rich and brilliant, and the ambience is ideal. Paita's own Philharmonic Symphony Orchestra produces playing of the first order, creating an immediate feeling of expectancy at the opening, moving to a climax of great excitement and then relaxing engagingly for the coda. There is comparable expressive fervour in the *Poco adagio*, and the lilting rhythms of the scherzo are matched by the thrust and vigour of the finale. This makes a clear first choice on disc; the cassette transfer is faithful but made at rather a low level.

Rostropovich's is a big, powerful reading which presents not the lovable genial Dvořák but the tough composer who, here more than in his other symphonies, was biting and unrelenting. The spaciousness of his speeds is designed not for lyrical self-indulgence – as one might expect from his highly romantic view of the solo part of the *Cello concerto*

– but to underline the symphonic weight. Even the slow movement is big and powerful rather than warm or refined, and the scherzo is emphatic rather than urgent, the most controversial point of an unconventional, challenging interpretation. The recording is big and full to match.

Kertesz's version of the *D minor Symphony* was one of the first to be recorded in his LSO series, following soon after his extremely successful version of the *Eighth*. However, whereas that performance has striking extrovert brilliance, the approach to the *Seventh* is essentially relaxed. The tension is well maintained, but the voltage is lower, and the climaxes do not catch fire with quite the same vividness as in the rest of the cycle. Even so, with warm orchestral playing there is much to give pleasure, and there is a burst of energy in the finale. For the Jubilee reissue Decca have added Kertesz's colourful and atmospheric portrayal of *The Noonday Witch* (the traditional ogress threatened to erring children by distraught mothers). With excellent sound this is certainly attractive at medium price, and the cassette transfer is of Decca's best quality, both full and lively. The symphonic poem – which opens the proceedings, with the first movement of the symphony following – has striking colour and warmth.

In Ormandy's reading, with the sound of the orchestra as recorded sweet and soft-grained, the Viennese qualities of the symphony are brought out. In places the first movement seems to be in waltz-time, and the Slavonic element is minimized. The finale starts with tremendous swagger, and despite some mannerisms later, with Philadelphia ensemble below its best, the thrust of the performance is well caught. The cassette transfer is disappointingly fierce, with little bloom on the upper strings.

Symphony No. 8 in G, Op. 88.
*** Ph. 9500 317/*7300 611* [id.]. Concg. O., Colin Davis.

*** Ph. Dig. 6514 050/7337 050 [id.].
Minnesota SO, Marriner.
(M) *** Decca Jub. JB/KJBC 71. VPO,
Karajan – TCHAIKOVSKY: Romeo and
Juliet.***
*** DG Priv. 2535/3335 397 [139181].
Berlin PO, Kubelik.
**(*) DG 2531/3301 046 [id.]. Chicago
SO, Giulini.

Symphony No. 8; Carnaval overture.
**(*) CBS 76893/40- [Col. M/MT 35865].
Philh. O., Andrew Davis.

Symphony No. 8; Scherzo capric-
cioso, Op. 66.
*(*) HMV ASD/TC-ASD 4058. LPO,
Rostropovich.

Symphony No. 8; Slavonic dances,
Op. 46/2, 4 und 6.
(M) **(*) Ph. Fest. 6570/7310 078 [id.].
Concg. O., Haitink.

Symphony No. 8; Slavonic dance, Op.
46/8.
*(*) HMV ASD/TC-ASD 3775 [Ang.
SZ/4ZS 37686]. Berlin PO, Karajan.

Symphony No. 8; The Water Goblin,
Op. 107.
(M) *** Decca Jub. JB/KJBC 117 [(d)
Lon. STS 15526]. LSO, Kertesz.

With the appearance of a number of
new recordings and the reissue of some
very successful older ones, the choice for
Dvořák's G major Symphony is wide and
varied. For those seeking a new recording
of the highest quality and prepared to pay
premium price even though no coupling
is offered, the outstanding new Philips
issue played by the Amsterdam Concertgebouw Orchestra under Sir Colin Davis
must receive the strongest advocacy. The
reading has Davis's characteristic directness, and the performance balances an
engaging zestful exuberance in the outer
movements with a beautifully played and
eloquent Adagio and a lightly pointed
scherzo. Here the Amsterdam strings
have a delightful lyrical freshness in the
trio, and there is a spontaneous burst of

sheer high spirits in the coda. The recorded sound is excellent in every way on
both disc and tape (in the latter a slight
bass cut improves the balance).

In the re-shuffling of Kertesz's Dvořák
series for the Jubilee reissues, the particularly apt pairing with the Scherzo
capriccioso has been abandoned in
favour of Dvořák's folk-tale setting
about a malevolent Water Goblin. Kertesz's reading of the G major Symphony
has long been famous for its freshly
spontaneous excitement, with well-
judged tempi throughout and an affectionately expressive account of the slow
movement. The sound balance is forward
and brightly lit, but is notable also for
the warmth of the middle and lower
strings. The performance of the symphonic poem too is highly evocative and
atmospherically and vividly recorded.
The cassette offers demonstration quality
in the symphony, admirably fresh and
vivid; in the symphonic poem the focus is
slightly less clean.

Marriner's is a performance which
more than any presents the smiling side
of Dvořák. In principle one might object
to the very relaxed espressivo manner in
the first movement, but Marriner is so
persuasive that the joy and felicity are
irresistible. The slow movement is both
genial and elegant, and the third has a
delectable Viennese lilt. The finale very
much breathes the air of the Slavonic
dances, with fine rhythmic bite and no
pomposity whatever. On this showing
Marriner and the Minnesota orchestra
have built up a superb rapport. The refinement of the playing goes with fresh,
clean-cut digital sound, finely balanced.

The other Jubilee issue, from Karajan
and the Vienna Philharmonic, is also
generously recoupled with an excellent
1961 recording of Tchaikovsky's Romeo
and Juliet. Karajan's performance has
the merit of superb orchestral playing,
with the Vienna strings at their creamiest.
There are moments of self-indulgence in
the scherzo, but for the most part this is a
most winning performance, blending

polish and spontaneity in almost equal measure. The orchestra sound as if they are enjoying this symphony – and so do we. The recording too still sounds wonderfully fresh and finely detailed. The cassette matches the disc closely, though fractionally drier in the bass.

Kubelik's Privilege reissue also still holds its place at the top of the list. Kubelik's recording is hardly less brilliant than Kertesz's Decca, yet the balance is slightly more distanced, so that the orchestral perspective is highly convincing. The performance is outstandingly fine. Without personal idiosyncrasy (except for a modest touch of indulgence for the string theme in the trio of the scherzo) this is a vibrant reading, very faithful to the composer's intentions, with the personality of the orchestra coming through strongly. The cassette transfer too is outstanding, one of DG's best, with fresh, vivid upper strings, plenty of bloom on the orchestra and excellent detail.

Giulini's new DG version made in Chicago is also an attractive performance, more relaxed than Sir Colin Davis's, the phrasing broader, the rhythmic articulation more positive. The recorded sound is of DG's best quality and naturally balanced. Giulini's less pressing momentum brings some lovely soft-grained woodwind playing in the slow movement and a general sense of spaciousness, with the folksy quality of the scherzo material made obvious. The DG cassette is of high quality, lighter in the bass than Davis's Philips tape, but admirably full and with plenty of bloom.

Andrew Davis's account with the Philharmonia is issued by CBS but was recorded at EMI's Abbey Road studios with Neville Boyling the balance engineer. It could hardly be more different in effect from the Giulini and Colin Davis accounts; the sound is very brightly lit, the strings given a brilliant sheen, the brass resplendent almost to the point of brashness, yet undoubtedly telling in the finale. The performance makes the very most of the music's dynamic contrasts, with high drama in the climaxes of the *Adagio* and a feeling of vibrant energy throughout the outer movements. The scherzo responds least well to this approach, but there is no doubt about the exhilaration of the reading as a whole, and the slow movement does not lack moments of expressive tenderness. The bonus is a splendid account of the *Carnaval overture*, with the middle section and its cor anglais melody hauntingly atmospheric. The cassette transfer is very lively to match the disc, though the warmth of the middle range is not lost. On tape, however, the overture sounds distinctly thinner.

Haitink offers three bright-eyed *Slavonic dances* as his encore. Philips have considerably improved the sound of the symphony in this Festivo reissue; there is some lack of body in the middle strings, but otherwise the orchestral timbres are naturally balanced and vivid (on disc and tape alike), even if the effect sounds slightly dated. The performance has an attractive lyrical vigour, and the playing of the Concertgebouw woodwind gives constant pleasure. The reading has an element of sobriety compared to Sir Colin Davis's version with the same orchestra, but in the third movement the phrasing of the lilting melody of the trio has a disarming naturalness. Those wanting a medium-price version of the symphony might consider this, but competition from Kertesz, Kubelik and Karajan is considerable.

Rostropovich has taken over Kertesz's old coupling of the *G major Symphony* and *Scherzo capriccioso*, but with slow tempi and a consciously *espressivo* manner the performance of the symphony refuses to catch fire, and in the slow movement Rostropovich sounds too studied and unspontaneous. The *Scherzo capriccioso* is far more incisive and energetic, but here, as in the symphony, the recording balance favours the treble and there is a marked absence of bass. The sound on cassette is also rather fierce and dry, although the *Scherzo capriccioso* is fuller in body than the symphony.

Karajan's newest HMV recording with the Berlin Philharmonic is disappointing. If in the earlier Vienna performance he had moments of self-indulgence he also projected a consistent degree of affection for the score which makes a constant communication with the listener. In Berlin he is straighter, and in the trio of the scherzo the Berlin strings achieve their portamenti with considerable subtlety. But the *Adagio*, so involving in the Vienna performance, is now curiously unaffecting, while the scherzo's coda is rhythmically square. The most attractive part of the performance is near the close of the finale, where the composer recalls his opening material; here Karajan is appealingly nostalgic before dashing away into the coda, which is raucously recorded. Indeed the sound is generally unattractive, with glassy string fortissimos and a blisteringly fierce first-movement climax. The quality in the *Slavonic dance* is explosive.

Symphony No. 9 in E min. (From the New World), Op. 95.

(M) *** DG Priv. 2535/3335 473 [2530 415]. Berlin PO, Kubelik.

*** Ph. 9500 511/7300 671 [id.]. Concg. O., Colin Davis.

*** HMV ASD/TC-ASD 3407 [Ang. S/4XS 37437]. Berlin PO, Karajan – SMETANA: *Vltava.****

*** DG 2531/3301 098 [id.]. VPO, Boehm.

(M) *** Decca Jub. JB/KJBC 37 [Lon. 21025/5-]. New Philh. O., Dorati.

**(*) DG 2530/3300 881 [id.]. Chicago SO, Giulini.

**(*) CBS 76817/40- [Col. M/MT 35834]. Philh. O., Andrew Davis.

**(*) HMV ASD/TC-ASD 3786 [Ang. SZ 37719]. LPO, Rostropovich.

**(*) Telarc Dig. DG 10053 [id.]. St Louis SO, Slatkin.

** Decca Dig. SXDL/KSXDC 7510 [Lon. LDR/5- 10011]. VPO, Kondrashin.

(i; ii) *Symphony No. 9;* (i; iii) *Carnaval overture;* (iv) *Slavonic dances, Op. 46/5 and 8; Op. 72/2.*

(B) *(*) HMV TC-IDL 501. (i) Philh. O.; (ii) Malko; (iii) Weldon; (iv) BBC SO, Schwarz.

Symphony No. 9; Othello overture.

(M) *** Decca Jub. JB/KJBC 118. LSO, Kertesz.

There are now some three dozen versions of the *New World symphony* listed in the American *Schwann Catalogue*. The *Gramophone Classical Catalogue*, because of recent pruning by the British companies, contents itself with about two thirds of those listings. The reissue of Kertesz's 1967 LSO recording on Jubilee must stand with Kubelik at the top of the list, one of the finest versions ever committed to record, with a vivid first movement (exposition repeat included) and a *Largo* bringing playing of hushed intensity to make one hear the music with new ears. Tempi in the last two movements are also perfectly judged, and the recording quality remains outstanding.

Kubelik's marvellously fresh account with the Berlin Philharmonic, recorded in the early 1970s, is certainly among the very finest. The hushed opening immediately creates a tension which is to be sustained throughout, and the approach to the gentle second subject of the first movement underlines the refinement which is the hallmark of the reading. The slow movement has a compelling lyrical beauty, with playing of great radiance from the orchestra. With a scherzo of striking character and a finale of great urgency – the forward impulse magically slackened as the composer is allowed to dreamily recall his earlier themes – the playing is throughout of the first rank. The recording is well up to the standard of Kubelik's DG Dvořák series, firm, smoothly blended and clear. There is a slight lack of resonance in the bass, but at medium price this has strong claims to.

be at the very top of a distinguished list.

Among the new versions, that by Sir Colin Davis and the Concertgebouw Orchestra stands high in general esteem. It is completely free from egotistic eccentricity. The music is allowed to unfold in the most natural way, its drama vividly projected, and with beautiful orchestral playing throughout and really outstanding recording (rich and full-blooded, clearly detailed yet with a natural bloom on the whole orchestra), this is very appealing. For some listeners Davis's very directness may have its drawbacks. The cor anglais solo in the slow movement has an appealing simplicity, yet the effect is not very resilient, and later, when the horns echo the theme at the end of the opening section, the impression is positive rather than seductively nostalgic. The cassette transfer is one of Philips' very best, the level higher than usual, balancing clarity with weight and richness.

A splendid alternative choice is provided by Karajan's newest recording for HMV, which has the advantage of a generous coupling, a highly successful account of *Vltava*. Karajan's view of the symphony is more romantic than Davis's, but it is refined too, and has an unselfconscious warmth. It may not have quite the polish that marked Karajan's earlier reading for DG (no doubt shortly to reappear on Accolade), but the result is robust and spontaneous-sounding, with the cor anglais solo of the *Largo* very fresh at a fractionally more flowing tempo than in the earlier version. The EMI sound is warmly atmospheric rather than analytical. Originally the cassette transfer was not entirely successful, lacking in refinement, but it is likely to have been remastered by the time we are in print.

The Viennese tradition is superbly captured in Boehm's version, with ripe, sweet playing and vivid recording. Though Boehm indulges in traditional speed changes, and tempi are on the slow side, his is a fresh and alert reading rather

than a moulded one. The folk-like quality of the themes emerges all the more refreshingly, with the great cor anglais of the *Largo* given a moving and tender simplicity, and the movement's closing pages are very hushed and beautiful. The cassette transfer is acceptable on side one, where the transfer level is comparatively low, resulting in some loss of brilliance; then on side two the level rises dramatically, with a corresponding increase in range and projection.

Dorati's version was originally recorded in 1968 using Decca's artificially balanced Phase Four system, with close microphones to bring everything vividly forward. Dorati's approach is straightforwardly direct, the outer movements vigorous and alert, the *Largo* expressive and simply presented, and the scherzo characterized strongly. The bold primary colours of the recording undoubtedly heighten the dramatic effect, although the sound, crisp and clear, now seems just a shade lacking in depth and bass resonance. There is little to choose between disc and tape, and those who like brightness and immediacy will find that the performance communicates strongly.

As in his Philharmonia version of the early 1960s, Giulini here takes a sympathetic but slightly detached view of the *New World*, and the high polish of the Chicago orchestra's playing ensures that this DG recording is most enjoyable. But by the highest standards – and that includes the earlier Giulini account – the new performance is slightly over-refined and lacking in spontaneity, with the last two movements biting less sharply than before. Fine full recording, if at a somewhat low level; the cassette matches the disc fairly closely, but has slightly more projection and bite on the second side. (Incidentally Giulini's earlier HMV version with the Philharmonia has also been reissued on cassette in a first-class transfer of striking immediacy. This HMV tape includes not only a sparkling performance of the *Carnaval overture* – as on disc – but also an attractive account of Bizet's *Jeux d'enfants:* TC-SXLP 30163.)

Andrew Davis gives a relaxed and direct reading, the opposite of inflated, with plenty of vigour and impulse in the outer movements, yet with folk inspiration rather than symphonic grandeur underlined. The *Largo* is played with attractive expressive simplicity; in the finale the intensity increases and more than usual provides a satisfying resolution. The CBS recording is somewhat hard and not too well-defined. The cassette transfer is bright and clean, if a little fierce. It sounds best with the equalization set for chrome rather than ferric tape.

Rostropovich directs the weightiest reading imaginable. The very opening chords of the slow introduction suggest an epic view, and from then on, with generally expansive tempi, the performance presents this as a genuine '*Ninth*', a culmination to the cycle. In the first movement the exposition repeat brings a slight modification of treatment the second time, and some will resist such inconsistencies as that. The conscious weight of even the *Largo* is controversial too, though in all four movements Rostropovich contrasts the big tuttis – almost Straussian at times – with light pointing in woodwind solos. The recording is ample to match, and the cassette transfer is generally a close match for the disc.

The St Louis Symphony plays for Slatkin with polish and refinement, the cor anglais solo of the slow movement is so velvety it hardly sounds like a reed instrument at all. One or two mannerisms apart, the reading is enjoyably direct, and the recording, though not one of Telarc's most spectacular digital offerings, brings out the sweetness of the string note even in the gentlest pianissimos.

Kondrashin gives a genial rather than a dramatic reading. At the very start the tension is low, with little sense of expectancy, and though in principle Kon-

drashin's preference for keeping a steady tempo even in the first movement is admirable, in places the result sounds perfunctory. The cor anglais solo in the slow movement is easy and songful but not fully expressive, and the disc's main claim to attention lies in the digital sound, warmly coordinated rather than brilliant. On cassette, side one offers a rather soft-grained orchestral image, but it increases in brilliance and projection (with a rise of level) to reach demonstration standard on side two.

One wonders why EMI chose the Malko version of the *New World* for their 'hour-long' cassette series. It is a routine performance and the recording lacks dynamic contrast and impact until the finale, which suddenly springs to life (after the side-turn). The rest of side two offers attractively lively performances of the *Carnaval overture* and three *Slavonic dances*, where the sound has both weight and sparkle.

Still recommended: Kertesz's 1951 VPO account is still quite competitive. It is relatively idiosyncratic but sympathetic and exciting (Decca SPA/*KCSP* 87 [Lon. STS/5- 15101]). But the 1967 LSO recording (see above) is maturely convincing in every way, and at Jubilee price it is now a more obvious choice.

Piano quintet in A, Op. 81.
** RCA RL 12240 [ARL 1/*ARK 1* 2240]. Ax, Cleveland Qt.

(i) *Piano quintet in A. String quintet in E flat, Op. 97.*
(M) *** Ph. 6570/7310 571. Berlin Philharmonic Octet (members), (i) with Bishop-Kovacevich.

It is surprising that these two masterly quintets have not been recorded more often. Paired generously together on the mid-price Philips disc – each work lasts over half an hour – they make a superb coupling. The Berlin players have a consistent freshness, an easy warmth which never develops into sentimentality. In that they are splendidly matched in the *Piano quintet* by Stephen Bishop-Kovacevich, whose clarity of articulation is a marvel. The recording is not as weighty as it might be, lacking a little in bass, but it is still satisfyingly balanced.

Extravagantly spread over two whole sides, the Cleveland Quartet's version of the rich and amiable *Piano quintet* is attractively relaxed, but fails to convey the full warmth of Dvořák's inspiration.

Piano trios Nos. 1 in B flat, Op. 21; 2 in G min., Op. 26; 3 in F min., Op. 65; 4 in E min. (Dumky), Op. 90.
(M) *** Ph. 6703 015 (3) [id.]. Beaux Arts Trio.
(M) *** Sup. 1411 2621/3. Suk Trio.

Piano trios Nos. 1–4; 4 Romantic pieces (for violin and piano), *Op. 78; Romance in G min.* (for cello and piano), *Op. 94.*
**(*) CRD CRD 1086/8/*CRDC 4086/8.* Cohen Trio.

The Beaux Arts versions of the trios come from the early 1970s but sound amazingly fresh and sparkling. The *F minor*, arguably the most magnificent and certainly the most concentrated of the four, is played with great eloquence and vitality; the splendours of the *Dumky* are detailed below under the individual mid-price disc. The recording is splendidly vivid and truthful.

The Suk Trio bring a special authority to this music (after all, Josef Suk can trace his ancestry back to the composer himself), and their readings have the benefit of concentration and intellectual grip. They hold the architecture of each movement together most impressively, and they also have the advantage of very good recorded sound. Perhaps the Beaux Arts Trio score in their wonderful pianist, Menahem Pressler, who brings such sen-

sitivity and imagination to his part; Jan Panenka is very good, but not quite so inspired. But honours are very evenly divided, and both these sets are at medium price.

The Cohen is a family trio, so opportunities for rehearsal should be unlimited! Their set also adds Opp. 78 and 94, which the two rival accounts do not include, but the price is higher. The playing is always thoroughly musical, though not quite as masterly as that of the Beaux Arts. The recording is very good, and collectors are unlikely to find much here to disappoint them. The cassettes are each available separately and offer faithful transfers, although one . notices slightly greater presence on the second sides of CRDC 4086 and 7 than the first. On CRDC 4088, which couples the *Dumky trio* with Opp. 75 and 94, the level is higher and this cassette is demonstrably more vivid.

Piano trio No. 4 (Dumky).
(M) *** Ph. 6833 231 [(d) 802918]. Beaux Arts Trio – HAYDN: *Piano trio No. 25.****
*** Pearl SHE 553. Beaux Arts Trio – MENDELSSOHN: *Piano trio No. 1.****

On its first appearance the Beaux Arts' Philips performance of the *Dumky trio* occupied two sides, which made it an expensive proposition at full price. Now it has the advantage of a fill-up as well as a reduction in cost. The performance has great sparkle and freshness and the quality of the recording is altogether exemplary, vivid and lifelike and with marvellously silent surfaces. This is arguably the best buy now at any price.

We associate the Beaux Arts Trio with Philips and therefore wonder whether we are dreaming when their names are clearly printed in black and white on the Pearl label. They have recorded both the *Dumky* and the Mendelssohn trio for Philips, and there is not a great deal to choose between these performances; perhaps surprisingly, there is also little difference in recorded quality. So the question of couplings and, of course, the cost – the Pearl disc is at full price – can be left to decide.

String quartet No. 12 in F (American), Op. 96.
*** Ph. 9500/7300 995 [id.]. Orlando Qt – MENDELSSOHN: *Quartet No. 1.****
** HMV ASD/TC-ASD 3694. Medici Qt – SMETANA: *Quartet No. 1.**(*)

The Orlando Quartet were new to the catalogue when the Philips issue appeared, and the sleeve-note of both disc and cassette concentrates on the artists rather than the music, which is familiar enough. They are based in Holland and have won wide acclaim for their concert appearances. The Dvořák is played with finely balanced and well-blended tone, excellent musical judgement and great sensitivity. Indeed this ranks among the very best versions of the quartet currently available and can stand comparison with the classic account by the Italian Quartet. The recording is completely natural and lifelike; the cassette transfer is admirable, wide-ranging, fresh and clean.

The Medici Quartet possess the virtues of honesty, but they do not present a serious challenge in this oft-recorded quartet. The sound they produce seems less fully integrated than that of many of their rivals, and though rhythms are well articulated and phrasing is musical, the reading is not sufficiently characterized to displace other recommendations. The recording as such has much to commend it, for it has a vivid and lively presence, with firm cello tone. The cassette matches the disc closely.

Slavonic dances Nos. 1–16, Opp. 46 and 72.
*** DG 2531/3301 349 [id.]. Alfons and Aloys Kontarsky.

Characteristically crisp and clean performances by the Kontarsky brothers of some of the most delectable piano duets ever written. More than they usually do, these pianists here allow themselves the necessary rubato, conveying affection and joy along with their freshness. Excellent recording and a splendid high-level cassette transfer, matching the disc closely.

4 Folksongs, Op. 73; Gipsy songs, Op. 55.
*** Mer. E 77042. Walker, Vignoles – BRAHMS: *Mädchenlieder* etc.***

Songs my mother taught me is the one everyone knows from the *Four Folksongs* (here sung in Czech). The others too, and the *Gipsy songs*, are beautifully suited to Sarah Walker's vibrant personality. An attractive coupling for the exactly comparable Brahms songs, with excellent accompaniment from Roger Vignoles and very good recording.

Requiem, Op. 89.
(M) **(*) DG Priv. 2726/3372 089 (2). Stader, Wagner, Haefliger, Borg, Ch., Czech PO, Ančerl.

Ančerl's version of the *Requiem* on the mid-price Privilege label makes an excellent alternative to Kertesz on Decca, and the 1960 recording still sounds remarkably good for its period, warm and atmospheric. The charming opening of the *Recordare* is beautifully sung by Ernst Haefliger, and the combination of a non-Czech quartet of soloists with a Czech conductor, chorus and orchestra has worked well, with purity and authenticity combined. Those who want a more brilliant, more incisive reading will find the Kertesz (Decca SET 416/7) marginally preferable. We have been unable to hear the DG tape.

Stabat Mater, Op. 58.
*** DG 2707 099 (2). Mathis, Reynolds, Ochman, Shirley-Quirk, Bav. R. Ch., and SO, Kubelik.

283

Dvořák's devout Catholicism led him to treat this tragic religious theme with an open innocence that avoids the sentimentality of other works which made their mark (as this one did) in Victorian England. Characteristically four of the ten movements are based on major keys, and though a setting of a relatively short poem which stretches to eighty minutes entails much repetition of words, this idiomatic performance, warmly recorded and with fine solo and choral singing and responsive playing, holds the attention from first to last.

The Jacobin (opera).
**(*) Sup. SUP 2481/3. Blachut, Machotková, Zitek, Přibyl, Tuček, Prusa, Kantilena Children's Ch., Kuhn Ch., Brno State PO, Pinkas.

The Jacobin dates from the most contented period of Dvořák's life, and though the background to the piece is one of revolt and political turmoil, he was more interested in individuals, so that this is more a village comedy than a tract for the times. Václav Zitek sings the heroic part of the Jacobin himself with incisive strength, but the role which one remembers is that of the old musician, Benda, charmingly portrayed here by the veteran tenor Benno Blachut. Vilem Přibyl is less dominant than usual in the other tenor role of Jiři, one of a first-rate team. The conducting of Jiři Pinkas could be more positive, but the richness and variety of inspiration in a muddled but warmly satisfying opera come out most persuasively, helped by very acceptable recording.

Kate and the Devil (opera).
(M) **(*) Sup. 1116 3181/3. Barová, Novák, Ježil, Šulcová, Brno Janáček Op. Ch. and O., Pinkas.

This delightful fairy-tale opera about the girl who literally makes life hell for the devil who abducts her has more in common with Smetana and *The Bartered Bride* than with Wagner, whose techniques Dvořák – writing in 1899, towards the end of his career – was here consciously using. The jolly folk atmosphere of the opening is established in peasant choruses with the tenor hero (a shepherd) slightly tipsy. The devil appears in the guise of a handsome gamekeeper, and in his wooing brings obvious Wagnerian references. It is charmingly effective to have the supernatural represented in more chromatic music and to have a distant imitation of Wagner's Nibelheim music for the scene in hell in Act 2. Kate naturally wins in her contest with the devil. Here the mezzo-soprano Anna Barová makes a formidable Kate, with Milos Ježil a sharply projected, Slavonic-sounding tenor as the shepherd and Richard Novák comparably Slavonic as the devil who makes a mistake. Pinkas directs a lively performance with his Brno forces. The recording is bright to the point of edginess, but can easily be tamed.

Eccles, Henry (1670–*c*. 1742)

Viola sonata in G min. (arr. Klengel).
(M) *** Sup. 1111 2694. Koďousek, Novotná – BRITTEN: *Lachrymae*; CLARKE: *Sonata.****

The interest of this record lies in the Britten and Rebecca Clarke works. The Eccles is not particularly individual, but it has dignity and makes an appealing makeweight in this eloquent performance.

Elgar, Edward (1857–1934)

Adieu (arr. Geehl). *Beau Brummel: Minuet. Sospiri, Op. 70. The Spanish*

Lady: Burlesco. The Starlight Express: Waltz. Sursum corda, Op. 11.
(M) *** Chan. CBR/*CBT* 1004. Bournemouth Sinf., Hurst – VAUGHAN WILLIAMS: *Collection.****

A collection of delightful Elgar rarities. Most unexpected is the *Sursum corda* for organ, brass, strings and timpani (no woodwind), an occasional piece written for a royal visit to Worcester in 1894, which has real *nobilmente* depth. The *Burlesco*, a fragment from the unfinished Elgar opera, is delightfully done, and each one of these items has its charms. Well coupled with rare Vaughan Williams, warmly performed and atmospherically recorded.

'The miniature Elgar': Bavarian dance No. 2. Beau Brummel: Minuet. Chanson de matin. Dream Children, Op. 43/1 and 2. Nursery suite. The Serious Doll. The Starlight Express: (i) *Organ Grinder's songs: My Old Tunes; To the Children. The Wand of Youth suites:* excerpts: *Serenade; Sun dance; The Tame Bear.*
(M) *** HMV Green. ESD/*TC-ESD* 7068. RPO, Collingwood, (i) with Harvey.

Inspired by the BBC TV *Monitor* film on Elgar's life, this wholly delightful anthology collects together some of the composer's most attractive contributions in the lighter field, including several of those fragile and nostalgic little portraits which give the *Nursery* and *Wand of Youth* suites their special character. Frederick Harvey joins the orchestra for two *Organ Grinder's songs* written as incidental music for *The Starlight Express*. These are splendidly alive, with as much interest in the orchestra as in the stirringly melodic vocal line. Throughout this very well recorded collection the orchestral playing under Lawrence Collingwood is especially sympathetic, and

the programme as a whole has been cleverly planned to make a highly enjoyable concert in itself. The cassette transfer is immaculate, first-class in every way.

Cockaigne overture, Op. 40; Falstaff, Op. 68.
(B) *** CfP CFP/*TC-CFP* 40313. LPO, Handley.
(M) *** CBS 61883/40-. LPO, Barenboim.

Vernon Handley directs a superb performance of *Falstaff*, one of Elgar's most difficult works, and the achievement is all the more remarkable because his tempi are unusually spacious (generally following the composer's markings), making the contrasted episodes more difficult to hold together. The playing of the LPO is warmly expressive and strongly rhythmic, and the recording is one of the finest to come from Classics for Pleasure. *Cockaigne* is also given a performance that is expansive yet never hangs fire. This is a richly enjoyable coupling, and the cassette transfer is of first-rate quality, matching the disc closely.

Barenboim's view of *Falstaff* is compelling in a quite different way. Rarely even under the composer has the storytelling element in the music been so captivatingly presented. Barenboim's habit in Elgar of moulding the music in flexible tempi, of underlining romantic expressiveness, has never on record been so convincing as here, where the big contrasts of texture, dynamic and mood are played for all they are worth. The Gadshill episode with its ambush is so vivid one can see the picture in one's mind's eye. *Cockaigne* also is given a colourful reading and though the recording is not ideally balanced, this is certainly the finest of the Barenboim Elgar series. The cassette transfer is one of CBS's best, the sound vivid and full-blooded with plenty of body and colour.

Cockaigne overture; Pomp and Circumstance marches, Op. 39/1–5; National anthem (arrangement).
*** Decca SXL/*KSXC* 6848 [Lon. 7072/5-]. LPO, Solti.

Solti's view of the marches is refined, with sharp pointing in the outer sections, spaciousness in the great melodies. The result is richly satisfying. *Cockaigne* too is sharply dramatic, and the recording quality gives a bloom to all the performances which few Elgarians will resist. The cassette transfer is first-class, with thrilling impact and weight.

(i) *Cockaigne overture;* (ii) *Pomp and Circumstance marches, Op. 39, Nos. 1, 2 and 4.*
(M) **(*) Ph. Fest. 6570/*7310* 763. (i) LSO, Colin Davis; (ii) Concg. O., Marriner – TIPPETT: *Birthday suite* ***; WALTON: *Crown Imperial.***

Sir Colin Davis's slightly controversial recording of *Cockaigne* and Marriner's spaciously sumptuous Amsterdam recordings of three of the *Pomp and Circumstance marches* (see below) are here economically recoupled in an anthology issued to celebrate the wedding of the Prince and Princess of Wales. The sound cannot be faulted, although the disc has a slightly more telling upper range than the cassette, which otherwise is well transferred.

Cockaigne overture; Enigma variations, Op. 36.
(M) ** Ph. Fest. 6570/*7310* 188 [id.]. LSO, Colin Davis.

Davis's reading of the *Enigma variations* is in the main a straightforward one, with each variation carefully shaped, and really first-rate playing from the LSO throughout. In *Cockaigne*, however, the conductor is more wilful in his choice of tempi, and this is less convincing than it can be. The Philips recording

is good, but only good. The snag is that this comes into competition with Barbirolli's superb disc for HMV (ASD 548 [Ang. S 36120]), which features the same coupling but with readings that are altogether riper.

Cello concerto in E min., Op. 85.
*** Decca SXL/*KSXC* 6965 [Lon. 7195/5-]. Harrell, Cleveland O., Maazel – TCHAIKOVSKY: *Rococo variations* etc.***
*(*) Chan. Dig. ABRD/*ABTD* 1007. Kirshbaum, SNO, Gibson – WALTON: *Concerto.***

(i) *Cello concerto. Elegy for strings, Op. 58; In the South, Op. 50.*
(B) *** CfP CFP/*TC-CFP* 40342. LPO, Del Mar, (i) with Robert Cohen.

Lynn Harrell's outstanding account of the Elgar *Cello concerto* with the Cleveland Orchestra is the first to challenge the Du Pré versions for HMV and CBS (see below). With eloquent support from Maazel and the orchestra (the woodwind plays with appealing delicacy), the reading, deeply felt, balances a gentle nostalgia with extrovert brilliance. The slow movement is tenderly spacious, the scherzo bursts with exuberance, and after a passionate opening the finale is memorable for the poignantly expressive reprise of the melody from the *Adagio*, one of Elgar's greatest inspirations. The recording of the orchestra is brightly lit in the American way; the solo cello is rich and firmly focused, a little larger than life but convincingly balanced. The cassette matches the disc closely: it is slightly smoother on top, mellowing the sheen on the orchestral strings.

The Classics for Pleasure disc is an outstanding bargain. Robert Cohen's performance is strong and intense, with steady tempi, the colouring more positive, less autumnal than usual, relating the work more closely to the *Second Symphony*. Yet there is no lack of inner feeling. The ethereal half-tones at the close of the first movement are matched by the gently elegiac poignancy of the *Adagio*. Del Mar's accompaniment is wholly sympathetic, underlining the soloist's approach. He also directs an exciting account of *In the South* (recorded in a single take), not quite as exhilarating as Silvestri's famous performance (HMV ESD 7013) but certainly spontaneous in effect. The *Elegy* makes an eloquent bonus. The recording is wide-ranging and brilliant but shows Cohen's tone as bright and well-focused rather than especially resonant in the bass. The cassette matches the disc, with slightly less edge at the top, rather more body.

Kirshbaum, a fine cellist, is disappointing here. At the very start the great double-stopped chords are anything but commanding, not helped by recessed recording, and the whole performance sounds tentative rather than expressing spontaneity. Originally issued as an analogue disc, this is now displaced by a digital version, which is crisper in outline but cannot cure the balance.

Still recommended: Jacqueline du Pré's inspired early HMV recording (with Barbirolli) is available coupled either to the *Sea Pictures* (ASD/*TC-ASD* 655) or to the Delius *Concerto* (ASD 2764 [(d) Ang. S 36338]); the later, more mature and no less compelling CBS version directed by her husband, Daniel Barenboim, is coupled to the *Enigma variations* (CBS 76529/40- [Col. M/*MT* 34530]).

Violin concerto in B min., Op. 61.
*** Decca SXL/*KSXC* 6842 [Lon. 7064/5-]. Kyung-Wha Chung, LPO, Solti.
*** DG Dig. 2532/*3302* 035 [id.]. Perlman, Chicago SO, Barenboim.
(B) **(*) CfP CFP 40322. Bean, Royal Liv. PO, Groves.
** HMV ASD/*TC-ASD* 3598. Haendel, LPO, Boult.

Kyung-Wha Chung's is an intense and deeply committed reading which rises to great heights in the heartfelt account of the slow movement – made the more affecting by its vein of melancholy - and the wide-ranging performance of the finale. At the start of that third movement Chung at a fast tempo finds a rare element of fantasy, a mercurial quality, and the great accompanied cadenza is commandingly done, ending on an achingly beautiful phrase from the third subject of the first movement. The first movement itself brings much beautiful playing too, but there are one or two tiny flaws of intonation, and here Solti's accompaniment does not have quite so firm a grasp. But as an illuminating alternative to the Zukerman performance (CBS 76528 [Col. M 34517]), awarded a rosette in the second edition of the *Penguin Stereo Record Guide*), this will be refreshing for any Elgarian. The brilliant Decca recording, giving first-class results on disc, sounds rather edgy in its cassette format.

Perlman's ease in tackling one of the most challenging violin concertos ever written brings a richly enjoyable performance, though he misses some of the darker, more intense elements in Elgar's inspiration. The solo instrument is forwardly balanced and the recording is bright and vivid rather than rich (especially on cassette), lacking some of the amplitude one expects in the Elgar orchestral sound.

Hugh Bean offers us the only modern recording of the Elgar concerto on a bargain label. He has not the outsize personality of his most eloquent rivals but there is much to be said for his playing. He studied with Albert Sammons and his reading has a nobility and reticence well attuned to this composer, and his selfless artistry is wholly dedicated to the music rather than to ego projection. The balance of the recording underlines his reticence, the solo instrument backward and pictured struggling against the weight of orchestral sound as in a live concert hall. The recording has great warmth and fidelity, and the perspective matches the undramatic yet convincing view of the concerto Mr Bean gives. His version may not have the authority of Perlman or Zukerman (at full price), but given the up-to-date recorded sound and the excellence of Groves's support, it is well worth considering. Indeed, in the quieter, more reflective passages, Hugh Bean has something quite special to say.

Ida Haendel adopts tempi so consistently spacious that they will amaze most Elgarians. She plays with all her usual firmness of tone, and with the most stylish of all Elgar conductors beside her as well as opulent recording the result is never less than interesting. But the finale in particular sounds in places like a practice run-through rather than a performance; other versions are preferable. The cassette transfer, is very successful, matching the disc closely.

Crown of India suite, Op. 66; In the South overture, Op. 50.
(M) *(*) CBS 61892/40- [(d) Col. M 32936; M/*MT* 35880]. LPO, Barenboim.

Both works have been recoupled in the UK. (The original couplings, discussed in the *Penguin Stereo Record Guide*, remain in the USA.) In the concert hall Barenboim has directed performances of *In the South* full of his most passionate commitment, but this recording disppointingly presents a performance which fails to add up to the sum of its parts, lacking concentration and impetus. He is more convincing in the *Crown of India suite*. The recording is lively but not especially rich, and the cassette is successful, matching the disc fairly closely.

(i) *Elegy for strings, Op. 58; Froissart overture, Op. 19; Pomp and Circumstance marches, Op. 39, Nos.* (ii) *1 in D;* (i) *2 in A min.; 3 in C min.;* (ii) *4 in G;* (i) *5 in C;* (i) *Sospiri, Op. 70.*

(M) *** HMV SXLP/*TC-SXLP* 30456 [Ang. S 36403]. (i) New Philh. O.; (ii) Philh. O.; cond. Barbirolli.

The five *Pomp and Circumstance marches* make a very good suite, with plenty of contrast in Nos. 2 and 3 to offset the Edwardian bombast of 1 and 4. The splendid *nobilmente* of No. 5 closes the set in rousing fashion. Barbirolli is obviously determined not to overdo the patriotism, and the studio recording suits this fresh approach. The sound is brilliant, but one notices that the recording of the string pieces offers more warmth in the middle range. The *Elegy* shows Barbirolli at his gentle best; *Sospiri* is contrastingly passionate, and the collection concludes with the early overture *Froissart*. Here the orchestral links with Brahms are strong, but the fingerprints of the Elgar to emerge later are everywhere, and if the piece is loose in structure it has a striking main theme. The cassette equivalent of this issue has been remastered and sounds lively and vivid. *Froissart* is marginally less full-blooded than the other items.

Falstaff, Op. 68; In the South, Op. 50.
** Decca SXL/*KSXC* 6963 [Lon. 7193]. LPO, Solti.
Falstaff; Enigma variations.
** RCA RL/*RK* 25206. SNO, Gibson.

The tensions of Solti and Elgar can be invigorating, and in these performances of two of the more problematic Elgar works there is much that is very exciting. But with Decca recording in which the brilliance is not matched by weight or body (as is essential in Elgar), the results are too nervy and unrelaxed, particularly in *Falstaff*. The playing is excellent. There is no appreciable difference in sound between disc and cassette.

Gibson's clean-cut account of *Falstaff* had the misfortune to appear in the same month as Vernon Handley's outstanding performance on Classics for Pleasure, which is altogether warmer and more expansive. The *Enigma variations* in an equally straight and unmannered performance make a generous coupling, but the recording lacks body and immediacy, with the cassette reflecting the disc fairly closely.

Introduction and allegro for strings, Op. 47.
(B) **(*) RCA VICS/*VK* 2001 [AGL 1/ *AGK 1* 3790]. Boston SO, Munch – BARBER: *Adagio;* TCHAIKOVSKY: *Serenade.***(*)

A striking performance from Munch, individual in that his tempo for the big *Sul G* unison tune must be the slowest on record. But otherwise the reading has plenty of vitality, and the recording is full, with only a touch of the characteristic Boston harshness found in recordings from the early stereo era. The chrome cassette is first-rate

King Arthur: suite; (i) *The Starlight Express, Op. 78: suite.*
(M) ** Chan. CBR/*CBT* 1001. Bournemouth Sinf., Hurst, (i) with Glover, Lawrenson.

The *King Arthur suite* is put together from incidental music that Elgar wrote in 1923 – well after his creative urge had fallen away – for a pageant-like play by Laurence Binyon. Though not great at all, it is full of surging, enjoyable ideas and makes an interesting novelty on record. *The Starlight Express suite* is similarly taken from music Elgar wrote in the First World War for a children's play, very much from the same world as the *Wand of Youth suites*, with a song or two included. Though the singers here are not ideal interpreters, the enthusiasm of Hurst and the Sinfonietta is well conveyed, particularly in the *King Arthur suite*. The recording is atmospheric if rather over-reverberant. The cassette transfer is acceptable but lacks range

(most noticeably in *King Arthur*). The solo voices are naturally caught.

Pomp and Circumstance marches, Op. 39/1–5; Empire march (1924); *Imperial march, Op. 32.*
*** HMV ASD/*TC-ASD* 3388 [Ang. S/ *4XS* 37436]. LPO, Boult – WALTON: *Marches.****
(M) ** CBS 61893/40- (without *Empire march*) [(d) Col. M 32936]. LPO, Barenboim.

Boult's approach to the *Pomp and Circumstance marches* is brisk and direct, with an almost no-nonsense manner in places. There is not a hint of vulgarity, and the freshness is most attractive, though it is a pity he omits the repeats in the Dvořák-like No. 2. The *Empire march*, written for the opening of the 1924 Wembley Exhibition, had not been recorded again since then. It is hardly a great discovery, but makes a good makeweight for the more characteristic pieces. Warm, immediate and resplendent recording; the cassette is not as sharply focused as the disc.

Barenboim's set of *Marches* was originally appropriately coupled with the *Crown of India suite* (it still is in the USA). The present mid-priced reissue is hardly generous. Barenboim's tempi are surprisingly fast (though Elgar's own tended to be fast too), and not all Elgarians will approve of his updating of Edwardian majesty. If only the recording were richer, the interpretations would emerge more convincingly than they do.

Serenade for strings in E min., Op. 20.
** Abbey ABY 810. Scottish Bar. Ens., Friedman – BRITTEN: *Simple symphony;* WARLOCK: *Capriol suite;* WILLIAMSON: *English lyrics.***(*)

The Scottish Baroque Ensemble give an alert if not especially elegant performance of Elgar's delightful *Serenade*, not as polished as some, but brightly recorded and interestingly coupled.

The Starlight Express (incidental music), Op. 78.

(M) *** HMV Green. ESDW/TC2-ESDW 711. Masterton, Hammond Stroud, LPO, Handley.

The Starlight Express was a children's play, adapted from a novel by Algernon Blackwood, which in 1916 its promoters hoped would prove a successor to Barrie's Peter Pan. Though the play failed to attract a comparable following, Elgar himself at the time recorded a whole sequence of numbers from it. Even that failed to keep the music alive, and it has been left to latter-day Elgarians to revive a score which reveals the composer at his most charming. On record in this dedicated reconstruction with even the linking fragments included (but without the spoken dialogue) one is conscious of an element of repetition, but the ear is continually beguiled and the key sequences suggest that this procedure would have won the composer's approval. Some of the words reflect the coy manner of the original libretto, but much of the orchestral music has that nostalgically luminous quality that Elgarians will instantly recognize. Both soloists are excellent, and the LPO plays with warmth and sympathy. The 1976 recording is excellent, and the glowing quality of the cassette transfer (the music all on a single double-length tape) makes this an ideal way to dip into a delightful score and discover Vernon Handley already emerging as a distinguished Elgarian.

Symphonies Nos. 1 and 2.

*** ASV ALHB 201 (2). Hallé O., Loughran.

Loughran directs deeply sympathetic performances of both symphonies, beautifully played, with the refinement of pianissimo from the Hallé strings more remarkable than from this orchestra in the past. Loughran, in the Boult tradition, takes a direct view, less overtly expressive or emotional than Handley on CfP, for example, so that, though the result may be less exciting, it has a reflective quality that is very satisfying too. The slow movement of No. 1 makes a culmination, with the third theme ravishingly beautiful in its tenderness. In No. 2 Loughran's feeling for climax is unerring, but his relatively slow tempi in the last two movements bring a slight lack of intensity, with the chains of sequential phrases sounding too unpointed, rhythmically heavier than they need be. Splendid recording, with the timpani vividly caught, but with a general distancing that matches the degree of reserve in the performances.

Symphony No. 1 in A flat, Op. 55.

(B) *** CfP CFP/TC-CFP 40331. LPO, Handley.
(M) *** Lyr. REAM 1. LPO, Boult
 − VAUGHAN WILLIAMS: Tallis fantasia.***
(M) ** CBS 61880/40-. LPO, Barenboim.
(M) ** HMV SXLP/TC-SXLP 30268. Philh. O., Barbirolli.
(B) ** RCA VICS/VK 2010. SNO, Gibson.

Vernon Handley directs a beautifully paced performance of Elgar's First. The LPO has recorded this symphony many times before, but never with more poise and refinement than here, and the Elgar sound is gloriously captured, particularly the brass. Not surprisingly Handley, a former pupil of Sir Adrian Boult, takes a direct view. As in his fine recording of Falstaff, there is sometimes a hint of restraint which then opens up, with power in reserve. It is in the slow movement, more spacious and lovingly expressive than Sir Adrian allows, that Handley scores above all. Even making no allowance for price (and Sir Adrian's Lyrita disc, although it has a generous coupling, costs about a pound more than the CfP issue) this is outstanding among current versions. The cassette transfer too is first-class, remarkable in its wide amplitude and range.

However, the inclusion on the Lyrita issue of the Vaughan Williams *Tallis fantasia* as a bonus makes it very striking value for money, particularly as it offers the most invigorating recording Sir Adrian ever made of the Elgar *First*. The opening movement is fierce and biting (reflecting perhaps the conductor's irritation at being pressured into having all the violins on the left); the scherzo is delicate in the fairy-like scampering at the start and in the trio, while the slow movement is light and tender, with the emotion understated before the heroic culmination of the finale. With its apt and particularly generous coupling it makes a fine alternative recommendation, brightly recorded.

Barenboim like Solti studied Elgar's own recording before interpreting the *First Symphony*, and the results are certainly idiomatic, though in the long first movement Barenboim overdoes the fluctuations, so losing momentum. The other three movements are beautifully performed, with the slow movement almost as tender as in Solti's reading with the same players. The recording is not as opulent or well-balanced as Elgar's orchestration really demands, and the tape transfer is disappointing, with restricted upper range.

Barbirolli's HMV reissue still sounds very well in its disc form, although the cassette has less body and amplitude, with papery string tone (especially in the first movement) and a lack of weight. Barbirolli's tempi are also controversial; apart from the very slow speed for the slow movement, there is a hint of heaviness in the first movement too, where after the slow march introduction the music should surge along.

Gibson draws a direct, intelligent performance from the Scottish National Orchestra, but he lacks the urgency and commitment of the finest readings on

record. At bargain price he competes directly with Handley's fine CfP issue, which is preferable not only as a performance but also as a recording. The RCA disc has less body, and Gibson's view of Elgar is rather literal, starting with a matter-of-fact view of the motto march-theme. The chrome tape is first-class.

Reminder: At full price Solti's Decca version (SXL/*KSXC* 6569 [Lon. 6789]), which earned a rosette in the *Penguin Stereo Record Guide*, has the same committed qualities that mark out the composer's own performance. Boult on HMV (ASD/*TC-ASD* 3330 [Ang. S 37240]) presents the symphony as a close counterpart of the *Second* with hints of reflective nostalgia amid the triumph. The HMV recording has an opulence that even outshines the Decca version.

Symphony No. 2 in E flat, Op. 63.
⊛ (B) *** CfP CFP/*TC-CFP* 40350. LPO, Handley.
*** HMV ASD/*TC-ASD* 3330 [Ang. S 37218]. LPO, Boult.
(M) **(*) Lyr. REAM 2. LPO, Boult.
(M) **(*) HMV SXLP/*TC-SXLP* 30287. Hallé O., Barbirolli.
(M) **(*) HMV SXLP/*TC-SXLP* 30539. USSR SO, Svetlanov.

Handley's is the most satisfying modern version of a work which has latterly been much recorded. It is broadly in the Boult mould, never forcing the pace (as Elgar himself did, and, following him, Solti) but equally adopting tempi such as Sir Adrian preferred at the height of his career, rather more urgent, less elegiac. What Handley conveys superbly is the sense of Elgarian ebb and flow, building climaxes like a master, and drawing excellent, spontaneous-sounding playing from the orchestra which more than any other has specialized in performing this symphony. The sound is warmly atmospheric, and vividly conveys the added organ part in the bass just at the climax of the finale (eight bars after

Fig. 165 in the score), which Elgar himself suggested 'if available': a tummy-wobbling effect. This would be a first choice at full price, and as a bargain there are few records to match it. The cassette is every bit the equal of the disc and in many ways preferable. It has slightly more warmth and body without loss of upper range.

For his fifth recording of the *Second Symphony* Sir Adrian Boult, incomparable Elgarian, drew from the LPO the most richly satisfying performance of all. Over the years Sir Adrian's view of the glorious nobility of the first movement has mellowed a degree. The tempo is a shade slower than before (and much slower than Solti's or the composer's own in the great leaping 12/8 theme), but the pointing of climaxes is unrivalled. With Boult more than anyone else the architecture is clearly and strongly established, with tempo changes less exaggerated than usual. The peak comes in the great *Funeral march*, where the concentration of the performance is irresistible. The LPO strings play gloriously, with the great swooping violin phrases at the climaxes inspiring a frisson as in a live performance. The scherzo has lightness and delicacy, with Boult very little slower than Solti but giving more room to breathe. In the finale, firm and strong, Boult cleverly conceals the repetitiveness of the main theme, and gives a radiant account of the lovely epilogue. With superb, opulent recording, this is a version to convert new listeners to a love of Elgar. The tape transfer too is admirably rich, yet with good detail, one of EMI's best cassettes.

Boult's earlier recording on Lyrita has been reissued at medium price, but unlike the *First Symphony* it has no extra coupling to tempt the prospective purchaser. As in the recording of the *First*, Sir Adrian was persuaded by the recording manager to have all the violins on the left – previously unheard-of in a Boult performance. The result was that the sessions had extra tensions which are reflected in the performance. But in this work the authority of Boult is even more unassailable, with a noble approach that puts even Barbirolli in the shade. The latter's version was originally issued as a two-disc set coupled to *Falstaff*. This reissue fits the performance on two sides without striking loss in the recording's amplitude. The cassette too is much more successful than the tape issue of Barbirolli's *First Symphony*, with good balance and detail and only marginally less ripeness of middle frequencies than the disc. Barbirolli's interpretation is a very personal one, the pace of the music often excessively varied, coarsening effects which Elgar's score specifies very precisely, and weakening the structure of the finale.

Only a political doctrinaire would suggest that the Soviet view of Edwardian grandeur is the one to prefer to all others, but Svetlanov's passionate and deeply sympathetic reading makes fascinating listening for any Elgarian. It is taken from a live performance in Moscow recorded in 1979, and though the ensemble is often imprecise, with brass whooping coarsely but excitingly, the conviction is what matters. Svetlanov takes a brisk view of the first movement, which yet does not sound breathless. Slavonic vibrato on some of the trumpet and trombone solos is hard to take, and the balance obscures much string detail, but as a document this is unique, the more attractive on a mid-price label.

Variations on an original theme (Enigma), Op. 36.

(M) *** Decca Jub. JB/*KJBC* 106. LAPO, Mehta – MUSSORGSKY: *Pictures.***(*)

*** HMV ASD/*TC-ASD* 3857 [Ang. SZ/*4ZS* 37627]. LSO, Previn – VAUGHAN WILLIAMS: *Tallis fantasia; Wasps.****

(i) *Enigma variations;* (ii) *Pomp and Circumstance marches Nos. 1–5.*

** Ph. 9500 424/*7300 642* [id.] (Marches 1, 2, 4 only). Concg. O., Marriner.

(M) ** Decca SPA/*KCSP* 536. LSO, (i) Monteux, (ii) Bliss.

Melita, born and brought up in India, has evidently not rejected all sympathy for the British Raj and its associations. Certainly he is a strong and sensitive interpreter of Elgar if this highly enjoyable account is anything to go by. There are no special revelations, although the transition from the spacious climax of *Nimrod* to a delightfully graceful *Dorabella* is particularly felicitous. The vintage Decca recording, with the organ entering spectacularly in the finale, is outstanding, and the cassette is excellent too, every bit as vivid and only marginally less rich.

Previn uniquely but imaginatively couples Elgar's most popular orchestral work with what are probably the two most popular pieces of Vaughan Williams. This *Enigma* is not entirely idiomatic, but it is refreshingly spontaneous. The points which may initially strike the Elgarian as unusual, particularly on the question of speed fluctuation, result from a literal reading of the score, the proverbial 'new look'. In some ways it is a similar reading to that of Monteux with the same orchestra, strong and consistent, noble rather than passionate. The recording is impressively ample, and the cassette transfer is comparably full-blooded.

Marriner's reading is commendably clean-cut, but it was perverse of Philips to record this piece with the Concertgebouw. For all the refinement of their playing, they fail to convey a consistent development of structure and tension. The finale starts on side two, and the coupling is limited to only three of the *Marches*. The recording is wide-ranging but has some unnaturally close balancing. The cassette transfer is bass-heavy, and there is a lack of brilliance and bite in the *Marches*.

Monteux's reading is as fresh as ever. Here it is recoupled with Bliss's account of the *Marches*, where rumbustious

vigour is leavened with a proper touch of *nobilmente*. Both recordings have been remastered and now show their age (they were made more than twenty years ago), with thin upper strings. The cassette tends to emphasize this more than the disc.

Violin sonata in E min., Op. 82.
(*) HMV ASD 3820. Y. and H. Menuhin – VAUGHAN WILLIAMS: *Sonata.*(*)

The Menuhins present a large-scale view of this sonata, the least ambitious of Elgar's three late chamber works but one which still brings echoes of the *Violin concerto*. Unfortunately, though slow speeds bring their moments of insight and revelation at the hands of a Menuhin, the result overall is too heavy, and is marred too by imperfect intonation. The recording is first-rate.

VOCAL AND CHORAL MUSIC

Songs: *After; As I laye a-thinkynge; Come, gentle night; In the dawn; Is she not passing fair; The language of flowers; The pipes of Pan; Pleading; Rondel; Shepherd's song; A song of autumn; A song of flight; Speak, music; Through the long days; The wind at dawn.*
(M) ** RCA Gold GL/*GK* 25205. Rayner Cook, Vignoles.

Elgar's songs more than his other music reflect a Victorian background. Their invention is only rarely individual, but they have their charm. Brian Rayner Cook gives somewhat cautious performances – the magic of the enchanting *Shepherd's song*, for example, is missed – but with commendably clear words and sensitive accompaniment this is a collection that is welcome on a mid-price issue, particularly with well-balanced recording on disc and cassette alike.

Angelus; Ave Maria; Fear not, O land; Give unto the Lord (Psalm 29); *Go, song of mine; Great is the Lord* (Psalm 48); *I sing the birth; O harken thou; O salutaris hostia; They are at rest.*
*** Abbey ABY 822. Worcester Cath. Ch., Hunt; Trepte; Hill (organ).

Framed by two very grand Psalm settings (designed for Westminster Abbey and St Paul's Cathedral respectively) this admirable selection of Elgar church music covers an area seriously neglected on record. The Worcester Cathedral Choir, faithfully and atmospherically recorded (but not in a washy cathedral acoustic), sings with fine fresh tone. Grandeur is given to the Psalms (both settings from the high peak of Elgar's maturity) and tenderness to the shorter pieces, of which *Go, song of mine* (not strictly religious) is the finest.

Ave verum corpus; Ecce sacerdos magnus; Great is the Lord (Psalm 48).
** Abbey LPB 813. Leeds Parish Church Ch., Lindley; Corfield (organ) – LISZT: *Via crucis.***

The *Ave verum corpus* is an early work, and so is *Ecce sacerdos magnus* (the latter is not otherwise available). *Psalm 48*, a later work, is rather more impressive; the early pieces do not wholly escape the charge of sounding sanctimonious, and they do not really show the master at his most inspired. Good choral singing and a decent accompaniment from the organist, Tom Corfield.

From the Bavarian Highlands, Op. 27.
*** HMV ASD/TC-ASD 4061. Bournemouth Ch. and SO, Del Mar – VAUGHAN WILLIAMS: *In Windsor Forest.****

The three *Bavarian dances* for orchestra, which Elgar extracted from this suite of part songs, are well known, but not the original choral work, which is as effective as it is enjoyable. Here, although the recording is agreeably rich and full-bodied, balances are not always ideal, with the choral descant in the *Lullaby* third movement outweighing the orchestral detail. However, the performances are infectiously spirited, conveying warmth as well as vigour. The cassette is rather less clean in focus than the disc, but still sounds well.

The Light of Life (oratorio), *Op. 29.*
*** HMV ASD/TC-ASD 3952. Marshall, Watts, Leggate, Shirley-Quirk, Royal Liv. Ch. and PO, Groves.

The Light of Life was one of the works immediately preceding the great leap forward which Elgar made with *Enigma* in 1899. This compact oratorio – telling the story of Jesus giving sight to the blind man – has many foretastes of *The Dream of Gerontius*, but with an uninspired libretto, the overall flavour has something of updated Mendelssohn rather than pure Elgar. The fine opening prelude, *Meditation*, is the only passage that is at all well-known, but that includes some of the finest, most memorable motifs. The tenor aria for the blind man is almost operatic in its intensity, but the attempt to dramatize the incident is so naive that the modern listener may well remain unconvinced. Otherwise there is a fine baritone aria for Jesus, *I am the good shepherd*, and much else to delight the committed Elgarian. Sir Charles Groves's understanding performance features four first-rate soloists and strongly committed, if not always flawless, playing and singing from the Liverpool orchestra and choir. The recording is warm and atmospheric in EMI's recognizable Elgar manner. The cassette transfer is good, but made at rather a modest level for EMI, especially on side two, where the choral climaxes have a reduced sharpness of focus and the soloists less presence.

Songs: *Pleading; The river; The torch; 3 Songs, Op. 59.*
*** HMV ASD/*TC-ASD* 3896. Tear, CBSO, Handley – BUTTERWORTH: *Love Blows as the Wind****; VAUGHAN WILLIAMS: *On Wenlock Edge.***(*)

At his most creative period in the early years of the century Elgar planned another song cycle to follow *Sea Pictures*, but he completed only three of the songs, his Op. 59. The other three songs here are even more individual, a fine coupling for the Vaughan Williams. Incisive and characterful performances from Tear, and good recording, warm and atmospheric on disc and cassette alike.

Sea Pictures, Op. 37.
(M) **(*) CBS 61891/40-. Minton, LPO, Barenboim – BERLIOZ: *La Mort de Cléopâtre.***(*).

(i) *Sea Pictures. Pomp and Circumstance marches, Op. 39/1–5.*
*** CfP CFP/*TC-CFP* 40363. LPO, Handley, (i) with Greevy.

Bernadette Greevy – in glorious voice – gives the performance of her recording career in an inspired partnership with Vernon Handley, whose accompaniments are no less memorable, with the LPO players finding a wonderful rapport with the voice. The singer's imaginative illumination of the words is a constant source of delight and her tenderness in the *Sea slumber song* and the delightfully idyllic *In haven* contrasts with the splendour of the big central and final songs, where Handley revels in the music's surging momentum. Here he uses a telling ad lib organ part to underline the climaxes of each final stanza. The recording balance is ideal, the voice rich and clear against an orchestral background shimmering with atmospheric

detail. The coupled *Marches* are exhilaratingly brilliant, and if Nos. 2 and (especially) 3 strike some ears as too vigorously paced, comparison with the composer's own tempi reveals an authentic precedent. Certainly the popular *First* and *Fourth* have an attractive gutsy grandiloquence. The recording is again excellent. The cassette matches the disc closely, but the *Sea Pictures* is slightly less refined on top (although the difference is marginal).

Yvonne Minton uses her rich tone sensitively in Elgar's orchestral song cycle. There is less passion and less subtlety in her reading than in Janet Baker's (HMV ASD/*TC-ASD* 655 or ASD 2721 [Ang. S 36796], coupled with the *Cello concerto* or Mahler *Rückert Lieder* respectively); but Barenboim is a persuasive Elgarian, and this makes a welcome medium-priced coupling with the Berlioz scena. Colourful recording, not ideally subtle, and a good tape transfer with the voice well caught.

Falla, Manuel de
(1876–1946)

(i) *Harpsichord concerto;* (ii) *Psyché;* (ii; iii) *Master Peter's puppet show (El retablo de Maese Pedro).*
*** Argo ZRG 921. (i) Constable, (ii) Jennifer Smith, (iii) Oliver, Knapp; L. Sinf., Rattle.
*** Erato STU 70713. (i) Veyron-Lacroix, (ii) Higueras-Aragon, (iii) Cabrera, Bermudez; Instrumental Ens., Dutoit.

Simon Rattle and the London Sinfonietta have exactly the same coupling as Dutoit on Erato. There is little to choose between them: the orchestral response in the Argo version is every bit as incisive, alive and characterful as Dutoit's, and the Argo singers – particularly Jennifer Smith as the boy – are if anything even better. John Constable is an admirable interpreter of the *Concerto*, though his instrument is more reticently balanced than Robert Veyron-Lacroix, who also recorded it in the early days of stereo as well as for Dutoit. Those who want the greater presence of a more forward harpsichord should choose the Erato, where Veyron-Lacroix plays with elegance and panache, but there is no doubting the truth and subtlety of the Argo balance, or the excellence of the performance. *Psyché*, also common to both discs, is a setting of words by Jean Aubry for voice and a small instrumental grouping of the size used in the *Harpsichord concerto*. Though honours are pretty evenly divided here, Rattle's Argo disc has a marginal lead over its distinguished rival.

El amor brujo (*Love, the Magician;* ballet): complete.
(M) *** Decca Jub. JB/*KJBC* 50 [Lon. STS 15358]. Mistral, New Philh. O., Frühbeck de Burgos – GRANADOS: *Goyescas*; RAVEL: *Alborada* etc.***
(M) **(*) RCA Gold GL/*GK* 13792 [AGL 1/*AGK 1* 3792]. Leontyne Price, Chicago SO, Reiner – BERLIOZ: *Nuits d'été.***

Frühbeck de Burgos provides us with a completely recommendable version of *El amor brujo*. His superbly graduated crescendo after the spiky opening is immediately compelling, and the control of atmosphere in the quieter music is masterly. Equally the *Ritual fire dance* is blazingly brilliant. Nati Mistral has the vibrant open-throated production of the real flamenco singer. She is less polished than Los Angeles in her HMV version, but if anything the music sounds more authentic this way. Brilliant sound, a trifle light in the bass, but offering luminous textures in the quieter sections. The cassette transfer, made at a high level, is admirably vivid.

Reiner's version, from a vintage period with the Chicago orchestra, is a fiery and colourful account, with recording well over twenty years old but still sounding amazingly good. But Leontyne Price's contribution finds her (as in the Berlioz coupling) well below her commanding best. The cassette transfer is bright and lively, but also slightly harsh.

The Three-cornered Hat: suites Nos. 1 and 2.
*** HMV Dig. ASD/*TC-ASD* 3902 [Ang. DS/*4ZS* 37742]. Phd. O., Muti – CHABRIER: *España*; RAVEL: *Rapsodie.***
(*) Decca SXL/*KSXC* 6956. LAPO, Lopez-Cobós – CHABRIER: *España*; RIMSKY-KORSAKOV: *Capriccio.*

Muti's reading of the colourful Falla ballet is characteristically thrustful, lacking just a little in rhythmic subtlety but making up for that in bite. The two suites incorporate the greater part of the ballet, with *The Corregidor*, *The Miller's Wife* and *The Grapes* sections complete. The recording, typically reverberant, is among the finest yet from Philadelphia. The chrome cassette transfer is astonishingly brilliant, the resonant acoustic having no detrimental effect on the inner detail.

Helped by an extremely vivid recording (the opening timpani are arresting) and understanding conducting from Jesus Lopez-Cobós, with nicely managed rhythmic inflections, the Decca version is undoubtedly enjoyable, as the orchestral playing is lively, though not absolutely first-class. But Muti's Philadelphia coupling is outstanding in every way and the glittering digital sound is even more spectacular. The Decca cassette is very well managed; if anything the sound is richer than the disc, without loss of sparkle.

Fauré, Gabriel (1845-1924)

Ballade for piano and orchestra, Op. 19; Berceuse for violin and orchestra, Op. 16; Caligula, Op. 52; Les Djinns (orchestral version), Op. 12; Élégie for cello and orchestra, Op. 24; Fantaisie for piano and orchestra, Op. 111; Masques et bergamasques (complete), Op. 112; Pelléas et Mélisande (incidental music), Op. 80; Pénélope: Prélude; Shylock, Op. 57.
*** HMV SLS 5219 (3). Collard, Yan-Pascal and Paul Tortelier, Von Stade, Gedda, Bourbon Vocal Ens., Toulouse Capitole O., Plasson.

Although Fauré's most deeply characteristic thoughts are intimate rather than public, and his most natural outlets are the mélodie, chamber music and the piano, this set of his orchestral music nonetheless contains much that is highly rewarding. It includes the delightful Masques et bergamasques and the Pelléas et Mélisande and Shylock music as well as such rarities as Les Djinns and Caligula. The Orchestre du Capitole de Toulouse may lack the finesse and bloom of the leading Parisian orchestras, but Michel Plasson gets an alert and spirited response and is blessed with very decent orchestral sound. He shows a genuine feeling for the Faurean sensibility, and the fine-spun lyricism of the Nocturne from Shylock is well conveyed. The two works from piano and orchestra are particularly valuable; Jean-Philippe Collard gives a really distinguished account of both the early Ballade and the seldom heard Fantaisie, Op. 111. This is a lovely set in every way, though the piano sound is a trifle hard (not the playing, of course); but it can be tamed with some treble cut. This collection contains many delights and cannot be too warmly recommended.

Ballade for piano and orchestra, Op. 19; Fantaisie for piano and orchestra, Op. 111; Pelléas et Mélisande, Op. 80: suite.
(M) * Turn. TVS 34587. Johannesen, R. Lux. O., Froment.

On the face of it this is a most useful coupling, bringing together Fauré's only two works for piano and orchestra, the Ballade of 1881 and the late Fantaisie of 1919, a subtle and aristocratic piece that is somewhat slower to reveal its secrets than the Ballade. Grant Johannesen recorded the Fantaisie with Goossens in the late 1950s and is thoroughly inside the Fauré style. Both pieces together occupy one side, while the other is given over to the suite from Pelléas et Mélisande. The playing is not quite as polished and refined as one would like, but the recording, which tends to compress dynamics and iron them out to a much narrower range, rarely falling to a real piano or pianissimo, does not help matters. Much of the delicacy and gentleness of Fauré's art are lost as a result of unrelieved stretches of mezzo forte.

Fantaisie for flute and orchestra (arr. Galway).
*** RCA RL/RK 25109 [ARL 1/ARK 1 3777]. Galway, RPO, Dutoit – CHAMINADE: Concertino; IBERT: Concerto; POULENC: Sonata.***

James Galway's arrangement of a Fantaisie for flute and piano that Fauré composed in the late 1890s makes an appealing fill-up to an enterprising collection of concertante flute works impeccably played and finely recorded. There are two genuine flute concertos here (Ibert and Chaminade) and two arrangements, this and Lennox Berkeley's expert orchestration of Poulenc's Flute sonata. A fine disc and a well-transferred tape that will give great pleasure.

(i) *Masques et bergamasques* (suite), *Op. 112;* (ii) *Pavane, Op. 50;* (i) *Pelléas et Mélisande, Op. 80: suite; Pénélope: Prélude;* (iii) *Impromptu, Op. 86.*

(M) *** Decca Eclipse ECS 805. (i) SRO, Ansermet; (ii) New SO (of London), Agoult; (iii) Ellis.

An admirable introduction to Fauré's orchestral music: Ansermet offers sympathetic and stylish accounts of *Masques et bergamasques* and *Pelléas et Mélisande,* both written for the theatre. The *Prélude* to *Pelléas* must be among the most eloquent and moving pieces written by any French composer, and it is affectingly played here. The disc also has the advantage of a Fauré rarity, the *Prélude* to *Pénélope,* a noble and impressive piece that is alone worth the price of the record, as well as the *Harp impromptu,* Op. 86, elegantly played by Osian Ellis, and the familiar *Pavane.*

(i) *Andante in B flat, Op. 28; Berceuse in D, Op. 16;* (ii) *Cello sonatas Nos. 1 in D min., Op. 109; 2 in G min., Op. 117; Élégie in C min., Op. 24;* (iii) *Fantaisie in C, Op. 79; Morceau de concours in F;* (i) *Morceau de lecture à vue in A;* (ii) *Papillon in A, Op. 77;* (iv) *Piano quartets Nos. 1 in C min., Op. 15; 2 in G min., Op. 45; Piano quintets Nos. 1 in D min., Op. 89; 2 in C min., Op. 115; Piano trio in D min., Op. 120;* (ii) *Romance in A, Op. 69; Serenade, Op. 98; Sicilienne, Op. 78;* (iv) *String quartet in E min., Op. 121;* (i) *Violin sonatas Nos. 1 in A, Op. 13; 2 in E min., Op. 108.*

*** EMI 2C 165 16331/6. Collard, with (i) Dumay, (ii) Lodéon, (iii) Debost, (iv) Parrenin Qt.

In 1971 Erato issued a five-record set of the complete chamber music of Fauré – Tortelier playing the *Cello sonatas,* Jean Hubeau the pianist throughout, Raymond Gallois-Montbrun the violinist, and the Via Nova Quartet – a set that has done excellent service and whose value is enhanced by the perceptive notes of Harry Halbreich. This new EMI survey is even more comprehensive in that it also includes some of the smaller pieces such as Opp. 16, 24, 28, 69, 77–79 and 98, and so runs to an extra record. It has the advantage of a more imaginative pianist in Jean-Philippe Collard as well as other gifted French artists of the younger generation, such as Augustin Dumay and Frédéric Lodéon. Normally there are disadvantages in this kind of compilation, but they are minimized here because so much of this rewarding and civilized music is not widely duplicated in the catalogue. True, there are excellent accounts of the *Violin sonatas* from the Grumiaux/Crossley and Amoyal/Queffélec partnerships and a fine set of the *Cello sonatas* from Tortelier and Heidsieck on HMV. Generally speaking, however, there are no strong rivals in the bigger works such as the *Piano quartets,* and neither of the *Quintets* is available separately. The attractions of the compilation are also enhanced by the generally admirable standard of performance and recording. There are masterpieces hidden away in this set, such as the *String quartet in E minor,* Fauré's last utterance, and it will yield enormous rewards.

Piano trio in D min., Op. 120; (i) *La Bonne Chanson, Op. 61.*

*** CRD CRD 1089/CRDC 4089. Nash Ens., (i) with Sarah Walker.

The characterful warmth and vibrancy of Sarah Walker's voice, not to mention her positive artistry, come out strongly in this beautiful reading of Fauré's early settings of Verlaine, music both tender and ardent. The passion of the inspiration is underlined by the use of a long-neglected version of the cycle in which the composer expanded the accompaniment by adding string quartet and double bass to the original piano. Members of the Nash Ensemble give dedicated performances both of that and of the late and rarefied *Piano trio*, capturing both the elegance and the restrained concentration. The atmospheric recording is well up to CRD's high standard in chamber music; on cassette there is a hint of edge on the voice in *La Bonne Chanson*, and in the *Piano trio* the resonance brings an inner focus that is slightly less sharp than on disc.

Violin sonatas Nos. 1 in A, Op. 13; 2 in E min., Op. 108.
⊛ *** Ph. 9500 534 [id.]. Grumiaux, Crossley.
*** Erato STU 71195. Amoyal, Queffélec.
(M) ** Sup. 1112 323. Kuronuma, Panenka.

Violin sonata No. 1; Berceuse, Op. 16.
** CBS 76813 [Col. M 35179]. Zukerman, Neikrug – DEBUSSY: *Sonata.***

Four decades separate the two Fauré sonatas and they make a perfect coupling. The *First* is a richly melodious piece which, strangely enough, precedes the César Franck sonata by a dozen or so years, while the *E minor* was written in the same year as Debussy's (1917). They are immensely refined and rewarding pieces, with strange stylistic affinities and disparities: the second movement of the *E minor* actually uses a theme intended for a symphony that Fauré had discarded more than thirty years earlier. Although they have been coupled before (by Barbizet and Ferras, and Gallois-Montbrun and Hubeau), they have never been so beautifully played or recorded as on the Philips issue. Indeed, this is a model of its kind: there is perfect rapport between the two artists, and both seem totally dedicated to and captivated by Fauré's muse. Moreover, they are accorded

recorded quality that is little short of superb. The two artists sound as if they are in the living room; the acoustic is warm, lively and well-balanced. The *Second* is not so readily accessible as the *First* and it is difficult to imagine more persuasive advocacy than this. Unfortunately Fauré is not and never will be a popular composer and it is doubtful whether this record will survive the lifetime of this *Guide*, so do not hesitate.

Pierre Amoyal and Anne Queffélec are hardly less successful in this coupling than Grumiaux and Crossley, but though their performance is just as impassioned (perhaps more so) and no less authoritative, it falls short of the distinction of the Grumiaux. Amoyal plays with great purity of tone and is the equal of Grumiaux in the *First Sonata* but less convincing in the more elusive half-lights of the *E minor*. Queffélec is a splendid player and the result of their partnership is undoubtedly satisfying, as well as being well-recorded. In the absence of the Grumiaux/Crossley disc, this would be a strong first choice.

Yuriko Kuronuma is a persuasive player and she is well supported by Jan Panenka in idiomatic and often eloquent performances. The recording is well-balanced but not particularly distinguished. The Philips issue remains first choice, and both that and the Erato are to be preferred.

Zukerman and Marc Neikrug give a frankly lyrical reading of Op. 13 that may seem to some listeners a little wanting in feeling for the subtleties of the Fauréan sensibility. Others, however, will revel in its wealth of expression and its evident warmth. There is no question of its accomplishment, nor of the excellence of the recording. The artists have a good rapport and both give pleasure. The *Berceuse* is also beautifully played.

Barcarolle No. 2, Op. 41; 8 Short Pieces, Op. 34: Nos. 1, Capriccio; 2, Improvisation; 5, Adagietto. 9 Prel-

udes, *Op. 103; Theme and variations,
Op. 73.*
(M) *** Saga 5466. Ferber.

Fauré's piano music is grievously neglected both in the concert hall and on the gramophone. Neither of the complete surveys, by Evelyne Crochet and (briefly available on Erato) by Jean Doyen, was wholly satisfactory, and it is good to report that this issue is a signal success. Albert Ferber is a sensitive player who penetrates far more deeply into Fauré's often elusive world than any of his rivals past or present on record. This disc is particularly valuable in making available the *Nine Preludes*, Op. 103, composed in 1909–10. These well repay the repeated attention the gramophone affords, for they are not immediately accessible yet are deeply rewarding. The *Theme and variations*, popular with students, is given a well-characterized and finely considered reading too, and there are some welcome smaller pieces. What a fine pianist Albert Ferber is: imaginative, poetic and content to let music speak for itself. He is well-recorded and at such a modest price, this is surely a record not to be missed.

Nocturnes (complete); *Theme and variations, Op. 74.*
*** EMI 2C 069 12575/6. Collard.

This is glorious music which ranges from the gently reflective to the profoundly searching. The *Nocturnes* are thirteen in number, composed over the best part of half a century: the first was sketched at the time of the *First Violin sonata* (1875–6) and the last dates from 1921. They offer a glimpse of Fauré's art at its most inward and subtle; and they take a greater hold of the listener at each hearing, the quiet-spoken reticence proving more eloquent than one would ever suspect at first. Immensely civilized yet never aloof, this music offers balm to the soul. There have been a few complete

recordings before (Eric Heidsieck, Jean Doyen and Evelyne Crochet) but none so wholly identified with the Fauréan sensibility as Jean-Philippe Collard's. His account of the *Theme and variations* is no less masterly, combining the utmost tonal refinement and sensitivity with striking keyboard authority. The recording, which dates from 1974, is good, though it has not the bloom and freshness of the very finest piano records.

La Bonne Chanson, Op. 61 (see also under *Piano trio*).
(M) **(*) Decca Eclipse ECS 810. Danco, Agosti – RAVEL: *Shéhérazade; Mélodies.* **(*)

Suzanne Danco made this recording of *La Bonne Chanson* in the early 1950s; it is in mono and has been transcribed to give a stereo effect in this transfer. Whatever its sonic limitations, collectors will not regret investing in this ravishing performance. It is, of course, true that Danco does not bring the dramatic variety to the cycle that other interpreters have, but the voice has such purity and beauty that criticism is disarmed. The coupling is an added and welcome attraction.

Pelléas et Mélisande (incidental music), *Op. 80.*
*** Ph. 6769 045 (2) [id.]. Gomez, Rotterdam PO, Zinman – SCHOENBERG and SIBELIUS: *Pelléas.* **(*)

To couple together three different orchestral works inspired by Maeterlinck's drama seems a good idea, although not everyone who responds to Fauré and Sibelius will be drawn to the more inflated symphonic poem of Schoenberg (which is also less effective here as a recorded performance). However, Fauré's incidental music is beautifully played, and to make the selection complete Jill Gomez gives a delightful account of the song *The three blind daughters*, not previously recorded.

David Zinman's refined approach suits Fauré admirably, and there is a pervasive tenderness and delicacy (the *Sicilienne* is memorable). The recording too is naturally balanced and of high quality.

Requiem, Op. 43.
(M) *(*) Decca SPA/*KCSP* 504 [Rich. 33168]. Danco, Souzay, L'Union Chorale de la Tour de Peilz, SRO, Ansermet.

Requiem; Cantique de Jean Racine, Op. 11.
*** HMV ASD/*TC-ASD* 3501. Burrowes, Rayner Cook, CBSO Ch. and O., Frémaux.
(M) *** RCA Gold GL/*GK* 25243. Thilliez, Kruysen, Caillard Chorale, Monte Carlo Op. O., Frémaux.

Requiem; Pavane, Op. 50.
*** CBS 76734/40- [Col. M 35153]. Popp, Nimsgern, Amb. S., Philh. O., Andrew Davis.

The directness and clarity of Andrew Davis's reading go with a concentrated, dedicated manner and a masterly control of texture to bring out the purity and beauty of Fauré's orchestration to the full. Moreover the fresh vigour of the choral singing achieves an admirable balance between ecstasy and restraint in this most elusive of requiem settings. The style of the phrasing is not so openly expressive as in some other versions, but that is in character with the intimacy of the reading, culminating in a wonderfully measured and intense account of the final *In Paradisum*. Lucia Popp is both rich and pure, and Siegmund Nimsgern (if less memorable) is refined in tone and detailed in his pointing. The recording, made in a church, matches the intimate manner, and the cassette transfer is one of the finest we have heard from CBS.

Frémaux's HMV version is attractively atmospheric, the recording comparatively recessed. Frémaux has a moulded style which does not spill over in too much expressiveness, and there is a natural warmth about this performance that is highly persuasive. Norma Burrowes sings beautifully; her innocent style is most engaging. On tape the backward balance means that the focus is not as clear as on the CBS version.

Frémaux's RCA recording comes from the 1960s (it was briefly available on World Records) and must be accounted one of the best. It was the first to use a boy treble instead of a female singer, a practice followed by Neville Marriner and David Willcocks. Denis Thilliez gives a touching account of the part, and Bernard Kruysen, who also recorded it later with Fournet, is in fresh and eloquent voice. This is a sensitive and unforced account that has a natural sincerity and dignity that are most appealing. The recording is altogether natural, and readers not prepared to go to a full-price version can rest assured that this modest account will give them much musical satisfaction. It offers the additional bonus of the *Cantique de Jean Racine*. The cassette transfer is acceptable but does not match the disc in clarity and bloom.

Ansermet's version is technically immaculate, but its clarity serves only to emphasize the rather thin-toned contribution of the chorus. The solo singing is still good (even if Danco is no match for Victoria de los Angeles in sheer spiritual beauty), and this may be considered fair value for money at its price. However, the Classics for Pleasure version with Los Angeles and Fischer-Dieskau under Cluytens remains a clear first choice in the bargain range: CFP/*TC-CFP* 40234.

Pénélope (opera; complete).
*** Erato STU 71386 (3). Norman, Taillon, Vanzo, Huttenlocher, Van Dam, LaForge Vocal Ens., Monte Carlo PO, Dutoit.

Pénélope, Fauré's only opera, is a rarity in the theatre and seldom surfaces on the radio. A concert performance mounted by the French Radio in the mid-1950s, with Régine Crespin in good voice and no less a conductor· than Inghelbrecht in charge, has recently appeared in a mono recording, but this Erato issue is the first commercial stereo set. The work itself is often haunting, nearly always noble and rarely uncompelling. Though it is overtly Wagnerian in its adoption of *leitmotiv*, it seldom sounds in the least Wagnerian, and as it was written in the years immediately before the First World War, it has all the harmonic subtlety and refinement of late Fauré. The title role is eloquently sung by Jessye Norman, a beautifully characterized performance, and the singing throughout is first-class. Charles Dutoit secures good ensemble and committed playing from his orchestra, and the only possible criticism would be one or two inconsistencies of balance. The work takes not much more than two hours and could have been accommodated on two records. But such are the musical rewards of this glorious work that readers will not begrudge the price of this set, which moreover has the advantage of an admirable essay by the French Fauré expert, Jean-Michel Nectoux, as well as the usual libretto.

Ferneyhough, Brian
(born 1943)

Transit.
*** Decca HEAD 18 [id.]. Hardy, Hurst, Harrison, Hall, Etheridge, Earle, L. Sinf., Howarth.

The complex and thorny textures of Brian Ferneyhough do not make easy listening, but for the unprejudiced ear there is no doubt of the concentration and depth of feeling in this ambitious work (with Heraclitus and Paracelus

among its sources of inspiration), which leads to a genuinely visionary climax. The impact of the music – strong enough to set the listener searching behind the expressionistic gestures to the inner logic – is greatly enhanced by the singers of the London Sinfonietta, under the dedicated direction of Elgar Howarth; the craggy lines, varied vibrato and glissando effects hold no terrors for them. Excellent recording.

Fibich, Zdeněk (1850–1900)

Symphony No. 2 in E flat, Op. 38.
(M) ** Sup. 4102 165. Brno State PO, Waldhans.

All three of the symphonies that Fibich composed during his fifty years have been recorded at one time or another. The *Second* is the most often played, and though its melodic inspiration is not as fresh or spontaneous as that of Dvořák and Smetana, it has considerable appeal. Fibich's phrase structures tend to be four-square, and the music proceeds at times in a somewhat predictable way, but it is nonetheless congenial and, at its best, as in the scherzo, it is stirring and colourful. The Brno orchestra under Jiří Waldhans give a straightforward performance, though the balance does not flatter the tone of the first desks. Indeed the recording is somewhat opaque, and tutti could be more cleanly defined. In some respects the earlier recording under Karel Sejna had more inner vitality, but this newcomer has more sense of space.

Šárka (opera; complete).
(M) *** Sup. 1416 2781/3. Děpoltová, Přibyl, Randová, Zítek, Brno Janáček Op. Ch. and State PO, Štych.

Much of Fibich's invention is prosaic

and predictable, but there is much that is both endearing and fresh too. *Šárka* is his sixth opera and was composed in 1896–7, during the last years of his short life. In addition to the nationalist element, there is a strong awareness of Wagner too. Although it has never caught on outside Czechoslovakia, it has been recorded before (by the Prague National Opera under Chalabala), but this new version has the advantage of far superior recording and an atmospheric and committed performance. Fibich, though a composer of the second order, is nonetheless far from unrewarding, and there are some colourful and melodically appealing episodes here, even if the quality of the inspiration is not consistent. The music is not as ardent and captivating as Novak's *The Storm* or as searching as the *Asrael symphony* of Suk (to name two lesser-known Czech pieces neglected on record) but readers will still find it worth investigation.

Field, John (1782–1837)

Nocturnes Nos. 1 in E flat; 2 in C min.; 3 in A flat; 4 in A; 5 in B flat; 6 in F; 9 in E flat; 10 in E min.; 12 in G; 13 in D min.; 17 in E.
(*) HMV ASD 3599. Adni.

In the history books Field is best-remembered for inventing the form which Chopin developed into the most poetic of piano genres. It is idle to compare Field's *Nocturnes* with those of Chopin, except in the broadest terms; but Daniel Adni's fresh and sensitive playing, though not always warm enough in its rubato, has one responding to the charm in this well-chosen selection. For samples try No. 4 in A major or the Russian-tinged No. 10. The piano tone is full and firm.

Finzi, Gerald (1901–56)

Cello concerto, Op. 40.
*** Lyr. SRCS 112. Ma, RPO, Handley.

Completed right at the end of Finzi's life, before his premature death at the age of fifty-five, the *Cello concerto* is one of the most ambitious as well as the most searching of all his works, notably in the long first movement, which pointed towards important stylistic developments that were to remain unfulfilled. The central slow movement has Elgarian nobility but also a poignancy that is typical of Finzi. The rondo finale is less concentrated than the other two movements, but completes a work which should certainly be in the repertory alongside the Elgar and Walton concertos. Yo Yo Ma is one of the outstanding cellists of his generation, and though he does not always convey the full power of Finzi's vision, he responds most sensitively, helped by first-rate playing from the RPO under Handley and recording of Lyrita's usual excellence.

Clarinet concerto, Op. 31.
*** Hyp. A/KA 66001. King, Philh. O., Francis – STANFORD: *Concerto.***

(i) *Clarinet concerto;* (ii) *Eclogue for piano and strings, Op. 10; Grand fantasia and toccata, Op. 38.*
(*) Lyr. SRCS 92. New Philh. O., Handley, with (i) Denman, (ii) Katin.

Finzi's *Clarinet concerto*, composed in 1948, is one of his finest works. If it lacks the contemplative qualities of the ambitious *Cello concerto*, its more extrovert character is no less compelling. The expressive intensity of the slow movement communicates immediately, and the joyous pastoral lyricism of the finale has a sharp memorability. On the Hyperion label, Thea King (pupil of the dedicatee of the concerto, Frederick Thurston, who gave the first performance and advised the composer during composition) gives a definitive performance, strong and clean-cut. Her characterful timbre, using little or no vibrato, is highly telling against a resonant (marginally too resonant) orchestral backcloth. The accompaniment of the Philharmonia under Alun Francis is sympathetic, bringing out the amiability of the finale in fine contrast to the eloquent *Adagio*. Even though the orchestral recording lacks sharpness of internal focus, there is a vivid overall projection. The cassette transfer is of demonstration quality, virtually identical with the LP. With Stanford's even rarer concerto this makes a most attractive issue.

The two works for piano and orchestra included on the Lyrita disc both date from the late 1920s and show a different side to Finzi's personality; they are less searching and individual than the *Clarinet concerto*, but they make an interesting coupling. John Denman gives an eloquent account of the work for clarinet, and the two earlier pieces are well served by Peter Katin and the orchestra under Vernon Handley. The Lyrita recording has clarity and definition to commend it and (apart from an ugly tape edit) is flawless.

The Fall of the Leaf (Elegy for orchestra), Op. 20. (i) *Introit for small orchestra and solo violin. Love's Labour's Lost (suite), Op. 28: 3 Soliloquies for small orchestra; Nocturne (New Year music), Op. 7; Prelude for string orchestra, Op. 25; Romance for string orchestra, Op. 11; A Severn rhapsody, Op. 3.*
*** Lyr. SRCS 84. LPO, Boult, (i) with Friend.

This collection of shorter orchestral works has some charming miniatures, the music reflecting the wistful, often death-obsessed side of Finzi's character: thus in the *Nocturne* the New Year brings regret rather than celebration. The pure beauty of the *Introit* (surviving movement from a violin concerto whose outer movements were withdrawn) and the easy Englishness of the *Severn rhapsody* are equally characteristic, implying more than they seem to. Boult's affectionate performances are superbly recorded, and Rodney Friend is an understanding soloist in the concerto movement.

Choral music: *All this night; God is gone up, Op. 27; Lo, the full, final sacrifice; Magnificat, Op. 36; 7 Partsongs, Op. 17; 3 Short Elegies, Op. 5.*
**(*) O-L DSLO 32. Exultate Singers, O'Brien; Farrell (organ).

Finzi's gentle art is beautifully represented in this collection of choral pieces, some of them mere fragments but all finely reflecting the cadences of English words, whether in religious or secular texts. Garrett O'Brien draws lively performances from the Exultate Singers, not always perfectly disciplined but very well recorded.

Dies natalis; For St Cecilia.
**(*) Argo ZRG 896 [id.]. Langridge, LSO Ch., LSO, Hickox.

Dies natalis is one of Finzi's most sensitive, deeply felt works, using contemplative texts on the theme of Chirst's nativity by the seventeenth-century writer Thomas Traherne. Finzi's profound response to the words inspires five intensely beautiful songs; only the central *Rapture*, subtitled *Danza*, provides vigorous contrast to the mood of contemplation. The cantata commissioned for the annual St Cecilia's Day celebration in 1947 is an altogether more external work, but even there Finzi was able to respond individually to the text specially written by his contemporary Edmund Blunden. The performances in their contrasted moods are both strong and convincing, though an earlier version of *Dies natalis* (now deleted) with the late Wilfred Brown was even more searching. The Argo recording is excellent.

(i) *Farewell to Arms, Op. 9;* (ii) *In Terra Pax;* (iii) *Let Us Garlands Bring, Op. 18;* (i) *2 Sonnets by John Milton, Op. 12.*
*** Lyr. SRCS 93. (i) Partridge; (ii) John Alldis Ch.; (iii) Carol Case; New Philh. O., Handley.

Very few composers, even those with the deepest insights into English lyric poetry, have been able to put great sonnets into a fitting musical setting. Finzi – who actually turned Wordsworth's *Intimations of Immortality* into a successful choral work – here sets highly compressed Milton sonnets in a way that genuinely intensifies the words, reflecting the composer's own intimations of death at the time of composition. They are beautifully sung by Ian Partridge, who is also the soloist in the introduction and aria *Farewell to Arms. In terra pax* is a Christmas cantata in miniature, charming in Finzi's most relaxed folk-based style; *Let Us Garlands Bring* has John Carol Case as soloist in five Shakespeare lyrics, delicate and individual. A valuable collection which helps to fill in the complex personality of a minor composer who is still under-appreciated. Excellent recording.

Flotow, Friedrich (1812–83)

Martha (complete).
⊛ *** Ar. Eur. 25422 (3)/*ZC 500217.* Popp, Soffel, Jerusalem, Nimsgern, Ridderbusch, Bav. R. Ch. and O., Wallberg.
**(*)EMI 1C 19730241/3. Rothenberger,

Fassbaender, Gedda, Prey, Weller, Bav. State Op. Ch. and O., Heger.

Martha is a charming opera that should be much better known in England than it is. The delicacy of its story, set in and around Richmond in the reign of Queen Anne, allows for moments of broader humour which are not so far distant from the world of Gilbert and Sullivan, and there are always the established favourite numbers to look forward to, culminating in the often repeated but still exquisite *Letzte Rose – The last rose of summer.*

The Eurodisc cast is as near perfect as could be imagined. Lucia Popp is a splendid Lady Harriet, the voice rich and full (her *Letzte Rose* is radiant) yet riding the ensembles with jewelled accuracy. Doris Soffel is no less characterful as Nancy, and Siegfried Jerusalem is in his element as the hero, Lionel, singing ardently throughout. Not only is his famous *Ach! so fromme* a superb highlight; the *Gute Nacht* sequence which becomes the *Mitternacht notturno* is glorious, a quartet to equal almost any rival in operatic magic. Siegmund Nimsgern is an excellent Lord Tristan, and Karl Ridderbusch matches his genial gusto, singing Plunkett's *Porter-Lied* with weight as well as *brio*. Wallberg's direction is marvellously spirited, and the opera gathers pace as it proceeds; the first-act finale is taken at a fizzing tempo, and the drama and passion of Acts 3 and 4 bring genuine grandeur. The Bavarian Radio Chorus sings with joyous precision and the orchestral playing sparkles. With first-class recording, full and vivid, this is highly recommended. The cassettes are very lively too, and even without a libretto it is a marvellously entertaining set, with the soaring choral finale leaving any romantically inclined listener in a state of satisfied exhilaration.

The Electrola recording (once available in the UK on HMV SLS 944) is not ideal, but captures the right atmosphere and still gives pleasure. Curiously, the veteran conductor Robert Heger, for all the

305

delicacy of his pointing, sometimes chooses slow tempi, and Gedda as Lionel is a little stiff; but otherwise there is a stylishness and a jollity all round, with Rothenberger in clear, fresh voice as the heroine and Brigitte Fassbaender excellent as Nancy. Prey, agreeably expressive in a light-toned way, makes a youthful-sounding Plunkett. Minimal cuts and bright, atmospheric recording.

Foerster, Josef (1859–1951)

Cyrano de Bergerac (suite), Op. 55.
(M) **(*) Sup. 1110 2456. Czech P.O, Smetáček.

Josef Bohuslav Foerster was a highly respected figure in Czech musical life during his long career. He died in Prague at the age of ninety-one. Though his music bears the same national stamp as Dvořák, Smetana and Janáček, his years in Hamburg and Vienna (where he was a friend of Mahler) lend his music a more cosmopolitan flavour. His *Fourth Symphony* (1905) has an Elgarian nobility, and its scherzo, which shows a delightful fecundity of invention, was recorded by both Kubelik and Smetáček. *Cyrano de Bergerac*, which bears an adjacent opus number to the symphony, caused something of a stir in the first decade of this century, and like the symphony it is the product of a refined and cultivated musical mind. There is a warm lyrical feel to the music which mingles Strauss and other post-romantic influences with Czech nationalism. As is the case with the symphony, the best movements are the first two; there is less concentration and more self-indulgence in the later movements. The playing of the Czech Philharmonic is alert and vital, but the recording is acceptable rather than distinguished; the climaxes tend to be a little opaque, and the overall image could be more

finely detailed. Nonetheless this is a record that will give pleasure.

Foulds, John (1880–1939)

String quartets Nos. 9 (Quartetto intimo), Op. 89; 10 (Quartetto geniale), Op. 97. Aquarelles, Op. 32.
⊗ *** Pearl SHE 564. Endellion Qt.

This superb first recording by the Endellion Quartet, one of the outstanding groups of its generation, brings an exciting rediscovery. John Foulds, born in Manchester, was early recognized for his serious work, not least by Hans Richter, conductor of the Hallé, but he later came to be known best for his light music. Then, withdrawing to India in the thirties, he continued the impressive series of string quartets he had begun in his youth. The *Quartetto intimo*, written in 1931, is a powerful five-movement work in a distinctive idiom more advanced than that of Foulds's British contemporaries, with echoes of Scriabin and Bartók. Also on the disc is the one surviving movement of his tenth and last quartet, a dedicated hymn-like piece, as well as three slighter pieces from earlier. Passionate performances and excellent recording.

Françaix, Jean (born 1912)

(i) *Piano concerto;* (ii) *Rhapsody for viola and small orchestra;* (iii) *Suite for violin and orchestra.*
(M) **(*) Turn. TVS 34552 [id.]. R. Lux. O., composer, with (i) Paillard-Françaix; (ii) Koch; (iii) Lautenbacher.

This useful disc fills a significant gap

in the catalogue. The music of Jean Françaix in unaccountably neglected; at its best, as in the delightful *Concertino* for piano and orchestra or the ballet *La Dame dans la lune*, it has an irrepressible charm and high spirits. The *Piano concerto*, which occupies the first side here, dates from 1936; the night-club exuberance in its first movement and its general air of carefree gaiety at times recall Milhaud, though the scoring is lighter than in many of the latter's works. It has the authority of the composer's direction and his daughter's advocacy at the keyboard; Françaix recorded it himself in the days of 78s, with Nadia Boulanger conducting, but this performance naturally is better-recorded and it has more charm. The second side is occupied by the early *Suite for violin and orchestra* (1932) and a post-war viola *Rhapsody* (mislabelled on the actual record as for violin instead of viola). There is a nice mixture of whimsy and a certain wistful melancholy throughout these pieces. The performances are good, though the orchestral playing could have a little more finish. The sound is reasonably well-balanced and has greater dynamic range than is sometimes encountered on this label. A rewarding and recommendable issue.

Wind quintet.
(M) *** Decca Ace SDD 555. V. Wind Soloists – TAFFANEL: *Quintet.****

Urbane and slight though Françaix may be, this *Wind quintet* from 1948 will give pleasure to all with a penchant for French music. It has wit and inventiveness to commend it and is refreshingly unpretentious. It is nicely played and recorded here.

Franck, César (1822–90)

Les Djinns; Symphonic variations (both for piano and orch.).

*** HMV ASD/*TC-ASD* 3960. Ortiz, Philh. O., Ashkenazy – GRIEG: *Concerto.***

The *Symphonic variations* show the best of the partnership between Ortiz and Ashkenazy, with its attractive combination of sparkle and expressive qualities; there is undoubted spontaneity here. *Les Djinns* does not quite live up to the promise of its powerfully evocative opening, but that is the composer's fault rather than that of the performers, who give a fully characterized reading, with telling delicacy in the closing section. The recording is vivid and brilliant; the cassette too is outstanding, bright and clear, yet with fine body and natural piano timbre. It is a pity that the coupling is much less recommendable.

Symphonic variations.
(M) *** Decca JB/*KJBC* 104 [Lon. STS 15407/5-]. Curzon, LSO, Boult – GRIEG: *Concerto*; LITOLFF: *Scherzo.****

(i) *Symphonic variations. Symphony in D min.*
(B) **(*) CfP CFP/*TC-CFP* 40347. Bournemouth SO, Berglund, (i) with Kersenbaum.
(M) **(*) Turn. TVS 34663 [id./*CT 2125*]. RPO, Dorati, (i) with Alpenheim.

Curzon's Decca performance of the *Symphonic variations* has stood the test of time. It is an engagingly fresh reading, without idiosyncrasy, and can be recommended unreservedly, particularly as the couplings are equally brilliantly done. The recording is beautifully clear and vivid; disc and cassette are very closely matched, and there is certainly no loss of quality or range on tape.
The reissue of the HMV Bournemouth coupling (recorded as recently as 1977) on Classics for Pleasure makes a formidable bargain. Berglund directs a rugged performance of a symphony which is

usually regarded as a product of the hot-house. There are even hints of Sibelius. It is an approach which to some ears grows the more attractive with repetition, strong and expressive in style of phrasing, with tempi evenly maintained. However, the comparatively slow speeds in the outer movements do bring a loss of romantic urgency, and some will find this lack of impulse a serious drawback. The playing is not always perfectly polished, but with a warm-blooded performance of the *Variations*, full of fantasy and poetry from the soloist, it makes an attractive coupling. The cassette has been re-mastered since the original full-priced issue, and there is now no appreciable difference in sound between disc and tape.

Dorati's approach in the *Symphony* is a good deal more volatile, and in essence his reading is straightforwardly vigorous. The slow movement is paced fairly quickly too, but there is effective delicacy from the RPO strings and wind soloists. The finale catches fire and has striking impetus. Ilse von Alpenheim's account of the *Variations* is essentially lyrical. It undoubtedly has poetry, but the closing pages lack the last degree of momentum and sparkle. The recording of the piano has more body and bloom than one expects on this label, and the *Symphony* too is clear and well-balanced.

Symphony in D min.
(M) *** HMV SXLP/*TC-SXLP* 30256 [Ang. Sera. S 60012]. Fr. Nat. RO, Beecham.
(M) *** DG 2535/*3335* 156 [id.]. Berlin RSO, Maazel.
** Ph. 9500 605/*7300 727* [id.]. Concg. O., De Waart.

Choice between Beecham and Maazel is not easy. Beecham's version dates from the early sixties, Maazel's from the late sixties and the DG recording has an advantage, although the HMV reissue sounds both robust and clear. With Beecham the sheer gusto of the outer

movements is exhilarating, and even though Sir Thomas's treatment of the second subject of the first movement is somewhat indulgent, the interpretation remains highly convincing. There are expressive mannerisms in the slow movement too, but Beecham conjures eloquent playing from the orchestra and maintains a high level of tension. In some ways Maazel's straighter version is more effective, but Beecham's magnetism is compelling, and this version – however idiosyncratic – will be first choice for all those who admire his special feeling for French music. The HMV tape transfer is lively if a little fierce.

Maazel's account is beautifully shaped both in its overall structure and in incidental details. Yet though each phrase is sensitively moulded, there is no sense of self-conscious striving for beauty of effect. Maazel adopts a fairly brisk tempo in the slow movement, which, surprisingly enough, greatly enhances its poetry and dignity; his finale is also splendidly vital and succeeds in filtering out the excesses of grandiose sentiment and vulgarity that disfigure this edifice. The work gains enormously from the strong control and deliberate understatement as well as the refinement of tone and phrasing that mark this reading. (Paray also used to be particularly impressive in this way.) The recording is admirably well-blended and musically balanced. The cassette transfer is splendid: the sound, full yet lively in range and detail, is every bit the equal of the disc.

Edo de Waart's performance is well-prepared and has undoubted romantic feeling, and the Concertgebouw Orchestra plays beautifully, especially in the slow movement. However, this version lacks the charisma of Beecham's (though it is much better-recorded) and the thrust of Maazel's; nor does it have the expressive power and weight of Karajan's (HMV ASD 2552 [Ang. S 36729]). The cassette matches the excellent recorded quality of the disc, vivid and well-balanced.

Cello sonata in A (trans. of *Violin sonata*).
(*) CRD CRD 1091/*CRDC 4091.* Robert Cohen, Vignoles – GRIEG: *Cello sonata.*(*)

Cohen gives a firm and strong rendering of the Franck *Sonata* in its cello version, lacking a little in fantasy in the outer movements but splendidly incisive and dashing in the second movement *Allegro.* The Grieg coupling is attractive and apt, but the recording is more limited than one expects from CRD, a little shallow. The high-level cassette transfer is impressively close to the disc in balance and range.

Piano quintet in F min.
**(*) HMV ASD 3546. Ortiz, Medici Qt.

Cristina Ortiz and the Medici Quartet give a vigorous, outward-going performance of a work which has often seemed to be cloaked in thick Victorian sentiment. The result is refreshing if not always idiomatic, rather missing the more poetic side of Franck's inspiration. There is no modern rival in the catalogue, only the aged but superbly sensitive account by Curzon and the Vienna Philharmonic Quartet (Decca SDD 277); so, with its full and firm recording, this makes a good stopgap.

String quartet in D.
⊛ *** O-L DSLO 46. Fitzwilliam Qt.

Franck's *Quartet*, highly ambitious in its scale, its almost orchestral textures and its complex use of cyclic form, always seems on the point of bursting the seams of the intimate genre of the string quartet. Yet as a very late inspiration it contains some of the composer's most profound, most compelling thought, and this magnificent performance by the Fitzwilliam Quartet, superbly triumphing over the technical challenge with totally dedicated, passionately convinced playing, completely silences any reservations. In every sense this is a work which seeks to take up the challenge presented by late Beethoven in a way that few nineteenth-century composers attempted, not even Brahms. Richly recorded, with the thick textures nicely balanced, this is one of the finest chamber records of the 1980s.

Violin sonata in A.
⊛ *** Decca SXL/*KSXC* 6944 [Lon. 7171]. Kyung-Wha Chung, Lupu – DEBUSSY: *Sonata.* ⊛ ***
*** DG 2531/*3301* 330 [id.]. Danczowska, Zimerman – SZYMANOWSKI: *Myths* etc.***
(*) Ph. 9500 568 [id.]. Grumiaux, Sebök – GRIEG: *Sonata.*

Kyung-Wha Chung and Radu Lupu give a superb account, full of a natural and not over-projected eloquence and most beautifully recorded. The slow movement has marvellous repose and the other movements have a natural exuberance and sense of line that carry the listener with them. The quality of the recorded sound is very distinguished indeed, completely natural in perspective and thoroughly lifelike in timbre and colour. The Franck is, incidentally, accommodated on one side: as the Debussy is so short, readers might well imagine it was split over two. The cassette also offers demonstration quality and is the equal of the disc. Among recent versions this undoubtedly stands out.

Kaja Danczowska was a pupil of Eugenia Uminska and the late David Oistrakh, and on the evidence of this record she is an artist to reckon with. Her account of the Franck is distinguished by a fine sense of line and great sweetness of tone, and she is superbly partnered by Krystian Zimerman. Indeed, in terms of dramatic fire and strength of line, this version can hold its own alongside the finest, and it is perhaps marginally better-balanced than the Kyung-Wha Chung and Radu Lupu recording, where the violinist is slightly backward. This issue also has a particularly interesting coupling and would be worth acquiring on that score alone. The cassette transfer is first-class, both atmospheric and with good range and clarity. Strongly recommended.

There is such plentiful competition in the Franck *Sonata*, though not in the Grieg, which is the coupling on the Philips disc, that one wonders whether a new recording, even from so distinguished an artist as Arthur Grumiaux, is worthwhile. Yet his version, if less fresh than Kyung-Wha Chung's, has nobility and warmth to commend it. He is slightly let down by his partner, who is not as imaginative as Lupu or Zimerman in the more poetic moments, including the hushed opening bars. And, while Grumiaux's purity of line is to be admired throughout, his playing is not quite as inspired as we remember from his earlier record, made in the 1960s with István Hajdu. The balance very slightly favours the violin, but the overall sound is thoroughly lifelike in the best tradition of the house.

Prelude, chorale and fugue.
*** RCA RL/*RK* 13342 [ARL/*A RK* 13342]. Rubinstein (piano) – BACH: *Chaconne*; MOZART: *Rondo*.***

In music such as this, strangely poised between classic form and romantic expression, between the piano and the organ loft, no one is more persuasive than Rubinstein. This performance, recorded (like the Bach) in Rome in 1970, has fire and spontaneity. The piano tone is a little clangy on both disc and cassette.

Organ music: *3 Chorales (in E; B min.; A min.); Interlude symphonique de Rédemption; 3 Pièces (Fantaisie in A; Cantabile; Pièce héroïque); 6 Pièces (Fantaisie No. 1 in C, Op. 16; Grande pièce symphonique, Op.*

17; Prélude, fugue et variation, Op. 18; Pastorale, Op. 19; Prière, Op. 20; Final, Op. 21).
*** Erato STU 71035/7 (without *Interlude*). Alain (organ of St-François-de-Sales, Lyons).
*** O-L D 165 D 3 (3). Steed (organs of Bath Abbey; Holy Rude, Stirling).

These two sets of records include all of Franck's most important works for the organ: the *Six Pieces* written between 1860 and 1862 (Op. 16–21), the *Three Pieces* of 1878 and the *Three Chorales* of 1890, written in the last year of the composer's life. Though they are so obviously designed for the Cavaillé-Coll instruments with which Franck was associated all his life, Graham Steed makes them sound highly effective at the organ of Bath Abbey; his fill-up on side six is devoted to a transcription by Marcel Dupré of the orchestral interlude from *Rédemption*, recorded on the organ of the Holy Rude, Stirling. Steed has devoted a lifetime of study to these works and plays with evident authority, though some may feel that he moves the music on a little too much in the *Chorales*, where phrases could afford to breathe more expansively. Textures, however, are always clear and beautifully focused, and the recording, engineered by the late Michael Smythe, offers most impressive detail and a vivid sense of presence.

Marie-Claire Alain uses a Cavaillé-Coll that is virtually unaltered since it was built in 1879. The Cavaillé-Coll instruments are as closely related to Franck's muse as, say, Peter Pears' voice was to Britten's, and in this respect Marie-Claire Alain enjoys a distinct advantage over her rival. And it is not only the instrument which makes the Erato issue so distinguished; the sympathy which this player brings to the music and the authority of the results give it a special claim on the allegiance of collectors. The quality of sound achieved by the engineers is very good.

Chorale No. 1 in E; Prière, Op. 20.
**(*) HMV Dig. ASD/*TC-ASD* 3994
[Ang. DS 37748]. Parker-Smith (organ
of St Francis de Sales, Philadelphia) –
LISZT: *Ad nos.***(*)

Two of Franck's most characteristic
organ works here make an apt coupling for the Liszt *Fantasia.* Less aptly
the hazy opulence of the sound puts an
impressionistic cloud round the music,
spectacular as its range is. The cassette
transfer is astonishingly successful in its
wide dynamic contrast and atmosphere,
even if the sound – as on the disc – is
not sharply defined.

Grande pièce symphonique, Op. 17.
**(*) Abbey LPB 792. Cleobury (West-
minster Abbey organ) – DURUFLÉ:
*Suite.***(*)

Apart from the collections of Franck's
major works for the organ, separate listings of the *Grande pièce symphonique*
have been relatively few. Stephen Cleobury's account of this powerful work
succeeds in evoking its sense of mystical
fervour, though here the somewhat
distant balance diminishes the impact of
the piece a little. The actual balance is
admirable, no attempt being made to
compress the wide dynamic range of the
instrument, and the attraction of the disc
is enhanced by the interest of the coupling.

Fried, Alexej (born 1922)

(i) *Clarinet concerto No. 2;* (ii) *Guer-
nica* (for soprano saxophone and
string quartet).
(M) ** Sup. 1110 2750. Slováček, with (i)
Prague SO, Valěk, (ii) Kocian Qt –
GLAZOUNOV: *Saxophone concerto.****

Fried is little-known outside his native
Czechoslovakia and apart from this disc
is unrepresented on record. The *Guernica*
quintet dates from 1978 and was inspired
by the Picasso painting. Its idiom is direct
and accessible, though it plumbs no great
depths. The *Second Clarinet concerto,* a
slightly earlier work (1975–6), has some
jazz elements that do not seem to be fully
integrated into the whole. The overall
effect of the piece is glib and hollow, like
a TV film sound-track. The performances are highly accomplished and well-
recorded.

Froberger, Johann (1616–67)

*Fantasia No. 2 in E min.; Lamenta-
tion sur la mort de Ferdinand III;
Suites Nos. 1 in A min.; 15 in A min.;
20 in D; Toccatas Nos. 3 in G; 10 in
F; 12 in A min.*
(M) *** HM HM 20360. Leonhardt.

An impressive disc that gives a good
idea of Froberger's range and achievement. A pupil of Frescobaldi, he was one
of the most exploratory and inward-
looking composers of the seventeenth
century, and his bold dissonances and
harmonic daring continue to surprise and
at the same time satisfy. Gustav Leonhardt uses a Ruckers harpsichord dating
from Froberger's lifetime, and it would
be difficult to imagine more authoritative
or imaginative readings. Those who
recall the Oiseau-Lyre disc of the late
Thurston Dart playing Froberger on a
clarichord will need no encouragement to
investigate this very different but no less
perceptive anthology, which makes an
admirable companion to it. Strongly recommended.

Gabrieli, Andrea (1520–86)

Ricercar ariosi (for organ), *Nos. 2
and 4; Ave regina; Heu mihi; Laudate
dominum; Sancta et immaculata.*
**(*) Argo ZRG 857 [id.]. Magdalen
College, Oxford, Ch., Bernard Rose;
Gowman (organ), trombone trio –
G. GABRIELI: *Collection.***(*)

In modern times the name Gabrieli has
usually suggested Giovanni, nephew of
Andrea, but this record including a fine
selection of the uncle's music helps to
explain why in their day they were both
held in equal esteem. The unaccompanied motet *Sancta et immaculata* is the
richest, most elaborate item by Andrea,
but it is good too to have the two *Ricercars* for organ, crisply played by Richard
Gowman. Aptly coupled with other
rarities and well-recorded, this fills an
important gap, though the performances
are without strong individuality.

Gabrieli, Giovanni
(1557–1612)

*Canzonas Nos. 1, 4, 7–8; Sonatas
Nos. 13, 19 and 21; Sacrae sym-
phoniae: Canzonas 2–3 and 13.*
**(*) DG 2533 406 [id.]. L. Cornett and
Sackbut Ens., Parrott.

Using authentic instruments, Andrew
Parrott and the London Cornett and
Sackbut Ensemble present stylish performances of a well-chosen collection of
Gabrieli's instrumental pieces, not as
dramatic or incisive as some we have
heard on modern brass instruments but
beautifully recorded in spacious stereo.
Best-known is the magnificent *Sonata
pian' e forte.*

*Diligam te; Ego sum; Hodie Christus;
Jubilemus; Plaudite; Virtute
magnam.* (With BASSANO: *Ave
Regina.*)
**(*) Argo ZRG 857 [id.]. Magdalen
College, Oxford, Ch., Bernard Rose;
Gowman (organ), trombone trio –
A. GABRIELI: *Collection.***(*)

This coupling of rare pieces by Giovanni Gabrieli as well as items by his
uncle Andrea is welcome and apt. The
Christmas motet *Hodie Christus natus est*
is justly the most celebrated, but the other
items too are most beautiful, notably
Plaudite for three separate choirs. The
performances, though finely controlled,
could be more positive and dramatic, but
they are well-recorded. With the *Ave
Regina* of the Gabrielis' contemporary
Giovanni Bassano as makeweight, this is
a valuable issue.

Symphoniae sacrae II (1615): *Buc-
cinate in neomania (a 19); In ecclesiis
(a 14); Jubilate Deo (a 10); Magnificat a 14; Magnificat a 17; Mis-
ericordia [a 12]; Quem vidistis
pastores (a 14); Surrexit Christus (a
11); Suscipe (a 12).*
**(*) O-L DSLO 537. Taverner Ch., L.
Cornett and Sackbut Ens., Parrott.

As principal composer of ceremonial
music at St Mark's, Venice, the younger
Gabrieli had to write all kinds of appropriate church music, and this fine collection contains some of the pieces of his
later years, when – relying on instrumentalists rather than choristers – he
came to include elaborate accompaniments for cornetts and sackbuts. Here,
for example, six sackbuts accompany the
six-part setting of *Suscipe*, with glowing
results; and although after modern brass
these more authentic instruments may
seem on the gentle side, with Gabrielian
panoply underplayed, the singing and

playing are most stylish and are helped by first-rate recording.

attractive in its reduction for the tape box than the LP original.

Gay, John (1685–1732)

The Beggar's Opera (arr. Bonynge and Gamley).
*** Decca Dig. D 252 D 2/*K 252 K 22* (2). Kanawa, Sutherland, Dean, Marks, Lansbury, Resnik, Rolfe Johnson, L. Voices, Nat. PO, Bonynge.

This entertaining new version of *The Beggar's Opera* creates the atmosphere of a stage musical. The spoken prologue comes before the overture (rather in the way some films complete the opening sequence before the main titles appear). With Warren Mitchell and Michael Hordern immediately taking the stage, the listener's attention is caught before the music begins. The musical arrangements are free – including an unashamedly jazzy sequence in Act 2, complete with saxophones – but the basic musical material is of vintage quality and responds readily to a modern treatment which is always sparkling and often imaginative. The casting is imaginative too. With Alfred Marks and Angela Lansbury as Mr and Mrs Peacham a touch of humour is assured, and if James Morris is not an entirely convincing Macheath, he sings nicely, and Joan Sutherland makes a spirited Lucy. The rest of the participants show themselves equally at home with singing and speaking, an essential if the piece is to spring fully to life. Kiri Te Kanawa as Polly undoubtedly steals the show, as well she should, for it is a peach of a part. She sings deliciously and her delivery of the dialogue is hardly less memorable. The whole show is done with gusto, and the digital recording is splendid, as spacious as it is clear. The chrome tapes too are admirably vivid, although the extensive libretto/booklet is much less

Geminiani, Francesco (1687–1772)

6 Concerti grossi, Op. 3.
*** O-L DSLO 526 [id.]. AcAM, Schröder; Hogwood.

Some of these concertos have been available in various anthologies, but this is the first complete set for some years, and it reveals the vigour and freshness of Geminiani's invention to admirable effect. Though Burney hailed Op. 3 as establishing Geminiani's character and placing him at the head of all the masters then living, it must be conceded that they are less inspired than Handel or the best of Vivaldi, though still melodious and resourceful. They are given performances of genuine quality by the Academy of Ancient Music under their Dutch leader, and readers normally resistant to the cult of authentic instruments can be reassured that there is no lack of vigour, body and breadth in these performances. They are also extremely well recorded.

Gerhard, Roberto (1896–1970)

Astrological pieces: Libra. (i) *Gemini (Duo concertante for violin and piano). Leo.*
*** Decca HEAD 11. L. Sinf., Atherton, with (i) Liddell, Constable.

In the last four years of his life Gerhard wrote – among much else – these astrological pieces, reflections for chamber forces of the dynamic works he was composing for orchestra in the fruitful years before his death. Without a score they are not always easy for the unprepared listener to take in, but like all later Gerhard works they have their own internal logic which conveys concentration from the start, notably in *Libra*, with its important concertante part for guitar. These recordings were made as a by-product of the Sinfonietta's monumental series of concerts juxtaposing Gerhard with Schoenberg, conveying the fervour of that great project. Excellent recording.

Gershwin, George
(1898–1937)

(i) *An American in Paris; Piano concerto in F; Cuban overture; I Got Rhythm variations; Porgy and Bess: Symphonic picture* (arr. Robert Russell Bennett); *Rhapsody in Blue;* (ii) *Second Rhapsody. 3 Piano Preludes.* (iii) Songs: *Aren't you kind of glad we did; Bidin' my time; He loves and she loves; I've got a crush on you; Looking for a boy; The man I love.*
(M) *** Ph. 6747 062 (3). (i) Haas, Monte Carlo Op. O., De Waart or (ii) Inbal; (iii) Sarah Vaughan, Hal Mooney and O.

This splendid mid-priced box assembles some excellent performances of Gershwin's music from the early seventies with Werner Haas a fine soloist and Edo de Waart achieving vivid and warmly attractive performances with the Monte Carlo Orchestra. The recording has a natural balance and appealing body and warmth, even though there is some lack of sheer brilliance at the top. The playing has plenty of vigour and rhythmic vitality, and atmosphere too. The *Concerto* is particularly successful (its

lyrical moments have a quality of nostalgic melancholy which is very attractive), and the big blues melody in *An American in Paris* is glamorously relaxed. There is a cultured, European flavour about the music-making that does not detract from its vitality, and indeed the performance of the *Porgy and Bess Symphonic picture* is superb, each melody given its own individuality and the sumptuous acoustic bringing evocative qualities as well as sonic splendour. This is every bit the match of Previn's HMV version (see below) and is less self-consciously brilliant. The last disc, with the *Second Rhapsody*, is of a more recent provenance and the sound increases its brilliance and range. The songs are slow and romantic, and are splendidly sung with a vibrant, smoky timbre by Sarah Vaughan to Hal Mooney's silky accompaniments. Miss Vaughan sounds a little like Cleo Laine with an extra half octave at the bottom of the voice.

(i; ii) *An American in Paris;* (iii; iv) *Piano concerto in F;* (v; ii) *Overtures: Funny Face; Girl Crazy; Let 'Em Eat Cake; Of Thee I Sing; Oh, Kay; Strike Up the Band;* (iv) *Porgy and Bess: Symphonic picture* (arr. Bennett); (vi; ii) *Rhapsody in Blue.*
(M) **(*) CBS 79329/40- (3). (i) NYPO, (ii) Tilson Thomas, (iii) Entremont, (iv) Phd. O., Ormandy, (v) Buffalo PO, (vi) composer (recorded from piano rolls), Columbia Jazz Band.

This collection is distinguished by including the composer's famous piano roll recording of *Rhapsody in Blue*, to which the accompaniment by the Columbia Jazz Band was added many years afterwards. The fast tempi adopted by Gershwin (who at the time of his recording had no need to consider the problems of an instrumental accompaniment) may raise a few eyebrows – some have suggested an untruthful reproduction of the original piano roll – but he was obviously enjoying himself. The result is audaciously extrovert and certainly exhilarating, if at times a little breathless. Tilson Thomas also directs *An American in Paris*, plus an exuberant collection of Broadway overtures (see below). Ormandy conducts the other two items and Philippe Entremont joins him in the *Concerto*, which is well played, the Philadelphia Orchestra being especially persuasive in the slow movement. But the recordings are not of recent provenance; the concerto suffers from twangy piano timbre, and both here and in the *Porgy and Bess Symphonic picture* the upper strings are excessively bright and unrefined in texture. The sound on cassette is smoother, but in the concerto the bass drum brings other problems, resulting in the occasional textural hiatus. However, generally the tapes are well-produced, the *Rhapsody*, *American in Paris* and (especially) the overtures all sound well.

An American in Paris.
(M) **(*) WEA PRIM 3. Wren O., Snell – COPLAND: *Appalachian Spring* etc.**(*)

(i) *An American in Paris;* (ii) *Rhapsody in Blue.*
(M) *** Decca SPA/KCSP 525. (i) LAPO, Mehta; (ii) Katchen, LSO, Kertesz – COPLAND: *Fanfare.****
**(*) Telarc Dig. DG 10058. Cincinnati SO, Kunzel, (ii) with List.

Howard Snell's is not the most brilliant available performance of the extrovert Gershwin overture, but it is beautifully recorded and well paired with the Copland work.

The coupling of Mehta's splendidly alive account of *An American in Paris* with the European-styled version of the *Rhapsody in Blue* from Katchen and Kertesz makes a real bargain in Decca's lower mid-price range. Katchen made this recording not long before he died, but listening to the vivid, exciting playing

no one would suspect that his health was anything other than robust. Although the performance is cultured and lacking something in idiomatic feeling, it is spontaneous and enjoyable. The sound is excellent on disc and cassette alike.

Eugene List has also recorded the *Rhapsody in Blue* for Turnabout. Then he used the original scoring; here he is accompanied by a full symphony orchestra and very sumptuously recorded indeed in a glowingly resonant acoustic. Some of the work's rhythmically abrasive qualities are submerged, but the pianist does not lose the skittish character of the work's scherzando section. The rich sound is ideal for those who like to wallow in the melodic richness of *An American in Paris*. The great blues tune certainly sounds sumptuous and there is no real lack of vitality, although in both works the hi-fi-conscious engineers have provided rather too much bass drum. Enjoyable but not so exhilarating as the famous CBS version with Gershwin himself (see above; it is also available separately on CBS 76509/40- [Col. XM/XMT 34205]).

Cuban overture. (i) *Second Rhapsody* (arr. McBride). *Porgy and Bess: Symphonic picture* (arr. Bennett).
*** HMV Dig. ASD/TC-ASD 3982. LSO, Previn, (i) with Ortiz.

Gershwin's *Cuban overture* is too long for its material, but the music has genuine vitality. Here Previn plays it with such gusto, and the digital recording is so infectiously brilliant, that one's reservations are almost swept aside. Similarly the *Second Rhapsody* cannot compare with the *Rhapsody in Blue* for melodic appeal (Gershwin, like Hollywood, was not good at sequels); but this performance is very persuasive. The highlight here is of course the brilliant arrangement by Robert Russell Bennett of themes from *Porgy and Bess*, which has established a separate identity of its own. At the opening one fears the performance is going to be too self-conscious (although one can understand Previn revelling in the gorgeous LSO playing – *Summertime* is ravishing). But the music soon takes wing and again the ear revels in the glittering sonics. The marvellous chrome tape is every bit as demonstration-worthy as the disc.

Broadway overtures: Funny Face; Girl Crazy; Let 'Em Eat Cake; Of Thee I Sing; Oh, Kay; Strike Up the Band.
*** CBS 76632/40- [Col. M/*MT* 34221]. Buffalo PO, Tilson Thomas.

Overtures: Funny Face; Let 'Em Eat Cake; Of Thee I Sing; Oh, Kay. Girl Crazy: suite. Wintergreen for President (orch. Paul). *3 Preludes* (orch. Stone). (i) *Second Rhapsody.*
** Decca PFS/*KPFC* 4438 [Lon. 21185/5-]. Boston Pops O., Fiedler, (i) with Votapek.

The Broadway overtures are given expert and idiomatic performances by Michael Tilson Thomas and the Buffalo orchestra. After the success of his last Gershwin record, one would expect no less from this brilliant conductor. The recording is well detailed, with good stereo definition and wide range. Balance and perspective are perfectly truthful and the strings reproduce cleanly and smoothly at the top of the aural spectrum. A first-class issue that will give wide pleasure, whether on disc or on the cassette, which is excellently transferred (at the highest level).

Fiedler's performances are played with obvious idiomatic understanding, but they lack the zip of the Tilson Thomas versions. However, there are some valuable novelties here. *Wintergreen for President* quotes glibly from a number of other sources (including *The Pirates of Penzance*), and Fiedler catches its circus-styled roisterous ambience. The *Second*

Rhapsody, one of Gershwin's near misses, is given considerable fervour in its advocacy here, with Ralph Votapek's solo contribution sparking off a good orchestral response, but even so it remains obstinately unmemorable. The three piano *Preludes* do not readily transcribe for orchestra. The recording is forwardly balanced and brightly vivid, and the cassette matches the disc in its impact and brilliance.

Orchestral arrangements of songs: Damsel in Distress: A foggy day. Funny Face: 'S wonderful. Girl Crazy: medley. Lady, Be Good; The man I love; Fascinating rhythm. Love Walked In. Of Thee I Sing: Wintergreen for President. Oh, Kay; Someone to watch over me. Porgy and Bess: medley. Shall We Dance: Promenade. Strike Up the Band.
** CBS 61449/40-. Kostelanetz and his O.

Though the performances are rather high-powered, and the glossy recording is brilliant to the point of fierceness (the cassette reflecting the disc in this respect), there is no denying that Kostelanetz's orchestra is first class and that he understands the demands of an orchestral approach to songs without words. The excerpts from *Porgy and Bess* provide an attractive atmospheric interlude while *Strike up the band* has a uniquely transatlantic exuberance. But turn down the treble before you start.

Piano concerto in F; Rhapsody in Blue (versions for 2 pianos).
**(*) Ph. 9500/*7300* 917 [id.]. Katia and Marielle Labèque.

Both the *Rhapsody in Blue* and the *Concerto* were originally sketched out on four staves, and the *Rhapsody* and two movements of the *Concerto* were first performed on two pianos. Katia and

Marielle Labèque are a highly accomplished duo actively interested in jazz, and they play with flawless ensemble and superb attack. These are sparkling accounts and are vividly recorded. The cassette is of excellent quality, matching the disc quite closely. Anyone with an interest in this repertoire should consider this issue, although both works undoubtedly lose a good deal of colour without the orchestral contrast.

Solo piano music: *Impromptu in 2 keys; Jazzbo Brown blues* (from *Porgy and Bess*); *Merry Andrew; Promenade; Preludes 1–3; Three quarter blues; 2 Waltzes in C.* Arrangements of songs: *Clap yo' hands; Do it again; Do, do, do; Fascinating rhythm; I got rhythm; I'll build a stairway to paradise; Liza; The man I love; My one and only; Nobody but you; Oh, Lady be good; Somebody loves me; Strike up the band; Swanee; Sweet and low-down; 'S wonderful; That certain feeling; Who cares.* (With W. DONALDSON: *Rialto ripples.*)
**(*) EMI EMD/TC-EMD 5538. Bennett.

Richard Rodney Bennett turns a composer's ear on Gershwin's piano music, including the composer's own arrangements of some of his most famous songs, and perhaps that is why the performances are not always fully idiomatic. Their rhythmic vigour is underpinned by considerable expressive conviction, yet the melodic exhilaration does not always come over, although there are undoubted insights. But such a comprehensive collection is welcome, especially as the recording – made in a resonant acoustic is first-class, with an excellent wide-ranging cassette to match the disc.

Songs: *But not for me; Embraceable you; I got rhythm; The man I love; Nice work if you can get it; Our love is here to stay; They can't take that away from me. Blue Monday: Has anyone seen Joe. Porgy and Bess: Summertime; I loves you, Porgy.*
**(*) Ph. 9500/7300 987 [id.]. Hendricks, Katia and Marielle Labèque.

An obvious follow-up to the Labèque duo's LP of the *Concerto* and *Rhapsody in Blue.* Here they are joined by Barbara Hendricks, a talented young coloured singer who studied at the Juilliard School of Music and played Clara in Maazel's set of *Porgy and Bess.* She is at her finest in the operatic numbers (*I loves you, Porgy* is particularly eloquent), and the warm beauty of the voice gives much pleasure throughout the programme. The performances of the songs are lushly cultured, often indulgently slow (even the faster numbers lack something in vitality), and create a sophisticated Hollywoodian image of late-evening cocktails and cigarette smoke, low-cut silky dresses and dinner jackets. The piano arrangements are elaborate; the playing is elegantly zestful, not out of style, but giving the presentation a European veneer that is in its way very beguiling. The sound is first-class and the stereo layout most realistic, with an excellent cassette equivalent.

(i) *Blue Monday* (chamber opera). (ii; iii) *Let 'Em Eat Cake:* choral scenes. (iv; v) Songs: *By Strauss; In the Mandarin's Chinese garden* (iii; v; vi) Madrigals: *The jolly tar and the maid; Sing of spring.*
(M) *** Turn. TVS 34638 [id.]. (i) Andrews, Mason, Richardson, Bogdan, Meyer; (ii) Bogdan, Magdamo; (iii) Gregg Smith Singers; (iv) Lees; (v) Cybriwsky (piano); (vi) Aks, Meyer.

Two years before he wrote *Rhapsody in Blue* Gershwin completed *Blue Monday,* his first sustained composition. As part of a revue it was a failure, but

Paul Whiteman was impressed enough to commission the *Rhapsody*. This performance, using a reduced orchestration (Gershwin never did one himself), brings out the tangy jazz-influenced flavour well, and the other rarities on the disc are well worth hearing, including the satirical choral scenes from *Let 'Em Eat Cake*; all are given clean and fresh performances and recording to match.

Porgy and Bess (complete).
*** RCA RL/*RK* 02109 (3) [ARL 3/ *ARK 3* 2109]. Ray Albert, Dale, Andrew Smith, Shakesnider, Marschall, Children's Ch., Houston Grand Op. Ch. and O., DeMain.

The distinction is readily drawn between Maazel's Cleveland performance (Decca SET 609/11/*K 3 Q 28* [Lon. 13116/ 5-]) and John DeMain's equally complete and authoritative account on RCA. Where Maazel easily and naturally demonstrates the operatic qualities of Gershwin's masterpiece, DeMain – with a cast which had a riotous success with the piece on Broadway and elsewhere in the United States – presents a performance clearly in the tradition of the Broadway musical. There is much to be said for both views, and it is worth noting that American listeners tend to prefer the less operatic manner of the RCA set. The casts are equally impressive vocally, with the RCA singers a degree more characterful. Donnie Ray Albert, as Porgy, uses his bass-like resonance impressively, though not everyone will like the suspicion of hamming, which works less well in a recording than on stage. That underlining of expressiveness is a characteristic of the performance, so that the climax of the key duet, *Bess, you is my woman now*, has a less natural, more stagey manner, producing, for some ears, less of a frisson than the more delicate Cleveland version. For others the more robust Houston approach has a degree of dramatic immediacy, associated with

the tradition of the American popular theatre, which is irresistible. This basic contrast will decide most listeners' approach, and although the RCA recording has not quite the Decca richness it is strikingly vivid and alive. The RCA tape transfer is not quite so sophisticated as the Decca, but it matches the records in presence, giving fine projection of the solo voices, although the chorus is sometimes less well focused.

Porgy and Bess: excerpts.
**(*) RCA Gold GL/*GK* 13654 [AGL 1 3654]. Price, Warfield, Boatwright, Bubbles, RCA Victor Ch. and O., Henderson.

This studio compilation, which was recorded in the mid-sixties, a decade before the complete versions appeared, uses a cast of the finest opera-house singers, rather than those trained in the American Musical tradition, to underline the clear claims of *Porgy and Bess* to be regarded as a work in the mainstream of opera. Both Price and Warfield sing magnificently and the supporting group is given lively direction by Skitch Henderson. One may miss favourite touches – the style is direct and full-blooded – but the impact of such committed singing is undeniable. The cassette transfer emphasizes the treble, and both voices and orchestra sound thin and fierce.

Gesualdo, Carlo
(*c.* 1560–1613)

Responsoria (1611; complete).
*** DG Arc. 2710 028 (3) [id.]. Escolania de Montserrat, Segarra.

Responsoria: Animam meam dilectam tradidi in manus iniquorum; Omnes amici mei dereliquerunt me et praevalerunt insidiantes mihi; Tam-

*quam ad latronem existis cum glau-
diis et fustibus comprehendere me;
Tenebrae factae sunt, Velum templi
scissum est; Vinea mea electa, ego te
plantavi.*
(M) *** HM HM 230. Deller Cons.,
Deller.

*Responsoria: Benedictus; Caligave-
runt oculi mei fletu meo; Feria sexta;
Jesum tradidit; Miserere; Tradide-
runt me in manus impiorum.*
(M) *** HM HMU 240. Deller Cons.,
Deller.

*Responsoria: Feria quinta; Re-
sponsoria et alia ad officium; Heb-
domadae Sanctae Spectantiae.*
(M) *** HM HM 220. Deller Cons.,
Deller.

The *Responses* for Holy Week of 1611
are as remarkable and passionately expressive as any of Gesualdo's madrigals,
and in depth of feeling they can be
compared only with the finest music of
the age. The idiom is less overtly chromatic than in the madrigals, yet dissonance
is used whenever it can heighten an
expressive effect, and one has the same
awareness of words that fires Gesualdo's
responses in the madrigals. The invention
is often unpredictable and nearly always
highly original. Now that his sacred
music is beginning to attract more attention, it is clear that he poured great feeling into this medium. The Deller Consort
bring to this music much the same approach that distinguishes their handling
of the madrigal literature. The colouring
of the words is a high priority yet it never
oversteps the bounds of good taste to
become precious or over-expressive. The
consort blends excellently, and intonation is excellent.

The Montserrat version offers the
Responses sung by a celebrated Spanish
choir in a resonant acoustic. The boys
have a purer yet more fervent tone than
the female voices in Deller's group, and
though they have difficulties with one or

two lines, these performances have a
splendid sense of passion and commitment even if words are not so strongly
projected as in the Deller set. (The latter
omit the music for Holy Saturday.) There
is a grandeur here that compensates for
the slightly unreal-sounding acoustic: a
building of this size naturally poses
problems. The three Montserrat discs
come in a well-annotated box, while
Deller's smaller Consort presents each
record separately. Both are impressive.

Gilles, Jean (1669–1705)

Requiem (with *Carillon* by Corrette).
*** DG Arc. 2533 461. Rodde, Nirouet,
Hill, Studer, Kooy, Ghent Coll.
Vocale, Col. Mus. Ant., Herreweghe.

Like his English contemporary Purcell,
the Provençal Jean Gilles died sadly
young. This *Requiem*, which for many
years was a favourite work in France, was
rejected by the two families who originally commissioned it, so Gilles decreed
that it should be used for his own funeral.
The rhythmic and harmonic vigour (with
plentiful false relations to add tang) is
well caught in this performance on original instruments. First-rate recording.

Giordano, Umberto
(1867–1948)

Andrea Chénier (complete).
*** RCA RL/*RK* 2046 [ARL 3/*ARK 3*
2046]. Domingo, Scotto, Milnes, John
Alldis Ch., Nat. PO, Levine.

Levine has rarely if ever displayed his
powers as an urgent and dramatic opera
conductor more potently than on this

splendid set, in almost every way a reading that will be hard to better. Giordano always runs the risk – not least in this opera with its obvious parallels with *Tosca* – of being thought of in the shadow of Puccini, but this red-blooded score can, as here, be searingly effective with its defiant poet hero – a splendid role for Domingo at his most heroic – and the former servant, later revolutionary leader, Gerard, a character who genuinely develops from act to act, a point well appreciated by Milnes. Scotto was here near the beginning of the intensive spell of recording which compensated for the record companies' neglect earlier, and though a few top notes spread uncomfortably, it is one of her most eloquent and beautiful performances on record. The bright recording intensifies the dramatic thrust of playing and singing. The cassettes are vivid and generally well focused, though the level rises on side five, bringing some fierceness. On sides one and two the review copy had some curious repeated clicking, but presumably this is isolated to a single batch.

Giuliani, Mauro (1781–1828)

Guitar concerto No. 1 in A, Op. 30.
(M) *** RCA Gold GL/*GK* 13883 [AGL 1/*AGK 1* 3883]. Bream, Melos Ens. – ARNOLD: *Concerto.****
(*) DG 2530 975 [id./*3300 975*]. Yepes, ECO, Navarro – RODRIGO: *Fantasia para un gentilhombre.*(*)

Giuliani's innocent concerto is uncommonly well played by Julian Bream, and the recording (dating originally from 1961) still sounds well. This issue also has the advantage of a very attractive coupling, Malcolm Arnold's *Guitar concerto*, one of his best works and certainly his wittiest. On cassette the high-level transfer produces a somewhat spiky upper range to the orchestra; although the sound is clean, it lacks warmth.

Yepes gives a lively and polished account, straightforward and not lacking in character. The balance is good and the accompaniment is stylish and alert. The performance certainly projects the music very positively, but it has not the smiling ambience of the Philips version by Pepe Romero and the St Martin's Academy under Marriner (coupled with Rodrigo's *Concierto madrigal*), to which we awarded a rosette in the second edition of the *Penguin Stereo Record Guide*; that must remain the first choice.

Gran overture, Op. 61; Gran sonata eroica in A, Op. 150; La Melanconia; Variations on a theme by Handel, Op. 107; Variations on 'I bin a Kohlbauren Bub', Op. 49.
*** DG 9500 513/*7300 660* [id.]. Pepe Romero.

As we know from his recordings of the concertos, Pepe Romero is fully at home in Giuliani's ingenuous yet rather engaging musical world, though perhaps at times here his style is a fraction too positive and purposeful. But he is rightly concerned with making each piece sound as substantial as possible, and his bravura is always at the service of the composer. There is subtlety of colour too, and the playing does not lack spontaneity. The Philips recording is very truthful, and the immaculate cassette matches the disc very closely.

Variations on a theme by Handel, Op. 107.
*** CBS 73745/*40*-. Williams – PAGANINI: *Terzetto* etc.***

The *Variations* are on the theme known as *The Harmonious Blacksmith*. Their construction is guileless but agreeable, and they are expertly played and well recorded here. This is only a very small part of a collection mostly devoted to music of Paganini.

tion It is short (about twelve minutes) and, unlike some Glazounov works, it does not outstay its welcome.

Glazounov, Alexander
(1865–1936)

Birthday Offering (ballet, arr. Irving).
(M) *** HMV Green. ESD/TC-ESD 7080. RPO, Irving – LECOCQ: *Mam'-zelle Angot.***(*)

The ballet *Birthday Offering* was arranged by Robert Irving for the silver jubilee of the Sadler's Wells Ballet in 1956. The music derives from a number of Glazounov's works, particularly *The Seasons, Ruses d'amour, Scènes de ballet* and the *Concert waltz No. 1*. It is tuneful and nicely varied in mood and is all thoroughly engaging when played with such wit and polish. The recording dates from 1959, and that shows a little in the upper strings, but otherwise the sound is full and vivid on disc and tape alike.

Saxophone concerto in E flat, Op. 109.
(M) *** Sup. 1110 2750. Slováček, Prague SO, Válek – FRIED: *Clarinet concerto No. 2 etc.***

The *Saxophone concerto*, as its opus number implies, is a late work, written for alto saxophone and string orchestra in 1934. Its performance here is more mellifluous, perhaps, than that by Lev Mikhailov which enjoyed a brief lifetime between the appearance of the *Penguin Stereo Record Guide* and this volume. Though not great music, it is more interesting than its neglect would imply, and it has a certain nobility that one does not associate with the instrument, and a witty fugal section that excites admira-

Violin concerto in A min., Op. 82.
*** Erato STU 71164. Amoyal, RPO, Scimone – BRUCH: *Concerto No. 1.***

Glazounov was an exact contemporary of Sibelius and composed his concerto at about the same time as did the Finnish master. Pierre Amoyal plays it quite superbly, and his reading must be accounted the best now before the public. He has the measure of Glazounov's sweetly effortless lyricism and aristocratic poise, and both in terms of purity of line and generosity of feeling he scores a real success. The soloist is slightly too forward but this does not diminish the strength of this record's attractions.

The Seasons (ballet), *Op. 67; Concert waltzes Nos. 1 in D, Op. 57; 2 in F, Op. 51.*
*** HMV ASD/TC-ASD 3601 [Ang. S/4XS 37509]. Philh. O., Svetlanov.

The Seasons is an early work, first performed at St Petersburg in 1900, the choreography being by the famous Petipa. With colourful orchestration, a generous sprinkling of distinctive melody, and, at the opening of *Autumn*, one of the most virile and memorable tunes Glazounov ever penned, the ballet surely deserves to return to the repertoire. Svetlanov's account is most beautifully played and recorded. His approach is engagingly affectionate; he caresses the lyrical melodies persuasively, so that if the big tune of the *Bacchanale* has slightly less thrust than usual it fits readily into the overall conception. The richly glowing HMV recording is outstanding in every way, and the cassette is only marginally less crisp in focus than the disc, without loss of warmth.

Stenka Razin, Op. 13.
*** HMV ASD 3660. USSR SO, Svet-
lanov – BALAKIREV: *Thamar*; RACH-
MANINOV: *The Rock*.***

Stenka Razin has been neglected since
Constant Lambert's set of 78s. The only
current alternative, by Ansermet, dates
from the mid-1950s. It is a colourful and
attractive piece, though the closing pages,
where the *Song of the Volga Boatmen*
swamps the score, will prove too much
for some listeners. Svetlanov has the
measure of its atmosphere and although
the Russian brass need to be tamed the
orchestral playing is generally of a high
standard, and totally committed in feeling.

Symphony No. 3 in D, Op. 33.
*** HMV ASD 3993. Moscow RSO,
Fedoseyev.

Glazounov actually published an
eighth symphony and the first movement
of a ninth. Yet unlike the symphonies of
his contemporary Sibelius, Glazounov's
in no way break new ground formally,
and they show little of the growth and
development of the Finn. However, they
offer a generous fund of melodic invention, attractively laid out and – for the
most part – pleasingly scored. The *Third*
possesses an excellent scherzo (often the
most memorable movement in a Glazounov symphony) and all four movements,
save possibly the finale, show him in the
best light. The performance and recording here are superior to the earlier HMV
Melodiya issue with the same orchestra
under Boris Khaikin, though neither
wind nor brass is as refined as that of
the finest European orchestra; nevertheless this is a thoroughly recommendable
issue.

*Barcarolle and Novelette, Op. 22; 3
Études, Op. 31; Prelude and fugue,
Op. 62; Prelude, caprice-impromptu*

*and gavotte, Op. 49; Variations on a
Finnish folksong, Op. 72.*
*** Pearl SHE 548. Howard (piano).

A useful companion disc to the two
sonatas that Leslie Howard has recorded
for this same company. The music can
all be found in the first volume of the
complete edition; nearly all of it is of interest and none is otherwise available in
modern recordings. The most substantial
piece is the *Variations on a Finnish folksong* (the same theme that crops up in
Glazounov's orchestral *Finnish Fantasy*,
Op. 88). Howard projects all these pieces
with admirable character and undoubted
fluency. He does not possess the refined
sensibility of a Gilels or Richter, but he
has the benefit of strength, intelligence
and sound musical judgement. He is admirably recorded.

*Piano sonatas Nos. 1 in B flat min.,
Op. 74; 2 in E min., Op. 75; Grand
concert waltz in E flat, Op. 41.*
**(*) Pearl SHE 538. Howard.

Both of Glazounov's piano sonatas
date from 1901 and neither is otherwise
available. Though not as distinctively
personal as Rachmaninov's, which are a
few years later, nor as impressively
wrought as Balakirev's superb essay in
this form, the Glazounov sonatas are well
worth investigating, particularly in performances as committed and as well-
recorded as these. Leslie Howard is a
devoted champion of neglected composers and his fine technique and fluent
fingers make out a strong case for both
pieces, and for the slighter concert waltz
that serves as fill-up. Howard does not
always make the most of the poetry here
and is not always consistent in observing
dynamic nuances, but there is more to
praise than to criticize. Admirers of
Glazounov's art should investigate this
issue.

Glière, Reinhold (1875–1956)

The Red Poppy (ballet): *suite, Op. 70.*
(M) (*) Turn. TVS 34644 [id./*CT 2224*].
Seattle SO, Katims – RIMSKY-KOR-
SAKOV: *Sadko*; SHOSTAKOVICH: *Age
of Gold.*(*)

This is the only available recording of
the ballet suite. Glière's scoring tends to
be rather noisy, and although the work is
not without melody and colour the *Russian sailors' dance* is justly remembered
best. The music is not well served by this
issue. The performance is acceptable, but
the thin, lustreless sound precludes a
recommendation.

*Symphony No. 3 in B min. (Ilya
Murometz), Op. 42.*
*** Uni. Dig. PCM/*UKC* 500/1. RPO,
Farberman.

Glière's massive programme symphony manages to stretch thin material
extraordinarily far, but those who respond to the composer's open, colourful
style will be delighted that Farberman,
unlike his predecessors in stereo, has
recorded the score absolutely complete.
His conducting cannot be described as
volatile, and he is never led into introducing urgent stringendos to add to the
passion of a climax, but his very patience,
helped by superb recording, makes for
very compelling results. Enterprisingly
Unicorn got in ahead of even the major
companies (except Decca) in bringing out
one of the first digital recordings, and
though the long finale is marginally less
clean in its textures, the sound from first
to last has natural balance and warmth.
If at the start of the main allegro of the
first movement the RPO cellos and
basses have limited resonance, that is
clearly a reflection of how the players
actually sounded in the hall. The cassette

transfer is acceptable, well balanced with
no obvious congestion. But compared to
the discs the upper range is restricted; the
violins lack freshness at the top and the
big climax of the last movement does not
match the LP sound in its feeling of
spectacle.

Glinka, Michail (1804–57)

*Ivan Susanin: Overture; Russlan and
Ludmilla: Magic dances.*
** HMV ASD/*TC-ASD* 3709. USS R
SO, Svetlanov – BALAKIREV: *Islamey*
etc.***; SCRIABIN: *Day Dreams.*"

Vital and lively accounts of the Glinka
pieces from the USSR Symphony
Orchestra, playing with genuine fire and
commitment under Yevgeny Svetlanov.
This forms part of an interesting anthology, which is well recorded, though
wanting the last ounce of clarity. The
transfers to tape are clear and sparkling,
the string timbre dry and bright but not
lustreless.

Russlan and Ludmilla: Overture.
(M) **(*) Ph. Fest. 6570/*7310* 176 [id.].
Concg. O., Haitink – DVOŘÁK:
Scherzo capriccioso; MUSSORGSKY:
Pictures; TCHAIKOVSKY: *Capriccio
italien.***(*)

An excellent performance of this
much-recorded overture, set within the
context of a generous collection. The
Concertgebouw Orchestra shows the
requisite energy, and Haitink points the
inner detail effectively. The sound is
equally good on disc and tape.

Goldmark, Karl (1830–1915)

*Violin concerto No. 1 in A min., Op.
28.*

(*) HMV ASD/*TC-ASD* 3408 [Ang.
S/*4XS* 37445]. Perlman, Pittsburgh
SO, Previn – SARASATE: *Zigeuner-
weisen.***
(M) ** Turn. TVS 37126 [Can. 31106].
Ricci, R. Lux. O., Froment – SPOHR:
*Concertante.***

Like the *Rustic Wedding symphony*,
this the first of Goldmark's two violin
concertos maintains a peripheral position
in the catalogue. It is a pleasing and
warm-hearted concerto in the romantic
tradition that deserves to be better
known. It could not be more beautifully
played than by Itzhak Perlman, whose
effortless virtuosity and lyrical poise even
challenge Milstein's aristocratic record of
the late 1950s (now deleted). The latter
was better balanced, for the EMI engineers have placed Perlman very much
in the foreground – so much so that
orchestral detail does not always register
as it should. The sound quality is fresher
in the newer recording, and Previn
accompanies sympathetically. This is
very charming and likeable music, and
Perlman plays it most winningly. The
cassette transfer matches the disc fairly
closely, though the climaxes could reproduce more smoothly.

An enjoyable account too from Ricci,
who is on excellent form – he plays the
second subject of the first movement very
appealingly and phrases the *Andante* with
equal sympathy. But he too is placed
much too forwardly, so that he dwarfs
the orchestra, and the spotlight on the
violin emphasizes every detail of his
playing. Otherwise the recording is
acceptable. The playing of the Radio
Luxembourg Orchestra is somewhat
wanting in polish, but Ricci has a considerable price advantage and the Spohr
coupling is more substantial than Perlman's Sarasate.

Rustic Wedding symphony, Op. 26.
⊛ *** HMV ASD/*TC-ASD* 3891 [Ang.
SZ/*4ZS* 37662]. Pittsburgh SO,
Previn.

** Decca Dig. SXDL/*KSXDC* 7528
[Lon. LDR 10000/5-]. LAPO, Lopez-
Cobós.

The *Rustic Wedding symphony* was one
of the three colourful works – the others
being the *Violin concerto No. 1* and the
opera *The Queen of Sheba* – which
appeared in quick succession in the mid-
1870s and which together have alone
sustained Goldmark's reputation to the
present day. 'Clear-cut and faultless',
Brahms called this large but consciously
unpretentious programme symphony,
wittily echoing what Schumann had once
said to Brahms himself, that 'it sprang
into being, a finished thing, like Minerva
from the head of Jupiter'. The opening
movement brings not a sonata-form
structure but a simple set of variations
with one or two pre-echoes of Mahler in
Wunderhorn mood, and though there are
no neurotic tensions whatever, with a tale
of a peasant wedding simply told, it seems
likely that Mahler learnt something from
the piece. Previn relishes the contrasts,
the rhythmic drive and the innocent lyricism, drawing excellent playing from the
Pittsburgh orchestra, as he did accompanying Perlman in the *Violin concerto
No. 1*. Warm, red-blooded recording to
match. The cassette offers similarly attractive sound, rich, glowing and atmospheric. Highly recommended.

Lopez-Cobós directs a refreshing and
attractive reading. The generally fast
tempi detract from the charm of the piece
– Previn's HMV is altogether more
colourful and persuasive – but with wide-
ranging digital sound which presents the
Los Angeles Orchestra untypically at a
distance it is a fair recommendation. The
cassette transfer is admirable, crisp and
clear to match the disc closely.

Die Königin von Saba (opera).
(M) **(*)** Hung. SLPX 12179/82. Nagy,
Gregor, Kincses, Jerusalem, Miller,
Takács, Hungarian State Op. Ch. and
O., Fischer.

Goldmark's most successful works came within a relatively short span in his career, of which this long opera is the most ambitious product. With the Queen of Sheba representing evil and the lovely Sulamit representing good, its theme links directly with that of Wagner's *Tannhäuser*, but in style Goldmark rather recalls Mendelssohn and Gounod, with a touch of Meyerbeer. In the tenor role of Asad, Siegfried Jerusalem gives a magnificent performance, not least in his aria *Magische Töne*. Klára Takács is dramatic and characterful as the Queen of Sheba, but on top the voice is often raw. Sándor Nagy is an impressive Solomon, and Adam Fischer, one of the talented family of conductors, draws lively performances from everyone. The recording is very acceptable.

Goodwin, Ron (20th century)

Film themes: *Miss Marple; Of Human Bondage; Operation Crossbow; 633 Squadron; Those Magnificent Men in their Flying Machines; The Trap. Girl with a Dream; The Headless Horseman; India; London serenade; Prairie serenade; Puppet serenade.*
(B) *** MfP MFP/*TC-MFP* 1025 (2). Goodwin and his O. – *Concert (Sounds superb).****

Of all the composers writing popular film themes over the last two decades (and especially in the sixties) Rod Goodwin stands out. His unfailing melodic gift is matched by an orchestral flair to compare with that of Malcolm Arnold. In *633 Squadron* it produced one of the most memorable horn calls since Richard Strauss, while the delicious neoclassical touch to the *Miss Marple* tune, with its switch from strings to harpsichord, is quite captivating. *The Trap* has another ripe horn melody, and all these 'themes'

are splendidly crafted to make miniature ternary structures. The short characteristic pieces are attractive too, sometimes slightly old-fashioned, like the fragile *Puppet serenade*. Goodwin is a superb exponent of his own music, and the brilliant recordings stem from EMI Studio Two masters. The tape transfer is tart, but this is ideal motorway background music, and the rest of the programme is very enjoyable too (see the Concerts section below).

Goossens, Eugene (1893–1962)

Symphony No. 1, Op. 58.
*** Uni. Kanchana KP 8000. Adelaide SO, Measham.

Between the wars Eugene Goossens was thought of as a composer of considerable talent: two of his operas were produced at Covent Garden and works like *Kaleidoscope* kept his name alive among pianists. The *First Symphony* was written in 1940 and it is appropriate that an Australian orchestra should record it, since Goossens spent many years there as conductor of the ABC Sydney Symphony Orchestra. The idiom is wholly accessible, and readers who enjoy the symphonies of Bax should investigate this well-constructed and finely paced score, which has variety both of colour and of substance. David Measham gets very impressive results from the Adelaide orchestra, and the warm acoustic, which is alive and spacious, helps the well-detailed and vivid recording. Strongly recommended.

Gould, Morton (born 1913)

Spirituals for string choir and orchestra; Foster Gallery.

** Crystal Clear CCS 7005 [id.]. LPO, composer.

A modern recording of Gould's *Spirituals* is most welcome, particularly one so rich and spacious and naturally balanced. But the composer's performance is disappointing. The elegiac quality of the slow movement, *Sermon*, is expressively caught, and the strident percussive effects of *Protest* are extremely telling; but there is a disappointing lack of wit in the miniature scherzo, *A little bit of sin*, with its sly humour and quotation of *Shortnin' bread*. The *Foster Gallery* derives its material from Stephen Foster melodies, but apart from a delicate appearance of *Jeannie with the light brown hair* it is surprisingly unmemorable. Walter Susskind's famous Everest recording of the *Spirituals* has greater point and spontaneity, and the sound, from the earliest days of stereo, is amazingly brilliant still, if a shade glossy. This bargain-priced disc (Everest 3002), coupled to an excellent version of Copland's *Appalachian Spring*, easily holds its own, even if the direct-cut Crystal Clear issue has obvious sonic advantages.

Gounod, Charles (1818–93)

Fantasy on the Russian National Hymn for piano and orchestra.
(M) (*) Turn. TVS 37127 [Can. 31088]. Dosse, Westphalian SO, Landau – MASSENET: *Piano concerto*; SAINT-SAËNS: *Africa fantasy*.(*)

Gounod's *Fantasy* on the Tsarist Hymn is repetitive and hardly worth preserving on record. Neither performance nor recording (which is thin) is persuasive.

Petite symphonie in B flat (for wind).

(M) *** Ph. Fest. 6570/7310 205. Neth. Wind Ens., De Waart – DVOŘÁK: *Serenade*; SCHUBERT: *Octet, D. 72* (excerpts).***
*** RCA RL/RK 25278. Athena Ens. – IBERT: *3 Pièces brèves*; POULENC: *Sextuor*.***

An astonishingly fresh and youthful work, the *Petite symphonie* in fact dates from Gounod's later years: he was nearly seventy when he wrote it for one of the celebrated Parisian wind ensembles of the day. The work has impeccable craftsmanship and is witty and civilized. It makes ideal listening at the end of the day, and its charm is irresistible, particularly in so crisp and vital a performance as Edo de Waart's. The Philips recording is altogether excellent, and the cassette transfer is first-class, matching the disc closely. The couplings further enhance the attractions of this issue.

The Athena performance is equally expertly played and lives up to the title of the RCA collection, 'Joie de vivre'. The other items are by twentieth-century French composers and this anthology is as successful in its way as the Philips one. The cassette transfer is immaculate, admirably clear and clean.

Symphonies Nos. 1 in D; 2 in B flat.
(M) **(*) HMV Green. ESD/TC-ESD 7093 [Ang. SZ/4ZS 37726]. Toulouse Capitole O., Plasson.

Gounod's two symphonies sound astonishingly youthful, though they were in fact composed in quick succession in his mid-thirties. Listening to No. 1, the Bizet symphony leaps to mind, and the effortless flow of first-rate ideas, the sunny Schubertian temperament and grace, and the mastery both of the orchestra, which is handled with the greatest expertise, and of symphonic form are memorable. The Orchestra of the Capitole, Toulouse, is not the Berlin Philharmonic and the playing is not as finished or accomplished as these delightful works deserve. Michel Plasson has the measure of this music, however, and the engineers have produced decent if less than distinguished sound. Ideally, this music deserves performances of comparable sparkle and polish, but there is far too much to enjoy here for reservations to carry undue weight. The cassette transfer is slightly 'fluffy' in focus in No. 1; No. 2 is clean and clear but has slightly less ambient warmth.

Faust (complete).
** HMV SLS/*TC-SLS* 5170 (4) [Ang. SZX/*4Z4X* 3868]. Freni, Domingo, Allen, Ghiaurov, Paris Op. Ch. and O., Prêtre.
*(*) Erato STU 71031 (4) [RCA FRL4 2493]. Caballé, Aragall, Plishka, Huttenlocher, Ch. of Op. du Rhin, Strasbourg PO, Lombard.

Even in French music Prêtre is an unpersuasive conductor. His four principals are all fine singers, aptly chosen for their roles, but without magic from the conductor they only fitfully produce their best singing, and too often the results are lumpy and unidiomatic. When Freni sings *Ah, je ris* at the beginning of the *Jewel song*, laughter is nowhere near. Domingo is less stylish than he usually is in French music; Ghiaurov is less rich and resonant than he was in the Bonynge set of 1967; and only Thomas Allen gives a performance which matches the best on rival sets. The recording is full and warm, and the cassette transfer captures the resonance with only marginal loss of crispness. The layout, with each act complete on a cassette side and side six given to the ballet music, is admirable.

The Erato version is disappointing, not one of Lombard's successes as an opera conductor. The unatmospheric recording and singing either unstylish or dull do not help. Caballé is the chief offender, plainly seeing herself as a prima donna whose vagaries and self-indulgences have to be

wooed. Aragall produces some beautiful sounds, but he does not seem completely happy in French, and Paul Plishka lacks flair and devilry as Mephistopheles. The Cluytens set with Los Angeles, Gedda, Blanc and Christoff remains the most attractive available version (HMV SLS 816 [Ang. S 3622]). The Bonynge set is now also available on cassette (Decca K 127 K 43 [Lon. 5-1433]).

Mireille (complete).
*** HMV SLS 5203 (3) [Ang. SX 3905]. Freni, Vanzo, Rhodes, Van Dam, Bacquier, Toulouse Capitole Ch. and O., Plasson.

Based on an improbable rustic epic in Provençal – a subject which had Gounod temporarily taking up residence in Provence – *Mireille* is nicely divided between scenes of country innocence (cue for airy tunes and skipping rhythms that to British ears suggest Sullivan) and high sentimental drama, including an excursion *à la Freischütz* into the supernatural when the villain is borne off by a phantom boatman. Gounod as ever is most memorable when he is not aiming too high, and one regrets that the freshness of the opening scenes has to give way to the heavy sentiment, which on the heroine's death at the end grows oppressive. Nonetheless, in so strong and committed a performance as Plasson's, with attractive and generally stylish singing, it makes a very welcome rarity. Vanzo, Bacquier and Van Dam are all in excellent form, and though Freni does not always sound comfortable in French, it is an appealing performance. It is a pity that in the interests of authenticity this recording of the original text excludes the most famous number, the coloratura waltz song.

Roméo et Juliet: highlights.
(M) *(*) HMV SXLP/*TC-SXLP* 30304. Carteri, Gedda, Paris Op. O., Lombard – BIZET: *Pêcheurs de perles highlights.**(*)

Gounod's Shakespeare opera is so poorly represented on record that any items are welcome, but these selections (including the *Waltz song* from Act 2, *Nuit d'hyménée* from Act 4, and the Act 5 tomb scene) are not very stylish, with even Gedda less impressive than usual. The recording is satisfactory on both disc and cassette.

Gowers, Patrick

(20th century)

(i) *Chamber concerto for guitar;* (ii) *Rhapsody for guitar, electric guitars and organ.*

(M) *** CBS 61790/40- [Col. M/*MT* 35866]. Williams, with (i) Chamber Ens., composer (organ), Salmon; (ii) composer (electric organ).

This coupling of two works previously available separately seems eminently sensible. Patrick Gowers is a highly intelligent and resourceful musician, and as long as you do not take it too seriously his *Chamber concerto* is crisp, enjoyable music. It is complete with parts for alto saxophone, bass guitar, electric organ and drums as well as string trio. The *Rhapsody* too has many imaginative effects, although it will not automatically enjoy universal appeal. Both are made to sound far more persuasive by the artistry of John Williams, a superb advocate. The recording is rather close, but, that apart, the coupling can be recommended. On tape the sound is restricted in range, but pleasingly intimate and well balanced.

Grainger, Percy (1882–1961)

Blithe Bells (Free ramble on a theme by Bach: Sheep may safely graze);

Country Gardens; Green Bushes (passacaglia); Handel in the Strand; Mock Morris; Molly on the Shore; My Robin Is to the Greenwood Gone; Shepherd's Hey; Spoon River; Walking tune; Youthful Rapture; Youthful suite; Rustic dance; Eastern intermezzo.

*** RCA RL/*RK* 25198. Bournemouth Sinf., Montgomery.

Among several new anthologies of Grainger's music, this one stands out for the sparkling, sympathetic playing of the Bournemouth Sinfonietta and an engaging choice of programme. Among the expressive pieces, the arrangement of *My Robin Is to the Greenwood Gone* is highly attractive, but the cello solo in *Youthful Rapture* is perhaps less effective. The passacaglia on *Green Bushes* is characteristically repetitive, yet the diversity in the inner parts shows Grainger's decorative imagination in full flight. Favourites such as *Country Gardens, Shepherd's Hey, Molly on the Shore* and *Handel in the Strand* all sound as fresh as paint, and among the novelties the *Rustic dance* and *Eastern intermezzo* (in musical style a cross between Eric Coates and Edward German) have undoubted period charm. The recording is first-class and the tape transfer is clear and clean.

Children's march; Colonial song; Country Gardens; Handel in the Strand; Immovable Do; Irish tune from County Derry; Mock Morris; Molly on the Shore; My Robin is to the Greenwood Gone; Shepherd's Hey; Spoon River.

(M) ** Mercury SRI 75102 [id.]. Eastman Rochester Pops O., Fennell.

Lively and sympathetic performances from Fennell, and a nicely balanced programme. But the Mercury sound (from the beginning of the sixties) is slightly abrasive, with pithy strings, almost giving an impression of baroque period instruments. The *Londonderry air* sounds the very opposite of sumptuous. The recording does not lack ambience, but some allowances will have to be made for the close positioning of the microphones.

Danish folk music suite; The Immovable 'Do'; In a Nutshell suite; Irish tune from County Derry; Molly on the Shore.
*** HMV ASD/TC-ASD 3651. E. Sinfonia, Dilkes.

The two suites make up the greater part of the record, supplemented on each side by a brief 'encore' item, the well-known *Molly on the Shore* and a piece inspired by the time when Grainger had a 'cipher' on his harmonium and the note C went on sounding through everything. *In a Nutshell* is an early work, a collection of tunes colourfully set, while the *Danish folk music suite* is equally attractive and unpretentious if less distinctive. Performances and recording are very compelling. The transfer to tape is admirably crisp and vivid, but has not quite the bloom of the LP (the strings in the *Londonderry air* are clear rather than rich).

Irish tune from County Derry; Lincolnshire Posy; Molly on the Shore; Shepherd's Hey.
*** ASV ALH/ZCALH 913. L. Wind O., Wick – MILHAUD and POULENC: *Suites françaises.****

First class playing and vivid recording, with the additional attraction of delightful couplings, make this highly recommendable. The Grainger pieces come off excellently, and the sound could hardly be better balanced. This is in the demonstration class.

Lincolnshire Posy; Shepherd's Hey.
*** Telarc Dig. DG 10050 [id.], Cleveland Symphonic Winds, Fennell –

ARNAUD: *Fanfares;* VAUGHAN WILLIAMS: *English folksongs suite* etc.***

Grainger scored *Shepherd's Hey* for wind band as a result of his experience as a recruited musician in the US Army during the First World War. The six-movement *Lincolnshire Posy* was written in New York in 1937. It is the highlight of this impressive compilation, played with marvellous bravura and understanding. The climax of *Rufford Park poachers* is splendidly made, and the nice wit of *The brisk young sailor*, which follows, makes a perfect foil. The recording has superb clarity and a real feeling of spectacle. A demonstration disc indeed, the pressing absolutely clean and surfaces immaculate.

(i) *Country Gardens.* (ii) *Brigg Fair; Died for Love; Dollar and a Half a Day; Green Bushes; The Hunter in his Career; Irish tune from County Derry; The Merry King; Molly on the Shore; The Power of Love; Shenandoah; Six Dukes Went A-fishin'; Stormy; The Three Ravens; Under a Bridge.*
*** Decca SXL 6872. (i) Composer (piano); (ii) Pears, Shirley-Quirk, Reynolds, Linden Singers, Wandsworth Boys' Ch., ECO, Bedford.

Grainger's quirky genius is splendidly portrayed in this richly varied record, linking some of his highly imaginative folksong settings in performances by varied voices and choirs with instrumental pieces, of which the prize here is *Country Gardens* recorded by the composer himself at the piano in 1927. The sound is fresh for its age but shows all too clearly that Grainger's high reputation as a virtuoso still involved a surprising proportion of wrong notes. The recordings of the 1970s are very vivid indeed, and the performances delightful.

Granados, Enrique
(1867–1916)

Goyescas: Intermezzo.
(M) *** Decca Jub. JB/*KJBC* 50. New Philh. O., Frühbeck de Burgos – FALLA: *El amor brujo*; RAVEL: *Alborada* etc.***

A lusciously brilliant performance, superbly recorded by Decca. The cassette transfer is also first-class.

Spanish dance, Op. 37/5: Andaluza.
(M) ** Decca SPA/*KCSP* 551. LSO, Gamba – RAVEL: *Boléro* etc.; SARASATE: *Carmen fantasy.***

Granados's most famous melody is here vividly performed and recorded (on disc and tape alike), but this is only a bonus item for a coupling of two of Ansermet's Ravel performances and Ricci's super-brilliant account of the Sarasate.

(i) *Piano quintet in G min. A la Cubana, Op. 36; Aparicion; Cartas de Amor – valses intimos, Op. 44; Danza caracteristica. Escenas poeticas* (2nd series).
*** CRD CRD 1035. Rajna (piano), (i) with Alberni Qt.

The *Piano quintet* is a compact work, neat and unpretentious, in three attractive movements, including a charming lyrical *Allegretto* and a vigorous finale where the piano is most prominent. Among the piano music here, the evocative pieces in the *Escenas poeticas II* are the most valuable, but even the more conventional colour-pieces which make up the rest of the disc are well worth hearing in such perceptive readings as Thomas Rajna's. The CRD recording is first-rate.

Danzas españoles Nos. 1–12 (Books 1–4).
(M) *** RCA Gold RL/*RK* 25242. Larrocha.

These performances are not of recent provenance, but Alicia de Larrocha, who studied with Frank Marshall, a pupil of Granados himself, has special authority in this repertoire. She plays these pieces with flair and temperament, more freely in fact than in her earlier recording from the 1950s. Her playing has an aristocratic poise that silences criticism; her departures from the printed score one assumes to spring from her teacher and presumably carry the composer's imprimatur. Although the recording is not distinguished, it is fresh and clean – just a shade wanting in range – but given the price the disc can be strongly recommended. But the cassette, with plummy timbre and more than a hint of wow on sustained passages, is not recommendable.

Goyescas (complete).
*** Decca SXL/*KSXC* 6785 [Lon. 7009/5-]. Larrocha.
(M) **(*) RCA Gold RL/*RK* 35301. Achucarro.

The Decca recording is most distinguished. Alicia de Larrocha brings a special authority and sympathy to the *Goyescas*; her playing has the crisp articulation and rhythmic vitality that these pieces call for, and the overall impression could hardly be more idiomatic in flavour. In every way these performances displace the alternative listings (Rajna on CRD and Mario Miranda on Saga), not least for the excellence of the recorded sound. It is remarkably firm and secure, though there is a marginally harder piano tone in the cassette format.

Achucarro is an impressive artist and much at home in this repertoire, which he plays with the right amount of flair and poetry. But the recording, though not unacceptable, is by no means as natural or truthful as Alicia de Larrocha's. The RCA sound is a little shallow and wanting in range, although this is more noticeable on cassette than on disc.

A la pradera; Barcarola, Op. 46; Bocetos; Cuentos de la Juventud, Op. 1; Mazurka, Op. 2: Mosque y Arabe; Sardana; Los soldados de cartón.
*** CRD CRD 1036/*CRDC 4036*. Rajna.

6 Estudios expresivos; Estudio, Op. posth.; Impromptu, Op. 39; 2 Marches militaires; Marche militaire; Paisaje, Op. 35; Pequena suite (In the garden of Elisenda).
*** CRD CRD 1037/*CRDC 4037*. Rajna.

Most of Granados's finest piano music comes in the earlier volumes recorded by Thomas Rajna for CRD. The *Danzas españoles* are complete on CRD1021/*CRDC 4021*; the *Goyescas, Escenas poéticas* and *Libro de horas* are on CRD 1001/2/*CRDC 4001/2*, and the balance on CRD 1022/3. These later volumes, excellently played and recorded, should nonetheless be acquired, and not merely for the sake of completeness. The *Seis Estudios* serve to point the formative influences in Granados's style – Schumann and, to a lesser extent, Fauré – while the other pieces, including the *Marches militaires* (in which Rajna superimposes the second piano part), are unfailingly pleasing. Obviously not essential Granados but certainly recommended for the enthusiast. The cassettes are of CRD's usual excellent quality, matching the discs closely.

Canciones amatorias: Gracia mía; Iban al pinar; Llorud corazón; Mananica era; Mira que soy Nina; No Lloreis ojuelos. Tonadillas: Amor y odio; Callejeo; Las Currutacas modestas; El majo discreto; El majo olvidado; El majo tímido; El Tra-lalá y el punteado; El mirar de la maja; La maja de Goya; La maja dolorosa, Nos. 1–3.
** Decca SXL 6866 [Lon. 26558/5-]. Lorengar, Larrocha.

With a celebrated Spanish soprano accompanied by the most vividly characterful of Spanish pianists, the casting in these colourful, finely wrought songs might seem ideal. But Lorengar's tone, never perfectly steady, has grown slacker with the years, not even vibrant in an aptly Spanish way. Thanks to the pianist, however, Spanish fire is rarely lacking for long, even if the partnership is unequal. The recording is very good indeed.

Graun, Johann Gottlieb
(1703–71)

Oboe concertos: in C min.; in G min.
*** DG Arc. 2533 412. Holliger, Camerata Bern, Van Wijnkoop – KREBS: *Double concerto.***(*)

The Camerata Bern and Holliger, responsible for the magnificent set of Zelenka's orchestral music, here turn to other neglected composers of Bach's period. This Graun was the brother of the better-known composer of the opera *Montezuma*, and the *C minor Concerto* is delectable in its originality. All three movements are highly inventive, and the briefer *G minor Concerto* has a beautiful slow movement with muted strings. Interestingly coupled and splendidly recorded, it makes a valuable baroque rarity, particularly with Holliger at his most sparkling.

Grechaninov, Alexander
(1864–1956)

The Lane (5 children's songs), *Op. 89.*
*** Decca SXL 6900 [Lon. 26579].
Söderström, Ashkenazy – MUS-
SORGSKY: *Nursery;* PROKOFIEV: *Ugly
Duckling.****

Grechaninov, much influenced by
Mussorgsky, wrote these songs in 1920,
and though they are far less original and
intense than the Mussorgsky cycle on the
reverse, they make an admirable fill-up
for a superb record, vividly performed
and recorded.

Gregorian chant

First Christmas Mass.
(M) *** DG Priv. 2535/*3335* 345.
Benedictine Monks' Ch. of St Martin's
Abbey, Beuron, Pfaff.

Third Christmas Mass.
(M) *** DG Arc. Priv. 2547/*3347* 001. Ch.
of St Martin's, Beuron, Pfaff.

Easter Sunday Mass.
(M) *** DG Arc. Priv. 2547/*3347* 016. Ch.
of St Martin's, Beuron, Pfaff.

The German tradition of plainsong
combines dedication with careful preparation. It is different in style and timbre
from the choirs of Italy and France, but
not less eloquent. These three recordings
made in the spacious acoustic of the
Abbey at Beuron demonstrate the skill
and devotion of the choir's director,
Father Maurus Pfaff. The recording,
from the early sixties, is first-class, and
the tape transfers are strikingly vivid
(though on 3347 016 there is at times a
hint that the level is fractionally too

high). This is music especially suited for
cassettes, with their freedom from background disturbances.

Requiem Mass.
*** DG Arc. Priv. 2547/*3347* 028. Ch. of
St Martin's, Beuron, Pfaff.

The liturgy for the *Missa pro defunctis*
dates back to the earliest days of the
Christian church. Besides its use at funerals, this *Requiem Mass* (which assumed
its present form in the Middle Ages) is
celebrated in the church calendar on All
Souls Day (2 November). The music is
understandably sombre, and its simplicity makes a powerful effect, especially
in a performance such as is given here
under Father Pfaff. The recording – as in
the rest of the Beuron series – is of high
quality, with sonorous choral tone, a
clear focus, and a convincing ambience.
The cassette transfer is outstandingly
well managed, and the tape, like the disc,
is provided with admirable notes and a
full translation.

Gregorian chants from Assisi:
*Laudes antiquae; In cena domini: De
missa solemni vespertina* (Plainsong
for the commemoration of the Lord's
Supper on Maundy Thursday).
(M) *** DG Priv. 2726/*3372* 004 (2).
Coro della Cappella Papale di San
Francesco d'Assisi, Ferraro.

The Medieval Lauds included here
come from the Cortona Book, which
dates from the thirteenth century. They
are written in short phrases and often
take the form of a dialogue, either a solo
with a refrain or answering stanzas from
a double choir. The music is expressive,
but more simple and direct in utterance
than much plainsong. Here the second
choir features trebles and they make an
attractively robust, even earthy contrast
with the all-male group. The Maundy
Thursday Liturgy is in a more traditional
plainsong style. The singing throughout

is eloquent, using dramatic contrasts, expansions and diminuendos of tone in an effectively musical way without robbing the music of its essential serenity. The recording was made in the church where St Francis of Assisi was buried (he is traditionally credited with the origination of the Lauds). Its acoustic is ideal, having splendid atmosphere without affecting the clarity of focus. The sound is equally beautiful on disc and cassette.

Collection: *Credo I; Magnificat; Tu es pastor ovium; Te Deum. Sequences: In Festa Septem Dolorum B.M.V.; In Festo Corporis Christi; Tempore Paschali; In honorem Sancti Sacramenti: Hymns, Antiphon; Sequence; Hostia. In Honorem B.M.V.: 4 Antiphons. In Festo Pentecost: Veni, creator.*
(M) ** Ph. Fest. 6570/*7310* 154. Benedictine Monks' Choirs of St Maurice and St Mazur, Clervaux.

This recording was made in 1959, but successfully combines a feeling of atmosphere with clarity, both on disc and on the excellent cassette. The singing style is devoted and the eloquence of the musical line produces an almost lyrical feeling in the longer phrases. Some may feel this is too romantic, and there is a discreet organ accompaniment throughout much of the recital, which many will count unnecessary; but less experienced ears may find that this adds colour to the musical effect without destroying its character. Other recordings offer singing of greater polish but are not necessarily more approachable.

Grieg, Edvard (1843–1907)

Piano concerto in A min., Op. 16.
(M) *** Decca Jub. JB/*KJBC* 104 [Lon. STS 15407/5-]. Curzon, LPO,

Fjeldstad – FRANCK: *Symphonic variations;* LITOLFF: *Scherzo.****
·(B) **(*) Con. CC/*CCT* 7506. Katchen, Israel PO, Kertesz – SCHUMANN: *Concerto.***
** HMV ASD/*TC-ASD* 3960. Ortiz, Philh. O., Ashkenazy – FRANCK: *Les Djinns*; *Symphonic variations.****
** HMV ASD/*TC-ASD* 3521 [Ang. S/ 4*XS* 37510]. Gutiérrez, LPO, Tennstedt – SCHUMANN: *Concerto.***
(M) *(*) Ph. Fest. 6570/*7310* 170 [id.]. Arrau, Concg. O., Dohnányi – SCHUMANN: *Concerto.*(*)

The sensitivity of Curzon in the recording studio is never in doubt, and the Jubilee compilation has been a favourite disc and cassette over a long period. The recording hardly shows its age and the coupling includes one of the finest versions of the Franck *Symphonic variations* to have appeared throughout the LP era. Curzon's approach to the Grieg is wonderfully poetic, and this is a performance with strength and power as well as freshness and lyrical tenderness. The sound on disc and cassette is virtually identical; indeed the tape offers demonstration quality in all respects.

Katchen's performance, reissued at bargain price on Contour, is strong and commanding, a touch of wilfulness tempered by a natural flexibility and a feeling for the work's poetry. Kertesz provides plenty of life in the accompaniment, and the recording is vivid and powerful in Decca's more spectacular manner. Some ears find that the sound here has a reverberant twang, and the effect is certainly somewhat highpowered. The cassette, with its slightly reduced upper range, is effectively mellower, but neither on disc or tape does this issue displace Solomon (see below).

The partnership between Cristina Ortiz and Ashkenazy is much less successful here than in the excellent Franck couplings. The performance has its moments: the opening of the slow movement is poetically phrased by Ashkenazy, and the appearance of the second subject of the first movement brings a fusion of · poetry between the two artists that is repeated at a similar point in the structure of the finale. But elsewhere there is a lack of spontaneity and forward thrust (the cadenza is particularly disappointing). The recording is brilliant on disc and tape alike.

Gutiérrez and Tennstedt are less controversial but also less individual in their approach; and in terms of poetry and musical insight this version does not match the finest. The recording is good.

The reflective, studied calm of Arrau's reading of the first movement, presented within a mellow recording, is seriously lacking in vitality and sparkle. Although this performance is not without romantic feeling and integrity, its heaviness is out of character.

Still recommended: Alongside Curzon, Bishop-Kovacevich still leads the field on disc (Ph. 6500 166); and Radu Lupu's account, which successfully combines freshness and warmth, has the advantage of an outstanding tape transfer (Decca SXL/*KSXC* 6624 [Lon. 6840]). But at bargain price Solomon's similar coupling with the Schumann *Concerto* (CfP CFP/ *TC-CFP* 40255) is almost irresistible, equally desirable on disc or cassette.

(i) *Piano concerto in A min. 4 Norwegian dances, Op. 35; Wedding Day at Troldhaugen, Op. 65/6.*
(M) **(*) Turn. TVS 34624 [id.]. Utah SO, Abravanel, (i) with Johannesen.

Those looking for an inexpensive version of the Grieg *Concerto* not coupled to the Schumann might well find this Turnabout disc very acceptable. The performance is fresh and alive, and shows an excellent rapport between Johannesen and Abravanel. There is a flexibility about the phrasing and an unexaggerated response to the work's poetry that is very satisfying. Abravanel's *Norwegian dances*

are strongly characterized, vividly spontaneous and show a feeling for atmosphere. The recording is closely balanced, but the piano timbre is more convincing than on many records from this source.

2 Elegiac melodies, Op. 34; Holberg suite, Op. 40.
(M) *(*) HMV Green. ESD/*TC-ESD* 7084. Polish CO, Maksymiuk – TCHAIKOVSKY: *Serenade.**(*)

The recording here is brilliant and very sharply focused; every strand of texture is clearly detailed. The outer movements of the *Holberg suite* are strongly articulated, and the sound matches Maksymiuk's approach. But the expressive *Sarabande* and *Air* and the *Elegiac melodies* respond less well to such analytical presentation.

Holberg suite, Op. 40.
*** DG Dig. 2532/*3302* 031 [id.]. Berlin PO, Karajan – *Concert.****

This is the outstanding item in a triptych of performances (the other composers represented are Mozart and Prokofiev) listed in the Concerts section below. The playing in the Grieg has a wonderful lightness and delicacy, with cultured phrasing not robbing the music of its immediacy. There are many subtleties of colour and texture revealed here by the clear yet sumptuous digital sound, and both on disc and on cassette this is among the finest available versions.

Holberg suite, Op. 40; Lyric suite, Op. 54; Sigurd Jorsalfar (suite), Op. 56.
** Ph. 9500 748/*7300 833* [id.]. ECO, Leppard.

Grieg's delightful *Lyric suite*, which is surprisingly under-represented in the catalogue, is the finest of the performances here, freshly played and warmly recorded. The *Holberg suite*, however, is made to sound rather bland; this performance does not match the lithe, alert articulation of the ASMF version under Marriner (Argo ZRG/*KZRC* 670). *Sigurd Jorsalfar* is reasonably vivid, but not memorable. The recording is naturally balanced; the cassette matches the disc fairly closely.

Symphony in C min.
*** Decca Dig. SXDL/*KSXDC* 7537. Bergen SO, Anderson.

The *Symphony* is a student work written while Grieg was living in Denmark and completed before he was twenty-one. The two inner movements were published in a piano-duet reduction in 1869 as his Op. 14, but Grieg forbade performances of the work after hearing Svendsen's *First Symphony* in 1867, and the score was bequeathed to Bergen Public Library on the understanding that it was never to be performed. Rumour has it that a copy was illicitly made and the score performed in the USSR. In any event the Bergen Harmonien, who played the work in 1865 for the first time under Grieg, have now recorded it in excellent digital sound. The piece takes just over thirty-seven minutes, and those expecting characteristic Grieg will be disappointed: it sounds like the work of any highly talented Leipzig student of the day, only one figure on the oboe towards the end of the second group of the first movement betraying signs of things to come. There are endearing moments but much of the material is uninspired. The scherzo is distinctly second-rate; the corresponding movement of Svendsen's *First* is in a wholly different league, sparkling, inventive and captivating. But although much of Grieg's symphony is pretty unmemorable, it is good to hear for ourselves the kind of music he composed in his youth, and the first movement is arguably as well put together as the first movement of the Op. 7 *Piano sonata*. In

some ways the finale is the most confident of the four movements, though its seams are clearly visible. The ideas are fresher than in the inner movements and though it is no masterpiece, it is uncommonly assured for a youth of twenty, and well laid out for the orchestra. The Decca recording is truthfully balanced, with good perspective and colour, and detail reproduces with fine definition. Like the disc, the excellent cassette has a wide range, plus an attractive ambient warmth.

Cello sonata in A, Op. 36.
(*) CRD CRD 1091/*CRDC 4091*. Robert Cohen, Vignoles – FRANCK: *Cello sonata*.(*)

With his clean, incisive style Cohen gives a strong performance of the rarely heard Grieg *Sonata*, sensitively accompanied by Roger Vignoles. In the folk element Cohen might have adopted a more persuasive style, bringing out the charm of the music more; but certainly he sustains the sonata structures well. The last movement is one of Grieg's most expansive. The recording lacks a little in range at both ends, but presents the cello very convincingly. The cassette transfer is of CRD's usual high quality.

Violin sonata No. 3 in C min., Op. 45.
*** Ph. 9500 568 [id.]. Grumiaux, Sebök – FRANCK: *Sonata*.**(*)

Grumiaux's earlier recording of this often charming sonata was also coupled with the Franck. Unlike the latter, however, the Grieg sonata is not generously represented on record, and at the time of writing this is its only modern version. Grumiaux plays with his usual blend of warmth and nobility and is given good support by György Sebök, even though memories of his earlier accompanist, Istvan Hajdu (and other pianists we have heard in this piece), are not obliterated. Lifelike recording.

Lyric pieces: Op. 12/1; Op. 38/1; Op. 43/1–2; Op. 47/2–4; Op. 54/4–5; Op. 57/6; Op. 62/4 and 6; Op. 65/5; Op. 68/2, 3 and 5; Op. 71/1, 3 and 6–7.
⊛ (M) *** DG Acc. 2542/*3342* 142 [2530 476]. Gilels.

A generous selection of Grieg's *Lyric pieces*, from the well-known *Papillon*, Op. 43/1, to the less often heard and highly poetic set Op. 71, written at the turn of the century. This excellently recorded survey is an admirable alternative to Daniel Adni's complete box, but the playing is of a wholly different order. Good though Mr Adni is, with Gilels we are in the presence of a great keyboard master whose characterization and control of colour and articulation are wholly remarkable. An altogether outstanding record in every way, and the cassette too offers first-class quality. At medium price this is irresistible.

Moods (Stimmungen), Op. 73/1–7; Norwegian peasant dances (Slåtter) Op. 72/1–17.
(M) **(*) RCA Gold GL/*GK* 25329. McCabe.

An imaginatively planned and welcome issue. Opp. 72 and 73 are the most neglected of all Grieg's piano pieces: the *Stimmungen*, placed first on the record, are to all intents and purposes a last set of *Lyric pieces*. They date from 1905, two years before Grieg's death. The *Slåtter* are among his boldest keyboard creations and though their percussive and astringent style was soon to be overtaken by Bartók and Prokofiev, at the time they were composed (1902), they had no real precedent. They derive their inspiration from the folk repertoire of the *hardingefele* (the hardanger fiddle), from which their harmonic daring springs. John McCabe plays all these with spirit and intelligence, though the recording is a shade over-reverberant. Eva Knardahl (on an imported BIS record) may bring slightly greater pianistic finesse to bear, but this coupling is more serviceable and has a distinct price advantage. The cassette transfer is reasonably close to the disc, though the timbre has rather more clang and less warmth and colour.

Landkjenning (Recognition of Land): cantata, Op. 31. (i) *Olav Trygvason* (operatic fragments), *Op. 50: Scenes 1–3.*
*** Uni. RHS/*UKC* 364. Hansli, Oslo Philharmonic Ch., LSO, Dreier, (i) with Carlsen, Hanssen.

Grieg was at the height of his fame when these excerpts from *Olav Trygvason* first saw the light of day in 1888. Olav was the Norwegian King from A.D. 995 to 1000 who converted his pagan countrymen to Christianity, and these three scenes scored a great success at their first performance. But neither they nor *Landkjenning*, an earlier cantata that portrays the Norwegian King sighting land as he returns from his travels to claim the throne, is vintage Grieg, though as always there are some appealing ideas, particularly in the third scene of *Olav*. The cantata was originally written for organ and scored some years later. The Norwegian soloists and chorus respond in exemplary fashion to Per Dreier, who also produces sensitive and idiomatic playing from the LSO. The recording is equally clean and well focused on disc and tape, and readers with a special interest in this eternally fresh composer need not hesitate.

Peer Gynt (incidental music), Op. 23 (complete).
⊛ *** Uni. RHS/*UKC* 361/2. Carlsen, Hanssen, Björköy, Hansli, Oslo Philharmonic Ch., LSO, Dreier.

Grieg's incidental music to *Peer Gynt* is far more extensive than the familiar suites. The score used at the first performance of the play with his music in Oslo in 1876 survives in the Norwegian Music Archives, and the Royal Library in Copenhagen possesses the revised version Grieg prepared for the 1886 production. This recording includes thirty-two numbers in all, including Robert Henriques's scoring of the *Three Norwegian dances* used in the 1886 production in Copenhagen. The score, whether familiar or unfamiliar, continues to astonish by its freshness and inexhaustibility. At one time Ibsen had wanted Grieg to replace Act 4 with a tone-poem describing Peer's wanderings over the globe. Grieg himself found many of these suggestions unmanageable and even went so far as to describe the famous *Hall of the Mountain King* in a letter to Ibsen thus: 'I have written something for the hall of the Troll king which smacks so much of cow-dung, ultra-Norwegianism and self-satisfaction that I literally cannot bear to listen to it.'

Hearing the complete score brings many delightful surprises and serves as a reminder that there is much more to Grieg than the 'sweetmeats filled with snow' of Debussy's image. There are occasional reminders even of Berlioz (*The thief and the receiver* is an instance in point, and *Scene on the upturned boat* could easily have come from Liszt). The scoring is often delicate and imaginative, while the two folk dances in the first act are immensely characterful and far removed from the familiar sweetness associated with Grieg. The playing and singing here are of a high order and though memories of Beecham are not banished in the familiar music, it must be said that the Norwegian conductor Per Dreier achieves very spirited results from his soloists, the Oslo Philharmonic Chorus and our own LSO, with some especially beautiful playing from the woodwind. The recording is generally first-class with a natural perspective between soloists, chorus and orchestra. There is no want of presence and range, though it could do with greater richness in the middle bass. This is perennially fresh and delightful music, and this issue

will almost double the amount of music most people know from *Peer Gynt*. The cassettes are splendidly managed, the sound always clear and well balanced and often reaching demonstration quality.

Peer Gynt (incidental music): extended excerpts.

(M) *** HMV SXLP/*TC-SXLP* 30423 [Ang. S 35445]. Hollweg, Beecham Ch. Soc., RPO, Beecham.

**(*) HMV ASD/*TC-ASD* 3640 [Ang. S 37535]. Valjakka, Thaullaug, Leipzig R. Ch., Dresden State O., Blomstedt.

**(*) Decca SXL/*KSXC* 6901. RPO, Weller.

(M) ** Ph. Seq. 6527/*7311* 086. Stolte, Leipzig GO, Neumann.

All the single-disc compilations from *Peer Gynt* rest under the shadow of Beecham's, which is not ideal as a recording (the choral contribution lacks polish and is rather fiercely recorded), but which offers moments of magical delicacy in the orchestral playing. Beecham showed a very special feeling for this score, and to hear *Morning*, the gently textured *Anitra's dance*, or the eloquent portrayal of the *Death of Aase* under his baton is a uniquely rewarding experience. Ilse Hollweg too is an excellent soloist. The orchestral recording shows its age in fortissimos, where there is a lack of weight in the upper strings, but this fault is minimized by the cassette transfer, which has a slightly smoother treble response than the disc. It is otherwise vivid and well detailed.

The HMV and Decca recordings are of course much more modern and there is some splendid orchestral playing from the Dresden State Orchestra, with Joachim Ulbricht's folksy violin solos especially effective in the *Prelude*. The Leipzig chorus is spirited and vigorous, although the choral recording is not quite as clean as that of the orchestra. But in most respects the sound is lovely, warm and full, although the cassette focus is less sharp than the disc in the heavier climaxes. The two soloists sing strongly and dramatically, not always seeking to charm the ear.

Weller's is a purely orchestral collection, very positively characterized and showing the RPO in excellent form. The Decca recording is of demonstration quality on disc; the cassette is a little fierce but otherwise excellent. It is clean at the top and responds to the controls.

Neumann's Leipzig version omits the *Prelude* and the *Dance of the Mountain King's daughter*, but it is at medium price (as, of course, is Beecham), and the playing is warm and attractive, and there is a fine soloist in Adele Stolte. The recording is pleasingly reverberant and (with a small bass cut) sounds especially well in its tape format, where there is more body given to the upper strings.

Peer Gynt: suites Nos. 1, Op. 46; 2, Op. 55.
(M) ** CBS 60105/40- [Col. MY 36718]. NYPO, Bernstein – SIBELIUS: *Finlandia* etc.**

The slightly mannered performance of *Anitra's dance* and the touch of melodrama in the *Second Suite* add individuality to Bernstein's performances, which are very well played and brilliantly recorded in CBS's brightly lit manner. The string tone in *Morning* lacks bloom in consequence, but the *Arab dance* is strikingly exotic.

Peer Gynt: suite No. 1; suite No. 2: Ingrid's lament; Arab dance.
(*) Telarc Dig. DG 10048 [id.]. St Louis SO, Slatkin – BIZET: *Carmen suites.*(*)

The Telarc digital recording is impressively vivid and clear. The over-resonant bass drum which muddies the fortissimos of the coupled incidental music from Bizet's *Carmen* is less troublesome here (although the climax of *In the hall of the*

Mountain King is not absolutely clean). The orchestral playing is good (*Morning* is not so evocative as in the finest versions) and the overall balance is natural. *Anitra's dance* is played by the first desks of the strings, which gives an intimate, chamber-scale presentation that is not ineffective.

(i) *Peer Gynt suite No. 1.* (ii) *Sigurd Jorsalfar: Homage march. Wedding Day at Troldhaugen, Op. 65/6.*
(M) * DG Priv. 2535/3335 635 [id.]. (i) Bamberg SO, Richard Kraus; (ii) Nordmark SO, Steiner – SIBELIUS: *Finlandia* etc.***

Richard Kraus's Bamberg version of the *First Peer Gynt suite* is well characterized, but the recording dates from 1959 and the lack of body to the upper strings is a serious drawback (it is even thinner on tape than on disc), although the recording is otherwise effectively balanced. The other performances under Steiner are less appealing, and the 1965 sound is no more beguiling. The coupling – Sibelius performances by the Berlin Philharmonic under Karajan – is of high quality.

Grofé, Ferde (1892–1972)

Grand Canyon suite.
(M) *** HMV Green. ESD/TC-ESD 7073 [Ang. S/4XS 37314]. Utah SO, Abravanel – COPLAND: *El Salón Mexico.****

Abravanel and his Utah orchestra understandably provide a most attractive account of the *Grand Canyon suite*, making the most of its melodic content and finding plenty of warmth and colour in the musical pictorialism. *On the trail* is wittily and affectionately done, and the spectacle of the storm scene, with its imitative thunder and lightning effects, is not overdone. The richly reverberant recording does not lack detail and has plenty of bloom. The tape transfer is very well managed and only marginally less crisply focused than the disc (the side-drum is not absolutely clean).

Guastavino, Carlos
(born 1912)

Las Presencias No. 6 (Jeromita Linares) for guitar quintet.
*** CBS Dig. 36671/41-. Williams, L. Qt – BOCCHERINI: *Quintets.****

Carlos Guastavino studied at the Buenos Aires conservatoire and later in London. He is best known, it would seem, for his vocal music, which reflects something of the character of his native Argentina. *Las Presencias No. 6* takes just over thirteen minutes and is conventional both in language and in layout, eminently unmemorable and really quite empty. The three stars are for the performance and a vivid (if somewhat forward) recording. The high-level chrome tape is full-bodied and clear.

Guilmant, Alexandre
(1837–1911)

Allegro in F sharp min.; Elevation in A flat; March on a theme of Handel; Sonata No. 1 in D min.; Wedding march.
*(*) Abbey LPB 794. Jackson (York Minster organ).

Guilmant is not generously represented on record at present, though he was a key figure in French organ music

during his lifetime and one of the founders of the Schola Cantorum. The *Organ sonata* is arguably his best work and certainly has greater interest than the other pieces on this record. The problems of York Minster are considerable, for the period of reverberation is long, yet the engineers have achieved no mean degree of clarity here. There is plenty of atmosphere, but the texture becomes clouded in the lower register. There is nothing spectacular about this music or the playing or the recorded sound, but there is still pleasure to be had for those with an interest in this repertoire, even if the York instrument is not wholly suited to the Gallic style.

Gurney, Ivor (1890–1937)

Ludlow and Teme (song cycle).
*** Hyp. A 66013. Hill, Johnson, Coull Qt – VAUGHAN WILLIAMS: *On Wenlock Edge.****

Gurney's setting of Housman poems uses exactly the same forces as the Vaughan Williams cycle, making the perfect coupling. Gurney, poet as well as composer, is tender and lyrical here, giving hints of tragic overtones by inference merely, himself unhinged by his experiences in the First World War. Martyn Hill with his clear-cut tenor gives understanding performances, admirably accompanied by Graham Johnson and the Coull Quartet. The recording is nicely atmospheric.

Hadley, Patrick (1899–1973)

(i) *One Morning in Spring* (rhapsody for small orch.); (ii) *The Trees So High* (symphonic ballad).

*** Lyr. SRCS 106. (i) LPO, Boult; (ii) Allen, Guildford Philharmonic Ch., New Philh. O., Handley.

For most of his working career Patrick Hadley was the archetypal Cambridge composer, seduced by the charms of life as a senior member of the university from writing the music he plainly had in him. *The Trees So High*, described as a symphonic ballad, is a wide-ranging choral work taking the folksong of that name as its base. The idiom is broadly in the Vaughan Williams school but spiced with invention eclectically drawn from later composers. Thomas Allen makes an outstanding soloist, and Vernon Handley draws persuasive singing and playing from his large forces. The fill-up is a short piece written for the seventieth birthday of Vaughan Williams, charming in its lack of pretension. Both works are beautifully recorded.

Handel, George Frideric
(1685–1759)

Ballet music from *Alcina* (including *Overture* and *Dream music*); *Ariodante* (including *Overture*); *Il Pastor Fido:* Hunting scene.
(M) *** Argo ZK/*KZKC* 68. ASMF, Marriner.

One of Sir Thomas Beecham's hobbies was exploring the lesser-known music of Handel to find items for his ballet suites. Here we have a generous selection using Handel's original scoring. The music from *Alcina* is particularly diverse in invention, and all is played with grace and marvellous rhythmic point by Marriner and his splendid orchestral group. The recording is of superlative quality, and the cassette transfer is admirable, offering warmth as well as Argo's characteristic bright clarity.

Concerto grosso in C (*Alexander's Feast*); Concerto a due cori No. 2 in F; Music for the Royal Fireworks.
(M) ** DG Arc. Priv. 2547/*3347* 006. Cappella Coloniensis or Schola Cantorum Basiliensis, Wenzinger.

These recordings were made in the early days of stereo, but the sound is not very dated and Wenzinger's performances are alert and stylish. The account of the *Fireworks music* has a splendid feeling for the open-air style of the writing, with crisp buoyant rhythms. The use of original instruments gives a suitably robust effect (together with less than perfect intonation). The cassette quality is less refined than the disc, especially in the *Concerto a due cori*, and the *Alexander's Feast Concerto grosso* is rather lacking in body and bloom.

Concerti grossi, Op. 3/1–6.
(M) *** HMV Green. ESD/*TC-ESD* 7089. Prague CO, Mackerras.
(M) *** Ph. 9502/*7313* 006. ECO, Leppard.
(M) *** DG Arc. Priv. 2547/*3347* 017. Cappella Coloniensis, Wenzinger.
(M) **(*) ASV ACM/*ZCACM* 2004. Northern Sinfonia, Malcolm.
** Erato STU 71367. E. Bar. Soloists, Gardiner.

Mackerras brings his usual blend of scholarship and vitality to bear on these inventive concertos and he draws good playing from the Prague orchestra. In a field that is already quite well filled, this set is still highly competitive and also has the advantage of excellent recorded sound. Mackerras is more robust than Leppard, and his recording has more body. The cassette transfer is vividly bright and immediate, first-rate in every way.

Lively, fresh performances too from Leppard on Philips and very good sound on both disc and cassette. Leppard includes oboes and bassoons and secures

excellent playing all round. At times one
wonders if he isn't just a shade too elegant, as if he were playing Arne, but these
are fleeting thoughts, and in general this
set ranks among the very best versions of
Op. 3.

Wenzinger was a pioneer of recording
baroque music using original instruments, and his 1960 record has a special
place in the catalogue. There are some
delightful sounds here, from soft-grained
oboes and recorder to 'woody' bassoons.
Horst Schneider provides some very distinguished oboe playing in No. 2; No.
6 includes a well-balanced organ solo
contribution from Eduard Müller. The
sound is generally very good on both disc
and cassette, although the tape transfer
drops in level on side two, with a consequent slight loss of range.

George Malcolm's performances are
spirited and stylish and not lacking
polish. The recording is vivid, but the
forward balance of the oboes makes them
sound rather larger than life and tends to
reduce the dynamic range, although the
contrasts of light and shade within the
strings are effective. Rhythms are sometimes jogging rather than sprightly, but
this is enjoyable music-making, and the
vivid cassette transfer has striking life
and detail.

There is some spirited playing from the
English Baroque Soloists under John
Eliot Gardiner, who give the Op. 3 concertos with no want of style. However,
there is a lack of finish in one or two
places, and some poor intonation in No.
2 in B flat. There are, of course, many
good things here – not least an admirably
balanced and fresh-sounding recording –
but this issue cannot be regarded as a first
choice.

*Concerti grossi, Op. 6/3, 5, 7, 9–10
and 12.*
(M) **(*) DG Priv. 2726 069 (2). Berlin
PO, Karajan.

(i) *Concerti grossi, Op. 6/3–4 and 8.*
(ii) *Music for the Royal Fireworks.*

(M) ** DG Priv. 2535/3335 269. Berlin
PO, (i) Karajan, (ii) Kubelik.

The two-disc Privilege set completes
Karajan's set of Op. 6 (the other concertos are on 2726 068). But with only
three concertos to a disc the format is not
very economical, even at medium price.
Karajan directs the performances from
the keyboard, and so, while a large body
of strings has been used in a reverberant
acoustic, the continuo comes through
clearly. The playing of the Berlin Philharmonic is lively and polished and there
is much to admire here; the performance
of No. 5 in D is particularly fine. If elsewhere the full baroque spirit is sometimes
a little submerged, there is still much to
enjoy, and the recording is only slightly
dated. Kubelik also uses a full orchestra
for the *Fireworks music* and there is some
predictably fine playing. The sound,
however, is not ideally transparent. The
quality on tape is acceptable but not outstanding because of the low transfer
level.

*Concerti a due cori Nos. 1 in B flat;
2–3 in F.*
(M) **(*) Ph. 9502/7313 021. ECO, Leppard.

The *Concerti a due cori* were almost
certainly written for performance with
the three patriotic oratorios (No. 1 with
Joshua, 2 with *Alexander Balus* and 3
with *Judas Maccabaeus*). Leppard gives
very stylish accounts of them and there is
some marvellous wind-playing. At times
one feels the need for a greater sense of
space or majesty, but the alertness and
brilliance of the playing are always a
source of pleasure. At medium price this
issue is competitive. The cassette transfer,
however, is made at an unexpectedly high
level, which brings a degree of congestion
from the horns in the two *F major Concerti.*

Harp concerto, Op. 4/6.
*** Argo ZRG/KZRC 930. Robles,

ASMF, Iona Brown – BOIELDIEU and DITTERSDORF: *Concertos.****

Handel's Op. 4/6 is well-known in both organ and harp versions. Marisa Robles makes an unforgettable case for the latter by creating the most delightful textures, yet never letting the work sound insubstantial. She is well served by the excellent Argo recording and the stylish and beautifully balanced accompaniment from the ASMF under Iona Brown. The cassette transfer is splendidly fresh and clean, retaining the luminous texture of the outstanding disc. This collection as a whole makes perfect late-evening listening.

Concerto for 2 lutes in B flat, Op. 4/ 6.
(*) RCA RL/*RK* 11180 [ARL 1/*ARK 1* 1180]. Bream, Spencer, Monteverdi O., Gardiner – KOHAUT and VIVALDI: *Concertos.*(*)

Here the ever-engaging Op. 4/6 appears in Thurston Dart's reconstruction for lute and harp, which Bream has further adjusted and elaborated, using a chitarrone for the slow-movement continuo. The performance is a fine one (Bream plays both solo parts), but it suffers from an unnatural recording balance, with the soloists placed forwardly so that their dynamic range approaches that of the orchestra, with very little contrast. The cassette transfer, made at the highest level, is extremely vivid.

Oboe concertos Nos. 1–2 in B flat; 3 in G min.
(M) *** HMV SXLP/*TC-SXLP* 30294 [Ang. S 3610]. Goossens, Bath Festival CO, Menuhin – BACH and VIVALDI: *Concertos.****

This is the star item in an attractive collection of baroque concertos recorded in the early sixties. Leon Goossens is

in ravishing form, and although his recorded image is not as forward as usual, this integration into the string texture, in the nature of a concerto grosso, in no way diminishes the projection of his personality. Menuhin accompanies sympathetically and the recording does not sound its age. The tape transfer is smooth and realistic.

Organ concertos Nos. 1–6, Op. 4/1– 6; 7 in F (The Cuckoo and the Nightingale); 8 in A (Set 2); 13–18, Op. 7/ 1–6; 19 in D min.; 20 in F.
*** Erato STU 71097 (4). Alain (organ of Collegiate Church), Paillard CO, Paillard.

Organ concertos Nos. 1–6, Op. 4; 13– 18, Op. 7.
**(*) Tel. FK6/*MH4* 35282 (3). Tachezi, VCM, Harnoncourt.

A French view of Handel might be expected to provide a new look, and in fact the Erato set is a highly successful venture on almost every count: the playing has breadth and an appropriate feeling of grandeur at times, as well as the expected elegance. The Op. 7 set is particularly successful. The solo playing is consistently alert and imaginative; the dance movements are delightful. Op. 7/1, after an impressively regal opening, has an enchanting closing *Bourrée*, while in No. 3 of the same set the contrasts of colour between soloist and ripieno in the fugal *Spiritoso* third movement are matched by the rhythmic grace of the minuet. The *Andante larghetto e staccato* of Op. 7/5 is a set of Handelian variations over an ostinato bass, and this brings some characterfully rhythmic articulation from the soloist, and the elegance of the closing *Gavotte* is no less striking. Among the four concertos without opus numbers, *The Cuckoo and the Nightingale* can surely never have been more winningly registered on disc, and its *Siciliano* slow movement is most graciously played. The *A major Concerto* is an arrangement of a *Concerto grosso* (Op. 6/ 11); the finale specializes in echoes which are realized stereophonically by the antiphonal use of two manuals. Marie-Claire Alain's creative contribution is unfailingly stylish and inventive, and it seems almost churlish to mention the slight reservation that the first four concertos of the Op. 4 set, although still enjoyable, seem to have marginally less life and spontaneity than the rest. On the other hand the registration at the opening of Op. 4/6 (also well-known in transcribed versions) is memorable. Taken as a whole, this set would seem to be a clear first choice in this repertoire.

Herbert Tachezi concentrates on the twelve concertos which make up Opp. 4 and 7, which he offers complete. We are told in the accompanying booklet that the ornamentation in these performances was essentially spontaneous and even varied from take to take. This may have made Harnoncourt and his accompanying group over-cautious, for they sometimes seem unadventurous, even square. The overall scale of the music-making is relatively modest, creating an agreeable chamber-music atmosphere. However, at times one feels that the more robust and grander qualities of Handel's inspiration are played down. Tachezi's registration and decorative flourishes give consistent cause for pleasure; his unnamed organ is a splendid instrument and obviously well chosen for this repertoire. It makes a strong contrast with the 'authentic' string group, which at times produce a rather sombre colouring. Their rhythmic pointing can sometimes be agreeably lively too. The recording is excellent on disc, and the use of chrome tape has produced a wide-ranging tape transfer (indeed the upper range needs smoothing). There are two cassettes against three LPs, which seems perverse; had three cassettes been used it would have been possible to have two works to each side.

Organ concertos Nos. 2 and 4, Op. 4/ 2 and 4; 7 in F (The Cuckoo and the Nightingale); 16, Op. 7/4.
**(*) Argo ZRG/KZRC 888. Malcolm, ASMF, Marriner.

Organ concertos Nos. 7; 13 and 15–16, Op. 7/1, 3–4.
(M) *** DG Priv. 2535/3335 264. Müller, Schola Cantorum Basiliensis, Wenzinger.

Organ concertos Nos. 7; 16–18, Op. 7/ 4–6.
(M) *** Ph. 9502/7313 022. Chorzempa, Concerto Amsterdam, Schröder.

Organ concertos Nos. 8 in A; 19 in D min.; 20 in F.
(M) *** Ph. 9502/7313 007. Chorzempa, Concerto Amsterdam, Schröder.

Excellent selections here from the Malcolm and Chorzempa complete sets, contrasted in sound and feeling: Malcolm's registrations are piquant and refined; Chorzempa, using a Dutch organ (and with the Concerto Amsterdam playing period instruments), is broader, more robust. Both are splendidly recorded on disc. The Argo cassette is clean and clear, but slightly dry in the bass; the Philips tapes are of demonstration quality, with a sparkling treble response.

Eduard Müller's Privilege collection is also very attractive, demonstrating the German approach to Handel at its most persuasive. The playing is sturdy rather than incandescent, but very satisfying, and the sound is both full and lively. For Op. 7/1 Müller plays the large organ of the Tituskirche in Basle; a less ambitious instrument is used elsewhere, and Müller's registration is admirable. The accompanying group uses period instruments to colourful effect. The recording quality on cassette is especially fine.

Overtures: *Agrippina; Alcina; Belshazzar; Deidamia; Jephtha; Radamisto; Rinaldo; Rodelinda; Susanna.*

(M) *** DG Priv. 2535 242. LPO, Karl Richter.

Richter is weighty, but his broadness of style is tempered by brilliantly alert orchestral playing, with allegros taken exhilaratingly fast. Those who admire the German tradition in Handel will find this partnership with a British orchestra fruitful and rewarding. The recording is first-class.

Music for the Royal Fireworks (original wind scoring).
⊕ *** Telarc Dig. DG 5038 [id.]. Cleveland Symphonic Winds, Fennell – HOLST: *Military band suites.* ⊕ ***

Music for the Royal Fireworks (original wind scoring); *Concertos Nos. 1 in F; 3 in D; Concerto a due cori No. 2 in F.*
*** HMV ASD/TC-ASD 3395 [Ang. S/4XS 37404]. LSO, Mackerras.

Music for the Royal Fireworks; Concerto grosso in C (Alexander's Feast); Overture in D.
**(*) Ph. 9500 868/7300 843. ASMF, Marriner.

(i) *Music for the Royal Fireworks;* (ii) *Berenice overture; Concerto a due cori No. 3 in F.*
*(*) CBS 76834/40- [Col. M/MT 35833].
(i) NYPO; (ii) Philh. CO, Boulez.

Music for the Royal Fireworks; Water music: extended suite.
(M) *** Ph. Seq. 6527/7311 047. ECO, Leppard.

In 1959 Mackerras made a historic recording of Handel's *Fireworks music* with an enormous band of wind, including twenty-six oboes. In 1977 HMV attempted to produce a comparable version with the benefit of modern stereo; a year later, in Severance Hall, Cleveland, Ohio, Frederick Fennell gathered together the wind and brass from the Cleveland Orchestra and recorded a new

performance to demonstrate spectacularly what fine playing and digital sound could do for Handel's open-air score. Not all the sound is massive, of course; there is some refreshingly sprightly articulation in the *Bourrée*. But in the *Overture*, *La Réjouissance* and the closing section of the *Minuet*, the effect is overwhelming, with marvellously telling use of the drums. Indeed one can shut one's eyes and imagine the fiery set-pieces and the rockets shooting up into the sky. The record also includes an inflated account of Bach's *Fantasia in G*, but that is not an asset. The performance of the Handel represents one of the first great classic successes of digital recording, and the reading itself has genuine grandeur.

On HMV too the martial music is formidably impressive, and the impact of Mackerras's version is vividly and powerfully caught. The *Concerto a due cori* is also impressive with its antiphonal wind effects, and the two other concertos with their anticipations of the *Fireworks music* make an apt fill-up. The sound on cassette is full-blooded, marginally less crisp and fresh than on the disc, but still impressive.

On the mid-price Philips Sequenza label Leppard's is an outstanding coupling. The resonance of the sound in the *Fireworks music* matches the broad and spectacular reading, while the substantial extract from Leppard's complete *Water music* recording has comparable flair, combining rhythmic resilience with an apt feeling for ceremony. The sound is excellent (the cassette full and lively too, if marginally less sharp in focus than the disc), and this is good value. But it must be remembered that at full price Marriner offers an outstanding coupling of the complete *Fireworks* and *Water music* (Argo ZRG/KZRC 697).

Using a relatively small band (more suitable for Handel's concert hall than for a grand occasion in the open air), Marriner directs an elegant performance of the *Fireworks music*, beautifully recorded. Energy is there as well as polish, as too in the attractive couplings; the *Overture in D* is hardly known at all but very much breathes the same air as the rest.

Boulez's direction of Handel is disappointing, inappropriately heavy and unsprung, and it is not helped by poor ensemble and indifferent recording. The *Berenice overture* is better played and recorded by the Philharmonia Orchestra, but that is little compensation. The cassette transfer is edgy and fierce.

Water music: suites Nos. 1–3 (complete).
*** O-L DSLO/*KDSLC* 543 [id.]. AcAM, Hogwood.
*** Ph. 9500 691/*7300 779* [id.]. ASMF, Marriner.
(M) *** Ph. Fest. 6570/*7310* 018 [6500 047/*7300 060*]. ECO, Leppard.
*** Ar. Eur. Dig. 203676. Lucerne Festival O., Baumgartner.
*** Delos Dig. DMS 3010 [id.]. LACO, Schwarz.
** HMV ASD/*TC-ASD* 3597 [Ang. S/ *4XS* 37532]. Prague CO, Mackerras.
** Tel. AW6/*CX4* 42368. VCM, Harnoncourt.
(M) *(*) RCA Gold GL/*GK* 25241. Paillard CO, Paillard.

The Academy of Ancient Music has made many records for Oiseau-Lyre but few more immediately appealing than this account of music familiar in less 'authentic' renderings. Though it may come as a surprise to hear the well known *Air* taken so fast – like a minuet – the sparkle and airiness of the invention have rarely been so endearingly caught on record. The unusual timbres of original instruments are here consistently attractive, with vibrato-less string tone never squeezed too painfully. It was with this work that the Academy made its Prom début in the summer of 1978, and the joy of that occasion is matched by this performance, in which scholarship and imagination are ideally joined. The cassette

transfer is lively but rather astringent in the treble. The upper partials could be cleaner, and the trumpets in the third suite are not free from discoloration.

The Philips version of the *Water music* brings Neville Marriner's second complete recording, and characteristically he has taken the trouble to correct several tiny textual points wrongly read before. The playing too is even finer than before, helped by full-ranging, refined recording. For anyone wanting a version using modern instruments this is highly recommendable, although one cannot forget that the Argo issue (ZRG/*KZRC* 697, which still sounds extremely well) offers the *Fireworks music* too. The Philips cassette is of excellent, natural quality but does not sparkle at the top like the Argo tape.

For anyone wanting the *Water music* alone, a medium-priced issue is undoubtedly attractive, and Raymond Leppard and the ECO give elegant, beautifully turned and stylish performances of all three suites on Festivo, with well-judged and truthful recording. Moreover the equivalent cassette, transferred at a high level, offers virtually demonstration quality, fresh, vivid and clean, with no problems from the brass entry in the third suite.

The first two digital recordings of the *Water music* appeared within a month of each other at the end of 1981. The Eurodisc version comes nearer to Leppard's set, with a warmly resonant acoustic, yet with clean lines and no blurring of inner detail. Tempi throughout are admirably chosen (the famous *Air* is nicely paced, expressive without being too slow). In many ways Baumgartner's approach is traditional, yet his predominantly young players prevent any heaviness, and rhythms are nicely buoyant. But it is the warm beauty of the sound that impresses the ear, although the continuo is reticent.

The Los Angeles performance under Gerard Schwarz is hardly less enjoyable, its character more athletic, with playing that is both polished and sprightly, less warmly elegant than Leppard. It has an attractive freshness of spirit, yet is without the abrasiveness of Hogwood's early instrumental timbres. In the second movement of the first suite the oboe soloist takes an extra degree of rhythmic freedom, yet still plays very stylishly. The sound is first-class; the horns are crisp and in the D major suite, which (as in the Lucerne recording) is placed second, the trumpets are bright and gleaming. The clear detail does not prevent an overall ambient warmth. However, this record is very much more expensive than its companions.

Mackerras is a lively Handelian, as many records have shown, including two of the *Fireworks music*. But this version of the complete *Water music* has a heavyweight quality in the string tone (hardly a question of recording), which weighs the music down too often and prevents it from sparkling. The recording is rich and vivid, but there are several finer versions. The tape transfer is well managed, smooth and vivid.

Harnoncourt's use of original instruments, however admirable on most of his records, is too often aggressively unpleasing in the *Water music* – for example in the raspberry effect of trilling horns in the famous *Allegro*. Fast speeds can be very apt and effective – as in the admirable version by the Academy of Ancient Music, also using original instruments – but here they often sound brutal and unsympathetic. The recording is of good Telefunken quality. The chrome tape is disappointing, with patches of coarseness at climaxes.

The performance by Jean-François Paillard and his chamber orchestra is acceptable but in no way remarkable or distinguished by special insights. In such a competitive field it hardly competes, even at medium price. The cassette transfer is ill-focused and has a limited dynamic range.

Water music (suite, arr. Harty).
*** Chan. DBR/*DBT* 2001 (2). Ulster O., Thomson – HARTY: *Violin concerto* etc.***
(M) *** Chan. CBR/*CBT* 1005 (as above) – HARTY: *John Field suite* etc.***

It was Sir Hamilton Harty's famous suite that introduced many listeners to Handel's *Water music*. It has fallen out of favour in recent years, though it still retains a foothold in the catalogue. Bryden Thomson gives a good account of it, but frankly the main interest here is the couplings. The two-disc set offers a substantial Harty work in the form of the *Violin concerto* (not on the medium-priced separate issue) and some lighter music from his pen, all well recorded. The tape transfer is vivid and well balanced, but the upper range is restricted compared with the LP version.

CHAMBER AND INSTRUMENTAL MUSIC

'Halle' Trio sonatas for 2 oboes and continuo Nos. 1–6.
*** Ph. 9500 671/7300 766 [id.]. Holliger, Bourgue, Sax, Jaccottet.

The so-called *'Halle' Trio sonatas* are among the very first works Handel ever wrote. Although no autograph survives, the flute player Weidemann copied them while in London and Handel acknowledged them as having been written while he was studying with Zachow. These are scrupulous and imaginative performances, beautifully balanced and elegant in every way. They are extremely well recorded and should appeal to all lovers of this period save those who feel strongly that baroque instruments are essential for this music.

Violin sonatas, Op. 1/1, 3, 10, 12–13 and 15.
(M) *(*) Ph. 9502 023 [id.]. Grumiaux, Veyron-Lacroix.

The slow movements are rather romanticized, which is not wholly unwelcome, but in the outer movements both Grumiaux and his partner do not sound wholly committed. Well-played and recorded though it is, this issue raises little real enthusiasm.

Recorder sonatas, Op. 1/2, 4, 7, 11; in B flat; in D min.
*** Tel. EX 6.35359 (2). Brüggen, Bylsma, Leonhardt – TELEMANN: *Essercizii musici.****

These recordings all come from the mid-1960s. Frans Brüggen is at his most effortless and inspired in the Handel, where he seems wholly untroubled by such considerations as taking breath! His sense of style matches his technical command, and the recording is fresh and immediate.

Harpsichord suites Nos. 1 in B flat; 2: Chaconne in G; 3 in D min.; 4 in D min.; 5 in E min.; 6 in G min.; 7 in B flat; 8 in G; 9: Prelude and Chaconne in G.
*(*) Ar. Eur. 300003 (2). Krapp.

Harpsichord suites Nos. 1–8.
(M) *** HM HM 447/8. Gilbert.

Harpsichord suite in D min.; Partitas: in A; in G; in C min. Pieces: Air in B flat; Air and Double in F; Allegro in D min.; 3 Allemandes; 2 Chaconnes in G min.; Entree in G min.; Fuge in F; Impertinence in G min.; Overture in G min.; Preludes: in D min.; F; G min.; Prelude and Capriccio in G; Sonata in G min.; Sonatinas: in A min.; B flat; G; G min. (2); Toccata in G min.
*(*) Ar. Eur. 300403 (2). Krapp.

The *Suites* are among Handel's most rewarding instrumental works, and recordings of them and his other keyboard music are not so thick on the ground that we can afford to pick and choose. Since 1977, Colin Tilney's Archive set has disappeared from the catalogue, which leaves Kenneth Gilbert's and Edgar Krapp's as the only recent versions. Gilbert is a scholar as well as a distinguished player, and his version of *Suites 1–8*, recorded on a copy of a Taskin harpsichord by Bedard, is well worth seeking out. Like the only available rival, Blandine Verlet, Gilbert observes most first-half repeats but not the second, and he is as imaginative in the handling of decoration and ornamentation as one would expect. If one were to quibble, it would be merely that some grandeur, some larger-than-life vitality, is missing; but so much else is there that there is no case for qualifying the recommendation. The recording is much better balanced and more natural than its recent rivals.

Krapp is an accomplished artist, though a trifle academic, perhaps. His instrument in the 1733 suites is a copy of a Kirckman, and in the second set he uses a fine 1620 Ruckers from the Brussels Conservatoire Museum. The playing does not eclipse memories of such artists as Anton Heiller and Thurston Dart and does not match their flair and imagination, but this is in some measure due to the close balance and high level at which he is recorded. This does not enable such variety of colour as there is to make itself properly felt, and as a result the ear tends rapidly to tire.

VOCAL AND CHORAL MUSIC

Acis and Galatea (masque).
*** Argo ZRG 886/7/*K 114 K 22* (2) [id.]. Gomez, Tear, Langridge, Luxon, Ch. and ASMF, Marriner.
*** DG Arc. 2708 020/*3375 004* (2) [id.]. Burrowes, Rolfe Johnson, Hill, Elliot, White, E. Bar. Soloists, Gardiner.

The refinement and rhythmic lift of the

Academy's playing under Marriner
makes for a lively and highly engaging
performance of *Acis and Galatea*, marked
by characterful solo singing from a
strong team. The choruses are sung by a
vocal quartet (not the same singers) and
with warmly atmospheric recording the
result is a sparkling entertainment.
Robert Tear's tone is not always ideally
mellifluous (for instance in *Love in her
eyes sits playing*), but like the others he
has a good feeling for Handel style, and
the sweetness of Jill Gomez's contribution is a delight. The cassette transfer,
made at a characteristically high level,
has plenty of range and detail, capturing
the resonant acoustic faithfully and placing soloists and chorus in realistic perspective.

Some of John Eliot Gardiner's tempi
are idiosyncratic (some too fast, some too
slow), but the scale of performance, using
original instruments, is beautifully
judged to simulate domestic conditions
such as they might have been in the first
performance for the Duke of Chandos,
with the vocal soloists banding together
for the choruses. The acoustic is far drier
than in the Argo version, and the soloists
are less characterful, though more consistently sweet of tone. The authentic
sounds of the English Baroque Soloists
are finely controlled so as not to offend
unprepared ears too blatantly, and those
who prefer vibrato-less string tone for
music of this period should certainly
select this. The DG cassette transfer is
made at a somewhat lower level than the
Argo, producing an extra smoothness in
the treble, although there is no lack of
life to the voices. The orchestra, in particular, has splendid presence and detail.

Alceste (overture and incidental
music).
*** O-L DSLO 581. Nelson, Kirkby,
Cable, Elliot, Thomas, AcAM, Hogwood.

Commissioned to write incidental
music for a play by Smollett (something

to associate with Purcell, not Handel),
the composer was stopped in his tracks
with the abandonment of the whole project. Nonetheless there is much to enjoy
here, not just solo items but also some
simple tuneful choruses, all introduced
by an impressive dramatic overture in D
minor. Hogwood draws lively performances from his usual team and as ever is
very well recorded.

Alexander's Feast.
*** HMV SLS/*TC-SLS* 5168 (2) [Ang.
SZ 3874]. Donath, Burgess, Tear,
Allen, King's College Ch., ECO,
Ledger.
**(*) Tel. EX 6.35330 (2) [id.]. Palmer,
Rolfe Johnson, Roberts, Stockholm
Bach Ch., VCM, Harnoncourt.

Philip Ledger directs an exhilarating
performance of one of Handel's most
concentratedly inventive choral works,
far shorter in span than the big oratorios
but here augmented by a duet and chorus
which Handel tacked on at the end, the
duet most prettily sung by Helen Donath
and Sally Burgess. But the meat of the
piece lies in such big arias as the bass's
Revenge, Timotheus cries, brilliantly and
heroically sung here by Thomas Allen.
Robert Tear in the tenor role sometimes
pushes heroic tone into roughness, but he
too is most compelling, while King's
College Choir sings both angelically and
incisively in the choruses. The recording
on both disc and cassette is warmly
atmospheric without being unclear, and
the presentation, including the notes by
Winton Dean, is exemplary.

Harnoncourt's version may be warmly
recommended to those who insist on a
version of this splendid work using original instruments, though in energy and
conviction it cannot really compare with
Ledger's outstanding version with King's
College Choir. Here Harnoncourt uses a
mixed choir (in any case less authentic,
since Handel plainly expected male
voices in the top line in the drinking

chorus, not contraltos), but it is a superb ensemble from Sweden. The soloists are first-rate; Anthony Rolfe Johnson has rarely sounded so resonant on record, though Stephen Roberts lacks the weight really needed for *Revenge, Timotheus cries.* First-rate recording, but inadequate documentation – surprising when linked to a performance aiming at the highest scholarship.

L'Allegro, il penseroso, il moderato.
*** Erato STU 71325 (2). Kwella, McLaughlin, Jennifer Smith, Ginn, Davies, Hill, Varcoe, Monteverdi Ch., E. Bar. Soloists, Gardiner.

Taking Milton as his starting point, Handel illustrated in music the contrasts of mood and character between the cheerful and the thoughtful. Then, prompted by his librettist, Charles Jennens, he added compromise in *Il moderato*, the moderate man. The final chorus may fall a little short of the rest (Jennens's words cannot have provided much inspiration), but otherwise the sequence of brief numbers is a delight, particularly in a performance as exhilarating as this, with excellent soloists, choir and orchestra. The recording is first-rate.

Anthem for the Foundling Hospital; Ode for the birthday of Queen Anne.
*** O-L DSLO/*KDSLC* 541. Nelson, Kirkby, Minty, Bowman, Hill, Thomas, Ch. of Christ Church Cath., Oxford, AcAM, Preston.

Two splendid examples of Handel's occasional music make an excellent coupling, superbly performed and recorded. The *Ode* is an early work, written soon after Handel arrived in England. It has its Italianate attractions, but it is the much later *Foundling Hospital Anthem* on the reverse which is much the more memorable, not just because it concludes with an alternative version of the *Hallelujah chorus* (sounding delightfully fresh on this scale with the Christ Church Choir) but because the other borrowed numbers are superb too. An extra tang is given by the accompaniment on original instruments. The tape transfer is of excellent quality, with plenty of bloom as well as clarity and a very good choral focus, considering the degree of resonance.

Cantata: *Crudel tiranno Amor.* Motet: *Silete venti. Giulio Cesare: E pur così in un giorno . . . Piangerò la sorte mia (Cleopatra's aria).*
*** Ph. Fest. 6570/*7310* 113 [id.]. Ameling, ECO, Leppard.

The delicacy, sparkle, precision and sweetness of Elly Ameling's voice make this a delightful record, with Leppard directing beautifully sprung accompaniments. One might object that *Cleopatra's aria* could be more dramatic, but as elsewhere the freshness here is most captivating, and the 1971 recording still sounds well in this mid-price reissue. The high-level cassette transfer is first-class in every way. An issue not to be missed, whichever format is chosen.

Dixit Dominus; Zadok the Priest.
*** Erato STU 71055. Palmer, Margaret Marshall, Brett, Messana, Morton, Thomson, Wilson-Johnson, Monteverdi Ch. and O., Gardiner.

Dixit Dominus.
(M) ** HMV SXLP/*TC-SXLP* 30444 [Ang. S 36331]. Zylis-Gara, Baker, Lane, Tear, Shirley-Quirk, King's College Ch., ECO, Willcocks.

Handel's *Dixit Dominus* dates from 1707 and was completed during his prolonged stay in Italy from 1706 to 1710. It divides into eight sections, and the setting, while showing signs of Handel's mature style in embryo, reflects also the baroque tradition of contrasts between small and large groups. The writing is extremely florid and requires bravura from soloists and chorus alike. John Eliot Gardiner catches all its brilliance and directs an exhilarating performance marked by strongly accented, sharply incisive singing from the choir and outstanding solo contributions. In high contrast with the dramatic choruses the duet for two sopranos, *De torrente*, here beautifully sung by Felicity Palmer and Margaret Marshall, is languorously expressive but stylishly so. Other soloists match that, and the recording is first-rate.

The performance on HMV is also alive and spirited, but one senses that the security that comes with complete familiarity is not always present. The intonation of the soloists is not above reproach, and the trio *Dominus a dextris*, which comes at the beginning of side two, is not very comfortable. The chorus seems not completely happy with the virtuoso running passages a little later; Sir David Willcocks might have achieved more security had he been content with a slightly slower pace. There is vigour and enthusiasm here but not always the last degree of finesse. The recording is atmospheric, but the focus is not absolutely sharp. The cassette matches the disc closely.

Funeral anthem for Queen Caroline: The Ways of Zion Do Mourn.

*** Erato STU 71173. Burrowes, Brett, Hill, Varcoe, Monteverdi Ch. and O., Gardiner.

Queen Caroline – whom Handel had known earlier as a princess in Hanover – was the most cultivated of the royal family of the Georges, and when she died in 1737 he was inspired to write a superb cantata in an overture and eleven numbers. He later used the material for the first acts of *Israel in Egypt*. Gardiner directs a performance which brings out the high contrasts implicit in the music, making the piece energetic rather than

elegiac. Excellent work from soloists, chorus and orchestra alike, all very well recorded.

Israel in Egypt.

**(*) Erato STU 71245 (3). Knibbs, Troth, Clarkson, Elliot, Varcoe, Monteverdi Ch. and O., Gardiner.

Israel in Egypt has been lucky on record. Gardiner's fine version with its bitingly dramatic and incisive choral singing follows on the versions of Mackerras (with chamber orchestra but large choir) and Simon Preston (with boy trebles in the authentically sized choir). On choir alone the Gardiner is probably the finest of the three, but unlike the other versions the soloists here come from the choir itself, and though they sing well they rarely match in imagination the star singers of the other two sets. Nonetheless the vigour and concentration of the performance are formidably convincing, helped by excellent recording.

Still recommended: The Argo set with Gale, Watson, Bowman, Partridge and McDonald and the Christ Church Cathedral Choir under Preston is on ZRG 817/8; the DG Archive set with Harper, Clark, Esswood, Young, Rippon and Keyte and the Leeds Festival Chorus, directed by Charles Mackerras, is on 2708 020.

Jephtha.

*** Argo D 181 D 4/*K 181 K 43* (4) [id.]. Rolfe Johnson, Margaret Marshall, Hodgson, Esswood, Keyte, Kirkby, Ch. and ASMF, Marriner.

** Tel. GK 6.35499 (4) [id.]. Hollweg, Gale, Linos, Esswood, Thomaschke, Sima, Moz. Boys' Ch., Schoenberg Ch., VCM, Harnoncourt.

Jephtha, the last oratorio that Handel completed, is a strange and not always very moral tale. With the threat of blindness on him the composer was forced to break off from writing for several months, but that threat seems only to have added to the urgency of inspiration, and Marriner's performance, helped by the bright tones of boy trebles in the choruses, is refreshing from first to last, well sprung but direct in style. The soloists are excellent, with Emma Kirkby nicely distanced in the role of the Angel, her clean vibrato-less voice made the more ethereal. It is a very long oratorio, but in this performance it hardly seems so, with such beautiful numbers as Jephtha's *Waft her, angels* given a finely poised performance by Rolfe Johnson. The recording is first-rate, and the cassette transfer has a fine sparkle, with lively presence and detail.

Harnoncourt's pursuit of extra authenticity, with an orchestra using original instruments, will make his version an automatic choice for many; but for the general listener it has its snags, not just in the acid timbres of the strings. Harnoncourt takes a more operatic view of the work than Marriner on the rival version, which appeared simultaneously, but he mars the impact of that by too frequently adopting a mannered style of phrasing. The soloists too are on balance far less impressive than those on the Marriner version. The recording acoustic, typically clean, is less helpful in its relative dryness next to the rival set.

Judas Maccabaeus.
*** DG 2723 050/*3376 011* (3) [id.]. Palmer, Baker, Esswood, Davies, Shirley-Quirk, Keyte, Wandsworth School Ch., ECO, Mackerras.

Judas Maccabaeus may have a lopsided story, with a high proportion of the finest music given to the anonymous soprano and contralto roles, Israelitish Woman (Felicity Palmer) and Israelitish Man (Dame Janet Baker), but the sequence of Handelian gems is irresistible, the more so in a performance as sparkling as this one under Sir Charles Mackerras. Unlike many versions, particularly those

which in scholarly fashion attempt to restore Handel's original proportions, this holds together with no let-up of intensity, and though not everyone will approve of the use of boys' voices in the choir (inevitably the tone and intonation are not flawless) it gives an extra bite of character. Hearing even so hackneyed a number as *See, the conquering hero* in its true scale is a delightful surprise. The orchestral group and continuo sound splendidly crisp, and when the trumpets come in at *Sound an alarm* the impact is considerable, just as it must have been for the original Handelian audience. Though some may regret the passing of the old-style fruity singing in the great tenor and bass arias, Ryland Davies and John Shirley-Quirk are most stylish, while both Felicity Palmer and Dame Janet crown the whole set with glorious singing, not least in a delectable sequence on the subject of liberty towards the end of Act 1. The recording quality is outstanding, ideally fresh, vivid and clear and the tape transfer too is of demonstration quality, indistinguishable from the discs.

Arias: *Judas Maccabaeus: Father of Heaven. Messiah: He was despised; O thou that tellest. Samson: Return, O God of hosts.*
(M) *** Decca SPA/*KCSP* 531. Ferrier, LPO, Boult – BACH: *Arias.****

The reissue of Kathleen Ferrier's outstanding recital of Bach and Handel arias, where the new stereo-recorded accompaniment was lovingly superimposed over the old mono orchestral contribution, is most welcome. The transfer to tape has also been well done; the voice is naturally caught.

Psalms: *Laudate Pueri in D; Nisi Dominus; Salve Regina.*
(M) **(*) HM HM 1054. Deller Cons., King's Musick, Mark Deller.

These psalm settings come from early in Handel's career, when he was still working in Italy. Though *Nisi Dominus* ends with a conventional fugue of the kind which marks out later Handel, there is a lightness characteristic of the period, well brought out in these fresh and urgent performances, brightly if rather aggressively recorded.

Messiah (complete).
*** O-L D 189 D 3/*K 189 K 33* [id.].
Nelson, Kirkby, Watkinson, Elliot, Thomas, Ch. of Christ Church Cath., Oxford, AcAM, Hogwood.
(M) **(*) RCA Gold GL 0244 (3). Vyvyan, Sinclair, Vickers, Tozzi, Ch., RPO, Beecham.
(M) ** CBS 79336 (3). Smith, King, Brett, Hill, Cold, Worcester Cath. Ch., Gr. Écurie, Malgoire.

Christopher Hogwood in aiming at re-creating an authentic version – based meticulously on material from the Foundling Hospital, reproducing a performance of 1754 – has managed to have the best of both worlds, punctilious but consistently vigorous and refreshing, never falling into dull routine. The boy trebles of Christ Church are superb, and though the soloists cannot match the tonal beauty of the finest of their rivals on other sets, the consistency of the whole conception makes for most satisfying results. As to the text, it generally follows what we are used to, but there are such oddities as *But who may abide* transposed for a soprano and a shortened version of the *Pastoral symphony*. The recording is superb, clear and free to match the performance, and the cassette transfer is exceptionally successful, virtually indistinguishable from the discs.

Beecham's *Messiah* sharply divided opinion when it first appeared in 1960. He uses a bold orchestration, with highly anachronistic percussion (cymbals, anvils etc.), heavy brass and a full body of strings. In modern stereo it would still keep its impact, and as a curiosity it is worth hearing; but in the latest transfer from RCA the sound is notably less bril-

liant than the performance, which at every point radiates the natural flair of the conductor. Plainly the soloists, chorus and orchestra, an impressive team, were all inspired by the challenge.

Malgoire's version, like Hogwood's, which appeared immediately before it, aimed at authenticity, but by comparison the results are rough and unappealing, not helped by recording which tends to be aggressive. There are one or two interesting but not very revealing textual variations (*How beautiful are the feet* as a *da capo* aria, for example); and all the soloists are first-rate, with Charles Brett singing most beautifully in *He was despised*.

Still recommended: *Messiah* is exceptionally well served on both record and cassette, first choice probably resting between Sir Colin Davis's Philips set (6703 001/*7699 009*), with Harper, Watts, Wakefield and Shirley-Quirk, and the HMV version with the Ambrosian Singers under Sir Charles Mackerras and Harwood, Baker, Esswood, Tear and Herincx in the solo roles (SLS/*TC-SLS* 774 [Ang, S 3705]). If Davis adopts the more exhilarating tempi, the choruses on HMV have a compensating body and richness. On Erato, Raymond Leppard presents a fine, enjoyable account which avoids the extremes of his two principal rivals; his soloists are Palmer, Watts, Davies and Shirley-Quirk (STU 70921/3). Sir David Willcocks at King's directs what has been described as the 'all male *Messiah*' (HMV SLS 845); a counter-tenor, James Bowman, takes over the contralto solos, and the full complement of trebles of the choir sings the soprano solos, with enchanting results. The bass is Benjamin Luxon, and the St Martin's Academy makes a splendid contribution too. On cassette first choice rests with the HMV Mackerras set, which has been most successfully transferred.

Messiah: highlights.
*** O-L DSLO/*KDSLC* 592 (from above set cond. Hogwood).

*** Argo ZRG/*KZRC* 879. Ameling, Reynolds, Langridge, Howell, Ch., ASMF, Marriner.

(M) ** Decca Jub. JB/*KJBC* 80. Sutherland, Bumbry, McKellar, Ward, LSO Ch., LSO, Boult.

Messiah: (i) *Behold the Lamb of God;* (ii) *He was despised;* (i) *Surely he hath borne; And with his stripes; All we like sheep.*

(M) *** Decca SPA/*KCSP* 588. (i) Ch., LSO; (ii) Ferrier, LPO; Boult BACH: *Passion excerpts.****

The Oiseau-Lyre issue makes a generous sampler of the 'new original look' *Messiah.* Indeed listeners may immediately judge their reactions from the opening *Comfort ye* with its florid decorations. The solo singing is always fresh, David Thomas's *The trumpet shall sound* giving a robust reminder of an enduring style of presentation of this justly famous item. The recording is excellent; the cassette transfer is not quite as clean as the disc in reproducing the chorus, because the resonance tends to blur the outlines a little.

A highlights disc or tape is probably also the best way to sample the Marriner performance, with its fresh sound and splendid solo and choral singing. The selection is generous. The same comment might apply to Boult's 1961 version, where Sutherland alone pays any attention to the question of whether or not to use ornamentation in the repeats of the *da capo* arias. One of the most enjoyable components of this set is the choral singing, and so it was a happy idea to extract choruses from this version to frame Kathleen Ferrier's famous account of *He was despised*, which is appropriately coupled to Passion music of Bach. The sound is excellent, with no perceptible difference between disc and tape.

Cantatas: *Nell'Africane selve; Nella stagion che, dio viole e rose.* Duets: *Quel fior che all'alba ride; No, di voi non vo' fidarmi; Tacete, ohimè, tacete!* Trio: *Se tu non lasci amore.*
*** O-L DSLO 580. Kirkby, Nelson, Thomas; Hogwood, Sheppard.

The most ear-catching items among these Italian cantatas are those which Handel later drew on in *Messiah* for such numbers as *His yoke is easy, For unto us a child is born* and *All we like sheep.* Emma Kirkby and Judith Nelson sing them brilliantly; and one of the less striking pieces yet presents an amazing virtuoso display from the bass, David Thomas, who is required to cope with an enormous range of three octaves. In the fast movements Hogwood favours breathtaking speeds (in every sense), yet the result is exciting, not too hectic, and the recording is outstanding.

Ode for St Cecilia's Day.
*** ASV DCA/*ZCDCA* 512. Gomez, Tear, King's College Ch., ECO, Ledger.
(M) **(*) Decca Ser. SA/*KSC* 9 [Argo ZRG 563]. Cantelo, Partridge, King's College Ch., ASMF, Willcocks.

An outstanding new version of Handel's splendid *Ode for St Cecilia's Day* from Ledger. With superb soloists – Jill Gomez radiantly beautiful and Robert Tear dramatically riveting in his call to arms, *The trumpet's loud clangour* – this delightful music emerges with an admirable combination of freshness and weight. Ledger uses an all male chorus, and the style of the performance is totally convincing without being self-consciously authentic. The recording is first-rate, rich, vivid and clear; the cassette is very good too, if not quite so sharp in its upper focus. Highly recommended.

The earlier Argo version also sounds bright and lively in the medium-priced Serenata reissue. This is a performance we have perhaps underrated in previous editions of this *Guide:* April Cantelo is not as beguiling as Jill Gomez on ASV, but she sings sensitively and accurately, and although Ian Partridge is less vibrant than Robert Tear in *The trumpet's loud clangour*, it is still a highlight of the Serenata performance. Willcocks is less energetic at the opening than Ledger, but his closing chorus (*As from the power of sacred lays*) is faster and brighter, and some may prefer this approach. Certainly elsewhere the choral singing is incisive, but generally the ASV version has more imaginative detail, and the sound is richer. However, the crisp Argo recording has transferred exceptionally well to cassette, where the focus is admirably sharp throughout.

La Resurrezione.
(M) ** Turn. TVS 3711/5. Gabry, Töpler-Marizy, Lisken, Fackert, Wenk, Ch. of Munster, Santini CO, Ewerhart.

This early oratorio of Handel, written for Rome in 1708, and first given there under Corelli, was rediscovered as recently as 1961 and here promptly recorded. It tells of the events between Good Friday and Easter Morning, with the confrontation between the Angel and Lucifer providing dramatic contrast to the lyricism of the rest. The chorus is limited to the very end of the work, a brief contribution, but most of the solo work in this lively performance is very acceptable, though the recording shows its age.

Samson.
*** Erato STU 71240 (4). Baker, Watts, Tear, Luxon, Shirley-Quirk, Burrowes, Lott, L. Voices, ECO, Leppard.

Leppard directs a highly dramatic account of Handel's most dramatic oratorio, one which translates very happily to the stage; its culmination, the exultant aria, *Let the bright seraphim,* is here beautifully sung by Felicity Lott, but for long was associated with Joan Sutherland at Covent Garden. The moment when the orchestra interrupts a soloist in mid-sentence to indicate the collapse of the temple is more vividly dramatic than anything in a Handel opera, and Leppard handles that and much else with total conviction. Robert Tear as Samson produces his most heroic tones – rather too aggressively so in *Total eclipse* – and the rest of the cast could hardly be more distinguished. Dame Janet Baker – not by nature a seductress in the Dalila sense – yet sings with a lightness totally apt for such an aria as *With plaintive notes*, and the others are in excellent voice. The recording is outstanding, atmospheric and well balanced.

Saul.
*** HMV SLS/*TCC-SLS* 5200 (3). Allen, Tear, Margaret Marshall, Esswood, Burgess, King's College Ch., ECO, Ledger.

With an excellent team of soloists and the choir of King's College, fresh-toned with trebles, Philip Ledger gives a compelling performance of this highly dramatic oratorio. His speeds are at times on the slow side, but not unconvincingly so. Thomas Allen makes a superb Saul, relishing his rage arias; Robert Tear is in fine voice as Jonathan; and the male alto Paul Esswood sings the castrato role of David freshly and incisively. Exceptionally Ledger gives the role of the Witch of Endor to a tenor, Martyn Hill. The two women soloists, Margaret Marshall and Sally Burgess, are both excellent. Good atmospheric recording; the chrome cassette transfer is acceptable but not one of EMI's finest. The choral focus loses something in crispness, and there is some peaking on Margaret Marshall's fortissimo top notes.

Solomon.
**(*) HMV SLS/*TC-SLS* 5163 (2). Cameron, Young, Morison, Lois Marshall, Beecham Ch. Soc., RPO, Beecham.

In his revision of *Solomon* Sir Thomas Beecham boldly left out sections which hold up the central plot involving the Queen of Sheba, omitting the Judgement scene but using the double chorus *From the censer curling rise* after the entertainment for the Queen. With Beecham magicking the music – however unauthentically – the performance can be warmly recommended to devotees of the conductor, and to Handelians too as long as they are tolerant. Lois Marshall is more effective here than as Constanze in Beecham's *Entführung*, and the other soloists are first-rate. The recording is fair for its mid-fifties vintage, and it has transferred to cassette well enough (though hardly refined in its choral focus).

Utrecht Te Deum and Jubilate.
*** O-L DSLO/*KDSLC* 582. Nelson, Kirkby, Brett, Elliot, Covey Crump, Thomas, Ch. of Christ Church Cath., Oxford, AcAM, Preston.

Utrecht Te Deum and Jubilate; Zadok the Priest.
(M) **(*) DG Arc. Priv. 2547/*3347* 022. Wolf, Watts, Wilfred Brown, Hemsley, Geraint Jones Ch. and O., Jones.

Handel wrote the Utrecht pieces just before coming to London, intending them as a sample of his work. Using authentic instruments and an all-male choir with boy trebles, Preston directs a performance which is not just scholarly but characteristically alert and vigorous, particularly impressive in the superb *Gloria* with its massive eight-part chords. With a team of soloists regularly associated with the Academy of Ancient Music, the disc can confidently be recommended; the cassette too is well managed, if marginally less refined at the top. However, the rival version of Geraint Jones, reissued on a mid-price Archive issue, has many points in its favour, particularly for those who resist a performance on original instruments. At a cheaper price it contains an extra item, *Zadok the Priest.* Although this dates from the earliest days of stereo, the recording is well balanced and clean. Small resources are used to great effect (the *Coronation anthem* is not as overwhelming as some like it to be) and with excellent soloists the result is vivid and lively, the choral focus marginally sharper on disc than on tape.

OPERA

Ariodante (complete).
*** Ph 6769 025/*7699 112* (4) [id.]. Baker, Mathis, Burrowes, Bowman, Rendell, Oliver, Ramey, L. Voices, ECO, Leppard.

Set improbably in medieval Scotland, Handel's *Ariodante* has a story far more direct and telling in simple emotional terms than most of his operas, even though the conflict between characters does not emerge until well into the second act. The libretto inspired Handel – who had just lost some of his finest singers to a rival opera company – to write an amazing sequence of memorable and intensely inventive arias and duets, with not a single weak link in the chain, a point superbly conveyed in this colourful, urgent performance under Raymond Leppard.

The castrato role of Ariodante is a challenge even for Dame Janet Baker, who responds with singing of enormous expressive range, from the dark agonized moments of the C minor aria early in Act 3 to the brilliance of the most spectacular of the three display arias later in the act. Dame Janet's duets with Edith Mathis as Princess Ginevra, destined to marry Prince Ariodante, are enchanting too, and there is a not a single weak link in the cast, though James Bowman as Duke Polinesso is not so precise as usual, with words often unclear. Though this long work is given uncut, it is perhaps the most riveting Handel opera recording available, helped by the consistently resilient playing of the English Chamber Orchestra and the refined, beautifully balanced recording, equally impressive on disc and cassette.

Giulio Cesare: arias.
(M) **(*) Decca Ace SDD 574. Sutherland, Horne, Sinclair, New SO, Bonynge.

With the items dotted in no particular order, this selection at medium price hardly represents a 'potted version' but is welcome for much brilliant and beautiful singing. In 1964 Sutherland's coloratura was magnificent, and though in the slow music she too readily adopts a swooning manner her six arias are most impressive. Equally welcome items include Cornelia's beautiful lament sung by Marilyn Horne and a stunning display from Monica Sinclair in Ptolemy's aria, spanning in range a full three octaves. Good reverberant recording.

Partenope (complete).
*** HM 1C 157 99855/8. Laki, Jacobs, York Skinner, Varcoe, Müller-Molinari, Hill, La Petite Bande, Kuijken.

By the time he wrote *Partenope* in 1730 Handel was having to cut his cloth in opera production rather more modestly than earlier in his career. This opera in its limited scale has few heroic overtones, yet a performance as fresh and alert as this amply demonstrates that the result can be even more involving. One problem for Handel was that his company at the time could call on only one each of soprano, tenor and bass, but with an excellent team of counter-tenors and contralto this performance makes light of that limitation. With the exception of René Jacobs, rather too mannered for Handel, the team of soloists is outstanding, with Krisztina Laki and Helga Müller-Molinari welcome newcomers. Though ornamentation is sparse, the direction of

Sigiswald Kuijken is consistently invigorating, and the recording is outstanding.

Rinaldo (complete).
*** CBS 79308/40- (3) [Col. M3 34592]. Watkinson, Cotrubas, Scovotti, Esswood, Brett, Cold, Gr. Écurie, Malgoire.

The vigour of Malgoire's direction of an opera which plainly for him is very much alive, no museum piece, will attract many who normally steer clear of Handel opera, particularly in performances like this which use authentic instruments. The elaborate decorations on *da capo* arias are imaginatively done, but most effectively the famous *Cara sposa* is left without ornamentation, sung beautifully by the contralto Rinaldo, Carolyn Watkinson. The finest singing comes from Ileana Cotrubas, but under Malgoire the whole team is convincing. The bright but spacious recording adds to the vigour, and the magic sounds associated with the sorceress Armida, such as the arrival of her airborne chariot, are well conveyed. Needless to say, the story about the crusader Rinaldo hardly matters at all, but Handel's invention is a delight. The cassettes are of unreliable technical quality, and in its tape format the set is poorly produced.

Serse (*Xerxes;* complete).
**(*) CBS 79325 (3). Watkinson, Esswood, Wenkel, Hendricks, Rodde, Cold, Studer, Bridier Vocal Ens., Gr. Écurie, Malgoire.

Malgoire's vigorous, often abrasive style in baroque music makes for a lively, convincing performance of one of Handel's richest operas, helped by a fine complement of solo singers. Carolyn Watkinson may not be the most characterful of singers in the high castrato role of Xerxes himself, but it is good to have the elaborate roulades so accurately sung. The celebrated *Ombra mai fu* is most beautiful. Paul Esswood is similarly reliable in the role of Arsamene (originally taken by a woman) and the countertenor tone is pure and true. Barbara Hendricks and Anne-Marie Rodde are both outstanding in smaller roles, and the comic episodes (most unexpected in Handel) are excellently done, Malgoire's generally heavy rhythmic pulse here paying dividends. There are detailed stylistic points one might criticize in his rendering (for example, the squeeze effects on sustained string notes), but the vitality of the performance is never in doubt, and the recording, somewhat close, is vivid too.

VOCAL COLLECTIONS

Arias: (i) *Acis and Galatea: I rage, I melt, I burn . . . O ruddier than the cherry.* (ii) *Alexander's Feast: Revenge, Timotheus cries.* (iii) *Atalanta: Care selve.* (ii) *Judas Maccabaeus: I feel the Deity within . . . Arm, arm, ye brave;* (iv) *Father of heaven;* (v) *My arms . . . Sound an alarm.* (vi) *Messiah: I know that my Redeemer liveth.* (v) *Ptolemy: Silent worship.* (vii) *Radamisto: Gods all powerful.* (v) *Semele: Where'er you walk.*
(M) *** Decca SPA/KCSP 566. (i) Brannigan; (ii) Forbes Robinson; (iii) Greevy; (iv) Ferrier; (v) McKellar; (vi) Armstrong; (vii) Flagstad.

Enticingly titled '*Where'er you walk*' this is an outstandingly successful popular anthology. Kenneth McKellar's warmly lyrical voice is heard at its most appealing in the title song and in the equally memorable *Silent worship*. Owen Brannigan's inimitably genial *O ruddier than the cherry* is unforgettable, and Forbes Robinson, another distinguished Handelian, makes several fine contributions. Kathleen Ferrier and Bernadette Greevy have comparable nobility of line,

matched by the eloquence of Sheila Armstrong's *I know that my Redeemer liveth.* The only comparative disappointment is Flagstad's 1957 recording of *Gods all powerful*, where the voice is not always fully in control. The recording is vivid throughout, and the high-level tape transfer matches the disc closely.

'*Great choruses': Coronation anthem: Zadok the Priest. Israel in Egypt: He spake the word; He gave them hailstones. Jephtha: When his loud voice. Judas Maccabaeus: See the conquering hero comes. Messiah: Hallelujah; For unto us a child is born; Worthy is the Lamb; Amen. Saul: Gird on thy sword. Solomon: May no rash intruder.*
(M) *** Decca SPA/KCSP 567. Handel Op. Soc. Ch. and O., Farncombe.

A most enjoyable concert, freshly sung and vividly recorded. It opens with an attractively buoyant account of *Hallelujah*, and there is an unexpected refinement in *For unto us a child is born*. Of the lesser-known choruses, *May no rash intruder* from *Solomon* with its evocative pastoral scene is particularly successful. The small orchestral group and indeed the excellent amateur choral singing readily make up in spontaneity for any lack of polish. The recording, originally made in Phase Four, is forward but has depth as well as impact, and the tape transfer is outstandingly successful, approaching demonstration quality in its vividness and clarity.

COLLECTIONS

Concerti grossi in B flat, Opp. 3/1 and 6/7. Oboe concerto No. 3 in G min. Organ concerto No. 7 in F (The Cuckoo and the Nightingale). Music for the Royal Fireworks. Water music (complete). Alcina: Dream music.

Berenice: Overture. Il Pastor fido: Hunting scene. Solomon: Arrival of the Queen of Sheba. (Vocal) *Acis and Galatea: I rage, I melt, I burn . . . O ruddier than the cherry. Jephtha: Scenes of horror; Waft her, angels. Messiah: Hallelujah. Ode for St Cecilia's day: The trumpet's loud clangour.* (Opera) *Alcina: Verdi prati. Ezio: Se un ball'ardire.*
(M) *** Argo D 242 D 3 (3)/*K 242 K 33.*
ASMF, Marriner, with Lord, Malcolm; Luxon, Hodgson, ASMF Ch; Partridge, King's College Ch.; Greevy, Forbes Robinson.

This engaging anthology should especially suit a small collection and invite further exploration. The *Fireworks* and *Water music* are complete, and no better versions are available. The selection of oratorio and opera excerpts on the final side is particularly enjoyable. Performances and recording are characteristically reliable, and the cassettes match the discs very closely (losing a very slight degree of refinement in the *Fireworks music*). At medium price this is thoroughly recommendable.

'The glory of Handel': (i; ii) *Concerto grosso in B min., Op. 6/6: Musette.* (i; iii) *Royal Fireworks music: Overture.* (iv) *Saul: Dead march.* (i; iii) *Water music: Overture; Hornpipe.* (v) *Harpsichord suite No. 5 in E min.: Air and variations (Harmonious Blacksmith).* (iv; vi) *Judas Maccabaeus: See, the conquering hero comes.* (vii) *Messiah: Hallelujah chorus; I know that my Redeemer liveth.*
(M) ** DG Priv. 2535/*3335* 247. (i) Berlin PO; (ii) Karajan; (iii) Kubelik; (iv) ECO, Mackerras; (v) Stadelmann; (vi) Wandsworth School Ch.; (vii) Donath, John Alldis Ch., LPO, Karl Richter.

A well-balanced collection on this DG Privilege issue, showing not just the

German way with Handel but the British view too. The selection is well made, and the generally excellent performances are matched by good recording, although on cassette the choral focus is marginally less sharp than on disc.

Hanson, Howard
(1896–1981)

Symphony No. 4.
(M) *** Mercury SRI 75107 [id.]. Eastman Rochester O., composer –
PISTON: *Symphony No. 3.****

Hanson wrote his *Fourth Symphony* in 1943 as an orchestral requiem for his father. The titles of the four movements show that it draws its inspiration from the church liturgy: *Kyrie eleison, Requiescat, Dies irae* and *Lux aeterna.* Even at a first hearing it is impossible not to be impressed by this powerful work, cyclic in thematic construction, compressed (it plays for only twenty minutes), but with clearly defined movements, the first agitated and impassioned, the second eloquently expressive, the scherzo full of energy and fire, and the finale reaching a moving apotheosis. The performance under the composer's direction is deeply committed, and though the Mercury recording is not ideally expansive, it is clear and vivid, and communicates instantly.

Harris, Roy (1898–1979)

Concerto for piano and strings; Cimarron (symphonic overture); *West Point symphony* (for band).
** Varese VC 81100 [id.]. J. Harris, International String Congress O., UCLA Wind Ens.; Westbrook or composer.

The important work here is the *Concerto*, which is an arrangement of the *Piano quintet* of 1937. Roy Harris was a dominant figure in American music in the 1930s and 40s, but his wider reputation rests almost exclusively on the *Third* and *Seventh Symphonies* – and this quintet-cum-concerto. Harris made a number of alterations in the score before recording the concerto version in 1960. It was given in Puerto Rico, and unfortunately the sound quality is wanting in transparency, and the piano itself sounds in poor condition. The composer's widow is certainly not able to secure the sensitive results that distinguished her earlier recording of it in its chamber form. The band symphony precedes the *Seventh*. It is a well-wrought piece that bears Harris's distinctive stamp, without perhaps having the freshness of his greatest work. However, this and *Cimarron* are still worth investigating, and both the performances and recordings are vital and bright.

(i) *Piano quintet. String quartet No. 3 (4 Preludes and fugues).*
** Varese VC 81123 [id.]. Blair Qt, (i) with J. Harris.

'Arguably the greatest single chamber work by any American composer', says the front cover of the record about the *Piano quintet*, and it is a claim that is well vindicated. Written in 1937 as a wedding present for Harris's wife Johana, who is the soloist here, this is powerful stuff, very much in the spirit of the *Third Symphony* (1938), with the same sense of span and feeling for line. It is a noble piece and among Roy Harris's finest works. So too is the *Third Quartet*, which dates from 1939, the year which saw the first performance of the *Third Symphony*. It is in the form of four preludes and fugues and is both learned (as befits a work premiered for an international convention of musicologists) and satisfying, sinuous and sinewy. This is a masterful work which

repays study. The Blair Quartet play well, though one would welcome a wider dynamic range and a more flattering recorded sound. The *Piano quintet* is not as well recorded as one could wish (the piano seems diffuse and a shade unreal), but the performance is authoritative enough.

Harty, Hamilton (1879–1941)

(i) *Violin concerto. A John Field suite; Londonderry air; Variations on a Dublin air.*
*** Chan. DBR/*DBT* 2001 (2). Ulster O., Thomson, (i) with Holmes – HANDEL: *Water music suite.****

(i) *Violin concerto. Variations on a Dublin air.*
*** Chan. ABR/*ABT* 1044 (as above).

A John Field suite.
(M) *** HMV Green. ESD/*TC-ESD* 7100. E. Sinfonia, Dilkes – *Concert (English music).****

A John Field suite; Londonderry air.
(M) *** Chan. CBR/*CBT* 1005. Ulster O. (as above) – HANDEL: *Water music suite.****

Sir Hamilton Harty is better remembered as an interpreter than as a composer; conducting gradually made such inroads into his life that he spent less time composing later in his career. The *Violin concerto* is an early work and comes from 1908; it was written for Szigeti, who gave the first performance. Though it has no strongly individual idiom, the invention is fresh and often touched with genuine poetry. Ralph Holmes gives a thoroughly committed account of the solo part and is well supported by an augmented Ulster Orchestra under Bryden Thomson. The other music in the Chandos collection is less impressive though thoroughly enjoyable, and readers who imagine that the orchestral playing will be indifferent (this is the début record of a provincial orchestra) will be pleasantly surprised. These are accomplished and well-recorded performances – and it is good to hear Harty's attractive arrangement of the John Field pieces again after so long an absence from the catalogue. The recording is excellent; the tape transfers are well balanced but lack the last degree of range and sparkle in the treble. As can be seen the collection has also been split up into separate issues, the second at medium price. However, those wanting the engaging *John Field suite* may prefer the excellent Dilkes version within an anthology of music by Bax, Bridge and Butterworth (see the Concerts section below).

An Irish symphony; A comedy overture.
*** Chan. Dig. ABRD/*ABTD* 1027. Ulster O., Thomson.

The *Irish symphony* dates from 1904 and arose from a competition for a suite or symphony based on traditional Irish airs, inspired by the first Dublin performance of Dvořák's *New World symphony*, 'founded upon negro melodies'! Harty's symphony won great acclaim for its excellent scoring and good craftsmanship. He revised it twice, and though it lays no claim to being a work of exceptional individuality, it is an attractive and well-wrought piece of light music. The scherzo is particularly engaging. It is extremely well played by the Ulster Orchestra under Bryden Thomson and the overture is also successful and enjoyable. The recording is absolutely first-class in every respect. The cassette is marginally less wide-ranging than the disc, but still yields excellent results.

Haslam, David (20th century)

Juanita, the Spanish lobster.
** CRD CRD 1032/*CRDC* 4032. Morris, Northern Sinfonia, composer – PROKOFIEV: *Peter and the Wolf.****

Johnny Morris's tale of how Juanita, the Spanish lobster, gets caught and rescued in the nick of time has more narrative detail than story-line. It is supported by a colourful and undoubtedly tuneful score by David Haslam, but the music is not really distinguished enough for re-hearing by way of a recording, although it is not without charm. The narrator is given some songs to provide variety within the spoken text, and they have something of an *Alice in Wonderland* flavour. Johnny Morris's personality is well projected by an excellent recording, and the performance is first-rate. The cassette matches the disc closely.

Haydn, Josef (1732–1809)

Cassation in G, H. II/2; (i) *Double concerto in F for violin, harpsichord and strings, H.XVIII/6.*
*** Ph. 9500 602/*7300 724* [id.]. I Musici, (i) with Carmirelli, Garatti.

The *Concerto* is an early work from the 1760s and pleasing rather than important. It is so attractively presented by Pina Carmirelli, Maria Teresa Garatti and I Musici that one does not think of it as being anything other than first-rate. The *Cassation* is even earlier: it dates from the 1750s and is very slight indeed, although it has an engaging *Adagio* (the fourth of six movements), not played too slowly here, which could easily become a classical 'pop' were it better known. Given performances of such charm and splendid recording quality (on disc and cassette alike), this can be strongly recommended.

Cello concertos in C and D.
**(*) CBS 76978 [Col. M 36674]. Ma, ECO, Garcia.
(M) *(*) Turn. TVS 34695 [id.]. Varga, Bamberg SO, Dorati.

Cello concerto in D.
(M) **(*) HMV SXLP/TC-SXLP 30273 [Ang. S 36580]. Du Pré, LSO, Barbirolli – MONN: Concerto.**(*)

Yo Yo Ma provides an attractive alternative to Rostropovich's recording (HMV ASD 3255 [Ang. S 37193]) of the two Haydn concertos, both of them works of the sharpest imagination. His approach is more restrained in expression, not so lovingly moulded in the lyrical slow movements, a degree more detached. The result is not so compellingly individual, but many will prefer directness in music firmly belonging to the classical eighteenth century. Apart from one or two odd points of balance, the recording is clean and full.

It is a pity that Jacqueline du Pré's performances of the two Haydn Cello concertos were not coupled together for the HMV reissue. She recorded the C major work – by now well accepted in the canon after its exciting rediscovery – rather earlier with Daniel Barenboim. With Barbirolli to partner her, the style is even more romantic, and though the purists may object, the conviction and flair of the playing are extraordinarily compelling. The recording is full and well balanced; the sound is fractionally less refined in orchestral tutti in the cassette transfer, but it is fully acceptable.

Laszlo Varga is a fine player and can hold his own with anyone – at least as far as technique is concerned. He is rather forwardly balanced, but his refinement is not echoed in the orchestral playing, which is not particularly imaginative.

Tempi throughout are just a shade on the measured side and the music, not Haydn's greatest, needs stronger persuasive advocacy. There is no real challenge here to Rostropovich or Yo Yo Ma.

Horn concertos Nos. 1 and 2 in D (ed. Steves).
*** HMV ASD/TC-ASD 3774 [Ang. SZ/4ZS 37569]. Tuckwell, ECO – M. HAYDN: Concertino.***

Barry Tuckwell has recorded these concertos before for Argo (ZRG 5498), but they are differently coupled, and the new HMV coupling, a Concertino by Michael Haydn, is a useful addition to the horn repertoire. These performances of the two concertos attributed to Josef (the second is of doubtful lineage) are every bit as good as before, with the solo line of the much superior First Concerto memorably eloquent. The orchestral playing is crisp and classical in feeling; the phrasing has less finesse than on the Argo disc (under Marriner) but is neat and musical. The sound is first-class and the cassette transfer strikingly clean.

(i) Horn concerto No. 1 in D; (ii) Organ concerto No. 1 in C; (iii) Trumpet concerto in E flat.
(M) *** Decca VIV/KVIC 12. ASMF, Marriner, with (i) Tuckwell, (ii) Preston, (iii) Stringer.

An appropriate budget-priced realignment of familiar performances, generally well recorded on disc (though the cassette focus of the solo instruments is less agreeable). Tuckwell plays the Horn concerto superbly, particularly the beautiful Adagio. The Organ concerto is not one of Haydn's most memorable works, but Simon Preston and Marriner are persuasive: the registration is vivid and the accompaniment spirited. Alan Stringer favours a forthright open timbre for the Trumpet concerto, but he plays the famous slow movement graciously and

361

the orchestral playing has striking elegance and finesse. Good value on disc, but the tape needs remastering.

Keyboard concertos

(i) *Fortepiano concertinos; in C, H.XIV/3, 11 and 12; in G, H.XIV/ 13; in F, H.XVIII/F2; Fortepiano concerto in C, H.XVIII/10.* (ii) *Organ concertos Nos. 1 in C, H.XVIII/1; 2 in C, H.XVIII/8; 3 in C, H.XVIII/5.* (i) *Divertimentos: in C, H.XIV/C2; in C, H.XIV/7; in C, H.XIV/8; in C, H.XIV/9.* (i) *Sonata in E for violin, cello, 2 horns and fortepiano.*
(M) ** Turn. TVS 37103/5 [SVBX 5141]. (i) Von Alpenheim, Instrumental Ens.; (ii) Lehrndorfer, Württemberg CO, Faerber.

These are competent, spirited performances of essentially lightweight music, which taken in small doses is agreeable enough. The tinkly fortepiano is well balanced, and the recordings are good if not distinguished. The three organ concertos are certainly successful and Franz Lehrndorfer is quite a persuasive soloist, although the sound is clear rather than rich. The most interesting work here is the *Sonata in E flat*, a kind of piano trio with ad lib horns – and they are by no means always conventional horn parts – which is given an extremely vigorous performance (although the sound is two-dimensional).

Organ concertos Nos. 1–3 in C, H.XVIII/1, 5 and 8.
(M) ** Turn. TVS 34694 [id.]. Lehrndorfer, Württemberg CO, Faerber.

This is a separate issue of performances first offered within a three-disc set (see above). Lehrndorfer registers effectively and he is well balanced. The per-

formances are alert and the recording is clean.

(i) *Organ concerto No. 1 in C, H.XVIII/1;* (ii) *Double horn concerto in E flat* (arr. Nys); (iii) *Trumpet concerto in E flat.*
(M) *** RCA Gold GL/GK 25238. Paillard CO, Paillard, with (i) Alain; (ii) Barboteu, Coursier; (iii) André.

An excellent collection, featuring distinguished soloists from the Erato catalogue. Marie-Claire Alain gives a vigorous, buoyant performance of the *Organ concerto*, with more character than Lehrndorfer's (see above), and Maurice André's account of the *Trumpet concerto* is first-class, with an elegant *Andante* and a sparkling finale. The *Double horn concerto*, whether or not it is by Haydn, is an interesting work, with extremely florid solo parts, closely intertwined. It is played with obvious bravura and the French french horn style is not too distracting. The recording throughout is very good, although on tape the focus is less clear and the dynamics seem compressed.

Piano concertos: in C; in F; in G; in D, H.XVIII/1, 3–4 and 11.
(M) (*) Sup. 1101 861/2. Kameniková, Virtuosi Pragenses, Hlaváček.

Although Valentina Kameniková's playing is both stylish and neat, this set is rather ruled out of court by some ugly pitch discrepancies between the piano and the orchestra; they are slight but important. The *C major Concerto* is familiar from other records as an *Organ concerto*. (It is described, incidentally, as *per il clavicembalo* and also on the manuscript as *per l'organo*.)

Piano concerto in D, H.XVIII/2.
*** Decca SXL/KSXC 6952 [Lon. 7180/ 5-]. Larrocha, L. Sinf., Zinman – BACH: *Concerto No. 5*; MOZART: *Concerto No. 12.****

With clean, crisp articulation, Alicia de Larrocha obviously seeks to evoke the fortepiano. The outer movements are strongly characterized, and the crisp rhythmic snap of the 'gipsy' finale is a joy. David Zinman's accompaniment is excellent and the scale of the recording is highly effective, the resonance giving breadth to the orchestral group. The cassette transfer is of high quality, a fraction over-bright.

Piano concertos: in D; in F; in G, H.XVIII/2–4; in G, H.XVIII/9; in D, H.XVIII/11; in C, H.XIV/4.
(M) ** Turn. TVS 37090/2. Von Alpenheim, Bamberg SO, Dorati.

Haydn's keyboard concertos may not show him at his most inspired, but there is some charming music in some of the quicker movements. The *G major Concerto* (H.XVIII/9) is one of the better ones, and it has an appealing slow movement. The recorded balance here is not very satisfactory, the soloist being placed far too forward. This is a set for those who must have everything, but it is not essential listening even for Haydn enthusiasts.

Keyboard concertos: in D; in F; in G, H.XVIII/2–3 and 9.
**(*) Erato STU 70989. Jaccottet (harpsichord), Lausanne Instrumental Ens., Corbóz.

Although the *D major Concerto* comes off much better on the piano, it is effectively played here by Christiane Jaccottet on the harpsichord. She is forwardly balanced, but that is inevitable given the realities of the instrument, and few would find it unacceptable. The *G major Concerto* is less successful, but the other works are so persuasive in the hands of these Swiss artists that collectors are unlikely to be disappointed by this issue. None of these pieces is essential Haydn, but of the recordings now on the market

this is the one that shows them in the best light. The sound is extremely good.

Violin concertos: in C; in A; in G, H.VIIa/1, 3 and 4; Double concerto for violin and harpsichord in F, H.XVIII/6; Sinfonia concertante in B flat, H.I/105.
*** Ph. 6769/7643 059 (3) [id.]. Accardo, Canino, Black, Sheen, Schiff, ECO.

The three *Violin concertos* are all early; the *C major*, written for Tomasini, is probably the best. The other two have only come into the limelight since the war. In the *G major*, Accardo follows the critical edition rather than the Melk autograph published by the Haydn-Mozart Presse, and omits the two horns listed in the Breitkopf 1771 catalogue. Not that this is of any great importance, for although Accardo plays with great elegance and charm, it would be idle to pretend that this is great music. The same goes for the *Double concerto for violin and harpsichord*, which is of relatively slender musical interest. The *Sinfonia concertante* is of course a totally different affair, and the playing here splendidly relaxed and musical. The soloists are a shade forward perhaps, but the quality is lifelike, with impeccable surfaces on the discs. The cassette transfers too are admirably faithful. The second tape, containing the *Violin concertos*, offers demonstration quality.

6 Scherzandi, H.II/33/38.
(M) ** Turn. TVS 37112 [(d) in SVBX 5108]. Piedmont CO, Harsanyi.

These are strange, hybrid works, each in four miniature sections, with the usual order of slow movement and minuet and trio reversed. Finales are very brief and lively. The invention is characteristically felicitous (although the music pre-dates the symphonies) and though not all the writing is very substantial it is well worth investigation. Performances are neat and apart from an insistent continuo the balance is good.

The Seven Last Words of Christ (original orchestral version).
*** HMV ASD 3451 [Ang. S 37480]. ASMF, Marriner.

These performances of Haydn's great sequence of slow movements completely give the lie to the idea that consistently slow tempi make for lack of variety. Marriner's way is both deeply felt and stylish, while the Academy plays with customary warmth and polish. Excellent, full recording too. Marriner with his finely chosen tempi makes a formidable case for regarding this original orchestral version of the score as even finer than those for string quartet, piano and accompanied chorus.

Symphonies Nos. 1 in D; 2 in C; 4, 10 and 15 in D; 18 in G; 37 in C.
(M) *** Saga HAYDN 1 (3). L'Estro Armonico, Solomons.

It is well known that the generally accepted numbering of Haydn's symphonies contains many anomalies. The composer himself stated very clearly which was No. 1, but a dramatic discovery after the Second World War – original parts for the first twenty-five symphonies, which had lain hidden in a castle library in Hungary – indicated the order of those at least. Derek Solomons directs a band of authentic music specialists (the membership overlapping with other groups in London) in performances that are alert and refreshing. The smallness of the string band and the intimacy of the acoustic are apt, adding to the bite of the performances, nicely sprung and with non-vibrato strings rarely if ever squeezing too painfully. What emerges from this sequence – as in Dorati's conventional cycle from his much larger-scaled readings – is that from the start Haydn's symphonic writing was fully mature and strongly imaginative.

Symphonies Nos. 3 in G; 5 in A; 11 in E flat; 27 in G; 32 in C; 33 in C; in B flat (Morzin symphonies).
(M) *** Saga HAYDN 2 (3). L'Estro Armonico, Solomons.

The second instalment of this series of early Haydn symphonies recorded in chronological order with authentically intimate forces is as successful as the first. In terms of musical vitality Dorati is more compelling in these works, but the rivalry is hardly direct. As before, L'Estro Armonico uses original instruments and vibrato-less string sound very convincingly, and generally sweetly, well caught by the excellent recording.

Symphonies Nos. 22 in E flat (Philosopher); 43 in E flat (Mercury); 44 in E min. (Trauersymphonie); 48 in C (Maria Theresia); 49 in F min. (La Passione); 55 in E flat (Schoolmaster); 59 in A (Fire); 85 in B flat (La Reine); 94 in G (Surprise); 96 in D (Miracle); 100 in G (Military); 103 in E flat (Drum Roll).
(M) *** Ph. 6768 003 (6). ASMF, Marriner.

This set is superbly recorded and splendidly played, and readers wanting this compilation of named symphonies need not hesitate. The orchestral playing is more polished and urbane than in rival accounts by Dorati and others, though ultimately there is an earthier quality in the music than Marriner perceives. But despite the hint of blandness, these are satisfying performances that will give much pleasure.

Symphonies Nos. 22 in E flat (Philosopher); 55 in E flat (Schoolmaster).
**(*) Ph. 9500 198 [id./7300 560]. ASMF, Marriner.

Very good performances, excellently recorded. The Philosopher comes off very well and, generally speaking, is to be preferred to Bernhard Klee's neat, well-trimmed account with the Prague Chamber Orchestra (now deleted). The *Schoolmaster* too is nicely characterized and has greater charm than in Dorati's version on Decca. There is a hint of blandness in the second movement, but the performance as a whole undoubtedly gives pleasure. The recording has freshness and refinement of detail, good perspective and a warm but not overreverberant acoustic.

Symphonies Nos. 31 in D (Hornsignal); 45 in F sharp min. (Farewell); 73 in D (Hunt); 82 in C (The Bear); 83 in G min. (The Hen); 92 in G (Oxford); 101 in D (Clock); 104 in D (London).
(M) **(*) Ph. 6768 066 (4). ASMF, Marriner.

Generally speaking, this set is distinguished by lively, musicianly playing that cannot fail to give satisfaction, even though none of these performances can be numbered among Marriner's best. He has set himself high standards, and though there is much to admire in each of these performances, all fall short of real distinction, just as, at the same time, they rise above the mere routine.

Symphonies Nos. 31 in D (Hornsignal); Symphony No. 73 in D (Hunt).
** Ph. 9500 518/7300 674 [id.]. ASMF, Marriner.

A logical pairing that has a certain wit. The performances are musicianly and well shaped, but a little faceless. Even on a second hearing the *Horn-signal* gave relatively little pleasure, though it would be difficult to fault the players. Excellent recording; the cassette transfer, made at a characteristically modest level, produces smooth natural sound, without quite the upper range of the LP.

Symphonies Nos. 43 in E flat (Mercury); 44 in E min. (Trauersymphonie).
(M) *** Decca Ace SDD 546. Philh. Hungarica, Dorati.

Dorati is at his very finest in the magnificent symphony of mourning, *Trauersymphonie*, one of the masterpieces of the *Sturm und Drang* period. The *Mercury symphony*, equally inspired, makes a fine contrast, with Dorati delicately pointing the rhythm in the minuet, taken slowly. Good, warm recording.

Symphonies Nos. 44 in E min. (Trauersymphonie); 49 in F min. (La Passione).
⊛***Ph. 9500 199 [id./7300 561]. ASMF, Marriner.

Superlative playing from Marriner and the Academy: even among their many fine Haydn couplings this stands out. The wonderfully expressive string phrasing of the opening *Adagio* of No. 49 is superbly contrasted with the genial and buoyant rhythms of the second-movement *Allegro*. There is some excellent horn-playing in both works, almost self-effacing in its delicacy. But perhaps the highlight of this splendid coupling is the tender way Marriner shapes the radiantly elegiac slow movement of No. 44, which Haydn is reported to have chosen for performance at his funeral (hence the title). A discreet harpsichord continuo is used in both symphonies. The contrast between repose and restless vitality which is at the heart of both these works is the hallmark of the performances, which are recorded with characteristic Philips naturalness and glow.

Symphonies No. 45 in F sharp min. (Farewell); 48 in C (Maria Theresia).
**(*) DG 2531/3301 091 [id.]. ECO, Barenboim.

There is sensitive playing in the *Farewell symphony*, and the DG engineers give Barenboim and the ECO a flattering sound. In the *Maria Theresia* there is also playing of much vitality, though Barenboim uses trumpets and drums instead of the alto horns in C favoured by Goberman and Marriner. A recommendable issue, nonetheless, even if it is not a first choice. The tape transfer is disappointing, bass-heavy and mushy in detail.

Symphonies Nos. 45 in F sharp min. *(Farewell); 101 in D (Clock).*
*** Ph. 9500 520/*7300 676* [id.]. ASMF, Marriner.

Very satisfactory accounts of the *Farewell* and the *Clock*, vital and intelligent. The Philips engineers produce outstanding quality, and the playing of the Academy is very spruce and clean. Marriner has slightly more finesse than Dorati but not quite so much character and earthiness; however, the honours are pretty evenly divided. The tape transfers are made at a moderate level, and a slight bass cut improves the balance. Then there is good detail and no lack of life at the top.

Symphonies Nos. 46 in B; 47 in G.
*** DG 2531/*3301* 324 [id.]. ECO, Barenboim.

Sweet-toned, cultured and vital performances of two of the so-called *Sturm und Drang* symphonies. No. 46 could perhaps with advantage be more severe than Barenboim makes it, but generally speaking there is no cause here to withhold a three-star recommendation, for both playing and recording are of the highest quality. The cassette transfer is smooth and pleasing; the sound is very slightly bland in the slow movements.

Symphonies Nos. 48 in C (Maria Theresia); 49 in F min. (La Passione).
*** Decca Ace SDD 547. Philh. Hungarica, Dorati.

La Passione, one of the masterpieces of Haydn's *Sturm und Drang* period with a moving opening *Adagio*, draws a fine performance from Dorati and his devoted orchestra. The much lighter-weight *Maria Theresia symphony* makes a well-contrasted coupling.

Symphonies Nos. 48 in C (Maria Theresia); 85 in B flat (La Reine).
** Ph. 9500 200 [id./*7300 536*]. ASMF, Marriner.

These symphonies share regal titles, the festive C major work being perhaps the more stately. Marriner gives fresh and in every way lively performances that have many sensitive touches yet are not free from a certain blandness. The slow movement of *La Reine*, for example, is just a shade too fast and under-characterized to grip the listener, and the trio of the minuet could do with more personality. Much the same can be said of the *Maria Theresia symphony*; but there is no denying the musicianship of the playing and the refined quality of the Philips recording. The sound quality has a pleasingly warm acoustic and a totally realistic perspective. Despite the reservation, these are enjoyable performances.

Symphonies Nos. 82–7 (Paris symphonies).
** DG Dig. 2741/*3382* 005 (3) [id.]. Berlin PO, Karajan.

Karajan's set is big-band Haydn with a vengeance; but of course the orchestra of the *Concert de la Loge Olympique* for which Haydn wrote these symphonies was a large band, consisting of forty violins and no fewer than ten double-basses. It goes without saying that the quality of the orchestral playing is superb, and Karajan is meticulous in observing repeats and in his attention to detail. There is no trace of self-indulgence or mannerisms. However, these are rather heavy-handed accounts, closer to Imperial Berlin than Paris; generally speaking, the slow movements are kept moving and the minuets are very slow indeed, full of pomp and majesty – and, at times, too grand! In spite of the clean if slightly cool digital recordings, which have splendid presence, these performances are too charmless and wanting in grace to be wholeheartedly recommended. There is no appreciable difference in quality between discs and cassettes.

Symphonies Nos. 82 in C (The Bear); 83 in G min. (The Hen).
(M) *** Decca Ace SDD/KSDC 482. Philh. Hungarica, Dorati.
**(*) Ph. 9500 519/7300 675 [id.]. ASMF, Marriner.

Symphonies Nos. 84 in E flat; 85 in B flat (La Reine).
(M) *** Decca Ace SDD 483. Philh. Hungarica, Dorati.

Symphonies Nos. 86 in D; 87 in A.
(M) *** Decca Ace SDD/KSDC 484. Philh. Hungarica, Dorati.

The separate reissue of Dorati's splendid performances of the *Paris symphonies* is most welcome. The readings almost always outshine their direct rivals on disc, the playing consistently fresh and stylish, the recording balance always vivid. Even the least-known of these symphonies, No. 84, has a first movement of the most delicate fantasy, and the whole set can be warmly recommended. The cassette transfers are clear and lively, though there is a degree of edge at the top. A slight treble cut and matching boost of bass restore the bloom to the sound.
From Marriner, good but not outstanding performances of *The Bear* and *The Hen*. There is more polish than in

Dorati's versions but ultimately less character. Excellent recorded sound is an inducement, but the Decca rival is also well recorded and has a price advantage over the newcomer. The usual moderate level of the Philips cassette transfer brings natural sound, if lacking the last bit of upper range. However, in the first movement of No. 82 the bass resonance seems to exaggerate the timpani, which overdominate the texture and rob it of freshness.

Symphonies Nos. 86 in D; 98 in B flat.
⊛ *** Ph. 9500 678/7300 773 [id.]. Concg. O., Colin Davis.

Superbly alive and refined playing from the Concertgebouw Orchestra and Sir Colin Davis. This Haydn series is one of the most distinguished things Davis has given us in recent years, and its blend of brilliance and sensitivity, wit and humanity gives these issues a special claim on the collector. There is no trace of routine in these performances and no failure of imagination. The recordings are first-class, and one is tempted to say that although both these symphonies have had outstanding performances on record (in the case of No. 86 one thinks of the pre-war Bruno Walter and for No. 98 there are Beecham and Jochum), these are second to none and arguably finer. The tape transfer is one of Philips' best, offering warm, rich sound with excellent bloom. The strings are fresh, and only the last degree of upper range is missing in comparison with the disc.

Symphonies Nos. 87 in A; 103 in E flat (Drum Roll).
*** Ph. 9500 303/7300 589 [id.]. Concg. O., Colin Davis.

No one sampling these performances will be in any doubt as to the distinction of the playing and the stature of the readings. Marriner's account of the *Drum*

Roll coupled with No. 100 (the *Military*) is superbly recorded and played with consummate musicianship, and might well be preferred by those who resist the big-band approach to Haydn. But Sir Colin Davis's account seems of an altogether higher order of sensitivity and imagination, almost in the Beecham tradition. Phrasing is the soul of music-making, and Davis inspires the great Dutch orchestra to playing that exhibits delicacy and vitality and phrasing that breathes naturally. The cassette is marginally less fresh and wide-ranging than the disc, but there is little to choose between them.

Symphonies Nos. 88 in G; 104 in D (London).
*** CRD CRD 1070/*CRDC* 4070. Bournemouth Sinf., Ronald Thomas.

A much admired record which has received wide acclaim both for the quality of the performances and for the sound. Although the orchestra is smaller than the Concertgebouw or LPO, the playing has great freshness and vitality; indeed it is the urgency of musical feeling that Ronald Thomas conveys which makes up for the last ounce of finesse. They are uncommonly dramatic in the slow movement of No. 88 and bring great zest and eloquence to the rest of the symphony too. In No. 104 they are not always as perceptive as Sir Colin Davis, but this brightly recorded coupling can be recommended alongside his version. The cassette is vividly transferred and matches the disc closely.

Symphonies Nos. 94 in G (Surprise); 96 in D (Miracle).
**(*) Ph. 9500 348 [id./*7300 594*]. ASMF, Marriner.

Another fine issue in the Academy series of Haydn symphonies. The freshness of the playing is matched by the natural warmth of the recordings. There is most delightful woodwind detail in No. 96 (the oboe solo in the trio of the minuet is a joy) and the genially resilient rhythms in the first movements are matched by the lightness of the finale. No. 94 has a particularly fine performance of the variations which form the slow movement (the 'surprise' itself most effective). The recording is well up to Philips' high standard.

Symphonies Nos. 94 in G (Surprise); 101 in D (Clock).
(B) ** Con. CC/*CCT* 7552 [DG 138782/ *923 033*]. Berlin PO, Karl Richter.

Karl Richter's approach is rather sober, but he secures excellent playing from the Berlin Philharmonic, with fine woodwind detail. The overall effect is straitlaced, but the recording is full and clear (the cassette slightly less transparent than the disc).

Symphonies Nos. 94 in G (Surprise); 103 in E flat (Drum Roll).
** HM 1C 065 99873. Coll. Aur., Maier.

The Collegium Aureum is a conductorless orchestra that uses authentic period instruments and is led from the front desk by Franzjosef Maier. The recording is made in the resonant acoustic of Schloss Kirchheim, so that readers fearing the worst (thin, vinegary string tone reminiscent of a school band) can be reassured. In fact the Collegium Aureum do not sound out-of-tune or inhibited, and are closer to the conventional orchestra than many other groups such as the Academy of Ancient Music. Dynamics tend to be more constricted than is either usual or desirable, but the performances are musicianly enough, even if they lack the stamp of personality. But rival accounts have far more character and are textually correct too.

*Symphonies Nos. 94 in G (Surprise);
104 in D (London).*
**(*) HMV ASD 3839 [Ang. SZ 37575].
Pittsburgh SO, Previn.

In a coupling of what are arguably
Haydn's two most popular symphonies,
Previn conducts lively performances,
very well played and recorded. The only
reservations are over the slow movements, which sound just a little perfunctory, lacking in poise.

*Symphonies Nos. 95 in C min.; 101 in
D (Clock).*
(B) *** RCA VICS/*VK* 2007 [AGL 1
1275]. SO, Reiner.

No. 95 is unlikely ever to be as popular
as the *Clock symphony*, yet it is a splendid
work, with a fine, graciously melodic
slow movement and an agile cello melody
to catch the ear in the trio of the minuet.
It is beautifully played here and makes
an outstanding coupling for a highly
individual account of the *Clock*. Some
may resist Reiner's slow tempo for the
Andante, but the playing itself is most
beguiling. At bargain price and with a
matching chrome cassette (there is no
appreciable difference in sound between
disc and tape), this is most attractive. The
mid-sixties recording sounds admirably
fresh.

*Symphonies Nos. 96 in D (Miracle);
99 in E flat.*
⊛ (M) *** Ph. Fest. 6570/*7310* 083 [id.].
Concg. O., Haitink.

A wholly delightful coupling, in which
the composite personality of the great
Concertgebouw Orchestra projects as
vividly as that of its conductor. Haitink's
approach is direct and unmannered, and
there is some wonderfully smiling playing
in the two slow movements and in the
minuet and trio of the *Miracle symphony*.
The outer movements have plenty of
impetus, and the finales are managed

with a touch that is at once light and
spirited. The sound is excellent, giving
lithe string textures and both detail and
warmth. Highly recommended on both
disc and cassette; they are almost indistinguishable.

*Symphonies Nos. 96 in D (Miracle);
101 in D (Clock).*
** Decca Dig. SXDL/*KSXDC* 7544.
LPO, Solti.

Solti gives brilliant performances,
rather too taut to convey much of
Haydn's charm. With wide-ranging
digital sound to match, they can be
recommended for demonstration rather
than for relaxed listening. The cassette
uses chrome tape and has the same brilliant qualities as the disc.

*Symphonies Nos. 100 in G (Military);
103 in E flat (Drum Roll).*
**(*) Ph. 9500 255 [id./*7300 543*].
ASMF, Marriner.

These are fine performances, with
beautifully sprung rhythms and excellent
detail. The atmosphere at the opening
of the *Drum Roll* is wonderfully caught,
and the first movement's second subject
shows the fine pointing and lightness
of touch which distinguish the music-
making throughout. The recording is
sophisticated in balance and natural in
timbre. In both symphonies Jochum
evinces slightly more personality, although there is not a great deal to choose
between them in terms of orchestral
execution. The Philips recording is
marginally smoother and more finely
detailed.

*Symphonies Nos. 100 in G (Military);
104 in D (London).*
*** Ph. 9500 510/*7300 670*. Concg. O.,
Colin Davis.
(M) *** DG Priv. 2535 347/*3335 347*
[2530 525]. LPO, Jochum.

Sir Colin Davis's coupling has genuine stature and can be recommended without reservation of any kind. It has better claims than any current rivals; the performances have breadth and dignity, yet are full of sparkle and character. The playing of the Concertgebouw Orchestra is as sensitive as it is brilliant, and Davis is unfailingly penetrating. The performances also benefit from excellent recorded sound, with fine clarity and definition. There is warmth and humanity here, and in either work collectors need look no further. The cassette, however, is disappointing, the sound opaque and bass-heavy, with congestion in the percussion effects of the *Military symphony*.

Jochum secures some fine playing from the LPO and is well recorded; but in spite of many felicitous touches, both his performances yield to Davis and the Concertgebouw in terms of sensitivity and refinement. The playing of the LPO in the finale of No. 100 is very good indeed, and at medium price this record deserves to do well. But the Davis is worth the extra money. Jochum's cassette transfer, however, is much better managed by the DG engineers than the Philips tape. There are no problems with the percussion in the *Military symphony*, and there is both detail and warmth.

Symphonies Nos. 101 in E (Clock); 102 in B flat.
*** Ph. 9500 679/7300 774. Concg. O., Colin Davis.
(M) *** HMV SXLP/TC-SXLP 30265. RPO, Beecham.

Sir Colin Davis's set of late Haydn symphonies strikes the most sympathetic resonances: it has the eloquence and strength of Jochum with the finesse of Beecham. It is big-band Haydn and of its kind very impressive. There is superb playing from the Concertgebouw, and the recording is excellent. The cassette is of demonstration quality, one of Philips' finest, with striking range as well as body and richness. The orchestral detail comes through splendidly.

Beecham's performances, however, are in a special class of their own. Phrasing is the soul of music, and these artists shape each phrase as naturally as they breathe. Perhaps not every detail is perfect: the chording in the introduction to No. 102 is not beyond reproach; but these performances penetrate the spirit of the music as do few others. Like Beecham's recordings of Symphonies Nos. 103 and 104, these were made before H. C. Robbins Landon's editions came into general currency. There is a drop of pitch in the slow movement of No. 102 caused by an edit of the master tape; but none of these small reservations detracts from the magic of the performances. The sound balance is an object lesson of its kind, even if the frequency range is a little limited by modern standards. The cassette transfer is made at a high level, and generally the quality is fresh and well detailed.

Symphonies Nos. 103 in E flat (Drum Roll); 104 in D (London).
(M) *** HMV SXLP/TC-SXLP 30257. RPO, Beecham.

Beecham's coupling is self-recommending. Haydn's last two symphonies have rarely, if ever, sounded so captivating and sparkling as they do here. Beecham does not use authentic texts – he was a law unto himself in such matters – but the spirit of Haydn is superbly caught, whether in the affectionately measured (but never mannered) slow movements or in the exhilarating rhythmic spring of the outer movements. The recording is warmly attractive, and the cassette transfer is admirably managed.

CHAMBER MUSIC

Baryton trios Nos. 37, 48, 70–71, 85, 96–7, 109, 113, 117, 121.

(M) *** HMV SLS 5095 (2) [Ang. S 6116]. Esterházy Baryton Trio.

Baryton trios Nos. 44, 52, 61, 96, 101.
*(*) DG Arc. 2533 405. Munich Baryton Trio.

Baryton trios Nos. 51, 70, 107, 113, 117.
*(*) DG Arc. 2533 444. Munich Baryton Trio.

Baryton trios Nos. 63–4, 82, 87–8, 107, 110.
(M) *** HMV HQS 1424. Esterházy Baryton Trio.

Prince Nikolaus Esterházy was an enthusiastic baryton player and Haydn composed some 126 trios for his noble patron. The baryton is a kind of large viola d'amore, with six or seven bowed strings and up to twenty-two sympathetic strings which can be plucked. It produces a beguiling sound and blends splendidly with the viola and cello. The HMV box offers us eleven of the trios in elegant performances by the Esterházy Baryton Trio (which is incidentally based in London and not Eisenstadt!). Not all of the music has the range or variety one would expect to find in Haydn – indeed, there is nothing here to match the string quartets – but taken in small doses these well-recorded performances will give pleasure. This group is far livelier than their Munich rivals on Archive.

The Munich recordings are well balanced and the performances are accomplished. But there is nothing here to make the heart beat faster. Generally speaking, the quality of invention in many of these trios does not match Haydn's best, and here, once the novelty of the baryton's sonority has worn off, the temptation to allow one's thoughts to wander is difficult to resist.

On HQS 1424, the personnel of the Esterházy Trio is not identical with that on the companion set: Roger Chase replaces the Hungarian violist, Csaba

Erdélyi. The playing, however, is no less expert and lively. Although Haydn did not pour his finest inspiration into this medium, there are some good moments in all these trios – and the minuets, generally speaking, are inventive and rewarding. Excellent recording.

Flute trio in D (for flute, cello and piano), *H.XV.*
(M) ** Turn. TVS 34575. NY Camerata – CLEMENTI: *Sonata*; HUMMEL: *Adagio.***

This engaging little work is given a freshly sympathetic account by the excellent New York players. The recording is good, clear and clean.

Guitar quartet in E, Op. 2/2.
(M) *** CBS 61842/40- [(d) Col. MS 7163]. Williams, Loveday, Aronowitz, Fleming – STRAUBE: *Sonatas.***(*)

This recording originally appeared in 1968 coupled with a Paganini *Terzetto.* John Williams's arrangement of the quartet draws both on the lute transcription and the original, and the compromise is a successful one. This is a beguiling performance, more appealing than the string quartet itself. The new coupling, however, is not an improvement on the old. The cassette transfer is full and clear, with plenty of range.

Piano trios (complete).
⊛ *** Ph. 6768 077 (14). Beaux Arts Trio.

Most of the performances in this set have been noticed individually in earlier volumes of the *Penguin Stereo Record Guide.* This is a remarkable and invaluable collection which is unlikely to be challenged, let alone surpassed. It is not often possible to hail one set of records as a 'classic' in quite the way that Schnabel's Beethoven sonatas can be so described. All too few performances attain that level of artistic insight, and such is the sheer proliferation of material that records have a greater struggle for attention. Yet this set can be described in those terms, for the playing of the Beaux Arts Trio is of the very highest musical distinction. The contribution of the pianist, Menahem Pressler, is little short of inspired, and the recorded sound is astonishingly lifelike. The performances follow the Critical Edition of H. C. Robbins Landon, whose indefatigable researches have increased the number of trios we know in the standard edition from thirty-one to forty-three. This is the kind of inflation one welcomes! Most collectors will find something new in this box, and its riches will stand us in good stead for many decades. Here is music that is sane and intelligent, balm to the soul in a troubled world.

Piano trios Nos. 1 in G min.; 37 and 39 in F; in G.
*** Ph. 9500 657 [id.]. Beaux Arts Trio.

These are early trios and of relatively little musical substance, but they are well worth having in such delightful and sparkling performances. The *F major*, H. XV/39 (No. 4 in H. C. Robbins Landon's chronological listing) is composed of transcriptions of individual movements from the early keyboard sonatas, and there is even doubt whether they are made by Haydn himself. All the others were published by the Dutch publisher Hummel in the 1760s.

Piano trios Nos. 2 and 6 in F; 8 in B flat.
*** Ph. 9500 325 [id.]. Beaux Arts Trio.
Piano trios Nos. 5 in G; 10 and 11 in E flat.
*** Ph. 9500 327 [id.]. Beaux Arts Trio.
Piano trio No. 25 in G.
(M) *** Ph. 6833 231. Beaux Arts Trio – DVOŘÁK: *Piano trio No. 4.****

A delightful performance and splendid recording make the appealing *Trio No. 25* a desirable fill-up for Dvořák's *Dumky trio.* The latter is arguably the best version on the market.

Piano trios Nos. 34 in E; 35 in A; 38 in B flat; 40 in F.
*** Ph. 9500 473 [id.]. Beaux Arts Trio.
Piano trios Nos. 36 in E flat; in C; in D; in F min.
*** Ph. 9500 472 [id.]. Beaux Arts Trio.
Piano trios in C and G, H.XV/C1 and C41.
*** Ph. 9500 658 [id.]. Beaux Arts Trio.

Both trios on 9500 658 are early and of little real significance. Haydn himself did not acknowledge the *C major* (H.XV/C1), but scholars seem to think it authentic. Sparkling performances and vivid recording make this a thoroughly pleasurable disc.

String quartets Nos. 13 in E; 14 in C; 15 in G; 16 in B flat; 17 in F; 18 in A, Op. 3/1–6; 50–56 (The Seven Last Words of Jesus Christ), Op. 51/1–7.
(M) *** Argo HDNV 82/4 [Lon. STS 15459/61]. Aeolian Qt (with Pears).

Though Haydn authorities claim that the Op. 3 quartets are by Romanus Hofstetter, not Haydn, it was wise of the Aeolian Quartet to include them in the collected edition, if only because the *Andante cantabile* of Op. 3/2 is so very popular, the so-called *Serenade* with its lovely melody of muted violin with pizzicato accompaniment. There are other treasures here, but the real reason for having this box is the magnificent quartet version of the *Seven Last Words*, here avoiding any risk of monotony from so many *Adagios* in succession by inserting poetry readings between movements. The texts are beautifully chosen and read by Sir Peter Pears. Excellent atmospheric recording.

String quartets Nos. 17 in F (Serenade), Op. 3/5; 67 in D (Lark), Op. 64/5; 76 in D min. (Fifths), Op. 76/2.
(M) *** Ph. 6570/7310 577. Italian Qt.

At first these performances strike one as slightly under-characterized, but on closer acquaintance they reveal qualities of insight that had escaped one. The first movement of the *Lark* is a bit too measured in feeling and could do with more sparkle, but the performance of the *Serenade quartet* is as fine as any available. The *D minor Quartet* is admirably poised and classical in feeling; this rivals if not outclasses the performance by the Janáček Quartet (Decca SDD 285 [Lon. 6385]). The recording is most musically balanced and emerges freshly in this Musica da Camera reissue. The cassette transfer is first-class.

String quartets Nos. 31 in E flat; 32 in C; 33 in G min.; 34 in D; 35 in F min.; 36 in A, Op. 20/1–6.
(M) ** CBS 79305 (3) [Col. M3 34593]. Juilliard Qt.

The Juilliard Quartet is among the most perfect of ensembles, yet the depth and the simplicity of this music elude them. There is some superb quartet playing – and the quality of the recorded sound, though far from distinguished, is better than on previous issues from this source – but the sheer virtuosity and brilliance of this ensemble draw attention to themselves. At no time does one think of a group of highly accomplished musicians making music for pleasure in a domestic situation – surely the whole point of chamber music. This is over-projected. Though far more polished than the Aeolian Quartet, this is less well recorded and ultimately less satisfying.

String quartets Nos. 34 in D, Op. 20/4; 74 in G min. (Rider), Op. 74/3.
*** RCA RL 13485 [ARL 1/ARK 1 3485]. Guarneri Qt.

Nowadays Haydn quartets tend to be recorded in groups and series, so it is good to welcome an excellent disc of two works which each represent the peak of a creative period – the Op. 20 work from 1772, the *Rider* of twenty-four years later when Haydn was writing for Salomon in London. Both have Hungarian elements – in the *Minuet alla zingarese* of the earlier quartet and in the finales of both. The *Rider*, so called because of its dashing first movement, is notable for its beautiful *Largo*, very well played here by the Guarneri Quartet, finely tuned and characterful. Good recording.

String quartets Nos. 44 in B flat; 45 in C, Op. 50/1–2.
⊛ (M) *** DG Priv. 2535/3335 464. Tokyo Qt.

Not since the Schneider Quartet in the 1950s, or perhaps even the pre-war 78s of the Pro Arte, have the quartets of Op. 50 been better served on record. The Tokyo Quartet play with impeccable style and a refreshing and invigorating vitality. They are admirably unaffected but phrase with real imagination. DG give them well-defined and excellently balanced recording and the usual impeccable surfaces. This is an outstanding issue, strongly recommended. The cassette transfers are immaculate, although Op. 50/1 would have benefited from a slightly higher level to match its companion. Even so the sound is fresh and clean.

String quartets Nos. 50–56 (The Seven Last Words), Op. 51; 57–9, Op. 54; 60–62, Op. 55; 63–8, Op. 64; 69–71, Op. 71; 72–4, Op. 74; 75–80, Op. 76; 81–2, Op. 77; in D min. Op. 103.
(B)**(*) DG 2740 250 (14). Amadeus Qt.

These fourteen records collect the last twenty-seven Haydn quartets plus the *Seven Last Words*, in recordings made by the Amadeus over the last eighteen years.

Most of them are from the 1970s, and there will be few quarrels with the quality of the sound. Apart from the Aeolian Quartet, no other ensemble has offered this repertoire in recent years, though older collectors will doubtless still cherish the Schneider and even the pre-war Pro Arte versions of some of them. The Amadeus do not always penetrate the depths of Haydn's slow movements, and Norbert Brainin's vibrato is not to all tastes, but reservations about individual movements should not temper admiration for the undertaking as a whole. Individually these performances may be surpassed by such ensembles as the Orlando, Italian and Tokyo quartets, but it would be curmudgeonly not to extend a warm welcome to this bargain-price reissue.

String quartets Nos. 57 in G; 58 in C, Op. 54/1–2.
*** Ph. 9500/*7300* 996 [id.]. Orlando Qt.

The Orlando Quartet is based in Holland and can boast four different nationalities among its members (Hungarian, Austrian, Rumanian and German). Their Haydn enhances their reputation: this is alert, sensitive and refined playing, scrupulous in its recognition of dynamic nuance (yet without ever being too self-conscious, as the Alban Berg Quartet have become) and superb in its accuracy of ensemble and tonal blend. These are marvellously fresh performances and cannot be too strongly recommended. The *C major Quartet*, with its unusual *Adagio* finale, is a particularly fine work. The cassette matches the disc closely in lively naturalness.

String quartets Nos. 69 in B flat; 70 in D; 71 in E flat, Op. 71/1–3; 72 in C; 73 in F; 74 in G (Rider), Op. 74/1–3.
*** DG 2709 090 (3). Amadeus Qt.

This fine set finds the Amadeus in better form than they have shown for some years; there is a sense of spontaneity as well as genuine breadth to these readings. Haydn's late quartets have much the same expansiveness and depth as the symphonies, and here the Amadeus succeed in conveying both their intimacy and their scale. The recordings have a warm acoustic and good range.

String quartet No. 77 in C (Emperor), Op. 76/3.
*** Ph. 9500 662 [id. *7300 762*]. Italian Qt. – MOZART: *Quartet No. 17.***(*)
(M) *** DG Acc. 2542/ *3342* 122. Amadeus Qt – MOZART: *Quartet No. 17.****

The Italian version of the *Emperor* is already available in a more sensible coupling (Haydn's Op. 76/4), but Philips have now coupled this relatively recent performance with the B flat Mozart, K. 458, recorded in the mid-1960s, without reducing it to medium price. Both are noble performances, and they are extremely well recorded; but the more competitive Amadeus, now on the mid-price DG Accolade label, may tempt some readers. The Amadeus version of the *Emperor* was always one of their best records from the mid-1960s, and it has breadth and warmth. The over-sweet vibrato of Norbert Brainin is less obtrusive here than in many other Amadeus records of this period. Though the Italians are more spacious and have greater nobility (and more modern recording), the excellent Mozart coupling and the competitive price are in the Amadeus's favour. The high-level cassette transfer makes this one of the most attractive string quartet couplings available on tape.

Piano sonatas Nos. 36 in C min. (H. XVI/20); 44 in E flat (H.XVI/49).
*** Ph. 9500 774/*7300 862* [id.]. Brendel.

If all Haydn sonata performances were of this quality, they would be more firmly entrenched in the catalogue. This is playing of real distinction, aristocratic without being aloof and concentrated without being too intense. Everything is cleanly articulated and finely characterized. Brendel observes all the repeats, and he is accorded lifelike and vivid recording. The cassette is particularly fine.

VOCAL MUSIC

The Creation (in German).
*** Ph. 6769 047/7699 154 [id.]. Mathis, Fischer-Dieskau, Baldin, Ch., ASMF, Marriner.
**(*) Decca D 50 D 2/K 50 K 22 [Lon. 12108/5-]. Popp, Hollweg, Dösc, Luxon, Moll, Brighton Festival Ch., RPO, Dorati.

The Creation has always been fortunate on record, and Marriner's version makes an excellent choice if you fancy the work on a relatively intimate scale. With generally fast tempi Marriner draws consistently lithe and resilient playing and singing from his St Martin's team. There is no lack of weight in the result. The great cry of *Licht* on a fortissimo C major chord when God creates light is overwhelming. You might even count Dietrich Fischer-Dieskau in the baritone role as too weighty, recorded rather close, but his inflection of every word is intensely revealing. The soprano is Edith Mathis, very sweet of tone if not always quite so steady as some of her rivals on record, with *Nun beut die Flur* (*With verdure clad*) very light and pretty. The one notable snag is that Aldo Baldin's tenor is not well focused by the microphones. Otherwise the recording is first-rate; so are the cassettes, which in spite of a modest transfer level offer sound that is both robust and clear.

Dorati, as one would expect, directs a lively and well-sprung account, but neither in crispness of ensemble nor in detailed imagination does it match the finest recorded performances. It is partly the fault of the recording that the chorus sounds less well defined than it ought,

and though the soloists make a good team, their singing is rarely distinguished. This joyful performance would be acceptable if the Marriner or the Karajan version (DG 2707 044) were not available, but as it is it falls short. The Decca cassettes, however, are exceptionally successful; technically this is the most enjoyable *Creation* in tape format.

Lieder; English songs and folksong settings (complete).
*** Ph. 6769 064 (3). Ameling, Demus.

'The unknown Haydn', says an essay accompanying this delightful set, but with Elly Ameling projecting these simple but often touching songs to perfection, that is hardly true any more. The celebrated ones like *The Sailor's Song* (with its improbable refrain of 'hurlyburly') and *My mother bids me bind my hair* are well matched by dozens of others almost equally charming, some with clear anticipations of nineteenth-century Lieder. The collection ends with the *Emperor's hymn*, first the Austrian and later the German national anthem: with Ameling even that is made moving in its simplicity. Joerg Demus is a brightly sympathetic accompanist, and the recording is first-rate.

Masses Nos. (i) *1 in F major* (*Missa brevis*); (ii) *4 in G major* (*Missa Sancti Nicolai*).
*** O-L DSLO/KDSLC 538. Nelson, Ch. of Christ Church Cath., Oxford, AcAM, Preston, with (i) Kirkby; (ii) Minty, Covey-Crump, Thomas.

Haydn wrote the early *Missa brevis* when he was seventeen. The setting is engagingly unpretentious; some of its sections last for under two minutes and none takes more than three and a half. The two soprano soloists here match their voices admirably and the effect is delightful. The *Missa Sancti Nicolai* dates from 1772 but has a comparable freshness of inspiration. The unconventional time-signature of the *Kyrie* established the composer's individuality, and the deeply expressive central section of the *Credo* is matched by the characterful opening of the *Sanctus* and the touch of melancholy in the *Agnus Dei*. This performance is first-rate in every way, beautifully sung, with spontaneity in every bar, and a highly characterful accompaniment. The recording is first-class, the cassette only marginally less clearly focused than the disc (because of the reverberation).

Mass No. 2 in E flat (Missa in honorem Beatissimae Virginis Mariae).
**(*) O-L DSLO/*KDSLC* 563 [id.]. Nelson, Watkinson, Hill, Thomas, Ch. of Christ Church Cath., AcAM, Preston.

In this early Mass Haydn followed the rococo conventions of his time, dutifully giving weight to the *Gloria* and *Credo* in culminating fugues but generally adopting a style featuring Italianate melody, which to modern ears inevitably sounds operatic. This first Haydn essay from Preston and his distinguished choir was not quite so crisp or enlivening as most of their records with the Academy of Ancient Music; but with fine, atmospheric recording it is well worth investigating. One intriguing point in the Mass is Haydn's use of a pair of cors anglais, which add a touch of darkness to the scoring. The recording is excellent on disc and cassette alike: there are some delightful sounds here.

Mass No. 3 in C (Missa Cellensis); Missa rorate coeli desuper: Gloria.
*** O-L DSLO 583/4. Nelson, Cable, Hill, Thomas, Ch. of Christ Church Cath., AcAM, Preston.

The *Missa Cellensis* (also known as the *Missa Sanctae Caeciliae*) is Haydn's long-

est setting of the liturgy; the *Gloria* alone (in seven cantata-like movements) lasts nearly half an hour. By contrast the *Gloria* of the little *Missa rorate coeli desuper* is only nine bars long, and with the words all jumbled together it lasts well under a minute. That miniature setting was written by Haydn when he was still a choirboy in Vienna, and it may well be his earliest surviving work. Not everything is perfunctory, for the *Agnus Dei* has a touching gravity. Nonetheless this two-disc set is chiefly valuable for presenting yet another unknown work of Haydn full of vigorous inspiration, with a setting of the *Benedictus* which is darker than one would expect from Haydn. Preston directs an excellent performance with fine contributions from choir and soloists, set against a warmly reverberant acoustic.

Masses Nos. 5 in B flat (Little organ Mass); 6 in C (Missa Cellensis): Mariazeller Mass. Mechanical organ pieces Nos. 3, 6–8.
*** Argo ZRG/*KZRC* 867 [id.]. Jennifer Smith, Watts, Tear, Luxon, St John's College Ch., ASMF, Guest; Scott (organ).

The *Little organ Mass* dates from 1775 and fares better here than in the rival version under Münchinger. There is some fine invention in this piece, though it is not by any means the equal of the *Mariazeller Mass* of 1782, which H. C. Robbins Landon called 'the most perfect large-scale work Haydn achieved' in this particular period. The singing is of excellent quality, and so too is the orchestral playing. Excellent recording and good balance make this a desirable issue for all Haydn lovers. The cassette transfer is of very good quality too.

Mass No. 10 in B flat (Theresien).
*** CBS Dig. 35839 [Col. IM/*HMT* 35839]. Popp, Elias, Tear, Hudson, LSO Ch., LSO, Bernstein.

Bernstein recorded the *Theresienmesse* at Henry Wood Hall immediately after a live performance at the Festival Hall, and the grand manner goes with playing and singing of infectious bounce and resilience, typical of this conductor. The soloists are first-rate, especially Lucia Popp, and with rounded, not specially analytical digital sound this can be warmly recommended to those who favour a large-scale view of this music.

Il ritorno di Tobia (oratorio).
*** Decca D 216 D 4/*K 216 K 44* [Lon. 1445/5-]. Hendricks, Zoghby, Della Jones, Langridge, Luxon, Brighton Festival Ch., RPO, Dorati.

Haydn's first commision from Vienna, written while he was still at Esterháza, is by modern standards a great stranded whale of a piece, full of marvellous material but absurdly long for concert conditions. Based on a subject from the Apocrypha, the story of Tobias and the Angel, it has a libretto which undermines dramatic interest, but on record this objection largely disappears and Haydn's inspiration can at last be appreciated once more. This is the equivalent in oratorio terms of *opera seria*, and though the arias are very long they generally avoid *da capo* form. Most invigorating are the coloratura arias for the Archangel Gabriel (here the dazzling Barbara Hendricks) and the arias for the other soprano, Sara (the radiant Linda Zoghby), which include a lovely meditation, accompanied unexpectedly by antiphonies between oboes and cors anglais in pairs. The other soloists do not quite match the sopranos but the Brighton Festival Chorus is lively and fresh-toned; and except in the rather heavy recitatives Dorati springs the rhythms beautifully, with the five magnificent choruses acting as cornerstones for the whole expansive structure. The recording is both brilliant and atmospheric, and the admirable cassette transfer catches the spacious acoustic without loss of clarity or breadth. A first-class achievement in either format.

The Seasons (in English).
*** Ph. Fest. 6770/7650 035 (3) [id.]. Harper, Davies, Shirley-Quirk, BBC Ch., BBC Ch. Soc., BBC SO, Colin Davis.
**(*) HMV SLS/*TC-SLS* 5158 (3). Morison, Young, Langdon, Beecham Ch. Soc., RPO, Beecham.

Like Marriner (see below), Sir Colin Davis directs a tinglingly fresh performance of Haydn's mellow last oratorio, and choice can safely be left to a preference for the original German text or an excellent English translation. In this work – based with flamboyant freedom on a German translation of James Thomson's English poem – there is more than usual reason for using a translation, and the excellent soloists and chorus attempt with fair success to get the words over clearly. Although the tape transfer seems to be at an unnecessarily low level, the cassettes produce bright fresh sound and a little treble cut is possible to minimize hiss. The choral sound is full and clear and the performance overall makes a good impact.

Beecham here even more than usual in Haydn is cavalier with the text, scoring the *secco* recitatives for strings, adding a tubular bell when the text at the end of *Summer* talks of the evening bell, and often adopting eccentric speeds. The very opening is so slow that Beecham decides to make a cut; but the result is magical. Anyone who did not know the work must inevitably be cajoled into loving this performance with its persuasive playing and singing. It is good to hear these vintage soloists: Elsie Morison in particular is in superb voice, and though the fifties recording is rather limited, it has been remastered effectively. The English translation is by Dennis Arundell. The tape transfer gives vivid presence to soloists and orchestra, but the choral sound is variable. The *Spinning chorus* on side four is poorly focused, and a rise in level on side two brings a patch of roughness.

The Seasons (in German).
*** Ph. Dig. 6769/7654 068 (3) [id.]. Mathis, Jerusalem, Fischer-Dieskau, Ch. and ASMF, Marriner.
**(*) Decca D 88 D 3/*K 88 K 32* (3) [Lon. 13128/5-]. Cotrubas, Krenn, Sotin, Brighton Festival Ch., RPO, Dorati.

Neville Marriner followed up the success of his resilient recording of *The Creation* with this superbly joyful performance of Haydn's last oratorio, effervescent with the optimism of old age. Edith Mathis and Dietrich Fischer-Dieskau are as stylish and characterful as one would expect, pointing the words as narrative. The tenor too is magnificent: Siegfried Jerusalem is both heroic of timbre and yet delicate enough for Haydn's most elegant and genial passages. The chorus and orchestra, of authentic size, add to the freshness. The recording, made in St John's, Smith Square, is warmly reverberant without losing detail. Highly recommended. The chrome cassette transfer has been made at a low level, and while the soloists sound fresh the chorus is less sharply focused than on disc.

Dorati brings to the work an innocent dedication, at times pointing to a folk-like inspiration, which is most compelling. This is not always as polished an account as others available, but with excellent solo singing and bright chorus work it is just as enjoyable. The choruses of peasants in Part 3, for instance, are strikingly robust, with accented rhythms to give a boisterous jollity. Textually there is the important advantage that, with the encouragement of H. C. Robbins Landon (who provides the excellent album notes), Dorati has restored the original version, notably the cuts in the introductions to *Autumn* and *Winter*, the latter with some wonderfully adventurous harmonies. The gains are marginal

but important, and the recording quality is of outstanding vividness, though the chorus might have been more sharply focused. The orchestral detail is well realized; the pictorial effects towards the end of Part 2 are highly effective. The performance as a whole is splendidly animated. With Dorati this is above all a happy work, a point made all the more telling by the immediacy of the sound, equally impressive on disc and tape.

The Seasons: choruses and arias: *Spring:* Nos. 2, 4, 6; *Summer:* Nos. 14–17; *Autumn:* Nos. 27, 31; *Winter:* Nos. 32, 35, 40, 44.
(M) *** DG Priv. 2535/3335 368. Janowitz, Schreier, Talvela, V. Singverein, VPO, Boehm.

This excellent and generous set of excerpts reminds us of the spirited spontaneity that makes Boehm's complete set (DG 2709 026/3371 028) so compelling. For those not wanting a complete recording the selection here is well-balanced, and on disc and tape alike the recording reflects the excellent qualities of its source.

Salve Regina; Stabat Mater.
*** Argo ZRG 917/8. Auger, Hodgson, Rolfe Johnson, Howell, L. Chamber Ch., Argo CO, Heltay.

Haydn's *Stabat Mater*, one of his first major masterpieces, showing him at full stretch, was written in his early years at Esterháza. Scored for strings with oboes, the work is far bigger in aim than that scale might suggest, and some of the choruses include harmonic progressions which in their emotional overtones suggest music of a much later period. On record as in the concert hall the work is scandalously neglected, and it is good that Heltay's reading conveys its essential greatness, helped by admirable soloists and atmospheric recording. The *Salve Regina*, another early work, comparable in its depth of feeling, is here given with full chorus, although solo voices were originally intended; the weight of the piece is better conveyed in this way.

OPERA

Armida (complete).
*** Ph. 6769 021 (3) [id.]. Norman, Ahnsjö, Burrowes, Ramey, Leggate, Lausanne CO, Dorati.

Armida, considered in Haydn's time to be his finest opera, was the last he produced at Esterháza and the one most frequently performed there. It is a piece in which virtually nothing happens. Rinaldo, a crusader seduced away from crusading by the sorceress Armida, heavily disguised as a goody, takes three acts to decide to cut down the myrtle tree which will undermine Armida's wicked power. But, more than most works in this stilted form, *Armida* presents a psychological drama, with the myrtle tree the most obvious of symbols. On record it makes fair entertainment, with splendid singing from Jessye Norman, even if she hardly sounds malevolent. Claes Ahnsjö as the indecisive Rinaldo does better than most tenors coping with the enormous range. The whole team of soloists is one of the most consistent in Dorati's Haydn opera series, with Norma Burrowes particularly sweet as Zelmira. As well as some advanced passages, *Armida* also has the advantage that there is relatively little secco recitative. The recording quality is outstanding.

L'Incontro improvviso (complete).
*** Ph. 6769 040 (3) [id.]. Zoghby, Margaret Marshall, Della Jones, Ahnsjö, Trimarchi, Luxon, Prescott, Lausanne CO, Dorati.

In eighteenth-century Vienna the abduction opera involving moorish enslavement and torture became quite a cult – strange masochistic taste when Turkish invasions were not that distant. The greatest example is Mozart's *Entführung*, but this example of the genre from Haydn, a light entertainment for Prince Esterházy's private theatre, is well worthy of comparison with its very similar story. In forty-seven generally brief numbers, but with finales of almost Mozartian complexity, it may lack depth of characterization (Haydn was using a libretto set by Gluck) but the result is musically delightful. The most heavenly number of all is a trio for the three sopranos in Act 1, *Mi sembra un sogno*, which with its high-flown legato phrases keeps reminding one of *Soave sia il vento* in *Così fan tutte*. The tenor's trumpeting arias are beautifully crisp and the vigorous canzonettas for the two buffo basses include a nonsense song or two. Benjamin Luxon and Domenico Trimarchi are delectable in those roles. Claes Ahnsjö is at his finest, resorting understandably to falsetto for one impossible top E flat; the role of heroine is superbly taken by Linda Zoghby, and she is well supported by Margaret Marshall and Della Jones. The secco recitatives are rather heavy, as ever contradicting Dorati's generally well-sprung style in Haydn. The recording conveys a most convincing theatre atmosphere.

L'Infedeltà delusa (complete).
** Hung. SLPX 11832/4. Kalmár, Pászthy, Rozsos, Fülöp, Gregor, Liszt CO, Frigyes Sándor.

L'Infedeltà delusa (complete). Arias from: *Acide e Galatea; Ifigenia in Tauride; I finti eredi; La Circe.*
*** Ph. 6769 061 (3). Mathis, Hendricks, Ahnsjö, Baldin, Devlin, Lausanne CO, Dorati.

This was the last of the admirable Philips series of Haydn operas, recorded with Antal Dorati and the Lausanne Chamber Orchestra, providing an important nucleus of the operas written for performance at Esterháza. This one, a simple rustic comedy, may not be the most imaginative dramatically, but by the standards of the time it is a compact piece, punctuated by some sharply memorable arias such as a laughing song for the hero Nencio (the admirable Claes Ahnsjö) and a song of ailments for the spirited heroine, Vespina (Edith Mathis lively and fresh). Vespina is first cousin to Despina in *Così fan tutte*, and there is a splendid Mozartian anticipation when in the finale of Act 1 she slaps Nencio's face, Susanna-style. Dorati draws vigorous, resilient performances from everyone (not least the delightful Barbara Hendricks), and the final side devoted to arias and ensembles that Haydn devised for other men's operas adds to the attractions, ending with an amazing eating-and-drinking trio. Splendid and full-bodied recording.

The Hungaroton version is quite a strong contender even in the face of Dorati's fine Philips recording of this delightful piece. Sándor's approach is a degree more relaxed, and though the vocal quality is not so consistent, it is plain that the singers have performed this music on stage together, and a sense of involvement comes over. The recording is good but cannot match the excellence of the Philips, and there is no fill-up.

L'Isola disabitata (complete).
*** Ph. 6700 119 (2) [id.]. Lerer, Zoghby, Alva, Bruson, Lausanne CO, Dorati.

By eighteenth-century standards *L'Isola disabitata* (*The Uninhabited Island*) is an extremely compact opera, and were it not for the preponderance of accompanied recitative over set numbers it would be an ideal one to recommend to the modern listener. As it is, many passages reflect the *Sturm und Drang* manner of the middle-period Haydn, urgently dramatic with tremolos freely used. But in Act 1 it is only after twenty minutes that the first aria appears, a delightful piece for the heroine with a hint of *Che farò* in Gluck's *Orfeo*. Vocally it is

the second soprano here, Linda Zoghby, who takes first honours, though the baritone, Renato Bruson, is splendid too. The piece ends with a fine quartet of reconciliation, only the eighth number in the whole piece. The direction of recitatives is unfortunately not Dorati's strong point – here as elsewhere in the series rather too heavy – but with excellent recording this makes a fascinating issue.

Il Mondo della luna (complete).
*** Ph. 6769 003 (4) [id./7699 078]. Auger, Mathis, Von Stade, Valentini Terrani, Alva, Rolfe Johnson, Trimarchi, Suisse Romande Ch., Lausanne CO, Dorati.

Il Mondo della luna (*The World on the Moon*) is better known (by name at least) than the other Haydn operas that the Philips series has progressively disinterred. Written for an Esterházy marriage, it uses the plot of a naive but engaging Goldoni comedy as its basis. A bogus astronomer (played by Luigi Alva) hoodwinks the inevitable rich old man (Domenico Trimarchi sparkling and stylish in comic vocal acting) into believing he has been transported to the moon. All this is in aid of getting the rich man's lovelorn daughter married to the hero of her choice, and though by the standards of the time the plot is simple it takes a long time in the resolving. Much of the most charming music comes in the brief instrumental interludes, and most of the arias are correspondingly short. That leaves much space on these records devoted to secco recitative, and as on his earlier Haydn opera issues, Dorati proves a surprisingly heavy and sluggish harpsichord continuo player. Nonetheless, with splendid contributions from the three principal women singers, this is another Haydn set which richly deserves investigation by anyone devoted to opera of the period. Excellent, finely balanced recording.

Orlando paladino (complete).
*** Ph. 6707 029 (4) [id.]. Auger, Ameling, Killebrew, Shirley, Ahnsjö,
Luxon, Trimarchi, Mazzieri, Lausanne CO, Dorati.

One might well infer from this delightful send-up of a classical story in opera
that Haydn in his pieces for Esterháza
was producing sophisticated charades for
a very closed circle. Though long for its
subject, this is among the most delightful
of all, turning the legend of Roland and
his exploits as medieval champion into
something not far from farce. Roland's
madness (*Orlando furioso*) becomes the
amiable dottiness of a Disney giant with
a club, and there are plenty of touches of
parody: the bass arias of the King of
Barbary suggests mock-Handel and
Charon's aria (after Orlando is whisked
down to hell) brings a charming exaggeration of Gluck's manner. Above all
the Leporello-like servant figure, Pasquale, is given a series of numbers which
match and even outshine Mozart, including a hilarious duet when, bowled
over by love, he can only utter mono-
syllables, cue for marvellous buffo singing from Domenico Trimarchi. The singing team is strong, with Arleen Auger as
the heroine outstandingly sweet and
pure. George Shirley as Orlando snarls
too much in recitative, but it is an aptly
heroic performance, and Elly Ameling
and Gwendolyn Killebrew in subsidiary
roles are both excellent. The recitatives
here, though long, are rather less heavily
done than on some other Dorati sets, and
the recording is first-rate.

Lo Speziale (complete recording of
surviving music).
** Hung. SLPX 11926/7. Fülöp,
Istvan, Kalmár, Kincses, Liszt CO,
Lehel.

Lo Speziale (*The Apothecary*), written
for the inauguration of the opera house at
the new palace of Esterháza, is a conventional buffo piece based on Goldoni.
Though Haydn had had little or no
experience of the stage, he produced individual numbers which are brilliantly
successful, notably when two bogus
notaries falsify a marriage contract as it
is being dictated. It gained currency in
Germany in the present century in a
garbled edition, but here Lehel seeks to
return to the original, and directs a lively
if not always polished performance. The
four young-sounding soloists (Fülöp
rather too young for the role of Apothecary) are fresh-toned, singing agreeably
if with little distinction. Fair recording.

Arias: *Acide e Galatea: Tergi i vez-
zosi rai. Il Disertore: Un cor si tenero.
La Scuola di gelosi: Dice benissimo.
La vera costanza: Spann' deine
lange Ohren.*
(M) *** Decca Jub. JB/KJBC 100.
Fischer-Dieskau, V. Haydn O., Peters
—MOZART: *Arias.***(*)

'Haydn and Mozart rarities', the disc
says, and very delightful they prove, even
if Haydn gets much less attention, with
comparatively lightweight and simple
pieces. Fischer-Dieskau is as thoughtfully stylish as ever, though it is a pity
that he did not take more advice about
the inclusion of appoggiaturas. Yet this
is a most enjoyable recital and well worth
investigating at Jubilee price. The recording is excellent on disc and tape alike.

Haydn, Michael (1737–1806)

*Concertino for horn and orchestra in
D* (ed. Sherman).
*** HMV ASD/TC-ASD 3774 [Ang.
SZ/4ZS 37569]. Tuckwell, ECO –
J. HAYDN: *Horn concertos.****

The *Concertino* is a curious work, beginning with a slow movement, followed

by a fast one and closing with a minuet and trio in which the soloist is featured in the middle section, with an ad lib contribution at the reprise of the trio. The music itself is attractive and of course brilliantly played and splendidly recorded, with an excellent cassette to match the disc.

Henze, Hans Werner
(born 1926)

Voices.
*** Decca HEAD 19/20. Walker, Sperry, L. Sinf., composer.

Voices outshines most of the other products of Henze's revolutionary fervour in the sharpness of detailed imagination. He sets a sequence of twenty-two texts in English, Spanish, German and Italian, using a wide variety of styles to match the variety of revolutionary protest which they contain. It matters little that echoes of Shostakovich rub shoulders with echoes of Weill along with unashamed lyricism of a kind that the composer has rarely allowed himself. The virtuosity of the writing is matched by the brilliance of the performance, designed as a whole evening of entertainment, here crisply caught on record, with the London Sinfonietta at its most inspired.

Herrmann, Bernard
(1911–75)

Film scores: *Beneath the Twelve-mile Reef;* (i) *Citizen Kane* (suites). *Hangover Square:* (ii) *Concerto macabre. On Dangerous Ground:*

Death hunt. White Witch Doctor: suite.
(M)*** RCA GL/*GK* 43441 [ARL 1/ *ARK 1* 0707]. Nat. PO, Gerhardt, with (i) Te Kanawa, (ii) Achucarro.

In 1940 Orson Welles chose Bernard Herrmann to write the background music for *Citizen Kane.* It established Herrmann's international reputation and was to remain one of the freshest and most original of all film scores, making a major contribution to the narrative atmosphere, but also providing a suite fully able to stand as music in its own right. It includes a fascinating pastiche aria from a fictitious opera, *Salammbô*, using a text loosely derived from Racine's *Phèdre*, eloquently sung by Kiri Te Kanawa. In the film the heroine was unable to pit her voice successfully against the Straussian orchestration, but – needless to say – that is not the case here. The collection opens with an exhilarating example of the composer's ferocious chase music, the *Death hunt* from *On Dangerous Ground.* With eight roistering horns and all the brass augmented to match (six trumpets, six trombones, two tubas), the effect is overwhelmingly brilliant. *Beneath the Twelve-mile Reef* shows Herrmann's soaring melodic gift and his equally impressive orchestral flair. The evocation of the *Undersea forest* with its menacing octopus (a tapestry backed by nine harps, with an imaginative amalgam of low woodwind, electric bass and organ pedals) is unforgettable, while in *White Witch Doctor* opportunities for exoticism and a wide range of drum effects are used with great colouristic skill. The Busoni–Liszt-derived *Concerto macabre* is brilliantly played by Joaquin Achucarro, and the orchestra under Charles Gerhardt is spectacularly sympathetic throughout. The wide-ranging recording is marginally less refined in transient sharpness in its tape format, and the cassette does not include the disc's insert leaflet of back-up information and pictures.

North by Northwest (film score).
**(*) Uni. Kanchana Dig. DKP 9000
[id.]. L. Studio SO, Lauric Johnson.

Although inventive and scored with Herrmann's usual feeling for atmosphere, this selection of incidental music is a bit thin. It has a distinctly attractive romantic strain, but much of the rest is unmemorable away from the visual images, which it seldom recalls. The playing is excellent and the digital recording is of high quality.

Hertel, Johann (1727–89)

Concerto à 6 for trumpet, oboe and strings.
*** CBS 76862/40- [Col. M/*M T* 35856].
Bernard, Holliger, ECO, Malcolm –
ALBINONI and HUMMEL: *Trumpet concertos.****

Hertel's *Concerto à 6* combines two solo instruments that do not easily balance together, and in spite of the efforts of the engineers with their microphones this awkwardness remains. Having said that, it must be admitted that with such a distinguished partnership this makes engaging listening in its offbeat manner. The Hummel coupling is also first-rate. The tape is well managed and thoroughly acceptable even though it has slightly less upper range than the disc.

Hindemith, Paul (1895–1963)

(i) *Concert music for piano, brass and harps, Op. 49. Concert music for strings and brass, Op. 50; Morning music for brass.*

*** Argo Dig. ZRDL 1000. Philip Jones Ens., Howarth, (i) with Crossley.

When he wrote these pieces in 1930 and 1931, Hindemith was at the peak of his powers, practising his *Gebrauchsmusik* as a practical musician but finding individual inspiration in the specific challenge of strange groupings of instruments as well as specific commissions. The *Concert music for Strings and Brass*, a powerful and inventive piece, is the more immediately attractive of the two big works, but thanks to the inspired playing of Paul Crossley, the poetry as well as the severe logic of the Op. 49 work comes over compellingly. The *Morgenmusik* for brass alone is a brief but worthwhile makeweight. The digital recording is outstanding, the perfect foil for the Ensemble's unfailing virtuosity.

Concert music for strings and brass; Symphonic metamorphoses on themes by Weber.
*** HMV ASD/*TC-ASD* 3743 [Ang. SZ 37536]. Phd. O., Ormandy.

The *Concert music for strings and brass* is here given a superb performance and recording; the Philadelphia Orchestra bring virtuosity and opulent tone to this rewarding score. The *Symphonic metamorphoses on themes by Weber* is more generously represented on record, and although these artists play with splendid panache and brilliance, the humour of the second movement is perhaps less effectively realized in their hands than in, say, Abbado's. In every other respect, however, this is first-class, and the recording too does justice to the quality of sound this great orchestra produces. The tape is clear and full-blooded, slightly sharper-edged and correspondingly less rich than the disc. But the sound is extremely vivid.

Viola concerto (Der Schwanendreher).

*** DG 2531 249 [id.]. Benyamini, Orchestre de Paris, Barenboim – BARTÓK: *Viola concerto*.***

(M) * Turn. TVS 34687 [id.]. Thompson, Boston MIT SO, Epstein – BLOCH: *Suite hébraïque*; MARTIN: *Sonata da chiesa*.*

On DG a superbly eloquent account of Hindemith's *Der Schwanendreher concerto*, a rewarding and inventive score which repays attention. According to Simon Streatfield, who played under the composer, the 'swan-turner' of the title is simply the man who turned the handle of the spit on which the swan was roasted! Daniel Benyamini must be among the most gifted of violists now before the public and he serves the score to perfection – without impairing the flavour of its texture by over-heating it. Barenboim gives excellent support, and although the violist is rather prominently focused, the overall sound is very natural. An enterprising and strongly recommendable coupling.

The alternative performance on Turnabout is simply not distinguished enough to warrant more than a qualified recommendation. The soloist is wanting in real warmth and personality, and the orchestral support is not in the first league either. The recording is equally lacklustre.

Kammermusiken: Nos. 1 for small orchestra, Op. 24/1; 2 for piano and 12 solo instruments; 3 for cello and 10 solo instruments; 4 for violin and chamber orchestra; 5 for viola and chamber orchestra, Op. 36/1–4; 6 for viola d'amore and chamber orchestra; 7, Organ concerto, Op. 46/1–2.

*** HM 1C 99 721/3. Ensemble 13, Baden-Baden, Reichert.

These chamber concertos for various instruments are from a vintage period and are full of rewarding invention both in terms of musical ideas and novel textures. Here we have music that is highly original and much lighter in touch than the name Hindemith would lead many collectors to expect. It is marvellously recorded, too, and will yield quite unexpected pleasures to those enterprising enough to invest in it. The performances are all highly accomplished and imaginative.

Mathis der Maler (symphony).

(M) *** HMV SXLP/*TC-SXLP* 30536 [Ang. S 35949]. Berlin PO, Karajan – BARTÓK: *Music for strings, percussion and celesta*.**(*)

Karajan's 1960 account of the *Mathis symphony* is beautifully spacious and among the very finest versions of the work ever made. Karajan succeeds in producing a more refined and transparent texture than we are accustomed to, and both dynamic nuances and details of phrasing are attentively followed without creating a sense of beautification. The first two movements in particular are fresh and atmospheric, and the opening of the finale is wonderfully dramatic. The recording is atmospheric too, but rather wanting in body. It is not the equal of Karajan's EMI recordings made much earlier in London with the Philharmonia, including the Stravinsky *Jeu de cartes* of 1952, which has far more detail and definition than this. However, the performance is so fine – and certainly the best on the market at the time of writing – that the recommendation must be unqualified.

Nobilissima visione (suite); *Symphonic metamorphoses on themes by Weber*.

(M) *(*) Sup. 4102 197. Czech PO, Delogu.

Nobilissima visione is one of Hindemith's most eloquent and approachable works, though records of it never seem to enjoy a long life in the catalogue. The more popular *Symphonic metamorphoses* has greater exuberance if less depth. Here Gaetano Delogu secures good results from the Czech Philharmonic Orchestra in terms of ensemble and vitality, though neither performance is particularly memorable or distinguished. Phrasing in the *Nobilissima visione* suite could be more imaginatively shaped, and dynamic nuances in the *Metamorphoses* are by no means as subtle here as they are in Abbado's LSO version. The recording is somewhat wanting in depth, so that the overall effect is somewhat two-dimensional. In the absence of an alternative *Nobilissima*, this will have to do, but it is a stop-gap recommendation.

Symphonic metamorphoses on themes by Weber.
(*) Telarc Dig. DG 10056/7 [id.]. Atlanta SO, Shaw – ORFF: *Carmina Burana.*(*)

Robert Shaw treats Hindemith's colourful variations almost neoclassically. His is a sharp, incisive performance that misses some of the bounce and charm, but makes a fair fill-up for a three-sided version of *Carmina Burana*. The recording here is not quite of the demonstration quality given to the Orff

Clarinet sonata.
* Merlin MRF 80701. Kelly, Pearson – POULENC: *Sonatas.*(*)

Full marks to Merlin for enterprise, but unfortunately the dry acoustic in which the Hindemith is recorded is not helpful. This sonata needs beauty of sound if it is to be persuasive.

Kleine Kammermusik, Op. 24/2.
*** Uni. RHS 366. Danish Wind Quintet – MILHAUD: *Cheminée du Roi René* *(*), NIELSEN: *Quintet.***

Alert and sensitive playing here from the Danish Wind Quintet, who are far more imaginative and responsive in the *Kleine Kammermusik* than in their native Nielsen. Dynamic nuances are scrupulously observed here, whereas in the latter they are not. Good recording of engaging music.

String quartets Nos. 2 in C, Op. 16; 3, Op. 22.
**(*) Tel. AW 6.42077. Kreuzberg Qt.

Hindemith was so prolific that the very size of his output deters the music-lover from investigating it. Yet at his best – and his six string quartets are among his finest works – he is enormously rewarding and often really moving. The *Third* is the most familiar of the quartets (save perhaps for the *Fifth*), and its centrepiece is an eloquent and dignified slow movement that is gravely beautiful and genuinely haunting. Inventive, resourceful, intelligent music, and very well played too by these young German musicians. The recording has the merit of clarity and good definition, though it could really have done with a more spacious acoustic.

When lilacs last in the dooryard bloom'd (Requiem).
(M) *** CBS 61890 [Odys. Y 33821]. Parker, London, NY Schola Cantorum, NYPO, composer.

Hindemith's *When lilacs last in the dooryard bloom'd* was written at the end of the last war as a commission from the Robert Shaw Chorale. With the recent death of Roosevelt in mind, Hindemith turned to Whitman's elegy on the death of Lincoln, and he produced a work of surpassing beauty and eloquence that must be numbered among his most impressive achievements. Why this work is not more often performed is a mystery indeed: right from the dignified and noble prelude through to the imposing finale, the inspiration is of the highest quality. Louise Parker and George London are committed soloists, though they are too forward in relation to the orchestra. Hindemith himself is at the helm, so the performance carries genuine authority; the recording has a warm and realistic acoustic, and reproduces far more satisfactorily than it did in the US pressings in which it first gained currency. Though the sound may not be absolutely ideal, it is perfectly acceptable, and the music can be recommended with all possible enthusiasm.

Mathis der Maler (opera; complete).
*** EMI 1C 165 03515/7. Fischer-Dieskau, Feldhoff, King, Schmidt, Meven, Cochran, Malta, Grobe, Wagemann, Bav. R. Ch. and SO, Kubelik.

There is little doubt that the opera *Mathis der Maler* is Hindemith's masterpiece. The fine symphony which he extracted from it gives only a partial idea of its quality, for here Hindemith's theorizing went with a deep involvement with the subject. There is no mistaking that behind the characteristic gruffness of manner, there is not just urgency but warmth. Fischer-Dieskau proves the ideal interpreter of the central role, the painter Mathias Grünewald, who in the troubled Germany of the sixteenth century joins the cause of the rebellious peasants – a subject with a very clear relevance to the times when the piece was written, during the rise of the Nazis. Other fine contributions come from James King as the Archbishop, Donald Grobe as the Cardinal, Alexander Malta as the army commandant and Manfred Schmidt as the Cardinal's adviser. The women principals are less happily chosen; Rose Wagemann as Ursula is rather squally. But with splendid playing and singing from Bavarian Radio forces under Kubelik, it is a highly enjoyable as well as an important set.

Holborne, Anthony
(died 1602)

Cradle pavane and galliard (The woods so wild); Countess of Pembroke's paradise; Holborne's almain (suite); Muy linda; Nowell's galliard; 2 Pavans and galliards; Quadro pavan and galliard. Suite: Galliard: Heres paternus; Heigh ho holiday; The wanton.
*** Mer. E 77027. Extempore String Ens., Weigland.

The Extempore String Ensemble attempts to live up to its name by playing spontaneously even in the recording studio. This Holborne disc does not have quite the expressive abandon which made the group's earlier record of consort music by different composers so compelling, but it presents an illuminating musical portrait of a long-neglected but fascinating Elizabethan, a key figure in spheres other than music. First-rate recording.

Pavanes and galliards (1599): Almayne; As it fell on a holie eve; Ecce quam bonum; The funerals; 3 Galliards; Heigh ho holiday; Heres Paternus; The Honiesuckle; Image of melancholy; Infernum; Muy Linda; Paradizo; Pavan; Pavana ploravit; The sighes; Sic semper soleo.
*** O-L DSLO 569 [id.]. Guildhall Waits, Cons. of Musicke, Trevor Jones or Rooley.

Holborne's *Pavanes and galliards* were published in 1599 and comprise sixty-five five-part dances, of which seventeen are included on this record. The music is very appealing indeed, and though it could easily sound unvaried, the planners of the record have achieved satisfactory results by contrasting the Guildhall Waits (cornetts and sackbuts) with the strings of the Consort of Musicke. The cornetts and sackbuts sound a shade inhibited at times, and generally speaking a little more abandon would not have come amiss in what is a lively anthology. The recording is cut at a high level but does not give trouble to pick-ups that are tracking properly. If there is end-of-side distortion (as stated in one or two reviews) you can be sure that it is not the fault of the record if the copy corresponds to the ones we have tried.

Short airs, both grave and light (suite).
(B) *** CfP CFP/TC-CFP 40335. Praetorius Cons., Ball – LAMBRANZI: *Dances*; PRAETORIUS: *Terpsichore.****

Another engaging selection from Holborne's collection of pavanes and galliards. As in the *Terpsichore* coupling, Christopher Ball's arrangements are recorder-dominated, and occasionally the ear craves a consort of viols, and perhaps voices too. But the skill of the scoring (*The last will and testament* is a poignant example) and the freshly alert and sympathetic performances are matched by the excellent CfP sound. There is no appreciable difference between the disc and the excellent cassette. Highly recommended in both formats.

Holbrooke, Josef (1878–1958)

The Birds of Rhiannon, Op. 87.
*** Lyr. SRCS 103. LPO, Handley – ROOTHAM: *Symphony No. 1.****

A recording of remarkable clarity, definition and depth. *The Birds of Rhiannon* is a shortish piece, lasting about fifteen minutes and drawing on Holbrooke's operatic trilogy on Welsh legends that occupied him from 1912 to 1920. Arthur Hutchings suggests that *The Birds of Rhiannon* may well bear much the same relationship to the operas as the *Siegfried idyll* does to the *Ring*. The piece ends with bird song, as does the opera *Bronwen*, when the seven heroes are so beguiled by the magical sounds that they remain at Harlech for seven years. The level of inspiration of Holbrooke's piece does not quite rise to the theme, and it would be idle to pretend that it is a masterpiece. The playing of the LPO under Handley is excellent, as also in the rather more interesting coupling.

Holmboe, Vagn (born 1909)

Symphony No. 10, Op. 105.
*** Cap. CAP 1116. Gothenberg SO, Ehrling – NYSTROEM: *Sinfonia breve.****

The Danish composer Holmboe possesses a powerful and inquiring mind; his music betrays a strong sense of purpose and establishes a sound world that is immediately identifiable. The *Tenth* of his eleven symphonies was written for Sixten Ehrling and the Detroit Orchestra, and dates from 1971. It is music of vision and individuality whose language will strike a responsive chord in any admirer of Nielsen, though Holmboe's music does not resemble that of his great countryman. It is well played and recorded and should not be overlooked by any collector with an interest in the Scandinavian symphonic tradition. The Swedish symphony with which it is coupled, though not of comparable stature, is also worth investigation.

Holst, Gustav (1874–1934)

Brook Green suite (for strings); *A Somerset rhapsody.*
*** HMV ASD/*TC-ASD* 3953. Bournemouth Sinf., Del Mar – VAUGHAN WILLIAMS: *The Wasps.****

Like the *St Paul's suite*, this *Brook Green suite* was originally written for the St Paul's School for Girls, where Holst was in charge of music. It emerged as far more than an exercise for students, as this dedicated performance demonstrates, most strikingly in the vigorous final dance. The *Somerset rhapsody*, one of Holst's most evocative pieces, is here most persuasively played, helped by recording of demonstration quality. Indeed this record with its delightful Vaughan Williams coupling is more than the sum of its parts, and the cassette is equally recommendable, offering warmly atmospheric textures, the resonance captured most naturally.

(i) *Egdon Heath, Op. 47; The Perfect Fool* (opera): *ballet suite, Op. 39;* (ii) *Hymn of Jesus, Op. 37.*
(M) *** Decca Jub. JB/*KJBC* 49. (i) LPO; (ii) BBC SO and Ch.; Boult.

Fine performances of the *Hymn of Jesus* and *Egdon Heath* are suitably leavened here with a brilliant and flashingly colourful account of the *Perfect Fool ballet suite* – Holst at his most vividly extrovert and colourful. Boult's performance of the *Hymn of Jesus* is undoubtedly a fine one, bringing out its mystical element as well as its atmosphere. The recording has a wide dynamic range and the work's climaxes are dramatically made. The bleak, sombre evocation of *Egdon Heath* is hauntingly conveyed and provides yet another contrast. Although the account of the *Hymn of Jesus* is perhaps not quite so penetrating as Groves's on HMV (see below),

there will be many who prefer the couplings on this excellent Decca disc. The cassette transfer is marvellously vivid, with a wide dynamic range and plenty of atmosphere in the *Hymn of Jesus* yet offering the most refined detail.

Hammersmith: Prelude and scherzo, Op. 32; Military band suites Nos. 1 in E flat; 2 in F, Op. 28.
*** ASV ACA/*ZCACA* 1002. L. Wind Soloists, Wick – VAUGHAN WILLIAMS: *English folksongs suite* etc.***

Military band suites Nos. 1–2.
⊛ *** Telarc Dig. DG 5038 [id.]. Cleveland Symphonic Winds, Fennell – HANDEL: *Royal Fireworks music.* ⊛ ***

Holst's two *Military band suites* contain some magnificent music – much underrated because of the medium – and they have been lucky on records. Frederick Fennell's famous Mercury recording, made at the beginning of the sixties, is remembered nostalgically by many collectors and was a landmark in its day. His new versions have more gravitas and perhaps less sheer *joie de vivre*. But they are magnificent nonetheless, and the recording is truly superb – digital technique used in a quite overwhelmingly exciting way. Perhaps there is too much bass drum, but no one with equipment to handle the climaxes adequately is going to grumble one bit. The *Chaconne* of the *First Suite* makes a quite marvellous effect here. The playing of the Cleveland wind group is of the highest quality, smoothly blended and full in slow movements, vigorous and alert and with strongly rhythmic articulation in fast ones.

The recording by the London Wind Soloists (a group drawn from the LSO) is enjoyable in quite a different way. The performances are altogether more lightweight, but they have great spontaneity. The music's lyrical feeling is displayed more readily: the *March* from the *Second Suite* is resilient; the *Fantasia on the*

Dargason has unmistakable sparkle and *Hammersmith* too has an attractive rhythmic freshness. The recording is altogether less massive than the Telarc disc, but still very good indeed, and with worthwhile couplings this is well worth investigating as an attractively different approach. The cassette is just a little disappointing, good but with only a modest transfer level; the transients are less sharp than on the disc.

The Planets (suite), *Op. 32.*
⊛ *** DG 2532/*3302* 019 [id.]. Berlin PO and Ch., Karajan.
*** HMV ASD/*TC-ASD* 3649. LPO, Mitchell Ch., Boult.
(M) *** Decca Jub. JB/*KJBC* 30 [Lon. 6244]. VPO, V. State Op. Ch., Karajan.
*** Decca SET/*KCET* 628 [Lon. 7110]. LPO and Ch., Solti.
*** Chan. Dig. ABRD/*ABTD* 1010. SNO and Ch., Gibson.
(M) **(*) RCA Gold GL/*GK* 13885 [AGL 1/*AGK 1* 3885]. Phd. O., Mendelssohn Club Ch., Ormandy.
**(*) HMV Dig. ASD/*TCC-ASD* 4047 [Ang. DS 37817]. Philh. O., Amb. Ch., Rattle.
**(*) CBS 61932/*40-* [Col. M/*MT* 31125]. NYPO and Ch., Bernstein.
**(*) Ph. 9500 425/*7300 643* [id.]. Concg. O., Amb. S., Marriner.
*(*) Ph. 9500 782/*7300 856* [id.]. Boston SO, Ozawa.
*(*) Turn. KTVS 34598 [id./*CT 2153*]. St Louis SO and Ch., Susskind.
(B) (*) Con. CC/*CCT* 7518 [Lon. 21049]. LPO and Ch., Herrmann.

On his newest DG digital record (and chrome tape) Karajan directs a thrilling performance that makes one hear Holst's brilliant suite with new ears. With the Berlin Philharmonic at peak form he improves even on the performance he recorded two decades earlier with the Vienna Philharmonic, modifying his reading to make it more idiomatic; for example in *Jupiter* the syncopated opening now erupts with joy and the big melody has a natural flow and nobility to make one long to hear Karajan conducting Elgar. *Venus* has sensuous string phrasing, *Mercury* and *Uranus* have beautiful springing in the triplet rhythms, and the climax of that last movement brings an amazing glissando on the organ, made clear by the thirty-two-channel recording. In sound as in interpretation, this is a stunning issue on disc and cassette alike.

It was Sir Adrian Boult who, over sixty years ago, first 'made *The Planets* shine', as the composer put it, and in his ninetieth year he recorded it for the last time. It sets the seal on a magnificent Indian summer in the recording studio, a performance at once intense and beautifully played, spacious and dramatic, rapt and pointed. If the opening of *Mars* – noticeably slower than in Boult's previous recordings – suggests a slackening, the opposite proves true: that movement gains greater weight at a slower tempo. *Mercury* has lift and clarity, not just rushing brilliance, and it is striking that in Holst's syncopations – as in the introduction of *Jupiter* – Boult allows himself a jaunty, even jazzy freedom which adds an infectious sparkle. The great melody of *Jupiter* is calculatedly less resonant and more flowing than previously but is more moving, and *Uranus* as well as *Jupiter* has its measure of jollity, with the lolloping 6/8 rhythms delectably pointed. The spacious slow movements are finely poised and the recording is of demonstration quality, gloriously full and opulent, with the tape measuring up well to the disc.

One must not forget Previn's attractive version, also on HMV (ASD/*TC-ASD* 3002 [Ang. S/*4XS* 36991]). This too has outstandingly fine sound, clear and vivid, although the acoustic is just a little dry; the performance also has an appealing freshness. But for many the alternative choice will lie with Karajan's earlier Vienna version, which even though it is twenty years old is still very impressive with its richly atmospheric Decca sound. Now reissued on Jubilee this easily leads the mid-price field and indeed remains near the top of the list on most counts. It was here we first heard Karajan's transformation of a work we had tended to think of as essentially English into an international score. There are many individual touches, from the whining Wagnerian tubas of *Mars*, the *Venus* representing ardour rather than mysticism, the gossamer textures of *Mercury* and the strongly characterized *Saturn* and *Uranus*, with splendid playing from the Vienna brass. The cassette like the disc is technically first-class.

With *Mars* opening with a brilliant cutting edge and at the fastest possible tempo, Solti's version could not be more contrasted with Boult's newest recording, which arrived simultaneously. Solti's pacing is exhilarating to the point of fierceness in the vigorous movements, and undoubtedly his direct manner is refreshing, the rhythms clipped and precise, sometimes at the expense of resilience. His directness in *Jupiter* (with the trumpets coming through splendidly) is certainly riveting, the big tune taken literally rather than affectionately. In *Saturn* the spareness of texture is finely sustained; here the tempo is slow, the detail precise, while in *Neptune* the coolness is even more striking when the pianissimos are achieved with such a high degree of tension. The recording has remarkable clarity and detail, and Solti's clear-headed intensity undoubtedly shows refreshing new insights into this multi-faceted score, even if some will prefer a more atmospheric viewpoint. The recording gives the orchestra great presence. The cassette too is very impressive, clearly detailed yet with plenty of atmosphere and striking weight and sonority in the bass.

Gibson's version with the Scottish National Orchestra had the distinction of being the first set of *The Planets* to be recorded digitally. The reading is characteristically direct and certainly well played. Other versions have more individuality and are more involving, but there is no doubt that the Chandos recording has fine bite and presence (slightly too much so in *Neptune*, with the chorus too positive and unethereal) and excellent detail (although the cassette is marginally less wide-ranging than the disc). With this vivid sound the impact of such a colourful score is undoubtedly enhanced.

Ormandy's version of *The Planets* was one of the finest records he made in the last few years before he retired as the principal conductor of the Philadelphia Orchestra. The playing has great electricity, and it is a pity that the recording is so fiercely brilliant (the orchestra does not sound like this in the flesh). Even so, this is a highly compelling reading, and the sound gives added edge to the ferocity of *Mars*, balanced by an eloquently peaceful *Venus* with rapt, translucent textures. Ormandy, like Bernstein, paces the central tune of *Jupiter* slowly and deliberately. (This seems almost to be an American tradition; transatlantic performances of Vaughan Williams's arrangement of *Greensleeves* show a similar gravity.) The performance is at its finest in *Uranus* (with crisply vigorous brass articulation) and the restrained melancholy of *Saturn*, deeply felt and somehow personal in its communication. *Neptune* too is beautifully tapered off at the close. The recording sounds much the same on disc and cassette and its super-brilliance responds quite well to the controls, without loss of the undoubtedly vivid detail.

For Simon Rattle, HMV's digital recording provides wonderfully atmospheric sound at the very opening (the *col legno* tapping at the start of *Mars*) and the very close of *Neptune* (the fading chords in endless alternation from the offstage women's chorus). The quality in *Venus* and *Mercury* is also very beautiful, warmly translucent. Otherwise it is not so distinctive a version as one might have expected from this leading young conductor; it is sensibly paced but neither so polished nor so bitingly committed as

Karajan, Previn or Boult, or for that matter Ormandy, who is at his finest on his Philadelphia record. The HMV chrome cassette matches the disc with impressive faithfulness; disappointingly, in *Jupiter* the Kingsway Hall resonance on both disc and cassette takes the edge of brilliance from the sound.

Bernstein, like Ormandy, suffers from a characteristically over-brilliant transatlantic sound balance, rather dry in the bass. Also like Ormandy's, the performance is charismatic, with moments of striking individuality. The choral singing in *Neptune* is most refined and the closing diminuendo very beautiful. The tape, which has a more limited range, softens the lighting of Holst's vivid score (some may think too much). Unfortunately in our review copy the texture in *Mars* was patchily insubstantial, fluctuating in body (not pitch); but other batches may not have this fault.

Marriner's account is marked by splendid orchestral playing and richly spacious recording. The opulence and beauty of the sound here are very striking. The performance is full of individual touches, which some will warm to more readily than others. At the very opening of *Mars* – taken more slowly than usual – a sudden crescendo on the timpani gives a sense of underlying menace, and the flamboyant use of the tam-tam increases the feeling of spectacle. The orchestral playing in *Venus* is richly refined (a ravishing horn solo and translucent flutes). Marriner's tempo is relatively fast, and the music's sensuousness is only hinted at: here the essential mood is one of innocence. The big tune in *Jupiter* is given a slow but gloriously rich presentation, but for some Marriner might seem too weighty. *Uranus* has a skittish quality (particularly its middle section) and is vividly coloured. There is beautiful singing from the Ambrosians in *Neptune*, although the final fade is not so distantly ethereal as in some versions. But even with the reservations noted this performance has many refreshing features. The

tape transfer is rather too heavily weighted in the bass, and lacks the last degree of range and sparkle in the treble.

Ozawa secures fine orchestral playing in Boston; both *Venus* and *Uranus* are impressive in this respect. But *Mercury* is curiously lacking in sparkle, and *Mars* is unmenacing. Altogether this is disappointingly under-characterized.

Walter Susskind's performance is alert and well played and is basically well recorded. The sound is both vivid and atmospheric, but the hall in which the recording was made is very resonant and this blurs the rhythms in *Mars* and tends to create an ugliness of effect not intended by the composer. The blurring adds to the sensuousness of *Venus* and the brass is enriched in *Saturn*. But in the faster music the reverberation causes an unwanted muddiness, and *Uranus* loses much of its edge. This is a great pity, since the music-making is sympathetic and spontaneous.

It is curious that Contour should have chosen the (originally Phase Four) Herrmann set of *The Planets* instead of reissuing the excellent Bournemouth performance under George Hurst. With unconventionally slow tempi Herrmann's is the only recorded version to have almost no virtues at all except good orchestral playing. Even the possibilities of an artificially close balance fail to make it project vividly, and the cassette is even less impressive than the disc. At budget price the versions by Sargent (see below) and Loughran (CFP/*TC-CFP* 40243) are far preferable.

(i) *The Planets, Op. 32;* (ii) *St Paul's suite, Op. 29/2.*
(M) ** HMV *TC-IDL 507.* (i) BBC SO and Ch ; (ii) RPO; Sargent.

This cassette is issued in HMV's tape-only series, which guarantees an hour of music at lower mid-price. Sargent's view of *The Planets* is a traditional one, but full of character. The recording has plenty of weight, and *Mars* makes an excellent impact. But the highlight is the glowingly exuberant version of *Jupiter*, with its richly expansive central melody. After the side turn the quality of the hitherto excellent tape transfer falls off slightly, and the pianissimo textures at the opening and close of *Saturn* and again in *Neptune* lack the last degree of focus. Within a few seconds of the closing diminuendo of *Neptune*, Sargent's colourful and ebullient account of the *St Paul's suite* positively bursts upon the listener. It is transferred at a higher level, and the sound is extremely vivid to match the lively performance.

Terzetto for flute, oboe and viola. Music for voices: Ave Maria, Op. 9b, H. 49; 6 Canons, H. 187; 2 Carols with oboe and viola, H. 91; 2 Carols for unaccompanied chorus, H. 130/1; The Evening Watch for unaccompanied choir, Op. 43/1, H. 159; Jesu, Thou the Virgin-born, Op. 20b, H. 82; 6 Medieval lyrics for men's voices and strings; 2 Part songs for unaccompanied female voices, H. 92, 119; 7 Part songs for women's voices and strings, Op. 44, H. 162; Song of the Blacksmith, H. 136; 4 Songs for voice and violin, Op. 35a, H. 132; 12 Songs, Op. 48, H. 174; This Have I Done for my True Love for unaccompanied voices, Op. 34/1, H. 128; 3 Welsh songs for unaccompanied chorus, H. 183.

(M) **(*) Argo ZK 74/5. Pears, Britten; Brainin (viola); Purcell Singers, ECO, Imogen Holst.

This set combines two records of unequal interest which were originally available separately at full price. The first is essentially a record for the Holst specialist rather than the general listener. Holst's earlier songs dating from 1900 are not always very individual, and some of

them are frankly very ordinary indeed. Even the 1929 settings of Humbert Wolfe are rather uneven in appeal, and the composer himself did not seem to arrive at a unifying style. Some seem deliberately bare, while others are much richer, and the words do not always provide the obvious clue to the composer's choice. Peter Pears and Benjamin Britten bring a characteristic creative quality to the performances, but this only serves to highlight the difference between the less interesting songs and the one or two masterpieces. The choral singing is excellent. The second disc is a collection of vocal and instrumental music made under the direction of the composer's daughter. It brings together an illuminating group of works, easy and difficult, simple and highly experimental. Technically the most interesting is the *Terzetto*. Holst wrote it right at the end of his career as an experiment in polytonality, with each of the three instruments using a different key signature. At the time he was not even sure whether he liked it himself, but as Imogen Holst pointed out – and the record bears witness – to ears thirty years later it sounds delightfully pointed and even charming, not least because of the endlessly fascinating rhythms. The choral pieces range from simple and imaginative carol-settings (plus a very long unaccompanied one, *This Have I Done*) to crisp canons which, like the *Terzetto*, experiment in lines following contrasted key signatures. The *Four Songs*, sung beautifully by Peter Pears, are also examples of Holst's austere style, but were written at roughly the same apparently expansive period of *The Planets*. Sensitive, committed performances and outstandingly clear recording.

Choral hymns from the Rig-Veda, Op. 26/4 (Second group); Festival Te Deum; Hymn of Jesus, Op. 37; Ode to Death, Op. 38.

*** HMV ASD/*TC-ASD* 3435. LSO Ch., Choristers of St Paul's Cath., LPO, Groves.

This recording of the *Hymn of Jesus* is basically finer than Boult's account (see above under *Egdon Heath*), which has served collectors well over the years. Sir Charles Groves brings great sympathy and conviction to this beautiful and moving score, whose visionary quality has never paled. He is moreover given a recording of great clarity and presence. Like *Hymn of Jesus*, the Short *Festival Te Deum* comes from 1919 but takes only a little over four minutes and is an 'occasional' piece, less original than the *Hymn*. The *Ode to Death* is from the same period, written in memory of Holst's friends killed in the 1914–18 war. A set ting of Whitman, it must be accounted one of Holst's most inspired and haunting scores, comparable in quality with the *Choral fantasia*, and it is eloquently performed here. Its neglect is unaccountable; this is its first recording. The second group of *Rig-Veda hymns* are less of a revelation: they were written in the immediate wake of Holst's Algerian visit of 1909, which also produced *Beni Mora*. These are on familiar Holstian lines, though they make considerable demands on the singers. A most welcome issue. (We find copies of the cassette tend to produce varying quality, though always good.)

Honegger, Arthur
(1892–1955)

Piano concertino.
(M) ** Sup. 1410 2705. Krajný, Prague CO, Macura – POULENC: *Aubade***(*); ROUSSEL: *Piano concerto.***

Honegger's engaging and fresh *Concertino* is not otherwise available at present, but Boris Krajný's version misses something of the sparkle and dash of its first section. Nonetheless, the performance is eminently serviceable and the only

real objection is some less than perfect orchestral intonation.

Pacific 231.
(M) *** Decca Jub. JB/*KJBC* 36 [Lon. 6367]. SRO, Ansermet – DUKAS: *L'Apprenti sorcier*; RAVEL: *Boléro; La Valse.****

The polyphonic climax of Honegger's orchestral portrayal of a railway locomotive needs reasonable clarity of recording to achieve its maximum impact. The reverberation is perhaps not quite perfectly judged here, but the power of the mighty engine is marvellously conveyed and its surging lyricism too, while the grinding tension of the final braking gives this mechanical monster an almost human personality. The cassette matches the disc closely.

Symphonies Nos. 1; 2 for strings and trumpet; 3 (Liturgique); 4 (Deliciae basiliensis); 5 (Di tre re). Chant de joie; Pacific 231; Pastorale d'été.
(M) *** Sup. 1101 741/3. Czech PO, Baudo.

Symphonies Nos. 1–5; Pacific 231.
** EMI 2C 167 16327/9. Toulouse Capitole O., Plasson.

Honegger's symphonies are currently much underrated, and their scant representation in the concert hall scarcely reflects their artistic standing. The *First* was commissioned by Koussevitzky for the fiftieth anniversary of the Boston Symphony (along with Stravinsky's *Symphony of psalms*, Prokofiev's *Fourth Symphony* and Roussel's *Third*). The *Second* is a probing, intense wartime composition that reflects something of the anguish Honegger felt during the German occupation. The Czech Philharmonic recording of this coupled with the *Third Symphony* (*Liturgique*), which dates from the end of the war, was made in the early 1960s. The performances are totally committed but the sound is very

393

reverberant and could do with more body. The *Fourth Symphony*, composed for Paul Sacher, makes use of Swiss folk material. It is perhaps the most under-rated of them all, for its delights grow fresher every time one hears it, and its melodic charm is irresistible. Underneath its pastoral, smiling surface, there is a gentle vein of nostalgia and melancholy, particularly in the slow movement. The finale is sparkling and full of high spirits, though even this ends on a bitter-sweet note. The *Fifth* is a powerful work, in-ventive, concentrated and vital, very well played too, though again the recording is a little pale. Generally speaking, the Czech versions of the symphonies and the three pieces coupled with the *Fifth Symphony* give such pleasure that reser-vations can be set aside. This is a most rewarding set.

Michel Plasson has the advantage of more modern recording: his set was made in the late 1970s whereas Baudo's cycle dates from the previous decade. How-ever, the performances do not have the same panache and virtuosity that the Czech orchestra brings to this music. The scherzo of the *Fifth Symphony*, for ex-ample, sounds very tame by the side of the Czech version, though the sound quality is richer and more transparent. One other point: in the *Symphony for strings* (the *Second*) the trumpet for which Honegger called to strengthen the chorale, but which he did not regard as mandatory, is omitted.

Symphonies Nos. 2 and 3.
⊛ (M) *** DG 2543 805. Berlin PO, Karajan.

On its first appearance we greeted this as a first recommendation in both works and as 'an altogether marvellous record'. There is no reason to modify this view: it is arguably the finest version of any Honneger works ever put on record. The playing of the Berlin strings in the war-time *Second Symphony* is superb, sump-tuous in tone and refined in texture. The *Third Symphony* (*Liturgique*) has never sounded more brilliant or poetic and the coda is quite magical. The quality of the recorded sound is in the highest bracket and with the welcome reduction of price, this is an indispensable issue.

Jeanne d'Arc au bûcher (complete).
*** Sup. 1121 651/2. Chateau, Rodde, Brachet, Proenza, Jankovsky, Loup, Kühn Children's Ch., Czech PO and Ch., Baudo.

The ear-catching effects and mixture of styles in this brilliant and dramatic ora-torio have tended to draw attention away from its musical strength. So plainsong and folksong on the one hand go with the ondes martenot on the other. Such a performance as this under the direction of Baudo, a Honegger specialist who has also recorded the symphonies, presents the piece at its most impressive, helped by outstanding choral singing, first-rate playing and a most touching rendering of the role of the Saint from Nelly Bor-geaud, with her youthful speaking voice. The recording is most atmospheric, with apt reverberation.

Le Roi David.
(B) **(*) Decca DPA 593/4 [(d) Lon. STS 15155/6]. Audel (nar.), Danco, De Montmollin, Martin, Hamel, SRO and Ch., Ansermet – MARTIN: *In terra pax.****

Le Roi David is better described as a dramatic mosaic rather than a sym-phonic psalm. It was for many years Honegger's best-known work (with the sole exception of *Pacific 231*), largely on account of its pageantry and atmosphere. This Decca recording, made under the authoritative guidance of Ernest An-sermet, dates from the mid-1950s and originally appeared in mono only. The sound lacks the range and body of the most modern recordings, but it wears its age lightly, and given the enormous interest and invention this score offers, and the interest of its coupling, readers need not hesitate to invest in it. Judged by the highest standards, the orchestral playing is a little wanting in finish, but there is now no alternative at any price, and no collector is likely to be dissatisfied with the distinguished cast, or this richly inventive tapestry of sound. A thoroughly rewarding set.

Hummel, Johann (1778–1837)

Trumpet concerto in E flat.
*** CBS 76862/40- [Col. M/*MT* 35856]. Bernard, ECO, Malcolm – ALBINONI: *Concerto*; HERTEL: *Concerto à 6.****

Hummel's *Trumpet concerto* is second only to Haydn's in its popular appeal – perhaps not even second, for its finale is irresistible when played with such flair as it is here by André Bernard, who, with Malcolm, sets a sparkling pace. The performance throughout is superb; there is none finer in the present catalogue, and the reverberant acoustic seems admirably judged for the music. The couplings are attractive (especially the Hertel *Concerto*) and this can be cordially recommended on disc or tape (which is quite well managed, if with rather less upper range than the LP).

Adagio, variations, and rondo on 'Schöne Minka', Op. 78.
(M) ** Turn. TVS 34575. NY Camerata – CLEMENTI: *Sonata*; HAYDN: *Flute trio.***

Hummel was good at variations: these are unpretentious and agreeably slight. They make a good foil for the more classically-minded trios by Clementi and Haydn. This adds up to an entertaining lightweight collection, well recorded.

Grand military septet in C, Op. 114.
*** CRD CRD 1090/*CRDC 4090*. Nash Ens. – KREUTZER: *Septet.****

Hummel's *Military septet* is not really as grand as its name implies. It features a trumpet, certainly, but that only makes a major contribution in the third movement, although in the first its fanfare-like interjections do bring in a somewhat refined reminder of the work's title. The invention throughout is ingenuous but attractive, particularly in such a delightfully spontaneous account as is provided by the Nash Ensemble. There is sparkle and warmth, and the playing itself has beguiling elegance. The recording is superb (with a demonstration-worthy cassette to mirror the disc), and the balance of the trumpet part (very nicely played by James Watson) is most felicitous. Highly recommended, especially in view of the apt coupling.

Septet in D min., Op. 74.
*** CRD CRD 1044/*CRDC 4044*. Nash Ens. – BERWALD: *Septet.****

An enchanting and inventive work with a virtuoso piano part, expertly dispatched here by Clifford Benson. The *Septet* is full of vitality, and its scherzo in particular has enormous charm and individuality. A fine performance and excellent recording make this a desirable issue, particularly in view of the enterprising coupling, which is not otherwise available. The cassette too is up to the usual high standard of CRD chamber-music tapes: the sound has warmth and bloom, with good detail.

Humperdinck, Engelbert
(1854–1921)

Hänsel und Gretel (complete).
(M) *** HMV SLS/*TC-SLS* 5145 (2).
Schwarzkopf, Grümmer, Metternich,
Ilosvay, Schürhoff, Felbermayer,
Children's Ch., Philh. O., Karajan.
*** CBS 79217/40- (2) [Col. M2-35898].
Cotrubas, Von Stade, Ludwig,
Nimsgern, Te Kanawa, Söderström,
Cologne Op. Children's Ch., Cologne
Gürzenich O., Pritchard.
**(*) Decca D 131 D 2/*K 131 K 22* [Lon.
12112]. Fassbaender, Popp, Berry,
Hamari, Schlemm, Burrowes, Gruber-
ova, V. Boys' Ch., VPO, Solti.

Karajan's classic 1950s set of Humperdinck's children's opera, with Schwarzkopf and Grümmer peerless in the name
parts, is enchanting; this was an instance
where everything in the recording went
right. The original mono LP set was
already extremely atmospheric – the
cuckoos in the wood, for example – but
the stereo transcription adds an irresistible further bloom without losing the
inner focus. One notices that the main
image stays fairly centrally situated between the speakers, but in all other respects the sound has more clarity and
warmth than rival recordings made in the
1970s. There is much to delight here; the
smaller parts are beautifully done and
Else Schürhoff's Witch is memorable.
The tape transfer too is splendid.

Beautifully cast, the Pritchard version
from CBS is the first in genuine stereo to
challenge the vintage Karajan set. Cotrubas – sometimes a little grainy as
recorded – and Von Stade both give
charming characterizations, and the supporting cast is exceptionally strong, with
Söderström an unexpected but refreshing
and illuminating choice as the Witch.
Pritchard draws idiomatic playing from
the Gürzenich Orchestra, and though the
recording has not the sharply focused

brilliance of Solti's Decca sound, it is
pleasingly atmospheric. Moreover the
CBS tape transfer is most effective, with
voices and orchestra very well balanced.

Solti with the Vienna Philharmonic
directs a strong, spectacular version,
emphasizing the Wagnerian associations
of the score. It is well sung – both principals are engaging – but just a little short
on charm. The solo singing is not so
steady in tone as on the EMI set, and the
lack of geniality in the atmosphere is a
drawback in a work of this nature.
Needless to say, Solti does the *Witch's
ride* excitingly, and the VPO are
throughout encouraged to play with consistent fervour. Edita Gruberova is an
excellent Dew Fairy and Walter Berry is
first-rate as Peter. Anny Schlemm's
Witch is a very strong characterization
indeed, and there are some imaginative
touches of stereo production associated
with *Hocus pocus* and her other moments
of magic. The recording is admirably
vivid, but its sense of spectacle does not
erase one's memory of the Karajan version. The cassette transfer is characteristically brilliant, with vivid detail but not
a great deal of warmth.

Hänsel und Gretel: favourite scenes.
**(*) Decca SET 633 (from above set
cond. Solti).

The Decca set of excerpts includes the
overture, the *Witch's ride*, *Dream pantomime*, gingerbread house scene and
finale. It reflects admirably the vivid
qualities of the complete set and the
slightly dry brilliance of the Decca recording.

Königskinder (complete).
*** EMI 1C 157 30698/700. Prey,
Donath, Ridderbusch, Ch. and O.,
Wallberg.

The success of *Hänsel und Gretel* has
completely overshadowed this second
fairy-tale opera of Humperdinck, which

contains much fine music, notably in the love duets (for the goose-girl who tragically falls in love with a prince); the fiddler's songs and the preludes to the three acts. Humperdinck had expanded his incidental music to a play to make this opera, which was given its première in New York in 1910. In an entertainment for children the sadness and cruelty of a typical German fairy-tale, not to mention the heavy vein of moralizing, are a serious disadvantage, but in a recording as fine as this it is a piece well worth investigation. Both the conducting and the singing of the principals is most persuasive.

Hurlstone, William

(1876–1906)

(i) *Piano concerto in D. Fantasie-variations on a Swedish air.*
*** Lyr. SRCS 100. LPO, Braithwaite, (i) with Parkin.

Hurlstone's was a tragic career. He was a prodigy as a composer and as a pianist, but ill-health and poverty prevented him from developing those talents, and he died at the age of thirty. Neither of these works has the formal strength of some of his chamber music (Lyrita ought to record the *Piano quartet* of 1898), but they are both distinctive, the *Concerto* the more positive, the *Variations* the more quirkily individual. Good performances and recording.

Ibert, Jacques (1890–1962)

Flute concerto.
*** RCA RL/RK 25109 [ARL 1/ARK 1 3777]. Galway, RPO, Dutoit – CHAMINADE: *Concertino*; FAURÉ: *Fantaisie*; POULENC: *Sonata*.***

Ibert's high-spirited and inventive concerto deserves the widest currency; it is full of charm and lyrical appeal, particularly when it is as well performed as it is here by James Galway and the RPO under Charles Dutoit. Moreover it has the distinct advantage of highly attractive couplings. There is no alternative in the catalogue, and it will be difficult to supersede this version, which enjoys a clear, spacious recording on disc, and has been skilfully transferred to tape.

Divertissement; Bacchanale.
(M) **(*) HMV Green. ESD/TC-ESD 7097. CBSO, Frémaux – BERLIOZ: *Damnation de Faust excerpts* **(*); SATIE: *Gymnopédies*.***

Frémaux's account of the *Divertissement* is warm-hearted and vigorous, with genuine exuberance in the 'police-whistle' finale. But Martinon's deleted Decca version [Lon. STE 15093] had an extra finesse and *joie de vivre*, and also a more appropriate recording acoustic. The Birmingham recording is somewhat over-reverberant, although that suits the *Bacchanale*, an empty piece to which Frémaux applies an appropriate degree of frenzy. The tape transfer copes with the resonance with little loss of focus.

Trois Pièces brèves.
*** RCA RL/RK 25278. Athena Ens. – GOUNOD: *Petite symphonie*; POULENC: *Sextuor*.***

This collection, appropriately entitled '*Joie de vivre*', includes a witty, polished account of Ibert's three miniatures within an entertaining and well-recorded collection of French wind music. The sound is equally sharply-focused on disc and cassette.

d'India, Sigismondo
(*c*. 1582–*c*. 1630)

Duets, laments and madrigals: *Amico,. hai vinto; Ancidetemi pur, dogliosi affani; Chi nudrisce tua speme; Giunto a la tomba; Langue al vostro languir; O leggiadr' occhi; Quella vermiglia rosa; Son gli accenti che ascolto; Torna il sereno Zefiro.*
(M) ** HM HM 1011. Concerto Vocale.

Sigismondo d'India was among the vanguard of the new movement founded by Monteverdi at the beginning of the seventeenth century, and his laments show him a considerable master of expressive resource. He is highly responsive to the emotions of the poetry, and the harmonies and the unpredictable lines make this music fascinating. The performances are authoritative, though there are moments of slightly self-conscious rubato that hold up the flow. The recording could be more spacious and warmer, but in spite of that qualification this is thoroughly recommendable.

d'Indy, Vincent (1851–1931)

La Forêt enchantée, Op. 8; Jour d'été à la montagne, Op. 61; Tableaux de voyage, Op. 36.
*** EMI 2C 069 16301. Loire PO, Dervaux.

The most substantial work on this record is *Jour d'été à la montagne*, composed just after Debussy's *La Mer*, and inspired by the beauties of the Vivarais region of central France, where d'Indy was born. He was a devoted Wagnerian, but that influence is more completely assimilated in this triptych

than in, say, *Fervaal* or the early tone poem *La Forêt enchantée* with which it is coupled. The latter is all the same a finely wrought and highly imaginative piece,. reminiscent of the best tone poems of Liszt and Franck, yet distinctively individual too. The make-weight is a delightful suite, *Tableaux de voyage*, originally written for piano. This is a most enjoyable collection that reveals d'Indy as a far richer and more rewarding composer than most people give him credit for, and the performances are in no sense secondrate, even though the Orchestre Philharmonique des Pays de Loire is hardly of international standing. The sound too is absolutely first-class. The sleeve (and *Grove*) describes *La Forêt enchantée* as Op. 8, but the annotator refers to it throughout as Op. 7. This is a distinguished and likeable release, well worth acquiring.

Ireland, John (1879–1962)

Concertino pastorale.
(M) **(*) Uni. UNS 260. Westminster Cath. String O., Mawby – L. BERKELEY: *Antiphon*; M. BERKELEY: *Meditations.***(*)

The *Concertino pastorale*, written for the Boyd Neel Orchestra in 1939, is a gently persuasive piece, rather long for its unambitious material but always attractive. It is an important addition to the limited range of Ireland's music on record, and is here well coupled.

A London overture.
(M) *** HMV Green. ESD/TC-ESD 7092 [Ang. S 36415]. LSO, Barbirolli – BAX: *Tintagel*; DELIUS: *Collection.****

One of Ireland's most immediately attractive works, and Barbirolli's performance of it is a great success. The main theme (rhythmically conjuring up the bus conductor's call 'Piccadilly') is made obstinately memorable, and the warm romanticism of the middle section is perfectly judged. The recording sounds remarkably fresh and vivid in this excellent Greensleeve reissue, the cassette as crisp and full as the disc.

The Overlanders: suite (arr. Mackerras).
*** Uni. Kanchana KP 8001. W. Australian SO, Measham – VAUGHAN WILLIAMS: *On Wenlock Edge.* ***

The Overlanders is not the best of Ireland, but it is as persuasively presented here as it is by Sir Adrian Boult on a Lyrita disc, where the couplings (other Ireland works) are perhaps less appealing than the Vaughan Williams offered by Unicorn Kanchana. The sound here is admirably vivid.

Phantasy trio in A min.; Piano trios Nos. 2 and 3 in E.
*** Lyr. SRCS 98. Neaman, Lloyd Webber, Parkin.

The *Phantasy trio* and the *Second Trio in E major* are accommodated on the first side. The former, an early piece dating from 1908, is not particularly individual; its companion has more substance, and the *Andante* section has a splendid sense of desolation. The finest of the three is the last, which began life as a trio for clarinet, violin and piano in 1913 but was totally rewritten in 1938. This has much greater imaginative vitality and a transparency of texture that calls to mind Ireland's great admiration for the Ravel *Trio.* Few pianists understand Ireland's piano writing better than Eric Parkin does, and he and his partners give an eloquent account of all three pieces. They are excellently recorded.

Cello sonata.
(*) ASV ACA/ZCACA 1001. Lloyd Webber, McCabe – BRIDGE: *Elegy*; BRITTEN: *Suite.* *

The *Cello sonata* is among Ireland's most richly inspired works, a broad-spanning piece in which ambitious, darkly intense outer movements frame one of his most beautiful slow movements. Julian Lloyd Webber, who has long been a passionate advocate of the work, here conveys its full expressive power. The piano is placed at a distance, but perhaps that is apt for a work in which the cello should be presented in full strength. The cassette matches the disc fairly closely, though the resonance means that the focus is marginally less sharp.

Piano music

The Almond Trees; April; Columbine; 3 Dances (Gypsy dance; Country dance; Reapers' dance); Decorations; Preludes, No. 3, The Holy Boy; Sarnia.
(M) *** HMV HQS 1414. Adni.

Daniel Adni's recital overlaps with Eric Parkin's on SRCS 89 in *Sarnia* but otherwise makes an admirable complement. Adni penetrates the atmosphere of this music to the manner born, and seems thoroughly inside the idiom. Eric Parkin's *Sarnia* is perhaps more concentrated and more deeply imaginative, but it would be curmudgeonly to give any but the warmest praise to Adni's playing, which is characterful and accomplished. He is accorded a natural and truthful recording.

Ballade; Greenways (3 Lyric pieces); Month's Mind; 2 Pieces (February's Child; Aubade); Sarnia; Sonatina
*** Lyr. SRCS 89. Parkin.

Ireland was arguably at his most natural when writing for the piano. He seems fully to have understood the instrument, and he poured into it some of his finest invention. *Sarnia*, subtitled *An island sequence*, is certainly among his best pieces; it was inspired by the Channel Islands, whose atmosphere Ireland evoked in many other works, including *The Forgotten Rite*. Eric Parkin plays all these pieces with complete sympathy and subtlety. Indeed, it is difficult to imagine his performances being surpassed, for he brings a command of colour and a temperamental affinity to this music. The recording is excellent.

Piano sonata; The Darkened Valley; Equinox; On a Birthday Morning; 2 Pieces (For Remembrance; Amberley Wild Brooks); 2 Pieces (April; Bergomask); Summer Evening.
*** Lyr. SRCS 88. Parkin.

Ireland made a distinctive and distinguished contribution to the language of twentieth-century piano music, and his *Sonata* is rightly admired as being among his finest compositions. It has a directness yet subtlety of appeal that seem as fresh today as when it was first committed to paper. Eric Parkin is an authoritative and sympathetic advocate of Ireland's always personal idiom, and both in the *Sonata* itself and in the shorter pieces on this record his playing carries the ring of real conviction. He also enjoys the benefit of good modern recording.

3 Arthur Symons songs; 3 Thomas Hardy songs. Songs: *Bed in Summer; Earth's Call; East Riding; Heart's Desire; The Land of Lost Content; Love Is a Sickness; Mother and Child; My True Love Hath my Heart; Remember Hawthorne Time; Sacred Flame; Three Ravens; The Trellis; What Art Thou Thinking?*
**(*) Lyr. SRCS 118. Hodgson, Mitchinson, Rowlands.

Earth's Call is the most ambitious of these songs – almost a dramatic scena – but most of them reflect the tinge of melancholy that was an essential part of Ireland's temperament, subtle miniatures which sensitively follow the cadences of English lyric poetry. These thoughtful performances (with the piano balanced rather backwardly) make an excellent companion to the earlier Lyrita issues covering the baritone songs that make up the rest of Ireland's contribution to the genre. *

Ives, Charles (1874–1954)

Symphony No. 3; Three Places in New England.
(M) **(*) Mercury SRI 75035 [id.]. Eastman Rochester O., Hanson.

Ives's quixotic genius is at its most individual in the *Three Places in New England*. Written between 1903 and 1914 this music is still able to shock the ear, especially the second movement, *Putnam's Camp, Redding, Connecticut*, with its phantasmagoric orchestral fantasy-images inspired by a child's dream at a site connected with the American War of Independence. The outer movements too are highly original and searingly atmospheric. The work is most understandingly presented here under Howard Hanson, but the recording is rather close and studio-bound (the bass drum too insistent). Similarly the *Third Symphony* is not ideal as sound; the quality is full-bodied but forward and lacking dynamic contrast, although again the performance is thoroughly sympathetic. This is a very worthwhile reissue, reasonably priced.

Jacob, Gordon (born 1895)

Clarinet quintet.
*** Hyp. A 66011. King, Aeolian Qt –
SOMERVELL: *Quintet.****

Gordon Jacob wrote his fine *Clarinet quintet*, an ambitious work lasting over half an hour, in 1942 for Frederick Thurston, one of the great clarinettists of his time who represented a more severe style of tone and technique than has become accepted more recently. Thea King, Thurston's widow and former pupil, plays with deep understanding, and is strongly matched by the Aeolian Quartet. Good recording.

Janáček, Leoš (1854–1928)

(i) *Sinfonietta;* (ii) *Taras Bulba* (rhapsody).
*** Decca Dig. SXDL/*KSXDC* 7519. VPO, Mackerras.
(M) *** HMV SXLP/*TC-SXLP* 30420.
(i) Chicago SO, Ozawa; (ii) RPO, Kubelík.

Mackerras's coupling comes as a superb supplement to his Janáček opera recordings with the Vienna Philharmonic. The massed brass of the *Sinfonietta* has tremendous bite and brilliance as well as characteristic Viennese ripeness, thanks to a spectacular digital recording. *Taras Bulba* too is given more weight and body than is usual, the often savage dance rhythms presented with great energy. The cassette has comparable brilliance and range, although on some machines the upper range is fierce and needs taming.

Kubelík's account of *Taras Bulba* dates from the late 1950s, though it is difficult to credit that, so vivid and full-blooded is the quality. His later version

made with the Bavarian Radio Orchestra is a little more refined but not less vital. This offers excellent value for money, particularly with Ozawa's brilliant account of the *Sinfonietta* on the reverse. In the mid-price range this is a highly competitive coupling on disc and tape alike, though one cannot deny the claims of Mackerras's recording, which is both authoritative and technically superb.

Taras Bulba (rhapsody).
(M) ** Sup. 1101 889. Ostrava Janáček PO, Trhlík – DVOŘÁK: *Golden Spinning Wheel.***

Taras Bulba; The Cunning Little Vixen: suite (arr. Talich).
*** CBS 76818/40- [Col. M 35117]. Toronto SO, Andrew Davis.

Andrew Davis and the Toronto Orchestra can hold their own with the competition in *Taras Bulba*, and are well recorded. This is the only version since Talich's own to couple *Taras* with his suite drawn from *Cunning Little Vixen*. The Toronto account is vital and fresh, and it reflects credit on all concerned. The quality of the recorded sound is very good indeed, and the only criticism that might be made is that it is slightly over-bright. The woodland magic of the *Vixen* came over better in the Talich record, perhaps because it was less sharply focused. Anyone wanting this coupling need not hesitate.

Trhlík and the Ostrava orchestra would probably not be the first choice for anyone who did not particularly want this coupling, though it is perfectly well played and recorded. This *Taras Bulba* is vigorous and full-blooded, though the orchestral playing is not quite as refined and polished as the most formidable of the rivals, nor is the recording any match for the best of them. The sound is a little thin on top and somewhat reverberant: in some ways it is scarcely an improvement on the Ančerl record Supraphon made in the 1960s, though the sound is marginally fresher.

(i; ii) *Capriccio for piano and 7 instruments; Concertino for piano and 6 instruments;* (iii; i) *Dumka for violin and piano;* (ii) *Mládi for wind sextet;* (iv; i) *Presto for cello and piano;* (iii; i) *Romance for violin and piano;* (v) *String quartets Nos. 1 and 2;* (iv; i) *A Tale for cello and piano;* (iii; i) *Violin sonata (for violin and piano).* (Piano) (i) *In the Mist; On an Overgrown Path; Recollection; Piano sonata; Theme and variations.* (vi; ii) *Rikadia for chamber choir and 10 instruments.*

(M) *** Decca D 223 D 5 (5). (i) Crossley; (ii) L. Sinf. (members), Atherton; (iii) Sillito; (iv) Van Kampen; (v) Gabrieli Qt; (vi) L. Sinf. Ch.

This five-record box offers the essential Janáček in absolutely first-class performances and recordings. The performances of the string quartets, which are discussed below, are the equal of any rivals. Paul Crossley is the impressive soloist in the *Capriccio* and the *Concertino*, performances that can be put alongside those of Firkusný – and no praise can be higher. This account of *Mládi* is to be preferred to the version by the Vienna Wind Soloists; the work's youthful sparkle comes across to excellent effect here. Crossley's survey of the piano music is both poetic and perceptive, and his mastery of keyboard colour and feeling for atmosphere is everywhere evident, and the sound that the engineers have achieved is very truthful and satisfying. The set brings a number of rarities to the catalogue too, the *Violin sonata* (which Suk and Panenka have also recorded) and the *Rikadia* for chamber choir and ten instruments. A distinguished set.

String quartets Nos. 1 (Kreutzer sonata); 2 (Intimate pages).

(M) *** Decca Ace SDD 527 [Lon. STS 15432]. Gabrieli Qt.

(M) *** HMV HQS 1433. Medici Qt.

Janáček's two string quartets come from his last years and are among his most deeply individual and profoundly impassioned utterances. The Gabrieli Quartet have the measure of this highly original music and give just as idiomatic an account of these masterpieces as did the Janáček Quartet in the 1960s. They have the advantage of a finely focused and beautifully balanced recording which has maximum clarity and blend as well as considerable warmth.

The Medici too give a thoroughly impassioned and imaginative account of both quartets, and are no less inside the music than the Gabrielis. Indeed honours are so evenly divided in places that it is difficult to say which is to be preferred. The Gabrielis have slightly greater polish and fervour, and their recording is better focused; the Medici are rather widely spread between the two speakers. But even though this new HMV issue does not displace the Gabrieli, it deserves a strong recommendation.

Male choruses: *Ach vojna (The Soldier's Lot); Ceská legie (Czech Legion); Coz ta nase bríza (Our Birch Tree); Kantor Halfar (Schoolmaster Halfar); Klekánica (The Evening Witch); Marycka Magdonova; Potulý sílenec (The Wandering Madman); Rozlouceni (Leavetaking); Sedmesát tisic (Seventy-thousand).*

(M) **(*) Sup. 112 0878. Moravian Teachers' Ch., Tucapský.

This is marvellous stuff. Janáček was a master of this medium and the Moravian Teachers' Choir was closely associated with him throughout his mature life. *The Evening Witch* was especially written for them after he first heard them in 1904. The singing has great eloquence and the music has both passion and inspiration to commend it. Strongly recommended, even though the recording is not ideally refined.

Amarus (lyric cantata).
(M) ** Sup. 1121 678. Gubauerová,
Zahradníček, Tuček, Czech PO Ch.,
Ostrava Janáček PO, Trhlík –
SUK: *Under the Apple Tree.***

Janáček's *Amarus*, though not a fully
mature piece, has many facets of the
familiar personality and some striking
invention in the course of its thirty-odd
minutes. It is a setting of a poem by Jaroslav Vrchlický that must have struck a
responsive chord in a composer whose
own upbringing had been entrusted to a
monastery. The hero of the poem is a
monk who pines for life and love, and
prays for deliverance from his earthly lot.
It is scored for three soloists, mixed
chorus and orchestra, and was first performed in 1900 under Janáček's own
baton. The performance is committed
enough, with some sensitive and responsive orchestral playing and some fine
choral singing. The tenor is unsympathetic, however, and the recording could
do with more opulence. Apart from the
slightly *can belto* singer, this is a useful
contribution to the Janáček discography.

The Diary of One Who Disappeared.
(M) **(*) Sup. 1112 2414. Márová, Přibyl,
Kühn Female Ch., Páleníček.

Janáček's narrative song cycle is based
on the diaries of an unknown son of a
peasant who disappeared from a Walla-
chian village. He left behind him verses
in which he avowed his love for a gipsy
girl by whom he had had a child and for
whose sake he left home. The burden of
the narrative is given to the tenor, but the
voice of the beloved is also heard in some
of the poems, and there are female voices
behind the scenes in parts IX and X. It is
left to the piano to provide the dramatic
background of the story and to evoke
atmosphere.
This is the only version now available
and was made in 1978. The tenor is an
impassioned singer, but the voice could
do with greater variety of colour and

timbre. Libuše Márová and the female
choir give a good account of themselves
and are well enough recorded. Josef
Páleníček is a capable pianist but he lacks
perhaps the last ounce of imagination in
his treatment of the quieter passages of
this demanding part. However, there is
much more to admire here than to cavil at.

Glagolitic Mass.
*** HMV Dig. ASD/*TCC-ASD* 4066
[Ang. DS 37847]. Palmer, Gunson,
Mitchinson, King, CBSO and Ch.,
Rattle.
(M) ** Sup. 1112 2698. Beňačkova-
Čápová, Randová, Přibyl, Kopčák,
Czech PO Ch., Brno State PO, Jílek.

Now that the earlier versions by Bre-
tislav Bakala and Karel Ančerl have long
disappeared, Jílek's is the only native account of Janáček's masterpiece on the
market. Very good it is too, with much
fervour and excitement to commend it,
and very decently recorded into the bargain. It is a good two-star recommendation, and it is only when one hears the
brilliant new HMV recording (with its
excellent chrome tape equivalent) that
one appreciates the greater sophistication
of Western digital recording. Rattle's
performance is strong and vividly
dramatic, with the Birmingham performers lending themselves to Slavonic
fervour. This is the finest version yet.

OPERA

The Cunning Little Vixen (com-
plete).
(M) *** Sup. 1121 181/2. Kroupa, Proch-
ázková, Hlavsa, Vonásek, Jedlicka,
Heriban, Tattermuschová, Dobrá,
Prague Nat. Th. Ch. and O., Gregor.

On the face of it, Janáček's choice of a
story of wild life in the countryside (a
gnat, a rooster and a grasshopper are
among the cast) sounds softly sentimental. In fact, with his characteristically

sharp and direct expression the result is just the opposite. It is a fascinating, totally original opera, given here with Slavonic warmth by the composer's compatriots. Some might prefer a more detached reading, but this shows very clearly the red-blooded nature of Janáček's inspiration even in a stylized subject. The part of the little vixen herself is charmingly sung by Helena Tattermuschová. Good recording.

Fate (complete).
(M) **(*) Sup. SUP 2011/2. Přibyl, Hajóssyová, Palivcová, Krejčík, Ch. and O. of Brno State Th. Op., Jílek.

Semi-autobiographical and including scenes at a spa and at a music academy, *Fate (Osud)* is a strange work. It took the composer four years to complete after he had written his first operatic masterpiece, *Jenůfa*. Though the story is quirky in the way one associates with Janáček's later operas, he was aiming at a wide popular appeal, and there are a few nods in the direction of Puccini. In the context of the rest of Janáček's work – now increasingly recognized as a unique *œuvre* – *Fate* has an important though secondary place among the operas. A performance as strong and well-recorded as this is very welcome, and it can be warmly recommended to the converted.

From the House of the Dead (complete).
⊛ *** Decca Dig. D 224 D 2/K 224 K 22 (2) [Lon. LDR 10036]. Zahradníček, Zídek, Janska, Zítek, V. State Op. Ch., VPO, Mackerras.

With fine digital recording adding to the glory of the highly distinctive instrumentation, the Decca recording of Janáček's last opera outshines even the earlier recordings in this Mackerras series. By rights this piece based on Dostoyevsky should in operatic form be intolerably depressing. In effect, as this magnificent

performance amply demonstrates, the mosaic of sharp response, with sudden hysterical joy punctuating even the darkest, most bitter emotions, is consistently uplifting. Apart from one exception the cast is superb, with a range of important Czech singers giving sharply characterized vignettes. The exception is the raw Slavonic singing of the one woman in the cast, Jaroslav Janska as the boy Aljeja, but even that fails to undermine the intensity of the innocent relationship with the central figure, which provides an emotional anchor for the whole piece. The cassette production is characteristic of Decca's usual high standard, although the transfer level is not as high as on some Decca sets, so that the transients are slightly sharper on disc. Even so the sound is extraordinarily vivid.

Jenůfa (complete).
(M) ** Sup. SUP 2751/2. Beňačková, Krejčík, Kniplová, Přibyl, Pokorná, Brno Janáček Op. Ch. and O., Jílek.

This Supraphon version of *Jenůfa* lacks the concentration of Mackerras's Janáček performances for Decca, but the performance is fresh, sharp and enjoyable. A strong cast is headed by two veteran singers, Vilém Přibyl as Laca and Nadejda Kniplová as the Kostelnitchka; their singing is most assured but their voices are often raw for the gramophone. So too with most of the singers in the smaller parts, though the role of Jenůfa has gone to a fine, creamy-toned soprano with no hint of Slavonic wobble, Gabriela Beňačková. As Stewa, the tenor Vladimir Krejčík confirms the excellent impression he made in the Decca set of *The Makropoulos Affair*. However, it would still seem advisable to wait for the promised Mackerras set to appear.

Kátya Kabanová (complete).
*** Decca D 51 D 2/K 51 K 22 (2) [Lon. 12109/5-]. Söderström, Jedlička, Dvorský, Márová, Kniplová, Svehla, V. State Op. Ch., VPO, Mackerras.

An altogether superb issue on all counts, and the first triumphant success for Sir Charles Mackerras in his Janáček opera series. He draws playing of great eloquence from the Vienna Philharmonic. *Kátya Kabanová* is based on Ostrovsky's play *The Storm*, which has inspired other operas as well as Tchaikovsky's overture, and was Janáček's first stage work after the First World War. (It is worth adding that this was the first recording of a Janáček opera ever made outside Czechoslovakia.) Elisabeth Söderström dominates the cast as the tragic heroine and gives a performance of great insight and sensitivity; she touches the listener far more deeply than did her predecessor on Supraphon, and is supported by Mackerras with an imaginative grip and flair that outstrip his Czech colleagues. The plot (very briefly) centres on Kátya, a person of unusual goodness whose marriage is loveless, and her husband, who is dominated by his mother. Her infatuation with Boris (Peter Dvorský), her subsequent confession of adultery and her ultimate suicide are pictured with music of the most powerful and atmospheric kind. The other soloists are all Czech and their characterizations suitably authentic. But it is the superb orchestral playing and the inspired performance of Söderström that make this set so memorable. The recording has a realism and truthfulness that do full justice to Janáček's marvellous score. The difference between disc and cassette is minimal.

The Makropoulos Affair (*Věc Makropulos;* complete).
*** Decca D 144 D 2/*K 144 K 22* (2) [Lon. 12116/5-]. Söderström, Dvorský, Zítek, Jedlička, Krejčík, Blachut, V. State Op. Ch., VPO, Mackerras.

Mackerras and his superb team provide a thrilling new perspective on an opera which is far more than the bizarre dramatic exercise it once seemed, with its weird heroine preserved by magic elixir well past her 300th birthday. In most performances the character of the still-beautiful Emilia seems mean past any sympathy, but here the radiant Elisabeth Söderström sees it rather differently, presenting from the first a streak of vulnerability. She is not simply malevolent: irritable and impatient rather, no longer an obsessive monster. Framed by richly colourful singing and playing, Söderström amply justifies that view, and Peter Dvorský is superbly fresh and ardent as Gregor. The recording, like the others in the series, is of demonstration quality, the cassettes only marginally less sharp in focus than the discs.

Jannequin, Clement
(*c*. 1485–1558)

Chansons nouvelles: L'amour, la mort et la vie; Baisez moy tost; L'espoir confus; Guillot ung jour; Il estoit une filette; J'atens le temps; Jehanneton fut l'aultre jour; Las qu'on congneust; M'amye a eu de Dieu; O fortune n'estois tu pas contente; Ou mettra l'on ung baiser; Plus ne suys; Secouez moy; Si come il chiaro sole; Sy celle la qui oncques; Une belle jeune espousée; Ung gay bergier; Ung jour Robin; Va rossignol.
**(*) Tel. AW 6.42120. Ens. Polyphonique de France, Ravier.

Jannequin is a good composer, well worth more than specialist interest: his invention is fresh, and he is resourceful and imaginative in setting words. Charles Ravier and the Ensemble Polyphonique de France give crisply defined accounts of these chansons, but they would have gained in aural variety had he chosen to use single voices in some and to make more imaginative use of the instruments at his command. As it is, they merely duplicate vocal parts, though occasionally they are heard on their own. Nevertheless, this repertoire is not so well served at present that we can afford to disregard this well-produced and finely performed disc. Providing that the listener takes a handful of pieces at a time rather than a whole side, this record will give much pleasure.

Jenkins, John (1592–1678)

Consort music: *Almain No. 9 in D; Fancy-air sett No. 6 in G min.; Fantasy in D min.; Lady Katherine Audley's Bells; A New Year's Gift to T.C.; Pavan in G min.; Suite in D min. (Divisions); Suite of 3-part ayres in C (Nos. 53–5); 4-part ayre No. 51.*
*** Mer. E 77020. Ars Nova, Holman.

The career of John Jenkins – who died at the age of eighty-six – spanned virtually the whole period between the two English giants, Byrd and Purcell. The New *Grove* suggests that in the mid-seventeenth century his consort music was the mainstay of the repertory; and so it deserved to be, if this fine collection is anything to go by. On record Jenkins has been shockingly neglected, but these first-rate performances, well recorded, should do much to rectify that.

Jones, Daniel (born 1912)

Symphonies Nos. 8–9; Dance fantasy.
*** BBC REGL 359. BBC Welsh SO, Thomson.

Three of Daniel Jones's ten symphonies have already been recorded

(Nos. 4, 6 and 7), and this brings the total to five. His is music of genuine integrity and power: he possesses the qualities of a real symphonist, a sense of movement and a feeling for growth. The two symphonies recorded here are both finely crafted and tersely argued. Purposeful music, very well played by the BBC Welsh Orchestra under Bryden Thomson and truthfully recorded. A valuable issue, well worth investigating.

Joplin, Scott (1868–1917)

Rags: *The Entertainer; Easy Winners; Gladiolus; Heliotrope Bouquet; Magnetic rag; Maple Leaf rag; Paragon rag; Pineapple rag; Solace – A Mexican serenade.*
*** HMV Dig. EMD/*TCC-EMD* 5534 [Ang. DS/*4ZS* 37331]. Rifkin (piano).

Joshua Rifkin's cool and relaxed approach to the Joplin *Rags* brings undoubted authenticity, with articulate rhythms and a deliberate manner. Some may feel that he sounds too calculatedly uninvolved, yet his steady tempi are what the composer himself advocated. The playing is alive, and it certainly has style; and the programme includes the obvious favourites. The digital recording is very good indeed, and the piano image has striking body and presence both on disc and on the excellent chrome tape.

Kabalevsky, Dmitri (born 1904)

Symphony No. 2, Op. 19.
(*) Uni. RHS 346. New Philh. O., Measham – MIASKOVSKY: *Symphony No. 21.**

Kabalevsky's *Second Symphony* enjoyed some popularity in the 1940s and is high-spirited, well crafted and far from unappealing. It has not the substance or depth of Miaskovsky with which it is coupled, but is nonetheless worth having as an example of the 'official' Soviet symphony. David Measham secures excellent results from the New Philharmonia, and although the sound is just a little wanting in transparency the overall picture is truthfully in focus, and the surface is exemplary.

Kalinnikov, Vassily
(1866–1901)

Symphony No. 1 in G min.
*** HMV ASD 3502. USSR SO, Svetlanov – TCHAIKOVSKY: *Coronation march* etc.**(*)

Kalinnikov was born a few months after Glazounov and died in penury at the beginning of this century. According to a note in the score, his *First Symphony* was written in 1895, shortly after he graduated. He sent it to Rimsky-Korsakov in the hope of moral encouragement or a performance, but received neither. It was, however, given with great success in Kiev two years later. Influenced by Borodin, it can best be described as an example of the post-nationalist symphony at its most appealing. The ideas are fresh and the whole work is infused with a vein of frank lyricism that should enjoy wide popularity. Its second group in the first movement is one of those tunes which, once heard, remains obstinately in the mind. There is, too, a poetic slow movement not unlike early Rachmaninov. The structural layout with its conventional and at times predictable treatment of the material reveals the composer's youth; but this is nonethe-

less a highly attractive work, and the performance by Yevgeny Svetlanov is every bit as good as its predecessor on this label under the late Kyril Kondrashin. The recording is lively and the orchestral response equally satisfactory.

Kálmán, Emmerich
(1882–1953)

Die Csárdásfürstin (*The Gypsy Princess;* abridged).
**(*) RCA RL 25167. Moffo, Kollo, Koller, Németh, Mensáros, Peter Comehlsen Ch., Rosi Singers, Gipsy Ens., Graunke SO, Grund.

This selection from Kálmán's classic operetta was taken from a 1971 television production which aimed at some musical updating. It is not so much a Viennese performance as one which cocks an eye at Kurt Weill. But the result is characterful and compelling, bringing out the dash of Kálmán's infectious gipsy rhythms and haunting tunes. Anna Moffo is not always beguiling in the topmost register, but she and René Kollo make a strong team, and the recording is fair.

Gräfin Mariza (abridged).
(M) ** RCA Gold GL/*GK* 30315. Hartung, Wunderlich, Görner, Hofmann, Kusche, Cologne R. Ch. and SO, Marszalek.
(M) ** Tel. AF 6.21311. Dahlberg, Németh, Minich, Prikopa, V. Volksoper Ch. and O., Paulik.

On RCA's mid-price label the Cologne performance, taken from a broadcast of 1962, is welcome, since the catalogue contains too little of this repertory. It is good to have the honeyed tones of the late Fritz Wunderlich in Tassilo's two songs, rather overshadowing the others.

Nonetheless the results are generally idiomatic and the recording fair for its period. The selection is generous, but does not (as is claimed) include all the music. The cassette transfer treats the solo voices well, but produces a curiously cavernous effect in the choruses.

The Telefunken cast is more evenly balanced, with a consistently lively and reliable contribution from the soloists and the Chorus and Orchestra of the Vienna Volksoper. The recording is vivid and not wanting in atmosphere. The presentation is in Telefunken's potpourri style, common to this series.

Kern, Jerome (1885–1945)

Songs (arr. R. R. Bennett): *All the things you are; Don't ever leave me; Go, little boat; I'm old-fashioned; Long ago and far away; Smoke gets in your eyes; Sure thing; Till the clouds roll by/Look for the silver lining; Up with the lark; The way you look tonight; Why do I love you; Yesterdays.*
*(*) HMV ASD/*TC-ASD* 3844 [Ang. SZ 37723]. Tuckwell, Instrumental Ens., Richardson.

An enticing-looking collection from the great American tunesmith proves in the event most disappointing. The instrumentations chosen by Barry Tuckwell and the small accompanying group under Neil Richardson are insubstantial, and the playing itself curiously unmemorable. At best this is usable (perhaps ideally in its cassette format, which is of excellent quality) as late-evening musical wallpaper. The sound itself is immaculate.

Ketèlbey, Albert (1875–1959)

Bells across the Meadow; Chal Romano (Gypsy Lad); The Clock and the Dresden Figures; In a Chinese Temple Garden; In a Monastery Garden; In a Persian Market; In the Moonlight; In the Mystic Land of Egypt; Sanctuary of the Heart.
*** HMV ASD/*TC-ASD* 3542 [Ang. S 37483]. Midgley, Temperley, Amb. S., Pearson (piano), Philh. O., Lanchbery.

A splendid collection in every way. John Lanchbery plainly has a very soft spot for Ketèlbey's tuneful music (and there are some very good tunes here), and he uses every possible resource to ensure that when the composer demands spectacle he gets it. *In the Mystic Land of Egypt*, for instance, uses soloist and chorus in canon in the principal tune (and very fetching too). *The Clock and the Dresden Figures* is deliciously done, with Leslie Pearson playing the concertante piano part in scintillating fashion. Perhaps in the *Monastery Garden* the distant monks are a shade too realistically distant, but in *Sanctuary of the Heart* there is no mistaking that the heart is worn firmly on the sleeve. The orchestral playing throughout is not only polished but warm-hearted – the middle section of *Bells across the Meadow*, which has a delightful melodic contour, is played most tenderly and loses any hint of vulgarity. Yet when vulgarity is called for it is not shirked – only it's a stylish kind of vulgarity! The *Chal Romano* has an unexpectedly vigorous melodic impulse, reminding the listener of Eric Coates. The recording is excellent, full and brilliant. The cassette is marginally less refined than the disc but still good.

Khachaturian, Aram
(1903–78)

Gayaneh: excerpts; *Masquerade: suite.*
(M) *** Sup. 1101 226. Brno State PO, Belohlávek.

A first-class coupling of an extended selection from *Gayaneh* and the suite from *Masquerade*, which is less indelible but still enjoyable in its lightweight way. The orchestral playing is full of verve and spirit and most sympathetic to the genuinely inspired lyrical music of *Gayaneh*. The recording is vivid and the acoustic has just the right degree of reverberation.

Masquerade: suite; Spartacus: suite.
**(*) Decca PFS 4434 [Lon. 21184/5-]. LSO, Black.

Characteristically direct, well played and vivid performances, very brightly and forwardly recorded in Decca's Phase Four manner. The measure is somewhat short, but the items all represent Khachaturian at his most communicative. Stanley Black handles the famous 'Onedin Line' sequence from *Spartacus* effectively.

Symphony No. 1 (revised version).
(***) RCA RL/*RK* 25203. LSO, Tjeknavorian.

Symphonic form always brought out the bombastic side of Khachaturian, and it was already so in 1934 when he wrote this first essay as a graduation exercise. One might extract a reasonably attractive suite from the incidental ideas which represent the simple lyrical side of the invention; but the attempts to build a big structure – forty-five minutes long are sadly unconvincing. Even Tjeknavorian's enthusiastic advocacy and good playing and recording (the cassette less

expansive than the disc) cannot prevent this from being a bore.

Symphony No. 3.
(M) (***) RCA Gold GL/*GK* 42923 [(d) LSC 3067]. Chicago SO, Stokowski – RACHMANINOV: *Vocalise*; RIMSKY-KORSAKOV: *Russian Easter Festival overture*.***

Khachaturian's *Third Symphony* might almost have been designed to demonstrate how not to write symphonically. The composer's chronic tendency to repeat a phrase ad nauseam, his refusal to appreciate that enough is enough – early in this symphony there is a truly terrible organ passage in mad triplets – are the antithesis of true development. Even so Stokowski's richly expressive direction and the virtuoso playing of the Chicago orchestra almost make the results tolerable, particularly as the recording is super-brilliant. The cassette matches the disc closely.

Knussen, Oliver
(born 1952)

Symphony No. 3; Ophelia dances, Book 1.
*** Uni. Dig. RHD 400. Philh. O. or L. Sinf., Tilson Thomas – BAINBRIDGE: *Viola concerto*.***

Oliver Knussen first attracted attention with his *Symphony No. 1,* written when he was only sixteen and first performed by the LSO with the boy composer conducting (in place of an indisposed Istvan Kertesz). He studied with John Lambert and Gunther Schuller. His *Third Symphony* was finished in 1979 and dedicated to Michael Tilson Thomas, who conducted its first performance at a Prom the same year. The idiom is accessible; its sound world is distinctive and reflects an alive, vivid imagination. The language itself seems to have grown from Messiaen – and even perhaps Britten and Henze – yet its accents are personal. It is a short fifteen-minute piece in one movement, and it is superbly performed and recorded. The *Ophelia dances* played by the London Sinfonietta which make up the side are from 1975; they are related to the symphony and are no less inventive and rewarding.

Kodály, Zoltán (1882–1967)

Dances of Galánta; Dances of Marosszék; Háry János: suite.
(M) *** CBS 61930/40-. Phd. O., Ormandy.

Dances of Galánta; Háry János: suite; (i) *Arias: Poor I am still; Once I had a brood of chicks.*
(M) *** Decca Jub. JB/*KJBC* 55. LSO, Kertesz, (i) with O. Szönyi.

Háry János: suite.
(M) *** RCA Gold GL/*GK* 42698. Boston SO, Leinsdorf – PROKOFIEV: *Lieutenant Kijé.***(*)

Ormandy plays these famous scores with great panache, and the Philadelphia Orchestra is in superb form. It is a pity that the balance is so close, reducing the dynamic range and producing a giant-sized cimbalom in *Háry János*. However, it is easy to forgive the faults of balance when everything is so vivid and the playing so zestful. The cassette matches the disc in brilliance but is less refined in the upper range; our copy had a degree of discoloration.

Háry János is also superbly played under Kertesz, who has the advantage of the very finest Decca recording. This has always been something of a demonstration piece, even in mono days, and once again *The battle and defeat of Napoleon*

proves an example of how much modern recording can offer in realism and clarity. There is a complete absence of pre-echo here in a passage notorious for this fault. In the *Viennese musical clock*, the percussion balance might ideally have achieved a crisper effect, especially from the side-drum, but some will be glad not to have the kitchen department exaggerated as it sometimes is. One certainly could not fault the balance of the cimbalom, which emerges as soloist in the *Intermezzo* without drowning everything. Throughout, the orchestral playing has great élan, something which the *Dances of Galánta* share; indeed they are so well played they almost rise to the stature of *János*. The two arias are short but attractive, and Miss Szönyi sings with such character that her Slavonic wobbles can be forgiven. The cassette is an example of the highest state of the art, offering demonstration quality, rich and vivid throughout.

Leinsdorf draws brilliant and colourful playing from the Boston orchestra in Kodály's witty and memorable suite. The recording – mid-sixties vintage – is excellent, and the coupling on the mid-price RCA reissue is ideal. The cassette transfer, however, is made at a relatively modest level; the reverberant acoustic tends to blur the transients.

(Unaccompanied) Cello sonata, Op. 8.
*** HMV ASD 3458. Tortelier – TOR-TELIER: *Suite.****
*(*) Nimbus 2117. Hocks – BRIDGE: *Sonata.***

Every cellist of distinction measures himself at some time against the challenge of Kodály's masterpiece. Tortelier's version has a quiet authority all its own: passion is controlled and disciplined, and though there is no absence of virtuosity, there is not the slightest trace of flamboyance. This is a dignified, penetrating and serene account of the work, very different from either of Starker's (mono) recordings, and musically most satisfying, with truthful and realistic recorded sound, and a particularly rich and sonorous bass.

Christian Hocks is a young cellist of mixed German and Russian parentage, who has studied with Fournier and Navarra. He plays the Kodály *Sonata* with fervour and commitment, but the recording lets things down. The acoustic is very resonant, and full justice is not quite done to this artist's tone, which sounds coarser than in the Bridge *Sonata* on the other side. An imaginative and enterprising coupling nonetheless, and it deserves support. Though it is not the equal of the Tortelier and Starker performances or that of Frans Helmersen (briefly available on BIS and coupled with a Bach suite), Hocks plays with an ardour that is refreshing.

String quartet No. 2, Op. 10.
(M) *** Decca Ace SDD 543. Küchl Qt – SUK: *Quartet No. 1;* WOLF: *Italian serenade.****

Kodály has been so completely overshadowed as a quartet composer by his compatriot Bartók that this record performs a valuable service. The rarity of the work does not reflect its importance, for it deserves to be heard as often as Bartók's early quartets, and is hardly less rewarding. It is beautifully played by the Küchl Quartet (now called the Musikverein), and the couplings are of exceptional interest. Altogether an excellent issue, particularly at so reasonable a price.

(i) *Hymn of Zrinyi;* (ii) *Laudes organi* (*Fantasia on a 17th-century sequence*); *Psalm 114* (*from the Geneva Psalter*).
*** Decca SXL 6878. (i) Luxon, (ii) Brighton Festival Ch., Heltay, with Weir.

This disc conveniently brings together three of the choral works which Kodály

wrote towards the end of his career. The most ambitious, the *Hymn of Zrinyi,* for unaccompanied chorus and baritone solo, celebrates a Magyar hero. The other two rest their interest as much on the organ as the choir. Even when Kodály took on dramatic subjects his was a relatively gentle art (totally in contrast to his friend Bartók). Heltay directs persuasive performances, with Gillian Weir brilliant at the organ; the recording is excellent.

Kohaut, Carl (Joseph)
(1736–93)

Lute concerto in F.
(*) RCA RL/*RK* 11180 [ARL 1/*ARK 1* 1180]. Bream, Monteverdi O., Gardiner – HANDEL and VIVALDI: *Concertos.*(*)

Kohaut, a Bohemian composer, was himself a lutenist, and this is a well-made little work, *galant* in style and with an attractively simple *arioso* forming the slow movement. The performance is excellent and the recording good except for the jumbo-sized solo instrument created by the unnaturally forward balance. The cassette matches the LP closely.

Korngold, Erich (1897–1957)

Film scores: *Adventures of Robin Hood: March and Battle. Anthony Adverse: No father, no mother. Between Two Worlds: Main title; Mother and son. Captain Blood: Overture. The Constant Nymph:* (i) *Tomorrow. Deception: Main title. Devotion: Death of Emily Brontë. Escape Me Never (suite). Juarez: Love theme. King's Row: Main title.*

*Of Human Bondage: Nora's theme.
The Sea Hawk: miniature suite.*
(M) *** RCA Gold GL/*GK* 43446 [AGL
1/*AGK 1* 3707]. Nat. PO, Gerhardt,
with (i) Procter, Amb. S.

Film scores: *Another Dawn: Night
scene. Anthony Adverse: In the forest.
Deception:* (i) *Cello concerto in C,
Op. 37. Of Human Bondage: suite.
The Prince and the Pauper: miniature
suite. The Private Lives of Elizabeth
and Essex: Overture. The Sea Wolf:
suite.*
(M) *** RCA Gold GL/*GK* 43438 [ARL
1/*ARK 1* 0185]. Nat. PO, Gerhardt, (i)
with Gabarro.

These two RCA anthologies,
splendidly played by the National Philharmonic Orchestra under the passionately sympathetic advocacy of Charles
Gerhardt, are admirably recorded, evoking a proper Hollywoodian sense of
spectacle, the spacious acoustic providing a brilliant panoply of brass and
strings. The cassettes are good too, with
only very slight loss of sparkle, and often
showing rather more middle-range richness. However, each disc has an insert
leaflet, with back-up documentation and
pictures, while the tapes provide nothing
at all! The music is nearly always in-
ventively rich, has much lyrical warmth
and sometimes splendour, with Hollywoodian hyperbole (heard at its most
overwhelming in the *Between Two
Worlds* sequence) but never coarsening
into vulgarity. Korngold's skill and professionalism are consistently apparent.
For *Deception* he invented a miniature
Cello concerto; the closing sequence of
The Constant Nymph (about a composer)
brings a characteristically flamboyant
setting for contralto soloist (here Norma
Procter) and chorus. *The Sea Wolf* contrasts a snarlingly pungent portrayal of
the main character (played by Edward G.
Robinson) with a tenderly nostalgic
romantic interlude. The elegy for *The

Death of Emily Brontë* (*Devotion*) is
touchingly direct, while the swashbuck-
ling *Captain Blood, Robin Hood* and *The
Sea Hawk* (all Errol Flynn vehicles) are
vigorously exhilarating. The opening
sequence of *Elizabeth and Essex* with its
vivid thrust admirably demonstrates the
vigour of Korngold's inspiration at its
most compelling.

King's Row (film score).
*** Chalfont Dig. SDG 305. Nat. PO,
Gerhardt.

Korngold's score for *King's Row*
shows characteristic craftsmanship and
flair. The invention is undoubtedly
memorable · in its way, its character
closely matched to the film's atmosphere
and melodramatic storyline. The material in the grandiloquent title sequence
has a germinal effect, and Korngold's
reworking of his melodic fragments
throughout is highly imaginative and
sufficiently interesting to give the score a
life of its own away from the visual
images. Near the end there is a (Richard)
Straussian apotheosis, and although the
effect has to be thrown away afterwards
to meet the needs of the closing narrative,
the composer's ready flexibility commands admiration. Charles Gerhardt is a
highly sympathetic advocate and the
National Philharmonic Orchestra plays
splendidly, obviously relishing the
moments of cinematic pathos. The digital
recording is suitably brilliant and clear.

Much Ado About Nothing: suite.
(M) ** Turn. TVS 37124 [Can. 31091].
Westphalian O., Landau – WEILL:
Quodlibet.**

Korngold's *Much Ado About Nothing*
is not new to the gramophone. It dates
from the end of the 1914–18 war and is
much indebted to the Strauss of *Till* and
Le Bourgeois Gentilhomme; but there is
much to admire even if the idiom seems
dated. There is a certain vitality and con-

fidence about its ideas, although some of them outstay their welcome. The performance and recording are not in the top drawer but are perfectly acceptable.

Symphony in F sharp, Op. 40.
(M) *** RCA Gold GL/*GK* 42919. Munich PO, Kempe.

This is a work of Korngold's last years, overtly and unashamedly romantic in idiom. Written in 1950, it was admired by Mitropoulos, who planned to conduct its first performance. His death intervened and its première, under Kempe, did not take place until 1972. Some of its ideas are freshly imagined, and the work is laid out with great expertise and impeccable craftsmanship. Whether its appeal can sustain its time-scale will inevitably be a matter for individual judgement (there are many post-romantic symphonies with stronger claims on the repertoire) but it is undoubtedly worth hearing, and Kempe's advocacy and the fine if reverberant recording could hardly be more persuasive. The cassette transfer too is first-class. It is slightly less expansive in the middle and bass, but otherwise matches the disc closely.

String quartets Nos. 1 in A, Op. 16; 3 in D.
*** RCA RL 25097. Chilingirian Qt.

Apart from the famous *Violin concerto*, Korngold is remembered for his operas and film music rather than instrumental pieces. The *First Quartet* was composed at the suggestion of Arnold Rosé, Mahler's brother-in-law, whose quartet first gave the piece in Vienna in 1924. The *Third* is a much later work, dedicated to Bruno. Walter and composed after Korngold's association with Hollywood. In fact, the piece is a little tarnished from the intervening experience (it incorporates ideas from the movies); the *First* is altogether fresher. It is well laid out for the medium, though at

times one wonders whether its lushness of idiom might not have made it more suitable for either full strings or even orchestra. It is Mahleresque in idiom, with a whiff of the French as well. Excellent playing by the Chilingirian Quartet and very good sound into the bargain.

Violanta (complete).
**(*) CBS 79229 (2) [Col. M2 35909]. Marton, Berry, Jerusalem, Stoklassa, Laubenthal, Hess, Bav. R. Ch., Mun. RO, Janowski.

Korngold was perhaps the most remarkable composer-prodigy of this century; he wrote this opera at the age of seventeen. It was given its first triumphant performance under Bruno Walter, and even Ernest Newman seriously compared Korngold to Mozart. The story of the piece is a sort of compressed version of *Tristan*, but there is more of Lehár and Puccini in the idiom than of Wagner. Though luscious of texture and immensely assured, the writing lets one down in an absence of really memorable melody, but with a fine red-blooded performance – the remarkable Siegfried Jerusalem showing enormous promise as the hero – it makes a fascinating addition to the recorded repertory. The Hungarian Eva Marton, not always beautiful of tone, combines power and accuracy in the key role of the heroine, suddenly floating high pianissimos with unexpected purity. The recording is warm if unsubtle.

Kozeluch, Leopold
(1747–1818)

Symphonies: in F; in G min.
(M) ** Sup. 1102 078. Prague SO, Hlaváček.

Kozeluch was a Bohemian contemporary of Haydn and Mozart, though he outlived them both. His music is far from negligible, and both these symphonies, written in 1787, after Haydn's *Paris symphonies*, are well constructed and – up to a point – inventive. Yet his melodic inspiration lacks the humanity and richness of his great contemporaries, and though the slow movements have a certain dignity, they seem by the side of Haydn to be going through the motions rather than achieving any real depth. The performances are lively enough and the recording perfectly acceptable.

Kraus, Joseph Martin
(1756–92)

Keyboard sonatas Nos. 1 in E; 2 in E flat.
*** Cap. CAP 1173. Negro (harpsichord).

Joseph Martin Kraus was German-born but settled in Sweden, becoming kapellmeister at the Royal Theatre. He has a Gluck-like breadth and an inquiring mind that suggests *Sturm und Drang* Haydn or C. P. E. Bach. The two sonatas recorded here on period instruments (one a Swedish instrument by Johan Söderberg and the other a south German instrument, both in the Stockholm Museum) are of more than just historical interest, and they are played with quite exceptional insight and sensibility by Lucia Negro. The sonatas come from 1785 and 1787, and are worthy to be compared only with the very finest examples of their kind by Haydn and C. P. E. Bach. Excellent recording. This is well worth the attention of a wide public.

Krebs, Johann (1713–80)

Double concerto in B min. for oboe, harpsichord and strings.
(*) DG Arc. 2533 412. Holliger, Jaccottet, Camerata Bern, Van Wijnkoop – GRAUN: *Oboe concertos.**

Krebs was a pupil of J. S. Bach who left Leipzig with a glowing testimonial from the master. One can understand why from this delightful *Double concerto*, which makes a good coupling for the two splendid oboe concertos of Graun on the reverse. Holliger as ever plays beautifully, but Christiane Jaccottet adopts too romantically expressive a style, undermining the stylishness of the Camerata's playing. First-rate recording.

Kreisler, Fritz (1875–1972)

Andantino in the style of Martini; Allegretto in the style of Boccherini; Caprice viennoise, Op. 2; Chanson Louis XIII and Pavane in the style of Couperin; La Gitana; Liebesfreud; Liebeslied; Recitativo and scherzo capriccioso, Op. 6; Rondino on a theme of Beethoven; Schön Rosmarin; Tambourin chinois, Op. 3. Arrangements: ALBÉNIZ: *Tango.* DVOŘÁK: *Slavonic dance No. 3 in G.* FALLA: *La Vida breve: Danse espagnole.*
*** HMV ASD 3258 [Ang. S/4XS 37171]. Perlman, Saunders.

Perlman is on sparkling form in these *morceaux de concert* of Fritz Kreisler, and the recording is of the highest quality. If the invention is lightweight it is never trivial, and much of this music is very entertaining, as it was meant to be.

(For his second anthology (ASD 3346) Perlman concentrated on transcriptions and arrangements, and that recital is listed in the Collections section below.)

Aubade provençale; Menuet (after Porpora); La Précieuse (after Couperin); Scherzo (after Dittersdorf); Siciliano and Rigaudon (after Francœur); Syncopation; Toy soldiers' march. Arrangements: CHAMINADE: *Sérénade espagnole.* LEHÁR: *Frasquita serenade.* PADEREWSKI: *Melody, Op. 16/2.* TCHAIKOVSKY: *Andante cantabile; Chanson sans paroles.* DVOŘÁK: *Slavonic dance No. 1 in G min.* PAGANINI: *Caprice No. 20.* GRAINGER: *Molly on the Shore.*
*** HMV ASD/TC-ASD 3980 [Ang. SZ/4ZS 37630]. Perlman, Saunders.

Perlman's third selection of Kreisler trifles is if anything even more captivating than the first two. Though there are fewer favourites, the original pieces here include such artless charmers as *Syncopation* (jauntily relaxed), while the arrangements bring such surprise items as *Molly on the Shore*. The recording is first-rate, and the cassette is extremely lively, matching the disc closely.

Caprice viennoise, Op. 2; La Gitana; Liebesfreud; Liebesleid; Polichinelle; La Précieuse; Recitativo and scherzo caprice, Op. 6; Rondo on a theme of Beethoven; Syncopation; Tambourin chinois; Zigeuner (Capriccio). Arrangements: ALBÉNIZ: *Tango.* WEBER: *Larghetto.* WIENIAWSKI: *Caprice in E flat.* DVOŘÁK: *Slavonic dance No. 10 in E min.* GLAZOUNOV: *Sérénade espagnole.* GRANADOS: *Danse espagnole.*
*** DG 2531/3301 305 [id.]. Mintz, Benson.

One can understand why DG chose to introduce Shlomo Mintz with this Kreisler programme, alongside his coupling of the Bruch and Mendelssohn concertos. He plays with a disarmingly easy style and absolute technical command to bring out the music's warmth as well as its sparkle. Try *La Gitana* to sample the playing at its most genially glittering. A very attractive programme, given first-class recording and a refined cassette equivalent (perhaps a little lacking in level for maximum impact).

Kreutzer, Conradin
(1780–1849)

Septet in E flat, Op. 62.
*** CRD CRD 1090/CRDC 4090. Nash Ens. – HUMMEL: *Military septet.****

Kreutzer's *Septet* is a delightful work, and it is given a thoroughly engaging performance here by the Nash Ensemble, whose playing is as lyrically elegant as it is full of refined detail. The care of the players over the use of dynamic graduation is matched by the warmth of their phrasing. The Hummel coupling too is most apt, as both works date from the same period (around 1830). The recording is first-class in every way and beautifully balanced, with a demonstration-worthy cassette to match the disc.

Krommer, Franz (František) (1759–1831)

(i) *Clarinet concerto in E flat, Op. 36;* (ii) *Oboe concerto in F, Op. 37.*
**(*) EMI 1C 065 03429. Prague CO, Vajnar, with (i) Zahradnik, (ii) Mihule.

A fluent composer rather than a profound one, the Moravian Franz Krommer (or František Kramár) bridges the classic and romantic eras, and this record has a foot in both camps. The *Oboe concerto* belongs firmly to the eighteenth century; the *Clarinet concerto* is of a more romantic sensibility. The performances are expert, and the recording, though a little lacking in warmth, has exemplary clarity. Pleasant music which is well worth investigation.

(i) *Bassoon quartet in E flat, Op. 46* (for bassoon, 2 violas and cello); (ii) *Oboe quartets Nos. 1 in C; 2 in F* (for oboe, violin, viola and cello).
(M) *** 1111 2824. Suk Qt (members), with (i) Seidl; (ii) Mihule.

The *Bassoon quartet* is a delight; it has warmth, individuality and a fund of good invention. The unusual combination of instruments produces a rich-bodied texture, and the playing of Jiri Seidl is sensitive both in its dynamic range and in its variety of colour. This *Quartet* makes thoroughly civilized listening; it dates from 1804, later than the two *Oboe quartets*, which are elegantly played and often witty (the finale of the F major even has a Haydnesque false ending). The recording has more body and colour than many from this source, and though it is a trifle on the close side, the timbre is natural and there is plenty of range. A thoroughly enjoyable record – and the *Bassoon quartet* is really something of a discovery.

Clarinet quartet in D, Op. 82.
*** O-L DSLO 553. Hacker, Music Party – WEBER: *Clarinet quintet.****

Krommer's *Clarinet quartet* is a pleasing and accomplished work written at much the same time as its Weber coupling. Alan Hacker plays a clarinet in A from 1825 and the quartet (led by Duncan Druce) use period instruments. The strings play without vibrato and

there is an inevitable loss of warmth. The clarinet is played with sensitivity and skill, and the recording is alive and splendidly balanced.

Kuhnau, Johann (1660–1722)

Der Gerechte kommt um (motet).
*** O-L DSLO/*KDSLC* 572. Ch. of Christ Church Cath., AcAM, Preston – BACH: *Magnificat.****

Kuhnau was Bach's predecessor in Leipzig. He wrote this charming motet with a Latin text; it was later arranged in a German version, and there are signs of Bach's hand in it. The piece makes an excellent makeweight to a fine version of the *Magnificat*.

La Guerre, Elisabeth de (1659–1729)

Harpsichord suite in D min.
(M) *** Argo ZK 64. Gilbert – CLÉRAMBAULT: *Suites.****

Elisabeth Jacquet de la Guerre is one of the earliest women of music, though it would be going too far to describe her as the Ethel Smyth of Versailles. Louis XIV took great delight in her playing, and she appeared at court when she was hardly fifteen, drawing much praise alike for improvisation and for compositions. Titon de Tillet wrote in *Le Parnasse François* (1732): 'A person of her sex has never before had such great gifts for composition and for amazing performance upon the harpsichord and the organ'. There are three volumes of cantatas, trio sonatas and even a full-scale opera, *Céphale et Procris*, in five acts from her pen. These pieces comprising the *D minor Suite* are full of personality (there is striking use of major/minor contrasts) and there is much delicacy and refinement. Kenneth Gilbert plays with obvious relish and authority and is beautifully recorded on a 1747 harpsichord of Sebastian Garnier.

Lalo, Édouard (1823–92)

Cello concerto in D min.
🅑 *** CBS Dig. 35848 [Col. IM/*HMT* 35848]. Ma, Orchestre Nat. de France, Maazel – SAINT-SAËNS: *Concerto No. 1.* 🅑 ***

Yo Yo Ma is an artist who eschews overstatement, and his account of the Lalo *Concerto* must rank as the finest now available. It has great sensitivity, beauty of tone and expressive feeling to commend it, and indeed it makes the work seem better than in fact it is. Moreover Maazel and the Orchestre National de France give magnificent support, matching the sensitivity of the soloist. The quality of the recorded sound is first-class, beautifully balanced and spacious, yet with detail well in focus.

Piano concerto in F min.
(M) *(*) Turn. TVS 37125 [Can. 31102]. Dosse, Stuttgart PO, Kuntzsch – PIERNÉ: *Concerto.* *(*)

Although it opens with a rather attractive *Lento* section, Lalo's *Piano concerto* is melodramatic rather than exciting, and not lyrically memorable. This performance is strong rather than coaxing, and the forward balance increases the feeling of over-projection, with a larger-than-life piano image. The sound is certainly vivid, though somewhat aggressive.

Namouna (ballet): *Rhapsodies Nos. 1 and 2; Cigarette waltz. Rapsodie norvégienne.*

(M) **(*) DG 2543 803. Paris ORTF O., Martinon.

There is much engaging music in *Namouna*, a ballet score much admired by Debussy and dating from 1882. The first movement opens with an unashamed Wagnerian crib from *Das Rheingold*, but elsewhere Lalo's music is more individual. He is at his finest in the gentler atmospheric writing: the *Sérénade*, the *Valse de la cigarette*, and the enchanting Bacchanesque lollipop, *La Sieste*. These are all memorable and nicely played. The *Pas des cymbales* is admirably crisp, although in the louder sections of the score the recording is inclined to fierceness, making the music sound noisier than necessary. Jean Martinon is a sympathetic exponent throughout, and he also gives us the attractively tuneful *Rapsodie norvégienne* in its adapted version for orchestra alone (1879). (The original, composed a year earlier, featured a concertante violin: see below.)

Rapsodie norvégienne.
(M) * Turn. TVS 34570 [id.]. R. Lux. O., Cao – CHABRIER: *Fête polonaise* *; MASSENET: *Scènes hongroises.**(*)

Cao's performance is spirited and reasonably well played, but the recording is shallow and artificially balanced, with close microphones intruding into a resonant acoustic.

Scherzo for orchestra.
(M) *** HMV Green. ESD 7048. Orchestre de Paris, Jacquillat – MESSAGER: *Deux pigeons*; PIERNÉ: *Marche* etc.***

Lalo's *Scherzo for orchestra* is a first-rate piece which enhances this splendid collection of French music. The compilation also includes Berlioz's arrangement of *La Marseillaise* (all verses included) for soloists, choirs and orchestra. Like everything else on the disc, this is presented with flair and excellently recorded.

Symphonie espagnole, Op. 21.

*** DG Dig. 2532/*3302* 011 [id.]. Perlman, Orchestre de Paris, Barenboim – BERLIOZ: *Romance.****

*** CBS 76726/40- [Col. M/*MT* 35132]. Zukerman, LAPO, Mehta – BRUCH: *Concerto No. 1.***(*)

(B) *** CfP CFP/*TC-CFP* 40364. Menuhin, Philh. O., Goossens – SAINT-SAËNS: *Havanaise* etc.***

*** Decca Dig. SXDL/*KSXDC* 7527 [Lon. LDR 71029/5-]. Kyung-Wha Chung, Montreal SO, Dutoit – SAINT-SAËNS: *Concerto No. 1.****

(M) **(*) CBS 61933/40- [Col. MS 7003]. Stern, Phd. O., Ormandy – BRUCH: *Concerto No. 1.***(*)

(M) **(*) Ph. Fest. 6570/*7310* 192 [id.]. Grumiaux, LOP, Rosenthal – SAINT-SAËNS: *Havanaise* etc.**(*)

(M) ** RCA Gold GL/*GK* 11329 [AGL 1 1329]. Perlman, LSO, Previn – RAVEL: *Tzigane.*(*)

Lalo's brilliant five-movement distillation of Spanish sunshine and dance rhythms is currently better served on disc than ever before. Perlman and Zukerman both play with great panache, and the vintage Menuhin and Stern versions show these artists at the peak of their form. Perlman's newest DG digital recording is both vivid and refined. The very opening sets the style of the reading, with a strongly articulated orchestral introduction from Barenboim that combines rhythmic buoyancy with expressive flair. The lyrical material is handled with great sympathy, and the richness and colour of Perlman's tone are never more telling than in the slow movement, which opens tenderly but develops a compelling expressive ripeness. The scintillating brilliance of the scherzo is matched by the dancing sparkle of the finale. The recording is extremely vivid – the chrome cassette matching the disc closely – and the forward balance of the soloist in no way obscures orchestral detail and impact.

Zukerman's performance too is outstandingly successful. He plays with great dash and fire yet brings a balancing warmth. The rhythmic zest of the scherzo, with its subtle control of dynamic shading, is contrasted with a richly expressive *Andante*, to be followed by a dazzling display of fireworks in the finale. Mehta accompanies with sympathetic gusto, and the reverberant, larger-than-life recording suits the style of the music-making, the soloist balanced forwardly. Zukerman's coupling is more generous than Perlman's, but the effect of the DG recording is to give Perlman's account slightly more romantic finesse.

Menuhin's recording, now reissued at bargain price on Classics for Pleasure, remains very competitive indeed. It dates from the earliest days of stereo, and its extreme liveliness brings a touch of fierceness to the upper range. However, with a treble cut and bass increase it can produce excellent results. The cassette is a shade less brightly lit than the disc and may be found preferable. It is a glittering performance, and the clean sound, with excellent woodwind detail, is especially effective in the delectable finale. Menuhin is on top form throughout and the warm spontaneity of his playing is matched by his feeling for the music's rhythmic character. The way he shapes the sinuous secondary theme of the first movement is wonderfully engaging. The accompaniment too is excellent, with the orchestra on its toes throughout. The Saint-Saëns couplings are superbly played.

Kyung-Wha Chung has the advantage of a first-class Decca digital recording (the cassette matching the disc closely), with a highly effective, natural balance. Hers is an athletic, incisive account, at its most individual in the captivatingly lightweight finale, with an element almost of fantasy. For some ears the lack of sumptuousness of style as well as timbre may be a drawback; Miss Chung does not have quite the panache of Zukerman or Perlman. But Charles Dutoit's accompaniment is first-class and the orchestral characterization is strong throughout.

Stern's version from the late sixties has all the rich, red-blooded qualities that have made this artist world-famous. Indeed this coupling with the Bruch *G minor Concerto* is one of his very finest records. Reservations are inevitable about the close balance (although Ormandy's fine accompaniment is not diminished), but the playing makes a huge impact on the listener and although the actual sound quality is far from refined (especially on the cassette, where tuttis are inclined to be explosive) the charisma of this performance is unforgettable.

Like Menuhin's before him, Grumiaux's performance is ideally coupled with the Saint-Saëns *Havanaise* and *Introduction and rondo capriccioso*. Grumiaux too is in good form and he gives a persuasive account of the *Symphonie*, not as extrovert as Stern's but with plenty of colour and an attractive, unforced bravura. The Lamoureux Orchestra is no match for the finest rivals, but it provides an alert accompaniment under Rosenthal and allows Grumiaux to dominate the proceedings. The Philips recording was made about the same time as Stern's and has more depth and warmth than the CBS version. There is also an attractive and lively cassette transfer.

Perlman's earlier recording for RCA is superseded by his new DG version. The 1969 account was brilliant enough, with Perlman sparkling in the bravura and relishing the expressive melodies. He was ably supported by Previn but the recording placed an aural spotlight on the soloist, sometimes at the expense of the orchestra so that accompanying detail is all but masked. The sound is very brilliant, with a lack of bloom (the cassette is slightly smoother than the disc). However, the performance is infectiously spirited and at medium price this might be considered if the coupling is suitable.

Lambert, Constant
(1905–51)

Pomona; Romeo and Juliet (ballets).
*** Lyr. SRCS 110. ECO, Del Mar.

The sparky invention of the extraordinarily precocious Lambert is well represented in these two ballet scores (he wrote most of *Romeo and Juliet* before he was twenty). In these crisp, unpretentious dances the brilliant young man showed how cleverly he could pick up tricks from those fashionable in Paris at the time, Stravinsky, Milhaud and others. It is not surprising that Diaghilev appreciated Lambert's talent enough to put on *Romeo* – though scandal followed the first production, with the composer forcibly prevented from recovering his score. Del Mar directs bright and persuasive performances, well recorded.

Lambranzi, Gregorio
(*fl. c.* 1640)

Dances from the School of Gregorio Lambranzi (arr. Ball).
(B) *** CfP CFP/*TC-CFP* 40335. Praetorius Cons., Ball – HOLBORNE: *Airs*; PRAETORIUS: *Terpsichore*.***

Gregorio Lambranzi was an Italian dancing master of whom very little is known. But the dances he used, which are arranged here by Christopher Ball into three short pot-pourris, are delightfully infectious and tuneful. Surprisingly, they seem to show some evidence of English derivation, even including a piquant reminder of *The British Grenadiers*. With sparkling performances and excellent recording this is in many ways the most interesting of the three groups of dances on this enterprising issue. The cassette transfer is of outstanding quality, offering sound identical with the LP. Highly recommended.

Langlais, Jean (born 1907)

Mass: Salve Regina.
(*) Argo ZRG 938. Richard Hickox Singers, Philip Jones Brass Ens., Hickox – DURUFLÉ: *Messe*.*

The Langlais Mass *Salve Regina*, which dates from 1949, is pure pastiche, but good clean fun all the same. It is scored for three choirs, two organs and two brass ensembles and would make an excellent score for a TV production set in Renaissance France. Both performance and sound are good, but the Duruflé Mass is more worthy to be taken seriously.

Lassus, Orlandus
(*c.* 1530–1594)

Chansons: *A ce matin; Avecques vous mon amour finira; Ardant amour; En un chasteau; Fleur de quinze ans; Je l'ayme bien; La nuict froide et sombre; Las, voulez-vous; L'heureux amour; Monsieur l'abbe; O vin en vigne; Quand mon many; Qui dort icy; Sauter danser, faire les tours; Se le long tems; Si je suis brun . . . Ne vous soit estrange; Si par souhait; Soyons joyeux; Un advocat dit à sa femme; Un jour vis un foulon.*
**(*) Tel. AW 6.41934. Paris Polyphonic Ens., Ravier.

Given his stature, Lassus is grievously neglected in the gramophone catalogues, only a fraction of his output being rep-

resented. This record offers an attractive anthology of his chansons, from the Susato collection of 1555 and many of the later books down to the mid-1570s. There is variety of character here, and much of Lassus's range as a composer of chansons is demonstrated. The excellent Paris ensemble under Charles Ravier sometimes does not make the most of this diversity, and intonation is not always flawless. All the same, we must be grateful for a record that explores this rewarding repertoire and does so proficiently.

Madrigals: *Al dolce suon'; Ben convenne; Bestia curvafia pulices; Ove d'alta montagna; Praesidium sara; Spent'è d'amor.* Motets: *Beati pauperes – Beati pacifici; Da pacem, Domine; Domine, quando veneris; Gloria patri et filio.* Chansons: *Lucescit jam o socii; Voir est beaucoup.*
** Tel. Dig. AZ 6/CX 4 42632. Alsfelder Vocal Ens., Helbich.

Expertly directed performances, with good intonation and tonal blend. Wolfgang Helbich does not vary the forces involved here, however; everything is done with full chorus, whereas many of the items would have benefited from greater variety of vocal texture. Thus the overall impact of this issue is less than the sum of the parts.

Lawes, William (1602–45)

Setts for one violin: Nos. 3 in A min.; 8 in D; Setts for two violins: Nos. 2 in G; 3 in A min.; 8 in D; Sett No. 1 in G min. for two division viols and organ.
*** O-L DSLO 564. Cons. of Musicke, Rooley.

William Lawes, the younger of the two composer brothers, the one who died fighting for Charles I at the Siege of Chester, was also the more prolific. These *Setts* (or suites) represent some of the works with viols accompanied by keyboard (here a chamber organ) as opposed to the consort music. Here too Lawes shows his mastery of contrapuntal writing, and though the bulging technique of the players here may at first be hard for the modern ear to appreciate, this selection is invaluable for bringing to life a long-neglected figure. Performances and recording are first-rate.

Setts for three lyra viols: Nos. 1 in D min.; 7 in A min.; 8 in C; Fantazia; Saraband.
*** O-L DSLO 573. Cons. of Musicke, Rooley.

These *Setts* include in their extended sequences of movements some that are as ambitious as any consort music of the period – for example, the sarabande in the first *Sett*, the superb contrapuntal *Fantazia*, and the pavan at the start of the *Eighth Sett*. With authentic performing practice (in other words, no vibrato) the modern ear may resist hearing more than one work at a time, and the three lyra viols hardly sound sweet in multiple stopping; but Rooley directs performances that it would be hard to beat, and the recording is excellent.

Viol consort music: *Setts Nos. 2 in A min.; 3 in C min.; 3 in F; 4 in B flat.*
*** O-L DSLO 560. Cons. of Musicke, Rooley.

These viol pieces show William Lawes more as a thoughtful, inward-looking composer rather than as precursor of the early baroque style. Particularly in the fantasies and the slower movements of these *Setts*, we find him as chromatic and bold as Jenkins. The example of his master Coperario and the chromaticism of the Italian madrigalists were a spur to his imagination, and the results are of

unfailing interest harmonically and full of bold and original touches. The Consort of Musicke plays with authority and virtuosity, and the recording is made in a sympathetic acoustic. A really outstanding record in every way.

Dialogues, psalms and elegies: *The cats as other creatures doe; Cease, O cease, ye jolly shepherds; Charon, O Charon; Charon, O gentle Charon, let me wooe thee; Come heavy heart; How like a widow; Musicke, the master of arts is dead; Orpheus, O Orpheus; Psalm 22; Tis not, boy; When death.* (Also includes: JENKINS: *Why is this shade of night?*; H. LAWES: *Psalm 22.*)
*** O-L DSLO 574. Cons. of Musicke, Rooley.

William Lawes was an inventive composer whose diversity and resource are well conveyed in this selection, which ranges from the elegiac to the comic. Good performances from the Consort of Musicke under Anthony Rooley.

Leclair, Jean-Marie
(1697–1765)

6 Concertos, Op. 7; 6 Concertos, Op. 10.
*** Erato STU 71093 (3). Jarry, Larde, Paillard CO, Paillard.

The twelve concertos recorded here make up Leclair's complete orchestral output. Op. 7 was composed in 1737 and Op. 10 in 1743–4; generally speaking, they are underrated, and their merits are considerable, although one cannot include among them a strongly individual lyrical power. But they are fresh, well-constructed, and often highly expressive, even if the ideas are not in themselves

421

memorable. These performances by the violinist Gérard Jarry and flautist Christian Larde are of exemplary style and virtuosity. Those who must have this music with the benefit of period sonorities can turn to Schröder's selection (see below), but there is nothing here that is wanting in stylistic sense or musical verve. The notes by Harry Halbreich are particularly thorough and helpful, and the recordings first-class.

Violin concertos in C, Op. 7/3; in A min., Op. 7/5; in G min., Op. 10/6.
*** Tel. AW 6.42180 [id.]. Schröder, Concerto Amsterdam.

Distinguished playing from Jaap Schröder and his colleagues, who make outstanding advocates of these concertos. Leclair is a stronger composer than he is often given credit for, and the *G minor Concerto* of Op. 10 is a work of real sensibility and imagination. The performances are all given on period instruments or copies, and can be recommended to *aficionados*. Good sound.

Overture in D for two violins and continuo, Op. 13/2; Sonatas (duos) for two violins: in G min., Op. 12/5; in B flat, Op. 12/6; Trio (overture) in A for two violins and continuo, Op. 14.
*** DG Arc. 2533 414 [id.]. Col. Mus. Ant., Goebel.

Leclair may have few records to represent him in the catalogue, but they are all first-rate; and none more so than this recital, which embodies scholarship, enthusiasm and virtuosity in full measure. Those whose hearts sink at the prospect of duos for two violins alone can rest assured that Leclair's invention and layout are so masterly that no sense of strain or thinness of texture is felt. Excellent in every way.

Lecocq, Alexandre
(1832–1918)

Mam'zelle Angot (ballet): *suite* (arr. Jacob).
(M) **(*) HMV Green. ESD/*TC-ESD* 7080. RPO, Irving – GLAZOUNOV: *Birthday Offering.****

La Fille de Madame Angot was a highly successful operetta of the 1870s. The ballet, which dates from 1943, follows the story of the operetta but also includes music from other works by Lecocq. The score is wittily arranged by Gordon Jacob in the manner of Constant Lambert's *Les Patineurs* (Meyerbeer). The spirits of both Adam and Offenbach occasionally hover in the background. The music is stylishly played and brightly recorded, although the age of the original issue (1959) shows in a lack of overall opulence. But this remains an attractive coupling, and the music is delightful. The cassette transfer is vivid, but the upper strings sound more obviously dated here than on the LP.

LeFanu, Nicola
(born 1947)

(i) *But Stars Remaining;* (i, ii) *The Same Day Dawns for soprano and five players;* (ii; iii) *Deva for cello and seven players.*
*** Chan. ABR/*ABT* 1017. (i) Manning; (ii) Nash Ens.; (iii) Van Kampen.

But Stars Remaining, a setting of Day Lewis for unaccompanied soprano, is beautifully sung by the formidably talented Jane Manning. More ambitious is *The Same Day Dawns*, a sequence of settings of oriental poems in different languages; LeFanu uses an ensemble of five players to provide a spare and free commentary on the vocal line. More beautiful than either is *Deva*, where the cello soloist is similarly the focus of a rather larger ensemble. Excellent performances and recording, the cassette admirably vivid and atmospheric to match the disc closely.

Lehár, Franz (1870–1948)

Friederike (complete).
*** HMV SLS 5230 (2). Fuchs, Donath, Dallapozza, Finke, Grabenhorst, Rüggeberg, Griendl-Rosner, Bav. R. Ch., Munich RO, Wallberg.

The idea of Richard Tauber inspiring Lehár to write an operetta with the poet Goethe as main character may sound far-fetched, but that is just what *Friederike* is, more ambitious than a genuine operetta and bringing the obvious snag for non-German-speakers that there is a great amount of spoken dialogue, the more disruptive because the libretto does not provide an English translation. In every other way this is a delightful issue, with Helen Donath charming and sensitive in the name part. Dallapozza has a light heady tenor, at times stressed by the weight of the part of Goethe, but rising above all to the great Tauber number, *O Mädchen, mein Mädchen!*, based (like other numbers) on a Goethe poem, *Mailied*. Heinz Wallberg is a lively and persuasive director, and the recording has the bloom one associates with German EMI (Electrola).

Der Graf von Luxemburg (abridged).
(M) **(*) Tel. AF 6.23067. Gueden, Kmentt, Pütz, Hoppe, Ch. and O.

No conductor is named here, but the direction is admirably vivacious, and with a tuneful score and Hilde Gueden and Waldemar Kmentt in excellent form the music is projected admirably. Kmentt's *Warst du's lachendes Glück* is a highlight. The recording is vivid; the presentation, in pot-pourri style, is effective enough.

The Merry Widow (complete).
** HMV SLS/*TC-SLS* 5202 (2) [Ang. S 3630]. Moser, Prey, Kusche, Donath, Jerusalem, Bav. R. Ch., Mun. RO, Wallberg.
*(*) DG 2725/*3374* 102 (2) [2707 070/ *3370 003*]. Harwood, Stratas, Kollo, Hollweg, Keleman, Grobe, German Op. Ch., Berlin PO, Karajan.

With the two principals (Edda Moser as Hanna Glawari, Hermann Prey as Danilo) both seriously lacking in charm, the Wallberg version is hardly a serious competitor, though the direction is idiomatic, the recording very good and the contributions of the second pair of lovers, Helen Donath as Valencienne and Siegfried Jerusalem as Camille, are outstanding.

'Brahms's *Requiem* performed to the tunes of Lehár' was how one wit described the Karajan version, with its carefully measured tempi and absence of sparkle. Though Harwood is an appealing Widow, she seems colourless beside Schwarzkopf. The recording has religious reverberation, and the tape transfer is even less well-defined than the discs.

Still recommended: The magical HMV set conducted by Matačić – one of Walter Legge's masterpieces as a recording manager – with Schwarzkopf, Gedda and Waechter, is unsurpassable, beautifully sung, and creating a sense of theatre that is almost without rival in gramophone literature (HMV SLS 823 (2) [Ang. S 3630]).

The Merry Widow (in an English version by Bonynge): highlights.
** Decca SET/*KCET* 629 [Lon. 1172/ *5*-]. Sutherland, Krenn, Resnik, Ewer, Nat. PO, Bonynge.

Although not everyone will take to Sutherland's Widow, this is generally an attractive English version. The exuberantly breezy overture (arranged by Douglas Gamley) sets the mood of the proceedings, and the slightly brash recording (the sheen on the strings sounding artificially bright) is determinedly effervescent. The chorus sings with great zest and the ensembles are infectious. The whole of the closing part of the disc – the finale of Act 2; Njegus's aria (nicely done by Graeme Ewer); the introduction of the girls from Maxims and the famous Waltz duet – is certainly vivacious; the Parisian atmosphere is a trifle overdone, but enjoyably so. Earlier Sutherland's *Vilja* loses out on charm because of her wide vibrato, but the Waltz duet with Krenn is engaging. There is little difference between disc and tape.

The Merry Widow (abridged, in an English version by Hassall).

(B) **(*) CfP CFP/*TC-CFP* 40276. Wilson, Blanc, Hay, Hillman, McCue, Sandison, Scottish Op. Ch., Scottish PO, Gibson.

Gibson is at his freshest and most inspired in this magic operetta. The 1977 recording is warm and full, and the selection of items is admirable, with several passages included which have often been missed in 'complete' recordings, the duet *Zauber der Häuslichkeit* and the Act 3 *Cakewalk*. Much of the singing is not distinguished, but it is the teamwork which makes this a sparkling entertainment, and at the price it can be warmly recommended. The cassette version is rather less clean in focus than the LP, but the solo voices are clear and there is no lack of bloom on the sound.

Der Zarewitsch (abridged).

(M) ** Tel. AF 6.21273. Di Stefano, Koller, Hanak, Holecek, Cossack and Operetta Ch., V. Operetta O., Scherzer.

Opening atmospherically with the chorus, and later introducing an effective version of the *Volga boat song* and balalaika effects, *Der Zarewitsch* establishes its locale in a kind of Ruritanian Russia. The score is lyrically pleasing, and Giuseppe di Stefano makes the most of his *Wolgalied* and *Kosende Wellen*. The rest of the cast are more than adequate, and the direction is lively and sympathetic.

'The world of Lehár': (i) *Giuditta: Meine Lippen, sie küssen.* (i; ii) *Der Graf von Luxemburg: Sind sie von sinnen . . . Lieber Freund . . .* Waltz: *Bist du's lachendes Glück.* (iii; iv) *Das Land des Lächelns: Dein ist mein ganzes Herz; Wer hat die Liebe uns ins Herz gesenkt.* (i; v) *Die lustige Witwe: Dance; Vilja; Waltz: Lippen Schweigen;* Finale: *Ja, das Studium der Weiber ist schwer.* (iv) *Paganini: Gern hab' ich die Frau'n geküsst.* (iii) *Schön ist die Welt: Ich bin verliebt.* (i; ii) *Der Zarewitsch: Wolgalied: Allein wieder allein! Kosende Wellen;* Finale. (i) *Zigeunerliebe: Hör ich Cymbalklänge.*

(M) *** Decca SPA/*KCSP* 517. (i–iv) V. Volksoper Ch. and O., various conductors; (i) Gueden; (ii) Kmentt; (iii) Holm; (iv) Krenn; (v) Grunden, V. State Op. Ch. and O., Stolz.

An excellent anthology, the best collection of Lehár's music on a single disc or tape. The compiler has drawn heavily on a stylish operetta duet recital of Renate Holm and Werner Krenn (his opening *Dein ist mein ganzes Herz* is splendid) and also on Hilde Gueden's vintage recordings from the late fifties and early sixties. Highlights include the delicious *Ich bin verliebt* (Renate Holm) from *Schön ist die Welt* and Hilde Gueden's enchanting waltz song from *Giuditta, Meine Lippen, sie küssen so heiss*. The excerpt from *Der Zarewitsch* has a splendidly atmospheric gipsy accompaniment. On side two there are some lively items from Decca's 1958 *Merry Widow*. The recordings come up surprisingly well, and the tape transfers are generally vivid.

Leigh, Walter (1905–42)

Agincourt overture.
*** Lyr. SRCS 95. New Philh. O., Braithwaite – *Concert (Overtures)*.***

Harpsichord concertino.
(M) *** HMV Green. ESD/TC-ESD 7101. Dilkes, E. Sinfonia – *Concert*.***

The overture forms part of an ingenious Lyrita collection using a variety of orchestras and conductors. It is well worth investigating, as is the engaging neoclassical *Harpsichord concertino*, which Neville Dilkes directs from the keyboard. Both recordings are first-class.

Le Jeune, Claude (1528–1600)

Mass in D.
(M) ** HM HMU 251. Deller Cons. – TITELOUZE: *Veni creator*.**

Claude le Jeune is best known for his chansons, and his only *Mass* was published posthumously. It was written for the Chapel of Henri IV, so that there can be little historical evidence to justify its performance by single voices. Much of the music is expressive, and there is a serenity, too, that is undeniably rewarding. The performance, given the above caveat, is accomplished enough, though reverberation is sometimes cut short. Otherwise this is a technically satisfactory record.

Leoncavallo, Ruggiero (1858–1919)

I Pagliacci (complete).
(*) HMV SLS/*TC-SLS* 5187 (3) [Ang. SZX 3895]. Scotto, Carreras, Nurmela, Amb. Op. Ch., Philh. O., Muti – MASCAGNI: *Cavalleria Rusticana*.(*)
Decca D 83 D 3/*K 83 K 32* (3) [Lon. D 13125]. Freni, Pavarotti, Wixell, L. Voices, Finchley Children's Group, Nat. PO, Patané – MASCAGNI: *Cavalleria Rusticana*.(*)

Under Muti's urgent direction both *Cav.* and *Pag.* represent the music of violence. In both he has sought to use the original text, which in *Pag.* is often surprisingly different, with many top notes eliminated and Tonio instead of Canio delivering (singing, not speaking) the final *La commedia è finita*. Muti's approach represents the opposite of Karajan's smoothness, and the coarse rendering of the *Prologue* in *Pag.* by the rich-toned Kari Nurmela is disappointing. Scotto's Nedda goes raw above the stave (more so than her Santuzza on the RCA *Cav.*), but the edge is in keeping with Muti's approach with its generally brisk speeds. Carreras seems happier here than in *Cav.*, but it is the conductor and the fresh look he brings which will prompt a first choice here. The sound is extremely vivid on disc and tape alike.

Pavarotti links the latest Decca recordings of *Cav.* and *Pag.*, both of them beefy performances, very well recorded. In *Pag.*, Pavarotti gives a committed performance, though in both operas he seems reluctant to sing anything but loud. Voices are recorded rather close, which exaggerates this fault, and Freni is not helped by the balance either, not as sweet as she usually is. Wixell as Tonio is somewhat out of character, giving a Lieder-style performance, full of detail.

The cassettes match the discs closely in vividness and clarity.

I Pagliacci: highlights.
** Decca SXL/*KSXC* 6986 (from above set cond. Patané) – MASCAGNI: *Cavalleria Rusticana* highlights.**(*)

A coupling of excerpts from *Cav.* and *Pag.* that is more generous than usual is welcome enough, even if the performances are flawed. The recording is as vivid as on the original set, and there is a brilliant cassette equivalent; but the most attractive pairing of highlights from these two operas is Karajan's La Scala issue centred around Bergonzi, with Joan Carlyle in *Pag.* and Fiorenza Cossotto in *Cav.*, which also has the advantage of economy (DG Priv. 2535/*3335* 199).

Liadov, Anatol (1855–1914)

Eight Russian folksongs, Op. 58.
(M) *** RCA Gold GL/*GK* 42960. LSO, Previn – TCHAIKOVSKY: *Symphony No. 2.****

Liadov is content to provide simple orchestral settings for these characteristic Russian melodies, piquant or charming to suit the character of each. The result is enchanting. Previn plays the music with obvious affection and warmth and is very well recorded. The cassette, however, is unrefined and is not recommended.

Liapunov, Sergei
(1859–1924)

Rhapsody on Ukrainian themes for piano and orchestra, Op. 28.

(M) * Turn. TVS 34645 [id.]. Ponti, Westphalian SO, Landau – BALAKIREV: *Piano concerto No. 2.**

Liapunov is probably best known for his set of *Transcendental studies,* but he composed a good deal of other music as well, including two symphonies, two piano concertos, a violin concerto and some tone poems. He also completed the finale of the Balakirev concerto with which this *Rhapsody* is coupled. The work dates from 1908 and is dedicated to no less an artist than Busoni. The score has much charm; but, though Michael Ponti copes manfully, the orchestral playing is lacklustre and the recording poor. It would be good to welcome this enterprising and interesting coupling, but it can be recommended, if at all, only as a stopgap.

Liszt, Franz (1811–86)

Ce qu'on entend sur la montagne (Bergsymphonie). (i) *Dante symphony. Festklänge; Hunnenschlacht; Die Ideale; Orpheus; Les Préludes; Tasso; Von der Wiege bis zum Grabe* (symphonic poems).
*** HMV SLS 5235 (4). Leipzig GO, Masur, with (i) Leipzig Thomanerchor.

(i) *A Faust Symphony. 2 Episodes from Lenau's Faust (Mephisto waltz No. 1; Der nächtliche Zug); Hamlet; Héroïde funèbre; Hungaria; Mazeppa; Mephisto waltz No. 2; Prometheus.*
*** HMV SLS 5236 (4). Leipzig GO, Masur, with (i) Leipzig R. Ch. Male Voices.

Apart from *Les Préludes,* the splendid *Mazeppa,* and to a lesser extent *Tasso,* Liszt's symphonic poems enjoy a fairly limited popularity if successive record catalogues are anything to go by, and even Liszt's most fervent champions are sparing in their praises of all but a handful of them. Some of the earlier pieces, such as *Ce qu'on entend sur la montagne* and *Festklänge*, suffer not only from formal weakness but also from a lack of interesting melodic invention. But elsewhere, in *Hamlet*, the *Héroïde funèbre* and *Prometheus* for example, there is a lot to admire. *Hamlet* has great dramatic intensity, particularly in the hands of Kurt Masur, who is a vivid and sympathetic exponent throughout. *Die nächtliche Zug*, the first of the *Two Episodes from Lenau's Faust*, strikes the listener immediately with its intent, brooding atmosphere. These performances – and, whatever one may think of it, this music – cast a strong spell, and with rare exceptions Masur proves as persuasive an advocate as any on record. It is the rich sonority of the lower strings, the dark, perfectly blended woodwind tone and the fine internal balance of the Leipzig Gewandhaus Orchestra that hold the listener throughout – for in the weaker pieces Liszt needs all the help the interpreters can give him.

Only in *Orpheus* does Masur let us down. He breezes through it at record speed and misses the endearing gentleness that Beecham brought to it in the early 1960s. In the two symphonies, which are allotted one to a box, Masur is impressive, though even in the *Gretchen* movement of the *Faust symphony* he moves things on, albeit not unacceptably, and there is no want of either delicacy or ardour. Masur's *Faust symphony* can certainly hold its own against all comers, and the *Dante symphony* has no current rival. The recordings are well balanced and refined, perhaps not as transparent as the finest 1982 Decca or Philips recordings, but still very good indeed. Liszt's influence was enormous in his lifetime – on Wagner, the Russians, the French – and listening to these records one realizes that the personality has lost none of its magnetism even in a field that he was slow to conquer.

Piano concertos Nos. 1–2; Fantasia on themes from Beethoven's The Ruins of Athens, G.122; Grande fantaisie symphonique on themes from Berlioz's Lélio, G.120; Malédiction, G.121; Polonaise brillante on Weber's Polacca brillante in E, G.367; Totentanz, G.126; Wanderer fantasia on Schubert's Wanderer fantasy, G.366.
***HMV SLS 5207 (3). Béroff, Leipzig GO, Masur.

Michel Béroff has won acclaim for his superb technique and his refined poetic sense, and this box, which collects Liszt's output for piano and orchestra, shows him to be a Lisztian of flair. Although the concertos have been recorded in abundance, other works here, such as the *Grande fantaisie* on themes from *Lélio* and the *Malédiction*, are rarities. Brendel's brilliant account of the latter is now showing its age, and the only current alternative versions of the *Polonaise brillante* on a theme of Weber and the *Fantasia on themes from The Ruins of Athens* are on Jerome Rose's Turnabout import (see below). Béroff's account of the two concertos can hold its own with most of the competition: here there is nothing routine or slapdash, as can sometimes emerge from him in a live performance. Indeed the flair and imagination that distinguish his Debussy and Prokofiev are in ample evidence, along with his remarkable technical prowess. These are exhilarating performances and are given the extra attraction of fine orchestral playing and vivid recording quality.

Piano concertos Nos. 1 in E flat, G.124; 2 in A, G.125.
*** Ph. 9500 780/*7300 854* [id.]. Arrau, LSO, Colin Davis.

(M) *** Ph. Seq. 6527/*7311* 048. Janis, Moscow PO, Kondrashin, or Moscow RO, Rozhdestvensky.

(M) *** Decca VIV/*KVIC* 11. Ivan Davis, RPO, Downes.

Claudio Arrau made a stunning record of the *E flat Concerto* with Ormandy and the Philadelphia Orchestra in the 1950s, and this new account, made in his mid-seventies, is scarcely less fine. Even though some of the youthful abandon is tamed, Arrau's virtuosity is transcendental. There is a greater breadth in No. 1 here than in the earlier version, and there are many thoughtful touches throughout. This artist's Indian summer shows no loss of fire, and he brings plenty of panache to the *A major Concerto*. This does not displace Brendel (Ph. 6500 374) or Berman (DG 2530/*3300* 770) among the top recommendations but takes its place beside them. First-class sound, although the cassette transfer lacks something in upper range (the triangle is almost inaudible in its famous solo passage in No. 1).

The reissue of Byron Janis's performances on Philips' mid-priced Sequenza label is most welcome, and while the versions by Brendel, Berman and Arrau are not overshadowed, this is a distinguished coupling. The partnership between the soloist and both his conductors is unusually close. In the slow movement of No. 1 Janis offers most poetic playing, and the scherzo is deliciously light, while the clipped martial rhythms of the finale are almost over-characterized. The reflective opening of the *Second Concerto* is another superb moment, and Rozhdestvensky's contribution throughout this concerto has an appealing lyrical feeling. The finale, as in No. 1, has an unashamed touch of melodrama about it and there is an exhilarating dash in the pianism at the closing pages. As so often with Philips, the tape does not always match the LP in immediacy, and pianissimo detail registers less well. This is more noticeable in the *First Concerto*,

which has a slightly lower transfer level.

Ivan Davis shows a genuine feeling for both concertos, revealing their poetry as well as their flamboyance. He is admirably accompanied by the RPO under Edward Downes, and the recording is, in its way, in the demonstration class. Originally made in Decca's Phase Four, it has vivid spotlighting of orchestral soloists, not quite natural but effective enough when the piano too is forwardly balanced and boldly recorded. There is little to choose between disc and cassette, and this reissue is excellent value.

Fantasia on themes from Beethoven's The Ruins of Athens, G.122; Wanderer fantasia on Schubert's Wanderer fantasy, G.366; Polonaise brillante on Weber's Polacca brillante in E, G.367.

(M) **(*) Turn. TVS 34708 [id.]. Rose, Philh. Hungarica, Kapp.

Jerome Rose plays with fine dash and is especially good in the *Beethoven Fantasia*. The accompaniments under Richard Kapp are commendably alert, and the Turnabout recording is bold and full, better-balanced than is usual on this label. An enjoyable and useful collection that fills an important gap in the catalogue for those not wanting to invest in Béroff's HMV box.

A Faust symphony, G.108.

*** DG 2707 100/*3370* 022 (2). Riegel, Tanglewood Festival Ch., Boston SO, Bernstein – BOITO: *Mefistofele: Prologue.***

Bernstein recorded this symphony in the mid-1960s, but this newer version, made in Boston, is both more sensitive and more brilliant. It is the first modern recording to offer a serious challenge to Beecham's classic account made in the late 1950s (HMV SXDW 3022 [Ang. Ser. S 6017]). The *Gretchen* movement is most beautifully played here, with finely delineated detail and refined texture. The tenor soloist in the finale is excellent, and the Boston orchestra produce some exciting and atmospheric playing. The recording too is extremely fine, and it has transferred well to cassette.

Symphonic poems: *Festklänge, G.101; Les Préludes, G.97; Prometheus, G.99.*
*** Decca SXL/*KSXC* 6863 [Lon. 7084/5-]. LPO, Solti.

Solti is just the conductor for Liszt's symphonic poems: he finds the right kind of intensity so that *Les Préludes* is exciting, without vulgarity, yet does not lose its flamboyant character. The closing pages are superbly rousing, but are not without dignity. There is plenty of drama in *Prometheus* and some beautifully refined orchestral playing in *Festklänge*, yet the tension is strongly held. The recording has superb life and colour, and the cassette transfer is one of Decca's best.

Hungarian rhapsodies for orchestra Nos. 1–6, G.359.
(M) *** Ph. Fest. 6570/*7310* 140. LSO, Dorati.

Hungarian rhapsodies Nos. 2–3 and 5; Mephisto waltz No. 1, G.110/2.
(M) **(*) HMV Green. ESD/*TC-ESD* 7058 [Ang. S/*4XS* 37278]. LPO, Boskovsky.

Hungarian rhapsodies Nos. (i) 2 and (ii) 4, G.359. (iii) Les Préludes, G.97.
(M) *** DG Priv. 2335/*3335* 628. (i) Bamberg SO, Richard Kraus; (ii) Berlin PO, Karajan; (iii) Berlin RSO, Fricsay – BRAHMS: *Hungarian dances.***(*)

Dorati's is undoubtedly the finest set of orchestral *Hungarian rhapsodies*. He brings out the gipsy flavour, and with lively playing from the LSO there is both polish and sparkle, but the music does not become urbane. The use of the cimbalom within the orchestra brings an authentic extra colouring. The recording has a Mercury source and is characteristically vivid if a little thin on top. The tape transfer is first-class.

Richard Kraus's account of Liszt's most famous *Hungarian rhapsody* has both sparkle and panache, while Karajan shows characteristic flair in No. 4, with its quixotic changes of mood and colour. But what makes the DG collection doubly attractive is the inclusion of Fricsay's superb *Les Préludes*. Fricsay had just the temperament for this fine piece, and his performance has enormous conviction and an extremely vivid recording. Indeed the sound throughout is excellent on disc and cassette alike.

Boskovsky's second collection is more successful than his first (also on Greensleeve). The *Second Hungarian rhapsody* is sumptuously done, and the *Third*, with its effective use of the cimbalom, has plenty of colour. The gipsy element too is quite well managed, and with excellent orchestral playing the *Mephisto waltz* (using the less often heard alternative version, with its more poetic ending) is suitably atmospheric. The rich recording has on the whole been well transferred to cassette, with only slight loss of focus.

Symphonic poems: *Orpheus, G.98; Les Préludes, G.97; Tasso, lamento e trionfo, G.96.*
(M) ** Ph. Fest. 6570/*7310* 056. LPO, Haitink.

The music of *Les Préludes* and *Tasso* creates its scenic backgrounds and unfolds its narrative with bold strokes of the brush. To realize the composer's intentions a full-blooded, committed approach from the conductor and players needs to be married to spectacular recording. Philips have certainly put more life into the sound of this Festivo reissue, but Haitink is most successful with the music's gentler poetic moments, less so with the melodrama. *Orpheus* is the finest performance here; the others will appeal most to those who dislike an extrovert approach to Liszt's orchestral music.

Les Préludes (see also above).
(M) *** HMV SXLP/*TC-SXLP* 30450 [Ang. S 35613]. Philh. O., Karajan – BERLIOZ: *Carnaval romain*; RESPIGHI: *Pines.****
Les Préludes; Tasso, lamento e trionfo.
(M) *** HMV SXLP/*TC-SXLP* 30447. Philh. O., Silvestri – RIMSKY-KOR-SAKOV: *May Night overture.****

Karajan's 1958 recording of *Les Préludes* found much favour in its day, as well it should. It still sounds thrilling even now, particularly given the superb quality of the EMI transfer and the fine musical judgement of the original engineers. This is the equal of any modern version you can name. The cassette transfer too is full-bodied and clear and satisfyingly balanced.

Silvestri's version, originally issued in the same year as Karajan's, is a highly distinguished account, with fine playing from the Philharmonia. The performance itself generates rather less adrenalin than Karajan's but has a balancing breadth. *Tasso* is also very well played, and the Rimsky-Korsakov coupling is attractive too. The cassette transfer is admirable, strikingly clear and clean.

Totentanz, G.126.
*** EMI 4E 063 32484. Solyom, Mun. PO, Westerberg – STENHAMMAR: *Piano concerto No. 2.****

A superb account of the *Totentanz* from Janos Solyom, whose brilliance and virtuosity are second to none. He is well supported by Westerberg and the Munich Philharmonic Orchestra and excellently recorded. For Liszt collectors, however, Brendel will remain first choice, since he offers superb performances of

the two concertos as well as a dazzling *Totentanz*. Solyom's record has a Stenhammar rarity.

Piano music

Années de pèlerinage: Book 1, 1st year: Switzerland, G.160; Book 2, 2nd year: Italy, G.161; Supplement: Venezia e Napoli, G.162; Book 3, 3rd year: Italy, G.163 (complete).
*** DG 2709 076 (3) [id.]. Berman.

Lazar Berman's is the only complete version of the *Années de pèlerinage*, and a very fine one it is. Berman's technique is fabulous, more than equal to the demands made by these twenty-six pieces. Even readers who do not normally respond to Berman's art should sample this set, for the playing is free from empty display and virtuoso flamboyance, even though its brilliance is never in question. Indeed Berman brings searching qualities to this music: much of the time he is inward-looking and thoughtful in pieces like *Angelus* and *Sunt lachrymae rerum*. In the slower pieces tension and concentration sometimes sag a little – but perhaps that is an illusion caused by listening to a number of these pieces at one sitting. The recording is excellent and does full justice to Berman's range of colour and dynamics.

Années de pèlerinage, 2nd year, G.616; 3 Sonetti del Petrarca (Nos. 47, 104, 125); Consolations Nos. 1–5, G.172; Liebesträume Nos. 1–3, G.541.
*** DG 2531/*3301* 318 [id.]. Barenboim.

The Liszt *Consolations* are not otherwise available at present and Barenboim proves an ideal advocate. His playing has an unaffected simplicity that is impressive, and throughout this compilation there is a welcome understatement and naturalness. The quality of the recorded sound is excellent and does full justice to the lyricism of these interpretations. The cassette matches the disc closely, though the transfer level is not especially high.

Concert paraphrases of Schubert Lieder: *Der Doppelgänger, G.560; Erlkönig, G.558/4; Die Forelle, G.563/6; Der Lindenbaum, G.561/7; Des Mädchens Klage, G.563/2; Morgenständchen, G.558/9; Der Müller und der Bach, G.565/2; Rastlose Liebe, G.558/10; Das Sterbeglöcklein, G.563/3; Die Taubenpost, G.560/13.*
**(*) Mer. E 77019. Bingham.

It is good to have John Bingham's fresh and distinctive talents recognized on record, though this first major recording from him does not quite convey the full intensity one witnesses in recital. This is an admirable choice from the fifty-eight transcriptions that Liszt made of Schubert songs, and Bingham is most persuasive in producing singing tone as well as pianistic sparkle. The piano tone is good if a little rough at climaxes.

3 Concert studies, G.144; 2 Concert studies, G.145; Concert paraphrase: *Réminiscences de Don Juan* (Mozart), *G.418.*
*** O-L DSLO, 41 [id.]. Bolet.

Jorge Bolet is still seriously underrepresented in the catalogues, and this Liszt offering is among his finest records yet, particularly valuable for the *Don Giovanni* paraphrase, a piece which itself is neglected on record. Bolet may convey even keener electricity in the concert hall, but here the combination of virtuoso precision and seeming spontaneity is most compelling. The recording captures his wide range of timbre very well.

Harmonies poétiques et religieuses, G.173; excerpts (*3, Bénédiction de Dieu dans la solitude; 4, Pensées des morts);* Prelude and fugue on the name BACH, G.260; Variations on Bach's 'Weinen, Klagen, Sorgen, Zagen', G.673.
*** Ph. 9500 286/7300 565 [id.]. Brendel.

The *Prelude and Fugue on the name BACH* and the *Variations on 'Weinen, Klagen, Sorgen, Zagen'* are better-known in their organ version but sound no less impressive on the piano, particularly when they are played so masterfully as by Brendel. This is a magnificent recital, and the recording is wide-ranging and realistic. The sound quality of the cassette yields little if anything to that of the disc, which is high praise indeed.

Hungarian rhapsodies, G.244, Nos. 2 in C sharp min.; 5 in E min. (Héroïde élégiaque); 9 in E flat (Carnival in Pest); 14 in F min.; 15 in A min. (Rákóczy march); 19 in D min.
(M) *** DG Priv. 2535/3335 420 [2530 441]. Szidon.

Roberto Szidon offers Liszt playing of the highest order, and recording quality to match. Szidon won acclaim some years ago with his début record (Prokofiev *Sixth Sonata,* Scriabin No. 4 and Rachmaninov No. 2), and his set of the complete *Hungarian rhapsodies* more than fulfilled the promise shown in his very first record. He has flair and panache, genuine keyboard command and, when required, great delicacy of tone. All six pieces here are of high musical quality, and the playing readily demonstrates Szidon's finely judged rubato, boldness of line, and sure sense of style. The recording is first-class on both disc and cassette.

Piano sonata in B min. G.178.
(M) **(*) Saga 5460. David Wilde – SCHUMANN: *Fantasia.***(*)

431

** Decca SXL/*KSXC* 6756 [Lon. 6989/5-]. Larrocha – SCHUMANN: *Fantasia.***

Piano sonata; Polonaise in E min., G.223; Réminiscences de Don Juan (Mozart), *G.418.*
(M) ** DG Priv. 2535/*3335* 270 [id.]. Vásáry.

David Wilde's account of the *Sonata* is impressive. He possesses technique in abundance and is completely inside this music. A dazzling performance that deserves a high place in any recommended list even though the quality of the recorded sound is not in the very first flight. There is a certain shallowness at times, particularly at the top end of the register, but given playing of such flair and the relatively modest price, this does not matter too much.

There is some formidable piano playing from Alicia de Larrocha here. She is recorded in a pleasing, open acoustic and there need be no reservation on the count of recording quality. Yet for all the many perceptive touches, her view of the *Sonata* is a little too idiosyncratic to take precedence over the finest available versions. Choice for cassette users is a little less wide but the excellence of the engineering of this Decca issue does not outbalance the claims of the less well-recorded alternatives.

Tamás Vásáry's record dates from the early 1960s and is perhaps wanting in dash and swagger. Yet for all that there is plenty of pianistic elegance to admire in the *Sonata* and the *Réminiscences.* The sound too has now been improved and gives satisfactory results. This is contained rather than flamboyant playing.

Weihnachtsbaum (Christmas Tree) suite, G.186.
** Chan. ABR/*ABT* 1006. Gillespie.

The *Christmas Tree suite* is a charming rarity which deserved a recording, and though the sound on this Chandos issue is disappointing, Rhondda Gillespie plays with obvious dedication.

Miscellaneous collections

Années de pèlerinage, 1st year, G.160: Au bord d'une source. Concert paraphrase of Schubert's Schwanengesang, G.560: Liebesbotschaft. Harmonies poétiques et religieuses, G.173: Funérailles. Hungarian rhapsodies Nos. 11 and 14, G.244, Die Loreley, G.531. Mephisto waltz No. 1, G.514.
** Ph. 9500 401 [id.]. Dichter.

Misha Dichter is an intelligent and sensitive pianist with a formidable technique well able to rise to the demands this music makes. One scarcely needs new versions of any of these pieces, but piano sound of the quality that the Philips engineers invariably achieve is always assured of a welcome. At the same time Misha Dichter does not achieve quite the high voltage and dash of the greatest Liszt players (put his *Mephisto waltz No. 1* alongside the Cziffra disc made in the mid-1950s, and there is no question of the greater excitement generated by the latter). This is highly musical, finely shaped and well phrased but never really distinctive.

Années de pèlerinage, 3rd year, G.163: Nos. 2, Aux cyprès de la Villa d'Este; 4, Jeux d'eau à la Villa d'Este; 5, Sunt lachrymae rerum. Csárdás macabre, G.224. Mosonyi's Funeral Procession, G.194. Schlaflos, Frage, und Antwort, G.203. Unstern, G.208. Valse oubliée No. 1, G.215. Schlummerlied.
*** Ph. 9500 775/*7300 863* [id.]. Brendel.

Brendel's reputation as a Lisztian dates back to the late 1950s and early 1960s. This anthology is among the very finest Liszt records he has ever made, and it also has the benefit of extraordinarily lifelike sound. There is something stark and bitter about some of these late pieces, and Brendel's playing is distinguished by a concentration and subtlety of nuance that are wholly convincing. This is a most distinguished issue, and an obligatory acquisition for all lovers of Liszt. The cassette has fractionally less range at the top but is still extraordinarily fine. If the richly resonant bass is cut back just a little, the balance is first-class.

Années de pèlerinage, 3rd year, G.163: Aux cyprès de la Villa d'Este. Hamlet, G.104 (arr. Nyiregyhazi). Harmonies poétiques et religieuses, G.173: Miserere after Palestrina. Hungarian rhapsody No. 3, G.244. March of the Three Holy Kings from 'Christus'; Mosonyi's Funeral Procession, G.194. Nuages gris, G.199. Weihnachtsbaum, G.186; Nos. 9, Abendglocken; 12, Pölnisch.
*(*) CBS 79219 (2) [Col. M2 34598]. Nyiregyhazi.

As a child prodigy Erwin Nyiregyhazi vied with young Claudio Arrau when they were both studying in Berlin. Later in America his career ran into trouble. He was 'rediscovered' in the seventies and brought back into the limelight, but from this sad, wilful and splashy collection one wonders why. There is evidence of great personality, but the technique has faded and the set can only be regarded as a curiosity – not just for the oddity of the playing but for the absurd superlatives that various commentators were persuaded to write. The sound is indifferent.

Consolation No. 3, G.172/2; Mephisto waltz No. 1, G.514.
*** RCA RL/RK 13433 [ARL 1/ARK 1 3433]. Horowitz – RACHMANINOV: *Barcarolle* etc.; SCHUMANN: *Humoreske.****

Even in his advanced years Horowitz remains very much a law unto himself. His *Mephisto waltz* quite dazzles the listener, silencing criticism, and throughout both the *Consolation* and the *Mephisto* one is sitting on the edge of the chair. The sound is a little hard but the ear rapidly adjusts. The cassette transfer is first-class, fully matching the disc.

Organ music

Fantasia and fugue on 'Ad nos, ad salutarem undam', G.259.
(*) HMV Dig. ASD/TC-ASD 3994 [Ang. DS 37748]. Parker-Smith (organ of St Francis de Sales, Philadelphia) – FRANCK: *Chorale No. 1* etc.(*)

Fantasia and fugue on 'Ad nos, ad salutarem undam'; Prelude and fugue on the name BACH, G.260; Variations on Bach's 'Weinen, Klagen, Sorgen, Zagen', G.673.
(M) *** ASV ACM 2008. Bate (Royal Albert Hall organ).

Jennifer Bate gives superb performances of these Liszt warhorses. The clarity and incisiveness of her playing go with a fine sense of line and structure; and even making no allowance for the Royal Albert Hall's acoustic problems the recording captures an admirable combination of definition and atmosphere.

Those who like wallowing in organ sound rather than listening to its details will enjoy Jane Parker-Smith's performance. The digital recording has wide range, but (on both disc and tape) it remains mushy because of the reverberant acoustic. The performance is characteristically flamboyant – as is the portrait of the soloist on the sleeve.

VOCAL MUSIC

Lieder: *Der Alpenjäger; Anfangs wollt ich fast verzagen; Angiolin dal*

biondo crin; Blume und Duft; Comment, disaient-ils: Die drei Zigeuner; Du bist wie eine Blume; Der du von dem Himmel bist; Enfant, si j'étais roi; Ein Fichtenbaum steht einsam; Es muss ein Wunderbares sein; Es rauschen die Winde; Der Fischerknabe; Gastibelza; Gestorben war ich; Der Hirt; Hohe Liebe; Ich möchte hingehn; Ihr Glocken von Marling; Im Rhein, im schönen Strome; In Liebeslust; J'ai perdu ma force; Kling leise, mein Lied; Lasst mich ruhen; Die Lorelei; Morgens steh' ich auf und frage; Oh! Quand je dors; O Lieb, so lang; Petrarch sonnets Nos. 1-3; Schwebe, schwebe blaues Auge; S'il est un charmant gazon; Die stille Wasserrose; Des Tages laute Stimmen schweigen; La tombe et la rose; Der traurige Mönch; Über allen Gipfeln ist Ruh; Die Vätergruft; Vergiftet sind meine Lieder; Le vieux vagabond; Wer nie sein Brot; Wieder möcht' ich dir; Wie singt die Lerche schon.
*** DG 2740 254 (4). Fischer-Dieskau, Barenboim.

As in a number of other fields Liszt has been severely underappreciated as a song-composer. This collection of forty-three songs plus an accompanied declamation should do much to right the balance. Fischer-Dieskau, so far from making such an enormous project sound routine, actually seems to gather inspiration and intensity with the concentration; for example, the most famous of the songs, the *Petrarch sonnets*, are here even more inspired than in his previous performances. The sheer originality of thought and the ease of the lyricism – not least in *O Lieb*, which everyone knows as the famous piano solo, *Liebestraum No. 3* – are a regular delight, and Barenboim's accompaniments could hardly be more understanding, though Liszt presented

surprisingly few virtuoso challenges to the pianist. The recording is excellent.

Lieder: *Du bist wie eine Blume; Der du von dem Himmel bist; Die drei Zigeuner; Es war ein König in Thule; Die Fischerstochter; Freudvoll und leidvoll; Im Rhein, im schönen Strome; Die Lorelei; S'il est un charmant gazon; Über allen Gipfeln ist Ruh; Vätergruft; Das Veilchen.*
*** HMV ASD/TC-ASD 3906. Baker, Parsons.

Dame Janet Baker's selection of songs – starting with the most ambitious and one of the most beautiful, *Die Lorelei* – brings out the wide range of Liszt in this medium. His style is transformed when setting a French text, giving Parisian lightness in response to Hugo's words, while his setting of the *King of Thule* from Goethe's *Faust* leaps away from reflectiveness in illustrating the verses. The glowing warmth of Janet Baker's singing is well matched by Geoffrey Parsons's keenly sensitive accompaniment. The recording is first-rate, even fuller on cassette than on disc.

Lieder: *Die drei Zigeuner; Enfant, si j'étais roi; Es muss ein Wunderbares sein; Es war ein König in Thule; Kling leise, mein Lied; Die Lorelei; Ne brany menya moy drug; Vergiftet sind meine Lieder.*
*** Decca SXL 6964. Sass, Schiff – BARTÓK: *5 Songs.****

The vibrant Sylvia Sass and the inspirational Andras Schiff give dedicated performances of eight Liszt songs. The occasional rawness in Sass's voice seems apt in performances which bring out the Hungarian flavours, and which with often weighty underlining convey operatic overtones. Next to Dame Janet Baker in some of the songs Sass sounds extrovert, if splendidly full of temperament. The recording is outstandingly clear.

Via crucis.
** Abbey LPB 813. Connolly, Holmes, Wheeler, Leeds Parish Church Ch., Lindley; Jackson (organ) – ELGAR: *Ave verum* etc.**

A stately, unaffected performance from Leeds, wanting only in the bite and emotional fervour that Hungarian artists would and have brought to it. The sound is musically balanced, and readers wanting this interesting and underrated score need not hesitate.

Litolff, Henri (1818–91)

Concerto symphonique No. 4, Op. 102: Scherzo.
(M) *** Decca Jub. JB/*KJCB* 104. Curzon, LPO, Boult – GRIEG: *Concerto*; FRANCK: *Symphonic variations.***
(M) *** Decca Jub. JB/*KJBC* 29. Curzon (as above) – TCHAIKOVSKY: *Concerto No. 1.***
** CBS 76910/40-. Entremont, Nat. PO, Kamu – DOHNÁNYI: *Nursery variations*; R. STRAUSS: *Burleske.***

Curzon's performance is available either in its original combination with Franck and Grieg or coupled with his 1960 recording of the Tchaikovsky *B flat minor Concerto*. Curzon provides all the sparkle Litolff's infectious *Scherzo* requires, and this is a delightful makeweight, whichever coupling is chosen. The fine qualities of the original sound, freshness and clarity, remain equally impressive on both disc and cassette; there is no appreciable difference between the two.
On CBS the Litolff piece makes an attractive fill-up for two more substantial

works, though the forward balance of the piano prevents it from having quite the delicacy it needs.

Lloyd Webber, Andrew
(born 1948)

Variations.
**(*) MCA MCF/*TC-MCF* 2824. Julian Lloyd Webber, Airey, Argent, Hiseman, Mole, More, Thompson, composer.

This fascinating hybrid work inhabits the world of 'pop' music of the late seventies yet draws inspiration from the classical mainstream of variations on Paganini's ubiquitous theme, which has inspired so many diverse compositions over the past century and a half. Andrew Lloyd Webber's piece began life as a comparatively short twenty-minute work, composed with his brother's brilliant cello-playing very much in mind. It was then expanded to the format here recorded, lasting about half an hour, and has since been blown up to even greater proportions for a concert performance at the Royal Festival Hall, which received a very mixed press. The vulgarity of the ambience of its 'pop' sections will exasperate many listeners, yet its sheer vitality cannot be ignored and the lyrical variations, featuring the flute and solo cello, are genuinely memorable. The recording is good, if inflated; the cassette is acceptable but does not match the disc in range and transient sharpness.

Tell Me on Sunday (song cycle).
⊛ *** Polydor POLD/*POLDC* 5031. Webb, LPO, Rabinowitz.

This inspired song cycle by Andrew Lloyd Webber with splendid lyrics by Don Black chronicles a disastrous series of love affairs of an English girl living in

America. (The eventual plan of the creators is to provide a mirror scenario for an American in England and join both into a Coward-like stage piece.) The theme of the songs is both nostalgic and life-enhancing, for the heroine gradually comes to terms with her failures and it is she who makes the final break. The music itself is totally memorable. One thinks of the lovely curving contour of *It's not the end of the world*, the steamy *Sheldon Bloom*, the witty tunefulness of *Capped teeth and Caesar salad*, with its repeated pay-off line 'Have a nice day', the sparklingly happy *I'm very you* (the lyrics of these songs continually recalling Cole Porter) and above all the haunting title melody. The communication throughout is of a kind one despairs of finding in so much of today's 'serious' music, and the marvellous performance by Marti Webb (for whom the cycle was written) cannot be too highly praised. She is splendidly accompanied by Harry Rabinowitz and members of the LPO, and there is much fine solo playing. The recording is first-class on disc and tape alike, and the only small snag is that the opening number, *Take that look off your face*, was stridently heated up to secure its entry into the charts as a hit single.

Locatelli, Pietro (1695–1764)

12 Flute sonatas, Op. 2.
*** O-L DSLO 578/9. Preston (with McGegan in No. 12), Pleeth, Hogwood.

Apart from the concertos the twelve *Flute sonatas* are perhaps the most important collection among Locatelli's works. Published in 1732, they take a traditional line in their use of binary form, but the amiable freshness of the writing is most persuasive in fine authentic performances like these. No. 12 here includes the optional rendering of the *Largo* as a canon, with Nicholas McGegan taking the second flute part. The recording is excellent.

Lotti, Antonio (1667–1740)

Crucifixus.
*** Argo ZRG 850. St John's College Ch., Guest – A. BONONCINI: *Stabat Mater*; CALDARA: *Crucifixus.****

This short *Crucifixus*, which takes less than four minutes, may well have inspired the noble Caldara setting that completes the second side. The Lotti setting is less elaborate in texture than Caldara's, but it is hardly less noble or affecting. Performance and recording are excellent.

Luigini, Alexandre
(1850–1906)

Ballet Egyptien: suite, Op. 12.
(M) *** HMV Green. ESD/*TC-ESD* 7115. RPO, Fistoulari – MEYERBEER: *Les Patineurs* **; PONCHIELLI: *Dance of the Hours* **(*); TCHAIKOVSKY: *Nutcracker suite.* **

Luigini's amiable and tuneful *Ballet Egyptien* suite was for many years regarded as salon music, and there is some doggerel about 'Dame Ella Wheeler Wilcox' which neatly fits the famous opening rhythm. However, the music is highly engaging especially when played as stylishly as it is here under that master conductor of ballet Anatole Fistoulari. The recording is lively, a little dry: the cassette is slightly softer-grained than the disc and preferable.

Lully, Jean-Baptiste
(1632–87)

Le Bourgeois Gentilhomme (incidental music; complete).
(M) *** HM HM 20320/1. Nimsgern, Jungmann, Schortemeier, Jacobs, Tölz Ch., La Petite Bande, Leonhardt.

Entertainment rather than musical value: in itself Lully's score offers no great musical rewards. The melodic invention is unmemorable and harmonies are neither original nor interesting; but if the music taken on its own is thin stuff, the effect of the entertainment as a whole is quite another matter. This performance puts Lully's music into the correct perspective of the stage, and with such sprightly and spirited performers as well as such good recording, these discs can hardly fail to give pleasure. The orchestral contribution under the direction of Gustav Leonhardt is distinguished by a splendid sense of the French style.

Lutoslawski, Witold
(born 1913)

(i) *Cello concerto. Concerto for orchestra; Jeux vénitiens; Livre; Mi-Parti; Musique funèbre; Postlude No. 1; Preludes and fugue for thirteen solo strings; Symphonic variations; Symphonies Nos. 1–2.* (ii) *5 Lieder for soprano and orchestra.* (iii) *Paroles tissées.* (iv) *3 Poèmes d'Henri Michaux.*
*** EMI 1C 165 03231/6. Polish Nat. RSO or Polish CO, composer with (i) Jablonski; (ii) Lukomska; (iii) Devos; (iv) Krakau Polish R. Ch., Michniewski.

Unbelievably Lutoslawski is a senior figure in contemporary music, fast approaching his seventieth birthday. This six-record set is a kind of 'retrospective', collecting most of his major orchestral pieces right from the early and wholly beguiling *Symphonic variations*, with their Szymanowskian palette and luminosity, to works like the *Second Symphony* (1966–7) and the *Preludes and fugue* (1972) which consolidate the new language he formed after his change of style in the mid-1950s. Lutoslawski has not been neglected on record, and individual performances of such works as the *Concerto for orchestra*, the *Paroles tissées* by its dedicatee, Peter Pears, the *Musique funèbre* and the *Cello concerto*, which Rostropovich recorded with the composer himself, have long been in circulation. Readers who have missed these but want to explore Lutoslawski's work in greater depth could not do better than to turn to this box. The performances and recordings are of a high standard, and show this imaginative composer's sound world to good advantage. Given so large a package, it would be idle to dwell on individual works at any length. Obviously this set is for collectors already committed to the cause, but others too will find many rewarding pieces to justify the considerable outlay.

Mi-Parti.
(M) *** Sup. 1410 2734. Prague RSO, Kasprzyk – BAIRD: *Elegeia*; PENDERECKI: *Anaklasis* etc.***

Mi-Parti is a relatively recent work, dating from 1976. To explain its title, the composer describes it as *composée de deux parties égales mais différentes* ('music composed of two equal but different parts'), though it must be said that the haunting atmosphere of the quieter lyrical section, with its luminous Szymanowskian colourings, exerts the stronger appeal. *Mi-Parti* is also available under the composer's own baton (see above), but this performance is thoroughly committed and will be welcomed by those who do not want to invest in the complete EMI box. The recording is perfectly acceptable and the interest of the coupling enhances the attractions of the disc.

Machaut, Guillaume de (*c.* 1300–1377)

Amours me fait desirer (ballade); *Dame se vous m'estes* (bagpipe solo); *De bon espoir – Puis que la douce* (motet); *De toutes flours* (ballade); *Douce dame jolies* (virelai); *Hareu! hareu! – Helas! ou sera pris confors* (motet); *Ma fin est mon commencement* (rondeau); *Mes esperie se combat* (ballade); *Phyton, le mervilleus serpent* (ballade); *Quant j'ay l'espart* (rondeau); *Quant je sui mis* (virelai); *Quant Theseus – Ne quier veoir* (double ballade); *Se je souspir* (virelai); *Trop plus est belle – Biauté paree – Je ne sui* (motet). (Also includes: LESCUREL: *A vous douce debonaire;* MOLLINS: *Amis tous dous;* ANON.: *La Septime;* ANDRIEU: *Armes amours; O flour des flours*.)
*** HMV ASD 3454. Early Music Cons. of L., Munrow.

This record, taken from the set '*Guillaume de Machaut and his age*', shows the work of David Munrow and his consort at its finest. Treasures here include cantatas with James Bowman and Charles Brett beautifully matched as soloists. Everything reveals the life and energy which Munrow brought to early music, even if in some items he arguably goes too far in pepping it up. Excellent recording.

Maderna, Bruno (1920–73)

Aura; Biogramma; Quadrivium.
*** DG 2531 272 [id.]. N. German RSO, Sinopoli.

This record usefully brings together three of Bruno Maderna's key works, among the last he wrote before his untimely death when still in his early fifties. Earliest is *Quadrivium*, for four orchestral groups, each with percussion, a work designed 'to entertain and to interest, not to shock the bourgeois'. In 1972 came *Aura* and *Biogramma*; the former won the composer (posthumously) the city of Bonn's Beethoven prize. Excellent recording for dedicated performances.

Mahler, Gustav (1860–1911)

Symphonies Nos. 1–9; Symphony No. 10: Adagio.
(M) ****(*) DG 2720 090 (14).** Bav. RSO, Kubelik.

Kubelik's is a fastidious and generally lyrical view of Mahler, most persuasive in the delightful performances of the least weighty symphonies, Nos. 1 and 4. In much of the rest these sensitive performances lack something in power and tension, tending to eliminate the neurotic in Mahler; but there is a fair case for preferring such an approach for relaxed listening at home. However, other sets more compellingly compass the full range of Mahler's symphonic achievement. The recordings (late sixties, early seventies vintage) are still very acceptable.

Symphony No. 1 in D (Titan).
*** DG 2530/3300 993 [id.]. Boston SO, Ozawa.

(M) *** Decca SPA/*KCSP* 521. RPO, Leinsdorf.

(M) **(*) Ph. Seq. 6527/*7311* 062 [6500 342/*7300 397*]. Concg. O., Haitink.

**(*) Lodia LOD/*LOC* 776. RPO, Paita.

**(*) HMV ASD/*TC-ASD* 3541 [Ang. S/*4XS* 37508]. LPO, Tennstedt.

(M) ** RCA VICS/*V̇K* 2027 [AGL 1 2941]. Boston SO, Leinsdorf.

Among newer versions of Mahler's *First*, Ozawa's must be considered the most successful. While Solti (Decca SX L/*KSXC* 6113 [Lon. 6401]), Kubelik (DG 2535/*3335* 172) and Horenstein (Uni. RHS/*UKC* 301 [None. 71240/Ad. *D 1019*]) hold their places at the top of the list, Ozawa's is certainly a refreshing contender, bringing out the youthful exhilaration of Mahler's inspiration. The first movement is fleet and resilient, lightly referring to the *Wayfaring Lad* theme, and the freshness as well as the polish of the Boston playing make for a result both electrifying and beautiful. In the second movement Ozawa is relaxed and lilting, while in the slow movement his shading of dynamic is wonderfully poised, and the double-bass soloist is outstandingly pure in tone. This is a performance which leans towards a consciously expressive style – maybe too much so in the great melody of the finale – but which still maintains its freshness. The recording gives warmth and clarity too; the high-level tape transfer is somewhat over-bright but responds to a treble cutback.

Taking sound quality as well as interpretation into account, Leinsdorf's Decca version might be considered best buy in the budget price-range. Although Leinsdorf may not be as poetic as Kubelik, his is a strong and colourful version, finely controlled and built with sustained concentration. The recording, with brass well forward, is one of the best made in Decca's Phase Four system. The transfer to tape is among the cleanest available of this symphony.

When Philips gathered together Haitink's recordings of Mahler symphonies, they took the trouble to make a new version of No. 1; and not only is it far more refined as a recording, the reading is if anything even more thoughtfully idiomatic than before in Haitink's unexaggerated Mahler style. Reissued now on Sequenza this makes a good medium-price recommendation for those finding Leinsdorf too extrovert. The cassette transfer is of good quality, with a brighter upper range than many Philips cassettes, if not as clean as the disc.

Carlos Paita's Latin view of Mahler is striking for its spontaneous qualities. This is a most enjoyable performance in spite of its extremes of tempo (particularly in the first movement, where there are some expressive lunges, whether in sudden rubatos or tenutos). The coda produces some scrambled ensemble, but otherwise the playing of the RPO is very good indeed, notably so in a beautiful account of the long-drawn melody in the finale. The recording is full and immediate and the transfer to tape highly sophisticated.

Tennstedt's manner in Mahler is somewhat severe, with textures fresh and neat and the style of phrasing generally less moulded than we have come to expect. This concentration on precision and directness means that when the conductor does indulge in rubato or speed-changes it does not sound quite consistent and comes as a surprise, as in the big string melody of the finale. Most Mahlerians will prefer a more felt performance than this, but for some it could be a good choice; its rich warm recording is first-class and has transferred surprisingly well to cassette, considering the resonance and the wide amplitude of the sound.

Leinsdorf's Boston version competes with his own later mid-priced RPO version, more idiomatic and better-recorded. The only advantage of the Boston version is that it includes the exposition repeat. The 1963 recording is none too clear.

Symphony No. 2 in C min. (*Resurrection*).
*** Decca Dig. D 229 D 2/*K 229 K 22* (2) [Lon. LDR 72006]. Buchanan, Zakai, Chicago Ch. and SO, Solti.
**(*) HMV Dig. SLS/*TCC-SLS* 5243 (2/*1*) [Ang. DS 3916]. Mathis, Soffel, LPO and Ch., Tennstedt.
** Symph. SYM/*CSYM* 7/8 [Peters PLE 064/5]. Ander, Hodgson, Amb. S., Symph. of L., Morris.

In digital sound of extraordinary power Solti re-recorded with the Chicago orchestra this symphony which with the LSO was one of the finest achievements of his earlier Mahler series. Differences of interpretation are on points of detail merely, with a lighter, more elegant rendering of the minuet-rhythms of the second movement. Though the digital recording is not always so well balanced as the earlier analogue (Isobel Buchanan and Mira Zakai are too close, for example) the weight of fortissimo in the final hymn, not to mention the Judgement Day brass are breathtaking. Interpretatively too the outer movements are as fiercely intense as before, but it is only in the concluding passage of the last movement that Solti really outshines the DG performance of Abbado with the same orchestra (DG 2707 094), a reading that is more affectionate in all five movements without ever sounding mannered, featuring playing just as brilliant. The Decca cassettes are outstanding, sparklingly clear, full and wide-ranging. However, for Tennstedt's set HMV fit the work conveniently on a single chrome tape, also of the highest quality. Tennstedt's is a dedicated performance, not quite as well played as the finest, conveying Mahlerian certainties in the light of day, underplaying neurotic tensions. Excellent recording.

Wyn Morris's version is uneven. In the first two movements the lack of bite in the ensemble (with some obvious exceptions, as in the brassy start of the recapitulation in the first movement) puts it well behind most rivals, but from the third movement onwards the whole concept is tauter, and though the choir is somewhat small to represent the Heavenly Host on Judgement Day, the dramatic urgency reflects Morris's Walter-like concept of Mahler. Well-matched soloists, but recording that is not ideally clear, with a limited top. The cassettes have a restricted dynamic range and are not recommended.

Reminder: Besides Abbado's splendid DG set, Klemperer's famous Philharmonia recording (HMV SLS 806 (2) [Ang. S 3634]) holds its place at the top of the list.

Symphony No. 3 in D min.
*** DG Dig. 2741/*3382* 010 (2) [id.]. Norman, V. State Op. Ch., V. Boys' Ch., VPO, Abbado.
*** HMV Dig. SLS/*TC-SLS* 5195 (2) [Ang. DS/*4Z 2S* 3902]. Wenkel, Southend Boys' Ch., ladies of LPO Ch., LPO, Tennstedt.
**(*) Decca D 117 D 2/*K 117 K 22* (2) [Lon. 2249]. Forrester, LAPO, Mehta.
(M) ** DG Priv. 2726 063 (2). M. Thomas, Bav. R. Women's Ch., Tölz Ch., Bav. RSO, Kubelik.

With sound of spectacular range, Abbado's performance is sharply defined and deeply dedicated. The range of expression, the often wild mixture of elements in this work, is conveyed with extraordinary intensity, not least in the fine contributions of Jessye Norman and the two choirs. This will be first choice for many, but Tennstedt too gives an eloquent reading, spaciousness underlined with measured tempi. With Ortrun Wenkel a fine soloist and the Southend boys adding lusty freshness to the bell music in the fifth movement, the HMV performance with its noble finale is very impressive, and it is splendidly recorded on both disc and cassette. On tape the quality only slips slightly at the choral entry, where the focus is marginally less sharp than on disc.

Mehta in his years in Los Angeles rarely recorded a performance so authentically Viennese as this Decca account of Mahler's *Third*. The crisp spring of the first movement leads to a fruitily Viennese view of the second and a carefree account of the third in which the *Wunderhorn* overtones come out vigorously. The singing is excellent, and the sharpness of focus of the reading as a whole is impressive, underlined by brilliant and rather too close recording. (On the strikingly vivid and clear tape version the post-horn solos seem much too near.) Yet the performance leaves a feeling of aggressiveness which detracts from the warmer side of the reading. This cannot compare with the finest available, for apart from Tennstedt there are outstanding versions by Levine (RCA RL 01757 [ARL 2 1757]), Horenstein (Uni. RHS 032/3 [None. 73203]) and Haitink (Ph. 6700 037).

There is a practical advantage in Kubelik's version: the first movement is squeezed without a break on to the first side, but this is bought at the expense of tempo. As in the later Mahler symphonies Kubelik is tempted to lighten the music with rushed speeds, and when there are such fine rival versions, his can only be commended to those who want his cycle complete.

Symphony No. 4 in G.

*** DG 2531/*3301* 205 [id.]. Mathis, Berlin PO, Karajan.
*** HMV ASD/*TC-ASD* 3783 [Ang. SZ 37576]). Ameling, Pittsburgh SO, Previn.
**(*) Decca Dig. SXDL/*KSXDC* 7501 [Lon. LDR 1004/*5-*]. Hendricks, Israel PO, Mehta.
**(*) Chan. Dig. ABRD/*ABTD* 1025. Margaret Marshall, SNO, Gibson.
** DG 2530/*3300* 966 [id.]. Von Stade, VPO, Abbado.
** Pearl SHE 552. Harper, Berlin RSO, Maazel.

With playing of incomparable refinement – no feeling of rusticity here – Karajan directs a performance of compelling poise and purity, not least in the slow movement, with its pulse very steady indeed, most remarkably at the very end. Karajan's view of the finale is gentle, wistful, almost ruminative, with the final stanzas very slow and legato, beautifully so when Edith Mathis's poised singing of the solo is finely matched. Not that this quest for refinement means in any way that joy has been lost in the performance, and with glowing sound it is a worthy companion to Karajan's other Mahler recordings. The cassette is of demonstration quality; the sound is full, natural and transparent and carries the widest dynamic range without a trace of congestion.

Previn recorded this symphony immediately before taking the Pittsburgh orchestra on a European tour, where they proved – as on this record – what an outstanding band they have become. Previn starts the first movement slower than usual, underlining the marked speed-changes very clearly, and the second movement is unusually light and gentle. But it is the spaciousness of the slow movement, at a very measured pace, that provides total fulfilment, followed by a light and playful account of the finale, with Ameling both sweet-toned and characterful. The recording has outstanding depth and range. The cassette transfer is vivid and full, and undoubtedly wide-ranging, but it has marginally less bloom than the LP.

Fresh and spontaneous-sounding, with an apt hint of rusticity, Mehta's reading with the Israel orchestra has excellent digital sound, cleanly defined if rather forward, so that individual players can occasionally be picked out in the string sections. The slow movement is unusually expansive, finely concentrated, and though Mehta occasionally indulges in an exaggerated espressivo, it is a performance which holds together in its amiability, not least in the finale, where Barbara Hendricks brings a hint of boyishness to the solo. The cassette transfer has very striking clarity, with luminous woodwind quality, although the sharpness of the detail tends to emphasize the slightly febrile timbre of the Israeli upper strings.

Gibson secures some delightfully fresh and stylish playing from his Scottish orchestra. His is a characteristically unmannered reading, slightly wanting in drama but not in tenderness. The finale, however, lacks some of the repose essential in this child-song, with Margaret Marshall sounding a little tense. The digital recording conveys the breadth and clarity of the sound impressively without lacking ambient bloom, and the cassette transfer is first-class.

After his superb performance of the Mahler *Second* with the Chicago orchestra, Abbado's record of the *Fourth* is disappointing, above all in the self-consciously expressive reading of the slow movement. There is much beauty of detail, but the Vienna Philharmonic has played and has been recorded better than this.

Maazel's version with the Berlin Radio Orchestra appeared first on Concert Hall, but on Pearl remains at full price. It is a clean-cut, forthright reading, brightly recorded and well played except that the slow movement, taken at a relatively fast tempo, sounds a little unsettled, failing to convey its emotional warmth. The song-finale too sounds unspontaneous, despite some beautiful singing from Heather Harper.

Symphony No. 5 in C sharp min.; Symphony No. 10 in F sharp: Adagio.
*** HMV SLS/*TC-SLS* 5169 (2) [Ang. SZ 3883]. LPO, Tennstedt.
**(*) RCA RL 02905 (2) [ARL 2/*ARK 2* 2905]. Phd. O., Levine.
** Decca SXL 6806/7/*KSXC2* 7048 [Lon. 2248/5-]. LAPO, Mehta.

Symphony No. 5; (i) *Lieder eines fahrenden Gesellen.*

** Symph. SYM/*CSYM* 3/4 [Peters PLE 100/1]. Symph. of L., Morris, (i) with Hermann.

Symphony No. 5; (i) *5 Rückert Lieder.*
**(*) DG 2707 128/*3370 040* (2) [id.]. Chicago SO, Abbado, (i) with Schwarz.

Rather like Barbirolli (see below) Tennstedt takes a ripe and measured view of this symphony, and though his account of the lovely *Adagietto* lacks the full tenderness of Barbirolli's (starting with an intrusive balance for the harp), this is an outstanding performance, thoughtful on the one hand, warm and expressive on the other. The first movement of the *Tenth Symphony* makes an acceptable fill-up; the recording, not quite as detailed as in Tennstedt's later digital Mahler recordings with the LPO, is warm and full to match the performance. The cassettes, however, are rather patchy, not as cleanly focused as the best EMI transfers. (The older Barbirolli set is preferable.)

Apart from a self-consciously slow account of the celebrated *Adagietto*, Levine directs a deeply perceptive and compelling performance, one which brings out the glories of the Philadelphia Orchestra. The other movements are beautifully paced, and the fourth side brings a wonderfully luminous account of the first movement of the *Tenth Symphony.*

Abbado's readings of Mahler with the Chicago orchestra are always refined but they are not consistently convincing. Unlike the superb account of No. 2, this version of No. 5 lacks something in spontaneity. The *Adagietto*, for example, is hardly at all slower than with Karajan (DG 2707 081) but the phrasing by comparison sounds self-conscious. Nonetheless it is a polished reading, with first-rate digital sound, which can be recommended to those collecting Abbado's Mahler series. The cassette transfer has an impressively wide range and matches the discs closely; it is a pity that on the first tape the opening trumpet solo is discoloured for a few bars, but this may not apply to later batches. The *Rückert Lieder* – beautifully sung by Hanna Schwarz – offer demonstration quality in both media.

Brilliant as the recording is of Mehta's Los Angeles version, and the playing too, it misses the natural warmth of expression that the same conductor found in his reading of No. 2 with the Vienna Philharmonic. Most impressive is the virtuoso scherzo, but in their different ways the opening *Funeral march* and the beautiful *Adagietto* both lack the inner quality which is essential if the faster movements are to be aptly framed. The brilliance of the finale is exaggerated by Mehta's very fast tempo, missing the *Wunderhorn* overtones of this most optimistic of Mahler's conclusions. The cassette transfer is cleanly focused, one of Decca's best.

Wyn Morris starts with a strikingly commanding account of the *Funeral march*, but then the second movement is a little cautious, lacking bite, with the ensemble less crisp than elsewhere. In the third movement Morris captures the Viennese lilt very winningly; he takes the *Adagietto* at a flowing tempo and the finale in a broad expansive sweep, not quite as sharply focused as it might be. It is a sympathetic reading, but not consistent in its success. Fair atmospheric recording. Roland Hermann's performance of the *Lieder eines fahrenden Gesellen* is fresh and intelligent, though his baritone is sometimes too gritty, and at times expressiveness is underlined too heavily. The cassette transfer has moments of congestion and is not recommended.

Still recommended: First choice remains with Barbirolli on HMV SLS/*TC-SLS* 785, one of the greatest, most warmly affecting performances he ever committed to record, and coupled with Dame Janet Baker's account of the *Rückert Lieder*, which achieves a similar degree of poetic intensity.

Symphony No. 6 in A min.
*** DG 2707 106/*3370 026* (2) [id.]. Berlin PO, Karajan.
**(*) DG 2707 117/*3370 031* (2) [id.]. Chicago SO, Abbado.

(i) *Symphony No. 6;* (ii) *Rückert Lieder Nos. 1 and 3–5.*
(M) **(*) DG Priv. 2726 065. (i) Bav. RSO, Kubelik; (ii) Fischer-Dieskau, Berlin PO, Boehm.

With superlative playing from the Berlin Philharmonic, Karajan's reading of the *Sixth* is a revelation, above all in the slow movement, which here becomes far more than a lyrical interlude. With this *Andante moderato* made to flower in poignant melancholy and with a simpler lyrical style than Karajan usually adopts, it emerges as one of the greatest of Mahler's slow movements. The whole balance of the symphony is altered. Though the outer movements firmly stamp this as the darkest of the Mahler symphonies, their sharp focus in Karajan's reading – with contrasts of light and shade heightened – makes them both compelling and refreshing. Significantly, in his care for tonal colouring Karajan brings out a number of overtones related to Wagner's *Ring*. The superb DG recording, with its wide dynamics, adds enormously to the impact. It is given a characteristically sophisticated cassette transfer, although on tape the bass response is a little dry.

Abbado's reading of No. 6 comes somewhere between his radiant account of No. 2 and the too contained rendering he gave of No. 4, all with the Chicago orchestra. Though the playing is superlative, Abbado cannot quite match the incandescence of Karajan on the same label in the first movement, starting at a lower level of tension; but in the third movement he matches Karajan in his measured view, and the finale is drawn tautly together. It is a performance to win admiration rather than move one deeply. The cassette transfer is sophisticated, although the modest transfer level brings some image recession at pianissimo levels, notably in the first movement. Each movement is complete on one side.

Kubelik in one of his most successful Mahler recordings directs a performance both refined and searching. Without ever coarsening the result he allows himself generous ritardandi between sections, though ultimately the fineness of control gives a hint of reserve. The 1969 sound remains very acceptable and the coupling – from five years earlier – restores to the catalogue a valuable Fischer-Dieskau performance, four of the five *Rückert Lieder*.

Symphony No. 7 in E min.
*** HMV Dig. SLS/*TC-SLS* 5238 (2). LPO, Tennstedt.

(i) *Symphony No. 7;* (ii) *Kindertotenlieder.*

(M) **(*) DG Priv. 2726 066 (2). (i) Bav. RSO, Kubelik; (ii) Fischer-Dieskau, Berlin PO, Boehm.

Tennstedt is predictably spacious in his approach to Mahler's least recorded symphony. The first movement's architectural span is given the kind of expansive structural unity that one associates with Klemperer; but the concentration of the LPO playing under Tennstedt brings more success here than Klemperer found in his disappointing New Philharmonia version. In the central movements Tennstedt is not so imaginative as Solti (Decca SET 518/9 [Lon. 2231]), who is more mercurial in the scherzo and enchantingly seductive in the second *Nachtmusik*. Haitink is straighter in this movement, with a faster tempo than Solti, but overall his is a finely wrought and intensely convincing reading, given one of Philips' finest Concertgebouw recordings (6700 036). Tennstedt is again at his most impressive in the

finale, showing his directness and strength and with vigorous support from the LPO players, who are on top form throughout the symphony. The HMV digital recording is characteristically clear in detail. The cassette equivalent is ideally laid out on a single chrome tape (presented in a box), with the first two movements on side one and the remainder on side two. The quality is beautifully clear and detailed, yet expands weightily in the finale.

Now coupled with Fischer-Dieskau's version of the *Kindertotenlieder*, Kubelik's *Seventh* is attractively introduced to the medium-priced range. Kubelik is at his most impressive in what can be described as Mahler's *Knaben Wunderhorn* manner. The start of the second movement has an open-air innocence, but conversely Kubelik produces no sense of nocturnal mystery in the second *Nachtmusik*. The outer movements are characteristically refined and resilient, but something of Mahler's strength is missing. Fine recording.

Symphony No. 8 in E flat (Symphony of 1000).
** Ph. Dig. 6769/*7654* 069 (2) [id.]. Robinson, Blegen, Quivar, Riegel, Luxon, Howell, Tanglewood Festival Ch., Boston Boys' Ch. and SO, Ozawa.

Though the Philips digital recording is very good indeed, Ozawa's Boston reading of the *Symphony of a Thousand* rather lacks the weight and intensity of its finest rivals. It is a performance which has one thinking back to earlier Mahler of *Wunderhorn* vintage rather than accepting the epic scale. There is much beautiful singing and playing, recorded in a mellow acoustic, but this work needs more sense of occasion. Solti's classic Decca set still stands head and shoulders above other recorded versions of this symphony, with the conductor at his most inspired. The Decca recording too is a triumph for all concerned, and the quality of the cassette transfer is little short of astonishing (SET 534/5/*KCET 2 7006* [Lon. 1295/5-]).

Symphony No. 9 in D.
*** DG 2707 125/*3370 038* (2) [id.]. Berlin PO, Karajan.
*** HMV SLS/*TC-SLS* 5188 [Ang. SZ 3899]. LPO, Tennstedt.
(M) **(*) DG Priv. 2726 067 (2). Bav. RSO, Kubelik – WOLF: *Penthesilea.***(*)
** RCA RL 03641 (2) [ARL 2/*ARK 2* 3641]. Phd. O., Levine.
** Symph. SYM 14/15 [Peters PLE 116/7]. Symph. of L., Morris.

Fine as Karajan's other Mahler recordings have been, his account of the *Ninth* transcends them. In the middle two movements there is point and humour as well as refinement and polish, but it is the combination of richness and concentration in the outer movements that makes for a reading of the deepest intensity. Helped by rich, spacious recording, the sudden pianissimos which mark both movements have an ear-pricking realism such as one rarely experiences on record, and the unusually broad tempi are superbly controlled. In the finale Karajan is not just noble and stoic; he finds the bite of passion as well, sharply set against stillness and repose. When this issue appeared, he was quoted as counting this the finest of all his recordings, and he is not far wrong. On cassette, although the recording generally sounds well, the pianissimos are less sharply focused than on disc. The climaxes, however, expand impressively.

Tennstedt directs a performance of warmth and distinction, underlining nobility rather than any neurotic tension, so that the outer movements, spaciously drawn, have architectural grandeur. The second movement is gently done, and the third, crisp and alert, lacks just a little in adrenalin. The playing is excellent and the recording rich. The cassette issue (on one double-length tape, but supplied in a box) is vivid and well detailed, although the upper range is a trifle over-bright and needs smoothing.

Kubelik's restraint in the first movement means that the performance remains on a relatively low pitch of intensity. Though the result is in every way beautiful, it is only in the serenity of the finale that Kubelik achieves the sublimity to equal his finest rivals on record. But with an unusual and unexpected coupling it makes an interesting alternative among mid-price versions, and the recording is still very acceptable.

After some of his other Mahler recordings Levine's account of the *Ninth* is disappointing. Not only is the sound thin and poorly defined; the slow tempi for the outer movements sound self-conscious, particularly in the finale. Nonetheless there is much fine playing.

Morris's spacious view of the outer movements has a nobility to match some of his other Mahler recordings, but beside the finest versions the playing lacks a degree of distinction, and in the third-movement scherzo one needs a sharper focus. The recording is atmospheric but poorly defined in much of its detail.

Symphony No. 10 in F sharp (Unfinished; revised performing edition by Deryck Cooke).
*** HMV Dig. SLS/*TC-SLS* 5206 (2) [Ang. DS 3909]. Bournemouth SO, Rattle.
**(*) RCA Dig. RL/*RK* 13726 (2) [CTC 2/*CTK 2* 3726]. Phd. O., Levine.

With digital recording of demonstration quality on both disc and tape, Simon Rattle's vivid and compelling reading of the Cooke performing edition has one more than ever convinced that a remarkable revelation of Mahler's intentions was achieved in this painstaking reconstruction. To Cooke's final thoughts Rattle has added one or two detailed amendments, and the finale in particular, starting with its cataclysmic hammer-blows and growling tuba line, is a deeply moving experience, ending not in neurotic resignation but in open optimism. In the middle movements too Rattle, youthfully dynamic, has fresh revelations to make. The Bournemouth orchestra plays with dedication, marred only by the occasional lack of fullness in the strings. On cassette the work is admirably laid out on a single double-length tape.

Levine's planned complete Mahler symphony cycle will be the first to include the full five-movement version of the *Tenth Symphony*. The performance typically reveals Levine as a thoughtful and searching Mahlerian; the spacious account of the first movement is splendid, with refined Philadelphia string tone, but the recording, digital or not, does not always do justice to the high violins, which lack something in bloom, not least in the epilogue to the finale. The sound lacks a little in bass too. Although the playing is more polished than that of the Bournemouth orchestra on the rival HMV version, Levine as a rule is less intense, relaxing well in the jolly second movement, for example, but not quite conveying the same range of emotion as the work develops.

Kindertotenlieder; 5 Rückert Lieder.
*** DG 2531/*3301* 147 [id.]. Ludwig, Berlin PO, Karajan.

Christa Ludwig's two performances came originally as fill-ups for Karajan recordings of Mahler symphonies, and it is the distinction and refinement of playing and conducting which stand out above all. Ludwig's singing is characterful too, with the poise and stillness of the songs beautifully caught, but the microphone conveys some unevenness in the voice. The recording is rich and mellow to match the performances; the tape has slightly less range than the disc, but is naturally balanced.

Des Knaben Wunderhorn.
*** Ph. 9500 316 [id./*7300 572*]. Norman, Shirley-Quirk, Concg. O., Haitink.

Some may prefer a more sharply characterful reading of these keenly imagined songs than this, but the results here are most refined and satisfying. With the help of superb recording – as impressive in the cassette version as on disc – the singing of both of Jessye Norman and John Shirley-Quirk brings out the purely musical imagination of Mahler at his finest, while Haitink draws superbly clean and polished playing from his own Concertgebouw Orchestra.

Lieder eines fahrenden Gesellen; Lieder from Des Knaben Wunderhorn; Lieder und Gesänge aus der Jugendzeit; 5 Rückert Lieder.
*** HMV SLS 5137 (3). Fischer-Dieskau, Bárenboim.

Though most of these songs are better known with orchestral accompaniment, Mahler regarded the piano originals as equally valid alternatives, certainly not arrangements. This fine set gathers together those as well as the other Mahler Lieder. Although in some items a baritone voice may seem too heavy, and Fischer-Dieskau cannot always lighten the characterization sufficiently, one cannot imagine another singer today beginning to match him. Above all the weight and incisiveness he brings to the songs with military overtones (*Revelge, Der Tambourg'sell* etc.) are masterly. What bite, one wonders, would Mahler have brought to the gentler *Shropshire Lad* exploitation of the same theme. Barenboim's accompaniment could not be more understanding and sympathetic, and though the recording is close, the performances lose little and gain in bite.

Lieder eines fahrenden Gesellen; 5 Rückert Lieder.
** Decca SXL/*KSXC* 6698 [Lon. 26578/5-]. Horne, LAPO, Mehta.

Horne and Mehta are disappointing. The unevenness of Horne's vocal production is exaggerated by close recording, and that balance undermines any refinement in the orchestral accompaniment. Yet the sheer power of Horne's voice can be exciting, as in the climax of *Um Mitternacht.*

Lieder eines fahrenden Gesellen; 5 Rückert Lieder; Des Knaben Wunderhorn: excerpts (*Rheinlegendchen; Wer hat dies Liedlein erdacht*).
**(*) CBS 76828/40- [Col. M/*MT* 35863]. Von Stade, LPO, Andrew Davis.

Von Stade, normally so assured and stylish, has moments of ungainliness in the taxing *Rückert Lieder*, the legato line not always even. However, both there and, more strikingly, in the highly enjoyable account of the *Wayfaring Lad* cycle, there is a hint of youthful ardour which contrasts with most other recorded performances. If the playing seems at times to lack refinement, it is partly the fault of close recording; but the cassette is one of CBS's best, with rich sound and a striking bloom on the voice.

Maldere, Pierre van
(1729–68)

Symphonies in A; in D; in D, Op. 5/1; in E flat.
(M) *** DG Arc. Priv. 2547/*3347* 052. Solistes de Liège, Jalkus.

Two of these symphonies were published during van Maldere's short lifetime. Born in Brussels, he was acclaimed in Paris during the last decade of his life, the 1760s, and published two sets of symphonies there. The *D major*, Op. 5/1, dates from the last year of his life, and the *A major* from the beginning of the

decade, while the other two come from the Milan Conservatory Library and remain unpublished. The style is direct, and there is a fresh melodic appeal. The clichés of the time are in evidence but the slow movements have a gentle charm that rises above the period. Lively and sympathetic playing from the Liège ensemble and good recording, dating from the mid-1960s; the cassette matches the disc closely. This entertaining collection is worth exploring at medium price.

Marais, Marin (1656–1728)

Folies d'Espagne; Suite in B min.; Les Voix humaines.
*** Tel. AW 6.42121. Savall, Gallet, Hopkinson, Smith.

Marin Marais is a sophisticated and subtle composer whose music deserves more than just specialist attention. This anthology should not be played at one sitting, for the tone colour of the viola da gamba, even in such masterly hands as Jordi Savall's, is not as rich as that of the modern cello. Although the *Folies d'Espagne* outstay their welcome, the other pieces of the Second *Livre de pièces de viole* (1701) are of undoubted interest. The continuo accompaniments are imaginatively handled (the addition of theorbo adds variety and sonority) and Savall is a player of great artistry. The lament on the death of Lully from the *B minor Suite* is most affectingly played. The recording throughout is clean, well balanced and truthful.

Recorder suites: in C and G min.
**(*) Tel. AW 6.42192. Quadro Hotteterre.
Recorder suites: in E min. and F.
**(*) Tel. AW 6.42035. Quadro Hotteterre.

Marais was a great master of the gamba, where his innate melancholy found a natural outlet. These recorder suites dating from 1692, a collection of *Pièces en trio pour le flute, violon et dessus de viole avec b.c.* (basso continuo), are played throughout by two recorders, cello and harpsichord. The performances are of the highest sensitivity and virtuosity, but it would be idle to pretend that this music always sustains attention. Unlike some of Marais's gamba music, these suites are of limited interest and belong among that repertoire that is greater fun to play than to hear. Aficionados can be assured of the excellence of both performance and recording.

Marcello, Alessandro
(1669–1747)

6 Oboe concertos (La Cetra).
*** DG Arc. 2533 462 [id.]. Holliger, Pellerin, Camerata Bern, Füri.

Alessandro, the brother of the better-known composer Benedetto Marcello, was an accomplished practitioner of the other arts, notably painting, engraving and poetry. The six concertos of *La Cetra* are concertante exercises rather than concertos in the accepted sense of the word, and reveal a pleasing mixture of originality and convention. At times there is a certain want of expertise (as in the *E minor Concerto*, the second of the set) and a reliance on relatively routine gestures, but elsewhere one is surprised by a genuinely alive and refreshing individuality. These performances are vital and keen (occasionally almost aggressively bright) but full of style and character, and the recording is very faithful.

Marcello, Benedetto
(1686–1739)

6 Cello sonatas.
*** O-L DSLO 546. Pleeth, Webb, Hogwood.

Marcello came from an old patrician family and spent much of his life in public affairs. He was a member of the Council of Forty in his native Venice for some fourteen years and ended his career as Papal Chamberlain at Brescia. If he described himself as 'Dilettante di contrappunto', the fact remains that his music is far from wanting in craftsmanship and polish. The six sonatas for cello and continuo probably appeared in Venice between 1712 and 1717; an English edition comes from 1732. They may lack the emotional scale of the finest baroque music, but they are nonetheless the work of a cultured musician. The melodic ideas are not without appeal and, though the music lacks depth, given such persuasive performances and excellent recording as this, it will undoubtedly give pleasure to connoisseurs of the period. Anthony Pleeth does not try to make this music more searching than it is, and plays with keen musicianship and intelligence. The six sonatas are best heard separately rather than at one sitting.

Marini, Biagio (died 1665)

Sinfonias for strings Nos. 2 and 5; Sonatas for strings Nos. 1–4; Balletto primo (Gagliarda prima; Corrente nona). (i) Le Lagrime d'Erminia (1623).
*** O-L DSLO 570. Cons. of Musicke, Rooley or Trevor Jones, (i) with Kirkby and Rogers.

Marini was a younger contemporary of Monteverdi, his life spanning the first half of the seventeenth century. The prize discoveries here are the string sonatas, lively and imaginative; the other instrumental items too are far from routine. The songs are less interesting, but with fresh, characterful singing from Emma Kirkby and Nigel Rogers, they help to fill out the picture of an interesting historical figure long neglected. Performances and recording are typical of the excellent Florilegium series.

Martin, Frank (1890–1974)

Petite symphonie concertante.
** HMV ASD 3732 [Ang. S 37577]. Ellis, Preston, Ledger, ASMF, Marriner – BLOCH: *Concerto grosso.* ***

Frank Martin's *Petite symphonie concertante* is arguably his masterpiece, and its highly resourceful contrast of sonorities makes it particularly appealing. It is a searching, inventive and often profound work, though inevitably it causes problems of balance between the three concertante instruments and the double strings. These were solved in its pioneering mono record under Ansermet (Decca LXT 2631), but they seem to have eluded the skills of the EMI team on this occasion. The harpsichord is far too reticent by the side of its two companions, and though artificiality in balance is not a desirable goal, some compromise with nature is necessary for this work if its character is not to be impaired. The performance is sympathetic enough and, were the balance satisfactory, this would warrant three stars

Sonata da chiesa for viola d'amore and strings.
(M) * Turn. TVS 34687 [id.]. Thompson, Boston MIT SO, Epstein – BLOCH: *Suite hébraïque*; HINDEMITH: *Viola concerto.**

Frank Martin is so scantily represented in the catalogue that this work is a welcome addition to his discography. It was composed in 1938 for viola d'amore and organ and arranged for strings in 1952. It has a grave beauty whose eloquence is diminished by the inadequacies of this performance. The viola d'amore is notoriously difficult, and impurities of intonation as well as a generally undistinguished orchestral performance make it impossible to recommend this with any enthusiasm. Nor is the sound particularly flattering.

In terra pax (oratorio).
(B) *** Decca DPA 593/4. Buckel, Höffgen, Haefliger, Mollet, Stämpfli, SRO and Ch., Ansermet – HONEGGER: *Le Roi David.***(*)

Frank Martin's beautiful score was commissioned by the Swiss Radio in preparation for the announcement of the end of the 1939–45 war, and it was first performed by Ansermet. Originally this score occupied a whole disc but here it has been accommodated without appreciable loss of quality on a side and a half. Martin's music has an appropriate eloquence and spirituality, and he is admirably served by these fine soloists. The score falls into four short sections, all with biblical texts, and its sincerity and sense of compassion leave a strong impression. Coupled to Honegger's atmospheric pageant *Le Roi David* in an almost equally fine performance, this is an outstanding bargain. The recording, from the mid-1960s, is of high quality.

Martinů, Bohuslav
(1890–1959)

Comedy on the Bridge: suite. Mirandolina: Saltarello. The Suburban Theatre: suite (arr. Řiha). *Les Trois Souhaits: Le départ* (intermezzo).
(M) *** Sup. 1110 1620. Brno State PO, Jílek.

The first side is occupied by a suite from Act 1 of *The Suburban Theatre* (1935–6) arranged by Milos Řiha, which is highly attractive and will appeal to Martinů's growing band of admirers. Like the suite from *Comedy on the Bridge*, which Martinů himself arranged, the music has directness and melodic appeal. *Mirandolina* is a light comedy based on Goldoni, dating from the mid-1950s. Perhaps the most interesting of the works here is the intermezzo from *Les Trois Souhaits* (1928–9). None of this music shows Martinů at his most substantial, but it is well played and tolerably well recorded, albeit in a reverberant acoustic.

(i) *Concertino for piano trio and small orchestra;* (ii) *Sinfonietta giocosa for piano and small orchestra.*
(M) *** Sup. 4102 198. Panenka, Czech PO, cond. (i) Neumann (with Suk, Chuchro), (ii) Košler.

The *Sinfonietta giocosa* is one of Martinů's most engaging scores, remarkably high-spirited and carefree given the fact that at the time he was fleeing from the Nazis and living in great privation. The work bubbles over with wit, good humour and an infectious love of life. It is frankly neoclassical in outlook, its opening having something of the gait of a concerto grosso theme. All the tunes sparkle, and if we were living in a just world the score would enjoy the widest popularity. The *Concertino for piano trio*

and orchestra is not quite top-drawer Martinů, but it is thoroughly attractive. It is an earlier work, dating from the 1930s, and its melodic inspiration is fresh, without being as memorable as that of its companion on this disc. The performances are lively and keen, and the recording has plenty of presence and clarity of detail, even if the upper strings have a certain edge that needs to be tamed. Strongly recommended all the same.

Sinfonietta La Jolla; Symphony No. 4.
*(*) HMV ASD/TC-ASD 3888. Royal Liv. PO, Weller.

Walter Weller is at his best in the scherzo of the *Fourth Symphony*, surely Martinů's most lovable essay in this form; he secures playing of real motoric drive and energy. Moreover, the quality of the recorded sound is impressively clean and well-defined; there is no want of presence or weight. At the same time, the Liverpool strings do not possess the glowing intensity for which this score calls, nor the homogeneity and richness of sonority; and one misses too the sweetness and refinement of the Czech woodwind. Ultimately, one is left with the feeling that the Liverpool players did not quite have the time to get really inside the music. Much the same must be said of the *Sinfonietta La Jolla*, though it comes off better than the *Symphony*. The tape transfer is clear and bright if a little fierce on top.

Symphony No. 1; Inventions.
(M) *** Sup. SUP 2166. Czech PO, Neumann.

The *First Symphony* dates from 1942, the year after Martinů arrived in the United States, and, like so much good music of the period, it was written in response to a commission from Koussevitzky. Virgil Thomson's panegyric has been much quoted (but rightly so): 'The

shining sounds of it sing as well as shine
. . . Personal indeed is the delicate but
vigorous rhythmic animation, the singing
(rather than dynamic) syncopation that
permeates the whole work.' The 'singing
syncopation' has indeed something of the
quality of Hopkins's 'sprung' rhythm,
and lends this music a forward thrust and
subtlety that are exhilarating. The three
Inventions are earlier, dating from 1934,
and are highly imaginative and appealing. In every way this is a welcome addition to the growing Martinů discography. The performance is excellent
and the recording fully acceptable.

*Symphonies Nos. 2; 6 (Fantaisies
symphoniques).*
(M) *** Sup. SUP 2096. Czech PO, Neumann.

Martinů's first five symphonies
followed each other at annual intervals.
The *Second* (1943) is the most relaxed of
the six; its ideas are unforced, its mood
easy-going and bucolic. Much of it is
exhilarating, particularly the delightful
finale, and it has much charm in its pastoral slow movement. The *Sixth* is much
later and was introduced to the gramophone by Charles Munch and the Boston
Symphony, to whom the work is dedicated. For some time Martinů was
doubtful about its symphonic status; he
subtitled it *Fantaisies symphoniques* and
even briefly asked for it not to be included
in his numbered symphonies. The vivid
colouring and exotic textures (the opening sounds for all the world like a cloud
of Amazonian insects) must for him have
outweighed the effect made by the musical cogency and sweep of the score.
Václav Neumann's performance has an
impressive spaciousness, though there
could be more urgency and fire in places.
The Czech orchestra plays splendidly,
but the recording, made in the somewhat
resonant House of Artists in Prague,
could perhaps be more sharply focused.
Yet detail, even if lacking the last ounce
of presence, has been kept in truthful

perspective. No reservations should qual-
ify the recommendation this disc must
have; and those who do not know the
Martinů symphonies should start here.

Symphonies Nos. 3–5.
(M) *** Sup. SUP 2771/2. Czech PO,
Neumann.

The *Third* is in some ways the weightiest of Martinů's wartime symphonies;
it is without doubt the most concentrated
and powerful of the cycle, with the possible exception of the *Sixth*. It has too
something of the dark purposefulness
and vision of the *Double concerto*; the
middle movement has great intensity of
feeling and real depth. Neumann gives an
authoritative reading, with well-shaped
phrasing, and his conception is more
spacious than was Sejna's in his post-war
set. The first two movements of the
Fourth Symphony (1945) serve as a fill-
up; the remainder spill over to the next
record, and the *Fifth* likewise bestrides
the end of one side and goes over to the
fourth – not an ideal arrangement, perhaps. (There is still enough first-rate
Martinů to serve as fill-up material if
each symphony had been more tidily
accommodated on one disc.) The *Fifth* is
a marvellous piece, whose closing pages
radiate an almost incandescent quality
and a life-enhancing power quite out-of-
tune with the bleak post-war years that
gave it birth. The *Fourth* is perhaps the
most immediately attractive and appealing of all six, and though Neumann's
performances do not in every respect displace previous accounts by Ančerl, Tur-
novský and others, they are eminently
recommendable in spite of the reverberance of the acoustic.

(i) *Madrigal sonata.* Piano music: (ii)
Butterflies and Birds of Paradise; (iii)
3 Czech dances; Les Ritournelles.
(M) ** Sup. Panton 110446. (i) Dostlova,
Motulkova, Kramska; (ii) Krajný; (iii)
Holena.

The *Butterflies and Birds of Paradise* date from 1920 and reflect the influence of Debussy. The other two piano pieces, the *Czech dances* and the 1932 *Ritournelles*, come from Martinů's Paris years; the latter has genuine depth. The *Madrigal sonata* for flute, violin and piano, a two-movement work dating from the war years, is diverting and inventive without being really memorable. All the same this is welcome – recommendable though not indispensable Martinů. Good performances and decent recording.

String quartets Nos. 5; 7 (*Concerto da camera*).
(M) *** Sup. 1111 2675. Panocha Qt.

The *Fifth* is the more substantial of the two quartets recorded here. It dates from 1938, the same year as the *Double concerto*, to which it is close in spirit (at least in the two middle movements), though it is not as powerful. The *Seventh*, a postwar work, is a slighter piece, written in the immediate wake of the *Fifth Symphony*. The same coupling was recorded in the 1960s, but these performances displace the earlier disc both artistically and technically. The Panocha Quartet, an excellent ensemble, will be recording all seven Martinů quartets during the lifetime of this book; if the rest are as good as this, the set will be very rewarding.

The Epic of Gilgamesh.
(M) *** Sup. 1121 808. Machotková, Zahradníček, Zitek, Prusa, Brousek, Czech PO Ch., Prague SO, Belohlavek.

The *Epic of Gilgamesh* is one of Martinů's finest achievements. It belongs to his last years and touches greater depths than almost any other of his later works, with the possible exception of *The Prophecy of Isaiah*. *Gilgamesh* predates the Homeric epic by at least 1,500 years, and Martinů's oratorio draws one into this remote world with astonishing power.

The second and third parts of the oratorio centre on the themes of death and immortality, and it is here that some of the most imaginative and mysterious music is to be found. Part 2 recounts the death of Enkidu and Gilgamesh's grief, his plea to the gods to restore Enkidu and his search for immortality; the third part records his failure to learn its secrets. But it is not only these sections that inspire music of great atmosphere and mystery; the whole work has a concentration of vision and feeling, and an imaginative resource which shows that this legend triggered off particularly sympathetic resonances in the composer. The performance is sympathetic and spacious (tempi are leisurely), though not enough is made of the drama. When Gilgamesh is granted a vision of the underworld and Enkidu rises to answer his questions with the simple words 'I saw', the atmosphere could be more chilling and haunting: it is a superb moment. The Czech narration is a small element and need not deter anyone. *Gilgamesh* is an inspiring and rewarding work, not to be missed by Martinů's admirers.

The Greek Passion (opera; in English).
⊛ *** Sup. Dig. 1116/*KSUP* 3611/2. Mitchinson, Field, Tomlinson, Joll, Moses, Davies, Cullis, Savory, Kuhn Children's Ch., Czech PO Ch., Brno State PO, Mackerras.

Written with much mental pain in the years just before Martinů died in 1959, this opera was the work he regarded as his musical testament. Based on a novel by Nikos Kazantzakis (author of *Zorba the Greek*), it tells in an innocent, direct way of a village where a Passion play is to be presented, and the individuals – tragically, as it proves – take on qualities of the New Testament figures they represent. At the very opening there is a hymn-like prelude of diatonic simplicity, and what makes the work so moving – giving occasional overtones of Janáček,

Mussorgsky and Britten – is Martinů's ability to simplify his message both musically and dramatically. On stage the degree of gaucheness might be hard to present effectively, but on record it is quite different. This superb recording was made by a cast which had been giving stage performances for the Welsh National Opera; the singing is not just committed but accomplished too. The Czechs were happy to record the opera (digitally, using Japanese equipment) in what in effect is the original language of Martinů's libretto, English. Virtually every word is crystal-clear and the directness of the communication to the listener is riveting, particularly as the choral perspectives are so tellingly and realistically managed. The combination of British soloists with excellent Czech choirs and players is entirely fruitful. As a Czech specialist Mackerras makes an ideal advocate, and the recorded sound is both brilliant and highly atmospheric. In its simple, direct way *The Greek Passion* makes a most moving experience, and this set is strongly recommended; it is a major achievement to rank alongside Mackerras's splendid Janáček opera recordings for Decca. The chrome tapes are of the highest quality; the sound is virtually identical with the discs. The only snag is the reduction of the size of the libretto booklet, which produces minuscule print.

Mascagni, Pietro (1863–1945)

L'Amico Fritz (complete).
(M) *** HMV SLS 5107 (2) [Ang. S 3737]. Pavarotti, Freni, Sardinero, ROHCG Ch. and O., Gavazzeni.

The haunting *Cherry duet* from this opera whets the appetite for more, and it is good to hear so rare and charming a piece, one that is not likely to enter the repertory of our British opera houses. Even so enthusiasm has to be tempered a little, because no other number in the opera approaches the famous duet in its memorability. The libretto too is delicate to the point of feebleness. This performance could be more refined, though Freni and Pavarotti are most attractive artists and this was recorded in 1969 when they were both at their freshest. The Covent Garden Orchestra responds loyally; the recording is warm and atmospheric, and it has transferred very successfully to tape. While the dramatic conception is at the opposite end of the scale from *Cavalleria Rusticana*, one is easily beguiled by the music's charm, and the Puccinian influences are by no means a disadvantage.

Cavalleria Rusticana (complete).
*** RCA RL/*RK* 13091 [CRL 1/*CRK 1* 3091]. Scotto, Domingo, Elvira, Isola Jones, Amb. Op. Ch., Nat. PO, Levine.
(*) HMV SLS/*TC-SLS* 5187 (3) [Ang. SZX 3895]. Caballé, Carreras, Manuguerra, Varnay, Amb. Op. Ch., Philh. O., Muti – LEONCAVALLO: *I Pagliacci.*(*)
(*) Decca D 83 D 3/*K 83 K 32* (3) [Lon. D 13125]. Varady, Pavarotti, Cappuccilli, Gonzales, L. Op. Ch., Nat. PO, Gavazzeni – LEONCAVALLO: *I Pagliacci.*

There is far more than its compact format on a single disc (libretto included) or tape to recommend the RCA version. On balance in performance it stands as the best current recommendation, with Domingo giving a heroic account of the role of Turiddù, full of defiance. Scotto, strongly characterful too, though not always perfectly steady on top, gives one of her finest performances of recent years, and James Levine directs with a splendid sense of pacing, by no means faster than his rivals (except the leisurely Karajan), and drawing red-blooded playing from the National Philharmonic.

The recording is very good (particularly remembering the long sides), and the cassette transfer is first-class, one of RCA's very best.

There are fewer unexpected textual points in the HMV *Cav.* than in *Pag.*, but Muti's approach is comparably biting and violent, brushing away the idea that this is a sentimental score, though running the risk of making it vulgar. The result is certainly refreshing, with Caballé – pushed faster than usual even in her big moments – collaborating warmly. So *Voi lo sapete* is geared from the start to the final cry of *Io son dannata*, and she manages a fine snarl on *A te la mala Pasqua*. Carreras does not sound quite so much at home, though the rest of the cast is memorable, including the resonant Manuguerra as Alfio and the veteran Astrid Varnay as Mamma Lucia, wobble as she does. The recording is forward and vivid on disc and cassette alike.

With Pavarotti loud and unsubtle as Turiddù – though the tone is often most beautiful – it is left to Julia Varady as Santuzza to give the Decca version under Gavazzeni its distinction. Though her tone is not heavyweight, the impression of youth is most affecting; the sharpness of pain in *Voi lo sapete* is beautifully conveyed, and the whole performance is warm and authentic. Cappuccilli's Alfio is too noble to be convincing, and as in the companion *Pag.* the main claim to attention lies in the brilliant, forward recording, equally impressive on disc and tape.

Cavalleria Rusticana: highlights.
(*) Decca SXL/*KSXC* 6986 (from above set cond. Gavazzeni) – LEON-CAVALLO: *Pagliacci* highlights.

These excerpts from *Cavalleria Rusticana* include *Santuzza's prayer* and *Voi lo sapete*, very welcome because Julia Varady is the most individual member of the cast in the complete set. The selections from both operas are rather more generous than usual, and the recording is

excellent. The cassette transfer too is extremely vivid.

Massenet, Jules (1842–1912)

Piano concerto.
(M) (*) Turn. TVS 37127 [Can. 31088]. Dosse, Westphalian SO, Landau – GOUNOD: *Fantasy*; SAINT-SAËNS: *Africa fantasy*.(*)

Marylène Dosse and the Westphalian orchestra under Siegfried Landau fail to make a case for Massenet's *Piano concerto*. Although it has an atmospheric opening, the melodic material is very slight, and the work needs more coaxing than it receives here. The recording too is unpersuasively thin.

Scènes alsaciennes; Scènes dramatiques; Cendrillon: Marche des Princesses.
*** Decca SXL 6827 [Lon. 7048]. Nat. PO, Bonynge.

Massenet's *Scènes alsaciennes* have a good deal of charm and vitality. Their pictorial qualities – the Sunday-morning scene, with its gently evocative church chorale, contrasting with the evening bustle and the military sounding the retreat in the distance – are ingenuously engaging. The *Scènes dramatiques* have Shakespearian connotations and might better be called 'melodramatic'; as in the Alsatian set the scoring is vividly effective, but the invention is less memorable. The march from *Cendrillon* makes a piquant bonus. All the music is very well played here and directed by Bonynge with an affectionate ear for detail. The recording is warmly resonant, but is brilliant too, with an attractive bloom on the wind.

Scènes alsaciennes; Scènes dramatiques; Scènes de féerie; Scènes pittoresques; Don Quichotte: Interludes; La Vierge: The last sleep of the Virgin.
** Erato STU 71208 (2). Monte Carlo Op. O., Gardiner.

The Erato box gathers together four out of Massenet's seven orchestral suites, plus a few encores, including one of Sir Thomas Beecham's favourites, *The last sleep of the Virgin*. In fact this is all music that would respond to the Beecham touch. John Eliot Gardiner secures quite impressively characterized performances; he finds more *gravitas* than Bonynge in the *Scènes dramatiques*, and the *Scènes pittoresques* are bright and fresh, the horns tolling the Angelus with resonant impact. But the Monte Carlo orchestra produces a rather thin-bodied tutti, and though the full, atmospheric recording minimizes this effect, the ear remains conscious that the playing lacks the last degree of polish and elegance. The sound is limited in range and colour alongside Bonynge's Decca coupling.

Scènes hongroises.
(M) *(*) Turn. TVS 34570 [id.]. R. Lux. O., Cao – CHABRIER: *Fête polonaise;* LALO: *Rapsodie norvégienne.**

The *Scènes hongroises* have the deft scoring and craftsmanship that characterize Massenet's sets of musical picture postcards. The second, *Intermède*, is brief and attractive; the third, *Adieu à la fiancée*, also has a gentle charm, and the final *Bénédiction nuptiale* is the most ambitious movement and somewhat melodramatic. The work appears to have a connection with the composer's own engagement and marriage. The performance here is acceptable but not distinguished; the recording is shallow and artificially balanced.

(i) *La Cigale* (divertissement-ballet; complete). *Valse très lente.*
*** Decca SXL 6932 [Lon. 7163]. Nat. PO, Bonynge, (i) with Hartle, L. Voices.

A late work written with Massenet's characteristic finesse, *Cigale* was totally neglected until Richard Bonynge revived it in this recording. The ballet tells, in somewhat sentimental terms the story of the La Fontaine fable about the grasshopper and the ant. The melodic invention does not match Massenet's finest, but the score is charming and colourful, and it is brightly played and sung and brilliantly recorded.

Cendrillon (complete).
**(*) CBS 79323 (3) [Col. M3 35194]. Von Stade, Gedda, Berbié, Bastin, Amb. Op. Ch., Philh. O., Rudel.

Julius Rudel directs a sparkling, winning performance of Massenet's Cinderella opera, less a pantomime than a fairy story in which the magic element (direct from Perrault) is vital. The Fairy Godmother is a sparkling coloratura (here the bright-toned Ruth Welting) and Cendrillon a soprano in a lower register. Von Stade gives a characteristically strong and imaginative performance, untroubled by what for her is high tessitura. The pity is that the role of the prince, originally written for soprano, is here taken by a tenor, Gedda, whose voice is no longer fresh-toned. Jules Bastin sings most stylishly as Pandolfe and the others make up a well-chosen team. The recording is more spacious than many from this source.

Don Quichotte (complete).
*** Decca D 156 D 3/*K 156 K 32* (3) [Lon. 13134/5-]. Ghiaurov, Bacquier, Crespin, Command, Fremeau, SRO and Ch., Kord.

Massenet's operatic adaptation of Cervantes' classic novel gave him his last

455

big success, written as it was with Chaliapin in mind for the title role. It is a totally captivating piece, with not a jaded bar in it, suggesting that Massenet might have developed further away from his regular romantic opera style. There is genuine nobility as well as comedy in the portrait of the knight, and that is well caught here by Ghiaurov, who refuses to exaggerate the characterization. Bacquier makes a delightful Sancho Panza, but it is Régine Crespin, as a comically mature Dulcinée, who provides the most characterful singing, flawed vocally but commandingly positive. Kazimierz Kord directs the Suisse Romande in a performance that is zestful and electrifying, and the recording is outstandingly clear and atmospheric, with a cassette transfer of matching quality.

Manon (complete).
(M) *** HMV SLS/*TC-SLS* 5119 (3). Los Angeles, Legay, Dens, Borthaye, Ch. and O. of Paris Opéra-Comique, Monteux.

It is strange that despite the growth of interest in Massenet's music there has been no fully recommendable version of this most popular of his operas – and arguably the finest – since this superb mono set from the mid-sixties. Pierre Monteux (who had still some years of active career before him) never recorded a more glowing opera performance, and he was aided by the most radiant of heroines, Victoria de los Angeles at her very peak, the voice meltingly beautiful and finely poised, the characterization unfailingly endearing. In the aria *Je suis encore tout étourdie*, it is not just that she convinces one totally of her emotional involvement and phrases magically but that the fluttering phrases at the end of each section are breathtakingly delicate. Try as sample the scene where Des Grieux first meets Manon: Henri Legay conveys the wonderment of the moment and Monteux's conducting ensures an authentic frisson. There is no improvement in this stereo transcription on the original mono issue (arguably thinner violin sound), but the result is faithful to the voices and will not distract from a magical account of a most moving opera. The cassettes are first-class.

Le Roi de Lahore (complete).
⊛ *** Decca D 210 D 3/*K 210 K 33* (3) [Lon. LDR 10025]. Sutherland, Tourangeau, Lima, Milnes, Morris, Ghiaurov, L. Voices, Nat. PO, Bonynge.

With a libretto that sets high melodrama against an exotic background – even introducing the supernatural with an act set in the paradise of Indra – *Le Roi de Lahore* was Massenet's first opera for the big stage of L'Opéra in Paris and marked a turning-point in his career. The characters may be stock figures out of a fairy tale, but in the vigour of his treatment Massenet makes the result redblooded in an Italianate way. This vivid performance under Bonynge includes passages added for Italy, notably a superb set-piece aria which challenges Sutherland to some of her finest singing. Massenet's idea of the exotic extends to a saxophone waltz (here made deliciously Parisian), but generally the score reflects the eager robustness of a young composer stretching his wings for the first time. Sutherland may not be a natural for the role of innocent young priestess, but she makes it a magnificent vehicle with its lyric, dramatic and coloratura demands. Luis Lima as the King is sometimes strained by the high tessitura, but it is a ringing tenor, clean of attack. Sherrill Milnes as the heroine's wicked uncle sounds even more Italianate, rolling his 'r's ferociously; but high melodrama is apt, and with digital recording of demonstration quality, rich and rounded, this shameless example of operatic hokum could not be more persuasively presented. The cassettes are as demonstration-worthy as the discs.

Werther (complete)
**♦♦♦ Ph. 6769/7654 051 (3). Carreras, Von
Stade, Allen, Buchanan, Lloyd, Children's Ch., O. of ROHCG, Colin
Davis.
*** DG 2709 091/3371 048 (3) [id.].
Domingo, Obraztsova, Auger,
Grundheber, Moll, Col. Children's
Ch. and RSO, Chailly.
** HMV SLS 5183 (3) [Ang. SZX/4Z3X
3894]. Kraus, Troyanos, Manuguerra,
Barbaux, Ch. and LPO, Plasson.

Sir Colin Davis has rarely directed a
more sensitive or more warmly expressive
performance on record than his account
of *Werther*. The magic of sound hits the
listener from the opening prelude onwards, and the refined recording, coupled
with a superbly cast performance based
on a stage production at Covent Garden,
makes for consistent compulsion. Frederica von Stade makes an enchanting
Charlotte, outshining all current rivals on
record, both strong and tender, conveying the understanding but vulnerable
character of Goethe's heroine. Carreras
may not be quite so clearly superior to all
rivals, but, like his compatriot Placido
Domingo on the DG set (marred by an
inadequate Charlotte), he uses a
naturally beautiful voice freshly and
sensitively. Others in the cast, such as
Thomas Allen as Charlotte's husband
Albert and Isobel Buchanan as Sophie,
her sister, are excellent too. This is one of
the finest of recent sets of French opera.
The tape transfer is well planned, using
two cassettes (against three discs), so that
each act finishes at the end of a side. Although not stated on the box, chrome
tape appears to have been used, so while
the transfer level is (as usual with Philips)
comparatively low, there is little loss in
definition compared with the discs, and
the orchestra and voices have a pleasing
naturalness and bloom. The accompanying booklet is clearly printed, but when it
comes to the libretto itself, the style of
the photo-reduction is ill-conceived and
the typeface is minuscule.

With a recording that gives a beautiful
bloom to the sound of the Cologne
orchestra, down to the subtlest whisper
from pianissimo strings, the DG version
stands at an advantage over its HMV
rival, particularly as Chailly proves a
sharply characterful conductor, one who
knows how to thrust home an important
climax as well as how to create evocative
textures, varying tensions positively. Placido Domingo in the name part sings with
sweetness and purity as well as strength,
coping superbly with the legato line of the
aria *Pourquoi me réveiller*. Elena Obraztsova is richer and firmer than she usually
is on record, but it is a generalized portrait, particularly beside the charming
Sophie of Arleen Auger. The others make
up a very convincing team. The DG cassette transfer is very successful, matching
the discs closely.
It is sad that Alfredo Kraus, one of the
most stylish of tenors as a rule, came to
record *Werther* so late in his career.
Listen to this account of *Pourquoi me réveiller*, and the effortful underlining, with
its chopping of the melodic line, is almost
unrecognizable as his work. Elsewhere
the strained tone is less distracting, and
his feeling for words is generally most
illuminating. Troyanos makes a volatile
Charlotte, but the voice as recorded is
grainy. Manuguerra produces rich tone
as the Bailiff, but the engineers have not
been kind to the LPO strings, which
sound rather thin, particularly when
compared with those on the DG set.
Plasson is a stylish conductor but at times
fails to present the full power of the
piece.

Maunder, John (1858–1920)

Olivet to Calvary (cantata).
(M) **(*) HMV ESD/TC-ESD 7051.
Mitchinson, Harvey, Guildford Cath.,
Ch., Barry Rose; Moorse (organ).

It is easy to be patronizing about music like this. Its melodic and harmonic flavour will for many tastes seem too highly coloured and sugary for the subject, but provided one accepts the conventions of style in which it is composed the music is effective and often moving. The performance has an attractive simplicity and genuine eloquence. Just occasionally the soloists overdo the drama in their enunciation, but for the most part they are sensitive to the text and the obvious dedication of the music. Frederick Harvey is particularly moving at the actual moment of Christ's death: in a passage that, insensitively handled, could be positively embarrassing, he creates a magical, hushed intensity. The choir sing beautifully, and in the gentler, lyrical writing (the semi-chorus *O Thou whose sweet compassion*, for example) sentimentality is skilfully avoided. The HMV recording is first-class in every way and the tape quality is for the most part equally fine.

Maw, Nicholas (born 1935)

Life studies Nos. 1–8.
*** Argo ZRG 899 [id.]. ASMF, Marriner.

Life studies for fifteen solo strings makes a formidable addition to the line of great string works by British composers. On one level the eight movements present virtuoso exercises in texture and sonority; but with their broad range of expression in Maw's uninhibited style their impact is above all emotional, particularly in so strong a performance as this. The passionate unison melody of the eighth movement makes a superb culmination. The recording is excellent.

(i) *La vita nuova* (for soprano and chamber ens.); (ii) *The Voice of Love.*

*** Chan. ABR/*ABT* 1037. (i) Christie, Nash Ens.; (ii) Walker, Vignoles.

These two song cycles represent Maw's work at different periods of his career, yet both give warm evidence of his exceptional sensitivity towards the voice. To words specially written by the poet Peter Porter, *The Voice of Love* tells of the love affair of a seventeenth-century authoress, surrounding romantic emotion with colour and point in a rather Britten-like way. Sarah Walker, accompanied by the pianist Roger Vignoles, characterizes superbly. Nan Christie in the more recent cycle – setting Italian Renaissance love lyrics – is less sweetly caught; but here too the natural expressiveness of Maw's writing comes over most persuasively, helped by first-rate recording. The tape transfer is also excellent; there is little to choose between disc and cassette.

Maxwell Davies, Peter (born 1934)

Symphony No. 1.
*** Decca HEAD 21. Philh. O., Rattle.

The appearance in 1978 of Davies's *First Symphony* marked a turning-point in his career, for in this massive, strongly argued work, with its rich and atmospheric textures, he was speaking with no inhibitions. Its strength, energy and beauty were immediately apparent to a far wider audience than is normally attracted to new music, and it was good that Decca promptly promoted a recording with the young Simon Rattle in charge, as at the première. Though this recorded performance does not quite convey the full excitement of that first performance, it is very well played and brilliantly recorded. It is remarkable that a work which begins with such headlong enthusiasm in the first movement should maintain its full concentration through the enigmatic second movement, the still, evocative *Lento*, and the series of sustained crescendos at high speed which make up the finale with a passing reference to Orcadean birdsong.

Ave Maris Stella; (i) *Tenebrae super Gesualdo.*
*** Uni. Kanchana KP 8002. Fires of L., composer, (i) with Walker (guitar), Mary Thomas.

These two elegiac pieces – dating from 1975 and 1972 respectively – find Maxwell Davies at his most severe and demanding. Based on the chant of that name, *Ave Maris Stella* is yet more than a ritual, conveying inner tensions in its sharp contrasts. The *Tenebrae*, less complex in their textures but equally extended, are also deeply felt. The composer's concentration is reflected in the performances of both works under his direction; both are beautifully recorded.

Eight songs for a mad king.
(M) *** Uni. UNS 261 [None. 71285]. Eastman (reciter), Fires of L., composer.

There are many levels of imagination at work in this extraordinary, unforgettable piece, probably the most successful example of music-theatre that Davies has written. It is at once a re-creation of George III's madness, the reciter/singer taking the role of the king with nerve-jangling realism; at once an extraordinary example of new expression in sing-speech, with vocal harmonics and double-notes produced as part of the king's raving; at once a dramatic fantasy with flute, clarinet, violin and cello representing birds in cages, the birds the king tried to teach; at once a musical fantasy on tunes played by a mechanical organ that the king actually possessed and which survives today. It is harrowing

in its surrealism, its playing on the hidden nerve, but the power of inspiration, superbly interpreted here and splendidly recorded, is undeniable.

Medtner, Nikolai (1880–1951)

(i) *Piano quintet in C, Op. posth. Stimmungsbilder, Op. 1/1, 4 and 7; Piano sonata in C min., Op. 25/1.*
* Camb. CAM 2. Binns, (i) with New L. Qt.

The repertoire is rare enough. Medtner recorded the *Piano quintet* himself in the last months of his life, but it was never issued; and the piano pieces too are not otherwise available. Nevertheless, a dry acoustic and rather tentative string playing make this an unpersuasive record; the string players lack real commitment.

Dithyramb, Op. 10/2; Elegy, Op. 59/2; Skazki (Fairy tales): No. 1 (1915); in E min., Op. 14/2; in G, Op. 9/3; in D min. (Ophelia's song); in C sharp min., Op. 35/4. Forgotten melodies, 2nd Cycle, No. 1. Meditation. Primavera, Op. 39/3; 3 Hymns in praise of toil, Op. 49; Piano sonata in E min. (The Night Wind), Op. 25/2; Sonata Triad, Op. 11/1–3.
*** CRD CRD 1038/9. Milne.

Medtner remains lamentably neglected in the recital room and in the catalogues. His art is as subtle and elusive as that of, say, Fauré, whose piano music has also never found the wider public favour it deserves. Far from being the Russian Brahms or Rachmaninov-without-the-tunes, Medtner is very much his own man. He shows an aristocratic disdain of the obvious, a feeling for balance and proportion, and a quiet harmonic refinement that offer consistent rewards. This two-record set of piano music by Hamish Milne forms an admirable introduction to his art. Milne wisely avoids the *G minor Sonata*, Op. 22, and the *Reminiscenza*, Op. 38 (which Gilels recorded in the 1960s), and concentrates on music new to the catalogue. The most substantial piece in this set is the *E minor Sonata* (*The Night Wind*), which should dispel any doubts as to Medtner's capacity to sustain an argument on the grandest scale; it is a one-movement sonata taking the best part of half an hour. Milne also includes the less ambitious single-movement sonatas, Op. 11, which are finely concentrated, elegantly fashioned works. There is hardly a weak piece in this set, and Milne is a poetic advocate whose technical prowess is matched by first-rate artistry. The recording too is very truthful and vivid.

4 Skazki, Op. 26; Sonata-Ballade in F sharp, Op. 27; Sonata minacciosa in F min. (Sonata orageuse), Op. 53/2.
*** Pearl SHE 535. Binns.

The *Sonata-Ballade* comes from 1913 and was recorded by the composer himself on 78s towards the end of his life. It is an eloquent and often subtle statement whose feeling is none the less potent for being restrained. The *Four Fairy tales* are full of fantasy, and the *Sonata minacciosa*, a later work dating from the 1930s, is also a find. Malcolm Binns is more than equal to the demands these pieces make, and his artistry is faithfully served by the engineers.

Mendelssohn, Felix
(1809–47)

Piano concertos Nos. 1 in G min., Op. 25; 2 in D min., Op. 40.

(M) *** DG Priv. 2535/*3335* 416. Gheorghiu, Leipzig RSO, Kegel.

Valentin Gheorghiu is well-known in his native Rumania and made an impressive record of the Liszt *Sonata* on HMV in the days of mono LP. These performances originally appeared as part of a Mendelssohn–Schubert package and were never issued separately on a full-price DG record. Gheorghiu's playing has both sensitivity and strength, and his readings make a characterful alternative to the imaginative and thoroughly idiomatic account by Murray Perahia on CBS. If anything, however, Gheorghiu is better recorded, and though his playing does not quite match Perahia's delicacy of feeling, this must be accounted a highly competitive issue. The clean cassette transfer matches the disc closely.

Violin concerto in E min., Op. 64.
*** CRD CRD 1069/*CRDC 4069*. Ronald Thomas, Bournemouth Sinf. – BEETHOVEN: *Romances*; SCHUBERT: *Konzertstück*.***
*** DG Dig. 2532/*3302* 016 [id.]. Mutter, Berlin PO, Karajan – BRUCH: *Concerto No. 1*.***
(M) *** Decca VIV/*KVIC* 4. Ricci, Netherlands RO, Fournet – TCHAIKOVSKY: *Concerto*.***
(M) **(*) HMV *TC-IDL 508*. Kogan, Paris Conservatoire O., Silvestri – TCHAIKOVSKY: *Concerto*.***
(*) DG 2531/*3301* 304 [id.]. Mintz, Chicago SO, Abbado – BRUCH: *Concerto No. 1*.*
(M) **(*) CBS 60111/*40*- [Col. MY 36724]. Stern, Phd. O., Ormandy – TCHAIKOVSKY: *Concerto*. **(*)
(B) ** CfP CFP/*TC-CFP* 40374. Milstein, Philh. O., Barzin – BRUCH: *Concerto No. 1*.**
(M) ** DG Priv. 2535/*3335* 294 [id.]. Yong Uck Kim, Bamberg SO, Kamu – BRUCH: *Concerto No. 1*.*(*)
*(*) Ph. 9500 321/*7300 583* [id.]. Szeryng, Concg. O., Haitink – TCHAIKOVSKY: *Concerto*.*(*)

Ronald Thomas's is in many ways the opposite of a dashing virtuoso approach, yet his apt, unforced choice of speeds, his glowing purity of intonation and the fine coordination with the orchestra he regularly leads (an amazing achievement in this often complex, fast-flowing music) put this among the most satisfying versions available. It is intensely refreshing from first to last, and is helped by excellent recording on disc and cassette alike.

Here even more than in her Bruch coupling, the freshness of Anne-Sophie Mutter's approach communicates vividly to the listener, creating the feeling of hearing the work anew. Her gentleness and radiant simplicity in the *Andante* are very appealing, and the closing pages have real magic, with Karajan catching the mood and scale in his accompaniment. Similarly the second subject of the first movement has great charm, and the light, sparkling finale (again with the orchestral balance superbly managed) is a delight. There is a greater spontaneity here than in Mintz's slightly riper version, and the recording is most realistically balanced on both disc and tape.

Ricci's Viva reissue was originally recorded in Phase Four. The performance is even finer than his successful earlier version with Gamba. The balance places him well forward and reveals plenty of orchestral detail by the close microphoning of the woodwind. In the finale the listener's pleasure is enhanced by Fournet's precision in matching the solo line with the accompaniment, which adds considerable extra sparkle. The slow movement has a disarming simple eloquence, and the reading as a whole is undoubtedly distinguished. The vivid recording is admirably transferred to the cassette, though the tape has a marginally less dramatic dynamic range.

Kogan's version is one of HMV's tape-only reissues. He plays with great fervour throughout, and Silvestri matches his approach by taking the opening movement at a fairly fast tempo and by pressing on the middle section of the slow

movement strongly. The finale sparkles vividly. The orchestral playing is good rather than outstanding, and the reverberation of the recording sometimes clouds inner detail. Nevertheless this is a distinguished account on the part of the soloist, and it makes a powerful impact.

Shlomo Mintz is a young violinist of the highest promise and strongest individuality. His version of the Mendelssohn *Concerto* is powerfully conceived, and his forward placing gives the impression of an outsize personality and tone. There are moments of less than perfect intonation, and one feels that this performance is not quite the equal of the Bruch coupling. The Chicago orchestra and Abbado give splendid support. This is perhaps less reticent than the Accardo account, less spontaneous than Perlman. The cassette is more opaque, orchestrally, than the disc.

Stern's performance with the Philadelphia Orchestra was made at a peak period in his recording career. It has great bravura, culminating in a marvellously surging account of the finale. The slow movement too is played with great eloquence and feeling, but when pianissimos are non-existent – partly, but not entirely, the fault of the close recording balance – the poetic element is diminished. It remains a stirring account, and the recording is vivid if not refined.

Milstein is not at his most fervently lyrical or totally committed in his performance of the Mendelssohn. There is some patchy intonation at one point in the first movement, but that is not enough in itself to cause more than a passing raised eyebrow. There is a certain quality of detachment here, and for all its fine musicianship (there is some good orchestral playing) this is not as memorable or characterful as the best versions in this highly competitive field. But it is good value at Classics for Pleasure price.

The Privilege performance by Yong Uck Kim is genuinely touching, with an unforced eloquence that carries conviction. Unfortunately the soloist is handicapped by less than first-class orchestral support, and as a whole the coupling does not challenge the finest of its rivals. However, this is a rewarding performance which was underrated on its first appearance; those who investigate it may well feel that the rewards of Yong's playing outweigh the drawback of the orchestral support. The recording is eminently satisfactory.

Szeryng's performance is sensitive and lyrical, but it has no specially individual qualities either from the soloist or in the accompaniment.

(i) *Double concerto in D min. for violin, piano and strings. Symphony No. 12 in G min. for string orchestra.*
*** HMV ASD 3628. Menuhin Festival O., Menuhin, (i) with Y. and H. Menuhin.

These works both date from Mendelssohn's boyhood, and are both delectable examples of his precocious genius. The *G minor String symphony*, with its slow opening movement and weighty fugal writing, has become relatively well-known on record, but just as valuable is the *Double concerto*, with its ambitious first movement (sometimes cut in performance, following the original unauthentic edition) and its sparkling finale. This was one of the last of Hephzibah Menuhin's recordings with her brother before her untimely death, and it represents their art at its peak.

Overtures: Calm Sea and Prosperous Voyage, Op. 27; Fair Melusina, Op. 32; The Hebrides (Fingal's Cave), Op. 26; A Midsummer Night's Dream, Op. 21; Ruy Blas, Op. 95.
(M) ** DG Priv. 2535/*3335* 460. LSO, Chmura.

Gabriel Chmura is clearly a talent to watch. He has won both the Cantelli and the Karajan competitions and is still only in his thirties. He is obviously on guard against the impetuosity of youth, and these performances tend towards the other extreme: he errs on the side of excessive caution in *The Hebrides*, where his tempo is a bit too measured. This could have more lightness of touch, and *Ruy Blas* too needs more zest if it is to be really exciting. Yet he pays scrupulous attention to detail and is plainly both conscientious in his approach and deeply musical. The orchestral playing is obviously well prepared and has real finish, while the recording is clean, well focused and bright without being over-lit. The cassette transfer is well balanced, but a lower level on side two (*Midsummer Night's Dream* and *Calm Sea*) brings a loss of range and immediacy.

Symphonies for string orchestra, Nos. 2 in D; 3 in E min.; 5 in B flat; 6 in E flat.
(M) *** HMV Green. ESD/*TCC-ESD* 7123. Polish CO, Maksymiuk.

Digitally recorded on a mid-price label, this collection of the boy Mendelssohn's early *String symphonies* (written when he was only twelve) is most invigorating. These earlier symphonies of the series of twelve may look to various models from Bach to Beethoven, but the boy keeps showing his individuality, and however imitative the style the vitality of the invention still bursts through. The slow movement of the *Symphony No. 2*, for example, is a Bachian meditation that in its simple beauty matches later Mendelssohn. The Polish strings are set in a lively acoustic, giving exceptionally rich sound both on disc and on the excellent chrome cassette.

Symphonies for string orchestra Nos. 6 in E flat; 7 in D min.; 10 in B min.
**(*) HM 1C 065 99823. Ens. 13 Baden Baden, Reichert.

Drawn from members of the South-West German Radio Orchestra, this ensemble plays as stylishly here as in its more customary twentieth-century repertoire. Tempi are at times eccentrically fast in what after all are easy-going boyhood inspirations, and Kurt Masur in his complete set of the symphonies is generally preferable, but this selection is most welcome.

Symphonies Nos. 1 in C min., Op. 11;
(i) 2 in B flat (Hymn of Praise), Op. 52.
(M) ** Ph. 6768 030 (2). New Philh. O., Sawallisch, (i) with Donath, Hansmann, Kmentt, New Philh. Ch. ·

Symphonies Nos. 1; 4 in A (Italian), Op. 90.
** Ph. 9500 708/7300 803 [id.]. LPO, Haitink.

Symphony No. 2 (Hymn of Praise).
*** Decca D 133 D 2 (2) [Lon. 2250]. Ghazarin, Gruberova, Krenn, V. State Op. Ch., V. Singverein, VPO, Dohnányi – Erste Walpurgisnacht.***

(i) Symphonies Nos. 2; (ii) 3 in A min. (Scottish), Op. 56.
*** Ph. 6769 042/7699 128 [id.]. (i) Price, Burgess, Jerusalem, LPO, and Ch.; (ii) LSO; both cond. Chailly.

Mendelssohn's Hymn of Praise was once a favourite work with Victorian choral societies, who often forgot to include the first three purely instrumental movements. Latterly it has been unduly neglected, because it so manifestly falls short of its great model, Beethoven's Ninth Symphony. Sawallisch's recording goes some way towards repairing the neglect, though unfortunately he is not really a committed enough Mendelssohnian to brazen through the less-than-inspired passages, and the New Philharmonia Chorus for once sounds tepid – a pity some of the old Victorian-trained chorus members were not about to help. The C minor Symphony, on the other hand, is anything but pretentious; with its delightful scherzo it is another

example of Mendelssohn's electrically precocious genius. Good clean recording.

One clear advantage of the Chailly version of Hymn of Praise lies in its outstanding trio of soloists, with Margaret Price soaring radiantly in Lobe den Herrn, meine Seele and the women of the London Philharmonic Choir matching her. Siegfried Jerusalem also sings gloriously, with tone both bright and sweet, not least in the duet with Price. The recording is exceptionally realistic and beautifully balanced, so that Chailly's fresh and unaffected interpretation has its maximum impact, helped by fine playing and choral singing from London Philharmonic sources. With the London Symphony Orchestra Chailly gives a comparably enjoyable performance of the Scottish symphony, though the distancing of the sound in a rather reverberant acoustic takes some of the bite away. But if you prefer this coupling, Chailly is a good recommendation.

Dohnányi, coupling his version of Hymn of Praise not with another symphony but with another Mendelssohn choral work, relates the piece more to the choral than to the symphonic tradition. The chorus, not particularly large, yet sings incisively, and the wide-ranging recording underpins the texture of the finale, with resonant and superbly focused organ sound. In refinement and delicacy of shaping Dohnányi yields to a conductor like Karajan, and the 6/8 second movement lacks charm (the tempo is a fraction too fast); but this is altogether a refreshing performance of a work too long dismissed as sentimentally Victorian.

The Italian symphony really needs more sparkle than Haitink brings to it in his LPO version. It is always fresh and honest, but magic never quite develops, though some may be attracted by the unusual – but very apt – coupling of the early Symphony No. 1. The recording is fair but not one of Philips' clearest; the high-level cassette transfer is excellent.

463

Symphony No. 3 in A min. (Scottish), Op. 56; Athalia: Overture and War march of the Priests.
**(*) Decca SXL/KSXC 6954 [Lon. 7184]. VPO, Dohnányi.

Symphony No. 3; Overture: Calm Sea and Prosperous Voyage.
*** Ph. 9500 535/7300 678 [id.]. LPO, Haitink.

Symphony No. 3; Overture: The Hebrides.
(B) *** CFP/TC-CFP 40270. SNO, Gibson.
**(*) DG 2531/3301 256 [id.]. Israel PO, Bernstein.

Symphony No. 3; String symphony No. 10.
(M)** RCA Gold GL/GK 25330. Leipzig GO, Masur.

Symphonies Nos. 3–4.
(M) *** Decca Jub. JB/KJBC 103. LSO, Abbado.
(M) *** ASV ACM/ZCAM 2012. O. of St John's, Lubbock.
**(*) Argo ZRG/KZRC 926 [id.]. ASMF, Marriner.

Haitink's Philips recording of the Scottish symphony has gloriously beautiful sound, the upper strings glowingly fresh and woodwind rich and luminous. Yet the sumptuous body of tone of the full orchestra does not bring clouded detail. Comparison with Muti's excellent Philharmonia version for HMV is inevitable, since Muti offers the same coupling (ASD 3183 [Ang. 37168]) and is also beautifully, if not so richly, recorded. Haitink sets a faster pace in the opening movement yet loses nothing of the music's lyrical power. There is a feeling of greater symphonic breadth too, helped by the resonant fullness of the recording. But Muti scores by observing the exposition repeat, which Haitink omits. In the other three movements the performances are remarkably alike, but the warmth and glow of the Philips recording are always

telling, especially at the opening of the scherzo, and for the dancing violins in the finale. The final peroration sounds magnificent. The evocation of the overture is similarly persuasive, but Muti's faster tempo for the ingenuous brass entry at the end is the more effective. The Philips cassette is slightly less sumptuous than the disc, but the sound is full, fresh and wide-ranging – one of Philips' very best tapes.

Dohnányi's record has also been much praised, particularly and justifiably for its superb recording, among the finest the Scottish symphony has received (though the timpani are too prominent). The cassette transfer too is outstandingly successful. The performance is fresh and alert and the recording helps to underline the stormy quality that Dohnányi aptly finds in the first movement, though in other movements this is a less characterful reading than the best rivals. Not all the woodwind playing is elegant, and the welcome fill-up, a march once deservedly popular, is given a square performance.

In the bargain range the CfP version, appropriately recorded in Scotland, is very competitive. Gibson and his orchestra are on top form and they play the piece with warmth and eloquence. The string phrasing is strikingly fresh, and among the wind soloists the clarinets distinguish themselves (as also in the overture). The reading is agreeably relaxed and its presentation is helped by the rich glowing recording, with its full body and natural perspective. The (high-level) tape transfer has marginally less range and transparency than the disc but is still very good. One must not forget Maag's very successful early LSO recording for Decca (SPA/KCSP 503 [Lon. STS 15091]), which offers the same coupling and a vivid recording that wears its years lightly; but that is in the lower-middle price-range.

Bernstein and the Israel orchestra, recorded live in Munich, give a loving performance whose expansive tempi run the risk of overloading Mendelssohn's fresh inspiration with heavy expressiveness, making the slow introduction and the slow movement sound almost Mahlerian. The rhythmic lift of the scherzo and finale make amends, and throughout the performance a feeling of spontaneity helps one to accept the exaggerations; but it is not a version to recommend for repeated listening. The recording is well-balanced and the coupling apt if ungenerous. The cassette is well managed, fresh, rich and clear.

For its mid-priced reissue, RCA have added the *String symphony in B minor* to Masur's Leipzig disc, but the performance of the *Scottish symphony*, although it has many virtues, does not match the finest alternative versions, and it cannot compete on price with Maag and Gibson.

Abbado's *Scottish symphony* is beautifully played, each phrase sensitively moulded, and the *Italian symphony* has a comparable lightness of touch, matched with lyrical warmth. The sound is first-class.

With a chamber-sized string section, Lubbock offers a refreshingly direct performance of the *Scottish symphony*, presenting Mendelssohn's refined textures with delightful lightness and clarity. The tempo for the first-movement allegro is very brisk indeed (the reading could not be further removed from Haitink's in its approach), but there is no sense of hurry and the effect is almost Mozartian. The other movements are a little lacking in individuality, but the performance as a whole is most enjoyable. The *Italian symphony* has extremely vivacious outer movements (room was found to include the first-movement exposition repeat) and a nicely paced, engagingly delicate *Andante*. The recording is bright and clean, with no lack of bloom (the cassette and disc a close match), and the balance brings out the extra woodwind detail that naturally emerges from a performance with reduced strings. The playing may be a shade less polished than with Abbado or Marriner, but it is attractively spirited.

In Marriner's Argo performance the *Adagio* of the *Scottish* is so spacious (arguably too much so, since the middle section grows heavy) that the finale has to be put on side two. The means that the *Italian* has to be given without the exposition repeat and the twenty-bar lead-back. The performances are stylish and well-sprung but have no more individuality than Lubbock's. Again the use of a smaller-scaled ensemble brings a crisper, more transparent effect than usual. The recording is excellent, although the cassette has a less cleanly focused upper range than the disc; Lubbock's ASV tape is much brighter and cleaner.

Symphonies Nos. 3–5; Overture Ruy Blas.
(M) ** Ph. 6768 031 (2). New Philh. O., Sawallisch.

Sawallisch's collection of Mendelssohn's last three symphonies makes a good mid-price package, but the performances – from his complete set of the late sixties – lack something in resilience and charm. Everything is a little too straight-faced and literal, and the recording (good for its period) adds no sparkle.

Symphony No. 4 in A (Italian), Op. 90.
(M) (***) World mono SH/TC-SH 290. Philh. O., Cantelli – SCHUBERT: *Symphony No. 8.* ⊛ ***
**(*) DG 2531 291 [id.]. Berlin PO, Karajan – SCHUBERT: *Symphony No. 8.* **(*)
(*) HMV Dig. ASD/TCC-ASD 3963 [Ang. DS/4ZS 37760]. Berlin PO, Tennstedt – SCHUMANN: *Symphony No. 4.*(*)

Symphony No. 4; Overtures: Calm Sea and Prosperous Voyage; The Hebrides.
*** Decca Dig. SXDL/KSXDC 7500 [Lon. LDR 10003/5-]. VPO, Dohnányi.

Symphony No. 4; Overtures: The Hebrides; A Midsummer Night's Dream; Ruy Blas.
*** HMV ASD/*TC-ASD* 3763 [Ang. SZ 37614]. LSO, Previn.

Symphony No. 4; Overture Ruy Blas.
(M) *** RCA Gold GL/*GK* 12703 [AGL 1/*AGK 1* 2703]. LSO, Previn – PRO-KOFIEV: *Symphony No. 1.****

(i) *Symphony No. 4; A Midsummer Night's Dream overture, Op. 21; Nocturne; Scherzo, Op. 61; Overtures:* (ii) *The Hebrides;* (iii) *Ruy Blas.*
(M) *** HMV *TC-IDL 502.* (i) Philh. O., Wallberg; (ii) RPO, Sargent; (iii) Royal Liv. PO, Groves.

Previn's later HMV version of the *Italian symphony* comes in what is in effect an ideal Mendelssohn coupling (perfect for recommending to anyone who just wants a single disc to represent the composer), his best-loved symphony matched against the three most popular overtures. Previn, always an inspired Mendelssohnian, gives exuberant performances. In the symphony he has modified the tempo of the *Pilgrims' march* very slightly from his earlier RCA reading, making it more clearly a slow movement, while the third movement has a cleaner culmination on the reprise. The outer movements as before are urgent without sounding at all breathless, and are finely sprung; the recording balance has the strings a little less forward than they might be, but the fullness of sound is impressive. The cassette too is first-class, rich and vivid and only fractionally less refined than the disc.

Previn's earlier RCA recording remains fully competitive at mid-price. It is a delightful performance, fresh and disciplined. Detail is beautifully articulated and the proceedings have a spontaneous yet well-controlled vitality. Previn makes no egocentric interpretative points: his view of the work is admirably unfussy

and straightforward, and the recording, though not as rich as the newer, full-priced HMV, is firm and well focused, with plenty of stereo information. The tape is much less recommendable, with the dynamics compressed.

Dohnányi, in one of the first digital recordings to be issued, gives a characteristically refreshing account of the *Italian symphony*, never pushed too hard, even though the *Saltarello* is taken exhilaratingly fast. It is a pity that – unlike many of the finest versions (both of Previn's, Leppard's and Abbado's) – this omits the exposition repeat in the first movement, so one misses the extended lead-back passage. No doubt it was decided that for so important a digital issue wide groove-spacing was essential, and the two overtures on the reverse bring sound even more impressive, with the whispered opening of *Meerestille* particularly evocative. *The Hebrides* is taken rather slowly and romantically.

What is it that makes Guido Cantelli's performances so memorable? There are no personal touches of the kind we are used to from Furtwängler, Koussevitzky or Toscanini. In many ways Cantelli was a self-effacing conductor, concerned largely with perfection of detail, ensemble and balance, yet never at the expense of the overall impression. He was an artist with a highly developed sense of proportion; the part never detracts from the beauty of the whole, yet no single detail fails to tell. Remarkably few allowances need be made for the sound quality here, even though it is more than a quarter of a century old. The Schubert symphony with which it is coupled is genuinely stereo, but this is mono. Nonetheless, it sounds as fresh and alive as do the performances themselves. There is little difference in quality between disc and tape.

For their 'hour-long' tape-only issue, HMV have used Wallberg's splendid Philharmonia coupling of the early sixties. Beautifully recorded, it sounds as fresh as the day it first appeared. The performance of the symphony is lively and stylish; admittedly Wallberg paces the slow movement rather stolidly, but this is redeemed by the lightness of the orchestral playing. The outer movements are beautifully judged – the first not too fast, so that the rhythm has an exhilarating lift to it, and the finale lithe and athletic in its *moto perpetuo*. The *Midsummer Night's Dream* excerpts are no less stylish, with the Philharmonia players on top form, and again one is impressed by the warmth and bloom of the recording. With Sir Charles Groves's resonantly exciting version of *Ruy Blas* and Sargent's atmospheric *Fingal's Cave*, this makes a very attractive collection.

Karajan's account was originally coupled with the *Reformation symphony*. It goes without saying that the playing of the Berlin Philharmonic is outstanding, but, finely shaped as this performance is, it lacks the last degree of spontaneity and sparkle. Most collectors would probably be less enthusiastic about a full-priced reissue of a 1966 recording of Schubert's *Unfinished* (with which it is now coupled), even though Karajan's performance has the merit of inspired and unaffected simplicity.

Tennstedt's account of the *Italian* is vividly articulated and obviously felt. He is not quite as spontaneous as Bernstein and the Israel Philharmonic (see below), though the quality of the Berliners' playing is finer. The digital sound has admirable body and clarity to recommend it (the chrome cassette is first-class too), and this is certainly a version to be considered.

Symphonies Nos. 4 (Italian); 5 in D min. (Reformation), Op. 107.
*** Erato STU 71064 [RCA ARL 1/ARK 1 2632]. ECO, Leppard.
*** DG 2531/*3301* 097 [id.]. Israel PO, Bernstein.
(M) *(*) RCA Gold GL/*GK* 25307. Leipzig GO, Masur.

Symphony No. 5.
*** HMV ASD/*TC-ASD* 3781 [Ang. S 37601]. Philh. O., Muti – SCHUMANN: *Symphony No. 1.***(*)

Leppard directs joyful performances of both symphonies. Consistently he shows how infectiously he can lift rhythms, so that the first movement of the *Italian* has exhilaration with no feeling of rush. The relatively small string section of the ECO may sound a little thin in the third movement of the *Italian*, but the *Saltarello* finale brings superbly clean articulation of triplets. In the *Reformation* the scale of the performance, coupled with Leppard's rhythmic flair, helps to lighten a work that can sometimes seem too heavy for its material. The *Allegro con fuoco* gets its fire not from high speed but from crisp precision; the scherzo too is beautifully lilting, and the *Allegro maestoso* of the finale firmly replaces pomposity with joy. The recording is airily atmospheric to match.

Bernstein's performances of both symphonies are also sparkling and persuasive, never falling into the rather exaggerated expressiveness which in places mars the companion account of the *Scottish symphony*. As with that work, the recordings were made at live concerts, and though the speeds are often challengingly fast, they never fail to convey the exhilaration of the occasion. In the *Reformation symphony* Bernstein encourages the flute to give a meditative account of the chorale *Ein feste Burg*, but he makes it a revelation, not a distraction. The recording is convincingly atmospheric without being ideally clear. The cassette transfer lacks the last degree of refinement, with a tendency for the bass to boom a little in the *Italian* and a touch of roughness in the finale of the *Reformation*.

Muti gives real fire to the *Allegro con fuoco* of the first movement of the *Reformation* and generally, with the Philharmonia in excellent form, this is a performance which sweeps away any

Victorian cobwebs, urgency never pressed too far. The recording is excellent too, although the cassette is not as refined as the disc.

No grumbles about the playing of the Leipzig Gewandhaus Orchestra on the mid-price RCA Gold label, and full marks to Kurt Masur for giving us the exposition repeat in the *Italian*. Taken on its own merits there is much to be said for this cultured performance, but the recording is distinctly subfusc and does not compete either in its disc or cassette form with the rival full-price accounts, which are worth the extra money.

Octet (for strings) *in E flat, Op. 20.*
** Decca Dig. SXDL/*KSXDC* 7506 [Lon. LDR 10009]. Israel PO, Mehta.

Octet; String symphonies Nos. 10 and 12.
(M) *** Ph. Seq. 6527/*7311* 076 [6580 103]. I Musici.

Octet; String quintet No. 2 in B flat, Op. 87.
*** Ph. 9500 616 [id.]. ASMF, Marriner.

The Academy's earlier Argo record of the *Octet*, with a Boccherini quintet as a fill-up, dates from the late 1960s, and, good though it was in almost every way, this newcomer is an improvement. The playing has greater sparkle and polish; the recorded sound is also far superior; and it has the advantage of an altogether excellent coupling. Whereas on the earlier disc the *Octet* spilt over to the second side, here it can be played without a break and room is left for an important work of Mendelssohn's later life, the *Second Quintet*. This is an underrated piece, and it too receives an elegant and poetic performance that will give much satisfaction and is unlikely to be surpassed for a long time.

The I Musici version of the *Octet* is also one of the finest available, smooth in contour but with a fine balance between vitality and warmth. The *String symphonies* are obviously smaller in scale than on the alternative full orchestral versions, but they are beautifully played. The recording is excellent and the tape transfer smooth and quite lively.

Mehta's account using a full complement of orchestral strings is brilliantly and clearly recorded, but the effect is glossy. The cassette is sweeter and smoother on top than the LP and is generally preferable. The playing itself emphasizes vitality at the expense of warmth.

Piano trio No. 1 in D min., Op. 49.
*** HMV ASD/*TC-ASD* 3894. Kyung-Wha Chung, Tortelier, Previn – SCHUMANN: *Trio No. 1.***
*** Pearl SHE 553. Beaux Arts Trio – DVOŘÁK: *Trio No. 4.****

Piano trios Nos. 1; 2 in C min., Op. 66.
(M) *** Ph. Fest. 6570/*7310* 075 [6580 211]. Beaux Arts Trio.
*** Erato STU 71025. Queffélec, Amoyal, Lodéon.

Mendelssohn's *D minor Trio* is one of his most richly inspired chamber works, challenging the sharply contrasted musical personalities of Chung, Tortelier and Previn to provide a fascinating interplay. If anyone leads, it is Previn, whose agility is remarkable in fast passage-work; but above all the emotional drive of a piece which can easily seem sentimental comes out magnificently in this exceptional matching of talent. The recording is excellent; on cassette the sound is full, but not quite so clear and refined as on the disc.

The Beaux Arts Trio offer an obvious and sensible coupling. Their playing is always splendidly alive and musical, and they are vividly recorded (the sound on cassette is first-class too). The playing in the *D minor Trio* is not quite in the same category as the Chung/Tortelier/Previn version, which shows greater drive and warmth, but nonetheless at medium price it is extremely acceptable and the coupling is a valuable one.

On Erato the excellent partnership of Anne Queffélec, Pierre Amoyal and Frédéric Lodéon provides expert, spontaneous and characterful performances with refreshing sparkle and zest. The recording too is first-class, well detailed and with plenty of presence. It has slightly more body than the Beaux Arts version (made in the late 1960s), and the playing is by no means inferior either. However, while the Philips version, with its considerable price advantage, is still available the Erato disc is likely to remain marginally second choice.

On Pearl the Beaux Arts offer a further alternative choice for those only requiring the *D minor Trio*. The two performances are of equal attractiveness and there is very little to choose between the Philips and Pearl recording quality. Of course the Pearl disc is premium-priced but it includes an excellent account of the *Dumky Trio* which many readers may want to have.

String quartet No. 1 in E flat, Op. 12.
*** Ph. 9500/7300 995 [id.]. Orlando Qt
– DVOŘÁK: *Quartet No. 12.****

String quartets Nos. 1; 2 in A min., Op. 13.
(M) *** Decca Ace SDD 544 [Lon. STS 15463]. Orford Qt.

The delightful *F flat Quartet* was composed when Mendelssohn was twenty, and the *A minor* (1827), despite the later opus number, precedes it by two years. Both are strong works, though the scherzo of Op. 12 has a close affinity with Cherubini's quartet in the same key, written in the previous decade. Mendelssohn's inspiration is fresh and spirited, and those requiring this coupling will find that the excellent performances by the Canadian Orford Quartet are straightforward and unfussy, with an admirable sense of continuity and pace. The re-

cordings are both faithful and the Decca pressings excellent.

The Orlando Quartet, a superb ensemble, has been widely acclaimed for its concert appearances – small wonder, if they are as accomplished and sensitive as this account of the *E flat Quartet*, which is among the very best ever put on record. It is played with lightness of touch, delicacy of feeling and excellent ensemble. The recording is totally natural and lifelike, and the cassette transfer is of Philips' best quality, matching the disc closely.

String quintets Nos. 1 in A, Op. 18; 2 in B flat, Op. 87.
(M) *** Decca Ace SDD 562. V. Philharmonic Quintet.

String quintet No. 2
*(*) RCA RL/*RK* 13354 [ARL 1/*ARK 1* 3354]. Guarneri Qt, Zukerman –
BEETHOVEN: *String Quintet.**(*)

The two *Quintets* come from either extreme of Mendelssohn's career. The first was composed when he was a youth of seventeen, only a year after the *Octet* – to which, it must be admitted, it is inferior. The second dates from 1845, two years before his death, and is the more rewarding of the two. The Vienna Philharmonic Quintet give performances of great suavity and finesse, though at times they do not observe the finer dynamic nuances. The logical coupling and the excellent recording are as strong a factor in this issue's favour as its medium price. However, there is no doubt that the Academy of St Martin-in-the-Fields bring a shade more imagination and feeling to the Op. 87 *Quintet*; their performance is coupled with the *Octet* (see above).

The version by the Guarneri Quartet with Pinchas Zukerman hardly competes at all in this field. There is a lack of charm and, more surprisingly, of refinement and polish too. Nor do these artists enjoy the advantage of sumptuous recorded sound. (The tape emphasizes the bright treble

469

and tends to fierceness, though it does not lack body.)

Violin sonata in F min., Op. 4.
*** O-L DSLO 571. Schröder, Hogwood – SCHUBERT: *Sonata, D. 574.****

As its opus number indicates, the Mendelssohn *Violin sonata* is an early piece, written when he was a boy of fourteen. It is not the most memorable of his early works, though it has many endearing moments and is here most persuasively presented on period instruments: Jaap Schröder plays a Stradivarius of 1709 and Christopher Hogwood a fortepiano of the mid-1820s. Beautifully alive and natural recording.

Scherzo from A Midsummer Night's Dream, Op. 61 (trans. Rachmaninov).
*** Hyp. A 66009. Shelley – RACHMANINOV: *Variations* etc.***

Rachmaninov's transcription was one of the composer–virtuoso's favourite party pieces, and Howard Shelley, with fabulously clear articulation and delectably sprung rhythms, gives a performance of which Rachmaninov himself would not have been ashamed. This is a delightful makeweight for an outstanding disc of Rachmaninov variations.

Songs without Words, Book 1, Nos. 1, 5, 6 (Venetian gondola song); Book 2, Nos. 9, 10, 12 (Venetian gondola song); Book 3, Nos. 14, 15, 17; Book 4, Nos. 20, 21; Book 5, Nos. 23, 29 (Venetian gondola song), 30 (Spring song); Book 6, Nos. 32, 34 (Spinning song), 35, 36; Book 7, Nos. 39, 42; Book 8, Nos. 43, 46, 48.
*** DG 2531 260 [id.]. Barenboim.

An admirable selection from Barenboim's fine complete set of the *Songs without Words* (2740 104), which is still

available. The playing is fresh and imaginative, and the recording maintains the excellent quality of the original.

Songs without Words Nos. 1, 3, 6, 7, 10, 12, 14, 17, 18, 20, 25, 26, 29, 30, 32, 34, 43, 45, 47.
(M) *(*) HMV Green. ESD/*TC-ESD* 7113. Adni.

Adni's selection is at medium price, but it is seriously lacking in charm. The recording is excellent on disc and cassette alike, but Barenboim's full-priced DG disc is far more rewarding.

6 Organ sonatas, Op. 65; 3 Preludes and fugues, Op. 37.
(M) **(*) O-L SOL 350/1. Fisher (organ of Chester Cath.).

Mendelssohn's *Organ sonatas* were commissioned by an English publisher (Coventry and Holland), so it seems slightly unreasonable to reflect that the registrations Roger Fisher conjures from his instrument at Chester sound too bland. Fisher obviously has the measure of the music and can produce bursts of power when called for, as in the exciting closing pages of the finale of Sonata No. 4. He is at his best in the *Preludes and fugues*. But the reverberation tends slightly to blur the articulation in fast passages (this is not the fault of the admirably truthful recording), and the lack of bite and piquancy of colour gives an impression of sympathetic scholarship rather than persuading the listener that these works offer the best of Mendelssohn.

Die erste Walpurgisnacht, Op. 60.
*** Decca D 133 D 2 (2) [Lon. 2250]. Lilowa, Laubenthal, Krause, Sramek, V. Singverein, VPO, Dohnányi – *Symphony No. 2.****

Die erste Walpurgisnacht; Overture: The Hebrides.

** RCA RL/*RK* 13460 [*ARL* 1/*ARK* 1 3460]. Taylor, Norman, Estes, Mendelssohn Club Ch., Phd. O., Ormandy.

Die erste Walpurgisnacht, with its un-expected anti-Christian stance (reflecting Goethe's sardonic tone of voice in his dramatic poem), is an oddity, but one full of interest for the modern listener. Witches and druids are angrily pursued by Christians on the Brocken, and some of the more dramatic moments suggest that had he been given the right libretto Mendelssohn might have made an opera composer. Squeezed by Decca on to a single side, with crisp, bright recording, it makes an excellent fill-up to Dohnányi's refreshing version of the choral *Second Symphony* (*Hymn of Praise*).

Eugene Ormandy and his excellent forces give a straightforward and well-conceived account of the work, though they do not perhaps achieve the refinement or sureness of touch that are needed in this piece. The cantata is spread over two sides, with *The Hebrides overture*, which most collectors will already have, as a fill-up. This is a useful issue for those who cannot abide the *Hymn of Praise*, but Dohnányi is undoubtedly the better recorded. The cassette is a bit fierce and needs a treble cut; the voices, however, have plenty of life and presence.

A Midsummer Night's Dream: Over-ture, Op. 21; Incidental music, Op. 61 (*1, Scherzo; 2, Melodrama; 2a, Fairy march; 3, You spotted snakes; 4, Melodrama; 5, Intermezzo; 6, Melodrama; 7, Nocturne; 8, Melodrama; 9, Wedding march; 10, Melodrama; 10a, Funeral march; 11, Dance of the clowns; 12, Melodrama; 13, Finale*).
*** Erato STU 71090 (complete). Gale, Murray, LPO and Ch., Leppard.
(M) *** DG Priv. 2535/*3335* 393 [138959] (omitting Nos. 2, 4, 6, 8, 10, 12). Mathis, Boese, Bav. R. Ch. and O., Kubelik.

(M) *** Ph. Fest. 6570/*7310* 021 [id.] (omitting Nos. 2, 4, 6, 8, 10, 12). Woodland, Watts, Ch., Concg. O., Haitink.
(M) **(*) Decca Jub. JB/*KJBC* 72 (complete). Bork, Hodgson, Amb. S., New Philh. O., Frühbeck de Burgos.

Like Previn's version of the *Midsummer Night's Dream* music (see below), Leppard's includes even the tiny frag-ments between scenes, not just the main items. Musically they may be of slight value, but they help to intensify the atmosphere of this most imaginative of incidental music. Leppard like Previn gives the music sparkle and resilience, taking the *Nocturne* with its horn solo more persuasively at a flowing tempo, though the *Wedding march* is here rela-tively heavy. There is also a case for pre-ferring Leppard's use of a women's choir instead of children's voices (as in the Previn), though the extra bite and edge of young voices in *You spotted snakes* makes the Previn refreshing and indivi-dual. Leppard's account of the lovely epilogue to the overture, later reproduced in the finale after the concluding chorus, is particularly beautiful. The Erato re-cording is admirably refined.

Among reissues, that by the Bavarian Radio Orchestra takes pride of place. The playing and recording (equally clear and clean on disc and cassette, yet not lacking atmosphere) are both strikingly fresh. Even with the advantage of economy, however, this does not displace Previn on disc (HMV ASD 3377 [Ang. S/*4XS* 37268]), where the performance, like Leppard's, has extra imagination and sparkle (the *Nocturne*, too, is more ro-mantic); but at medium price the DG version is still very attractive.

The playing on Haitink's Concertge-bouw issue is also wonderfully felicitous, the musical characterization sensitive (the *Wedding march* is especially fine). The mellow sound that Philips provide may be preferred by some, but the acous-tic also brings a lack of internal clarity

471

(especially on tape), which must be counted a drawback. This is very rewarding in many ways, but it does not displace Previn, Leppard or Kubelik.

The reissue at medium price of the Frühbeck de Burgos version is also attractive; the sound, though reverberant, is beautiful on disc and tape alike, with a striking bloom overall. The orchestral playing is very fine, and although the overture is not quite so evocative as under Leppard and Previn, this is the only mid-priced issue to present the score complete.

A Midsummer Night's Dream: Overture, Op. 21; Scherzo; Nocturne; Wedding march, Op. 61.
(M) *** Ph. Seq. 6527/7311 056. Concg. O., Szell – SCHUBERT: *Rosamunde.****

Superlative playing from the Concertgebouw Orchestra under Szell. He seldom recorded in Europe, but when he did the results were always impressive. Here the lightness and clean articulation of the violins in the overture are a delight; the wonderfully nimble wind playing in the *Scherzo* is no less engaging, and there is a fine horn solo in the *Nocturne*. The recording has been freshened for this reissue and sounds admirably clear, without loss of bloom. Szell's Schubert performances are equally rewarding, and there is no better version of this attractive coupling. The cassette transfer is good.

Psalms Nos. 42: Wie die Hirsch schreit (As pants the hart), Op. 42; 95: Kommt, lasst uns anbeten (Come, let us worship), Op. 46.
*** Erato STU 71101. Baumann, Silva, Blaser, Lisbon Gulbenkian Foundation Ch. and O., Corbóz.

Choral works like these may characteristically glide over the problems of religious faith in an easy and sweet setting of texts (*Psalm 42* begins with what is

suspiciously close to a waltz); but in fine performances they are still worth hearing. The best inspirations in each of these cantatas point directly back to Mendelssohn's great model, J. S. Bach. Recording is full and atmospheric.

Psalms Nos. 98: Singet dem Herrn ein neues Lied, Op. 91; 115: Nicht unserm Namen, Herr, Op. 31. Lauda Sion, Op. 73.
*** Erato STU 71223. Brunner, Ihara, Ramirez, Huttenlocher, Lisbon Gulbenkian Foundation Ch. and O., Corbóz.

The two psalm settings inspire Mendelssohn to some of his most effectively Bach-like writing. The text of Psalm 98 inspired Bach too, and though austerity periodically turns into sweetness, both pieces are most welcome in performances as fresh and alert as these. *Lauda Sion* is less varied in its expression, a persistent hymn of praise.

Die Heimkehr aus der Fremde.
*** EMI 1C 065 30741. Donath, Schreier, Fischer-Dieskau, Bavarian R. Ch., Munich RO, Wallberg.

The German title conceals what we generally know in English-speaking countries (from the overture at least) as *Son and Stranger*. That inspired piece, much admired by Richard Strauss among others, leads to a *Singspiel* which was written with charm and tenderness for the silver wedding of the composer's parents, being presented to them (aptly, since the title means *The Return from Abroad*) on his return from a lengthy stay in England. Apart from the overture one of the arias was once also well-known in its English translation, *I am a rover*. In the drama it is sung by a disagreeable grocer – a splendid vehicle here for Fischer-Dieskau. Although the plot is predictable, with troubles for the returning soldier finally being solved, the piece is enchanting in a performance such as this, at once effervescent and touching, and helped by excellent recording.

Die beiden Pädagogen.
*** HM 1C 065 45416. Laki, Fuchs, Dallapozza, Fischer-Dieskau, Bavarian R. Ch., Munich RO, Wallberg.

This little *Singspiel* about the quarrels of pedagogues – a subject on which the young Mendelssohn had personal experience – makes a charming entertainment, an amazing piece of work for a twelve-year-old. Tongue in cheek, he uses academic devices like fugue with the assurance of a master, never making the joke too heavy. The ensemble in which rival pedagogues argue their different ideas of education and shout their allegiance with cries of *Pestalozzi* and *Basedow* is hilarious. Fischer-Dieskau is only one of the excellent soloists in this superbly produced recording, a sparkling performance to match the boy Mendelssohn's inspiration.

Messager, André (1853–1929)

Les Deux Pigeons (ballet): suite; *Isoline* (ballet): suite.
(M) *** HMV Green. ESD 7048. Orchestre de Paris, Jacquillat – LALO: *Scherzo*; PIERNÉ: *Marche* etc.***

What an enchanting score is Messager's *Two Pigeons* ballet; and there is some lovely music in *Isoline* too. Part of a wholly recommendable concert of French music, this can be welcomed with the utmost enthusiasm. The recording is most successful, offering plenty of warmth and colour as well as sparkle.

Messiaen, Olivier (born 1908)

Turangalîla symphony.
*** HMV SLS/*TC-SLS* 5117 (2) [Ang. S 3853]. Béroff (piano), Loriod (ondes martenot), LSO, Previn.

Messiaen's *Turangalîla symphony* was written at a time (1946–8) when – Shostakovich notwithstanding – the symphonic tradition seemed at its lowest ebb. Yet it is unquestionably a masterpiece: an uneven masterpiece perhaps, but a work of great magnetism and imaginative power. Its characteristc mysticism is balanced by its strongly communicative nature – even at a first hearing it evokes a direct and immediate response in its audience. Messiaen's conception is on an epic scale, to embrace almost the totality of human experience. This is immediately implied in the Sanskrit title, a complex word suggesting the interplay of life forces, creation and dissolution, but which is also divisible: *Turanga* is Time and also implies rhythmic movement; *Lila* is Love, and with a strong inspiration from the Tristan and Isolde legend Messiaen's love music dominates his conception of human existence. The actual love sequences feature the ondes martenot with its 'velvety glissandi'. This fascinating texture is a truly twentieth-century sound, and at times it has an unearthly quality suggesting Man looking out into a universe which is almost his to grasp. The piano obbligato is also a strong feature of the score, and the balance here is skilfully managed so that it is integrated within the orchestral tapestry yet provides a dominating decorative influence. The spirit of Debussy hovers over the piano writing, while the Stravinsky of *Le Sacre* is clearly an influence elsewhere. But this is by no means an eclectic work; it is wholly original and its themes (with their element of vulgarity as well as mysticism) are undoubtedly haunting.

The essence of the symphony is more readily captured in the concert hall than in the recording studio, but Previn's vividly direct approach, helped by recording of spectacular amplitude and dynamic range, certainly creates tingling electricity from the first bar to the last. Perhaps the music's atmospheric qualities are marginally less well captured here than in Ozawa's earlier RCA set (now long deleted), which was softer-grained. Previn is at his very best in the work's more robust moments, for instance the jazzy fifth movement, and he catches the wit at the beginning of *Chant d'amour 2*. The idyllic *Garden of the sleep of love* is both serene and poetically sensuous, and the mysterious opening of the third movement is highly evocative. The apotheosis of the love theme in the closing pages is jubilant and life-enhancing. The bright, vivid detail of the recording is also captured extraordinarily well on tape, which on an A/B comparison with the discs reveals fractionally more sharpness of detail, but, correspondingly, marginally less depth. However, the differences are minimal.

Quatuor pour la fin du temps.
*** DG 2531 093 [id.]. Yordanoff, Tetard, Desurment, Barenboim.
*** Ph. 9500 725 [id.]. Beths, Pieterson, Bylsma, De Leeuw.

Barenboim and his colleagues recorded the *Quatuor pour la fin du temps* in the presence of the composer. Messiaen's visionary and often inspired piece was composed during his days in a Silesian prison camp. Among his fellow-prisoners were a violinist, clarinettist and cellist, who with the composer at the piano made its creation possible. Barenboim is a strong personality who carries much of this performance in his hands, and inspires his colleagues with his own commitment to the music. The performance is certainly better recorded than any of its rivals so far, and readers wanting

to invest in this strange and often haunting work need have no doubts as to its excellence.

The Dutch team are also given good recording. Indeed their account has the merit of outstanding team-work, and Reinbert de Leeuw has a keen sense of atmosphere, though he does not dominate the proceedings. There is some superbly eloquent playing from George Pieterson and Anner Bylsma too. Honours are pretty evenly divided between this and the DG record, and choice can be safely left to personal taste and availability.

Chants de terre et de ciel; Harawi (Chants d'amour et de la mort); Poèmes pour Mi; Trois Mélodies.
**(*) EMI 2C 167 16226/8. Command, Petit.

These three records offer Messiaen's complete vocal output in performances of considerable power and authority. The early songs (the *Trois Mélodies* of 1930 and the two sets from the mid-1930s, *Poèmes pour Mi* and *Chants de terre et de ciel*) are given with great sensitivity and eloquence, even if the voice sometimes seems too big for these settings. *Harawi* dates from the post-war years; the title is a Peruvian-Indian word meaning a love song leading to the lovers' death. It forms part of the *Tristan*-inspired pieces which engaged Messiaen in the late 1940s and also include the *Turangalîla symphony* and the *Cinq Rechants*. The performances were presumably recorded over a longish period and there is some inconsistency in balance, the piano varying in prominence from the reticent to the forward. So far Michèle Command is the only French artist to have given us a comprehensive survey of Messiaen, and collectors with an interest in this key figure in post-war French music can invest in this set with confidence.

Meyerbeer, Giacomo
(1791–1864)

Les Patineurs (ballet suite, orch. Lambert).
(M) ** HMV Green. ESD/*TC-ESD* 7115. Philh. O., Mackerras – LUIGINI: *Ballet Egyptien* ***; PONCHIELLI: *Dance of the Hours* **(*); TCHAIKOVSKY: *Nutcracker suite.* **

Les Patineurs was arranged by Constant Lambert using excerpts from Meyerbeer's operas. Sir Charles Mackerras here directs a characteristically vivacious performance of the suite, but the 1960 recording, though vivid, is rather dry both on disc and on tape.

Miaskovsky, Nicolai
(1881–1950)

Symphony No. 11 in B flat min., Op. 34; 2 Pieces for string orchestra, Op. 46b.
*** HMV ASD 3879. Moscow RSO, Dudarova.

The *Eleventh* of Miaskovsky's twenty-seven symphonies dates from 1931–2 and deserves a wider hearing. Before the First World War Miaskovsky had been identified with the progressive Western-influenced musical trends, but during the 1920s and 30s his was a conservative voice in the new music. Yet the language is often unpredictable: there are suggestions of Reger even, and a distinctive melodic style, particularly evident in the finale. Miaskovsky touches a vein of nostalgia that is very much his own, and there is a gentle melancholy that is very appealing. This surfaces in the *Two Pieces for strings*, which Miaskovsky transcribed from his *Nineteenth Symphony,* written in 1939 for the Red Army band. This is dignified and eloquent music that readers should lose no time in searching out, for the deletions axe treats Miaskovsky with consistent cruelty. Good performances from the Radio Orchestra and fully acceptable sound too.

Symphony No. 21, Op. 51.
*** Uni. RHS 346. New Philh. O., Measham – KABALEVSKY: *Symphony No. 2.* **(*)

The *Twenty-first* is Miaskovsky's most recorded symphony and arguably his finest. David Measham has the measure of Miaskovsky's blend of melancholy and nostalgia, and in both the contemplative opening and the poetic closing pages he does this score full justice. Though it is conservative in idiom, this symphony stands the test of time remarkably well, and Miaskovsky's elegiac musings ring far truer than many more overtly 'modern' scores of the early 1940s. The timbre of the various instruments reproduces truthfully and the recording is fully acceptable, though it is a little wanting in transparency and range at the top.

Milan, Luis (c. 1500–c. 1561)

El Maestro: Fantasias Nos. 8, 9, 12 and 16; Pavanas Nos. 1, 4, 5 and 6; Tento No. 1.
*** RCA RL/*RK* 13435 [ARL1/*ARK1* 3435]. Bream – NARVAEZ: *Collection.* ***

Julian Bream seeks nobility of feeling in this repertoire and often chooses slow, dignified tempi. The music was originally written for the vihuela, a hybrid instrument popular in sixteenth-century Spain, looking like a guitar but tuned like a lute.

However, it all sounds splendid here on a proper lute, especially when so beautifully recorded. The cassette transfer is immaculate too.

Milhaud, Darius (1892–1974)

Le Bœuf sur le toit (ballet); *La Création du monde* (ballet); *Saudades do Brazil Nos. 7–9 and 11.*
**(*) HMV ASD 3444 [Ang. S/4XS 37442]. Orchestre Nat. de France, Bernstein.

Milhaud was essentially a Mediterranean composer whose scores radiate a sunny, relaxed charm that is irresistible. The *Saudades do Brazil* come from the period when he served as Claudel's secretary in Rio de Janeiro, while the two ballet scores come from the 1920s. As one would expect, Bernstein finds this repertoire thoroughly congenial, though his performance of *La Création du monde* disappoints slightly: the French orchestra do not respond with the verve and virtuosity that the Boston orchestra give Munch in the RCA recording (see below). Nor does *Le Bœuf sur le toit* have quite the sparkle and infectious gaiety that the music ideally demands. This is not to deny that these are good performances and well worth acquiring, particularly as the recordings are well balanced and vividly detailed.

La Création du monde; Suite provençale.
(M) ** RCA Gold GL/GK 12445 [AGL 1 2445]. Boston SO, Munch – POULENC: *Organ concerto.***

These delightful Milhaud pieces originally occupied a side each when these recordings first appeared twenty years ago, and their compression on to one side has not resulted in any improvement in sound quality. The performance of *La Création du monde* has great brilliance and virtuosity to commend it, though Charles Munch uses larger forces than those specified for the original production. The acoustic is reverberant, so that textures are less transparent than is ideal. Much the same must be said for the *Suite provençale* based on themes by André Campra, a marvellous score that ought to enjoy much wider popularity than it does. It is not otherwise available at present, and even if the sound is not of the very first order by modern standards, it is nonetheless acceptable. The tape transfers are undistinguished; the sound has a restricted dynamic and frequency spectrum.

Music for wind: *La Cheminée du Roi René, Op. 105; Divertissement en trois parties, Op. 399b; Pastorale, Op. 47; 2 Sketches, Op. 227b; Suite d'après Corrette, Op. 161b.*
**(*) Chan. ABR/ABT 1012. Athena Ens., McNicol.

La Cheminée du Roi René.
*(*) Uni. RHS 366. Danish Wind Quintet – HINDEMITH: *Kleine Kammermusik ***; NIELSEN: *Quintet.***

Two of these pieces were derived from film music: *La Cheminée du Roi René* is based on a score Milhaud wrote to *Cavalcade d'Amour*, set in the fifteenth century; and the *Divertissement* draws on material composed for a film on the life of Gaugin. The *Suite d'après Corrette* features music written for a Paris production of *Romeo and Juliet*, using themes by the eighteenth-century French master, Michel Corrette. Though none of this is first-class Milhaud, it is still full of pleasing and attractive ideas, and the general air of easy-going life-loving enjoyment is well conveyed by the alert playing of the Athena Ensemble. One's only quarrel with this issue is the somewhat close balance, which picks up the mechanism of the various keys, and does less than justice to the artists' pianissimo tone. However, this can be remedied a little by a lower level setting, and there is far too much to enjoy here to inhibit a recommendation. The cassette transfer is excellent, matching the disc closely.

The Unicorn recording also suffers from a limited dynamic range; but, more seriously, there is also a lack of the kind of charm and sparkle that might persuade doubters.

Suite française.
*** ASV ALH/ZCALH 913. L. Wind O., Wick – GRAINGER: *Irish tune* etc.; POULENC: *Suite française.****

The *Suite française* is an enchanting piece, full of Mediterranean colour and an earthy vitality. It would be difficult to imagine a more idiomatic or spirited performance than this one, which has excellent balance and blend. Vivid recording. This is an extraordinarily appealing work and ought to be far more popular than it is.

Millöcker, Karl (1842–99)

Der Bettelstudent (complete).
*** EMI 1C 30162/3. Streich, Holm, Litz, Prey, Unger, Bav. R. Ch., Graunke SO, Allers.

Der Bettelstudent: highlights.
(M) **(*) Tel. AF 6.21287. Koth, Bartos, Bartel, Schutz, Böhme, Ch. and O., Michalski.

With a first-rate cast and excellent team-work (the charming trio at the beginning of the third act is a good example) the EMI set offers a consistently vivacious account of *Der Bettelstudent.* The plot, with its extraordinary mixture of Polish patriotism, mistaken identities and the triumph of true love, is supported by an attractively lyrical score, which is

admirably presented and well recorded here. It is a pity that the libretto booklet, although it gives a synopsis of the story-line in English, does not provide a translation; but there is only a comparatively small amount of linking dialogue.

Some may well decide that a single-disc selection is more suitable and the alternative Telefunken issue serves this purpose very well. The selection is well made, with a good deal of music from Act 2. The duets *Nur das Eine bitt' ich dich* and *Ich setz' den Fall*, give the four principals a chance to shine, and their response is delightful. Then follows a series of lively numbers for the chorus (including *Glückliche Braut, Trink uns zu* and *Heidahi*), and although there is some rather cavalier fading in and out of the music for the sake of continuity, the sparkle is in no doubt. The recording is lively and the acoustic well judged. There is spoken dialogue to link the musical numbers.

Gasparone (abridged).
(M) *** Tel. AF 6.21288. Barabas, Badorek, Lins, Schutz, Bartos, Ch. and O., Michalski.

Karl Millöcker's three big successes were written within a period of five years, 1879–84. *The Dubarry* came first, then *Der Bettelstudent* (1882) and finally *Gasparone.* The score of *Gasparone* is highly engaging, with the waltz song *Im dunklen Wald* (beautifully sung here by Sari Barabas) an obvious highlight. The Act 1 finale is particularly infectious, with a string of attractive tunes in different rhythms and styles. Act 2 offers another lyrical waltz melody (*Dunkelrote Rosen*), which is nicely done by Wilfried Badorek, and the same rhythm predominates in the operetta's closing pages. This performance is first-rate in every way, and all the important numbers are included, with judicious linking dialogue. The recording is lively and atmospheric. The presentation (both here and in *Der Bettelstudent*) is in Telefunken's usual potpourri style.

477

Moeran, Ernest J.
(1894–1950)

Violin concerto.
*** Lyr. SRCS 105. Georgiadis, LSO, Handley.

Moeran, whose composing career never quite flowered as it should have done – whether or not as cause or result of personal instability – yet wrote some delectably rewarding works. This one, dating from 1942, reflects his devotion to Delius more than most; two lyrical movements frame a central scherzo with something of an Irish flavour. It receives a superb performance from John Georgiadis, one-time leader of the London Symphony Orchestra, strongly backed by his former colleagues under Handley. The recording is excellent.

Lonely Waters; Whythorne's Shadow.
(M) *** HMV Green. ESD/*TC-ESD* 7101. E. Sinfonia, Dilkes – *Concert* (*English idyll*).***

These lovely orchestral miniatures are most beautifully played and recorded (the cassette matching the disc in warmth and bloom). They are part of an outstanding collection of mainly gentle English music (see the Concerts section below).

Monn, Georg Matthias
(1717–50)

Cello concerto in G min.
(M) **(*) HMV SXLP/*TC-SXLP* 30273 [Ang. S 36580]. Du Pré, LSO, Barbirolli – HAYDN: *Concerto in D.***(*)

Monn's highly attractive *Cello concerto* has the distinction of arriving in an edition prepared by Arnold Schoenberg, though the harpsichord continuo player Valda Aveling has in fact modified what he wrote. The work follows very much the traditions established in the preceding generation by J. S. Bach and Vivaldi, with alternating ritornelli and solo passages in the outer movements and a siciliano-like *Adagio* for slow movement. Very positive playing from Du Pré, sympathetically accompanied by Barbirolli and the LSO, and good recording, with a smooth, fresh tape transfer.

Monteverdi, Claudio
(1567–1643)

MADRIGALS

Madrigals for 5 voices, Book 3 (complete).
(M) **(*) Ph. 9502 008 [id.]. Armstrong, Eathorne, Watson, Hodgson, Collins, English, Partridge, Dean, Keyte; Leppard.

Monteverdi's *Third Book of Madrigals*, dating from 1592, was the one where the sharpness of his originality began to make itself felt to the full – not just musically but in his serious treatment of subjects, breaking away from formality. Outstanding among the soloists here is Ian Partridge, but too much of the rest lacks the bite which generally marks Leppard's performances of Monteverdi. The result is a little too smooth, though the quality of the music itself and its rarity are enough to make this a most attractive issue, particularly at medium price; and it is very well recorded.

Ah dolente partita; Al lume delle stelle; Amor, che deggio far; Chiome d'oro; Damigella tutta bella; Dolci miei sospiri; Eccomi pronta ai baci;

La piaga ch'ho nel core; Lamento della ninfa; Non vedro mai le stelle; O come sei gentile; Sfogava con le stelle; Si ch'io vorrei morire.

(M) *** Argo ZK 66. Purcell Cons., Grayston Burgess.

Ever since Nadia Boulanger made her historic recording of Monteverdi madrigals in the late thirties, the Nymph's Lament, *Lamento della ninfa*, has been a favourite, and here again it stands at the centre of the collection. With Eileen Poulter as soloist, this is a less personal reading than Boulanger's, but at a slower tempo and with a purer-toned soprano this is if anything even more beautiful. *Chiome d'oro* is another which coincides with the original Boulanger collection, here more authentically allotted to two sopranos instead of Boulanger's tenors (one of them the incomparable Hugues Cuénod) and not nearly so witty. But the wonder is that these performances stand comparison so well with that classic example. This is cleaner and straighter in style than Raymond Leppard's Contour collection (see below), and it is a wonderful record for anyone simply wanting to sample the irresistible glories of this great musical revolutionary. It is beautifully recorded.

Bel pastor; Della bellezza le dovute lodi; Dolci miei sospiri; Fugge il verno; Gira il nemico insidioso; Lamento della ninfa; Lidia spina del mio core; Non così; Ohimè ch'io cado; O Rosetta; La pastorella; Si dolce è il tormento.

(B) *** Con. CC/*CCT* 7534. Wolf, Tear, English, Keyte, ECO, Leppard.

This was the first of Raymond Leppard's madrigal anthologies, dating from the mid-sixties, and at bargain price it still makes a splendid introduction to this wonderful repertoire. Not since Nadia Boulanger made her first, historic recording of Monteverdi madrigals in Paris

in the thirties (imagine it, a piano continuo!) had the most sensuously beautiful of the works in this form, *Lamento della ninfa*, been recorded with such feeling. For that item alone the record would be worth the price, for with wonderfully clear recording and imaginative direction by Leppard, its beauty is irresistible. Some who know the Boulanger version may feel it is taken too slowly, but that only prolongs the ecstasy. Not only this but all the other items here are most welcome. The singing is fresh, and in its new bargain-priced format this collection cannot be too highly recommended. The cassette is nearly as lively as the disc.

CHURCH MUSIC

Ab aeterno ordinata sum; Confitebor tibi, Domine (3 settings); *Deus tuorum militum sors et corona; Iste confessor Domini sacratus; Laudate Dominum, O omnes gentes; La Maddalena: Prologue: Su le penne de venti. Nisi Dominus aedificaverit domum.*

⊛ *** Hyp. Dig. A/*KA* 66021. Kirkby, Partridge, Thomas, Parley of Instruments.

There are few records of Monteverdi's solo vocal music as persuasive as this. The three totally contrasted settings of *Confitebor tibi* (Psalm 110) reveal an extraordinary range of expression, each one drawing out different aspects of word-meaning. Even the brief trio *Deus tuorum militum* has a haunting memorability – it could become to Monteverdi what *Jesu, joy of man's desiring* is to Bach – and the performances are outstanding, with the edge on Emma Kirkby's voice attractively presented in an aptly reverberant acoustic. The accompaniment makes a persuasive case for authentic performance on original instruments.

Laudate pueri; Mass in 4 parts (1640); Mass in 4 parts (1651); Ut queant laxis.

479

(M) **(*) Argo ZK 15. Turner, Odom, Birts, Bishop, Keen, St John's College Ch., ASMF, Guest.

There is a finer version of the 1640 *Mass* on a Oiseau-Lyre disc conducted by George Malcolm (SOL 263). But this is well sung, and the other items include much fine music that is well worth having. At medium price this is worth investigating; the recording is excellent.

Selva morale e spirituale (excerpts); *Gloria; Laudate Dominum omnes gentes. Laudate pueri; Mass in 4 parts.*
*(*) Tel. AW 6.42163. Coll. Vocale, Mus. Ant., Koopman.

Only two of the items come from the *Selva morale* (the *Gloria* and the invigorating *Laudate Dominum*), but all are splendid examples of Monteverdi's choral music. The performances, well recorded in a reverberant acoustic, are only variably successful, lacking in contrast and expressiveness. Most of the pieces have been better recorded elsewhere.

OPERA AND OPERA-BALLET

Il Combattimento di Tancredi e Clorinda. L'Arianna: Lasciatemi morire (Ariadne's lament). *Lamento d'Olimpia.* (With FARINA: *Sonata in G min.*)
*** DG Arc. 2533 460 [id.]. Kwella, Watkinson, Rogers, Thomas, Col. Mus. Ant., Goebel.

Under Reinhard Goebel the Cologne Musica Antiqua using original instruments has built up a formidable reputation on record, and these tasteful performances of a masterly set of Monteverdi pieces, well coupled with the sonata by Monteverdi's contemporary Carlo Farina, are most welcome. Carolyn

Watkinson's singing of the two laments is finely controlled, and after initial uncertainty positively dramatic. Excellent recording.

L'Incoronazione di Poppea, Act 1: *Disprezzata Regina* (Ottavia's lament); Act 3: *Addio Roma* (Ottavia's farewell). *L'Arianna: Lasciatemi morire* (Ariadne's lament).
(M) *** HMV SXLP/TC-SXLP 30280. Baker, ECO, Leppard – A. and D. SCARLATTI: *Cantatas.***

In the operatic field Leppard's approach to Monteverdi and his school has sometimes raised scholarly temperatures, but the general listener can revel in the richness and elaboration. In any case, in these extended Monteverdi offerings the artistry of Dame Janet Baker provides the cornerstone, and the flowing *arioso* of these classically inspired scenes inspires her to bring out the living, human intensity of each situation. There is not quite the variety of expression one finds in the madrigals – inevitably so with operatic *arioso* – but the range of emotion is if anything greater. Highly recommended; fine recording, with a vivid cassette equivalent.

Il Ritorno d'Ulisse in patria (arr. Leppard; complete).
*** CBS 79332 (3) [Col. M3 35910]. Von Stade, Stilwell, Power, Lewis, Parker, Murray, Bryson, Glyndebourne Ch., LPO, Leppard.

Scholars may argue about the lush sounds which Leppard draws from his forces – especially here in Henry Wood Hall, very different from the dry Glyndebourne acoustic where these same artists were appearing at the time of the sessions – but no one will miss the depth of feeling behind this performance. The role of the faithful Penelope is superbly taken here by Von Stade, one of her very finest performances on record, while

Richard Stilwell gives a noble account of Ulisse's music. Some may prefer a more detached view of an early-seventeenth-century opera, but the freshness and life, the immediacy and involvement of the drama set this apart among recordings of Monteverdi operas; for Leppard both as conductor and editor holds together what can easily seem a very long opera, here expertly tailored for a modern audience. With lavish and exotic continuo, the strings of the LPO have rarely sounded sweeter. The voices are balanced rather close but not objectionably so.

Montsalvatge, Xavier

(born 1912)

Concerto breve for piano and orchestra.
*** Decca SXL 6757 [Lon 6990/5-]. Larrocha, RPO, Frühbeck de Burgos – SURINACH: *Piano concerto.***(*)

Xavier Montsalvatge's *Concerto breve* is dedicated to Alicia de Larrocha, who plays it here with authority and conviction. She is sympathetically accompanied by the RPO under Frühbeck de Burgos and is given excellent Decca engineering. The work itself has facility and good workmanship to commend it, but it would be idle to pretend that its thematic substance was particularly memorable or distinguished (or for that matter that the work evinced strong personality). However, the recording is spectacularly brilliant.

Morgan, David (born 1933)

(i) *Violin concerto. Contrasts.*
*** Lyr. SRCS 97. RPO, Handley, (i) with Gruenberg.

David Morgan is an unashamed traditionalist. His *Violin concerto*, dating from 1967, is a warmly lyrical work in an expressively Waltonian idiom, and it comes as quite a surprise that the composer relates his inspiration darkly to the destruction of the individual, for ostensibly this is a work of protest. *Contrasts* consists of two movements merely, the first slow, with a central scherzando section, the second a toccata-like finale. It almost makes a symphony but not quite, for though the seriousness of Morgan's purpose is never in doubt (the Shostakovich initials D–S–C–H an important motif) the balance of sections is odd. Performances here are admirable, not least from the soloist in the *Concerto*, Erich Gruenberg, and the recording is well up to Lyrita's high standard.

Morley, Thomas (1557–1603)

Ballets, Madrigals, Pavanes: *About the maypole new; Arise, awake; Barlowe; Frog galliard; Hard by a crystal fountain; Ho! who comes here; Love took his bow and arrow; Now is the month of Maying; O mistress mine; Pavane; You that wont to my pipes.* Sacred music: *Agnus Dei; Galliard to the Sacred End; I call with my whole heart; Let my complaint come before Thee; Nolo mortem peccatoris; O amica mea; Out of the deep; Sacred End pavane.*
(M) *** HM HMU 241. Deller Cons., Deller Instrumental Ens., Munrow.

It was shrewd of Alfred Deller to go to David Munrow and his then newly formed Early Music Consort to accompany this record of Morley's music, one of the few specifically devoted to that Italianate Elizabethan. This anthology, well recorded, provides not just a beautifully contrasted programme but one which, like a concert, ends with the finest item of all, the *Sacred End pavane*. Deller, long neglected by the British record companies, here showed that his band of singers was as lively as ever.

Moszkowski, Moritz
(1854–1925)

Suite in G min. for two violins and piano, Op. 71.
*** HMV ASD 3861 [Ang. SZ 37668]. Perlman, Zukerman, Sanders – PRO-KOFIEV: *Sonata*; SHOSTAKOVICH: *Duets*.***

The Moszkowski *Suite* is something of a find, and will reward anyone investing in this disc. It has charm and character, and is splendidly played. This is an interesting collection on all counts.

Mozart, Leopold (1719–87)

Cassation in G (includes Toy sym-phony, attrib. Haydn).
** DG 2531/*3301* 275 [id.]. ECO, Barenboim – PROKOFIEV: *Peter*.**(*)

This *Cassation* seems an insubstantial coupling for *Peter and the Wolf*, even though it is well enough played and recorded. There is an alternative version of the *Toy symphony* on ASV ACM/ *ZCACM* 2033: see below under Pou-lenc's *Babar*.

Mozart, Wolfgang
(1756–91)

Adagio and fugue in C min., K.546; 3

Divertimenti for strings, K.136/8; Serenade No. 13 in G (Eine kleine Nachtmusik), K.525.
**(*) Abbey ABY 809. Scottish Bar. Ens., Friedman.

No complaints about the Scottish Baroque Ensemble, who give alert per-formances on this record. Their attack is clean and their ensemble good, and the playing has sensitivity without ever showing too much sophistication. They are quite well recorded, and though the performances do not displace Bosk-ovsky or Marriner (see below), and do not quite match them in elegance, they are thoroughly recommendable all the same.

Cassations Nos. 1 in G, K.63; 2 in B flat, K.99.
(M) *** Decca Jub. JB/*KJBC* 66. V. Moz. Ens., Boskovsky.

The delightful *First Cassation* has two enchanting slow movements. The first is a delicate *Andante* (nicely atmospheric here), which is reminiscent of *Così fan tutte* in its mood and colour; the second introduces a cantilena for solo violin. K.99 is almost equally attractive. Bos-kovsky's performances are excellent in every way. The playing is marvellously alive and stylish, investing these com-paratively lightweight works with con-siderable stature. The recording is flaw-less; the cassette transfer is immaculate too, if slightly dry.

(i) *Bassoon concerto in B flat, K.191;*
(ii) *Clarinet concerto in A, K.622.*
** DG 2531/*3301* 254 [id.]. Boston SO, Ozawa, with (i) Walt, (ii) Wright.

(i) *Bassoon concerto;* (ii) *Clarinet concerto;* (iii) *Adagio and rondo for glass harmonica, K.617.*

(M) ** DG Priv. 2535/*3335* 188. (i) Allard, LOP, Markevitch; (ii) Leister, Berlin PO, Kubelik; (iii) Zabaleta, Kuentz CO.

(i) *Bassoon concerto;* (ii) *Clarinet concerto. March in D major, K.249; Thamos, King of Egypt* (incidental music), *K.345: Entr'acte No. 2.*
(M) *** HMV SXLP/*TC-SXLP* 30246 [Sera. 60197]. RPO, Beecham, with (i) Brooke; (ii) Brymer.

The early HMV coupling of the *Bassoon* and *Clarinet concertos* is one of Beecham's most beguiling recordings. Both his soloists play with great character and beauty, and the affectionate accompaniment is wonderfully gracious. The recording in no way sounds its age, and current copies of the cassette match the disc closely. The bonuses are a pair of most welcome 'lollipops'.

The Boston performances from DG are thoroughly musical and beautifully recorded on disc and tape alike. The warm tone of the clarinet soloist is especially appealing. However, Ozawa's accompaniments, though well fashioned and neatly laid out, are rather matter-of-fact, and the overall effect is accomplished rather than inspired.

On the Privilege issue Karl Leister gives a thoughtfully sensitive and musical performance of the *Clarinet concerto,* but with his gentle, introvert style and lack of a forceful personality the effect is rather too self-effacing. However, Kubelik's attention to detail and gracious phrasing mean that the orchestral contribution gives special pleasure. The recording is excellent. When one turns over for the *Bassoon concerto* the orchestral quality is thinner. But Maurice Allard plays a characterful bassoon; his timbre is attractively woody (it suggests a French instrument, certainly) and his reading shows imagination and humour. The transcription of Mozart's *Adagio and rondo,* K.617, for harp with flute, oboe, viola and cello, is most engaging; it is

beautifully played and recorded. The tape transfers are well managed throughout.

Clarinet concerto in A, K.622.
(*) Mer. E 77022. King, ECO, Francis – SPOHR: *Concerto No. 4.**

Clarinet concerto; Bassoon concerto, K.191 (arr. for clarinet).
* RCA RL/*RK* 13934 [ARL 1/*ARK 1* 3934]. Stoltzman, ECO, Schneider.

(i) *Clarinet concerto;* (ii) *Flute and harp concerto in C, K.299.*
(M) *** Ph. Fest. 6570/*7310* 146 [id.]. LSO, Colin Davis, with (i) Brymer, (ii) Barwahser, Ellis.

Thea King, who earlier recorded an outstandingly sensitive account of the *Clarinet quintet* for Saga, sounds a degree less assured in the *Concerto.* Where the *Quintet* brought deeply expressive playing in the meditative slow movement, there is less sense of repose here, and the strength of the performance lies in its brightness, its rhythmic qualities, notably in the finale. The recording is generally well-balanced, and this version can be considered by anyone who fancies the coupling.

On Philips Jack Brymer plays his concerto beautifully, conveying a most eloquent, autumnal serenity. The reading has a soft lyricism that is especially appealing in the slow movement. Barwahser (the first flute of the Concertgebouw) and Ellis give a sparkling account of the *Flute and harp concerto,* and Sir Colin Davis accompanies both with the greatest sprightliness and sympathy. The recording is smooth to match and this is unquestionably a fine coupling. The cassette is well managed but tends to emphasize the slightly bland quality of the Philips recording.

Richard Stoltzman's version of the *Clarinet concerto* is put out of court by the harsh, grainy recording, which makes the solo instrument sound unappealingly hard and dry in timbre. This is a pity, for Stoltzman's performance is imaginative, especially in matters of light and shade, and he plays the slow movement beautifully. The *Bassoon concerto*, however, loses much of its character in this transcription, and the unevocative sound does not help. The high-level tape if anything emphasizes the fierceness of the sound, especially in K.191, which is strident.

(i) *Clarinet concerto;* (i; ii) *Sinfonia concertante in E flat, K. 297b.*
(M) (***) HMV mono XLP/*TC-XLP* 60004. Philh. O., Karajan, with (i) Walton, (ii) Sutcliffe, James, Brain.

Bernard Walton's slightly reserved, patrician reading of the *Clarinet concerto* has considerable character, but the mono recording from the early fifties sounds rather dated here. The sound in the *Sinfonia concertante* is first-class, however, and beautifully balanced so that the ear hardly notices that it is mono. The brilliant interplay of the famous wind soloists in this work is sheer delight, and Karajan's direction is most felicitous.

(i) *Clarinet concerto;* (ii) *Sinfonia concertante for violin and viola in E flat, K.364.*
(M) **(*) Decca Jub. JB/*KJBC* 48. (i) De Peyer, LSO, Maag; (ii) I. and D. Oistrakh, Moscow PO, Kondrashin.

Gervase de Peyer's performance of the *Clarinet concerto* is as fine as any available, fluent and lively, with masterly phrasing in the slow movement and a vivacious finale. It was a happy idea to recouple it on Jubilee with the Oistrakhs' version of the *Sinfonia concertante*. This performance also offers distinguished solo playing and is notable for its relaxed manner. Everything is shaped most musically, but sometimes the listener might feel that the performers, in their care for

detail, are less involved with the music itself. However, the outer movements have plenty of vitality, and the sound is good, the cassette tending to show up the date of the original recording of the *Sinfonia concertante* (1964) more strikingly than the disc.

Flute concertos Nos. 1 in G; 2 in D, K.313/4.
(B) *** Pick. SHM 3010 [id.]. Galway, New Irish C. Ens., Prieur.
*** Argo ZRG/*KZRC* 910 [id.]. Bennett, ECO, Malcolm.

Flute concertos Nos. 1–2; Andante in C, K.315.
(M) *** Ph. Fest. 6570/*7310* 091 [id.]. Barwahser, LSO, Colin Davis.
**(*) Erato STU 71144 [RCA ARL 1 3084]. Rampal, Jerusalem Music Centre CO, Stern.
**(*) HMV ASD/*TC-ASD* 4056. Solum, Hanoverian O., Holloway.

To have modern recordings of Mozart's two *Flute concertos* played by James Galway available in the cheapest price range is bounty indeed. Moreover the accompaniments, ably directed by André Prieur, are polished and stylish, and the recording (although it gives a rather small sound to the violins) is excellent, clear and with good balance and perspective. It might be argued that Galway's vibrato is not entirely suited to these eighteenth-century works, and that his cadenzas too are slightly anachronistic. But the star quality of his playing disarms criticism. The slow movement of the *First Concerto* is beautifully paced; the timbre and phrasing have exquisite delicacy, and the pointed articulation in the finale (nicely matched by the orchestra) is a delight. In No. 2 Galway again floats the melodic line of the first movement with gossamer lightness, and after another enchanting slow movement the finale sparkles joyously, with the orchestra once more on top form.

William Bennett gives a beautiful account of the concertos, among the finest to have appeared in recent years. Every phrase is shaped with both taste and affection, and the playing of the ECO under George Malcolm is fresh and vital. The recording is clean, well detailed and with enough resonance to lend bloom to the sound. The cassette matches the LP closely, although on tape there is an excess of bass resonance in the *First Concerto* that needs attenuating. On disc Galway's performances are available at half the price of this Argo issue, and it must inevitably take second place.

The Barwahser versions date from the mid-sixties, but the recording still sounds full and fresh on disc and cassette alike. It is in the medium price-range and has the advantage of including the *Andante for flute and orchestra, K.315*. The performances are consistently polished and elegant, helped by the attractive warmth of the sound balance, with the soloist naturally caught. Barwahser's phrasing is unfailingly beautiful; his playing of the *G major Concerto* recalls Gluck in its delicacy of line. Some might feel that the style of the soloist evokes something of a French classical feeling, that it is too cool. But though his manner is slightly detached at times (in the *Andante* of K.314, for instance), this certainly does not reflect any lack of sensibility, and the finale of that same D major work has an attractive lightness and sparkle.

Jean-Pierre Rampal gives a performance of the highest distinction, as one would expect from an artist of his stature. His is playing of vital imagination, and his record also has the advantage of including the *Andante*. The orchestral contribution is not perhaps of the same order of sensitivity, though it is perfectly acceptable. Rampal is too closely balanced in relation to the orchestra, but in other respects the sound is very good.

John Solum uses a period instrument — or, more accurately, three, one for each of the works recorded here. The results are inevitably not as full-blooded as they

are on modern instruments. However, the performances are both accomplished and persuasive, and the Hanoverian Orchestra, a group of about twenty players also using originals or copies of period instruments, show genuine spirit and seem free from the slightly inhibited quality that at times assails practitioners of authenticity (as if fearful that their wigs will fall off). The recordings are natural and and well balanced, and although most collectors would not want this as their only version, it is an invaluable complement to the conventional modern view. The cassette is both lively and vivid, but the upper strings sound rather spiky.

(i) *Flute concerto No. 1, K.313;* (ii) *Flute and harp concerto in C, K.299.*
(M) **(*) DG 2535/3335 477. (i) Linde, Mun. CO, Stadlmair; (ii) Zöller, Zabaleta, Berlin PO, Märzendorfer.

There are no strictures about the Zöller/Zabaleta account of the *Flute and harp concerto*. The flautist is a most sensitive player, and his phrasing is a constant source of pleasure, while Zabaleta's sense of line knits the overall texture of this solo-duet most convincingly. Märzendorfer conducts with both warmth and lightness; the outer movements have an attractive rhythmic buoyancy. The recording is clear and clean, if not as rich as we would expect today. The performance of the *Flute concerto* is described below.

(i) *Flute concerto No. 1, K.313;* (ii) *Oboe concerto in C, K.314.*
(M) **(*) DG Arc. Priv. 2547/3347 015. Mun. CO, Stadlmair, with (i) Linde, (ii) Holliger.

Impeccably played and neatly recorded, Linde's performance of the *Flute concerto* has a hint of rhythmic stiffness in the outer movements. The

485

highlight is the slow movement, where the playing is beautifully poised, and the melody breathes in exactly the right way. Holliger's account of the *Oboe concerto* is, needless to say, first-class, his tone appealing and his style and technique serving the music's grace and elegance. But Stadlmair's accompaniment is crisply straightforward rather than especially imaginative, and though this makes a good medium-priced coupling (with a faithful cassette alternative) Holliger's later, full-priced Philips version, coupled with Richard Strauss's *Concerto* (6500 174/*7300 119*), is more masterly, more refined.

Readers should also be reminded that Claude Monteux's sunny performance of the flute version of this concerto (K.314) is available on a bargain-priced Contour reissue (CC/*CCT* 7504). It is part of a concert also including music of Bach and Gluck (see the Concerts section below).

(i) *Flute and harp concerto in C, K.299. Flute concerto in G, K.622G* (arrangement of *Clarinet concerto*, ed. Galway).
**(*) RCA RL/*RK* 25181 [ARL 1/*ARK 1* 3353]. Galway, LSO, Mata, (i) with Robles.

The *Flute and harp concerto* has seldom sounded so lively in a recording as it does here, with an engaging element of fantasy in the music-making, a radiant slow movement, and an irrepressibly spirited finale. Marisa Robles makes a characterful match for the ubiquitous Galway. The balance of the soloists is forward, but not unrealistically so. The *Flute concerto* arranged from Mozart's masterpiece for clarinet is more controversial; the key of G major as well as Galway's silvery flute timbre make for even lighter results than one might have anticipated. The scintillating finale is especially successful. The recording is admirably bright and clear, the cassette slightly less refined than the disc.

Horn concertos Nos. 1–4, K.412, 417, 447, 495. Concerto No. 5 (fragment).
(M) *** Decca Jub. JB/*KJBC* 70 [Lon. 6403]. Tuckwell, LSO, Maag.
**(*) DG 2531/*3301* 274 [id.]. Hogner, VPO, Boehm.

Tuckwell's earlier recording of the four *Horn concertos*, plus the fragment from *No. 5 in E major* (which ends where Mozart left it at bar 91) continues to stand up against all competition. The solo playing is vigorous, spontaneous, and lyrically exuberant. Peter Maag's accompaniments are admirably crisp and nicely scaled, giving the soloist buoyant support. The recording is excellent on disc and tape alike, and the Jubilee reissue is attractively priced.

Gunter Hogner also plays with much character, and no one will be disappointed with the DG issue, which is beautifully recorded and has splendid accompaniments from the VPO under Boehm. However, this would not be a first choice in a very competitive field.

(i) *Horn concerto No. 4, K.495;* (ii) *Piano concerto No. 21 in C, K.467;* (iii) *Serenade No. 13 (Eine kleine Nachtmusik), K.525.*
(M) **(*) HMV *TC-IDL 510.* (i) Tuckwell, ASMF, Marriner; (ii) Annie Fischer, Philh. O., Sawallisch; (iii) Philh. O., Kempe.

This tape-only compilation, otherwise very attractive, is let down a little by Kempe's account of *Eine kleine Nachtmusik*, which, though elegantly phrased and given a warm, clear recording, has a flaccid minuet and shows a similar lack of sparkle in the finale. The *Horn concerto* shows Tuckwell in first-class form, and Annie Fischer's silken touch in the K.467 *Piano concerto* (which has a distinguished accompaniment from the Philharmonia under Sawallisch) makes delightful listening, particularly as the recording matches the playing in its refinement of timbre and detail.

Oboe concerto in C, K.314; Oboe concerto in E flat, K.App.294b (attrib. Mozart and ed. Jensen-Maedel).
**(*) HMV ASD/*TC-ASD* 3553 [Ang. S 37534]. De Vries, Prague CO, Kersjes.

The oboe sound that Han de Vries creates is small and neat, light in timbre and texture, but beautifully articulated. If the slender image lacks a degree of tonal opulence, the playing is consistently alert, at once expressive and delicate, the phrasing and style above all classical in manner. This certainly works well in Mozart, particularly as the accompaniment is crisp and in scale. The *E flat Concerto*, at best a Mozart attribution, is a pleasant, sprightly, but uninspired *galant* work, more Weberian than Mozartian and with a hint of Hummel. Han de Vries plays it nimbly and eloquently. The recording is fresh and clean on both disc and tape, with excellent presence and detail.

Piano concertos Nos. 5 in D, K.175; 9 in E flat, K.271.
(M) *** HMV SXLP/*TC-SXLP* 30418. Barenboim, ECO.

Barenboim's recording of K.175 is delightful and played with great spirit. Some may find that his version of K.271 displays too great awareness of refinements of tone and dynamics that are strictly speaking anachronistic. Faced with such masterly pianism, however, and such alert and musical direction, few are likely to grumble. The most serious reservation concerns the minuet of the last movement, which is far too measured. On balance Ashkenazy's sparkling account on Decca (SXL/KSXC 6259 [Lon. 6501/5-]) is still the finest in the current catalogue and it is better recorded; but those who want the Barenboim coupling can rest assured that this is a distinguished record. The tape transfer is not one of EMI's best; a bass

cut improves the sound balance, but inner detail is not ideally clean.

Piano concertos Nos. 8 in C, K.246; 22 in E flat, K.482.
*** CBS 76966/40- [Col. M/*MT* 35869]. Perahia, ECO.

Murray Perahia's version of the great *E flat Concerto* is second to none. He has the measure of its scale, and yet every phrase is lovingly shaped too. Perahia is an artist who blends unusual qualities of spirit with wonderful sensuousness; not only does he draw magical sounds from the keyboard, he also inspires the wind players of the ECO, who invest the serenade-like episodes in the slow movement with great eloquence. This is a reading of real stature. It is well recorded, though there is not quite the range and depth that distinguished Perahia's slightly earlier coupling of K.414 and K.595. The early *C major Concerto* is unfailingly fresh and elegant in his hands. The cassette, on chrome tape, is of good quality.

Piano concertos Nos. 8, K.246; 26 in D (Coronation), K.537.
**(*) HM 1C 065 99699. Demus, Coll. Aur.

Joerg Demus's record has a special appeal in that it uses period instruments and will give at least some idea of what tonal resources were at Mozart's command during his lifetime. The timbre of the fortepiano that Demus uses is beautifully captured here, and he plays it with consummate taste and artistry. The warm acoustic makes the Collegium Aureum sound fresher and more pleasing than is often the case, and readers wanting an example of Mozart in period dress, very well played and recorded, could do no better than to turn to this disc or its companion (*Concertos Nos. 21 and 23*).

Piano concertos Nos. 9 in E flat,
K.271; 11 in F, K.413; 14 in E flat,
K.449; 20 in D min., K.466; 21 in C,
K.467; 24 in C min., K.491.
⑧ *** CBS 79317/40- (3). Perahia, ECO.

These are among the most distinguished Mozart performances in the
catalogue. They are not unblemished
(there is some less than perfect intonation
from the wind in K.271 and K.466), but
Perahia offers playing of a consistent
excellence and distinction. He has the
power to draw from the keyboard a
quality of sound that few of his rivals can
begin to approach. In K.413 and K.466
the recording does justice to the quality
and range of colour that he commands,
and elsewhere the sound is eminently
satisfactory. These are searching and
poetic performances that only gain by
repetition, and the reservations mentioned in some of the individual reviews
melt away as one gets to know these
beautiful readings more closely. Perahia's blend of sensuousness and spirituality is very special. This set earns a
rosette in its disc format, and the cassette
transfers are among the best to come
from CBS. They are slightly variable in
level, and the orchestral quality is not
always as rich and detailed as on disc (the
upper strings noticeably lack bloom in
K.271); but the piano timbre is consistently natural.

Piano concertos Nos. 9, K.271; 27 in
B flat, K.595.
**(*) HMV ASD/TC-ASD 3776. Esch-
enbach, LPO.

Christoph Eschenbach, the latest
pianist to direct Mozart from the keyboard, succeeds in accommodating the
early Jeunehomme concerto and the B
flat, K.595, on one disc. There is much
excellent playing here, for Eschenbach is
an artist of the utmost sensitivity and
refinement. He secures a good sense of
movement and line, and the orchestral

playing is taut and lively. Perhaps these
readings lack the ultimate sparkle and
character that Perahia, Barenboim and
Brendel have achieved in recent years,
but they are still to be reckoned with and
are given sound quality of considerable
distinction. Anyone wanting this particular coupling will surely not be disappointed. The cassette transfer is lively and
clear; the brightness of the upper strings
needs a little softening, but otherwise the
vivid orchestral sound is well matched by
a piano image with plenty of colour and
depth.

Piano concerto No. 9, K.271; (i)
Double concerto in E flat, K.365.
*** Ph. 9500 408/7300 616 [id.]. Brendel,
ASMF, Marriner, (i) with Cooper.

Alfred Brendel gives us a finely proportioned and cleanly articulated account of the Jeunehomme concerto, with
a ravishing performance of the slow
movement. The finale has great sparkle
and finesse, and the recording has exemplary clarity. In the eight-record box
in which this first appeared it occupied
two sides, but Philips have sensibly accommodated it on one here. The other
side gives us a spirited version of the
Double piano concerto, in which Brendel
is joined by Imogen Cooper. This is an
alert and finely recorded performance,
but it does not quite efface memories of
the DG recording with Gilels et fille
under Karl Boehm, which has slightly
more repose. Yet there is no ground for
complaint about anything on this issue,
and the cassette transfer is of excellent
quality: the Double concerto is strikingly
full and vivid.

Piano concertos Nos. 11 in F, K.413;
16 in D, K.451.
*(*) Tel. AW 6.42162. Engel, Salz.
Mozarteum O., Hager.

Sobriety is the keynote of Karl Engel's
approach, and although the playing both

of soloist and orchestra is immaculate and the quality of the recorded sound lifelike and truthful, these performances remain somewhat earthbound. Engel is an intelligent player but neither of these performances is as poetic or imaginative as the best on the market.

Piano concertos Nos. 11, K.413; 20 in D min., K.466.
*** CBS 76651/40- [Col. M/*MT* 35134]. Perahia, ECO.

This is the most impressive of Perahia's Mozart concerto records so far. He plays both works with abundant artistry and imagination and is well served by the CBS engineers. These are finely integrated readings: the solo entry in the first movement of K.413 could hardly emerge more organically from the texture, and in the slow movement he is more withdrawn, more private than many of his colleagues. Here he is at the other end of the spectrum from Barenboim, whose reading is more outgoing and life-loving. Perahia brings less dramatic fire to K.466 than some of his colleagues, but there is a strong case for this; too many artists view the work from the vantagepoint of *Don Giovanni* rather than seeing it in terms of its own unique sensibility. None of the disturbing undercurrents goes unnoted, but at the same time the spiritual dimensions remain within the period: not the only way of looking at this work but a most convincing one. The cassette is not as wide-ranging as the disc but is satisfactorily balanced.

Piano concerto No. 12 in A, K.414.
*** Decca SXL/*KSXC* 6952 [Lon. 7180/ 5-]. Larrocha, L. Sinf., Zinman – BACH: *Concerto No. 5*; HAYDN: *Concerto in D.***

An outstanding account of the *A major Concerto* from Alicia de Larrocha and David Zinman, who form a splendid partnership. The opening movement is

graciously phrased yet has an engaging momentum and resilience. The slow movement is beautifully played and the finale is full of rhythmic character and sparkle. Excellent recording too, with no appreciable difference between cassette and disc. If the couplings are suitable this can be recommended highly.

Piano concertos Nos. 12, K.414; 27 in B flat, K.595.
⊛ *** CBS 76731/40- [Col. M/*MT* 35828]. Perahia, ECO.

Murray Perahia has the capacity to make the piano breathe and to persuade the listener that the sound he produces is almost independent of any physical agent. Yet this spiritual dimension harmonizes with a flesh-and-blood intensity and strongly classical instincts. Both these performances have great sparkle and a sense of naturalness and rightness: listening to the finale of K.414, one feels it could not be taken at any other speed or phrased in any other way. In K.595 Perahia produces some wonderfully soft colourings and a luminous texture, yet at the same time he avoids underlining too strongly the sense of valediction that inevitably haunts this magical score. There is a sublime simplicity to the slow movement in these artists' hands – for the ECO too seem as inspired as the soloist-director. The CBS sound is excellent, freshtoned and well balanced. The cassette has less upper range than the disc, but with a bass cut the sound balance is pleasing, and there is no muffling of the strings.

Piano concertos Nos. 13 in C, K.415; 14 in E flat, K.449.
*** Ph. 9500 565/7300 714. Brendel, ASMF, Marriner.

The *E flat Concerto*, K.449, is distinguished by beautifully clean and alive passage-work, and there is superb control and poise. The main ideas are well shaped without being overcharacterized.

Tempi are wisely chosen and perfectly related, though the finale is a little less playful than Perahia's. Indeed, with Brendel one views the landscape with all the clarity of high noon, every detail sharply in focus, while with Perahia there are many pastel colourings and all the sparkle and freshness of early morning. In the *C major Concerto* there is no want of surface elegance yet it is never allowed to obscure the music's depths or to attract attention to itself. A refreshingly classical reading without a trace of self-indulgence; indeed in the second group of the first movement Brendel might have allowed himself something of the beguiling eloquence that Barenboim brought to this idea. However, these are most distinguished performances and beautifully recorded too, on disc and tape alike.

Piano concertos Nos. 14, K.449; 26 in D (Coronation), K.537.
**(*) DG 2531/*3301* 207 [id.]. Vásáry, Berlin PO.

Yet another pianist directing the orchestra from the keyboard. Tamás Vásáry is a fine Mozartian, with exemplary taste and judgement, though ultimately these performances do not sparkle quite so much as the finest of their rivals. The *D major*, K.537, is the better of the two, and has grandeur as well as vitality. The quality of the recorded sound is very good indeed, and the difference between disc and cassette is minimal.

Piano concerto No. 15 in B flat, K.450; Symphony No. 36 in C (Linz), K.425.
(M) **(*) Decca Jub. JB/*KJBC* 95 [Lon. 6499/5-]. Bernstein, VPO.

Such a record as this claims Leonard Bernstein as a European at heart. In the performance of the *Linz symphony* one may keep recognizing the characteristic Bernstein touches that we know from his

New York performances – the glowing violin lyricism in the slow introduction, the bristling manner of the *Allegro* – but somehow a carefree quality is there too, such as one finds only rarely in his American records. In addition the recording quality provided by the Decca engineers, not to mention the comparatively small forces used, gives a transparency to the sound of a kind one may hear from Bernstein in the concert hall but rarely on record. The concerto, even more than the symphony, conveys the feeling of a conductor enjoying himself on holiday. Bernstein's piano playing may not be as poised in every detail as that of full-time virtuoso pianists, but every note communicates vividly. So much so that in the slow movement he even manages to make his dual tempo convincing – faster for the tuttis than for the more romantic solos. The finale is taken surprisingly slowly, but Bernstein brings it off. Some may resist his individuality but it is only too easy to come under the spell of this engagingly spontaneous music-making, especially as the sound is first-rate on both disc and cassette.

Piano concertos Nos. 17 in G, K.453; 18 in B flat, K.456.
*** CBS Dig. 36686/*41-*. Perahia, ECO.

Perahia's cycle goes from strength to strength, and his account of the *G major Concerto* must rank among the very finest now before the public. It has all the sparkle, grace and finesse that one expects from him, and like its companion offers a thoroughly integrated view of the score. He has established a rapport with his players that recalls Edwin Fischer or Adolf Busch. An indispensable issue for Mozartians even if they already have other versions of these concertos. Good sound, clean yet not in any way lacking in warmth, and the chrome cassette offers a first-class transfer.

Piano concertos Nos. 17, K.453; 21 in C, K.467.
*** Decca SXL/*KSXC* 6881. [Lon. 7104/5-]. Ashkenazy, Philh. O.

Vladimir Ashkenazy's first Mozart concerto records made a great impression in the 1960s, and this coupling is in every way a worthy successor. Both performances are directed from the keyboard, and combine a refreshing spontaneity with an overall sense of proportion and balance. There is a fine sense of movement and yet nothing is hurried; detail is finely characterized, but nothing is fussy. Moreover the recording is clear and lucid, with the balance between soloist and orchestra finely judged. The cassette transfer is made at the very highest level, and although the sound is rich, very full and has striking range, there is just a hint of the refinement slipping marginally in tuttis.

Piano concertos Nos. 19 in F, K.459; 24 in C min., K.491.
*** Decca SXL/*KSXC* 6947 [Lon. 7174/5-]. Ashkenazy, Philh. O.

Ashkenazy's account of the *C minor Concerto* is a strong one, and must be numbered among the very finest now on the market. He has the measure of the work's breadth and emotional power, and his playing, while showing all the elegance and poise one could desire, never detracts from the coherence of the whole. His is a balanced view of the first movement which avoids investing it with excessive intensity yet never loses impact. He is every bit as sensitive as his most formidable rivals (Barenboim and Perahia) in the middle movement and highly characterful in the finale. The *F major Concerto* also comes off effectively; it is subtle and sparkling. Clean, well-focused recording and an orchestral response that does almost as much credit to the pianist as his solo contribution. The cassette transfers are of Decca's highest quality:

the *C minor Concerto* sounds particularly beautiful.

Piano concertos Nos. 19, K.459; 27 in B flat, K.595.
(M) ****(*)** DG Priv. 2525/*3335* 244. Anda, Salz. Mozarteum Cam. Ac.

Géza Anda's performance of K.595 is among the finest accounts of this work now available, and it is beautifully recorded, with fresh clear sound and a natural image of the piano. The sound is rather less clear and free on the second side – although still good – and the piano tone is less well focused here. But, as always, Anda's playing is deft and lively, and this can certainly be recommended. The cassette matches the disc closely.

Piano concertos Nos. 20 in D min., K.466; 22 in E flat, K.482.
** RCA Dig. RL 13457 [ARL 1/*ARK 1* 3457]. Ax, Dallas SO, Mata.

Good performances of both concertos from Emanuel Ax, who plays with keen sensitivity and elegant musicianship. He does not bring the qualities of poetic insight that mark both Perahia and Brendel, and he is not quite as vividly recorded as they. But this coupling offers good value in that the main rival versions of the *E flat Concerto* tend to spread the work on to a second side.

Piano concertos Nos. 20, K.466; 23 in A, K.488.
(M) ******* Ph. Fest. 6570/*7310* 023. Brendel, ASMF, Marriner.
**(*) Ph. 9500 570/*7300* 703 [id.]. Bishop-Kovacevich, LSO, Colin Davis.

As a sampler for Brendel's Philips cycle, the Festivo issue could hardly be more enticing, coupling what always used to be regarded as the two most popular Mozart concertos – that is before K.467 was elevated by the inescapable film

Elvira Madigan. Brendel here sounds more spontaneous than on some of his other Mozart records, notably in K.488, which is given a performance both strong and lyrical, with the F sharp minor slow movement intensely beautiful. The sound is up to Philips' usual high standard. The cassette is well balanced, but the modest transfer level brings a rather bland quality to the upper strings, though the piano timbre is hardly affected.

There is a clarity and directness about the combination of Bishop-Kovacevich and Davis in Mozart concertos which is always refreshing. If their coupling of the *D minor* and the *A major* lacks the magic of the earlier coupling of the two *C major Concertos* from the same artists, it is largely that the playing of the LSO is less polished, the strings often edgy. Nonetheless the minor-key seriousness of the outer movements of K.466 and the F sharp minor *Adagio* of K.488 comes out superbly. It is a token of the pianist's command that without any expressive exaggeration the K.488 slow movement conveys such depth and intensity. The recording is bright and clear, although the definition at the top is slightly less sharp on tape than on disc.

Piano concerto No. 20, K.466; (i) *Double concerto in E flat, K.365.*
*(*) HMV ASD/TC-ASD 3337 [Ang. S 37291]. Previn, LSO, (i) with Lupu.

André Previn is the soloist in the great *D minor Concerto,* not Radu Lupu. With the best will in the world, his reading of the solo part cannot be said to match those of Ashkenazy, Brendel, Barenboim or Perahia. Needless to say, everything is musical enough, but the performance as a whole lacks real personality. It is fluent, intelligent and far from unenjoyable, yet ultimately bland. The recording is admirably detailed and well balanced, as is also the case in the *Double concerto.* Again this version does not possess the sparkle and distinction of Gilels and his daughter on DG or the well-engineered

Brendel/Cooper account on Philips (see above). In a cruelly competitive field this issue, for all its merits, does not stand out.

Piano concertos Nos. 21 in C, K.467; 22 in E flat, K.482.
(M) **(*) DG Priv. 2535/3335 317. Anda, Salz. Mozarteum Cam. Ac.

Géza Anda's account of the *E flat major Concerto,* K.482, has previously occupied a side and a half, so that there is some loss of level in this new but competitive transfer. There are compelling accounts of this concerto from Brendel and Perahia at the top end of the catalogue, but Anda's is one of the most impressive of his cycle. Even though the strings do not sound as fresh as they did, this version is still able to hold its own and in this coupling with Anda's poetic account of the *C major Concerto,* K.467, it can surely be said to offer very good value. In the *E flat Concerto,* moreover, Anda's cadenzas are thoroughly idiomatic and appropriate – which is more than can be said for Annie Fischer's famous recording, good though that is. Thoroughly recommendable in both disc and cassette format.

Piano concertos Nos. 21, K.467; 23 in A, K.488.
*** HM 1C 065 99628. Demus, Coll. Aur., Maier.
(B) **(*) Con. CC/CCT 7505. Vered, LPO, Segal.

In one sense the Harmonia Mundi performances have no competitors, because Joerg Demus is the only artist to have used a period instrument in these concertos. Those whose hearts sink at the prospect of Mozart concertos on the fortepiano should nonetheless try this issue: it is generally very well played and the special colour and timbre of the instrument are in their way quite haunting. The fortepiano is unlikely to drive out the modern grand as the harpsichord displaced Bach on the piano, but it is revealing to hear Mozart concertos on the scale on which they were conceived. Good recording.

Ilana Vered plays with the spontaneity of youth, phrasing most persuasively. In K.488 she takes a dangerously slow tempo for the central *Adagio* and does not avoid heaviness, but that is an exception. Close-up recording, originally Decca Phase Four, and generally well balanced and full. At bargain price, this is good value on disc but not on tape, where the transfer has a boomy bass and limited upper range, especially in K.467.

Piano concerto No. 22 in E flat, K.482; Concert rondos Nos. 1 in D, K.382; 2 in A, K.386.
*** Ph. 9500 145 [id./7300 121]. Brendel, ASMF, Marriner.
*** Decca SXL/KSXC 6982 (without *Rondo No. 2*). Ashkenazy, Philh. O.

A very distinguished account of the *E flat Concerto* from Brendel and the Academy, beautifully recorded by the Philips engineers. Brendel's earlier account with Paul Angerer, like his K.503, enjoyed a well deserved celebrity in its day, but the newer version has more sparkle and greater depth and is infinitely better recorded. Brendel's first movement has breadth and grandeur as well as sensitivity, while the slow movement has great poetry. There have been some impressive accounts of this concerto in recent years but it is fair to say that there is none finer than this, nor any that is more beautifully recorded. The two *Concert rondos* – the first (K.382) is the Viennese alternative to the *Salzburg concerto* (K.175) – are no less elegantly performed.

Ashkenazy's account of the *E flat Concerto* also belongs at the top of the list. He has the measure of its strength and enjoys the advantage of rich and finely detailed recorded sound; in this he

is better served than either Brendel or Perahia. Both of them give performances of the greatest distinction, but Ashkenazy is scarcely less thoughtful or lyrical. He evidently does not use the *Neue Mozartausgabe* edition, as he leaves out two bars in the first movement, but that is hardly likely to weigh heavily in the balance for most collectors. This is thoroughly recommendable and nicely recorded too; the cassette matches the disc closely but the resonance has brought a very slight loss of refinement at the top in the orchestral tuttis. The piano is most naturally caught.

Piano concertos Nos. 23 in A, K.488; 25 in C, K.503.
(M) *(*) DG Priv. 2535/3335 245. Anda, Salz. Mozarteum Cam. Ac.

Anda's account of the *C major Concerto* misses something of its grandeur (the first movement is inclined to be insufficiently spacious). Needless to say, there is much to admire in both performances (the *A major* is particularly sunny), but the sound is beginning to show its age. The upper strings have lost their freshness, and given the really distinguished rival accounts of both concertos now on the market, the recommendation here must be qualified.

Piano concertos Nos. 25 in C, K.503; 27 in B flat, K.595.
** Decca SXL/KSXC 6887. Larrocha, LPO, Solti.

Neither concerto finds Alicia de Larrocha in her best form. The *C major*, K.503, is distinctly wanting in grandeur, though Sir Georg Solti sets an impressive stage for her in the orchestral ritornello. There is just a slight lack of range and character in the *B flat Concerto*, though the soloist does not succumb to the temptation to sentimentalize. The recorded sound is in the best traditions of the house, but this is not a really distinguished issue.

Piano concerto No. 25, K.503; Concert rondo No. 1 in D, K.382.
(M) *** Ph. Seq. 6527/7311 085 [id.].
Brendel, ASMF, Marriner.

This is a more elegant and finished account of the C major Concerto than Brendel's Turnabout version made in the early 1960s with Angerer. Yet that had fine concentration and a sense of pace which compelled admiration, even though the orchestral playing and the quality of the recorded sound were not top-drawer. However, there is the same keen intelligence here, and the Academy of St Martin-in-the-Fields under Marriner is alert and supportive, while the recording has ample bloom and finesse. The cassette is warm and agreeable, but the focus is not particularly sharp.

Piano concertos Nos. 26 in D (Coronation), K.537; 27 in B flat, K.595.
(B) **(*) CfP CFP/TC-CFP 40357.
Orozco, ECO, Dutoit.

Rafael Orozco is an accomplished and intelligent artist, but there is a certain pallor about these readings. One feels the need for greater characterization and vitality, though Orozco is never insensitive. Given the excellence of the orchestral support and the quality of the recording, with no appreciable difference between disc and cassette, this is good value at bargain price. Yet artistically it must yield to the fine performances by Perahia, Barenboim and (in K.595) Gilels.

Violin concertos Nos. 1–5; Adagio in E, K.261; (i) Concertone in C, K.190; Rondos Nos. 1–2, K.269 and 373; (ii) Sinfonia concertante, K.364.
(M) *** Ph. 6746 376 (4). Szeryng, New Philh. O., Gibson, with (i) Poulet, (ii) Giuranna.

This set, which originally appeared just over ten years ago, now makes its return as part of the Mozart Complete Edition and offers excellent value. The performances are all on a high level though some find Henryk Szeryng's playing a shade cool. For the most part, however, these excellently recorded performances give pleasure, particularly the Sinfonia concertante, in which Szeryng is splendidly partnered with the violist Bruno Giuranna.

Violin concertos Nos. 1 in B flat, K.207; 3 in G, K.216; Rondos Nos. 1 in B flat, K.269; 2 in C, K.373.
(M) *** RCA Gold GL/GK 25288. Suk, Prague CO.

Suk gives us playing of the highest distinction, and the only possible objection that some collectors might have concerns the response of the Prague Chamber Orchestra, which has less warmth and sensitivity than is ideal. The recording brings them into sharper focus than does the Philips for Szeryng and the New Philharmonia, but having made this reservation one should stress that these are still performances that give much delight, and at medium price they can be strongly recommended. The cassette transfer is clear and clean, but the upper range is raw, and a strong treble cut is needed, though side two gives a fuller impression than side one.

Violin concertos Nos. 1, K.207; 4 in D, K.218; Adagio in E, K.261; Rondo No. 1, K.269.
(M) *** Ph. Fest. 6570/7310 109 [id.].
Szeryng, New Philh. O., Gibson.

The merits of Szeryng's accounts of both concertos are well known, and at medium price this makes an appealing collection. The recordings still sound warm and well balanced, and Szeryng's playing is of a high order. Anyone wanting this coupling will be rewarded with satisfying performances, not perhaps so Mozartian in scale as Iona Brown's version of K. 218 (see below), but thoroughly stylish all the same. The high-level tape transfer is excellent, clear and clean. With a slight reduction of treble and comparable increase of bass (an unusual recipe for Philips) it yields excellent results.

Violin concertos Nos. 2 and 4 in D, K.211 and 218.
** CBS 76681 [Col. M/*MT* 35111]. Stern, ECO, Schneider.

Isaac Stern has the benefit of good recorded sound, and his playing is always full of personality. At the same time one would hesitate to call these performances really inspired, for all the distinction of soloist and conductor; indeed the former's intonation is (surprisingly) not always beyond reproach.

Violin concertos Nos. 2, K.211; 5 in A (Turkish), K.219.
** HMV ASD/*TC-ASD* 3639 [Ang. SZ 37511]. Spivakov, ECO.

Vladimir Spivakov is a highly accomplished young Soviet master, and his playing in both concertos is wonderfully polished. But there is little about either performance that really lingers long in the memory. Clean, well-articulated playing in good style but perhaps a shade deficient in personality. The orchestral balance is excellent and the playing responsive. We shall surely hear more of this artist.

Violin concerto No. 2, K.211; Rondo No. 2, K.373; (i) *Sinfonia concertante in E flat, K.364.*
(M) *** Ph. Fest. 6570/*7310* 175 [id.]. Szeryng, New Philh. O., Gibson, (i) with Giuranna.

Violin concerto No. 2, K.211; (i) *Sinfonia concertante, K. 364.*
(M) *** RCA Gold GL/*GK* 25284. Suk, Prague CO, (i) with Koďousek.

Henryk Szeryng and Bruno Giuranna give a beautifully polished and musically refined account of the *Sinfonia concertante* and have the advantage of a natural and well-balanced recording. The orchestral playing is fresh and spontaneous – and in this respect probably has the edge on the RCA version with the Prague Chamber Orchestra, though the latter is very well drilled. Szeryng's account of the *D major Concerto*, K.211, has the benefit of a short fill-up. There is nothing much to choose between the two rival accounts on disc. The Philips cassette transfer is characteristically smooth, with a refined solo image and good balance.

The RCA performances also offer exemplary value. Both are highly distinguished, and Suk's contribution has character and warmth, while his partner in the *Sinfonia concertante* is hardly less impressive. Good, well-focused and clean recording. The RCA cassette transfer is unrefined, both at the top and in the internal texture (the horns give trouble in the *Sinfonia concertante*).

Violin concertos Nos. 3 in G, K.216; 4 in D, K. 218.
*** Argo ZRG/*KZRC* 880 [id.]. Iona Brown, ASMF, Marriner.
*** CRD CRD 1041/*CRDC 4041.* Thomas, New L. Soloists Ens.

Iona Brown gives a particularly successful account of these two concertos and is well able to hold her own with the most celebrated rivals. There is a spring-like freshness about the outer movements of the *G major* and a sultry Mediterranean warmth in the middle movement. Beautifully integrated performances, with recording to match. The cassette transfer is crisp and clean, of Argo's best quality.

Choice between this and the alternative coupling from CRD is by no means straightforward. Ronald Thomas has a warm, clear tone and plays very sensitively, with no romantic overtones yet plenty of feeling. His approach is extremely stylish. The accompaniments are alert and sparkling, crisply small-scale (a continuo is used in the orchestra) and strictly in period. One of the pleasures of the coupling is the gracious phrasing by soloist and orchestra alike of both slow movements. The spirited finales provide excellent contrast. Besides directing the orchestra, Thomas plays his own admirable cadenzas. The balance is undoubtedly realistic and the sound excellent on both disc and tape.

Violin concertos Nos. 3, K.216; 5 in A (Turkish), K.219.
(M) *** HMV SXLP/TC-SXLP 30449 [Ang. S 35745]. Menuhin, Bath Festival CO.
*** DG 2531/3301 049 [id.]. Mutter, Berlin PO, Karajan.
(M) *** Ph. Fest. 6570/7310 024 [id.]. Szeryng, New Philh. O., Gibson.

This coupling is exceptionally well served, and any of these performances will give satisfaction. Menuhin's versions, recorded at the beginning of the sixties, have an attractively intimate air. The orchestra is authentic in scale and the clear, lively recording is excellently detailed (the cassette is very bright, and side one needs some treble cut). Menuhin is in good form and finds characteristic warmth in the slow movements. However, he uses his own cadenzas, and some may feel that they are not entirely Mozartian. But this is the only reservation; the music-making has both charisma and spontaneity.

Extraordinarily mature and accomplished playing from Anne-Sophie Mutter, who was a mere fourteen years of age when this recording was made. Her playing has polish but artistry too, and it goes without saying that she receives the most superb orchestral support from the Berlin Philharmonic and Karajan. With a well-balanced and finely detailed

modern recording this is an eminently recommendable issue; but in the cassette transfer the forward placing of the soloist means that, although the timbre and detail of the violin are admirably clear (if very bright), the recessed orchestral detail is less clean, notably in the finale of No. 5.

Those collecting the Philips Festivo recordings sponsoring the partnership of Szeryng and Gibson will find this issue well up to the high standard set by the series. The performance of the so-called *Turkish concerto* is first-class, and K.216 is hardly less impressive. Gibson accompanies as sensitively as Szeryng plays, and the recording does justice to them both, with a smooth, clear cassette transfer to match the disc fairly closely.

Violin concerto No. 3, K.216; (i) Sinfonia concertante in E flat, K.364.
** HMV ASD/TC-ASD 3859. Spivakov, ECO, (i) with Bashmet.

There is admirably fluent playing here from Vladimir Spivakov yet little real sense of great personality. Nonetheless, he is an alert and sensitive artist with a good sense of style. His partner in the *Sinfonia concertante* is an artist of greater warmth and obviously someone to watch. Well-balanced recording both here and in the concerto, although on tape the sound seems rather plushy and thick. At full price, this playing is not quite memorable enough to displace any of the first recommendations.

Violin concertos Nos. 4 and 6 in D, K.218 and 271a.
(M) *** HMV SXLP/TC-SXLP 30454. Menuhin, Bath Festival O.

Menuhin's performance of K.218 is well-knit and lively, with his Bath Festival Orchestra at their sympathetic best. The first movement sounds dignified yet sufficiently ebullient, thanks to a nice choice of tempo, and the seraphic melody of the slow movement has seldom floated more gracefully and effortlessly than it does here. In the finale everyone is alert and extrovert. K.271a is almost certainly spurious, but if accepted by the listener simply as a late-eighteenth-century concerto of better than average quality it can be enjoyed for its own sake rather than as a work that might or might not be Mozart's. Menuhin makes the very most of its qualities. The recording is rather bright and sharply focused, but responds to the controls. The cassette transfer is admirably clean and clear.

Collection of Contredanses; German dances; Marches; Minuets; Les Petits Riens (ballet), K.299b.
(B) *** Decca D 121 D 10 (10). V. Moz. Ens., Boskovsky.

This series encompassing Mozart's complete marches and dances is one of the triumphs of the modern gramophone. Much of the credit for it should go to its expert producer, Erik Smith, who provides some of the most informative and economically written sleeve-notes that have ever graced a record. On its completion H. C. Robbins Landon cabled his praises and hailed 'the most beautiful Mozart playing and most sophisticated sound I know'; and one cannot imagine that anyone would dissent from this view. Now reissued in a bargain-priced boxed set of ten discs, each offering a generous sample of delightful and often inspired music, this makes a superb investment to dip into at will, especially for playing on a summer evening (or indeed at any time of the year).

Collection: 'Mozart in London' (arr. and orch. Smith): 3 Contredanses in F; 2 Contredanses in G; 6 Divertimenti (from 2nd London Notebook), K.15.
(M) *** Ph. 6833 222. ASMF, Marriner.

The recording producer and Mozart scholar Erik Smith had the brilliant idea of orchestrating some of the very earliest of the boy Mozart's pieces for keyboard, mostly written in London when with his father ill he began to write intensively. The results sound amazingly authentic, regularly surprising one with the vigour of the invention. Performances and recording are immaculate.

4 Contredanses, K.267; Contredanse in G (Les filles malicieuses), K.610; 2 Marches in D, K.290 and 445; Minuets: in E flat, K. 122; in D and G, K.164/3–4; 5 Minuets, K.461; 2 Minuets with a Contredanse, K.463; Overture and 3 Contredanses, K.106.
(M) *** Saga 5478. Angerer Ens., Angerer.

Paul Angerer directs a talented group of solo strings in stylish performances of an appetizing group of Mozart dances. The sound is a little forward, but the more involving for that.

3 Divertimenti for strings, K.136/8; Serenade No. 6 in D (Serenata notturna), K.239.
(M) *** Decca Ser. SA/KSC 1. ASMF, Marriner.

The reissue of Marriner's set of String Divertimenti on Decca's mid-priced Serenata label tends to sweep the board. The playing is marvellous, and Marriner's choice of tempi is equally apt. The same warm stylishness distinguishes the Serenata notturna, where timpani are added to the strings. The Argo recording, rich in texture and detail, sounds admirably fresh here, and the cassette transfer is splendid too. The sparkle of this music-making is irresistible.

Divertimento No. 1 for strings in D, K.136; Serenades Nos. 5 in D, K.204; 6 in D (Serenata notturna), K.239.

(M) *** Decca Jub. JB/*KJBC* 88. V. Moz. Ens., Boskovsky.

This is a new recording in Decca's series of *Divertimenti* and *Serenades* by Boskovsky and the Vienna Mozart Ensemble which began way back in the 1960s. The *Serenata notturna* receives a sparkling and delightful performance, as good as any ever made, and the fine *D major Serenade* is elegantly done. (The only rival, by Edo de Waart and the Dresden State Orchestra, is in the ten-record set of the *Serenades* in the Philips Complete Mozart Edition.) The performance has a smiling, captivating quality that should win this piece many admirers. A first-rate record in every respect; the cassette too is excellent, the sound clear and transparent, yet with plenty of body and warmth.

Divertimenti for strings Nos. 1–2, K.136/7.
*** HMV Dig. HQS 1432. Berlin PO Octet (members).

Although the measure is short and it is a pity that room could not have been found for the third *Divertimento* of the set, K.138, these performances by members of the Berlin Philharmonic are both lively and stylish, with solo strings giving extra bite to the ensemble. They were recorded in Japan and the digital recording is outstandingly vivid and realistic.

Divertimento No. 2 for strings in B flat, K.137; Divertimento No. 15 in B flat, K.287.
(M) *** Decca Jub. JB/*KJBC* 90. V. Moz. Ens., Boskovsky.

The K.287 *Divertimento* occupies the larger part of this record and is given a performance that has both charm and elegance. Like the *F major Divertimento*, K.247, this piece was intended for solo instruments (and is so recorded by the Vienna Octet on Decca Ace of Dia-

monds). Here even the solo line at the beginning of the fourth movement is done by several players, though the cadenza at the end is not. In any event, there is nothing here that lets down the high standard achieved by the Boskovsky series, both in terms of playing and recording. The *B flat Divertimento*, K.137, provides a short fill-up. As on disc, the quality of sound on tape is superb, with splendid life and bloom and excellent detail.

Divertimento No. 3 for strings in F, K. 138; Divertimento No. 10 in F, K.247; Serenade No. 8 in D for four orchestras, K.286.
(M) *** Decca Jub. JB/*KJBC* 89. V. Moz. Ens., Boskovsky.

Like the *Divertimenti in B flat*, K.287, and *D major*, K.334, the *F major*, K.247, is for solo instruments and sounds much better in that form. However, if one is to have it in orchestral dress, none could be more elegant than this. Boskovsky draws playing of great finesse from the Vienna Mozart Ensemble, and few collectors will want to grumble at the results. (Single-instrument versions exist on Decca played by the Vienna Octet and in the Philips Mozart Edition played by the Berlin Philharmonic Octet.) The *Serenade for four orchestras* gains immeasurably from stereo and comes off beautifully in this new recording. (Many of the Decca Jubilee issues of the *Serenades* and *Divertimenti* derive from the series of superb recordings Boskovsky made in the late 1960s, but this one is quite new.) The tape transfer is strikingly rich and spacious, one of Decca's finest cassettes, with a wide amplitude and plenty of range.

Divertimenti Nos. 1 in E flat, K.113; 2 in D, K.131.
(M) *** Decca Jub. JB/*KJBC* 67. V. Moz. Ens., Boskovsky.

Beecham's performance (mono only) of the *Divertimento in D major* remains firmly in the memory, but even by Beecham's standards these are fine performances, offering grace as well as sparkle. The playing itself is of the highest standard, as is the recording. The cassette matches the disc in bloom and clarity, except that the focus of the horns is inclined to spread somewhat.

Divertimenti Nos. 7 and 11 in D, K.205 and 251.
(M) *** Decca Jub. JB/*KJBC* 65 [Lon. STS 15416]. V. Moz. Ens., Boskovsky.

This, the eighth volume in the series of Mozart *Divertimenti* and *Serenades* from this source, is as sparkling and enjoyable as the others. Indeed, like the Beaux Arts Trio's accounts of Haydn's *Piano trios*, or these same artists' set of Mozart *Dances* and *Marches*, the series is one of the great achievements of the gramophone in the 1970s. The playing is so totally idiomatic and masterly that one scarcely thinks of the artists at all, only of the music. Decca provide a recording that is as delightfully fresh as the music itself; detail is excellently captured and yet the aural perspective remains consistent and truthful. The tape transfer too is excellent, warmer and richer than in some of the other Jubilee reissues, and also with slightly less edge on the treble.

Divertimento No. 17 in D, K.334.
(M) *** Decca Jub. JB/*KJBC* 64 [Lon. STS 15417]. V. Moz. Ens., Boskovsky.

The K.334 *Divertimento* is a captivating piece scored for string quintet (including double-bass) and two horns (used sparingly but effectively). There is a famous minuet which everyone knows, but the whole work offers Mozartian melody at its most attractive. Boskovsky's performance is outstanding; it is

superbly recorded and offers sparkling, unaffected playing of great spontaneity. The cassette is no less successful, with a lively upper range and no lack of warmth and bloom.

Wind divertimenti Nos. 8 in F, K.213; 9 in B flat, K.240; 13 in F, K.253; 14 in B flat, K.270.
⊛ *** DG 2531 296 [id.]. VPO Wind Soloists.

This is utterly enchanting playing, beautifully blended in tone and matched in terms of phrasing. These artists play with the utmost sensitivity and refinement, and they are beautifully recorded too.

17 Epistle sonatas (for organ and orchestra), *K.67–9; K.144–5; K.212; K.224–5; K.241; K.244–5; K.263; K.274; K.278; K.328–9; K.336. Adagio and allegro in F min., K. 594; Andante in F, K.616; Fantasia in F min., K.608.*
**(*) HMV SLS 5218 (2). Rogg (organ of Lutry Reformed Church), Lausanne CO, Gerecz.

Mozart's *Epistle sonatas* are miniatures, the organ taking a concertante role within the instrumental group rather than acting as extrovert soloist, although the final *Sonata in C*, K.336, is more ambitious in this respect. The solo items were conceived for mechanical instruments, but Lionel Rogg, as is the usual practice today, plays them on a larger scale. The elegant charm of the *Sonatas* is nicely caught (none is much longer than five minutes) and the playing is sympathetic and stylish. These are hardly among the most important of Mozart's works but their diminutive charm makes for agreeable late-evening listening. The recording is excellent.

A Musical Joke, K.522; Serenade No. 1 in D, K.100.

(M) *** Decca Jub. JB/*KJBC* 51 [Lon. STS 15301]. V. Moz. Ens., Boskovsky.

With playing of such elegance and sparkle, and recording well up to the high standard of this Decca series, it is not surprising that Boskovsky and his Viennese group provide yet another highly delectable coupling. They even succeed with a piece like the *Musical Joke*, making it appear as an almost unqualified masterpiece.

A Musical Joke, K.522; Serenade No. 13 in G (Eine kleine Nachtmusik), K.525.
*** DG 2531/*3301* 253 [id.]. Augmented Amadeus Qt.

Eine kleine Nachtmusik has rarely sounded so refreshing and exhilarating as here; the finale in particular is delectably resilient. The musical clowning in the *Musical Joke*, which can so often seem heavy and unfunny, is here given charm. The horn players, Gerd Seifert and Manfred Klier, are from the Berlin Philharmonic. The recording is first-rate, although on the cassette the horns create slight problems of focus in the *Musical Joke* when they are playing loudly.

Overtures: Apollo et Hyacinthus; Ascanio in Alba; Bastien und Bastienne; La Clemenza di Tito; Idomeneo; The Impresario; Lucio Silla; Mitridate; Il Re pastore; Il Sogno di Scipione.
(M) **(*) Turn. TVS 34628 [id./*CT 2162*]. Württemberg CO, Faerber.

Faerber and his Württemberg orchestra give brisk and enjoyable performances of a generous list of rare Mozart opera overtures, most of them early but all of them with endearing ideas. The sound is sometimes edgy and the performances are not always perfectly polished, but at budget price this is well worth investigating.

Overtures: La Clemenza di Tito; Così fan tutte; Don Giovanni; Die Entführung aus dem Serail; Idomeneo; Lucio Silla; Le Nozze di Figaro; Der Schauspieldirektor; Die Zauberflöte.
*** Ph. 9500/*7300* 882 [id.]. LPO, Haitink.

Essentially concert performances, with a warm, resonant acoustic emphasizing the weight and giving suitable *gravitas* to the introductions for *Don Giovanni* and *Die Zauberflöte.* The acoustic suits *Le Nozze di Figaro* less well, but the warmth and richness of the sound always give pleasure. Haitink lavishes special care on the less well-known pieces, *Der Schauspieldirektor, La Clemenza di Tito* and *Lucio Silla*, which the LPO strings play with elegance and sparkle, while the woodwind shine in *Così fan tutte.* Most enjoyable, but not for those who favour the more astringent approach to Mozart of the Academy of Ancient Music. The cassette transfer is well balanced but lacks the last degree of upper range.

Serenade No. 4 in D (Colloredo), K.203; (i) *Concert rondo in E flat for horn and orchestra, K.371* (arr. Smith).
(M) *** Decca Jub. JB/*KJBC* 54 [Lon. STS 15077]. V. Moz. Ens., Boskovsky, (i) with Berger.

This *Serenade* dates in all probability from the year 1774, when Mozart was eighteen, and the suggestion by Mozart's first biographer that it was written for the name-day of Archbishop Colloredo has resulted in it being called the *Colloredo serenade.* Like many of the other serenades, the work embraces a violin concerto (preceding the independent concertos by several months), the solo part being played here with great distinction by Alfred Staar. The music – in particular the *Night music* for muted strings – is altogether delightful. The *Rondo*, K.371, is the earliest of Mozart's horn pieces. It survives in a fragmentary condition, and the arrangement here is by the producer of the Decca Mozart series, Erik Smith. The recording is first-class, although (as with some of the other earlier Jubilee tape transfers) the sound on cassette is a little dry compared with the disc.

Serenades Nos. 6 in D (Serenata notturna), K.239; 13 in G (Eine kleine Nachtmusik), K.525; Symphony No. 29 in A, K.201.
**(*) CRD 1040/CRDC 4040. New L. Soloists Ens., Thomas.

A pleasingly gracious account of *Eine kleine Nachtmusik* is matched by an equally elegant *Serenata notturna*. The symphony is given an alert, genial performance of considerable character. The music-making is authentic in scale, but it seems stretching the point a little to use a harpsichord continuo in *Eine kleine Nachtmusik*. The sound is spaciously resonant, but on tape the levels vary between sides and the *Night music* is not as vividly projected as the symphony.

Serenades Nos. 7 in D (Haffner), K.250; 9 in D (Posthorn), K.320; 2 Marches in D, K.335/1–2.
(M) *** Ph. 6770 043 (2). Dresden State O., De Waart.

We are well served with separate issues of the *Haffner* and *Posthorn serenades*, with Boskovsky's admirable accounts available separately on Decca's mid-priced Jubilee label (see below). Though not quite so well recorded, Edo de Waart's Dresden version of the *Haffner* is perhaps the only one that can be mentioned in the same breath. It has rhythmic poise and delightful spontaneity and warmth; moreover the same artists' account of the *Posthorn serenade* is in some ways preferable even to Boskovsky's,

though the recorded sound is not as fresh. The Dresden orchestra displays superb musicianship and the effect reminds one a little of some of Bruno Walter's pre-war Mozart records. With sparkling playing and very well disciplined, the reading also uses the marches that Christa Landon includes in her edition of the score, which preface and round off the performance. This set is well worth considering alongside Boskovsky.

Serenade No. 7 in D (Haffner), K.250.
(M) *** Decca Jub. JB/KJBC 31 [Lon. STS 15414]. V. Moz. Ens., Boskovsky.

Serenade No. 7, K.250; March in D, K.249.
*(*) HMV Dig. ASD 4013. Berlin RIAS Sinf., Kühn.

Boskovsky's version of the *Haffner serenade* is marvellously alive, full of sparkle and elegance, with admirable phrasing and feeling for detail. The recording too is outstanding, fresh and vivid, although the cassette is a little dry and lacking in bloom (it benefits from a treble cut and balancing bass lift).

Gustav Kühn is a conductor of much promise who is beginning to make a considerable name in his own country. His account of the *Haffner serenade* has the advantage of a clean digital recording, though it is not greatly superior to its analogue rival from Decca. The performance is not a particularly distinguished one, and things remain distinctly earthbound most of the time; Boskovsky is much to be preferred.

Serenade No. 9 in D (Posthorn), K.320.
(M) *** Decca Jub. JB/KJBC 34 [Lon. STS 15415]. V. Moz. Ens., Boskovsky.
*** HM 1C 065 99697. Coll. Aur., Maier.

The Jubilee issue upholds the fine tradition set by the Decca series. Boskovsky's performance, with its natural musicality and sense of sparkle, has the advantage of superb Decca recording and is recommendable in every way. The cassette transfer is a little dry in the matter of string tone compared with the disc, but there is plenty of bloom on the wind and detail is crisp and clean. Aficionados should also not overlook the Collegium Aureum version, recorded in the warm acoustic of Schloss Kirchheim. The playing is sensitive and vital, and never sounds pedantic. About twenty-five instrumentalists take part, playing period instruments or copies, and the inevitable problems of intonation are altogether minimal. The tempo of the two concertante movements is a little leisurely, but on the whole the playing is so musical that this seems of little account. This is one of the most successful of the Collegium Aureum's records.

Serenades Nos. 10 in B flat, K.361; 11 in E flat, K.375; 12 in C min., K.388.
(M) *** Ph. 6770 047 (2). Neth. Wind Ens., De Waart.
(M) *** HMV SXDW/TC-SXDW 3050 (2). L. Wind Quintet and Ens., or New Philh. Wind Ens., Klemperer.

The Dutch players offer performances that are marvellously fresh and alive. They are admirably sensitive both in feeling for line and in phrasing but never linger too lovingly over detail. This is both refreshing and satisfying and apart from the sheer quality of the playing, the discs are enhanced by the presence and sonority of the recording, which is beautifully balanced and combines rich homogeneity of timbre with crispness of focus. The performance of the famous *B flat major Serenade* for thirteen wind instruments does not erase memories of the outstanding Barenboim version (which has the advantage of being available separately: see below), but anyone investing in the Philips box will find its

qualities are very special indeed. The pressings are immaculate.

Admirers of Klemperer will find the alternative HMV double-album no less worthwhile in gathering together this great conductor's memorable performances of Mozart's great wind masterpieces. Though tempi tend to be on the slow side, the rhythmic control and fine ensemble make for performances which despite their magisterial weight are bright and refreshing, not heavy. They are far from being conventional readings but as the expression of a great Mozart interpreter they are endlessly illuminating. The mid-sixties recording still sounds first-rate. The tape transfers too are excellent, although, reflecting the records, the inner detail is slightly less sharply defined in K.388.

Serenade No. 10 in B flat for 13 wind instruments, K.361.
*** HMV ASD/TC-ASD 3426. ECO, Barenboim.
(M) **(*) Decca Ace SDD 579. V. Wind Soloists.
** Argo ZRG 919. L. Sinf., Atherton.

The Barenboim ECO reading is undoubtedly the most stylish of recent years. It is most distinguished and only the old Furtwängler Vienna account (mono) matches it in terms of warmth and humanity. Here we have expertly blended wind tone, free from the traces of self-indulgence that occasionally mar Barenboim's music-making. Tempi are a little on the brisk side (especially in the first movement) but none the worse for that when the playing itself is so resilient, and the quality of the recorded sound is beautifully focused, with no want of body and definition. The cassette too reproduces extremely well, and there is little to choose between the quality in either format.

The freshness of the new Vienna recording is also very striking. The sound is of demonstration quality, wonderfully vivid and clear yet with a natural overall blend. The alert, strongly characterized allegros are attractively buoyant here, and there is much delightful colouring. If in the *Adagio* and *Romanze* the playing is a shade literal and overall the performance does not quite have the incandescence of Barenboim's version, at medium price this remains well worth considering.

The London Sinfonietta's reading lacks fire. The results are not mannered, as in their companion record of K.375 and K.388, and the slow movements here are naturally expressive; but there are finer versions available. Unlike Barenboim this group does not use the latest amended edition of the score. The recording is nicely balanced.

Serenades Nos. 11 in E flat, K.375; 12 in C min., K.388.
** Argo ZRG/*KZRC* 911. L. Sinf., Pay.

This coupling is disappointing, lacking the alertness and bite one expects of the London Sinfonietta and with expressive mannerisms sounding intrusive. The recording is first-class on disc and cassette alike.

Serenades Nos. 11, K.375; 13 in G (Eine kleine Nachtmusik), K.525.
*(*) O-L DSLO 549. Music Party.

The *Serenade*, K.375, which we know as a wind octet, was originally conceived for wind sextet with pairs of clarinets, horns and bassoons but no oboes. The Music Party gives a performance on original instruments with plenty of spirit, but collectors are warned that the tone is often raw. Textually one difference between this and the octet version is that repeats are included in both halves of the first movement (neither of which the Music Party observes). The account of *Eine kleine Nachtmusik*, also on original instruments, is an even less persuasive example of authentic performance; quite

apart from intonation problems without the help of vibrato, the tempi tend to be deliberate and the repeats many.

Symphonies Nos. 1, 4–6, 7a, 8–20, 42–7, 55; in C, K.208/102; in D, K.45, 111/120, 141a and 196/121; in G.
(M) *** Ph. 6769 054 (8). ASMF, Marriner.

The two DG boxes of Mozart symphonies under Boehm were ultimately let down by a certain dourness and want of sparkle. In a sense, Günter Kehr's earlier set, some of which are still in circulation (see below), shows a more Mozartian spirit, and they are far from second-rate recordings. (Indeed they stand up well to competition from 1970 sound.) Marriner's survey has a splendid Mozartian vitality and seems to combine the best qualities of both its predecessors. The Academy play with great style, warmth and polish, while the Philips engineers respond with alive and vivid recording. These are altogether delightful records and can be strongly recommended.

Symphonies Nos. 1 in E flat, K.16; 4 in D, K.19; 5 in B flat, K.22; 6 in F, K.43.
(M) *** Turn. TVS 34087 [in SVBX 5119]. Mainz CO, Kehr.

These recordings date from the 1960s but in many respects remain superior to later rivals. They have a spontaneity and vitality that make them preferable to the Boehm set on DG, and the sound is no less fresh and well-detailed. No. 1 dates from Mozart's London visit when he was only eight, and, like the companion works here, it is lightly scored: strings, two oboes and two horns. No. 5 in B flat was composed in the Netherlands and like all these symphonies is modelled on the Italian sinfonia or overture.

Symphonies Nos. 7 and 8 in D, K.45 and 48; in G, K.45a (Anhang 221); in B flat, K.45b (Anhang 214).
(M) *** Turn. TVS 37088 [in SVBX 5119]. Mainz CO, Kehr.

Another delightful disc in the Kehr series of Mozart symphonies recorded in the 1960s. The *Symphony No. 7 in D* was composed in January 1768, a few days before Mozart's thirteenth birthday, and makes use of trumpets and timpani. Its successor has no lack of drama and charm. The *Lambacher Sinfonia*, K45a, is so called because Leopold Mozart is supposed to have presented the autograph to the Benedictine monastery at Lambach when he and the young Mozart visited it in 1769. A delightful issue.

Symphonies Nos. 9 in C, K.73; 10 in G, K.74; 42 and 43 in F, K.75 and 76.
*** Turn. TVS 37089 [in SVBX 5119]. Mainz CO, Kehr.

These performances continue to have a charm that eludes many subsequent rivals. Günter Kehr draws stylish and vital playing from his Mainz orchestra, which is eminently well recorded. The earliest of these symphonies is No. 43 (K.76 or 42a), whose finale draws on a Rameau *Gavotte*, and which dates from about 1766. The others come from 1770–71, though the editors of the latest *Köchel* give No. 9, K.73, an earlier date. This can be warmly recommended.

Symphonies Nos. 9 in C, K.73; 14 in A, K.114; 15 in G, K.124; 16 in C, K.128; 17 in G, K.129; in C, K.35; in D K.38; in D, K.62a/K.100; (42) in F, K.75; in G, K.75b/K.110.
*** O-L D 168 D 3/K 168 K 33 (3). AcAM, Schröder.

The fourth volume to appear in the Academy of Ancient Music series (see below) deals with the earliest Salzburg symphonies (those that Mozart composed before 1770 were written in London). The work in D, K.62a, is also known and played as the *Serenade No.1*, K.100, which Boskovsky has recorded very stylishly. His approach reveals much more expressive warmth, for it is vitality and sharpness of articulation which dominate the reading here. In the later symphonies textures are sometimes thinned ever further by the use of solo strings in sections of the music, which produces the feeling of a chamber ensemble, and seems a questionable practice. However, Schröder and his group are nothing if not consistent, and those collecting this series can be assured that this volume is as vigorous and dedicated as the others. The recording too is lively, although the acoustic at times seems somewhat over-resonant, especially in the earlier works. This brings problems for the tape transfer, where with a high level (probably too high) there are moments of roughness and a recurring degree of congestion in tuttis.

Symphonies Nos. 18 in F, K.130; in D, K.141a; 19 in E flat, K.132; 20 in D, K.133; 21 in A, K.134; in D, K.135; 26 in E flat, K.161a; 27 in G, K.161b; 22 in C, K.162; 23 in D, K.162b; 24 in B flat, K.173dA.
*** O-L D 169 D 3/K 169 K 33 (3) [id.]. AcAM, Schröder; Hogwood.

This was the first box of the Academy of Ancient Music's projected complete recording of Mozart symphonies using authentic texts and original instruments; and very invigorating it proved. The series, meticulously planned under the guidance of the American Mozart scholar Neal Zaslaw, aims to reproduce as closely as possible the conditions of the first performances. It includes not just the symphonies in the regular numbered series but works which might have been compiled as symphonies (the overture to *Lucio Silla*, for example), and the variety of scale as well as of expression makes it a very refreshing collection, particularly as the style of performance, with its non-vibrato tang, is so bright and clean, sharply picking out detail of texture rather than moulding the sound together. The recording is excellent, and the sophisticated tape transfer catches the wide amplitude of the sound without loss of range and focus.

Symphonies Nos. 21 in A, K.134; 31 in D (Paris), K.297.
** HMV Dig. ASD 4014. Berlin RIAS Sinf., Kühn.

Kühn's coupling is hardly generous, and although the performances are extremely well recorded, they lack something in brio and individuality. The simple *Andante* that Mozart wrote as an alternative for the usual *Andantino* is included in this account of the *Paris symphony*.

Symphonies Nos. 22–41.
(M) *** Ph. 6769 043 (8) [id.]. ASMF, Marriner.

Marriner, following up the success of his splendid volume of the early symphonies, here presents the later works in comparably stylish, well-recorded performances. Perhaps when he reaches the *Jupiter* he fails quite to capture the full weight of Mozart's argument (exposition repeat not observed in the finale); but the wonder is that so many of the symphonies have been performed with no hint of routine. Nos. 35 and 40 were recorded (in original instrumentation) in 1970, but they marry well with the refined sounds of the recordings from the late 1970s.

Symphonies Nos. 25 in G min., K.183; 28 in C, K.200; 29 in A, K.201; 30 in D, K.202; in D, K.203, 204 and 196/121.
*** O-L D 170 D 3/K 170 K 33 (3) [id.]. AcAM, Schröder; Hogwood.

With this second batch of Salzburg works the Academy of Ancient Music come to symphonies that have long been established in the regular modern repertory. It is a revelation to find that a symphony such as the *G minor* (No. 25) is not a 'little *G minor*' at all, for with repeats all observed (even those in the minuet the second time round), it acquires extra weight; and in so lively and fresh a performance as this the extra length from repetition proves invigorating, never tedious. The *A major* – another 'big' symphony – also has a new incisiveness and clarity, without losing anything in rhythmic bounce; so too with the less well-known works. Though it is confusing not to have the regular numbers appended – particularly when the series is so liberally supplied with rarities – the notes by Neal Zaslaw add enormously to the excitement of new discovery. As in the other volumes, the recording is superb, and the cassettes match the discs closely. Sometimes the string timbre seems slightly drier on tape than on disc, and there is just a hint of overloading from the horns in the finale of No. 29; but the resonance does not cloud over the detail as it sometimes can on cassette.

Symphonies Nos. 25 in G min., K.183; 29 in A, K.201.
*** Decca SXL/KSXC 6879. ECO, Britten.

Several years before his untimely death Benjamin Britten recorded these exhilarating performances of the two greatest of Mozart's early symphonies. Inexplicably the record remained unissued, finally providing a superb codicil to Britten's recording career. It is striking that in many movements his tempi and even his approach are very close to those of Neville Marriner on his excellent Argo disc (ZRG 706); but it is Britten's genius along with his crisp articulation and sprung rhythms to provide the occasional touch of pure individual magic. Britten's slow movements provide a clear contrast, rather weightier than Marriner's, particularly in the little *G minor*, where Britten, with a slower speed and more expressive phrasing, underlines the elegiac quality of the music. Rich, well-balanced recording and a first-class cassette transfer.

Symphonies Nos. 25, K.183; 29, K.201; 32 in G, K.318.
(M) **(*) Ph. Fest. 6570/7310 207 [id.].
LSO, Colin Davis.

The 'little *G major Symphony*' almost steals the show here, so vivaciously alert is the playing. But the spontaneity of the other performances is striking too, and Davis achieves a splendid rhythmic spring in the opening *Allegro* of the early *G minor Symphony*. The character of the first movement of No. 29 is also well caught by this polished, stylish approach, and both slow movements have an appealing fragile delicacy. The recording (from the mid-sixties) is warm and full, not as freshly transparent and wide-ranging as Philips' best, but fully acceptable. The cassette is well managed but needs a high-level playback.

Symphonies Nos. 26 in E flat, K.184; 31 in D (Paris), K.297; 38 in D (Prague), K.504.
(M) **(*) DG Acc. 2542/3342 127. Berlin PO, Boehm.

This is a recoupling. Symphonies Nos. 26 and 31 come from the mid-sixties, but the *Prague* is much earlier and the upper strings are recorded with less body and bloom. The performances, however, are alert and sensitive. The playing is first-class, as one would expect, and show Boehm on his best Mozartian form. The sound is lively and well balanced on disc and cassette alike.

Symphonies Nos. 29 in A, K.201; 35 in D (Haffner), K.385; 3 German dances, K.605.
(B) **(*) CfP CFP/TC-CFP 40306. LPO, Davison.

An attractive coupling at bargain price. Spontaneous performances, with tempi well judged, are given excellent modern recording, brilliant and well detailed yet with an attractive ambient bloom. The *A major Symphony* comes off especially well; the relaxed warmth of Davison's approach is appealing, yet he still keeps a grip on the overall structure. The *Haffner* contrasts athletic outer movements with an elegant and nicely pointed *Andante*. Some will count it a drawback that the first-movement exposition repeat is not observed; but instead we are offered three *German dances*, including the justly famous *Sleighride*. The full, resonant recording is equally well caught on the vivid cassette.

Symphonies Nos. 29, K.201; 35 (Haffner), K.385; Masonic funeral music, K.477.
** DG 2531/3301 335 [id.]. VPO, Boehm.

These performances, which appeared not long before Boehm's death, are distinguished by finely groomed playing from the Vienna Philharmonic. The first movement of the *A major Symphony* is on the slow side, but there is some lovely expressive playing in the second. However, there is none of the sparkle and spontaneity of Sir Colin Davis's LSO account, and the overall impression both here and in the *Haffner* is a shade dour. Refined playing, dignified readings, excellent recording – but all just a shade wanting in charm. The disc and cassette are closely matched; the sound is slightly cleaner on LP.

*Symphonies Nos. 31 in D (Paris),
K.297; 32 in G, K.318; 39 in E flat,
K.453.*
(B) *** CfP CFP/*TC-CFP* 40354. LPO,
Macal.

The Classics for Pleasure series of the
mature Mozart symphonies is well represented in Macal's sympathetic readings
of an attractive coupling. The recording
is bright but rather reverberant, at times
obscuring rapid passage-work; but the
playing of the LPO is most stylish, with
joyfully affectionate – but unmannered –
accounts of such movements as the first-
movement *Allegro* of No. 39 and the
dashing finale of the *Paris*. The cassette
is of high quality, slightly smoother on
top, but otherwise there is no appreciable
difference between disc and tape.

*Symphonies Nos. 32 in G, K.318; 33
in B flat, K.319; 34 in C, K.338; 35 in
D (Haffner), K.385; 36 in C (Linz),
K.425; in C, K.213c/208; in D,
K.248b/250 and 320.*
*** O-L D 171 D 4/*K 171 K 44* (4) [id.].
AcAM, Schröder; Hogwood.

This volume of the Academy of Ancient Music's collected edition of Mozart
symphonies includes the works that
Mozart wrote between 1775 and 1783,
not just those in the regularly numbered
series (Nos. 32 to 36) but two other
symphonies extracted from large-scale
serenades (the *Haffner serenade* and the
Posthorn serenade) as well as a short
Italian-style *Sinfonia* taken from the
overture to *Il Re pastore*. As before, using
authentic performance style with all repeats observed, the readings are always
fresh and illuminating, the speeds often
brisk but never rushed, though some will
prefer a more relaxed, less metrical style
in slow movements. The recordings –
with Hogwood's harpsichord presented
clearly against the full ensemble – strings
9.8.4.3.2 – are superbly faithful to the aim
of re-creating the sounds Mozart origi-

nally heard. The cassette transfer offers
the finest tape quality in this series so far;
the sound is full and resonant and has a
striking life and upper range. Only on
the last side is there a hint of stridency
in the upper strings; otherwise this is
demonstration-worthy.

*Symphonies Nos. 32, K.318; 35 in D
(Haffner), K.385; 36 in C (Linz),
K.425; 38 in D (Prague), K.504; 39
in E flat, K.543; 40 in G min., K.550;
41 in C (Jupiter), K.551.*
*** DG 2740 189/*3371 038* (3) [id.].
Berlin PO, Karajan.

It is difficult to conceive of better big-
band Mozart than these beautifully
played and vitally alert readings. There
are details about which some may have
reservations: the minuet and trio of the
Linz may seem too slow, and the opening
of the *G minor*, which is a shade faster
than in Karajan's Vienna performance,
may not be quite dark enough for some
tastes. In general, however, these are such
finely proportioned readings, so exquisitely paced and shaped, that it is hard to
see how they could be surpassed. As recordings they are well balanced, alive and
yet smooth. Either as a complete set or
as individual issues (listed below), these
hold their own with the best; and the cassette transfers are altogether excellent.

*Symphonies Nos. 32, K.318; 35
(Haffner); 36 (Linz).*
*** DG 2531/*3301* 136 [id.]. Berlin PO,
Karajan.
(M) **(*) DG Acc. 2542/*3342* 119. Berlin
PO, Boehm.

Boehm's 1967 recording of the *Linz* is
one of his finest Mozart performances,
balancing vitality with warmth, and the
vivacious account of the 'Italian overture', K.318, is no less attractive. The
Haffner dates from 1960, and the recording has just a hint of stridency in the
upper string timbre (though this is

507

smoothed slightly in the cassette transfer). The performance is a good one, though less imaginative than the other two. The recorded sound is generally good, slightly warmer and fuller on cassette than on disc.

Symphonies Nos. 33 in B flat, K.319; 39 in E flat, K.543.
(M) ** Decca Eclipse ECS 823. VPO, Kertesz.

Kertesz's Mozart was inclined to be a little faceless. Beautiful orchestral playing, warm Decca recording of mid-sixties vintage and a gracious feeling for Mozartian phrasing distinguish this enjoyable but not outstanding reissue. The earlier symphony, played in a simple, relaxed way, comes off very well, but the great *E flat Symphony* is somewhat under-characterized.

Symphonies Nos. 34 in C, K.338; 35 in D (Haffner), K.385.
**(*) Tel. Dig. AZ6/CX4 42703. Concg. O., Harnoncourt.

With bright, clear digital recording – quite different from the sound which Philips engineers get from this orchestra – the Harnoncourt coupling provides refreshing, directly dramatic performances of these two symphonies, marked by unforced tempi. Charm is rather missing, and the coupling provides rather short measure; but the immediacy of sound is what compels attention.

Symphonies Nos. 35 (Haffner); 36 in C (Linz), K.425.
** HM 1C 065 99903. Coll. Aur., Maier.

Good performances for those whose interest lies in re-creating the 'original' instrumental sound of Mozart's time (although here the timbres are much more like a modern group than those of, say, the Academy of Ancient Music). Franzjosef Maier's direction is thoroughly

musical, and tempi are well judged. The recording is full-bodied and has good detail.

Symphonies Nos. 35 (Haffner); 40 in G min., K.550; March in D, K.408/2.
(M) *** Ph. Fest. 6570/7310 022. ASMF, Marriner.

Marriner's stylish coupling uses original scorings of both works – minus flutes and clarinets in the *Haffner*, minus clarinets in No. 40. The *March* is included as makeweight, since (having the same K. number) it has long been associated with the *Haffner symphony*. Marriner's readings are finely detailed but dynamic too, nicely scaled against refined recording. The cassette is well managed, although the bass needs cutting back for a satisfactory balance.

Symphonies Nos. 36 in C (Linz), K.425; 38 in D (Prague), K.504.
(B) *** CfP CFP/TC-CFP 40336. LPO, Mackerras.

Mackerras's splendid bargain coupling has appeared before on CfP and was withdrawn. In this reissue it now sounds freshly minted. The inclusion of a harpsichord continuo may seem slightly eccentric to some, but these are fine, stylish performances, polished and full of life. The new cassette transfer is first-class, and whether heard on disc or tape the sheer vitality of these performances is irresistible.

Symphonies Nos. 38 (Prague); 39 in E flat, K.543; 40 in G min., K.550; 41 in C (Jupiter), K.551.
(M) **(*) DG Acc. 2725/3374 104. Berlin PO, Boehm.

This mid-price two-disc folder neatly couples the last four symphonies from Boehm's complete series recorded in Berlin in the 1960s. With generally slowish tempi there is an attractive honesty and strength about them. The weight of sound from a relatively large band is not obtrusive, and though they may be a little short on charm and some of the finales lack sparkle, there is a comfortable quality of inevitability here, perpetuating a long Mozart tradition. The recordings still sound very well, although on cassette the lively upper range needs cutting back a little.

Symphonies Nos. 38 (Prague); 39, K.543.
*** DG 2531/*3301* 206 [id.]. VPO, Boehm.
*** DG 2531/*3301* 137 [id.]. Berlin PO, Karajan.
**(*) HM 1C 065 99786. Coll. Aur., Maier.

Boehm's recordings made when he had reached his mid-eighties are sunnier and more genial than those he made as part of his complete Mozart series in the sixties. The tempi are again spacious, but the results are less markedly magisterial. The glow of the performances is helped by warm DG sound. The cassette is of demonstration quality, full-bodied, clear and splendidly balanced, with a fine bloom on the strings. Karajan, who offers the same coupling, is also strongly recommendable (see the entry for his set above), but Boehm shows himself an even more understanding Mozartian.

The Harmonia Mundi issue is recommendable mainly to those for whom 'authenticity' of scale and timbre is of prime importance. Maier has been responsible for some excellent performances on original instruments, and though interpretatively these may seem a little cautious, playing and recording are first-rate.

Symphonies Nos. 39 in E flat, K.543; 40 in G min., K.550.
(M) *** Ph. Fest. 6570/*7310* 143. LSO, Colin Davis.
(M) **(*) HMV SXLP/*TC-SXLP* 30527. Berlin PO, Karajan.

Sir Colin Davis's much praised coupling returns once more to the catalogue on Festivo. The performances are strong and straightforward, refreshingly alive and stylish. This version of the *G minor Symphony* is one of the most recommendable ever issued, and the sound retains its bloom. The cassette is particularly successful, although it needs a small bass cut to achieve a proper balance.

Karajan offers us big-band Mozart – but what a band! Tempi are sensible and entirely free from egocentric touches. Karajan's views about both symphonies have remained consistent over the years and there is the same high regard for detail and beauty and refinement of tone. The only reservation might be the tempo for the *Andante* of No. 39, somewhat faster than listeners brought up on Beecham or Bruno Walter might like. To some ears the first movement of 39 might seem overgroomed, but its breadth and sense of stature command admiration. The sound is slightly more opaque than in Karajan's more recent DG set, but it is still very good indeed. On tape the quality is rather dry and harsh.

Symphony No. 40, K.550; Serenade No. 6 in D (Serenata notturna), K.239.
(M) *** Decca Jub. JB/*KJBC* 107. ECO, Britten.

Symphony No. 40, K.550; Serenade No. 13 in G (Eine kleine Nachtmusik), K.525.
(B) **(*) Con. CC/*CCT* 7507. VPO, Kertesz.
** Decca SXL/*KSXC* 6844 [Lon. 7066/5–]. Israel PO, Mehta.

Britten takes *all* repeats (the slow movement here is longer than that of the *Eroica*); but there are a composer's insights and he is almost totally convincing. The *Serenade* is enchanting. With the rich Maltings sound to give added breadth to the symphony, and at Jubilee price, this is well worth trying. The cassette is outstandingly full and wide-ranging in the *Symphony*; the *Serenade* has rather less body and refinement.

Kertesz underlines the richness of the music of the *G minor Symphony*, tempi on the slow side (except in the finale), with dramatic underlining of dynamic contrasts. The orchestral playing is first-class and with a warmly elegant account of *Eine kleine Nachtmusik* this is attractive at bargain price, especially as the recording is of vintage Decca quality, full and clear. The cassette transfer lacks range, especially in the symphony.

Mehta directs a refined and athletic account of the *G minor Symphony*, with rhythms well sprung in the outer movements at tempi marginally slower than usual. With exposition repeats observed in both, the weight of argument is reinforced, while Mehta uses the sparer version of the score, without clarinets. The recording is among the best that Decca has made with the Israel orchestra, but *Eine kleine Nachtmusik*, attractive as a coupling, is not nearly so recommendable. The phrasing of the Israel strings is not so refined, although the reading is strong and stylish enough. On tape, however, the recording of the *Serenade* is full and pleasing, and the transfer of the *Symphony* is also vivid and clear.

Symphonies Nos. 40, K.550; 41 in C (Jupiter), K.551.
*** DG 2531/*3301* 138 [id.]. Berlin PO, Karajan.
(M) **(*) Decca VIV/*KVIC* 6. VPO, Karajan.
*(*) DG 2531/*3301* 273 [id.]. LSO, Abbado.

Some ears find the DG Karajan recordings, made in Berlin in 1979, rather streamlined, and the opening of the *G minor Symphony* is here not as subtle in colour and feeling as in some versions. But the orchestra plays superbly and the *Jupiter* has weight and power as well as

surface elegance. The sound is wholly admirable on disc and cassette alike. Karajan's earlier Vienna recordings, dating from the early sixties, remain good value in the medium price-range. In the *G minor* every detail is beautifully in place, each phrase nicely shaped and in perspective. The exposition repeat in the first movement is observed, though the chords linking it to the development are prominent at a slightly higher level and the balance thereafter appears to be closer. Beautifully articulate and suave, this performance has a genuine dramatic power, even though one feels that it all moves within carefully regulated emotional limits. Karajan does tend to beautify detail without adding corresponding stature. The reading of the *Jupiter* is a strong one, one of the best things Karajan did in his short period in the Decca studios. The performance is direct and has breadth as well as warmth. The orchestral playing is excellent, and with first-rate sound this is certainly enjoyable, although there is no exposition repeat in the first movement. There is no appreciable difference in sound between disc and cassette.

Abbado directs the orchestra of which he is principal conductor in generally immaculate but curiously faceless performances of Mozart's last symphonies. The *Jupiter* is marginally more convincing, but there are far better versions of this coupling, notably Sir Charles Mackerras's with the LPO on CfP (CFP/*TC-CFP* 40253, which is a real bargain on either disc or cassette). The recording is bright and full, with little perceptible difference between disc and tape.

Symphony No. 41 (Jupiter), K.551.
(M) *** HMV SXLP/*TC-SXLP* 30443. RPO, Beecham – SCHUBERT: *Symphony No. 6.****

Symphony No. 41; Rondo No. 2 in C for violin and orchestra, K.373.
*** HM 1C 065 99673. Coll. Aur., Maier (violin).

Characteristically Beecham makes the *Jupiter* an elegant work rather than a magisterial one, and the minuet is a classic example of Beechamesque nuance, inimitably shaped at a slowish tempo. The outer movements are crisp and immediate, the slow movement gracious. Already this has become a period performance. The 1950s recording sounds well enough and its slightly dry quality has transferred very successfully to cassette.

Maier directs (from the leader's desk) a refined and sensitive performance of the *Jupiter* using original instruments, and with wide groove-spacing the sound is outstandingly vivid. This may miss some of the full power of the finest versions, but unless you insist on the original flat pitch, it is an admirable example of authentic performance, not so abrasive as those by the Academy of Ancient Music. However, with only the (well played) *Rondo*, K.373, for coupling this seems a very expensive issue, particularly compared with Beecham's *Jupiter* at the medium price coupled to a delectable Schubert symphony, or indeed Mackerras's stylish LPO version (see under the *G minor Symphony* above).

CHAMBER AND INSTRUMENTAL MUSIC

Adagio and rondo in C. min., K.617 (for glass harmonica etc.); *Oboe quartet in F, K.370; Oboe quintet in C min., K.406* (arr. of *Serenade No. 12, K.388*).
*** Ph. 9500 397/7300 607 [id.]. Hoffmann (glass harmonica), Holliger, Nicolet, Krebbers, Schouten, Munk-Gerö, Decross.

With such a distinguished roster it is not surprising that these performances are first-class. Moreover they are beautifully recorded, and the tape transfer too, which is made at quite a high level, has splendid immediacy; Holliger's bright

clear timbre dominates the strings without too forward a balance. The curiosity is Mozart's own arrangement of his *Wind serenade*, K.388, which some might feel sounds best in its original format. However, the playing here is undoubtedly persuasive, and of course the account of the *Oboe quartet* is peerless. Finally and certainly not least is the work for glass harmonica played on Bruno Hoffmann's set of drinking glasses (with moistened fingers). It is an unforgettably piquant sound and the result is delightful (the piece does not outstay its welcome).

Clarinet quintet in A, K.581; (i) *Clarinet trio in E flat, K.498.*
(M) *(*) Decca Ace SDD/KSDC 558. Schmidl, New V. Octet (members), (i) with Medjimorec.

Clarinet quintet; Horn quintet in E flat, K.407; Oboe quartet in F, K.370.
*** Ph. 9500 772/7300 848 [id.]. Pay, Black, Timothy Brown, ASMF Chamber Ens.

(i) *Clarinet quintet;* (ii) *Oboe quartet.*
(M) **(*) DG Priv. 2535/3335 287. Berlin PO soloists, with (i) Leister, (ii) Koch.

(i) *Clarinet quintet;* (ii) *Piano and wind quintet in E flat, K.452.*
(B) ** Con. CC/CCT 7544. V. Octet (members), with (i) Alfred Boskovsky, (ii) Panhoffer.

Antony Pay is a mellifluous and sensitive artist, and the account of the *Clarinet quintet* by the Academy of St Martin-in-the-Fields players must be numbered among the strongest now on the market. Contours are beautifully shaped, and the performers convey a strong sense of enjoyment. Neil Black's playing in the *Oboe quartet* is distinguished, and again the whole performance radiates pleasure. This issue gives excellent value in also including the *Horn quintet* in a well-projected and lively account with Timothy

Brown. The full-price Harmonia Mundi and Telefunken versions (see below) both offer only the *Horn quintet* and the *Oboe quartet*: here we have another major work besides – and all three are beautifully finished and musically alive performances. On cassette the sound is pleasingly warm and mellow yet does not lack range and detail.

The Privilege reissue offers fine playing but a somewhat suave atmosphere in the central movements of the *Clarinet quintet*. Karl Leister, the clarinettist, does not emerge as a strong individual personality, but he plays most musically and this performance undoubtedly gives pleasure. Lothar Koch shows a sweetly pointed timbre and a most sensitive feeling for the style of the *Oboe quartet*, though this is not quite so distinguished as his later Amadeus version. The recording is very good and the tape transfers are of excellent quality; the *Clarinet quintet* is especially vivid, the level unusually high for DG. However, the full-priced DG issue of these two works (2530/3300 720), where members of the Amadeus Quartet support Gervase de Peyer and Koch respectively, is splendid in every way and well worth the extra cost.

It is difficult to fault the playing in the Viennese performances by Peter Schmidl and members of the New Vienna Octet, but both in the *Clarinet quintet* and in the *Trio* the overall effect is of blandness. Cassette and disc are closely matched in quality.

Boskovsky's account of the *Clarinet quintet* is gracious and intimate, a little lacking in individuality, but enjoyable in its unforced way. The closing pages of the work are given a real Viennese lilt. The recording is warm and sympathetic. The account of the *Piano and wind quintet* might best be described as sturdy. Not all the subtleties of Mozart's part-writing are fully revealed, and the playing is rather earth-bound. The recording is a fairly old one but sounds remarkably fresh, although the stereo has not a great deal of inner separation when the group

are all playing together. This is excellent value in the bargain price-range.

Divertimento in E flat for string trio, K.563.
(M) *** Ph. 6570/7310 572. Grumiaux Trio.

The reappearance of this famous record in Philips' Musica da Camera series is particularly welcome. Arthur Grumiaux has long been remarkable even among the most outstanding virtuosi of the day for his purity of intonation, and here he is joined by two players (Georges Janzer and Eva Szabo) with a similar refined and classical style. They may only be an ad hoc group, but their unanimity is striking, and Grumiaux's individual artistry gives the interpretation very special claims on the collector. The hushed opening of the first-movement development – a visionary passage – is played with a magically intense half-tone, and the lilt of the finale is infectious from the very first bar. The title *Divertimento* is of course a monumental misnomer, for this is one of the richest of Mozart's last-period chamber works, far too rarely heard in the concert hall. The recording, outstandingly vivid in its day, emerges with striking freshness on disc and tape alike.

Flute quartets Nos. 1 in D; 2 in G; 3 in C, K.285/1–3; 4 in A, K.298.
*** DG 2530/3300 983 [id.]. Blau, Amadeus Qt.
*** HM 1C 065 99653. Barthold Kuijken, Coll. Aur.

Mozart professed an aversion for the flute (partly because at the time its intonation was suspect), yet he wrote some delightful music for it, none more so than these delicious lightweight quartets. Both the playing and the recording balance on this DG disc bring out their delicacy of texture. The solo wind instrument is beautifully integrated with the strings, and though the flute dominates, the other instruments are in no way over-weighed. The phrasing throughout breathes naturally. The enchanting slow movement of the *D major Quartet*, where the flute cantilena is floated over a pizzicato accompaniment, is very beautifully done, and the ear is caught by the gracious shaping of the *galant* themes used as the basis for variations in the second movement of No. 3 or the no less charming opening movement of No. 4. Andreas Blau is a splendid artist and the Amadeus accompany him with subtlety and distinction. The cassette transfer is not made at the highest level but is clear and refined in detail.

The Collegium Aureum version is the only one using period instruments. Kuijken plays a beguilingly soft instrument from Dresden, made by August Grenser in 1789, and the effect has great charm even to ears not much enamoured of authentic instruments. The playing of the three string instruments is no less accomplished and is beautifully recorded. The pitch is lower by a semitone, and the flute is not able to negotiate every interval perfectly, but this disc will nonetheless give much pleasure.

(i) *Horn quintet in E flat, K.407*; (ii) *Oboe quartet in F, K.370.*
** HM 1C 065 99695. Coll. Aur., with (i) Hucke, (ii) Luxutt.
** Tel. AW 6.42173 [id.]. Esterhazy Qt, with (i) Baumann, (ii) Piguet.

Both these records use period instruments. On Harmonia Mundi, Helmut Hucke uses a copy by Tutz of Innsbruck of a Grenser, *c.* 1790, and produces a sparkling account of the *Oboe quartet*. His colleague Walter Luxutt copes as best he can with the natural horn. These are good performances and well recorded, if anything better than their rivals on Telefunken. Here Michel Piguet plays an oboe of Delusse dating from 1785, only four years later than the *Quartet* itself, and Hermann Baumann uses a valveless horn

of about 1800 from Bohemia. The latter produces some pretty uneven scales but a delightfully soft tone. However, with less than a half-an-hour's playing time, both these issues seem unduly expensive when at about the same price there is a Philips record (see above) offering the *Clarinet quintet* as well.

(i) *Horn quintet, K.407. A Musical Joke, K.522; Serenade No. 13 in G (Eine kleine Nachtmusik), K.525.*
(M) ** Ph. Fest. 6570/7310 147. Berlin PO Octet, (i) with Klier.

A modestly priced and well-recorded set of performances which appeared in various couplings in the late 1960s. The *Horn quintet* is admirably played, and *Eine kleine Nachtmusik* is also given with some spirit and genuine refinement. Good, albeit not outstanding performances, with excellent sound. But the *Musical Joke* needs a more imaginative performance than it receives here, and it rather weakens the attractions of this issue. The tape transfer is well managed, but the horn tone tends to spread a little.

Oboe quartet in F, K.370.
(B) *** CfP CFP/TC-CFP 40356. Wilson, Gabrieli Qt – SCHUBERT: *String quartet No. 14.****

Ian Wilson's fresh, unmannered performance of Mozart's *Oboe quartet* is projected by a forwardly vivid recording (the cassette matching the disc closely), and the oboe timbre is bright and crisp to match the pert style of the playing. This makes an excellent filler for the fine Schubert performance on the reverse. However, the finest available version of the *Oboe quartet* is by Ray Still with three famous string virtuosi; see p.941.

Piano quartets Nos. 1 in G min., K.478; 2 in E flat, K.493.
*** Decca SXL 6989. Previn, Musikverein Qt.

513

**(*) DG 2531/*3301* 368 [id.]. Klien, Amadeus Qt.

**(*) RCA RL/*RK* 12676 [ARL 1/*ARK 1* 2676]. Rubinstein, Guarneri Qt.

Previn's sparkling playing gives these parallel masterpieces – especially the *G minor* – a refreshing spontaneity. Though the tuning of the Musikverein Quartet is not as sweet as that of the Amadeus on DG, this Decca coupling is preferable for the extra vitality.

The DG performances, with a straighter, less individual pianist, are well played and very well recorded (with disc and tape very closely matched). But in sheer electricity the performance of No. 2 markedly outshines that of No. 1, which sounds less spontaneous.

The pity is that Rubinstein's bright and invigorating playing with members of the Guarneri Quartet has its brightness and forwardness exaggerated in the recording. This is not so much a tasteful rendering of two of Mozart's most delectable chamber works as a mercurial recreation at the hands of a pianist who is nothing if not an individualist. Details matter less than the overall sweep of spontaneous expression. The liveliness of Rubinstein even in his eighties enjoying himself with fellow-musicians is ample reason for hearing this coupling, either on disc or on the cassette, which is equally clear and vivid.

Piano trios Nos. 1 in B flat, K.254; 2 in G, K.496; 3 in B flat, K.502; 4 in E, K.542; 5 in C, K.548; 6 in G, K.564.

⊛ (M) *** Ph. 6768 032/*7650 017* (2). Beaux Arts Trio.

Although these performances were recorded in the late 1960s, they still sound amazingly vivid and wonderfully fresh. Even if there were an alternative version – and at present this is the only contender – the Beaux Arts would be difficult to beat either artistically or in terms of recording. This set sounds exceptionally

well in its tape format, which is beautifully transferred, the quality fresh and clear and perfectly balanced.

Piano and wind quintet in E flat, K.452.

*** CRD CRD 1067/*CRDC 4067*. Nash Ens. – BEETHOVEN: *Piano and wind quintet.***

Vital and fresh playing makes the Nash Ensemble's version of the Mozart *Quintet* most desirable. Mozart thought this one of his best works, yet its representation in the catalogue is relatively slender. This version, which offers some good playing from the pianist Ian Brown, does not displace the Ashkenazy account, but it is worthy to stand alongside it. It has the advantage of an excellent cassette transfer, the quality vivid and clear.

Sonata for bassoon and cello in B flat, K.292.

(M) ** DG Priv. 2535/*3335* 328. Berlin PO Octet (members) – BEETHOVEN: *Septet.***

The *Sonata for bassoon and cello* is a rarity, not otherwise obtainable on record. It was probably written at the beginning of 1775 for Baron Thaddeus von Dürnitz, who was obviously an accomplished player. Like the *Bassoon concerto*, K.191, the *Sonata* gives the instrument a greater virtuoso role and expressive power than is usual in the period. Nonetheless, this is not great music and will hardly weigh in the balance for collectors choosing between the various Beethoven *Septets* on offer.

String quartets Nos. 14–19.

*** CRD CRD 1062/4/*CRDC 4062/4*. Chilingirian Qt.

**(*) DG 2740 249 (3). Melos Qt.

The set of six quartets dedicated to Haydn contains a high proportion of Mozart's finest works in the genre, music which uncharacteristically he took (for him) a long time to complete, writing without the compulsion of a commission. The Chilingirian Quartet plays with unforced freshness and vitality, avoiding expressive mannerism but always conveying the impression of spontaneity, helped by the warm and vivid recording. International rivals in these works may at times provide more poise and polish, but none outshines the Chilingirians in direct conviction, and their matching of tone and intonation is second to none. Unlike most quartets they never sound superficial in the elegant but profound slow movements. The equivalent cassettes are each packaged separately and offer demonstration quality, every bit the equal of the discs in presence and natural clarity.

Taken by and large the Melos Quartet set offers performances which are soundly conceived and finely executed. There are disappointments (see the reviews below), but the playing is unmannered, thoughtful and usually vital, and the recording is first-class.

String quartets Nos. 14 in G, K.387; 15 in D min., K.421.
*(*) DG 2530/3300 898 [id.]. Melos Qt.

Well-shaped and finely proportioned readings, played with good ensemble and internal balance. At times one feels the Melos could play with greater spontaneity: the outer movements of the *D minor Quartet* come close to being square, and more could be made of the slow movement, which is wanting in repose and is just a little prosaic. The *G major Quartet* is finely played, but here and there one feels the need of greater freshness and imagination. The disc is cut at a fairly high level, so that dynamic peaks could be smoother. The cassette transfers well, though it is not quite as fresh as the disc.

String quartets Nos. 16 in E flat, K.428; 17 in B flat (Hunt), K.458.

(M) *** Decca Ace SDD/KSDC 559. Musikverein Qt.
**(*) Tel. AW 6.42348 [id.]. Alban Berg Qt.

The Ace of Diamonds issue is as good as any Mozart quartet recording on the market. The Musikverein Quartet used to be named after its leader, Rainer Küchl, and all four players are members of the Vienna Philharmonic. There is a relaxed, unforced quality about their playing which is impressive, though there is no want of brilliance either. Even those who possess the Italian Quartet versions, either on single records or in the boxed set still in circulation, should investigate this splendid issue. It is moderately priced and splendidly recorded; the tape transfer has admirable clarity and immediacy.

The Alban Berg Quartet give a thoroughly stylish and deeply musical account of both quartets which can also be recommended on all counts, artistic and technical. There are none of the expressive exaggerations of dynamics and phrasing that marred this group's later records of Beethoven's *Rasumovsky quartets* for EMI. Were there no alternative this would be thoroughly recommended; but the Musikverein is even finer, and it is also cheaper!

String quartet No. 17 in B flat (Hunt), K.458.
(M) *** DG Acc. 2542/3342 122. Amadeus Qt – HAYDN: *Quartet No. 77.***
(*) Ph. 9500 662 [id./7300 762]. Italian Qt – HAYDN: *Quartet No. 77.*

The Amadeus, recorded in the mid-1960s, will have the edge on the Italians for some listeners. Their performance is slightly more characterized, and though there are some touches that will not have universal appeal (in the slow movement, for example, these artists do not always allow the music to speak for itself), it is, generally speaking, a most satisfying version – and well recorded too, on disc and cassette alike.

The Italian Quartet gives a fine and

unaffected account of the *Hunt*. Some may feel that it is a shade under-characterized in places, and it is certainly overpriced, even though it is coupled with a modern recording of the *Emperor*. Most companies offering records from the mid-1960s these days make a reduction in price.

String quartets Nos. 18 in A, K.464; 19 in C (Dissonance), K.465.
(M) *** Decca Ace SDD/*KSDC* 560. Musikverein Qt.
**(*) DG 2530 891 [id.]. Melos Qt.

The playing of the Musikverein Quartet in both quartets is characterized by great brilliance and sensitivity. They bring an imaginative vitality to bear on both scores that makes one forgive the way in which they succumb to the temptations of their own virtuosity in the outer movements of the *Dissonance*. Musically, however, this is a most satisfying issue, arguably the best versions of both quartets now before the public. The sound is extremely good.

The Melos Quartet of Stuttgart also give an admirably shaped account of both works, with finely integrated tone and much beauty of phrasing. They are a little less poetic and spontaneous than is ideal; perhaps their concentration on beauty of sound accounts for this. However, given the excellent quality of the recording and the well-thought-out and finely articulated performances, there is no need for any real reservation to inhibit a welcome for this issue.

String quartets Nos. 19 in C (Dissonance), K.465; 20 in D min. (Hoffmeister), K.499.
(M) *** Decca Ace SDD 561. Gabrieli Qt.

The Gabrieli Quartet's recording of the *Dissonance* comes from the same label as the version by the Musikverein group (see above); and even has an adjacent catalogue number, though it is at least differently coupled. The Gab-

rielis are also first-class (if not quite as brilliant or as superbly integrated as the Musikverein) and give expressive and eloquent performances of both the *Dissonance* and the *Hoffmeister*. They are a little too robust perhaps in the trio section of K.465 but for the most part their playing is of a high order, as is the Decca recording. In the *Dissonance* the Musikverein are to be preferred, but in the *Hoffmeister* the Gabrieli probably lead the field.

String quartets Nos. 20 (Hoffmeister), K.499; 21 in D, K.575; 22 in B flat, K.589; 23 in F, K.590 (Prussian Nos. 1–3).
(M) *** Ph. 6770 042 (2) [id.]. Italian Qt.

String quartets Nos. 22–3.
*** DG 2531/*3301* 320 [id.]. Melos Qt.
*** Tel. AW 6.42042 [id.]. Alban Berg Qt.

Philips have reissued the Italian Quartet's versions of the last four Mozart quartets as a double-record set at medium price, giving it an advantage over the Melos and Alban Berg Quartets. The performances originally appeared in the early 1970s and were rightly hailed at the time as among the very finest. We still hold the view stated in the first edition of the *Penguin Stereo Record Guide* that in terms of musical distinction these superbly shaped and balanced performances are unlikely to be surpassed for a very long time, and they certainly hold a special place in the Mozart discography. The recordings still sound remarkably lifelike and are in no way inferior to more recent rivals.

The Melos Quartet's coupling of the *Second* and *Third Prussian quartets* is the most attractive of their Mozart recordings. These works were written for the Prussian King Friedrich Wilhelm II, who was a keen cellist, and the Melos group possesses a particularly fine cellist, with a strong personality and a keen sense of characterization. In the slow movements of both quartets these artists bring more warmth even than the Italians, and they have the benefit of a slightly richer and fresher recording. On balance, however, there is not a great deal to choose between the two. The cassette transfer of the Melos coupling is outstanding. This is very much demonstration quality, natural in timbre and cleanly focused, one of the finest string quartet tapes yet issued.

The Alban Berg Quartet are at their best in Mozart's last two quartets. Their performances have an honesty and directness that are enhanced by polish and finesse. Their ensemble cannot be faulted, and though competition is strong, their claims still rank very high. It is a happy embarrassment these days that in some couplings collectors cannot go wrong; and late Mozart quartets in general are uncommonly well served at present.

String quintets Nos. 1 in B flat, K.174; 6 in E flat, K.614.
(M) ** Argo ZK 18. Aeolian Qt (augmented).

With Kenneth Essex as extra viola here as in their other Mozart quintet recordings, the Aeolians attractively couple the first and last of the cycle. K.174 brings an amazingly mature slow movement, and it is the performance of the slow movement in K.614 too which stands out from the rest. These are thoughtful, intelligent performances, not always ideally refined but always enjoyable and very well recorded. However, other issues in this Argo series are less recommendable and readers wanting a complete set of Mozart's *Quintets* are advised to consider the admirable Philips box (6747 107), recorded by an ensemble led by Arthur Grumiaux, which in general eclipses other recent accounts.

String quintets Nos. 2 in C min., K.406; 5 in D, K.593.
(M) *(*) Argo ZK 12. Aeolian Qt (augmented).

It was a good idea to record the *D major Quintet* with its alternative finale, but neither of these performances is really distinguished. These are good, workmanlike readings and well recorded, but they fall short of being memorable.

String quintet No. 3 in C, K.515.
(M) * Argo ZK/KZKC 17. Aeolian Qt (augmented).

The *C major Quintet*, an undoubted masterpiece, is not generously represented on record. The Aeolian Quartet and Kenneth Essex give a spirited but unsubtle reading of this great work. They do not make the most of dynamic contrasts, and in terms of tonal beauty they do not command the finesse of Grumiaux's team.

String quintets Nos. 3; 4 in G min., K.516.
(M) *** Ph.6570/7310 574. Grumiaux Ens.

These performances by the Grumiaux team sweep the board. Immensely civilized and admirably conceived readings, they have the advantage of refined and truthful recording on both disc and cassette.

String quintet No. 4 in G min., K.516.
(M) * Argo ZK/KZKC 35. Aeolian Qt (augmented).

A most disappointing performance of Mozart's most famous string quintet. The playing is expressive, with some sensitive detail, but there is a lack of finesse and certainly no hint of magic.

Piano duet

Andante and variations, K.501.
*** Ph. 9500 434/7300 644 [id.]. Argerich, Bishop-Kovacevich – BARTÓK: *Sonata;* DEBUSSY: *En blanc et noir.****

The charming *Andante and variations* is here taken at a rather brisker tempo than usual, but the playing of this duo is unfailingly sensitive and vital. The companion works by Bartók and Debussy are unlikely to be surpassed either artistically or as recordings. The cassette does not match the disc in range, though the Mozart suffers less from the low-level transfer than the two couplings.

Andante and variations, K.501; Fugue, K.426; Sonatas for piano duet: in D, K.381; in C, K.521.
(M) *** Decca Ace SDD 549. Eden, Tamir.

Fantasias Nos. 1 in F min., K.594; 2 in F min., K.608; Fugue, K.401; Sonatas: in C, K.19d; in G, K.357(497a); in B flat, K.358 (186c) (all for piano duet).
(M) *** Decca Ace SDD 550. Eden, Tamir.

Larghetto and allegro in E flat for 2 pianos; Double piano sonata in D, K.448; Sonata in F for piano duet, K.497.
(M) *** Decca Ace SDD 548. Eden, Tamir.

These three records encompass Mozart's output for piano duet and two pianos. They cover a wide period, the last disc ranging from the juvenile *C major Sonata* composed in London and the four-hand versions of the clockwork organ fantasies written towards the end of his life. The most important and rewarding of these pieces is the *D major Duo sonata*, K.448, and the *F major* and *C major Sonatas for piano duet* (K.497 and 521). The glorious *G major Andante and five variations*, K.501, is another masterpiece; but some of the other pieces are more fun to play than to listen to. Eden and Tamir give elegant and sensitive performances of all these pieces, and only the most joyless will fail to respond.

At times one might want more sparkle and less polish – one of the dangers when sophisticated players turn their attention to music of modest ambitions – but for the most part they offer music-making of much distinction. Excellent recording. Readers not wanting to collect all three discs should give priority to SDD 548 which offers two of the most substantial of Mozart's essays in this medium.

Solo piano music

Adagio in B min., K.540; Allegro in G min., K.312; Minuet in D, K.355; Sonata in F, K.533/494; Variations on a Dutch song, K.24.
**(*) Mer. E 77023. Ward.

David Ward provides an unusual and attractive collection of pieces, including the *Variations on a Dutch song* written when Mozart was a boy of ten. That is one of the shorter pieces on side two. Side one is devoted to the least-heard of the late sonatas, which Ward characteristically plays with fine clarity and directness. If the readings are just a little lacking in character, it is good to hear a pianist distinguishing himself with playing that is so naturally thoughtful and purposeful. The recording is a little light in bass but not inappropriately so.

Rondo in A min., K.511.
*** RCA RL/*RK* 13342 [ARL/*ARK* 13342]. Rubinstein – BACH: *Chaconne*; FRANCK: *Prelude, chorale and fugue.****

Rubinstein plays Mozart's *Rondo*, with its chromatic inflections, as though it were Chopin. Stylistically it may be indefensible, but the magic is irresistible. A charming makeweight, recorded in 1959 but lost for twenty years among bigger issues.

Piano sonatas Nos. 1–17; Fantasia in C min., K.475.
(M) *** Decca D 226 D 6 (6). Schiff.

Andras Schiff is a first-class artist whose fingerwork and sense of colour excite admiration. He takes a rather more romantic view of Mozart than Christoph Eschenbach, who was the last to give us a comprehensive survey (on DG), and he is slightly prone to self-indulgence in the handling of some phrases. This is a fine achievement all the same, and splendidly recorded. Taking the excellent sound balance into account, this set can be recommended as probably the most satisfying way of acquiring this repertoire.

Piano sonatas Nos. 2 in F, K.280; 3 in B flat, K.281; 9 in D, K.311; 10 in C, K.330.
⊛ *** DG 2531/3301 052 [id.]. Zimerman.

Marvellous playing. Krystian Zimerman makes no pretence of playing a fortepiano, using a wide range of tonal shading and phrases delicately echoed in the baroque manner. Yet the playing is essentially robust, and the slow movements of K.311 and K.330 are performed with great eloquence, without ever taking the music outside the period of its natural sensibility. The recording is flawless, absolutely natural in balance, and the cassette also offers superbly realistic piano tone, rich, clear in detail, and perfectly focused.

Piano sonatas Nos. 4 in E flat, K.282; 8 in A min., K.310.
*** Decca SXL/KSXC 6951 [Lon. 7179]. Larrocha – BEETHOVEN: *Bagatelles.****

Alicia de Larrocha plays the early *E flat Sonata* simply, yet with an attractive balance between warmth and poise. She is at her finest in the A minor work, with

its memorable slow movement, which she plays beautifully. The Decca recording is first-class (there is little or nothing to choose between disc and cassette), and if the Beethoven coupling is suitable this can be recommended.

Piano sonatas Nos. 12 in F, K.332; 15 in C, K.545; 17 in D, K.576.
*** Decca SXL/KSXC 6865 [Lon. 7085]. Larrocha – BACH: *Chorale preludes.****

Alicia de Larrocha's clean style, strong yet never rigid, showing sensibility and control and a natural understanding, is matched by an admirably truthful recording. Her pellucid touch is particularly effective in the famous *C major Sonata,* K.545, which is a highlight of an excellent collection. The cassette transfer is immaculate, of demonstration quality.

VOCAL AND CHORAL MUSIC

(see also 'Miscellaneous Vocal Recitals' section below)

Lieder: *Abendempfindung; Als Luise die Briefe; Die Alte; An Chloë; Dans un bois solitaire; Im Frühlingsanfange; Das Kinderspiel; Die kleine Spinnerin; Das Lied der Trennung; Oiseaux, si tous les ans; Ridente la calma; Sehnsucht; Das Traumbild; Das Veilchen; Der Zauberer; Die Zufriedenheit.*
*** HMV ASD/TC-ASD 3958. Schwarzkopf, Gieseking.

Elisabeth Schwarzkopf's art brings out the variety of Mozart's often underprized Lieder, and in these 1955 recordings with Gieseking as the most imaginative of accompanists she has an artist at the piano to reinforce the point. *Die kleine*

MOZART

Spinnerin, for example, might seem just a simple strophic song, but pianist as well as singer give it an unsuspected range of expression. And when it comes to the more ambitious songs, the gravity of *Das Lied der Trennung* and the radiant beauty of *Abendempfindung* have never on record been captured with such intensity. The reissue brings a stereo version not previously published, the sound given extra spaciousness and realism. The cassette too is of outstanding quality, clear and free and most natural in tone and balance.

Adoramus te, K.Anh.109/3; Ave verum corpus, K.618; De profundis clamavi, K.93; Ergo, interest, an quis; God is our refuge, K.20; Justum deduxit Dominus, K.93d; Kyrie (for 5 sopranos), K.73k; Regina coeli, K.74d.
** Abbey LPB 773. Jill Gomez, St Bartholomew's Ch., Morris; St Bartholomew's Hospital Ch. Soc., Anderson; Sinfonia of St Bartholomew; Brockless (organ).

There are rarities here: the *Regina coeli*, K.108/74d, is one, and quite a number of the others are not available in alternative versions. Jill Gomez sings with her usual accomplishment and warmth, while the forces assembled here produce musical and pleasing results. The sound is acceptable. (The proceeds of the disc go to cancer research.)

Concert arias: *Ah se in ciel, K.538; Mia speranza adorate . . . Ah, non sai, K.416; Nehmt meinen Dank, K.383; No, che non sei capace, K.419; Popoli di Tessaglia! . . . Io non chiedo eterni Dei, K.316/300b; Vado, ma dove, K.583; Vorrei spiegarvi, K.418.*
(M) *** DG Priv. 2535/3335 465. Streich, Bav. RSO, Mackerras.

Though her voice is not really large enough for the more dramatic items, Rita

Streich gives delightful performances of this attractive collection of Mozart concert arias. The agility in this often florid music is amazing, and though the performances date from 1959 the sound remains relatively fresh. The cassette transfer is disappointing, emphasizing the age of the recording, with a tendency to peakiness in the voice and without lustre in the orchestral accompaniment.

La Betulia liberata (oratorio), *K.118.*
*** DG 2740 198 (3). Schwarz, Cotrubas, Schreier, Berry, Fuchs, Salz. Mozarteum Chamber Ch. and O., Hager.

Though this early oratorio has its inevitable *longueurs*, it contains so much delightful material and is here so beautifully performed that this set can be warmly recommended. The story – set at a very leisurely pace – tells of Judith's killing of Holophernes and the conversion of the heathen general Achior. In Germanic style the harpsichord continuo is somewhat bald, but the line-up of soloists could hardly be bettered, with Peter Schreier outstanding in the big role of Ozias, and Ileana Cotrubas enchanting in the role of Amital. Hanna Schwarz as Judith (Giuditta) is more variable, at times rather heavy for Mozart, but with excellent recording and well-paced conducting from Leopold Hager, this is an excellent example of the important Mozart series made in the Salzburg Mozarteum.

Davidde penitente (cantata), *K.469.*
** Turn. TVS 37141 [Can. 31107]. Csapo, Koban, Baldin, Württemberg Chamber Ch. and O., Kurz.

Mozart never completed his most ambitious setting of the Mass, the great work in C minor, K.427, which happily remains in the repertory as an inspiring torso. But in 1785 he decided to use eight movements from that masterpiece for a

520

dramatic oratorio, adding two extra arias. The result is *Davidde penitente*. The Mass settings are in no way improved by the new texts here, but neither do they lose in the transformation. The extra arias are for soprano and tenor, ambitious pieces if not quite on the same exalted level of inspiration as the rest. On a budget label Dieter Kurz directs a capable rather than inspired performance, with variable soloists, quite well recorded.

Masonic funeral music, K.483; Gesellenreise, K.468; Dir Seele des Weltalls, K.429; Die ihr des unermesslichen Weltalls Schöpfer ehrt, K.619; Ihr unsere neuen Leiter, K.484; Laut verkünde unsre Freude, K.623; Die Maurerfreude, K.471; Maurergesang, K.623; O heiliges Band, K.148; Zerfliesset heut' geliebte Brüder, K.483.
(M) *** Ph. 6570/*7310* 063 [id.]. Hollweg, Partridge, Dean, Amb. S., New Philh. O., De Waart.

Mozart's *Masonic funeral music* (written in 1785 to commemorate the death of two aristocratic fellow-masons), although only sixty-nine bars long, is an extraordinarily eloquent piece. It is splendidly played here, its dark colouring and sombre dignity well brought out; and it serves as introduction to an excellent compilation of Mozart's Masonic music. This ranges from the song *O heiliges Band*, a setting of a Masonic text composed when Mozart was only sixteen (and with no direct Masonic implications, for it was originally intended for soprano voice), to the cantata, K.619, written concurrently with *Die Zauberflöte* and the *Requiem* in the summer of 1791. The choral items (six are included) are all memorable, and they are impressively sung by the Ambrosian group. The solo items are good too and the recording is excellent, with no appreciable

difference between disc and cassette. Well worth exploring.

Masses Nos. 10 in C (Spetzenmesse), K.220; 13 in C (Organ solo), K.259; Ave verum corpus, K.618.
(M) ** Ph. Fest. 6570/*7310* 079 [id.]. Behan, Raninger, Resch, Buchbauer, V. Boys' Ch., V. Dom O. and Ch., Grossman.

These two early Masses plus the lovely *Ave verum corpus* appeared in the Philips Mozart Edition, but the recording dates from earlier than that. Ferdinand Grossman directs sympathetic performances which lack something in polish, and not everyone will like boy soloists in soprano and alto parts, even ones as accomplished as those from the Vienna Boys' Choir. But at medium price this makes an attractive and unusual coupling. The cassette needs a bass reduction, but then the balance is excellent, clear and full: the *Ave verum* sounds especially well.

Masses Nos. 11 in C (Credo), K.257; 16 in C (Coronation), K.317.
(M) *** Ph. Fest. 6570/*7310* 025 [6500 234/*7300* 161]. Donath, Knight, Ryland Davies, Grant, Dean, John Alldis Ch., LSO, Colin Davis.

Sir Colin Davis relishes the youthful high spirits of the *Coronation Mass*, here given a vital performance with a strong team of soloists. The *Credo Mass*, a much rarer work, is equally spirited here – a performance to get new listeners discovering this dramatic, often secular-sounding music. Good, reverberant recording and a reasonably vivid cassette equivalent; in spite of the modest transfer level, the chorus is not muffled.

Mass No. 12 in C (Spaur), K.258; Vesperae solennes de confessore, K.339.
*** Argo ZRG/*KZRC* 924. Palmer, Cable, Langridge, Roberts, St John's College Ch., Wren O., Guest.

The *Spaur Mass* is not among Mozart's most inspired, but in a vigorous performance like this, with trombones justifiably doubling some of the choral lines, it is most enjoyable. The coupling is a masterpiece, and though this does not always match the version by Sir Colin Davis, for example – Felicity Palmer is a less poised soloist than Kiri Te Kanawa – this has the advantage of authenticity in the use of boys in the chorus. The recording is warmly atmospheric and the cassette transfer first-class, bright and lively with no loss of choral focus; indeed the treble may need a little softening.

Reminder: The Davis version of the *Vespers* (on Philips 6500 271) is part of a delightful collection of Mozart's choral music also including *Ave verum corpus, Exsultate jubilate* and the *Kyrie,* K.341.

Mass No. 18 in C min. (Great), K.427.
** Ph. 9500 680/*7300 775* [id.]. Margaret Marshall, Palmer, Rolfe Johnson, Howell, Ch. and ASMF, Marriner.
*(*) Erato STU 71100. Masterson, Baumann, Klietmann, Brodard, Lisbon Gulbenkian Foundation Ch. and O., Corbóz.

Neville Marriner secures a good response from his artists, though this performance falls short of being really inspired. Marriner's is a well-thought-out and conscientious reading, and there is some fine singing. His account does not quite communicate the sense of stature this music calls for, but he is not helped by less than transparent recorded sound on disc and tape alike. A serviceable rather than distinguished issue, then, which does not challenge existing recommendations.

There is some good singing in the Lisbon performance directed by Michel Corbóz, particularly from the two sopranos, and the overall conception is sound in every way. But the gramophone is a cruel taskmaster and good though

this might seem at a public performance, it falls short of those qualities that would compel one to return to it time and again. The recording is serviceable but not distinguished. Again no challenge to either the Leppard or the Davis versions (available on HMV ASD 2959 [Sera. S 60257] and Philips 6500 235 respectively).

Requiem Mass (No. 19) in D min., K.626.
(M) **(*) HMV SXLP/*TC-SXLP* 30237. Mathis, Bumbry, Shirley, Rintzler, New Philh. Ch. and O., Frühbeck de Burgos.
**(*) HMV ASD/*TC-ASD* 3723 [Ang. SZ 37600]. Donath, Ludwig, Tear, Lloyd, Philh. Ch. and O., Giulini.
**(*) Argo ZRG/*KZRC* 876 [id.]. Cotrubas, Watts, Tear, Shirley-Quirk, Ch. and ASMF, Marriner.
(M) ** DG Priv. 2535/*3335* 257. Lipp, Rössl-Majdan, Dermota, Berry, V. Singverein, Berlin PO, Karajan.

The glory of Frühbeck's HMV reissue is the singing of the New Philharmonia Chorus, and with the choral music very much the centre of interest, that gives it an edge over Sir Colin Davis's version on Philips. This is unashamedly big-scale Mozart, and that is perhaps apt for a work that has less need for apology than was once thought. (Research suggests that Süssmayr's contribution was smaller than was once believed, and certainly the aesthetic test is clear: very little indeed falls below what one would expect of a Mozart masterpiece, and much is of supreme greatness.) Frühbeck does not have a very subtle Mozart style, and on detail some of his rivals outshine him; for instance, Davis's *Recordare* is much more relaxed and refined. But as an interpretation it stands well in the middle of the road, not too romantic, not too frigidly classic, and quite apart from the choral singing – recorded with beautiful balance and richness – the soloists are all first-rate. The cassette transfer has caused some loss of refinement in the larger choral climaxes, but otherwise it is effective in capturing the spaciousness and immediacy of the disc.

Giulini directs a large-scale performance which brings out both Mozartian lyricism and Mozartian drama, and anyone who fancies what by today's standards is an unauthentic approach may consider this version. The choir is in excellent incisive form, and the soloists are a first-rate quartet. As one would expect, what Giulini's insight conveys is the rapt quality of such passages as the end of the *Tuba mirum* and the *Benedictus*. The recording is warm rather than brilliant; the cassette is well balanced but slightly opaque.

Marriner, who can usually be relied on to produce vigorous and sympathetic performances on record, generates less electricity than usual in the *Requiem*. It is interesting to have a version which uses the Beyer Edition and a text which aims at removing the faults of Süssmayr's completion, amending points in the harmony and instrumentation; but few will register any significant differences except in such points as the extension of the *Osanna*. Solo singing is good, but the chorus could be more alert. Excellent, atmospheric recording and a first-class cassette transfer, the chorus sounding clean and incisive.

Karajan's earlier, 1962 reading, now reissued on Privilege, took a suave view of the work. The chief objection to this version is that detail tends to be sacrificed in favour of warmth and atmosphere. The solo quartet are wonderfully blended, a rare occurrence in this work above all, and though the chorus lacks firmness of line they are helped out by the spirited playing of the Berlin Philharmonic. The sound is good on disc, acceptable on cassette. But Karajan's newer full-priced version (DG 2530/*3300* 705) is well worth the extra cost; indeed it is outstandingly fine, deeply committed and with a finely balanced quartet of soloists and superbly vivid recording (the

cassette only marginally less sharply focused than the disc). This is a clear first choice until Davis's version is reissued by Philips at medium price.

Thamos, King of Egypt (incidental music), *K.345*.
(M) ** Turn. TVS 34679. Charlotte Lehmann, Scheible, Pfaff, Abel, Heilbronn Vocal Ens., Württemberg CO, Faerber.

The music for the play *Thamos, King of Egypt* is now thought to come from 1776–7 (rather than two years later on). Joerg Faerber's version is welcome: the singing is fully acceptable; the orchestral playing is thoroughly musical, and the performance as a whole has life and spontaneity. The textures are not ideally transparent on this recording (the string quality above the stave is wanting in freshness, and the sound fails to expand). Given the interest of the music and the modest price, this is worth investigating.

OPERA

Ascanio in Alba (complete).
** DG 2740 181 (3) [id.]. Sukis, Baltsa, Mathis, Schreier, Auger, Salz. Mozarteum Chamber Ch. and O., Hager.

Though issued in 1981, the set of *Ascanio in Alba*, a court entertainment rather than an opera, written for Milan when Mozart was fifteen, was among the first of Leopold Hager's series of recordings of the dramatic works. The singing cast is excellent, with Agnes Baltsa outstanding as Ascanio, but Hager's direction is generally uninspired and the playing is routine. In any case by Mozartian standards this is not a fully imaginative score. The best music is that for the two lovers, with Edith Mathis, a charming Silvia, contrasting well with Baltsa. Good recording.

La Clemenza di Tito (complete).

*** Ph. 6703 079/*7699 038* (3) [id.]. Baker, Minton, Burrows, Von Stade, Popp, Lloyd, ROHCG Ch. and O., Colin Davis.

*** Ph. 2709 092/*3371 049* (3) [id.]. Berganza, Varady, Mathis, Schreier, Schiml, Adam, Leipzig R. Ch., Dresden State O., Boehm.

It was a revelation, even to dedicated Mozartians, to find in the 1970s Covent Garden production that *La Clemenza di Tito* had so much to offer. Sir Colin Davis's superb set, among the finest of his many Mozart recordings, sums up the achievement of the stage production and adds still more, for, above all, the performance of Dame Janet Baker in the key role of Vitellia has deepened and intensified. Not only is her singing formidably brilliant, with every roulade and exposed leap flawlessly attacked; she actually makes one believe in the emotional development of an impossible character, one who develops from villainy to virtue with the scantiest preparation. Whereas earlier Dame Janet found the evil hard to convey on stage, here the venom as well as the transformation are commandingly convincing. The two other mezzo-sopranos, Minton as Sesto and Von Stade in the small role of Annio, are superb too, while Stuart Burrows has rarely if ever sung so stylishly on a recording as here; he makes the forgiving emperor a rounded and sympathetic character, not just a bore. The recitatives add to the compulsion of the drama – here they are far more than mere formal links – while Davis's swaggering manner in the pageant music heightens the genuine feeling conveyed in much of the rest, transforming what used to be dismissed as a dry *opera seria*. Excellent recording, which loses a little in brightness and immediacy in cassette form because of the relatively low level of the Philips transfer.

In his mid-eighties Karl Boehm at last managed to record *La Clemenza di Tito*.

Even more than rival versions he gave the work warmth and charm, presenting the piece more genially than we have grown used to. The atmospheric recording helps in that, and the cast is first-rate, with no weak link, matching at every point that of Sir Colin Davis on his Philips set. Yet ultimately even Julia Varady for Boehm can hardly rival Dame Janet Baker for Davis, crisper and lighter in her coloratura. Davis's incisiveness too has points of advantage; but in sum any Mozartian can safely leave the preference to his feelings about the two conductors, the one more genial and glowing, the other more urgently dramatic. Tape collectors will find that the DG cassettes have more range and presence than the Philips set (although there is a hint of edginess on the ladies' voices).

Così fan tutte (complete).

**(*) Erato STU 71110 (3). Te Kanawa, Stratas, Von Stade, Rendall, Huttenlocher, Bastin, Strasbourg PO, Lombard.

*(**) Ar. Eur. 80408XGR (3)/*500 213*. Casapietra, Geszty, Burmeister, Schreier, Leib, Adam, German State Op. Ch., Berlin State O., Suitner.

Alain Lombard's sextet of young soloists together make up a team that rivals almost any. Outstanding is Kiri Te Kanawa, rich and creamy of tone, commanding in *Come scoglio* and tenderly affecting in *Per pietà*. Frederica von Stade's Dorabella is almost as distinguished, with fine detail and imaginative phrasing. David Rendall is a fresh-toned tenor, and the others too give firm, clean performances. Lombard is not the most perceptive of Mozartians, and some of the tempi are on the slow side; but for any who follow the singers in question this set is very desirable indeed, and it is well recorded.

The specially attractive quality about the Eurodisc version is its lightness of touch. With a chamber-sized orchestra and a very good balance, the intimacy of this most delightful opera comes across to counterpoint its warmth and charm. The *recitativo* exchanges are nicely paced, and (even without a libretto) the listener is taken into a real world of human frailty, gently and wittily observed, with its changes of mood from ardour and despair to ironic acceptance and ultimate happiness. The duets, trios and ensembles which arrive in delicious profusion give much pleasure, even though all the singing is not ideally polished. The duet which serves to introduce Fiordiligi (Celestina Casapietra) and Dorabella (Annelies Burmeister), *Ah guarda, sorella*, sounds nervous and insecure and should have been remade; but the performance soon settles down. There is a superb contribution from Peter Schreier as Ferrando, and he is stylishly partnered by Günther Leib's Guglielmo. Sylvia Geszty's portrayal of Despina is one of the set's highlights; her arias are captivating in their lightness and character. Casapietra's *Come scoglio* is bold and dramatic, even if it lacks the bite of Schwarzkopf's famous account on the HMV Boehm set. Taken as a whole this recording will give much pleasure, not least because of the recorded sound and its natural acoustic, with an agreeable resonance and bloom. But it cannot possibly be recommended as a first choice because of the incomprehensible omission of Fiordiligi's great Act 2 aria, *Per pietà*. The cassettes match the discs closely. Unaccountably the level rises on side three, bringing a slight feeling of strain in *Come scoglio*; otherwise the quality is remarkably fresh and clean.

Still recommended: The classic HMV Boehm recording with Schwarzkopf, Ludwig and Walter Berry heading an outstanding cast remains a bargain without parallel in its HMV mid-priced reissue (SLS/*TC-SLS* 5028 [Ang. S 3631).

Così fan tutte: highlights.
(M) *** HMV SXLP/*TC-SXLP* 30457 [Ang. S 36167]. Schwarzkopf, Ludwig, Steffek, Kraus, Taddei, Berry, Philh. O., Boehm.
(M) *** Ph. Fest. 6570/*7310* 099. Caballé, Cotrubas, Baker, Gedda, Ganzarolli, Van Allan, ROHCG Ch. and O., Colin Davis.

It is impossible to assemble on a single disc or cassette all the many delectable highlights of the Boehm recording of *Così*, and it seems almost perverse to recommend the HMV selection (even though it contains much to give great pleasure) when the complete set is so reasonably priced. However, the sound certainly maintains the quality of the original, and the cassette transfer is crisp and clean.

For those who already possess the Boehm set, the collection of excerpts from the almost equally captivating Davis version should prove very attractive. The names of the three women principals are guarantee enough of the quality. The challenge between Caballé and Baker is always a delight. The choice of items is sensible and generous, and the recording is, as on the original set, refined. The cassette transfer is also especially lively, giving excellent presence to the solo voices.

Don Giovanni (complete).
**(*) DG 2740 194/*3371 042* [2709 085/ *3371 042*]. Milnes, Tomowa-Sintow, Zylis-Gara, Mathis, Schreier, Berry, V. State Op. Ch., VPO, Boehm.
**(*) CBS 79321/40- [Col. M3 35192]. Raimondi, Moser, Te Kanawa, Berganza, Riegel, Van Dam, Paris Op. Ch. and O., Maazel.
** Decca D 162 D4/*K 162 K 42* [Lon. 1444/5-]. Weikl, Sass, Price, Popp, Bacquier, Burrows, Moll, LPO, Solti.

Recorded in 1977 at a sequence of live performances in the Kleines Festspielhaus at Salzburg, Karl Boehm's second recording of this opera has an engaging vigour. The tempi are sometimes on the slow side, but the concentration is unfailing, and the whole reading centres round an assumption of the role of the Don which is richly heroic and far more sympathetic in characterization than is common. Sherrill Milnes sings with a richness and commitment which match his swaggering stage presence. Anna Tomowa-Sintow as Donna Anna is generally creamy-toned, only occasionally betraying a flutter, while Teresa Zylis-Gara as Elvira controls her warm voice with delicacy. These are stylish performances without being deeply memorable. Edith Mathis sings with her usual intelligence, but the tone is not always perfectly focused. Firm reliable performances from the men. Unlike Boehm's Salzburg Così fan tutte, where the ensembles were distractingly ragged, this live Giovanni presents a strong and consistently enjoyable experience distinct from that on any other set. The recording – favouring the voices but amazingly good under the conditions – is especially vivid in the culminating scene. This set has one savouring the unique flavour of Mozart opera in Salzburg with remarkable realism and with few distractions. The cassette transfer, made at a fairly high level, has plenty of immediacy, but the upper range is not too cleanly focused.

Whatever the inhibitions and influences of preparing his CBS recording as a soundtrack for the Losey film of Don Giovanni, Lorin Maazel directs a strong and urgent performance, generally very well sung. An obvious strength is the line-up of three unusually firm-toned basses: José van Dam a saturnine Leporello, not comic but with much finely detailed expression; Malcolm King a darkly intense Masetto, and Ruggero Raimondi a heroic Giovanni, not always attacking notes cleanly but on balance one of the very finest on record in this role. Among the women Kiri Te Kanawa is outstanding, a radiant Elvira; Teresa Berganza as

a mezzo Zerlina generally copes well with the high tessitura; and though Edda Moser starts with some fearsome squawks at her first entry, the dramatic scale is certainly impressive and she rises to the challenge of the big arias. Unfortunately the recording, made in a Paris church, has the voices close against background reverberation. Considering this, the cassettes are well enough focused, although on tape the orchestral sound is thin in the overture.

Solti directs a crisp, incisive performance, with generally fast tempi and very well-directed recitatives. If it shows no special signs of affection, it contains one glorious performance in Margaret Price's Anna, pure in tone and line but powerfully dramatic too, always beautiful. Next to her Sylvia Sass as a somewhat gusty Elvira sounds rather miscast, characterful as her singing is. The two baritones, Bernd Weikl and Gabriel Bacquier, are clearly contrasted as Giovanni and Leporello respectively, though the microphone is not kind to either. The recording is brilliant in its realistic clarity on disc and tape alike (the pair of cassettes offer the ideal presentation, one act complete on each side).

Still recommended: First choice remains the mid-priced HMV set. Not only is the singing cast (including Waechter, Schwarzkopf, Sutherland and Taddei) more consistent than in any other version; the direction of Giulini and the playing of the vintage Philharmonia Orchestra carry all before them (SLS/TC-SLS 5083 [Ang. S 3605]).

Don Giovanni: highlights.
*** CBS 73888/40- [Col. M/MT 35859] (from above set cond. Maazel).
(M) *** HMV SXLP/TC-SXLP 30300 [Ang. S 35642]. Schwarzkopf, Sciutti, Sutherland, Taddei, Waechter, Alva, Philh. O., Giulini.
(M) *** Ph. Fest. 6570/7310 097. Wixell, Arroyo, Te Kanawa, Freni, Ganzarolli, Burrows, Van Allan, ROHCG Ch. and O., Colin Davis.

**(*) DG 2537/*3306* 050 (from above set cond. Boehm).

The CBS highlights disc from the Maazel version, containing an hour of music, presents a far more coherent idea of the opera's shape than any other, completing each side with a substantial slice of each finale. Choice of individual items is very good, though many will regret that Kiri Te Kanawa has – apart from her contribution to the finales – only one of her arias, *Mi tradi*. As in the complete set the recording is flawed, because of an over-reverberant acoustic, but again the cassette is well balanced (there is a slight lack of upper range, but it is not too serious); and undoubtedly this issue matches value with genuine enjoyment.

On performance grounds alone, although it is much less generous in content, first choice would be the mid-price HMV issue, which makes an excellent sampler of the outstanding set under Giulini. Not surprisingly it concentrates on Sutherland as Anna and Schwarzkopf as Elvira, and the Don and Leporello get rather short measure. But Sciutti's charming Zerlina is also given fair due, and with the recording sounding well, it can be recommended to those who already own a different complete set. The sound is excellent on disc and cassette alike.

The mid-price highlights from Sir Colin Davis's set are also most attractive, a generous selection, well chosen, well performed and well recorded. Wixell's Don is intelligent and stylish if not always seductive in tone, and there is no serious weakness in the cast, though Arroyo's weight does not always go with Mozartian delicacy. Davis's direction is fresh and invigorating.

Edited from live performances, Karl Boehm's Salzburg recording of 1977 has qualities of vigour and imagination rarely found in studio accounts, but there are inevitable flaws too, and many will prefer to have a selection only. This highlights disc admirably fills the bill; the voices are recorded relatively close, but, considering the problems of the engineers, the sound is amazingly vivid on disc (somewhat less so on cassette).

Arrangements for wind: *Don Giovanni: Overture* and excerpts (arr. Triebensee).
**(*) Chan. ABR/*ABT* 1015. Athena Ens.

Arrangments for wind: excerpts from: *Don Giovanni* (arr. Triebensee); *Die Entführung aus dem Serail* (arr. Wendt).
(M) *** Ph. 6833 251. Neth. Wind. Ens.

Here are arrangements for wind octet of music from *Don Giovanni* and *Die Entführung aus dem Serail*. The first was made by Johann Georg Triebensee: fourteen numbers from his potpourri are included on the Netherlanders' record; the second, which runs to eight numbers, mostly from the second act, was made by Johann Wendt. There are some delicious noises, particularly in the latter, where Wendt uses cors anglais instead of the clarinets of Triebensee's ensemble. The playing of the Netherlands group is flawless and the Philips recording beautifully smooth. The Athena Ensemble also give a thoroughly delightful account of the *Don Giovanni* arrangements, with plenty of spirit and no want of sensitivity. They are crisply and brightly recorded, just a shade too close for some tastes, with the result that the odd click of a key mechanism can be heard. They have less finesse perhaps than the Netherlands Ensemble, whose recording is superbly balanced.

Die Entführung aus dem Serail (*Il Seraglio;* complete)
(M) **(*) HMV SLS/*TC-SLS* 5153 (2). Lois Marshall, Hollweg, Simoneau, Unger, Frick, Beecham Ch. Soc., RPO, Beecham.

** Ph. 6769 026/*7699 111* [id.]. Eda-

Pierre, Burrowes, Burrows, Tear, Lloyd, Jurgens, John Alldis Ch., ASMF, Colin Davis.

Despite some textual oddities and flawed casting in the principal soprano role – Lois Marshall is neither commanding nor sweet-toned – the magic of Beecham makes his set a classic. The famous rehearsal record for the Janissaries' chorus and for Osmin's *Ach, wie will ich triomphieren*, superbly sung by Gottlob Frick, has long given evidence of the conductor's fervour in his project, and that is consistently confirmed in the complete set, a total and captivating entertainment, in spite of the strange order of items that Beecham devised. Both tenors are outstanding, and so is Ilse Hollweg. Even Marshall's is a voice one can get used to, especially as the direction is so persuasive. The sound is surprisingly good for its period, and the cassette transfer too is most successful (after a degree of fierceness in the overture).

Sir Colin Davis, using a smaller orchestra, the St Martin's Academy, than he usually has in his Mozart opera recordings, produces a fresh and direct account, well but not outstandingly sung. There are no performances here which have one remembering individuality of phrase, and even so characterful a singer as Robert Tear does not sound quite mellifluous enough in the role of Pedrillo, while Robert Lloyd as Osmin is outshone by a number of his rivals, especially the incomparable Gottlob Frick in the Beecham set. Crisp as the ensembles are, Davis's reading rather lacks the lightness and sparkle, the feeling of comedy before our eyes, which made the Boehm version on DG (2740 102) such a delight from beginning to end. The Philips set justifies its three discs by including five alternative arias and duets. The recording is clear and refined on disc, but the low-level tape transfer robs the orchestra of transient crispness (as can be heard immediately in the Turkish music of the overture). The solo voices are naturally caught.

La finta giardiniera (complete).
*** DG 2740 234 (4). Conwell, Sukis, Cesare, Moser, Fassbaender, Ihloff, McDaniel, Salz. Mozarteum O., Hager.

By the time Leopold Hager recorded *La finta giardiniera* in his Mozart series with Salzburg Mozarteum forces, the text of the original recitatives in Italian had been rediscovered, so avoiding the clumsy transformation into a German Singspiel which had to be adopted for the first complete recording a few years earlier. This is a strong vocal team, with three impressive newcomers taking the women's roles – Jutta Renate Ihloff, Julia Conwell (in the central role of Sandrina, the marquise who disguises herself as a garden-girl) and Lilian Sukis (the arrogant niece). Brigitte Fassbaender sings the castrato role of Ramiro, and the others are comparably stylish. It is a charming – if lengthy – comedy, which here, with crisply performed recitatives, is presented with vigour, charm and persuasiveness. The recording, made with the help of Austrian Radio, is excellent.

Idomeneo (complete).
*** DG 2740 195 (4)/*3371 043* (3) [id.]. Ochman, Mathis, Schreier, Varady, Winkler, Leipzig R. Ch., Dresden State O., Boehm.
**(*) Tel. GX6/*MU4* 35547 (3) [id.]. Hollweg, Schmidt, Yakar, Palmer, Zürich Op. O., Harnoncourt.

Textually Karl Boehm's version of *Idomeneo* gives grounds for regrets. The score is snipped about in the interests of a staged production, and, like previous recordings, it opts for a tenor in the role of Idamante. But once that is said, this is an enormously successful and richly enjoyable set, completing Boehm's incomparable series of Mozart's operatic masterpieces with a version of this *opera seria* which as a dramatic experience outshines all previous ones. Boehm's conducting is a delight, often spacious but never heavy in the wrong way, with lightened textures and sprung rhythms which have one relishing Mozartian felicities as never before. Even where the tempi are unconventional, as in the hectic speed for the final chorus, Boehm conveys fresh delight, and his singing cast is generally the best ever recorded. As Idomeneo, Wieslaw Ochman, with tenor tone often too tight, is a relatively dull dog, but the other principals are generally excellent. Peter Schreier as Idamante too might have sounded more consistently sweet, but the imagination is irresistible. Edith Mathis is at her most beguiling as Ilia, but it is Julia Varady as Elettra who gives the most compelling performance of all, sharply incisive in her dramatic outbursts but at the same time precise and pure-toned, a Mozartian stylist through and through. Hermann Winkler as Arbace is squarely Germanic, and it is a pity that the secco recitatives are heavily done; but whatever incidental reservations have to be made this is a superbly compelling set which leaves one in no doubt of the work's status as a masterpiece. The recording is first-class on disc and cassette alike.

Using a text very close to that of the Munich première of Mozart's great *opera seria*, and with the role of Idamante given to a soprano instead of being transposed down to tenor register, Harnoncourt presents a distinctive and refreshing view, one which in principle is preferable to general modern practice. The vocal cast is good, with Hollweg a clear-toned, strong Idomeneo, and no weak link. Felicity Palmer finds the necessary contrasts of expression as Elettra. Exaggerated by aggressive digital recording (though the chrome cassettes, without loss of range and presence, are smoother than the discs), the voices are sometimes given an unpleasant edge, and the sharp articulation of the recitatives is initially

disconcerting. It is surprising that in an account which aims at authenticity appoggiature are so rarely used. This is hardly a performance to warm to, but it is refreshing and alive.

Idomeneo: highlights.
*** DG 2537/*3306* 051 (from above set cond. Boehm).

Karl Boehm more than any other Mozart conductor showed consistently that, whatever the dramatic stiffness of this *opera seria*, the whole work bubbles with Mozartian delight. His text for the complete recording can be criticized, but no such doubts apply to this intelligently chosen selection of highlights. Outstanding is Julia Varady as Elettra; her fine attack goes with an ability to soften and sweeten the voice for lyrical passages, and she is matched by the charming Ilia of Edith Mathis. The recording is warm rather than brilliant, with little to choose in quality between disc and tape formats.

Lucio Silla (complete).
*** DG 2740 183 (4) [id.]. Schreier, Auger, Varady, Mathis, Donath, Krenn, Salz. Mozarteum and R. Ch. and O., Hager.

The sixteen-year-old Mozart wrote his fifth opera, on the subject of the Roman dictator Sulla (Silla), in double quick time; and although the formal story has its *longueurs* (the total timing is 3¼ hours) the speed of composition is electrically communicated, with most of the arias urgently fast and strong symphonic ideas developed at surprising length. There are many pre-echoes of later Mozart operas, not just of the great *opera seria, Idomeneo,* but of *Entführung* and even *Don Giovanni.* Though the formal limitations inhibit ensembles, there is a superb one at the end of Act 1, anticipating the Da Ponte masterpieces. A rousing chorus is interrupted by an agonized G minor lament for the heroine and leads finally to an ecstatic reunion duet. The castrato roles are here splendidly taken by Julia Varady and Edith Mathis, and the whole team could hardly be bettered. The direction of Hager is fresh and lively and the only snag is the length of the secco recitatives. The recording quality is excellent.

Mitridate, re di Ponto (complete).
**(*) DG 2740 180 (3) [2711 021]. Auger, Hollweg, Gruberova, Baltsa, Cotrubas, Salz. Mozarteum Cam. Ac., Hager.

Mozart at fourteen attempted his first full-scale *opera seria*, and showed that he could fully compass the most ambitious of forms. Not all of the twenty-two arias are of the finest quality. Some are too long for their material, and the Metastasio libretto is hardly involving dramatically. But a fresh and generally lively performance (the rather heavy recitatives excepted) brings splendid illumination to a long-hidden area of the boy Mozart's achievement. Two of the most striking arias (including an urgent G minor piece for the heroine, Aspasia, with Arleen Auger the ravishing soprano) exploit minor keys most effectively. Ileana Cotrubas is outstanding too as Ismene, and the soloists of the Salzburg orchestra cope well with the often important obbligato parts. This makes a fine addition to an important series, well recorded if lacking a little in atmosphere.

Le Nozze di Figaro (complete).
(M) *** HMV SLS/*TC-SLS* 5152 (3) [Ang. S 3608]. Schwarzkopf, Moffo, Cossotto, Taddei, Waechter, Philh. Ch. and O., Giulini.
** Decca D 132 D 4/*K 132 K 42* [Lon. 1443]. Cotrubas, Tomowa-Sintow, Von Stade, Van Dam, Krause, V. State Op. Ch., VPO, Karajan.

Giulini's set with its star-studded cast, unavailable for some years, is now reissued at medium price in an excellent transfer on to six sides instead of eight. If Giulini misses some of the fun of the comedy, his is a beautifully paced, consistently stylish reading which provides an admirable frame for the extraordinary team of soloists. Taddei with his dark bass may be an odd choice as Figaro, but he amply justifies it, and the trio of women singers has rarely if ever been matched, with Schwarzkopf the most patrician of Countesses and Moffo at her freshest and sweetest. The cassette transfer is clear and clean but just a little lacking in warmth. On disc this will be first choice for many, but Erich Kleiber's superb Decca set with Gueden, Danco, Della Casa, Siepi, and Poell still makes an outstanding recommendation on cassette (✿ *K 79 K 32*), the warm, honeyed quality of the sound matching the lyrically vivacious and consistently stylish singing. With each act complete on a single cassette side the compelling onward flow of Kleiber's shaping of each act becomes even more apparent than on the equivalent discs, with their inevitable mid-act side breaks.

With Karajan the speed and smoothness of the overture establish the character of the whole performance. Too much is passed over with a deftness which quickly makes the result bland, despite superb singing and playing. Only Frederica von Stade as Cherubino establishes the sort of individuality of expression that is the very stuff of operatic drama; she alone emerges as a rounded character. With a bloom on the sound (equally striking on both disc and cassette) the performance is a joy to the ear but is likely to leave any Mozartian unsatisfied.

Le Nozze di Figaro: highlights.
(M) *** Decca SPA/*KCSP* 514. Della Casa, Peters, Elias, London, Tozzi, V. State Op. Ch., VPO, Leinsdorf.
(M) *** Ph. Fest. 6570/*7310* 164 [6500 434]. Freni, Norman, Minton, Ganzarolli, Tear, Wixell, BBC SO and Ch., Colin Davis.

(M) **(*)HMV SXLP/*TC-SXLP* 30303
[Ang. S 35640] (from above set cond.
Giulini).
**(*) Decca SXL/*KSXC* 6987 (from
above set cond. Karajan).

The excellent and thoroughly enjoyable Decca sampler reminds us of the
many qualities of Leinsdorf's *Figaro* recording. The selection is generous (52
minutes); it is subtitled 'Scenes and arias',
and thus makes no attempt to provide a
potted opera, which is impossible with a
work so teeming with highlights. It
rightly concentrates on the contributions
of the ladies, who stand out in a generally
good cast, Roberta Peters a sparkling
Susanna, and Lisa della Casa characteristically fine as the Countess. Their
famous *Letter duet* (*Cosa mi narri?*)
shows how delightfully the voices match,
and the beauty of Della Casa's *Porgi
amor* and *Dove sono* are complemented
by Susanna's charming *Deh vieni*, while
Rosalind Elias as Cherubino provides a
no less memorable *Voi che sapete*. But
there are fourteen numbers here and they
give an excellent sampler of the fresh,
alert qualities of the performance as a
whole. The recording is vivid and lively
on disc and tape alike. It dates from 1960
and only shows its age slightly in the
timbre of the upper strings.

The selection from Sir Colin Davis's
outstanding complete set is well balanced
and attractive – though what disc could
possibly contain every favourite item
from such an opera? The sound is good.

In the selection from the Giulini recording, which is not particularly
generous, arias have been preferred to
ensembles. That brings many splendid
performances, including Figaro's three
arias (intensely sung by Taddei) and the
Countess's two (given with rare poise by
Schwarzkopf), but it seems a pity that the
overture was included instead of one or
other of the ensembles. The recording is
clear and bright, although in the cassette
transfer there is a noticeable lack of
warmth in the orchestral balance.

Though overall Karajan's reading,
with its wilful speeds, is too slick for so
fizzing a comedy as *Figaro*, such polish
and refinement deserve to be sampled –
notably Frederica von Stade's Cherubino. This selection, beautifully recorded,
does the job admirably.

Il Re pastore (complete).
*** DG 2740 182 (3). Schreier, Mathis,
Auger, Ghazarian, Krenn, Salz.
Mozarteum O., Hager.

Hager directs a bright and well-sprung
reading of one of the most charming of
Mozart's early dramatic works. It may
not even have been intended for full stage
presentation when he originally wrote it,
but on record with an excellent cast –
Arleen Auger outstanding in the well-
known soprano aria *L'amerò*, Peter
Schreier unfailingly stylish in the role of
Alexander the Great – it makes a delightful entertainment. The recitatives might
have been brisker (an earlier version
squeezed the whole piece on to two instead of three discs), but with excellent
recording, this is fully worthy of a first-
rate series.

Il Sogno di Scipione (complete).
*** DG 2740 218 (3). Popp, Gruberova,
Schreier, Ahnsjö, Moser, Salz. Mozar-
teum Chamber Ch. and O., Hager.

Mozart described this early piece as a
serenata or *azione teatrale* rather than an
opera; it was written for the enthrone-
ment of Colloredo, the Archbishop with
whom Mozart had his celebrated dispute.
It presents an allegorical plot with Scipio
set to choose between Fortune and
Constancy, and in effect it consists of a
sequence of eleven extended arias using
three tenors and two sopranos. As a
modern entertainment it outstays its welcome, but a recording as stylish and well-
sung as this certainly has its place. Given
the choice of present-day singers, this
cast could hardly be finer, with Edita

Gruberova, Lucia Popp and Edith Mathis superbly contrasted in the women's roles (the last taking part in the epilogue merely), and Peter Schreier is joined by two of his most accomplished younger colleagues. Hager sometimes does not press the music on as he might, but with fine recording this set is not likely to be surpassed for many years.

Die Zauberflöte (complete).
*** HMV Dig. SLS/*TCC-SLS* 5223 (3). Popp, Gruberova, Lindner, Jerusalem, Brendel, Bracht, Zednik, Bav. R. Ch. and SO, Haitink.
*** DG Dig. 2741/*3382* 001 (3) [id.]. Mathis, Ott, Perry, Araiza, Hornik, Van Dam, German Op. Ch., Berlin PO, Karajan.
**(*) Ar. Eur. 80584/*500 221* (3). Donath, Geszty, Schreier, Adam, Hoff, Leib, Leipzig R. Ch., Dresden State O., Suitner.
** RCA RL 03728 (4) [CTC4 4124]. Donat, Cotrubas, Kales, Tappy, Talvela, Boesch, V. State Op. Ch., VPO, Levine.

Haitink in his first ever opera recording directs a rich and spacious account of *Zauberflöte*, superbly recorded in spectacularly wide-ranging digital sound. There is a sterling honesty in Haitink's approach to every number. With speeds generally a shade slower than usual, the point of the playing and the consistent quality of the singing present this as a Mozart masterpiece that is weighty as well as sparkling. The dialogue – not too much of it, nicely produced and with sound effects adding to the vividness – frames a presentation that has been carefully thought through. Popp makes the most tenderly affecting of Paminas (as she did in the Salzburg production) and Gruberova has never sounded more spontaneous in her brilliance than here as Queen of the Night: she is both agile and powerful. Jerusalem makes an outstanding Tamino, both heroic and

sweetly Mozartian; and though neither Wolfgang Brendel as Papageno nor Bracht as Sarastro is as characterful as their finest rivals, their personalities project strongly and the youthful freshness of their singing is most attractive. The Bavarian chorus too is splendid, and the recording's perspectives featuring the chorus are extraordinarily effective, particularly in the superb Act 1 finale. The chrome cassettes are no less outstanding technically than the discs, offering sound of remarkable range, body and presence. Some readers will certainly prefer Karajan's more urgent, more volatile Berlin version, but the *gravitas* of Haitink's approach does not miss the work's elements of drama and charm, though nothing is trivialized.

Zauberflöte has also inspired Karajan to one of his freshest, most rhythmic Mozart performances, spontaneous-sounding to the point where vigour is preferred to immaculate precision in ensembles. The digital recording is not always perfectly balanced, but the sound is outstandingly fresh and clear, on disc and chrome cassettes alike. There are numbers where the tempi are dangerously slow (Tamino's *Dies Bildnis*, both of Sarastro's arias and Pamina's *Ach, ich fühl's*), but Karajan's concentration helps him to avoid mannerism completely. The choice of soloists may seem idiosyncratic, and in principle one would want a darker-toned Sarastro than José van Dam, but the clarity of focus and the fine control, not to mention the slow tempi, give the necessary weight to his arias. Francisco Araiza and Gottfried Hornik make impressive contributions, both concealing any inexperience. Karin Ott has a relatively weighty voice for the Queen of the Night, but in his tempi Karajan is most considerate to her; and the Pamina of Edith Mathis has many beautiful moments, her word-pointing always intelligent.

The Eurodisc is well cast, directed with breadth and spirit, and vividly recorded. Indeed, considering the recording was made over a decade ago it sounds remarkably well, although with a forward balance there is not the subtlety of perspective one finds in the HMV or DG digital sets. There are no real flaws here. The finest performance comes from Peter Schreier, an outstanding Tamino, ardent and stylish; Sylvia Geszty's Queen of the Night is fierce to the point of shrillness, but it is a forceful projection and balances with Donath's somewhat ingenuous portrayal of Pamina, prettily sung but no match for Lucia Popp on HMV. Theo Adam is a commanding Sarastro, though not as impressive vocally as José van Dam on the Karajan recording. Renata Hoff and Günther Leib make an attractive team as Papagena and Papageno, but while the orchestral playing is first-rate the contribution of the Leipzig Radio Choir is less impressive. There is a minimum of dialogue. The cassette transfer is lively and well projected and this makes an enjoyable tape set for use in the car; but it can hardly be regarded as a first choice.

RCA's project to record the memorable Salzburg Festival production of this opera was an admirable one, but only a German-speaker will want as much dialogue as is given here – spreading the opera on to eight instead of the usual six sides. Christian Boesch – an enchanting Papageno in the Felsenreitschule – is more an actor than a singer, and two of the singers who latterly made the production a delight – Lucia Popp as Pamina and Edita Gruberova as Queen of the Night – are on the Haitink HMV version, not this. Levine is not at his most sparkling, and neither is the recording.

Die Zauberflöte: highlights.
*** DG 2532/*3302* 004 [id.] (from above set cond. Karajan).

This selection from the Karajan set concentrates on the major arias, and very impressive it is. The buoyancy as well as the spaciousness of Karajan's reading come over well, helped by the bright

digital recording. The cassette transfer is not made at the highest level but retains the immediacy and range of the complete set.

MISCELLANEOUS VOCAL RECITALS

Arias: *La Betulia liberata: Quel nocchier che in gran procella. Exsultate, jubilate, K. 165. Grabmusik, K. 42: Betracht dies Herz. Die Schuldigkeit des ersten Gebots: Ein ergrimmter Löwe brüllet; Hat der Schöpfer dieses Leben. Vesperae solennes de confessore: Laudate Dominum. Vesperae solennes de dominica: Laudate Dominum.*
*** DG 2530/*3300* 978 [id.]. Mathis, Dresden Ch. and State O., Klee.

Edith Mathis gives sweet, sympathetic performances, beautifully sprung, of an attractive collection of early Mozart pieces from a nice range of sources. The most substantial item is the well-known cantata *Exsultate, jubilate*, with its final exultant *Alleluia*. The recording and accompaniments are immaculate to match, although on the (otherwise vivid) cassette, the vocal line is not always absolutely smooth, with hints of peakiness at fortissimo.

Arias: *Ch'io mi scordi di te, K. 505. Exsultate, jubilate, K. 165: Alleluia. Vorrei splegarvi, K. 418. Le Nozze di Figaro: Porgi amor; Voi che sapete; Dove sono; Deh vieni, non tardar. Il Re pastore: L'amerò, sarò costante. Die Zauberflöte: Ach, ich fühl's.*
**(*) Decca SXL/*KSXC* 6933 [Lon. 26613]. Sutherland, Nat. PO, Bonynge.

It is a pity that this Mozart recital was not recorded earlier, for by 1980 when it was issued Sutherland's voice, as recorded, had acquired a beat that in this precise, classical writing was obtrusive; and her habit of attacking first notes of phrases from below was damaging too. The coloratura remains a delight, with *Alleluia* one of the highspots of the recital. *Ach, ich fühl's* brings the purest singing here, a fair reminder of one of the first roles which at Covent Garden in the fifties first alerted perceptive opera-lovers to the arrival of a major star. The recording is of good Kingsway Hall vintage.

Arias: *Così dunque tradisci . . . Aspri rimorsi atroci, K. 432. Un bacio di mano, K. 541. Mentre ti lascio, K. 513. Ein deutsches Kriegslied, K. 539: Ich möchte wohl der Kaiser sein. La finta giardiniera: Nach der welschen Art. Le Nozze di Figaro: Hai già vinta la causa; Vedrò mentr'io sospiro. Warnung, K. 433; Männer suchen stehts zu naschen.*
(M) **(*) Decca Jub. JB/*KJBC* 100. Fischer-Dieskau, V. Haydn O., Peters – HAYDN: *Arias.****

The Mozart rarities on this disc are more numerous and more interesting than the Haydn items, and it is particularly fascinating to hear the Count's aria from *Figaro* in a version with a high vocal line which the composer arranged for performances in 1789. There is also a beautiful aria from two years earlier, *Mentre ti lascio*, which reveals Mozart's inspiration at its keenest. The other items too bring their delights. Fischer-Dieskau sings most intelligently, if with some pointing of word and phrase that is not quite in character with the music. The sound is first-class, the cassette matching the disc closely.

COLLECTION

(i) *Violin concerto No. 3 in G, K. 216. Serenades Nos. 6 in D (Serenata not-*

turna), K. 239; 13 in G (Eine kleine Nachtmusik), K. 525. (i; ii) *Sinfonia concertante for violin and viola, K. 364. Symphonies Nos. 25 in G min.; 29 in A. Exsultate, jubilate. Litaniae lauretanae: Sancta Maria. Coronation Mass: Agnus Dei.*
(M) **(*) Argo D 243 D 3/*K 243 K 33* (3). Soloists, Ch. and ASMF, Marriner, with (i) Loveday, (ii) Shingles.

This anthology, centred on recordings by the St Martin-in-the-Fields Academy, is attractive if rather arbitrary. Alan Loveday's intimate reading of the *Violin concerto* is balanced with an account of the *Sinfonia concertante* that goes for elegance rather than any stronger Mozartian qualities, the slow movement wistfully refined. But *Eine kleine Nachtmusik* is outstandingly successful, fresh and unaffected, and the two symphonies have splendid life and polish. The pointing of the phrases of the 'little *G minor*' is done with a superb sense of style, and the scale of No. 29 is broad and forward-looking, with an exuberant finale. The recording tends to be reverberant, though not unattractively so. The vocal items are welcome and enjoyable, acting merely as a sampler of this side of Mozart's output. The cassettes are for the most part very successful, although the resonance in the last movement of No. 29 causes a momentary problem at the climax.

Muffat, Georg (1653–1704)

Exquisitioris harmoniae: Bona nova (Concerto in D min.). Florilegium II: Indissolubilis amicitia (Suite in E).
(M) **(*) DG Arc. Priv. 2547/*3347* 004. VCM, Harnoncourt – BIBER: *Battalia* etc.**(*)

Georg Muffat was a pupil of Lully, and *Indissoluble Friendship* pays homage to his illustrious master. The music itself, however, is rather bland, and it is not helped by the introvert and comparatively unprojected style of the playing here, on period instruments. The *Good News concerto* is another matter. It was written after a visit to Rome, where Muffat was greatly impressed by the works of Corelli. The scoring mixes strings with oboes, and a bassoon is included in the continuo. The result is delightful, with lively invention throughout. The recording is good, especially in the *Bona nova*, which is given vivid projection on disc and cassette alike.

Mundy, William
(*c.* 1529–*c.* 1591)

Vox Patris caelestis.
(B) *** CfP CFP/*TC-CFP* 40339. Tallis Scholars, Phillips – ALLEGRI: *Miserere*⊛; PALESTRINA: *Missa Papae Marcelli.***(*)

Mundy's *Vox Patris caelestis* was written during the short reign of Queen Mary (1553–8). While it is almost exactly contemporary with Palestrina's *Missa Papae Marcelli*, its florid, passionate polyphony is very different from that of the Italian composer. This is emphasized by Peter Phillips's eloquent performance, which presses the music onwards to reach an exultant climax in the closing stanza with the words '*Veni, veni, veni, caelesti gloria coronaberis*'. The work is structured in nine sections in groups of three, the last of each group being climactic and featuring the whole choir, with solo embroidery. Yet the music flows continuously, like a great river, and the complex vocal writing creates the most spectacular effects, with the trebles soaring up and shining out over the underlying cantilena. The imaginative force of the writing is never in doubt, and the Tallis Scholars

give an account which balances linear clarity with considerable power. The recording is first-class and the reverberant acoustic adds bloom and richness without blurring the detail. The sound on disc and cassette is virtually identical.

Mussorgsky, Modest
(1839–81)

The Capture of Kars (march). *St John's Night on the Bare Mountain. Scherzo in B flat. Khovantschina: Prelude to Act 1;* (i) *Introduction to Act 4. The Destruction of Sennacherib.* (i; ii) *Joshua.* (i) *Oedipus in Athens: Temple chorus. Salammbô: Priestesses' chorus.*
*** RCA RL/*RK* 31540 [ARL 1/*ARK 1* 3988]. LSO, Abbado, with (i) LSO Ch., (ii) Zehava Gal.

To commemorate the centenary of Mussorgsky's death Abbado and the LSO came up with this attractive and revealing anthology of shorter pieces. Some of the orchestral items are well enough known, but it is good to have so vital an account of the original version of *Night on the Bare Mountain*, different in all but its basic material from the Rimsky-Korsakov arrangement. Best of all are the four choral pieces; even when they are early and untypical (*Oedipus in Athens*, for example) they are immediately attractive, and they include such evocative pieces as the *Chorus of Priestesses* (intoning over a pedal bass) from a projected opera on Flaubert's novel. The chorus is rather recessed, but not inappropriately so, and the orchestra is given refined recording. The high-level cassette transfer is one of RCA's best, and there is little appreciable difference in sound between disc and tape; if anything the chorus has more immediacy on the latter.

The Capture of Kars; Intermezzo in modo classico; Scherzo in B flat. Pictures at an Exhibition (orch. Tushmalov).
**(*) Acanta DC 22128. Munich PO, Andreae.

The special interest of this record is its inclusion of an early orchestration of Mussorgsky's *Pictures* by Michail Tushmalov. He was a pupil of Rimsky-Korsakov, who conducted the première of this arrangement in 1891 (the original piano work dates from 1874). Not unexpectedly, Tushmalov's scoring is strongly influenced by his master; it favours full washes of orchestral sound rather than the comparatively sharp and more vivid textures familiar from Ravel's version of 1922. *Gnomus*, *Tuileries* and *Bydlo* are omitted, and the work plays for some twenty-four minutes, ending with a sumptuous version of *The Great Gate of Kiev* using hammered percussive strokes to increase the impact. This performance is a fine one, with a warmly resonant recording to bring out the orchestral colours vividly. Among the fillers, the *Intermezzo*, dedicated to Borodin, is undoubtedly memorable. This record is worth exploring, though hardly a first choice for the principal work.

Night on the Bare Mountain (arr. Rimsky-Korsakov).
*** DG 2536/3336 379 [id.]. Chicago SO, Barenboim – BORODIN: *Polovtsian dances* ***; RIMSKY-KORSAKOV: *Capriccio* etc.**(*)
(M) *** Decca Eclipse ECS 838 [Lon. STS 15530]. SRO, Kletzki – RACHMANINOV: *Symphony No. 3.***
(B) *(*) CfP CFP 40309. LPO, Susskind – BORODIN: *In the Steppes* etc.*(*)

Barenboim gives a powerful account of the Mussorgsky/Rimsky-Korsakov piece (the original version is available in an excellent RCA recording, conducted by Abbado; see above), and it is vividly and

weightily recorded on both disc and cassette.

Kletzki's version is also brilliantly done and the Decca recording is first-class. The coupling, however, is not a primary recommendation for Rachmaninov's *Third Symphony*. Susskind's account is well played and is given a vivid modern recording; but the performance refuses to catch fire, and only really comes to life in Rimsky's lyrical coda.

In the lower-medium price-range there is a superb collection of Russian music played by the Berlin Philharmonic under Sir Georg Solti (Decca SPA/KCSP 257), which includes not only a gripping account of *Night on the Bare Mountain* but also the beautiful *Khovantschina Prelude*, with the *Persian dance* from the same opera for good measure. The other items – no less recommendable – are Glinka's overture for *Russlan and Ludmilla* and Borodin's for *Prince Igor*. The recording is first-class in every way.

Night on the Bare Mountain (arr. Rimsky-Korsakov); *Pictures at an Exhibition* (orch. Ravel).
⊛*** Telarc Dig. DG 10042 [id.]. Cleveland O., Maazel.
(M) **(*) RCA Gold GL/GK 42702 [(d) LSC 2977]. Chicago SO, Ozawa.
(M) ** CBS 60113/40- [Col. MY 36726]. NYPO, Bernstein.
*(*) Ph. Dig. 9500 744/7300 829 [id.]. Concg. O., Colin Davis.

All current versions of this coupling rest under the shadow of the magnificently recorded Telarc disc, one of the first great successes of the early digital era and still much prized by collectors of audio demonstration records. The quality of the recording is apparent at the very opening of *Night on the Bare Mountain* in the richly sonorous presentation of the deep brass and the sparkling yet unexaggerated percussion. With the Cleveland Orchestra on top form the *Pictures* are very strongly characterized; this may not be the subtlest reading available, but each of Mussorgsky's cameos comes vividly to life. The opening trumpets are more robust than in the Philadelphia version (see below), and *The old castle* is particularly evocative. The chattering children in the Tuileries are matched in presence by the delightfully pointed portrayal of the cheeping chicks, and if the ox-wagon (*Bydlo*) develops a climax potent enough to suggest a juggernaut, the similarly dramatic brass in the *Catacombs* sequence cannot be counted as in any way overdramatized. After a vibrantly rhythmic *Baba-Yaga*, strong in fantastic menace, the closing *Great Gate of Kiev* is overwhelmingly spacious in conception, and quite riveting as sheer sound. Technically there are few better records of a big symphonic climax than this, with the clean pressing and immaculate surface enhancing the realism and impact. The rosette goes to the producer, Robert Woods, and sound engineer, Jack Renner, but must also be shared by the mastering engineer, Stan Ricker. The sleeve, however, while waxing enthusiastic about the technical background of the recording, omits to provide a simple list of the titles of the pictures (although they are discussed in the musical notes).

Above all Ozawa shows his feeling for orchestral colour in his undoubtedly successful version of *Pictures at an Exhibition*. Moreover the orchestra is on top form; yet the virtuosity is always put to the service of the music's pictorialism and atmosphere. Ozawa does not force the pace or make unnecessary underlining; he lets the work unfold naturally, though with excellent incidental detail. The coupling is strikingly vivid, with plenty of electricity, and the recording is full and atmospheric, lacking only the last degree of clarity. The cassette, however, has less transient crispness than the disc.

The New York Philharmonic is on top form for Bernstein's performance of the *Pictures*, with crisp ensemble and vivid solo playing, so that the conductor can relax, yet each of Mussorgsky's pictures is strongly characterized. The recording is spacious, but its rather fierce upper range becomes more apparent when one turns over for *The Great Gate of Kiev* (presented very grandly) and the *Night on the Bare Mountain*.

This first digital recording from Philips was technically a disappointment. The recording, refined enough, lacked body and immediacy, and the performance too is strangely short on brilliance. The speeds are often on the slow side, which makes the music fragile and undercharacterized rather than weighty. A performance like this sounds like a run-through, and though some may like the total absence of vulgarity in the *Night on the Bare Mountain*, it too sounds disappointingly tame. The cassette transfer is bass-heavy, and detail is muffled.

Pictures at an Exhibition (orch. Ravel).
*** HMV ASD/TC-ASD 3645 [Ang. S/4XS 37539]. Phd. O., Muti
STRAVINSKY: *Firebird suite.****
*** Decca Dig. SXDL/KSXDC 7520 [Lon. LDR 10040/5-]. Chicago SO, Solti – RAVEL: *Tombeau de Couperin.***
(M) **(*) Ph. Fest. 6570/7310 176 [id.]. Concg. O., Haitink – GLINKA: *Russlan overture*; DVOŘÁK: *Scherzo capriccioso*; TCHAIKOVSKY: *Capriccio italien.***(*)
(B) **(*) CfP CFP/TC-CFP 40319. LPO, Pritchard – PROKOFIEV: *Symphony No. 1.*(*)

Pictures at an Exhibition. Khovantschina, Act 4: Entr'acte and Dance of the Persian slaves.
(M) *** HMV SXLP/TC-SXLP 30445 [(d) Ang. S 35430]. Philh. O., Karajan – BORODIN: *Polovtsian dances.****

Muti's reading is second to none. Any comparison is only with the finest previous versions (Toscanini, Koussevitzky,

Karajan), and given the excellence of its recorded sound, it more than holds its own. Moreover it is one of the first records to do justice to the Philadelphia sound (although the balance is forward and perhaps not all listeners will respond to the brass timbres at the opening). But it is a far richer and more full-blooded quality than we have been used to in recent years from this source. The lower strings in *Samuel Goldenberg and Schmuyle* have extraordinary body and presence, and *Baba-Yaga* has an unsurpassed virtuosity and attack as well as being of demonstration standard as a recording. The richly glowing colours, the sheer homogeneity of the strings and the perfection of ensemble are a consistent source of admiration. The coupling is no less thrilling. The focus on the cassette is marginally less clean than the disc, but remains impressive.

Karajan's Philharmonia recording dates from the earliest days of stereo, yet here also the quality of the sound is astonishing, another tribute to the immense skill of Walter Legge and his early Philharmonia recording team. There is extraordinary clarity and projection, and it is matched by the brilliantly polished detail of the orchestral playing – the vintage Philharmonia offering breathtaking standards of ensemble and bite. The characterization of each picture is outstandingly vivid, and *The Great Gate of Kiev* is a frisson-creating climax of great splendour. The main work is framed by the two excerpts from *Khovantschina*, which are played most seductively, and the Borodin *Polovtsian dances* are hardly less riveting. This is not to be missed, even if purchased as a second version. The cassette transfer is first-class, full-bodied, clear and clean, without a trace of distortion at climaxes.

Solti's performance is fiercely brilliant rather than atmospheric or evocative. He treats Ravel's orchestration as a virtuoso challenge, and with larger-than-life digital recording it undoubtedly has demonstration qualities. The cassette is

one of Decca's very finest, matching the disc closely, but softening the edge of the sound picture very slightly without losing detail. It is no less demonstration-worthy than the disc, and many might feel that its focus is more natural. But whether heard on LP or tape this is a listening experience that tingles with energy and electricity. The Ravel fill-up makes an original coupling, although here the brilliantly forward sound balance is less appropriate.

Haitink's account is part of a rather generous anthology. It has not the electricity of Solti's version, but the playing of the Concertgebouw Orchestra is evocative and cultured. The recording is warm yet well detailed, and there is plenty of atmosphere, each picture caught with considerable skill. *Cum mortuis in lingua mortua*, which comes immediately before the side-break, is wonderfully serene. The cassette transfer, made at a high level, matches the disc in being spacious and weighty rather than strikingly brilliant.

The Classics for Pleasure issue offers at bargain price a brilliant account from the LPO under Pritchard, in which the personality of the orchestra comes over strongly, the players obviously enjoying themselves and their own virtuosity. The very clear, dry recording makes every detail of the orchestration glitter, even if it lacks atmosphere, and the conductor's characterization of each picture is equally positive. The building of the *Great Gate of Kiev* finale is vividly exciting. This recording has been remastered and recoupled, and its sharpness of detail is now even more striking, both on disc and on tape (which approaches demonstration standard). Unfortunately the Prokofiev coupling has less attractive sound.

Pictures at an Exhibition (arr. for brass ensemble by Elgar Howarth).
*** Argo ZRG/*KZRC* 885 [id.]. Jones Brass Ens., Howarth.

There is no reason why Mussorgsky's

famous piano work should not be transcribed for brass as effectively as for a full symphony orchestra, and Elgar Howarth's inspired arrangement fully justifies the experiment. There is never any feeling of limited colour; indeed the pictures of the unhatched chicks and the market place at Limoges have great pictorial vividness, and the evocation of the dead has an almost cinematic element of fantasy. *The Great Gate of Kiev* is as thrilling here as in any orchestral recording, and elsewhere the deep brass effects are superbly sonorous. The disc version has already acquired 'collector' status as a demonstration record, and the tape transfer is hardly less impressive. Either format will give great satisfaction.

Pictures at an Exhibition (original piano version).
*** DG 2531/*3301* 096 [id.]. Berman –
SHOSTAKOVICH: *Preludes.***
(*) Decca SXL/*KSXC* 6840 [(d) Lon. 6559/5-]. Ashkenazy – TCHAIKOVSKY: *Concerto No. 1.*
(B) ** Con. CC/*CCT* 7516 [DG 2535/*3335* 272]. Firkusny – RACHMANINOV: *Preludes.***(*)

Lazar Berman opens his account of the original piano version of the *Pictures* with an uncompromisingly fast pacing of the *Promenade*. One can picture him striding round the exhibition brusquely, hands behind his back, only stopping to admire those pictures which take his fancy. The ox-wagon (*Bydlo*) certainly does, and undoubtedly *Catacombs* and *Cum mortuis* make a very direct communication, for the playing here has arresting power and atmosphere. On the other hand the *Ballet of the unhatched chicks* finds him more concerned with articulation (the playing is superb) than evocation. *The Great Gate of Kiev* makes a riveting (if not overwhelming) climax, and with splendid sound this is undoubtedly the most compelling account of the work to have been recorded in recent

years. The coupling too is first-rate, and the cassette transfer is of DG's finest quality.

Ashkenazy's account is distinguished by poetic feeling, but lacks something of the extrovert flair with which pianists like Richter or Berman can make one forget all about the orchestral transcription. Decca have recoupled this with the Tchaikovsky *B flat minor Piano concerto* and have taken the opportunity to improve the sound still further. If the coupling is attractive, this cannot be faulted on technical grounds.

At bargain price Firkusny's version deserves to be considered. The playing is spontaneous, and the music sounds fresh and well characterized, even if there is some lack of extrovert bravura at the end. The piano tone on tape is firm and realistic; the cassette has marginally less range than the disc but is fully acceptable.

Pictures at an Exhibition (arr. for organ by Wills).
(M) ** Hyp. Dig. A/*KA* 66006. Wills (organ of Ely Cath.).

Arthur Wills's registration is effective enough, if showing no especial creative flair, and the performance too is competent rather than inspired. The problem is the articulation of the quick music: the children playing in the Tuileries, the chicks, and *Baba-Yaga* all lack the sharpness of attack that the piano (or orchestral instruments) can readily provide. *Bydlo*, the Polish ox-wagon, comes off splendidly, and *The Great Gate of Kiev* is massive, if not overwhelming. The recording is spectacularly realistic, and the disc has been advocated for demonstration by some hi-fi magazines. The cassette transfer too is impressively free from congestion.

The Nursery (song cycle).
*** Decca SXL 6900 [Lon. 26579]. Söderström, Ashkenazy – GRECHANINOV: *Láne*; PROKOFIEV: *Ugly Duckling.***

Elisabeth Söderström's series of song recordings with Vladimir Ashkenazy has mainly concentrated on Rachmaninov, but here she chooses an illuminating group of pieces about children, which, with thrillingly imaginative accompaniment, are characterized with vivid intensity. The Mussorgsky cycle has one registering the different voices – nurse or child – with extraordinary immediacy. There are few records of Russian song as refreshing and exciting as this. The recording of both voice and piano is outstanding.

Songs and Dances of Death (song cycle). *Song of the Flea.*
*** Decca SXL 6974. Talvela, Gothoni – RACHMANINOV: *Songs.* **(*)

Martti Talvela's magnificent bass is superbly caught in brilliant Decca sound to make his account of Mussorgsky's dark, intense cycle vividly immediate and involving. A singer with an operatic background gains enormously here, and there has not been a finer version since Boris Christoff's many years ago. Gothoni's imaginative accompaniment is not nearly so well caught, but it is the voice which compels attention.

Sunless (song cycle).
*** HMV ASD 3700. Nesterenko, Krainev – SHOSTAKOVICH: *Songs.* ***

Yevgeny Nesterenko made his London début with an outstandingly memorable concert at Wigmore Hall, and this record brings it home that he not only possesses a superbly dark-toned and finely focused bass voice, typically Russian in timbre, but has a rare ability to use it for intensifying word meaning. Here he presents Mussorgsky's sombre cycle with a power and feeling for detail that relate it directly to the finest of Lieder cycles; and Krainev's accompaniment adds an almost orchestral weight, well caught in the recording.

Boris Godunov: scenes (*Prologue; Coronation scene;* Act 2: *Recitative and aria of Boris; Clock scene;* Act 4: *Pimen's narration and Death of Boris*).
**(*) HMV ASD 4006. Nesterenko, Sokolov, Bolshoi Th. Ch. and O., Simonov.

When generations of basses singing this part snarl and bark, it is a joy to hear the even vocalization of Nesterenko, by far the richest of Russian basses today. His emphasis on purely musical values, on firm tone and even legato, on flowing phrasing, means that extrovert characterization is not part of the experience in these excerpts. There are many niceties of expression that Nesterenko misses when compared with Boris Christoff, and the very evenness might be counted too predictable; but it is a voice of such magnificence as to send shivers through one, and though on disc the Russian recording as a whole is disappointingly thin (the cassette is fuller, but the resonance brings a degree of clouding at climaxes), the principal voice is glorious from first to last. Until Nesterenko tackles a complete recording of this unique masterpiece – as surely he must before long – this makes a valuable stopgap.

Salammbo (arr. Pesko).
** CBS 79253 (2). Schemchuk, Seleznev, Stone, Surjan, Arena, Italian R. and TV Ch. and SO, Pesko.

The chorus of Libyan warriors here brings a sudden reminder that Mussorgsky raided such early works as this when he came to write his masterpiece, *Boris Godunov:* the high priest in the Carthaginian temple with chorus presents the great melody which later became Boris's Act 2 monologue. Mussorgsky was in his early twenties when he attempted to turn Flaubert's exotic novel into an opera and sketched out some five scenes, mostly in piano score merely.

Zoltan Pesko, the conductor here, has completed these to produce a sort of cantata. Indifferently recorded at a live concert presented by Italian Radio, it can be recommended to anyone curious about a composer too often unable to carry his strokes of genius to real fulfilment.

Narvaez, Luis de
(1500–c. 1555)

El Delphín de Musica, Book 1: *Fantasia No. 5;* Book 2: *Fantasias Nos. 5–6;* Book 3: *La canción del Emperador;* Book 4: *O gloriosa domina (Seys diferencias);* Book 5: *Arde coracón, arde; Ye se asiente el Rey Raminor;* Book 6: *Conde claros; Guárdame las vacas; Tre diferencias por otra parte; Baxa de contrapunto.*
*** RCA RL/*RK* 13435 [ARL 1/*ARK 1* 3435]. Bream (lute) – MILAN: *Fantasias* etc.***

This collection of music by Narvaez is more diverse than the coupled representation of his distinguished contemporary Luis Milan, and includes arrangements of popular songs of the time and some of the earliest known sets of *diferencias* (variations). Bream is in his element in this repertoire, and each piece is eloquently felt and strongly characterized; the music's nobility is readily conveyed. The recording is first-class, with the cassette matching the disc closely.

Newman, Alfred (1901–70)

Film music: *20th Century-Fox fanfare. Airport: Main title. Anastasia: Main title. Best of Everything:*

London calling. The Bravados: Main title (The Hunters). Captain from Castile: Pedro and Cataña; (i) *Conquest. Down to the Sea in Ships: Hornpipe. How to Marry a Millionaire: Street scene.* (i; ii) *The Robe: suite.* (ii) *The Song of Bernadette: Prelude; The vision. Wuthering Heights: Cathy's theme.*
(M) ** RCA Gold GL/*GK* 43437 [ARL 1/*ARK 1* 0184]. Nat. PO, Gerhardt, with (i) Grenadier Guards Band, (ii) Amb. S.

Alfred Newman is guaranteed immortality as the composer of the famous 20th Century-Fox trademark fanfare. Unlike Korngold, Rózsa and Waxman he had no European background, but (born in Connecticut) was Hollywood's own man. Indeed the Hollywood hyperbole was an intrinsic part of his musical nature. He was good at rumbustious, rather empty marches (as in *Captain from Castile*) and tended to overscore (as in the *Hornpipe* from *Down to the Sea in Ships*). The very first piece here (after the fanfare) is genuinely memorable: *Street scene,* a Gershwinesque idea originally written in 1931 for a film of the same name but more recently made familiar by its re-use as an introduction to *How to Marry a Millionaire.* For the rest there is sentimentality (*Cathy's theme* for *Wuthering Heights*), orchestral inflation, the occasional touch of brilliant fantasy (the vision sequence in *The Song of Bernadette,* effective even though essentially tasteless) and luscious religiosity, epitomized by the score for *The Robe.* Charles Gerhardt's committed advocacy (and the splendid orchestral playing) ensures maximum impact throughout, and there is something endearing about such ingenuous vulgarity when the end result so obviously provided what directors and producers required. The sound is well up to the brilliant standard of this RCA series; the cassette, however, has rather fuzzy transients, although it is otherwise acceptable. The cassette does not include the insert LP leaflet with documentation and movie stills.

Nicolai, Otto (1810–49)

Die lustigen Weiber von Windsor (The Merry Wives of Windsor; complete).
*** Decca D 86 D 3 (3) [Lon. 13127]. Ridderbusch, Donath, Schmidt, Brendel, Malta, Ahnsjö, Bav. R. Ch. and SO, Kubelik.

Kubelik's performance may not have quite the dramatic ebullience which made Bernhard Klee's DG recording so exhilarating, but in many ways his extra subtlety brings more perceptive results – as in the entry of Falstaff in Act 1, for example, where Kubelik conveys the tongue-in-cheek quality of Nicolai's pomposo writing and Klee takes it seriously. In quality of singing there is little to choose between this cast and the outstanding one on DG, though Ridderbusch here is straighter and nobler, Moll on DG more sparkling. The dialogue here is more crisply edited without the device of the Garter Inn waiter, and the recording, fairly reverberant, is vividly atmospheric.

Nielsen, Carl (1865–1931)

Flute concerto.
*(*) Erato STU 71272. Rampal, Sjaellands SO, Frandsen – NØRBY: *Illuminations.***

The *Flute concerto* is a late work written at about the same time as Sibelius's *Tapiola* – and, moreover, in the same country, Italy. It is a wonderfully subtle and affecting piece whose light spirits hide a vein of keen poetic feeling. Strange that such artists as James Galway, William Bennett and Karlheinz Zöller have not committed it to disc. Jean-Pierre Rampal plays with predictable aplomb and virtuosity, but he is handicapped on two counts: first, the balance favours him too much, so that his tone is larger than life and his pianissimo playing does not register as it should; secondly, and more seriously, the quality of the orchestral playing is lacklustre. The strings of the Sjaellands orchestra are wanting in real body and sonority. Frantz Lemsser's version in Blomstedt's EMI box is in every respect to be preferred and may well appear separately during the lifetime of this volume.

Symphony No. 1 in G min., Op. 7.
(M) ** Uni. KPM 7001/*UKC 7130* (*with Symphony No. 3*). LSO, Schmidt.
Symphony No. 1; Saul and David: Prelude to Act 2.
(M) *** RCA Gold GL/*GK* 42872. LSO, Previn.

Nielsen's *First Symphony* is a delight. Its seams may be clearly visible but its musical ideas have such warmth, freshness and imagination that any doubts are instantly banished. Nielsen rightly retained a strong affection for it. André Previn's recording is relaxed and spacious, and he draws an excellent response from the LSO. Indeed, this must count as among the best records he made with them during this period. Moreover, it has the advantage of a fill-up and it is attractively priced. The cassette offers a very bright and vivid side one (the first two movements), but a lower transfer level on side two brings a warmer sound, with less range and impact. The disc is preferable.

Ole Schmidt is a Nielsen conductor of vital instinct, but he is by no means so self-effacing as such distinguished predecessors as Thomas Jensen and Erik

Tuxen, who recorded this composer in the 1950s. The *First* was composed while Nielsen was still a member of the Royal Orchestra, and its youthful freshness is not enhanced by a number of agogic distortions that Schmidt makes in the inner movements. The recording is not as well-balanced as the RCA version, but the cassette version is much superior. It is offered complete on one side, backed by the *Third Symphony*. The sound is full, clear and vivid.

Symphony No. 2 (*The Four Temperaments*), Op. 16.
(M) *** Uni. KPM 7002/*UKC 7250* (*with No. 5*). LSO, Schmidt.

The *Second* is one of Nielsen's most appealing scores, and Ole Schmidt's account with the LSO is quite simply the best to have been recorded since Thomas Jensen's pioneering 78s. He characterizes each of the four temperaments enshrined in the work to excellent effect, and every detail comes to life. The brass could perhaps have been more discreetly balanced in relation to the wind and strings, but this small reservation should not deter collectors. The cassette version is complete on a single side, coupled with the *Symphony No. 5*. The transfer is lively and the sound vivid, though slightly over-bright on top.

Symphony No. 3 (*Sinfonia espansiva*), Op. 27.
(M) **(*) Uni KPM 7003/*UKC 7130* (*with No. 1*). Gomez, Rayner Cook, LSO, Schmidt.

The *Sinfonia espansiva* is given a good performance even if it falls short of the highest distinction. The first movement is a little wanting in momentum, but, generally speaking, tempi are well judged and there is evidence of sensitivity and breadth. Memories of earlier Danish performances of the 1950s from Erik Tuxen and John Frandsen are not wholly banished, but there is no serious reason

to withhold a recommendation. The recording is not as refined or as transparent as the best modern engineering can produce but it is fully acceptable. On cassette the symphony is coupled with No. 1. The transfer is well managed, though a high-level playback is needed.

Symphony No. 4 (*Inextinguishable*), Op. 29.
*** DG Dig. 2532/*3302* 029 [id.]. Berlin PO, Karajan.
(M) *** Uni. KPM 7004/*UKC 7460* (*with No. 6*). LSO, Schmidt.

Symphony No. 4; An Imaginary Journey to the Faroe Islands; Pan and Syrinx, Op. 49.
** RCA RL/*RK* 25226. SNO, Gibson.

By far the best performance of Nielsen's *Fourth* ever recorded comes from Karajan. The orchestral playing is altogether incomparable and there is both vision and majesty in the reading. The strings play with passionate intensity at the opening of the third movement, and there is a thrilling sense of commitment throughout. The wind playing sounds a little over-civilized by comparison with the pioneering record from Launy Grøndahl and the Danish State Radio Orchestra, made in the early 1950s, but what exquisitely blended, subtle playing this is. It is excellently recorded, too. The sound on cassette is bright and vivid but rather light in the bass.

Schmidt gives a vital and invigorating account of the *Fourth Symphony* that captures its spirit as completely as any on record. Only a minor reservation has to be made: the wind are a little recessed, though the balance between them and the strings is well judged; but the brass are in a closer perspective and this is occasionally disturbing. On cassette the coupling is with No. 6; the sound is very brilliant and needs a little taming.

At full price the Scottish National Orchestra offers two rarities as a fill-up, and these may well sway some collectors in its favour. There is no want of commitment from the players, and Sir Alexander Gibson has well-judged tempi and an obvious sympathy for this work. Perhaps the strings do not have the weight that is required, and one misses the last ounce of fire. Yet there is much to admire, including a well-balanced sound picture. Both *Pan and Syrinx* and the much later 'rhapsodic overture', one of Nielsen's last works, dating from 1927, are given perceptive readings that realize much of the mystery these scores evoke. The cassette transfer is made at a low level, and the reverberation offers minor problems.

Symphony No. 5, Op. 50.
(M) *** Uni. KPM 7005/*UKC 7250* (*with No. 2*). LSO, Schmidt.

Ole Schmidt's account of the *Fifth* is probably the best now available. He brings freshness and authenticity of feeling to this music, and the LSO respond positively to his direction. Minor reservations about balance apart, this is a well-recorded and highly recommendable version. The cassette transfer too is impressive; there is plenty of bite and impact at climaxes yet no congestion and beautifully refined string pianissimos.

Symphony No. 6 (Sinfonia semplice).
(M) *** Uni. KPM 7006/*UKC 7460* (*with No. 4*). LSO, Schmidt.

Nielsen's *Sinfonia semplice* is one of his strangest and most haunting utterances. The first and third movements in particular must rank among his most remarkable and visionary achievements. As with No. 5, Ole Schmidt scores a resounding success here, and his version is closer to the spirit and the letter of this work than any of the current rivals. Much the same reservations apply to the recorded sound as we have noted in the companion discs, but they are not serious enough to inhibit a strong recommenda-

tion. The cassette version (coupled with No. 4) needs a little smoothing on top but is vivid and clear.

Canto serioso; Fantasias for oboe and piano, Op. 2; The Mother (incidental music), *Op. 41; Serenata in vano; Wind quintet, Op. 43.*
** Chan. ABR/*ABT* 1003. Athena Ens.

A most useful record which collects Nielsen's output for wind instruments in chamber form. The Athena Ensemble give a thoroughly lively account of the *Wind quintet*; they earn gratitude for observing the exposition repeat in the first movement but none for ignoring some of the dynamic markings! The ostinato figure at letter D in the first movement is marked *pp* but does not really sound it here, though the close balance does not help matters. The balance is rather more disturbing in the *Serenata in vano*, where the clarinet is in your lap, and similar points could be made about the other pieces. But none of them is otherwise available and all are beautiful; they are also very well played. The cassette transfer is of good quality, smooth and refined.

Wind quintet, Op. 43.
** Uni. RHS 366. Danish Wind Quintet – HINDEMITH: *Kleine Kammermusik* ***; MILHAUD: *Cheminée du Roi René*.*(*)

Well recorded though they are, the Danish Wind Quintet do not play with quite the same sensitivity as their namesakes who made the pioneering set of this work. There are felicitous touches, of course, but dynamic inconsistencies – the absence of really soft playing – and a certain want of poetry diminish the impact of this performance. It would be wrong to place too much weight on its shortcomings, for we are not well served at present (the Melos version is deleted); but this remains a stop-gap that falls short of the ideal.

Maskarade (opera; complete).
*** Uni. RHS 350/2. Hansen, Plesner, Landy, Johansen, Serensen, Bastian, Brodersen, Haugland, Danish R. Ch. and SO, Frandsen.

Maskarade is new to the gramophone: only the overture and a handful of interludes have been recorded before. It is Nielsen's second and last opera and must be accounted a triumphant success in this recording. The libretto derives from Holberg's comedy of 1724, which Nielsen himself shaped into operatic form with the literary historian Vilhelm Andersen as collaborator. The plot is straightforward and simple, and to recount it would do scant justice to the charm and interest of the opera. *Maskarade* is a buoyant, high-spirited score full of strophic songs and choruses, making considerable use of dance and dance rhythms, and having the unmistakable lightness of the *buffo* opera. It is excellently proportioned: no act outstays its welcome, one is always left wanting more, and the scoring is light and transparent. The performance here is delightful and is distinguished by generally good singing and alert orchestral support. The sound is well focused and the singers well blended; even if they are a trifle forward in relation to the orchestra, this is in no way obtrusive. Above all, the sound is musical, the images well located and firm. There are none of the awkward edits that disfigured *Saul and David*, and the sound is altogether more vivid.

Nono, Luigi (born 1924)

A floresta è jovem e cheja de vida (1965/6) for soprano, voices, clarinet, copper plates and magnetic tape; . . . sofferte onde serene . . . (1976) for piano and magnetic tape.

*** DG 2531 004 [id.]. Poli, Pollini, Bove, Vicini, Troni, William Smith, cond. Canino.

sofferte onde serene represents Nono's direct response to the playing of Pollini, his sympathy and admiration heightened by family bereavements suffered by composer and pianist. The concentration of the performance helps one to make light of the difficulty of idiom. The other work has a frankly political purpose, containing as it does a setting of words by an Angolan guerrilla and an appeal against the war in Vietnam. For full appreciation it plainly requires a degree of political involvement matching that of the composer, but the vitality of the writing is not in doubt, with shouting and gasping of texts set against regular singing. Performances and recording here are excellent.

Nørby, Erik (born 1936)

Illuminations (Capriccio for flute and orchestra).
** Erato STU 71272. Rampal, Sjaellands SO, Frandsen – NIELSEN: *Flute concerto.**(*)

Erik Nørby is a Danish composer best-known perhaps for *The Rainbow Snake*, which the Danish Radio Symphony Orchestra brought to England on a recent tour. *Illuminations* was commissioned by Jean-Pierre Rampal and is full of imaginative sonorities. It is impressionistic in character, easily accessible in idiom and quite convincing in layout. The distinguished soloist is in excellent form, and the playing of the Sjaellands Orchestra sounds better rehearsed and more sensitive than on the Nielsen side. The soloist is too forwardly balanced but otherwise the recording is good.

Nordheim, Arne (born 1931)

Epitaffio (for orchestra and magnetic tape); *Greening* (for orchestra); (i) *Doria* (for tenor and orchestra).
**(*) Decca HEAD 23. RPO, Dreier, (i) with Pears.

Arne Nordheim is generally thought of as one of the brightest luminaries in modern Norwegian music and a leading composer of the middle generation. Of the three works recorded here with much dedication and skill the best is *Doria* (1975), in which the soloist is Peter Pears. It is a setting of words by Ezra Pound and has a distinctive atmosphere and feeling that its companions on this record do not wholly sustain. *Greening*, which comes from the early 1970s, outstays its welcome and has little concentration or real coherence. The performances are expert and the recording superb.

Novák, Vitezslav
(1870–1949)

The Storm, Op. 42; Ranoša, Op. 19/1.
(M) *** Sup. 1112 3231/2. Soloists, Czech Ch. and PO, Košler.

The Storm is arguably Novák's finest composition and this is its first stereo recording. It was briefly available in mono in a fine performance by Jaroslav Krombholc, and this newcomer is long overdue. It is a work of great beauty and imagination, scored with consummate mastery and showing a lyrical gift of a high order. It has warmth and genuine individuality; the idiom owes something to Richard Strauss as well as the Czech tradition, and there is an impressive command of both melody and structure.

This is noble, moving and powerful music – very different from, say, Janáček but recognizably from the same part of the world and equally fresh. This is a fine recording and performance, though the sound is just a shade wanting in real depth. *Ranoša* is a miniature cantata for chorus and orchestra based on a Moravian folk poem. It is a straightforward, attractive piece and makes a good fill-up for the major work. Strongly recommended.

Nystroem, Gösta (1890–1966)

Sinfonia breve.
*** Cap. CAP 1116. Gothenburg SO, Ehrling – HOLMBOE: *Symphony No. 10*.***

Gösta Nystroem studied painting and music as a young man, and spent his formative years in Paris. His music shows something of the influence of Honegger, and though it is deficient in melodic vitality, he is able to project a certain atmosphere. The *Sinfonia breve* comes from the period 1929–31, thus preceding by a few years his finest work, the *Sinfonia espressiva*, which enjoyed a brief vogue in this country after the war. It is well played and recorded here, though it must be conceded that the main attraction of this disc is the Holmboe symphony, a most powerful and cogently argued work.

Obrecht, Jacob (c. 1453–1505)

Motets: *Beata es Maria; Salve crux; Salve Regina.*
*** DG Arc. 2533 377 [id.]. L. Pro Cantione Antiqua, L. Cornett and Sackbut Ens., Turner – RUE: *Motets*.***

Pierre de la Rue and Jacob Obrecht are two of the major contemporaries of Josquin. The Obrecht *Salve Regina* is particularly beautiful and has a tender austerity that is both original and moving. The performances are among the best that this ensemble has given us, and the recordings too are excellent: a worthwhile addition to the catalogue.

Missa fortuna desperata. (Also includes ANON.: *Fortuna desperata.*) (M) *(*) HM HM 998. Clemencic Cons.

Obrecht is often thought of as the most austere of the Flemish contemporaries of Josquin, though his music can often attain an expressive purity that transcends the severe and aloof quality of his invention. Finely wrought though it is, the *Missa fortuna desperata* remains a cold exercise in polyphony, even though this performance is far from insensitive or unpersuasive. The record also includes the chanson *Fortuna desperata*, on which the Mass is based.

Offenbach, Jacques

(1819–80)

Gaîté Parisienne (ballet, arr. Rosenthal): *Suite.*
(*) CBS 76909/40- [Col. M/*MT* 35843]. Orchestre Nat. de France, Maazel – DUKAS: *L'Apprenti sorcier* **(*); SAINT-SAËNS: *Danse macabre.**
(M) ** HMV Green. ESD/*TC-ESD* 7152. Monte Carlo Op. O., Rosenthal – ROSSINI: *Boutique fantasque.***(*)

With the French orchestra making a suitably tangy sound, Maazel's is a highly vivacious account, brilliant without being driven too hard. The brightly lit recording (a little harder-edged on tape than on disc) suits the music. Manuel

Rosenthal's own selection is very brightly recorded, and the orchestral playing is enthusiastically lively.

Overtures: La Belle Hélène; Blue-beard; La Grande-Duchesse de Gér-olstein; Orpheus in the Underworld; Vert-vert. Barcarolle from Contes d'Hoffmann.
*** DG Dig. 2532/*3302* 006 [id.]. Berlin PO, Karajan.

Other hands besides Offenbach's helped to shape his overtures. Most are on a potpourri basis, but the tunes and scoring are so engagingly witty as to confound criticism. *La Belle Hélène*, by Haensch, is well constructed, and the delightful waltz tune is given a reprise before the end. Karajan's performances racily evoke the theatre pit, and the brilliance is extrovert almost to the point of fierceness. But the Berlin playing is marvellous, and with so much to entice the ear this cannot fail to be entertaining. The demonstration item is *Vert-vert*, which is irresistibly tuneful and vivacious. The digital sound is extremely vivid and there is no appreciable difference between disc and cassette: both have marvellous range and immediacy.

Overtures: La Belle Hélène; La Grande-Duchesse de Gérolstein; Orpheus in the Underworld. Les Belles Américaines: Waltz (orch. Bennett). Contes d'Hoffmann: suite. Geneviève de Brabant: Galop. La Périchole: Potpourri. (i) Musette (Air de ballet).
(M) ** RCA Gold GL/*GK* 43193. Boston Pops O., Fiedler, (i) with Mayes (cello).

Fiedler's selection is interesting and generous, and if, after listening to Karajan's Berlin Philharmonic disc, one feels he is fielding a second team, these performances are lively and their brashness is not unattractive. The sound is vivid enough on disc, in the American manner, but the cassette is not recommended: the quality is undistinguished and the dynamic range severely restricted.

Cello duos, Op. 54: Suites Nos. 1 and 2.
*** HM HM 1043. Pidoux, Peclard.

This Harmonia Mundi issue is an unexpected and delightful surprise. Offenbach was himself a very accomplished cellist, and these two works are bristling with bravura, but tuneful too and imaginatively laid out to exploit the tonal possibilities of such a duo. The two works offer plenty of contrast and Offenbach's natural wit is especially apparent in the *First Suite in E major.* The performances here are excellent and so is the recording.

Orphée aux enfers (Orpheus in the Underworld; 1874 version).
*** HMV SLS 5175 (3) [Ang. SZX 3886]. Sénéchal, Mesplé, Rhodes Burles, Berbié, Petits Chanteurs à la Croix Potencée, Toulouse Capitole Ch. and O., Plasson.

Plasson recorded his fizzing performance – the first complete set in French for thirty years – in time for the Offenbach centenary. He used the far fuller four-act text of 1874 instead of the two-act version of 1858, so adding such delectable rarities as the sparkling *Rondo* of Mercury and the *Policemen's chorus.* Mady Mesplé as usual has her shrill moments, but the rest of the cast is excellent, and Plasson's pacing of the score is exemplary. The recording is warmly atmospheric and the leavening of music with spoken dialogue just enough.

'The world of Offenbach': Overtures: (i; ii) *La Belle Hélène;* (iii; iv) *La Fille du tambour-major;* (i; ii) *Orpheus in the Underworld.* (iii; iv) *Le Papillon:*

Valse des rayons. Les Contes d'Hoffmann: (v; i; iv) *Ballad of Kleinzach;* (vi; i; iv) *Doll's song;* (vi; vii; i; iv) *Barcarolle. La Grande-Duchesse de Gérolstein:* (viii; i; ix) *Piff-paff-puff;* (x–xii) *Portez armes . . . J'aime les militaires. La Périchole:* (x; i; xii) *Air de lettre; Ah! quel dîner.*
(M) *** Decca SPA/*KCSP* 512. (i) SRO; (ii) Ansermet; (iii) LSO; (iv) Bonynge; (v) Domingo; (vi) Sutherland; (vii) Tourangeau; (viii) Corena; (ix) Walker; (x) Crespin; (xi) V. Volksoper O.; (xii) Lombard.

A characteristically felicitous Decca anthology, as generous as it is wideranging. The performances cannot be faulted; Ansermet and Bonynge offer much character in the overtures, and the vocal numbers – which come from a wide variety of sources – are no less colourful. The recording throughout is immensely vivid on disc and tape alike. Ansermet incidentally takes the final *Can-can* of the *Orpheus overture* (which closes the concert) slower than usual, but invests it with such rhythmic vigour that the music sounds freshly minted.

Orff, Carl (1895–1982)

Carmina Burana (cantata).
*** HMV ASD/*TC-ASD* 3900 [Ang. SZ/*4ZS* 37666]. Auger, Summers, Van Kesteren, Southend Boys' Ch., Philh. Ch. and O., Muti.
(*) Telarc Dig. DG 10056/7 [id.]. Blegen, W. Brown, Hagegard, Atlanta Ch. and SO, Shaw – HINDEMITH: *Symphonic metamorphoses.*(*)
**(*) RCA Dig. RL 13925 [ATC 1/*ATK 1* 3925]. Hendricks, Aler, Hagegard, Boys of St Paul's Ch., LSO and Ch., Mata.
(M) **(*) Decca Jub. JB/*KJBC* 78. Burrows, Devos, Shirley-Quirk, Brighton

Festival Ch., Southend Boys' Ch., RPO, Dorati.
(B) **(*) CfP CFP/*TC-CFP* 40311 [Sera. S/4XG 60236]. Babikian, Hager, Gardner, Houston Chorale and Boys' Ch., Houston SO, Stokowski.

Partly because of recording which dramatically brings out the fullest weight of bass (timpani and bass drum most spectacular at the opening) Muti's is a reading which underlines the dramatic contrasts, both of dynamic and tempo. So the nagging ostinatos are as a rule pressed on at breakneck speed, and the result, if at times a little breathless, is always exhilarating. The soloists are first-rate; Arleen Auger is wonderfully reposeful in *In trutina* and Jonathan Summers in his first major recording characterizes well. The Philharmonia Chorus is not quite at its most polished, but the Southend Boys are outstandingly fine. This is a performance which may lose something in wit and jollity but is as full of excitement as any available. On cassette the choral sound is satisfyingly full-blooded but the wide dynamic range has brought serious recession of image when the soloists are singing quietly.

Spreading *Carmina Burana* on to three sides instead of the usual two makes for wide groove spacing, and Telarc characteristically present exceptionally full and brilliant sound, though hardly more so than the analogue sound given to Muti on HMV. Like Muti, Robert Shaw – who was for some years Toscanini's choirmaster – prefers speeds on the fast side, though his manner is more metrical. In *The Court of Love* one wants more persuasive treatment, though the choral singing – recorded rather close in analytical sound – is superb. The soloists are good, but the Atlanta boys cannot quite match their rivals on most European versions.

Mata's is a volatile performance, not as metrical in its rhythms as most, which at times means that the LSO Chorus is

not as precise in ensemble as it is for Previn. The choristers of St Paul's Cathedral sing with perfect purity, perhaps not boyish enough, and though the soloists are first-rate (with John Adler coping splendidly, in high refined tones, with the roast swan episode), the recording – digital but lacking a little in bass – does not put a very persuasive bloom on their voices.

Dorati's Jubilee version was originally recorded in Phase Four. It is a beefy, vibrant account with good singing and playing. Despite some eccentric speeds, Dorati shows a fine rhythmic sense, but the performance cannot quite match the best available. Moreover the high-level recording has hints of over-modulation at peaks, noticeable both on disc and on cassette (which is otherwise successfully transferred).

Rhythmic relentlessness is a quality much in demand in Orff's cantata, and though Stokowski brings to this unexpected repertory his usual flair and individuality, he does not have the bite one really needs for such music to have its full impact. The recording, originally from Capitol, is not as bright as some from that source, but at the price this is a more than acceptable record on which to get to know a work that has defied the pundits in remaining genuinely popular. Moreover, any doubts about the rather recessed effect of the Capitol recording on disc (which appears to come from the original masters) is dispelled on tape, which offers quite different sound, brilliant at the top, with incisively vivid projection for the chorus.

Still recommended: Previn's version (HMV ASD/*TC-ASD* 3117 [Ang. S/4XS 37117]) remains a first-class recommendation, richly recorded and strong on both humour and rhythmic point. All in all this is hard to beat, and the cassette has recently been remastered to match the disc closely in vibrant projection and sharpness of focus.

Catulli Carmina (cantata). *
(M) *** DG Priv. 2535/*3335* 403 [id.].
Auger, Ochman, German Op. Ch.,
four pianos and percussion, Jochum.

Though in sheer memorability it
cannot match *Carmina Burana*, Orff's
sequel (using much the same formula) has
its nagging attractions. For anyone hyp-
notized by the earlier and more popular
work, *Catulli Carmina* is the Orff piece
to recommend next. Jochum's version is
as fine as any available. His chorus sings
with sharp rhythmic point, and if imagination is called for in such music,
Jochum matches flexibility with a spark
of humour in control of mechanistic
rhythms. His soloists are individual and
sweet-toned. In this Privilege reissue the
recording is outstanding, although on
side two the evocative pianissimo section
is a shade over-recessed. There is no appreciable difference between disc and
cassette; both need to be played at a high
level for maximum impact.

Antigonae (opera; complete).
(M) **(*) DG 2740 226 (3). Borkh,
Hellman, Alexander, Stolze, Uhl,
Haefliger, Plümacher, Borg, Engen,
Bav. R. Ch. and SO, Leitner.

Antigonae was the first of three works
in which Orff sought to relate opera back
to Greek origins. Using an orchestra full
of percussion (including grand pianos) he
reminds one on the one hand of Stravinsky's *Les Noces*, on the other of Stravinsky's much greater operatic setting of
the Oedipus legend. The baldness of the
writing brings few of the delights of such
a work as *Carmina Burana*, but the
splendid performance here of Inge Borkh
– one of her finest on record – makes it
an important set. The recording, dating
from 1960, is a little rough in places, but
hardly hampers enjoyment.

Oedipus Tyrannus (opera; complete).

(M) **(*) DG 2740 227 (3). Stolze,
Harper, Varnay, Alexander, Kohn,
Bav. R. Ch. and SO, Kubelik.

This is a rather more colourful example
of Orff's later style (1959) than the first
of the trilogy of Greek-based operas,
Antigonae. But musically it is a scrappy
piece, and with no English translation
given, only the original text (Hölderlin's
translation of Sophocles), it is recommendable only to those who readily
understand German. The performance,
persuasively conducted by Kubelik, is
dominated by the Oedipus of Gerhard
Stolze, a virtuoso performance well
balanced by the characterful Jokasta of
Astrid Varnay. The 1969 recording still
sounds well.

Paer, Ferdinando (1771–1839)

Leonora (complete).
**(*) Decca D 130 D 3 (3) [Lon. 13133].
Koszut, Gruberova, Jerusalem,
Tadeo, Brendel, Bav. SO, Maag.

Paer's treatment of the story which
inspired Beethoven's later masterpiece
makes an interesting historical curiosity.
It was written in 1804, only just before
the first version of the Beethoven opera,
but it inhabits an altogether more conventional operatic world. Being an
Italian opera it has recitatives, and the
formal arias rely to a great degree on
florid writing. Knowing Beethoven – and
remember, even he got his timing wrong
first time – one registers the occasional
ineptitude rather than the felicities, but
Peter Maag makes a most persuasive
case, and it is a pity that, except for Siegfried Jerusalem as Florestano and Gior-
gio Tadeo as Rocco, the singing is not of
the highest standard, though Gruberova's coloratura is a model compared
with the clumsy singing of Ursula

Koszut. Excellent recording and lively playing.

Paganini, Niccolò (1782–1840)

Violin concerto No. 6 in E min., Op. posth.

(M) *** DG Priv. 2535/*3335* 421 [2530 467/*3300 412*]. Accardo, LPO, Dutoit.

This further newly discovered concerto is entirely characteristic, tuneful and bristling with bravura. This Privilege reissue comes from Salvatore Accardo's complete set recorded in the mid-seventies. The performance demonstrates the effortless wizardry of the soloist, who is beautifully accompanied and most naturally recorded. However, even at medium price this seems short measure. The cassette is transferred at a high level and is slightly over-brilliant.

24 Caprices for solo violin, Op. 1; Duo Merveille; Sonata for solo violin; Variations on God save the King; Variations on Nel cor più non mi sento.

*** DG 2707 107 (2) [id.]. Accardo.

Accardo succeeds in making Paganini's most routine and empty phrases sound like the noblest of utterances, and he invests these *Caprices* with an eloquence far beyond the sheer display they offer. There are no technical obstacles and both in richness of tone and grandeur of conception these are peerless. Accardo observes all the repeats (Perlman on HMV ASD 3384 [Ang. S 36860] observes some but not others, though he accommodates the set on two sides, while Accardo spills over on to a third). As in Accardo's Paganini concerto records made in the early to mid-1970s, the fill-ups are of equal interest, and they are performed with effortless and spectacular virtuosity. The recording is first-class.

(i) *Terzetto for violin, cello and guitar. Caprice No. 24, Op. 1/24; Sonata in A* (arr. Williams).
*** CBS 73745/40-. Williams, with (i) Loveday, Fleming – GIULIANI: *Variations.****

The *Terzetto* is a small-scale but very charming work, and it is beautifully played here. John Williams is also in excellent form in the makeweights, the *Sonata* and *Caprice*, both originally for violin. The CBS recording is of high quality though forwardly balanced.

Palestrina, Giovanni da (c. 1525–1594)

Alma Redemptoris Mater (antiphon); *Missa Papae Marcelli; Peccantem me quotidie* (motet); *Stabat Mater.*
(M) **(*) ASV ACM 2009. L. Pro Cantione Antiqua, Turner.

In this record of well-known masterpieces Bruno Turner uses small forces, and the gain in clarity is at the expense of a certain radiance of texture. The acoustic is clear and precise. Yet it should be emphasized that these are most beautiful performances of all four pieces, offering both intelligence and sensitivity in the handling of each line. Rather forward recorded balance enhances clarity of texture. This is not the only way of performing Palestrina, but it is nonetheless impressive.

Exsultate Deo; Hymnus in adventu Dei; Jesu Rex admirabilis (hymn); *Magnificat VI toni; Tua Jesu dilec-*

tio; Veni sponsa Christi (antiphon; mass and motet).
(M) *** Argo ZK 69. St John's College Ch., Guest.

Dignified performances, well recorded, of some fine Palestrina works. Although these performances are firmly in the Anglican tradition and lack some of the fervour one would find on the Continent, they have great purity of tone and beauty of phrasing. Moreover the acoustic has atmosphere, yet detail is not lost.

Missa Papae Marcelli.
(B) **(*) CfP CFP/TC-CFP 40339. Tallis Scholars, Phillips – ALLEGRI: *Miserere*⊛; MUNDY: *Vox Patris caelestis.****

Palestrina's *Missa Papae Marcelli* has a famous historical reputation for its influence on decisions made at the Council of Trent. The Catholic hierarchy had become concerned that the elaborate counterpoint of much church music, and the interpolation of non-liturgical texts, was obscuring the ritual purpose of the Mass itself. Palestrina's work, with its syllabic style and clear text, supposedly demonstrated that great music need not cover the religious message and so influenced the decision not to ban polyphony altogether. If the story is apocryphal, there is no doubt that Palestrina's settings satisfied the authorities, while the quality of his music, and the memorability of the *Missa Papae Marcelli* in particular, are equally certain. With its apparent simplicity of line and serene beauty which disguises an underlying fervour, it is not a work which lends itself readily to performers with an Anglican background. This account is certainly the finest at present available on record, catching the music's cool dignity and much of its expressive richness. The singing has purity of tone, a refined control of dynamics and beauty of phrasing. It is

splendidly recorded within the admirably reverberant acoustic of Merton College, Oxford. The cassette transfer too is of the highest quality, and in this music freedom from extraneous background noises is essential.

Missa Tu es Petrus. Motets: *Ave Maria; Quam pulchri sunt; Tu es Petrus.*
*(*) HM 1C 065 99685. Tölz Boys' Ch., Schmidt-Gaden.

There is no lack of life here in the six-part Mass, but pleasure is somewhat diminished by the less than secure intonation of the boys. For all the keenness of musical intention, this does not really merit a strong recommendation, and the same applies to the rest of the collection.

The Song of Songs.
(M) ** Sup. 4122 141/2. Czech Philharmonic Ch., Veselka.

Palestrina's motet cycle drawing on words from the *Song of Songs* must be numbered among his most glorious works. Josef Veselka's approach distances him from that of some colleagues who view Palestrina's *Song of Songs* as ardent, passionate celebrations of love not dissimilar from contemporary Italian madrigalists. Veselka's reading underlines the sacred dimension in these motets and he eschews the expressive detail and word-colouring favoured by those who use smaller forces. The singing of the Czech Philharmonic Choir is of high quality, and the recording sounds natural enough. This is a useful alternative to Michael Howard's recording with the Cantores in Ecclesia (Oiseau-Lyre SOL 338/9), but it in no sense displaces it.

Panufnik, Andrzej
(born 1914)

Concerto festivo; (i) *Concerto for timpani, percussion and strings. Katyń epitaph; Landscape.*
*** Uni. Kanchana Dig. DKP 9016. LSO, composer, (i) with Goedicke and Frye.

Andrzej Panufnik's music is invariably approachable, finely crafted and fastidiously scored. This superbly recorded disc gives a good example of his feeling for atmosphere and colour; the textures are always transparent and clean, and there is an alert and refined sensibility. Perhaps the only criticism one could make is of a certain motivic economy that borders dangerously on paucity. The *Katyń epitaph* is powerfully eloquent and, oddly enough, is reminiscent at one point of the atmosphere of the last pages of Britten's *A Time There Was*, though the Panufnik was written some years earlier. The LSO play well for the composer himself; the recording is excellently balanced and in the demonstration class. The best of this music is deeply felt.

Sinfonia rustica (Symphony No. 1); Sinfonia sacra (Symphony No. 3).
(M) **(*) Uni. UNS 257. Monte Carlo Op. O., composer.

The *Sinfonia rustica* was the work which first attracted attention to Panufnik shortly after the war. It is the more individual of the two works recorded here and has plenty of character, though its invention is less symphonic than in the style of a sinfonietta. The performances of both works under the composer's baton are alert and spirited, though the Monte Carlo orchestra is not in the first flight. The recording, made by EMI, is excellent: the stereo is very much in the demonstration class.

Sinfonia di sfere (Symphony No. 5); Sinfonia mistica (Symphony No. 6).
*** Decca HEAD 22. LSO, Atherton.

Both these works date from the late 1970s and exploit Panufnik's increasing preoccupation with geometrical forms as his source of musical inspiration. The *Sinfonia di sfere*, his fifth symphony, consists of three movements in ternary form representing a journey through three concentric spheres. The *Sinfonia mistica*, his sixth symphony, takes the number six as its root in a single movement of six sections, with each parameter dominated by that division into sixths. Though the cerebration of the scheme sometimes has one questioning the intensity of emotion conveyed, the idiom is not difficult, and the structural firmness adds very plainly to the immediate sense of conviction in each sharp contrast as it develops. Excellent performances and recording.

(i) *Thames Pageant. Invocations for Peace.*
(M) *** Uni. UNS 264. King's House School Ch., Thames Youth Ens., Stuckley, (i) with Amis.

Thames Pageant, a choral suite written for children to perform, ends riotously with a musical representation of the Oxford and Cambridge boat race (with John Amis the commentator). There is an engaging directness too about the earlier movements, which include a march representing Julius Caesar and a nicely pointed portrait of Alexander Pope. Inevitably the performance has its rough edges, but the spirit is what matters. The *Invocation* is in a sparer style, with trebles accompanied by brass and bells. The recording is commendably clear.

Parry, Hubert (1848–1918)

Symphony No. 5 in B min.; Symphonic variations; Elegy to Johannes Brahms.
*** HMV ASD/*TC-ASD* 3725. LPO, Boult.

This was the last record made by Sir Adrian Boult, whose recording career was longer than that of any important rival. The *Fifth Symphony*, the last that Parry wrote, is broadly Brahmsian in style but with the four movements linked in a Lisztian cyclic manner; the slow movement is particularly beautiful. Equally impressive is the *Elegy*, not merely an occasional piece but a full-scale symphonic movement which builds to a powerful climax. The sharply inventive *Symphonic variations* – also recorded by Boult for an earlier Lyrita disc – complete the Parry portrait. Recording and performances are exemplary, a fitting coda to Sir Adrian's recording career. The cassette needs playing back at a high level; then the quality is good, with a bright upper range and plenty of weight and body, so necessary for these Elgarian textures.

Shulbrede tunes Nos. 1–2 and 4–7; Theme and 19 variations.
** Pearl SHE 546. Parry (piano) – STANFORD: *3 Rhapsodies.***

Parry's *Theme and variations* dates from 1885 and is fashioned with predictable expertise. It is not music of great personality or character, but nor is it without merit. The *Shulbrede tunes* are short, rather Schumannesque vignettes, written just before the First World War and portraying family members and life at his daughter's house. John Parry plays with commitment and makes out a good case for these neglected pieces.

Songs of Farewell.
(M) *** Argo ZK 58. Louis Halsey Singers, Halsey – STANFORD: *Part songs.****

The *Songs of Farewell* make a splendid set, one of Parry's finest works, demonstrating in rich polyphonic writing the composer's feeling both for words and for voices. The setting of Donne's *At the round earth's imagined corners* in seven parts is the richest of all, while the last, *Lord, let me know mine end*, is the most expansive. Louis Halsey draws fine singing from his choir, the recording is most atmospheric and the only snag about this issue is that no texts are provided. Admirers of Parry should buy this record quickly, for the companion Argo disc (ZK 44) including a fine selection of miscellaneous songs, splendidly sung by Robert Tear, which was only issued in October 1979, has already been deleted.

Patterson, Paul (born 1947)

(i) *Kyrie and Gloria;* (ii) *Fluorescences; Trilogy for organ; Visions.*
*** HMV CSD 3780. (i) L. Chorale, Wales (with piano); (ii) Wills (organ of Westminster Cath.).

Of the younger generation of British composers, Paul Patterson is one of the most approachable, and these organ pieces as well as the *Kyrie and Gloria* give ample evidence of his ability to communicate directly and attractively. The *Kyrie and Gloria*, with their unconventional piano accompaniments, even have a hint of pop in their idiom, and Roy Wales directs spirited performances. Arthur Wills is equally committed in the solo organ works, with their elaborate rhetoric and dramatic contrasts. Excellent recording.

Payne, Anthony (born 1936)

(i) *Phoenix Mass;* (ii) *Paean;* (iii) *The World's Winter.*
*** BBC REH 297. (i) BBC Singers, Jones Brass Ens., Poole; (ii) Bradshaw; (iii) Manning, Nash Ens., Friend.

Payne's music, thoughtful and closely argued, is well represented by these three works. *The World's Winter*, a setting for soprano and instrumental ensemble of two poems by Tennyson, uses Payne's personal brand of numerical serialism. The *Mass* relies on more complex textures, but in its contrasts of expression is just as communicative. The piano piece *Paean*, written for Susan Bradshaw, makes an apt fill-up. The BBC recordings are very acceptable, though the *Mass* is a little too reverberant for full clarity.

Peeters, Flor (born 1903)

Missa festiva, Op. 62.
*** Argo ZRG 883 [id.]. St John's College Ch., Guest – POULENC: *Exultate Deo* etc.***

The Belgian composer and organist Flor Peeters is now in his eightieth year and his output includes eight Masses and more than two hundred organ works, some of which are available on specialist labels. The *Missa festiva* is a highly accomplished work, more severe than the Poulenc pieces with which it is coupled but no less inventive and dignified. The relative unfamiliarity of this composer should not deter readers from investigating this Mass, which is well balanced and cleanly recorded.

Penderecki, Krysztof (born 1933)

Anaklasis for strings and percussion; The Awakening of Jacob.
(M) *** Sup. 1410 2734. Prague RSO, Kasprzyk – BAIRD: *Elegeia;* LUTO-SLAWSKI: *Mi-Parti.****

The two Penderecki complete each side: *The Awakening of Jacob* follows the *Mi-Parti* on side one, and *Anaklasis*, an inventive piece for strings and percussion, comes after the *Elegeia*. Neither is longer than about six minutes, and both hold the listener. *Anaklasis* is the earlier piece, dating from 1959–60; its companion comes from 1974. With fine, committed performances and good sound this makes a thoroughly worthwhile anthology.

Violin concerto.
*** CBS 76739 [Col. M 35150]. Stern, Minnesota SO, Skrowaczewski.

This concerto, written for Isaac Stern in 1977, marked Penderecki's return to a more conservative idiom. Even so his fingerprints are clearly identifiable, and the compression of thematic material, combined with spare, clean textures, makes for memorable results. The single movement, which lasts almost forty minutes, contains within it the traces of a funeral march, a scherzo and a meditative adagio. The performance here is passionately committed, with Stern at his most inspired, and the recording is splendidly detailed.

St Luke Passion.
*** HM 1C 157 99660/1. Woytowicz, Hiolski, Ladysz, Bartsch (speaker), Tölz Boys' Ch., Col. R. Ch. and SO, Czys.

The *St Luke Passion*, written between

1963 and 1965, is the key work in Penderecki's career, the one which firmly launched him as an international figure. Taking a broadly Bachian view of setting the Passion, Penderecki with great virtuosity uses an enormously wide spectrum of choral and orchestral effects. The result is powerfully dramatic in a way which communicates directly to audiences unused to hearing advanced music. That drama is splendidly conveyed in this recording under the direction of the conductor who has specialized in Penderecki's music. Ensemble and solo singing are admirable, and so is the recording.

Pergolesi, Giovanni
(1710–36)

Miserere No. 2 in C min.
*** Argo ZRG 915. Wolfe, James, Covey-Crump, Stuart, Magdalen College Ch., Wren O., Rose.

Pergolesi's *Miserere* was long listed under doubtful or spurious works, but modern opinion seems to favour its probable authenticity. In his sleeve-note, Dr Rose argues its similarity to the *Stabat Mater*, where there are striking parallels in melodic lines, motifs and harmonic progressions. Whatever the case, this work is both ambitious and moving. It consists of fifteen numbers, seven solo arias, two trios and six choruses. The singers are all of quality, particularly Richard Stuart, and Bernard Rose secures expressive and persuasive results from the Magdalen College Choir and the Wren Orchestra. The recording, made in Magdalen College Chapel, Oxford, is warm and atmospheric.

Stabat Mater; Concertino armonico No. 2 in G.
** Argo ZRG/*KZRC* 913 [id.]. Palmer, Hodgson, St John's College Ch., Argo CO, Guest.
Stabat Mater; Salve Regina in C min.
**(*) Erato STU 71119. Cotrubas, Valentini Terrani, Sol. Ven., Scimone.

Well-coupled with a rare *Salve Regina*, the Scimone version of the *Stabat Mater* makes an excellent choice. It is a performance which brings out the devotional side of the work, even in music which has many secular, even theatrical overtones. Though the portamento style of both soloists is at times distracting, the voices are sweet and blend well, and the playing of I Solisti Veneti is admirable, though the recording is not ideally clear.

George Guest directs a sensible, unaffected performance that misses much of the music's variety, and neither soloists nor choir are at their liveliest. The fill-up is attractive, and far more resiliently performed. Good recording, and an excellent cassette transfer, the richly expansive acoustic caught without problems.

La Serva padrona (complete).
**(*) HM 1C 065 99749. Bonifaccio, Nimsgern, Coll. Aur., Maier.

Maier directs an admirably lively performance of a comic opera which can easily seem over-long. Though the soprano has her moments of shrillness she takes the role of the servant very characterfully, and Nimsgern, stepping out of his usual repertory, proves admirable in the buffo role of Uberto, never resorting to unmusical exaggerations of character. The recording is first-rate, though it dates from 1970.

Perugia, Matteo da
(died 1418)

Belle sans per (virelai); *Dame d'honour* (rondeau); *Dame que j'aym; Dame souvrayne* (virelais); *Gia de rete d'amour* (ballata); *Helas merci* (rondeau); *Ne me chaut* (virelai); *Pour bel accueil* (rondeau); *Pres du soleil; Se je me plaing* (ballades); *Seta que, zorno mai* (ballata); *Trover ne puis* (rondeau).
*** O-L DSLO 577. L. Medieval Ens., P. and T. Davies.

Matteo da Perugia was the first *maestro di cappella* of Milan Cathedral and one of the leading figures of the period between Machaut and Dufay. His songs, which number two dozen in all, constitute the largest surviving secular output by any composer of that period (the beginning of the fifteenth century). Although he was presumably from Perugia, his secular music is predominantly French in style, and all but two of the songs on this disc are to French texts. Yet although this period is relatively unexplored on record, this disc is by no means just for specialists. It is thoroughly accessible and enjoyable, and the performances are of a high level of accomplishment throughout. So, too, is the recording, which does credit to all concerned. This is an issue that would give great pleasure to many readers who do not realize its potential.

Peterson-Berger, Wilhelm
(1867–1942)

Symphony No. 2 in E flat (*Sunnanfärd*).
*** EMI 7C 061 35455. Swedish RSO, Westerberg.

Peterson-Berger is remembered in his native Sweden for his smaller instrumental pieces in folk idiom and as a lively critic of Shavian stamp. He composed five symphonies, however, the second, subtitled '*Journey to the Sun*', dating from the first decade of the present century. It is not in the same league as Stenhammar's *Second Symphony*, nor is it as assured as those of Atterberg. Yet for all its naïvistic touches and moments of inelegance, there is something worthwhile here. It opens promisingly, and the reflective dreamlike episode in the second movement is altogether haunting, though taken as a whole it lacks cohesion and concentration. Yet it strikes more sympathetic resonances than Alfvén or Rangström. Not a well-argued symphony, perhaps: the three stars are for the excellent performance and recorded sound.

Pettersson, Allan (1911–80)

Violin concerto No. 2.
*** Cap. CAP 1200. Haendel, Swedish RSO, Blomstedt.

The Swedish composer Allan Pettersson suffered neglect in his native country during the 1950s and enjoyed a subsequent popular vogue in the last decade or so of his life. His musical language is predominantly diatonic and direct in utterance, though some of his gestures are strongly Mahlerian in character and not wholly free from self-pity and self-indulgence. It is the kind of music that excites the allegiance of some and the impatience of others. His *Second Violin concerto* is no exception. Like many of his symphonies (there are thirteen in all) it is long; its one movement takes the best part of an hour, and it wears its heart very much on its sleeve, as does so much of his music. Admiration for Pettersson's work is tempered by the note of self-pity that he strikes and by its sheer garrulity.

557

As always with this composer, there are moments of eloquence when one is touched, and Ida Haendel, for whom the work was written, braves its difficulties gallantly. The three stars are for the performance and the recording.

Pierné, Gabriel (1863–1937)

Les Cathédrales: No. 1, Prélude. Images, Op. 49. Paysages franciscains, Op. 43.
*** EMI 2C 069 16302. Loire PO, Dervaux.

Gabriel Pierné was a leading figure in French musical life during the years of Debussy and Ravel. The music recorded here is urbane, civilized and charming, and should make him many friends, particularly in view of the persuasive accounts of these scores given by Pierre Dervaux and the Orchestre Philharmonique des Pays de Loire. The first side is occupied by Images, a late work composed in 1935 only two years before Pierné's death. It derives from a divertissement of a pastoral character which shows not only Pierné's virtuosity as an orchestrator but his subtlety as a composer. The score is full of touches of pastiche – a reference to Dukas's La Péri in the opening, an allusion to Debussy's Gigues and so on – and there is also a set of pieces in which he developed two of the numbers of his Divertissement under the title Viennoise et Cortège blues! The Paysages franciscains (1920) on the reverse side betrays the composer's love of Italy, and was inspired by a Danish writer, Johannes Joergensen (1866–1956), much influenced by French symbolism and Catholic culture. The Prélude to Les Cathédrales (1915) is an evocation of the desolation caused by war. Rewarding music in the best French tradition and extremely well played and recorded. Pierné ought to be a popular composer.

Piano concerto in C min.
(M) *(*) Turn. TVS 37125 [Can. 31102].
Dosse, Stuttgart PO, Kuntzsch –
LALO: Concerto.*(*)

Pierné's Piano concerto in C minor has a highly engaging scherzando second movement which might become a favourite 'lollipop' if it were better known. The finale is vivacious too, although without a slow movement the piece lacks a central area of repose. The performance is quite well done, the scherzo played lightly and pleasingly. The recording is vivid rather than especially refined, with a forward balance.

Cydalise et le chèvre-pied (ballet): suite; Ramuntcho overture.
*** EMI 2C 069 14140. Paris Op. O., Mari.

Everyone will recognize the opening of Cydalise et le chèvre-pied, for as the Entry of the Little Fauns it enjoyed great popularity in the 1940s and 50s. Indeed, its fame has helped to keep Pierné's name alive and led to the current resurgence of interest in him in France. The whole ballet dates from 1919 and was first produced in 1923. The ideas are fresh, often modal, beautifully fashioned though ultimately not really distinguished. Nonetheless, this is music that deserves the widest circulation, and even the Ramuntcho overture, an earlier piece dating from 1907 and based on popular Basque themes, has vitality and charm. The Paris Opéra Orchestra responds with enthusiasm to this music and Jean Baptiste Mari secures excellent results. The recording is bright and well-detailed, and the presentation in a gate-folder sleeve is exceptionally informative; the cover, Zuccarelli's Bacchanale, is most attractive.

Marche des petits soldats de plomb.
(M) *** HMV Green. ESD 7048.
Orchestre de Paris, Jacquillat – LALO:
Scherzo; MESSAGER: *Deux Pigeons*
etc.***

Pierné's *March of the little lead soldiers*
sounds deliciously piquant here, and with
attractive couplings and excellent recording, this is a delightful disc on all
counts.

Piston, Walter (1894–1976)

The Incredible Flutist (ballet): suite.
(M) ** Turn. TVS 34670 [id.]. (Boston)
MIT SO, Epstein – COPLAND: *Dance
symphony.***

Walter Piston's ballet *The Incredible
Flutist* is probably his best-known work
and has reached a wider public than any
of his eight symphonies. It was written in
the 1930s after his studies with Nadia
Boulanger in Paris, and some of the
episodes are distinctly Gallic in atmosphere. *The Incredible Flutist* is a highly
attractive score that deserves wide popularity, and this performance by the
orchestra of the Massachusetts Institute
of Technology, though not of the highest
order of virtuosity, is eminently acceptable; and there is no current alternative.
This score would suit Bernstein and we
must hope his CBS version will be issued
here: he was a pupil of Piston in the
1940s. The recording could be warmer
and richer but on the whole this is more
successful than the Copland side.

Symphony No. 3.
(M) *** Mercury SRI 75107 [id.]. East-
man Rochester O., Hanson – HANSON:
Symphony No. 4.***

Piston's *Third Symphony* is a more
ambitious canvas than its Hanson coup-

ling (thirty-four minutes against twenty).
It was commissioned by the Koussevitzky Music Foundation and completed in 1947. The music, which has no
stated programmatic implications, is
nevertheless deeply subjective, often
sombre in mood, with a searching quality
in the first and third movements and an
abrasively biting scherzo. The finale is
positive and vigorous, and the work
stands out among twentieth-century
American symphonies.

Hanson's performance is eloquent and
committed and although the Mercury
sound is not ideally expansive, it is not
without body and has good detail.

Play of Daniel (medieval)

The Play of Daniel (liturgical
drama).
*** Argo ZRG/*KZRC* 900 [id.]. L. Pro
Cantione Antiqua, Landini Cons.,
Mark Brown.

The Play of Daniel first became widely
known thanks to the re-creation by the
American Noah Greenberg; his dramatic
view of a medieval miracle play made an
understandably strong impact on record.
This version under Mark Brown is much
more austere and far more authentic.
There is a simplicity and restraint in both
the performance and the treatment which
with such sensitive, felt singing and playing is most affecting. The recording is
excellent. The cassette transfer, made at
a very high level, is extremely vivid (with
a tendency to fierceness).

Ponce, Manuel (1882–1948)

Hace ocho meses; Marchita el alma;

3 Mexican folksongs; La Valse; Variations on 'Folia de España' and fugue; Yo adoro a mi madre.
⊛ *** CBS 76730/40- [Col. M 35820]. Williams.

Aficionados will welcome John Williams's record devoted to the music of Manuel Ponce, and those not normally drawn to the guitar repertoire should investigate it. The *Variations on 'Folia de España'* are subtle and haunting, and their surface charm often conceals a vein of richer, darker feeling. The writing is resourceful and imaginative (perhaps it is least successful when Ponce attempts imitative textures), and there is a refined harmonic awareness in some of the more reflective variations. The second side is given over to smaller pieces, all of which are played with consummate mastery. The CBS engineers have produced sound that is more natural and lifelike than has often been the case with this artist, and though the balance is far from distant, there is no distortion of perspective and no feeling that the instrument is larger than life; and adjustment of the level enables one to set the image further back should one so desire. The sound is admirably clean and finely detailed yet at the same time warm. The cassette too is excellent.

Ponchielli, Amilcare
(1834–86)

La Gioconda (complete).
*** Decca Dig. D 232 D 3/*K 232 K 33* (3). Caballé, Baltsa, Pavarotti, Milnes, Hodgson, L. Op. Ch., Nat. PO, Bartoletti.
(M) *** HMV SLS/*TC-SLS* 5176 (3) [Ang. S 6031]. Callas, Cossotto, Ferraro, Vinco, Cappuccilli, Companeez, Ch. and O. of La Scala, Milan, Votto.
(M) ** Decca D 63 D 3 (3) [Lon. 13123].

Milanov, Di Stefano, Warren, Elias, Ch. and O. of St Cecilia Ac., Previtali.

The colourfully atmospheric melodrama of this opera gives the Decca engineers the chance to produce a digital blockbuster, one of the most vivid opera recordings yet made by this process. The casting could hardly be bettered, with Caballé just a little overstressed in the title role but producing glorious sounds. Pavarotti, for long immaculate in the aria *Cielo e mar*, here expands into the complete role with equally impressive control and heroic tone. Commanding performances too from Milnes as Barnaba, Ghiaurov as Alvise and Baltsa as Laura, firm and intense all three. Bartoletti proves a vigorous and understanding conductor, presenting the blood and thunder with total commitment but finding the right charm in the most famous passage, the *Dance of the hours*. The chrome cassettes match the discs closely (there is very little loss of focus, in spite of the resonance), but the smaller libretto supplied with the tape box is much less attractive to read.

In the title role in Ponchielli's highly melodramatic opera, Maria Callas gave one of her most vibrant, most compelling, most totally inspired performances on record, with vocal flaws very much subdued. The challenge she presented to those around her is reflected in the soloists – Cossotto and Cappuccilli both at the very beginning of distinguished careers – as well as the distinctive tenor Ferraro and the conductor Votto, who has never done anything finer on record. The recording still sounds well, though it dates from 1960. The cassette transfer is exceptionally successful, the solo voices vibrant and the choral detail clear, with an atmospheric perspective; the break between sides one and two is ill-chosen, but Acts 3 and 4 are each given a cassette side.

The Previtali set is worth hearing for a vintage performance from Zinka Milanov, rather past her best, with raw tone both above and below, but she floats a glorious top B flat on *Come t'amo*. Leonard Warren was another favourite singer at the Met., but his somewhat woolly baritone never recorded really well. Di Stefano produces much heroic tone, and the recording is fair for its late-fifties vintage.

Reminder: Tebaldi much admired the Callas recording and there is evidence that it influenced her own, made towards the end of her recording career. Callas of course remains unique but no one should miss hearing Tebaldi's Decca set, with Horne, Bergonzi and Merrill under Gardelli, which has superlative recorded quality (SET 364/6 [Lon. 1388]).

La Gioconda: Dance of the hours.
(M) **(*) HMV Green. ESD/TC-ESD 7115. Philh. O., Mackerras – LUIGINI: *Ballet Egyptien* ***; MEYERBEER: *Les Patineurs* **; TCHAIKOVSKY: *Nutcracker suite.***(*)

Walt Disney's *Fantasia* gave the short ballet sequence from Ponchielli's opera worldwide popularity, and interestingly it was the only piece in the film that Stokowski extended to fit the animated narrative (much of the other music had to be truncated). Here is the original in a vivacious performance under Sir Charles Mackerras, with the Philharmonia in brilliant form. The bright 1960 recording is not without bloom but is slightly lacking in body. There is little appreciable difference between disc and tape.

Poulenc, Francis (1889–1963)

Aubade (for piano and 18 instruments).
(M) **(*) Sup. 1410 2705. Krajný, Prague CO – HONEGGER: *Concertino* **; ROUSSEL: *Piano concerto.***

The *Aubade* shows Poulenc at his most Stravinskian and wittily self-conscious, and Krajný and the Prague Chamber Orchestra capture its spirit admirably. Indeed, this is as good a performance as any past accounts, though the reverberant acoustic presents problems to the engineers. But the sound is far from unattractive, and as there are no alternative accounts of this charming piece (or either of its companions here) this disc is welcome.

Babar le petit éléphant. (Also includes L. MOZART: *Toy symphony;* MOZART: *3 German dances, K. 605.**(*)
(M) ** ASV ACM/ZCACM 2033. Rippon, Parkhouse.

Poulenc's *Babar*, an entertainment for children, is heard here in the original version for narrator and piano. The music is unambitious but has moments of gentle charm, notably in the expressions of unforced melancholy when things are not turning out quite as Babar expected. David Parkhouse makes the very most of the piano part, playing with commitment and character. Angela Rippon, however, seems not always at home in the narrative and does not readily find a balance between the melodrama (there are two moments of sudden death) and the more congenial events. But her direct friendly style certainly communicates to younger listeners. The recording is excellent (the cassette, the most suitable medium for children, is admirably clear and faithful). The fill-ups, played by the Orchestra of St John's under John Lubbock, are not memorable: the *Toy symphony* is rather lacking in vitality.

(i) *Les Biches* (ballet; complete). *L'Éventail de Jeanne: Pastourelle. La Guirlande de Campra: Matelot provençale. Variations sur le nom de Marguerite Long: Bucolique.*

⊛ *** HMV Dig. ASD/*TCC-ASD* 4067. Philh. O., Prêtre, (i) with Amb. S.

Georges Prêtre recorded *Les Biches* in the 1960s but not in its complete form or with the choral additions that Poulenc made optional when he came to rework the score. The title is untranslatable: it means 'female deer' and is also a term of endearment. Noel Goodwin's sleeve-note defines the *biches* as 'young girls on the verge of adventure in an atmosphere of wantonness, which you would sense if you are corrupted, but which an innocent would not be conscious of'. The music is a delight, and so too are the captivating fill-ups here: a gravely touching tribute to Marguerite Long, which comes close to the Satie of the *Gymnopédies*, and the charming *Pastourelle* from *L'Éventail de Jeanne*. High-spirited, fresh, elegant playing and sumptuous recorded sound enhance the claims of this issue. The strings have wonderful freshness and bloom, and there is no lack of presence. The chrome cassette too is of outstanding quality, matching the disc in its tonal richness and brilliance. The chorus is beautifully focused.

Concert champêtre for harpsichord and orchestra; Concerto in G min. for organ, strings and timpani.
*** HMV ASD/*TC-ASD* 3489 [Ang. S/ 4XS 37441]. Preston, LSO, Previn.
*** Argo ZRG/*KZRC* 878 [id.]. Malcolm, ASMF, Iona Brown.

On HMV each of the recordings is realistically balanced, and Simon Preston, who plays the solo parts in both concertos (the first artist to have done so in the recording studio), produces readings of great fluency and authority. Previn, too, has a genuine feeling for the music, though in the finale of the *Concert champêtre* there are odd moments when the phrasing might be more characterful. But there need be no real reservations here; the playing is always musical, often

sparkling, and the recording is first-class, setting new standards. On cassette the *Concert champêtre* is beautifully managed, with everything natural and in perspective, but the *Organ concerto* is less refined, with a degree of coarseness at fortissimo levels.

George Malcolm follows Simon Preston's example in playing both concertos and does so with considerable success. The engineers have not succumbed to the temptation of making the harpsichord sound larger than life in the *Concert champêtre* – indeed, for some tastes they may have gone too far in the other direction. (Aimée van der Wiele's first stereo LP struck perhaps the right compromise.) George Malcolm rather rushes things in the finale, but in every other respect his is an exemplary account that can well be recommended alongside the Preston. The playing of the Academy of St Martin-in-the-Fields is splendidly crisp and vital, both here and in the *Organ concerto*. The sound on both disc and cassette is first-class.

Concerto in G min. for organ, strings and timpani.
(M) ** RCA Gold GL/*GK* 12445 [AGL 1 2445]. Zamkochian, Boston SO, Munich – MILHAUD: *Création du monde* etc.**

Poulenc's endearing and inventive concerto is not otherwise available at medium price, though it cannot be long before EMI reissue the Duruflé version they made with Prêtre at about the same time as this Boston account appeared. The recording shows its age a little, but the performance still proves a convincing one. The versions by George Malcolm and Simon Preston at full price have, of course, the advantage of modern and vivid recording; the RCA disc has two of Milhaud's most appealing scores as an added attraction. The cassette is not recommended: it has compressed dynamics and undistinguished sound.

Sonata for flute and orchestra (orch. Berkeley).
*** RCA RL/*RK* 25109 [ARL 1/*ARK 1* 3777]. Galway, RPO, Dutoit – CHAM-INADE: *Concertino*; FAURÉ: *Fantaisie*; IBERT: *Concerto*.***

Poulenc's *Flute sonata*, composed in the mid-1950s towards the end of his life, deserves to be widely popular, so beguiling is its delightful opening theme. Yet so far it remains relatively neglected in the British catalogue (though not the American one) and this is the only version currently available. Let us hope that Sir Lennox Berkeley's delightful arrangement and James Galway's persuasive advocacy will bring it to a larger public. The performance is elegant and polished and the orchestration highly successful. The recording is admirably spacious and well detailed and the tape transfer is clear and clean.

Suite française.
*** ASV ALH/*ZCALH* 913. L. Wind O., Wick – GRAINGER: *Irish tune* etc.; MILHAUD: *Suite française*.***

This engaging suite is based on themes by the sixteenth-century composer Claude Gervaise, which Poulenc scored for a small ensemble of wind instruments for a production of a play of Édouard Bourdet called *La Reine Margot*. They are dance pieces which Poulenc has freely transcribed and which come up very freshly in these artists' hands. Excellent recording and couplings. Thoroughly recommendable.

Clarinet sonata; Sonata for clarinet and bassoon.
*(*) Merlin MRF 80701. Kelly, Pearson, Gatt – HINDEMITH: *Clarinet sonata*.*

Good performances of the Poulenc sonatas, more persuasive than the Hindemith on the reverse. Thomas Kelly plays sensitively, though the dry ac-

coustic diminishes the appeal of this disc. Leslie Pearson is a fine pianist, but the instrument does not sound in perfect condition.

Sextuor for piano and wind.
*** RCA RL/*RK* 25278. Ian Brown, Athena Ens. – GOUNOD: *Petite symphonie*; IBERT: *3 Pièces brèves*.***

An excellent performance of Poulenc's *Sextuor*, well recorded on both disc and cassette (the slightly dry piano image suits the music), forms part of a recommendable anthology which is more than the sum of its parts.

Exultate Deo; Mass in G; Salve Regina.
*** Argo ZRG 883 [id.]. Bond, St John's College Ch., Guest; Scott (organ) – PEETERS: *Missa festiva*.***

The Choir of St John's College, Cambridge, offers the pre-war *Mass in G major* with two motets, finely wrought pieces, in performances of great finish. There is little to choose between this version of the *Mass* and that of the Uppsala forces on Erato (see below). The more logical coupling on Erato is likely to exert the stronger appeal on collectors, though the Flor Peeters Mass is excellent. The St John's College forces cope with the delicacy and sweetness of Poulenc's chromatic harmony, and the recorded sound is eminently realistic and truthful.

Figure humaine (cantata); *Mass in G; Quatre petites prières de Saint-François d'Assise.*
*** Erato STU 70924. Mellnäs, Sunnegärdh, Uppsala Academic Chamber Ch., Kfum Chamber Ch., Stenlund.

Figure humaine is a wartime work written during the occupation to words of Paul Éluard. It is perhaps Poulenc's most substantial and deeply felt work in this medium, and these Swedish forces convey its eloquence to good effect. The pre-war *Mass in G major* is less intense but contains a moving soprano solo, which is beautifully done here. The four male-voice settings are post-war and are effectively projected by these fine Uppsala singers. A strongly recommended disc, which offers atmospheric sound.

Gloria.
*** CBS 76670 [Col. M/*MT* 34551]. Blegen, Westminster Ch., NYPO, Bernstein – STRAVINSKY: *Symphony of Psalms.****
(M) ** Turn. TVS 37134 [Can. 31104]. Lovaas, Stuttgart Vocal Ens. and PO, Zanotelli – BIZET: *Te Deum.***

The *Gloria* is one of Poulenc's last compositions and among his most successful. Bernstein perhaps underlines the Stravinskian springs of its inspiration and produces a vividly etched and clean-textured account which makes excellent sense in every way and is free from excessive sentiment. Judith Blegen is an appealing soloist, and the recording, though not the last word in refinement, is really very clear, well detailed and spacious. With its outstanding Stravinsky coupling this is a very attractive issue.

Though the Turnabout version cannot compare with its principal rivals in subtlety, it is well worth considering on a budget label and with such an unusual coupling. There is a splendidly strong contribution from the soprano soloist, Kari Lovaas, and the enthusiasm and vigour of the chorus are in no doubt. The sound is forward and vivid.

Praetorius, Michael
(1571–1621)

Dances from Terpsichore.
(M) *** DG Arc. Priv. 2547/*3347* 003 [198166]. Coll. Terpsichore – SCHEIN: *Banchetto*; WIDMANN: *Dances.****

(B) *** CfP CFP/*TC-CFP* 40335. Praetorius Cons., Ball – HOLBORNE: *Airs*; LAMBRANZI: *Dances.****

Terpsichore is a huge collection of some three hundred dance tunes used by the French court dance bands of Henry IV. They were enthusiastically assembled by the German composer Michael Praetorius, who also harmonized them and arranged them in four to six parts. Moreover he left plenty of advice as to their manner of performance, although he would not have expected any set instrumentation – this would depend on the availability of musicians. Any selection is therefore as arbitrary in the choice of items as it is conjectural in the matter of their orchestration. Perhaps the most imaginative arrangements are to be found on the late David Munrow's outstanding HMV disc (CSD 3761 [Ang. S 37091]), but a warm welcome must be given to the mid-priced reissue of the pioneering Archive recording, offering performances that are both robust and scholarly and orchestrations that are as stylish as they are exhilarating. The sound is not seriously dated, and the couplings are admirably chosen. Unfortunately the Archive cassette has not quite the range and sparkle at the top that make the disc so attractive.

On Classics for Pleasure Christopher Ball has arranged his suite skilfully, although the consort he uses tends to be marginally too recorder-dominated. The playing is alive and spontaneous and has a real sense of fun. The ready tunefulness of the music is most engaging. At times the ear might wish for rather more use of viols, although variety is provided by employing lute and crumhorns etc. to vary the colouring. The CfP recording is crisp and clean, of demonstration quality, and there is no discernible difference between the disc and cassette. What makes this issue especially attractive is the fascinating Lambranzi coupling.

Premru, Raymond
(born 1934)

Music from Harter Fell.
*** Argo ZRG/*KZRC* 906 [id.].
Jones Brass Ens. – ARNOLD: *Symphony* **(*); SALZEDO: *Capriccio.***

Raymond Premru is one of the trombonists in this ensemble, and his *Music from Harter Fell* is expertly laid out for three trumpets and three trombones. The invention is fresh and the style adventurous, and though it is slow to take wing, there is genuine inspiration and vision here. The playing and recording are both superb.

Previn, André (born 1929)

A Different Kind of Blues (*Look at him go; Little face; Who reads reviews; Night thoughts; A different kind of blues; Chocolate apricot; The five of us: Make up your mind*).
*** HMV Dig. ASD/*TCC-ASD* 3965 [Ang. DS 37780]. Perlman, Previn, Manne, Hall, Mitchell.

Perlman, unlike his colleagues here, is no jazz musician, and he had to have the 'improvisations' written out for him; but the challenge of this project, with Previn's colourful and appealing pieces dividing sharply between brilliant and sweet, is very clear from first to last. There are not many better examples of 'middle-of-the-road' records, and the haunting *Chocolate apricot* could become a classic. No information is given on which critic gave rise to *Who reads reviews*. The digital recording is immediate and vivid, and the chrome cassette matches the disc closely.

It's a Breeze (*It's a breeze; Rain in my head; Catgut your tongue; It's about time; Bowing and scraping; A tune for Heather; Quiet diddling; The red bar*).
*** EMI Dig. EMD/*TCC-EMD* 5537. Perlman, Previn, Manne, Hall, Mitchell.

This second instalment of Previn's jazz pieces written for Perlman is if anything even more persuasive than the first, recorded at Heinz Hall, Pittsburgh, as a relaxed supplement to more serious sessions. Such sweet numbers as *A tune for Heather* are particularly attractive, with a tingle of Walton. The digital recording presents balances that are closer to those preferred in pop than to those one would expect in a semi-classical issue, but the sound is very vivid. The chrome cassette is marginally less refined on top than the disc.

Prokofiev, Serge (1891–1953)

Chout (*The Buffoon;* ballet)*: Suite, Op. 21; Romeo and Juliet* (ballet)*. Suite, Op. 64.*
(M) *** Decca Jub. JB/*KJBC* 56 [Lon. STS 15477]. LSO, Abbado.

It is difficult to see why a well-selected suite from *Chout* should not be as popular as any of Prokofiev's other ballet scores. It is marvellously inventive music which shows Prokofiev's harmonic resource at its most delicious. Abbado's version with the LSO offers a generous part of the score, including some of the loosely-written connecting tissue, and Abbado reveals a sensitive ear for balance of texture. The excerpts from *Romeo and Juliet* are well chosen: they include some of the most delightful numbers that are normally omitted from the suites, such as

---

PROKOFIEV

the *Dance with mandolins*, the *Aubade* and so on. The *Dance of the girls* is very sensuous but too slow, far slower than Prokofiev's own 78s. But despite a slight want of intensity and fire, there is an admirable delicacy and lightness of touch that are most captivating. The recording is a model of its kind, with a beautifully balanced perspective and no lack of stereo presence. The cassette transfer too is of Decca's top quality, splendidly vivid and detailed. Highly recommended.

(i) *Piano concerto No. 1 in D flat major, Op. 10. Romeo and Juliet: Scene and dance of the young girls* (arr. for piano by the composer).
⊛ *** HMV ASD/*TC-ASD* 3571 [Ang. S 37486]. Gavrilov, (i) with LSO, Rattle – RAVEL: *Concerto for left hand*; *Pavane.****

A dazzling account of the *First Concerto* from the young Soviet pianist Andrei Gavrilov, who replaced Richter at Salzburg in 1975 and has astonished audiences wherever he has appeared. This version is second to none for virtuosity or for sensitivity: it is no exaggeration to say that this exhilarating account is the equal of any we have ever heard and superior to most. Apart from its brilliance, this performance scores on all other fronts too; Simon Rattle provides an excellent orchestral support and the EMI engineers offer vivid recording. An outstanding issue which commands a rosette in its LP issue. On tape, as the opening *tutti* shows, the reverberation causes some blurring in the orchestral focus, but the piano quality is excellent and the general detail of the recording is good in all but the most expansive fortissimos.

(i) *Piano concerto No. 1;* (ii) *Sinfonia concertante for cello and orchestra, Op. 125.*

(M) ** Turn. TVS 34585 [id.]. R. Lux. O., Froment, with (i) Tacchino, (ii) Varga.

Laszlo Varga gives a fine account of the *Sinfonia concertante* that Prokofiev fashioned from his pre-war *E minor Cello concerto*, dedicating the result to Rostropovich. Varga plays with conviction and power (and, when called for, restraint), and the Radio Luxembourg Orchestra, though not the equal of the RPO or the Boston Symphony, who have recorded it in the past, give lively enough support. There are times when one feels the need for greater mystery, but there is no lack of grip here. The second movement in particular is splendidly vital and crisp. As a fill-up, Gabriel Tacchino gives an expertly delivered performance of the *First Piano concerto*, though he does not possess quite the flair or wildness of a Gavrilov or Richter.

Piano concertos Nos. 2 in G min., Op. 16; 3 in C, Op. 26.
*** HMV ASD 3871. Alexeev, RPO, Temirkanov.

Dmitri Alexeev, the Leeds prizewinner in 1975, is a Prokofiev interpreter of the highest quality. The *Second Piano concerto* is a noble and spacious work, originally composed before the First World War but subsequently lost; the present score is a reconstruction that Prokofiev made in the United States. No one wanting this particular coupling need hesitate, for these performances must be accounted first-rate by any standards. Moreover the recordings have clarity, presence and detail, and the orchestral playing under Yuri Temirkanov is excellent. This more than holds its own with the current competition: it is comparable to Ashkenazy in the *Second Concerto* and arguably superior in the *Third*.

Piano concerto No. 3.
(M) *** DG Acc. 2542/*3342* 149 [139349]. Argerich, Berlin PO, Abbado – RAVEL: *Concerto in G.****

Martha Argerich made her outstanding coupling of the Prokofiev and Ravel concertos in 1968, while still in her twenties, and this record helped to establish her international reputation as one of the most vital and positive of women pianists. There is nothing ladylike about the playing, but it displays countless indications of feminine perception and subtlety. The Prokofiev *C major Concerto*, once regarded as tough music, here receives a sensuous performance, and Abbado's direction underlines that from the very first, with a warmly romantic account of the ethereal opening phrases on the high violins. When it comes to the second subject the lightness of Argerich's pointing has a delightfully infectious quality, and surprisingly a likeness emerges with the Ravel *G major Concerto* (given on the reverse), which was written more than a decade later. This is a much more individual performance of the Prokofiev than almost any other available and brings its own special insights. The recording remains excellent and the cassette transfer too is first-class, matching the disc closely. A highly recommendable mid-priced reissue.

.(i) *Piano concerto No. 4 in B flat for left hand, Op. 53. Symphony No. 4, Op. 47.*
(M) **(*) CBS 61435 [(d) Col. MS 6405; Y 32226]. Phd. O., Ormandy, (i) with Rudolf Serkin.

The *Fourth* is the most rarely heard of the Prokofiev concertos. Written for, but never played by, the pianist Paul Wittgenstein, this is a challenging and often sparkling work. Not all of its charms emerge in Serkin's reading, but much of its brilliance does. Ashkenazy (Decca SXL 6769 [Lon. 6964]) has its measure, but his disc is at full price. The *Fourth Symphony* is also a work seldom heard in either concert hall or recording studio. Ormandy uses the fuller post-war revision that Prokofiev made in the last years

of his life. His is a well-paced version, with orchestral playing of the highest quality, even though there is some want of spontaneity. The sound is perfectly acceptable without being particularly distinguished, but at medium price it is undoubtedly a bargain, especially with such a generous filler.

Violin concertos Nos. (i) *1 in D, Op. 19;* (ii) *2 in G min., Op. 63.*
(M) **(*) CBS 61796/40- [Col. MS 6635]. Stern, Phd. O., Ormandy.
(M) **(*) RCA Gold GL/*GK* 42917. Boston SO, Leinsdorf, with (i) Friedman, (ii) Perlman.

Violin concerto No. 2.
(M) *** Ph. Seq. 6527/*7311* 041 [Quin. 7150]. Szeryng, LSO, Rozhdestvensky
– SIBELIUS: *Violin concerto.***(*)

Stern is extrovert in his romanticism, holding little back; these are confident and ripely perceptive performances, revelling in and bringing out the lyricism in these fine concertos. Stern's warmly expressive approach is matched by Ormandy, who provides an orchestral texture well suited to the soloist's needs. However, the forward balance and the consequent lack of a really hushed quality precludes the element of mystery. Kyung-Wha Chung in her Decca coupling (SXL 6773 [Lon. 6997]) finds a tenderness and sense of fantasy that are not part of Stern's conception. The CBS sound is extremely vivid and the playing often makes a dazzling impact. The cassette matches the disc fairly closely, with only marginal loss of refinement (more noticeable in No. 2).

Erik Friedman is an artist better known in the USA than Europe. A pupil of Heifetz, he demonstrates here a rock-firm technique, a fine tone and considerable subtlety of feeling. His account of the *D major Concerto* is altogether impressive, and the recording allows him some magical pianissimo playing. His radiant timbre at the openings of both the first and the final movements is matched by superb spiccato bowing in the scherzo. The balance favours the soloist, but orchestral detail comes through readily. Friedman's performance was originally coupled to an unattractive version of the *Fifth Piano concerto*, but now it has been recoupled to what was Itzhak Perlman's début recording on RCA. Surprisingly, in the opening movement of the *G minor Concerto* Perlman shows less obvious individuality than Friedman. But his playing remains impressive and has undoubted sensitivity and fire. Leinsdorf is not so naturally understanding an accompanist as Ormandy for Stern, but this RCA issue remains competitive. The sound on cassette is thinner and spikier than on disc.

Szeryng's account of the *Second Concerto* is in every way first-class. Perhaps it has less powerful projection than Stern's version, but Szeryng finds a greater degree of tenderness and he is more poetic in the slow movement. Rozhdestvensky accompanies sensitively and the overall impression is eloquent and committed. The balance of the Philips recording is admirable; the sound has warmth as well as presence. The cassette transfer is one of Philips' best, matching the disc closely.

Lieutenant Kijé (incidental music): Suite, Op. 60.
(M) **(*) RCA Gold GL/*GK* 42698. Chatworthy, Boston SO. Leinsdorf – KODÁLY: *Háry János.****

Leinsdorf, always a sharp and stylish interpreter of Prokofiev, directs a sparkling performance of *Lieutenant Kijé* complete with the part for baritone. The late-sixties recording remains one of the finest from this source, and the coupling is ideal. This is not the most distinctive version available, but it is good value at medium price. The tape transfer lacks the clean sharpness of outline of the disc, but the sound remains attractively vivid.

Lieutenant Kijé: Suite; The Love of Three Oranges (opera): *Suite; Symphony No. 1 in D (Classical), Op. 25.*
*** Ph. 9500/*7300* 903 [id.]. LSO, Mariner.

Good playing and recording; if you want this particular coupling, there is little here to disappoint. Individually these pieces are available in other versions that are as good as (if not superior to) this compilation, but these are lively performances in well ventilated sound.

Peter and the Wolf, Op. 67.
(M) *** HMV Green. ESD/*TC-ESD* 7114. Flanders, Philh. O., Kurtz – BRITTEN: *Young Person's Guide*; SAINT-SAËNS: *Carnival.****
(M) *** ASV ACM/*ZCACM* 2005. Rippon, RPO, Hughes – SAINT-SAËNS: *Carnival.****
*** CRD CRD 1032/*CRDC 4032.* Morris, Northern Sinfonia, Haslam – HASLAM: *Juanita.***
(B) *** Con. CC/*CCT* 7519. Connery, RPO, Dorati – BRITTEN: *Young Person's Guide.***(*)
(*) RCA RL/*RK* 12743 [ARL 1/*ARK 1* 2743]. Bowie, Phd. O., Ormandy – BRITTEN: *Young Person's Guide.*
(*) DG 2531/*3301* 275 [id.]. Du Pré, ECO, Barenboim – L. MOZART: *Cassation.*

Of the many fine versions of *Peter and the Wolf*, Sir Ralph Richardson's vivid narration remains a top favourite; it is still available coupled to an excellent version of the *Classical symphony* (Decca SPA/*KCSP* 90 [Lon. STS/5- 15114]). However, the HMV Greensleeve reissue of the 1959 Michael Flanders recording now tends to sweep the board of the single-disc versions in offering not only Saint-Saëns's *Carnival of the Animals*, but a very lively account under Sir Charles Groves of Britten's *Young Person's Guide to the Orchestra* as a bonus. Michael Flanders adds a touch or two of his own to the introduction and narration, and, as might be expected, he brings the action splendidly alive. The pace of the accompaniment under Kurtz is attractively vibrant, and the Philharmonia are first-rate. The recording is crisply vivid on disc and cassette alike.

Angela Rippon narrates with charm yet is never in the least coy; indeed she is thoroughly involved in the tale and thus involves the listener too. The accompaniment is equally spirited, with excellent orchestral playing, and the recording is splendidly clear, yet not lacking atmosphere. Anyone attracted to this coupling will find it a first-class investment. The cassette matches the disc closely.

Johnny Morris provides a completely new and extended text. The narration continues with the music far more than in the standard version, the characterizations are filled out and the narrator becomes more integrated with the story. For instance Grandfather wears slippers and they go 'Sl-ip, sl-op' beautifully to Prokofiev's music. At the very end it is suggested that the tale does not end happily ever after for everyone; the Wolf is now in the zoo and the Duck (in spite of the ghostly 'Quack') is almost certain not to see the light of day again. It is all very vivid and convincing, and although obviously aimed at younger children it is never arch. The wind players add to the effect of the new version by superb musical characterization, and they are beautifully recorded; the cassette is excellent, like the disc. It is a pity that the coupling is less recommendable, for undoubtedly this 'new-look' *Peter and the Wolf* is a great success.

Sean Connery uses a modern revision of the narrative by Gabrielle Hilton. This exchanges economy of words for a certain colloquial friendliness and invites the narrator to participate more than usual in the narrative. Sean Connery does this very well. His relaxed style, the vocal colour like brown sugar, is certainly attractive from the very beginning (if you can accept such extensions as a 'dumb duck' and a pussy-cat who is 'smooth, but greedy and vain') and when the tale reaches its climax he joins in the fray most enthusiastically. Dorati supports him well and the pace of the orchestral contribution quickens appropriately (in tension rather than tempo). The recording, originally Phase Four, is clear, brilliant and colourful, the spotlight well used. Children of all ages who have no preconceived notions about the words of the narrative will enjoy this. Both sides start attractively with the orchestra tuning-up noise, and here the introductory matter is entirely fresh and informal. The cassette transfer is acceptable but not as crisply focused as the disc.

David Bowie's narration has undoubted presence and individuality. He makes a few additions to the text, and colours his voice effectively for the different characters. He has the face to say 'Are you sitting comfortably?' before he begins, and on the whole the narration seems aimed at a younger age group. The manner is direct and slightly deadpan, but definitely attractive. Ormandy accompanies imaginatively, and the orchestral players enter fully into the spirit of the tale. The recording is generally excellent (David Bowie's voice is very close, but admirably real), although at times the cassette transfer has slight blurring caused by the reverberation. However, with so many versions available at less than full price this issue seems expensive.

Jacqueline du Pré's is a leisurely and intimate account, like a bedtime story. That is not to suggest she is uninvolved, but with her husband pacing the accompaniment in similar mood, the story unfolds without a great deal of excitement, although the narrative line is not without individuality and colour. Yet after the moral of the tale has been rather nicely pointed the orchestral postlude fails to reflect Peter's self-congratulatory high spirits. The coupling too is in no way memorable. Excellent sound on both LP and cassette.

Romeo and Juliet (ballet), *Op. 64:* highlights.
**(*) HMV Dig. ASD/*TC-ASD* 4068. Phd. O., Muti.
(M) **(*) RCA Gold GL/*GK* 42699 [AGL 1 1273]. Boston SO, Leinsdorf.

Muti plays the first *Suite* complete and five of the seven movements comprising the second. In the latter he omits the two lighter and alluring dances, including the *Dance of the girls*. There is impressive virtuosity from the Philadelphia Orchestra and a vivid recording, particularly rich and full-blooded in the bass. There are some magical things, such as the opening of the *Romeo and Juliet* movement in the first suite, but elsewhere there is a certain rigidity and want of charm. The opening of the *Montagues and Capulets* has superb tension and drama but rhythms (though not inflexible) are a little unyielding and accents are heavy. This does not displace the Maazel selection (see below).

Leinsdorf's selection is generous – effectively following the narrative line of the ballet – and well recorded. He shows a good ear for the composer's characteristic sonorities, and with tempi often on the broad side he brings out the nobility and depth of Prokofiev's score. Maazel's Decca selection from his complete set is even finer and superbly recorded (SXL/*KSXC* 6688 [Lon. 6865]), but that is at full price; this RCA disc is good value. On tape the dynamic range is compressed, though otherwise the quality is acceptable.

Romeo and Juliet, Op. 64: Suite No. 1: excerpts.
(M) *** DG Priv. 2535/*3335* 422 [2530 308/*3300 284*]. San Francisco SO, Ozawa – BERLIOZ: *Roméo et Juliette: Love scene;* TCHAIKOVSKY: *Romeo and Juliet.****

The Prokofiev items make an attractive contrast to the other two very romantic evocations of Shakespeare on the same theme. Ozawa draws from his 'other' orchestra warmly committed playing, helped by rich recording quality. There is no appreciable difference between disc and cassette.

Sinfonietta, Op. 48.
*** HMV SLS 5110 (2) [Ang. S 3851]. Philh. O., Muti – *Ivan the Terrible.****

This excellent performance and recording of a first-class work makes a good bonus for a superb account of *Ivan the Terrible*.

(i) *Summer Day* (children's suite for small orchestra), *Op. 65a;* (ii) *A Winter Camp-fire* (suite), *Op. 122.*
(M) *** Sup. 50773. (i) Prague CO (without conductor); (ii) Prague RSO and Children's Ch., Klima.

A wholly delightful and unexpected coupling which will give great pleasure to all those who love *Peter and the Wolf*. The *Summer Day* suite has seven short characteristic movements of great charm. Each sets the other off: the opening *Morning*, lazily atmospheric, is contrasted with *Tag*, which shows the composer at his wittiest, and is played and recorded with irresistible crispness; then comes a beguilingly gentle miniature waltz, and so on. The alert playing of the Prague Chamber Orchestra is a joy. Side two offers a work obviously primarily aimed at boys, with its opening and closing patrol and an enchanting central chorus round the camp-fire, infectiously sung here. The music is presented with great affection; the recording is excellent throughout.

Symphony No. 1 in D (Classical), Op. 25.

(M) *** RCA Gold GL/GK 12703 [AGL 1/AGK 1 2703]. LSO, Previn MEN-DELSSOHN: *Symphony No. 4* etc.***

(B) *(*) CfP CFP/*TC-CFP* 40319. LPO, Davison – MUSSORGSKY: *Pictures.***(*)

* HMV ASD 3872. USSR SO, Svetlanov – RACHMANINOV: *Piano concerto No. 2.**

A neatly turned account from Previn and the LSO, and well recorded into the bargain. The performance is not quite as distinguished as that of the Mendelssohn *Italian symphony* on the reverse side, but it is still highly competitive in this mid-priced format. The dynamic range of the cassette is compressed, but the sound remains vivid (better than the coupling).

An artificially bright sound balance detracts from Davison's modern LPO recording. The brightness here is even less appropriate because the performance is basically genial and relaxed. But when the piccolo joins the violins the shrillness is piercing, and the sound is much the same on both disc and cassette.

Svetlanov could perhaps bring a lighter touch to this perennially fresh score, though he secures a lively enough response from the USSR Symphony Orchestra. However, the Soviet orchestra has not the polish or elegance of its international rivals, and those looking for a good recording of this delightful symphony have better versions to choose from, more sensibly coupled too – Marriner, for instance (Argo ZRG/*KZRC* 719), who chooses Bizet's *Symphony*).

Symphony No. 1; Lieutenant Kijé: Troika; The Love of Three Oranges: March.

(M) ** CBS 60112/40- [Col. MY 36725]. NYPO, Bernstein – BIZET: *Symphony.***(*)

In the first two movements Bernstein's homage to the *Classical symphony*'s eighteenth-century ancestry produces

a slightly self-conscious stiffness of manner, but even so the bassoon manages a gentle smile in his solo and the poise of the strings in the slow movement's upper cantilena is superb. The finale is exhilarating, yet played with admirable precision. The original bonus (Dukas's *L'Apprenti sorcier*) has been replaced with two of Prokofiev's most famous lollipops, brilliantly played. The sound is very bright but not harsh.

Symphonies Nos. 1 (Classical); 7 in C sharp min., Op. 131; The Love of Three Oranges: Suite.

(M) *** HMV SXLP/*TC-SXLP* 30437. Philh. O., Malko.

Malko's performances were recorded in 1955, and the accounts of the two symphonies were the first stereo EMI ever made. (They did not appear at the time.) All the performances are quite excellent, and the *Seventh Symphony*, of which Malko conducted the UK première, is freshly conceived and finely shaped. What is so stunning is the range and refinement of the recording. The engineers have now accommodated the *Seventh Symphony* on one side without any loss of immediacy, and the excellence of the balance and the body of the sound are remarkable. No less satisfying is the *Suite* from *Love of Three Oranges*, an additional bonus making this outstanding value. The reverberation brings minor problems in the cassette transfer, notably in *The Love of Three Oranges*, which lacks sharpness of focus. There is a touch of harshness in the *Seventh Symphony*.

Symphonies Nos. 1 and 7.

*** HMV ASD/*TC-ASD* 3556 [Ang. S/ 4XS 37523]. LSO, Previn.

In both symphonies (a popular coupling since the earliest days of LP) Previn is highly successful. He produces much inner vitality and warmth, and the EMI engineers provide a strikingly realistic and integrated sound. The *Classical symphony* is more successful here than in Previn's earlier version on RCA (see above); it is genuinely sunlit and vivacious, and the ripe recording is entirely appropriate. Previn is obviously persuaded of the merits of the underrated and often beguiling *Seventh Symphony*. The sound on tape is not quite as crisply focused as on disc (the percussive transiences are less sharp), but the quality remains rich and vivid.

Symphony No. 2 in D, Op. 40; The Love of Three Oranges: Suite.
*** Decca SXL 6945. LPO, Weller.

The *Second* is undoubtedly the most dissonant and violent of the Prokofiev symphonies. Its first movement more than vindicates the composer's avowed intention of writing a work 'made of iron and steel'. Indeed it leaves the impression of being an interminably sustained *fortissimo* – relieved from time to time by a *forte*. In sheer density of sound Prokofiev never surpassed it. Formally the work is modelled on Beethoven's Op. 111 and is in two movements, the second being a theme and variations. One or two of the variations may be overscored, but the movement as a whole is full of fantasy and invention. At times in his cycle of the symphonies for Decca, Walter Weller has shown a certain want of bite and concentration, but he gives an altogether impressive account of this problematic score, and he draws from the LPO playing of great refinement and finesse. The second variation of the second movement is rushed, but otherwise this is a remarkably fine performance. So, too, is that of the fill-up. The recording is of demonstration standard.

Symphony No. 3 in C min., Op. 44; Scythian suite, Op. 20.
* Decca SXL 6852. LPO, Weller.

Prokofiev's *Third Symphony*, like its successor, derives from a stage work, in this case the opera *The Fiery Angel*. Walter Weller's recording couples it with the vividly coloured and much underrated *Scythian suite*. Every detail in these complex scores is beautifully observed; there is great richness of sonority, naturalness of perspective and splendid presence, for these are not the easiest of scores to encompass on vinyl. The performances do not arouse the same enthusiasm, however. Weller's accounts of both the symphony and the suite are pale and flaccid, without real momentum and savour; in the slow movement of the symphony, and in *Night* from the *Scythian suite*, there is scant atmosphere. These are all too literal and offer no challenge, except technically as recordings, to Abbado or Rozhdestvensky, who recorded them in the 1970s.

Symphony No. 4, Op. 47; Overture russe, Op. 72.
**(*) Decca SXL 6908. LPO, Weller.

Walter Weller and the LPO have elected to record the revised version of the *Fourth Symphony*, which Prokofiev originally composed in response to a commission from the Boston Symphony Orchestra. Its thematic substance draws on the ballet *The Prodigal Son*, which Prokofiev had written for Diaghilev in 1928. The revision dates from 1947, a year before the Zhdanov affair brought disfavour on nearly all the established Soviet composers, and some time after Prokofiev had suffered a fall that impaired his health. The 1947 version is substantially longer, and the results are not always as convincing. The Decca recording has remarkable clarity and refinement, with excellent body and impact. The performance could do with more bite and edge, but there is no question about the polish and accomplishment of the orchestral response. Had this reading been tauter, it would have earned an unqualified recommendation.

Symphony No. 5 in B flat, Op. 100.
(M) *** HMV SXLP/*TC-SXLP* 30315
[Ang. S 37100]. LSO, Previn.
**(*) Decca SXL/*KSXC* 6875 [Lon.
7099/5-]. Cleveland O., Maazel.
** CBS Dig. 35877/*41*- [Col. M/*4MT*
35877]. Israel PO, Bernstein.

Previn takes a weighty view of a wide-spanning symphony. His first-movement tempo is spacious, and the contrasts are strongly underlined, with Prokofiev's characteristic use of heavy brass, notably the tuba, superbly brought out by the LSO players, not to mention the EMI engineers. The slow movement too is firmly placed in the grand tradition of Russian symphonies. The scherzo and later the finale have fractionally less brilliance than one expects from this source, but with rich recording the result is still formidably powerful. The cassette transfer too is first-class, encompassing the wide dynamic range of the recording full-bloodedly.

Maazel takes a broader, squarer view of Prokofiev's most approachable symphony than is common. He lets the melodies sing for themselves, and with fine ensemble from the Cleveland players the result is certainly refreshing, though the performance misses on the one hand some of the work's tenderness and even more of its wit on the other. The recording is outstandingly brilliant and full on disc and cassette alike.

Bernstein's digital version, edited from live performances, is disappointing. He overloads Prokofiev's free-flowing melodies with romantic expressiveness in a way which undermines the natural freshness of the inspiration. Bernstein is superb at building climaxes, but there is too much heaviness of the wrong kind. On disc the recording is bass-heavy to exaggerate that fault. The chrome tape is better balanced and offers striking range and detail, although the upper strings are somewhat lacking in body.

5 Melodies, Op. 35b (for violin and piano).
(M) *** Ph. Fest. 6570/*7310* 206 [id.]. D. Oistrakh, Bauer – DEBUSSY, RAVEL and YSAŸE: *Sonatas.* ***

The Prokofiev pieces are rarities, surprisingly so considering their appeal. They are inventive and charming, and an admirable makeweight in an outstanding recital record. Wonderful playing from Oistrakh and Frida Bauer, and excellent recording too. The cassette transfer is first-rate, with striking presence.

Violin sonatas Nos. 1 in F min., Op. 80; 2 in D, Op. 94a.
(B) *** RCA VICS/*VK* 2008 [AGL 1/ AGK 1 3912]. Perlman, Ashkenazy.

Both of the *Violin sonatas* date from the years immediately after Prokofiev returned to the Soviet Union. The *F minor Sonata* is one of his very finest works, and the *D major*, originally written for the flute and sometimes heard in that form, has a winning charm and melodiousness. Both works are masterly and rewarding, and Perlman and Ashkenazy play them superbly. The recording is well balanced, slightly dry in timbre, but otherwise truthful and fully acceptable. Perhaps some machines will respond more warmly to it than others, and reservations on this score should not deter anyone from investing in this issue, especially when it is in the lowest price-range. The sound on the chrome cassette is identical with that on the disc

Sonata for two violins, Op. 56.
*** HMV ASD 3861 [Ang. SZ 37668]. Perlman, Zukerman – MOSZKOWSKI: *Suite*; SHOSTAKOVICH: *Duets.* ***

The *Double violin sonata* is a rarity and not otherwise available (though that also goes for the other pieces on this record). It dates from 1932, when Prokofiev was still living in Paris, and is lyrical in feeling. Sonatas for two violins rarely possess depth or charm, but this offers something of both. The playing is as excellent as one has every right to expect.

Piano sonata No. 2 in D min., Op. 14; Romeo and Juliet: Suite.
*** DG 2531/*3301* 095 [id.]. Berman.

With the *Second Sonata* one can say that Prokofiev found himself as a keyboard master. It is succinct, beautifully laid-out for the instrument, and highly original. It bristles with opportunities for virtuoso brilliance, and Lazar Berman deserves credit for the restraint which marks his approach; he elects for that kind of virtuosity that seems unconcerned with sheer display. Prokofiev made these piano transcriptions of the *Romeo and Juliet* music before the Bolshoi ballet itself was staged, and played them in public in 1937. Berman characterizes each piece to excellent effect and is well served by the engineers, who produce clean and well-focused tone. The cassette too is first-class, natural and well-focused to match the disc closely.

Piano sonata No. 8 in B flat, Op. 84; Romeo and Juliet: Suite.
*** HMV ASD/*TC-ASD* 3802. Gavrilov.

Andrei Gavrilov gives a pretty dazzling account of the wartime *Eighth Sonata*. This is among Prokofiev's most admired piano works and is certainly the most recorded of his sonatas. Few performances, however, really succeed in persuading the listener that this is Prokofiev at his very best, though Gilels and Ashkenazy have come close to doing so. The *Eighth* does not seem as concentrated, as explosive or as strong in profile as its immediate predecessor, but Gavrilov's brilliance has one sitting on the edge of one's chair. His playing has intensity and dash with just enough of that wayward poetry to make one revise

one's judgement. Even the *Romeo and Juliet* pieces in their monochrome form sound abundantly characterful in his hands. The recording is very good indeed, with a demonstration-worthy cassette to equal the disc.

Alexander Nevsky (cantata), *Op. 78.*
*** DG 2531/*3301* 202 [id.]. Obraztsova, LSO Ch., LSO, Abbado.
(M) **(*) HMV SXLP/*TC-SXLP* 30427 [Ang. S 40010]. Avdeyeva, RSFSR Russian Ch., USSR SO, Svetlanov.
(M) ** Turn. TVS 37135 [Can. 31098/*CT 2182*]. Carlson, St Louis Ch. and SO, Slatkin.

With playing and singing of great refinement as well as of great power and intensity, Abbado's performance is one of the finest he has ever recorded with the LSO. One might argue that a rougher style is needed in what was originally film music, but the seriousness underlying the work is hardly in doubt when it culminates in so deeply moving a tragic inspiration as the lament after the battle (here beautifully sung by Obraztsova) and when the battle itself is so fine an example of orchestral virtuosity. The chorus is as incisive as the orchestra, and the recording is exceptionally brilliant to match. The cassette transfer is most successful, refined in its warmth, detail and atmosphere yet creating the fullest spectacle in the *Battle on the ice.* A folded booklet provides notes and a translation; indeed the presentation is a model of its kind.

Svetlanov's is a vigorous, earthy performance which gains enormously from the authentic sounds of a Russian chorus. The recording, though not really refined, has admirable weight and body, and though the ensemble cannot match that of the best performances from the West, the urgency of inspiration is most compelling. At medium price it makes an excellent recommendation. The cassette is clear and vivid, with an incisive edge on the choral tone, but it is light in bass and is not as rich as one would ideally like.

Slatkin's Turnabout version does not lack vividness, and Claudine Carlson is an eloquent soloist. The recording has a wide dynamic range and the battle sequence makes a fine climax. This is effective enough, but the Russian recording on HMV is worth the small extra cost.

Ivan the Terrible, Op. 116 (film music arr. in oratorio form by Stasevich).
*** HMV SLS 5110 (2) [Ang. S 3851].
Arkhipova, Mokrenko, Morgunov (narrator), Ambrosian Ch., Philh. O., Muti – *Sinfonietta.****

This oratorio was put together long after Prokofiev's death by the scholar Abram Stasevich, and it lacks the sharp sense of drama which made the comparable cantata *Alexander Nevsky* so strikingly successful. That work, which the composer himself arranged from earlier film music, is crisply dramatic, but with Prokofiev/Stasevich the result is diffuse, and the device of adding a spoken narration (in Russian) could well prove irritating on repetition. Nevertheless Riccardo Muti's enthusiasm for the piece is hardly misplaced, for, with fine playing and choral singing, there are many imaginative ideas here to relish, not least those using broad, folk-like melodies (including one which also served for Kutuzov's great aria in the opera *War and Peace*). The recording is rich and spacious, and though the histrionic style of the narrator, Boris Morgunov, is unappealing, the two other soloists are both excellent in their limited roles. The *Sinfonietta* makes a highly welcome filler for side four.

The Ugly Duckling, Op. 18.
*** Decca SXL 6900 [Lon. 26579].
Söderström, Ashkenazy – GRECH-ANINOV: *Lane*; MUSSORGSKY: *Nursery.****

Prokofiev's extended song-narrative on the Hans Andersen story makes a vivid item in Elisabeth Söderström's splendid collection of Russian songs about children, sharp in its focus thanks not just to the singer but to the pianist too. The recording is excellent.

Puccini, Giacomo
(1858–1924)

Capriccio sinfonico; Prelude sinfonico in A; Prelude to Edgar. (Also includes: MERCADANTE: *Sinfonia on themes from Rossini's Stabat Mater*; VERDI: *La Battaglia di Legnano:* overture.***)
*** Erato STU 71040. Monte Carlo Op. O., Scimone – BOITO: *Sinfonia.****

These Puccini rarities, aptly coupled with equally rare works by other Italian composers, make up an attractive collection. Puccini's *Preludio sinfonico*, written when he was eighteen, is amazingly assured, sounding rather like Mascagni. The *Capriccio sinfonico* is the source of the theme Puccini used at the very opening of *La Bohème*, and it is fascinating to follow the improbable symphonic developments of it here, though the piece rather winds down before the end. The *Prelude to Edgar* is a separate piece that develops the material used in the final approved score of the opera. First-rate recording and stylish performances.

Crisantemi for string quartet.
*** CRD CRD 1066/*CRDC 4066*.
Alberni Qt DONIZETTI: *Quartet No. 13*; VERDI: *Quartet.****

Puccini's brief essay in writing for string quartet dates from the late 1880s; three years later he used the main themes in his first fully successful opera, *Manon Lescaut*. It is given a warm, finely controlled performance by the Alberni Quartet and makes a valuable makeweight for the two full-scale quartets by fellow-opera-composers. The cassette transfer is of demonstration quality, admirably vivid and clear.

OPERA

La Bohème (complete).
(M) **(*) HMV SLS/*TC-SLS* 5059 (2). Callas, Di Stefano, Moffo, Panerai, Zaccaria, Ch. and O. of La Scala, Milan, Votto.
** HMV SLS/*TC-SLS* 5192 (2). [Ang. SZBX/*4Z2X* 3900]. Scotto, Kraus, Milnes, Neblett, Plishka, Manuguerra, Trinity Boys' Ch., Amb. Op. Ch., Nat. PO, Levine.
** Ph. 6769 031 (2)/*7699 116* [id.]. Ricciarelli, Carreras, Wixell, Putnam, Hagegard, ROHCG Ch. and O., Colin Davis.

Neither of the most recent versions of *La Bohème* earns more than a qualified recommendation, and these recordings will appeal most to collectors especially interested in the artists concerned. The Callas set of 1958, however, reissued in a stereo transcription of excellent quality, has some unforgettable moments and is an essential purchase for her many admirers. Our principal recommendations remain with Beecham's classic 1956 recording with De Los Angeles and Bjoerling, which still earns a rosette (HMV SLS/*TC-SLS* 896 [Sera. S/*4X2G* 6099]), and, for those seeking sumptuous modern stereo, Karajan's spacious yet electrically intense version, with Freni a seductive Mimi and Pavarotti an inspired Rodolfo (Decca SET 565/6/*K 2 B 5* (Lon. 1299/5-]).

Callas, flashing-eyed and formidable, may seem even less suited to the role of Mimi than to that of Butterfly, but characteristically her insights make for a vi-

brantly involving performance. The set is worth getting for Act 3 alone, where the predicament of Mimi has never been more heartrendingly conveyed in the recording studio. Though Giuseppe di Stefano is not the subtlest of Rodolfos, he is in excellent voice here, and Moffo and Panerai make a strong partnership as the second pair of lovers. Votto occasionally coarsens Puccini's score – as in the crude crescendo in the closing bars of Act 3 – but he directs with energy. The stereo transcription captures the voices well and the tape transfer is of very high quality. The comparatively restricted dynamic range means that the singers appear to be 'front stage', but there is no lack of light and shade in Act 2. The orchestra sounds full and warm, and the voices are clearly and vividly caught.

On the newest HMV set, conducted by James Levine, Alfredo Kraus's relatively light tenor sets the pattern at the very start for a performance that is strong on comedy. One registers the exchanges more sharply than usual on record, and though Kraus (no longer so sweet of timbre as he was) tends to overpoint in the big arias, it is a stylish performance. Scotto – who first recorded the role of Mimi for DG in 1962 – is not flatteringly recorded here, for the rawness and unevenness which affect her voice at the top of the stave are distracting, marring an affectionate portrait. Milnes makes a powerful Marcello and Neblett a strong Musetta, a natural Minnie in *Fanciulla* transformed into a soubrette. Levine, brilliant in the comic writing of Acts 1 and 4, sounds less at home in the big melodies. The recording has wide range but lacks a little in stage atmosphere. The tape transfer reflects the LP sound faithfully and is both rich and well focused. It is a pity there had to be a turnover for the last few minutes of Act 1; on cassette the avoidance of such breaks should be taken for granted. The libretto provided with the cassette box also earns a black mark for its small print and not very dark registration.

As in *Tosca*, Sir Colin Davis here takes a direct view of Puccini, presenting the score very straight, with no exaggerations. The result is refreshing but rather lacks wit and sparkle; pauses and hesitations are curtailed. Ricciarelli's is the finest performance vocally, and Davis allows her more freedom than the others. *Sì, mi chiamano Mimì* is full of fine detail and most affecting. Carreras gives a good generalized performance, wanting in detail and in intensity and rather failing to rise to the big moments. Wixell makes an unidiomatic Marcello, rather lacking in fun, and Robert Lloyd's bass sounds lightweight as Colline. Ashley Putnam makes a charming Musetta, and the recording quality is typically refined. The cassette transfer is acceptable but less sharply focused than the discs.

Edgar (complete).
** CBS 79213 (2) [Col. M2 34584]. Scotto, Bergonzi, Sardinero, Killebrew, NY Schola Cantorum and Op. O., Queler.

'What is wanted is a subject which palpitates with life and is believable', wrote Puccini after one performance of *Edgar*, his second opera, a work which, as we can see now, took him in the wrong direction, away from realism towards this medieval fantasy in which the knightly hero has to choose between the loves of the symbolically named Fidelia and Tigrana (a Carmen figure without the sparkle). The motivation was made even less convincing by the cutting which Puccini carried out in later editions; but, as this recording makes plain, there is much to enjoy. The melodies are not quite vintage Puccini, but Scotto as Fidelia, Killebrew as Tigrana and Bergonzi as Edgar give them compelling warmth. Eve Queler proves a variably convincing conductor, with Act 3 in need of more rehearsal. But this set, edited from live performances at Carnegie Hall and commendably well recorded, makes a welcome stopgap.

La Fanciulla del West (*The Girl of the Golden West;* complete).
⊛ *** DG 2709 078/*3371 031* (3) [id.]. Neblett, Domingo, Milnes, Howell, ROHCG Ch. and O., Mehta.

Like *Madama Butterfly*, 'The Girl', as Puccini called it in his correspondence, was based on a play by the American David Belasco. The composer wrote the work with all his usual care for detailed planning, both of libretto and of music. In idiom the music marks the halfway stage between *Butterfly* and *Turandot*, and the first audience must have been astonished at the opening of an Italian opera dependent on the whole-tone scale in a way Debussy would have recognized as akin to his own practice. Nevertheless it produces an effect wildly un-Debussian and entirely Puccinian. DG took the opportunity of recording the opera when Covent Garden was staging a spectacular production in 1977. With one exception the cast remained the same as in the theatre and, as so often in such associated projects, the cohesion of the performance in the recording is enormously intensified. The result is magnificent, underlining the point that – whatever doubts may remain over the subject, with its weeping goldminers – Puccini's score is masterly, culminating in a happy ending which brings one of the most telling emotional coups that he ever achieved.

Mehta's manner – as he makes clear at the very start – is on the brisk side, not just in the cakewalk rhythms but even in refusing to let the first great melody, the nostalgic *Che faranno i viecchi miei*, linger into sentimentality. Mehta's tautness then consistently makes up for intrinsic dramatic weaknesses (as, for example, the delayed entries of both heroine and hero in the first act). Sherrill Milnes as Jack Rance was the newcomer to the cast for the recording, and he makes the villain into far more than a small-town Scarpia, giving nobility and understand-

. ing to the first-act *arioso*. Domingo, as in the theatre, sings heroically, disappointing only in his reluctance to produce soft tone in the great aria *Ch'ella mi creda*. The rest of the Covent Garden team is excellent, not least Gwynne Howell as the minstrel who sings *Che faranno i viecchi miei*; but the crowning glory of a masterly set is the singing of Carol Neblett as the Girl of the Golden West herself, gloriously rich and true and with formidable attack on the exposed high notes. Rich atmospheric recording to match, essential in an opera full of evocative offstage effects. These very distant effects have only fractionally less sharpness of focus on tape than on disc, and this is one of DG's very finest opera recordings in this medium.

Madama Butterfly (complete).
*** CBS 79313/40- (3) [Col. M3 35181].
  Scotto, Domingo, Knight, Wixell, Amb. Op. Ch., Philh. O., Maazel.
(M) **(*) HMV SLS/*TC-SLS* 5128 (3) [Ang. S/*4X3S* 3604]. Los Angeles, Bjoerling, Pirazzini, Sereni, Rome Op. Ch. and O., Santini.
(M) **(*) HMV SLS/*TC-SLS* 5015 (3). Callas, Gedda, Borriello, Danieli, Ch. and O. of La Scala, Milan, Karajan.

Eleven years after her recording with Barbirolli (HMV SLS 927 [Ang. S 3702]), Renata Scotto recorded this role again with Maazel, and the years brought nothing but benefit. The voice – always inclined to spread a little on top at climaxes – had acquired extra richness and was recorded with a warmer tonal bloom. In perception too Scotto's singing is far deeper, most strikingly in Butterfly's *Un bel dì*, where the narrative leads to special intensity on the words *Chiamerà Butterfly dalla lontana*. Maazel is warmly expressive without losing his architectural sense; he has not quite the imaginative individuality of a Karajan or a Barbirolli, but this is both powerful and unsentimental, with a fine feeling for

Puccini's subtle orchestration. Other contributors are incidental, even Placido Domingo, who sings heroically as Pinkerton but arguably makes him too genuine a character for such a cad. Wixell's voice is not ideally rounded as Sharpless, but he sings most sensitively, and Gillian Knight makes an expressive Suzuki. Among the others Malcolm King as the Bonze is outstanding in a good team. The recording is rich and warm without having the bloom of Karajan's Decca set (see below), and the voices are balanced relatively, though not uncomfortably, close. The cassette transfer, however, while clear and immediate, is disappointingly lacking in warmth and cannot compare with the discs.

In the late fifties and early sixties Victoria de los Angeles was incomparable in the role of Butterfly, and her 1960 recording displays her art at its most endearing, her range of golden tone colour lovingly exploited, with the voice well recorded for the period, though rather close. Opposite her Jussi Bjoerling was making one of his very last recordings, and though he shows few special insights, he produces a flow of rich tone to compare with that of the heroine. Mario Sereni is a full-voiced Sharpless, but Miriam Pirazzini a disappointingly wobbly Suzuki, while Santini is a reliable, generally rather square and unimaginative conductor who rarely gets in the way. With recording quality very acceptable this is an excellent mid-priced recommendation. There is a tiny accidental cut at the start of the suicide aria, eliminating three of the heroine's cries of *Tu!* The cassette transfer is excellent, clear in detail yet with plenty of body.

The idea of the flashing-eyed Maria Callas playing the role of the fifteen-year-old Butterfly may not sound convincing, and certainly this performance will not satisfy those who insist that Puccini's heroine is a totally sweet and innocent character. But Callas's view, aided by superbly imaginative and spacious conducting from Karajan, gives extra dimension to the Puccinian little woman, and with some keenly intelligent singing too from Gedda as Pinkerton (a less caddish and more thoughtful character than usual) this is a set which has a special compulsion. The mono recording has been given a useful face-lift in this stereo transcription. On tape there is a more noticeable lack of range than on disc, and the choral climaxes lack definition.

Still recommended: First choice (on both disc and tape) remains with the resplendently recorded Karajan Decca set with Freni and Pavarotti (SET 584/6/*K 2 A 1* [Lon. 13110/5-]). Karajan inspires singers and the Vienna Philharmonic Orchestra to a radiant performance which brings out all the beauty and intensity of Puccini's score, sweet but not sentimental, powerfully dramatic but not vulgar.

Madama Butterfly: highlights.
(M) **(*) HMV SXLP/*TC-SXLP* 30306 [Ang. S/*4XS* 35821] (from above set cond. Santini).
(M) **(*) Decca Jub. JB/*KJBC* 32 [Lon. 25084/5-]. Tebaldi, Bergonzi, Cossotto, Ch. and O. of St Cecilia Ac., Serafin.

The well-chosen selection from the warmly compelling HMV set is most welcome. For a generation De Los Angeles was the most tenderly affecting of Butterflies, golden-toned; and Bjoerling plainly enjoyed this late trip to the recording studio. The recording is good for its late-fifties vintage, although there are a couple of uncomfortably quick cut-offs at the end of excerpts. The cassette transfer is lively, though the voices show a touch of harshness at climaxes.

There are many fine moments too in Tebaldi's performance, even if here she rarely shows the creative insight of characterization that Freni and Scotto bring to the part. Yet vocally this recording was one of Tebaldi's finest achievements. Few

sopranos can float a soft note with such apparent ease, and her rich creamy tone is often all-enveloping in its beauty. The recording is vivid on both disc and tape, though its age is betrayed by the sound of the upper strings.

Manon Lescaut (complete).
(M) (***) HMV mono RLS/*TC-RLS* 737. Callas, Di Stefano, Fioravanti, Ch. and O. of La Scala, Milan, Serafin.

First choice for *Manon Lescaut* in stereo remains with the HMV recording conducted by Bartoletti, with Caballé as Manon and Placido Domingo singing strongly and sensitively as her lover, Des Grieux (SLS 962 [Ang. S 3782]), but the early La Scala mono set partnering Callas and Di Stefano has even more individuality and dramatic power. It is typical of Callas that she turns the final scene – which usually seems an excrescence, a mere epilogue after the real drama – into the most compelling part of the opera. Serafin, who could be a lethargic recording conductor, is here electrifying, and Di Stefano too is inspired to one of his finest complete opera recordings. The cast list even includes the young Fiorenza Cossotto, impressive as the singer in the Act 2 madrigal. The recording – still in mono, not stereo transcription – minimizes the original boxiness and gives good detail. The cassettes are well transferred and match the discs closely.

Suor Angelica (complete).
**(*) Decca SET/*KCET* 627 [Lon. 1173/5-]. Sutherland, Ludwig, Collins, London Op. Ch., Finchley Children's Music Group, Nat. PO, Bonynge.

Puccini's atmospheric picture of a convent is superbly captured here, with sound of spectacular depth. Bonynge's direction is most persuasive, and Dame Joan Sutherland rises superbly to the big dramatic demands of the final scenes. With Sutherland, Angelica is in no sense a 'little woman' or even an inexperienced girl, but a formidable match for the implacable Zia Principessa, here superbly taken by Christa Ludwig, detailed and unexaggerated in her characterization. The supporting cast is outstanding, and the pity is that Sutherland did not record the piece rather earlier, before the beat developed in her voice. The first offstage entry and opening scene catch it rather distractingly. The cassette transfer is first-class.

Il Tabarro (complete).

** CBS 76641 [Col. M 34570]. Scotto, Domingo, Wixell, Amb. Op. Ch., Nat. PO, Maazel.

Maazel takes a characteristically direct view of Puccini's evocative score, concentrating less on atmospheric effects (in which it abounds) than on musical cogency. The result may initially be a shade disconcerting, but need not deter anyone who wants to hear Scotto and Domingo in this music; both of them are very powerful, even if Domingo's voice is less flatteringly recorded (rather close) than in his RCA set under Leinsdorf, now deleted. The snag is Wixell's portrait of the cuckolded bargemaster, thoughtful and intelligent, full of detail, but lacking the tragic bite and earthiness essential if the murder is to carry conviction. The supporting singers are a good team, and the recording is bright and forward.

Tosca (complete).

⊛(M)(***) HMV SLS/TC-SLS 825 (2). Callas, Di Stefano, Gobbi, Calabrese, Ch. and O. of La Scala, Milan, De Sabata.

*** DG 2707 121/3370 033 (2) [id.]. Ricciarelli, Carreras, Raimondi, Corena, German Op. Ch., Berlin PO, Karajan.

(M) *** RCA Gold GL 20105 (2) [ARL 2/ARK 2 0105]. Price, Domingo, Milnes, John Alldis Ch., Wandsworth School Boys' Ch., New Philh. O., Mehta.

**(*) HMV Dig. SLS/TCC-SLS 5213 (2). Scotto, Domingo, Bruson, Amb. Op. Ch., St Clement Danes School Boys' Ch., Philh. O., Levine.

** Decca D 134 D 2/K 134 K 22 (2) [Lon. 12113/5-]. Freni, Pavarotti, Milnes, Wandsworth School Boys' Ch., L. Op. Ch., Nat. PO, Rescigno.

There has never been a finer recorded performance of Tosca than Callas's first, with Victor de Sabata conducting and Tito Gobbi as Scarpia. One mentions the prima donna first because in this of all roles she was able to identify totally with the heroine, and turn her into a great tragic figure, not merely the cipher of Sardou's original melodrama. Gobbi too makes the unbelievably villainous police chief into a genuinely three-dimensional character, and Di Stefano as the hero, Cavaradossi, was at his finest. The conducting of de Sabata is spaciously lyrical as well as sharply dramatic, and though the recording (originally mono, here stereo transcription) is obviously limited, it is superbly balanced in Walter Legge's fine production. The cassette transfer too is very successful, vivid and atmospheric. In both media the ear can easily forget the mono source.

Karajan's superbly unified reading presents Tosca as very grand opera indeed, melodrama at its most searingly powerful. For Karajan the police chief, Scarpia, seems to be the central character, and his unexpected choice of singer, a full bass, Raimondi, helps to show why, for this is no small-time villain but a man who in full confidence has a vein of nobility in him – as in the Te Deum at end of Act 1 or the closing passage of the big solo addressed to Tosca, Già mi dicon venal. Detailed illumination of words is most powerful, and Karajan's coaching is evident too in the contribution of Katia Ricciarelli – another singer who had not taken the role on stage before the recording. She is not the most individual of Toscas but the beauty of singing is consistent, with Vissi d'arte outstanding at a very slow tempo indeed. Carreras is also subjected to slow Karajan tempi in his big arias, and though the recording brings out an unevenness in the voice (this is not as sweet a sound as in the performance he recorded with Colin Davis for Philips), it is still a powerful, stylish one. The recording is rich and full, with the stage picture clearly established and the glorious orchestral textures beautifully caught. The difference between discs and tapes is only marginal (the discs are fractionally sharper in focus).

Leontyne Price made her RCA recording of *Tosca* ten years after her 1963 Decca set (5BB 123/4/*K 59 K 22* [Lon. 1284/5-]). The interpretation remained remarkably consistent, a shade tougher in the chest register – the great entry in Act 3 is a magnificent moment – a little more clipped of phrase. That last modification may reflect the relative manners of the two conductors, Karajan on Decca more individual in his refined expressiveness, Mehta on RCA more thrustful. On balance, taking Price alone, the preference is for the earlier set, which still sounds splendidly vivid on disc or cassette. But Mehta has even more modern recording (no more refined than the earlier one) and his set boasts a spectacular cast, with the team of Domingo and Milnes at its most impressive. At medium price this reissue is very competitive.

With extreme speeds, both fast and slow, and fine playing from the Philharmonia Orchestra, Levine directs a red-blooded performance which underlines the melodrama. Domingo here reinforces his claim to be the finest Cavaradossi today, while the clean-cut, incisive singing of Renato Bruson presents a powerful if rather young-sounding Scarpia. Renata Scotto's voice is in many ways ideally suited to the role of Tosca, certainly in its timbre and colouring; but as caught on record the upper register is often squally, though not so distressingly so as in some other recent records. The digital recording is full and forward.

The action of the drama is superbly caught in the vividly recorded Decca version under Nicola Rescigno. The three principals were originally lined up for a Karajan recording on Decca, but plans turned in other directions. Pavarotti is a bright-eyed Cavaradossi, but it is only in Act 3 that the voice acquires its full magic. As Tosca, Freni sounds rather taxed, so that even *Vissi d'arte* produces her stressed tone rather than even, lyrical sound. Milnes as Scarpia gives a fresh, direct performance, with words finely enunciated, a fine characterization. The big snag is Rescigno's conducting, for his control of rubato sounds forced and unspontaneous, strange from an Italian conductor. The Decca cassettes offer demonstration quality: the projection of voices and orchestra is superbly vivid, with the *Te Deum* scene memorable in its amplitude and impact.

Tosca: highlights.
(M) *** Ph. Fest. 6570/*7310* 158. Caballé, Carreras, Wixell, Ramey, ROHCG Ch. and O., Colin Davis.
** Decca SXL/*KSXC* 6984 (from above set cond. Rescigno).
** DG 2537/*3306* 044. Vishnevskaya, Bonisolli, Manuguerra, Fr. Nat. O. and Ch., Rostropovich.

An excellent selection from the Davis set, with both Caballé and Carreras at the height of their vocal powers and Wixell a credible Scarpia. The recording is excellent, the cassette matching the disc: the *Te Deum* and the execution scene are given a splendid sense of spectacle.

The generous selection from Rescigno's set reflects its qualities, including the vivid recording, and will be useful for those wanting a sampler of Pavarotti's assumption of the role of Cavaradossi.

The selection from the Rostropovich set moves straight from *Vissi d'arte* to *E lucevan le stelle*, omitting the electrifying scene where Scarpia is murdered, which is the dramatic highlight of this particular recording. Otherwise this is a fair disc. The cassette has generally less immediacy.

Il Trittico: (i) *Il Tabarro;* (ii) *Suor Angelica;* (iii) *Gianni Schicchi.*
(*) CBS 79312 (3) [Col. M3 35912]. Maazel, (i; ii) Scotto, (i; iii) Domingo, (i) Wixell, Sénéchal, (ii) Horne, (ii; iii) Cotrubas, (iii) Gobbi, Amb. Op. Ch., (ii) Desborough School Ch., (i; ii) Nat. PO, (iii) LSO.

Hearing Maazel's performances of the three *Trittico* operas together underlines his consistency. *Il Tabarro* may most seriously lack atmosphere, but his directness is certainly refreshing, and in the other two operas it results in powerful reading; the opening of *Gianni Schicchi,* for example, has a sharp, almost Stravinskian bite. In the first two operas, Scotto's performances have a commanding dominance, presenting her at her finest. In *Gianni Schicchi* the veteran Tito Gobbi gives an amazing performance, in almost every way as fine as his HMV recording of twenty years earlier – and in some ways this is even more compelling. The generally close recording has a pleasantly full range.

Le Villi: complete.
*** CBS 76890 [Col. M/*MT* 36669]. Scotto, Domingo, Nucci, Gobbi, Amb. Op. Ch., Nat. PO, Maazel.
*(*) Chan. ABR/*ABT* 1019. Richardson, Parker, Christiansen, Adelaide Festival Chorale, Corinthian Singers, Fredman.

Maazel directs a performance so commanding, with singing of outstanding quality, that one can at last assess Puccini's first opera on quite a new level. Its weaknesses have always been the feeble, oversimplified story and the cardboard characterization. With such concentration, and with musical qualities emphasized, the weaknesses are mini-mized, and the result is richly enjoyable. Puccini's melodies may be less distinctive here than they later became, but one can readily appreciate the impact they had on early audiences, not to mention Puccini's publisher-to-be, Giulio Ricordi. Scotto's voice tends to spread a little at the top of the stave, but like Domingo she gives a powerful performance, and Leo Nucci as the hero's father avoids false histrionics. A delightful bonus is Tito Gobbi's contribution reciting the verses which link the scenes; he is as characterful a reciter as he is a singer. The recording is one of CBS's best.

The Chandos version cannot compare with the CBS, though John Culshaw's production brings with it sound even clearer and more brilliant. The conducting is persuasive but at times languid, and the spoken verses between the scenes are omitted. None of the soloists, as recorded, is of full international standard. The cassette transfer is vividly full-blooded, although the overall range is not as refined as the disc and on side two of the review copy there were patches of discoloration in the woodwind. A folded libretto is provided which does not fit inside the cassette case.

Arias: *La Bohème: Sì, mi chiamano Mimì; Donde lieta uscì. La Fanciulla del West: Laggiù nel Soledad. Gianni Schicchi: O mio babbino caro. Madama Butterfly: Un bel dì; Con onor muore. Manon Lescaut: In quelle trine morbide; Sola, perduta. La Rondine: Sogno di Doretta. Suor Angelica: Senza Mamma. Tosca: Vissi d'arte. Turandot: Signore, ascolta!; In questa reggia; Tu che di gel sei cinta.*
(M) *** Decca GRV 3. Tebaldi.

It was understandable that Decca should choose a Puccini recital to represent Tebaldi in their *Grand voci* series, for in this repertoire her glorious voice with its creamy richness of tone is consistently telling. Hearing a series of arias like this (recorded between 1958 and 1965, mostly taken from complete sets, and very well edited) reminds the listener that characterization was not her strong point. The assumption of both soprano roles in *Turandot* brings primarily a contrast of drama and lyricism, although she identifies most readily with Liù, as she does with Manon and Mimì, producing ravishing phrases and engaging the listener's sympathy with her natural warmth. She was never finer on record than in *Butterfly*, and *Con onor muore* makes a powerful impact. The sound is consistently vivid and generally kind to the voice itself.

Arias: *La Bohème:* (i) *Che gelida manina;* (ii) *Sì, mi chiamano Mimì;* (iii) *Musetta's waltz song.* (iv) *La Fanciulla del West: Ch'ella mi creda.* (v) *Gianni Schicchi: O mio babbino caro. Madama Butterfly: Un bel dì.* (i) *Manon Lescaut: Donna non vidi mai.* (vi) *Tosca: Recondita armonia;* (vii) *Vissi d'arte;* (vi) *E lucevan le stelle. Turandot:* (viii) *In questa reggia;* (ix) *Nessun dorma.*
(M) **(*) Decca SPA/KCSP 574. (i) Bergonzi, (ii) Chiara, (iii) Zeani, (iv) Bjoerling, (v) Weathers, (vi) Di Stefano, (vii) Cerquetti, (viii) Tebaldi, (ix) Prevedi.

Highlights here are Felicia Weathers's contributions (a vibrant *One fine day* and a characterful *Oh my beloved father*) and Maria Chiara's ravishing *Sì, mi chiamano Mimì.* Bergonzi's *Che gelida manina* is very effective too; otherwise this is a stock anthology, and neither Jussi Bjoerling nor Tebaldi are heard at their very best. The recording is characteristically vivid on both disc and cassette.

'Famous operatic duets': La Bohème: (i; ii) *O soave fanciulla;* (ii; iii) *O Mimì, tu più non torni. Madama Butterfly:* (i; ii) *Love duet;* (i; iv) *Flower duet. Tosca:* (i; v) *Mario, Mario!*
(M) **(*) Decca SPA/KCSP 496. (i) Tebaldi, (ii) Bergonzi, (iii) Bastianini, (iv) Cossotto, (v) Del Monaco – VERDI: *La Forza del destino* excerpt. **(*)

Although it opens with *Solenne in quest'ora* from Verdi's *Forza del destino*, this is primarily a collection based on the Tebaldi recordings of the three key Puccini operas. Decca are understandably proud of these recordings, and indeed most of the excerpts are already available in other anthologies. However, the present rejigging works well enough; the voices have admirable presence and freshness, and the age of the recordings shows only in the string tone. The one small snag is that the final item – the *Flower duet* from *Madama Butterfly* – ends cadentially in the air, and makes an unsatisfactory close to the recital. This could surely have been avoided by rearrangement of the excerpts.

Punto, Giovanni (1748–1803)

Horn concertos Nos. 5 in F; 6 in E flat; 10 in F; 11 in E.
⊛ *** HMV ASD 4008 [Ang. SZ 37781]. Tuckwell, ASMF, Marriner.

Giovanni Punto was a Bohemian, born a serf on the estate of Count Johann von Thun. In early youth he showed such a prodigious talent on the horn that the Count was willing to finance his studies in Prague, Dresden and Munich with the finest players of the day. Punto returned a great virtuoso in his own right, but after serving as a court musician for a period he became restless and escaped bondage (being unsuccessfully pursued by troops with orders to knock out his teeth when he was captured!) His reputation spread throughout Europe; Mozart composed his *Sinfonia concertante*, K.297b, with Punto in mind, and Beethoven wrote the *Horn sonata*, Op. 17, for him. This disc shows a successful and highly cultivated composer, and the four concertos recorded here are most engaging if eclectic in style. Interestingly they establish the three most effective keys in which the horn was to make its reputation as a solo instrument during the nineteenth century. The music itself is fluent and tuneful, demonstrating the tasteful elegance for which Punto's playing was famous. The finale of No. 5 bristles with bravura (Tuckwell here in his element) but, as in the florid minuet variations which form the finale of No. 11, the writing avoids empty note-spinning. No. 6 is a splendid work, Mozartian in feeling and line, with a fine, eloquent *Adagio* and a delightful rondo finale. The *Tenth* has a Hummelian opening movement, with an attractive dotted main theme (the playing of the ASMF under Marriner presents it with memorable grace) and a catchy finale that could readily become famous.

This record was issued to celebrate the fiftieth birthday of Barry Tuckwell, one of the great horn virtuosi of our own time, and it is fully worthy of the occasion. The solo playing is warmly eloquent and excitingly secure; the accompaniments are as stylish as they are sympathetic. The recording is of outstanding demonstration quality; the horn, understandably, is balanced a little forward, but there is splendid presence and life overall.

Purcell, Henry (1658–95)

Chacony in G min.; Fantasia in three parts on a ground in D; 5 Pavans; Trio sonata for violin, viola da gamba and organ.
*** O-L DSLO 514. AcAM, Hogwood – *Elegies*.***

Fantasia (Chaconne) in three parts on a ground in D; Overtures in D min. and G min.; Pavans in A min. and B; Pavan of four parts in G min.; Sonata in A min.; Suite in G: Overture. Keyboard pieces: *Ground in D min.; New Ground in E min.; Sefauchi's farewell in D min.; Suite in D.*
(M) *** Tel. AQ6/CQ4 41222. Leonhardt Cons., Leonhardt.

The outstanding Leonhardt anthology, with harpsichord solos interpolated between the consort pieces to bring variety of texture, sounds as fresh today as when it was originally issued at the end of the sixties. The Dutch ensemble gets right inside the spirit of Purcell's music, playing with taste and finesse. The *Fantasia on a ground* is a brilliant work exploiting the special sound of three violins over a repeated bass motive. The performances throughout balance expressive qualities with sparkle, and Leonhardt's interpretation of the harpsichord pieces leaves little to be desired. The stereo sound is full and lively, and the cassette offers demonstration quality in its crisp clarity.

The Academy of Ancient Music also offer first-class performances, with a slightly more abrasive style. On original instruments the sharpness of Purcell's inspiration comes over very compellingly, though the Academy tends to prefer tempi faster than one might expect. The *Chacony* is well-known, and the set of five *Pavans* also contains much splendid music. The full, bright recording captures the impact of the playing, as at the dramatic start of the four-part *Pavan in G minor* (also included in Leonhardt's collection).

15 Fantasias for viols.
*** DG Arc. 2533 366 [id.]. Ulsamer Collegium.

The Purcell *Fantasias* are among the most searching and profound works in all music, and their neglect by the gramophone – and the public – is quite unaccountable. The Ulsamer Collegium do not shrink from investing them with an expressive eloquence that does not seem one whit out of place or out of period, and play with a warmth that is welcome. Extraordinary though it may be, this is the only complete set of these masterpieces currently available. Fortunately, it is beautifully played and recorded, and no one who cares about English music – or indeed any music – can afford to pass this record by.

Overtures: Abdelazer; Bonduca; Dido and Aeneas; Distressed Innocence; The Fairy Queen; The Indian Queen; King Arthur; The Married Beau; The Old Bachelor; The Rival Sisters; Timon of Athens.
**(*) Chan. ABR/*ABT* 1026. Bournemouth Sinf., Thomas.

It was a good idea to collect Purcell overtures on a single disc, and Ronald Thomas directs lively performances, well recorded. His editing makes for varied repeats in some of the overtures, and the range of expression comes out well, not just a matter of extrovert energy but of heartfelt chromatic writing in adagios (as in *Bonduca*). The cassette offers uneven quality. Side one, which includes *Bonduca*, *The Fairy Queen*, *Dido and Aeneas*, *King Arthur* and *The Married Beau*, is transferred at a high level and offers the most vivid quality, with regal trumpets; on side two, the level drops and the sound becomes disappointingly recessed.

Harpsichord suites Nos. 1–8.
*** DG Arc. 2533 415 [id.]. Tilney (spinet).

Harpsichord suites Nos. 1–8. 2 Grounds in C min.; Lessons (suite);

Musick's Handmaid, Part 2: 18 Pieces. 2 Trumpet tunes. Airs: *Canary; Gavottes; Grounds; Hornpipe; Jig; Minuet; Prelude (from Suite No. 4); Round.*
(M) *** Saga 5458/9. Woolley (harpsichord).

Robert Woolley is a young player, still in his mid-twenties. He plays copies of two eighteenth-century instruments by Benjamin Slade and his pupil Thomas Hitchcock, both of which sound well; they are not recorded at too deafening a level and produce crisp yet full-bodied sound. The playing itself is vital and far from unimaginative, and Woolley can hold his own against senior and better-known rivals. His two records include some music that is not otherwise available, which makes them even more competitive.

Colin Tilney, who uses a spinet dating from the end of the seventeenth century, is in excellent form. His record is full-price, but both sound and documentation are of high quality, and the playing is extremely fine. Choice between Tilney and Woolley rests on whether you want the additional pieces at the small extra outlay involved. Robert Woolley's playing is delightfully fresh.

MISCELLANEOUS
VOCAL MUSIC

Ayres: *Awake, awake, ye dead! (Hymn for Day of Judgement). Birthday ode for Queen Mary: Strike the Viol. Diocletian: Chaconne. Elegy on the death of Queen Mary. Evening hymn. The Fairy Queen: One charming night. How pleasant is this flowery plain (ode). If ever I more riches (cantata): Here let my life. The Indian Queen: Why should men quarrel. King Arthur: Shepherd, shepherd, leave decoying. King Richard II: Retir'd*

*from any mortal's sight. The Old
Bachelor: Thus to a ripe consenting
maid. There ne'er was so wretched a
lover as I* (duet). *Timon of Athens:
Hark how the songsters.*
(M) **(*) HM HMU 214. Deller Cons.
and Ens., Deller.

Deller here put together what you
might regard as a sampler of Purcell's
vocal music, a varied collection which
includes some of his most beautiful inspirations. Lively performances and fair
recording.

*Benedicite; I Was Glad; Jehova,
quam multi sunt hostes. Voluntary for
double organ.*
** Mer. E 77013. Ely Cath. Ch., Wills
(organ) – BLOW: *Collection.***

Coupled with motets and voluntaries
by Purcell's mentor Blow, these magnificent motets are given heartfelt performances under Arthur Wills, not as
polished as some but very enjoyable. The
Organ voluntary too (though it may not
be by Purcell) is well worth having on
disc.

Blow up the Trumpet (anthem);
*Psalms Nos. 80, O Lord God of hosts;
89, My song shall be alway; 102,
Hear my prayer;* (i) *106, O give
thanks. O, Solitude* (arioso).
(M) *** HM HM 247. Deller Cons.,
Deller, (i) with string ens.

As well as a group of fine anthems, vigorously sung by the Deller
Consort, this excellent record has a valuable rarity in *O, Solitude,* a long arioso
over ground bass set to a religious text.
This inspires Deller to one of his finest
performances on record, restrained but
moving. The setting of *Psalm 89* too is
a solo piece providing textural contrast. The recording is clear if a little
hard.

Songs: *Come, let us drink; A health
to the nut brown lass; If ever I more
riches; I gave her cakes and I gave her
ale; Laudate Ceciliam; The miller's
daughter; Of all the instruments;
Once, twice, thrice I Julia tried; Prithee ben't so sad and serious; Since
time so kind to us does prove; Sir
Walter enjoying his damsel; 'Tis
women makes us love; Under this
stone; Young John the gard'ner.*
(M) **(*) HM HM 242. Deller Cons.,
Deller.

One side of this charming and stylish
disc has a selection of Purcell's catches,
some of them as lewd as rugby-club songs
of today, others as refined as *Under this
stone* – all of which the Deller Consort
take in their stride. The two final pieces
are extended items; *If ever I more riches,*
a setting of Cowley, has some striking
passages. The voices are not always perfectly caught, but the recording of the
instruments is first-rate.

*Come, ye Sons of Art; Funeral music
for Queen Mary* (1695).
*** Erato STU 70911. Lott, Brett, Williams, Allen, Monteverdi Ch. and O.,
Equale Brass Ens., Gardiner.

Come, ye Sons of Art, the most celebrated of Purcell's birthday odes for
Queen Mary, is splendidly coupled here
with the unforgettable funeral music he
wrote on the death of the same monarch.
With the Monteverdi Choir at its most
incisive and understanding, the performances are exemplary, and the recording,
though balanced in favour of the instruments, is clear and refined. Among the
soloists Thomas Allen is outstanding,
while the two counter-tenors give a
charming performance of the duet *Sound
the trumpet.* The *Funeral music* includes
the well-known *Solemn march* for trumpets and drums, a *Canzona* and simple
anthem given at the funeral, and two of

Purcell's most magnificent anthems setting the *Funeral sentences.*

3 Elegies (*On the death of John Playford; On the death of Matthew Locke; On the death of Thomas Farmer*).
*** O-L DSLO 514. Hill, Keyte, AcAM, Hogwood – *Chacony* etc.***

The three *Elegies*, each written on the death of a friend and colleague, are particularly fine, and the performances here are first-rate, with eloquent soloists in Martyn Hill and Christopher Keyte.

Songs: *Evening hymn: Fairest isle; From rosy bow'rs; I attempt from love's sickness to fly; If music be the food of love; Music for a while; Not all my torments; O lead me to some peaceful gloom; The plaint; Retired from any mortal's sight; Since from my dear Astrea's sight; Sweeter than roses; Thrice happy lovers.*
(M) *** HM HM 249. Deller.

In one of his last records before his untimely death, Deller here collected solo items suitable for counter-tenor and gave characteristically expressive performances, his voice amazingly well-preserved, more distinctive than any successor. The recording is first-rate.

In Guilty Night (*Saul and the Witch of Endor*); **Man that is Born of Woman** (*Funeral sentences*); **Te Deum and Jubilate in D.**
(M) **(*) HM HM 207. Deller Cons., Stour Music Festival Ch. and O., Deller.

In Guilty Night is a remarkable dramatic scena depicting Saul's meeting with the Witch of Endor. The florid writing is admirably and often excitingly sung by Alfred Deller himself as the King and Honor Sheppard as the Witch. The *Te*

Deum and Jubilate are among Purcell's last and most ambitious choral works; the *Funeral sentences* from early in his career are in some ways even finer in their polyphonic richness. The chorus here is not the most refined on record, but with sensitive direction this attractive collection is well worth hearing. The recording is fair.

Love's Goddess sure (*Ode for the birthday of Queen Mary*); **Ode on St Cecilia's Day** (*Welcome to all the pleasures*).
** HM HMU 222. Deller Cons., Stour Music Festival CO, Deller.

These odes make an attractive coupling, two works which in spite of doggerel texts yet inspired Purcell to some striking and memorable ideas, as for example the duet for two counter-tenors, *Sweetness of nature*, in the St Cecilia Ode. The performances are not ideal, with rhythms a little heavy, and the recording is limited, though quite acceptable if you fancy this coupling.

Anthems: *O Lord, rebuke me not; Praise the Lord, O Jerusalem; Praise the Lord, O my soul; Save me, O God; Why do the heathen.*
(M) **(*) HM HMU 223. Deller Cons., Instrumental Ens., Deller.

Deller and his choir here give five verse anthems, products of Purcell's last years, two with organ accompaniment merely, three with strings and continuo also. Most striking is *Praise the Lord, O Jerusalem*. The singing here is fresh and alert if not always impeccably tuned, and the recording is atmospheric enough.

(i) **Te Deum in D;** (ii) **Yorkshire Feast.**
*** CBS 76925/40-. Esswood, Partridge, St Martin's, Warwick, Ch., Pro Cantione Antiqua, Gr. Écurie, Malgoire,

with (i) Beverley, Grenat, Brett, (ii) Georges.

The poet D'Urfey said that Purcell's *Yorkshire Feast* of 1690 was 'one of the finest compositions he ever made and cost £100 the performing'. More modern commentators have been less enthusiastic, but Malgoire with his vigorous performing style confirms that any inadequacy tends to be in the paltry words rather than the music. This is a fine rarity to set against the *Te Deum in D*, also given with sharp focus and fine panache. The recording is first-rate, but the cassette, with generally poor-quality sound and discoloured trumpet timbre, is not recommended.

STAGE WORKS

Amphitryon or The Two Sosias: Overture and suite; The Old Bachelor: Overture and suite; The Virtuous Wife or Good Luck at Last: Overture and suite.
*** O-L DSLO 550. AcAM, Hogwood.

Purcell wrote some of his most attractive music for plays now long-forgotten, and the pieces revived here from three such Restoration entertainments make a delightful collection, refreshingly if abrasively played on original instruments. The overtures are the most extended of the pieces and the most valuable, but the slow numbers in particular are also very fine. The songs are sung very stylishly by Judith Nelson, Martyn Hill and Christopher Keyte, and the recording is excellent.

Bonduca: Overture and suite. Circe: suite. Sir Anthony Love: Overture and suite.
**(*) O-L DSLO 527. Nelson, Lane, Lloyd, Bowman, Hill, Elliott, Byers, Bamber, Keyte, Taverner Choir, AcAM, Hogwood.

Purcell's theatre music, virtually buried along with the plays for which it was written, comes up with wonderful freshness in these performances using authentic instruments. As well as the charming dances and overtures, this disc contains songs and more extended scenas with soloists and chorus, which provide the meatiest items. Tastes may differ on style of baroque performances, but the vigour of Hogwood and his team is hard to resist. Excellent recording.

Dido and Aeneas (complete).
*** Decca SET/*KCET* 615 [Lon. 1170/ 5-]. Baker, Pears, Burrowes, Reynolds, London Op. Ch., Aldeburgh Festival Strings, Bedford.
*** Chan. ABR/*ABT* 1034. Kirkby, Nelson, Thomas, Taverner Ch. and Players, Parrott.
(M) **(*) DG Arc. Priv. 2547/*3347* 032. Troyanos, Armstrong, Johnson, McDaniel, Hamburg Monteverdi Ch., N. German R. CO, Mackerras.
(B) ** CfP CFP/*TC-CFP* 40359 [Ang. 36359]. Los Angeles, Harper, Johnson, Glossop, Amb. S., ECO, Barbirolli.
** Erato STU 71091. Troyanos, Stilwell, Johnson, E. Chamber Ch., ECO, Leppard.

With many individual touches in sharp pointing and unexpected tempi that suggest earlier consultation with Benjamin Britten, the Decca version is the recording that Britten himself should have made. Steuart Bedford proves an admirable deputy, and the Britten/Holst edition, with its extra items completing Act 2, is most effective. With Norma Burrowes a touchingly youthful Belinda, with Peter Pears using Lieder style in the unexpected role (for him) of Aeneas, with Anna Reynolds an admirable Sorceress and other star singers even in supporting roles, there is hardly a weak link, and the London Opera Chorus relishes the often unusual tempi.

As for Dame Janet Baker, here returning to the area of her earliest success in the recording studio, the portrait of Dido is even fuller and richer than before, with more daring tonal colouring and challengingly slow tempi for the two big arias. Some will still prefer the heartfelt spontaneity of the youthful performance (Oiseau-Lyre SOL 60047), but the range of expression on the newer version is unparalleled, and the rich modern recording quality adds to the vividness of the experience. The cassette transfer is generally of high quality, with plenty of presence to the voices and the atmosphere of the recording admirably caught.

Andrew Parrott's concept of a performance on original instruments has one immediately thinking back to the atmosphere of Josias Priest's school for young ladies where Purcell's masterpiece was first given. The voices enhance that impression, not least Emma Kirkby's fresh, bright soprano, here recorded without too much edge but still very young-sounding. It is more questionable to have a soprano singing the tenor role of the Sailor in Act 3, but anyone who fancies the idea of an authentic performance need not hesitate. The cassette transfer is fresh and clean, retaining the recording's bloom. There is just the faintest hint of peaking on one of two of Miss Kirkby's high notes.

The other different versions of Purcell's compressed operatic masterpiece make for tantalizing comparisons. Sir Charles Mackerras gives perhaps the most satisfying direction, for as well as being scholarly it is very vital, with tempi varied more widely and – as he himself suggests – more authentically than usual. There is also the question of ornamentation, and as a whole Mackerras manages more skilfully than any of his rivals, with shakes, backfalls, forefalls, springers and so on, all placed authentically. Even so, his ideas for ornamenting Dido's two big arias are marginally less convincing than Anthony Lewis's on the Oiseau-Lyre disc, with many appoggiaturas and com-

paratively few turns and trills. He has the edge over Lewis in using Neville Boyling's edition based on the Tatton Park manuscript, and he adds brief extra items from suitable Purcellian sources to fill in the unset passages of the printed libretto. As to the singing, Tatiana Troyanos makes an imposing, gorgeous-toned Dido, and Sheila Armstrong as Belinda, Barry McDaniel as Aeneas, and Patricia Johnson all outshine the rival performances, but ultimately the Dido of Janet Baker is so moving it more than compensates for any relative shortcomings, and Thurston Dart's continuo-playing on the Oiseau-Lyre disc is much more imaginative than the Hamburg harpsichordist's. The DG cassette transfer is made at a rather modest level, and although the solo voices sound fresh and clear the choral focus is not as sharp as on the disc.

Barbirolli – not the most likely conductor in this opera – takes some trouble with his text, using the Neville Boyling edition that Mackerras also prefers. But on questions of authenticity other versions have every advantage, and Barbirolli finds fewer moments of high emotional intensity such as would justify a 'personality' reading than one would expect. The tempi are generally perverse, with slow speeds predominating – sometimes grotesquely slow – but with Dido's *When I am laid in earth* beautifully sung but taken equivalently fast. Victoria de los Angeles makes an appealing Dido, but she does not have anything like the dramatic weight of Janet Baker or Tatiana Troyanos, and the tone sometimes loses its bloom on top. The other singers are good, but with keen competition this version commands only a qualified recommendation. The sound is excellent both on disc and tape (closely matched), and this is good value at bargain price.

On the Erato disc Leppard directs a consistently well-sprung, well-played performance, as one would expect, but the overall impression is disappointing, largely because the climax of the opera fails to rise in intensity as it should. Tatiana Troyanos, stylish elsewhere, misses the tragic depth of the great lament of Dido, and without that focus the impact of the rest falls away. Having had a tenor Aeneas (Peter Pears) in Benjamin Britten's version, it is interesting here to have a baritone instead of a tenor (Richard Stilwell) singing the Sailor's song. The recording is excellent.

Don Quixote: Overture and incidental music.

*** O-L DSLO/*KDSLC* 534 [id.]. Kirkby, Nelson, Bowman, Hill, David Thomas, AcAM, Hogwood.

Purcell was one of the contributors of incidental music to the three plays which Thomas D'Urfey based on Cervantes's famous novel. The music was written at high speed, but, as this charming recording demonstrates, much of it was attractively lively and it richly deserves to be resurrected in such stylish and brightly recorded performances as these. This is one of the most successful of Hogwood's enjoyable series; there is some quite enchanting singing from both the soprano soloists, and the instrumental contribution has splendid bite. The quality of the recording is first-class, and the cassette transfer is crisp and clean.

The Double Dealer: Overture and suite. Henry II: In vain I strove. The Richmond Heiress: Behold the man. The Rival Sisters: Overture; 3 songs. Tyrannic Love: Ah! how sweet (duet and song).

*** O-L DSLO 561. Nelson, Kirkby, Hill, Thomas, AcAM, Hogwood.

This collection of music which Purcell wrote for a whole range of Restoration plays uncovers yet more charming examples of his spontaneous genius, with French-style overtures (pressed rather hard here), many dances and songs and a delightful duet from *The Richmond Heiress* representing a flirtation in music. Hogwood directs vigorous performances on original instruments, with bright-toned singing from the soloists, all superbly recorded.

The Indian Queen (incidental music; complete).

**(*) Erato STU 71275. Hardy, Fischer, Harris, Smith, Stafford, Hill, Elwes, Varcoe, Thomas, Monteverdi Ch., E. Bar. Soloists, Gardiner.

The Indian Queen; Timon of Athens (masque).

(M) **(*) HM 243 (2). Knibbs, Sheppard, Mark and Alfred Deller, Elliot, Bevan, Deller Singers, King's Musick, Deller.

The Indian Queen is one of the entertainments that fit into no modern category, a semi-opera. The impossible plot matters little, and Purcell's music contains many delights; indeed the score seems to get better as it proceeds. The Erato disc is fully cast, and uses an authetic accompanying baroque instrumental group. The choral singing is especially fine, the close of the work movingly expressive. John Eliot Gardiner's choice of tempi is apt and the soloists are all good, although the men are more strongly characterful than the ladies. Yet the lyrical music comes off especially well. The advantage of having all the music on one record recommends this issue above Deller's set, although that performance has its own special felicities. The recording is spacious and well balanced.

Deller's group is at its liveliest and most characterful in both works. In *The Indian Queen, Ye twice ten hundred deities* is splendidly sung by Maurice Bevan; and the duet for male alto and tenor, *How happy are we* (with Deller himself joined by Paul Elliot), as well as the best-known item, the soprano's *I attempt from Love's sickness to fly* (Honor Sheppard), are equally enjoyable. The masque that Purcell wrote for Shakespeare's *Timon of*

Athens makes a delightful supplement. However, the Oiseau-Lyre version of *The Indian Queen* (SOL 294, with Cantelo, Wilfred Brown, Tear, Keyte and the St Anthony Singers under Mackerras), like the Erato issue, has squeezed all the music on a single disc, and at medium price it remains an obvious first choice.

King Arthur (complete).
(M) **(*) HM HM 252/3. Sheppard, Knibbs, Hardy, Alfred and Mark Deller, Elliot, Nixon, Maurice Bevan, Nigel Bevan, Deller Ch., King's Musick, Deller.

King Arthur contains some of Purcell's most memorable inspirations, not just his most famous song, *Fairest isle*, but a whole range of lively and atmospheric numbers like the *Frost chorus* and the enchanting duet *Hither this way* (very brightly done here). The score is incomplete and is a hunting-ground for musicological discussion, but Deller's solutions to performing problems will satisfy almost everyone, and though the solo singing is not always polished, the performance has a refreshing vigour, and the recorded quality is good. However, while the marvellous Oiseau-Lyre set (SOL 60008/9), with a first-rate cast under Anthony Lewis, is still available, Deller's set must take second place.

The Tempest (incidental music).
*** Erato STU 71274. Jennifer Smith, Hardy, Hall, Elwes, Varcoe, David Thomas, Earle, Monteverdi Ch. and O., Gardiner.

Whether or not Purcell himself wrote this music for Shakespeare's last play (the scholarly arguments are still unresolved), Gardiner demonstrates how delightful it is, a masterly collection, in performances both polished and stylish and with excellent solo and choral singing. At least the overture is clearly Purcell's, and that sets the pattern for a very varied collec-

tion of numbers including three *da capo* arias and a full-length masque celebrating Neptune for Act 5. The recording is full and atmospheric.

Rachmaninov, Sergei
(1873–1943)

Piano concertos Nos. 1–4; Rhapsody on a theme of Paganini, Op. 43.
(M) *(*) Ph. 6747 397 (3). Orozco, RPO, De Waart.

Rafael Orozco is a powerful and often impressive player, as one would expect of a Leeds prizewinner, but his performances of the Rachmaninov concertos cannot really be accounted much of a success, in spite of some brilliant playing. His readings, though in many ways creditable, are in no way special; both soloist and conductor could be more responsive to the poetry and atmosphere of this music. There are undoubtedly good things in this set, but, given the competition, it is not a strong contender.

Still recommended: The partnership of Ashkenazy and the LSO under Previn has proved particularly fruitful in this repertoire; their Decca set stands out as a major achievement (SXLF 6565/7/K 43 K 33 [Lon. 2311/5-]).

Piano concertos Nos. 1 in F sharp min., Op. 1; 2 in C min., Op. 18.
(M) *** RCA Gold GL/GK 25291 [(d) Quin. 7052; 7006]. Wild, RPO, Horenstein.

Earl Wild recorded his cycle of the Rachmaninov concertos for the Reader's Digest record club, and it was only many years later that the quality of the series compelled RCA to issue it on the mid-price Gold Seal label. With Horenstein an inspired accompanist, Wild gives performances which have great emotional weight as well as dazzling virtuoso brilliance. Each performance conveys total spontaneity, and though the sixties recording sounds limited by today's standards, it is well-balanced, making this an issue to cherish. The cassette, however, is less recommendable; the transfer is clear, but the orchestra lacks richness and bloom and the piano timbre is rather clattery.

Piano concerto No. 2 in C min., Op. 18.

(M) *(**) Decca VIV/*KVIC* 16 [Lon. STS 15542/5-]. Vered, New Philh. O., Andrew Davis – TCHAIKOVSKY: *Concerto No. 1.***(*)

** RCA RL/*RK* 10031 [ARL 1/*ARK 1* 0031]. Rubinstein, Phd. O., Ormandy.

*(*) Decca SXL/*KSXC* 6978. Larrocha, RPO, Dutoit – SCHUMANN: *Concerto.**(*)

* HMV ASD 3872. Petrov, USSR SO, Svetlanov – PROKOFIEV: *Symphony No. 1.**

Piano concerto No. 2; Études-tableaux, Op. 33/7–8, 11.

(M) ** Decca Jub. JB/*KJBC* 52 [Lon. 6390]. Ashkenazy, Moscow PO, Kondrashin.

(i) *Piano concerto No. 2. Preludes Nos. 3, 5–6, 8, 12–13.*

(M) *** DG Priv. 2535/*3335* 475 [138076/ *923059*]. Sviatoslav Richter, (i) with Warsaw Nat. PO, Wislocki.

(i) *Piano concerto No. 2. Preludes Nos. 4, 7, 23.*

*(*) HMV ASD 3457. Alexeev, (i) with RPO, Fedoseyev.

After nearly two decades in the catalogue at full price, Richter's famous recording of Rachmaninov's *Second Concerto* has at last reverted to DG's medium-priced Privilege label. Coupled with marvellous performances of six of the *Preludes*, it remains a classic account,

even though Richter has strong, even controversial ideas about speeds in this concerto. The long opening melody of the first movement is taken abnormally slowly, and it is only the sense of mastery which Richter conveys in every note which prevents one from complaining. One ends by admitting how convincing that speed can be in Richter's hands, but away from the magic one realizes that this is not quite the way Rachmaninov himself intended it. The slow movement too is spacious – with complete justification this time – and the opening of the finale lets the floodgates open the other way, for Richter chooses a hair-raisingly fast allegro, which has the Polish players scampering after him as fast as they are able. Richter does not, however, let himself be rushed in the great secondary melody, so this is a reading of vivid contrasts. Good recording of the piano, less firm of the orchestra, but an atmospheric acoustic adds bloom overall. The tape transfer is good, but like the disc it lacks the last degree of sharpness of focus of the orchestra.

Ilana Vered is a naturally expressive interpreter of Rachmaninov, and the Decca Viva issue is the first to combine successful performances of the Rachmaninov *Second* and the Tchaikovsky concertos. The reading of the first movement reaches an impressive climax and the finale is undoubtedly exciting, but there is an element of languor in the slow movement which some may find overdone. However, the real drawback here is the recording balance, with an elephantine piano projected right into the room. The orchestra makes a fair impact, but the effect is artificial, even though it is certainly telling. There is no appreciable difference in quality between disc and tape.

Ashkenazy's earlier recording with Kondrashin is a relaxed, lyrical reading which rises to the climaxes but is seldom as compelling as the best versions. The *Études-tableaux* make an attractive bonus and are, needless to say, very well played. The sound is generally excellent, although the massed string tone here is not as convincing as on Ashkenazy's later Decca recording (SXL/*KSXC* 6554 [Lon. 6774/5-], coupled to the *First Concerto*), which is well worth the extra cost.

Rubinstein's performance, which dates from the early seventies, can hardly be counted a real competitor at full price, spread over two full LP sides. The sound is good (especially on the cassette, which is remarkably fresh and clear); the performance is essentially lyrical, with a relaxed first movement which does not achieve the fullest degree of electricity at its climax. The slow movement is beautiful and the finale spirited without being rushed.

Alicia de Larrocha's partnership with Charles Dutoit produces unexpectedly disappointing results. The Rachmaninov performance is lethargic, the first-movement climax unconvincing. There is no lack of poetry in the slow movement, but in spite of first-class sound on disc and cassette alike, this reading fails to convince, and the Schumann coupling is only marginally more successful.

Dmitri Alexeev won the 1975 Leeds Competition, and this was his first concerto record. He is a more exciting and perceptive player than this performance would lead one to believe. Here he is inclined to be brilliant but a shade literal, and although the RPO under Vladimir Fedoseyev give good support, and they are well recorded, this is no match for the best versions on the market.

Nicolai Petrov's version has even weaker claims. There are musicianly touches (in the second group of the first movement, for example) but for the most part there is nothing about this performance that would tempt one to return to it often. Nor does the orchestral playing rise to any heights of distinction under Yevgeny Svetlanov, it is sound but not particularly inspired.

(i) *Piano concerto No. 2;* (ii) *Rhapsody on a theme of Paganini, Op. 43.*

(M) *** Decca SPA/*KCSP* 505 [(d) Lon. STS 15086, 15406]. Katchen, (i) LSO, Solti, (ii) LPO, Boult.

(M) **(*) HMV Green. ESD/*TC-ESD* 7076. Collard, Toulouse Capitole SO, Plasson.

(M) *(*) CBS 60109/*40-* [Col. MY 36722]. Graffman, NYPO, Bernstein.

Katchen gives a dramatic and exciting account of the *C minor Concerto* such as we would expect from this pianist. He had a fabulous technique, and generally in this recording that leads to the highest pitch of excitement; but there are a number of passages – notably the big climax as well as the coda of the first movement – where he plays almost too fast. Miraculously he gets round the notes somehow but the result inevitably seems breathless, however exciting it is. The stereo recording is in Decca's best manner and manages to be brilliant and well co-ordinated at the same time. The account of the *Rhapsody* with Boult is superbly shaped and is notable not only for its romantic flair and excitement but for the diversity and wit displayed in the earlier variations. There is no question of anti-climax after the eighteenth, for the forward impetus of the playing has tremendous power and excitement. The recording comes from a vintage Decca period and is bold and vividly coloured. The piano timbre is particularly firm and rich. The cassette transfer too is one of Decca's best, clear and full-bodied.

The partnership of Jean-Philippe Collard and Michel Plasson also brings performances of great intensity but less in the way of romantic delicacy. The slow movement of the concerto is not wanting in lyrical ardour, but it misses the balancing sense of repose that is not lacking in the Katchen version. The opening of the finale has an almost explosive brilliance, to which it is impossible not to respond, yet ultimately this unrelenting vigour tends to overstate the case. The *Rhapsody* responds more readily to this degree of charismatic brilliance, with strong characterization throughout. The eighteenth variation is played with passionate fervour, and the work's closing pages undoubtedly have a cumulative excitement. The recording is super-brilliant and clear, the balance effective but not quite natural. The cassette transfer is first-class and tempers the very bright treble without losing detail.

The Graffman/Bernstein coupling is ultimately undistinguished. The *Concerto* performance is not convincing; the climax of the first movement is studied and unspontaneous. The *Rhapsody* is far more impressive, with striking bravura from Graffman, but here and in the *Concerto* the exaggerated forward balance of the piano negates any possibilities of dynamic contrast between orchestra and soloist. The sound too is lacking in warmth and bloom.

Piano concerto No. 3 in D min., Op. 30.
**(*) RCA RL/*RK* 12633 [CRL 1/*CRK 1* 2633]. Horowitz, NYPO, Ormandy.
(M) *** RCA Gold GL/*GK* 25292 [Quin. 7030]. Wild, RPO, Horenstein.
(M) *** Decca Jub. JB/*KJBC* 53. Ashkenazy, LSO, Fistoulari.
**(*) CBS 76597/40- [Col. M/*MT* 34540]. Berman, LSO, Abbado.

The new Horowitz/Ormandy performance (recorded in Carnegie Hall in January 1978) must certainly go to the top of the list. Horowitz's legendary association with this work daunted even the composer himself, and certainly this new version is masterly. Inevitably, perhaps, with rosy memories of the famous 78 r.p.m. recording, there is a slight element of disappointment. Some of the old magic seems to be missing; this is partly due to the clear, clinical recorded sound. Every detail of the piano part is revealed, and the dryness of timbre is matched by the orchestral texture, which has little expansive richness. All the more credit to Ormandy for creating a genuinely ex-

pansive romanticism in the great slow movement. The outer movements have undoubted electricity, but it is the fascination of the detail that makes one want to return to this remarkable recorded document. Not quite all the playing is immaculate, and there is some rhythmic eccentricity in the finale; but for those who can accept the 'bare bones' of the recorded sound (if anything slightly smoother and warmer on cassette than on disc) this issue will be indispensable.

Earl Wild's version dates from 1965 and cannot boast the finest modern sound; but the recording is vivid and full-blooded and the reading both scintillatingly brilliant and warmly expressive, product of real joy in virtuosity. The first movement's second subject brings a surge of romantic feeling, and a similar ardour permeates the *Adagio*, while the finale is very exciting indeed. Wild favours the less elaborate version of the first-movement cadenza and plays it with compelling bravura. Horenstein proves a most understanding partner, and though there are three brief cuts, which would no longer be sanctioned today, the insight has rarely been matched in this music. The cassette transfer is well managed, matching the disc closely in quality.

Ashkenazy's later reading of the *Third Concerto* with Previn is the controversial performance in his complete set. In some ways this earlier account with Fistoulari is fresher, and in its Jubilee reissue the richly immediate recording sounds first-rate, with little appreciable difference between disc and cassette. Ashkenazy's approach to the first movement is less extrovert than Wild's and there is more imaginative delicacy here, which some will prefer.

For all the eloquence and authority of Lazar Berman's playing, his performance is in the last analysis disappointing. In spite of the English venue the recording is comparatively shallow; not only does the piano lack the richness of sonority one would like, but the orchestra, notably at the climax of the slow movement, also lacks body and depth. It is thus in the work's reflective moments (as at the end of the cadenza in the first movement) that Berman's playing is at its most appealing, although the undoubtedly exciting finale has great force and bravura. Abbado accompanies attentively but is let down by the thin-textured recorded sound. The balance on the cassette is generally preferable to the disc. The recording has less range and refinement of detail but is mellower and more sympathetic in tonal quality.

Piano concerto No. 4 in G min., Op. 40; Rhapsody on a theme of Paganini, Op. 43.
(M) *** RCA Gold GL/*GK* 25293 [Quin. 7053]. Wild, RPO, Horenstein.
**(*) DG 2530 905. Vásáry, LSO, Ahronovitch.

In the Wild/Horenstein coupling, the sweep of the opening movement of the *G minor concerto* and the surprising degree of expressive power generated in the slow movement are matched by the exhilaratingly fast pacing of the *Rhapsody*, which makes the lyrical variations at the centre a greater contrast than usual. The resonant, full-blooded recording suits the style of the music-making, and if the actual recorded sound of the strings in the famous eighteenth variation is not so ripe as in some other versions, there is no lack of passion in the playing itself. An irresistible conclusion to this splendid series, so memorable for its spontaneous romantic flair. The cassette, transferred at a high level, sounds shallower and less refined than the LP.

It is possible to underrate the qualities of the series of recordings by Vásáry and Ahronovitch. The impetuous style certainly carries excitement with it, and the forward thrust of the *Rhapsody* (the opening faster than usual and with strong contrasts of tempo and mood between brilliant and lyrical variations) certainly does not lack adrenalin. The first move-

ment of the *Concerto* too has a strong forward impulse, with relaxation of tempo for the lyrical music. There is poetry in the slow movement, even if the brilliance of the finale carries also a lack of poise. Both these performances are highly involving, and they are well recorded. But at full price the Decca Ashkenazy version of the same coupling (SXL/*KSXC* 6556 [Lon. 6776/5-]) is still first choice.

The Rock (fantasy), *Op. 7.*
*** HMV ASD 3660. USSR SO, Svetlanov – BALAKIREV: *Thamar*; GLAZOUNOV: *Stenka Razin.****

This early work by Rachmaninov, sometimes known as *The Crag*, has enjoyed something of a vogue in recent years: Previn, Weller, De Waart and Rozhdestvensky have all recorded it (see below), though it rarely if ever features in concert programmes. Svetlanov is very persuasive here, more full-blooded and impassioned than most of his rivals. He makes a great deal of wide dynamic contrasts, and, despite the coarse brass tone of the USSR Symphony Orchestra, he secures an impressive response from them. This anthology is a particularly interesting one and should be investigated by all with a taste for romantic Russian music.

Symphonies Nos. 1–3; The Isle of the Dead, Op. 29; The Rock, Op. 7.
(M) ** Ph. 6768 148 (3). Rotterdam PO, De Waart.

Symphonies Nos. 1–3; Aleko: Intermezzo and Dance.
(M) *** HMV SLS/*TC-SLS* 5225 (3). LSO, Previn.

Previn's readings of Rachmaninov's *Second* and *Third Symphonies* have never been outshone, while his softer-grained view of the long *First Symphony* is also powerful, if not always sensuous or exciting. The seventies recordings are all first-rate, the transfers of Nos. 1 and 3 made cleaner – though not warmer – than on their original issue by the elimination of SQ quadraphonic information. The two pieces from *Aleko* make an attractive if hardly generous fill-up for the *Third Symphony*. The cassettes offer richly textured sound throughout, a little lacking in ultimate range at the top. In No. 2 the bass line is not so clean as on disc, but the strings are so sumptuous that most listeners will be content to luxuriate without criticism.

Edo de Waart secures excellent results from the Rotterdam Philharmonic; these performances are all well shaped and proportioned, fresh in conception and refined in phrasing and sonority. What they lack, perhaps, is the all-pervasive melancholy and sense of rapture that lie at the core of Rachmaninov's sensibility. No complaints about the quality of the orchestral response at any point in this set; nor could one fault the excellence and truthfulness of the Philips recording.

Symphony No. 1 in D min., Op. 13.
(M) **(*) CBS 61991/40- [Col. MS 6986]. Phd. O., Ormandy.
(M) **(*) Decca Jub. JB/*KJBC* 91. SRO, Weller.
** Ph. 9500 445/*7300 651* [id.]. Rotterdam PO, De Waart.

Ormandy's was the first stereo recording of Rachmaninov's *First Symphony*, dating from the mid-sixties, and in many ways it remains the strongest performance in the catalogue of a work that is notoriously difficult to hold together. Ormandy's thrustful view of the outer movements is supported by superbly committed Philadelphia playing, with the orchestra on top form, and although the slow movement and scherzo are not quite so fine, Ormandy's sympathy remains obvious. The sound is bright and forward, with woodwind solos spotlighted. The overall effect is unrefined

but has a strong impact on the listener. The cassette transfer is full-blooded and clear.

Weller's version is undoubtedly distinguished but suffers from the fact that the Suisse Romande Orchestra is unable to produce the body and richness of tone that the slow movement ideally demands. The performance has a fine feeling for the music's atmosphere (both inner movements show this readily). The recording is quite splendid, the finest available; its range and impact tell in the outer movements and never more vividly than in the work's dramatic closing pages. The cassette transfer is of excellent quality, and the tape holds the climaxes of the finale with aplomb.

The Rotterdam performance under Edo de Waart is freshly literal, but somewhat under-characterized. Comparing the swaggering brass fanfare which opens the finale (once famous as the signature tune for BBC TV's *Panorama* programme) with Ormandy's splendidly telling version, there is inevitable disappointment, even though the Philips sound is generally richer and more refined than that of the CBS disc.

Symphony No. 2 in E min., Op. 27.
(M) *** Decca Jub. JB/*KJBC* 92. LPO, Weller.
**(*) Chan. Dig. ABRD/*ABTD* 1021. SNO, Gibson.
**(*) Ph. 9500 309/*7300 653* [id.]. Rotterdam PO, De Waart.
** HMV ASD/*TC-ASD* 3606 [Ang. S/*4XS* 37520]. RPO, Temirkanov.
(M) ** ASV ACM 2016. Philh. O., Ling Tung.
(M) *(*) RCA Gold GL/*GK* 12877 [AGL 1 2877]. LSO, Previn.
(M) *(*) Decca Eclipse ECS 837 [Lon. STS 15530]. SRO, Kletzki.

All recordings of Rachmaninov's *Second Symphony* are overshadowed by Previn's outstanding version (HMV ASD/*TC-ASD* 2889 [Ang. S/*4XS* 2889]), one of the finest Rachmaninov records in the catalogue, vividly and sumptuously recorded. Its balance between extrovert romanticism and melancholy is particularly telling. Weller's performance, however, is a very fine one, and his Decca disc is undoubtedly competitive in its medium-price reissue, with an outstandingly rich, clear cassette to match the LP closely. Weller's reading is more restrained but genuinely symphonic in stature, with a dreamy poetic quality in the slow movement. Here the LPO strings do not quite match those of the LSO under Previn in fervour, but the relative reserve of the playing is not unattractive for repeated hearings, and the Decca recording is superb, finer even than the HMV, with greater inner detail, achieved without loss of body and weight.

Gibson and the Scottish National Orchestra have the advantage of an excellent digital recording, made in the Henry Wood Hall in Glasgow. The brass sounds are thrilling, but the slightly recessed balance of the strings is a drawback and there is not the body of tone demonstrated by both the HMV and Decca versions mentioned above. But this is a freshly spontaneous performance and overall the sound is admirably natural, even if it includes some strangely unrhythmic thuds at climaxes (apparently the conductor in his excitement stamping on the podium). The cassette transfer is clear and immediate, with crisply focused detail, but even more than on the LP the ear notices that the upper strings are not sumptuously rich in texture.

Edo de Waart's reading is attractively volatile, bringing out the music's freshness. With generally fast tempi the effect is emotionally lightweight, although the slow movement is very beautiful and the refined orchestral playing is naturally expressive throughout. The recording is full and well balanced. The cassette transfer, made at a rather low level, has not quite the inner clarity of the LP, nor its range at the top.

Temirkanov regularly adopts a free rubato style, which in the outer movements gives his reading an attractive expressive warmth. He carries that style a fraction too far in the big melody of the scherzo's first episode, making the result soupy, but by contrast the slow movement – at a relatively fast tempo which tends to get faster – runs the risk of sounding perfunctory. The recording is splendidly rich and full and the playing generally brilliant, though the ensemble cannot match that of Previn and the LSO on the same label. The cassette is brilliant but gives less body to the upper strings than the disc.

Ling Tung directs a warm and generally understanding reading, but neither the playing nor the recording matches up to the standards of other versions, with the Philharmonia violins somewhat backwardly balanced.

Previn's earlier RCA version, now at medium price, was recorded in the Kingsway Hall, and the sound has a fine glow; but the reading, although gloriously affectionate, is not as fine as Previn's later one and it is disfigured by cuts. The cassette sounds rich but has a relatively compressed dynamic range compared with the disc.

Kletzki shows more of a feeling for this score than his orchestra. When vigour and forward drive can make an effect, as in the scherzo or the climax of the slow movement, the music blossoms fully. But unfortunately the orchestral playing lacks refinement, and the second subject of the first movement has little charm. The clarinet solo in the slow movement is the very opposite of luscious, and Decca's close, vivid recording seems to emphasize the orchestra's faults instead of covering them in a warm glow of kindly reverberation.

Symphony No. 3 in A min., Op. 44.
(M) ** Decca Eclipse ECS 838 [Lon. STS 15530]. SRO, Kletzki – MUSSORGSKY: *Night.****

Symphony No. 3; The Rock, Op. 7.
(M) *** Decca Jub. JB/*KJBC* 93. LPO, Weller.
** Ph. 9500 302/*7300 596* [id.]. Rotterdam PO, De Waart.

Symphony No. 3; Vocalise, Op. 34/14.
(M) **(*) CBS 61994/40-. Phd. O., Ormandy.

At full price Previn's HMV version (ASD/*TC-ASD* 3369 [Ang. S/*4XS* 32760]) is unsurpassed, but at medium price both Ormandy and Weller have much to offer. Weller's performance is superbly recorded. There may be some slight sacrifice of detail to atmosphere, but the beautiful sound the orchestra consistently yields deserves this kind of richness and sense of space. The reading is an essentially lyrical one, showing great delicacy of feeling, notably in the preparation of the first movement's memorable second subject, but also in the sense of stillness that pervades the opening of the *Adagio* to make an absolute contrast with the *scherzando* middle section. The finale too responds to such spacious treatment, though its basic tempo has no lack of urgency. Weller's performance of *The Rock* is no less impressive, with a splendidly moulded climax. Like the disc, the cassette offers exceptionally sophisticated sound, rich, brilliant and detailed.

But, fine though Weller's performance is, Ormandy's is even more distinguished. The drawback to the CBS issue is the recorded sound, which, although brilliant, has a tendency to fierceness and lacks the body of tone the Decca engineers afford to the LPO strings. (This is even more noticeable on the CBS cassette, where the upper range becomes strident.) But with a cutback of treble the quality is fully acceptable; and the performance itself has memorable dedication and fervour. The orchestral response achieves an irresistible balance between subtlety of detail and tenderness

and romantic passion. The playing itself is marvellous and this warmth of feeling carries over into the touchingly shaped *Vocalise.*

An admirably shaped and well-played, if rather lightweight, account from Edo de Waart and the Rotterdam Philharmonic, which in his hands has developed into a first-class orchestra. The tension is not very strongly held in the first movement, and here de Waart omits the exposition repeat, whereas both Previn and Weller observe it. He is at his most persuasive in the outer sections of the slow movement, with some tender playing from the strings, but elsewhere there is a lack of fervour. The Philips recording is beautifully spacious and the balance finely integrated. The cassette, though acceptable, is less robust in effect than the disc.

Kletzki secures some fine playing from the Suisse Romande Orchestra and they are handsomely served by the Decca engineers. However, it must be admitted that in terms of orchestral polish and opulence of tone this orchestra is no match for its competitors.

Cello sonata in G min., Op. 19; Prelude; Danse orientale, Op. 2/1–2.
*** ASV ALH/*ZCALH* 911. Lloyd Webber, Yitkin Seow – DEBUSSY: *Cello sonata.****

Rachmaninov's *Cello sonata,* one of the most ambitious written in this genre, was an inspiration of the period of the *Second Piano concerto* when he was cured of the deep depression that followed the failure of his *First Symphony.* Its exuberant flow of arresting and powerful ideas is splendidly caught by Julian Lloyd Webber and Yitkin Seow, and they are equally persuasive in the two brief works of Op. 2, written over a decade earlier. The recording is firm and immediate rather than atmospheric. The cassette focus is diffuse.

PIANO MUSIC

Barcarolle; Humoresque, Op. 10/3 and 5.
*** RCA RL/*RK* 13433 [ARL 1/*ARK 1* 3433]. Horowitz – LISZT: *Consolation* etc.; SCHUMANN: *Humoreske.****

Horowitz uses the composer's revised edition for the *Barcarolle*, but both here and in the *Humoresque* he is so masterly and powerful that the listener is totally in his hands. The recording is good, and the cassette matches the disc closely.

Preludes Nos. 1 in C sharp min., Op. 3/2; 2 in F sharp min.; 3 in B flat; 5 in D, Op. 23/1–2 and 4; 22 in B min.; 24 in G sharp min., Op. 32/10 and 12; Variations on a theme of Corelli, Op. 42.
*** DG 2531 276 [id./*3301 276*]. Berman.

As one would expect, Lazar Berman gives a distinguished account of the fine *Corelli variations*, the last work Rachmaninov composed for solo piano – and, indeed, the only solo piano piece he composed during his quarter-of-a-century exile in America. It dates from the same year as the *Paganini Rhapsody* and at last appears to be coming into its own. Berman is restrained and classical in his approach, and gives a performance of some of the more popular *Preludes* on the reverse side that has finesse and great care for detail. The recorded sound is not as warm or rich as Decca's for Ashkenazy, who couples the *Corelli variations* with the *Études-tableaux* (SXL 6604 [Lon. 6822]), but it is nonetheless very clean, and can be recommended alongside its rival and Howard Shelley (see below).

Preludes Nos. 3 in B flat; 5 in D; 6 in G min.; 8 in C min., Op. 23/2, 4–5 and 7; 12 in C; 13 in B flat min., Op. 32/1–2.

(B) *** Con. CC/*CCT* 7516 [DG 2535/ *3335 272*]. Sviatoslav Richter – MUSSORGSKY: *Pictures.***

Richter's marvellous performances make one hope that one day we shall have a complete set of the *Preludes* from him in stereo. The recording here is good; the cassette has rather less range than the disc but is fully acceptable.

Russian rhapsody; Symphonic dances, Op. 45.
*** Decca SXL/*KSXC* 6926 [Lon. 7159/ 5-]. Ashkenazy, Previn.

The two-piano version of the *Symphonic dances* – Rachmaninov's last major work – was written not as an arrangement of the orchestral score but as a preparation for it. The ingenuity of his handling of a difficult medium produced a work which in pianistic detail as well as sharpness of argument is masterly. Ashkenazy and Previn are challenged to a dazzling performance, superbly recorded with bright, realistic piano sound. The coupling is an early work, musically rather naive but well worth hearing in a performance as persuasive as this. The cassette, unusually for Decca, has not quite the upper range of the disc: the warmly resonant acoustic has accentuated the bass response.

Piano sonatas Nos. 1 in D min., Op. 28; 2 in B flat min., Op. 36.
(M) *** RCA Gold GL/*GK* 42867. Ogdon.

An obvious coupling yet one which no other artist seems to have attempted. The *First Sonata* is the rarity, dating from 1907; John Ogdon is more than equal to its considerable demands. The *Second* was composed in 1913 but Ogdon chooses the revision that Rachmaninov published in the early 1930s. (Horowitz and Jean-Philippe Collard, the only others to have recorded it as far as the

UK catalogue is concerned, both play a compromise version of the two.) Recorded in the late 1960s, the sound quality is perfectly acceptable even if it falls short of being really distinguished, and given the interest of the coupling and the vitality of Ogdon's playing, few will be dissatisfied. The cassette is disappointing, with a restricted dynamic range and lack-lustre timbre.

2 Suites for two pianos, Opp. 5 and 17.
*** DG 2531 345 [id.]. Güher and Süher Pekinel.

Güher and Süher Pekinel are Turkish sisters who studied at the Juilliard School and also in West Germany. They are an accomplished duo and give sensitive and musicianly accounts of these delightful pieces, and they are admirably recorded. This can be recommended alongside but not in preference to the Ashkenazy/Previn recording of this same coupling, which has the benefit of warm, vivid sound quality (Decca SXL/*KSXC* 6697 [Lon. 6893/5-]).

Variations on a theme of Chopin, Op. 22; Variations on a theme of Corelli, Op. 42; Mélodie in E, Op. 3/3.
*** Hyp. A 66009. Shelley – MENDELSSOHN: *Scherzo.****

Rachmaninov's two big sets of variations for solo piano make an excellent coupling, and Howard Shelley gives dazzling, consistently compelling performances, full of virtuoso flair. The *Corelli variations* are the better-known set (see above), product of Rachmaninov's years in exile, sharply imagined but far less passionate than his earlier music. Strangely the more expansive *Chopin variations* have been seriously neglected on record, but on any count they represent the composer at his most masterly, written as they were at the same rich period as the *Second Piano concerto*, the

Second Symphony and the *Cello sonata.* The grouping of variations brings a kind of sonata balance, with the climax of the final section superbly built by Shelley, helped by first-rate piano sound.

VOCAL AND CHORAL MUSIC

Songs: *Again you leapt, my heart!; All at once I gladly owned; Beloved, let us fly; Brooding; C'était en avril; Christ is risen; Come, let us rest; Daisies; The heart's secret; How few the joys; I came to her; I shall tell you nothing; Like blossom dew-freshed to gladness; Morning; Oh stay, my love, forsake me not!; A prayer; Twilight has fallen; The water lily.* (i) *Two partings.* (Piano) *Daisies.*
*** Decca SXL 6869 [Lon. 26559]. Söderström, Ashkenazy, (i) with Shirley-Quirk.

This fourth volume of Söderström and Ashkenazy's unique series contains fewer masterpieces (the highly characteristic *Brooding* is certainly one of them), but it presents rarities which make essential listening for those interested in the composer. Sonia's final speech in Chekhov's *Uncle Vanya* here becomes a song which nicely skirts sentimentality, and John Shirley-Quirk joins the soprano for the wry dialogue *Two partings*. Both singer and pianist are again intensely compelling in their inspired performances, and the recording is outstanding.

Songs: *All things depart; As fair as day in blaze of noon; By the gates of the holy dwelling; Do you remember the evening?; A flower fell; From St John's Gospel; Let me rest here alone; Love's flame; Night; O, do not grieve; Song of disappointment; The soul's concealment; 'Tis time; Thy pity I*

implore; Were you hiccoughing; When yesterday we met; With holy banner firmly held. Letter to Stanislavsky. (Piano) *Lilacs.*
*** Decca SXL 6940 [Lon. 26615]. Söderström, Ashkenazy.

Filling in the gaps from the previous records in their outstanding series, Söderström and Ashkenazy here range over the wide span of Rachmaninov's career as well as his whole emotional range. So you find the richly intense *O, do not grieve* on the one hand and on the other a comic skit on a drinking song, *Did you hiccough, Natasha?*; also a letter in music sent to Stanislavsky on the tenth anniversary of the Moscow Arts Theatre and the solo piano version of *Lilacs*. Model performances and recording.

Songs: *The answer; Before my window; Before the image; By the grave; The fountains; The lilacs; Loneliness; Melody (On slumberladen wings); Night is mournful; No prophet; On the death of a linnet; Powder'd paint; The ring; Sorrow in springtime; To the children; Twilight.*
*** Decca SXL 6832 [Lon. 26433]. Söderström, Ashkenazy.

This volume of Söderström and Ashkenazy's outstanding series contains all of the superb Op. 21 collection of songs (except for two included on earlier discs) as well as five masterly items from Op. 26, including the ecstatically beautiful *Before my window*, a mere twenty-three bars long. The Op. 21 songs, typically gloomy of mood, yet reflect the rare sense of confidence which came over the composer in the early years of the century. Most memorable is *The lilacs*, which Rachmaninov also arranged for solo piano; but the accompaniments here all provide the necessary challenge to Ashkenazy's virtuosity as well as his im-

agination, while Söderström's singing is equally compelling. A charming makeweight is the folksong, *Powder'd paint*, also known from the *Three Russian folksongs* for chorus and orchestra. Excellent recording.

The Bells (cantata), *Op. 35.*
** HMV ASD 4005. Pisarenko, Maslennikov, Yakoveno, RSFSR Yurlov Academic Russian Ch., USSR SO, Svetlanov.

There is much to be said for a Russian choir and soloists in this work, but Svetlanov's performance rather lacks the freshness and urgency which mark the finest versions in the past, including Previn's recorded in London (HMV ASD 3284 [Ang. S 37169]). The heaviness extends to the final *Lento lugubre*, where for all the expressive underlining the emotional intensity is too low. The Russian recording is wide in range, but the chorus sounds insubstantial and the vibrato of the soloists is distractingly caught.

Songs: *Christ is risen; A dream; The harvest of sorrow; How fair this spot; Night is mournful; Oh, never sing to me again; Oh, stay my love; When yesterday we met.*
**(*) Decca SXL 6974. Talvela, Gothoni
– MUSSORGSKY: *Songs and Dances of Death* etc.***

Talvela modifies his dark timbre, so apt for the Mussorgsky cycle, to suit the softer, gentler lines of these Rachmaninov songs, but as recorded – very vividly – the voice acquires a plaintive quality which is not quite pleasing. Nonetheless this is expressive and thoughtful singing, imaginatively accompanied, and the repertory is not so common that one can overlook this issue, particularly when it is so attractively coupled.

3 *Russian folksongs, Op. 41;* (i)
Spring cantata, Op. 20.
(M) *** RCA Gold GL/*GK* 42924
[*LSC 3051*/*RK 1115*]. Amb. S., New
Philh. O., Buketoff, (i) with Shaw –
TCHAIKOVSKY: *1812.***(*)

The *Spring cantata*, a delightful piece,
dates from 1902, the period of the *Cello
sonata*, the *Second Suite for two pianos*
and the *Second Piano concerto*. It is for
solo baritone, mixed chorus and orchestra and is persuasively done by these
artists and well recorded. This is the only
recording of the work in the current
catalogue. The *Three Russian folksongs*
for chorus and orchestra come from 1926
and were written for Stokowski, who
conducted their première the following
year in Philadelphia. Evocative and delightfully inventive pieces they are too,
heavy with nostalgia. Good performances, freshly sung and excellent recording on disc; the tape is disappointing,
with an edginess to the voices and poor
focus, especially towards the end of the
Spring cantata.

Vocalise, Op. 34.
(M) ** RCA Gold GL/*GK* 42923.
Moffo, American SO, Stokowski –
KHACHATURIAN: *Symphony No.
3* (***); RIMSKY-KORSAKOV: *Russian
Easter Festival overture.****

Rachmaninov's *Vocalise* was a favourite showpiece of Stokowski, usually in a
purely orchestral arrangement. Here with
Anna Moffo at her warmest it is good to
have the vocal version so persuasively
matching the accompaniment. The sound
is good and the cassette is notably rich
and sensuous, very like the disc in quality.
An attractive coupling for those with a
sweet tooth.

Rameau, Jean Philippe
(1683–1764)

Hippolyte et Aricie: orchestral suite.
⊛ *** HM 1C 065 99837. La Petite
Bande, Kuijken.

There were three productions of *Hippolyte et Aricie* during Rameau's lifetime,
in 1733, 1742 and 1757, for which various
instrumental additions were made. This
record collects virtually all the orchestral
music from the three, in performances so
lively and winning that the disc is irresistible. Sigiswald Kuijken gets delightful
results from his ensemble; the melodic
invention is fresh and its orchestral presentation ingenious. In every way an
outstanding release – and not least in the
quality of the sound.

Complete keyboard works: *Première
livre* (1706); *Pièces de clavecin*
(1724): *Première partie; Deuxième
partie; Nouvelles Suites de pièces de
clavecin* (1728): *Première partie;
Deuxième partie; Cinq pièces* (Nos.
1–4, 1741; No. 5, 1747).
*** DG Arc. 2710 020 (3) [id.]. Gilbert.

An impressive set which is unlikely to
be surpassed. Rameau's keyboard music
is among the finest of the whole baroque
era, and Kenneth Gilbert is not only a
scholar but an artist of genuine insight
and stature. He uses three harpsichords,
all from the Paris Conservatoire and all
from the period: a Goujon (1749), a
Hemsch (1761), and a third by Dumont
(1679) restored by Pascal Taskin in 1789.
They are superb instruments and are
excellently recorded too, without being
too close or cut at too high a level. There
is no need to dwell on details here, for
this is an indispensable set.

Les Indes galantes: excerpts (harpsichord transcriptions).
*** HM HM 1028. Gilbert.

These transcriptions are Rameau's own, made some time after the success scored by his first opera-ballet, *Les Indes galantes*, in 1735. He grouped a number of items into four suites or '*concerts*', and these included not only dance numbers and orchestral pieces but arias as well. Kenneth Gilbert, playing a fine instrument in contemporary tuning, reveals these miniatures as the subtle and refined studies that they are. He could not be better served by the recording engineers.

OPERA-BALLET
AND OPERA

Castor et Pollux: highlights.
(M) *** Tel. AQ6/CQ4 42024. Scovotti, Vandersteene, Lerer, Souzay, Villisech, Stockholm Chamber Ch., VCM, Harnoncourt.

An excellent and generous mid-priced selection from Rameau's second *tragédie lyrique*. The complete set from which it is taken runs to four discs (HF 6.35048), and this is a tempting sampler. The cast, including Scovotti and Souzay, is a strong one and Harnoncourt's directness is certainly refreshingly lively, even if he gives less emphasis to the music's lyrical elegance. The recording is bright and clear, although on cassette (with a drop in level) side two is softer-grained than side one.

Dardanus (complete).
**(*) Erato STU 71416 (2). Eda-Pierre, Von Stade, Gautier, Devlin, Soyer, Van Dam, Paris Op. Ch. and O., Leppard.

For the production at the Paris National Opéra Leppard prepared a satisfying conflation of the very different versions of this important work (which Rameau revised): not just the 1739 score but the score for the 1744 revival, which involved radical rewriting of the last two acts. Though the French chorus and orchestra here fail to perform with quite the rhythmic resilience that Leppard usually achieves on record, the results are refreshing and illuminating, helped by generally fine solo singing and first-rate recording. José van Dam as Ismenor copes superbly with the high tessitura, and Christiane Eda-Pierre is a radiant Venus. The story may be improbable (as usual), but Rameau was here inspired to some of his most compelling and imaginative writing.

Les Fêtes d'Hébé: 3rd Entrée: La Danse.
*** Erato STU 70189. Gomez, Rodde, Orliac, Monteverdi Ch. and O., Gardiner.

Les Fêtes d'Hébé was first staged in 1739 in Paris, and was the fourth major work Rameau had composed for the lyric stage. It was his second in the opera-ballet genre, *Les Indes galantes* being the first. In its complete form, *Les Fêtes d'Hébé* consists of a prologue and three acts dedicated to poetry, music and finally the dance. This last is a pastoral interspersed with dances in which Mercury courts the shepherdess Églé. Few people have done more in recent years for Rameau's music than John Eliot Gardiner, and this performance is distinguished by his great feeling for this composer and an alive sensitivity. He secures excellent playing and singing from his forces and is very well recorded too, with natural sound. The music itself is inventive and delightful; in short, a record not to be missed.

Hippolyte et Aricie (complete).
*** CBS 79314 (3). Calcy, Auger, Watkinson, Cold, Moser, Rodde, Van Egmonde, Goldthorpe, E. Bach Festival Ch., Gr. Écurie, Malgoire.

There are impressive things in this

set which outweigh its shortcomings. Anthony Lewis's set (Oiseau-Lyre SOL 286/8) uses the 1733 edition, and follows Rameau's own precedent in the 1757 performance of omitting the Prologue. Malgoire retains it, thus restoring some excellent music, but omits other things (for instance, the opening scenes of Act 5, which Anthony Lewis includes); he also uses the second form of the *Trio des Parques* (Act 2, scene 4), which Rameau had omitted because of the inadequacy of the performers. Malgoire in short uses a *mélange* of the 1733, 1742 and 1757 performances, plus or minus various bits and pieces, so that in one sense his account complements rather than displaces the older set. He has the advantage of excellent singers and a thoroughly idiomatic approach. Moreover, the orchestra is composed of authentic instruments and thus has real period flavour. Yet Lewis has greater breadth – and has the advantage of Janet Baker at her best. Both versions are well recorded, and such are the musical rewards of this work that neither should be ignored. This can be recommended alongside the Oiseau-Lyre. It is a very crude generalization, but readers more interested in the sound than the sense should turn to this newcomer; those less concerned with period presentation should stay with the older set.

Naïs (complete).
**(*) Erato STU 71439 (2). Russell, Jennifer Smith, Mackay, Parsons, Caley, Caddy, Jackson, Ransome, Tomlinson, E. Bach Festival Singers and Bar. O., McGegan.

Rameau's opera *Naïs* was commissioned by the Opéra to commemorate the Treaty of Aix-la-Chapelle and first appeared in 1749. It tells of Neptune's courtship of the water-nymph Naïs and is full of bold invention. The overture has some astonishing dissonances and syncopations, and the opening battle scenes

in which the Heavens are stormed by the Titans and Giants are quite striking. The melodic invention later in the work is not perhaps as elevated or inspired as the very finest Rameau, but it is still of fair quality and at times is very beautiful indeed. The performance, based on the 1980 English Bach Festival production, is full of spirit and uses authentic period instruments to good effect. The work is not long, occupying only four sides, and its rewards are such as to counterbalance any reservations one might have as to imperfections in ensemble or the like. Admirers of Rameau will need no prompting to acquire this set; the unconverted should sample the opening, which will surely delight and surprise. Good, well-balanced sound.

(i) *Pigmalion* (complete). *Les Indes galantes: troisième concert.*
(M) ** DG Arc. Priv. 2547/*3347* 047. Esposito, Lamoureux CO, Couraud, (i) with Marion, Collart, Selig, Raymond St-Paul Ch.

The opera-ballet *Pigmalion* dates from 1748 and, like so much of Rameau's music, is a mine of melodic invention. The action tells simply how Pygmalion falls in love with a statue he has sculpted and how the latter comes to life and returns his affection, whereupon the triumph of love is celebrated in music and dance. Eric Marion is an impressive singer and copes with the difficulties of the part admirably, but Couraud and his orchestra are inclined to tread with less than ideal lightness. The record was first issued nearly twenty years ago and is bottom-heavy; but as there is no current alternative, and the music is full of charm, it must be recommended. The cassette, like the disc, is slightly opaque and has too much bass, but it responds to the controls. The solo voices have presence but the choral quality lacks the last degree of refinement.

Rangström, Ture (1884–1947)

Symphony No. 1 in C sharp min. (In memory of Strindberg).
*** EMI 7C 061 35712. Swedish RO, Segerstam.

Ture Rangström was an almost exact contemporary of Arnold Bax or Ernest Bloch, though he did not possess the craftsmanship and orchestral expertise of either. His strength lies in his songs, which are among the finest in twentieth-century Swedish music. The first of his four symphonies, inspired by the death of Strindberg, is a lush, self-indulgent score in the post-national romantic idiom. It receives the most eloquent and persuasive advocacy from the Swedish Radio Orchestra under Leif Segerstam, though not even that can redeem the banality of some of its themes. First-class recording enhances the attractions of a disc introducing a composer who, for all his shortcomings, is well worth attention.

Symphony No. 3 in D flat (Song under the stars); Songs of King Erik; 2 Songs in the olden style.
*(*) EMI 7C 061 35774. Hagegård, Halsingborg SO, Frandsen; Fürst.

The *Third Symphony* dates from 1929 and is pure kitsch. It is also indifferently performed here. But the disc is worth considering for the sake of Håkan Hagegård's golden voice in the *King Erik Songs*. Rangström's scoring is occasionally inexpert but his invention is far better here than in the *Symphony*. All the songs are superbly sung, though the orchestra is less than first-class.

Ravel, Maurice (1875–1937)

Alborada del gracioso; Une Barque sur l'océan; Boléro. (i) Daphnis et Chloé (complete ballet). Fanfare pour l'Éventail de Jeanne; Menuet antique; Ma Mère l'Oye (ballet); Pavane pour une infante défunte; Rapsodie espagnole; Shéhérazade; Overture de féerie; Le Tombeau de Couperin; La Valse; Valses nobles et sentimentales.
(M) *** CBS 79404 (4). Cleveland O. or NYPO, Boulez, (i) with Camerata Singers.

Boulez's survey of Ravel's orchestral music achieves clarity but never at the expense of atmosphere. Detail is beautifully observed yet never seems coldly analytical. *Daphnis et Chloé* is particularly impressive; it has the essential ingredient, a sense of ecstasy and enchantment, and an ability to transport the listener into the enchanted landscape this work inhabits. Much the same goes for the *Valses nobles et sentimentales* and for *Une Barque sur l'océan* – a particularly atmospheric account – and his account of the less familiar music, the *Shéhérazade* overture and the *Fanfare*, is no less sympathetic. Perhaps *La Valse* – and certainly *Le Tombeau de Couperin* – are more magical in other hands, but generally speaking, this is an impressive and well-recorded set. It is *not* to be preferred to Martinon's set with the Orchestre de Paris (HMV SLS 5016), but that takes five discs and includes the two piano concertos, which some readers may not want. There are other individual recordings of equal or superior quality (Karajan's *Le Tombeau* and *La Valse* are examples, and Charles Dutoit's *Daphnis* is an outstanding contender, too); but those wanting a complete boxed set can be assured that the Boulez is eminently satisfying.

(i) *Alborada del gracioso;* (ii) *Boléro;* (i: iii) *Daphnis et Chloé: Suite No. 2;* (i) *La Valse.*
(M) **(*) CBS 60101/40-. (i) NYPO; (ii) Orchestre Nat. de France; (iii) Schola Cantorum; cond. Bernstein.

These are works at which Bernstein excels. He has recorded *Boléro* three times and here secures a first-class response from the French orchestra. The NYPO gives a glittering account of the *Alborada*, and *La Valse* has the expected panache. Only in the *Daphnis suite* (also superbly played, using the choral version of the score) is the ear left unsatisfied by the lack of sumptuousness in a recording which is elsewhere not without atmosphere, although brightly lit.

Alborada del gracioso; Boléro; Menuet antique; Rapsodie espagnole; Le Tombeau de Couperin.
(B) *** CfP CFP/TC-CFP 40375. Paris Conservatoire O., Cluytens.

In this Classics for Pleasure reissue Cluytens's highly regarded Ravel performances have been reshuffled, and this collection, like its companion (see below), is exceptionally generous. Cluytens gives a brilliant account of the *Alborada,* and room has now been found for his excellent version of *Rapsodie espagnole.* In *Boléro* he maintains a consistent tempo: this is a vivid and unaffected account but in the last analysis not as exciting as some. *Le Tombeau de Couperin* is eminently stylish. With about an hour's music this is a real bargain. The recording is atmospheric, and the cassette is only slightly less refined than the disc.

Alborada del gracioso; Boléro; Rapsodie espagnole.
**(*) RCA Dig. RL 13686 [ARC 1/ARK 1 3686]. Dallas SO, Mata.

Mata has helped to build the Dallas orchestra into a splendid band, and it gives impressive performances of these virtuoso showpieces. There are more distinguished accounts of each work, but the coupling is certainly recommendable, helped by digital recording of great range. *Boléro* develops from a whisper of pianissimo at the start to a formidably loud climax, though the detailed balancing is not always consistent.

Alborada del gracioso; Boléro; La Valse.
**(*) CBS 76513/40- [Col. XM/ẊMT 35103]. Orchestre Nat. de France, Bernstein.

There is no cause for complaint on the grounds of performance here; Bernstein secures a first-class response from the Orchestre National (the old Orchestre National de l'ORTF), and the engineers rise to the occasion. *La Valse* has a genuinely intoxicating quality and there is no doubt about the success of its companions. Yet, given the competition in this repertoire, this issue offers short measure: *Boléro* takes 15'35", and the other side only just exceeds twenty minutes. Were the sides well filled, these performances would merit a three-star recommendation. Because of the reverberation, the cassette is poorly focused and does not match the disc in quality.

Alborada del gracioso; Menuet antique; Rapsodie espagnole; Valses nobles et sentimentales.
**(*) Ph. 9500 347/7300 573 [id.]. Concg. O., Haitink.

The playing of the Amsterdam orchestra is eminently polished and civilized, and all four works are finely shaped. The *Rapsodie espagnole* lacks the last ounce of atmosphere when set alongside Karajan with the Orchestre de Paris, and likewise the *Valses nobles et sentimentales* just fall short of the magic that Cluytens or Martinon achieved. But to say this is not to deny the excellence of the orchestral response or the general sensitivity of Haitink's direction. Fine performances, very well recorded indeed, though the cassette is not the equal of the disc in terms of presence and impact.

Alborada del gracioso; Pavane pour une infante défunte.

(M) *** Decca Jub. JB/KJBC 50 [Lon. STS 15358]. New Philh. O., Frühbeck de Burgos – FALLA: El amor brujo; GRANADOS: Goyescas.***

Frühbeck de Burgos's *Alborada* is glitteringly brilliant, helped by one of Decca's best and most transparent recordings. The lovely *Pavane* is hardly less attractive, but this piece almost always seems to come off well in the recording studio. The cassette transfer is characteristically vivid and clear.

Alborada del gracioso; Rapsodie espagnole; Le Tombeau de Couperin; La Valse.

(M) *** HMV SXLP/TC-SXLP 30446 [Ang. S/4XS 36939]. Orchestre de Paris, Karajan.

These are superb performances. The Orchestre de Paris responds splendidly to Karajan's sensuous approach to these scores, and only the saxophone-like quality of the french horns gives cause for complaint. The dynamic range is extremely wide and the acoustic somewhat too resonant. The atmospheric quality of these performances is not wholly free from a trace of self-consciousness, as if Karajan were admiring his own enormously subtle control of texture and colour. Still there is no doubt about the mastery of *La Valse*, which is extremely fine, or the *Rapsodie espagnole*, the best performance since Reiner's. The *Alborada* is a bit too slow (doubtless the reverberant acoustic prompted this). The cassette transfer too is very sophisticated. The resonance brings a degree of mistiness in pianissimo detail (noticeable at

the opening of *La Valse*) and the upper range is marginally less refined, but the overall focus is impressive and the climaxes expand excitingly. An outstanding issue in every way.

Une Barque sur l'océan (from Miroirs). (i) Daphnis et Chloé: Suite No. 2. Pavane pour une infante défunte; La Valse; Valses nobles et sentimentales.

(B) *** CfP CFP/TC-CFP 40376. Paris Conservatoire O., Cluytens, (i) with Duclos Ch.

This second re-issued Cluytens collection is, if anything, even more attractive than the first. *Une Barque sur l'océan* sounds totally magical in Cluytens's hands, every bit as good as with Martinon or Boulez, and his performance of the *Valses nobles et sentimentales* is second to none: it has fine atmosphere and a genuine feeling for movement and rubato as well as elegance. Moreover it is very well recorded. The suite from *Daphnis et Chloé* is taken from the complete ballet (Cluytens never recorded the suite separately) and thus includes chorus. It is poetically conceived, and the recording still sounds astonishingly vivid. Some may find the wide horn vibrato, both here and in the *Pavane* a little off-putting, but apart from this there is a great deal to enjoy. At the price this is amazingly good value: the recording is atmospheric and well defined and has plenty of presence. The cassette has marginally less sharpness of focus.

Boléro.

(M) *** DG Acc. 2542/3342 116. Berlin PO, Karajan – DEBUSSY: La Mer; Prélude.***

*** HMV ASD/TC-ASD 3431 [Ang. S/4XS 37438]. Berlin PO, Karajan – DEBUSSY: La Mer; Prélude.**

** Decca SXL/KSXC 6813 [Lon. 7033/5-]. Chicago SO, Solti – DEBUSSY: La Mer; Prélude.**

Karajan's 1964 *Boléro* (reissued here on DG Accolade) is marvellously controlled, hypnotic and gripping, with the Berlin Philharmonic at the top of its form. The sound is astonishingly good, though Karajan's re-make for EMI is even better in terms of presence. The EMI *La Mer*, however, is not so inspired as the performance with which this is coupled. Both cassettes are well managed, with only slight loss of crispness of focus at the pianissimo opening of *Boléro*.

Metrically rigorous, Solti builds up the nagging climax with superb relentlessness. Though it lacks seductive touches, the performance is beautifully poised and pointed. Brightly analytical recording, and a faithful cassette transfer giving the clearest sound of all three tapes listed here.

Boléro; Daphnis et Chloé (ballet): *Suite No. 2; Pavane pour une infante défunte.*
*** HMV ASD/*TC-ASD* 3912 [Ang. SZ/4ZS 37670]. LSO, Previn.

Though an analogue recording, Previn's coupling of favourite Ravel pieces provides wonderfully rich, full and atmospheric sound for performances full of sparkle and flair. *Daphnis and Chloé* is sensuously beautiful (good augury for the complete recording of the ballet which Previn was scheduled to make within months), and *Boléro*, at a slow, very steady tempo rather like Karajan's, sounds splendidly relentless. The cassette quality too is outstandingly good, clear and full-bodied at the big climax of *Boléro*.

Boléro; Ma Mère l'Oye (ballet; complete); *La Valse.*
(M) **(*) Ph. Seq. 6527/*7311* 038. LSO, Monteux.

Monteux's complete version of *Ma Mère l'Oye* is a poetic, unforced reading,

given a naturally balanced sound, though the recording is not quite so vivid as that given to Boulez by CBS or as translucent as Haitink's Philips account. But at medium price this can be recommended on disc, even though Monteux's reading of *Boléro* has a slight quickening of tempo in the closing pages. The cassette has been remastered, and now matches the disc quite closely.

Boléro; Pavane pour une infante défunte; (i) *Daphnis et Chloé: Suite No. 2.*
*(*) Telarc Dig. DG 10052 [id.]. St Louis SO, Slatkin, (i) with Ch.

Slatkin directs capable performances of the Ravel showpieces, but they are lacking in rhythmic flair and the digital recording is, by Telarc standards, unspectacular, with a relatively limited range of dynamic.

Boléro; Pavane pour une infante défunte; Le Tombeau de Couperin; La Valse.
** Ph. 9500 314/*7300 571* [id.]. Concg. O., Haitink.

Fine performances, distinguished by instinctive good judgement and taste. The orchestral playing has refinement and finish, and the engineers produce a sound to match; the perspective is truthful and the overall effect most pleasing. Yet Haitink's *La Valse* fails to enchant and captivate the listener as did Cluytens's recording, made in the early 1960s but sounding every bit as vivid as this (it was remarkable for its period); and there is not quite enough atmosphere in *Le Tombeau de Couperin*. The cassette is not as vivid as the disc.

Boléro; Pavane pour une infante défunte; La Valse.

(B) **(*) Con. CC/CCT 7521. RPO, Claude Monteux.

Claude Monteux, more familiar as a flautist, shows himself an able exponent of this repertoire, and the performances here are excellent, both polished and exciting. The recording has a Decca Phase Four source, and although basically well balanced it has vivid spotlighting of solos which will not be to all tastes. However, on disc this is undoubtedly excellent value at bargain price, but the cassette, with a compressed frequency and dynamic range, is not recommended.

Boléro; Rapsodie espagnole.
(M) ** Decca SPA/KCSP 551. SRO, Ansermet – GRANADOS: *Spanish dance*; SARASATE: *Carmen fantasy.***

Boléro; La Valse.
(M) *** Decca Jub. JB/KJBC 36 [Lon. 6367]. SRO, Ansermet – DUKAS: *L'Apprenti sorcier*; HONEGGER: *Pacific 231.****

Ansermet's Jubilee reissue offers outstanding performances, characteristically vivid, with excellent recording on both disc and tape and equally desirable couplings.

The Eclipse reissue replaces *La Valse* with a more than serviceable account of the *Rapsodie espagnole*. However, with Karajan's version also available in the medium price-range (see above), this seems a much less attractive choice unless the other couplings are especially suitable. In the *Rapsodie* the upper strings sound rather smoother on tape than on disc.

Piano concerto in G.
(M) *** DG Acc. 2542/3342 149 [139349]. Argerich, Berlin PO, Abbado – PROKOFIEV: *Concerto No. 3.***

Argerich's half-tones and clear fingerwork give the *G major Concerto* unusual delicacy, but its urgent virility – with jazz

an important element – comes over the more forcefully by contrast. Other performances may have caught the uninhibited brilliance in the finale more fearlessly, but in the first movement few other versions can match Argerich's playing. The compromise between coolness and expressiveness in the slow minuet of the middle movement is tantalizingly sensual. With fine recording and an admirable high-level cassette transfer, very close to the quality of the disc, this coupling is a first-rate recommendation at medium price. However, Michelangeli's famous HMV recording (coupled to Rachmaninov No. 4) should not be forgotten; cassette collectors will be glad to know that it is now available in a splendid new transfer (SXLP/TC-SXLP 30169 [Ang. S 35567]).

Piano concerto in G; Piano concerto for the left hand in D.
⊛*** HMV ASD/TC-ASD 3845 [Ang. SZ 37730]. Collard, Orchestre Nat. de France, Maazel.

Superb recording quality – indeed, it is arguable that these works have never been better served by the engineers, who here produce marvellously transparent orchestral textures and splendidly truthful piano tone. The performances are no less successful: Jean-Philippe Collard gives a meticulous, sparkling and refined account of the *G major Concerto* and a marvellously brilliant and poetic account of the *Left-hand Concerto*. He brings great *tendresse* to the more reflective moments and there is real delicacy of feeling throughout. Lorin Maazel gives thoroughly sympathetic support (anyone who knows his accounts of the Ravel operas will know how keenly attuned he is to this composer) and the Orchestre National play superbly. In the *Left-hand Concerto* Collard does not quite match the dash and swagger of Gavrilov's altogether dazzling account (see below), but he runs him pretty close. This is

609

undoubtedly the best version of this coupling to have appeared for many years and will be difficult to surpass. The cassette transfer is of demonstration standard, extraordinarily vivid in projection with impressively crisp transients.

(i) *Piano concerto for the left hand.*
Pavane pour une infante défunte.
*** HMV ASD/*TC-ASD* 3571 [Ang. S 37486]. Gavrilov, (i) with LSO, Rattle
– PROKOFIEV: *Concerto No. 1; Romeo and Juliet.*⊛***

Gavrilov's recording of the *Concerto for the left hand* is altogether dazzling. He plays with effortless virtuosity, brilliance and, when required, great sensitivity. This is at least the equal of any of the classic accounts either on 78s or LP, and is magnificently recorded. The *Pavane* is also very distinguished; apart from the strangely impulsive closing bars, this too is beautiful playing. Gavrilov has superb dash and impeccable style. The tape transfer has some problems with the resonance, notably in the main climax of the concerto; otherwise the sound and balance are good.

Daphnis et Chloé (ballet; complete).
⊛*** Decca Dig. SXDL/*KSXDC* 7526 [Lon. LDR 71028/5-]. Montreal SO and Ch., Dutoit.
*** HMV Dig. ASD/*TCC-ASD* 4099 [Ang. DS 37868]. LSO and Ch., Previn.
(M) *** Decca Jub. JB/*KJBC* 69 [Lon. STS 15090]. ROHCG Ch., LSO, Monteux.
**(*) RCA Dig. RL 13458 [ARC 1/*ARK 1* 3458]. Dallas SO and Ch., Mata.

The sound on the Dutoit Montreal version is ravishing, and it is matched by a sumptuously evocative performance. Dutoit adopts an idiomatic and flexible style, observing the minute indications of tempo change but making every slight variation sound totally spontaneous. The final *Danse générale* finds him adopting a dangerously fast tempo, but the Montreal players – combining French responsiveness with transatlantic polish – rise superbly to the challenge, with the choral punctuations at the end adding to the sense of frenzy. The digital recording is wonderfully luminous, with the chorus ideally balanced at an evocative half-distance, and the demonstration-worthy cassette matches the disc closely.

With rhythm more important than atmosphere, Previn directs a superbly vivid and very dramatic performance, an exciting alternative to the superlative Dutoit version, with equally spectacular sound on disc and chrome tape.

Monteux's version remains strongly recommendable at medium price. He conducted the first performance of *Daphnis et Chloé* in 1912, and it is a matter for gratitude that his poetic and subtly shaded reading should have been made available in such an outstanding recording. The performance was one of the finest things Monteux did for the gramophone, and the richly sensuous and atmospheric orchestral and choral sheen Decca have provided is fully worthy of such distinguished and memorable music-making. The cassette transfer is made at a relatively modest level.

Mata directs a warmly atmospheric reading for which RCA produced one of the very finest of their early digital recordings. This version was quickly overtaken by others even in the digital field, but it has fine rhythmic pointing and an easy freshness in every scene.

(i) *Daphnis et Chloé: Suites Nos. 1 and 2. Ma Mère l'Oye* (complete).
(M) *** Turn. TVS 34603 [id./*CT 2131*]. Minnesota O., Skrowaczewski, (i) with St Olaf Ch.

The first *Daphnis suite* is absolutely magical in Skrowaczewski's hands, and in terms of sheer atmosphere and imaginative vitality these performances can well stand comparison with their most prestigious rivals. Though the Minnesota Orchestra is not so superlative an ensemble as the Amsterdam Concertgebouw Orchestra or the French Orchestre National, there is absolutely nothing second-rate about its playing, and the recording is beautifully balanced and wide-ranging. Skrowaczewski conveys every subtlety of texture and colour, and he shapes phrases not only with the good taste and fine musical judgement that Haitink gives us in his Philips records, but with a genuine feel for the sensuous, sumptuous qualities of these scores. His *Ma Mère l'Oye* is complete, like Monteux's and Boulez's, and stands comparison with either. There are finer accounts of the second *Daphnis et Chloé suite* at full price (Karajan or Previn, for example), but this is still amazingly good.

Daphnis et Chloé: Suite No. 2.
(*) Centaur Dig. CRC 1007 [id.]. LSO, Mackerras – DEBUSSY: *La Mer.*(*)
** HMV ASD/TC-ASD 3705. Leningrad PO, Temirkanov – STRAVINSKY: *Petrushka.***(*)

Mackerras's reading has all his characteristic energy and intensity, but with recording less clear and vivid than one expects of digital sound – particular when the side length is so short – it need be recommended only to those who want this particular coupling.

There is no want of character in Temirkanov's *Daphnis et Chloé* though it does not match the refinement and delicacy of the very finest versions. The Leningrad wind are less elegant than, say, the Berliners or the Philharmonia, and much will depend on whether readers want this coupling, whose logic resides in the Diaghilev connection and the close proximity of the gestation of the two ballets. The forward balance of the wind will not appeal to all tastes, but otherwise the recording is acceptable. The tape transfer is dramatically vivid, although

there is a patch of distortion with the forwardly balanced trumpets near the end of the ballet.

Ma Mère l'Oye: suite; Rapsodie espagnole.
*** DG 2531/*3301* 264 [id.]. LAPO, Giulini – DEBUSSY: *La Mer.****

The Giulini Los Angeles performance conveys much of the sultry atmosphere of the *Rapsodie espagnole*. Indeed some details, such as the sensuous string responses to the cor anglais tune in the *Feria*, have not been so tenderly caressed since the intoxicating Reiner version of the early 1960s. The *Ma Mère l'Oye suite* is beautifully done too, though it is not superior to Giulini's Philharmonia version; no one would guess that the recordings were separated by twenty years. The cassette transfer is disappointing, not matching the LP in range or detail.

Ma Mère l'Oye: suite; Le Tombeau de Couperin; Valses nobles et sentimentales.
(M) ** Decca Eclipse ECS 815. SRO, Ansermet.

Eminently serviceable accounts, with the usual distinguished recording from the Decca engineers. The sound is a little dated now and the playing lacks the last ounce of polish and refinement, but at its price the disc is well worth considering if this coupling is required.

Rapsodie espagnole.
*** HMV Dig. ASD/*TCC-ASD* 3902 [Ang. DS/*4ZS* 37742]. Phd. O., Muti – CHABRIER: *España*; FALLA: *Three-cornered Hat.****

Muti directs a performance which is aptly refined in its textures and also strikingly vigorous in the sharp definition of the dance rhythms. The work here sounds more like Spanish music than

RAVEL

French, so is well matched with the other items on the disc. The digital recording in the reverberant Philadelphia acoustic is first-rate, and the chrome cassette is excitingly vivid.

Le Tombeau de Couperin.
** Decca Dig. SXDL/*KSXDC* 7520 [Lon. LDR 10040/5-]. Chicago SO, Solti – MUSSORGSKY: *Pictures.****

Recorded with very different microphone placing from the main Mussorgsky work on the disc, *Le Tombeau de Couperin* in Solti's reading sounds hard and brilliant rather than classically elegant. The recording is partly to blame, with close-up sound reducing the sense of ambience. Nonetheless it makes an original coupling for the Ravel arrangement of Mussorgsky. The cassette transfer is softer-edged than the disc and the effect more atmospheric; many will prefer it.

Tzigane (for violin and orchestra).
*** Decca SXL/*KSXC* 6851 [Lon. 7073/5-]. Kyung-Wha Chung, RPO, Dutoit – CHAUSSON: *Poème*; SAINT-SAËNS: *Havanaise* etc.***
(M) *(*) RCA Gold GL/*GK* 11329 [AGL 1 1329]. Perlman, LSO, Previn – LALO: *Symphonie espagnole.***

With its seemingly improvisatory solo introduction, *Tzigane* is a work which demands an inspirational artist, and Kyung-Wha Chung is ideally cast, coupling this elusive piece with other concertante works too often neglected. Accompaniments and recordings are both excellent; the cassette needs a slight smoothing of the treble to sound its best.

Perlman's performance is a brilliant one and Previn accompanies imaginatively, but the exaggeratedly close balance of the soloist robs the music of subtlety and atmosphere in spite of the fine playing.

CHAMBER MUSIC

Piano trio in A min.
** HMV ASD 3729. De la Pau, Yan-Pascal and Paul Tortelier – SAINT-SAËNS: *Piano trio.****

Piano trio; Violin sonata in G; Violin sonata (1897).
*** EMI 2C 069 73024. Collard, Dumay, Lodéon.

(i) *Piano trio;* (ii) *Violin sonata in G; Tzigane.*
(M) **(*) Ph. Fest. 6570/*7310* 177 [id.].
(i) Beaux Arts Trio; (ii) Grumiaux, Hajdu.

The three young French musicians, Augustin Dumay, Frédéric Lodéon and Jean-Philippe Collard, give as convincing an account of the *Trio* as any of their rivals. They are eminently well recorded, though perhaps not as vividly as the Tortelier group. The particular attraction of this performance is its combination of strength and repose, brilliance and *tendresse*. The value of the issue is enhanced by its couplings: a good account of the *Violin sonata* written in the mid-1920s along with the only recording of an early sonata in one movement dating from 1897. Though this is far from distinctive Ravel, it is nonetheless fastidiously crafted, elegant and poised. Dumay plays it and the *Sonata in G* excellently and is most sensitively partnered by Collard: a useful alternative to the Grumiaux version of the *G major Sonata*, though not perhaps as aristocratic.

The Beaux Arts give a predictably fine account of the *Trio*, and even though the recording is not of the most recent provenance – it dates from the 1960s – the sound is extremely good and the price a strong advantage. The only slight criticism would be an occasional want of charm on the part of Daniel Guilet, but that is a very small reservation. In the *Violin sonata in G*, Grumiaux's playing has great finesse and beauty of sound, and the recording is very natural too. The fill-up is the popular *Tzigane*, where both Grumiaux and his partner, István Hajdu, display appropriate panache. A good record. On cassette the unnecessarily low level of transfer of the *Trio* and the *Sonata* robs the music-making of presence and impact; the *Tzigane* is slightly better.

Tortelier *père et fils* and Maria de la Pau enjoy the advantage of the most vivid recorded sound; the upper end of the piano is particularly clean and lifelike, and there is real presence here. It is a vital and thoroughly enjoyable performance (and has the advantage of an enterprising coupling) even if it does not displace earlier rivals. Maria de la Pau is an intelligent and agile pianist, but the softest dynamics do not always register, and, though too much should not made of this small point, at the end of the first movement there is a lack of magic and sense of repose.

String quartet in G min.
✵*** DG 2531/*3301* 203 [id.]. Melos Qt –
  DEBUSSY: *Quartet.*✵***
(M) * Argo ZK/*KZKC* 46. Aeolian Qt –
  DEBUSSY: *Quartet.**

For many years the Italian Quartet held pride of place in this coupling. The Melos Quartet of Stuttgart brings artistry of the highest order to this magical score. The slow movement offers the most refined and integrated quartet sound; in terms of internal balance and blend it would be difficult to surpass it, and the reading has great poetry. In both the scherzo and finale the Melos players evince the highest virtuosity, and there is not the slightest trace of the prosaic phrasing that marred their Mozart *D minor Quartet*, K. 421. They also have the advantage of superbly truthful recording. Highly imaginative playing touched with a complete identification with Ravel's sensibility. The cassette matches the disc closely, though there is a touch of fierceness in the treble which needs softening with the controls.

More polish and finesse would be welcome in the Aeolian performance. Given the competition this is not really a contender.

Violin sonata in G.
(M) *** Ph. Fest. 6570/*7310* 206 [id.]. D. Oistrakh, Bauer – DEBUSSY and YSAŸE: *Sonatas*; PROKOFIEV: *5 Melodies.****

Oistrakh's account of the Ravel *Sonata* is a beautiful one, and though it faces strong competition from Grumiaux (see under the *Piano trio* above), the quality of this account and the interest of the couplings give it the stronger claim. The recording is good on both disc and cassette.

PIANO MUSIC

À la manière de Borodin; A la manière de Chabrier. (i; ii) *Frontispiece. Gaspard de la Nuit; Jeux d'eau; Menuet antique; Menuet sur le nom de Haydn.* (i) *Ma Mère l'Oye. Miroirs; Pavane pour une infante défunte; Prélude; Sérénade grotesque.* (i) *Sites auriculaires. Sonatine; Le Tombeau de Couperin.* (i) *La Valse. Valses nobles et sentimentales.*
*** EMI 2C 167 73025/7. Collard, with (i) Béroff, (ii) Labèque.

Jean-Philippe Collard has already recorded outstanding performances of the Ravel concertos. His survey of the piano music is hardly less distinguished and is touched with much the same sensitivity. The three records include a version of *La Valse* for two pianos (with Michel Béroff) and the *Sites auriculaires*, which are not included in Pascal Rogé's survey. Collard has a strong sense of line and a keen rhythmic backbone. His *Valses nobles et sentimentales* are splendidly crisp, and his playing in *Gaspard de*

la Nuit is finely characterized. He is
recorded in a less flattering acoustic than
was Rogé, whose set has great sensitivity
and a sophisticated sense of keyboard
colour. Put his *Le gibet* alongside Collard's, and the comparison is to his advantage which was not the case in the
concert hall! Collard has undoubted
style, however, and his set can be strongly
recommended. The earlier editions of the
Penguin Stereo Record Guide underrated
the Rogé set: repeated hearing has
revealed its strengths. Collard can be
recommended alongside it, for he has a
tautness and rhythmic strength that are
appealing as well as a fine sense of texture
and tenderness.

*À la manière de Borodin; À la man-
ière de Chabrier; Gaspard de la Nuit.*
(i) *Habanera. Jeux d'eau; Menuet
antique; Menuet sur le nom de
Haydn.* (i) *Ma Mère l'Oye. Miroirs;
Pavane pour une infante défunte;
Prélude; Sonatine; Le Tombeau de
Couperin; Valses nobles et sentimentales.*
(M) (***) CBS mono 77346 (3). Robert
(and (i) Gaby) Casadesus.

These mono performances recorded in
the early 1950s deserve an enthusiastic
welcome back to the catalogue. They still
sound remarkably fresh, and the quality
is excellent for its period. Casadesus was
a great exponent of this repertoire, and
in many of these works he is still unsurpassed: the *Valses nobles et sentimentales, Miroirs,* and the *Toccata* from
Le Tombeau de Couperin are very special.
Other pieces are less sensitive; *Jeux d'eau*
and even *Gaspard de la Nuit* find him less
responsive to dynamic nuance, a shade
routine. However, there is so much that
is memorable that this surely ranks as an
indispensable set for all lovers of piano
music, particularly given the modest
price.

*À la manière de Borodin; À la
manière de Chabrier; Prélude; Le
Tombeau de Couperin; Valses nobles
et sentimentales.*
** Nimbus 2103. Perlemuter.

*Gaspard de la Nuit; Jeux d'eau;
Menuet antique; Pavane.*
** Nimbus 2101. Perlemuter.

*Menuet sur le nom de Haydn; Mir-
oirs; Sonatine.*
** Nimbus 2102. Perlemuter.

As a pupil of Ravel, Vlado Perlemuter
enjoys some authority, but it would be
idle to suggest that this survey, recorded
in his seventies, is an unqualified success.
The piano is somewhat distantly
balanced and the resulting textures,
though lifelike, could be cleaner and
more strongly defined. The playing is
natural enough and free from idiosyncrasy, but there is little real magic
now. In recent years Perlemuter has
become something of a vogue pianist in
certain circles, but this set left a feeling of
disappointment.

Gaspard de la Nuit. (i) *Ma Mère
l'Oye. Valses nobles et sentimentales.*
** RCA RL 12530 [ARL 1/*ARK 1*
2530]. Ax, (i) with Yoko Nozaki.

Emanuel Ax is an impressive artist
and, taken on its own merits, his version
of *Gaspard de la Nuit* has striking refinement and control of keyboard colour.
Yet he can be a little wayward at times,
and though his technique is more than a
match for *Scarbo*, his account has not the
electricity or intensity which are required
– and which one finds in Gavrilov's Ravel
performances. Indeed, his *Gaspard* is not
as convincing as Pascal Rogé's, which has
perhaps been underrated; it wears well
and has genuine atmosphere, and Rogé
enjoys the charming distinction of being
the only pianist to have recorded *Mother
Goose* with his mother! Emanuel Ax records it with his wife – and very well, too.

VOCAL MUSIC

(i) *Chansons madécasses.* (ii) *Cinq Mélodies populaires grecques: Le réveil de la mariée; Tout gai!* (only); *Deux Mélodies hébraïques; Shéhérazade* (song cycle).
*** CBS 36665/41- [Col. IM/HMT 36665]. Von Stade, with (i) Dwyer, Eskind, Katz, (ii) Boston SO, Ozawa.

The distinctive timbre of Frederica von Stade's voice and her yearning expressiveness make for sensuous performances not just of *Shéhérazade* – here as evocatively beautiful as it has ever been on disc – but also of the often strikingly original songs which make up the apt coupling. In these, Ravel was writing unpredictably, and they need persuasive handling, which Ozawa and the Boston forces richly provide too. The digital recording is not of the most brilliant but is admirably atmospheric. The chrome cassette is also well managed.

Deux Mélodies hébraïques; Shéhérazade (song cycle); *Trois Poèmes de Stéphane Mallarmé.*
(M) **(*) Decca Eclipse ECS 810 |(d) Lon. STS 15155/6]. Danco, SRO, Ansermet – FAURÉ: *La Bonne Chanson.***(*)

The excellent (no, magical) account of *Shéhérazade* is among the classics of the gramophone, and age has not diminished its power to enchant. Though it first appeared in 1955, it is genuine stereo, as is the recording of the *Deux Mélodies hébraïques.* Suzanne Danco sings these as beautifully as she does the exquisite and much neglected Mallarmé settings (which are transcriptions from mono). Though there are more modern (and more sumptuously recorded) versions to claim the collector's first allegiance, this Danco record remains an indispensable part of the Ravel discography.

Shéhérazade.
(*) Ph. 9500 783/7300 857 [id.]. Norman, LSO, Colin Davis – BERLIOZ: *Nuits d'été.*(*)

Jessye Norman seems more at home in Ravel's song cycle than in the coupled account of the Berlioz, although she and Sir Colin Davis are languorous to the point of lethargy in *L'indifférent.* With the voice very forward, the balance is less than ideal, though otherwise the sound is rich and atmospheric. Danco, Baker and Crespin, however, each have special qualities to offer which Miss Norman does not match. The Philips tape transfer is faithful, but made at a rather low level.

L'Enfant et les sortilèges.
*** HMV Dig. ASD/TCC-ASD 4167 [Ang. DS 37869]. Wyner, Auger, Berbié, Langridge, Bastin, Amb. S., LSO, Previn.

(i) *L'Enfant et les sortilèges;* (ii) *L'Heure espagnole* (operas; complete).
(M) **(*) DG Priv. 2726 076 (2). (i) Ogéas, Collard, Berbié, Gilma, RTF Ch. and O.; (ii) Berbié, Sénéchal, Giraudeau, Bacquier, Van Dam, Paris Op. O.; cond. Maazel.

Given digital sound of demonstration quality (on both disc and tape), Previn's dramatic and highly spontaneous reading of *L'Enfant* brings out the refreshing charm of a neglected masterpiece. Helped by a strong, stylish team of soloists, this makes superb entertainment.

Maazel's recordings of the two Ravel one-act operas were made in the early sixties (*L'Enfant* in 1961, *L'Heure espagnole* four years later), and though the solo voices in the former are balanced too close, the sound is vivid and the performances are splendidly stylish. Neoclassical crispness of articulation goes with refined textures that convey the tender poetry of the one piece, the ripe humour of the other.

Rawsthorne, Alan (1905–71)

Piano concertos Nos. 1–2.
*** Lyr. SRCS 101. Binns, LSO,
Braithwaite.

Both of Rawsthorne's concertos are
among the most memorable written by
British composers, providing a Proko-
fiev-like contrast between jagged figuration and lyrical warmth. Without losing
the necessary edge in the writing, Malcolm Binns brings out the expressiveness
of the music, particularly in the *First
Concerto*, with its hushed slow movement and interlude in the middle of the
final *Tarantella*. There is plenty of vigour
in both dance finales (the second has its
quota of Latin American rhythms).
Good orchestral playing and recording.

Street Corner: overture.
*** Lyr. SRCS 95. LPO, Pritchard –
*Concert (Overtures).****

The *Street Corner overture* is one of
Rawsthorne's more familiar short pieces.
The performance here is first-class and
the recording excellent. It is part of a
highly recommendable anthology discussed in the Concerts section below.

Rebel, Jean-Fery (1661–1747)

Les Éléments (ballet).
*** O-L DSLO 562 [id.]. AcAM, Hogwood – DESTOUCHES: *Suite.****

Rebel, a contemporary of Bach and
Handel, was in his seventies when he
wrote his ballet on the elements emerging
out of Chaos, startling even twentieth-
century listeners with the massive discord
illustrating Chaos at the start. The sequence of dances, beautifully performed
on original instruments by Hogwood's

Academy, is consistently sharp and
refreshing, helping to revive an un-
deservedly neglected name.

Reger, Max (1873–1916)

Piano concerto in F min., Op. 114.
(M) **(*) CBS 61711/40-. Serkin, Phd.
O., Ormandy.

Reger's *Piano concerto* is a remarkable
and powerful composition. Its dark
opening momentarily suggests Shostakovich! No one but Reger, however, could have conceived the rugged
Brahmsian piano writing. The slow
movement is a contemplative, rapt piece
that touches genuine depths. Less successful writing, perhaps, in the rhetorical
finale. Serkin gives a magisterial performance and is well supported by the
Philadelphia Orchestra under Ormandy.
The recording is not outstanding but
eminently satisfactory. Worth exploring.

*Benedictus, Op. 59/2; Fantasia on a
chorale 'Halleluja! Gott zu loben,
bleib meine Seelenfreud', Op. 52/3;
Fantasia and fugue on B.A.C.H., Op.
46; Toccata and fugue in D min./
major, Op. 59/5–6.*
*** Mer. E 77004. Sanger (organ of St
Jude-on-the-Hill, London).

Reger, one of the most Germanic of
composers, requires persuasive handling if he is not to sound lumpy and
heavy, and that particularly applies to
the organ music. David Sanger, using
a moderate-sized, clean-textured instrument of fine quality, does wonders
with these heavyweight works. With
fine recorded sound this can be recommended to others besides organ enthusiasts.

Reich, Steve (born 1936)

Six Pianos; (i) *Music for mallet instruments, voices and organ.*
(M) (***) DG Priv. 2535/*3335* 463.
Chambers, Preiss, Hartenberger, Becker, Reich, Velez, with (i) Ferchen, Harms, Jarrett, LaBarbara, Clayton.

This disc might be entitled 'Stuck in a groove'. Both pieces exploit Reich's technique of endlessly repeating a very brief fragment which gradually gets transformed, almost imperceptibly, by different emphases being given to it. The result is mesmeric, though of very limited expressive value. No doubt the drug culture provides parallels. *Six Pianos* is the longer piece (no less than twenty-four minutes) and by its very texture more aggressive. With gentler marimbas the other side is far less wearing. The 1974 recording is by all reckonings faithful, though not as weighty as it might be. The cassette matches the disc closely. Frankly, this is music that some listeners will not be able to take seriously.

Respighi, Ottorino
(1879–1936)

Ancient airs and dances: Suites Nos. 1–3.
⊛ (M) *** Mercury SRI/*MRI* 75009. Philh. Hungarica, Dorati.
*** Decca SXL 6846. LPO, Lopez-Cobós.
**(*) DG 2530/*3300* 891 [id.]. Boston SO, Ozawa.

Dorati's famous and very distinguished Mercury recording of the sixties has been in and out of the British catalogue over the years and now returns as an import, pressed in Holland, but using the original masters. The performance, one of the first recordings by this group of Hungarian expatriates based in Vienna, is of the utmost distinction. It combines brilliance with great sensitivity – the delicacy of articulation of the principal oboe is a special delight – to display a remarkable feeling for the colour and ambience of the Renaissance dances on which Respighi's three suites (the last for strings alone) are based. The refinement and warmth of the playing (and the sound) are very striking, particularly in the *Third Suite*, where the string textures are very beautiful. Dorati finds in this music a nobility and graciousness that make it obstinately memorable. Marriner's fresh and sunny account with the Los Angeles Chamber Orchestra is perhaps even more beautifully recorded (HMV ASD 3188 [Ang. S 37301]), but Dorati's version has very special claims on the collector, quite irrespective of its lower price. The cassette is first-class.

The Decca version by the LPO under Lopez-Cobós, however, is by no means an also-ran. It is superbly recorded, and the Kingsway Hall acoustic, with its characteristic warmth, gives the orchestra an enticing bloom. The Decca cassette matches the disc closely. The performance is not as elegant as Marriner's but it has striking intensity. The third movement of the *Second Suite* and the central movements of the *Third* demonstrate this readily. The LPO strings produce playing of considerable fervour, and there is plenty of sparkle in the lighter sections throughout.

Ozawa is rhythmically very positive, and the Boston orchestra is on excellent form. The DG recording is brightly vivid and strongly projected (it sounds especially good on tape, where the edges are fractionally softer). Ozawa is at his best in the *Second Suite*, where the luminous wind playing combines with strong contrasts of dynamic and tempo to dramatic effect. The *Third Suite* is rather less memorable.

Ancient airs and dances: Suite No. 3 (for strings).

(M) **(*) Ph. Fest. 6570/7310 181 [id.]. I Musici – BARBER: *Adagio*; BARTÓK: *Rumanian folk dances*; BRITTEN: *Simple symphony.***(*)

A warmly gracious if rather leisurely approach to the *Third Suite*, helped by the rich Philips recording and polished playing. Other versions have more vitality; but this is certainly very agreeable.

The Birds (suite); *Brazilian impressions.*

(M) *** Mercury SRI 75023 [id.]. LSO, Dorati.

Respighi wrote his *Brazilian impressions* after spending a summer in Rio de Janeiro in 1927. The music is colourful and atmospheric and the triptych obviously recalls Debussy's *Ibéria*. The second impression sinisterly invokes the *Dies irae*, for it is named after Butantan, famous for its reptile institute where poisonous snakes are bred in vast numbers for the production of serum. Respighi's finale, *Canzone e danza*, does not match Debussy's festive morning scene, but is still highly evocative. Dorati's performance is vividly characterized, and it is coupled to a spirited account of *The Birds*, with its dance rhythms strongly projected and its pictorial piquancy well realized by the excellent LSO wind playing. The recording (from the beginning of the sixties) is more forwardly balanced and makes a stronger impact than Kertesz's Decca version of *The Birds*, yet it has plenty of ambient warmth and does not sound dated. Recommended.

The Birds; The Fountains of Rome; The Pines of Rome (symphonic poems).

(M) *** Decca Jub. JB/KJBC 59. LSO, Kertesz.

The special attraction of Kertesz's disc is the inclusion of *The Birds*, an evocative

and beautifully scored work, given a first-class performance and rich recording. In the two symphonic poems Kertesz is again at his finest. These are strongly characterized and deeply musical performances; the elements of spectacle (the turning on of the Triton fountain) and grandeur (the Trevi climax, with its evocation of Neptune's heavenly processional) are balanced by a magical sense of atmosphere in the central movements of *The Pines*, although in the finale of this work other performances find more excitement. The Decca engineers provide outstanding sound quality, the cassette matching the disc and handling the climaxes with aplomb. At medium price this is outstanding value.

3 Botticelli Pictures; (i) *Deità silvane*; (i; ii) *Lauda per la Natività del Signore.*

*** Argo ZRG 904. London Chamber Ch., Argo CO, Heltay, with (i) Tear, (ii) Gomez, Dickinson.

Here is a totally different side to Respighi from the familiar lush opulence of the Roman trilogy. This music is fastidiously scored for small forces, and the effect is of refinement and great skill in the handling of pastel colourings. The most familiar is the *Three Botticelli Pictures* (1927), a delicate and affecting piece well played by these artists, and already available on record. The two rarities are no less appealing. The *Lauda per la Natività del Signore* (1929) is a setting of words attributed to Jacopone da Todi, a Franciscan of the thirteenth century, and is ingeniously scored for two flutes, piccolo, oboe, cor anglais, two bassoons, piano (four hands) and triangle, while the voices are wonderfully handled. The *Deità silvane* (1917) was originally for soprano and piano but the composer scored it in 1926 for single wind, horn, percussion, harp and strings – to great effect. An enterprising and rewarding issue which reflects credit on all concerned and has the benefit of excellent sound too.

Feste romane.
(B) **(*) RCA VICS/*VK* 2006 [AGL 1/*AGK 1* 1276]. LAPO, Mehta – R. STRAUSS: *Don Juan.***(*)

This was one of Mehta's first recordings with the orchestra of which he became principal conductor in his twenties. Its flair for display in one of Respighi's most brilliant – if musically empty – showpieces is very striking. The recording is extremely bright and vivid, with an element of brittleness in the treble, common to both the disc and the excellent chrome cassette.

Feste romane; The Fountains of Rome.
**(*) CBS 76920 [Col. M/*MT* 35846]. LAPO, Tilson Thomas.

Michael Tilson Thomas secures a highly sensitive response from the Los Angeles Philharmonic, with string playing of the greatest delicacy. The closing bars of the *Fountains* are hauntingly atmospheric in his hands, and the CBS engineers produce tone quality that is completely truthful in timbre though not in perspective. This is nonetheless a competitive issue, and though it is not as sumptuous as the Karajan *Fountains* (see below), it may still be worth considering. However, Ozawa's excellent DG record provides an extra work for a similar outlay.

Feste romane; The Fountains of Rome; The Pines of Rome.
*** DG 2530/*3300* 890 [id.]. Boston SO, Ozawa.
☮ (M) (***) RCA mono VL 46000. NBC SO, Toscanini.

The combination of Respighi's Roman trilogy on a single LP is an obvious coupling and although the DG sides are well-

filled the quality of the recording does not suffer. Indeed this stands up well beside Karajan's DG disc (see below) which offers only two of the three symphonic poems. Ozawa is at his finest in *The Fountains of Rome*: this is the most impressive recorded performance since Reiner's RCA version dating from the very earliest days of stereo; and the other works have plenty of atmosphere too. *Feste romane* is vivid without being noisy, even if there is not quite the stereoscopic clarity of pictorial detail that distinguishes Maazel's Decca version (see below). The orchestral playing is very fine throughout, and DG's recording is splendid, with a demonstration-worthy cassette matching the disc very closely indeed. The climax of *The Pines* makes an overwhelmingly powerful effect in both media.

Toscanini's accounts of the *Fountains* and *Pines* fall into a special category. They were made in the early 1950s and were among his best recordings technically. Their refinement and definition have been greatly enhanced in these new transfers, mastered at half speed and giving a more subtle response in the upper register. The performances are legendary, and the virtuosity of the NBC in the 1949 record of *Feste romane* is quite stunning. This performance is startlingly well recorded and has never been surpassed on disc. The quality of the strings in the quieter passages is beautifully lush, and the engineers have succeeded in removing the hard edges that distinguished the earlier transfers without any loss of brilliance.

Feste romane; The Pines of Rome.
*** Decca SXL/*KSXC* 6822 [Lon. 7043/5-]. Cleveland O., Maazel.

Maazel's account of *Feste romane* (musically the least interesting of Respighi's three symphonic poems inspired by the capital city) is something of a revelation. The Decca recording is extremely sophisticated in its colour and detail, and Respighi's vividly evocative sound pictures are brought glitteringly to life. The orchestral playing shows matching virtuosity, and the final festival scene (*The night before Epiphany in the Piazza Navona*), with its gaudy clamour of trumpets and snatches of melody from the local organ-grinder, is given a kaleidoscopic imagery exactly as the composer intended. Elsewhere the superbly stylish playing has an almost baroque colouring, so wittily is it pointed. *The Pines of Rome* is given a strong, direct characterization, undoubtedly memorable, but without quite the subtlety or electricity of Karajan's two versions (see below). But the Decca recording throughout this disc (and especially in *Feste romane*) has a breathtaking, demonstration vividness, finer than many digital issues. The cassette is only fractionally less clear in *Feste romane*, but in *The Pines* the focus is appreciably sharper on the LP.

The Fountains of Rome; The Pines of Rome.
*** DG 2531/*3301* 055 [id.]. Berlin PO, Karajan.
(B) *** CfP CFP/*TC-CFP* 40348. New Philh. O., Frühbeck de Burgos – STRAVINSKY: *Circus polka* etc.***

The Fountains of Rome; The Pines of Rome; Belfagör overture.
**(*) HMV ASD 3372 [Ang. S 37402]. LSO, Gardelli.

Karajan is in his element in this music, and the playing of the Berlin Philharmonic is wonderfully refined. The evocation of atmosphere in the two middle sections of *The Pines of Rome* is unforgettable. A distanced and magically haunting trumpet solo is matched by the principal clarinet, who is hardly less poetic. This is all projected against a ravishingly sensuous background of string tone, and when the nightingale begins his song the effect is uncannily real. To set the scene of *The pines of the*

Appian Way Karajan creates a riveting pianissimo and slowly builds a climax of tremendous grandeur. In *The Fountains* the tension is rather less tautly held, but the pictorial imagery is hardly less telling when the playing is so beautiful. But here Ozawa (see above) is even more impressive, and his disc has the advantage of offering an extra work. The Karajan cassette is of DG's highest quality, with only very fractionally less range than the LP.

The extraordinarily vivid Classics for Pleasure coupling dates from 1969. Originally made in EMI's hi-fi-conscious Studio Two technique it combines brilliance with atmosphere. The opening of *The pines of the Villa Borghese* makes an electrifying impact, and the power of the Appian Way climax is matched by the spectacle of Neptune's procession in the evocation of the Trevi fountain. The orchestral playing is extremely fine; Frühbeck de Burgos finds a haunting elegiac quality for the central sections of *The Pines* and creates a romantically beautiful Villa Medici sunset. The lustrous sheen of the New Philharmonia strings and woodwind is superbly caught by the engineers both on disc and on the quite outstanding cassette, which loses almost nothing in range and detail. The Stravinsky encores make a delightful bonus.

Gardelli's are atmospheric performances, sympathetic and finely played, with much atmospheric warmth if less of a feeling of drama. There are some lustrous sounds here, and the HMV recording quality is both rich and refined. The *Belfagor overture* is a dramatic and lively piece, strongly characterized and vivid, but it is not of sufficient interest to make this issue strongly recommendable in such a competitive field.

The Pines of Rome.
(M) *** HMV SXLP/*TC-SXLP* 30450 [Ang. S 35613]. Philh. O., Karajan – BERLIOZ: *Carnaval romain*; LISZT: *Les Préludes.****

Karajan's earlier EMI recording of *The Pines of Rome* dates from 1958. The performance is absolutely superb, with the Philharmonia strings producing refined and sumptuous tone. So for that matter do the wind and brass; even the nightingale sounds enchanted with the proceedings. What never ceases to amaze is the way these early Philharmonia records sound so fresh. The various departments of the orchestra blend among themselves and with each other. This version holds its own remarkably well with Karajan's later recording with the Berlin Philharmonic (see above), issued in late 1978, though comparison reveals that the latter has a little more range at either end of the spectrum and a somewhat more open acoustic. However, this is really superb. The cassette transfer is admirable, to match the disc closely.

Rossiniana (suite arr. from piano pieces by Rossini: *Quelques riens pour album*).

(M) **(*) Decca Jub. JB/*KJBC* 79. RPO, Dorati – ROSSINI: *La Boutique fantasque*.**(*)

It is perhaps curious that this work is usually catalogued under Respighi, whereas *La Boutique fantasque*, which Respighi also based on Rossini's music, is more often found under Rossini. *Rossiniana* is not so inspired a score as *La Boutique fantasque*, but it is beautifully played here and Dorati's affection is most persuasive. The recording is first-class. It has more atmosphere than in the coupling, although on cassette the difference is rather less striking than on disc.

Rimsky-Korsakov, Nikolas (1844–1908)

Capriccio espagnol, Op. 34.
** Decca SXL/*KSXC* 6956. LAPO,

Lopez-Cobós – CHABRIER: *España* **; FALLA: *Three cornered Hat*.**(*)

Lopez-Cobós is rather relaxed at the opening, and in the variations the Los Angeles string section is not ideally sumptuous (though the horns are splendid). The wind acquit themselves well in the cadenza section, and the closing *Fandango* really catches fire. The sound is characteristically vivid in the Decca manner, although at the very opening of the cassette (which otherwise matches the disc closely) the quality is not absolutely clean.

Capriccio espagnol; Le Coq d'or: suite; Russian Easter Festival overture, Op. 36.
*** Decca SXL/*KSXC* 6966 [Lon. 7196]. Cleveland O., Maazel.

Maazel's famous early stereo recording of the *Capriccio espagnol* with the Berlin Philharmonic is not quite equalled by this new Cleveland version in charisma and excitement, but the other works included here come off splendidly. The performance of the *Russian Easter Festival overture* is full of imaginative touches, so that one has the sense of hearing the score for the first time. *Le Coq d'or* is gorgeously played and sumptuously recorded (the Queen of Shemakha's memorably sinuous theme is given a telling combination of delicacy and sensuous colour). Perhaps Maazel tends to indulge himself somewhat, luxuriating in the aural magic of Rimsky's scoring, but his warmth of affection communicates, and he creates a superb climax with *The marriage feast and lamentable end of King Dodon*. Even though the *Capriccio* is lacking in thrust, this is an indispensable collection, for the other two works have never been presented on record more enticingly. The Decca sound is of demonstration standard throughout, and the tape has only marginally less transient sparkle than the disc.

Capriccio espagnol; Russian Easter Festival overture, Op. 36.
(*) DG 2536/*3336* 379 [id.]. Chicago SO, Barenboim – BORODIN: *Polovtsian dances*; MUSSORGSKY: *Night.**

After an arresting start to the *Capriccio*, Barenboim adopts a rather leisurely pace in the variations, and although the orchestral playing is first-class, this is not a performance to set the adrenalin racing. But it is not wanting in colour, and the *Russian Easter Festival overture* is splendidly dramatic and full of atmosphere. The recording is spectacular, with very effective percussion. The cassette matches the disc fairly closely.

Capriccio espagnol; The Snow Maiden: Dance of the tumblers.
(M) ** CBS 60115/40- [Col. MY 36728]. NYPO, Bernstein – TCHAIKOVSKY: *Capriccio italien* etc.**

Bernstein's CBS record favours a coupling familiar from the early days of LP, with bonus items as makeweight. The opening of the *Capriccio espagnol* is rather slow and positive, but later the New York orchestra is given plenty of opportunities to display its virtuosity, and the closing *Fandango* is very brilliant indeed. The *Dance of the tumblers* must be the fastest performance on record, and the effect is exhilarating, although here the tendency to fierceness in the recording's upper range is even more marked than earlier.

Concert fantasy for violin and orchestra, Op. 33.
(M) ** Turn. TVS 34629 [id./*CT 2133*]. Rosand, R. Lux. O., Froment – ARENSKY: *Concerto ***; WIENIAWSKI: *Concert polonaise.***

Rimsky-Korsakov's *Concert fantasy* dates from the mid-1880s, immediately after the revision of the *Third Symphony*, at a time when he had become interested in the violin and its technique. The superb playing of Aaron Rosand cannot disguise the fact that this is a shallow piece whose invention is thin; the overall impression is amiable but unmemorable. However, this disc is worth having for the sake of the Arensky concerto, which is a charmer.

Le Coq d'or: suite.
(M) *(*) RCA Gold GL/*GK* 42700 [AGL 1/*AGK 1* 1528]. Boston SO, Leinsdorf – STRAVINSKY: *Firebird suite.*(*)

Rimsky-Korsakov's exotic and attractive orchestral suite from *Le Coq d'or* is ill-served by this rather undistinguished reissue. The recording is unattractively resonant and although the playing is not without atmosphere there is little magic.

Le Coq d'or: Introduction and (Act 3) *Procession. The Invisible City of Kitezh: Eulogy to the wilderness and Entr'acte* (Act 3). *May Night: overture. Mlada: Procession of the nobles. Tsar Saltan: suite.*
*** HMV ASD 3710. USSR SO or Bolshoi Th. O., Svetlanov.

All these recordings are new, save for the *May Night overture*, which dates from the 1960s. The music is colourful and most of it popular, and the playing of the USSR Symphony Orchestra in all these items is full of fire and panache. As the recordings are also of high standard, this disc ought to enjoy wide appeal. The only less familiar pieces are from *Kitezh*, Rimsky's last opera, and they are beautifully done.

May Night: overture.
(M) *** HMV SXLP/*TC-SXLP* 30447. Philh. O., Silvestri – LISZT: *Les Préludes* etc.***

This is only a makeweight for some fine Liszt performances, but the playing and recording (from the beginning of the sixties) are strikingly vivid and colourful. The cassette matches the disc closely.

Russian Easter Festival overture, Op. 36.

(M) *** RCA Gold GL/GK 42923 [(d) LSC 3067]. Chicago SO, Stokowski – KHACHATURIAN: *Symphony No. 3* (***); RACHMANINOV: *Vocalise*.**

(M) **(*) Ph. Fest. 6570/7310 191 [id.]. Concg. O., Markevitch – BORODIN: *Polovtsian dances*; TCHAIKOVSKY: *1812*.**(*)

Stokowski's performance of this work has been famous since the days of his black-label 78 discs, when he substituted a human voice for the trombone solo. The present performance is not eccentric but broad and sympathetic, with plenty of colour and excitement. The recording is rich, but lacks something in sparkle in the upper register. The cassette transfer has emerged with slightly more brilliance on top than the LP, yet retains its body and bloom.

An excellent performance from Markevitch, with fine orchestral playing to bring out the score's glowing colour. There is no lack of character and electricity; the recording is relatively modern (if not in the very top flight) and it has transferred acceptably to cassette. The couplings are recommendable too.

Sadko, Op. 5.

(M) (*) Turn. TVS 34644 [id./CT 2224]. Seattle SO, Katims – GLIÈRE: *Red Poppy*; SHOSTAKOVICH: *Age of Gold*.(*)

Rimsky-Korsakov's *Sadko* needs warmth and colour to make its full effect. Here the lively playing in Seattle is set at naught by the thin recording.

Scheherazade, Op. 35.

(B) *** CfP CFP/TC-CFP 40341. Philh.

O., Kletzki – TCHAIKOVSKY: *Capriccio italien*.**(*)

*** Ph. 9500 681/7300 776 [id.]. Concg. O., Kondrashin.

(M) **(*) HMV SXLP/TC-SXLP 30253 [Ang. S/4XS 35505]. RPO, Beecham.

(B) **(*) Con. CC/CCT 7501 [(d) Lon. 6212]. SRO, Ansermet.

**(*) Chalfont Dig. SDG 304. LSO, Tjeknavorian.

(B) **(*) HMV TC-IDL 505. Philh. O., Matačic – BORODIN: *Polovtsian dances* etc.**(*)

(M) **(*) DG Priv. 2535/3335 474 [2530/3300 972]. Boston SO, Ozawa.

** HMV ASD/TC-ASD 3779. [Ang. SZ/4ZS 37558]. LSO, Svetlanov.

Scheherazade; Capriccio espagnol.

(M) *(*) Ph. Fest. 6570/7310 148 [id.]. LSO, Markevitch.

Scheherazade; Tsar Saltan: Flight of the bumble bee; March.

(M) **(*) RCA Gold GL/GK 42703 [AGL 1/AGK 1 1330]. LSO, Previn.

Kletzki's famous recording of Rimsky-Korsakov's orchestral showpiece was a best-seller on HMV's Concert Classics label for over fifteen years. The recording has an attractively spacious acoustic, and the Philharmonia solo playing is superb, with highly distinguished violin solos from Hugh Bean. Kletzki's reading is broad in the first movement, and he makes the second glow and sparkle (the famous brass interchanges having the most vivid projection). The richness of the string playing in the third movement is matched by the exhilaration of the finale. The recording has been brightened in the new transfer and now sounds remarkably clear, though lacking something in sumptuousness, especially in the first movement. The second remains as demonstration-worthy as ever. The finale has rather more weight, but generally the sound balance is enhanced by a slight treble cut and comparable bass boost. As so often with CfP, there is minimal difference in sound between disc and cassette. The latter has fractionally less edge at the top but slightly more warmth, which makes the slow movement sound even more lustrous.

Kondrashin's version with the Concertgebouw Orchestra has the advantage of marvellous recorded sound, combining richness and sparkle within exactly the right degree of resonance. Here the personality of Hermann Krebbers (the orchestra's concertmaster) very much enters the picture, and his gently seductive portrayal of Scheherazade's narrative creates a strong influence on the overall interpretation. His exquisite playing, especially at the opening and close of the work, is cleverly used by Kondrashin to make a foil to the expansively vibrant contribution of the orchestra as a whole. The first movement, after Krebbers' tranquil introduction, develops a striking architectural sweep; the second is vivid with colour, the third beguilingly gracious, while in the finale, without taking unusually fast tempi, Kondrashin creates an irresistible forward impulse leading to a huge climax at the moment of the shipwreck. Alongside the other famous Philips record by Haitink and the LPO (6500 410/7300 226) this must count among the very finest of modern recordings. Unfortunately the cassette transfer, although well balanced, lacks the ultimate range and sparkle of the disc.

Beecham's record was originally issued at full price at the same time as Kletzki's. It is a fine performance, notable for superlative wind playing and the solo violin contribution of Steven Staryk. Sir Thomas's reading has both glamour and panache, and if some other versions have more drama (especially in the first movement) there is a compensating elegance and warmth. The slight snag is the recording, which, on disc, lacks voluptuousness and is rather hard on top and light in the bass. The cassette has rather more breadth and body.

Ansermet's version (shorn of its original *Polovtsian dances* coupling in this Contour bargain-priced reissue) was famous as a recording for its crystal clarity and vividness, rather than for any sensuous qualities. Thus the outer movements, with their undoubted sparkle, are the finest: the first is dramatic, and in the last the final climax makes a great impact. In Ansermet's hands the music's sinuous qualities are not missed and every bar of the score is alive. With a clean new master this is excellent value, though the cassette is not the equal of the disc, with boomy bass on side two.

Tjeknavorian's Chalfont digital record costs a great deal more than its competitors. Undoubtedly it is an arresting performance, and, with a notably clean pressing and extremely brilliant and detailed recording, its sharpness of detail will certainly appeal to some ears. The overall sound balance is bright rather than richly sumptuous, yet the bass response is strong and clear. Tjeknavorian paces the music briskly throughout; the first movement has a strong, passionate climax, and the slow movement has less repose than usual, sounding more elegant, less sensuous, its 6/8 rhythmic pattern readily apparent. The finale has a furious basic tempo, but the LSO players obviously revel in their virtuosity and the result is consistently exhilarating, with (for the most part) amazingly clear articulation. The climax has a brilliance to make the ears tingle, with a hint of fierceness in the recording itself.

At expansive tempi Previn's view of the first three movements is unexpectedly cool, the very opposite of vulgar. With rhythmic pointing which is characteristically crisp the result grows attractive on repetition, while the finale brings one of the most dramatic and brilliant performances ever recorded of that showpiece. The fill-ups provide a charming makeweight, particularly the *Tsar Saltan march* with its reminders of Walton's *Henry V* and Vaughan Williams's *Wasps*. The recording is outstanding for its late-sixties vintage, making this an attractive mid-price issue. The tape transfer fully conveys the richness and warmth of the recording; it has some slight lack of range in the treble, but this is not serious.

Matačić's cassette-only version on HMV offers a considerable bonus (this series guarantees an hour of music) and is reasonably priced. The Philharmonia playing is of the highest quality and the music-making throughout is alive, often dramatic. The sound is very good indeed, sparkling, yet with plenty of atmosphere, and offering a wide dynamic range. This is not the most distinctive and individual version available, but it is certainly worth considering in its price-range.

Ozawa's is an attractive performance, richly recorded. The first movement is strikingly spacious, building to a fine climax, and if the last degree of vitality is missing from the central movements the orchestral playing is warmly vivid. The finale is lively enough if not earthshaking in its excitement; but the reading as a whole has plenty of colour and atmosphere, and it is certainly enjoyable. The tape transfer is sophisticated.

Svetlanov's HMV version is disappointing, in spite of John Georgiadis's subtly seductive image of Scheherazade. The broad, powerful opening movement is balanced by a finale which is almost aggressively brilliant. The inner movements are extremely volatile, with much ebb and flow of tempo, so that they are less contrasted than usual. The LPO wind solo playing is impressive, but the strings sometimes have an almost febrile timbre which is less than glamorous. Svetlanov's conception undoubtedly brings out the Russianness of the score and it is certainly vivid, but in such a competitive field this could hardly be a first choice.

On Philips Festivo, Markevitch offers a generous coupling (though not more generous than Kletzki), but neither work generates the degree of vivid colour or sheer excitment that the music needs, although the slightly dry recording does not lack immediacy. There is some good orchestral playing here, but it is doubtful

if Scheherazade would have lasted 1001 nights at this temperature. The cassette matches the disc closely.

Symphonies Nos. (i; ii) 1 in E min., Op. 1; (i; iii) 2 (Antar), Op. 9; (i; iv) 3 in C, Op. 32. (v) Capriccio espagnol, Op. 34; (i; vi) Fantasia on Serbian themes, Op. 6; Sadko, Op. 5; Sinfonietta on Russian themes, Op. 31.
(M) ** HMV SLS 5150 (3). (i) Moscow RSO; (ii) Khaikin; (iii) Ivanov; (iv) Rozhdestvensky; (v) USSR SO, Svetlanov; (vi) Maxim Shostakovich.

Some of this music is very thin indeed: neither the first nor the third symphonies can bear too much repetition. Many of the performances emanate from the early 1960s, though the sound quality is perfectly acceptable. *Antar* and *Sadko* are probably the most rewarding pieces here, and it is a pity that the charming *Skazka* (*A Fairy Tale*) was not included in the package.

Tsar Saltan: suite; Flight of the bumble bee.
(M) **(*) Ph. Fest. 6570/7310 105 [id.]. Monte Carlo Op. O., Benzi – BORODIN: *Symphony No. 2.***

Benzi secures a strong and cohesive performance of Rimsky-Korsakov's colourful suite (although the vibrato from the brass colours the texture in a French way). The recording is vivid, bright and glittering at the top, and with as much body as the orchestra itself can provide. The cassette is very well managed, having slightly more 'middle' without noticeable loss of brilliance.

Robles, Marisa (20th century)

Narnia suite.
*** ASV Dig. DCA/ZCDCA 513.

Composer, Hyde-Smith, Robles Harp Ens.

This incidental music was commissioned for the integral recording of the C. S. Lewis *Narnia Chronicles*. Even though it consists entirely of a series of miniatures for harp, with the flute of Christopher Hyde-Smith used sparingly but to great effect, the music stands up well away from the narrative. Its freshness and innocence are entirely in keeping with the wondrous world of princes and lords, fauns and dryads, talking animals and dwarfs, ruled over by High King Peter and Queen Susan under the ever-watchful eye of Aslan. Lewis never overdoes the Christian allegory; he is first and foremost a marvellous story-teller, and similarly Marisa Robles's music, with its indelible leitmotives for Narnia and Aslan, is memorable without being too insistent in characterization. The themes for *The Voyage of the Dawn Treader*, perhaps the most imaginative of all the tales, are particularly attractive. With the composer so admirably partnered, the music cannot fail to project, particularly as the digital recording is both lustrous and atmospheric as well as beautifully clear. The cassette too offers first-class quality. The actual *Chronicles* (including the incidental music) are available as follows: SWD/ZCSWD 351 (*The Magician's Nephew*); SWD/ZCSWD 352 (*The Lion, the Witch and the Wardrobe*); SWD/ZCSWD 353 (*The Horse and his Boy*); SWD/ZCSWD 354 (*Prince Caspian*); SWD/ZCSWD 355 (*The Voyage of the Dawn Treader*); SWD/ZCSWD 356 (*The Silver Chair*); SWD/ZCSWD 357 (*The Last Battle*). Michael Hordern proves an ideal narrator, colouring his voice with great skill to represent the multitude of characters, while his range of tone and expression is compellingly wide. Indeed his presentation is a *tour de force*, and the characters spring to vigorous life, not least the Sons of Adam and Daughters of Eve on whom the tales centre.

Rochberg, George
(born 1918)

Violin concerto.
*** CBS 76797 [Col. M 35149]. Stern, Pittsburgh SO, Previn.

George Rochberg, a much admired figure in American music, is more respected on this side of the Atlantic than he is played. For many years he wrote in the twelve-note idiom, then subsequently rediscovered tonality. His *Violin concerto* instantly proclaims that it is earnest and modern, opening with a suitably astringent gesture from the soloist before relapsing into a neo-romanticism redolent of Bartók and Szymanowski. (Not that this is any bad thing, save for the fact that Gunther Schuller's *Violin concerto* does it far more impressively!) The sentiment in the Rochberg *Concerto* is mawkish and the sequences hollow. It is beautifully played by Isaac Stern and the Pittsburgh orchestra under Previn and is well recorded, with fine detail and good balance. At a time when we need good recordings of such concertos as the Piston, the Frank Martin or the William Schuman, it is difficult to rouse enthusiasm for this release. Those who must have it and who believe in it can rest assured that this is a three-star effort.

Rodrigo, Joaquín
(born 1902)

(i–iv) *Concierto Andaluz;* (i; iv) *Concierto de Aranjuez;* (i; ii; v) *Concierto madrigal;* (i; v) *Fantasia para un gentilhombre.*

(M) *** Ph. 6747 430 (?) (i) Angel Romero; (ii) Pepe Romero; (iii) Celedonio and Celin Romero; (iv) San Antonio SO, Alessandro; (v) ASMF, Marriner.

It was an excellent idea to gather these four first-class performances together in a medium-priced box. Rodrigo's music wears marvellously well: the melody is unpretentious yet obstinately memorable; the structures, though involving a good deal of repetition, show a natural craftsmanship. Some might feel that the first movement of the *Andaluzian concerto* is less imaginative than the composer's best music, but it has a hauntingly atmospheric slow movement, and the finale is typically felicitous and spirited. The other works are undoubtedly inspired. Both the *Concierto de Aranjuez* and the *Concierto madrigal* were written for the Romero family, and the performances here are definitive and beautifully recorded. Marriner's contributions to the latter work and the graciously noble *Fantasia para un gentilhombre* have real distinction, and the sound is superb. The pressings here are immaculately silent-surfaced.

(i) *Concierto Andaluz* (for four guitars and orchestra); (ii) *Concierto de Aranjuez*.
*** Ph. 9500 563/*7300 705* [id.]. ASMF, Marriner, with (i) Los Romeros; (ii) Pepe Romero.

Los Romeros and the Academy under Marriner make the very most of the *Concierto Andaluz*, with infectious life and spirit in the outer sections and plenty of romantic atmosphere in the slow movement. Pepe Romero's account of the *Concierto de Aranjuez* is second to none. The famous *Adagio* is memorable, with the opening and closing sections delicately rhapsodic, and a glamorous climax, bursting with Mediterranean feeling. The orchestral playing is a

delight, more elegant and polished than in the earlier Philips version (see above), although both are very enjoyable. The recording is of demonstration quality on disc and tape alike (although on cassette there is a slight excess of bass in the finale of the *Concierto Andaluz*).

Concierto de Aranjuez.
(B) *** Con. CC/*CCT* 7510. Behrend, Berlin PO, Peters – CASTELNUOVO-TEDESCO: *Concerto.***

A first-rate bargain version of Rodrigo's famous *Guitar concerto*, immensely alive and vivid both as a performance and for the bright-as-a-button recording. The cassette is only marginally less lively. This excellent performance was available at medium price (DG Privilege 135117), coupled to the *Concierto serenata* for harp; but the present coupling has undoubted charm and is no less effectively presented.

Concierto de Aranjuez; Fantasia para un gentilhombre.
⊛*** Decca Dig. SXDL/*KSXDC* 7525. Bonell, Montreal SO, Dutoit.
*** HMV ASD/*TC-ASD* 3415 [Ang. S/ *4XS* 37440]. Angel Romero, LSO, Previn.
(M) *** CBS 60104/*40-* [Col. MY 36717]. Williams, Phd. O., Ormandy, or ECO, Barenboim.
**(*) Erato STU 71128. Santos, French Nat. Op. O., Scimone.
(M) ** DG Acc. 2542/*3342* 150 [139440/ *3300 172*]. Yepes, Spanish R. and TV O., Alonso.
(M) *(*) Ph. Seq. 6527/*7311* 058 [6500 454]. Lagoya, Monte Carlo Op. O., Almeida.

The great success of the newest Decca issue is due not only to the exceptionally clear and well-balanced digital recording (as realistic and demonstration-worthy on cassette as on disc) and Bonell's imaginative and inspired account of the solo part, but equally to the strong characterization of the orchestral accompaniments by Charles Dutoit and his excellent Montreal orchestra. In the *Concierto* the series of vivid interjections by the orchestral wind soloists (cor anglais, bassoon and trumpet) is projected with the utmost personality and presence, and a feeling of freshness pervades every bar of the orchestral texture. Soloist and orchestra combine to give an outstandingly eloquent account of the famous slow movement, and the climax retains its clarity of texture as it does in no other version. The finale has irresistible sparkle. In the *Fantasia* the balance between warmly gracious lyricism and sprightly rhythmic resilience is no less engaging and here again the orchestral solo playing makes a strong impression. This is a clear first choice for this coupling.

The Previn/Romero issue is undoubtedly very successful too and might be considered by those who prefer a recording that favours atmospheric warmth to crystal clarity (though the Decca version does not lack ambient effect). Angel Romero does not emerge as such a strong personality as his brother Pepe (see above), but the skill and sensibility of his playing are in no doubt, and Previn is obviously so delighted with the orchestral scores that he communicates his enthusiasm with loving care for detail. Thus, although the solo guitar is slightly larger than life in relation to the orchestra, Previn is still able to bring out the delightful woodwind chatter in the outer movements of the *Concierto*. The famous slow movement is very beautifully played indeed; the opening is especially memorable. The approach to the *Fantasia* is vividly direct, missing some of the essentially Spanish graciousness that marks the Marriner version (see above), but its infectious quality is more than enough compensation. The warmly spacious recording has transferred well to tape (the short patch of less than perfectly focused *tutti* at the end of the slow

movement of the *Concierto* is common to tape and disc).

John Williams's first recording of the *Concierto* with Ormandy is a red-blooded romantic reading, with the tension well held throughout. The recording is vivid and not lacking atmosphere, and the orchestral detail is telling, even though the soloist is balanced forwardly. The *Fantasia* too is impeccably played and thoroughly enjoyable, with Barenboim making the most of the vivid orchestral colouring. At medium price this is very competitive.

Santos's Erato recording is slightly more reverberant than the HMV version. This brings a sumptuously rich quality to the opening string melody in the *Fantasia*, but it means that in both works the inner orchestral detail is less sharply focused. Santos does not project a strongly individual personality (that again may be partly the effect of the acoustic) but he is very musical, and both performances are warmly sympathetic, with plenty of expressive feeling in the *Adagio* of the *Concierto*. However, this could not be recommended as a first choice in this coupling.

Yepes's 1970 DG version is disappointing. His much earlier identical coupling for Decca (SPA 233 [Lon. STS 15199]) had the advantage of extremely lively accompaniments, directed by Argenta and Frühbeck de Burgos respectively, and vintage Decca sound. Alonso is much less imaginative, as is readily apparent in the *Concierto*'s outer movements (the finale is rhythmically stiff), and though Yepes is at his finest in the *Adagio* and plays nobly in the *Fantasia* (which is generally more successful), the dry DG recording does not help, although it ensures a clean and vivid cassette transfer.

Lagoya is a good player but he does not project strongly, except perhaps in the slow movement of the *Concierto*, which he plays with considerable feeling. The outer movements lack the sprightly momentum which distinguishes the best versions. The recording is fair, but the cassette is seriously lacking in range and sparkle at the top.

Concierto de Aranjuez; (i) *Concierto madrigal* (for two guitars).
**(*) DG 2531/*3301* 208 [id.]. Yepes, Philh. O., Navarro, (i) with Monden.

Yepes's 1980 version of the *Concierto de Aranjuez* is an improvement on his recording of a decade earlier (see above), mainly because of the superior accompaniment. But even here there is a lack of vitality in the outer movements, although the poetic element of the *Adagio* is well realized. The account of the *Concierto madrigal* (with Godelieve Monden the excellent second guitarist) is first-class; each of the twelve delightful miniatures which make up this engaging work springs vividly to life. The recording is excellent, with the cassette matching the disc very closely (indeed the *Concierto* has slightly more projection on tape). This is the only available record and cassette offering this coupling.

(i) *Concierto de estío* (for violin); (ii) *Concierto en modo galante* (for cello).
*** HMV Dig. ASD/*TCC-ASD* 4198. LSO, Bátiz, with (i) Cohen, (ii) Ara.

The cello concerto dates from 1949 and the *Summer concerto* for violin ('conceived in the manner of Vivaldi') from 1943. We have waited an unconscionable time for these première stereo recordings, but HMV now makes amends with a really outstanding coupling. Agustín Léon Ara's account of the *Concierto de estío* catches its neoclassical spikiness admirably in the outer movements, and the central *Sicilienne* with its set of simple variations is most sympathetic. But it is the cello concerto that is the major addition to the repertoire, and it is given a masterly performance by Robert Cohen; he combines elegance of phrasing with

warm beauty of timbre in the lovely secondary theme (*in tempo di minuetto galante*) of the first movement and the no less haunting melody which dominates the *Adagietto.* His spirited articulation of the opening ostinato idea and the lively *Zapateado* rondo finale is matched by Enrique Bátiz, who secures playing of fire and temperament from the LSO, all its members sounding as if they had just returned from a holiday in the Spanish sunshine. The digital recording is forward and at times brilliant to the point of fierceness, but it has excellent detail and an attractive ambient warmth, and the over-emphasis at the top is easily softened with the controls. The outstanding chrome tape is just as vivid but smoother on top.

Concierto pastoral (for flute and orchestra); *Fantasia para un gentilhombre* (arr. Galway for flute and orchestra).
*** RCA RL/*RK* 25193 [ARL 1/*ARK 1* 3416]. Galway, Philh. O., Mata.

The *Concierto pastoral* was composed for James Galway in 1978. Its spikily brilliant introduction is far from pastoral in feeling, but the mood of the work soon settles down. At first hearing, the material seems thinner than usual but Rodrigo's fragmented melodies and rhythmic ostinatos soon insinuate themselves into the listener's memory. The slow movement is especially effective, with a witty scherzando centrepiece framed by the *Adagio* outer sections. James Galway's performance is truly superlative, showing the utmost bravura and matching refinement. He is beautifully recorded (and the tape transfer is immaculately truthful), and the small accompanying chamber orchestra is well balanced. The arrangement of the *Fantasia* is a very free one, necessitating reorchestration, exchanging clarinet and horn instrumentation for the original scoring for trumpet and piccolo. The solo part too has been rewritten and even extended, apparently with the composer's blessing. The result is, to be honest, not an improvement on the original. But Galway is very persuasive, even if there is a persistent feeling of inflation.

Fantasia para un gentilhombre.
(*) DG 2530 975 [id./*3300 975*]. Yepes, ECO, Navarro – GIULIANI: *Concerto No. 1.*(*)

Like the Giuliani coupling, this performance has character and refinement, and the recording balance is clear and immediate. But Yepes comes into competition with other very attractive versions, notably the graciously amiable account by Pepe Romero on Philips (9500 042, coupled to a different Giuliani work), with a smiling accompaniment from the St Martin's Academy under Marriner and superbly warm and atmospheric recording.

Bajando de la Meseta; Fandango; Junto al Generalife; 3 Petites pièces; Por los campos de España; En los trigales; Romance de Durandarte; Sonata a la española; Tiento antigua.
*** Ph. 9500/*7300* 915 [id.]. Pepe Romero.

An excellent anthology of Rodrigo's shorter works for solo guitar, distinguished by informative and articulate sleeve-notes from the composer himself. He tells us, for instance, that the Spanish subtitle for the *Sonata* has a certain irony, which Pepe Romero does not miss in his performance. Indeed he is strikingly responsive to the changing moods and colours of all these pieces, his rubato free but convincing and his evocation of atmosphere – as in the central section of *En los trigales* – telling. The closing *Romance de Durandarte* (originally written for the ballet *Pavana Real*) is particularly haunting. The Philips recording

is close but realistic on disc and cassette alike.

Rootham, Cyril (1875–1938)

Symphony No. 1 in C min.
*** Lyr. SRCS 103. LPO, Handley – HOLBROOKE: *Birds of Rhiannon.****

Cyril Rootham, who was born in Bristol in 1875 and died the year before the outbreak of the Second World War, spent the bulk of his life at Cambridge, where his pupils included Arthur Bliss. The first of his two symphonies was composed in 1932 and leaves no doubt as to his expertise and powers of craftsmanship. Rootham was a serious and dedicated musician, though it must be said that his is not a distinctive voice in English music. His orchestration is very fine and it is reproduced by the engineers in sound of quite remarkable realism. Indeed, this is a demonstration record, with impressive clarity, definition and depth. Readers should investigate this record for themselves, for there is much to admire, even if few would claim that the symphony is a powerfully original work.

Rossini, Gioacchino (1792–1868)

La Boutique fantasque (ballet, arr. Respighi; complete).
⊛*** CBS Dig. 35842/*41*-[Col. M/*HMT* 35842]. Toronto SO, Andrew Davis.
(M) **(*) HMV Green. ESD/*TC-ESD* 7152 (slightly abridged). LSO, Gardelli – OFFENBACH: *Gaîté Parisienne.*

La Boutique fantasque: suite.
(M) *** Chan. CBR/*CBT* 1003. SNO,

Gibson – DUKAS: *L'Apprenti sorcier*; SAINT-SAËNS: *Danse macabre*.***
(M) **(*) Decca Jub. JB/*KJBC* 79. RPO, Dorati – RESPIGHI: *Rossiniana*.**(*)

At last we are given an absolutely complete version of *La Boutique fantasque*, one of the great popular triumphs of Diaghilev's Ballets Russes. The new CBS digital recording is arrestingly brilliant, yet its surface sparkle is balanced by a glowing ambient warmth. Respighi's masterly scoring, glitteringly vivid and sumptuous, transmutes his relatively slight source material into a magical tapestry. In the sympathetic hands of Andrew Davis there is not a dull bar, for Respighi's linking passages (usually omitted) are marvellously crafted. The Toronto orchestra is in superb form, playing with matching bravura and affection: the gentler second half of the ballet is particularly beautiful. The recording has the widest dynamic range; the actual opening is a mere whisper and the first climax expands gloriously. A demonstration disc for the digital era, recalling Ansermet's famous Decca mono LP of the early fifties (which was not complete). The chrome tape is acceptable but has not quite the sparkle of the disc.

Gardelli's performance was originally recorded complete, but was quickly withdrawn and is here reissued in a slightly abridged single-sided format, coupled with a generous selection from *Gaîté Parisienne*. Gardelli's performance is both spirited and sympathetic, but the sound of the reissue has a very brilliant treble which needs taming, and there is less atmosphere than on the original disc. The cassette, however, offers warmer sound (on both sides), but here the upper range is somewhat short on sparkle. However many will feel this is competitive at medium price; all the most important music is included.

For those content with the highlights Gibson's Chandos reissue, with its excellent couplings, can be strongly recommended. Gibson's performance sounds for all the world as if he had been listening to Ansermet's famous record. Tempi are similar, and the opening is cunningly slow, with much of the magic that Ansermet found. The Scottish National Orchestra is on its toes, and the sound on disc is excellent. The cassette transfer would have been improved by a more ambitious level; as it is, the upper range lacks the last degree of glitter compared with the disc.

Dorati's performance has plenty of life and colour, but the recording acoustic is a little lacking in atmosphere: the very opening of *La Boutique fantasque* is made to sound rather dry and unevocative by the relative lack of ambient glow. However, it is easy to make too much of this. The vivacity and point of the orchestral playing are often exhilarating, and on cassette, where the sound is slightly richer than on the LP, the dryness is much less obvious.

Overtures: Armida; Il Barbiere di Siviglia; Bianca e Faliero; La Cambiale di matrimonio; La Cenerentola; Demetrio e Polibio; Edipo a Colono; Edoardo e Cristina. (i) *Ermione. La Gazza ladra; L'Inganno felice; L'Italiana in Algeri; Maometto II; Otello.* (i) *Ricciardo e Zoraide. La Scala di seta; Semiramide; Le Siège de Corinthe; Il Signor Bruschino; Tancredi; Il Turco in Italia; Torvaldo e Dorliska; Il Viaggio a Reims; William Tell. Sinfonia al conventello; Sinfonia di Bologna.*
*** Ph. 6768 064/7699 136 (4). ASMF, Marriner, (i) with Amb. S.

Marriner's four discs aim to collect Rossini's 'complete' overtures, but of course not everything is here. The early Neapolitan operas, with the exception of *Ricciardo e Zoraide* and *Ermione*, make do with a simple prelude, leading into the opening chorus. Sometimes Rossini uses the same overture for more than one opera, and there are extensive quotations of material from one to another. Even so, twenty-four overtures make a delightful package in such sparkling performances, which eruditely use original orchestrations. Rossini's earliest overture, *Demetrio e Polibio*, written when he was only fifteen (and later providing a theme for *Il Signor Bruschino*), is a charmer, and *Ermione* has offstage contributions from a male chorus. Clean, bright and atmospheric recording on disc; the cassettes are variable, often lacking transient sparkle on top.

Overtures: Il Barbiere di Siviglia; La Gazza ladra; La Scala di seta; Semiramide; William Tell.

(M) *** Decca Jub. JB/*KJBC* 33 [Lon. 6204]. LSO, Gamba.

This is a very good collection. The performances are taut and exciting and the orchestral playing splendidly alive and polished, even at the very fast speeds sometimes chosen for the allegros. A strong disciplining force – not unlike Toscanini's style – is felt in every piece, and care in phrasing is noticeable at every turn. Particularly captivating is the string cantilena at the introduction of *The Barber of Seville*, which is phrased with a wonderful sense of line. Decca's recording is very good. The only quality perhaps missing is a touch of geniality. The tape transfer, made at a high level, tends to be somewhat fierce in the treble.

Overtures: Il Barbiere di Siviglia; La Gazza ladra; La Scala di seta; Le Siège de Corinthe; Il Signor Bruschino; William Tell.

(M) * Decca SPA/*KCSP* 538 [Lon. STS 15307]. New Philh. O., Gardelli.

A disappointingly mundane set of performances, surprising from such an experienced conductor. *La Scala di seta* has

curious tempo changes that sound almost like unmatched tape-joins. Even the recording is below Decca's usual sparkling standard in this kind of music. The cassette, however, is strikingly rich and vivid, even if the forward balance reduces the dynamic contrast to some extent.

Overtures: Il Barbiere di Siviglia; La Gazza ladra; William Tell.

(M) *** DG Priv. 2535/*3335* 629. Berlin PO, Karajan – SUPPÉ: *Overtures.****

This Privilege selection is extracted from Karajan's full-priced disc (2530 144, still available). The performances offer supreme polish and extrovert bravura. Karajan takes the main allegro of *La Scala di seta* very fast indeed, but the playing is beautifully light and assured, and the oboe playing gives no suggestion of breathlessness. The recording is both lively and atmospheric on disc, but on tape the reverberation has produced roughness at climaxes, especially in *La Gazza ladra* and in the brilliant account of *William Tell*. Those favouring a coupling with some swaggering Suppé performances should choose the disc.

Overtures: Il Barbiere di Siviglia; La Scala di seta; Semiramide; Le Siège de Corinthe; Il Viaggio a Reims; William Tell.

**(*) HMV ASD/*TC-ASD* 3903 [Ang. SZ 37750]. Philh. O., Muti.

Muti, following the Rossini style of his great compatriot Toscanini, generally adopts fast tempi for these sparkling overtures. The performances are brilliant and thrustful, helped by large-scale recording, but at times they are just a little short on wit and delicacy. The cassette is full-blooded and lively, matching the disc closely.

Overtures: La Cenerentola; La Gazza ladra; Le Siège de Corinthe;

Semiramide; Il Viaggio a Reims; William Tell.
*** Ph. 9500 349/7300 595 [id.]. ASMF, Marriner.

Sparkling, lively performances that should give wide pleasure to collectors. The sound is pleasing and the balance musically judged. There is no shortage of recommendable anthologies of Rossini overtures, but this is certainly among them. *The Siege of Corinth* and *The Journey to Rheims* are particularly delectable. The cassette transfer too is successful, clean and clear, although on tape the *Galop* from *William Tell* lacks something in sheer sonic brilliance.

Overtures: Elisabetta, Regina d'Inghilterra; La Scala di seta: Semiramide; Tancredi; Il Turco in Italia; William Tell.
**(*) RCA RL/RK 31379 [ARL 1/ARK 1 3634]. LSO, Abbado.

Zestful performances from Abbado, with exhilaratingly fast tempi, the LSO players kept consistently on their toes and obviously revelling in their own virtuosity. The exuberance comes especially to the fore in *Tancredi* – there is even a brief clarinet glissando – in a revised version by Philip Gosset. But some might feel that *La Scala di seta* would be more effective if a fraction more relaxed. *William Tell* opens with elegant cellos, then offers an unashamedly vulgar storm sequence and a final *Galop* taken at a breakneck pace. *Elisabetta, Regina* is our old friend *The Barber of Seville* but with a subtle change (a triplet consistently repeated in the first theme of the allegro): again stylish but fast. Excellent recording and a good tape, which has a very slightly compressed dynamic range.

Overtures: La Gazza ladra; L'Italiana in Algeri; La Scala di seta; Il Signor Bruschino; Il Turco in Italia; Il Viaggio a Reims; William Tell.

*** Decca Dig. SXDL/KSXDC 7534. Nat. PO, Chailly.

Generous measure here and first-class Decca recording, brilliantly vivid, yet with a natural ambience. The solo playing is first-rate too: the cellos at the opening of *William Tell* and the principal oboe and horn in *The Italian Girl* and *The Turk in Italy* (respectively) all demonstrate that this is an orchestra of London's finest musicians. The wind articulation, in *La Scala di seta* is admirably clean, although the bow tapping at the opening of *Il Signor Bruschino* is rather lazy. Just occasionally elsewhere the ensemble slips when the conductor, Riccardo Chailly, lets the exhilaration of the moment triumph over absolute discipline and poise. But if you want precision and virtuosity alone, go to Karajan; under Chailly the gusto of the music-making conveys spontaneous enjoyment too, especially in *The Thieving Magpie* and the nicely paced account of *William Tell*. Incidentally *Il Viaggio a Reims* had no overture at its first performance, but one was put together later, drawing on the ballet music from *Le Siège de Corinthe*.

String sonatas Nos. 1–6.
(M) *** Argo ZK 26/7. ASMF, Marriner – DONIZETTI: *String quartet No. 4.****
String sonatas Nos. 1–6; Duet in D for cello and double bass; Une larme; Un mot à Paganini.
*** Ph. 6769 024 (2). Accardo, Gazeau, Meunier, Petrachi, Canino.

Unbelievably, the *String sonatas* were written when Rossini was only twelve, yet their invention is consistently on the highest level, bubbling over with humour and infectious spontaneity. The playing of the St Martin's group under Marriner is marvellously fresh and polished, the youthful high spirits of the writing presented with glowing affection and sparkle. On Philips these youthful pieces are given by single strings, and it would be difficult to imagine them being better done. The playing has an effortless virtuosity and elegance that are wholly captivating. All the rival accounts, including those of I Musici (at present deleted) and the Academy of St Martin-in-the-Fields, are for larger forces. But given such spontaneous playing and excellent recording, this set will be the first choice for many.

String sonatas Nos. 2–5.
**(*) HMV ASD 3464. Polish CO, Maksymiuk.

Generally fine playing from the Polish chamber group, with some impressive scalic bravura and warm phrasing in the slow movements. There is plenty of character here, but in the last analysis the ensemble does not show the immaculate ease of execution of Marriner's Academy, and though the allegros are spirited, with the rhythms nicely pointed, they have not the effervescent wit of the Argo set. The recording is agreeably warm and rich.

Petite Messe solennelle.
** Argo ZRG 893/4/*K 118 K 22* [id.]. Marshall, Hodgson, Tear, King, London Chamber Ch.; Holford, Constable, Birch.
(M) *(*) Decca Ace SDD 567 (2). Freni, Valentini, Pavarotti, Raimondi, Ch. of La Scala, Milan, Gandolfi.

Rossini's *Petite Messe solennelle* must be the most genial contribution to the church liturgy in the history of music. The description *Petite* does not refer to size, for the piece is comparable in length to Verdi's *Requiem*; rather it is the composer's modest evaluation of the work's 'significance'. But what a spontaneous and infectious piece of writing it is, bubbling over with characteristic melodic, harmonic and rhythmic invention. The composer never overreaches himself. 'I

was born for *opera buffa*, as well Thou knowest,' Rossini writes touchingly on the score. 'Little skill, a little heart, and that is all. So be Thou blessed and admit me to paradise'.

The Argo version must be regarded as a stopgap until the Ariola Eurodisc recording under Sawallisch reappears. It was issued here on RCA and is still available in the USA (ARL 2/*ARK 2* 2626). The recording on Argo is of the highest quality and has striking vividness and presence on disc and cassette alike (the choral entry of the *Gloria* is arresting in its impact and realism), but the reading is much too literal and lacks geniality. Both Margaret Marshall and Alfreda Hodgson sing eloquently; there is some finely shaped and expressive choral singing, and good support from the two pianists, with John Birch on the harmonium; and the clean well-balanced sound is a constant source of pleasure. But the music-making does not fully catch the music's spirit and can give only limited satisfaction.

Gandolfi unfortunately takes a coarse view of a work which demands some refinement, letting his famous soloists have their head. Freni has some beautiful moments in the *Crucifixus* and *O salutaris*, but Pavarotti and Raimondi are both well below their best, and the chorus is fruity-sounding in the wrong way.

Stabat Mater.
(M) *(*) Turn. TVS 34634 [id.]. Lee, Quivar, Riegel, Plishka, Cincinnati Ch. and SO, Schippers.

The Turnabout version of the *Stabat Mater* is disappointing. Schippers presses too hard for comfort, and the women soloists are poorly cast for this music; but Kenneth Riegel's *Cujus animam* is memorable, though hardly Italianate. The recording is limited. The Decca version under Kertesz (SXL 6534 [Lon. 26250]) is the one to go for, with a cast of soloists including Lorengar, Minton and Pavarotti. Some may understandably complain that Kertesz under-plays the work in removing the open-hearted vulgarity, but he certainly makes one enjoy the music afresh and the recording is excellent.

OPERA

Il Barbiere di Siviglia (complete).
(M) **(*) HMV SLS/TC-SLS 5165 (3). Los Angeles, Alva, Cava, Wallace, Bruscantini, Glyndebourne Festival Ch., RPO, Gui.
(M) *(*) Decca D 38 D 3 (3). Simionato, Bastianini, Misciano, Corena, Siepi, Ch. and O. of Maggio Musicale Fiorentino, Erede.

Victoria de los Angeles is as charming a Rosina as you will ever find: no viper this one, as she claims in *Una voce poco fa*. Musically it is an unforceful performance – Rossini's brilliant *fioriture* done lovingly, with no sense of fear or danger – and that matches the gently rib-nudging humour of what is otherwise a recording of the Glyndebourne production of the early sixties. It does not fizz as much as other Glyndebourne Rossini on record, but with elaborate stage direction in the stereo production and with a characterful line-up of soloists, it is an endearing performance, which in its line is unmatched. The recording still sounds well; the cassette transfer is generally first-class, indeed for the most part almost demonstration-worthy. The only small drawback is that the high transfer level has brought slight peaking on just one or two of Victoria de los Angeles's high fortissimos in her key arias. It is a tiny blemish but a pity.

Although the cast of soloists in the Decca set looks strong on paper, with four out of the five principals stylish, characterful artists (the exception is the tenor), this is a variably successful version, with Erede a generally uninspiring conductor. The 1957 recording is fair for its period. First choice for this opera

remains with the classic Callas set from the very beginning of the stereo era (HMV SLS 853 [Ang. S/4XS 35936]). Callas and Gobbi were here at their most inspired, and Alva is in good form too. The recording quality has been refurbished.

Guglielmo Tell (*William Tell*; complete).
*** Decca D 219 D 4/K 219 K 44 [Lon. 1446/5-]. Pavarotti, Freni, Milnes, Ghiaurov, Amb. Op. Ch., Nat. PO, Chailly.

Rossini wrote his massive opera about William Tell in French, and the first really complete recording (under Gardelli on HMV) used that language. But Chailly and his team put here forward a strong case for preferring Italian, with its open vowels, in music which glows with Italianate lyricism. Chailly's is a forceful reading, particularly strong in the many ensembles, and superbly recorded. Milnes makes a heroic Tell, always firm, and though Pavarotti has his moments of coarseness he sings the role of Arnoldo with glowing tone. Ghiaurov too is in splendid voice, while subsidiary characters are almost all well taken, with such a fine singer as John Tomlinson, for example, finely resonant as Melchthal. The women singers too are impressive, with Mirella Freni as the heroine Matilde providing dramatic strength as well as sweetness. To fit this epic piece on to eight sides requires close-grooving, but the sound is superb, rich and atmospheric as well as brilliant. The cassette transfer is of outstandingly sophisticated quality; at times the choral sound might be fractionally more sharply focused on disc, but the vibrant projection of the soloists and the depth and atmosphere of the overall sound picture are consistently demonstration-worthy. The libretto/booklet too is admirably clear.

L'Italiana in Algeri (complete).

*** Erato STU 71394 (3). Horne, Palacio, Ramey, Trimarchi, Battle, Zaccaria, Prague Ch., Sol. Ven., Scimone.

Scholarship as well as Rossinian zest have gone in to Scimone's highly enjoyable version, beautifully played and recorded with as stylish a team of soloists as one can expect nowadays. The text is complete, the original orchestration has been restored (as in the comic duetting of piccolo and bassoon in the reprise in the overture) and alternative versions of certain arias are given as an appendix. Marilyn Horne makes a dazzling, positive Isabella, and Samuel Ramey is splendidly firm as Mustafa. Domenico Trimarchi is a delightful Taddeo and Ernesto Palacio an agile Lindoro, not coarse, though the recording does not always catch his tenor timbre well. Nonetheless the sound is generally very good indeed, and the only regret is that the booklet includes no English translation – a pity when there is more unfamiliar material here than usual.

Otello (complete).
*** Ph. 6769 023 (3)/7699 110 (2) [id.]. Carreras, Von Stade, Condò, Pastine, Fisichella, Ramey, Amb. S., Philh. O., Lopez-Cobós.

Quite apart from the fact that the libretto of Rossini's *Otello* bears remarkably little resemblance to Shakespeare – virtually none at all until the last act – the layout of voices is odd. Not only is Otello a tenor role; so is Rodrigo (second in importance), and Iago too. It is some tribute to this performance, superbly recorded on both disc and cassette, and brightly and stylishly directed by Lopez-Cobós, that the line-up of tenors is turned into an asset, with three nicely contrasted soloists. Carreras is here at his finest – most affecting in his recitative before the murder – while Fisichella copes splendidly with the high tessitura of Rodrigo's role, and Pastine has a distinctive timbre to identify him as

the villain. Frederica von Stade pours forth a glorious flow of beautiful tone, well-matched by Nucci Condò as Emilia. Samuel Ramey is excellent too in the bass role of Elmiro. *Otello* Rossini-style is an operatic curiosity, but this recording helps to explain why it so ensnared such a sensitive opera-lover as the novelist Stendhal.

Tancredi (complete).
** Arion ARN 338 010 (3). Patricia Price, Francis, Stokes, Lewis, McDonnell, Jeffes, Ch. and O., Perras.

Written when Rossini was still only twenty-one, *Tancredi* – unbelievably, his ninth opera – was his first really serious one, a *melodramma eroico*, a tale of medieval chivalry in which the part of the hero, following the tradition of the *opera seria*, is a travesty role given to a mezzo-soprano. Here Patricia Price makes a firm-toned hero, a mezzo who can yet cope with a sudden top C; but neither she nor the other members of a largely British cast quite measures up to the fearsome technical demands of early Rossini with its elaborate *fioriture*. The orchestral playing is only just adequate, and with dry recording the set must be regarded as a stopgap only, valuable for illuminating a work that is full of superbly memorable ideas, not least the aria which at once made Rossini a star, *Di tanti palpiti*.

Il Turco in Italia (complete).
(M) ** HMV SLS/TC-SLS 5148 (2). Callas, Gedda, Rossi-Lemeni, Calabrese, Stabile, Ch. and O. of La Scala, Milan, Gavazzeni.

Callas was at her peak when she recorded this rare Rossini opera in the mid-1950s. As ever, there are lumpy moments vocally, but she gives a sharply characterful performance as the capricious Fiorilla, married to an elderly, jealous husband and bored with it. Nicola

Rossi-Lemeni as the Turk of the title is characterful too, but not the firmest of singers, and it is left to Nicolai Gedda as the young lover and Franco Calabrese as the jealous husband to match Callas in stylishness. It is good too to have the veteran Mariano Stabile singing the role of the Poet in search of a plot. Walter Legge's production has plainly added to the sparkle, and the stereo transcription recording sounds well for its period. The tape transfer is smooth and quite well balanced: the sound reflects the limited range of the discs.

Arias: *La Cenerentola: Nacqui all'affano. Guglielmo Tell: S'allontano alfin!; Selva opaca. Semiramide: Bel raggio lusinghier.*
*(*) HMV ASD/*TC-ASD* 3984. Callas, Paris Conservatoire O., Rescigno – DONIZETTI: *Arias.***

These recordings made in the mid-sixties show a degree of cautiousness that rarely marked Callas's earlier work. She was obviously very conscious of all the criticisms and did her utmost to avoid the worst blots. She generally succeeds, but there is something far less positive about the end result, and, more serious, the performances do not have that refinement of detail that at her peak lit up so many phrases and made them unforgettable. The recording is vivid; on cassette there are one or two moments of peaking on high fortissimos.

Roussel, Albert (1869–1937)

Piano concerto, Op. 36.
(M) ** Sup. 1410 2705. Krajný, Prague CO, Macura – HONEGGER: *Concertino***; POULENC: *Aubade.***(*)

Roussel's textures are often congested and unrelieved in busier movements, and

the somewhat reverberant acoustic of the House of Artists does not lend this score greater transparency. However, this is a reflective and intelligent performance which does more justice to the score than many earlier versions. At the time of writing there is no alternative recording of either the Roussel or the couplings.

Symphony No. 4 in A, Op. 53.
(M) (***) HMV mono XLP/*TC-XLP* 60003. Philh. O., Karajan – STRAVINSKY: *Jeu de cartes.*(***)

This 1949 recording leads the field at present! The transfer is of exceptional quality and the sound, though lacking the body and range of more modern stereo recording, is remarkably vivid. Karajan gives a powerful yet sensitive account of Roussel's inventive score. The strings have splendid firmness and bite, and the Philharmonia wind playing is beautiful. The cassette transfer is smooth and clean, but it reveals the recording date by its relative lack of amplitude.

Serenade for flute, violin, viola, cello and harp, Op. 30; Trio for flute, viola and cello, Op. 40; Impromptu for harp, Op. 30.
*** HM HM 735. Marie-Claire Jamet Quintet (members).

A welcome addition to the all-too-meagre Roussel discography. The inventive and charming *Serenade* is elegantly played, even if it does not efface memories of the Melos Ensemble version, coupled with the Debussy *Trio sonata*, Ravel's *Introduction and allegro* and some Ropartz – a favourite record (Oiseau-Lyre SOL 60048). The value of this issue lies in its including the only account of Roussel's powerful, original and beautifully-wrought *Trio for flute, viola and cello*, dating from 1929, not long before the *Third Symphony*. The performance is sensitive; Christian Lardé is particularly eloquent. Marie-Claire

Jamet gives an elegant account of the *Impromptu for harp*, and the recording is eminently satisfactory. Self-recommending.

Rózsa, Miklós (born 1907)

Ben Hur (film score): extended excerpts.
*** Decca PFS 4394 [Lon. 21166]. Nat. PO and Ch., composer.

Rózsa's score for *Ben Hur* is a potent mixture of orchestral spectacle and choral kitsch. There is an appealing lyrical theme for the love story, an exciting sequence for the galley slaves rowing into battle, and a stirring *Parade* for the famous chariot race. But towards the end the religiosity, with its lavish panoply of chorus and orchestra, overwhelms the listener in an ocean of sumptuous vulgarity. Certainly it is all presented here with great conviction, and the Decca Phase Four techniques create the maximum impact, with rich sonorities and a sparklingly brilliant upper range.

Film scores: *Double Identity:* excerpts; *The Four Feathers:* excerpts; *Ivanhoe Overture: The Jungle Book:* (i) *Song of the Jungle; Knights of the Round Table: Scherzo; The Lost Weekend* (*suite*); (i) *The Red House* (*suite*). *Spellbound* (*Dream sequence; Mountain lodge); The Thief of Baghdad: The Love of the Princess.*
(M) **(*) RCA Gold GL/GK 43443 [ARL 1/ARK 1 0911]. Nat. PO, Gerhardt, (i) with Amb. S.

The most celebrated piece here is *Spellbound*, in which Rózsa scores for the theremin (a sound very like that of the ondes martenot) to evoke a feeling of paranoia; the result is undoubtedly arresting. For the rest the composer's powerful orchestral command is balanced by an attractive if not always memorable lyrical flow. His invention is at its most diverse in the suite from *The Red House*. The scoring of the brief *Scherzo* from *Knights of the Round Table* shows great imaginative skill, while on a larger scale, the spacious jungle evocation for *Jungle Book* is more than equalled by the elaborate imagery of *The Lost Weekend*. The performances are well up to the standard of this distinguished series, and the recording too is spectacular, the tape nearly matching the disc in range and impact. The cassette does not, however, provide the documentary support which is included with the LP and is essential.

Piano sonata, Op. 20; Bagatelles, Op. 12; The Vintner's Daughter, Op. 23; Variations, Op. 9.
(M) *** Uni. UNS 259. Parkin.

The Hungarian Miklós Rózsa, well-known for such scores as *Quo Vadis, Ben Hur* and other film spectaculars, is also a serious composer for the concert platform, and these accessible pieces show him to possess more than mere fluency. The *Sonata* is a powerful work of widely contrasting moods and well-integrated ideas. The piano writing is thoroughly idiomatic, and the playing of Eric Parkin is persuasive and commanding. Rózsa is not so deeply individual in his musical language as Bartók or Kodály, but he repays investigation none the less. Good recording.

Rubbra, Edmund (born 1901)

(i) *Soliloquy for cello and orchestra, Op. 57;* (ii) *Symphony No. 7 in C, Op. 88.*

*** Lyr. SRCS 119. (i) Saram, LSO, Handley; (ii) LPO, Boult.

The Rubbra *Seventh Symphony* originally appeared in harness with the *Tallis fantasia*, and its reappearance in this coupling may well attract collectors reluctant to duplicate the Vaughan Williams. The *Soliloquy*, a decade earlier than this *Symphony*, was written just before the *Fifth*. It has been described by Ronald Stevenson as 'a saraband, symphonically developed in flexible tempo ... a meditation with flashes of interior drama', and its grave beauty exerts a strong appeal. Rohan de Saram plays with a restrained eloquence that is impressive, and he has excellent support from the LSO under Vernon Handley. The *Soliloquy* is placed after the *Symphony* on side two and takes about fifteen minutes. The *Symphony* itself is a considerable piece and Rubbra's admirers will surely be attracted to this new coupling. The recording is up to the high standards we expect from Lyrita.

Symphony No. 2 in D, Op. 45; Festival overture, Op. 62.
*** Lyr. SRCS 96. New Philh. O., Handley.

The *Second Symphony* dates from 1937 and like its predecessor showed Rubbra a symphonist of a rather special order, an artist able to think on a large scale and in long-breathed paragraphs, yet at the same time apparently indifferent to the orchestral medium. He subsequently thinned out the scoring and made a cut in the middle of the first movement in 1950, not long after the composition of his *Fifth Symphony*. Rubbra's symphonies do not offer the cut-and-thrust of dramatic contrast but rather unfold in an overall organic flow whose incidental beauties are subservient to the general structural plan. His music lays stress on matter rather than manner, and attaches scant importance to surface appeal. The

listener who seeks will find, and will not need to be drawn by colour or texture to the musical substance. It is the slow movement that offers the deepest musical experience here. We have writing of a deep originality that has evolved from Holst and Sibelius, that inhabits a northern but not a Scandinavian landscape, and is unlike anything else in the British music of its time. This and the finale are the most successful movements; the latter is inventive and original, and has overtones of the *Perigourdine* movement of the *First Symphony*, though its accents are very English. Not the most flawless of Rubbra's symphonies, perhaps, for the score is undoubtedly overladen with contrapuntal detail, and the orchestration is thick in the first movement. Good performances of both symphony and the overture, which bears an adjacent opus number to the *Fifth*. The recording is up to the high standard of realism and presence one expects from this source.

Symphony No. 5 in B flat, Op. 63.
(*) Chan. ABR/*ABT* 1018. Melbourne SO, Schönzeler – BLISS: *Checkmate.*(*)

Rubbra's *Fifth Symphony* is a noble work which grows naturally from the symphonic soil of Elgar and Sibelius. Although the Melbourne orchestra is not in the very first flight, they play this music for all they are worth, and the strings have a genuine intensity and lyrical fervour that compensate for the opaque effect of the octave doublings. The introduction is grander and more spacious here than in Barbirolli's pioneering record with the Hallé, made in the early 1950s, and the finale has splendid lightness of touch. More attention to refinement of nuance would have paid dividends in the slow movement, whose brooding melancholy does not quite emerge to full effect. Altogether, though, this is an imposing performance which reflects credit on all concerned. The recording is well balanced and lifelike; on tape its sonority comes over effectively, but the ear perceives that the upper range is rather restricted.

Piano music: *Introduction, aria and fugue, Op. 104; Introduction and fugue, Op. 19; 9 Little pieces, Op. 74; 8 Preludes, Op. 131; Prelude and fugue, Op. 69; 4 Studies, Op. 139.*
*** Phoenix DGS 1009. Moore.

Edmund Rubbra was a fine pianist, as older readers will recall, but his output for the instrument is so small that it can be accommodated on one record: half-a-dozen opus numbers in an *œuvre* comprising more than 150. Yet the music, quite apart from being well laid out for the piano, as one would expect, is far from uncharacteristic or insubstantial. Perhaps the most impressive of the pieces are the *Eight Preludes*, Op. 131, which are both inventive and atmospheric; but rewards are to be found in practically all this music. Edward Moore is a convinced and convincing advocate, and though he is not particularly well recorded, the sound is good enough to allow the interest of this issue to carry an unreserved recommendation.

Rubinstein, Anton

(1829–94)

Piano sonatas Nos. 1 in F min., Op. 12; 3 in F, Op. 41.
*** Hyp. Dig. A 66017. Howard.

Leslie Howard is a fine virtuoso who has made a speciality of the music of Anton Rubinstein. One can hardly imagine more persuasive performances than these, though the actual invention is barely enough to sustain interest over ambitious spans. Rubinstein wrote these

display works for himself to play in his recitals, and no doubt his personality helped to persuade early listeners. The digital recording is first-rate.

Rue, Pierre de la
(*c.* 1460–1518)

Motets: *Gaude Virgo; Laudate Dominum; Pater de caelis; Salve Regina.*
*** DG Arc. 2533 377 [id.]. L. Pro Cantione Antiqua, L. Cornett and Sackbut Ens., Turner – OBRECHT: *Motets.****

Pierre de la Rue was a Flemish master who studied with Ockeghem and ranks among the leading contemporaries of Josquin. Bruno Turner successfully uses instruments to enliven and enrich the textures of these motets, which are of striking beauty. The recordings are admirable in every respect, and readers with an interest in this period can investigate this issue with confidence.

Ruggles, Carl (1876–1971)

(i) *Angels for brass* (two versions). (ii) *Evocations; Men; Men and Mountains; Organum; Portals* (for strings); *Sun-Treader.* (iii) *Evocations* (original piano version). (i; iv) *Exaltation for brass, chorus and organ.* (v) *Toys for voice and piano.* (vi) *Vox clamans in deserto* (for chamber orchestra and mezzo-soprano).
*** CBS 79225 (2) [Col. M2 34591] (i) Brass Ens., Schwarz; (ii) Buffalo PO, Tilson Thomas; (iii) Kirkpatrick; (iv) Gregg Smith Singers; Raven; (v)

Blegen, Tilson Thomas; (vi) Morgan, Speculum Musicae.

Carl Ruggles was in his way as striking an original among American composers as the more fêted Charles Ives. These two discs bring together all that he wrote, giving, with the help of dedicated performances, a complete portrait of a fascinating figure, whose experiments in atonality have a communicative directness to make them more essentially 'modern' than much more recent music. *Sun-Treader* is the biggest piece here, but every one of these often craggy items is important, with *Evocations* given in both its solo piano and orchestral form. With informative if idiosyncratic notes, this collection can be strongly recommended to any adventurous listener.

Saint-Saëns, Camille

(1835–1921)

Africa fantasy (for piano and orchestra), *Op. 89.*
(M) (*) Turn. TVS 37127 [Can. 31088]. Dosse, Westphalian SO, Landau – GOUNOD: *Fantasy*; MASSENET: *Piano concerto.*(*)

Saint-Saëns's exotic *Africa fantasy* is given a lively if unsubtle performance here, but the Turnabout recording is thin and lustreless, and readers not insistent on acquiring these couplings are advised to look elsewhere.

Allegro appassionato for cello and orchestra, Op. 43; Caprice in D major for violin and orchestra (arr. Ysaÿe); *Carnival of the Animals: Le cygne; Cello concerto No. 1 in A min., Op. 33; Wedding Cake (Caprice-valse) for piano and strings, Op. 76; Le Déluge: Prelude, Op. 45.*

**(*) HMV ASD 3058. Yan Pascal Tortelier, De la Pau, Paul Tortelier, CBSO, Frémaux.

Paul Tortelier gives an assured account of the *A minor Cello concerto*, but fails to make much of the busy but uninspired *Allegro appassionato*. Yan Pascal Tortelier plays with charm in the *Caprice* and catches the *salon* element in the music without vulgarizing it. He plays with pleasing simplicity in the *Prelude* to the oratorio *Le Déluge*, which has a concertante part for the solo violin. The *Wedding Cake caprice* is also nicely done, even though Maria de la Pau does not reveal a strong personality. With *Le Cygne* (Paul Tortelier accompanied by a harp) thrown in as a bonus, this is quite an attractive anthology, well recorded.

Carnival of the Animals.
(M) *** HMV Green. ESD/*TC-ESD* 7114. Hephzibah Menuhin, Simon, Philh. O., Kurtz – BRITTEN: *Young Person's Guide*; PROKOFIEV: *Peter.****
(M) *** ASV ACM/*ZCACM* 2005. Goldstone, Ian Brown, RPO, Hughes – PROKOFIEV: *Peter.****
(M) ** Turn. TVS 34586 [id.]. Dosse, Petit, Württemberg CO, Faerber – CHABRIER: *Valses*; SÉVERAC: *Le Soldat de plomb.***

The bargain-priced Classics for Pleasure version of Saint-Saëns's delightful zoological fantasy (CFP/*TC-CFP* 40086) remains highly competitive, the solo pianists, Peter Katin and Philip Fowke, entering fully into the spirit of the occasion and Gibson directing the SNO with affectionate, unforced humour. With excellent recording on disc and cassette alike and good couplings (Ravel's *Ma Mère l'Oye suite* and Bizet's *Jeux d'enfants*) this is very attractive indeed. However, HMV's Greensleeve reissue of Kurtz's splendid version from the end of the fifties has even more generous couplings and offers some vintage solo contributions from members of the Philharmonia Orchestra. The recording too is first-class, although, curiously, the definition is poor for the double basses in their portrayal of *Tortoises*. Elsewhere orchestral detail is admirably firm and vivid, and *The Swan* is memorably serene. The two pianists are spirited, and Kurtz's direction is witty and attentive.

The two pianists on ASV play with point and style, and the accompaniment has both spirit and spontaneity. *The Swan* is perhaps a trifle self-effacing, but otherwise this is very enjoyable, the humour appreciated without being underlined. The recording is excellent, both atmospheric and vivid, with the cassette matching the disc closely.

There is no lack of freshness on Turnabout, and the playing, if deadpan, has plenty of life. The balance is characteristically forward, with soloists spotlighted, and there is an element of shallowness in the sound. This is mainly of interest to those seeking the couplings.

(i) *Carnival of the Animals;* (ii) *Septet in E flat* (for trumpet, strings and piano), *Op. 65.*
** HMV ASD/*TC-ASD* 3448. Collard, Instrumental Ens., with (i) Béroff, (ii) André.

A bright-eyed chamber performance of the *Carnival*, recorded intimately within a comparatively dry acoustic. There is some good playing, but the lack of atmosphere is a drawback, and while there is sparkle there is little charm. The *Septet* is similarly unexpansive, although clear, and the curious instrumentation of trumpet, strings and piano does not seem to gell here, although the performance is lively enough. The cassette transfer is clean, but seems to have more edge than the disc.

Cello concerto No. 1 in A min., Op. 33.

⊛ *** CBS Dig. 35848 [Col. IM/*HMT* 35848]. Ma, Orchestre Nat. de France, Maazel – LALO: *Concerto.*⊛***
** HMV ASD/*TC-ASD* 3452 [Ang. S/ 4XS 37457]. Rostropovich, LPO, Giulini – DVOŘÁK: *Concerto.**(*)

Yo Yo Ma's performance of the Saint-Saëns *Concerto* is distinguished by fine sensitivity and beautiful tone. As in the Lalo, one is tempted to speak of him being 'hypersensitive', so fine is his attention to light and shade; yet there is not a trace of posturing or affectation. The Orchestre National de France respond with playing of great refinement throughout. Superb recorded sound which reflects great credit on the engineers.

Rostropovich's performance serves as a filler for the Dvořák *Concerto* and is more successful than its coupling, though not as impressive as his earlier version (now deleted). There is less rhetorical intensity here than in the Dvořák, and the performance is warmly and atmospherically recorded, with a quite well detailed cassette transfer.

Piano concertos Nos. 1–5; La Jeunesse d'Hercule, Op. 50.
*** Decca D 244 D 3/*K 244 K 33* (3). Rogé, Philh. O., LPO or RPO, Dutoit.

Piano concertos Nos. 1–5; Africa fantasy, Op. 89; Rapsodie d'Auvergne, Op. 73; Wedding Cake (Caprice-valse), Op. 76.
(M) ** Turn. TVS 37106/8 [SVBX/*CBX* 5143]. Tacchino, R. Lux. O., Froment.

The first of these concertos dates from 1858, and the last, written in the closing years of the last century, is every bit as fluent and engaging without being in any way deeper. Played as they are here, these concertos can exert a strong appeal: Pascal Rogé brings delicacy, virtuosity and sparkle to the piano part, and he receives expert support from the various London orchestras under Dutoit. Altogether delicious playing and excellent piano sound from Decca, who secure a most realistic balance. On the sixth side there is a rarity in the shape of *La Jeunesse d'Hercule*, Saint-Saëns's final tonepoem. In every respect, this set outclasses Aldo Ciccolini's survey of the early 1970s, good though that was. The cassettes sound splendid too, although the resonant acoustic, while creating an attractively rich and spacious effect, does bring a very marginal loss of focus, most noticeable at the evocative opening of the *Third Concerto*. Even so, tape collectors need not hesitate: this is still very sophisticated quality.

In none of the Turnabout performances does Gabriel Tacchino seriously challenge Rogé or Aldo Ciccolini's brilliant HMV set (SLS 802 [Scra. S/4X3G 6081]), but he is very good indeed. He has the appropriate keyboard presence and plays with great flair. There is vivid orchestral support, and if the orchestral playing itself lacks the last degree of distinction the performances have such spirit and spontaneity that reservations need not be serious. The bonus items on the third disc are all well worth having; the *Wedding Cake caprice* is given a most agreeable lightness of texture. The recording is of generally good quality, crisp and clear and with bold, firmly focused piano timbre and good orchestral detail. There is a degree of shallowness but not enough to detract from the general attractiveness of this set.

Violin concerto No. 1 in A, Op. 30.
*** Decca Dig. SXDL/*KSXDC* 7527 (Lon. LDR 71029/5-]. Kyung-Wha Chung, Montreal SO, Dutoit – LALO: *Symphonie espagnole.****

Saint-Saëns's *First Violin concerto* is a miniature, playing for only eleven and a half minutes. It was written for Sarasate, and if it seems somewhat insubstantial,

Kyung-Wha Chung makes the most of the lyrical interludes and is fully equal to the energetic bravura of the outer sections. With a clear yet full-blooded digital recording and an excellent accompaniment from Charles Dutoit, this is persuasive. The cassette is of very good quality, matching the disc closely.

Danse macabre, Op. 40.
*** CBS 76909/*40*- [Col. M/*MT* 35843]. Orchestre Nat. de France, Maazel – DUKAS: *L'Apprenti sorcier;* OFFENBACH: *Gaîté Parisienne.***(*)
(M) *** Chan. CBR/*CBT* 1003. SNO, Gibson – DUKAS: *L'Apprenti sorcier;* ROSSINI: *Boutique fantasque.****

Maazel himself plays the solo violin, with appropriate flair, in the excellent CBS account of Saint-Saëns's genially melodramatic piece. It is well recorded (although slightly less brilliant on tape than on disc), and the Offenbach coupling is attractive too; the Dukas is less memorable.

Gibson's performance has slightly less panache than Maazel's but it is vividly played and very well recorded (the cassette only marginally less brilliant than the disc). The couplings are both equally attractive.

Danse macabre; La Jeunesse d'Hercule, Op. 50; Marche héroïque, Op. 34; Phaéton, Op. 39; Le Rouet d'Omphale, Op. 31.
⊛*** Decca SXL/*KSXC* 6975. Philh. O., Dutoit.

Beautifully played performances, recorded in the Kingsway Hall with splendid atmosphere and colour. Charles Dutoit shows himself an admirably sensitive exponent of this repertoire, revelling in the composer's craftsmanship and revealing much delightful orchestral detail. *La Jeunesse d'Hercule* is the most ambitious piece, twice as long as its companions; its lyrical invention is both sensuous and elegant. The *Marche héroïque* is flamboyant but less memorable, and *Phaéton*, a favourite in the Victorian era, now sounds slightly dated. But the delightful *Omphale's Spinning Wheel* and the familiar *Danse macabre* show the composer at his most creatively imaginative. The slightly bizarre pictorial realization of the imagery of the *Danse macabre* by M. Jean Paul Veret makes a striking sleeve design. The cassette is of demonstration quality, quite the equal of the disc. On both LP and tape the various elements of the orchestra are ideally balanced and proportioned, and the sound is vivid, truthful and atmospheric, with wonderfully rich brass and light, feathery strings.

Havanaise, Op. 83; Introduction and rondo capriccioso, Op. 28.
(B) *** CfP CFP/*TC-CFP* 40364. Menuhin, Philh. O., Goossens – LALO: *Symphonie espagnole.****
*** Decca SXL/*KSXC* 6851 [Lon. 7073/5-]. Kyung-Wha Chung, RPO, Dutoit – CHAUSSON: *Poème*; RAVEL: *Tzigane.****
(M) **(*) Ph. Fest. 6570/*7310* 192 [id.]. Grumiaux, LOP, Rosenthal – LALO: *Symphonie espagnole.***(*)

Menuhin was at the peak of his form when he recorded these superb performances at the end of the fifties. The opening of the *Havanaise* is quite ravishing, and the shaping of the coda is no less seductive. Similarly he emphasizes the contrasts in Op. 28 by playing the *Introduction* with heart-warming beauty of tone and producing brilliant spiccato bravura at the end of the *Rondo capriccioso*. Goossens accompanies with considerable flair and the recording sounds freshly minted, the cassette marginally softer in outline than the disc.

On Decca the fireworks in two Saint-Saëns showpieces provide the necessary contrast for the more reflective works with which they are coupled. In both

Kyung-Wha Chung shows rhythmic flair and a touch of the musical naughtiness that gives them their full charm. As in the other nicely matched pieces Dutoit accompanies most sympathetically, and the recording is excellent on disc and tape alike.

Excellent performances from Grumiaux, purer and less romantic in style than some. The opening of the *Havanaise* is beautifully played but less sensuous than with Menuhin (or Perlman, who offers the same couplings as Kyung-Wha Chung in performances of splendid panache and virtuosity: HMV ASD 3125 [Ang. S 37118]). Grumiaux is given lively orchestral support, and the Philips recording is good, with plenty of life in the equivalent cassette transfer.

Symphony No. 3 in C min., Op. 78.
*** Chalfont Dig. SDG 312 [id.]. Rawsthorne, Royal Liv. PO, Tjeknavorian.
*** HMV ASD/*TC-ASD* 3674. Fr. Nat. RO, Martinon.
(M) **(*) CBS 61914/*40*- [Col. MS 6469]. Phd. O., Ormandy.
(M) ** Ph. Fest. 6570/*7310* 149 [id.]. Hague PO, Benzi.
*(*) Telarc Dig. DG 10051 [id.]. Phd. O., Ormandy.

Symphony No. 3; (i) *Wedding Cake (Caprice-valse), Op. 76.*
** Ph. 9500 306/*7300 597* [id.]. Rotterdam PO, De Waart, (i) with Chorzempa.

Saint-Saëns's *Third Symphony* is exceptionally well represented in the current catalogue. Barenboim's Chicago recording for DG, to which we gave a rosette in the second edition of the *Penguin Stereo Record Guide*, is a superlative performance, superbly recorded on disc and tape alike (2530/*3300* 619) while in the mid-price bracket Frémaux's splendid version with the City of Birmingham orchestra is also impressively recorded on disc, and the performance is as warm-hearted as it is brilliant (HMV ESD 7038).

The new Chalfont digital recording, made in Liverpool Cathedral, is perhaps the most sumptuous and spectacular so far, with an overwhelming climax at the close of the finale, organ pedals effectively underpinning the spacious orchestral tutti. Tjeknavorian's reading has plenty of energy in the first movement and the scherzo (which brings minor ensemble problems near the opening, caused by the resonant acoustic), and in the slow movement he balances repose and eloquence. The playing of the Liverpool orchestra is excellent and the reading as a whole is highly enjoyable, even if Tjeknavorian's pacing and interpretative control sound less natural and spontaneous than the Barenboim and Frémaux versions.

Martinon's account, which comes from his boxed set containing all the symphonies (HMV SLS 5053), is ripely expansive, and very well recorded, although the first entry of the organ in the finale is not as dramatic as in some versions. The cassette accommodates the histrionics of the last movement without congestion, although at the expense of some loss of bloom on the upper strings.

Ormandy's CBS reissue offers a fresh and vigorous performance, with the conductor's affection fully conveyed. The alert, polished Philadelphia playing brings incisive articulation to the first movement and scherzo, while the slow movement is expressive without being sentimentalized. The recording is vivid but rather dry, however, although this has meant that the tape transfer successfully avoids congestion.

Benzi's Hague version is eminently serviceable, and has excellent recording to commend it; but the performance is a little under-powered, and in the mid-price range Frémaux is much to be preferred.

Polished as the playing of the Rotterdam orchestra is, helped by refined Philips recording (if at a disappointingly low level in the tape version), the De Waart performance cannot compare in excitement with the finest accounts. Some may be swayed by the attractive fill-up, though after the organ glories at the end of the symphony few will want to go on at once to such relative triviality.

Ormandy's Telarc performance is curiously lacking in vitality. It is not helped by the recessed, over-resonant recording, in which the microphones place the organ in a forward, concerto-like position. Orchestral detail is poor and the piano contribution barely audible. In the finale the closing climax is effectively balanced, but elsewhere the performance makes little real impact.

Piano trio in F, Op. 18.
*** HMV ASD 3729. De la Pau, Yan-Pascal and Paul Tortelier – RAVEL: *Piano trio.***

The *Piano trio* is an early work, written when Saint-Saëns was twenty-eight, before his disastrous marriage. He wrote it during a holiday in the Auvergne, and the invention is fresh and smiling. Here it has the advantage of superb recorded sound and a good, keenly alert performance. Though not a masterpiece, the *Trio* is well worth getting to know, and the Ravel coupling is attractive, though the Torteliers' performance here is not quite as sensitive as its rivals.

Messe à quatre voix, Op. 4.
**(*) Argo ZRG 889. Colston, Rivaz, John Vickers, Owen, Harvey, Worcester Cath. Ch., Hunt; Massey (grand organ), Trepte (small organ).

Donald Hunt directs an enjoyable performance of an early rarity of Saint-Saëns. Written when he was only twenty-one, this *Mass* shows how well he had learnt his academic lessons, for at various points he uses with total freshness what at the time were archaic techniques, as in the beautiful *Agnus Dei* at the end.

The organ writing is characteristically French, and though one finds few signs of deep feeling, the piece is well worth hearing. The soloists here are variable, but the choir is excellent and the recording atmospheric.

Samson et Dalila (opera; complete).
*** DG 2709 095/*3371 050* (3) [id.].
Obraztsova, Domingo, Bruson, Lloyd, Thau, Ch. and Orchestre de Paris, Barenboim.

DG's recording sessions were held in conjunction with live performances at the Orange Festival, and that is reflected in the tingling electricity of the result, for Barenboim proves as passionately dedicated an interpreter of Saint-Saëns here as he did in the *Third Symphony*, sweeping away any Victorian cobwebs. It is important too that the choral passages, so vital in this work, are sung with this sort of freshness, and Domingo has rarely sounded happier in French music, the bite as well as the heroic richness of the voice well caught. Renato Bruson and Robert Lloyd are both admirable too, but sadly the key role of Dalila is given an unpersuasive, unsensuous performance by Obraztsova, with her vibrato often verging on a wobble. The recording is as ripe as the music deserves; the cassette transfer is very successful, wide-ranging and clear, following the layout of the discs.

Collection: (i; ii) *Danse macabre, Op. 40;* (iii) *Havanaise, Op. 83; Introduction and rondo capriccioso, Op. 28;* (i; ii) *Le Rouet d'Omphale, Op. 31. Samson et Dalila:* (iv) *Mon cœur s'ouvre à ta voix;* (i; v) *Bacchanale.*
(M) *** Decca Eclipse ECS 808. (i) Paris Conservatoire O.; (ii) Martinon; (iii) Ricci, LSO, Gamba; (iv) Resnik; (v) Fistoulari.

This is a characteristically well-made Decca anthology. The Martinon perfor-

mances of *Danse macabre* and *Le Rouet d'Omphale* are notably successful, and Ricci shows splendid form and plenty of personality in the works featuring the solo violin. Regina Resnik's performance of *Softly awakes my heart* is splendidly rich and resonant, and the collection ends vividly with Fistoulari's account of the *Bacchanale.*

Salieri, Antonio (1750–1825)

Double concerto for oboe, flute and orchestra in C.
(M) *** DG Priv. 2535/*3335* 417 [139152]. Holliger, Nicolet, Bamberg SO, Maag – BELLINI, CIMAROSA, DONIZETTI: *Concertos.****

Heinz Holliger and Aurèle Nicolet make an expert partnership, and Salieri's *Double concerto* is a pleasant little work. All the couplings are first-class, as is the recording in both disc and cassette formats.

Salzedo, Leonardo (born 1921)

Capriccio for brass quintet.
** Argo ZRG/*KZRC* 906 [id.]. Jones Brass Ens. – ARNOLD: *Symphony* **(*); PREMRU: *Music.* ***

The playing and recording here are altogether magnificent, and it is only Leonard Salzedo's piece that falls short of the highest quality. His music is nothing if not accomplished: it is effectively laid out for a quintet of two trumpets, horn, trombone and tuba, and has considerable facility. It stretches the players and is an excellent showpiece, but its invention is not particularly distinguished or memorable. The cassette transfer is exceptionally successful, resonant and clear; a bass plus and a treble minus improve the quality still further.

Sarasate, Pablo (1844–1908)

Carmen fantasy, Op. 25.
(M) ** Decca SPA/*KCSP* 551. Ricci, LSO, Gamba – GRANADOS: *Spanish dance*; RAVEL: *Boléro* etc.**

Ricci's account of Sarasate's *Carmen* potpourri has immense dash and virtuosity, but he is recorded very near the microphone and the resiny contact of bow on string is exaggerated. The cassette is marginally smoother than the disc.

Zigeunerweisen, Op. 20/1.
** HMV ASD/*TC-ASD* 3408 [Ang. S/ *4XS* 37445]. Perlman, Pittsburgh SO, Previn – GOLDMARK: *Violin concerto No. 1.***(*)

Perlman's account of Sarasate's *Zigeunerweisen* is both virtuosic and idiomatic. The engineers have placed the distinguished soloist rather too close to the microphone, but he survives any amount of scrutiny, and in any event the results are in no way disturbing. This makes an attractive fill-up to Goldmark's charming concerto, and in spite of the spotlight on the soloist the orchestral sound is full-blooded. The cassette transfer is well managed.

(i) *8 Spanish dances: Malagueña; Habanera, Op. 21/1–2; Romanza andaluza; Jota navarra, Op. 22/1–2; Playera; Zapateado, Op. 23/1–2; Nos. 7–8, Op. 26/1–2.* (ii) *Navarra for two violins, Op. 22.*

*** O-L DSLO 22. Campoli, with (i) Ibbott, (ii) Blunt.

Campoli is in excellent form here, and with the art that disguises art he makes these dances sound effortless yet brilliant. The record contains the first four books of the *Spanish dances* and the *Navarra*, in which Campoli is joined by Belinda Blunt. Popular light music this may be, but it is all thoroughly enjoyable when the playing is of this quality. The recording, too, is very good indeed, and although at times it is a little close, this is never troubling.

Satie, Erik (1866–1925)

Gymnopédies Nos. 1 and 3 (orch. Debussy).
(M) *** HMV Green. ESD/*TC-ESD* 7097. CBSO, Frémaux – BERLIOZ: *Damnation de Faust excerpts*; IBERT: *Divertissement* etc.**(*)

Beautiful orchestral playing and rich, resonant recording which suit Debussy's indulgent scoring perfectly. The cassette matches the disc closely.

Gymnopédies Nos. 1 and 3; Parade; Relâche (Parts 1 and 2).
(M) **(*) CBS 61992/*40*- [Col. M 30294]. RPO, Entremont.

Entremont presents the *Gymnopédies* sympathetically and brings plenty of bite and point to the other two scores, though he rather overdoes the humour in *Parade*. Still his *Relâche* is very good, and the recordings are fully acceptable both on disc and on the tape (which has the body of the LP but slightly less edge).

Monotones (ballet, arr. Lanchbery); *Jack in the Box* (orch. Milhaud); *Deux Préludes posthumes* (orch.

Poulenc); *Trois Morceaux en forme de poire* (orch. Désormière). (M) *(*) HMV Green. ESD/*TC-ESD* 7069. ROHCGO, Lanchbery.

The music for Sir Frederick Ashton's ballet *Monotones* is principally based on Satie's *Gnossiennes* and *Gymnopédies*. The music is fairly static, and although it is gracefully played there is a lack of momentum here: the best-known third *Gymnopédie* is extended by repetition and at Lanchbery's slow, stately pace almost outlasts its welcome. The arrival of the more lively *Jack in the Box* comes as a relief, but side two returns to the somewhat languid mood of the opening, and the two posthumous *Préludes* seem almost totally lacking in vitality. No doubt this issue will be sought after by balletomanes but it cannot be generally recommended with any enthusiasm. The recording is suitably atmospheric, although on tape the sound is not especially refined in detail, and *Jack in the Box* could do with more glitter.

PIANO MUSIC

Avant-dernières pensées; Chapitres tournés en tous sens; Cinq Grimaces; Deux Rêveries nocturnes; Le Fils des étoiles; Gnossiennes Nos. 2–3; Je te veux – valse; Nocturnes Nos. 3 and 5; Les Pantins dansent; Pièces froides; Le Piège de Méduse; Première Pensée Rose et Croix; Prélude de la porte héroïque du ciel; Rêverie du pauvre; Trois Valses distinguées du précieux dégoûté; Valse-ballet.
(M) **(*) Saga 5472. McCabe.

This entertaining and attractive anthology is well played and recorded, and ranges from relatively neglected early works like the *Valse-ballet*, Satie's first published piano piece, dating from 1885, to the *Rêverie du pauvre* (1900) and the *Deux Rêveries nocturnes* (1911), pub-

lished as late as 1968. This is all intelligently played, as one expects from this artist.

Avant-dernières pensées; Embryons desséchés; Gymnopédies Nos. 1–3; Gnossiennes Nos. 1–5; Nocturne No. 1; Sarabandes Nos. 1–3; Sonatine bureaucratique; Trois Valses distinguées du précieux dégoûté.
(M) ** CBS 61874. Varsano.

A good, cleanly focused but too closely balanced recording of the piano. Daniel Varsano has the measure of these pieces and plays admirably. Perhaps the first of the *Embryons desséchés* could have greater delicacy and wit, and there could be greater melancholy in the second of the *Gymnopédies*. The latter are spread out on the second side, the *Embryons desséchés* and *Sonatine bureaucratique* being sandwiched between them, and all five works being in turn placed between the fourth and fifth *Gnossiennes*. Likewise the first three *Gnossiennes* are distributed over the first side with other pieces interspersed. There are good things here, and it is a pity that the slightly dry sound and inelegant presentation (there are no notes) diminish the appeal of this issue.

Chapitres tournés en tous sens; Croquis et agaceries d'un gros bonhomme en bois; Gnossiennes Nos. 2 and 4; Trois Gymnopédies; Heures séculaires et instantanées; Nocturnes Nos. 2 and 4; Nouvelles pièces froides; Passacaille; Le Piège de Méduse; Prélude No. 2 (Le Fils des étoiles); Sonatine bureaucratique.
(B) ** CfP CFP/*TC-CFP* 40329. Lawson.

Satie's deceptively simple piano writing poses problems for the interpreter; it has to be played with great sensitivity and subtlety if justice is to be done to its special qualities of melancholy and irony. Peter Lawson is very well recorded both on disc and on tape (there is little difference between them, except for the virtually silent background of the cassette). The recital opens with the famous *Gymnopédies*, played coolly but not ineffectively. The highlight is a perceptive and articulate characterization of *Le Piège de Méduse*, seven epigrammatic *morceaux de concert*, originally written as incidental music for a comedy in which Satie himself took the lead. Elsewhere Lawson's playing is fresh and clean but lacking in individuality. His way is quietly tasteful, and though he catches something of Satie's gentle and wayward poetry he is less successful in revealing the underlying sense of fantasy. There are more distinguished and memorable recordings available at full price; but the present issue is a good deal more than serviceable for those with a limited budget.

Danses gothiques; Fête donnée par des Chevaliers Normands en l'honneur d'une jeune demoiselle; Six Gnossiennes; Cinq Gymnopédies; Ogives; Petite Ouverture à danser; Pièces froides; Prélude d'Eginhard; Prélude de la porte héroïque du ciel; Deux Préludes de Nazaréen; Prière; Trois Sarabandes; Trois Sonneries de la Rose Croix.
**(*) Ph. 6768 269 (3). De Leeuw.

This three-record set concentrates on Satie's earlier music and collects the bulk of his output from 1885 to 1900, much of it otherwise unobtainable. Reinbert de Leeuw is a sensitive player and thoroughly attuned to Satie's personality. He takes him at his word by playing many of the pieces *très lent*; indeed he overdoes this at times, though this impression may be caused by listening to too much at once. But if one

occasionally feels the need for more movement (and on occasion greater dynamic nuance), these are still admirable performances, and they are beautifully recorded.

Gnossiennes Nos. 1, 4 and 5; Trois Gymnopédies; Nocturne No. 1; Passacaille; Six Pièces (Désespoir agréable; Effronterie; Poésie; Prélude canin; Profondeur; Songe creux); Ragtime (from Parade, arr. Ourdine); Sarabandes Nos. 1 and 3; Sonatine bureaucratique; Sports et divertissements; Véritables préludes flasques; Vieux sequins et vieilles cuirasses.
(M) ** Saga 5387 McCabe.

Although Satie is often overrated by his admirers there is a desperate melancholy and a rich poetic feeling about much of this music which are altogether unique. The *Gymnopédies* show such flashes of innocence and purity of inspiration that criticism is disarmed. John McCabe's performances are cool, even deliberate, but they are not heavy, and his sympathy is never in doubt. He is quite well recorded.

Scarlatti, Alessandro
(1660–1725)

6 Concerti grossi.
*** Ph. 9500 603/7300 725 [id.]. I Musici.
(M) ** DG Arc. Priv. 2547/3347 020. Scarlatti O. of Naples, Gracis.

These noble and elevated works were first published by Benjamin Cooke in 1740, fifteen years after Scarlatti's death. Though far from radical in style, they have invention of quality to commend them; I Musici give performances of some eloquence and warmth, and great transparency. The latter is welcome in the fugal movements, which are numerous (eleven out of twenty-three). These very well recorded performances are unlikely to be surpassed for a very long time. The cassette transfer is first-class, full, with plenty of life and detail.

Ettore Gracis's recording was made in the 1960s and has the advantage of a mid-range price as well as more detailed documentation from Malcolm Boyd. The performances are workmanlike but not as fresh or as accomplished as those of I Musici, and the recording is less impressive; the latter is well worth the extra outlay. The DG cassette matches the disc closely.

Sinfonias Nos. 6 and 10 in A min.; 7 and 9 in G min.; 8 in G; 11 in C.
(M) ** RCA Gold GL/*GK* 25197. Cantilena, Shepherd.

The five *Sinfonie di concerto grosso* recorded here come from 1715 and are far from unappealing, though the invention is not always of the most memorable. The playing of this group is fresh and alert, but tempi are often extreme: slow movements are very broad indeed, and fast movements are a shade too brisk. The oboe, oddly enough, is chosen to replace the recorder in at least three of the sinfonias, the flute being used elsewhere. There is no want of feeling in the slow movements, and the sound is good on both disc and cassette, although on tape the dynamic range is more restricted. This may not be for purists, but there is still enjoyment to be had here.

Cantata pastorale per la Natività di Nostro Signore Gesù Cristo.
(M) *** HMV SXLP/*TC-SXLP* 30280. Baker, ECO, Leppard – MONTEVERDI: *L'Incoronazione di Poppea excerpts;* D. SCARLATTI: *Salve Regina.****

The cooler enchantments of Alessandro Scarlatti make an admirable foil for the intense Monteverdi offerings on this issue, and Janet Baker's depth of expression brings vividness to this *Cantata pastorale* written for Christmas. The recording is excellent on disc and cassette alike.

Il Giardino di amore (The Garden of Love; cantata).
(M) *** DG Arc. Priv. 2547/*3347* 033 [2535/*3335* 361]. Gayer, Fassbaender, Mun. CO, Stadlmair.

Scarlatti called this delightful work a serenata, for there are only two characters and the orchestra is basically a string group, with colourful obbligatos for recorder, violin and trumpet. The names of the two principal characters, Venus and Adonis, will recall the somewhat earlier work by Blow. Here the originally castrato role of Adonis is attractively sung by a soprano, Catherine Gayer, with Brigitte Fassbaender providing a foil in her portrayal of Venus. The two voices are well matched and the singing has both charm and character. Repeats are skilfully ornamented and the whole production has an engaging spontaneity to match its stylishness. There are some delightful pictorial touches in Scarlatti's word settings, and they are imaginatively realized. The nightingale song (with recorder obbligato) is especially memorable, as is the aria *Con battaglia di fiero tormento,* which has a trumpet obbligato worthy of Handel. The recording from the mid-sixties is excellent and the cassette is vividly bright and clear.

St Cecilia Mass.
*** Argo ZRG/*KZRC* 903 [id.]. Harwood, Eathorne, Cable, Evans, Keyte, St John's College Ch., Wren O., Guest.

In this celebratory setting of the Mass, the most elaborate and expansive that Scarlatti wrote, he applied to church music the techniques he had already used in opera. This is far more florid in its style than Scarlatti's other Masses, and it receives from Guest a vigorous and fresh performance. The soloists cope with their difficult *fioriture* very confidently, and they match each other well. The recording is warmly atmospheric to set choir and orchestra nicely in place. The cassette is good too, coping with the reverberation with only very minor loss of focus of the chorus.

Scarlatti, Domenico
(1685–1757)

Keyboard sonatas, Kk. 3, 52, 184–5, 191–3, 208–9, 227, 238–9, 252–3.
*** RCA RL 30334. Leonhardt.

Very distinguished playing from Gustav Leonhardt on a copy of a Dulcken harpsichord: characterful performances in every way and well-focused, clean sound recorded in a pleasant acoustic. Vigilance is required with the documentation: the second band offers Kk. 185 and 184 (as listed above), not Kk. 184 and 183, as the label and sleeve have it.

Keyboard sonatas, Kk. 46, 87, 99, 124, 201, 204a, 490–92, 513, 520–21.
*** CRD CRD 1068/*CRDC 4068.* Pinnock.

No need to say much about this: the playing is first-rate and the recording outstanding in its presence and clarity. There are few better anthologies of Scarlatti in the catalogue, and this has the advantage of including a half-dozen sonatas not otherwise available. The excellent cassette matches the disc closely.

Keyboard sonatas, Kk. 111, 129, 142,

148–9, 160–61, 170, 176, 183–4, 199–200, 213–14, 225–6, 266–7, 274–6, 279–80, 283–4, 310–11, 322–5, 331–2, 335–6, 343–4, 352–3, 370–71, 376–7, 380–81, 424–5, 462–3, 474–5, 485–7, 503–4, 507–8, 514–15, 536–7, 540–41.
*(*) Erato ERA 92222 (4). Sgrizzi.

This box includes sixty-five sonatas, all of which bear witness to Luciano Sgrizzi's fine technique and vital musicianship. But four records is a lot to buy all at once, and in a number of the sonatas Sgrizzi's enthusiasm runs away with him and the performances are less keenly controlled than is ideal; and some of the rubato does not wholly convince. The sound is vivid and the harpsichord (by Anthony Sidey) reproduces well.

Keyboard sonatas, Kk. 123–4, 147, 198, 326–7, 428–9, 454, 466–7.
*(*) O-L DSLO 567. Tilney.

Colin Tilney's recital is not an unqualified success, though the harpsichord on which he records is undoubtedly of interest: it is a Sodi of 1782 which is particularly warm and rich at the bass. Some of these pieces come off well, but others have a somewhat pedantic air and a stiffness out of key with Scarlatti's mercurial temperament. The sound is truthful enough and a number of these pieces are not obtainable elsewhere.

Salve Regina (arr. Leppard).
(M) *** HMV SXLP/*TC-SXLP* 30280. Baker, ECO, Leppard – MONTEVERDI: *L'Incoronazione di Poppea excerpts*; A. SCARLATTI: *Cantata pastorale*.***

This *Salve Regina* has conventional passages, but Janet Baker and Leppard together hardly let you appreciate any weakness, so intense is the performance.

The recording too is admirably vivid on both disc and cassette.

Scheidt, Samuel (1587–1654)

Tabulatura nova, Vol. 1: 12 Passamezzo variations.

⊛ (M) *** Argo ZK 65. Weir (organ of Clare College, Camb.) – BRUHNS: *Preludes.*⊛***

These *Variations* demonstrate Scheidt's mastery of variation technique, with imaginative invention throughout. Gillian Weir helps a great deal, not only by playing the music splendidly but by choosing registrations with great flair and a marvellous sense of colour. The piquancy of several of her combinations is unforgettably apt. She is superbly recorded, and this disc of pre-Bach German organ music is quite outstandingly attractive.

Schein, Johann (1586–1630)

Banchetto musicale: 3 Suites.

(M) *** DG Arc. Priv. 2547/3347 005 [198166]. Coll. Terpsichore – PRAETORIUS: *Terpsichore*; WIDMANN: *Dances.****

Johann Schein's *Banchetto musicale* is an obvious precursor of Telemann's *Tafelmusik*. The invention is pleasing if not quite so memorable as the coupled Praetorius dance music. Here the scholarly instrumental re-creation is imaginatively supported by agreeably volatile playing. The recording is good too, though the cassette has not quite the upper range and bite of the LP.

Schoeck, Othmar (1886–1957)

Élégie, Op. 36; 3 Hesse Lieder; 6 Eichendorff Lieder.

** Jecklin DISCO 0510/11. A. Loosli, CO, Hug; Grenacher (piano).

Nachhall, Op. 70; 12 Lenau Lieder; O du Land.

** Jecklin DISCO 0535. A. Loosli, Bern RCO, T. Loosli.

Der Postillon, Op. 18; 15 Lieder.

** Jecklin DISCO 0505. Haefliger, Wettinger Ch. and CO with Zürich Wind Ens., Grenacher; Grenacher (piano).

The Swiss composer Othmar Schoeck is more praised than played, but those who know his work testify to its rare qualities. He is arguably the finest song composer after Wolf (his only rival being the Finn, Yrjö Kilpinen), yet despite the advocacy of such an artist as Dietrich Fischer-Dieskau, who has made several records of his work, his cause has made little headway. Like his younger contemporary, Frank Martin, he creates a concentrated and powerful atmosphere, and he has a highly developed feeling for language. His early music shows the influence of Richard Strauss, but he soon developed an individual style, expressionist in feeling, assimilating the chromaticism of Berg into a language that is basically traditional yet thoroughly personal. He is a composer who stands aloof from the mainstream of the twentieth century, yet those who seek him out are rewarded with music that has both subtlety and substance. The records listed above give a fair sample of his large output of songs and (in the last record) choruses. The last disc dates from the late 1960s but no one with a serious interest in song should fail to explore this composer—the *Élégie*, settings of Lenau and Eichendorff, is a masterpiece. The performances are idiomatic and on the whole reasonably well recorded

Schoenberg, Arnold
(1874–1951)

Accompaniment to a cinematographic scene, Op. 34; 5 Pieces for orchestra, Op. 16; Variations for orchestra, Op. 31, (i) A Survivor from Warsaw, Op. 46.
*** CBS 76577 [Col. M/MT 35882]. BBC SO, Boulez, with (i) Reich, BBC Singers.

Boulez's choice of four key works gives on a single disc a splendid conspectus of Schoenberg's achievement as a writer for orchestra. This is a record which should win converts, for all these works communicate directly and immediately. Boulez's account of the thornily complex *Variations* may lack both the warmth and the polish of Karajan's celebrated version, but Boulez's earthiness is compelling too, unrelentingly forceful. The *Five Pieces for orchestra*, once regarded as difficult, now emerge as colourful and expressive, hardly more elusive than Debussy, while the *Film scene* is as atmospheric as one would expect, if not as emotionally involved as *A Survivor from Warsaw*, illustrating a tragic scene from the siege of that city in 1945, with a narrator telling the story and the chorus entering movingly to illustrate the defiance of the doomed Jews. Boulez's performances are strong and spontaneous-sounding, and are given large-scale, immediate recordings.

Chamber symphony, Op. 9.
*** DG 2531 213 [id.]. Boston Chamber Players BERG: *Chamber concerto: Adagio*; DEBUSSY: *Prélude.****

For a concert tour of Spain, Webern

arranged Schoenberg's *Chamber symphony* for the quintet of instruments used in *Pierrot Lunaire*. Here members of the Boston Symphony Orchestra give a powerfully convincing performance, beautifully recorded, though even they cannot quite make one forget the richness of the original scoring.

Pelleas und Melisande (symphonic poem), *Op. 5.*
(*) Ph. 6769 045 (2) [id.]. Rotterdam PO, Zinman FAURÉ: *Pelléas* *; SIBELIUS: *Pelléas.***(*)

In a useful anthology of music inspired by Maeterlinck's play, Zinman's reading of Schoenberg's somewhat inflated symphonic poem is strongly characterized and very well played. But the Rotterdam orchestra cannot match the opulence of Karajan's ravishing Berlin Philharmonic version (DG 2530 485), and the reverberant Philips recording is not always kind to Schoenberg's sometimes pungent scoring.

Verklaerte Nacht.
(*) CBS 76305/40- [Col. M 35166]. NYPO, Boulez – BERG: *Lyric suite.*(*)

Boulez secures responsive playing from the strings of the New York Philharmonic and has the measure of Schoenberg's poetic essay. But this performance in no respect matches Karajan's superbly fashioned and sensitive account with the Berlin Philharmonic, coupled with the *Variations*, Op. 31 (DG 2530 627), and is not as richly recorded. There is no other alternative on cassette, but on record Boulez's version must yield not only to the Karajan but also to Marriner's Argo disc with the Academy of St Martin-in-the-Fields (ZRG 763) and contend with the London Sinfonietta's Decca Ace of Diamonds version, coupled with the *Chamber symphony*, Op. 9, and played in its solo-string form (SDD 519).

The CBS cassette is smoothly transferred and full in texture.

String quartets Nos. 1 in D min., Op. 7; 2 in F sharp min., Op. 10; 3, Op. 30; 4, Op. 37; in D (1897).
** CBS 79304 (3) [Col. M3 34581]. Juilliard Qt.

The Juilliard Quartet offer performances of all Schoenberg's quartets, including the *D major* of 1897. The playing is powerful and accurate but the recording rather dry and forward. Comparing these performances with the Juilliard mono set made in the 1950s, one is struck by the hardness and efficiency of these newcomers: there is an unrelieved intensity and a want of real pianissimo here, for which the recording may in part be responsible. The LaSalle set on DG was better recorded and more sensitively played, but it is no longer available, and the Juilliards must be recommended *faute de mieux*. There is no lack of expertise and forcefulness in their approach to these scores.

(i) *String quartet No. 2, Op. 10, with soprano;* (ii) *Verklaerte Nacht (for string sextet), Op. 4.*
(M) *** Ph. 6570/7310 576. New V. Qt, (i) with Lear, (ii) augmented.

At medium price this is a specially generous coupling of works which each last over half an hour. Though the matching of the New Vienna Quartet is not always flawless, these passionate performances will do much to persuade the unconverted that Schoenberg – at least early in his career – could be warmly sympathetic, not just in the post-Wagnerian *Verklaerte Nacht* but in the rather later *Second Quartet* too. Its last two movements (both slow) are intensified by the contribution of a soprano, here the admirable Evelyn Lear. First-rate recording and an excellent cassette, lively yet full-bodied.

Gurrelieder.
*** Ph. 6769 038/7699 124 [id.]. McCracken, Norman, Troyanos, Arnold, Scown, Tanglewood Festival Ch., Boston SO, Ozawa.

Ozawa directs a gloriously opulent reading of Schoenberg's massive score, one which relates it firmly to the nineteenth century rather than pointing forward to Schoenberg's own later works. The playing of the Boston Symphony has both warmth and polish and is set against a warm acoustic; among the soloists Jessye Norman gives a performance of radiant beauty, reminding one at times of Flagstad in the burnished glory of her tone colours. As the wood-dove Tatiana Troyanos sings most sensitively, though the vibrato is at times obtrusive, and James McCracken does better than most tenors at coping with a heroic vocal line without barking. Other versions have in some ways been more powerful – Boulez's, for one – but none is more sumptuously beautiful than this. The cassettes match the discs closely, encompassing the wide dynamic range without difficulty until the short but massive closing chorus, which lacks the open quality of the LP.

Pierrot Lunaire, Op. 21.
**(*) CBS 76720. Minton, Zukerman, Harrell, Debost, Pay, Barenboim, Boulez.

Boulez's performance has a most distinguished group of instrumentalists, but the result lacks the expressive intensity one expects of this conductor in this music. With Yvonne Minton eschewing sing-speech, the vocal line is precisely pitched but with frequent recourse to half-tones. It is a most musical result but hardly conveys the cabaret associations which are important in this highly coloured melodramatic work. Unlike some of the finest rivals, this version has no coupling. The recording is forward and clean, if lacking in bloom.

Schubert, Franz (1797–1828)

Konzertstück for violin and orchestra in D, D. 345.

*** CRD CRD 1069/*CRDC 4069.*
Thomas, Bournemouth Sinf. –
BEETHOVEN: *Romances*; MENDELS-
SOHN: *Concerto.****

The *Konzertstück* is hardly vintage Schubert, but Ronald Thomas's refreshing playing and direction make it well worth hearing along with the excellent Mendelssohn and Beethoven. The cassette transfer matches the first-class recording of the disc.

Konzertstück, D. 345; Polonaise in B flat, D. 580; Rondo in A, D. 438.

*** DG 2531 193 [id.]. Kremer (violin), LSO, Tchakarov – BEETHOVEN: *Concerto movement* etc.***

Like Beethoven in the *Concerto movement* Schubert was twenty when he wrote these three concertante pieces, none of them specially individual, but all attractive in performances so sweetly sympathetic. Excellent recording.

(i) *Marche militaire, D.733/1;* (ii) *Overtures in the Italian style, D.590, D.591;* (iii) *Rosamunde: Overture (Die Zauberharfe, D.644); Entr'acte in B flat; Ballet music No. 2, D.797. Symphony No. 8 in B min. (Unfinished), D.759.*

(M) *** HMV *TC-IDL 504.* (i) Philh. O., Kurtz; (ii) Menuhin Festival O., Menuhin; (iii) RPO, Sargent.

This is a generous and attractive medium-priced anthology on tape only. Sargent was a highly musical if perhaps slightly square Schubertian, but his reading of the *Unfinished symphony* matches warm lyricism with a satisfying architectural control. The playing of the

Rosamunde music is unpretentiously attractive, and Menuhin's account of the two Rossini imitations is fresh, brightly played and recorded. Indeed the sound throughout is bright, clean and full-bodied.

Overtures: Fierrabras, D.796; Die Freunde von Salamanka, D.326; Rosamunde (Die Zauberharfe, D.644); Der vierjährige Posten, D.190; Die Zwillingsbrüder, D.647; Overtures in the Italian style: in B flat, D.470; in D, D.590.

(M) ** HMV Green. ESD/*TC-ESD 7086.* Bournemouth SO, Schwarz.

An attractive anthology. Several of these charming overtures are not otherwise available on record. The playing is unaffected and fresh, let down only by the rather thin quality of the strings (as recorded here). The recording needs to expand at climaxes but is otherwise very good. Not high-powered accounts but thoroughly musical and enjoyable all the same. On cassette the sound is slightly thick in the middle range and lacks something in freshness on top.

Overtures: Fierrabras, D.796; in the Italian style in C, D.591; Des Teufels Lustschloss, D.84.

(M) *** Decca Jub. JB/*KJBC 76* [Lon. STS 15476]. VPO, Kertesz – *Symphony No. 8.****

These overtures provide an enterprising coupling for a first-rate account of the *Unfinished symphony*. *Des Teufels Lustschloss* is a juvenile work, and its bright-eyed freshness shows much in common with the music of the young Mendelssohn. *Fierrabras* is more melodramatic but lively in invention; and Schubert's Rossini imitation nearly comes off here with such neat, sparkling playing. Excellent recording too on both disc and cassette.

*Symphonies Nos. 1–9. Rosamunde:
Overture, D.644; incidental music,
D.797.*
**(*) HMV SLS/*TC-SLS* 5127 [Ang. S
3862]. Berlin PO, Karajan.

*Symphonies Nos. 1–9; 2 Overtures in
the Italian style, D.590, D.591.*
(M) ** Ph. 6747 491 [6770 015]. Dresden
State O., Sawallisch.

Karajan presents the most polished
and in many ways the most beautiful set
of the Schubert symphonies. The point
and elegance of the Berliners' playing in
the early symphonies is most persuasive,
yet the results are never mannered. One
might criticize the reverberant acoustic
for giving the impression of too large a
band, one which rather lacks the brightness one associates with Schubert's songful writing; and the *Fourth Symphony*, the
Tragic, finds Karajan less compelling. So
does the *Great C major*, though this is a
far less superficial reading than the one
he recorded earlier for DG. The culmination of the set comes not in No. 9 but
in the *Unfinished*, which with Berlin refinement at its most ethereal has an
other-worldly quality, rapt and concentrated. Other versions convey more
Schubertian freshness, but this set plainly
earns a high place. The cassettes match
the discs fairly closely, although in tuttis
the upper range is not quite so clean.

Sawallisch gives refined, somewhat
reticent readings of all the Schubert symphonies. He misses some of the fun in the
early works and some of the weight of
the later symphonies, but with polished
playing from the Dresden orchestra it
remains an enjoyable set, nowhere
seriously disappointing. The recorded
sound, of late-sixties vintage, is somewhat cautious, but Sawallisch's ability to
compel attention on a pianissimo – so
important when most of these symphonies begin with slow introductions –
is most impressive, evidence of his
unforced concentration and the beauty of
the Dresden string section.

*Symphonies Nos. 1 in D, D.82; 2 in B
flat, D.125.*
(M) **(*) Decca Jub. JB/*KJBC* 73 [Lon.
STS 15473]. VPO, Kertesz.
** Decca SXL/*KSXC* 6892 [Lon. 7114/
5-]. Israel PO, Mehta.

Kertesz's performances are stylishly
played and very well recorded on disc and
cassette alike (the tape benefits from a
slight treble cut). They also have the advantage of economy; but in the last analysis they lack sparkle, and Boehm's disc
remains first choice in this coupling (DG
2530 216).

Mehta's performances are direct and
refreshing, but lack the lift and style of
the finest readings; the playing of the
Israel orchestra is rather less polished
than that of the finest rivals. The recording is full and brilliant, the tape matching
the disc closely.

*Symphonies Nos. 3 in D, D.200; 5 in
B flat, D.485.*
**(*) HMV ASD/*TC-ASD* 3860 [Ang.
SZ 37754]. Berlin PO, Karajan.
** Decca SXL/*KSXC* 6799 [Lon. 7020/
5-]. Israel PO, Mehta.

Beecham made this coupling his own
with his magical record from the beginning of the sixties, sunny, sparkling performances given a recording which is
quite perfectly balanced, and which
sounds equally impressive in its new cassette format (HMV SXLP/*TC-SXLP*
30204): a treasurable issue which no
newer version can match.

Indeed Karajan's performances of
what are Schubert's two most attractive
early symphonies lack the geniality that
was the hallmark of Beecham's approach. Yet the beauty of the Berliners'
playing is appealing too, with wit as
well as refinement convincingly caught.
Few players can match the precision of
the Berliners in the scampering triplets of
the finale of No. 3. The reverberant recording adds to the beauty even if it

makes the orchestra sound rather large for this intimate music. The cassette offers admirable quality, both rich and refined in detail.

Mehta has often demonstrated on record his Viennese sympathies, but here, except in the minuet of No. 5, his rhythmic manner is notably less persuasive than that of Beecham. Sensitive as Mehta unfailingly is, the results are heavy by comparison, and even the recording – made in the Mann Auditorium – is not in every way an improvement on the vintage EMI, though it is bright and full (slightly less rich on tape than on disc).

Symphonies Nos. 3; 6 in C, D.589.
(M) ** Decca Jub. JB/*KJBC* 74. VPO, Kertesz.

Good performances, though they lack the last ounce of character or distinction; the Vienna Philharmonic play well for Kertesz but not memorably. The recording is very good, with the cassette transfer lively if with slightly less bloom than the disc.

Symphonies Nos. 3; 8 in B min. (Unfinished), D.759.
**(*) DG 2531/*3301* 124 [id.]. VPO, Carlos Kleiber.

Carlos Kleiber is a refreshingly unpredictable conductor, but sometimes his imagination goes too far towards quirkiness, and that is certainly so in the slow movement of No. 3, which is rattled through jauntily at breakneck speed. The effect is bizarre even for an *Allegretto*, if quite charming. The minuet too becomes a full-blooded scherzo, and there is little rest in the outer movements. The *Unfinished* brings a more compelling performance, but there is unease in the first movement, where first and second subjects are not fully coordinated, the contrasts sounding a little forced. The recording brings out the brass sharply, and is of pleasantly wide range. On cassette

the pianissimos of the *Unfinished* tend to recede a little; otherwise the transfer is of sophisticated quality and strikingly clear.

Symphonies Nos. 4 in C min. (Tragic), D.417; 5 in B flat, D.485.
(M) **(*) Decca Jub. JB/*KJBC* 75. VPO, Kertesz.

Apart from a few extreme tempi – a fast minuet in No. 4, a fast first movement and a slow start to the second in No. 5 – this coupling offers attractive, stylish Schubert playing. Kertesz does not always find the smile in Schubert's writing, but the playing of the Vienna Philharmonic is beyond reproach and the recording exemplary. The cassette transfer, remastered for this Jubilee issue, is first-class, rich and full, yet with plenty of range at the top.

Symphonies Nos. 4; 8 in B min. (Unfinished), D.759.
(M) ** Ph. Fest. 6570/*7310* 150. Dresden State O., Sawallisch.
** DG 2531/*3301* 047 [id.]. Chicago SO, Giulini.
*(*) Decca SXL 6845 [Lon. 7067/5-]. Israel PO, Mehta.

Sawallisch's view of the *Unfinished* is spacious, a thoughtful, lyrical reading rather than a dramatic one, unforcedly compelling because of the refinement and concentration of the Dresden playing. The *Tragic symphony* is less successful if only because it is slightly faceless, even a little prosaic. The recording is refined for its late-sixties vintage. On cassette the sound in No. 4 is if anything fuller than on disc and the *Unfinished* is attractively warm and atmospheric.

Giulini's account of the *Tragic* is controversial in its choice of tempi. He makes heavy weather of the first-movement allegro (at roughly minim 92), adopting a speed which offers insufficient contrast with the *Andante*, and which impedes a proper sense of flow. In the second movement he applies the brakes just before the return of the main theme (bar 110) and passes some less than perfect intonation in the ensuing section. The scherzo is not remotely *vivace*, and the finale is only a little less pedestrian. The recording is full-blooded and the transfer tape has good detail and range, although the bass needs cutting back somewhat. Mehta chooses sensible tempi in the *Tragic* and secures decent enough playing from the Israel orchestra; the performance has an almost rustic bounce and energy. The same goes for his account of the *Unfinished*, and the Decca sound throughout is characteristically bright and vivid. Giulini offers a deeply-felt reading of the latter, with much carefully considered detail. There are some magical things, such as the phrasing of the opening of the development of the first movement. By comparison Mehta seems markedly less refined and imaginative, but even so Giulini does not match here his earlier (1962) Philharmonia performance (now deleted).

Symphony No. 5 in B flat, D.485.
*** DG 2531/*3301* 279 [id.]. VPO, Boehm – SCHUMANN: *Symphony No. 4.****

Boehm in his mid-eighties returned to Schubert's *Fifth Symphony* with his favourite orchestra, and the result glows with freshness, warmth and energy. As a performance this is sharper and tauter than Boehm's earlier reading with the Berlin Philharmonic, and it is much more fully recorded on disc and tape alike, a splendid version well coupled with an outstanding account of the Schumann.

Symphonies Nos. 5; 8 in B min. (Unfinished), D.759.
(B) *** CfP CFP/*TC-CFP* 40370. LPO, Pritchard.

The reissue of Pritchard's coupling in an attractive new sleeve is most timely.

These are superbly refreshing performances. Pritchard's reading of the *Unfinished* is unusually direct, establishing the first movement as a genuine symphonic *allegro* but with no feeling of breathlessness, even in the melting lyricism of the incomparable second subject. The high dramatic contrasts – for instance in the development – are fearlessly presented, with fine intensity; and the second movement too brings purity and freshness. In the *Fifth Symphony* Pritchard's directness allows for nudging delicacy, particularly at the very start, and the playing of the LPO is again superbly refined, With glowing recording to match, this coupling in no way falls short of the full-price versions, yet on the CfP label it costs merely a fraction as much. There is no appreciable difference in quality between disc and cassette.

Symphony No. 6 in C, D.589.
(M) *** HMV SXLP/*TC-SXLP* 30443. RPO, Beecham – MOZART: *Symphony No. 41.****

Symphony No. 6; Rosamunde: Overture (Die Zauberharfe, D.644); Entr'acte in B flat; Ballet music Nos. 1 and 2, D.797.
**(*) Decca SXL/*KSXC* 6891 [Lon. 7115/5-]. Israel PO, Mehta.

Few conductors have ever been as persuasive as Beecham in the 'little' *C major symphony*. The rhythmic point and high spirits of the first movement and scherzo are irresistible, while the finale, taken rather more gently than usual, is delectably sprung. The fifties recording still sounds well, and the coupling is most attractive. The cassette transfer is of excellent quality, the sound slightly dry but clear and clean and not lacking weight.

Mehta's account is attractively direct and very well recorded. It can be recommended to those who want the *Rosamunde* coupling, though there are more subtly pointed readings of the symphony. The cassette offers first-class quality, rich and detailed; a small bass cut may be useful.

Symphony No. 8 in B min. (Unfinished), D.759.

⊛ (M) *** World SH/*TC-SH* 290. Philh. O., Cantelli – MENDELSSOHN: *Symphony No. 4.*(***)

(M) *** HMV SXLP/*TC-SXLP* 30513. Philh. O., Karajan – BRAHMS: *Symphony No. 2.****

(M) *** Decca Jub. JB/*KJBC* 76 [Lon. STS 15476]. VPO, Kertesz – *Overtures.****

(B) *** Con. CC/*CCT* 7503. VPO, Krips – BEETHOVEN: *Symphony No. 8.****

(M) **(*) CBS 60106/40- [Col. MY 36719]. NYPO, Bernstein BEETHOVEN: *Symphony No. 5.***

(*) DG 2531 291 [id.]. Berlin PO, Karajan – MENDELSSOHN: *Symphony No. 4.*(*)

Cantelli's moving account of the *Unfinished* was recorded in 1956, a year before his premature death. It was made in genuine stereo and few allowances have to be made for its age. As always with Cantelli, the playing is remarkably fresh and alive. There are no 'interpretative touches' of the kind favoured by 'great' conductors, and yet for all that (or perhaps because of it) it is deeply personal and committed. The orchestral blend is an object lesson for its kind, and every phrase is carefully thought out yet at the same time spontaneous. This takes its place among the recorded classics. The cassette transfer is beautifully managed, well balanced and clear.

Karajan's earlier *Unfinished* with the Philharmonia dates from the late 1950s. It is without any question a most beautiful account, and yet there is no attempt at beautification. The quality of the playing is remarkably fine and can hold its own against most of the mid-priced alternatives – and some of the full-price competition too. There is no question about a best version of this work – Can-

telli with the same orchestra – but nor is there any doubt that this Karajan record belongs among the finest, and given the coupling (Brahms's *Second Symphony*) this must be accounted an outstanding bargain. The cassette has rather less range and refinement than the disc: the bass is a little muddy.

Kertesz's reading is one of the finest of his Schubert cycle, spacious and unaffected and supported by fine orchestral playing. The recording is of the highest quality, with a wide dynamic range so that the woodwind solos in the second movement tend to sound a little distant. The pianissimo at the opening, however, immediately creates a degree of tension that is to be sustained throughout the performance. The cassette transfer is notably clear and vivid in Decca's best manner.

Krips recorded the *Unfinished* in the very early days of LP in a gentle, glowing performance, and here again he directs an unforced, wonderfully satisfying account, helped by excellent playing and recording. It may lack some of the bite which even this symphony should have, but anyone wanting this coupling will not be disappointed. The new Contour pressing sounds first-rate, but on cassette the sound lacks transparency and has an ill-defined bass.

Bernstein's is a highly dramatic account and an exciting one, with a great surge of energy in the first-movement development. Yet there is lyrical warmth too and at times a sense of mystery. The playing of the New York orchestra is first-class – the rich yet cleanly focused sound of the lower strings tells at the very opening – and this makes a memorable coupling for a fine version of Beethoven's *Fifth*. The recording is not strikingly lustrous but is fully acceptable.

The Karajan DG account first appeared in 1966, and its merits of simplicity and directness have been well detailed in past editions. Artistically it rates three stars, but DG are ungenerous in offering it at full price, given the competition – including Karajan's own Philharmonia version from the late 1950s. If this version of the *Unfinished* is still moving and free from affectation and artifice, it is nonetheless overpriced.

Symphonies Nos. 8; 9 in C (Great), D.944; Rosamunde: Overture (Die Zauberharfe, D.644); Ballet music Nos. 1 and 2, D.797.
(M) *** DG Acc. 2725/*3374* 103 (2). Berlin PO, Boehm.

This mid-price folder gives an alternative format for the last two symphonies in Boehm's Berlin cycle of 1961. If you want this collection of Schubert works – with the *Rosamunde* items, recorded ten years later, filling the fourth side – it is highly recommendable; all of the performances are ripely persuasive in Boehm's very Austrian, at times almost rustic, style of Schubert interpretation. There are few accounts of the *Great C major* which glow so warmly as this. The *Unfinished* too is freshly radiant rather than brooding. The recordings of both vintages are very good, and the cassettes match the discs closely (although the transfer level is modest).

Symphony No. 9 in C (Great), D.944.
*** DG 2531/*3301* 352 [id.]. Dresden State O., Boehm.
(M) *** HMV SXLP/*TC-SXLP* 30267 [Sera. S. 60194]. Hallé O., Barbirolli.
(B) *** Con. CC/*CCT* 7512 [Quin. 7100]. Bav. RSO, Jochum.
(M) *** Decca Jub. JB/*KJBC* 77 [Lon. STS 15505]. VPO, Kertesz.
**(*) Decca SXL 6729 [Lon. 6948]. Israel PO, Mehta.
(M) **(*) Ph. Fest. 6570/*7310* 054 [id.]. Dresden State O., Sawallisch.
**(*) ASV ALH/*ZCALH* 905. Hallé O., Loughran.
** DG 2530/*3300* 882 [id.]. Chicago SO, Giulini.
*(*) Ph. 9500/*7300* 890 [id.]. Boston SO, Colin Davis.

(M) * DG Priv. 2535/*3335* 290. Berlin PO, Karajan.

Boehm's Dresden performance was recorded live in January 1979, and presented marvellous evidence of his continuing energy in his mid-eighties. If anything, this is a more volatile performance than the glowing one included in his cycle of the Schubert symphonies, with a marked relaxation for the second subject in the first movement and extreme slowing before the end. The slow movement is fastish, with dotted rhythms crisply pointed and a marked slowing for the cello theme after the great dissonant climax. The scherzo is sunny and lilting, the finale fierce and fast. It may not be quite so immaculate as the studio-recorded version, but it is equally a superb document of Boehm's mastery as a Schubertian, and the recording, though a little edgy on brass, has fine range. The tape is lively but slightly fierce on side two.

Barbirolli's is a warm, lyrical reading, with the speeds perfectly chosen to solve all the notorious interpretative traps with the minimum of fuss. The Hallé playing may not be quite so polished as that of, say, the Concertgebouw on the Haitink version (see below); but it is far more important that the Barbirollian magic is conveyed at its most intense. Barbirolli is completely consistent, and although, characteristically, he may always indulge in affectionate phrasing in detail, he is usually steady in maintaining tempi broadly throughout each movement. The second subject of the first movement, for example, brings no 'gear-change', but equally no sense of the music being forced; and again with the tempo changes at the end of the movement, Barbirolli's solution is very satisfying. The recording on disc is full and ample, but the high-level cassette transfer, while clear and well detailed, is a little lacking in richness.

Jochum's recording dates from 1958, but one would hardly guess it from this splendidly vivid disc, which, though bright and detailed and with strong impact, has no lack of depth. The reading is immensely dramatic, with great vitality and unleisurely tempi that are varied flexibly with the ebb and flow of the music. The slow movement has less repose than usual (although there is no suggestion of hurry) and it has a climax of great power. The compelling thrust of the reading extends through the exhilarating scherzo to a finale which has an irresistible onward impulse. Jochum's use of light and shade is never more effective than here. The cassette transfer has not quite the range of the disc but it is acceptably lively.

Kertesz's disc is also in its way outstanding. It is remarkably well recorded, with a splendid overall warmth, yet plenty of bite and clarity. One is made conscious that the symphony is scored for trombones as well as horns, something that does not emerge clearly in many recordings. The performance is fresh, dramatic and often very exciting. Kertesz's springlike approach counteracts any feeling that each movement is just a shade too long. The cassette is bright and immediate, but has a tendency to fierceness in the upper register.

Mehta's is a sunny performance, well-paced and well-sprung, with the Israel orchestra in amiable form. The very start brings a full *mezzo forte* in the opening horn melody, but that sign of insensitivity is an exception, and generally Mehta solves all the many interpretative problems of the work naturally and convincingly, observing the exposition repeat in the first movement, but then in the scherzo omitting the second repeat, as is common. The recording is beefy, with a boosted bass to balance a brilliant treble, not quite so refined in sound as some other versions.

Sawallisch's reading, like his other recordings of the Schubert symphonies, is refreshingly direct. In this symphony some will find the result undercharacterized, but with refined playing from the Dresden orchestra and recording refined for its age it can be recommended

at medium price. The cassette is one of Philips' best, clean and bright yet with plenty of warmth.

Loughran was the first conductor to record the *Great C major* with every single repeat observed. His reading is characteristically plain and direct, but its communication is helped by the lyrical warmth of the orchestral playing and the fullness of the recording. The reading has a leisurely feeling throughout, and such a performance may tend to outstay its welcome when the rhythms are not always quite resilient enough. Nevertheless this is a performance of distinct character. The cassette has a rather low transfer level, but the sound is pleasingly balanced, with an attractive overall bloom.

Giulini's is a distinctive reading, generally relaxed but with a dramatic finale. He seeks to establish a modular tempo through different sections, so that the slow introduction leads into the *Allegro* without any change of pulse. He draws the most beautiful playing from the Chicago orchestra, and the result, if somewhat self-conscious, is often persuasive. The recording is good on both disc and tape.

With rather bottom-heavy sound on disc (the cassette is better balanced), Sir Colin Davis's Boston version does not avoid dullness. From the slow introduction onwards Davis tends to prefer slow tempi, which, with every single repeat observed, even in the finale, and a very straight approach to the notorious problems in the score (except for an over-expressive cello line after the climax of the slow movement), make the work outstay its welcome for once. The oboe in the slow movement sits under the note, but the ensemble of the Boston strings is superb.

Karajan's 1971 DG recording, reissued on Privilege, is an intense disappointment, with the ruggedness of the writing smoothed over to a degree surprising even from this conductor. The tempi are fast; but, as other conductors have shown, that does not necessarily mean that the work need be weakened. But Karajan skates over the endless beauties. There is no impression of glowing expansiveness: this is a tour of a chromium heaven.

Reminder: Josef Krips never made a finer record than his LSO recording of Schubert's *Great C major symphony* with its direct, unforced spontaneity, and this medium-priced disc is not surpassed in the present catalogue (Decca SPA 467 [Lon. STS 15140]). Haitink's Philips recording with the Concertgebouw Orchestra (9500 097/*7300 510*) is also fresh and beautiful, and is marked by superb orchestral playing; this is equally recommendable on disc and cassette.

CHAMBER AND INSTRUMENTAL MUSIC

Cello sonata in A min. (originally for arpeggione), *D.821.*
** Nimbus 2111. Fleming, Parsons –
BRAHMS: *Cello sonata No. 1.**(*)

Amaryllis Fleming uses an Amati of 1610 with five strings, much closer than the normal cello to the six-stringed arpeggione for which Schubert originally composed this sonata. She plays with strong feeling and an acute sense of line, though neither she nor her admirable partner ever steps over the bounds of expressive propriety. The *Adagio* is a bit on the slow side, but few will cavil at the musical perception and the quality of the phrasing here. Unfortunately the recording is less than first-class, though it is natural enough. The sound needs to be better focused and more expansive.

Octet in F, D.803.
*** Ph. 9500 400/*7300 613* [id.]. ASMF Chamber Ens.
(M) *** Decca Ace SDD/*KSDC* 508. New V. Octet.

*** DG 2531/*3301* 278 [id.]. V. Chamber Ens.
*(*) ASV ACA/*ZCACA* 1004. Music Group of L.

The Chamber Ensemble of the Academy of St Martin-in-the-Fields offer one of the very best versions of this endearing work. Everything is vital yet polished and sensitive. The recording is beautifully balanced, and the performance has a warmth and freshness that justify the acclaim with which this issue was greeted. There is a high-level tape transfer of good quality, not quite as refined as the disc – there are hints at times that the level is fractionally too high.

The Vienna Chamber Ensemble do not overlap in personnel with the New Vienna Octet, though the performances have a similar polish and suavity. Mellifluous is the word for both performances, and those who adore the Viennese approach to this repertoire will find satisfaction in these elegant, highly finished accounts. The Vienna Chamber Ensemble produce a beautifully blended sound and are accorded excellent recording. There is so little difference between the two in quality of sound – the Decca is slightly brighter – or in the characterization of the playing that choice can be safely left to the reader. Given the price advantage enjoyed by the Decca, there seems no reason to prefer the DG newcomer. Those who find the Viennese approach too sweet should turn to the Academy, or to the Melos Ensemble on HMV (ASD 2417 [Ang. S 36529]) which is still highly competitive. This is not available on tape, but both the Decca and DG cassettes are of good quality.

The Music Group of London get off to a rather sluggish start. There is some musical phrasing and some warmth in this performance, but it remains untouched by real distinction. In terms of vitality and alertness it does not really compare with the best available, and at full price it is somewhat uncompetitive. It is well enough recorded, though the violins sound a little thinner than they need do; the cassette transfer is first-class. But these accomplished musicians are a shade wanting in real intensity.

Octet for wind, D.72: Minuet and finale in F.

(M) *** Ph. Fest. 6570/*7310* 205 [id.]. Neth. Wind Ens., De Waart – DVOŘÁK: *Serenade*; GOUNOD: *Petite symphonie*.***

Two charming little miniatures from Schubert's youth, crisply and attractively played. An admirable fill-up to the delightful Gounod piece. The cassette transfer matches the disc closely.

Piano quintet in A (Trout), D. 667.

*** Ph. 9500 442/*7300 648* [id.]. Brendel, Cleveland Qt.

*** HMV Dig. ASD/*TCC-ASD* 4032 [Ang. DS 37846]. Richter, Borodin Qt.

(M) **(*) Ph. Fest. 6570/*7310* 115 [id.]. Haebler, Grumiaux, Janzer, Czako, Cazauran.

(M) ** HMV SXLP/*TC-SXLP* 30523 [(d) Ang. S. 35777]. H. Menuhin, Amadeus Qt – BEETHOVEN: *Piano trio No. 4*.**

*(*) RCA RL 11882 [ARL 1 1882]. Peter Serkin, Tashi.

Piano quintet in A; Notturno in E flat, D.897.

**(*) CRD CRD 1052/*CRDC 1052*. Nash Ens.

(M) ** DG Priv. 2535/*3335* 332. Eschenbach, Koeckert Qt.

(i) *Piano quintet in A*; (ii) *Violin sonatina No. 2 in A min., D.385.*

(B) *(*) Con. CC/*CCT* 7525 [DG 2535/ 3335 225]. (i) Demus, Schubert Qt; (ii) Schneiderhan, Klien.

(i) *Piano quintet in A;* (ii) *Die Forelle.*

(M) *** Ph. Seq. 6527/*7311* 075. (i) Beaux Arts Trio, Rhodes, Hortnagel; (ii) Prey, Hokanson.

From the Beaux Arts Trio comes one of the most delightful and fresh *Trouts* now available. Every phrase is splendidly alive, there is no want of vitality and sensitivity, and a finely judged balance and truthful recording make it a most desirable version. The Sequenza reissue offers the small but happy bonus of the song itself, sung by Hermann Prey. On the cassette the focus of the upper strings is a little fluffy; otherwise the sound is good, with a firm piano image.

Richter dominates the HMV digital recording of the *Trout quintet*, not only in personality but in balance. Yet the performance has marvellous detail, with many felicities drawn to the attention that might have gone unnoticed in other accounts. The first movement is played very vibrantly indeed, and the second offers a complete contrast, gently lyrical. The variations have plenty of character, and taken as a whole this is very satisfying, even though other versions are better balanced and are stronger on Schubertian charm. The cassette, like the disc, gives striking presence to the piano, but adds just a hint of edginess to the strings, although this is more noticeable on the first side.

The Brendel/Cleveland performance may lack something in traditional Viennese charm, but it has a compensating vigour and impetus, and the work's many changes of mood are encompassed with freshness and subtlety. The second movement *Andante* is radiantly played, and the immensely spirited scherzo has a most engagingly relaxed trio, with Brendel at his most persuasive. His special feeling for Schubert is apparent throughout: the deft pictorial imagery at the opening of the variations is delightful. The recording is well balanced and truthful on disc and tape alike, although on the cassette there is a hint of edginess in the upper strings.

From Haebler a small-scale performance which is nonetheless very enjoyable. There is some admirably unassertive and deeply musical playing from Miss Haebler and from the incomparable Grumiaux, and it is this freshness and pleasure in music-making that render this account memorable. These artists do not try to make 'interpretative points' but are content to let the music speak for itself. The balance is not altogether perfect, but the quality of the recorded sound is good and the cassette transfer is natural in timbre and detail. The smoothness in the upper range is pleasing.

The Nash Ensemble version has spontaneity – indeed there is something of the quality of a live performance here – and the distinction of Clifford Benson's playing. There is a buoyant spirit and a freshness and vigour that are refreshing. Perhaps this does not match the Beaux Arts version in terms of imagination and flair, but it is still well worth considering. The account of the *Notturno* (a more intense piece than the title might suggest) is no less sympathetic. The recording is fully acceptable and well balanced; the cassette transfer lacks the last degree of range, but the sound is more refined on top than in many of the other tape versions and has good body and detail.

The HMV version at medium price has a generous coupling in the shape of Beethoven's *Ghost trio*. The record is produced in tribute to the late Hephzibah Menuhin and the performance dates from 1960. The balance is not wholly ideal, though the recording wears its years lightly. There are moments of charm here and the performance will give much pleasure. Hephzibah Menuhin was an intelligent but not always subtle player, and repeats have been excised from this performance so as to accommodate an ample fill-up. This is not a disc that displaces the existing mid-price or newer recommendations. The cassette transfer is clear, but rather dry.

An enjoyably alert performance from Christoph Eschenbach and members of the Koeckert Quartet. There is a good deal of sparkle and character – the variations are given plenty of individual interest, the outer movements striking momentum – and Eschenbach himself plays with genuine elegance. The recording acoustic is clear and rather dry; some may find it a trifle unexpansive. The *Notturno* has the advantage of a warmer acoustic and is most sympathetically played. The cassette transfer is strikingly clear and clean in the *Quintet*. This issue still yields to the Haebler/Grumiaux version, but it remains an attractive alternative, particularly in view of the fill-up.

An agreeable performance on Contour, with Demus dominating, partly because the piano recording and balance are bold and forward and the string tone is thinner. There is – as befits the name of the string group – a real feeling for Schubert, and the performance has spontaneity. The first movement is especially arresting, and the *Theme and variations* are well shaped. The tape transfer, however, seems to emphasize the thinness of the strings, although the piano image is lifelike. The *Violin sonatina*, a most acceptable bonus, is well played and recorded.

Tashi, a distinguished group of instrumentalists, and Peter Serkin give a thoroughly conscientious and carefully prepared account of the score, and are well recorded. There is no exposition repeat in the first movement, and no fill-up either. The performance has much refinement and polish, though a little more sparkle would not come amiss in the scherzo. Civilized playing but not quite the whole story.

Piano trio No. 1 in B flat, D. 898; Notturno in E flat, D. 897.
(M) *** Sup. 1111 1896. Suk Trio.

There need be no reservations here. Josef Suk, Jan Panenka and Josef Chuchro give an account of the *Trio* that is alive, sensitive and joyful. The *Notturno*, which was in all probability the original slow movement, is given with the same attentiveness that marks the performance of the *Trio*. The quality of the recorded sound is excellent, and this is as good as if not better than any version currently on the market.

String quartets Nos. 7 in D, D.94; 13 in A min., D.804.
(M) **(*) Argo ZK 88. Allegri Qt.

The Allegri players give a very musical account of the *A minor Quartet*, less pensive perhaps than that of the Italian Quartet (see below) but eminently concentrated and coherent. They are well recorded too. They observe the exposition repeat in the first movement, and the quartet spreads on to the second side. The early *Quartet in D major* has an affecting charm that comes over well in their hands, and this issue is competitively priced, though for the *A minor Quartet* the Italians would be worth the extra outlay.

String quartets Nos. 8 in B flat, D.112; 10 in E flat, D.87.
**(*) DG 2531/*3301* 336 [id.]. Amadeus Qt.

These two quartets date from Schubert's mid-teens and are a delight. Those who recall the pre-war Busch records may not be surprised to learn that the Amadeus account (particularly in the finale of the *B flat Quartet*) is not quite as elegant. In fact these performances are not as fresh and unmannered as one would like, and Norman Brainin's portamenti are occasionally disturbing. But of course there are many good things here too, and the recorded sound is excellent. The cassette is first-class, with plenty of range at the top and a natural balance.

String quartets Nos. 10 in E flat, D.87; 13 in A min., D.804.
*** Ph. 9500 078. Italian Qt.

The Italians get the *A minor Quartet* on

to one side by omitting the exposition repeat in the first movement. The sound quality achieved is excellent, even though the side is not short. The slow movement is beautifully paced – though some may find it a bit too slow – and has an impressive command of feeling. These players' understanding of Schubert is reflected throughout, and the early *E flat Quartet* (the old Op. 125) also comes off beautifully. Altogether a lovely disc, arguably the best version of both quartets.

String quartets Nos. 11 in E, D.353; 13 in A min., D.804.
** DG 2530 962. Melos Qt.

It is a pity that the quality of the recorded sound is not more appealing in this coupling. The *A minor Quartet* includes the first-movement exposition repeat, so it spills over on to the second side for the finale. Generally speaking, the Melos Quartet's playing is expert enough but they occasionally wear their hearts a little too much on the sleeve; the slow movements are just a shade too sentimental.

String quartet No. 12 in C min. (Quartettsatz), D.703.
*** CRD CRD 1034/*CRDC 4034*. Alberni Qt – BRAHMS: *String sextet No. 1*.***

A fresh and agreeably warm account of this fine single-movement work, originally intended as part of a full string quartet but finally left by Schubert to stand on its own. The coupling with the Brahms *Sextet* is appropriate, for it was Brahms who in 1870 arranged for the first publication of the *Quartettsatz*. The recording is first-class, and the cassette transfer is of excellent quality; this can be highly recommended.

String quartets Nos. 12 (Quartett-

satz); 14 in D min. (Death and the Maiden), D.810.

*** Ph. 9500 751 [id.]. Italian Qt.

(M) *** Ph. Fest. 6570/*7310* 180 [id.]. Italian Qt.

(M) **(*) Argo ZK/*KZKC* 77. Allegri Qt.

(M) **(*) DG Priv. 2535/*3335* 314. Amadeus Qt.

** DG 2530 533 [id.]. Melos Qt.

(M) *(*) Sup. 1111 1997. Prague Qt.

The Italian Quartet have made two recordings of this coupling, and both are currently available. The 1966 record was counted the finest available in its day, going much deeper than the Amadeus version. The slow movement is particularly impressive, showing a notable grip in the closing pages. Technically the playing throughout is quite remarkable. The lyrical intensity of the *Quartettsatz* is perhaps slightly overstated, but in the medium-price range this Festivo issue remains very highly competitive. The recording has plenty of impact and body and wears its years lightly. The high-level cassette transfer is first-class in every way.

The full-priced 1981 successor is hardly less impressive, and has the advantage of superior sound. The Italians again bring great concentration and poetic feeling to this wonderful score and they are free of the expressive point-making occasionally to be found in such rivals as the Melos Quartet of Stuttgart. Any newcomer will have to be very special to displace this.

The Allegris are straightforward in the *Death and the Maiden quartet*, and though not always as polished as the Italians or the Melos Quartet they have much to recommend them. They are often perceptive and thoughtful, and score points by observing the exposition repeat in the first movement. This is a very sound performance, decently recorded and reasonably priced. The tape transfer is both full-bodied and extremely lively, approaching demonstration standard in its combination of body and clarity.

The Amadeus Quartet gives a wonderful impression of unity as regards the finer points of phrasing, for example at the very beginning of the variations in D.810. This is a worthwhile issue, even if this account of *Death and the Maiden* cannot match that of the Italians in the same price-range. The recording still sounds well, and the cassette transfer is smooth and pleasing.

The Melos Quartet's record comes from their complete set, which appeared in the mid-1970s. Highly accomplished and expertly played, both *Death and the Maiden* and its companion have many points of interest, even if there are some mannered touches. The recording, however, is a little hard and close and it inhibits a whole-hearted recommendation.

The Prague Quartet give us a reading of D.810 marked more by technical expertise than poetic feeling. Workmanlike, extremely good playing, but rarely touching or inspired.

String quartets Nos. 12 (Quartettsatz); 15 in G, D.887.

(M) *** Decca Ace SDD 512 [Lon. STS 15418]. Gabrieli Qt.

The *G major Quartet* is one of Schubert's most profound and searching utterances, and it is a pleasure to record that the Gabrieli players have its measure. Their performance is compelling from beginning to end and has genuine sensitivity and depth of feeling. Moreover, the Decca engineers have achieved a natural balance and the most realistic quality of sound. Indeed as quartet sound this is one of the best records yet. The Gabrielis also give an eloquent account of the splendid C minor *Quartettsatz*.

String quartets Nos. 13 in A min., D.804; 14 in D min. (Death and the Maiden), D.810; 15 in G, D.887.

**(*) Nimbus 2301/3. Chilingirian Qt.

The Chilingirian Quartet offer the three greatest Schubert quartets in a box, not available separately. They are fine players and can hold their own in the best company. A minor lapse of intonation in the *D minor* and another elsewhere are of no account, and the performances throughout are compelling. However, taken individually these records would not displace the Italian Quartet in this repertoire, nor are they as beautifully recorded.

String quartet No. 14 in D min. (Death and the Maiden), D.810.
(B) *** CfP CFP/*TC-CFP* 40356. Gabrieli Qt – MOZART: *Oboe quartet.****

At the beginning of its concert career the Gabrieli Quartet made this excellent version of *Death and the Maiden* for the Classics for Pleasure bargain label, challenging all comers with a plain but sensitive reading, particularly impressive in the slow movement with its poise and delicate tonal shading. This reissue – with the sound still first-rate – provides an attractive coupling. The cassette transfer is excellent, full, clean and well balanced.

String quartet No. 15 in G, D.887.
*** Ph. 9500 409/*7300 617* [id.]. Italian Qt.
*** HMV ASD 3882. Alban Berg Qt.
(M) *** Argo ZK/*KZKC* 78. Allegri Qt.
**(*) CBS 76908 [Col. M/*MT* 35827]. Juilliard Qt.

Having lavished many plaudits on the Gabrieli account of the *G major Quartet* (see above), one hardly expected so strong a challenge to appear hot on its heels. Yet though the Italians are at full price and do not offer the *Quartettsatz* or any other makeweight, they are a strong front runner in this field. The conception is bolder, the playing is distinguished by the highest standards of ensemble, into-

nation and blend, and the recording is extremely fine. The Italians take an extremely broad view of the first movement, and they shape the strong contrasts of tempo and mood into an impressively integrated whole. The playing is no less deeply felt elsewhere in the work, making this one of the most thought-provoking accounts of the quartet now before the public. The cassette transfer is first-class; there is little to choose between disc and tape.

In some ways the Alban Berg players are the most dramatic and technically accomplished of all in this marvellous work. Indeed they tend to over-dramatize: pianissimos are the barest whisper and ensemble has razor-edge precision. They are marvellously recorded, however, and beautifully balanced; but it is the sense of over-projection that somehow disturbs the innocence of some passages. Like the Juilliards they do not observe the exposition repeat in the first movement.

The Allegri are recorded in a somewhat resonant acoustic, but theirs is a far from negligible account. They observe the first-movement exposition repeat and are less given to extremes of tempo than are the Italians. The playing is both alive and sensitive, and as this is so modestly priced it could well appeal to those who find the Italians just a shade too self-conscious in their search for depth in the slow movement. The excellent cassette approaches demonstration standard.

The Juilliard Quartet play superbly and in many ways are very impressive. They have no want of insight, and they are not given to expressive indulgence. However, though their technical finish is second to none, they are accorded a less than ideal, but by no means poor, recording; the sound tends to be a bit hard and cold.

Choice really lies between the Italians and the Berg, both self-conscious in different ways but the Italians more searching. At medium price the Allegri can be recommended alongside the Gabrieli, though the latter offer the *Quartettsatz* too.

String quintet in C, D.956.
(B) *** CfP CFP/*TC-CFP* 40355. Chilingirian Qt, J. Ward Clark.
(M) *** HM HM 980. Bulgarian Quintet.
**(*) DG 2530/*3300* 980 [id.]. Melos Qt, Rostropovich.
**(*) DG 2531 209 [id.]. LaSalle Qt, Harrell.
(M) ** Argo ZK 83. Allegri Qt, Welsh.
** Ph. 9500 752 [id.]. Arthur Grumiaux Qt.
(M) * DG Acc. 2542/*3342* 139 [139105]. Amadeus Qt.

Vividly recorded, with clear placing of instruments in a smallish but not dry hall, the Chilingirian version presents a most compelling account, totally unmannered and direct in style but full of concentration and spontaneity. So one has the consistent sense of live performance, and the great melody of the second subject emerges without any intrusive nudging or overexpressiveness. The slow movement too has natural intensity, though the closeness of the recording rather prevents one from registering a really soft pianissimo. An outstanding bargain on disc, but the cassette is slightly disappointing; one notices the reduced dynamic contrasts more, and there is less range at the top. Probably the best recommendation for tape collectors is the CRD issue by the Alberni Quartet and the late Thomas Igloi, a richly enjoyable and highly communicative reading (CRD 1018/*CRDC 4018*). On disc one must also remember the famous Aeolian version on Saga (5266), a performance of memorable intensity and concentration. Current pressings are immaculate and though the recording is not always of the clearest, the profundity of the music-making compensates for any deficiencies: the *Adagio* holds the listener breathless through hushed pianissimos of the most intense beauty.

The Bulgarian Quartet with Roland Pidoux as second cellist give a most compelling, forthright performance, very well played and with fine matching and excellent pacing. On a mid-price label it makes a first-rate recommendation, though it cannot quite compete with the equally refreshing version of the Chilingirian Quartet, cheaper still.

Rostropovich plays as second cello in the Melos performance, and no doubt his influence from the centre of the string texture contributes to the eloquence of the famous *Adagio*, which like the performance as a whole is strongly, even dramatically characterized. The emphasis of the rhythmic articulation of the outer movements leaves no doubt as to the power of Schubert's writing, and while there is no lack of atmosphere in the opening and closing sections of the slow movement, the performance is in the last analysis less persuasive than the Chilingirian version with its greater emotional resilience and flexibility. The DG recording is live and immediate. On cassette the upper strings are sometimes a little husky in focus, but there is a good balance.

The LaSalle version presents a refined but somewhat cool reading, the antithesis of the spacious but somewhat over-expressive reading of the Melos Quartet. Lynn Harrell makes an outstandingly positive second cellist, but there are more compelling readings than this, if few more refined. The recording is clean and faithful.

The Allegri version has the merit of including the exposition repeat – making the first side exceedingly long – but generally, with intonation and ensemble not always immaculate, it cannot quite match the finest versions, sensitive as the playing is. The recording too has some odd balances.

Grumiaux and colleagues give a consciously expressive performance which runs the risk of sounding mannered in its marked rubato and hesitations. The ensemble is most refined, but there are more rewarding performances than this just as well recorded.

Many find the playing of the Amadeus so refined and perfect in technique that this outweighs any reservations they harbour on points of interpretation. But not here. This performance of the *C major Quintet*, Schubert's sublimest utterance, is perfumed, mannered and superficial. The recording is good on disc and tape alike.

Violin sonata (Duo) in A, D.574; Fantaisie in C, D.934; Violin sonatinas Nos. 1 in D, D.384; 2 in A min., D.385; 3 in G min., D.408.
** Decca D 195 D 2 (2). Goldberg, Lupu.

Szymon Goldberg and Radu Lupu give us the complete violin and piano music (except for one small piece) in unaffected and well-recorded performances. Indeed Goldberg is vulnerable in that he almost undercharacterizes the line: the *Fantasy* is just a shade wanting in freshness, and one could do with a greater variety of dynamic nuance and tonal colour. Yet the presence of Radu Lupu ensures that these performances give pleasure, and his playing has a vitality and inner life that are undoubtedly rewarding. In the *Duo* and the *Sonatinas*, however, the Grumiaux/Crossley partnership (see below) is to be preferred.

Violin sonata (Duo), D.574.
*** O-L DSLO 571. Schröder, Hogwood – MENDELSSOHN: *Violin sonata*.***

The Schubert *Duo* is not otherwise available on period instruments and makes interesting listening, particularly in the sympathetic hands of these artists. Jaap Schröder uses a Stradivarius and Christopher Hogwood a piano from about 1825 by Georg Haschka, which he plays with exemplary skill and artistry. It does not produce the range of nuance and

tonal subtlety of which the modern piano is capable, but its lightness of colour has its special charm. Jaap Schröder plays with characteristic authority and artistry, and both artists are beautifully recorded. Modern performances will enjoy the wider appeal – probably rightly – but this is undoubtedly a version to hear.

Violin sonata (Duo), D.574; Violin sonatinas Nos. 1–3.
*** Ph. 9500 394 [id.]. Grumiaux, Crossley.
*** O-L DSLO 565 [id.]. Schröder, Hogwood.

These are lovely performances. Grumiaux has a supple sense of line and an aristocratic quality that communicates freshness and light, while his partner, Paul Crossley, is sensitive and imaginative, as one has come to expect. Rightly, they do not observe repeats, and they eschew any kind of egocentric interpretative point-making. The recording balance could scarcely be improved upon. Grumiaux recorded this coupling in the early 1970s with Robert Veyron Lacroix, but this is even better.

Those interested in hearing what this music sounded like in Schubert's own period should investigate the well-played Oiseau-Lyre disc, where the performance of the *Duo* is apparently the same as the one reviewed above in an alternative coupling.

Piano duet

Allegro in A min. (Lebensstürme), D.947; Divertissement à la française in E min., D.823; Divertissement à la hongroise in G min., D.818; Fantasia in F min., D.940; Grand Rondeau in A min., D.951.
*** HMV SLS 5138 (2). Eschenbach, Frantz.

This collection of Schubert duet music,

including the greatest work ever written for the genre, the *F minor Fantasia*, can hardly be recommended too strongly. The delicate interplay between the two pianists is a constant delight, whether in the cimbalom imitations of the Hungarian-style *Divertissement* or in the sprung rhythms of the *Fantasia*. The opening of the *Fantasia* might suggest that the performance is too reticent, but that is deceptive, and, with full, rounded piano tone, well recorded, this is as powerful a reading as any available, made the more attractive by the relative rarities with which it is coupled.

Andantino varié in B min., D.823; Duo in A min., D.947; Fantasia in F min., D.940; Grand duo sonata in C, D.812; 3 Marches militaires, D.733; 6 Polonaises, D.824; Rondo in A, D.951; Variations on an original theme in A flat, D.813.
*** Erato STU 71044 (3). Queffélec, Cooper.

Gilels and his daughter gave us one record (below); Eschenbach and Frantz offer a set of two; and this album consists of three but includes the *Grand duo*, which Eschenbach and Frantz give us on a separate record (see below). Choice in all these instances will depend on how much of this repertoire you want in your collection, for the playing of Anne Queffélec and Imogen Cooper is no less eloquent than their rivals, and they are very well recorded. Perhaps Eschenbach and Frantz score in terms of sheer freshness, yet there is so little in it that no one considering the present issue need worry too much.

Andantino varié in B min., D.823; 6 Ecossaises, D.145; Fantasia in F min., D.940; Grand Rondeau in A min., D.951.
*** DG 2531 079 [id.]. Emil and Elena Gilels.

In the works for piano, four hands, Schubertians are almost equally well served whichever choice they make. Gilels *et fille* give us a recital that is distinguished by any standards and also beautifully recorded. They bring a blend of strength and tenderness to this music, and the only reservation one might possibly have is that they offer short measure: some forty minutes. They include the *F minor Fantasia*, and the *Andantino varié* from the *Divertissement à la française*, whereas Eschenbach and Frantz offer the whole piece. All the same, a desirable and enjoyable issue.

Fantasia in F min., D.940; Grand duo sonata in C, D.812.
*(*) DG 2531 050 [id.]. Alfons and Aloys Kontarsky.

This ideal coupling of Schubert's two greatest works for piano duet brings bright, aggressive performances of both works, almost totally lacking in charm and poetry. The technique is formidable, as is the unanimity between two players who in twentieth-century music have few rivals; but here they make Schubert sound relatively heartless, whatever the incisive strength of the performances. The recording is bright to match.

Grand duo sonata in C, D.812; German dance with 2 trios in G, D.618; 2 Ländler in E, D.618; 4 Ländler, D.814.
**(*) HMV ASD/*TC-ASD* 3814. Eschenbach, Frantz.

Eschenbach and Frantz give an almost over-spacious performance of the *Grand duo*, revelling in the chances it gives them of drawing out phrases lovingly, of making the piano sing seductively in the widest range of tone-colours. The control is so sure that the result does not lack strength, and the pianists even sustain the enormous length involved when at a slow speed the first movement has its exposition repeated. The *Ländler* too bring performances of great charm, and the recording is ample and full. The cassette matches the disc closely in its depth, clarity and presence, but adds a little edge at the top.

Solo piano music

Allegretto in C min., D.915; Moments musicaux Nos. 1–6, D.780; 2 Scherzi, D.593; 12 Valses nobles, D.969.
** DG 2530/*3300* 996 [id.]. Barenboim.

Some of the finest playing here comes in the *Two Scherzi*. In the first, Barenboim's pointing is a delight, and he is equally persuasive in the trio of the second. The *Allegretto in C minor* is given an effective improvisatory quality, but the *Twelve Valses nobles* are played too forcefully for their full charm to be revealed. In the *Moments musicaux* there is much to admire: Barenboim's mood is often thoughtful and intimate; at other times we are made a shade too aware of the interpreter's art, and there is an element of calculation that robs the impact of freshness. There are good things, of course, but this does not challenge such artists as Brendel or Kempff. The piano tone on DG has impressive presence and weight but does not often display the richness of timbre Schubert's music ideally calls for. The cassette transfer is of high quality, clear and clean.

Fantasia in C (Wanderer), D.760; Piano sonata No. 13 in A, D.664.
(M) *** HMV SXLP/*TC-SXLP* 30297 [Ang. S 36150]. Sviatoslav Richter.

This is a famous record, one of Richter's finest, and its restoration to the catalogue offers an irresistible medium-price coupling of two of Schubert's greatest keyboard works. In the *Wand-*

erer fantasia Richter uses a new edition by Paul Badura-Skoda, which corrects many errors, in some cases altering harmony as well as individual notes. Richter's dynamism is heard at its most impressive in the opening pages, but he sustains the emotional curve throughout with effortless ease. The performance of the *Sonata* is no less telling, extracting the last ounce of Schubertian lyricism. The affectionate moulding of Schubert's innocent yet subtle melodic line is balanced by a striking rhythmic control and forward thrust. The recording, which dates from 1963, is excellent, and the cassette is first-class too, with bold, full timbre, giving excellent presence.

Impromptus Nos. 1–4, D.899; 5–8, D.935.
⊛*** Ph. 9500 357/*7300 587*. Brendel.
*** Hyp. A 66034. Ferber.
(M) *** Decca Ace SDD 563. Schiff.
**(*) DG 2530 896 [id.]. Barenboim.
**(*) DG Acc. 2542/*3342* 111 [139109]. Kempff.

Brendel's complete set of *Impromptus* on Philips was previously split into two separate groups (each coupled with other music of Schubert). Now they are joined and the result is truly magical. The recording is quite superb, rich with a glowing middle range and fine sonority. It is difficult to imagine finer Schubert playing than this; to find more eloquence, more profound musical insights, one has to go back to Edwin Fischer, and even here comparison is not always to Brendel's disadvantage. The cassette is no less recommendable than the disc, the focus a little softer. A superb issue in every way.

Albert Ferber is an underrated artist whose 78 rpm set of Beethoven's *Les Adieux sonata* is still remembered and who has championed Fauré of late. His account of the *Impromptus* is effortless, musical and eloquent, and he is very truthfully recorded. Others may colour detail with more sophistication, but Ferber has a naturalness and an unaffected quality that are most appealing. This is a highly attractive version.

At medium price Andras Schiff's Ace of Diamonds set is also very competitive. The clarity and evenness of his articulation in the *E flat Impromptu* are a delight, the scales in triplets physically tickling the ear. His are refreshing, unmannered readings, superbly recorded (in Japan), which convey poetry in their songful openness. There are subtler readings on record, but none more engaging.

Daniel Barenboim plays the *Impromptus* with characteristic sensitivity and refinement. His tempi are often rather slow (as were Eschenbach's in his now deleted DG record), and there are occasional touches of self-consciousness. Barenboim's touch is quite ethereal at times, and whatever one's response may be, the playing is enormously positive and full of character. The recording is admirable, with presence and clarity to commend it.

Predictably fine playing from Kempff, although here the magic comes more unevenly than usual. The D.899 set is beautifully done, and all the pieces are well characterized. DG's recording is faithful but a little dry in acoustic, so that the piano's middle register does not glow as perhaps it might. The cassette – transferred at rather a low level – matches the disc faithfully in this respect.

Moments musicaux Nos. 1–6, D.780; Impromptus (Klavierstücke), D.946, Nos. 1–3.
(M) *** Ph. Seq. 6527/*7311* 110. Brendel.

Brendel gives superb performances of the *Moments musicaux*. These are the most poetic readings now in the catalogue, and the recording is exemplary. Brendel recorded this same coupling earlier for Turnabout, but this reissue offers marginally more natural sound. The three *Klavierstücke* are a pleasing bonus.

Piano sonatas Nos. 1 in E, D.157; 3 in E, D.459; 6 in E min., D.566; 14 in A min., D.784; 17 in D, D.850; 21 in B flat, D.960.
(M) *(*) Turn. TVS 37121/3 [in SVBX 5465/7]. Klien.

Walter Klien is an understanding Schubertian, and in the rarities, notably the five-movement *E major Sonata*, D.459, and the *E minor*, D.566, there is evident sympathy and refinement. The set also includes a powerfully shaped and naturally expressive reading of the *D major*, D.850. However, Klien is surprisingly self-indulgent in the *B flat Sonata*. He disturbs the natural flow of the left-hand quavers at the opening and does not allow the theme to speak for itself. Here and elsewhere in the first movement there are moments of 'sophistication', where Klien invests detail with too much expressive significance. The recording sounds bottom-heavy, the treble bright and a little clangorous; the resonant acoustic is not helpful.

Piano sonatas Nos. 1 in E, D.157; 16 in A min., D.845.
*** Decca SXL 6931. Lupu.

Radu Lupu's version of the *A minor Sonata* of 1825 spreads on to the second side; the fill-up is the early *E major Sonata*, written in 1815. Its finale was never composed, and only three movements survive. Lupu is searching and poetic throughout. His is the only version of the *A minor Sonata* to have appeared in recent years, apart from Walter Klien's box, and it has formidable qualities. Brendel's account (Philips 6500 929) is more passionate and has, perhaps, more charm, yet Lupu brings tenderness and classical discipline to bear on this structure, and is in his way no less impressive. This does not displace Brendel but can be recommended alongside him. The recording is extremely fine.

Piano sonatas Nos. 2 in C, D.279; 4 in A min., D.537; 5 in A flat, D.557; 11 in F min., D.625; 19 in C min., D.958; 20 in A, D.959.
(M) ** Turn. TVS 37109/11 [in SVBX 5465/7]. Klien.

Some allowance has to be made for the recording quality here, for it is a little clangorous in fortissimo passages and not particularly natural elsewhere. Yet the playing is very good; indeed at times it is touched by real distinction. The editions that Walter Klien uses are not the most modern. The *C major Sonata*, D.279, is given without the *Allegretto in C minor*, D.346, which is nowadays taken to be its finale. The *F minor*, D.625, is also without the piece long thought to be its slow movement – the *Adagio in D flat*, D.505. Klien is a true Schubertian and unconcerned about making anything of the 'ineffective' passages; for the most part he allows these sonatas to unfold naturally.

Piano sonatas Nos. 2 in C, D.279; 21 in B flat, D.960.
(M) *** DG Priv. 2535/3335 240. Kempff.

It is a tribute to Kempff's artistry that with most relaxed tempi he conveys such consistent, compelling intensity in the *B flat major Sonata*. Hearing the opening one might feel that this is going to be a lightweight account of Schubert's greatest sonata, but in fact the long-breathed expansiveness is hypnotic, so that here quite as much as in the *Great C major Symphony* one is bound by the spell of heavenly length. Rightly Kempff repeats the first-movement exposition with the important nine bars of lead-back, and though the overall manner is less obviously dramatic than is common, the range of tone-colour is magical, with sharp terracing of dynamics to plot the geography of each movement. Though very much a personal utterance, this interpretation is no less great for that. It belongs to a tradition of pianism that has almost disappeared, and we must be eternally grateful that its expression has been so glowingly captured. The unfinished early *Sonata in C major* is given an appropriately direct performance. Here the recording is somewhat lacking in lustre, and there is a touch of hardness. Disc and tape are fairly closely matched.

Piano sonata No. 4 in A min., D.537.
** DG Dig. 2532/3302 017 [id.]. Michelangeli – BRAHMS: *Ballades.***

Michelangeli's Schubert is less convincing than the Brahms coupling. He rushes the opening theme and rarely allows the simple ideas of the first movement to speak for themselves. Elsewhere his playing, though aristocratic and marvellously poised, is not free from artifice, and the natural eloquence of Schubert eludes him. Splendid recording on both disc and chrome cassette.

Piano sonatas Nos. 5 in A flat, D.557; 20 in A, D.959.
*** Decca SXL 6771. Lupu.

The particular beauty of Radu Lupu's fine performance of the *A major Sonata* lies in the outer movements, which are wholly unmannered and free from expressive or agogic distortion. Lupu strikes the perfect balance between Schubert's classicism and the spontaneity of his musical thought, and at the same time he leaves one with the impression that this achievement is perfectly effortless. The scherzo has great sparkle and delicacy, and the slow movement has an inner repose and poetic feeling that remain memorable long after the record has stopped. Yet the strength of the interpretation lies in its sensitivity to detail and appreciation of the structure as a whole. The companion sonata is no less persuasively presented, and the recording is as natural and fresh as the performances themselves.

Piano sonatas Nos. 6 in E flat, D.568; 8 in B, D.575; 13 in A, D.664; 15 in C (La Relique), D.840; 16 in A min., D.845; 18 in G, D.894.
(M) ** Turn. TVS 37096/8 [in SVBX 5465/7]. Klien.

Walter Klien's survey of the sonatas makes no attempts to finish incomplete pieces; and the series is also handicapped in that the quality of the sound calls for some tolerance. It takes a little while to adjust to the slightly artificial and in climaxes clangorous tone. Nonetheless, there is much pleasure to be had from the performances themselves, which are most sensitive and unaffected. The pace is unforced, phrases breathe, and the right balance is maintained between strength and tenderness.

Piano sonata No. 13 in A, D.664; Impromptu in A flat, D.899/4.
*** Decca SXL/KSXC 6910 [Lon. 7134/5-]. Larrocha – SCHUMANN: *Carnaval.***(*)

A fresh and unaffected performance of the *Sonata* from Alicia de Larrocha, and one which has warmth too. She does not displace Ashkenazy (Decca SXL 6260 [Lon. 6500]) or Richter (see above) but can be recommended alongside them if this coupling appeals. The cassette is of excellent quality, full in timbre yet clear.

Piano sonatas Nos. 15 in C (Relique), D.840; 21 in B flat, D.960.
**(*) DG 2530 995 [id.]. Barenboim.

To say that Barenboim gives a Kempff-like reading of Schubert's greatest sonata, D.960, is not to deny his characteristic individuality but to point out that his is a reflective, lyrical view of the work, marked by exquisitely clean semiquaver passage-work and strong sharp dynamic contrasts. Yet the slightest sense of artifice is destructive in this

composer, and Barenboim's delivery of the first movement's opening statement is just a shade self-conscious. The artless grace and Blake-like innocence of this idea do not quite come across here. The second movement is slow and concentrated, the scherzo light and sparkling, with a real sense of joy. The finale is sharpened with clear-cut contrasts, yet there is a curious inelegance in the second subject, an obtrusive left-hand staccato at the end of the first half of the theme. But this issue remains attractive for its imaginative coupling, the unfinished *C major Sonata*, a formidably large-scale argument, presented in its full stature by Barenboim. The recording is truthful, bold and clear.

Piano sonata No. 18 in G, D.894.
** HMV ASD 3620 [Sera. S 60285]. Zacharias.

Christian Zacharias is an intelligent and accomplished artist at the beginning of what will no doubt be a distinguished career. It is bold to play Schubert on a début record, and he does not plumb all of the composer's depths, even though he brings many insights. There are more poetic and inspired accounts on the market. The EMI sound quality is excellent.

Piano sonata No. 21 in B flat, D.960
(M) **(*) CBS 61946 [Col. M 33932]. Rudolf Serkin.

Serkin's account comes from a live recital recorded at Carnegie Hall in 1977. The sound quality is not quite as finely detailed or wide in range as its studio rivals; but it is neither as brittle nor as shallow as live piano recitals can be from this source. Needless to say, there are searching things in this performance even if there are some of the moments of inelegance that are often to be found with this great artist. For Serkin's admirers, however, his shallows are more interesting than many younger artists' depths. The pursuit of truth rather than beauty sums up so much in his more recent recordings.

VOCAL MUSIC

Lieder: *Abendbilder; Am Fenster; Auf der Bruck; Auf der Donau; Aus Heliopolis; Fischerweise; Im Frühling; Liebesläuschen; Des Sängers Habe; Der Schiffer; Die Sterne; Der Wanderer; Wehmut; Das Zügenglöcklein.*
*** DG 2530 988 [id.]. Fischer-Dieskau, Sviatoslav Richter.

Recorded live, this beautifully balanced selection of Schubert songs displays the singer's enormous range of expression as well as the acute sensitivity of the pianist in responding. The songs have been grouped almost in a cycle, starting with a biting expression of self-torment (perhaps too aggressively sung here), but gradually the mood lightens from melancholy to brighter thoughts. Not many of these songs are well-known, but it is a programme to delight aficionado and newcomer alike, atmospherically recorded with remarkably little interference from audience noises.

Lieder anthology: *Abendlied der Fürstin; An die Nachtigall; An die Sonne; Ariette der Claudine; Berthas Lied in der Nacht; Blanca, das Mädchen; Delphine; Du bist die Ruh; Ellens Gesänge; Fischerweise; Der Fluss; Die Forelle; Die gefangenen Sänger; Gesang der Norna; Gretchen am Spinnrade; Gretchens Bitte; Hagars Klage; Heimliches Lieben.* (i) *Der Hirt auf dem Felsen. Im Freien; Im Frühling; Iphigenia; Die junge Nonne; Klage der Ceres; Klaglied; Kolmas Klage; Der König in Thule;*

Lambertine; Die Liebende schreibt; Lied der Anne Lyle; Lieder der Mignon, D.877/2-4; Lilla an die Morgenrote; Des Mädchens Klage, D.6, D.191, D.389; Die Männer sind méchant; Mignons Gesang; Die Rose; Schwestergruss; Suleika 1 and 2; Thelka, eine Geisterstimme, D.73, D.595; Vergissmeinnicht; Vom Mitleiden Marias; Wiegenlied, D.498, D.867.
(M) *** DG 2740 196 (5). Janowitz, Gage, (i) with Rodenhauser (clarinet).

Gundula Janowitz here tackles the formidable task of providing a counterpart for female voice of the massive collection of Schubert songs recorded for DG by Dietrich Fischer-Dieskau and Gerald Moore. This collection starts with what is probably Schubert's first vocal work, written when he was fourteen, *Hagars Klage.* Many of the earlier items are extended works, complete scenas or songs of many stanzas. They require persuasive handling, and Janowitz is enormously helped by the sympathetic, concentrated accompaniments of Irwin Gage. She cannot match Fischer-Dieskau in range of expression, but with a voice so naturally beautiful, and used with such easy musical intelligence, the results are consistently compelling, whether in the rarities or the many popular songs such as *Die Forelle* or *Gretchen am Spinnrade* (somewhat idiosyncratic in its speed variations). The recording is first-rate.

'Favourite songs': (i) *Abschied;* (ii) *An die Musik;* (iii) *An Sylvia;* (iv) *Du bist die Ruh;* (iii) *Erlkönig;* (v) *Die Forelle; Gretchen am Spinnrade;* (iv) *Heidenröslein;* (iii) *Im Abendrot;* (ii) *Der Musensohn;* (i) *Ständchen* (*Leise flehen*); (vi) *Ständchen* (*Zögernd leise*).
(M) ** Decca SPA/KCSP 524. (i) Krause, Gage; (ii) Ferrier, Spurr; (iii)

675

Prey, Engel; (iv) Burrows, Constable; (v) Price, Lockhart; (vi) Watts, Elizabethan Singers, Halsey; Tunnard.

Certainly these are favourite songs, and the recital is enjoyable, with its vividly projected recording. One assumes that such a concert is aimed at the inexperienced listener, so it would have been more helpful to provide the texts; or at the very least a synopsis of what each song is about should have been included. The performances are mixed in appeal. The opening items (*Die Forelle* and *Gretchen am Spinnrade*), sung by Margaret Price, are full of character, and Hermann Prey's group has plenty of atmosphere (especially *Im Abendrot*, with its beautiful pianissimo ending). Stuart Burrows's contributions are direct but not very subtle; on the other hand Tom Krause is on top form, and his *Abschied*, which ends side two, is most attractively sung. A good but not really outstanding anthology.

Secular vocal music: *Die Advocaten; An den Frühling; Andenken; Bardengesang; Bergknappenlied; Bootgesang; Coronach; Die Entfernten; Dessen Fahne Donnerstürme wallte; Das Dörfchen; Dreifach ist der Schritt der Zeit* (2 versions); *Ein jugendlicher Maienschwung; Die Eisiedelei; Erinnerungen; Ewige Liebe; Fischerlied; Flucht; Frisch atmet; Frühlingsgesang; Frühlingslied* (2 versions); *Geist der Liebe; Der Geistertanz; Gesang der Geister über den Wassern; Gold'ner Schein; Der Gondelfahrer; Gott in der Natur; Grab und Mond; Hier strecket; Hier umarmen sich; Hymnus an den heiligen Geist; Im gegenwärtigen Vergangenes; Jünglingswonne; Klage um Ali Bey; Lacrimosa son io* (2 versions); *Liebe; Liebe säuseln die Blätter; Lied im Freien; Lutzows wilde Jagd;*

Mailied (3 versions); *Majestät'sche Sonnenrose; Mirjams Siegesgesang; Mondens chein; Der Morgenstern; Die Nacht; Nachtgesang im Walde; Nachthelle; Die Nachtigall; Nachtmusik; Naturgenuss; La Pastorella; Psalm 23; Psalm 92; Punschlied: Im Norden zu singen. Räuberlied; Ruhe; Ruhe, schönstes Glück der Erde; Schlachtgesang; Der Schnee zerrinnt; Sehnsucht; Selig durch die Liebe; Ständchen; Das stille Lied; Thronend auf erhabnem Sitz; Totengräberlied; Trinklied* (4 versions); *Trinklied aus dem 16. Jahrhundert; Trinklied im Mai; Trinklied im Winter; Unendliche Freude* (2 versions); *Vorüber die stöhnende Klage; Wehmut; Wein und Liebe; Wer die steile Sternenbalm; Widerhall; Widerspruch; Willkommen, lieber schöner Mai; Zum Rundetanz; Zur guten Nacht; Die zwei Tugendwege.*

*** HMV SLS 5220 (5). Behrens, Fassbaender, Schreier, Fischer-Dieskau, Bav.R.Ch. and SO, Sawallisch.

This outstanding five-disc box, superbly performed and recorded, uncovers many rare treasures. Indeed just looking through the list of contents must intrigue and entice any true Schubertian. Some of the bigger items, such as *Mirjams Siegesgesang* and *Nachtgesang im Walde*, both memorable pieces, have been recorded before, but much here is virtually unknown, including fragments from Schubert's workbench, drinking songs and the like, which were written for singing with friends round the table. However trivial the pieces, these dedicated, stylish performers produce magical results, and much of the content is far from trivial, showing the composer at his most imaginative. Highly recommended to any Schubertian eager for new discovery.

Lieder: *An die Musik; An Sylvia; Auf*

dem Wasser zu singen; Du bist die Ruh; Die Forelle; Frühlingsglaube; Gretchen am Spinnrade; Heidenröslein; Die junge Nonne; Litanei; Der Musensohn; Nacht und Träume; Rastlose Lied; Der Tod und das Mädchen.

*** HMV ASD/*TC-ASD* 4054. Baker, Parsons.

Take a poll of favourite Schubert songs, and a high proportion of these would be on the list. With a great singer treating each with loving, detailed care, the result is a charmer of a recital record. At the very start Dame Janet's strongly characterized reading of *Die Forelle* makes it a fun song, and similarly Parsons's naughty springing of the accompaniment of *An Sylvia* (echoed later by the singer) gives a twinkle to a song that can easily be treated too seriously. One also remembers the ravishing *subito piano* for the second stanza of *An die Musik* and the heart-felt expression of *Gretchen am Spinnrade*. The recording is of good EMI vintage, but does not quite catch the voice at its most rounded. The cassette is comfortably transferred, but there is some loss of projection and sharpness of focus.

Lieder: *An die Musik; An Sylvia; Auf dem Wasser zu singen; Ganymed; Gretchen am Spinnrade; Im Frühling; Die junge Nonne; Das Lied im Grünen; Der Musensohn; Nachtviolen; Nähe des Geliebten; Wehmut.*
⊛(***) HMV mono ALP/*TC-ALP* 3843. Schwarzkopf, E. Fischer.

At the very end of his career Edwin Fischer partnered Elisabeth Schwarzkopf near the beginning of hers, and the result was magical. The radiance of the voice, the control of line and tone (vibrato an important element, varied exquisitely) set this apart even among the finest Schubert recitals. The simplest of songs inspire intensely subtle expression

from singer and pianist alike, and though Fischer's playing is not always perfectly tidy, he left few records so endearing as this. The mono sound has been beautifully refreshed, and the cassette transfer is clear and full.

Part-songs: *Das Dörfchen; Der Gondelfahrer; Grab und Mond; Im gegenwärtigen Vergangenes; Liebe; Lied im Freien; Mondenschein; Die Nacht; Nachthelle; Die Nachtigall; Nachtmusik; Ständchen; Trinklied aus dem 16. Jahrhundert; Wein und Liebe.*
*** Pearl SHE 549. Baccholian Singers, J. Partridge.

Atmospherically recorded, this is a delightful record, bringing together a sequence of rarities that have one imagining the Schubertiades which for long had to satisfy the young composer, otherwise starved of live performances of his music. Many of the items are relatively late, but most of them keep a sense of fun; much of this male-voice music is for friends drinking together. The Baccholian Singers give beautifully resilient, crisp performances, with their voices finely matched. Sometimes they sing unaccompanied; in other songs Jennifer Partridge admirably provides the piano accompaniment.

Lazarus (cantata), *D.689; Mass in G, D.167.*
*** Erato STU 71442 (2). Armstrong, Welting, Chamonin, Rolfe Johnson, Hill, Egel, Ch. and New Fr. R. PO, Guschlbauer.

Lazarus is a rarity both on the gramophone and in the concert hall. Schubert put the score on one side in February 1820 and never returned to it; perhaps he realized that it was too wanting in contrast and variety. About eighty minutes or so survive, and then the work comes to an abrupt ending in the middle of a soprano solo. Yet for all its uniformity of mood and pace, *Lazarus* is well worth having on record. Some of it is as touching as the finest Schubert and other sections are little short of inspired; there are some thoroughly characteristic harmonic colourings and some powerful writing for the trombones. Much of it is very fine indeed, though it would be idle to pretend that its inspiration is even or sustained. Nonetheless, no Schubertian will want to be without it, for the best of it is quite lovely. The singers and the French Radio forces are thoroughly persuasive and it would be difficult to fault Theodore Guschlbauer's direction or the warm quality of the sound achieved by the engineers. The *G major Mass*, an earlier piece, written when Schubert was only eighteen, has less depth and subtlety than the best of *Lazarus*. But there are some endearing moments, and the *Agnus Dei* is poignant. Again the performance and recording here are more than acceptable.

Magnificat, D.486; Offertorium, D.963; Stabat Mater, D.383.
**(*) Erato STU 71262. Armstrong, Schaer, Ramirez, Huttenlocher, Lausanne Vocal Ens. and O., Corbóz.

Schubert's setting of the *Stabat Mater* (in Klopstock's German translation) is a real rarity, and this well-sung performance (the chorus incisive both in counterpoint and in simple chordal writing) makes an excellent case for it. Philippe Huttenlocher has a sweet baritone, not quite dark enough for the solo *Sohn des Vaters*; the tenor, Alejandro Ramirez, gives a stylish performance of his very Bach-like aria. The other lesser pieces make a good coupling, also persuasively directed by Corbóz, though the recording is not as clear as it might be.

Mass No. 5 in A flat, D.678.
**(*) Argo ZRG/KZRC 869 [id.].

Eathorne, Greevy, Evans, Keyte, St John's College Ch., ASMF, Guest.

This is not quite so successful a performance as George Guest's earlier version of Schubert's *E flat Mass*. The present work dates from 1822, though it was probably begun a few years earlier and was certainly revised later. It has many beauties, and in a fervently inspired reading can sound most impressive. This performance is faithful but just lacks the distinction that marked Guest's recordings of the Haydn Masses on this label; neither the singing nor the playing is in the least routine, but it lacks the personality that these musicians brought to the Haydn and the later Schubert. The recording is very fine, though not every strand of texture comes through. The cassette transfer is of good quality.

Mass No. 7 in C, D.961; Gesang der Geister über den Wassern (Song of the Spirits over the Water), D.714; Eine kleine Trauermusik, D.79. Minuet and finale in D, D.72 (for wind).
**(*) Argo ZRG 916. Bryn-Julson, DeGaetani, Rolfe-Johnson, King, Ch. and L. Sinf., Atherton.

Schubert was strangely trivial when setting this version of the Mass, not noticeably inspired by any of the detailed sentiments of the liturgy. But in a lively performance this last of the four early Masses has refreshment to offer. On the reverse, secular music brings more memorable inspiration, above all in Schubert's last setting of Goethe's *Song of the Spirits over the Water*, a magical piece. The mourning music is very early indeed, remarkable for its solemn brass writing. The recording is not ideally clear but nicely atmospheric.

Rosamunde: Overture (Die Zauberharfe, D.644); incidental music, D.797 (complete).

(M) *** Ph. Fest. 6570/*7310* 053 [id.]. Heynis, Neth. R. Ch., Concg. O., Haitink.

** HMV Dig. ASD 4012. Montgomery, St Hedwig's Cath. Ch., Berlin RSO, Kuhn.

Haitink shows the simple eloquence and musical sensitivity that he found also for his companion Festivo version of the incidental music for Mendelssohn's *A Midsummer Night's Dream*. The recording is a trifle resonant for scoring that was expressly (and skilfully) designed for the theatre-pit, but the tape transfer is well managed and the reverberation overhang is only really noticeable in the overture. Haitink does the third *Entr'acte* and the second *Ballet* quite beautifully, and Aafje Heynis is in fine voice as soloist in the lovely *Romance* (*The full moon shines on mountain peaks*). The chorus is excellent in the music for Spirits, Shepherds and Weberian Huntsmen, although the focus lacks something in crispness here. For the most part the sound is clear and vivid, with disc and tape fairly closely matched. However, at full price Münchinger's beautifully recorded Decca version, made in Vienna (SXL/*KSXC* 6748 [Lon. 26444/5-], is still marginally first choice.

Kuhn, heard conducting Mozart at Glyndebourne, is, on the evidence of this Schubert record, better at refining textures than sustaining sprung rhythms. The *B flat Entr'acte* and the *Ballet in G* lack charm, and though the recording is very faithful (even to a certain thinness on the violins) there are finer versions of the *Rosamunde* music than this.

Rosamunde: Overture, D.644; Ballet in G; Entr'acte in B flat, D.797.

(M) *** Ph. Seq. 6527/*7311* 056. Concg. O. Szell – MENDELSSOHN. *Midsummer Night's Dream.****

Those wanting the most famous numbers from *Rosamunde* with the traditional

Mendelssohn coupling could hardly do better than this reissue, with recordings dating from the end of the sixties and sounding admirably fresh here. The orchestral playing is first-class: the *Overture* has a striking resilient spring, and the *Ballet* and *Entr'acte* match polish with charm. Particularly engaging is the way Szell quickens the pace of the middle section of the *Entr'acte* so that the effect of the reprise of the famous principal melody is heightened. Recommended.

Song cycles: (i) *Die schöne Müllerin, D.795*; (ii) *Schwanengesang, D.957*; (iii) *Die Winterreise, D.911.*

(M) **(*) Ph. 6767 300 (4). Prey, (i) Hokanson, (ii) Moore, (iii) Sawallisch.

With Sawallisch providing keenly imaginative accompaniment, Prey's performance of *Winterreise* is most impressive, though the range of expression in the voice is far more limited than with his obvious rival, Fischer-Dieskau. In *Schwanengesang* too, much of the success of the performance is owed to the accompaniment of Moore. These are all reliable performances, well recorded, and can be recommended to those for whom the timbre of Prey's voice is of special appeal.

Reminder: The set by Fischer-Dieskau and Moore (DG 2720 059/*3371 029* (3)), to which we gave a rosette in the *Penguin Cassette Guide*, makes an obvious first choice in this repertoire; it is equally desirable on disc and tape.

Schwanengesang (song cycle), *D.957.*

(M) *** DG Acc. 2542/*3342* 144. Schreier, Olbertz.

*(*) DG 2531 325 [id.]. Prey, Hokanson.

A tenor might not seem ideally suited to these often dark songs, but one has to remember that even the great song cycle *Die Winterreise* was written with the tenor voice in mind, and Peter Schreier,

679

as a keenly sensitive Lieder-singer, provides intensity and detail in place of weight. He is well accompanied and well recorded on an attractive mid-price reissue which comes with texts and translations. On cassette the quality is natural, but a lower transfer level on side one brings a slight recession of the piano image; on side two the recording approaches demonstration quality.

Prey's recording of *Schwanengesang* was made live at a recital at the 1978 Hohenems Festival. It gains little in intensity from that and suffers from inevitable vocal shortcomings (the early songs a little cautious) and rather humdrum accompaniment. The performance in Prey's boxed set (above) is far preferable.

Die Winterreise (song cycle), *D.911.*
*** DG 2707 118 (2)/*3301 237* [id.]. Fischer-Dieskau, Barenboim.
Die Winterreise. Lieder: *Frühlingslied; Jägers Liebeslied; Der Kreuzzug; Schiffers Scheidelied; Vor meiner Wiege; Das Weinen.*
(M) *** DG Priv. 2726 058 (2) [2707 028]. Fischer-Dieskau, Demus.

Fischer-Dieskau's fifth and latest recording of Schubert's greatest cycle, with the voice still in superb condition, is the most inspirational, prompted by Barenboim's spontaneous-sounding, almost improvisatory accompaniment. In expression this is freer than the earlier versions, and though some idiosyncratic details will not always please everyone, the sense of concentrated development is irresistible. The cycle is extravagantly spread over four sides, but the recording quality is excellent. On cassette the cycle is fitted on one double-length tape offered at normal price, an obvious bargain compared with the discs. The quality is very natural but a low transfer level on side one brings recession of the piano image; on side two the recording has slightly more presence.

There are those who regard Fischer-Dieskau's third recording of *Winterreise* as the finest of all, such is the peak of beauty and tonal expressiveness that the voice had achieved in the mid-sixties, and the poetic restraint of Demus's accompaniment. Certainly it makes an excellent recommendation in this medium-price Privilege reissue on three sides with six extra songs on the fourth side, none of them particularly well known. The recording still sounds well.

OPERA

Alfonso und Estrella (complete).
*** EMI 1C 157 30816/8 [Ang. SX 3878]. Schreier, Mathis, Prey, Adam, Fischer-Dieskau, Berlin R. Ch. and State Op. O., Suitner.

It is strange that Schubert, whose feeling for words in lyric poetry drew out emotions that have natural drama in them, had little or no feeling for the stage. Had his operas been produced, no doubt he would have learnt how to use music more positively; as it is, this tale of royal intrigue in medieval times goes its own sweet way without ever buttonholing the listener, as opera should. Once that is said, it contains a stream of delightful music, Schubert at his most open and refreshing, and under Suitner's direction it here receives a sparkling performance, excellently cast. Helen Donath makes a sweet heroine, and Peter Schreier sings radiantly, as if in an orchestrated *Schöne Müllerin.* The reconciliation duet between the hero's father and his usurper is most touching as sung by Fischer-Dieskau and Prey. The recording is richly atmospheric.

Alfonso und Estrella: Könnt'ich ewig hier verweilen. Lazarus: So schlummert auf Rösen. Rosamunde: Der Vollmond strahlt; Zögernd leise.
*** Ph. 9500 307 [id./*7300 582*]. Baker,

Ch., ECO, Leppard – BEETHOVEN: *Ah! perfido* etc.***

Schubertians may question some of the tempi for these rare orchestral songs, but Dame Janet's beautiful singing and Leppard's alert accompaniment make them an attractive coupling for the Beethoven items on the reverse. Excellent recording.

Schumann, Robert

(1810–56)

Cello concerto in A min., Op. 129.
(*) HMV ASD/*TC-ASD* 3728. Paul Tortelier, RPO, Yan-Pascal Tortelier – BOËLLMANN: *Symphonic variations*; BRUCH: *Kol Nidrei.**

Tortelier's is a characteristically inspirational performance, at its most concentrated in the hushed rendering of the slow movement. The soloist's son matches the warmth of his father's playing in the accompaniment, and although this version is not the most distinguished available, it can be recommended to those who fancy the unexpected coupling. The cassette is acceptable, though it has not quite the upper range of the disc.

Still recommended: The youthful ardour of Jacqueline du Pré's HMV version (coupled with Saint-Saëns) provides an impulsively spontaneous performance, with Barenboim the sympathetic accompanist (HMV ASD 2498 [Ang. S 36642]). Alternatively Rostropovich's earlier account on DG – superb in every way – is still available on Privilege, but it is coupled to Sviatoslav Richter's somewhat idiosyncratic performance of the *Piano concerto* (DG 2538 025/*3318 009*). However, it is also available in an excellent Accolade double album (see the Concers section below, p. 916).

Piano concerto in A min., Op. 54.

*** Ph. 9500 677/*7300 772* [id.]. Brendel, LSO, Abbado – WEBER: *Konzertstück.****

** DG 2531/*3301* 042 [id.]. Argerich, Nat. SO of Washington, Rostropovich – CHOPIN: *Concerto No. 2.***

(B) ** Con. CC/*CCT* 7506. Katchen, Israel PO, Kertesz – GRIEG: *Concerto.***(*)

** HMV ASD/*TC-ASD* 3521 [Ang. S/ *4XS* 37510]. Gutiérrez, LPO, Tennstedt – GRIEG: *Concerto.***

*(*) Decca SXL/*KSXC* 6978. Larrocha, RPO, Dutoit – RACHMANINOV: *Concerto No. 2.*(*)

(M) *(*) Ph. Fest. 6570/*7310* 170 [id.]. Arrau, Concg. O., Dohnányi – GRIEG: *Concerto.*(*)

Of recent accounts Brendel's is easily the best. It is a thoroughly considered yet fresh-sounding performance, with meticulous regard to detail. There is some measure of coolness, perhaps, in the slow movement, but on the whole this is a most distinguished reading. The orchestral playing under Abbado is good, and the occasional lapse in ensemble noted by some reviewers on its first appearance is not likely to worry anyone. The recorded sound is up to the usual high standards of the house. The cassette offers rather less transparent sound than the disc. This does not efface memories of the fresh and poetic account by Bishop-Kovacevich and Sir Colin Davis (Philips 6500 166), nor indeed the magic that Solomon found in this most elusive of romantic concertos (CFP/*TC-CFP* 40255).

The partnership of Rostropovich and Argerich produces a performance which is full of contrast – helped by a recording of wide dynamic range – and strong in temperament. There is an appealing delicacy in the *Andantino*, and the outer movements have plenty of vivacity and colour. Yet in the last analysis the work's special romantic feeling does not fully blossom here, although the playing is not without poetry. The recording is admirably lifelike and well balanced, and the cassette transfer has excellent life and detail, even though on tape both piano and orchestral images tend to recede somewhat in pianissimos.

Katchen is given a clear, brilliant (perhaps slightly too brilliant) recording. This is essentially a virtuoso reading, but Katchen's wilfulness does not eschew romantic charm and there is a pervading freshness. The opening movement has a number of tempo changes and sounds more rhapsodical than usual. In the finale, which is basically very spirited, the fast main tempo hardly relaxes for the bumpy little second subject. The cassette is mellower than the disc, and although it has less range some will prefer it. However, in this price-area Solomon is an easy first choice.

The performance by Horacio Gutiérrez is well played and recorded, and the recording is of first-class quality, the bold piano image matched by the clarity, depth and brilliance of the orchestra. But the reading fails to satisfy, and this cannot compete with the most imaginative and poetic alternative versions.

The reading by Alicia de Larrocha and Charles Dutoit is very relaxed indeed; it also has touches of wilfulness, as in the ritenuto before the recapitulation of the first movement. Poetry is certainly not absent: the exchanges between the piano and the clarinet are beautifully done, but the lack of overall vitality becomes enervating in the finale, where the approach is spacious, but the basic tempo too lazy to be convincing. The recording is first-class on disc and cassette alike.

Arrau's mood in this most romantic of all piano concertos is serious almost to the point of gruffness. His weighty manner in the dialogues of the first movement is surely too unyielding, and the performance as a whole lacks any feeling of incandescence. The recording is full, but lacks something in sparkle.

(i) *Piano concerto; Concert allegro in A min., Op. 134;* (ii) *Introduction and* *allegro appassionato in G (Konzertstück), Op. 92.*
*** Decca SXL/*KSXC* 6861 [Lon. 7082). Ashkenazy, LSO, cond. (i) Segal, (ii) Ashkenazy.

Ashkenazy's reading of the *Concerto* has the aptest of couplings – and a generous one – in Schumann's two other works for piano and orchestra. In the *Concerto* Ashkenazy balances the demands of drama against poetry rather more in favour of the former than one might expect, but it is a refined reading as well as a powerful one, with the finale rather more spacious than is usual. The other two works receive bright, incisive performances, although musically the late *Concert allegro* cannot match its predecessors. The cassette transfer is brilliant but has some lack of bloom at the top in the *Concerto*; side two is warmer and smoother.

(i) *Konzertstück in F for four horns and orchestra, Op. 86. Symphony No. 3 in E flat (Rhenish), Op. 97.*
**(*) HMV ASD/*TC-ASD* 3724 [Ang. SZ 37655]. Berlin PO, Tennstedt, (i) with Hauptmann, Klier, Kohler, Seifert.

The *Konzertstück*, with its brilliant horn writing, and the *Rhenish symphony*, with its whooping horn passages, make an excellent coupling, and these fine, ripe readings are welcome. The account of the symphony is firmly based on the strong symphonic structures of the outer movements, and the *Konzertstück* too is given an urgent performance. The recording is opulent on disc and cassette alike; the latter is well focused.

Symphonies Nos. 1–4; Konzertstück in F, Op. 86; Manfred overture, Op. 115.
**(*) DG 2740 174 (3) [2709 075]. Chicago SO, Barenboim.

Symphonies Nos 1–4; Overture, scherzo and finale, Op. 52; Julius Caesar overture, Op. 128.

(M) **(*) Decca D 190 D 3 (3). VPO, Solti.

Symphonies Nos. 1–4; Overtures: The Bride of Messina, Op. 100; Hermann und Dorothea, Op. 136.

**(*) HMV SLS 5199 (3). Philh. O., Muti.

Symphonies Nos. 1–4; Manfred overture, Op. 115.

(M) ** CBS 79324 (3) [Col. M 3-35199]. Bav. RSO, Kubelik.

In this repertoire Karajan still reigns supreme, and his boxed set of the *Symphonies* with the Berlin Philharmonic Orchestra (DG 2740 129 (3) [2709 036]) remains first choice. Solti, like Karajan, offers also the *Overture, scherzo and finale*, and he is at his best here, alongside the two middle symphonies. Anyone who has ever doubted whether Solti could convey genuine *Innigkeit*, with unwanted tensions removed and a feeling of spontaneous lyricism paramount, should hear the slow movement of his magnificent account of the *Second*. The *Rhenish* too is splendidly buoyant; its first movement hoists one aloft on its soaring melodies, and the *Fourth Symphony* is given full force without ever falling into excessive tautness. The *First Symphony* does not quite match the glowing inspiration of its companions, but Solti's springing of the rhythms is always a pleasure, and with first-class VPO playing and good Decca recording from the beginning of the seventies, this set is worth considering at medium price.

Barenboim takes an overtly romantic view of the Schumann symphonies. His are weighty performances which yet bring out the lyrical, poetic warmth, underlining dramatic contrasts. The Chicago orchestra plays with extrovert brilliance, but the recording is variably successful in bringing that out; in the

Fourth Symphony the violins are made to sound thin. The three well-packed discs include two important makeweights; the *Konzertstück* for four horns is given the most memorable performance of the whole set, Dale Clevenger's horn section playing with stunning virtuosity.

Muti is a spirited and warm-hearted interpreter of Schumann, and all four symphonies are most enjoyable. The very opening of No. 1 brings what is probably the most controversial speed in the whole set, so hectic that the spring-like lightness is rather missed. But it is a purposeful reading, and Muti brings out the reserve of the *Second Symphony*, the dark inward quality. No. 3 is given a noble reading, and No. 4 (recorded first) an exhilarating, glowing one. Though the Philharmonia strings are not always as polished as they have since become, both playing and recording are warm and ripe.

In his CBS set Kubelik was recording the complete Schumann symphonies for the second time. The readings display the same bright and alert sensitivity to Schumann style as his set for DG, but neither in the playing, which in places is rather rough, nor even in the recording, which is wide-ranging but rather coarse in music which needs its textures refining, can it match the earlier versions.

Symphony No. 1 in B flat (Spring), Op. 38.

(*) HMV ASD/*TC-ASD* 3781 [Ang. S 37601]. Philh. O., Muti – MENDELSSOHN: *Symphony No. 5.**

Muti, sparkling in Mendelssohn, forces Schumann rather hard in the first movement of the *Spring symphony*. He underlines his view of the work as a powerful symphonic structure with exposition repeats in both the outer movements, presenting the middle two movements almost as intermezzi. It is not the most persuasive of his Schumann recordings, but stands quite well in an otherwise excellent series, warmly recorded. The cassette transfer is generally good, though not always absolutely crisp in focus; it has plenty of body and good detail.

Symphony No. 1; Overture, scherzo and finale, Op. 52.
(M) *(*) RCA Gold GL/*GK* 25285. Leipzig GO, Masur.

Surprisingly, this is a shade dull. The Gewandhaus Orchestra is one of the finest in the world, but the performances here are sound rather than inspired, and Masur is not at his most vital or imaginative. Perhaps the less than ideal recording underlines this impression. Karajan, Kubelik or Sawallisch are all much more worth while in the symphony. The cassette transfers are acceptable, made at a rather low level: Op. 52 sounds fresher than the symphony.

Symphonies Nos. 1; 4 in D min., Op. 120.
(M) *** HMV SXLP/*TC-SXLP* 30526. Dresden State O., Sawallisch.
(B) **(*) Con. CC/*CCT* 7532 [DG 2535/ 3335 116]. Berlin PO, Kubelik.

Sawallisch is a clear front runner in this coupling now that his issue is at medium price. These are distinguished performances, finely played, as one would expect from this great orchestra, and charged with great vitality and imagination. The recording, too, is really very good, the treble rather brightly lit but not excessively so. The cassette transfer is first-class: there is little appreciable difference between tape and disc – if anything the cassette makes a slightly mellower impression.

Kubelik's accounts are beautifully played and well recorded. They have not the drive of Sawallisch's versions, and this is especially noticeable in No. 4, but they are direct in manner and certainly enjoyable. The recording still sounds well, and at bargain price this is competitive. The sound on cassette is agreeably full but has less upper range than the disc.

Symphony No. 2 in C, Op. 61; Genoveva overture, Op. 81.
*(*) Decca SXL/*KSXC* 6976. VPO, Mehta.

Mehta directs a totally un-Viennese performance of the *Second Symphony*, beautifully played but lacking in charm. Even Schumann's stronger qualities are diminished by Mehta's aggressive, baldly direct approach, in which the speeds – in principle well chosen – never sound quite right. Excellent recording; the cassette is full-bodied and lively, but the resonance brings a hint of congestion at climaxes.

Symphony No. 2; Overture: Hermann und Dorothea, Op. 136.
**(*) HMV ASD/*TC-ASD* 3648 [Ang. S 37602]. Philh. O., Muti.
(M) *(*) RCA Gold GL/*GK* 25286. Leipzig GO, Masur.

A sensitive performance of the *Second Symphony* from Muti, with orchestral playing of the highest quality. In no sense does the playing here compare unfavourably with that of the Vienna Philharmonic for Solti, and Muti is less concerned to push things along. Yet there is no want of vitality or momentum. The engineers are not always entirely successful in clarifying the admittedly dense textures Schumann favours, although the balance has a convincing enough perspective. The *Hermann und Dorothea overture* is not one of Schumann's stronger works, but it includes an engagingly lightweight quotation from the *Marseillaise*. The cassette transfer is well managed, the quality bright and full, although sometimes the focus is not absolutely clean.

Given the excellence of the Gewandhaus Orchestra and its conductor, it is a pity that their account of the *Second*

Symphony cannot be more warmly recommended. However, the recording lacks bloom and clarity (the cassette is no better than the disc), and the performance is not particularly distinguished either. Masur makes *Hermann und Dorothea* sound rather dull, whereas Muti's version persuades us that it is fresh. The latter is at full price, but this does not offer a challenge to it.

Symphony No. 3 in E flat (Rhenish), Op. 97; Overture: The Bride of Messina, Op. 100.
**(*) HMV ASD/TC-ASD 3696 [Ang. SZ 37603]. Philh. O., Muti.

Riccardo Muti has the measure of the nobility and breadth of Schumann's *Rhenish symphony* and secures eloquent playing from the Philharmonia. His account is of particular value in offering *The Bride of Messina*, an overture to Schiller's play composed in the last few years of Schumann's life (1850–51). Muti gives a fresh and invigorating account, and the only reason for withholding three stars is the somewhat reverberant and opaque recorded sound. On cassette the quality is full and bright, but there is a hint of roughness in the loudest climaxes.

Symphony No. 3; Manfred overture, Op. 115.
(B) **(*) Con. CC/CCT 7538 [DG 2535/3335 118]. Berlin PO, Kubelik.

In the *Rhenish symphony*, again Kubelik's straightforward, unmannered approach, coupled to a natural warmth, provides a musical and thoroughly enjoyable account. The overture too is apt and very well played, and the recording is up to the high standard of this series.

Symphony No. 4 in D min., Op. 120.
*** DG 2531/3301 279 [id.]. VPO, Boehm – SCHUBERT: *Symphony No. 5*.***

(*) HMV Dig. ASD/TCC-ASD 3963 [Ang. DS/4ZS 37760]. Berlin PO, Tennstedt – MENDELSSOHN: *Symphony No. 4*.(*)

In his mid-eighties Boehm's view of Schumann's *Fourth Symphony* was as weighty as Klemperer's a decade or so earlier; but equally, with ripely sympathetic playing from the Vienna Philharmonic, it is a performance which is full of energy and concentration, ending with an exhilarating account of the finale. The recording is excellent, and those who want this coupling need not hesitate. The tape transfer is made at rather a low level: it is well balanced but has slightly less upper range than the disc.

Tennstedt gives a finely shaped account of this work, which is alive and vibrant in every bar, and the Berliners respond to his direction with keen sensitivity. Yet the overall impression is not entirely convincing. The *Romance* could be more expansive and ruminative, and the opening of the finale could have a shade more mystery and atmosphere. The recording is rich and full-bodied as well as brilliant, and there is a first-class chrome tape to match the disc closely. This is among the better versions of this symphony before the public, but it is not the whole story. For that one must turn to such conductors as Cantelli (World SH 315), Furtwängler, Karajan and Klemperer. The latter offers the same coupling, and his outstanding HMV reissue is now available in an excellent, wide-ranging cassette transfer, matching the disc closely (HMV SXLP/TC-SXLP 30178 [Ang. S 35629]).

CHAMBER MUSIC

Abendlied, Op. 85/12 (arr. Joachim); Adagio and allegro in A flat, Op. 70; Fantasiestücke, Op. 73; 3 Romances, Op. 94; 5 Stücke im Volkston, Op. 102.

*** Ph. 9500 740/*7300 847*. Holliger, Brendel.

On this delightful record Heinz Holliger gathers together pieces written in 1849, the most fruitful of composing years for Schumann. The three *Romances* are specifically for oboe, but Holliger – pointing out that Schumann never heard any of the pieces except on the violin – suggests that the others too are suitable for the oboe, since the composer himself gave different options. One misses something by not having a horn in the *Adagio and allegro*, a cello in the folkstyle pieces, or a clarinet in the *Fantasiestücke* (the oboe d'amore is used here); but Holliger has never sounded more magical on record, and with superb recording and deeply imaginative accompaniment the result is an unexpected revelation. The cassette transfer is first-class, matching the disc closely.

Adagio and allegro in A flat, Op. 70.
*** DG 2531/*3301* 201 [id.]. Rostropovich, Argerich – CHOPIN: *Cello sonata* etc.***

The *Adagio and allegro* are normally given to the horn, but like other pieces from 1849 they can as well be played on the cello – or for that matter other instruments. Rostropovich is memorably expressive, making this an attractive coupling for the Chopin, very well recorded on disc and cassette alike.

Piano quintet in E flat, Op. 44.
*(*) DG 2531/*3301* 343 [id.]. Levine, LaSalle Qt – BRAHMS: *String quartet No. 3.**(*)

A rather hard-driven opening does not endear one to this version of the *Piano quintet*, although there is some sensitive playing from James Levine. It wants the spontaneity and freshness of the Beaux Arts team (Philips 9500 065) or the urgency and unforced eloquence of the

alternative CRD version by Thomas Rajna and members of the Alberni Quartet (CRD 1024/*CRDC 4024*). Both these issues are more appropriately coupled with the *Piano quartet*, Op. 47; the CRD tape is first-class in every way. The DG tape transfer is clear and clean, and whether on disc or cassette the sound has excellent presence.

Piano trio No. 1 in D min., Op. 63.
*** HMV ASD/*TC-ASD* 3894. Kyung-Wha Chung, Tortelier, Previn – MENDELSSOHN: *Trio No. 1.****

Schumann's *D minor Piano trio* makes an attractive and apt coupling for Mendelssohn's *Trio* in the same key. It is a more elusive work but in a performance as powerfully characterful as this – each individual constantly challenging the others – it emerges as a match for the other great Schumann chamber pieces with piano. As in the Mendelssohn, Previn's strongly rhythmic playing underpins the lyrical outpouring of the string players. The recording is first-rate, though the quality on the cassette is less transparent than the LP.

String quartet No. 1 in A min., Op. 41/1.
(M) *** Decca Ace SDD 510. Musikverein Qt – BRAHMS: *String quartet No. 3.****

The Musikverein Quartet (formerly known as the Küchl after the first violin) made a great impression with their recording of two late Mozart quartets, and this fine performance of the Schumann maintains their reputation for fine ensemble and natural musicality. There is a total absence of affectation here; the dynamic shading arises as a natural part of the music and never seems painted on. This is in some ways fresher than the fine Italian Quartet recording of all three quartets (Philips 6703 029) and the engineering is beyond reproach. A rewarding issue.

Violin sonatas Nos. 1 in A min., Op. 105; 2 in D min., Op. 121.
(M) *** HM HM 489. Oleg, Rault.

The *Violin sonatas* are products of Schumann's last years, composed at a period when he was fighting off insanity. Both are rewarding pieces and have been neglected by the gramophone since the Ferras/Barbizet DG recording from the mid-1960s. Raphael Oleg and Yves Rault are extremely young artists; the former was not twenty when this record was made, and the latter was still on the right side of twenty-one. They play these pieces well and deserve plaudits for their enterprise in offering a coupling that well-established artists have shunned. Good recording too.

PIANO MUSIC

Arabeske in C, Op. 18; Fantasia in C, Op. 17; Kinderscenen (Scenes from Childhood), Op. 15.
*** DG 2531/*3301* 089 [id.]. Barenboim.

Barenboim's account of the *Fantasia* is fervent and impressive, worthy to rank alongside the best available. This powerful reading is coupled with a sensitive yet unmannered version of *Kinderscenen* and a thoroughly recommendable *Arabeske*. Good recording; the cassette transfer does not quite match the disc, and on side one (the *Fantasia*) there is a degree of edge on the treble.

Blumenstück, Op. 19; Kinderscenen, Op. 15; Papillons, Op. 2; Romanzen, Op. 28.
*** Ph. 6500 395. Arrau.

As always the great Chilean pianist brings both intensity and devotion to these pieces. Every detail of phrasing is carefully thought out, and Arrau produces a characteristically warm and richly coloured sonority. Some of the *Kinderscenen* are perhaps invested with a little too much significance, and there are a few moments when one might take issue with this or that expressive touch. However, this is playing of real stature, and it is beautifully recorded.

Bunte Blätter, Op. 99; Fantasiestücke, Op. 12/9; 4 Fugues, Op. 72; Humoreske in B flat, Op. 20; 4 Klavierstücke; Kreisleriana, Op. 16; Nachtstücke, Op. 23; New Album for the Young; Papillons, Op. 2; 6 Studies, Op. 3.
(M) ** Turn. TVS 37118/20 [in SVBX 5468/72]. Frankl.

This set ranges from early Schumann – *Papillons* and the *Studies* (after Paganini), Op. 3 – to the *Bunte Blätter*, and it mingles rarities such as the *Fugues* with repertory pieces like the *Humoreske* and *Kreisleriana*. As usual, Peter Frankl evinces sound musicianship and fine intelligence, though the last ounce of poetic feeling seems to elude him. There are magnificent things here, but the recording lets it down; though some pieces are well served, there is pre-echo elsewhere and insufficient range.

Carnaval, Op. 9.
(*) Decca SXL/*KSXC* 6910 [Lon. 7134/5-]. Larrocha – SCHUBERT: *Piano sonata No. 13* etc.*

Alicia de Larrocha gives a strongly characterized if somewhat wayward account of *Carnaval*. Not every choice of tempo and turn of phrase will command universal acclaim, but hers is a committed personal view and she is beautifully recorded. The cassette transfer has plenty of colour, body and sparkle.

Carnaval, Op. 9; Faschingsschwank aus Wien, Op. 26.
⊛*** DG 2531/*3301* 090 [id.]. Barenboim.

Barenboim's reading of *Carnaval* is magical. His lively imagination lights on the fantasy in this quirkily spontaneous sequence of pieces and makes them sparkle anew. It is as if he were in process of improvising the music, yet his liberties of expression are never too great. He may allow himself free rubato in such a piece as *Valse noble*, but the result remains noble, not sentimental. The *Masked ball* piece on the reverse is more problematic, but the challenge inspires Barenboim, and here too he is at his most imaginative and persuasive, bringing out the warmth and tenderness as well as the brilliance. The recording is excellent. The cassette transfer of *Carnaval* is of demonstration quality; on side two the level is lower and the piano image has slightly less presence.

Davidsbündlertänze, Op. 6; Humoreske in B flat, Op. 20.
*** Chan. ABR/*ABT* 1029. Artymiw.

Lydia Artymiw attracted attention at the 1978 Leeds Piano Competition as a player of temperament and personality. Her finely delineated accounts of the *Davidsbündlertänze* and the *Humoreske* can both hold their own with the best now on the market. In both works Artymiw shows her finesse as a Schumann interpreter, drawing together music which in its very structure presents problems. Never exaggerating, she conveys consistent intensity as in a live concert. She is perhaps not as touching in the *Davidsbündlertänze* as Murray Perahia (on CBS 73202 [Col. M 32299], coupled with the *Fantasiestücke*, Op. 12), but she has the advantage of better recording. Her cleanly articulated playing has true artistry to recommend it alongside the naturally balanced sound image, equally impressive on disc and cassette.

5 Études, Op. posth.; Études symphoniques, Op. 13; Papillons, Op. 2.
*** CBS 76635/40- [Col. M/*MT* 34539]. Perahia.

Beautifully poetic accounts of all these works that can be strongly recommended. Murray Perahia has a special feeling for the *Symphonic studies* which is in evidence both on the concert platform and here, and makes every expressive point in the most natural and unfussy way. He plays the additional five studies that Schumann omitted from the published score as an addendum rather than inserting them among the other studies as do Ashkenazy and Richter. The *Papillons* are unrivalled on record at present and are unlikely to be surpassed. The engineers give Perahia too close a balance to be ideal, but the sound has distinct clarity and with adjustment of the controls it yields a generally pleasing quality. The cassette is less distinguished, the quality at times somewhat opaque, at others rather hard on top.

Études symphoniques, Op. 13; Fantasia in C, Op. 17.
** Ph. 9500 318/*7300 590*. Dichter.

Misha Dichter is served by recording of great naturalness and warmth (although the cassette is not as fresh as the disc), and his playing commands considerable admiration. There is fervour and at the same time discipline, and taken in pure isolation this record will give satisfaction. Yet in neither work does Dichter eclipse memories of his rivals. There are some mannerisms in the *Fantasy*, which is by no means as concentrated here as with Pollini or Richter. In the *Études symphoniques* Dichter restores the variations subsequently omitted by Schumann in a different order from Ashkenazy and Perahia; he intersperses the fourth rejected variation immediately after the theme, the third between the first and second studies, and the second and first (in that order) between Nos. 9 and 10 etc. Perahia breathes greater poetry into all these pieces, but his version is coupled with the *Papillons*; in this coupling of Opp. 13 and 17 Ashkenazy is to be preferred, even if he is not quite as well recorded (Decca SXL 6214 [Lon. 6471]).

Études symphoniques; Toccata, Op. 7.
(*) DG Dig. 2532/*3302* 036 [id.]. Pogorelich – BEETHOVEN: *Piano sonata No. 32.*(*)

Pogorelich opens his performance of the *Études symphoniques* with a self-conscious and studied presentation of the theme. This is pianism of the first order, but the listener's attention tends to be drawn from the music to the quality of the pianism. Yet this remains a performance to be reckoned with, even if it is not as fine as the fresh and ardent version by Murray Perahia. The recording is vivid and truthful.

Fantasia in C, Op. 17.
(M) **(*) Saga 5460. Wilde – LISZT: *Sonata.***(*)
** Decca SXL/*KSXC* 6756 [Lon. 6989/5-]. Larrocha – LISZT: *Sonata.***

David Wilde's account of the *C major Fantasy* is as powerful as the Liszt coupling. It is finely controlled and has splendid panache, and even though the recording falls short of the highest distinction, the playing ensures a high rating for this disc.

Alicia de Larrocha is an artist of temperament and personality, and her performance of the *Fantasy* is perhaps too personal for a strong recommendation; but there are many good things in its favour, not least its excellent recording. However, there are many outstanding rival versions available, for instance by Pollini, Richter, Arrau and Ashkenazy, and collectors cannot be recommended to acquire this in preference to them. This is not to say that Larrocha's playing is not eminently worth hearing.

Fantasia in C, Op. 17; Fantasiestücke, Op. 12.

**(*) CBS 76713 [Col. M 35168]. Argerich.

A rather exaggerated beginning to the *Fantasia* from Martha Argerich, with wide dynamic range, slightly mannered rubato but fabulous tone production. She is always a fascinating artist, but here there are too many agogic distortions and impetuous touches to make one feel entirely happy with it as an only version for one's collection. There are many beautiful moments throughout this record but her view is too personal to be recommended without reservation. The recording is reasonably fresh and warm but slightly too close.

Fantasia in C, Op. 17; Gesänge der Frühe, Op. 133; Novelletten, Op. 21; 7 Pieces in the form of fughettas, Op. 126; Piano sonata No. 1 in F sharp min., Op. 11; Theme and variations in E flat; Waldscenen, Op. 82.
(M) *(*) Turn. TVS 37131/3 [in SVBX 5468/72]. Frankl.

A blend of the familiar and less familiar Schumann, the centrepiece being the *C major Fantasy.* Again there is some thoroughly idiomatic playing, but Frankl tends to be better in the smaller rather than the bigger-boned pieces. He is always musicianly but rarely distinguished in this set. The recording is only fair, and the piano itself does not sound in the best condition.

Fantasia in C, Op. 17; Novelletten, Op. 21/1–2.
*** RCA RL/*RK* 13427 [ARL 1/*ARK* 1 3427]. Rubinstein.

Rubinstein at the very end of his career recorded this glowing account of the *Fantasia.* In the first movement he adopts a speed more relaxed than usual, but the compulsion of his playing is magnetic and there is no dragging. As for the slow finale, it finds Rubinstein at his most poetic. With the *Fantasia* spreading on to the second side, the fill-up is not generous, but the *Novelletten*, recorded much earlier, make an apt and poetic supplement. The recording of the *Fantasia* is bright and clear. There is little difference in quality between cassette and disc.

Faschingsschwank aus Wien, Op. 26; Piano sonata No. 2 in G min., Op. 22; Waldscenen, Op. 82: Vogel als Prophet.
(M) ** Argo ZK 91. Van Barthold.

The appeal of Kenneth van Barthold's record lies in the fact that he uses a period instrument, a Graf, for which Schumann is known to have had affection. Its pitch is, of course, lower than present-day concert grands, and the want of colour and range may be a drawback for some collectors. Modern instruments can more readily convey expressive range, and non-specialists may find this record more interesting than musically rewarding. But Kenneth van Barthold plays well enough, and he is well recorded too.

Humoreske in B flat, Op. 20.
*** RCA RL/*RK* 13433 [ARL 1/ ARK 1 3433]. Horowitz – LISZT: *Consolation* etc.; RACHMANINOV: *Barcarolle* etc.***

Horowitz conveys Schumann's volatile temperament to better effect than almost any other pianist. There is tremendous concentration about this playing and yet nothing is out of focus or larger than life. Masterly in every way, though the recording is just a shade on the hard side. The disc and cassette are closely matched.

Kinderscenen (Scenes from Childhood), Op. 15; Kreisleriana, Op. 16.
*** Ph. 9500/*7300* 964. Brendel.

Keenly intelligent and finely characterized playing from Brendel here. He is better recorded than most of his rivals, and though certain details may strike listeners as less spontaneous the overall impression is strong. The *Kinderscenen* is the finest for some years and is touched with real distinction. On cassette the sound has slightly less sharpness of focus than on disc, but remains very good.

Kinderscenen, Op. 15; Piano sonata No. 2 in G min., Op. 22.
(M) ** DG Acc. 2542/*3342* 155. Kempff.

Although nothing that Kempff does is without insights, neither of these is among his more compelling Schumann performances. The opening of *Kinderscenen* is cool; even the famous *Träumerei* sounds curiously literal, and it is only in the closing section of the work that the Kempff magic appears. The *Sonata* too, rather dryly recorded, is in no way memorable. The cassette transfer is faithful; the sound is warmer in *Kinderscenen*.

VOCAL MUSIC

Lieder: *Aufträge; Er ist's; Erstes Grün; Frage; Jasminenstrauch; Die Kartenlegerin; Das Käuzlein; Die letzten Blumen; Loreley; Marienwürmchen; Die Meerfee; Mein schönster Stern; Der Nussbaum; Der Sandmann; Schmetterling; Schneeglöckchen; Sehnsucht nach der Waldgegend; Die Sennerin; Waldesgespräch; Widmung.*
*** HM 1C 065 99631. Ameling, Demus.

The sweetness of Elly Ameling's singing in Lieder may sometimes suggest superficiality, but here is a record which in its quiet unforced musicality brings consistent delight, far more intense than the easy expression may initially suggest.

Ideally one would like more variety – *Loreley*, for example, can convey more magic – but the delight of Schumann in song is never far away, and the accompaniment and recording are most sympathetic.

2 Balladen, Op. 122; 6 frühe Lieder, Op. posth.; 4 Gesänge, Op. 142/1–2, 4; 5 heitere Gesänge, Op. 125/3–5; 4 Husarenlieder, Op. 117; 6 Lieder, Op. 89; 6 Lieder, Op. 90; 3 Lieder, Op. 96; Lieder und Gesänge aus 'Wilhelm Meister', Op. 98/2, 4, 6, 8; 10 Spanische Liebeslieder, Op. 138/2–3, 5, 7. Miscellaneous Lieder: *Abendlied; An den Mond; Dein Angesicht; Der Einsiedler; Es leuchtet meine Liebe; Der Gärtner; Der Handschuh; Mein schöner Stern; Minnespiel; Nachtlied; Provenzalisches Lied; Des Sängers Fluch; Schön Hedwig; Warnung.*
*** DG 2740 200 (3) [2709 088]. Fischer-Dieskau, Eschenbach.

This is the third volume in Fischer-Dieskau's projected recording of all the Schumann songs suitable for a male voice. Many of the songs in this volume date from late in Schumann's career, and normally their inspiration is regarded as suspect. But singer and pianist here transform their materials, revealing depths of expression not often recognized. A valuable supplement to the other volumes, beautifully recorded.

Dichterliebe, Op. 48; Kerner Lieder, Op. 35; Liederalbum für die Jugend (excerpts): *Zigeunerliedchen; Marienwürmchen; Die wandelnde Glocke; Des Sennen Abschied; Er ist's; Schneeglöckchen; Lied Lynceus des Türmers; Liederkreis, Op. 24; Spanisches Liederspiel: Melancholie; Geständnis; Der Kontrabandiste.*

Lieder: *Abends am Strand; Auf dem Rhein; Aufträge; Der arme Peter I–III; Die beiden Grenadiere; Belsatzar; Blondels Lied; Die feindlichen Brüder; Loreley.*
*** DG 2740 185 (3) [2709 079]. Fischer-Dieskau, Eschenbach.

With *Dichterliebe* and the Op. 24 *Liederkreis* among the items, this second volume forms a centrepiece to the Fischer-Dieskau/Eschenbach series; those well known works emerge as fresh as the many rarities also included. Eschenbach, a fine solo Schumann interpreter, steers an ideal course, offering his own individual touches yet always matching the singer. Excellent recording.

Dichterliebe; Liederkreis, Op. 24.
(M) *** DG Acc. 2542/3342 156. Schreier, Shetler.

Often the market in Lieder recordings of the male voice seems to be so dominated by Dietrich Fischer-Dieskau that other artists must inevitably rest in the shadow of the great baritone. But here is a record of tenor Lieder-singing which, while fully reflecting the Fischer-Dieskau art and technique, yet shows the singer able to bring an added inspirational quality of his own to the songs. These performances have marvellous spontaneity and feeling – the impression is of being at a live recital. The contrasts of emotion behind the song sequence of *Dichterliebe* are strongly brought out, underlying tensions given an almost painful degree of poignancy. Similarly Schreier treats the Heine *Liederkreis* as a unified whole by giving it satisfying emotional shape. With the voice at its freshest the vocal quality combines tonal beauty with tenderness, while the colouring achieves consistent subtlety. The result involves the listener from the first song to the last. The recording is first-class, and the cassette too is of demonstration realism. Highly recommended, especially to those new to this repertoire.

Dichterliebe; Liederkreis, Op. 39.
*** DG 2531 290 [id.]. Fischer-Dieskau, Eschenbach.

These two performances, taken from Fischer-Dieskau's boxes of Schumann Lieder, are most impressive when considered in detail against other versions of these much-recorded works. As his career has developed, so Fischer-Dieskau's readings have acquired a sharper edge, with the darkness and irony in some of these songs more specifically contrasted against the poetry and expressive warmth. The tone may not be so fresh as it once was, but Eschenbach's accompaniment is superb, consistently imaginative, and the recording is excellent: there are no finer versions of either cycle.

4 Duets, Op. 34; Duets, Op. 37/7, 12, Op. 74/2–4; 4 Duets, Op. 78; Duets, Op. 79/10, 16, 19, 21, Op. 101/3, 7, Op. 138/4, 9; Ländliches Lied, Op. 29/1; Die Lotusblume, Op. 33; Sommerruh; 3 zweistimmige Lieder, Op. 43.
*** DG 2531 204. Varady, Schreier, Fischer-Dieskau, Eschenbach.

As a supplement to Fischer-Dieskau's collected sets of Schumann songs, this disc of duets is a delight. In these sparkling performances all three singers, not to mention the pianist, are plainly relishing music which is generally on an unpretentious, domestic scale. The problems of balancing have been admirably judged.

Frauenliebe und Leben, Op. 42.
Lieder: *Die Blume der Ergebung; Frühlingslust; Hinaus ins Freie; Kinderwacht; Die letzten Blumen; Liebeslied; Lieder der Suleika; Mond meiner Seele Liebling; Reich' mir die Hand; Der Sandmann; Schmetterling; Singet nicht in Trauertönen; Weit! Weit!*
*** DG 2531/3301 323 [id.]. Mathis, Eschenbach.

With her fresh tone and delicately poised manner, Edith Mathis brings out the girlish feelings implied by the *Frauenliebe* songs. These are finely detailed performances, always refreshing and with keenly sensitive accompaniment from Eschenbach. Inevitably Mathis lacks a little weight in the last song of bereavement, but there is no lack of intensity, and the attractions of this version are enhanced by the coupling of more Schumann songs, an imaginative selection including neglected late songs. The recording is first-rate on disc and cassette alike.

Frauenliebe und Leben; Liederkreis, Op. 39.
** Ph. 9500 110. Norman, Gage.
* Chan. ABR/ABT 1009. Lear, Vignoles.

The richness and power of Jessye Norman's voice are well caught in both cycles, but in *Frauenliebe* she is not quite at her happiest or most spontaneous. It has its quota of mawkish words, and Miss Norman does not seem naturally to identify. Richer in its poetry, the Eichendorff *Liederkreis* is more sympathetic for her, but other versions are even more sensitive. Accompaniments and recording are most refined.

Evelyn Lear's coupling is disappointing; the readings lack projection, and the voice sounds uncomfortable in the upper register and poorly recorded. The cassette transfer is faithful.

3 Gedichte, Op. 30; 6 Gedichte, Op. 36; Gedichte aus Rückerts 'Liebesfrühling', Op. 37/1, 5, 8–9; 3 Gesänge, Op. 31; 5 Lieder, Op. 40; Lieder und Gesänge, Op. 27; Liederkreis,

Op. 39; Myrthen, Op. 25/1–3, 5–8, 13, 15 19, 21 2, 24 6; Romanzen und Balladen, Op. 45/1–2; Der frohe Wandersmann.
*** DG 2740 167 (3) [2709 074]. Fischer-Dieskau, Eschenbach.

This was the first volume of the projected collection of all the Schumann songs suitable for male voice, and it can be warmly recommended. Fischer-Dieskau's voice has remained amazingly consistent over the years, and the extra refinement of his readings of songs he has often recorded before goes with consistent sense of spontaneity. These readings are not self-conscious in the wrong way, for Eschenbach, a subtle Schumann interpreter, provides his matching imagination without ever forcing himself forward. The recording slightly favours the voice, but is tonally excellent.

6 Gedichte und Requiem, Op. 90; 5 Lieder, Op. 40; Liederkreis, Op. 39.
**(*) CBS 76815 [Col. M/MT 36668]. Pears, Perahia.

After Benjamin Britten's death Murray Perahia was the pianist who came to accompany Sir Peter Pears in his song recitals. Perahia may be of a totally different generation, but like Britten himself he is an inspirational pianist, able to snatch magic out of the air in Schumann's piano writing, not least in his important postludes. Unfortunately the rather close recording catches Pears's voice uncomfortably. At the very end of his singing career it had its measure of unevenness, which is exaggerated here; but the detailed perception and intensity in all these songs, matched by Perahia's playing, can be recommended to all admirers.

Liederalbum für die Jugend, Op. 79; Liederkreis, Op. 39.
*** Ph. 6769 037 (2) [id.]. Ameling, Demus.

The album of songs for the young contains many delightful inspirations, often so slight that in the world of significant Lieder-singing they are totally neglected. They are almost ideally suited to the light and sweet voice of Elly Ameling, and some of the most enchanting items of all come when with technical sleight of hand she is given the chance to sing duets with herself. The lightness of her voice is arguably less apt for the Op. 39 songs; there have been deeper readings on record, but by bringing out the vein of girlish freshness Ameling gives a special illumination. The accompaniment and recording are first-rate.

Schütz, Heinrich (1585–1672)

Musikalische Exequien.
(M) *** Ph. 9502 025 [id.]. Dresden Kreuzchor, Mauersberger.

Schütz's *Mass for the dead* is one of his most austere and serious masterpieces. This performance eschews any of the compromises that are sometimes made – fleshing out the texture so as to make it correspond to Schütz's Venetian style. This is as austere as the music itself, and the forces involved (the continuo consists of a tenor viola da gamba, violine and organ) are eminently well balanced. The soloists include two fine boy trebles (Friedemann Jäckel and Andreas Göhler) and the tenor Peter Schreier. Good recorded sound (the disc comes from 1970), with excellent perspective. There is no alternative version at present in the catalogue, but this is thoroughly recommendable at this price.

St Matthew Passion.
(M) *** Decca Ser. SA/KSC 3. Pears, Shirley-Quirk, Luxon, Schütz Ch., Norrington.

693

Schütz's setting of the *St Matthew Passion* is an austere one. The story is told for the most part in a series of unaccompanied recitatives, eloquent but restrained in style. The drama is suddenly heightened at the choral entries, but these are comparatively few, and the work relies on the artistry of the soloists to project itself on the listener. The solo singing here is of a high order and the choral contribution fine enough to make one wish there was more of it. The closing chorus, *Glory be to Thee*, is more familiar than the rest of the work, for it is sometimes extracted to be sung on its own. The recording is excellent, and it is understandable that the original language is used. Even so, one feels the work would communicate more readily when sung in English. The cassette transfer is admirable, full, yet clearly focused.

Scriabin, Alexander
(1872–1915)

Poème de l'extase, Op. 54.
(*) Decca SXL/KSXC 6905 [Lon. 7129/5-]. Cleveland O., Maazel – DEBUSSY: La Mer.(*)

Maazel's account of Scriabin's heavily scented and erotic score is a shade too efficient to be really convincing. The playing is often brilliant, but others succeed in communicating the atmosphere of this music more effectively. The recording is superbly detailed and well-lit (on tape as well as disc), though the trumpets are somewhat forward and strident. While Mehta's version with the Los Angeles Philharmonic Orchestra (Decca SXL 6325 [Lon. 6552]) is still in circulation, there is little to detain the collector here.

Day Dreams, Op. 24.
** HMV ASD/TC-ASD 3709. USSR SO, Svetlanov – BALAKIREV: *Islamey* etc.***; GLINKA: *Ivan Susanin* etc.**

Day Dreams is a short nostalgic piece written just before the *First Symphony*, and lasts only five minutes. Rozhdestvensky recorded it in the early 1970s, but this account is equally committed and forms part of an interesting compilation well worth investigation even if the recording, though rich, could be cleaner. The cassette transfer is clear but less sumptuous than the disc.

Symphonies Nos. 1 in E, Op. 26; 2 in C min., Op. 29; 3 in C min. (Le divin poème), Op. 43; Poème de l'extase, Op. 54; Prometheus, Op. 60.
*** Ph. 6769 041 (4). Soffel, Tenzi, Frankfurter Kantorei, W. Saschowa (piano), Frankfurt RSO, Inbal.

Yevgeny Svetlanov's box devoted to the Scriabin symphonies included the early *F sharp minor Piano concerto* and the *Rêverie* but omitted *Prometheus*. In any event this Philips set has the field to itself, now that Svetlanov has succumbed to the deletions axe. The Frankfurt recordings are moreover a good deal smoother than the older set, and the playing of the Radio Orchestra under Eliahu Inbal is rather more refined, albeit less intoxicating than the Russian performances. The *Poème de l'extase* is not quite so voluptuous as it was in Abbado's hands (his record is now deleted), but it is still eminently persuasive, as is the performance of *Prometheus*. A valuable and recommendable set that deserves wide currency.

Piano sonatas Nos. 2 (Sonata-fantasy) in G sharp min., Op. 19; 7 in F sharp (White Mass), Op. 64; 10 in C, Op. 70; Deux Danses, Op. 73; Deux Poèmes, Op. 32; Quatre Morceaux, Op. 56.
*** Decca SXL/KSXC 6868 [Lon. 7087/5-]. Ashkenazy.

This issue fulfils the high expectations engendered by Ashkenazy's earlier Scriabin recital (Decca SXL/*KSXC* 6705 [Lon. 6920/5-]). Ponti, Ogdon and Roberto Szidon have all given us complete Scriabin sonata cycles on disc, but none has matched Ashkenazy's commanding authority and sense of vision in this repertoire. Whether one likes this music or not, there is no questioning the demonic, possessed quality of the playing. The cassette faithfully reproduces the sound one finds on the disc; indeed there is remarkably little to choose between the two formats.

Séverac, Déodat de
(1872–1921)

Le Soldat de plomb.
(M) ** Turn. TVS 34586 [id.]. Dosse, Petit – CHABRIER: *Valses*; SAINT-SAËNS: *Carnival.***

This miniature suite (for piano, four hands) draws on Hans Andersen's *The Brave Tin Soldier* for its inspiration. It is highly engaging and very nicely played. The recording is good too, although some ears might find the acoustic overresonant.

Shankar, Ravi (born 1921)

Improvisations (Tenderness; Twilight mood; The enchanted dawn; Morning love).
*** HMV ASD 3357. Y. Menuhin, composer, Rampal, Géliot, Indian percussion ens.

While the Far East has produced violinists and pianists of undoubted stature, the West has yet to produce a great koto

player or a great exponent of the sarod or the shanai. The violin, of course, has a place in Indian music, and these improvisations, which bring together eminent musicians of different cultures, will give pleasure to those with an open mind. Others may well find the mixture incongruous and not wholly satisfying. One must be guided wholly by one's own predilections and curiosity: this is a disc that readers should sample for themselves. For many its rewards will be very limited.

Raga Jogeshwari (Alap; Jor; Gat I and II).
*** DG 2531 280 [id.]. Composer, Rakha, Jiban, Widya.

Jogeshwari is a morning *rāg*. The note series itself is revealed only gradually; the ascending line is composed of larger intervals, the descending is partly diatonic and in part chromatic. At first the *rag* is unfolded in the *Alap*, which is reflective and rhythmically free; the *Jor* which follows is metric yet still unaccompanied. Only on the second side of the record is Alla Rakha's virtuosity in evidence. Ravi Shankar is his usual masterly self and is eminently well recorded. There are helpful notes on the sleeve for the listener unversed in the procedures of Indian classical music.

Sheppard, John
(*c.* 1515–*c.* 1559/60)

Cantate Mass; Respond: Spiritus Sanctus.
*** Cal. CAL 1621. Clerkes of Oxenford, Wulstan.

John Sheppard's claims to musical mastery have only recently come to be widely appreciated, and this fine record could hardly be better designed to show why this contemporary of Tallis deserves a place next to that long-acknowledged master. The *Cantate Mass*, sung here a third higher than the manuscript indicates, and involving the sopranos in formidable problems of tessitura, is among the most distinctive works of its time, presenting surprises in a way uncommon in civilized polyphonic writing. The textures are refreshingly clear, helped by the superb performances of the Clerkes of Oxenford. The five-part *Spiritus Sanctus* is less striking but makes an excellent coupling, equally well recorded.

Shostakovich, Dmitri
(1906–75)

The Age of Gold (ballet): *suite, Op. 22.*
(M) (*) Turn. TVS 34644 [id./*CT 2224*]. Seattle SO, Katims – GLIÈRE: *Red Poppy*; RIMSKY-KORSAKOV: *Sadko*.(*)

The *Age of Gold suite* is given a lively and sympathetic reading by the Seattle orchestra (the *Polka* is not wanting in wit); but the recording is thin and the orchestral strings lack body.

(i) *Cello concerto No. 1 in E flat, Op. 107;* (ii) *Violin concerto No. 1 in A min., Op. 99.*
*** HMV ASD/*TC-ASD* 4046 [*Violin concerto* (d) Ang. S 36964]. (i) Tortelier, Bournemouth SO, Berglund; (ii) David Oistrakh, New Philh. O., Maxim Shostakovich.

Tortelier's reading of the first of Shostakovich's two cello concertos is both tough and passionate. In sheer precision of bravura passages it does not always quite match the example of the dedicatee and first performer, Rostropovich, but in

the urgency and attack of his playing Tortelier even outshines the Russian master, who made his recording before his interpretation really matured. Berglund and the Bournemouth orchestra provide colourful and committed accompaniment, and the recording is rich and vivid. David Oistrakh made three records of the *First Violin concerto*, which was written for him. The first, with Mitropoulos, had the most powerful atmosphere, and this latest version of the three does not dim memories of that. This is not so keenly characterized or as deeply experienced (in the mid-1950s the work was fresh), but it is only fair to add that it is a fine performance for all that. It also benefits from well-balanced and finely detailed EMI recording. Maxim Shostakovich does not display so firm a grip on proceedings as did Mitropoulos or Mravinsky, but the New Philharmonia plays with no want of commitment. This version is still highly recommendable. On cassette the resonant recordings lead to some slight loss of orchestral clarity, but both solo instruments are well focused.

Piano concertos Nos. 1 (for piano, trumpet and strings) *in C min., Op. 35; 2 in F, Op. 101.*
**(*) CBS 76822 [Col. MS 6124]. List, Moscow R. and TV O., Maxim Shostakovich.

Piano concertos Nos. 1–2; 3 Fantastic dances, Op. 5.
**(*) HMV ASD 3081 [Ang. S 37109]. Ortiz, Bournemouth SO, Berglund.

Eugene List plays the *First Concerto* with splendid dash and brilliance, underlining its brittle sonorities and brash swagger. He takes the finale of the *Second Concerto* very much up to speed, and throughout there is plenty of character and spirit. The strings of the Moscow Radio Orchestra are somewhat wanting in bloom and lustre, and in the slow movement of No. 1 the solo trumpet is not heard to best advantage; he is rather forwardly balanced, as is the rest of the orchestra. The sound on the CBS record is not quite as fresh and truthful as on Christina Ortiz's less well characterized but freshly enjoyable version on HMV. Both are recommendable but neither is ideal. List scores as a performance and has the authority of Maxim Shostakovich's direction; Ortiz has better-engineered sound and an enjoyable fill-up in the shape of the *Three Fantastic Dances*.

Piano concerto No. 2.
(M) *** HMV SXLP/TC-SXLP 30514. Ogdon, RPO, Foster – BARTÓK: *Concerto No. 3.***(*)

John Ogdon, at the height of his powers, gives a splendidly idiomatic account of this concerto written originally for Shostakovich's son, Maxim. The playing is full of character, the outer movements striking for their wit and dash, and the beautiful slow movement richly romantic without being sentimentalized. There is no better version of this work available, and the 1971 recording sounds as vivid as the day it was made. The cassette too offers demonstration quality. Although the coupling does not display quite the same degree of excellence, this medium-priced reissue is worth considering for the Shostakovich alone.

Symphonies Nos. 1 in F min., Op. 10; 9 in E flat, Op. 70.
*** Decca Dig. SXDL/KSXDC 7515 [Lon. 71017/5-]. LPO, Haitink.

Haitink's reading of the brilliant *First Symphony* may lack something in youthful high spirits (the finale does not sound quirky enough in the strange alternation of moods), but it is a strong, well-played performance nonetheless, and it is coupled with a superb account of No. 9, a symphony that has long been written off as trivial. Without inflation Haitink

gives it a serious purpose, both in the poignancy of the waltz-like second movement and in the equivocal emotions of the outer movements, which here are not just superficially jolly, as so easily they can seem. The recording is outstandingly clean and brilliant, with the cassette matching the disc closely.

Symphony No. 4 in C min., Op. 43.
*** HMV ASD/TC-ASD 3440 [Ang. S 37284]. Chicago SO, Previn.
**(*) Decca SXL/KSXC 6927 [Lon. 7160]. LPO, Haitink.

From Previn an eminently straightforward, superlatively played and vividly recorded account of the problematic *Fourth Symphony*, whose publication Shostakovich withheld from 1936 to the early 1960s. Before Previn, Ormandy and Kondrashin had recorded this anguished score, but neither version can be said to match Previn's in terms of the sheer quality of the orchestral response (the Chicago orchestra is untroubled here by the problems of woodwind intonation that have occasionally beset them elsewhere) or the body and presence of the recording. This powerful and well-prepared performance is unlikely to be superseded for a very long time. The quality on tape has plenty of amplitude and warmth and certainly does not lack an edge of brilliance, although occasionally under pressure the clarity slips a little.

If the *Fourth Symphony* usually seems overweight in its scoring, with the vehement brutality explaining why it remained on the shelf for so long, Haitink brings out an unexpected refinement in the piece, a rare transparency of texture. He is helped by recording of demonstration quality on both disc and tape. Detail is superbly caught; yet the earthiness and power, the demonic quality which can make this work so compelling, are underplayed. One admires without being fully involved.

Symphony No. 5 in D min., Op. 47.
*** CBS 35854/*41*- [Col. M/*HMT*
35854]. NYPO, Bernstein.
(M) *** RCA Gold GL/*GK* 42690. LSO,
Previn.
(B) *** CfP CFP 40330. Bournemouth
SO, Berglund.
*(*) HMV ASD/*TC-ASD* 3443 [Ang. S/
4XS 37285]. Chicago SO, Previn.

Symphony No. 5; Festival overture,
Op. 96.
**(*) HMV ASD/*TC-ASD-* 3855.
USSR SO, Svetlanov.

Recorded in Tokyo in 1979, when
Bernstein and the New York Philharmonic were on tour there, the CBS
version is the weightiest on record,
partly because of the interpretation
but also because of the digital sound,
which is particularly rich in bass.
Unashamedly Bernstein treats the work
as a romantic symphony. The very
opening makes an impact rarely possible
in the concert hall, and then exceptionally
in the cool and beautiful second-subject
melody Bernstein takes a slightly
detached view, though as soon as that
same melody comes up for development
after the exposition, the result is
altogether more warmly expressive. Yet
the movement's central climax, with its
emphasis on the deep brass, injects a
powerful element of menace, and the
coda communicates a strongly Russian
melancholy, which is perhaps why the
composer admired Bernstein above other
American interpreters of his music. The
Allegretto becomes a burlesque, but its
Mahlerian roots are strongly conveyed.
The slow movement is raptly beautiful
(marvellously sustained pianissimo playing from the New York Philharmonic
strings), and the finale is brilliant and
extrovert, with the first part dazzlingly
fast and the conclusion one of unalloyed
triumph, with no hint of irony. The
chrome cassette is one of CBS's finest,
carrying all the brilliance and weight of
the disc.

Previn's RCA version with the LSO,
which dates from the mid-sixties, is an
altogether superlative account. The recording too was outstanding in all departments of the orchestra. The freshness
and vitality of the reading and the first-
class orchestral playing combine to produce a performance that is literal without
lacking spontaneity. The kind of radiance that the strings achieve at the opening of the great slow movement is totally
memorable; and throughout there is
great intensity and eloquence. The buoyancy of the scherzo and the élan of the
finale are highly exhilarating. Unfortunately the cassette transfer – although it
generally sounds well – has a compressed
dynamic range (the climax of the first
movement is very much less telling here
than on the disc).

Berglund's recording, reissued on
Classics for Pleasure, dates from as
recently as 1976, and the quality is
superb, full-bodied, rich and atmospheric. The performance, however,
seeks breadth and nobility rather than
extrovert excitement, and although it has
both atmosphere and eloquence some
will find Berglund's approach too sober.
However, it is splendidly played, and at
bargain price it still has considerable
appeal.

Svetlanov's reading with a Russian
orchestra has an earthy, thrustful quality
that makes it most compelling in such
passages as the climax of the first-movement development, with the trumpets
exaggerating the dotted rhythm of the
brazen march theme. The scherzo too has
a footstamping rustic quality about it,
but the obverse of this is that Svetlanov underplays the tenderness and
lyrical poetry of the work, though
happily the great long-legged melody of
the second subject in the first movement
in its understated way is most beautiful.
Apart from the forward woodwind balance, this is one of the best, most
wide-ranging recordings to come to us
on the Russian Melodiya label. The *Festi-*
val overture makes an enjoyable bonus.

The cassette matches the disc fairly closely.

Previn's second recording of the *Fifth*, made in Chicago, does not match his earlier RCA version in intensity. His view of the work does not appear to have changed greatly in the intervening years, and although the playing of the Chicago orchestra is of the highest quality, there is little sense of freshness and urgency. The first movement is a good deal slower than usual, so much so that one feels the want of momentum. The scherzo is impressively played, but the slow movement is without a sense of forward movement and the climax, so impressive in the earlier version, lacks real urgency. The recorded sound is extremely impressive, and the cassette transfer is vividly detailed, with plenty of range and impact.

Symphony No. 6 in B min., Op. 54; The Age of Gold: suite, Op. 22.
(M) *** RCA Gold GL/*GK* 42916. Chicago SO, Stokowski.

Stokowski made the first-ever recording of Shostakovich's *Sixth*, over forty years ago. His expressive moulding of the composer's long-breathed melodic lines is naturally spontaneous, and the powerful first movement makes a memorable impression. The control of tempo throughout is wholly convincing – flexible without being over-indulgent – and the finale has a fine rhythmic point and sparkle. The characterization of the *Age of Gold suite* is no less vivid, the *Adagio* richly expressive to contrast with the famous *Polka*, which has never sounded wittier. Excellent recording, atmospheric and with a wide dynamic range. There is no mistaking the Stokowskian upper string sheen. Though this is essentially a romantic view, finding little of the bitterness that underlies Berglund's reading, the underlying poignancy of feeling is not lost when expressed in this more optimistic way.

Symphonies Nos. (i) *6;* (ii) *9 in E flat, Op. 70.*
**(*) HMV ASD/*TC-ASD* 3706. (i) Leningrad SO, Temirkanov; (ii) USSR SO, Svetlanov.

The coupling of these two symphonies is unexpectedly illuminating, for No. 9 starts where No. 6 leaves off, in a mood of seeming flippancy, which, as we know now, concealed bitter irony. It is a pity that the parallel is not heightened here by having the same conductor for both. Temirkanov gives a strong, urgent performance, missing at a fastish tempo the inner tragedy of the first movement. With Svetlanov in the lighter-weight symphony (No. 9) the playing of the USSR Symphony Orchestra is not really delicate enough; this is music which should sparkle. But he gives real emotional weight to the darkly austere *Moderato* which takes the place of a slow movement. The Russian recordings are forward and bright but inclined to coarseness; the tape transfers are generally first-rate, vividly clear and wide-ranging.

Symphonies Nos. 6; 11 in G min. (1905), Op. 103.
*** HMV SLS 5177 (2). Bournemouth SO, Berglund.

Berglund gives new tragic depth to the *Sixth*, and with similar rugged concentration demonstrates the massive power of the *Eleventh*, a work which with its programme based on the abortive 1905 uprising in Russia usually seems far too thin in material. Shostakovich's pessimism in both works is underlined, with hardly a glimmer of hope allowed. In the *Sixth* the very measured tempo for the first movement, taken direct and with little *espressivo*, points the link with the comparable movement of the *Eighth Symphony*, and the remaining two movements are made ruthlessly bitter by not being sprung as dance movements, as is more usual. No Soviet optimism here.

In the *Eleventh* too, even more daringly, Berglund lets the music speak for itself, keeping the long opening *Adagio* at a very steady, slow tread, made compelling by the hushed concentration of the Bournemouth playing. Superlative recording. Berglund's art has never been more powerfully conveyed on record.

Symphony No. 7 in C (Leningrad), Op. 60; Age of Gold: suite, Op. 22.
*** Decca Dig. D 213 D 2/*K 213 K 22* (2) [Lon. LDR 10015/5-]. LPO, Haitink.

Symphony No. 7; (i) The Execution of Stepan Razin, Op. 119.
**(*) HMV SLS 5109 (2). Moscow PO, Kondrashin, (i) with Gromadsky, RSFSR Ch.

With his characteristic refinement and avoidance of bombast Haitink might not seem an apt conductor for the most publicized of Shostakovich's wartime symphonies, but in effect he transforms it, bringing out the nobility of many passages. One sees that the long first-movement *ostinato* – now revealed as having quite different implications from the descriptive programme suggested by the Soviet propaganda machine in the war years – is almost an interlude in a work which otherwise in its deep seriousness challenges comparison with the other wartime symphony, the epic *Eighth*. The recording is of demonstration quality, and the fill-up, the joky *Age of Gold suite*, provides comparable brilliance. The cassette transfer is equally sophisticated, though the focus of the thundering side-drums slips just a little in the first-movement climax.

Kondrashin conducts a strong, even volatile reading of the *Leningrad symphony*, lacking a little in refinement but helped by one of the brightest of Russian recordings. The power of the piece is never in doubt, and the big climaxes are superbly thrustful, but he tends to miss the very qualities of refinement and inner intensity which are so convincing in the

very different Haitink version on Decca. In the cantata on side four, which dates from Shostakovich's final period, a sardonic element is intermingled with the predictable patriotism; we can now appreciate that such works expressed more than approved Soviet emotions. The performance here is exciting and idiomatic.

Symphony No. 10 in E min., Op. 93.
*** DG Dig. 2532/*3302* 030 [id.]. Berlin PO, Karajan.
**(*) Decca SXL/*KSXC* 6838 [Lon. 7061/5-]. LPO, Haitink.
(M) (***) CBS mono 61457. NYPO, Mitropoulos.

Already in his 1967 recording Karajan had shown that he had the measure of this symphony, and this newer version is if anything even finer. In the first movement he distils an atmosphere as concentrated as before, bleak and unremitting, while in the *Allegro* the Berlin Philharmonic leave no doubts as to their peerless virtuosity. Everything is marvellously shaped and proportioned. The *allegro* section of the finale is taken up to speed (176 crotchets to the minute), faster than Mitropoulos and much faster than most other rivals. The digital sound is altogether excellent, and this must now rank as a first recommendation. It has greater intensity and grip than Haitink (the LPO's playing is not quite in the same league), and though Mitropoulos's pioneering account is still to be treasured, this 1982 Berlin version is marvellously powerful and gripping. The cassette too is of demonstration quality; it has splendid range, body and detail.

As a recording Haitink's Decca version is in the demonstration class. It has impressive body, range and definition: the balance is very natural, yet every detail of Shostakovich's score registers, and the climaxes are astonishingly lifelike. Haitink really has the measure of the first movement, whose climaxes he paces with an admirable sense of architecture, and he secures sensitive and enthusiastic playing from the LPO both here and in the scherzo. In the third movement he adopts a slower tempo than usual, which would be acceptable if there were greater tension or concentration of mood. But here and in the slow introduction to the finale the sense of concentration falters, though this must not be allowed to detract from the overall integrity and eloquence that Haitink largely achieves. The sound quality from the cassette is hardly less impressive than that of the disc.

Mitropoulos's 1954 recording was the first made of Shostakovich's *Tenth.* It has all the freshness of new discovery, and the playing has tremendous intensity and power. While some allowances have to be made for the CBS mono recording, the communication of the music-making is riveting from the first bar to the last.

Symphony No. 13 in B flat min. (*Babi Yar*), Op. 113.
*** HMV ASD/*TC-ASD* 3911 [Ang. SZ 37661]. Petkov, LSO Ch., LSO, Previn.

This troubled work, inspired by often angry poems of Yevtushenko, is presented here at its most stark and direct. More usually the mood-painting of the poems is underlined, but Previn takes a relatively literal view of the sprung rhythms in the ironic second movement, *Humour*, and makes the picture of peasant women queueing for food in the snow less atmospheric than it sometimes is. The result is that this becomes a genuine symphony, not just an orchestral song cycle. One might even relate the overall shape to that of the *Eighth Symphony*, starting with a bald slow movement punctuated by cliff-like dynamic contrasts and ending in wistfulness on a final *Allegretto*, *A Career*, with weaving flutes and gently lolloping pizzicato rhythms. Playing and recording are superb, among the very finest from this source. The cassette transfer is first-class, outstandingly clean and vivid.

Symphony No. 14, Op. 135.
*** Decca Dig. SXDL/*KSXDC* 7532. Varády, Fischer-Dieskau, Concg. O., Haitink.

The *Fourteenth* is Shostakovich's most sombre and dark score, a setting of poems by Lorca, Apollinaire, Rilke, Brentano and Küchelbecker, all on the theme of death. It is similar in conception (though not in character) to Britten's *Nocturne* or *Spring symphony*, and is in fact dedicated to him. Earlier recordings under Barshai, Ormandy and Rostropovich have all been in Russian, but this version gives each poem in the original. This is a most powerful performance under Haitink, and it is impressively recorded. All but the Barshai have now disappeared from circulation, but in any case this fine reading would displace earlier recommendations. The outstanding recording is equally impressive on disc and the excellent chrome tape.

Symphony No. 15 in A, Op. 141.
⊛*** Decca SXL/*KSXC* 6906 [Lon. 7130]. LPO, Haitink.

The second issue in Haitink's Shostakovich series brings a performance which is a revelation. Early readings of the composer's last symphony seemed to underline the quirky unpredictability of the work, with the collage of strange quotations – above all the *William Tell* galop, which keeps recurring in the first movement – seemingly joky rather than profound. Haitink by contrast makes the first movement sound genuinely symphonic, bitingly urgent. He underlines the purity of the bare lines of the second movement, and after the Wagner quotations which open the finale his slow tempo for the main lyrical theme gives it heartaching tenderness, not the usual easy triviality. The playing of the LPO is excellent, with refined tone and superb attack, and the recording is both analytical and atmospheric, as impressive on cassette as on disc. Although the textures are generally spare, the few heavy tuttis are difficult for the engineers, and Decca sound copes with them splendidly.

Piano quintet in G min., Op. 57.
(*) CRD CRD 1051/*CRDC 4051.* Benson, Alberni Qt – BRITTEN: *String quartet No. 1.*(*)

A vigorous and finely conceived account of the *Quintet* from Clifford Benson and the Alberni Quartet. On disc it is a good alternative to the version by the Melos Ensemble with Lamar Crowson on Oiseau-Lyre (SOL 267), coupled with the Prokofiev *Quintet*, but in the cassette field there is no current alternative. Moreover the cassette is transferred at the highest level and has striking range and presence: it is of demonstration standard.

String quartets Nos. 1–15.
⊛*** O-L D 188 D 7 (7). Fitzwilliam Qt.

Shostakovich concentrated on the symphony earlier in his career; the *First Quartet* was not written until 1938, a year after the *Fifth Symphony*, but into this medium he then poured some of his most private and inspired musical thinking. Here perhaps more than in the symphonies is the record of the real man. As is well known, the Fitzwilliam Quartet played to Shostakovich himself and gave the UK premières of his last three quartets, and they bring to the whole cycle complete and total dedication. They are splendid players and their accounts of these works have won wide acclaim and a number of awards, well deserved. They are given first-class recording too, with great presence and body; a rather forward balance is chosen but the results are wholly natural. There are minor criticisms, but they are too trivial to weigh in the balance, for this set is by any standards a formidable achievement.

String quartets Nos. 1 in C, Op. 49; 2 in A, Op. 68.
*** O-L DSLO 31 [id.]. Fitzwilliam Qt.

The *First Quartet* is a slight but charming work, fluent, sunny and lyrical. The *Second* is a wartime work, like the *Eighth Symphony* and the *Piano trio*, which immediately precede it. It is less appealing than its predecessor – understandably so – and less concentrated. The slow movement is problematic, and its recitative can easily seem to hang fire. The darker overtones of the waltz and the richness of the variation movement are well conveyed in this excellent performance. The recording has splendid presence and body.

String quartets Nos. 3, Op. 73; 11 in F min., Op. 112.
*** O-L DSLO 28 [id.]. Fitzwilliam Qt.

The *Third* is a five-movement work written in the immediate wake of the *Ninth Symphony* (also in five movements) and completed in 1946. It is a powerful piece whose central *Allegro* movement almost foreshadows the scherzo of the *Tenth Symphony*. The Fitzwilliam players give a searching and thoughtful performance, with sensible tempi and total commitment. The quartet is split over two sides and prefaced on side one with the relatively lightweight *Eleventh Quartet* of 1966, a seven-movement piece of little more than a quarter of an hour's duration. This too is given an elegant performance, which can well hold its own with the Borodin Quartet's version once coupled with Maxim Shostakovich's account of the *Fifteenth Symphony*.

String quartets Nos. 4 in D, Op. 83; 12 in D flat, Op. 133.
*** O-L DSLO 23 [id.]. Fitzwilliam Qt.

These quartets come from widely different periods in Shostakovich's career: the *Fourth* was composed in 1949 in the immediate wake of the Zhdanov affair; the *Twelfth* was written in the late 1960s, a year before the *Fourteenth Symphony*. The *Fourth* is the most recorded (and possibly the most immediately attractive) of all the quartets, apart from No. 1. It is a measure of the Fitzwilliam players' achievement that they compare very favourably with competition past and present, and their account of the *Twelfth Quartet* is very impressive indeed. They pay scrupulous attention to dynamics, their tone is finely blended, and their intonation is admirably secure. The *Twelfth* is a profound and searching piece, and this account of it is powerful, often haunting.

String quartets Nos. 5 in B flat, Op. 92; 6 in G, Op. 107.
*** O-L DSLO 29 [id.]. Fitzwilliam Qt.

Two quartets from a vintage period. The *Fifth*, arguably the finest of the whole cycle, was composed immediately before the *Tenth Symphony*, and like the symphony it makes use of the autobiographical motivic fingerprint (DSCH). Its three movements have an emotional intensity that leaves no doubt that it meant a great deal to Shostakovich – as it obviously does to these young players. The *Sixth*, which immediately pre-dates the *Eleventh Symphony*, is a sunny and delightful work, finely proportioned and beautifully fluent. The Fitzwilliam Quartet gives strong, powerfully wrought performances, recorded with splendid presence.

String quartets Nos. 9 in E flat, Op. 117; 10 in A flat, Op. 118.
*** O-L DSLO 30 [id.]. Fitzwilliam Qt.

The *Ninth* and *Tenth Quartets* both come from the same year (1964) and find Shostakovich at his most private and eloquent. The *Tenth*, in particular, is deeply powerful and intensely felt, and it ranks among the very finest of his works

after the *Tenth Symphony*. These young English players exhibit the same sense of commitment and musicianship that has distinguished their whole cycle. Both quartets are superb and the players obviously have them in their blood. The forward balance of the recording secures body and presence, but as a result it tends to sacrifice real *pianissimo* tone, which imposes on the players a need to project *pianissimi* rather more than in fact they do. But this is only a small reservation and in no way dampens enthusiasm for this issue.

3 Violin duets.
*** HMV ASD 3861 [Ang. SZ 37668]. Perlman, Zukerman – MOSZKOWSKI: *Suite*; PROKOFIEV: *Sonata*.***

The Shostakovich trifles are entertaining (there is a salon piece, a gavotte and some waltzes), all betraying some measure of wit. They are excellent make-weights in an unusually successful record, likely to be overlooked but deserving of every attention.

Preludes, Op. 34, Nos. 1, 4, 10, 12, 14–16, 19, 22, 24.
*** DG 2531/3301 096 [id.]. Berman (piano) – MUSSORGSKY: *Pictures*.***

A thoroughly worthwhile coupling for Mussorgsky's *Pictures at an Exhibition*. Berman obviously has great sympathy for these diverse miniatures, and his characterization is highly imaginative. The playing has more warmth than on some of Berman's other recordings; indeed it is very distinguished. The consistent element of spontaneity brings the music fully to life. The recording is splendid, and the cassette transfer is admirably balanced.

Ballad; King Lear: Song of the Fool; Preface to the Complete Collection of my Works, and Brief Reflections, Op.

123; 5 Romances on texts from 'Krokodil' magazine, Op. 121; 4 Verses of Captain Lebyadkin, Op. 146.
*** HMV ASD 3700. Nesterenko, Shenderovich – MUSSORGSKY: *Sunless.****

The very humour of Shostakovich's songs here makes a sharp contrast to the dark intensity of Mussorgsky on the reverse. Yevgeny Nesterenko with his glorious bass voice relishes the contrast, underlining the sardonic character of many of the items with fine feeling for detailed word-meaning. The recording is very good.

The Gamblers (unfinished opera).
*** HMV ASD 3880. Rybasenko, Byelykh, Tarkhov, Kurpe, Sarkisov, Radivonik, Leningrad PO, Rozhdestvensky.

'I didn't need a libretto: Gogol was the best librettist.' Shostakovich's determination to set the Gogol play with no amendment was laudable in principle, but in wartime, just after the *Leningrad symphony*, this was not the sort of opera welcomed by the Soviet authorities. In any case the very length involved may after a time have daunted the composer, even though he adopted a much simpler, more direct style than that of his earlier Gogol opera, *The Nose*. The first eight scenes are all that he completed, but those were sufficiently advanced to be performable. Rozhdestvensky directs a reading with total commitment, sharp-edged as this music must be, and the recording is one of the best from Russia.

Lady Macbeth of Mtsensk (opera; complete).
⊛*** HMV SLS 5157 (3) [Ang. SX 3866]. Vishnevskaya, Gedda, Krenn, Petkov, Meoz, Tear, Finnilä, Malta, Amb. Op. Ch., LPO, Rostropovich.

Rostropovich's recording proves with thrilling conviction that this first version of Shostakovich's greatest work for the stage is among the most original operas of the century. In text *Lady Macbeth* may not be radically different from the revised version, *Katerina Ismailova*, but it has an extra sharpness of focus that transforms what is much more than just a sordid love story involving three murders by the heroine. Here the brutality of the love affair between the rich merchant's wife and Sergei, the roving-eyed workman, has maximum punch, and Rostropovich, helped by superlative recording, gives a performance of breathtaking power. Vishnevskaya in her finest ever performance on record provides moments of great beauty alongside aptly coarser singing, and Gedda matches her well, totally idiomatic. As the sadistic father-in-law, Petkov is magnificent, particularly in his ghostly return, and there are fine contributions from Robert Tear, Werner Krenn, Birgit Finnilä and Alexander Malta.

Shukur, Salman
(20th century)

Ghazal (Romance); Húriyyat al-Jabal (The Mountain Fairy); Improvisations on a theme of Hajji' Abdul-Ghaffár from a takya in Tikrit; Mahraján fi Baghdád (Festival in Baghdad).
*** Decca HEAD 16. Composer.

Salman Shukur is an eminent exponent of the *oud*, the Arab lute, and a distinguished theoretician. He has made a special study of medieval Arab music and is professor of oud at Baghdad. His compositions go beyond the accepted conventions of the Arab classical maqam system; they incorporate various Western elements, but the hybrid that results does not seem in any way unconvincing. The oud is a quiet instrument, and this music, which is eloquently played and beautifully recorded, can be recommended for late-night listening.

Sibelius, Jean (1865–1957)

Violin concerto in D min., Op. 47.
*** HMV ASD/*TC-ASD* 3933 [Ang SZ/*4ZS* 37663]. Perlman, Pittsburgh SO, Previn – SINDING: *Suite.****
(M) **(*) Ph. Seq. 6527/*7311* 041 [Quin. 7150]. Szeryng, LSO, Rozhdestvensky – PROKOFIEV: *Concerto No. 2.****
(***) RCA Dig. RL 13972. Jenson, Phd. O., Ormandy (with SAINT-SAËNS: *Introduction and rondo capriccioso* (***)).

(i) *Violin concerto. Finlandia, Op. 26; Karelia suite, Op. 11.*
(B) ** CfP CFP/*TC-CFP* 40360. Hallé O., Schmidt, (i) with Sarbu.

Violin concerto; 6 Humoresques, Op. 87/1–2, Op. 89/1–4.
*** Ph. 9500 675/*7300 770* [id.]. Accardo, LSO, Colin Davis.

Violin concerto; 2 Serenades, Op. 69/1–2; 2 Serious melodies, Op. 77/1–2.
**(*) Decca SXL/*KSXC* 6953 [Lon. 7181]. Belkin, Philh. O., Ashkenazy.

Itzhak Perlman first recorded this concerto in the mid-1960s with Leinsdorf and the Boston Symphony for RCA. Here he plays the work as a full-blooded virtuoso showpiece, and the Pittsburgh orchestra under André Previn support him to the last man. In the first movement his tempo is broader than that of Heifetz (on RCA), and in the rest of the work he seems more expansive than he was in the earlier record (the new version takes 32'00" and spills over to the second side, whereas his Boston performance took

29'15" and fitted on one side). He is at his stunning best in the first cadenza and makes light of all the fiendish difficulties in which the solo part abounds. The balance places Perlman rather forward, but on both disc and cassette the sound is marvellously alive and thrilling. He takes a conventional view of the slow movement, underlining its passion (unlike Accardo, who is more inward-looking), and gives us an exhilarating finale.

Salvatore Accardo brings a different perspective to bear on the whole work; the world of feeling he evokes is purer, its colours gentler and more subtle. His is a more broadly proportioned reading, though one never feels that tempi are too measured or that there is any want of momentum. Yet he conveys a greater sense of space and brings to the slow movement a quite special stillness and poetry, particularly in the closing bars. Sir Colin Davis fashions this movement in what seems to be complete harmony of spirit with his distinguished soloist, and the brass produce exactly the right kind of power and sonority. The finale is played with effortless brilliance by all concerned. On disc the recording is beautifully natural; the high-level tape transfer, however, is less refined on top, especially in the orchestral tuttis. Accardo also gives us the *Six Humoresques*, Opp. 87 and 89, and brings to them a fine sense of atmosphere and rapture. His readings have the full measure of their dreamy rhapsodizing and the 'white nights' and haunting landscape of the northern summer.

Boris Belkin is a powerful and sensitive player and brings a fiery temperament to the concerto. There are moments of exaggeration that might prove irritating, and although his playing has a Slavonic ardour and flamboyance, a boldness of attack and a spontaneity that are appealing, there are infelicities that do not improve on repetition: an ugly scoop at fig. 1 in the finale, and some less than true intonation in the sixths just after fig. 10 in the first movement. He inspires warm support from the Philharmonia under Vladimir Ashkenazy, and is very well recorded on disc and tape alike. But he resorts to an expressive distortion at the very beginning (playing *pp* instead of the *mf* marked) in aspiring to a rapt, other-worldly quality, then he suddenly exaggerates the earthiness of the G-string writing a couple of dozen bars later. However, the appeal of this issue is enhanced by the fill-ups, which are rarities: the *Two Serenades*, written just before the 1914–18 war, and the *Two Serious melodies*, Op. 77. These are marvellous works and are beautifully played here, with none of the zigeunerisms that mark the finale of the concerto. The two *Serenades* have been recorded by Ida Haendel, but the Op. 77 pieces are not otherwise available. The concerto, however, is not really as good as Kyung-Wha Chung's immaculate reading, as poetic as it is brilliant and thoroughly idiomatic. Moreover Miss Chung's coupling is an equally outstanding version of the Tchaikovsky concerto (Decca SXL/ KSXC 6493 [Lon. 6710].

From Szeryng, a spacious reading full of imaginative touches. Szeryng plays beautifully throughout and one's only quarrel is with his rather too measured tempo for the finale. Tovey spoke of this as 'a polonaise for polar bears', but it can hardly be said to suggest this here. Rozhdestvensky is a true Sibelian (if only someone would ask him to record a complete cycle), and the LSO play well for him. The recording has the usual Philips characteristics, a concert-hall balance, and a warm acoustic; in short it is excellent. The cassette too is one of Philips' best, with plenty of body and warmth and no constriction in the upper range. If the coupling is suitable this is a most competitive mid-priced version.

Dylana Jenson is a young American violinist, born in 1961, who has the full measure of this concerto. She hardly puts a foot wrong anywhere and her account has all the sense of space, nobility and warmth that one could want. The vir-

tuosity she commands seems quite effortless and is completely at the service of the music. Her tone is fine-spun and vibrant, and she communicates the sense of atmosphere and mystery in the opening to splendid effect. Alas, the sound on the recording lets her down. There is little top and transparency, and the bass is distinctly woolly. It is difficult to believe that this represents digital sound, since it has far less presence and clarity than the Accardo, Perlman, Haendel, Sarbu and other versions.

Eugene Sarbu is a young Rumanian, now in his early thirties, who is making quite a name. His vibrato is a little wide and intonation is not always impeccable, though he has plenty of dash and power. He makes the most of every expressive point and underlines romantic fervour rather than spirituality. His is a zigeunerlike approach without the purity and refinement of tone which are ideal – and which emerge in such performers as Kyung-Wha Chung and Accardo. There is a nobility in this music that Sarbu does not always convey. But he is well supported by the Hallé, who give Ole Schmidt sensitive and responsive playing, and they are heard to excellent effect in the *Karelia* and *Finlandia* makeweights. The recording is first-class, and the disc and cassette are closely matched (although in *Finlandia* and *Karelia* the percussion transients are less sharp on tape than on LP). Sarbu is a formidable artist, and at CfP price this vibrant collection is excellent value.

(i) *Violin concerto. Finlandia, Op. 26. Kuolema: Valse triste, Op. 44. Legend: The Swan of Tuonela, Op. 22/2. Symphonies Nos. 4–7. Tapiola, Op. 112.*

(B) *** DG 2740 255 (4). Berlin PO, Karajan, (i) with Ferras.

This box offers all the Sibelius recordings made by Karajan with the Berlin Philharmonic in the mid-1960s – at bargain price, so that there is a gain in purchasing them together rather than separately. An additional attraction is the Ferras account of the *Violin concerto* here coupled with the powerful version of *Tapiola* – originally this appeared with the *Fifth Symphony*. The strengths of the other performances are discussed below under the symphonies, but briefly the *Fourth*, *Fifth* and *Sixth* are among the very best performances on record, and the same goes for *Tapiola*. An outstanding bargain.

Finlandia; Kuolema: Valse triste; Legend: The Swan of Tuonela.
(M) *** DG Priv. 2535/3335 635 [id.]. Berlin PO, Karajan – GRIEG: *Peer Gynt* etc.*
(M) ** CBS 60105/40- [Col. MY 36718]. NYPO, Bernstein – GRIEG: *Peer Gynt*.**

It is curious that instead of reissuing Karajan's vintage collection of Sibelius's short orchestral pieces, three only should here have been coupled with some much earlier Grieg recordings under other conductors, where the sound is rather thin and uninviting. The Sibelius items sound very well on both disc and cassette.
Bernstein's account of *Finlandia* is brilliant and exciting, but the recording sounds rather brash. *The Swan of Tuonela*, however, is beautifully played, with finesse as well as a fine sense of brooding atmosphere, and the recording here is quite spacious.

Finlandia; Legend: The Swan of Tuonela; En Saga, Op. 9; Tapiola.
*** HMV ASD/TC-ASD 3374 [Ang. S/ 4XS 37408]. Berlin PO, Karajan.

This almost duplicates Karajan's earlier DG Sibelius anthology, except that *En Saga* replaces *Valse triste*. This is Karajan's third recording of *Tapiola* but his first of *En Saga*, where he is a brisk story-teller, more concerned with narrative than atmosphere at the beginning;

but the *lento assai* section and the coda are quite magical. *Finlandia* is superbly played and most realistically recorded. The *Tapiola* is broader and more expansive than the DG version, and at the storm section beginning at bar 513 the more spacious tempo is vindicated. The effect is altogether electrifying. The newer HMV recording is more forward and possesses great body and presence, so much so that some listeners may prefer the slightly more recessed yet atmospheric sound in the DG version. In any event both are great performances and totally committed. There is an ugly blemish in bar 598, where some of the cellos play D sharp and others D natural. This should have been corrected. The cassette produces impressive results and has ample body and firmness.

Karelia: suite, Op. 11; Kuolema: Valse triste, Op. 44; Pohjola's Daughter, Op. 49; En Saga, Op. 9.
** Ph. 9500/7300 893 [id.]. Boston SO, Colin Davis.

Beautifully refined and imaginative performances from the Boston orchestra, with a particularly distinguished account of *Pohjola's Daughter*; indeed, the latter ranks with the very finest performances ever recorded, though it is different from Koussevitzky's or Bernstein's. Sir Colin's maiden has real allure, Väinämöinen's struggles with his various tasks have never been more heroic. Unfortunately, the recording is (by Philips' standards) relatively wanting in clarity and detail. Put Ashkenazy's *En Saga* alongside Sir Colin's, and one removes a gauze veil – and brightens the picture. A pity, for artistically this is first-rate.

4 Legends, Op. 22 (Lemminkäinen and the Maidens of Saari; The Swan of Tuonela; Lemminkäinen in Tuonela; Lemminkäinen's Return).
*** HMV ASD/TC-ASD 3644 [Ang. S/ 4XS 37537]. Phd. O., Ormandy.

707

** Decca SXL 6973. SRO, Stein.

Ormandy's version must now be the first recommendation for the *Four Legends*. It offers an extremely fine recording that comes near to doing justice to the Philadelphia sound (though it is not so spectacularly successful as the *Pictures at an Exhibition* recording with Muti). In the first of the *Legends*, the wind are more closely observed than is ideal, and the sound would benefit from greater depth. Ormandy's account of the first *Legend* is not as spacious as Jensen's pioneering disc, but it is marvellously passionate. (These Maidens of Saari must have given Lemminkäinen quite a wild time!) Ormandy's *Swan of Tuonela* is among the very finest, full of atmosphere and poetry, and the third *Legend* is brooding and menacing. In *Lemminkäinen's Return*, he comes close to the famous headlong excitement generated in Beecham's old 78 set. The tape transfer is slightly sharper in detail than the LP and rather less rich in the middle range; but the difference is not great.

Horst Stein gives a far from unimpressive account of the *Four Legends* with a hell-for-leather performance of *Lemminkäinen's Return*. The recording, too, is absolutely first-class, having splendid clarity, body and definition. But, good though the playing of the Suisse Romande Orchestra is, it would be idle to pretend that it is in the highest flight – it is not as good here as in the coupling of *The Tempest* and *Pelléas* (see below). The strings are simply not as rich as those of the Philadelphia, and their want of tonal finesse tells in the magical middle section of *Lemminkäinen in Tuonela*, and again in the closing bars, where dynamic markings are far more scrupulously observed by Ormandy. There are good things nevertheless, in particular a well-shaped and often exciting account of the first *Legend*.

Pelléas et Mélisande (incidental music), *Op. 46*.

(*) Ph. 6769 045 (2) [id.]. Rotterdam PO, Zinman – FAURÉ: *Pelléas* *; SCHOENBERG: *Pelleas*.**(*)

The complete score is included here (including *At the seashore*) and the orchestral playing is of high quality. Zinman is undoubtedly sympathetic, but the music is just a shade under-characterized. Nevertheless the couplings are pertinent (although not all lovers of Fauré and Sibelius are likely to respond to Schoenberg) and this is quite an attractive package.

Pelléas et Mélisande, Op. 46; The Tempest (incidental music): *Prelude; Suite No. 1.*
*** Decca SXL 6912. SRO, Stein.

This record finds the Suisse Romande Orchestra in far better shape than it was in the late 1960s and early 1970s. Horst Stein secures a fine woodwind blend and a more firmly based and richer string sonority. Intonation may not be as impeccable as in the Concertgebouw – or our own Philharmonia – but it is very good. In *Pelléas et Mélisande* Horst Stein secures splendid results and (like Berglund, in his now deleted version, and Zinman) he includes *At the seashore*, intended to be played at the end of Act I and leading directly into *By the spring in the park*, which opens Act II. This is atmospheric, though without the magic of Beecham. *The Tempest* is impressive too, though we only get the *Prelude* and the *First Suite*. However, there is plenty of atmosphere, and even if the *Oaktree* is taken on the fast side, everything else is splendidly judged. The recording is of demonstration standard.

Symphonies Nos. 1–7.
(B) **(*) Decca Jub. JBB 506/9/*K 3 E 9*. VPO, Maazel.

Symphonies Nos. 1–7; The Bard, Op. 64; En Saga, Op. 9; Scènes historiques, Op. 25; (i) *Kullervo, Op. 7.*

** HMV SLS/*TC-SLS* 5129 (7). Bournemouth SO, Berglund, (i) with Kostia, Viitanen, Helsinki University Ch.

Symphonies Nos. 1–7; Finlandia; Legend: The Swan of Tuonela; Tapiola.
*** Ph. 6709 011 (5) [id.]. Boston SO, Colin Davis.

The Davis set is impressive and arguably the finest of the collected editions – though Karajan's new cycle, which has yet to appear, will probably be a strong competitor. These versions of the *Third, Fourth* and *Sixth* are among the best – if not *the* best – before the public, and the remaining symphonies are all finely played and in general given excellent sound. Davis's feeling for Sibelius is usually matched by the orchestral response. Whatever individual reservations there may be, this is a cycle to be reckoned with, and the performances are more consistently vital and powerful than those of Berglund and even Maazel.

Maazel's set from the 1960s is now at bargain price and still sounds astonishingly good. The sound is brighter and warmer than in some of the Boston records of Sir Colin Davis. The strengths of the set are the *First, Fourth* and *Seventh*; less impressive are the *Third* and *Fifth*, though there are some powerful things in them. The only performance that seems to miss the point is that of the *Sixth*. Even so, at the price this represents very good value. The cassette transfers, however, are disappointing, well below Decca's usual high standard; the climaxes produce fierceness and tonal unsteadiness. The layout too is extremely clumsy, with several of the symphonies commencing mid-side. Readers are advised to stick to the records.

Berglund's is the only boxed set to include Sibelius's very first symphonic venture, *Kullervo*. This is an impressive five-movement piece on a Mahlerian scale: it precedes *En Saga* and contains

some vividly imaginative choral writing. As for the symphonies themselves, the performances have their merits, but in almost every instance one can do better elsewhere. As recordings it would be difficult to improve on this set, and the orchestral playing is of high quality too. But judged by the highest standards, these conscientious and well-prepared versions remain just a shade too literal and earthbound to be recommended without qualification. The cassette transfers are clear and vivid. There is less warmth and richness of string timbre than on disc, and sometimes the upper range lacks something in bloom, but the choral focus in *Kullervo* is first-class, even clearer than on the LP version.

Symphony No. 1 in E min., Op. 39: The Bard, Op. 64.
(M) **(*) DG Priv. 2535/*3335* 457. Helsinki RO, Kamu.

Symphony No. 1; Karelia suite, Op. 11.
(M) *** Decca Jub. JB/*KJBC* 42. VPO, Maazel.

Symphony No. 1; Legend: The Swan of Tuonela, Op. 22/2.
*(*) RCA RL/*RK* 25316. LPO, Tieknavorian.

Maazel's version of the *First Symphony* leads the field. It has freshness of vision to commend it, along with careful attention both to the letter and to the spirit of the score. The Vienna Philharmonic responds with enthusiasm and brilliance, and the Decca engineers produce splendid detail. The performance of the *Karelia suite* is first-rate. The cassette transfer is fairly sophisticated, but it seems not to have been remastered for its Jubilee reissue, and although the quality is full-blooded it lacks the crispness of detail of the others in this series.

Okko Kamu and the Helsinki orchestra give a spacious account of the symphony, with a particularly impressive finale. The orchestral playing is good, and DG's recording has fine amplitude and richness on disc and tape alike. This is less distinctive than Maazel's version, but the fill-up is an exceptionally fine account of *The Bard*, which is given a beautifully atmospheric recording.

Loris Tjeknavorian's version with the LPO is decently played and recorded, but in such a strongly competitive field it needs to have special claims. It is free from any idiosyncratic touches: there are no mannerisms or interpretative indulgences. The playing is accurate – woodwind intonation is not absolutely perfect in the scherzo, but there is no need to exaggerate this. Ultimately the performance just lacks real distinction and personality. The cassette transfer, made at a low level, tends to lack range and detail.

Symphonies Nos. 1; 7 in C, Op. 105.
(M) **(*) HMV Green. ESD/*TC-ESD* 7095 [No. 1 (d) Sera. S 60289]. Bournemouth SO, Berglund.

This medium-priced reissue is exceptionally generous, and the full sides have not impaired the splendidly vivid and realistic sound quality. The high-level cassette transfer also offers an impressively rich and well-detailed orchestral tapestry. Berglund's approach, rugged and steady, misses the last degree of intensity, but not the underlying nobility of Sibelius's inspiration. In the *Seventh* Berglund corrects a number of small mistakes that have crept into the Hansen score, mostly dynamic and expressive indications affecting tonal balance. As a result his performance is smoother in contour, and the warm, spacious acoustic serves to Latinize this starkest and most powerful of Sibelius's symphonies.

Symphony No. 2 in D, Op. 43.
*** HMV Dig. ASD/*TC-ASD* 4060 [Ang. DS/*4ZS* 37816]. Berlin PO, Karajan.

**(*) Decca Dig. SXDL/*KSXDC* 7513 [Lon. LDR 10014/5-]. Philh. O., Ashkenazy.

(M) *** Decca Jub. JB/*KJBC* 43. VPO, Maazel.

(M) *** HMV SXLP/*TC-SXLP* 30414. Philh. O., Karajan.

(M) **(*) DG Priv. 2535/*3335* 458. Berlin PO, Kamu.

(M) ** RCA Gold GL/*GK* 42868 [AGL 1/*AGK 1* 3785]. Phd. O., Ormandy.

** HMV ASD/*TC-ASD* 3497. Bournemouth SO, Berglund.

*(*) HMV ASD/*TC-ASD* 3414 [Ang. S/*4XS* 37444]. Pittsburgh SO, Previn.

(i) *Symphony No. 2;* (ii) *Finlandia, Op. 26.*
(M) *** Ph. Seq. 6527/*7311* 111 [(d) 6570/*7310* 054]. Concg. O., (i) Szell, (ii) Beinum.

The *Second Symphony* is exceptionally well represented on records, but the choice for a single version is essentially subjective. Not all listeners will warm to the grand (and measured) approach to the finale in Karajan's newest digital recording; Ashkenazy's performance also provokes a mixed response (as will be seen below), while Maazel's splendidly recorded Jubilee version will appeal to some more than others for its sumptuous Tchaikovskian romanticism.

Karajan's 1981 version with the Berlin Philharmonic is more spacious than his earlier reading with the Philharmonia. Tempi in all four movements are fractionally broader; nevertheless, the first movement is still a genuine *Allegretto* – much faster than with Maazel, Barbirolli or Ashkenazy – and basically in the brisker tradition of Kajanus, whose pioneering 1930 records were probably closer to Sibelius's intentions than most others. Throughout all four movements there is splendour and nobility here – and some glorious sounds from the Berlin strings and brass. The oboe theme in the trio section of the scherzo is most expressively moulded, and the finale is slower and grander than its rivals, though there is no loss of lyrical fervour. It is not as beautifully recorded as the Ashkenazy/Philharmonia account on Decca, but it is undoubtedly a performance of stature – and probably the finest of the full-price issues currently before the public. The chrome cassette transfer is faithful and wide-ranging but tends to emphasize the slightly lean orchestral textures, for the upper strings are given less amplitude and richness by EMI than on either of the Decca recordings.

We are divided in our response to the Ashkenazy version. There are no doubts about the quality of the recorded sound, which is superb. It is atmospheric, beautifully rounded in tone, and has splendid clarity, definition and depth. As for the performance, it is a passionate, volatile reading, in many ways a very Russian view of Sibelius, with Ashkenazy finding a clear affinity with the Tchaikovsky symphonies. At the very opening the quick, flexible treatment of the repeated crotchet motif is urgent, not weighty or ominous as it can be. Ashkenazy's control of tension and atmosphere makes for the illusion of live performance in the building of each climax, and the rich digital sound (recorded in the ideal acoustic of the Kingsway Hall) adds powerfully to that impression. Yet some listeners may find it more difficult to respond positively to this reading, and, like R.L., they may feel the performance is wanting in firmness of grip, especially in the slow movement, with the dramatic pauses lacking spontaneity and unanimity of response. The cassette matches the disc in richness and bloom, but the biggest climaxes seem marginally less expansive on tape.

Maazel's account is more traditionally lush: it is sumptuously recorded and beautifully played by the Vienna Philharmonic, but his reading leans more to the romantic view of the work favoured by some virtuoso conductors. The Tchaikovskian inheritance is stressed, rather than the classical forebears. The cassette transfer of this performance offers Decca's very best quality, and at medium price this issue is very competitive.

In its latest incarnation Szell's performance comes with a fill-up in the shape of *Finlandia*, excellently played by the Concertgebouw under Eduard van Beinum and recorded in the late 1950s. Szell's account of the *Second* still impresses by its tautness and grasp of architecture, though there is no want of feeling. It ranks among the best mid-price versions. It is not as richly recorded as Maazel's Jubilee version, but the quality is full and lively and makes an excellent impact. Barbirolli's marvellously alive RCA mid-price record with the RPO should also be considered (GL 25011 [Quin. 7008]); its spontaneity and vitality have all the qualities of a live concert performance, and the recorded sound has both immediacy and presence.

Karajan's Philharmonia recording dates from 1960 and shows him very much at his best. It has dramatic intensity, a feeling for line and texture, and a grasp of the architecture. It is not in the least self-indulgent or excessively Italianate, and perhaps lacks the last ounce of spontaneity that marks the Barbirolli version. Yet it is freer, more expressively eloquent than Szell's version with the Concertgebouw. It goes without saying that it is extremely well played, indeed superbly played, and the sound quality is remarkably vivid, rich and sonorous. The tape transfer too is first-rate; the sound is slightly dry in the bass, but with excellent detail and striking impact.

Okko Kamu secures highly polished and superbly refined playing from the Berlin Philharmonic; he indulges in some impulsive touches – the odd attention-seeking speed-up or slow-down – but these are not destructive. The recording here is first-class, both on disc and on cassette, bringing out the spacious sweep of the finale to great effect.

Ormandy's version first appeared in quadraphonic form. Reissued at medium price in ordinary stereo, it still makes a considerable impact and is marvellously played. However, the reading rarely sheds new light on this wonderful score. The overall impression is of a superbly disciplined response from the Philadelphians, well recorded, but wanting that extra degree of freshness and character to justify the exposure that repeated hearing will give it. The cassette generally sounds well but there is a degree of coarsening at the climax of the finale (in spite of the relatively modest level of the transfer).

Berglund's is essentially a broad view. The lack of urgency is immediately felt at the opening of the first movement, and while the scherzo has plenty of impetus, and the finale provides a satisfyingly broad culmination, the tension is slackly held in the slow movement. Overall the lack of dynamism must be counted a drawback in a symphony which is justly famous for engendering a high level of excitement. The recording is rich and spacious, and the tape transfer is of first-class quality, virtually indistinguishable from the disc.

Previn's version too is very well recorded, but unfortunately the quality of the orchestral playing is not comparable with that of the finest international orchestras, and while Previn eschews any egocentric interpretative gestures, his performance is not wholly free from the charge of under-characterization. Put bluntly, this has less personality and conviction than its rivals.

Symphony No. 3 in C, Op. 52; En Saga, Op. 9.
(M) *** DG Priv. 2535/*3335* 459. Helsinki RO, Kamu.

Among modern accounts of the *Third Symphony*, Kamu's has strong claims to be considered among the finest. Tempi are well judged and the atmosphere is thoroughly authentic, particularly in the slow movement, whose character seems to have eluded so many distinguished conductors since Kajanus's pioneering account with the LSO, fortunately available once again on World Records (SH 173/4). The recording is excellent and most musically balanced. Readers requiring this bracing and rewarding symphony should turn to this in preference to Maazel. The performance of *En Saga* is also admirable and justifies Kamu's growing reputation. Like the disc, the cassette sounds resonantly spacious and full; *En Saga* approaches demonstration quality.

Symphonies Nos. 3; 5 in E flat, Op. 82.
(M) *** HMV Green. ESD/*TC-ESD* 7094. Bournemouth SO, Berglund.

Berglund's is a generous coupling, the more attractive at medium price. The *Fifth Symphony* is given a rugged, lustily exuberant performance, lacking a little in atmosphere and bite, with the slow movement a shade heavy, but with a superb build-up to the blazing coda of the finale. The *Third* emerges even more than usual as Sibelius's *Pastoral*, springy and genial in the first movement, freshly rustic in the slow movement, joyful and easy-going in the finale. The recording is remarkably opulent considering the length of sides. The cassette too, transferred at a high level, matches richness and body with excellent range and detail; moreover the brass has striking presence.

Symphonies Nos. 3; 6 in D min., Op. 104.
(M) *(**) Decca Jub. JB/*KJBC* 44. VPO, Maazel.

In the *Third Symphony* Maazel keeps a firm grip on the proceedings. He moulds phrases naturally and without affectation, and his build-up in the finale is most impressive. The slow movement is not quite poetic or reflective enough; he has little success in achieving the tranquillity and rapture (at fig. 6) that made Kajanus's set such a memorable experience. The *Sixth* is much less successful than the *Third*; Maazel does not penetrate beneath the surface and seems to have little sympathy for this most elusive and refined of Sibelius's scores. It is a pity that this issue is only partly successful; on disc the recording is first-class, and apart from a short passage where the timpani cause a little muddle in the climax of the first movement of No. 3, the cassette transfer is sophisticated.

Symphonies Nos. 3; 7 in C, Op. 105.
** HMV ASD 3671. Moscow RSO, Rozhdestvensky.

Gennady Rozhdestvensky is an *echt*-Sibelian and his performance of the *Third Symphony* is as finely paced as Sir Colin Davis's or Okko Kamu's. Only in the slow movement is he a shade brisker than they, but there is no lack of power or poetic feeling. His earlier version of the *Seventh Symphony*, made in the days of mono, was impaired by a ruinous trombone vibrato, and though things are better in this new version, made in 1975, the Soviet trombonist is still sufficiently wanting in nobility to rob the reading of its full majesty. Rozhdestvensky's conception is superb, but the Moscow Radio Orchestra is not in the same class as the finest of its competitors. Nor, to be frank, is the Soviet recording.

Symphony No. 4 in A min; Op. 63; Finlandia, Op. 26. (i) *Luonnotar, Op. 70.*
*** Decca Dig. SXDL/*KSXDC* 7517 [Lon. LDR 71019/5-]. Philh. O., Ashkenazy, (i) with Söderström.

Ashkenazy achieves great concentration of feeling in the *Fourth*. The brightness of the Philharmonia violins and the cleanness of attack add to the impact of this baldest of the Sibelius symphonies, and Ashkenazy's terracing of dynamic contrasts is superbly caught in the outstanding digital recording. Like his other Sibelius readings this one has something of a dark Russian passion in it, but freshness always dominates over mere sensuousness, and as ever Ashkenazy conveys the spontaneity of live performance. There is splendid drama and intensity throughout, and though some might feel that the spiritual landscape of the slow movement is more completely in focus in Sir Colin Davis's version (Philips 9500 143/*7300 520*) this is still a very impressive performance. The couplings add to the special attractions of this issue; *Finlandia* is made fresh again in a performance of passion and precision, and Elisabeth Söderström is on top form in *Luonnotar*, a symphonic poem with a voice (although some ears may find her wide vibrato and hard-edged tone not entirely sympathetic). The cassette offers impressively rich sound but has slightly less range at the top: the transients in *Finlandia* are less telling.

Symphony No. 4; Legend: The Swan of Tuonela, Op. 22/2.
(M) *** DG Acc. 2542/*3342* 128 [2535/ *3335* 359]. Berlin PO, Karajan.

Karajan's Berlin account from 1965 gains in stature with every hearing. This music offers no false consolation, and like many great works of art has a serious, forbidding exterior that dispenses with any gesture towards the listener. No performance surpasses this in splendour of orchestral sound and magnificence of colour. At first, one feels that its very opulence is not a useful tool in uncovering the secrets of this strange world; instead of the well-modulated, rich tone of the Berlin strings one longs for the cold, disembodied sound that Beecham evoked in his famous performance in the 1930s. But over the years, this reading haunts one – and it is to the Karajan that one turns for certain qualities: perhaps most of all the intensity with which he feels this music. It still sounds superb and the scherzo comes off more successfully than in the later HMV version. The tape transfer is made at a high level, and the richness and body of the orchestral texture are matched by the overall clarity. This is first-class.

Symphony No. 4; Tapiola, Op. 112.
(M) *** Decca Jub. JB/*KJBC* 45. VPO, Maazel.
**(*) HMV ASD/*TC-ASD* 3485 [Ang. S 37462]. Berlin PO, Karajan.

The *Fourth* is the most impressive of Maazel's Sibelius cycle. The orchestral tone is less richly upholstered than that of the Berlin Philharmonic in Karajan's HMV account, and Maazel brings to the music great concentration and power: the first movement is as cold and unremitting as one could wish, and throughout the work Maazel comes as close to the atmosphere and mystery of this music as almost anyone since Beecham. Apart from the slow movement, which could be a little more poetic, and one or two small points, there are no real reservations to be made. The recording here is superbly opulent and vivid. Maazel also gives a most impressive account of *Tapiola*. It is not so atmospheric as Karajan's at the outset, but it grows in power and impact as it proceeds. Maazel takes the famous storm section very slowly, and it gains immeasurably from this. But Sir Colin Davis's Boston account is superior to Maazel's in terms of sheer mystery and power, although the storm section is not as effectively done. The cassette transfer of Maazel's performances is of Decca's highest quality, with the most refined detail, the orchestral sound given splendid weight and atmosphere.

In some ways Karajan's re-recording of the *Fourth Symphony* for HMV must be counted controversial. He gives broadly spacious – and highly atmospheric – accounts of the first and third movements, a good deal slower than in his earlier DG version (see above). He conveys eloquently the other-worldly quality of the landscape in the third movement, even if in atmosphere the Davis account is more natural and intense. The first movement undoubtedly has great mystery and power. The recording is superb and the tape transfer is highly successful (one of HMV's best cassettes). Karajan's *Tapiola*, which is discussed above under its alternative coupling with *Finlandia* (ASD/*TC-ASD* 3374), is hardly less impressive, despite the error in bar 598.

Symphony No. 5 in E flat, Op. 82; Finlandia, Op. 26; Kuolema: Valse triste.
(M) *** DG Acc. 2542/*3342* 109. Berlin PO, Karajan.

Symphony No. 5; Night-ride and Sunrise, Op. 55.
*** HMV Dig. ASD/*TCC-ASD* 4168. Philh. O., Rattle.

Symphony No. 5; En Saga, Op. 9.
*** HMV ASD/*TC-ASD* 3409 [Ang. S/ 4XS 37490]. Berlin PO, Karajan.
*** Decca Dig. SXDL/*KSXDC* 7541. Philh. O., Ashkenazy.

Although the current catalogues list fifteen or so different versions of the *Fifth Symphony*, Simon Rattle's account has strong claims to be considered among the very finest. He secures a more refined response from the Philharmonia than does Ashkenazy, and he is every bit as well recorded. His tempo for the first movement is broad – not dissimilar in breadth to Karajan's 1978 HMV version, though he does not follow Karajan in making so rapid a transition to the scherzo or adopting so extreme a tempo. Indeed, the most remarkable thing about this performance is its control of the transition between the two sections, which is beautifully judged. There is a wonderful sense of mystery and power in the development section and in the slow movement, and detail is beautifully placed – the dynamic markings being scrupulously observed. Perhaps Rattle lacks the sense of excitement that Bernstein achieves in the first and last movements, but there is a splendour and vision that are most impressive. This is the finest record of the *Fifth* to appear since Karajan's 1965 Berlin version, and the digital recording is superb. The fill-up is generous – a Sibelius rarity, *Nightride and Sunrise*, which may not have the stature of the other performance, but is still thoroughly idiomatic. The tape sound is rather soft-grained.

Karajan's DG version of the Sibelius *Fifth* is a great performance. We have tended to underrate it in the past, but the 1965 recording sounds even fresher and more vivid in this new Accolade transfer. The orchestral playing throughout is glorious, and the effect is spacious and atmospheric. Karajan finds an engrossing sense of mystery in the development section of the first movement, and there is jubilation in the finale. Karajan has now recorded this symphony four times (1952, 1960, 1965, 1978), but this third version strikes us as the most successful all round, though there are many impressive qualities in the others. At medium price and with a superb *Finlandia* and *Valse triste*, this is quite a bargain. The sound on cassette too is admirably full and clear.

The first movement of the symphony is broader and more spacious in Karajan's HMV version, and he achieves a remarkable sense of its power and majesty. His transition from the work's first section to the 'scherzo' is slightly more abrupt than in the 1965 recording, and the tempi generally in the work's first half are rather more extreme. The variety of tone-colour and above all the weight of sonority that the Berlin Philharmonic have at their command are astonishing, and the bassoon lament in the development section finds the Berlin strings reduced to the merest whisper. Both the slow movement and finale are glorious

and have real vision, and the recording is excellent (as indeed it is in the 1965 DG version too). Some Sibelians are worried by the richness and sensuousness that Karajan brings to this score, but the sheer power and depth of this reading should convince. The performance of *En Saga*, which is discussed above under its alternative coupling with *Finlandia*, is no less compelling. The transfer to tape offers satisfyingly rich orchestral sound; although the detail of climaxes lacks the last degree of definition, the refinement does not slip.

Ashkenazy's performance is outstandingly well recorded, with fine, spacious and well-detailed digital sound. His reading is a thoroughly idiomatic one and falls short only in terms of the balance of tempi between the two sections of the first movement. This is a fine rather than a great performance. Ashkenazy's *En Saga* is the best version of that work now in the catalogue, and so, when one considers also the outstanding excellence of the recording, this issue will obviously have strong appeal. The chrome cassette is also very impressive, although in *En Saga* the bass is not so cleanly focused as on the disc.

Symphonies Nos. 5; 6 in D min., Op. 104.
*(*) HMV ASD 3780. Moscow RSO, Rozhdestvensky.

Rozhdestvensky couples the *Fifth* and *Sixth* symphonies, but neither reading is as good as the best. He is let down by coarse brass playing and a wide horn vibrato, though there are good things too: the development section of the first movement of the *Fifth* has majesty and vision. The *Sixth* is spoiled by the recording balance, which places some of the first desks of the strings too far forward. Rozhdestvensky shapes the introduction lovingly, but though the cellos are in better focus, the resonant acoustic produces an almost raw sound.

Symphonies Nos. 5; 7 in C, Op. 105.
(M) **(*) Decca Jub. JB/*KJBC* 46. VPO, Maazel.
(M) ** HMV SXLP/*TC-SXLP* 30434 (No. 7 mono). Philh. O., Karajan.

Maazel's *Fifth Symphony* is terribly fast, though it sets out at the same tempo as Karajan's. His second movement is twice as fast as Karajan's versions; hence there is little sense of space or breadth – or for that matter mystery – in this performance. The *Seventh*, on the other hand, is marvellous: this is the greatest account of the work since Koussevitzky's 78 r.p.m. recording, and has a rugged, epic power that is truly thrilling. Indeed the closing pages are as fine as Koussevitzky's, and no praise could be higher. The recording is superlative, with an excellent cassette transfer of striking range and definition – well up to the high standard of this excellent Jubilee series.

Karajan's second account of the *Fifth Symphony* with the Philharmonia was recorded in 1960, while the *Seventh* comes from 1955 and is in mono. The actual sound quality in both is excellent and the playing of the Philharmonia is really distinguished. This version of the *Fifth* is not to be preferred to the 1965 Berlin recording but nonetheless runs it very close. In the *Seventh*, however, there is some loss of intensity. Karajan's tempi are broad and spacious and more measured in the faster sections than we are accustomed to. The C major idea (at the *allegro molto moderato* section just after fig. N) will be a shade too *dolce* for some tastes. The later Berlin reading is stronger in this respect though there are, of course, many good things here all the same. The cassette transfer is satisfactory, the sound lean and bright on side one, slightly fuller on side two. The focus is generally slightly less refined than on the disc.

Symphonies Nos. 6 in D min., Op. 104; 7 in C, Op. 105.

(M) *** DG Acc. 2542/*3342* 137 [139032]. Berlin PO, Karajan.

Despite a certain pallor in the recording of the *Sixth*, it is highly recommendable. Karajan gives a poetic and committed account of this elusive symphony, and his reading has stood the test of time very well. There is concentration here, and an ability to convey the pale sun of the Finnish summer landscape. The *Seventh* too comes off well, though Karajan's is a spacious view that misses the intensity and electricity of Koussevitzky's famous early recording in the quicker sections. However, this is a more powerful and convincing reading than Karajan's Philharmonia version from the 1950s. The cassette is of DG's top quality, matching the disc closely.

Symphony No. 7; The Oceanides, Op. 73; Tapiola, Op. 112.
(M) **(*) HMV SXLP/*TC-SXLP* 30290 [Ang. S.35458]. RPO, Beecham.

Beecham's account of *The Oceanides*, made at the express wish of the composer, is one of the classics of the gramophone, and first appeared in harness with the *Symphony* and *Pelléas*. It is now recoupled with a splendidly powerful *Tapiola* – a version to rank alongside the finest ever made (Koussevitzky, Kajanus and Karajan), and some would argue that it is the finest ever. But the symphony was not the wholehearted success one had every right to expect from Beecham and the RPO. In the present transfer it occupies a whole side to itself, so that there is greatly enhanced impact and presence (on disc and cassette alike), but the performance is still relatively low-powered. *Tapiola* and *The Oceanides* are still available coupled with the *Pelléas* and should not be missed in that form (HMV SXLP 30197).

String quartet in F min. (Voces intimae), Op. 56.

*** O-L DSLO 47. Fitzwilliam Qt –
DELIUS: *Quartet*.***

Although there is an early quartet in B
flat, Op. 4, and some other juvenilia,
Sibelius composed only one mature
quartet. The title *Voces intimae* refers to
the three *ppp* chords of E minor in the
slow movement which pinpoint the withdrawn, rapt quality of the piece. Since its
pioneering recording by the Budapest
Quartet in 1933 (now reissued on World
Records SH 285 and sounding quite
stunning) there have been a number of
others; but none is in the same league as
this record. These young players give a
deeply felt and no less deeply considered
account. In their hands the work becomes
bigger in scale and more symphonic in
feeling (Sibelius's diaries reveal dis-
satisfaction with one or two passages as
quartet-writing). There is a wide range of
sonority and a scrupulous regard for
dynamic gradations. The opening is
played very much *con amore*, but it is evident from the cello entry (bar 18) that this
is going to be a big-boned account that
declares its proximity to the *Fourth Symphony*. The generally measured tempo is
justified in the sleeve-note by Alan
George, the violist of the quartet, who
bases their choice of tempi on metronome
markings that the composer himself gave
to the Griller Quartet. The 34'10"
Fitzwilliam take (as opposed to the
Budapest's 27'00") has been splendidly
accommodated by the Oiseau-Lyre engineers, for the recording is superb. This is
a thought-provoking and impressive record which deserves the widest currency.

This superb reissue should not be
missed. Robert Simpson is a powerful
symphonist, and his series of string quartets, which now number no fewer than
eight, is arguably the finest to appear in
post-war Britain. The *Clarinet quintet*
(1968), a searching and thoughtful piece,
is eloquently played here. The *Symphony*,
also from the 1960s, previously occupied
two sides, but here it has been accommodated on one without any loss of quality.

Sinding, Christian
(1856–1941)

Suite, Op. 10.
*** HMV ASD/*TC-ASD* 3933 [Ang. S/
4ZS 37663]. Perlman, Pittsburgh SO,
Previn – SIBELIUS: *Concerto*.***

Heifetz recorded this dazzling piece in
the 1950s, and it need only be said that
Perlman's version is not inferior. Sinding's A minor *Suite* was originally
composed in 1888 for violin and piano,
and subsequently scored for double
woodwind, two horns, strings and (in
the finale) a harp. Its blend of archaism
and fantasy sounds distinctively Scandinavian of the 1890s yet altogether fresh
– and quite delightful. Such is the velocity
of Perlman's first movement that one
wonders whether the disc is playing at the
right speed. Stunning virtuosity and
excellent recording; the cassette too is
brilliantly clear, its forward balance
matching the disc.

Simpson, Robert (born 1921)

(i) *Symphony No. 3;* (ii) *Clarinet
quintet.*
(M) *** Uni. UNS 225. (i) LSO, Horenstein; (ii) Walton, Aeolian Qt.

Smetana, Bedřich
(1824–84)

Má Vlast (complete).
*** HMV SLS/*TC-SLS* 5151 (2) [Ang.
S 3870]. Dresden State O., Berglund –

DVOŘÁK: *Scherzo capriccioso* etc.***
(M) **(*) DG Priv. 2726 111 (2)/*3300 895*
[2707 054]. Boston SO, Kubelik.
(M) ** Sup. 410 2021/2. Czech PO, Neumann.

Paavo Berglund's complete *Má Vlast*
with the Dresden Staatskapelle is undoubtedly the finest recording of this
elusive cycle of symphonic poems to have
appeared in stereo. Whereas so many
recorded performances have done well by
Vltava and *From Bohemia's Woods and
Fields* and then fallen short on the other
four pieces, it is in these less well-known
works that Berglund is most impressive.
Indeed if there is a criticism of this set
it is that *Vltava*, although splendidly
played, seems slightly under-characterized alongside the other sections of the
score. The opening *Vyšerad* is most
beautifully played, full of lyrical evocation and atmosphere, while *Sárka* is
arrestingly dramatic. *Tábor* and *Blanik*
are played together and so often in previous accounts they have become engulfed
in rhetoric: but not here. Berglund never
lets the forceful rhythms hammer the
listener into the ground, and the national
feeling that is the basis of their inspiration
here sounds surgingly jubilant. The closing pages of *Tábor* are beautifully
managed, and the pastoral interlude in
Blanik is engagingly lightweight, so that
when the closing chorale appears it has a
lilting step and conjures up memories of
The Bartered Bride rather than bombastic militarism. The end of the work has a
joyous release. Berglund does not shirk
the melodrama, but he never lets it get
the better of him. The Dresden orchestra
plays magnificently and the recording is
rich and full-blooded, the sound on tape
virtually indistinguishable from the LPs.
The two Dvořák bonuses are no less engagingly played (the *Third Slavonic rhapsody* is delightfully fresh), and the recording is equally successful here.

Kubelik's DG performance is much
more perceptive and penetrating than his
earlier Decca set. He is careful to temper
the bombast which too readily comes to
the surface in this music (in *Tábor* and
Blanik especially), and his skill with the
inner balance of the orchestration brings
much felicitous detail. The performances
of the two unquestioned masterpieces of
the cycle, *Vltava* and *From Bohemia's
Woods and Fields*, are very well made,
and the orchestral playing throughout is
first-class. Just occasionally a touch more
flair would have brought the orchestral
colours out more vividly, but this lack of
colour is partly caused by the DG sound,
which, although admirably brilliant and
clear, rather lacks sumptuousness and
warmth of texture. However, this has
the advantage that the louder, brassy
passages are not allowed to degenerate
into noise. The tape issue is fairly economically priced, since it offers the content
of two LPs on one full-priced cassette,
and the quality is good, full-bodied (in
some ways more so than in the equivalent
discs) but slightly below DG's highest
standards. There is a marginal lack of
range in the treble.

The account on Supraphon is not
without character, and the playing of the
Czech Philharmonic adds a certain idiomatic colouring and rhythmic feeling to
the performances. But Neumann's readings are sound rather than inspired, although the patriotism in the two final
works is not overdone. The recording,
though an improvement on Ančerl's
made in the 1960s, is not the equal of the
EMI or DG sets.

Má Vlast: Vltava.
*** HMV ASD/*TC-ASD* 3407 [Ang. S/
4XS 37437]. Berlin PO, Karajan –
DVOŘÁK: *Symphony No. 9.****

As a fill-up for an excellent version
of Dvořák's *New World symphony*
Karajan's account of Smetana's most
popular piece is comparably warm and
expressive, characteristically refined but richly spontaneous-sounding.
The recording is warm to match rather

than analytical. The lack of refinement of detail is more noticeable on cassette than on disc.

String quartet No. 1 in E min. (From my life).

*(*) HMV ASD/*TC-ASD* 3694. Medici Qt – DVOŘÁK: *Quartet No. 12*.**

String quartets Nos. 1; 2 in D min.

(M) *** Decca Ace SDD 529. Gabrieli Qt.

(M) *** Sup. 4112 130. Smetana Qt.

The Medici players give a good account of themselves in the *First Quartet* but they are not as committed or as idiomatic in this piece as one would wish. Their dance rhythm in the second movement is a shade too measured, and this is not as penetrating or as characterful as the versions by the Gabrieli and the Smetana Quartets, both of which are, more logically, coupled with Smetana's *Second Quartet*. The recording is vivid and rather forward; there is plenty of presence and a firm bass. The cassette transfer is vivid and full; now that the Decca cassette has been withdrawn this is the only version available on tape.

Artistically both the Gabrieli performances are first-class; technically they offer vivid and well-balanced recorded sound and moreover they are at medium price. The *Second Quartet* is not the equal of the more popular autobiographical *E minor*, but it is attractive nonetheless. This issue will give great satisfaction.

The personnel of the Smetana Quartet has remained the same for a quarter of a century, and their playing here is authoritative, idiomatic and fresh. There is little to choose between this issue and the Gabrielis': the opening of the *Second* is perhaps more convincing here, with more scrupulously observed dynamic shading, and there are other moments where the Smetana players seem bolder and more abandoned. Yet in other places the Gabrielis are equally sensitive, and the recording on Decca is marginally

smoother. Both are thoroughly recommendable, and choice can safely be left to individual whim.

10 Czech dances: Furiant; Slepička; Oves; Medved; Cibulička; Dupak; Hulán; Obkrocák; Sousedská; Skočná.

(M) ** Turn. TVS 34673 [id.]. Firkusny (piano).

These ten dances comprise Smetana's second set, written in 1879, some five years after the onset of his deafness, and they include some remarkably fine music. The piano recording is not of the first class: the balance is close and it tends to be slightly bottom-heavy. Yet with suitable adjustment of the controls it can be made to yield pleasing results.

The Bartered Bride (opera; complete, in German).

*** EMI 1C 149 30967/9. Lorengar, Wunderlich, Frick, Ch. and Bamberg SO, Kempe.

The Bartered Bride sung in German seems an unlikely candidate for a top recommendation, yet in the event this vivacious set is a remarkable success. This is an opera where the choruses form a basic platform on which the soloists can build their performances, and here they are sung with splendid lilt and gusto, Kempe's warm, guiding hand maintaining the lyrical flow perfectly. The discipline of the chorus and the lack of rigidity in the melodic line almost completely compensate for the absence of the idiomatic colouring that the Czech language can bring, and certainly the soloists here offer far more sophisticated singing than is likely from a Czech cast. Pilar Lorengar is most appealing as Mařenka and Fritz Wunderlich is on top form as Jeník. Gottlob Frick gives a strong, earthy characterization of Kecal, the marriage broker. The whole production goes with a swing, and the high spirits do not drown the lyricism – Wunderlich and Lorengar see to that. The recording is bright and vivid, yet has plenty of depth. This is not an opera that calls for much 'production', but the entry of the comedians is particularly well managed.

The Two Widows (opera; complete). (M) ** Sup. 1122 041/3. Sormová, Machotková, Zahradniček, Svehia, Horáček, Prague Nat. Th. Ch. and O., Jílek.

Rather cloudy recording mars what would otherwise be an endearingly bright and vigorous account of Smetana's country comedy about two widows. Though so Czech in its flavour, it was in fact drawn from a French source, and amid the rustic atmosphere there is something of Gallic sparkle. The two widows are here well contrasted, Sormová clear and agile if at times a little shrill, Machotková darker of tone but with an edge as well. The tenor Zahradniček is not so fresh-toned as the role of Ladislav really requires, but Jílek's direction is lyrical as well as energetic.

Soler, Antonio (1729–83)

Concertos for two keyboard instruments Nos. 1–6.
**(*) DG Arc. 2533 445 [id.]. Gilbert, Pinnock.

These Soler concertos are described in the surviving autograph as for two organs, but Kenneth Gilbert and Trevor Pinnock use either two harpsichords (copies of Florentine instruments 'after Vincenzio Sodi, 1782') or two forte-pianos (copies by Adlam Burnett of Heilmann, *c.* 1785), and very attractive they sound too! The music itself is not very substantial and does not possess the character of some of Soler's solo harpsi-chord music. Most of the concertos are in two movements, the second being minuets plus variations. These are highly skilful performances, well recorded, and if the music is not of outsize personality, it is far from unpleasing.

Sonatas: in C min.; in C sharp min.; in D; in D min.; in D flat; in F sharp; Concerto in G; Fandango.
(M) *** Mercury SRI 75131. Puyana.

Rafael Puyana uses a modern harpsi-chord which features, alongside the damping 'harp' stop, a means of creating dynamic contrast without altering the timbre. He plays flamboyantly, with very free rubato, the articulation demonstrating the greatest bravura, not just in the sparkling passage-work but also in the subtle changes of colour and light and shade within phrases. This is not a recital for eighteenth-century purists, but Soler's music springs vividly to life, its melodic resource and its Spanish qualities emphasized equally. Try the opening *F sharp major Sonata* with its Catalonian folk influence or the exciting *Fandango*, which makes an evocative flamenco-style mid-side interlude, and which, even more than the *Sonatas*, suggests affinities with the guitar. The recording is admirably faithful, but it is essential to cut the volume well back; the character of the instrument then emerges fully, with its bright treble and resonantly pungent lower registers.

Somervell, Arthur (1863–1937)

Clarinet quintet.
*** Hyp. A 66011. King, Aeolian Qt – JACOB: *Clarinet quintet.****

Sir Arthur Somervell, knighted by King George V for his work as a civil servant in charge of musical education, here shows what a skilful composer he was within his chosen Brahmsian idiom. This is just the sort of work (first performance 1919) which deserves resurrection on record when fashion no longer matters. The bubbling finale is a special delight, with Thea King and the Aeolian Quartet at their most persuasive, helped by very good recording.

Sor, Fernando (1778–1839)

Étude in A, Op. 6/12; Fantasia, Op. 7; Fantasia elegiaca, Op. 59; Fantasia on 'Ye banks and braes', Op. 40; Sonata in C, Op. 15b.
*** Mer. E 77006. Artzt.

Alice Artzt is an outstandingly compelling guitarist, whose range of tone on a 1931 Hauser instrument is exceptionally beautiful. This collection of works by Sor – most of them rarities – gives an excellent idea why this composer, a Spanish contempory of Beethoven, is regarded as the father of the modern guitar repertory. First-rate recording.

Spohr, Louis (1784–1859)

Clarinet concertos Nos. 1 in C min., Op. 26; 2 in E flat, Op. 57.
*** Argo ZRG 920. Pay, L. Sinf., Atherton.

Antony Pay and the London Sinfonietta give fluent, expert and thoroughly musical accounts of these concertos. The performances have the requisite lightness and wit, and do justice to the charm these concertos possess. Good recording.

Clarinet concerto No. 4 in E min.
*** Mer. E 77022. King, ECO, Francis – MOZART: *Clarinet concerto.***(*)

Spohr's *Fourth Clarinet concerto* admirably illustrates his amiable and facile invention, above all in the *Rondo al espagnol* finale, a witty bolero which gives Thea King a splendid opportunity for display. So does the elaborate *Larghetto* slow movement, though there the performance sounds less spontaneous. Nonetheless so stylish an account of so rare a work, well coupled with the Mozart and well recorded, is most welcome.

Violin concerto No. 8 in A min. (Gesangszene), Op. 47; Concertante in A flat for violin, harp and orchestra.
*** Erato STU 71318. Amoyal, Nordmann, Lausanne CO, Jordan.

Pierre Amoyal gives a fine-spun, lyrical yet intense account of the *Gesangszene concerto*, by far the best of those currently available – and the only one really worth listing. The *Concertante in A flat*, which Spohr wrote for his wife, the harpist Dorette Schneidler, makes an attractive fill-up, and again supersedes the rival version (see below). Amoyal is perhaps rather more forward than he would be if the balance were ideal, and tutti sound a little opaque; but there is no need to withhold a full three-star recommendation here. The *A minor Concerto* is one of Spohr's best-proportioned and most classically conceived works in spite of its innovatory features.

Concertante in A flat for violin, harp and orchestra.
(M) ** Turn. TVS 37126 [Can. 31106]. Mildonian, Ricci, R. Luxembourg O., Froment – GOLDMARK: *Violin concerto.***

This engaging piece, with its agreeable dotted rhythms in the finale, is played here with plenty of resilience. The performance throughout is alert and sympathetic, and it is a pity that the balance is artificial, with both soloists (and especially the violin) right on top of the listener. The Erato version (see above) is to be preferred.

Nonet in F, Op. 31; Octet in E, Op. 32.
*** CRD CRD 1054/*CRDC 4054*. Nash Ens.

These works are both otherwise available in Viennese performances, but not coupled together. They are inventive and charming pieces – and by no means mere note-spinning. They are very elegantly played here; the Nash Ensemble do not attempt to invest this music with more expressive feeling than it can bear. Quality throughout is natural and lifelike. This is civilized music, well worth having. The cassette is naturally balanced and agreeably smooth, lacking only the last fraction of upper range compared with the disc.

Stamitz, Karl (1745–1801)

Flute concertos: in A min.; in D.
(*) RCA RL/*RK* 25315 [ARL 1/*ARK 1* 3858]. Galway, New Irish CO, Prieur – C. P. E. BACH: *Sonata*.*

The *G major Flute concerto* (not the same work as that recorded by Wanausek on Turnabout TVS 34093) is quite an ambitious piece, well wrought and with an expressive *Andante* and a genial rondo finale. The other concerto here is shorter and less individual. James Galway lends his charisma to both, and the accompaniments are admirably stylish; but this is not great music. The recording is good, the flute forward, the orchestra bright and clear if lacking the last degree of warmth.

Stanford, Charles (1852–1924)

Clarinet concerto in A min., Op. 80.
*** Hyp. A/*KA* 66001. King, Philh. O., Francis – FINZI: *Concerto*.***

This Hyperion issue offers a particularly attractive coupling of a masterpiece by Gerald Finzi and this lighter but highly engaging work by Stanford. He wrote his *Clarinet concerto* for Richard Mühlfeld, the artist who inspired the late clarinet works of Brahms, but it remained unpublished for nearly a century and was totally neglected. In three linked sections it shows Stanford characteristically fastidious in developing his ideas; the clarinet repertory is not so rich that such a well-written piece should be neglected, particularly as the final section throws aside inhibition and presents more sharply memorable themes in a warm, late-romantic manner. Thea King's crisp-toned playing is most stylish, and the accompaniment thoroughly sympathetic. The recording is rather reverberant but otherwise attractively full and vivid; there is no appreciable difference in sound quality between disc and cassette.

3 Rhapsodies for piano, Op. 92.
** Pearl SHE 546. John Parry – PARRY: *Shulbrede tunes* etc.**

The *Three Rhapsodies* are as ambitious as they are neglected. They make considerable demands on the player, though only the *Francesca movement* rhapsody really justifies the effort. The *Beatrice portrait* (the work is inspired by Dante's *Inferno*) is pretty thin. The music dates from the first decade of the present century, and though it would be an exaggeration to hail it as important, there is no doubt that lovers of English music will find it of real interest.

Part-songs: *Chillingham; Heraclitus;*

My love's an arbutus; Shall we go dance; Sweet love for me; Veneta.
(M)*** Argo ZK 58. Louis Halsey Singers, Halsey – PARRY: *Songs of Farewell.****

The Stanford songs make an excellent coupling for the magnificent set of Parry pieces, also for unaccompanied choir. *Heraclitus* is superb, and so is the charming setting of the Irish folksong *My love is an arbutus.* Performances and recording are exemplary.

Stanley, John (1712–86)

6 Organ concertos, Op. 10.
*** CRD CRD 1065/*CRDC 1065*. Gifford, Northern Sinfonia.

John Stanley published these six concertos in 1775, towards the end of his long career as organist and composer. He gave the option of playing the solo part on the harpsichord or fortepiano, but this is essentially organ music, and these bouncing, vigorous performances, well recorded as they are on the splendid organ of Hexham Abbey, present them most persuasively. No. 4, with its darkly energetic C minor, is particularly fine. The cassette is of first-class quality, matching the disc closely.

Steiner, Max (1888–1971)

Film scores: *The Big Sleep* (suite); *The Charge of the Light Brigade: The charge; The Fountainhead* (suite); *Four Wives:* (i) *Symphonie moderne.* (ii) *The Informer* (excerpts); *Johnny Belinda* (suite); *King Kong* (excerpts); *Now Voyager* (excerpts); *Saratoga Trunk: As long as I live; Since You Went Away: Title sequence.*
(M) **(*) RCA Gold GL/*GK* 43447 [ARL 1/*ARK 1* 0136]. Nat. PO, Gerhardt, with (i) Earl Wild, (ii) Amb. S.

Max Steiner, like his famous colleagues Korngold and Waxman, exerted enormous influence on the development of orchestral background music during Hollywood's golden years. Born in Vienna, he emigrated to the USA in 1914, and after working as conductor-arranger-pianist on the East Coast he was lured to the West with the coming of sound movies in 1929. He worked first for RKO (providing music for some 135 pictures), then moved to Selznick and on to Warner Bros., where he wrote scores for another 155 films. Selznick 'borrowed' him back for *Gone with the Wind.*

Steiner would wait until a film was complete and edited before producing his ideas, quickly and spontaneously developing the finished work but leaving the orchestration to others. He understood that music could slow up as well as enhance a scene, and his professionalism was greatly admired. His style is unashamedly eclectic, but his gifts were prodigious and his music never sounds thin in ideas. This selection is typically diverse in mood and atmosphere. Sumptuous Tchaikovskian romanticism there is in plenty, with the luscious theme tune for *Now Voyager* approaching the famous *Gone with the Wind* melody in memorability. *As long as I live* from *Saratoga Trunk* is also lushly telling, while in *King Kong* and *The Big Sleep* there are appropriate elements of menace. In *The Informer* the Ambrosian Singers provide a highly effective burst of Hollywood religiosity at the final climax (the death of the principal character). It is all gorgeously played and recorded. The cassette is brilliant but is not as refined as the disc in the extreme treble; the record also has rather more body of tone and offers an elaborate illustrative leaflet, which the cassette omits.

Film scores: *Casablanca* (suite); *The Big Sleep: Love Theme; The Caine Mutiny: March; Key Largo* (suite); *Passage to Marseilles: Rescue at Sea; The Treasure of the Sierra Madre* (suite); *Virginia City* (excerpts). (Also includes: WAXMAN: *To Have and Have Not* (excerpts); *The Two Mrs Carrolls* (excerpts). HOLLANDER: *Sabrina* (excerpts). YOUNG: *The Left Hand of God: Love theme*. ROZSA: *Sahara: Main title sequence*.)
(M) ** RCA Gold GL/*GK* 43439 [AGL 1/*AGK 1* 3787]. Nat. PO, Gerhardt.

This collection concentrates on the key Humphrey Bogart movies and certainly shows Steiner's versatility. The changes of mood in the five brief sequences from *The Treasure of the Sierra Madre* are mirrored most imaginatively. However, the evocative piano solo so famous in *Casablanca* is not very successful here, although there is some touchingly romantic lyrical writing in the *Key Largo* sequence. Among the items by other composers the Waxman excerpts and the eloquent Victor Young melody written for *The Left Hand of God* stand out. But this is one of the least repeatable of Gerhardt's compilations. Performances and recordings are well up to standard; the cassette is not as refined as the disc at both ends of the spectrum in some of the biggest climaxes. It also omits the illustrated notes supplied within the LP sleeve.

Gone with the Wind: extended excerpts.
(M) *** RCA Gold GL/*GK* 43440 [ARL 1/*ARK 1* 0452]. Nat. PO, Gerhardt.

In 1939 Max Steiner wrote for *Gone with the Wind* the first really memorable romantic theme tune to be indelibly associated in the public mind with an epic movie. As introduced here in the title sequence, played with sweeping grandiloquence and sumptuously recorded, it cannot fail to involve the listener. It was imaginative of Steiner not to associate his most potent musical idea with one or more of the principal characters, but instead to centre it on Tara, the home of the heroine. Thus he could work it as a leitmotive and have it return again and again through a complex score of some two and half hours to remind the audience nostalgically that Tara represented permanence and continuity against a complex backcloth of changing human fortunes. It says something for the quality of Steiner's tune that its ability to haunt the memory remains after its many reappearances. The rest of the music is professionally tailored to the narrative line and makes agreeable listening, although the quality of the lyrical invention inevitably becomes more sentimental as the film nears its close. As ever, Charles Gerhardt is a splendid advocate and he secures fine playing and obvious involvement from his orchestra. The recording is both rich and brilliant, although there is less body of sound on the cassette than the LP. The cassette also omits the illustrated leaflet giving the film's background and synopsis.

Stenhammar, Wilhelm
(1871–1927)

Piano concerto No. 2 in D min., Op. 23.
*** EMI 4E 063 32484. Solyom, Mun. PO, Westerberg – LISZT: *Totentanz*.***

Stenhammar was a pianist as well as a composer and conductor, and in his youth he was a formidable exponent of the Brahms *D minor Concerto*. Brahms can be discerned here and there in this concerto, though his is not the only influence; there are moments when one is reminded of Mendelssohn and, more particularly, Saint-Saëns. There is no want of brilliant keyboard writing, though the ballad-like figure that dominates the first movement is not one of Stenhammar's strongest ideas. There is also an excessive reliance on sequence that draws attention to itself, notably in the delightful scherzo. But if the concerto has less depth than the *Second Symphony*, there are moments of genuine individuality that shine through some of the conventional and less fresh invention. This performance is worth three stars, as is the recording. The work, however, is not as rewarding as the other Stenhammar works below.

Serenade for orchestra, Op. 31; (i) *Florez and Blanzeflor* (ballad), *Op. 3.*
⊛*** EMI 4E 061 35148. Swedish RSO, Westerberg, (i) with Wixell.

The *Serenade for orchestra*, written during the First World War, shows Stenhammar's invention and his mastery of orchestral resource at their very best. The newcomer to Stenhammar's music will find traces of Brahms and Reger in the Swedish composer as well as something of the gentleness of Fauré and the dignity of Elgar. His sensibility is distinctly northern, however, and his personality, though not immediately assertive, becomes more sympathetic and compelling as one comes to grips with his music. He was a man of the orchestra, and his experience shows in every bar of this work, and there is an exuberance about these ideas as well as a vein of poetry and fantasy. The *Romance* is a beautifully wrought movement, full of nostalgia and that gentle melancholy so characteristic of the Swedish sensibility. This performance is committed and eloquent; the

Swedish Radio Symphony Orchestra is a very fine body. The recording is impressive, with much greater clarity and definition than in the old Kubelik record on DG. The fill-up is an early piece whose pages are crossed by the shadows of *Parsifal* and *Tristan*. It is beautifully sung by Wixell. This is the kind of record that deserves to reach a wide audience, who would surely respond if they only had the opportunity of making its acquaintance.

Symphony No. 2 in G min., Op. 34.
*** Cap. CAP 1151. Stockholm PO, Westerberg.

This is a marvellous symphony. It is an exact contemporary of Nielsen's *Fourth* and Sibelius's *Fifth* but resembles neither. It is direct in utterance; its ideas have splendid character and spirit; and there is a sense of forward movement, and the breadth and spaciousness of a symphonist with firm, secure roots. Stenhammar's classical sympathies lend his symphony strength; his feeling for nature gives it a distinctive sense of vision. Some of his music has a quality of reserve that masks his underlying warmth, but that is not the case here: the melodic invention is fresh and abundant, and the generosity of spirit it radiates is heart-warming. The Stockholm Philharmonic under Stig Westerberg play with conviction and eloquence; the strings have warmth and body, and they sing out as if they love playing this music. The wind are very fine too. The recording is vivid and full-blooded even by the digital standards of today: as sound, this record is in the first flight, and in terms of musical interest, its claims are scarcely less strong.

(i) *String quartet No. 6 in D min, Op. 35;* (ii) *Visor och Stämmingar, Op. 26.*
*** EMI 4E 053 35116. (i) Frydén Qt; (ii) Saeden, Ribera.

725

It is good to see that the last few years have brought a renaissance of interest in Stenhammar's music. Four other quartets of his are now on record but not available at present in the UK. This issue gives us the *Sixth* and last of the quartets, written in the 1920s – a finely wrought piece, well worth investigating, but slow to yield its rewards, rather as is Fauré's late chamber music, yet profoundly satisfying when one has come to terms with it. *Visor och Stämmingar* (*Songs and Moods*) is earlier – from the period 1908–9 – and is inventive and often charming. It is beautifully sung by Erik Saeden and the recording, though not new (it was made in 1970), is perfectly acceptable. The *Quartet* recording is of later provenance and sounds excellent.

Stockhausen, Karlheinz
(born 1928)

Sternklang (*Park music for 5 groups*).
*** DG 2707 123 (2) [id.]. Various artists dir. composer.

Sternklang, lasting over two hours, is designed as an extended ritual of meditation. Ideally the five groups of instruments are spread around an open-air setting, and a stereo recording can only approximate to what the composer intended towards 'sinking the individual into the cosmic whole, a preparation for beings from the stars and their arrival'. If that sounds pompous, Stockhausen does at least vary the mood more sharply than usual, with even some humour intended when perfect cadences are piled on each other in dance-like patterns. The virtuoso performance has the right tension and commitment, recorded as well as it can be in a conventional studio.

Straube, Rudolf
(1717–*c*. 1785)

Sonatas Nos. 1–3 for guitar and continuo.
(M) **(*) CBS 61842 [(d) Col. M 31194]. Williams, Puyana – HAYDN: *Guitar quartet.****

This is routine stuff, eighteenth-century musical wallpaper, far from unpleasing but totally inconsequential. It is all expertly played and well though forwardly recorded. The cassette transfer is lively, but here even more than on the disc the resonant recording of the harpsichord is slightly tiresome.

Straus, Oscar (1870–1954)

Ein Walzertraum (*A Waltz Dream*; operetta; complete).
**(*) EMI 1C 157 29041/2. Rothenberger, Gedda, Fassbaender, Brokmeier, Anheisser, Moser, Bav. State Op. Ch., Graunke SO, Mattes.

Oscar Straus had no connection with the famous Strauss family: his more natural affinity is with Franz Lehár. They were born in the same month and year, and *A Waltz Dream* was specifically written to challenge the success of *The Merry Widow*. It is not its equal, of course, but the score is tuneful and vivacious, and although this recording contains more dialogue than is ideal (and no libretto is provided, only a synopsis of the plot), it remains good entertainment, especially with such a distinguished cast. The recording is lively, but the voices are very forward, so that some of the offstage effects are rather primitive and not well focused.

Strauss, Johann, Snr
(1804–49)

Strauss, Johann, Jnr
(1825–99)

Strauss, Josef
(1827–70)

Strauss, Eduard
(1835–1916)

(All music listed is by Johann Strauss Jnr unless otherwise stated)

Cinderella (*Äschenbrodel*; ballet, rev. and ed. Gamley; complete); *Ritter Pásmán* (ballet music).
**(*) Decca Dig. D 225 D 2/*K 225 K 22* (2) [Lon. LDR 72005/5-]. Nat. PO, Bonynge.

Strauss did not live to finish his only full-length ballet. Most of the first act was completed, but the rest was pieced together and scored by Joseph Bayer. This version has been further revised and edited by Douglas Gamley. It would be nice to have discovered a hidden master-piece, but this is not it (Mahler was so unimpressed that he even doubted the score's authenticity, though he revised that view later). Bonynge does his utmost to engage the listener and secures warm, elegant and sparkling playing. He is superbly recorded; both discs and cassettes offer demonstration quality. But as the *Ritter Pásmán* ballet suite, which is much more memorable, shows, *Cinderella* is inconsequential, though pleasing enough for background listening.

Graduation Ball (ballet, arr. Dorati).
**(*) Decca SXL/*KSXC* 6867 [Lon. 7086/5-]. VPO, Dorati.

Since Dorati arranged the music for *Graduation Ball* it was understandable that Decca should choose him to direct their third recording of this attractive score (the first, and best, was conducted by Fistoulari in the mono era). In his sleeve-note Dorati tells us that he regards the work (written in partnership with the choreographer David Lichine for the Ballets Russes de Monte Carlo) as a 'youthful prank' or 'escapade', and his musical direction follows this mood. It is immensely spirited, even exhilarating, but barely hints at the charming ro-manticism with which the ballet itself is imbued. Both the opening of the work and the nostalgic closing section lack a sense of atmosphere, not helped by Decca's brilliantly lit recording. How-ever, many of the flamboyant solo dances come off vividly, and the waltzes are not without lilt, so that in its zestful exube-rance this is enjoyable enough, and Dorati welds the seams between the indi-vidual items skilfully. The cassette trans-fer is extremely vivid and full-blooded, but it needs some treble cut if the upper strings are not to sound slightly fierce.

COLLECTIONS OF
WALTZES, POLKAS, etc.

(Listed in alphabetical order under the name of the conductor and then in numerical order using the manufacturers' catalogue numbers)

Polkas: *Banditen galop; Explo-sionen; Im Sturmschritt; Leichtes Blut; Unter Donner und Blitz.* Waltzes: *Accelerationen; Lagunen; Morgenblätter; Schatz.* STRAUSS, Josef: *Feuerfest polka.*
**(*) HMV Dig. ASD/*TCC-ASD* 4041. Johann Strauss O. of V., Boskovsky

A genial digital supplement to the Boskovsky Strauss discography, without the electricity and sharply defined pres-ence of the Decca double album (see

727

below). Boskovsky is especially good in the polkas, which have genuine exuberance; there is a hint of blandness in the waltzes, but the resonant warmth of the recording makes for enjoyable listening nonetheless. There is not a great deal of difference in sound between the disc and the chrome cassette.

'A Strauss Gala': Marches: *Egyptian; Napoleon; Persian.* Overtures: *Die Fledermaus; Der Zigeunerbaron. Perpetuum mobile.* Polkas: *Annen; Auf der Jagd; Banditen galop; Champagne; Eljen a Magyar; Explosionen; Leichtes Blut; Neue Pizzicato; Pizzicato* (with Josef); *Tritsch-Tratsch; Unter Donner und Blitz.* Waltzes: *Accelerationen; An der schönen blauen Donau; Frühlingsstimmen; Geschichten aus dem Wiener Wald; Kaiser; Künstlerleben; Morgenblätter; Rosen aus dem Süden; 1001 Nacht; Wein, Weib und Gesang; Wiener Blut; Wiener Bonbons; Wo die Zitronen blühn.* STRAUSS, Eduard: *Bahn frei polka galop.* STRAUSS, Johann, Snr: *Radetzky march.* STRAUSS, Josef: Polkas: *Eingesendet; Feuerfest; Jockey; Plappermäulchen.* Waltzes: *Mein Lebenslauf ist Lieb und Lust; Sphärenklänge.*
(B) *** Decca D 145 D 4/*K 145 K 44* (4). VPO, Boskovsky.

With Boskovsky making many of his newer recordings for HMV, Decca are taking the opportunity to reissue his earlier versions in a more economical format. This four-disc (and four-tape) compilation uses material from recordings made during the sixties. It is remarkably comprehensive and very reasonably priced. The rearrangement of items is most successful, with a judicious selective order, so that polka and waltz alternate engagingly. The first group,

opening with a particularly vivacious account of the *Die Fledermaus* overture, gets the set off to an excellent start, and there are generally very few disappointments among the performances. The inclusion of four polkas by Josef Strauss, together with two of his finest waltzes, is particularly welcome. The recording seldom sounds really dated and is often very good; the cassette transfers are remarkably consistent too, generally full, bright and well focused.

'New Year's Day concert in Vienna' (1979): Polkas: *Auf der Jagd; Bitte schön; Leichtes Blut; Pizzicato* (with Josef); *Tik-Tak.* Waltzes: *An der schönen blauen Donau; Bei uns z'Haus; Wein, Weib und Gesang.* STRAUSS, Johann, Snr: *Radetzky march; Loreley-Rhein-Klänge waltz.* STRAUSS, Eduard: *Ohne Bremse* (polka). STRAUSS, Josef: Polkas: *Die Emancipierte; Moulinet; Rudolfsheimer.* Waltz: *Sphärenklänge.* (Also includes SUPPÉ: *Beautiful Galathea overture;* ZIEHRER: *Hereinspaziert waltz.*)
*** Decca Dig. D 147 D 2/*KSXC2 7062* [Lon. LDR 10001/2/5-]. VPO, Boskovsky.

Decca chose to record Boskovsky's 1979 New Year's Day concert in Vienna as one of their very first digital issues, and this has remained a demonstration recording, notably in the *Radetzky march,* where with the audience participation included the presence of the sound is almost uncanny. But the clarity, immediacy and natural separation of detail are very striking throughout, although the upper strings of the Vienna Philharmonic at times seem to have their upper partials slightly exaggerated, so that there is some lack of bloom at the top. In all other respects the recording is first-class and the excellence applies to the cassette as well as the discs. One notices the naturalness of the sound immediately in the very well-focused audience applause at the opening, and the crispness of the side-drum is another striking feature, to say nothing of the freshness of the woodwind. The music-making itself gains much from the spontaneity of the occasion: its relaxed style is persuasive throughout, but one can feel the tension rising as the concert proceeds, and in the second half (and especially the encores) the electricity is very apparent. The performances are generally first-class and this is highly recommended, provided one can accept the applause and audience participation. The sound on disc and tape is almost identical.

'Family concert': Spanish march. Polkas: Demolirer; Pizzicato (with Josef). Du und du (Fledermaus waltz). STRAUSS, Johann, Jnr, Josef, and Eduard: Schützenquadrille. STRAUSS, Eduard: Bahn frei polka galop. STRAUSS, Johann, Snr: Radetzky march. STRAUSS, Josef: Brennende Liebe polka. Transaktionen waltz.
(M) ** Decca Jub. JB/KJBC 28. VPO, Boskovsky.

In this further reshuffling of earlier Boskovsky/VPO material for Decca's Jubilee label there seems to be too great a proportion of music in duple or quadruple time; there are only two waltzes. But the collection is valuable for the inclusion of the Schützenquadrille, to which all three brothers contributed (it was written for a Viennese shooting contest in 1868). Of course the performances are lively and vivid and the recording good (though not so refined on tape as on disc); but unless these items are particularly wanted collectors will find many of Boskovsky's other issues more rewarding.

'World of the Strauss family': Napo-
leon march; Champagne polka; Wo die Zitronen blühn waltz. STRAUSS, Johann, Jnr, Josef and Eduard: Schützenquadrille. STRAUSS, Johann, Snr: Kaiser Franz Josef I Rettungs-Jubel march; Loreley-Rhein-Klänge waltz. STRAUSS, Josef: Polkas: Feuerfest; Jockey. Dorfschwalben aus Österreich waltz.
(M) **(*) Decca SPA/KCSP 589. VPO, Boskovsky.

An agreeably lively family album, with characteristically vivid playing from the VPO and brilliant Decca sound. The three waltzes combine affection and sparkle, but elsewhere (as the Napoleon march demonstrates) the recording acoustic is sometimes very reverberant and this offers a degree of smudging on the cassette transfers.

'The Spirit of Vienna': Eine Nacht in Venedig overture. Polkas: Champagne; Eljen a Magyar; Im Krapfenwald; Neue Pizzicato. Waltzes: An der schönen blauen Donau; Geschichten aus dem Wiener Wald; Kaiser; Künstlerleben; Rosen aus dem Süden; Wiener Blut; Wo die Zitronen blühn.
(B) ** HMV TC2-MOM 102. Johann Strauss O. of V., Boskovsky.

The Boskovsky recordings offered on this 'Miles of Music' double-length tape date from the early seventies. The performances are genial and stylish; there is no lack of lilt in the phrasing, and the control of rubato is effective. Yet the playing is somewhat less memorable and individual than in Boskovsky's Decca VPO series. With warm, agreeably resonant recording, the effect in the ear (for which this series, offering nearly an hour and a half's music, is primarily intended) is richly pleasing, and this makes entertaining and undistracting background entertainment for a long journey. At home the reproduction lacks something in brilliance and detail, but still sounds very acceptable.

Waltzes: *An der schönen blauen Donau; Frühlingsstimmen; Geschichten aus dem Wiener Wald; Künstlerleben; Wein, Weib und Gesang.*
(M) ** Decca VIV/*KVIC* 2 [Lon. STS 15545]. LPO, Dorati.

These are highly invigorating rather than romantic performances, supported by an extremely brilliant recording (originally made in Phase Four). Of its kind this is a good record, and those for whom the Viennese style is too droopy will not find a hint of slackness here. *Tales from the Vienna Woods* uses a zither, and the balance is never gimmicky. On cassette there is marginally less energy in the upper range in climaxes, and the effect is slightly smoother; however, Dorati's Hungarian liveliness still projects admirably.

Polkas: *Czech; Pizzicato* (with Josef). Waltzes: *Kaiser; Rosen aus dem Süden; Sängerlust; Wiener Blut; Wiener Bonbons.* STRAUSS, Johann, Snr: *Radetzky march.* STRAUSS, Josef: Polkas: *Feuerfest; Ohne Sorgen.*
(M) *** ASV ACM/*ZCACM* 2019. LSO, led Georgiadis (violin).

Among the new generation of Strauss recordings led in the authentic style by violinist-conductor, this collection from John Georgiadis, a brilliant virtuoso in his own right, is easily the most successful. The LSO is on top form, and the rhythmic feel of the playing combines lilt with polished liveliness. There is delicacy (the *Czech polka* is enchanting) and boisterousness, as in the irresistible anvil effects in the *Feuerfest polka.* The closing *Radetzky march* is as rousing as anyone

could wish, while the waltzes combine vitality and charm. With first-class recording in a suitably resonant (but not over-reverberant) acoustic, this is highly recommendable, especially at medium price. The cassette transfer is slightly less sharply focused than the disc; side two seems to have more range than side one.

Polkas: *Annen; Auf der Jagd. Geschichten aus dem Wiener Wald waltz.* Overtures: *Die Fledermaus; Der Zigeunerbaron.* STRAUSS, Josef: *Delirien waltz.*
(M) *** Decca Jub. JB/*KJBC* 68 [Lon. STS 15163/*5*-]. VPO, Karajan.

Warmly recorded, presumably in the same hall where the Boskovsky records are made, this early stereo collection is distinguished. Karajan's touch with the *Gypsy Baron overture* is irresistible, and *Tales from the Vienna Woods* is really beautiful, one of the very finest recorded performances of this piece, with a perfectly judged zither solo. The polkas have the panache for which this conductor at his best is famous. Highly recommended: this is among the best popular Strauss collections available on disc. The cassette is a little disappointing; it is obviously made from an early master, and although the sound is lively there are hints of minor discoloration in the upper partials of the woodwind.

Die Fledermaus overture. Persischer Marsch. Polkas: *Eljen a Magyar; Leichtes Blut; Unter Donner und Blitz.* Waltzes: *Accelerationen; An der schönen blauen Donau; Künstlerleben.*
*** DG. Dig. 2532/*3302* 025 [id.]. Berlin PO, Karajan.

A superbly played selection taken from Karajan's DG digital box (see below). The virility and flair of the waltzes (especially *Künstlerleben*) are matched by the exuberance of the polkas, and the *Fledermaus overture* sparkles so vividly it sounds like a new discovery. The sound is well matched on disc and chrome tape.

Der Zigeunerbaron overture. Polkas: *Annen; Auf der Jagd; Tritsch-Tratsch.* Waltzes: *Kaiser; Rosen aus dem Süden; Wein, Weib und Gesang.*
**(*) DG Dig. 2532/*3302* 026. [id.]. Berlin PO, Karajan.

This is less attractive than the first selection from Karajan's DG box. After a refined introduction, the *Emperor* does not achieve the zest of some of the other waltzes, and although the playing is not without elegance, the noble contour of the principal melody is less potent here than in some versions. The polkas go well, and the overture is a highlight. The digital sound is full and brilliant, and the chrome tape is of excellent quality.

Napoleon march. Perpetuum mobile. Die Fledermaus: Quadrille. Waltzes: *Geschichten aus dem Wiener Wald; Wiener Blut.* STRAUSS, Johann, Snr: *Radetzky march.* STRAUSS, Josef: Waltzes: *Delirien; Sphärenklänge.*
*** DG Dig. 2532/*3302* 027 [id.] Berlin PO, Karajan.

A splendid distillation from Karajan's Strauss box, with magically evocative openings to each of the four waltzes, and outstanding performances of *Sphären-klänge, Delirien* and (especially) *Wiener Blut. Perpetuum mobile* and the engaging *Fledermaus quadrille* make a piquant contrast as centrepieces of each side. The brilliant digital recording is equally impressive on disc and cassette.

Polkas: *Annen; Tritsch-Tratsch; Unter Donner und Blitz.* Waltzes: *An der schönen blauen Donau; Geschichten aus dem Wiener Wald; Wiener Blut.*

(M) **(*) DG Acc. 2542/*3342* 143. Berlin PO, Karajan.

Karajan is nothing if not consistent, and these earlier Strauss recordings are basically very little different in conception from those in the later digital set. There is less vitality here, but the performances are beautifully played; the recording does not sound its age, and the cassette transfer to is of DG's best quality. Many will like a selection which includes both *The Blue Danube* and *Tales from the Vienna Woods* (the latter performance is only marginally less distinguished than the one in Karajan's Decca Jubilee concert). The polkas are lively and make a suitable contrast.

Overtures: *Die Fledermaus* (and *Quadrille*); *Der Zigeunerbaron. Musicalischer Scherz.* Marches: *Napoleon; Persian. Perpetuum mobile.* Polkas: *Annen; Auf der Jagd; Cagliostro in Wien; Eljen a Magyar; Leichtes Blut; Tritsch-Tratsch; Ungarische; Unter Donner und Blitz.* Waltzes: *Accelerationen; An der schönen blauen Donau; Geschichten aus dem Wiener Wald; Kaiser; Künstlerleben, Rosen aus dem Suden; Das Spitzentuch der Königin; Wein, Weib, und Gesang; Wiener Blut.* STRAUSS, Johann, Snr: *Radetzky march.* STRAUSS, Josef: Waltzes: *Delirien; Sphärenklänge.*
*** DG Dig. 2741/*3382* 003 (3) [id.]. Berlin PO, Karajan.

Karajan's new three-disc (or three-tape) set of music of the Strauss family is a major achievement. The digital recording is full and brilliant, and there is no great difference between discs and chrome tapes: the former have a fractionally cleaner focus, the latter a marginally softer image for the upper strings. The performances are splendid; the waltzes have a stirring virility, yet their evocative introductions have never been more effectively prepared. *Künstlerleben, Wiener Blut, Sphärenklänge* and *Delirien* are superbly done, and on *The Blue Danube* Karajan lavishes special care, opening atmospherically and building to a climax of striking lyrical power. Yet one section is cunningly repeated with an arresting drop to pianissimo – a device he also used in his earlier recording, now on Accolade (see above). The Berlin Philharmonic playing is glorious, with precise ensemble not interfering with the Viennese-style lilt, to underline the sheer beauty of the music. The two overtures are no less compelling; Karajan must have given them many times, but here they sound freshly minted, and the sheer vigour of the waltz introduction to *Die Fledermaus* is irresistible. The polkas, played with great zest and panache, are nicely placed between the waltzes to provide exhilarating contrast. Above all the set has a flowing spontaneity, and if you start at side one and play right through to the end, the music-making seems to become more spirited and involving as it proceeds.

Pizzicato polka (with Josef). Waltzes: *Accelerationen; An der schönen blauen Donau; Kaiser; Rosen aus dem Süden.*

(B) ** Con. CC/*CCT* 7522 [Lon. STS 15012/5-]. VPO, Josef Krips.

Krips's performances with their gentle rhythmic emphasis, are attractively affectionate, and with the VPO in good form the result is bound to be enjoyable. The waltzes have spirit, and the *Pizzicato polka* comes off especially well (the recording here is strikingly live). This dates from the earliest days of stereo, but the acoustic is warm and the sound is surprisingly good. The cassette sounds richer than the disc but has a more restricted upper range.

'New Year in Vienna 1981': *Ägyp-*

tischer Marsch; Einzugsmarsch. Polkas: *Explosionen; Leichtes Blut; Stürmisch in Lieb' und Tanz; Tritsch-Tratsch; Pizzicato* (with Josef). Waltzes: *Accelerationen; Frühlingsstimmen; Rosen aus dem Süden.* STRAUSS, Johann, Snr: *Seufzer Galop.* STRAUSS, Josef: Polkas: *Frauenherz; Ohne Sorgen. Transaktionen waltz.*

** DG Dig. 2532/*3302* 018 [id.]. VPO, Maazel.

This record does not convey the electricity of Boskovsky's 1979 Decca digital concert (see above); indeed the audience response seems remarkably cool and well-behaved. Their presence is most felt in the *Pizzicato polka*, where one can sense the intercommunication as Maazel manipulates the rubato with obvious flair. He also gives a splendid account of *Transaktionen*, which has striking freshness and charm. For the rest these are well-played performances of no great memorability. The orchestra makes two rather self-conscious vocal contributions, and of course the playing itself is first-class. The digital sound is brilliant and clear, somewhat lacking in resonant warmth. Cassette and disc are closely matched.

Kaiser Franz Josef Marsch. Polkas: *Annen; Auf der Jagd; Fata Morgana; Tritsch Tratsch.* Waltzes: *An der schönen blauen Donau; Kaiser; Morgenblätter; Wiener Bonbons.* STRAUSS, Johann, Snr: *Cachucha Galop.* STRAUSS, Josef: Polkas: *Moulinet; Ohne Sorgen. Aquarellen waltz.*

** Chan. Dig. ABRD/*ABTD* 1039. Johann Strauss O., led Rothstein (violin).

Digital recording is not everything, and here it serves to emphasize the rather thin sound of the upper strings, although there is no lack of overall bloom. The playing is spirited and more infectious than Maazel's New Year digital concert (see above); indeed the spontaneity of the music-making is the strongest feature of this collection.

'Vienna in waltztime', Vol. 1: Perpetuum mobile; Persischer Marsch. Polkas: *Demolirer; Vergnügungszug.* Waltzes: *Accelerationen; An der schönen blauen Donau; Künstlerleben; Morgenblätter; Wiener Bonbons.*
(M) **(*) RCA Gold GL/*GK* 25263. Berlin SO or VSO, Stolz.

At the beginning of the seventies the German Eurodisc company produced a comprehensive boxed set of twenty LPs of Viennese dance music under the direction of the distinguished veteran Robert Stolz. Nine of these records were devoted to the music of Johann Strauss, Junior, and they are the source of this series of RCA reissues. Although the strings of the Berlin and Vienna Symphony Orchestras lack the polished veneer of the VPO, the playing has plenty of vigour. This collection opens with an infectious account of *Accelerationen* and closes with an equally spirited *Künstlerleben*. The polkas and the *Perpetuum mobile* are especially vivid. Stolz solves the problem of ending the latter with a slow diminuendo. The recording is warmly reverberant, but shows its age somewhat in the massed upper string tone. However, this is enjoyable and good value. The cassette is slightly overmodulated on side one, which brings moments of coarseness. Side two is better.

'Vienna in waltztime', Vol. 2: Marches: *Ägyptischer; Indigo.* Polkas: *Eljen a Magyar; Freikugeln.* Waltzes: *Freuet euch des Lebens; Geschichten aus dem Wiener Wald; 1001 Nacht; Wein, Weib und Gesang; Wiener Blut.*

(M) **(*) RCA Gold GL/*GK* 25264. Berlin SO or VSO, Stolz.

An enjoyable collection, including a pair of attractive novelties among more familiar fare. The performance of *Tales from the Vienna Woods* is appealing, and if Stolz's rubato is sometimes a little mannered, in general these performances combine warmth with vitality. The reverberant recording is well judged, and it has transferred quite well to tape at a noticeably lower level than the first volume.

'Vienna in waltztime', Vol. 3: Banditen galop; Ritter Pásmán csárdás; Im Krapfenwald'l polka; Russischer Marsch. Waltzes: *Frühlingsstimmen; Kaiser; Lagunen; Rosen aus dem Süden; Schatz.*
(M) *** RCA Gold GL/*GK* 25265. Berlin SO or VSO, Stolz.

This is the most successful of the Stolz Strauss collections so far. The performances combine vigour with an attractive Viennese lilt, and the csárdás, galop and polka bring a balancing exuberance. Stolz's affectionate phrasing of the waltzes never slips into blandness, and the whole concert is very enjoyable. The recording is lively and resonant; a little control of the treble is useful. The cassette has marginally less range than the disc, but this slight smoothing at the top is not disadvantageous.

Waltzes transcribed by Schoenberg, Webern and Berg: *Kaiser; Rosen aus dem Süden* (both trans. Schoenberg); *Schatz waltz* (from *Der Zigeunerbaron;* trans. Webern); *Wein, Weib und Gesang* (trans. Berg).
**(*) DG 2530/*3300* 977 [id.]. Boston SO Chamber Players.

A fascinating curiosity. Schoenberg, Berg and Webern made these transcriptions for informal private performances. Schoenberg's arrangements of the *Emperor* and *Roses from the South* are the most striking, though Berg's *Wine, Women and Song* is sweetly appealing with its scoring for harmonium. As might be expected, Webern's *Schatz waltz* is aptly refined. With the Boston Chamber Players taking rather too literal a view and missing some of the fun, the lumpishness of some of the writing is evident enough, but the very incongruity and the plain love of these three severe atonalists for music with which one does not associate them is endearing. Good, fresh recording and a well-balanced cassette transfer, lacking the final degree of range.

Polkas: *Bitte schön; Leichtes Blut; Sängerlust; Unter Donner und Blitz; Vergnügungszug.* Waltzes: *An der schönen blauen Donau; Geschichten aus dem Wiener Wald; Kaiser; Rosen aus dem Süden; Wiener Blut.*
** RCA RL/*RK* 12754 [ARL 1/*ARK 1* 2754. V. Boys' Ch., Gillesberger; Farnberger, Froschauer (pianos).

Understandably the Vienna Boys' Choir bring an infectiously idiomatic lilt to their singing of these famous waltzes, although occasionally Gillesberger is a shade over-emphatic in his rhythmic control. The singing is always fresh and readily conveys enjoyment, even if it is not always polished. If an orchestra had been provided instead of the piano-duet accompaniment, this would have been more strongly recommendable; when the keyboards substitute for the orchestral horns at the opening of *The Blue Danube*, the effect is very much second-best. However, admirers of the choir will find that their youthful enthusiasm often carries the day; *Tales from the Vienna Woods* is especially successful. Preludes and codas are often abbreviated, sensibly enough with the available resources. The recording is good both on disc and on tape.

OPERETTA

Die Fledermaus (complete).
(M) (***) HMV mono RLS/*TC-RLS* 728 (2). Schwarzkopf, Streich, Gedda, Krebs, Kunz, Christ, Philh. Ch. and O., Karajan.
(B) ** Eurodisc 88610 XDE (2). Lipp, Holm, Schock, Nicolai, Berry, Curzi, Steiner, V. State Op. Ch., VSO, Stolz.

If the catalogue has never been infested with Fledermice, that is a recognition of the quality of earlier sets, notably Karajan's 1955 version (originally issued on Columbia), produced by Walter Legge and now reissued on HMV. This version has great freshness and clarity along with the polish which for many will make it a first favourite. Tempi at times are unconventional, both slow and fast, but the precision and point of the playing are magical and the singing is endlessly delightful. Schwarzkopf makes an enchanting Rosalinde, not just in the imagination and sparkle of her singing but also in the snatches of spoken dialogue (never too long) which leaven the entertainment. Needless to say she makes a gloriously commanding entry in the party scene, which is in every sense a highspot of Walter Legge's production. As Adèle, Rita Streich (like Schwarzkopf a pupil of Maria Ivogün) produces her most dazzling coloratura; Gedda and Krebs are beautifully contrasted in their tenor tone, and Erich Kunz gives a vintage performance as Falke. The original mono, crisply focused, has been given a brighter edge but otherwise left unmolested. However, the tape transfer softens this considerably, yet loses none of the vocal presence and detail. Indeed the atmosphere and naturalness of the recording balance are splendidly caught.

Robert Stolz, himself a distinguished operetta composer, directs a sparkling performance of *Fledermaus*, bright and atmospheric if not as subtle in expression as, say, Karajan's. The jollity of the *Woe is me* trio (*O je, o je*) emerges in each stanza just a little too soon, for example. The cast represents a good sample of Viennese singers, but Wilma Lipp at the very end of her career is disappointingly shrill as Rosalinde, and not well contrasted with the charming Adèle of Renate Holm. The recording is vivid and immediate, the production excellent, and in spite of the reservations this makes congenial listening. However, first choice in stereo is still Boskovsky's HMV set (SLS 964 [Ang. S 3790]), with Anneliese Rothenberger a sweet, domestic-sounding Rosalinde, relaxed and sparkling, and an excellent supporting cast, among whom the Orlofsky of Brigitte Fassbaender must be singled out as quite the finest on record. The stereo is ripe and pleasing.

Die Fledermaus: highlights (in English).

(M) ** HMV Green. ESD/*TC-ESD* 7083. Studholme, Pollak, Elliot, Young, John Heddle Nash, Sadler's Wells Opera, Tausky.

The Sadler's Wells Company often showed in the theatre that it was second to none in capturing Viennese gaiety, and on this record the whole production moves with great vigour. The chorus in particular has an incisiveness which will disappoint no one, but it must be admitted that the soloists, while always reliable, are not particularly memorable in their singing. Marion Studholme, for example, as Adèle sings with great flexibility, but there is a 'tweety' quality to her voice, as caught by the microphone, which prevents the final degree of enjoyment. Anna Pollak is the one serious disappointment. In the theatre this highly intelligent singer rarely failed to give dramatic as well as understanding performances, but here as Prince Orlofsky she sounds too old-womanly by far, and her attempts at vocal acting – effective in the theatre – sound over-mannered and only add to the womanliness. The re-cording is brilliant, with a clarity of definition and numerous directional effects which are most realistic. The cassette transfer is strikingly lively and vivid, with plenty of sparkle and projection. The high level brings hardly any peaking.

Wiener Blut (complete).

(B) **(*) Eurodisc 88616 XDE (2). Schock, Schramm, Gueden, Lipp, Kusche, Kunz, V. State Op. Ch. and SO, Stolz.

This scintillating performance under the direction of Robert Stolz, with a first-rate singing cast headed by Rudolf Schock, Hilde Gueden and Erich Kunz, can be strongly recommended. Though the voices are balanced forward the production (with sound effects) is very atmospheric, making this Strauss confection – drawn from various earlier numbers with the blessing of the composer – a fizzing Viennese entertainment. It is a delight to hear the famous *Morning Papers* waltz, for example, turned into a song for Gabriele in Act 1; and here Gueden sings it charmingly, though hardly with the finesse of Schwarzkopf, whose performance in Walter Legge's medium priced mono set of the mid-fifties is, of course incomparable; but that is at present out of the catalogue.

Strauss, Richard
(1864–1949)

An Alpine symphony, Op. 64.

*** DG Dig. 2532/*3302* 015 [id.]. Berlin PO, Karajan.

*** Decca SXL/*KSXC* 6959 [Lon. 7189]. Bav. RSO, Solti.

(M) *** RCA Gold GL/*GK* 42697. RPO, Kempe.

Karajan's account is recorded digitally, but orchestral detail is less analytical than in Solti's Decca version. Indeed the latter is fresher and more transparent, and has not the slight edge to the upper strings that is a feature of the DG digital recording. But it would be wrong to give the impression that the DG sound is less than first-class, and as a performance, the Karajan is in the highest flight. It is wonderfully spacious, beautifully shaped and played with the utmost virtuosity. This is arguably the finest account now available, though Kempe's version has an equal breadth and majesty and no less atmosphere. The DG chrome cassette matches the disc closely, although side one has fractionally less sparkle at the top than side two. However, the edge noticeable on the disc is softened on tape.

The Bavarian Radio orchestra under Solti, recorded in the Herkulessaal in Munich, could hardly sound more opulent, with brass of incomparable richness. That warmth of sound and the superlative quality of recording tend to counterbalance the generally fast tempi. Many of them are in principle too fast, but with such sympathetic and committed playing in such a setting the results are warm rather than frenetic. The cassette matches the disc in depth and richness, although the LP has slightly more energy in the highest frequencies.

At medium price, Kempe's Gold Seal version makes an excellent recommendation, no less warm and committed than his later, Dresden performance on HMV, and on balance a shade more spontaneous-sounding. The recording quality is very good for its mid-sixties vintage, but on cassette the relative lack of bass detracts from the fullness, and the treble lacks real sparkle too.

Also sprach Zarathustra, Op. 30.
**(*) CBS Dig. 35888 [Col. M/*HMT* 35888]. NYPO, Mehta.
*(**) HMV ASD/*TCC-ASD* 3897 [Ang. DS 37744]. Phd. O., Ormandy.

Neither of the two new digital single-

disc versions of *Also sprach Zarathustra* is completely satisfactory, and as an example of sumptuously brilliant orchestral sound as well as a demonstration of instrumental virtuosity of the highest order, the DG version by the Berlin Philharmonic Orchestra under Karajan still earns a rosette as arguably the most electrifying recording ever made (2530 402/*3300 375*).

Mehta's NYPO version is predictably exciting and the recording is brilliantly clear and positive, with more tonal substance than the Ormandy HMV disc. There is some superbly eloquent horn playing, and the forceful thrust of Mehta's reading brings undoubted exhilaration at climaxes; the appearance of the midnight bell at the apotheosis of the *Tanzlied* makes a spectacular effect, and the closing *Nachtwanderlied* is tenderly played. But Karajan finds more mysticism in the score than Mehta, and the bright sheen on the New York strings is less telling than the Berlin string timbre in the 'Yearning' and 'Passion' sequences.

The very opening of the Ormandy disc is riveting in its clarity and impact, but elsewhere the massed Philadelphia strings are made to sound brittle by the crystalline brilliance of the lighting of the overall sound picture. Yet in all this sharpness of focus Nietzsche's midnight bell tolls without impact, all but buried in the middle of the orchestra. The performance is not without fire and virtuosity, but the sound tires the ear, though the cassette is slightly smoother and fuller than the disc.

Also sprach Zarathustra; Don Juan, Op. 20; Till Eulenspiegel, Op. 28.
(m) *** Decca Jub. JB/*KJBC* 77. VPO, Karajan.

With superlative performances of Strauss's three most popular symphonic poems squeezed on to a single disc, the Jubilee issue is an outstanding bargain at medium price. In Strauss no one can quite match Karajan in the flair and point of his conducting, and these Vienna performances of the early sixties make up in warmth what they may slightly lack in polish compared with Karajan's later Berlin versions for DG. The sound, though not as full as the DG recordings, is extremely good for its period. The cassette is generally satisfactory, although the spectacular opening is slightly more secure on the disc.

Also sprach Zarathustra; Salome: Dance of the Seven Veils.
(B) **(*) CfP CFP/*TC-CFP* 40289. LPO, Del Mar.

Norman Del Mar's performance of *Also sprach Zarathustra* lacks something in thrust and warmth, but it is a refined reading, which shows how perceptive an interpreter of Strauss he is. There is no hint of vulgarity here, and playing and recording (late-seventies vintage) are excellent. On cassette the treble needs cutting back if the upper strings are not to lack body, but the powerful opening is well caught, and the sinuous performance of *Salome's Dance* sounds especially vivid.

Also sprach Zarathustra; Salome: Dance of the Seven Veils; Till Eulenspiegel.
(M) *** HMV Green. ESD/*TC-ESD* 7026. Dresden State O., Kempe.

Kempe's stature as a Strauss conductor has been challenged only by Karajan. His *Also sprach Zarathustra* is completely free of the sensationalism that marks so many newer performances, though in sheer opulence and virtuosity it must yield to the Karajan DG version (see above), which offers more vivid sound but has no fill-ups. Kempe's *Till Eulenspiegel* is excellent, though it does not obliterate memories of his marvellous early Berlin Philharmonic account (used

as a fill-up to *Don Quixote*; see below). By the side of that, the present version seems rather square and earthbound, lacking in humour; but this remains an eminently recommendable collection, well recorded on both disc and tape, and offering the advantage of *Also sprach Zarathustra* complete and uninterrupted on one side.

Also sprach Zarathustra; Till Eulenspiegel.
(B) **(*) Con. CC/*CCT* 7542. RPO, Henry Lewis.

Lewis gives a glowing, warm-hearted performance of *Also sprach Zarathustra*, not lacking excitement, and a broad-paced but nicely sprung performance of *Till Eulenspiegel*. The recordings, originally made for Decca's Phase Four label, have a boldly spectacular sound that makes plenty of impact. The cassette matches the disc fairly closely; it has slightly less brilliance at the top and is not quite so secure in the famous opening climax of *Also sprach Zarathustra*. A good bargain in the lowest price-range.

(i) *Le Bourgeois Gentilhomme* (incidental music); (ii) *Oboe concerto in D.*
*** CBS 76826/40- [Col. M/*MT* 35160]. ECO, Barenboim, with (i) Frankl, (ii) Black.

Barenboim, directing an outstandingly crisp and elegant performance of Strauss's incidental music with its element of pastiche, makes it less sugary than it often is. The *Oboe concerto*, a work from much later in Strauss's career but also with a tinge of neoclassicism, draws a comparably sympathetic performance from Neil Black. The CBS recording is not quite so refined as the performances, but on disc this coupling is highly recommendable. The cassette is disappointingly lacking in range, and there is poor orchestral detail. The solo oboe is truthfully caught, but this cannot compare with the disc.

Burleske in D min. for piano and orchestra, Op. 11.
** CBS 76910/40- [Col. M/*MT* 35832]. Entremont, Nat. PO, Kamu – DOH-NÁNYI: *Nursery variations;* LITOLFF: *Scherzo.***

The close balance of the piano and the beefy recording quality work better in this Strauss rarity than in the couplings, and this is an energetic performance of music which is all youthful brilliance. The tape transfer is impressively lively and wide in range.

Horn concertos Nos. 1 in E flat, Op. 11; 2 in E flat.
(M) ** Sup. 1110 2808. Bělohlávek, Prague SO, Tylšar.

Jiri Bělohlávek is a fine player. He phrases musically, produces an agreeably rich timbre and articulates the finales of both these concertos with an attractively light touch. His romantic approach is persuasive, and the only drawback is that for some ears his use of vibrato, though subtly controlled, is at times intrusive, as in the bold central climax of the *Andante* of the *First Concerto.* The accompaniments are well made, and the integration of soloist and orchestra in No. 2 is striking. This is certainly enjoyable.

Death and Transfiguration, Op. 24; Don Juan, Op. 20; Till Eulenspiegel, Op. 28.
*** CBS Dig. 35826/41- [Col. M/*MT* 35826]. Cleveland O., Maazel.
**(*) Decca Dig. SXDL/*KSXDC* 7523. Detroit SO, Dorati.
(M) *(**) CBS 60108/40- [Col. MY 36721]. Cleveland O., Szell.
**(*) HMV Dig. ASD/*TCC-ASD* 3913 [Ang. DS/*4ZX* 37753]. VPO, Previn.

Maazel repeats a coupling made famous by George Szell at the peak of his era with the Cleveland Orchestra, but Maazel's approach is entirely different.

With superbly committed support from his players, he takes an extrovert view of *Death and Transfiguration;* the mortal struggle is frenzied enough, but there is comparatively little feeling of menace, and when the transformation comes, the opulent climax is endearingly rose-tinted. The portrayal of *Till* is warmly affectionate, but the reading is exhilaratingly paced and has excellent detail. *Don Juan* too is made totally sympathetic, with Maazel relishing every moment. In the famous love scene the oboe solo is glowingly sensuous, and the final climax is ecstatic, the tempo broadened when the strings rapturously take up the great horn tune. The CBS digital sound is sumptuous, richly glowing, but does not lack clarity, and the brass has telling bite and sonority. The chrome cassette too (transferred at a high level) has comparable body and brilliance, with a wide range.

Dorati's Decca recording is also digital, and its internal clarity is striking. Dorati's approach to *Death and Transfiguration* is more austere than Maazel's; there is plenty of atmosphere, a certain dignity in the struggle and a sense of foreboding before the release at the end, where the climax has real splendour (and a magnificent breadth of sound). Dorati's view of *Don Juan* is heroic, the sensuality played down by the sound balance, brilliant rather than sumptuous. After a central love scene which is tenderly delicate, there is satiety and disillusion at the end. *Till* is essentially a picaresque portrait, not without humour and well paced, but a little lacking in affectionate involvement. In spite of a transfer level that is lower than usual from Decca, there is no appreciable difference in sound between disc and cassette.

Szell's version of *Death and Transfiguration* has tremendous electricity. The opening creates striking atmosphere, and the triumphant closing pages are the more telling for Szell's complete lack of indulgence. *Till* is irrepressibly cheeky, his characterization created from the most polished and vivid orchestral playing, so that every detail is crystal-clear. *Don Juan* is impetuously passionate in the thrustful urgency of his sexuality. Superb playing, the whole interpretation founded on a bedrock of virtuosity from this remarkable orchestra. The recording here is brilliant but rather dry. For those willing to accept the dated sound, this is a fine disc. The cassette has rather less range than the disc but sounds richer if less refined.

Previn's coupling was the first product on record of his new relationship with the Vienna Philharmonic. Like Bernstein before him he has established a special rapport with these formidable players, and plainly their response is whole-hearted; one might well mistake this (as recorded) for the LSO. These are not at all Viennese-type performances, relatively direct, strong and urgent rather than affectionate, refreshing rather than idiomatic, but lacking something in ultimate spontaneity. Their qualities are matched by the full and bright digital recording. The chrome cassette is of good quality, but the relatively modest transfer level means that the upper range is less sparkling than on some EMI chrome issues.

Death and Transfiguration; Meta morphosen for 23 solo strings.
(M) *** DG Acc. 2542/*3342* 164. Berlin PO, Karajan.

Death and Transfiguration is stunningly played here and very well recorded. Karajan made the very first recording of *Metamorphosen* in the late 1940s, and this Berlin account is sumptuous in every way. Given its competitive price, this must now be a first recommendation in both works. The cassette is of good quality, though slightly less refined than the disc; it benefits from a treble cut.

Don Juan, Op. 20.
(B) *** Con. CC/ *CCT* 7528. VPO,

Karajan – TCHAIKOVSKY: *Romeo and Juliet.****
(B) **(*) RCA VICS/*VK* 2006 [AGL 1/*AGK 1* 1276]. LAPO, Mehta – RESPIGHI: *Feste romane.***(*)

Karajan's early Decca version of *Don Juan*, now reissued on Contour, is an outstanding bargain, for the performance is superbly played, and Karajan is as beguiling in the love music as he is exhilarating in the chase. The recording is excellent for its period (1961), and the Tchaikovsky coupling is equally exciting. The Contour cassette transfer lacks the lively upper range of the LP.

Extrovert brilliance is very much the principal quality of Mehta's version (one of the first records he made with the Los Angeles Philharmonic), but he relaxes expansively in the rich music of the love scene, drawing hushed and intense playing from the orchestra. With bright, atmospheric, but slightly brittle recording this might well be considered an alternative in the same price-range if the coupling is more suitable. The chrome tape mirrors the disc.

Don Juan; (i) *Don Quixote, Op. 35.*
**(*) Ph. 9500 440/*7300 647.* Concg. O., Haitink, (i) with De Machula.

Haitink's recording of the two Dons of Richard Strauss (an apt and surprisingly rare coupling) brings superb examples of Concertgebouw playing dating from different periods. *Don Juan*, which originally appeared as fill-up to Haitink's version of Elgar's *Enigma variations*, has refinement as well as panache. *Don Quixote* brings an even more striking performance, one which without exaggeration or mannerism makes Strauss's often fragmented textures cohere much more lyrically than is common. Tibor de Machula does not quite touch the depths in Quixote's dying peroration, but he has great dignity and beauty of tone; and the performance overall is strongly coordinated, consistently compelling, even if it has not the intoxicating flamboyance of either of the Karajan versions (HMV ASD/*TC-ASD* 3118 [Ang. S/*4XS* 37057] and DG 2535/*3335* 195). The Philips cassette is a little lacking in range in *Don Quixote*, but opens up impressively in *Don Juan*.

Don Juan; München (commemorative waltz); *Der Rosenkavalier: Suite*.
(M) **(*) RCA Gold GL/*GK* 42871 [AGL 1/*AGK 1* 2940]. LSO, Previn.

As a medium-price reissue Previn's coupling is most attractive. In principle one must disapprove of the rescoring of favourite extracts from *Rosenkavalier* (including the famous trio), but Previn here indicates what a persuasive opera conductor he might be. *Don Juan* is splendid too, and the waltz specially written for Munich is a charming and rare makeweight. The recording, late-sixties vintage, is excellent for its period. The cassette too is agreeably sumptuous.

Don Juan; Till Eulenspiegel, Op 28; Salome: Dance of the Seven Veils.
(M) **(*) HMV SXLP/*TC-SXLP* 30298. Philh. O., Klemperer.

Not everyone will respond to Klemperer's spacious approach to these symphonic poems. His account of *Salome's Dance* is splendidly sensuous, but the ennobled *Till* lacks something in boisterousness and sheer high spirits, and *Don Juan* is clearly seen as 'the idealist in search of perfect womanhood'. But with marvellous Philharmonia playing and a recording which still sounds strikingly sumptuous and yet has excellent detail on disc and tape alike, this collection is certainly not lacking in strength of characterization.

(i) *Don Quixote. Der Rosenkavalier: Waltz sequence*.
(M) *** HMV SXLP/*TC-SXLP* 30428.

Dresden State O., Kempe, (i) with Tortelier.

(i) *Don Quixote. Till Eulenspiegel*.
⊛ (B) *** CfP CFP/*TC-CFP* 40372. Berlin PO, Kempe, (i) with Tortelier.

The first of Kempe's two recordings of *Don Quixote* with Tortelier for EMI, the version with the Berlin Philharmonic Orchestra – unbelievably recorded as early as 1958 – is one of the great classics of the gramophone. It has been remastered for this CfP reissue, retaining its ambient warmth yet revealing every smallest detail of Strauss's magical score. The solo cello is admirably balanced, yet Tortelier's splendid contribution is still able to take a leading role in the performance. Kempe's reading is essentially traditional, yet the wit is pointed with delicious lightness of touch which suggests complete rapport with every member of the orchestra. There is the most refreshing spontaneity throughout, and the Dulcinea passages have a sweetness and lyrical beauty that do not sound out of keeping with the humour of the work. *Till Eulenspiegel* more than almost any other recorded performance conveys the sparkle of the work in playing that is brilliant but never forced. Both these picaresque symphonic poems, with their frequent changes of tempo, require the right degree of flexibility, and this Kempe achieves supremely well. Again the recording combines breadth with sparkle, although the upper range is more soft-grained. The cassette matches the disc closely, only fractionally less sharply focused and very well balanced.

Kempe's later Dresden recording is also highly recommendable. The recording – from the mid-seventies – is obviously richer and more sumptuous than the earlier one, but the balance gives the cello an exaggerated forward projection. Nevertheless Tortelier plays with great eloquence, and the performance overall is wholly satisfying. If the coupling is suitable (and Kempe's view of the *Rosen-*

kavalier waltzes is certainly beguiling) this is excellent value at medium price. On cassette the upper strings have slightly less body than on the disc; otherwise the sound is vivid and wide in range.

Fanfare for Music Week in Vienna (1924); *Fanfare for the Vienna Philharmonic; Feier Einzug der Ritter des Johanniterordens; Festmusik der Stadt Wien; Olympic hymn* (1936); *Parade marches Nos. 1 and 2* (arr. Locke).
*** Chan. ABR/*ABT* 1002. Locke Brass Cons., Stobart.

Not all this music is of equal interest. The two *Parade marches*, which date from 1905, offer agreeable invention but were scored by others. On the other hand the *Festmusik* is a considerable piece in the grand manner, using antiphonal effects to acknowledge its baroque heritage, although this is not emphasized by the recording layout. Otherwise the sound is first-class, rich and sonorous and spacious in feeling. On tape a relatively low-level transfer has lost a fraction of the upper range, but the body and amplitude of sound remain impressive. An attractive if hardly essential collection.

Ein Heldenleben, Op. 40.
(M) *** Ph. Seq. 6527/*7311* 128 [6500 048]. Concg. O., Haitink.
(M) ***HMV SXLP/*TC-SXLP* 30293 [Scra. S 60041]. RPO, Beecham.
(M) *** Decca Jub. JB/*KJBC* 101. LAPO, Mehta.
**(*) Decca SET/*KCET* 601 [Lon. 7083/5-]. VPO, Solti.
(M) ** DG Acc. 2542/*3342* 153. VPO, Boehm.
** CBS 76675 [Col. M 34566]. Cleveland O., Maazel.

Haitink's 1971 version of *Ein Heldenleben* is one of his finest records. He gives just the sort of performance, brilliant and swaggering but utterly without bombast, which will delight those who normally resist this rich and expansive work. With a direct and fresh manner that yet conveys consistent urgency, he gives a performance which makes even such fine rival versions as Mehta's or Karajan's sound a little superficial. In the culminating fulfilment theme, a gentle, lyrical 6/8, Haitink finds a raptness in restraint, a hint of agony within joy, that links the passage directly with the great Trio from *Der Rosenkavalier*. The Philips sound – freshened in this reissue – is admirably faithful, refined but full and brilliant too.

Beecham made a much praised mono recording of *Ein Heldenleben* in 1947 (available within World Records SHB 100), and in some respects this 1961 stereo version – the last major work he recorded – is not quite its equal. But the advantages of stereo in this score are very considerable, and the overall sound here is remarkably fresh and detailed: it has richness, warmth and greater clarity than the Karajan Privilege issue (DG 2535/*3335* 194). Beecham liked to work on a large scale, and the 1961 performance is immensely vigorous yet tender and sensuous when the music calls for it. There is also a marvellously unforced sense of naturalness in the phrasing, together with refined playing from strings and wind and an excellent solo contribution from the leader, Steven Staryk. Haitink's disc must be a first recommendation in this price-range, but the Beecham magic exercises its own special pull, and the HMV version remains highly competitive. The cassette transfer is well managed. The upper strings are slightly wanting in bloom, but there is no lack of body, and the bass is full and clean. Detail remains excellent.

Mehta's is an extrovert and extremely exciting account to impress the Straussian weaned on the opening of *Also sprach Zarathustra*. It may miss some of the subtler qualities of a richly varied score, but its thrust is undeniable. It is superbly recorded, and the cassette has all the breadth and amplitude of the LP; both approach demonstration quality.

Solti characteristically gives a fast-moving performance, tense to the point of fierceness in the opening tutti and elsewhere. It underlines the urgency rather than the opulence of the writing, and though many Straussians will prefer a warmer, more relaxed view, Solti finds his justification in a superb account of the final coda after the fulfilment theme, where in touching simplicity he finds complete relaxation at last, helped by the exquisite playing of the Vienna Philharmonic's concertmaster, Rainer Küchl. The Decca recording is formidably wide-ranging to match this high-powered performance. The cassette transfer is made at the highest level and has an obvious feeling of spectacle. But when one turns over for the 'battle' sequence there is a hint of congestion, although for the most part the sound is brilliant and vivid.

Boehm's version is superbly played by the Vienna Philharmonic, but his reading lacks the dash and fire of the others. He is a shade dour and a little too conscious of his dignity by comparison with the swaggering hero of Karajan. DG provide splendidly detailed recording, with no lack of impact and presence, but the performance is ultimately uncompelling. The cassette transfer is clear and full-bodied.

Maazel's reading brings splendid playing from the Cleveland Orchestra (the solo violin and first horn are outstanding), but the reading is strangely inconsistent, unexpectedly relaxed in the first half, very tense indeed in the second from the encounter with the critics onwards. The recording, unlike most from CBS, is very expansive, unanalytical to the point of being washy.

Metamorphosen for 23 solo strings (see also above); *Capriccio: Introduction.*

(*) Erato STU 71333. Lausanne CO, Jordan – WAGNER: *Siegfried idyll.**

Armin Jordan directs an impressively controlled account of *Metamorphosen*. The playing of the Lausanne Chamber Orchestra is excellent, though not quite as refined as in the ASMF version under Marriner, which has a similar coupling (Argo ZRG 604). The *Capriccio Introduction* is played by the full string section with considerable ardour. The sound is full-bodied and clear, and the coupling is attractive.

CHAMBER MUSIC

Serenade for wind instruments, Op. 7; Sonatina No. 1 in F; Symphony for wind; Suite in B flat for 13 wind instruments, Op. 4.

(M) *** Ph. 6770 048 (2). Neth. Wind Ens., De Waart.

A highly attractive set of wind music spanning the whole of Strauss's creative career. The *Serenade* was composed while he was still at school, and its accomplished writing and easy melodic flow are immediately engaging. The *Symphony* is a late work, and is given a marvellously alert performance here. The *Sonatina*, also a late work, was written while Strauss was recovering from an illness, and is subtitled 'From an invalid's workshop'. It is a richly scored piece, as thoroughly effective as one would expect from this master of wind writing. (The scoring is for double wind, a C clarinet, a corno di bassetto, bass clarinet and double bassoon, and marvellously sonorous it is.) The *B flat Suite* was written in 1884 but not published until 1911. These delightful pieces are given beautifully characterized accounts here, and they are crisply and cleanly recorded.

VOCAL MUSIC

Vier letzte Lieder (Four Last Songs);

Lieder: *Befreit; Morgen; Mutter-
tändelei; Ruhe, meine Seele; Wiegenlied; Zueignung.*
**(*) CBS 76794 [Col. M/*MT* 35140]. Te
Kanawa, LSO, Andrew Davis.

Kiri Te Kanawa gives an open-
hearted, warmly expressive reading of the
Four Last Songs. If she misses the sort
of detail that Schwarzkopf uniquely
brought, her commitment is never in
doubt. Her tone is consistently beautiful,
but might have seemed even more so if
the voice had not been placed rather too
close in relation to the orchestra. The
orchestral arrangements of other songs
make an excellent coupling (as a comparable selection does in the Schwarzkopf stereo version), and Andrew Davis
directs most sympathetically if not with
the sort of rapt dedication that Szell gave
to Schwarzkopf. The latter's similar
stereo collection is still available on
ASD/*TC-ASD* 2888 [Ang. S 36347],
with the newly issued cassette matching
the disc closely. The CBS tape is smooth
on top, but lacks something in expansive
richness in the middle range.

(i) *Vier letzte Lieder.* (ii) *Arabella:*
excerpts. (i) *Capriccio:* closing
scene.
(M) (***) HMV mono RLS 751 (2).
Schwarzkopf, Philh. O., cond. (i)
Ackermann, (ii) Von Matačic, with
Metternich, Gedda.

The separate mono recordings of
Richard Strauss which Schwarzkopf
made in the 1950s form a superb pendant
to her two supreme complete opera recordings with Karajan, *Rosenkavalier*
and *Ariadne auf Naxos.* Rarely if ever has
the character of Arabella been conveyed
so sparklingly yet with such tenderness
as in these generous and well-chosen excerpts, helped by the fine singing of a
baritone seldom heard on record, Josef
Metternich, a magnificent Mandryka.
The *Capriccio* last scene and the *Four*

Last Songs are a degree lighter than
Schwarzkopf's later recordings, but just
as detailed and searching, putting a
different gloss on interpretations unlikely
ever to be outshone. The transfers are
first-rate.

OPERA

Die ägyptische Helena (complete).
*** Decca D 176 D 3/*K 176 K 33* (3)
[Lon. 13135]. Gwyneth Jones, Kastu,
Hendricks, Willard White, Detroit SO,
Dorati.

Last of the six operas in which Strauss
collaborated with Hugo von Hofmannsthal, this grand classical ex-
travaganza was initially designed as a
vehicle for the glamorous soprano Maria
Jeritza (famous above all for her pro-
vocative *Tosca*) and the tenor Richard
Tauber. Hofmannsthal's device of ming-
ling two Helen legends has an element of
jokiness in it, but Ancient Greece, as so
often with Strauss, prompted some
heavyweight orchestral writing (echoes
of *Elektra*), and Dorati, using the original Dresden version of the score, draws
magnificent sounds from the Detroit
orchestra, richly and forwardly recorded.
The vocal sounds are less consistently
pleasing. Gwyneth Jones has her squally
moments as Helen, though it is a commanding performance. Matti Kastu
manages as well as any Heldentenor
today in the role of Menelaus, strained at
times but with a pleasing distinctive
timbre. The others too are not always
helped by the closeness, but with excellent documentation it is a richly
enjoyable as well as a valuable set. The
tape transfer is one of Decca's best,
with full-bodied, sumptuous orchestral
sound, splendidly achieved perspectives
for the solo voices and chorus, and
the most spectacular feeling of breadth
for the powerful closing section of the
work.

Arabella (complete).
*** HMV Dig. SLS 5224 (3) [Ang. SX 3917]. Varady, Fischer-Dieskau, Donath, Dallapozza, Schmidt, Berry, Bav. State Op. Ch. and O., Sawallisch.

It was high time that the magic of one of Strauss's sweetest inspirations was caught at full intensity on record. Fine as Sir Georg Solti's set was with Lisa della Casa, recorded in the late fifties, this splendid digital recording is in every way superior, not just in sound but in the warmth and understanding of Sawallisch, the characterful tenderness of Julia Varady as the heroine, and Fischer-Dieskau's fine-detailed characterization of the gruff Mandryka, *der Richtige* (Mr Right) according to the heroine's charmingly romantic view. Helen Donath too is charming as the younger sister, Zdenka, though the voice might be more sharply contrasted. If there are unappealing elements in an opera which would reach a happy ending far too quickly but for uncongenial twists of plot, this recording clothes them with an entirely Straussian glow of richness and charm. Highly recommended.

Ariadne auf Naxos (complete).
(M) (***) HMV mono RLS 760 (3). Schwarzkopf, Schock, Streich, Donch, Seefried, Cuénod, Philh. O., Karajan.
**(*) Decca D 103 D 3 (3)/*K 103 K 32* [Lon. 13131]. Leontyne Price, Gruberova, Kollo, Troyanos, Berry, Kunz, LPO, Solti.

In mono only and with a transfer that removes the fullness of bass, this classic reading of Strauss's most equivocal opera still surpasses any ever recorded in its power to captivate. Schwarzkopf makes the richest of Ariadnes, bringing an aching sense of tragedy to the great lament, while in the vignette of the prima donna in the Prologue she touches in a delectable caricature. Rita Streich's Zerbinetta is not just sparkling; she conveys total joy in her coloratura, and Irmgard

Seefried as the Composer is in some ways the most moving of all, imprinting for ever her distinctive tones on the radiant solo *Musik ist eine heilige Kunst* ('Music is a holy art'). Rudolf Schock is a capable Heldentenor, and the rest of the cast includes some masterly performances in the small roles, such as the Harlequinade characters. Most magical of all is Karajan, here giving a performance that even he has rarely matched in its glowing ardour, with the Philharmonia Orchestra at its very peak.

Brilliance is the keynote of Solti's set of *Ariadne*. This extraordinary confection has so many elements that within its chosen limits this reading is most powerful and compelling, with brilliant playing and recording as well as some strong singing. What the performance is short of is charm and warmth. Everything is so brightly lit that much of the delicacy and tenderness of the writing tends to disappear. Nonetheless the concentration of Solti in Strauss is never in doubt, and though Leontyne Price has given more beautiful performances on record, she makes a strong central figure, memorably characterful. Tatiana Troyanos is affecting as the Composer, and Edita Gruberova establishes herself as the unrivalled Zerbinetta of her generation, though here she is less delicate than on stage. René Kollo similarly is the best Bacchus available, but not of all time. The cassette transfer is clear and sparkling, with plenty of bloom on the voices. The sound of the strings, however, is a trifle dry. The Prologue is accommodated complete on the first of two tapes, with the second containing the rest of the opera.

Daphne (complete).
(M) *** DG 2721 190 (2) [2726 090]. Gueden, King, Wunderlich, Schöffler, Little, Braun, Streich, V. State Op. Ch., VPO, Boehm.

Daphne can be regarded as the first work of Strauss's 'classical' last period culminating in *Metamorphosen*, the *Oboe concerto* and the *Four Last Songs*. It tells the story of Daphne wooed by Apollo and finally turned into a tree, and though it has points in common with *Ariadne* the style is mellower. On record the long single act makes an attractive entertainment, in some ways more effective than on stage, as the final transformation scene is better imagined. This recording of a live performance could hardly be better cast, with the tenors, James King as Apollo and Fritz Wunderlich as Leukippos, both magnificent. Hilde Gueden gives one of her finest performances on record, and Karl Boehm, the opera's dedicatee, is unmatchable, bringing out the work's mellowness.

Elektra: Soliloquy; Recognition scene; Finale.
(B) *** RCA VICS/*VK* 2009 [AGL 1/*AGK 1* 3879]. Borkh, Schoeffler, Yeend, Chicago SO, Reiner.

Inge Borkh never sang *Elektra* at the Met., but this record of excerpts made in the early days of stereo gives a tantalizing indication of what such a performance would have been like. With Borkh singing superbly in the title role alongside Paul Schoeffler and Francis Yeend, this is quite a collector's piece. Reiner provides a superbly telling accompaniment; the performances of the Recognition scene and final duet are as ripely passionate as Beecham's old 78 excerpts and outstrip the complete versions. The balance by no means projects the singers at the expense of orchestral detail, and the recording, though dated, still sounds full and clear. The splendid chrome tape is if anything even more vivid than the disc.

Intermezzo (complete).
*** HMV SLS 5204 (3). Popp, Brammer, Fischer-Dieskau, Bav. RSO, Sawallisch.

What other composer but Strauss could turn an absurd little incident in his married life into an opera as enchanting as *Intermezzo*? He made no secret of the fact that the central character of Storch, the composer, was himself and the nagging but loving wife his own Pauline. That is very much the central role – the name Christine the flimsiest of disguises – involving a virtuoso performance which scarcely lets up for an instant. It was originally designed for the dominant and enchanting Lotte Lehmann, but I doubt if even she can have outshone the radiant Lucia Popp, for she brings out the charm of the character, which for all his incidental trials must have consistently captivated Strauss and provoked this strange piece of self-revelation. The piece inevitably is very wordy, but with this scintillating and emotionally powerful performance under Sawallisch, with fine recording and an excellent supporting cast, this set is as near ideal as could be, a superb achievement.

Der Rosenkavalier: excerpts (Act 1: *Introduction; opening scene; Marschallin's monologue, Duet, closing scene;* Act 2: *Presentation of the silver rose; Duet;* Act 3: *Marschallin's meeting with Sophie; Trio and final duet*).
(M) *** Decca Jub. JB/*KJBC* 57. Crespin, Söderström, Gueden, Holecek, VPO, Varviso.

It was hard luck on Régine Crespin being limited to a disc of excerpts instead of singing the Marschallin in a complete *Rosenkavalier*, but on this showing she would not in any case outshine the achievement of Elisabeth Schwarzkopf. This is a much plainer performance than Schwarzkopf's (some may prefer it on that account) and the projection of character is less intense. But even so Crespin has rarely, if ever, made a better record, and she is beautifully supported by Söderström and Gueden. The selection is most generous and well-chosen, and the recording is first-class, from a vintage Decca period. The tape transfer too is of high quality and approaches demonstration standard on side two, where the level is considerably higher than on side one.

Der Rosenkavalier: highlights.
(M) **(*) Ph. Fest. 6570/*7310* 101. Lear, Von Stade, Welting, Bastin, Hammond-Stroud, Neth. Op. Ch., Rotterdam PO, De Waart.

The glory of the complete set (now deleted) conducted by Edo de Waart was the singing of Frederica von Stade as Octavian, a fresh, youthful performance, full of imagination. Next to her the others are generally pleasing but rarely a match for the finest performances on other sets, though the vignette of Derek Hammond-Stroud's Faninal gives special pleasure, Bastin is a virile Ochs; the disappointment is the Sophie of Ruth Welting, often shallow of tone. Evelyn Lear produces her creamiest, most beautiful tone, but spreads uncomfortably in the Act 3 Trio. The selection here is generous and the recording excellent. The cassette transfer is rich and full, but there is some loss of presence when the level drops on side two.

Salome (complete).
*** HMV SLS/*TC-SLS* 5139 (2) [Ang. SBLX/*4X2X* 3848]. Behrens, Böhm, Baltsa, Van Dam, VPO, Karajan.

Recorded for EMI by Decca engineers in the Sofiensaal in Vienna, Karajan's sumptuously beautiful version faithfully recaptures the flair and splendour of the Salzburg production, which Karajan produced as well as conducted. It was daring of him when preparing both recording and stage production to choose for the role of heroine a singer then relatively unknown, but Hildegard Behrens is triumphantly successful, a singer who in the early scenes has one actively sym-

pathizing with the girlish princess, and who keeps that sympathy and understanding to a stage where most sopranos have been transformed into raging harpies. The sensuous beauty of tone is ravishingly conveyed, but the recording – less analytical than the Decca set under Solti, also recorded in the Sofiensaal – is not always fair to her fine projection of sound, occasionally masking the voice. All the same the feeling of a live performance has been well captured, and the rest of the cast is of the finest Salzburg standard. In particular José van Dam makes a gloriously noble Jokanaan, and in the early scenes his offstage voice from the cistern at once commands attention, underlining the direct diatonic strength of his music in contrast to the exoticry representing Salome and the court. Karajan – as so often in Strauss – is at his most commanding and sympathetic, with the orchestra, more forward than some will like, playing rapturously. This is a performance which, so far from making one recoil from perverted horrors, has one revelling in sensuousness. The tape transfer is less well focused than the discs, producing a degree of congestion at climaxes.

Still recommended: Solti's Decca version (SET 228/9/*K* 111 K 22 [Lon. 1218/5-]) remains a major achievement, arguably more authentic in its projection of horror and depravity. One's spine tingles even as one squirms. Birgit Nilsson's portrayal of Salome is unforgettable. In the final scene she rises to new heights, compelling one to accept the horror of it, while the uncleanness is conveyed more vividly than on any other recorded version. John Culshaw's 'Sonicstage' recording, with its remarkable combination of clarity and opulence, is outstanding; the disc and tape versions both rivet the ear in dramatic impact.

Salome: Dance of the Seven Veils; Closing scene. Lieder: *Cäcilie; Ich liebe dich; Morgen; Wiegenlied; Zueignung.*

**(*) DG 2530/*3300* 963 [id.]. Caballé,
Fr. Nat. O., Bernstein.

One of Caballé's earliest and most refreshingly imaginative opera sets was
Strauss's *Salome* with Leinsdorf conducting. This version of the final scene,
recorded over a decade later with a very
different conductor, has much of the
same imagination, the sweet innocent girl
still observable next to the blood-
thirsty fiend. The other side of the disc
is less recommendable, partly because
Caballé underlines the expressiveness
of works that remain Lieder even with
the orchestral accompaniment. Bernstein
too directs an overweighted account of
the *Dance of the Seven Veils*. The recording is warm and full, but the transfer to
tape is top-heavy: the strings have an
over-accented upper range and are
fierce.

Die schweigsame Frau (complete).
**(*) HMV SLS 5160 (3) [Ang. SZX
3867]. Adam, Burmeister, Scovotti,
Schmidt, Haseleu, Dresden State Op.
Ch., Dresden State O., Janowski.

Strauss was already seventy when he
tackled this exuberant comic opera, with
its libretto by Stefan Zweig based on Ben
Jonson's *Epicoene*. It is evidence of
Strauss's energy that he revelled in the
heavy task of composing and scoring so
much fast, brilliant and complex music,
with the ensembles pointed by touches of
neoclassicism. You might count it all a
lot of fuss over not very much, and this
version is not quite as persuasive as the
Glyndebourne production, with a church
acoustic giving bloom but blurring some
detail. Janowski conducts an efficient
rather than a magical performance, and
Theo Adam's strongly characterized rendering of the central role of Dr Morosus
is marred by his unsteadiness. Jeanette
Scovotti is agile but shrill as the Silent
Woman, Aminta. A valuable set of mixed
success.

STRAVINSKY

Stravinsky, Igor
(1882–1971)

Agon (ballet).
*** Argo ZRG 937. L. Sinf., Atherton –
BERG: *Chamber concerto.****

Agon was written in the mid-fifties,
when Stravinsky was beginning to turn
his attention to what had once been an-
athema to him, serialism. There are
already signs here of the developments in
idiom which were to mark his last period,
but in every bar the sharp, bright focus
of the argument with its distinctive
colourings is both memorable and immediately identifiable as the work of
Stravinsky. Atherton directs a splendid
performance, which without trying to
soften any edges gives an emotional
thrust to these formalized movements
designed for an abstract ballet. As a coupling for the Berg *Chamber concerto* it is
an unexpected but excellent choice, and
the recording is very vivid indeed.

Apollo (*Apollon Musagète*; ballet).
(M) *** DG Acc. 2542/*3342* 134 [2530
065]. Berlin PO, Karajan – BARTÓK:
*Music for strings, percussion and cel-
esta.***(*)

Apollo; Orpheus (ballet).
(M) *** ASV ACM/*ZCACM* 2025.
[None. 71401]. Orch. of St John's,
Lubbock.

The ASV issue offers an ideal and
generous coupling with refined performances and excellent recording. The delicacy of rhythmic pointing in *Apollo* gives
special pleasure, and there is a first-rate
solo violin contribution from Richard
Deakin. This is one of Stravinsky's most
appealing later scores, as readily accessible as the more famous ballets of his early
years. The cassette transfer is smooth and
natural and matches the disc closely.
Though Stravinsky tended to dis-

747

parage Karajan's approach to his music as not being rugged enough, here is a work where Karajan's moulding of phrase and care for richness of string texture make for wonderful results. This neoclassical score is strong enough to stand such individual treatment, and the writing is consistently enhanced by the magnificent playing of the Berlin Philharmonic Orchestra. The recording is first-class on disc and cassette alike.

(i) *Circus polka.* (ii) *Dumbarton Oaks concerto in E flat.* (i) *4 Études for orchestra.* (ii) *Greeting prelude.* (i) *8 Instrumental miniatures for 15 players.* (i) *Suites 1 and 2 for small orchestra.*
(M) *** CBS 61839 [Col. M 31729]. Members of (i) CBC SO, (ii) Columbia SO, cond. composer.

This medium-price reissue of some of Stravinsky's shorter and lighter pieces gives real point to CBS's 'Meet the Composer' series, underlining a sense of humour which came out more readily in the writings than in the music. Sharpest and most colourful are the two suites, but even the *Circus polka* for the Barnum and Bailey elephants and the *Greeting prelude* for Pierre Monteux (on *Happy birthday to you*) have the jewel of genius in them. The composer's own recordings, made when he was in his eighties, have not just unique historic interest but great vigour too, notably the delightful *Dumbarton Oaks concerto*, like a *Brandenburg* updated. The sound is bright but a little coarse.

Circus polka; Fireworks, Op. 4.
(B) *** CfP CFP/*TC-CFP* 40348. New Philh. O., Frühbeck de Burgos – RESPIGHI: *Fountains* and *Pines of Rome.****

Fireworks is a Rimskian scherzo, written in 1908 when Stravinsky was still studying in St Petersburg. It is scored for a large orchestra and caught the attention of Diaghilev, with historic consequences. The *Circus polka* quotes outrageously from Schubert's *Marche militaire.* Both are played here with considerable panache – the Philharmonia articulation in *Fireworks* creates a most exhilarating effect. The recording is reverberant but effectively so; the cassette matches the disc closely.

Violin concerto in D.
*** DG 2531/*3301* 110 [id.]. Perlman, Boston SO, Ozawa – BERG: *Violin concerto.****

Perlman's precision, remarkable in both concertos on this disc, underlines the neoclassical element in the outer movements of the Stravinsky. The two *Aria* movements are more deeply felt and expressive, presenting the work as a major twentieth-century concerto. The balance favours the soloist, but no one will miss the commitment of the Boston orchestra's playing, vividly recorded. The cassette transfer is first-rate, matching the disc closely. Kyung-Wha Chung's version for Decca (SXL/*KSXC* 6601 [Lon. 6819]) can be recommended with enthusiasm alongside Perlman's: its coupling is a splendid account of the Walton *Concerto.*

Ballets: *The Firebird: suite* (1919 score)*; Jeu de cartes; Petrushka* (1911 score). (i) *Pulcinella. The Rite of Spring* (all complete).
(M) *** DG 2740 257 (4) [id.]. LSO, Abbado, (i) with Berganza, Ryland Davies, Shirley-Quirk.

An attractive compilation of essential Stravinsky. The highlight is *Petrushka*, while both the *Firebird suite* and *Jeu de cartes* are given stunning performances of great vitality and sensitivity. The LSO plays with superb virtuosity and spirit; moreover the DG recording is of demonstration standard. This coupling was awarded a rosette in our last edition. There is a degree of detachment in Abbado's reading of *The Rite of Spring*, although his observance of markings is meticulous and the orchestra obviously revels in the security given by the conductor's direction. The recording here is multi-miked, and the effect is less exciting than one would have expected. Nevertheless this is a worthwhile investment taken as a whole.

The Firebird (ballet; complete).
*** Ph. 9500 637/*7300 742* [id.]. Concg. O., Colin Davis.
(M) *** Mercury SRI 75058 [id.]. LSO, Dorati.
(B) *** Con. CC/*CCT* 7500. New Philh. O., Ansermet.
**(*) Decca Dig. SXDL/*KSXDC* 7511 [Lon. LDR 10012/5-]. VPO, Dohnányi.

With superb analogue sound Sir Colin Davis directs a magically evocative account of the complete *Firebird* ballet, helped not just by the playing of the Concertgebouw Orchestra (the strings outstandingly fine) but by the ambience of the hall, which allows the finest detail but gives a bloom to the sound, open and spacious, superbly coordinated. This is finer even than Haitink's splendid LPO version (Philips 6500 483), and is probably the most satisfying account of the *Firebird* score ever committed to disc. The cassette is of good quality, but, as so often with Philips, the transfer level is unadventurous, and in some of the pianissimo passages the tape has not the sharpness of focus of the disc.

Dorati's electrifyingly dramatic 1960 recording remains a classic version. This reissue of the original Mercury disc sounds as fresh and vivid as the day it was made; the brilliant detail and enormous impact suggest a modern digital source rather than an analogue master tape made over twenty years ago. The stereo has remarkable atmosphere too,

and the balance is superb. The performance sounds completely spontaneous, and the LSO wind playing is most sensitive. At medium price this can still compete with the best of modern versions. Only the sound of the massed upper strings slightly hints at its age: the bite of the brass and the transient edge of the percussion are thrilling, especially in the finale.

Ansermet's New Philharmonia version makes a marvellous bargain on Contour in a strikingly clean pressing. It offers more polished playing than the performance Ansermet recorded earlier with his own Suisse Romande Orchestra, but generally the interpretations are amazingly consistent. At times one suspects that the new version is a degree slower, but on checking you find that the difference lies in the extra flexibility and polish of the London players. The recording is of vintage Decca quality and remains demonstration-worthy on disc, though not on cassette, where the bass is over-resonant at the opening and the upper range is restricted.

For a score as magical as *Firebird* a recording can actually be too clear, and the digital sound in Dohnányi's version tends to be too analytical, separating the threads in a way that prevents the music from making its full evocative effect. In any case the reading is on the chill side. The cassette matches the disc very closely indeed; if anything the tape quality is slightly more atmospheric and thus preferable.

The Firebird: Suite (1919 version).
*** HMV ASD/*TC-ASD* 3645 [Ang. S/*4XS* 37539]. Phd. O., Muti – MUSSORGSKY: *Pictures*.***
(*) Telarc Dig. DG 10039 [id.]. Atlanta SO, Shaw – BORODIN: *Prince Igor excerpts*.*

Muti secures superb playing from the Philadelphia Orchestra here. There have been many excellent accounts of this .

score in recent years, from Abbado, Giulini and others, but in terms of magic and poetry this surpasses them all. The pianissimo tone Muti draws from the Philadelphia strings is ravishing. This is a wonderful coupling, and the transfer to tape is first-class; the difference in sound between disc and cassette is minimal.

The *Firebird suite* has been recorded by the finest orchestras in the world, and excellent as is the Atlanta Symphony, it would not claim to be of their number. Nevertheless Robert Shaw, the thoroughly musical conductor, achieves an atmospheric and vivid reading of Stravinsky's famous suite. The *Round dance of the princesses* is played very gently to maximize the shock of the entry of Kastchei. The very wide dynamic range of the digital recording achieves the most dramatic impact both here and in the closing pages of the finale. With its spectacular coupling this issue is designed to appeal to those wanting to show off their reproducer, and that it will certainly do. The surfaces too are completely silent and the pressing very clean.

The Firebird: Suite (1919 version); *Symphony in 3 movements.*
*** RCA Dig. RL 13459 [ARC 1 4306]. Dallas SO, Mata.

The Mata coupling, helped by excellent, finely coordinated digital sound, is chiefly valuable for the vigorous and understanding account of the *Symphony in 3 movements*, a work under-represented on record. The *Firebird suite* in the popular 1919 version is also presented with colour and flair, a fine demonstration of the prowess of the Texas orchestra.

The Firebird: Suite (1945 revised version).
(M) *(*) RCA Gold GL/*GK* 42700 [AGL 1/*AGK 1* 1528]. Boston SO, Leinsdorf – RIMSKY-KORSAKOV: *Le Coq d'or.**(*)

Leinsdorf uses the revised 1945 score with the extra movements (and the *Dance with the golden apples* is one of the most effective numbers here). The over-resonant sound clouds the vivid detail of Stravinsky's orchestration, although in some ways the cassette has rather more impact than the disc. There is fine playing and atmosphere, but this cannot compare with the finest versions of the 1919 suite.

Jeu de cartes (ballet).
(M) (***) HMV mono XLP/*TC-XLP* 60003. Philh. O., Karajan – ROUSSEL: *Symphony No. 4.*(***)

Jeu de cartes was recorded in mono in 1952 and is little short of amazing given its date, with clarity and range that compare well with some modern records. The performance too is of high quality, and there is no want of sensitive and vital playing. In one or two places there could perhaps be greater tautness and concentration, but as a whole this is a satisfying and often exciting account. Altogether an outstanding issue. The cassette matches the disc fairly closely; there is some lack of body in the sound, but it is fully acceptable.

(i) *Jeu de cartes;* (ii) *Scènes de ballet;* (iii) *Bluebird pas de deux* (arr. for chamber orch. from Tchaikovsky's *Sleeping Beauty* ballet).
(M) **(*) CBS 61840 [Col. M 31921]. (i) Cleveland O.; (ii) CBC SO; (iii) Columbia SO; all cond. composer.

It is good to welcome these performances, which have the authority of the composer's direction, back into circulation even if the sound is not of the very highest quality. The CBS *Jeu de cartes*, which originally appeared in the mid-1960s, is inferior to Karajan's 1952 record in mono sound; admittedly the latter is a remarkably fresh and beautifully balanced disc. The *Scènes de ballet* is well worth having too, and the performances have plenty of humour and character even if they may fall short of the ideal in terms of finesse.

Petrushka (ballet; 1911 score; complete).

*** DG Dig. 2532/*3302* 010 [id.]. LSO, Abbado.

(M) *** DG Priv. 2535/*3335* 419. LSO, Dutoit.

Petrushka (1947 score; complete).

*** Decca Dig. SXDL/*KSXDC* 7521 [Lon. LDR 71023/5-]. Detroit SO, Dorati.

*** Ph. 9500 447/*7300 653* [id.]. Concg. O., Colin Davis.

**(*) Decca SXL 6883 [Lon. 7106/5-]. VPO, Dohnányi.

**(*) CBS Dig. 35823/*41*- [Col. M/*HMT* 35823]. NYPO, Mehta.

(*) HMV ASD/*TC-ASD* 3705. Leningrad PO, Temirkanov – RAVEL: *Daphnis Suite No. 3.*

** HMV Dig. ASD/*TCC-ASD* 4069. Phd. O., Muti.

*(*) RCA RL 12615 [ARL 1 2615]. Chicago SO, Levine.

Petrushka (1947 score); *Scherzo à la russe.*

**(*) CBS Dig. 37271/*40*- [Col. IM/*IMT* 37271]. Philh. O., Tilson Thomas.

Abbado's version of the 1911 *Petrushka* has the advantage of extremely fine digital sound, even though it is not quite as overwhelming sonically as Decca's for Dorati. The performance is strongly characterized, and the LSO play marvellously. Abbado combines refinement and a powerful sense of dramatic atmosphere (he is especially sympathetic in the central tableaux) with a kaleidoscopic brilliance of colour. The recording has impressive range and colour, with the chrome tape very close to the disc.

Dorati's account of *Petrushka*, also digital, is based on the 1947 version, though at certain points Dorati reverts to the original 1911 scoring in accordance with his recollections of a conversation he had with Stravinsky himself. *Petrushka* has always been a vehicle for the virtuosity of recording engineers, right from the early days of LP, when Decca put the famous first Ansermet mono LP on to the market. Dorati's version creates a comparable digital landmark. The sound is breathtakingly vivid and clean, yet remains naturally balanced and transparent. The performance does not always have the refinement of Abbado's, but it is immensely dramatic and also very telling in the scene where the frustrated Petrushka is confined to his cell. Dorati is at his finest in the final tableau, bringing out the robust Russian earthiness of the dancing peasants. Abbado's account also has splendid physical exuberance here, but the projection of the Decca sound is even more striking. The Decca cassette is up to the highest standards of the house, extraordinarily vivid and clear to match the disc very closely indeed, even though, unlike the DG Abbado cassette, it uses ferric tape.

At medium price the DG Privilege version remains very competitive indeed. It is brilliantly conducted by Charles Dutoit and is extremely vivid as a recording. Interestingly it was made almost impromptu: a planned opera recording fell through and sessions were hastily reallotted with little advance planning. The result is triumphantly spontaneous in its own right, with rhythms that are incisive yet beautifully buoyant, and a degree of expressiveness in the orchestral playing that subtly underlines the dramatic atmosphere, and is especially magical in the Third Tableau. The final section too is strongly coloured, so that the gentle closing pages make a touching contrast to the gaiety of the early part of the scene. The recording is rich and sparkling, the only fault of balance being the prominence of the concertante piano soloist, Tamás Vásáry, who (ably as he plays) is given a ridiculously out-of-proportion star billing. The tape transfer is extremely brilliant; it has plenty of bite and detail, but the treble needs cutting back or the upper strings sound shrill.

Sir Colin Davis's Philips version of the 1947 score combines brilliant and rich recording with a performance which to an exceptional degree makes a positive case for the 1947 score over the original. The recording has some curious and not always perfectly balanced spotlighting of instruments (most unexpected from Philips), but it reveals details of the rich texture that are normally obscured. From first to last Davis makes it clear that he regards this as fun music, drawing brilliantly precise playing from the Concertgebouw and rarely if ever forcing the pace, though always maintaining necessary excitement. The piano solo starts a little cautiously in the Russian dance, but that is an exception in an unusually positive reading. The cassette transfer is slightly soft-grained in the treble, and the tone of the upper strings is somewhat lacking in body compared with the rest of the orchestra; otherwise the quality is vivid.

Dohnányi directs a genial and well-paced reading, slightly lacking in sparkle and imagination but revealing the Vienna Philharmonic as a band very sympathetic to repertory not normally associated with it. Though the piano and trumpet might with advantage have been placed closer, the analogue sound comes near to matching in refinement some of the more recent digital versions.

Mehta's was the first digital recording issued of *Petrushka*, but the clarity and separation of the different strands seemed to be achieved by bringing everything a little too close. It is a clean, energetic performance, lacking a little in rhythmic spring and dramatic flair. The chrome cassette transfer is first-class; made at a high level, it produces wide-ranging, vivid sound, yet slightly mellows the overall effect with positive results.

Tilson Thomas brings more humanity to *Petrushka* than Muti does, though

CBS engineers do not achieve the same transparency and presence as their rivals. (One has to play this disc at high level for its impact to register.) Tempi are sensible and there is no want of character or sensitivity. The *Scherzo à la russe* comes off splendidly.

Temirkanov gets some good playing from the Leningrad orchestra, who respond enthusiastically to his direction. His reading is fresh and characterful, though not quite as polished as some of his best rivals. The cassette transfer is very bright and sharply focused. There is some distortion of the (forwardly balanced) trumpets in the final tableau.

Muti secures playing of stunning virtuosity from the Philadelphians; but if their response is breathtaking, his reading can best be described as breathless. There is unremitting drive here, with the *Danse russe* taken at breakneck speed and everything far too regimented. The recording has splendid impact and clarity, but there is too little tenderness and magic in this overdriven account.

Levine's version is ruled out by the strange congestion of the recording, not at all up to RCA's finest standards. The reading is colourful and vigorous.

Pulcinella: Suite; Scherzo fantastique; Symphonies of wind instruments.
*(*) CBS 76680. NYPO, Boulez.

Boulez, usually a fine Stravinsky interpreter, here misses both the neoclassical point of the *Pulcinella suite* and the darkly detached strength of the *Wind symphonies*, aptly weighty but with the woodwind lacking bite at times. The rare *Scherzo fantastique*, an early work, makes a welcome and brilliant coupling, the most successful performance of the three. The CBS engineers, with their close-up sound, have not helped.

The Rite of Spring (ballet; complete).

*** HMV ASD/*TC-ASD* 3807 [Ang. SZ 37646]. Phd. O., Muti.

*** DG 2530/*3300* 884 [id.]. Berlin PO, Karajan.

*** Decca Dig. SXDL/*KSXDC* 7548. Detroit SO, Dorati.

*** Ph. 9500 323/*7300 585* [id.]. Concg. O., Colin Davis.

**(*) Ph. 9500 781/*7300 855* [id.]. Boston SO, Ozawa.

(M) **(*) ASV ACM/*ZCACM* 2030. Nat. Youth O., Rattle.

** RCA RL 25130. LSO, Tjeknavorian.

In a Philadelphia line stretching back to Stokowski, Muti directs a performance of Stravinsky's barbaric masterpiece which is aggressively brutal yet presents the violence with red-blooded conviction. Muti generally favours speeds a shade faster than usual, and arguably the opening bassoon solo is not quite flexible enough, for metrical precision is a key element all through. There are signs that Muti has studied the last of Stravinsky's own recordings of the *Rite* (by far the most convincing of the three he made), and it is good to have the amendment to the horn part sanctioned in it in the *Sacrificial dance* (two bars before Fig. 75). The recording, not always as analytically clear as some rivals, is gloriously full and dramatic, with brass and percussion exceptionally vividly caught. Like the disc the tape has stunning body and impact: the timpani on side two are transferred without distortion and the effect is very exciting indeed.

Karajan's earlier recording of Stravinsky's masterpiece came in for much snide criticism from the composer, who described one passage as being a *'tempo di hoochie-koochie'*, and doubted whether Berlin Philharmonic traditions could compass music from so different a discipline. In this more recent recording, tougher, more urgent, less mannered, Karajan goes a long way towards rebutting Stravinsky's complaints, and the result is superb, Karajan at his very finest, persuasive still but never obtrusively so, and above all powerfully dramatic. Outstanding recording quality. There is little to choose between tape and disc, and both are spectacular in their vividness and wide range.

However, in terms of recorded sound, Dorati's *Rite* with the Detroit orchestra scores over its rivals. This has stunning clarity and presence, exceptionally lifelike and vivid sound, and the denser textures emerge more cleanly than ever before. It is a very good performance too, almost but not quite in the same league as those of Karajan and Muti, generating plenty of excitement. The only let-down is the final *Sacrificial dance*, which needs greater abandon and higher voltage. The Detroit strings too are not as sumptuous as those of the Berlin and Amsterdam orchestras and sound distinctly undernourished in places. Yet too much should not be made of this. Although Dorati does not match the atmosphere of his finest rivals, the performance is so vivid that it belongs among the very best – and for those primarily concerned with recorded sound, it will probably be a first choice.

Sir Colin Davis has his idiosyncrasies in this Stravinsky score (one of them is his strange hold-up on the last chord), but generally he takes an unusually direct view, and the result is strong, forthright and powerful. Some will prefer a more obviously involving reading, but with the opulent sound of the Concertgebouw Orchestra richly recorded the physical impact of this version is still irresistible. Its richness and body are well transferred to tape, but the cassette's upper range has less sparkle than the disc.

Ozawa directs a distinguished performance which, with superb playing from the Boston orchestra, has plenty of weight but lacks a little in barbaric bite and dynamism. It is rather too well-behaved, and the mellowness of the acoustic adds to that impression, faithful as the Philips sound is.

The performance of the National Youth Orchestra in this once-feared showpiece is not just 'good considering' but 'good' absolute; the youngsters under their young conductor produce warm and spontaneous playing. The conviction of the performance is the more evident because it was recorded in long takes, and the penalty of having a few imprecisions and errors is minimal. At medium price and with full and atmospheric sound this is well worth considering. The cassette transfer is excellent, matching the disc closely.

Tjeknavorian directs a rather sober account of a score that should by rights have an element of wildness, and he is not helped by sound which lacks something in brilliance. It is a capable reading, but cannot match the finest in a very long list which also includes Boulez (CBS 72807 [Col. MS 7293]), Haitink (Philips 6500 482), Solti (Decca SXL/KSXC 6691 [Lon. 6885/5-]), Abbado (DG 2530/3300 635) and Markevitch's excellent bargain version with the Philharmonia Orchestra (CfP CFP 129).

The Soldier's Tale (*L'Histoire du soldat*; complete, in English).
(M) *** DG Priv. 2535 456 [2530 609]. Gielgud, Moody, Courtenay, Boston Chamber Players.

The Boston Chamber Players offer an eminently well-characterized and civilized reading, and they are superbly recorded, even if the spoken element, admirably produced by Douglas Cleverdon, does occupy the foreground when speech and music are mixed.

Symphony in E flat, Op. 1; Symphony in C; Symphony in 3 movements; Ode (*Elegiacal chant in 3 parts*).
*** Chan. Dig. DBRD/*DBTD* 2004 (2). SNO, Gibson.

Even compared with the composer's own performances this collection by the Scottish National Orchestra – in excellent form – under Sir Alexander Gibson stands up well. The vividness of the digital recording makes up for any slight lack of sparkle, and while the *Symphonies for wind instruments* might have seemed a more obvious makeweight for the three major works, it is good to have the *Ode* in memory of Natalia Koussevitzky, which has an extrovert rustic scherzo section framed by short elegies.

VOCAL MUSIC

(i) *Mass;* (ii) *Les Noces.*
*** DG 2530 880 [id.]. (i) Trinity Boys' Ch., E. Bach Festival O.; (i; ii) E. Bach Festival Ch.; (ii) Mory, Parker, Mitchinson, Hudson; Argerich, Zimerman, Katsaris, Francesch (pianos), percussion; cond. Bernstein.

Bernstein directs characterful performances of both works, unexpectedly but imaginatively coupled. He reinforces the point that both the *Mass* and the much earlier ballet illustrating a folk wedding ceremony are intensely Russian in their inspiration. In the *Mass* the style is overtly expressive, with the boys of Trinity Choir responding freshly, but it is in *Les Noces* that Bernstein conveys an electricity, a dramatic urgency which at last on record give the work its rightful stature as one of Stravinsky's supreme masterpieces, totally original and even today unexpected, not least in its black-and-white instrumentation for four pianos and percussion. The star pianists here make a superb imaginative team. Good atmospheric recording.

(i) *Les Noces;* (ii) *Ragtime for 11 instruments;* (iii) *Renard.*
(M) **(*) CBS 61975/*40*-. (i) Barber, Copland, Foss, Sessions (pianos), soloists, Ch., Columbia Percussion Ens.; (ii) Koves (cimbalom), Columbia CO; (iii) Koves, Columbia Chamber Ens.; all cond. composer.

Stravinsky missed some of the barbaric bite of *Les Noces* when he came to record it in his eighties, and the translation into English hardly helps. But there remains a unique authority in this performance, not least with four such distinguished composers at the pianos, and the coupling of two lesser works of the same period, *Ragtime* and *Renard*, makes an attractive package. It is a pity that no text of *Renard* is given, and the recording is hardly refined, but these are issues of historic importance that should be permanently available and will give much pleasure. The cassette transfers of *Renard* and *Ragtime* are lively and vivid, but *Les Noces* (on side two) has less bite and edge because of the lower transfer level.

Oedipus Rex (opera-oratorio; complete).
**(*) Decca SET 616 [Lon. 1168/5-]. McCowen (narrator), Pears, Meyer, McIntyre, Dean, Ryland Davies, Luxon, John Alldis Ch., LPO, Solti.

Solti's view of this highly stylized work is less sharp-edged than one would expect, and the dominant factor in the performance is not so much the conductor's direction as the heartfelt singing of Sir Peter Pears in the title role. It was he who sang the part in the composer's first LP recording twenty years earlier, and here the crispness and clarity of his delivery go with an ability to point the key moments of deep emotion with extraordinary intensity. The rest of the vocal team is good, if not outstanding, and the narrations (in English) of Alec McCowen are apt and undistracting. The recording is outstandingly full and brilliant.

Pulcinella (ballet after Pergolesi; complete).
*** DG 2531/*3301* 087 [id.]. Berganza, Ryland Davies, Shirley Quirk, LSO, Abbado.

Abbado in his outstanding Stravinsky

series with the LSO gives a vividly high-powered reading of this neoclassical ballet score. If he is in danger of over-colouring, the bite and flair are entirely and convincingly Stravinskian, with rhythms sharply incisive. Not only the playing but the singing and recording are outstandingly fine. It is worth remembering, however, that Simon Rattle's more relaxedly pointed reading on HMV (see below) is more clearly in scale and includes a valuable fill-up. On the DG cassette the reverberant acoustic makes the focus less than completely clean in fortissimos, but the sound is generally vivid.

(i) *Pulcinella* (complete); *Suites Nos. 1 and 2.*
*** HMV ASD/*TC-ASD* 3604. Northern Sinfonia, Rattle, (i) with Jennifer Smith, Fryatt, King.

Simon Rattle, helped rather than hindered by a somewhat dry recording acoustic which gives the flavour of a small theatre, conveys far more than usual the links between this score and the much later neoclassical opera *The Rake's Progress.* As one hears this genial theatrical entertainment, Rattle might be directing it as an adjunct to *The Rake's Progress* at Glyndebourne. With lively colourful playing from the Northern Sinfonia (the solos strong and positive) and with first-rate contributions from the three soloists, all of them artists who deserve to record much more, the high spirits of this score come over superbly. The recording has a wide range and gives orchestra and voices alike the most vivid presence and detail. The two *Orchestral suites* are equally successful and make a valuable bonus. The cassette matches the disc closely, but it is a little sharp-edged on top and benefits from a smoothing of the treble.

Symphony of Psalms.
*** CBS 76670 [Col. M/*MT* 34551]. E.

Bach Festival Ch., LSO, Bernstein –
POULENC: *Gloria.****
** DG 2531/*3301* 048 [id.]. German Op.
Ch., Berlin PO, Karajan – BACH: *Magnificat.***

Bernstein's account of the *Symphony*
ranks among the best, though his view of
the work is not as austere and ascetic as
the composer's own. Yet there is grandeur and a powerful sense of atmosphere
as well as first-class singing and playing
from the Bach Festival Chorus and the
LSO. The recording, too, is distinguished
by clarity and range. Though this is not
an all-Stravinsky record it remains an
indispensable item in the Stravinsky discography of recent years.

Even in Stravinsky Karajan keeps
some of his characteristic smoothness –
as the composer himself noted in waspish
comments. This remains an unidiomatic
version, the less recommendable because
the coupling is disappointing, but the
greatness of this masterpiece can stand
the deviation, and the final *Alleluias*
are most beautifully done. The cassette
transfer is admirably faithful.

COLLECTION

'The Recorded Legacy' (anthology of
major works).
(M) **(*) CBS GM 31 (31) [Col. LXS
36940]. Various artists and groups,
cond. the composer or Craft.

For the Stravinsky centenary CBS
brought out one of the most lavish
packages ever published. These thirty-one records – in fourteen two-disc folders
and a three-disc box for *The Rake's Progress*, all handsomely presented – include
virtually all the later recordings Stravinsky made of his own music. The sound
is rarely very refined, but it comes up
well, and the closeness helps to intensify
the dynamic vigour which Stravinsky
retained to the last. Only a tiny proportion of the performances – *Les Noces*

unfortunately among them – is disappointing; otherwise the liveness of the
man comes over vividly. It is a pity that
some of the piano recordings Stravinsky
made for Columbia in the thirties on 78
rpm discs are not included, but in the
United States they are already available
on the Seraphim label.

Suk, Josef (1874–1935)

(i) *A Fairy Tale* (suite), *Op. 16.*
Scherzo fantastique, Op. 25.
(M) *** Sup. 1410 2699. Prague SO, Bĕlohlávek, (i) with Suk.

A Fairy Tale is drawn from the music
Suk composed to Zeyer's dramatic tale
Radúz and Mahulena (and is not to be
confused with *A Summer Fairy Tale* of
1907–9, which bears a later opus
number). The music shows Suk a master
of colour and a highly imaginative and
inventive composer, and serves as a reminder that his neglect in the concert hall
and on the gramophone is our loss. There
is no modern recording of *Asrael* or
Ripening, and this issue is the first of *A
Fairy Tale* since Zdeněk Mácal's of 1967.
That too was coupled with the delightful
Scherzo fantastique, which ought to be
every bit as popular as the *Scherzo capriccioso* of Suk's father-in-law, Dvořák.
The latter acclaimed *A Fairy Tale* as
'music from Heaven', and he might well
have said the same of the *Scherzo*, which
has a captivating tune that once heard is
difficult to dislodge from one's mind.
This vivid and warm music is splendidly
played and recorded and can be strongly
recommended. The violin solo, incidentally, is played by the composer's
grandson – very beautifully, too.

String quartet No. 1 in B flat, Op. 11.
(M) *** Decca Ace SDD 543. Küchl Qt –
KODÁLY: *Quartet No. 2;* WOLF: *Italian
serenade.****

The Küchl (now Musikverein) Quartet give an account of the *B flat Quartet* which can hold its own against the Smetana Quartet's recording of the 1960s, and is much superior as sound. This early work, written before the tragedy that overtook Suk in his thirties, is as sunny and fresh as any work of Dvořák. The attractions of the couplings make this a most rewarding issue.

Under the Apple Tree (cantata).
(M) ** Sup. 1121 678. Jelinková, Czech PO Ch., Ostrava Janáček PO, Trhlík – JANÁČEK: *Amarus.***

Under the Apple Tree is new to the catalogue and like the Janáček coupling comes from the turn of the century; it predates the *Asrael symphony*, the outpouring of grief on the deaths of Suk's father-in-law, Dvořák, and his wife, Otilia. This cantata may lack the depth of his later works, but it has some marvellous music in it. Not all the influences are fully digested: Dvořák and the Czech nationalists come to mind at the opening, Bruckner at the end, and there are moments of Lisztian-derived harmony that point towards Debussy in between. But Suk had a distinctive voice, even if in this work it was not yet fully developed. The performance is persuasive enough but the recording does not cope so well with the choral climaxes at the end of the side. However, this is well worth investigating.

Sullivan, Arthur
(1842–1900)

HMS Pinafore (complete, without dialogue).
(M) *** HMV SXDW/*TC-SXDW* 3034 (2) [(d) Ang. S., 3589]. George Baker, Cameron, Lewis, Brannigan, Morison, Sinclair, Glyndebourne Festival Ch.,Pro Arte O., Sargent – *Trial by Jury*. ***

It is to Owen Brannigan's great credit that, little as he had to do here, without the dialogue, he conveyed the force of Deadeye's personality so strongly. For those who find the dialogue tedious in repetition this is a very happy set, offering some good solo singing and consistently lovely ensemble singing and chorus work. The whole of the final scene is musically quite ravishing, and throughout if Sir Malcolm fails to find quite all the wit in the music he is never less than lively. George Baker is of course splendid as Sir Joseph, and John Cameron, Richard Lewis and (especially) Monica Sinclair, as Buttercup, make much of their songs. Elsie Morison is rather disappointing; she spoils the end of her lovely song in Act 1 by singing sharp. However, she brings plenty of drama to her *Scena* in Act 2. The male trio near the end of Act 1 is quite outstandingly well sung – full of brio and personality. The coupling with *Trial by Jury* makes this a fine bargain. The recording is bright and lively and does not lack atmosphere. For the cassette issue – unlike the rest of this series – two separate tapes are provided in a box. The transfer is of good quality, missing only the last touch of refinement.

Iolanthe (complete, without dialogue).
(M) **(*) HMV SXDW/*TC2-SXDW* 3047 (2). G. Baker, Wallace, Cameron, Young, Brannigan, Sinclair, Morison, Glyndebourne Festival Ch., Pro Arte O., Sargent.

There is much to praise in this HMV set, and EMI have refurbished the recording very successfully; it suits the studio-based performance and projects the music brightly without loss of inner warmth. The climax of Act 1, the scene of the Queen of the Fairies' curse on members of both Houses of Parliament, shows most excitingly what can be achieved with the 'full operatic treatment': this is a dramatic moment indeed. George Baker too is very good as the Lord Chancellor; his voice is fuller and more baritonal than the dry monotone we are used to from John Reed, yet he provides an equally individual characterization. For some listeners John Cameron's dark timbre may not readily evoke an Arcadian Shepherd, although he sings stylishly. The Peers' chorus is not a highlight. It is treated lyrically, and the tenors are not very incisive; some might wish for a more robust effect here. Nevertheless there is much to enjoy. The two Earls and Private Willis are excellent, the famous *Nightmare song* is very well and clearly sung, and all of the second act (except perhaps Iolanthe's recitative and ballad near the end) goes very well. The famous *Trio* with the Lord Chancellor and the two Earls is a joy. The opening scene of Act 1 is effectively atmospheric, with Monica Sinclair a splendid Fairy Queen. The tape version is on a single double-length cassette, an ideal format, and the lively yet spacious effect of the discs is generally mirrored faithfully.

The Pirates of Penzance (complete, without dialogue).

(M) *** HMV SXDW/*TC2-SXDW* 3041 (2). G. Baker, Milligan, Cameron, Lewis, Brannigan, Morison, Glyndebourne Festival Ch., Pro Arte O., Sargent.

This was one of the finest of Sir Malcolm Sargent's Gilbert and Sullivan sets. Besides a performance which is stylish as well as lively, conveying both the fun of the words and the charm of the music, the HMV recording has more atmosphere than usual in this series. Undoubtedly the star of the piece is George Baker; he is a splendid Major-General. Here is an excellent example of a fresh approach yielding real dividends, and Sargent's slower than usual tempo

for his famous patter song means that the singer can relax and add both wit and polish to the words. As in the Decca D'Oyly Carte set (SKL 4925/6/*K 61 K 22* [Lon. 1277]), Owen Brannigan gives a rich portrayal of the Sergeant of the Police. The performance takes a little while to warm up: Sargent's accompaniment to the Pirate King's song is altogether too flaccid. Elsie Morison is a less than ideal Mabel: her opening cadenza of *Poor wandering one* is angular and overdramatic, and she is not relaxed enough throughout. However, elsewhere she is much more convincing, especially in the famous duet, *Leave me not to pine alone*. The choral contributions (the opening of Act 2, for instance) are pleasingly refined, yet have no lack of vigour. *Hail poetry* is resplendent, while the choral finale is managed with poise and a balance which allows the inner parts to emerge pleasingly. The whole performance is in fact more than the sum of its parts. The recording has transferred smoothly and vividly to tape, and the reverberation has been successfully contained, so the focus is nearly always clean. A little treble cut may be useful, for the voices and chorus have plenty of presence. The single-tape format is doubly attractive here, as the two acts are given a complete side each.

Trial by Jury (complete).

(M) *** HMV SXDW/*TC-SXDW* 3034 (2). G. Baker, Cameron, Lewis, Brannigan, Morison, Sinclair, Glyndebourne Festival Ch., Pro Arte O., Sargent – *HMS Pinafore.****

An outstanding, thoroughly musical account, with a shade more 'production' than usual in the HMV series. The casting is excellent, and George Baker makes a fine judge. The recording is one of the best HMV have given us so far for G. and S.: it is clear, spacious and bright, and has some good but unexaggerated stereo effects. In many ways this is the finest available recording of *Trial by*

Jury. It is well transferred to tape, but it is a great pity that it could not have been given side four of this boxed tape set to itself. Not a great deal of tape has been saved by setting the beginning of the work clumsily just before the end of side three.

The Yeomen of the Guard (complete, without dialogue).
(M) *** HMV SXDW/*TC2-SXDW* 3033 (2). Thomas, Morison, Evans, Lewis, Brannigan, Carol Case, Sinclair, Glyndebourne Festival Ch., Pro Arte O., Sargent.

The singing on Sargent's HMV recording (which dates from 1960) is very persuasive. As on his more expensive Decca set, the trios and quartets with which this score abounds are most beautifully performed and skilfully balanced, and the ear is continually beguiled. Owen Brannigan's portrayal of Wilfred is splendidly larger than life and Monica Sinclair is a memorable Dame Carruthers. The finales to both acts have striking breadth, and the delightfully sung trio of Elsie, Phoebe and the Dame in the finale of Act 2 is a good example of the many individual felicities of this set. *Strange adventure*, too, is most beautifully done. As in the Decca recording there is very little feeling of humour, but the music triumphs. The sound is excellent on disc. On cassette there is less absolute refinement at the highest levels, but this is only marginal; generally the voices have warmth and presence, and the music-making sounds vivid.

'The Best of Gilbert and Sullivan': excerpts from *The Gondoliers; HMS Pinafore; Iolanthe; The Mikado; The Pirates of Penzance*.
(B) ** HMV *TC2-MOM 106* (from above Pro Arte series cond. Sargent).

This first 'Miles of Music' cassette, designed for in-car listening, includes somewhat over-generous excerpts from the two least successful Sargent sets, *The Mikado* and *The Gondoliers* (including the unattractively lethargic *Cachucha* from the latter opera, which is used to end side one). Some of the 'best' of the other Sargent recordings is included in the rather piecemeal selections from the remaining three operas. The sound is consistently good, however, and with some eighty minutes of music this is entertaining enough.

'The Best of Gilbert and Sullivan': excerpts from *HMS Pinafore; The Mikado; Patience; The Pirates of Penzance; Trial by Jury; The Yeomen of the Guard*.
(M) *** CBS 61437/40-. Eddy, Green, Rounseville, Meister, Randall, Groucho Marx, Ch. and O., Armbruster; Engel; Voorhees.

A collectors' item, not to be missed. Apart from including some vintage Martyn Green versions of the patter songs and showing Nelson Eddy totally at sea in this repertoire (he is hilariously ineffective in the Mikado's song, *My object all sublime* – with an awful stage laugh), the collection features Groucho Marx, no less, doing a vaudeville version of the *Little list* (from *Mikado*) and joining Barbara Meister and Susan Randall as one of the *Three little maids*. Some of the items are in artificially enhanced mono; some in genuine early stereo.

'Favourites': from *The Gondoliers; HMS Pinafore; Iolanthe; The Mikado; Patience; The Pirates of Penzance; Ruddigore; Trial by Jury; The Yeomen of the Guard*.
(B) *** HMV *TC2-MOM 114* (from above series cond. Sargent).

This second 'Miles of Music' selection includes excerpts from the nine most popular Savoy operas. It was a mistake to open with *The Mikado*, but the excerpts generally are unfailingly enjoyable, especially the selections from *Patience* (also included on CFP/TC-CFP 40282; see below), *Iolanthe* and *Ruddigore*. There is a clumsy fade after George Baker's *Judge's song* from *Trial by Jury*, but for the most part the editing is well managed and the sound is first-class, vividly demonstrating EMI's transfer technology at its best. There is nearly an hour and a half of music here, equally suitable for car or home listening.

'More Favourites': from *The Gondoliers; The Mikado; Patience; The Pirates of Penzance; Trial by Jury; The Yeomen of the Guard.*
(B) ** HMV *TC2-MOM 124* (from above series cond. Sargent).

The editors of this series seem determined to open each selection with items from Sargent's least effective set, and here the excerpts include the lukewarm finale to Act 1 of *The Mikado*. After this disappointing start the programme immediately improves, and side two is especially lively. The choices from *Pirates,* ` *Yeomen of the Guard* and *Patience* are all well made, even if the order is not always especially felicitous. The sound is very clear but rather dry. It projects well in the car, but the relative lack of bloom is more noticeable at home.

'Highlights', Vol. 3: from *The Gondoliers; HMS Pinafore; The Mikado; Patience; Ruddigore; The Yeomen of the Guard.*
(B) *** CfP CFP/TC-CFP 40282 (from above series cond. Sargent).

This is easily the most attractive of the collections of highlights from the Sargent recordings. The selection could not have been better made. Each of the six gener-

ous groups is beautifully balanced to match lyricism with fun, and the standard of singing is stunningly high. One especially remembers George Baker's *Flowers that bloom* and *Tit Willow* (from *Mikado*) and his performance of Sir Joseph Porter's autobiographical monologue from *Pinafore*. The selection from *Patience* is enchanting: *Prithee, pretty maiden, A magnet hung, If Saphir I chose to marry* – with a deliciously pointed accompaniment – and *When I go out of door* follow one another in rollicking inspirational profusion. The lyrical numbers from *Yeomen* provide ballast on side one. The recording is first-rate throughout and the tape has only fractionally less freshness and range than the disc (and that only noticeable on an A/B comparison). Very highly recommended.

'Highlights', Vol. 4: from *The Gondoliers; Iolanthe; The Mikado; The Pirates of Penzance; Ruddigore; Trial by Jury.*
(B) ** CfP CFP/TC-CFP 40338 (from above series cond. Sargent).

The collection here is enjoyable enough, but selected and arranged with no special perception. Owen Brannigan demonstrates that he was indeed a more humane Mikado than most, and though his words in the famous song are articulated with superb clarity, the characterization is too soft-centred. The attractive excerpts from *Trial by Jury* are spoiled by fades: it would have been better to offer one continuous excerpt. The *Ruddigore* items come off well, especially the patter trio, and the other distinctive group is from *The Pirates of Penzance*, although this ends side two and the closing number could have been more cleverly chosen to make a good finale. The recording is excellent on both disc and cassette.

'Gilbert and Sullivan spectacular': excerpts from *HMS Pinafore; The*

Mikado; The Pirates of Penzance; Ruddigore.
(B) **(*) Con. CC/*CCT* 7508. Reed, Adams, Sandford, Masterson, soloists, D'Oyly Carte Opera Ch., RPO, Sargent.

Basically the recording is certainly spectacular, with a rich overall ambience and the soloists spotlighted well forward. The choral sound, however, is somewhat grainy. The conducting is musical and solid, without the wit of Isidore Godfrey (outstanding among D'Oyly Carte musical directors), but genial in its way. The memorable items are *A wandering minstrel*, very nicely turned by Philip Potter, and Donald Adams's superb versions of the Mikado's famous song (that laugh sounds even more horrifying than usual) and the *Policeman's song* from *Pirates* (which he did not usually sing). John Reed's contributions are very closely microphoned indeed and reveal a break in the voice occasionally. The reverberation produces a lack of clarity of focus on cassette, especially in the ensembles.

Suppé, Franz von

(1819–95)

Overtures: Beautiful Galathea; Boccaccio; Light Cavalry; Morning, Noon and Night in Vienna; Pique Dame; Poet and Peasant.
** Ph. 9500 399/*7300 612* [id.]. LPO, Marriner.

Marriner's collection is certainly well played (although the LPO violins do not show the virtuosity of the Berlin Philharmonic the ensemble in *Light Cavalry*, for instance, is not as clean as it might be). Marriner is at his best in the overtures where elegance can add an attractive outer veneer to the music-making.

Other versions of *Light Cavalry* are rhythmically more exhilarating, and the reprise of the fanfare theme in the coda is awkwardly managed. The opening of *Poet and Peasant* is so broad that it is almost sluggish. The warmly reverberant recording is agreeable enough on disc, but produces a smudged cassette transfer, with patches of uncomfortable congestion at climax.

Overtures: Light Cavalry; Pique Dame; Poet and Peasant.
(M) *** DG Priv. 2535/*3335* 629. Berlin PO, Karajan – ROSSINI: *Overtures.****

On disc this generous Privilege recoupling is a bargain, with Karajan's swaggeringly brilliant Suppé performances attractively coupled to Rossini. The resonant recording is highly effective. But on tape the reverberation brings problems: the opening fanfare of *Light Cavalry* blisters, and elsewhere climaxes are fierce and uncomfortable.

Surinach, Carlos

(born 1915)

Piano concerto.
(*) Decca SXL 6757 (Lon. 6990/5-]. Larrocha, RPO, Frühbeck de Burgos – MONTSALVATGE: *Concerto breve.**

Carlos Surinach's *Piano concerto* was written for Alicia de Larrocha. The writing is not particularly individual though it is often far from ineffective. Ultimately, however, it is an obstinately unmemorable work, though it would be difficult to imagine a more persuasive advocate than Mme Larrocha, who enjoys excellent support from the RPO under Frühbeck de Burgos. The recording too has admirable clarity and warmth, and readers with a specialist interest in Spanish music might well want to investigate it. The coupling, a not-so-short *Concerto breve* by Xavier Montsalvatge, a composer of the same generation, is well worth hearing, even though it is not of compelling originality.

Szymanowski, Karol
(1882–1937)

Violin concertos Nos. 1, Op. 35; 2, Op. 61
**(*) EMI 1C 065 03597. Kulka, Polish RSO, Maksymiuk.

These marvellous concertos have not been as well served on record as the Bartók or Prokofiev. The performances here are committed and highly finished; they convey much of the ecstasy, longing and sensuousness of these luminous scores. Both works are rich in atmosphere, full of the exotic colours and the sense of rapture that permeate Szymanowski's very finest scores. The acoustic is reverberant, and that adds to the overheated impression conveyed in the *Second*, which is powerfully played though it is not quite as refined in character here as in Szeryng's version made in the early 1970s. Kulka and Maksymiuk could perhaps have brought greater poignancy and longing to the *First Concerto*. The multi-mike balance produces vivid sound but the perspective is not completely natural, and the overall effect is one of glare. However, these performances are both persuasive enough to be recommendable.

Symphonies Nos. 2, Op. 19; (i) 3 (Song of the Night), Op. 27.
*** Decca Dig. SXDL/KSXDC 7524 [Lon. LDR 71026/5-]. Detroit SO, Dorati, (i) with Karczykowski, Jewell Chorale.

This is the first western commercial record of either of these Szymanowski symphonies. *The Song of the Night* is one of his most beautiful scores, a setting made in the period 1914–16 of a poem by the great Persian Sufi mystic Djelaleddin Rumi. In recent years it has become fashionable to use a soprano rather than the tenor specified in the score (the composer apparently authorized performances without chorus, but the tenor was mandatory). The soprano has, of course, the ecstatic other-worldly quality that matches this score with its luminous textures, the heady, intoxicated – and intoxicating – atmosphere, the extraordinarily vivid colours and sense of rapture. Much of this is conveyed in the present performance, and the detail and opulence of the orchestral texture are revealingly captured by the digital recording. Rowicki brought an earthier more sensual atmosphere to the score in his 1962 version, but Dorati's is the finer recording. The *Second* is not so rewarding a symphony as the *Third*. It dates from 1909–11 and is unusual formally: there are two movements, the second being a set of variations culminating in a fugue. The influences of Strauss and Scriabin are clearly audible and not altogether assimilated. But this is a most valuable issue. The cassette is of very good quality if not quite as sharply focused as the disc (especially in the choral symphony), although its slightly mellower upper range has its own appeal. There is no lack of vividness.

(i) *Symphony No. 4 (Sinfonia concertante for piano and orchestra), Op. 60. 2 Études, Op. 4; 2 Mazurkas, Op. 50; 2 Preludes, Op. 1; Theme and variations in B flat min., Op. 3.*
** Uni. RHS 347. Blumenthal, (i) with Polish RSO, Kord.

The *Fourth Symphony* is a puzzling work, often haunting, though it is not altogether Szymanowski at his best. The opening idea is appealing, but as a whole the work lacks the richness of invention and distinctive profile of the two *Violin concertos*. The textures are unrelieved, and their density tends to diminish the impact of the work. Felicia Blumenthal is a persuasive exponent, though her performance is sound rather than inspired, and the playing of the Polish orchestra is committed. The second side gives us some of the earlier piano pieces, written at the turn of the century, and a couple of the Op. 50 *Mazurkas*. Let us hope that Szymanowski's centenary year will inspire a complete set of these remarkable pieces.

Myths, Op. 30. Kurpian folk song; King Roger: Roxana's aria (both arr. Kochanski).
*** DG 2531/*3301* 330 [id.]. Danczowska, Zimerman – FRANCK: *Violin sonata.****

There is no alternative version of the *Myths* currently available, but it is difficult to imagine any other rivalling, let alone surpassing, this issue. The violinist, Kaja Danczowska, a pupil of Eugenia Uminska and David Oistrakh, brings vision and poetry to the ecstatic, soaring lines of the *Fountain of Arethusa*. Her intonation is impeccable, and she has the measure of these other-worldly, intoxicating scores. There is a sense of rapture here that is totally persuasive, and Krystian Zimerman plays with a virtuosity and imagination that silence criticism. An indispensable issue, and very well recorded on both disc and cassette.

Taffanel, Paul
(1844–1908)

Wind quintet in G min.
(M) *** Decca Ace SDD 555. V. Wind Soloists – FRANÇAIX: *Wind quintet.****

Taffanel was born in Bordeaux, studied in Paris, and became one of the most respected flautists of his day. He was for many years a member of the Paris Opéra orchestra and became its conductor in 1890, moving two years later to take charge of the Paris Conservatoire Orchestra. The *Wind quintet in G minor*, his best-known work, is expertly laid out for the medium. Its invention is slight, pleasing and not particularly memorable; but there is no lack of wit in the finale, and the writing throughout is always fresh and vital. If no masterpiece, it is a civilized, sunny piece that repays an occasional airing, and the Vienna Wind Soloists give a persuasive and pleasing account of it, well recorded.

Takemitsu, Toru
(born 1930)

A Flock Descends into the Pentagonal Gardens; (i) *Quatrain.*
*** DG 2531 210 [id.]. Boston SO, Ozawa, (i) with Tashi.

In *Quatrain* Takemitsu contrasts his solo concertino of clarinet, violin, cello and piano with the full orchestra in a way that might suggest neoclassicism, except that Takemitsu's music is essentially sensuous and evocative. One might almost count him a Japanese Debussy. The other piece, which is purely orchestral, is overtly impressionistic. Both are superbly played and recorded; the outstanding Tashi group is ideally suited to *Quatrain*.

Tallis, Thomas
(c. 1505–1585)

Audivi vocem de Caelo; Honor virtus et potestas; O sacrum convivium; Salvator mundi; Sancte Deus.
*** CRD CRD 1072. Ch. of New College, Oxford, Higginbottom – TAVERNER: *Western Wynde* etc.***

A welcome addition to Tallis's representation on record. The Choir of New College produces a clean and well-blended sound, and given the attractions of the valuable Taverner coupling, this disc should have a strong appeal for those interested in the period.

Derelinquat impius; Ecce temptus idoneum. In ieiunio et fletu; In manus tuas; The Lamentations of Jeremiah the Prophet; O nata lux; Salvator mundi; Sancte Deus; Spem in alium (40-part motet); *Te lucis ante terminum* (2 settings); *Videte miraculum; Veni redemptor genitem. Organ Lesson.*
(M) *** Argo ZK 30/1. King's College Ch., Camb. University Musical Soc., Willcocks; Andrew Davis (organ).

This medium-priced set joins together two previously full-priced collections (originally ZRG 5436 and 5479). The King's College Choir are in their element in this music, for the most part written for Waltham Abbey and the Chapel Royal. The highlight of the first disc is the magnificent forty-part motet *Spem in alium*, in which the Cambridge University Musical Society joins forces with King's. But the simple hymn settings are no less impressive, and the performance of *The Lamentations of Jeremiah*, authentically using men's voices only, has the right element of restraint without being inexpressive. The two motets *Sanctus*

Deus and *Videte miraculum* are for full choir and here the balance is less than ideal, giving too much prominence to the trebles. The recording throughout is distinguished, natural and atmospheric.

Mass: *Puer natus est.* Motets: *Salvator mundi; Suscipe quaeso domine.*
*** Cal. CAL 1623. Clerkes of Oxenford, Wulstan.

An outstanding record. The Mass is a reconstruction by David Wulstan and Sally Dunkley prompted by the researches and speculations of Joseph Kerman and Jeremy Noble. The details are too complex to be outlined here, but the results are so beautiful that readers should not miss this record. The Mass is among the finest Tallis and, for that matter, the finest music of the period, and it is performed with dedication and authority by these singers. There is no need to hesitate here: this is one of the most important recent issues of English music of this period and it is also one of the most successful artistically and technically.

Tartini, Giuseppe
(1692–1770)

Cello concerto in A.
*** DG 2530/*3300* 974 [id.]. Rostropovich, Zürich Coll. Mus., Sacher – BOCCHERINI and VIVALDI: *Concertos.****
(M) ** DG Arc Priv. 2547/*3347* 046. Mainardi, Lucerne Festival Strings, Baumgartner – BOCCHERINI: *Concerto***; VIVALDI: *Concerto.***(*)

As with the other works in his collection, Rostropovich's view of Tartini's concerto is larger than life, but the eloquence of the playing disarms criticism, even when the cellist plays cadenzas of his own that are not exactly in period. The lively accompaniment is matched by bright, vivid recording, and this has transferred to tape with plenty of presence.

Mainardi's performance is on a smaller scale, but he plays with warmth and colour and is clearly recorded, although the tonal balance favours the upper range of his instrument. Here the cassette is preferable to the disc, offering slightly more body of timbre and a smoother upper range.

(i) *Cello concerto in A.* (ii) *Violin concertos: in D min, for violin and strings, D.45; in D min. for violin, 2 horns and strings, D.21. Sonata in D for strings.*
*** Erato STU 70970. Sol. Ven., Scimone, with (i) Zannerini, (ii) Toso.

This collection was recorded in the mid-seventies but has only recently appeared here. Tartini's invention is at times almost romantic in character, and there are moments of vision that leave no doubt that he is underrated. The two *Violin concertos* are well worth investigation as is the *Cello concerto*, whose slow movement is quite striking. The playing is committed and persuasive, and the recording fully acceptable. A very worthwhile issue.

Violin sonatas: in A, Op. 1/1; in G. min., Op. 1/10; in F, Op. 1/12; in C; in A min., Op. 2/6–7; in G min. (Devil's Trill).
*** Erato STU 71023/4. Amoyal, Moses, Farina.

Violin sonatas: in A, Op. 1/3; in A min., Op. 1/5; in G min., Op. 1/10; in G min. (Devil's Trill).
(M) *** Ph. 9502 009. Michelucci, Walter, Sibinga.

Tartini's sonatas take their virtuosity for granted: there is none of the sheer display that his reputation as a great violinist and innovator would lead one to expect, yet they call for playing of the greatest technical finesse and musicianship. Spanning as he did both halves of the eighteenth century, Tartini possesses the lyrical purity of Corelli and Vivaldi with a forward-looking sensibility that is highly expressive. Pierre Amoyal plays them superbly; he makes no attempt to adapt his style to contemporary practice, but there is in a sense no need for him to do so. His playing has sweetness of tone and expressive eloquence to commend it, and though he is forwardly placed, the sound throughout is eminently acceptable. A most desirable pair of records.

Some of the sonatas in the Philips Michelucci collection overlap with Amoyal's Erato set, but this is on a single mid-price disc whereas its rival comprises two full-price records. Michelucci is a most beautiful player even if he sounds a shade bland by comparison with Amoyal. In its own right, however, this is a thoroughly enjoyable and often distinguished record, and Michelucci's partners have exemplary taste and musicianship. Excellent sound.

Taverner, John
(*c.* 1495–1545)

Mass in 4 parts: *The Western Wynde. Mater Christi.*
*** CRD CRD 1072. Ch. of New College, Oxford, Higginbottom – TALLIS: *Audivi vocem* etc.***

This is the only version of Taverner's Mass to appear since the King's College, Cambridge, record of 1962. It is a worthy successor, and the acoustic is, if anything, superior to that of King's, producing results of greater clarity and definition. Higginbottom's choir sings with great feeling but with restraint and splendid control both of line and of ensemble. Although the King's version is not completely superseded, this newcomer is to be preferred.

Tchaikovsky, Peter
(1840–93)

Capriccio italien, Op. 45.
(B) **(*) CfP CFP/*TC-CFP* 40341. Philh. O., Kletzki – RIMSKY-KOR-SAKOV: *Scheherazade.****
(M) **(*) Ph. Fest. 6570/*7310* 176 [id.]. Concg. O., Haitink – DVOŘÁK: *Scherzo capriccioso;* GLINKA: *Russlan overture;* MUSSORGSKY: *Pictures.***(*)

Kletzki's performance is very enjoyable. It offers superb Philharmonia playing and is well recorded (1960 vintage), making a good bonus for an outstanding version of *Scheherazade*.

Haitink's account is warm-blooded, with some elegantly turned string playing from the Concertgebouw Orchestra. The restatement of the main theme at the end is given tremendous weight, and to be honest it sounds rather phlegmatic played like this: it also means that the coda gets under way too slowly. But this is enjoyable in its fashion, and the acoustic, warm and spacious, matches the reading. The couplings add up to a generous mid-priced concert, and the orchestral playing throughout is distinguished.

Capriccio italien; 1812 overture, Op. 49; Marche slave, Op. 31.
** Decca SXL/*KSXC* 6895 [Lon. 7118/5-]. Detroit SO, Dorati.
** DG Dig. 2532/*3302* 022 [id.]. Chicago SO, Barenboim.

The Decca issue marked the return of the Detroit orchestra to the international recording scene at the beginning of 1979.

It is a somewhat brash début; Dorati was to go on to make more distinguished records than this. The somewhat aggressive brilliance may be partly contributed by the sound balance, which is obviously aimed at the hi-fi demonstration market, with an eruption of specifically American gun fire and bells at the end of *1812.* The performance of the *Capriccio* is not without elegance, but *Marche slave* seems excessively sombre until the change of mood at the coda, which is taken briskly. The music-making has plenty of confidence throughout and no lack of direct excitement, but in the last analysis it is unmemorable. The cassette transfer is not really successful, and the end of *1812* brings coarseness.

Barenboim gives a slinkily persuasive account of the *Capriccio,* but *1812* is disappointingly done and by Chicago standards poorly played. The chrome cassette matches the disc fairly closely, although the opening trumpet fanfare of *Capriccio italien* is not quite clean.

Capriccio italien; 1812 overture; Mazeppa: Cossack dance.
**(*) Telarc Dig. DG 10041. Cincinnati SO, Kunzel.

This famous disc offers performances where the sense of spectacle is paramount. In the *Capriccio italien* this is achieved by a substantial contribution from the bass drum, while the performance of *1812* is subordinate to the cannon at the end, which completely dwarf the orchestra. One hesitates to reproduce the latter work at full volume, for fear of what the wide amplitude of the cannon fusillade will do to one's loudspeaker cones. However, those with the largest, most accommodating equipment will not have this problem, and certainly the climax is ear-splitting. The orchestral contribution to both works is lively but not memorable, and the sound is generally spacious. The *Cossack dance* makes an attractive bonus.

(i; ii) *Capriccio italien;* (ii; iii) *1812 overture;* (i; iv) *Romeo and Juliet* (fantasy overture); *The Sleeping Beauty: Waltz;* (i; ii) *Eugene Onegin: Polonaise.*

(M) ** *TC-IDL 506.* (i) RPO, (ii) Weldon: (iii) Philh. O., Royal Marines Band; (iv) Sargent.

This tape-only compilation offers strong if not distinctive performances, well played and recorded. *Romeo and Juliet* shows Sir Malcolm Sargent at his most effective; it is not an overtly romantic performance, but telling in its drama and detail. The sound is good throughout, very good in *Romeo and Juliet*, a trifle dry in *1812.* As often with cassette transfers of this work the cannonade brings a momentary disturbance of the quality, although it is not serious enough to spoil the collection.

Capriccio italien; Eugene Onegin: Polonaise; Waltz.

(M) ** CBS 60115/*40-* [Col. MY 36728]. NYPO, Bernstein – RIMSKY-KOR-SAKOV: *Capriccio espagnol.***

Bernstein is somewhat indulgent in the *Capriccio italien,* with freely fluctuating tempi, but the structure holds together, and the closing pages match splendour with weight. The New York orchestral playing is strikingly brilliant, both here and in the dances from *Eugene Onegin,* which are vigorously rhythmic. The sound is quite spacious but over-brilliant.

Capriccio italien; Nutcracker suite; (i) *Andante cantabile for cello and string orchestra* (arr. Rostropovich from 2nd movt of *String quartet No. 1*).

⊛ *** DG 2531/*3301* 112 [id.]. Berlin PO, Rostropovich (cond. and (i) cello).

An enchanting performance of the

Nutcracker suite, quite the finest in the present catalogue, the characteristic dances played with engaging colour and charm. The *Sugar Plum Fairy* is introduced with ethereal delicacy, and the *Russian dance* has marvellous zip. The *Waltz of the Flowers* balances warmth and elegance with an exhilarating vigour. The *Capriccio italien* is highly successful too, and the vulgarity inherent in the principal theme (which Tchaikovsky thought was a folksong but which proved to be a local Italian 'pop' of the time) evaporates entirely, so decoratively elegant is the playing of the Berlin Philharmonic. There is a touch of rhythmic heaviness at the final climax, but otherwise this is first-rate. As an encore, Rostropovich indulges himself affectionately in a concertante arrangement of one of Tchaikovsky's loveliest melodies. The balance – all cello with a discreet orchestral backing – reflects his approach. The recording is spectacularly resonant, and the dynamic range extremely wide, with a rather low level of cut, meaning that this disc will be prone to any surface imperfections. But the pianissimos are very telling. The cassette transfer is first-class, encompassing the wide dynamic contrasts without problems.

Capriccio italien; Nutcracker suite; Eugene Onegin: Polonaise; Waltz.

(M) ** Ph. Seq. 6527/*7311* 079 [6500 766/*7300 332*]. LPO, Stokowski.

This reissue offers recordings made as recently as 1974, with resonant, full-blooded sound. But though nothing Stokowski did is without touches of magic, some fairly strong reservations must be expressed here. *Capriccio italien,* in spite of occasional nudges, has genuine panache, and the two *Eugene Onegin* dances have characteristic flair. But in the *Nutcracker* music (which he played so beautifully for Disney in *Fantasia*), after the introduction of a string tremolando at the opening of the *Dance of the Sugar*

Plum Fairy Stokowski indulges in very mannered phrasing; few will find this comfortable to live with. The reverberant sound brings some clouding of detail and a lack of transient sharpness to the cassette transfer.

Piano concertos Nos. 1, 2 (original version), *3*.
(M) ** Ph. 6768 037 (2). Haas, Monte Carlo Op. O., Inbal.

Werner Haas is an intelligent and masterly player whose accounts of these concertos, particularly given the finely recorded sound, is highly competitive. Unfortunately the Monte Carlo Opera Orchestra is not his equal, and their playing under Inbal cannot be described as distinguished.

Piano concerto No. 1 in B flat min., Op. 23.
*** CBS Dig. 36660/*41*- [Col. M/*HMT* 36660]. Gilels, NYPO, Mehta (with BACH: *Well-tempered Clavier: Prelude No. 10, BWV 855*, arr. Siloti ***).
(M) *** DG Priv. 2535/*3335* 295 [id.]. Argerich, RPO, Dutoit.
*** Decca SXL/*KSXC* 6840 [(d) Lon. 6360/5-]. Ashkenazy, LSO, Maazel – MUSSORGSKY: *Pictures*.**(*)
**(*) HMV ASD/*TC-ASD* 3818 [Ang. S 37679]. Gavrilov, Philh. O., Muti.
(M) **(*) Decca VIV/*KVIC* 16 [Lon. STS 15542/5-]. Vered, LSO, Kord – RACHMANINOV: *Concerto No. 2*.*(**)
**(*) Ph. 9500 695/*7300 783* [id.]. Arrau, Boston SO, Colin Davis.
(M) **(*) Decca Jub. JB/*KJBC* 29 [(d) Lon. STS 15471/5-]. Curzon, VPO, Solti – LITOLFF: *Scherzo*.***

Any Gilels record is an event, and this recording appears a quarter of a century after his first account with Fritz Reiner and the Chicago Symphony Orchestra. Gilels has an outsize musical personality and his is a performance of leonine calibre, with nobility and fire. There is no want of virtuosity – the double octaves leap off the vinyl – and there are the inward-looking qualities we associate with Gilels too. The performance was recorded live at Carnegie Hall, and the claims of Gilels's artistry have to be weighed against less than distinguished recorded sound and second-rate orchestral playing. The wind (bar 186) are not in tune and do not blend, and at no point does the orchestra respond as alertly or sensitively as it did in the days of Bernstein. The digital recording reproduces clean detail – the high-level tape transfer has striking range and brilliance, although the upper string timbre is rather crude – and the relationship between soloist and orchestra is well balanced. But the sound is not top-drawer. However, Gilels is Gilels, and the quality of his playing cannot be too highly praised. The Siloti arrangement of the Bach *Prelude* was his encore on the occasion of the recording, and it is affecting in its direct eloquence.

Gilels's playing is in the same league as Horowitz's famous version of this concerto with Toscanini, but one must remember that Lazar Berman's thrilling and poetic DG account (2530/*3300* 677) is hardly less compelling and has the considerable advantage of highly polished yet ripely committed playing from the Berlin Philharmonic Orchestra under Karajan and a massively brilliant recording, equally effective on disc or cassette.

Hardly less competitive is Martha Argerich's mid-priced version on DG's Privilege label in partnership with Charles Dutoit. Here the sheer weight of the opening immediately sets the mood for a big, broad performance, with the kind of music-making where the personalities of both artists are complementary. The recording too is first-class, full-bodied, wide in dynamic range, and yet with a natural balance. Argerich's conception encompasses the widest range of tonal shading. In the finale she often produces a scherzando-like effect; then the orchestra thunders in with the Russian dance theme to create a real contrast. The quality of Dutoit's contribution to the music-making is never in doubt. The tempo of the first movement is comparatively measured, seeking power rather than surface excitement, and again when the build-up begins for the final statement of the great lyrical tune of the finale, the conductor creates his climax in deliberate, measured fashion. The slow movement is strikingly atmospheric, yet delicate, its romanticism lighthearted. A most satisfying account in every way. The tape transfer is at a fairly high level and has plenty of body and good piano tone, though the treble range is less open than on the disc. The cassette offers a bonus, the *Waltz of the Flowers* elegantly played by the Berlin Philharmonic Orchestra under Leitner.

Originally issued spread uneconomically over two cassette sides, Ashkenazy's version now occupies only one, and is coupled to Mussorgsky. The remastering is highly successful on both disc and cassette. The piano sounds splendidly bold and clear, while the orchestral balance is most realistic. Ashkenazy's essentially lyrical performance offers a genuine alternative to those of Gilels, Berman and Argerich. They remain more obvious first recommendations, but there are many who will enjoy Ashkenazy's thoughtfulness and his refusal to be stampeded by Tchaikovsky's passionate rhetoric. The biggest climaxes of the first movement are made to grow out of the music, instead of being part of a sweeping forward momentum, and the lyrical side of the writing associated with the beautiful second subject is distilled with obvious affection. In the *Andantino* too, Ashkenazy refuses to play flashily and thus uses the middle section as a contrasting episode to set in the boldest relief the return of the opening tune, which is played very beautifully. The finale is very fast and brilliant, yet the big tune is broadened at the end in a most convincing way.

Gavrilov is stunning in the finale of the concerto, which at a very fast tempo is scintillating from first to last. The *prestissimo* middle section of the slow movement too goes like quicksilver, equally displaying the vein of spontaneous imagination that we recognize in Gavrilov's other records. The element of daring, of naughtiness even, is not so convincing in the first movement, where contrasts of dynamic and tempo are so extreme they sound self-conscious. Nor is the recording one of EMI's best; the piano is close yet not well focused. The cassette, however, is extremely well managed, if anything cleaner than the disc, with no loss of body and impact.

Ilana Vered's Decca Viva disc offers an exceptionally generous coupling. The recording, originally Phase Four, is extremely brilliant. The larger-than-life sound (the piano very forward and real, so that one almost feels able to touch it) is immensely dramatic, and if the overall balance is not natural, one can forgive that when the immediacy is given to such exciting playing. Alongside the bravura, there are many imaginative touches from the soloist and a freshness in the orchestra which is similarly appealing. The refinement of piano tone at the opening and close of the slow movement, played with the utmost delicacy, gives much pleasure, and the finale has no lack of brilliance and power. The coupling is not quite so successful (and here the balance is even more exaggerated), but it undoubtedly increases the interest of this issue. The cassette transfer is of Decca's best quality, with little distinguishable difference between tape and disc.

Arrau, splendidly accompanied, gives a direct and unexaggerated performance which is in general most refreshing. The temperature is not high, excitement is shunned, and with a seventy-year-old soloist double octaves do not run quite so freely as once they did. There is also a strange agogic hesitation in Arrau's enunciation of the main theme of the finale, but with clean recording this version will appeal to those who like a thoughtful reading. The high-level cassette transfer matches the disc fairly closely.

Sir Clifford Curzon's 1969 recording has been freshly remastered and made to sound well (especially in the bold, full-blooded cassette transfer). Some faults of balance remain, and there are one or two obvious joins in the master tape. But Curzon matches thoughtfulness to unostentatious bravura, and the performance has fine zest and spontaneity. The coupling is not generous, but the performance is as scintillating as the recording, which is of demonstration quality.

(i) *Piano concerto No. 1;* (ii) *Violin concerto in D, Op. 35.*
(M) *(*) Ph. Fest 6570/*7310* 028. Rotterdam PO, De Waart, with (i) Orozco, (ii) Fujikawa.

Orozco's version of the *Piano concerto* is flamboyant enough, but in spite of the bravura, and although it is well recorded, this performance fails to be memorable. The *Prestissimo* central section of the slow movement is certainly intended by the composer as an opportunity for the soloist to show his mettle, but the lack of refinement here is unattractive. Mayumi Fujikawa's account of the *Violin concerto* has a great deal more finesse, and in the slow movement her warmly lyrical phrasing gives much pleasure, particularly as the supporting woodwind detail is nicely played. But the first movement lacks impetus, and in spite of the attraction of the coupling this record is not such a bargain as it looks. The cassette transfers are made at a modest level, and the *Violin concerto* in particular lacks vividness unless the playback level is set very high.

(i) *Piano concerto No. 1;* (ii) *Variations on a rococo theme for cello and orchestra, Op. 33.*

*** Decca SXL 6955. LAPO, Dutoit, with (i) Myung-Whun Chung, (ii) Myung-Wha Chung.

The brother and sister of Kyung-Wha Chung prove in this most attractive Tchaikovsky coupling that the family's musical inspiration extends to them too. Myung-Whun, nowadays equally well-known as a conductor, here shows why he won a piano prize at the Tchaikovsky Competition in Moscow. There is a hint of restraint, and the recording balances him naturally with the orchestra, not in front of it. It means that this is not a rip-roaring account, but rather a thoughtful and poetic one. Similarly the cellist Myung-Wha holds back until the later variations draw out her full expressiveness. Beautifully played and recorded, and a very apt coupling; it can be warmly recommended.

Piano concertos Nos. 2 in G, Op. 44 (with abridged Siloti version of *Andante*); *3 in E flat, Op. 75.*
(M) CBS 61990/*40-* [Col. MS 6755]. Graffman, Phd. O., Ormandy.

Graffman uses Tchaikovsky's original for the outer movements of the *Second Concerto* but reverts to Siloti's abridged version of the *Andante*, thus cutting about half the music. Perhaps it was a sensible decision, for the orchestral cello and violin soloists find little charm in the passages that remain. The outer movements are played strongly but aggressively, and there is no sense of geniality in the finale. The *Third Concerto* fares no better, and this coupling will be unlikely to persuade any music-lover that either work deserves more frequent appearances in the concert hall. The recording is excessively brilliant, with clattery piano timbre and a harsh, thin orchestral texture, although (especially on side one) the cassette is more agreeable than the disc. Not recommended.

Violin concerto in D, Op. 35.
(M) *** Decca VIV/*KVIC* 4. Ricci, Neth. RO, Fournet – MENDELSSOHN: *Concerto.****
(B) *** CfP C̆FP/*TC-CFP* 40349. Hoelscher, New Philh. O., Kamu – DVOŘÁK: *Concerto.****
(M) *** HMV *TC-IDL 508.* Kogan, Paris Conservatoire O., Silvestri – MENDELSSOHN: *Concerto.***(*)
(M) **(*) Ph. Seq. 6527/*7311* 067. Grumiaux, Concg. O., Haitink.
(M) **(*) CBS 60111/*40-* [Col. MY 36724]. Stern, Phd. O., Ormandy – MENDELSSOHN: *Concerto.***(*)
*(*) Ph. 9500 321/*7300 583* [id.]. Szeryng, Concg. O., Haitink – MENDELSSOHN: *Concerto.**(*)

(i) *Violin concerto. Capriccio italien.*
(M) **(*) DG Acc. 2542/*3342* 162 [139028/*923031*]. Ferras, Berlin PO, Karajan.

Violin concerto; Meditation, Op. 42.
** CBS 76725/*40-* [Col. XM/*XMT* 35126]. Stern, Nat. SO, Rostropovich.

Violin concerto; Sérénade mélancolique, Op. 26.
*** HMV ASD/*TC-ASD* 3726 [Ang. SZ 37640]. Perlman, Phd. O., Ormandy.
** DG Dig. 2532/*3302* 001 [id.]. Kremer, Berlin PO, Maazel.

Violin concerto; Valse-scherzo, Op. 34.
*** Decca SXL/*KSXC* 6854 [Lon. 7076/*5-*]. Belkin, New Philh. O., Ashkenazy.

Although the coupling is not generous, the newest Decca recording of Tchaikovsky's concerto by Boris Belkin with the LSO under Ashkenazy lays fair claim to a position at the top of the list of available versions, particularly as the recording is of such outstanding quality, with no appreciable difference between disc and cassette. This is a performance of genuine distinction and strong personality. Belkin brings temperament and flair to the solo part besides great sympathy, and everything he does rings true; one feels he is discovering the beauties of the score for the very first time. There is no trace of routine either in his playing or in the orchestral accompaniment under Ashkenazy, and the freshness and spontaneity that they communicate, as well as the Slavonic authenticity of feeling, make this a memorably winning account. The Decca recording is beautifully focused and well defined: there is splendid body and no want of smoothness and refinement. One or two extraneous noises are present on both cassette and disc, but these are of minor account. A most poetic and imaginative account, as fine as any now before the public. The charming *Valse-scherzo* makes an admirable fill-up. However, in making a choice one must not forget that the alternative full-priced Decca version from Kyung-Wha Chung, with the LSO under Previn, is also extremely well recorded on both disc and cassette, and has the advantage of being coupled to an equally distinguished account of the Sibelius concerto (SXL/*KSXC* 6493 [Lon. 6710]). Chung's performance of the Tchaikovsky has warmth, spontaneity and discipline; every detail is beautifully shaped and turned, without a trace of sentimentality.

The expressive warmth of Perlman goes with a very bold orchestral texture from Ormandy and the Philadelphia Orchestra. The focus of sound is not quite so clean as this work ideally needs, and the coupling is less than generous, but anyone who follows Perlman – in so many ways the supreme violin virtuoso of our time – is not likely to be disappointed. The cassette is admirably clear and realistic, marginally less rich than the disc but still excellent.

Ricci made an outstanding record of this concerto in the early days of mono LP. He then recorded it in stereo with rather less success, but his newer (originally Phase Four) recording with Fournet restores his reputation fully. The characteristic intense vibrato may not be to all tastes, but the ear readily submits to the compulsion and colour of the playing, which shows a rock-steady technique and a splendid lyrical feeling. Even though Ricci is very near the microphone, so secure is his left hand that the rich stream of tone is always securely based, and the larger-than-life image is attractive when the orchestral impact and detail are so vividly conveyed. The cassette transfer matches the disc closely, although the dynamic range is very slightly reduced.

Hoelscher with his clean timbre never makes an ugly sound, and his hushed inward account of the central *Canzonetta* is outstandingly beautiful. If the effect in the outer movements is a little lightweight, this makes an excellent bargain version, warmly and fully recorded and with a generous coupling in the Dvořák concerto. The cassette transfer is first-class, well up to the usual CfP standard.

Kogan's splendid account was coupled with the *Meditation* in its original full-priced format. In this reissue (available only on cassette) it is paired with the Mendelssohn concerto; both recordings date from the beginning of the sixties. Kogan plainly enjoys the Tchaikovsky concerto enormously. Spontaneity and sincerity are written in every bar of his interpretation; the finale is especially infectious. There he allows himself a lilt in the rhythm, but in the first two movements he is steadier. His build-up of tension when the main theme is developed in the first movement is most exciting, through his very refusal to slacken the basic speed. His tone is impressively full, and in this tape transfer the sound of both soloist and orchestra has plenty of sparkle.

Grumiaux's account with Haitink also dates from the early sixties and was originally coupled with the Mendelssohn. Its reissue at medium price, spread over two sides, seems distinctly ungenerous, although it is a distinguished performance, intimate but unfailingly enjoyable.

The orchestral support is polished and musical: Haitink moulds the opening phrase beautifully and accompanies throughout with obvious warmth. The *Canzonetta* is very fine indeed, and the finale sparkles. The sound is good on disc and cassette alike, but the quality is very slightly dated, not as rich as we would expect today.

Consideration of the Ferras/Karajan performance must be affected by personal reactions to Ferras's characteristic tone, with its rather close vibrato in lyrical passages and tendency to emphasize the schmalz on the G string. One finds too that Ferras's playing tends to lack charm, but some may react differently, and this is a well-conceived reading, with Karajan shaping the work as a whole very convincingly. The recording is excellent, the brilliance emphasizing the style of the soloist. The fill-up is an exciting account of the *Capriccio italien*, the Berlin brass telling especially well.

Stern was on peak form when he made his first stereo recording with Ormandy, and it is a powerfully lyrical reading, rich in timbre and technically immaculate. The playing has undoubted poetry but is not helped by the very close balance of the soloist, so that pianissimos consistently become mezzo fortes. The orchestral sound is vivid but lacks amplitude. Stern's later recording with Rostropovich is also played with his usual impeccable technique, and this too is a distinguished and often sensitive account. The orchestral response is more than adequate and often responsive, though Rostropovich is not free from the charge of over-emphatic accentuation in one or two places. The balance somewhat favours the soloist, but in general the sound is very satisfactory. Like Milstein and Kogan before him, Stern includes the *Meditation*, Op. 42, which Tchaikovsky had originally intended as the slow movement of the concerto. Good though this version is, it does not displace such trusted accounts as those of Kyung-Wha Chung and Boris Belkin, and the recording is not quite as refined as theirs.

Kremer's is the first digital recording of the concerto. This artist blends keen nervous energy with controlled lyrical feeling, and it goes without saying that his virtuosity is impressive. Self-regarding agogic distortions are few (bars 50–58 and the first-movement cadenza are instances), and there is no lack of warmth. Yet both here and in the *Sérénade mélancolique*, there is something missing. A great performance of this work refreshes the spirit and resonates in the mind. Here, although the recording, and the playing of the Berlin Philharmonic for Maazel, are undoubtedly excellent, there is not the humanity and perception of a special kind that are needed if a newcomer is to displace the superb versions already available.

Szeryng is sweetly lyrical, but he is not helped by Haitink, who provides a rather slack accompaniment. The relaxed manner of the performance of the first movement is in some ways like the Belkin version on Decca, but that performance has strikingly more forward momentum and impulse. In the finale too Belkin shows a fire that Szeryng, although spirited, misses.

Coronation march in D; Overture in C min. (1866).
(*) HMV ASD 3502. USSR SO, Lazarev – KALINNIKOV: *Symphony No. 1.**

Neither the early *C minor Overture* nor the *Coronation march* written for the accession of Tsar Alexander III in 1883 is inspired Tchaikovsky, but there is still much pleasure to be derived from them. The *Overture* was a prentice work written while Tchaikovsky was a young professor at Nicholas Rubinstein's Conservatoire in Moscow. It precedes the Kalinnikov *Symphony No. 1*. It is a good fill-up to what must be one of the most likeable of minor Russian symphonies.

1812 overture, Op. 49.
(M) *** RCA Gold GL/*GK* 42924 [LSC 3051/*RK 1115*]. New Philh. O., RAF Central Band, Children's Ch., Amb. S., Buketoff – RACHMANINOV: *3 Russian folksongs* etc.**(*)
(M) **(*) Ph. Fest. 6570/*7310* 191 [id.]. Concg. O., Markevitch – BORODIN: *Polovtsian dances;* RIMSKY-KOR-SAKOV: *Russian Easter Festival overture.***(*)

Buketoff's performance of *1812* is different in including a children's chorus to sing a children's folksong that is one of the themes Tchaikovsky interpolated into his score. The effect is pleasingly fresh. The full chorus sings at the opening and joins in again in the finale. The cannon of the Royal Artillery are placed backwardly, and the closing pages have an attractive air of jubilation with the combination of orchestra, voices and victory bells. The recording accommodates it all without strain and the listener is left exhilarated rather than overwhelmed. The cassette is not recommended: the treble is edgy and thin.

Markevitch's performance is supported by first-class playing from the Concertgebouw Orchestra and well-balanced recording. There is no lack of character and excitement, though the absence of cannon at the end reduces the feeling of spectacle. However, this means there are no problems for the cassette transfer, which is free of congestion.

1812 overture; Marche slave; Romeo and Juliet.
(M) *(**) CBS 60110 [Col. MY 36723]. NYPO, Bernstein.
(B) * Con. CC/*CCT* 7551. LSO, Ahronovitch.

Bernstein's performances undoubtedly have charisma. There are one or two idiosyncrasies in *1812*, but the performance of *Romeo and Juliet* is thrillingly intense, while the coda of *Marche slave* has a similar projection of adrenalin. At the end of *1812* the fusillade is impressively spectacular, and the orchestral playing throughout is expert and totally committed. The snag is the recording, excessively brilliant, lacking sumptuousness in *1812* and harsh in the loud climaxes of *Romeo and Juliet*. Frankly this is not very congenial listening, for all the brilliance of the music-making itself.

Ahronovitch's performances are wilfully eccentric, and though the recording is lively and the record is cheap it cannot be recommended with any confidence. Previn's record of this combination of works is the one to go for (HMV ASD 2894 [Ang. S 36890]).

1812 overture; Romeo and Juliet.
(M) **(*) Decca Jub. JB/*KJBC* 96 [Lon. 6670/5-]. LAPO, Mehta.

Mehta's *1812* is spectacular and vivid, and moreover it is easy to reproduce. The performance itself, like that of *Romeo and Juliet*, is straightforward and exciting. Certain other accounts of *Romeo* are more individual, but this one, which lets the music speak for itself, is certainly effective. The cassette transfer is acceptable in *Romeo and Juliet*, but the explosive climax of *1812* is uncomfortable.

1812 overture; Serenade for strings in C, Op. 48.
**(*) HMV Dig. ASD/*TCC-ASD* 3956. Phd. O., Muti.

An urgent, crisply articulated version of *1812* (obviously more distinguished as a performance than the Kunzel Telarc digital version above), concentrated in its excitement. The Philadelphia Orchestra takes the fast speed of the main allegro in its stride, with immaculate ensemble. Perhaps a sense of genial high spirits is missing, but, with a splendidly evocative sense of anticipation, the coda produces a spectacular closing climax which is accommodated as easily on the chrome tape as on the disc. The digital recording is a

little fierce on top, and the ear notices this even more when the first movement of the *Serenade* begins on side one, after the end of the overture. Again in Tchaikovsky's string piece the articulation of the Philadelphia strings is very impressive, with freshness and resilience a feature of the *Waltz* and a strongly expressive *Elegy*. But other versions of the *Serenade*, notably Leppard's, are more smiling (see below).

Festival overture on the Danish national anthem, Op. 15. (i) Hamlet: Overture and incidental music, Op. 67 bis. Mazeppa: Battle of Poltava and Cossack dance; Romeo and Juliet (fantasy overture; 1869 version); Serenade for Nikolai Rubinstein's saint's day.
⊛*** Chan. Dig. DBRD/*DBRT* 2003 (2). LSO, Simon, (i) with Janis Kelly, Hammond-Stroud.

The credit for the appearance of this enterprising set, indispensable for any true Tchaikovskian, lies with Edward Johnson, a keen enthusiast and Tchaikovsky expert. He spent many months trying to persuade one of the major recording companies to make an investment in this repertoire, and it was Chandos which finally responded, producing a resplendent digital recording fully worthy of the occasion. Tchaikovsky himself thought his *Danish Festival overture* superior to *1812*, and though one cannot agree with his judgement it is well worth hearing. The *Hamlet* incidental music is another matter. The overture is a shortened version of the *Hamlet Fantasy overture*, but much of the rest of the incidental music (which occupies two well-filled LP sides) is unknown, and the delightful *Funeral march* and the two poignant string elegies show the composer's inspiration at its most memorable. Ophelia's mad scene is partly sung and partly spoken, and Janis Kelly's performance is most sympathetic, while

Derek Hammond-Stroud is suitably robust in the *Gravedigger's song*. The music from *Mazeppa* and the tribute to Rubinstein make engaging bonuses, but the highlight of the set is the 1869 version of *Romeo and Juliet*, very different from the final 1880 version we know so well. It may be less sophisticated in construction, but it uses its alternative ideas with confidence and flair. It is fascinating to hear the composer's early thoughts before he finalized a piece which was to become one of the most successful of all his works. The performances here under Geoffrey Simon are excitingly committed and spontaneous; the orchestral playing is nearly always first-rate, and the digital recording has spectacular resonance and depth to balance its brilliance. Edward Johnson provides the excellent notes and a translation of the vocal music, which is sung (as the original production of *Hamlet* was performed) in French.

Francesca da Rimini (fantasy), *Op. 32.*
(M) *** HMV SXLP/*TC-SXLP* 30509 [(d) Sera. S/*4XG* 60311]. Philh. O., Giulini – *Symphony No. 2.***(*)
(B) ** Con. CC/*CCT* 7533. SRO, Varviso – BORODIN: *Symphony No. 2.***(*)

Francesca da Rimini; Romeo and Juliet.
*** HMV ASD/*TC-ASD* 3567 [Ang. S/*4XS* 37528]. LPO, Rostropovich.
** DG 2531/*3301* 211 [id.]. Israel PO, Bernstein.
*(*) Ph. Dig. 9500 745/*7300 830* [id.]. Concg. O., De Waart.

Rostropovich's coupling of *Francesca da Rimini* and *Romeo and Juliet* is outstanding in every way. The readings are intensely individual and full of poetic feeling, with a loving concern for orchestral detail, yet they are underpinned by the drama of the narrative. The ebb and flow of tension have the spontaneity of live performances, and although Rostropovich's pacing is as free as his

moulding of the melodic lines, the listener is carried along by the expressive vitality of the orchestral playing. At the opening of *Romeo and Juliet* there are bold accents in the lower strings; later there is a compulsive *accelerando* before the final romantic climax, but the love theme is introduced with the greatest tenderness. It is an epic rather than a romantic approach, and *Francesca* has a similar sense of scale and high drama, with a breathtaking finale, yet touching delicacy in the work's central section, with radiant sounds from the LPO woodwind. The recording is resonant and spacious, with great body and impact, altogether thrilling. The cassette is fractionally less well focused, but still first-class.

Giulini's classic performance of *Francesca* comes from the early sixties, with marvellous playing from the Philharmonia in peak form. The coupled *Little Russian symphony* is disfigured by a very arbitrary cut in the finale, but is otherwise memorable. *Francesca* has a compelling forward sweep, with a sense of foreboding strongly conveyed at the opening and the lovers' passion urgently contrasted on the strings with delicately poised woodwind evocation in the central section. The ferocity of the whirlwinds frames the romantic narrative very convincingly, and the recording is suitably atmospheric, although we would expect a more sumptuous upper string sound today.

Bernstein's approach to *Francesca* certainly conveys the passion of the story, but the Israel Philharmonic is no match for the LPO in the idyllic central section; moreover Bernstein's pacing is idiosyncratic and unconvincing here. *Romeo and Juliet* is only moderately exciting, in spite of a brilliant sound balance. The cassette transfer has problems with the closing climax of *Francesca* and produces congestion.

The Philips digital recording for Edo de Waart has none of the clarity one usually associates with these new techniques; indeed the sound is muddy and bass-heavy. The performances are well played but not in any way distinctive. The cassette has almost no upper range at all.

Varviso has the advantage of vintage Decca sound. The performance is well made, but the Suisse Romande Orchestra does not produce the kind of glowing colours in the middle section of the work that distinguish the Rostropovich version. However, the inferno music is superbly managed by the recording, and its subtlety is revealed by the clever way the tam-tam is balanced, so that it adds its sombrely sinister warnings, as Tchaikovsky intended, and then at the end does not drown the orchestra in the final chords of the coda. The cassette transfer has a woolly bass and is not recommended.

Hamlet (fantasy overture), Op. 67a.
(M) ** Decca Jub. JB/*KJBC* 20 VPO, Maazel – *Symphony No. 1*.**(*)

Tchaikovsky's fantasy overture *Hamlet* did not repeat the success of *Romeo and Juliet*, but, as Stokowski has shown (Everest SDBR 3011), it can be made to sound an inspired piece even if the secondary lyrical material is less memorable (and less felicitously scored) than the famous 'love theme' of the better-known work. *Hamlet* is, however, very strong on atmosphere, and the opening and closing pages have a sombre colouring which catches the essence of Shakespeare's tragedy remarkably well. It is here that Maazel's directness is simply not imaginative enough to bring out the full character of the writing, although the performance as a whole is not without drama and excitement. The recording is excellent, and it has been vividly transferred to cassette. A more than generous coupling for a fine performance of the *Winter Daydreams symphony*.

Manfred symphony, Op. 58.
*** HMV Dig. ASD/*TCC-ASD* 4169. Philh. O., Muti.

*** Decca SXL/*KSXC* 6853 [Lon. 7075/5-]. New Philh. O., Ashkenazy.
*** HMV ASD/*TC-ASD* 3730 [Ang. SZ/*4ZS* 37297]. LPO, Rostropovich.
*** Ph. 9500 778/*7300 853* [id.]. Concg. O., Haitink.
**[*] CBS 76982 [Col. M/*MT* 36673]. LSO, Tilson Thomas.
[M] ** Decca Jub. JB/*KJBC* 26. VPO, Maazel.
(M) *(*) Ph. Fest. 6570/*7310* 162. LSO, Markevitch.
(M) (*) DG Priv. 2535/*3335* 476. LSO, Ahronovitch.

At last Tchaikovsky's glorious and underrated *Manfred symphony* has received its due in the recording studios. The 1970s saw five new recordings (including Previn's – HMV ASD/*TC-ASD* 3018 [Ang. S 37018] – which, though not as successful as the four top versions listed above, is by no means inconsiderable). Choice is not easy; each version has its own virtues, and each throws new light on a masterly score, one that is much less uneven in inspiration than hitherto suspected and in its finest moments shows Tchaikovsky at his most orchestrally and melodically imaginative.

Undoubtedly Muti's thrilling new HMV recording (made in the Kingsway Hall) is in a special class – one of the most impressive digital records yet issued. At the close of the first movement, Tchaikovsky's memorable climatic statement of the principal Manfred theme heard on the massed strings (*sul G*) brings a tremendous physical excitement, and when it is similarly reprised in the finale, capped with cymbals, the effect is electrifying. The weight of the sound emphasizes the epic style of Muti's reading, forceful and boldly dramatic throughout. Muti's scherzo has a quality of exhilarating bravura, rather than concentrating on delicacy; the lovely central melody is given a sense of joyous vigour. The *Andante*, after a refined opening, soon develops a passionate forward sweep; in the finale the amplitude and brilliant detail of the recording, combined with magnificent playing from the Philharmonia Orchestra, brings a massively compulsive projection of Tchaikovsky's bacchanale and a richly satisfying dénouement. The tape is thinner on top.

Under Ashkenazy the atmosphere and power of the opening movement are fully realized, and the scherzo has the most refined lyrical impulse, with wonderfully fresh string playing and sparkling articulation in the outer sections. The *Andante* is even finer; indeed in Ashkenazy's hands it is revealed as one of Tchaikovsky's most successful symphonic slow movements, full of lyrical fervour when the playing shows such strength of feeling yet is completely without exaggeration. The reading culminates in a stunning account of the finale, Ashkenazy opting for a fast tempo and providing a tremendous forward momentum. The *fugato* section is especially incisive, and the work's closing pages are given a satisfying feeling of apotheosis. The recording is immensely full-blooded and brilliant, yet natural in perspective; the tape transfer is highly sophisticated, both rich and detailed, with splendid weight and impact. A comparison with the disc, however, shows that (as in Ashkenazy's version of the *Fifth Symphony*) the climaxes on cassette are marginally less richly expansive, although elsewhere the sound is almost identical.

By comparison with Ashkenazy, Rostropovich is weightier, more symphonic, yet the element of fantasy is not lost; the delightful chimerical detail of the scherzo inspires some marvellously polished LPO playing. Even more than Ashkenazy, Rostropovich catches the mood of brooding Byronic melancholy in the first movement, and the introduction of the lovely *Astarte* brings a moment of great poignancy, the rhythmic pulse tenderly volatile. Rostropovich's approach to the *Andante* is also more measured, the lyrical feeling intense to match the powerful mood of despair in

the finale before the beginning of the *fugato*. Ashkenazy's greater vigour and momentum are more bitingly brilliant here, but at the close Rostropovich's weight and breadth are telling. The HMV recording is rich and full (slightly less immediate than the other symphonies in Rostropovich's complete cycle), and the cassette is if anything finer than the disc, gloriously rich yet without loss of sparkle at the top.

Haitink's account of *Manfred* is characteristically fresh and incisive. Where others bring out the rhapsodic expressiveness of a work which has close parallels with Berlioz's comparably Byronic *Harold in Italy*, Haitink more clearly relates it to the other symphonies. There is no want of urgency, but there is less spontaneous lyricism than under Ashkenazy and Rostropovich: in the passage depicting the vision of Astarte, Haitink misses some of the tenderness and sense of rapture, and the third movement is less passionate, more refined in line and texture. But there is genuine authority and grip, and the playing of the Concertgebouw is immaculate. The sound is superb, bringing out both the delicacy and the power of the piece. The cassette is well balanced, rich and full-bodied, but is slightly less brilliant at the top.

Michael Tilson Thomas is an understanding and perceptive Tchaikovskian, and he too has insights to offer in this fascinating score. He secures polished and committed playing from the LSO, at its finest in the eloquent central section of the scherzo and the zestful energy of the finale. The reading overall is structurally sound and impressive both in its romanticism and in its feeling for the work's Byronic atmosphere. But the slow movement, passionately volatile though it is, does not match Ashkenazy in spontaneity or Muti in thrust; and the CBS recording, though full and well balanced, and certainly clear, is not as rich as the finest of its competitors.

Maazel's is a fresh, straightforward

performance and by no means to be dismissed. At Jubilee price it is excellent value, for the recording is first-class, vividly detailed, with brilliant, expansive climaxes. The music is quite strongly characterized and well played, though the reading lacks the distinctive qualities that make the Ashkenazy, Rostropovich and Haitink versions so memorable. The cassette matches the disc closely.

Markevitch made the pioneering stereo recording of *Manfred* in the mid-sixties, but it is less successful than the rest of his symphonic cycle (see below). With so ardently romantic a subject, a more uninhibited approach is required, one that will provide the driving force in the fast movements and the coaxing delicacy in more relaxed moments. On neither count does Markevitch come out well, although the playing is of high quality. The recording is good but not outstanding, and the cassette transfer lacks sharpness of focus.

Ahronovitch is superbly recorded by DG, but his narcissistic *ritenuto* style, with constant agogic distortion of the rhythmic pulse, is totally unsatisfactory for repeated listening.

The Nutcracker (ballet), *Op. 71:* highlights.
**(*) Decca SXL/*KSXC* 6821 [Lon. 6890/5-]. Nat. PO, Bonynge.
(M) ** RCA Gold GL/*GK* 42869 [ARL 1/*ARK 1* 0027]. Phd. O., Ormandy.

The Nutcracker: suite, Op. 71a; Suite No. 2.
*** Ph. 9500 697/*7300 788* [id.]. Concg. O. (with chorus), Dorati.

Nutcracker suite.
(M) ** HMV Green. ESD/*TC-ESD* 7115. Philh. O., Malko – LUIGINI: *Ballet Egyptien* ***; MEYERBEER: *Les Patineurs* **; PONCHIELLI: *Dance of the Hours*.**(*)

Dorati offers a second suite to supplement Tchaikovsky's own selection. This

is taken from the splendid Philips complete set (6747 364/ *7505 076*), and with refined playing and Dorati's warm attention to detail, this makes a clear first choice for a single-disc compilation. It was recorded in the ample acoustic of the Concertgebouw, and the resonance has brought a low-level tape transfer, which reduces the sparkle of the cassette sound.

Bonynge's Decca selection is generous and superbly recorded. The playing is first-rate, although the characterization sometimes has less individuality than on the Dorati disc. The sound, however, is almost in the demonstration class, although the cassette is not quite so dynamically expansive as the LP.

Ormandy's mid-priced issue is also fairly competitive, although the bright recording is not as impressive as either the Philips or the Decca engineering. The performances offer characteristic Philadelphia finesse, although in the *Waltz of the Flowers* Ormandy unnecessarily takes the violins up an octave in repeating the swinging secondary string melody. The cassette transfer is vivid on side one, but on side two the level drops and the range is more restricted.

Nicolai Malko's performance dates from the earliest days of stereo, and the 1955 recording has surprising bloom and colour (it is richer than other items in this collection which were recorded more recently). The playing is polished and colourful; the characteristic dances are strikingly vivid. There is little to choose between disc and cassette.

Nutcracker suite; Romeo and Juliet.
**(*) Telarc Dig. DG 10068 [id.]. Cleveland O., Maazel.

With vivid orchestral playing and bright, crisply focused recording within a natural ambience, Maazel's *Nutcracker suite* is enjoyably colourful. His manner is affectionate (especially in the warmly lilting *Waltz of the Flowers*), and the only idiosyncrasy is the sudden *accelerando* at the close of the *Russian dance*. *Romeo and Juliet* is given a spaciously romantic performance, reaching a climax of considerable passion. However, the almost overwhelming impact of the percussion in the undoubtedly exciting feud music is obviously designed for those who like to say 'Listen to that bass drum!' Others may feel that the balance is not exactly what one would experience in the concert hall.

Nutcracker suite; Romeo and Juliet; The Sleeping Beauty: suite, Op. 66; Swan Lake: suite, Op. 20.
(M) **(*) DG 2725/3374 105 (2). Berlin PO, Karajan.

This medium-price double album recouples recordings from the late sixties and early seventies. Karajan's DG version of *Romeo and Juliet* is very telling, with passion and dignity nicely blended. The *Nutcracker suite* is superbly played, but its piquancy of colour is slightly smoothed over. The *Sleeping Beauty* and *Swan Lake* suites show Karajan at his finest, with a high level of tension and playing that is imaginative as well as exciting. The recording is suitably brilliant, though the cassettes seem less sumptuous than the discs.

Nutcracker: suite and No. 14a: Pas de deux; The Sleeping Beauty: suite.
(B) *** CfP CFP/TC-CFP 40369. RPO, Boult.

Sir Adrian Boult did not make many Tchaikovsky records, but this coupling is highly successful. Originally made in EMI's hi-fi-conscious Studio Two system, the sound is very brilliant indeed, but there is an attractive hall ambience, and detail remains crystal-clear. The characteristic dances in the *Nutcracker* are especially vivid, and the addition of the great Act 2 *Pas de deux*, played with swirling passion, was a fine idea. The *Sleeping Beauty suite* is Boult's own selection and includes one or two attrac-

tive surprise items, but not all the familiar ones. The cassette transfer is of CfP's usual high quality; indeed there is little discernible difference between disc and tape. The latter is perhaps slightly softer-grained at the top, which is in no sense a disadvantage.

(i) *Nutcracker suite.* (ii) *The Sleeping Beauty: suite.* (iii) *Swan Lake: suite.*
(M) ** Ph. Seq. 6527/7311 065. (i) Minneapolis SO, Dorati; (ii) LSO, Fistoulari; (iii) LSO, Monteux.
(M) *(*) Decca SPA/KCSP 594. SRO, Ansermet.

Nutcracker suite; The Sleeping Beauty: excerpts; Swan Lake: suite.
*** HMV ASD/TC-ASD 3584. LSO, Previn.

The HMV issue offers the complete *Nutcracker suite*, the usual concert suite from *Swan Lake* and four items from *The Sleeping Beauty* (including the *Panorama*, which Previn floats magically). The performances show Previn's view of these works in the best light: the *Nutcracker suite* has glowing orchestral colours, well caught in the warmly vivid sound. The 'plushy' effect characteristic of the other complete sets is not minimized here by the recording balance, which is rich and full rather than especially brilliant. But this makes very congenial listening on either disc or cassette, which sound very much the same.

The Philips Sequenza issue draws on three different sources. The *Nutcracker suite* comes from Dorati's earlier complete set (so the *Dance of the Sugar Plum Fairy* has the extended ballet ending). The performance is alert and has no lack of sparkle. The sound has more freshness and range than in the previous incarnation of these excerpts (on Universo), but the upper strings lack body. The sound improves markedly for Monteux's excerpts from *Swan Lake*, which are characteristically vivid (one does not forget that he conducted for Diaghilev), and is really excellent for Fistoulari in the suite from *The Sleeping Beauty* (taken from one of his best records). This is a generous compilation and is certainly enjoyable; it sounds well on cassette too.

Ansermet's rather similar collection (drawn from his early stereo complete sets) is, surprisingly, spoiled by the sound, which is clear but lacks the warmth and sumptuousness of the originals. The music-making too is less impressive when items are reassembled like this than when heard in context, and the ear is made more aware of the inadequacies of some of the orchestral playing, especially by comparison with Previn's highly polished selections.

Nutcracker suite; Swan Lake: suite.
*(*) Decca Dig. SXDL/*KSXDC* 7505 [Lon. LDR 10008/5-]. Israel PO, Mehta.

Decca's crystal-clear digital recording here throws a spotlight on playing that is less than distinguished. The recording is indeed very brightly lit, and solos sound slightly larger than life, with rather buzzy lower strings in the *Waltz of the Flowers*. (The Mann Auditorium of Tel Aviv has a somewhat lifeless acoustic, and this gives a curiously dry sound to the bass drum that sounds slightly bizarre.) Everything is alert, but there is little or no charm. The cassette matches the disc, though in climaxes the latter has more dynamic energy in the upper range.

Romeo and Juliet (fantasy overture).
*** HMV ASD/*TC-ASD* 3488 [Ang. S/*4XS* 37472]. Philh. O., Muti – *Symphony No. 2*.***
(M) *** DG Acc. 2542/*3342* 113 [(d) 2530 137]. Boston SO, Abbado – *Symphony No. 2*.**(*)
(M) *** DG Priv. 2535/*3335* 422 [2530 308/*3300 284*]. San Francisco SO, Ozawa – BERLIOZ: *Roméo et Juliette: Love scene*; PROKOFIEV: *Romeo and Juliet: excerpts*.***

(M) *** Decca Jub. JB/*KJBC* 71. VPO, Karajan – DVOŘÁK: *Symphony No. 8*.***
(B) *** Con. CC/*CCT* 7528. Karajan (as above) – R. STRAUSS: *Don Juan*.***
(M) (***) World mono SH/*TC-SH* 287. Philh. O., Cantelli – WAGNER: *Siegfried idyll*.(***)
(M) ** Decca Jub. JB/*KJBC* 21. VPO, Maazel – *Symphony No. 2*.**

Muti's *Romeo and Juliet* is distinguished, one of the finest available, and full of imaginative touches. The opening has just the right degree of atmospheric restraint and immediately creates a sense of anticipation; the great romantic climax is noble in contour yet there is no lack of passion, while the main allegro is crisply and dramatically pointed. The repeated figure on the timpani at the coda is made to suggest a tolling bell, and the expressive woodwind playing which follows gently underlines the feeling of tragedy. The full, rich recording suits the interpretation admirably, and the cassette transfer has plenty of weight and generally good detail.

Abbado's too is a noble reading. At the first appearance of the love theme he shows considerable restraint, and there is great delicacy in the articulation of the secondary idea on muted strings. But the reprise brings a welling up of passion. The allegros have tremendous power and impact, and the coda – after a thunderous timpani roll – is wonderfully eloquent. A performance to live with: its spellbinding qualities increase with familiarity. The recording is splendid, very brilliant as well as full; there is no appreciable difference between cassette and disc.

In the DG collection of musical evocations of *Romeo and Juliet* it was inevitable that the Tchaikovsky fantasy overture should be included. This is a thoroughly worthwhile anthology and Ozawa draws from the San Francisco orchestra warmly committed playing, very well recorded on disc and cassette alike; this should not disappoint anyone who likes the idea of having three Romeos contrasted.

Karajan's account of the *Romeo and Juliet* overture is among the best of its period. It has dramatic fire and excitement and, when the music calls for it, tenderness. The recording is from the early 1960s and is not quite as rich as one would expect today. Yet this is well worth considering if you want a Dvořák *G major Symphony*. The cassette is less refined in tuttis than some Decca transfers. This performance is also available on the Contour bargain label in an excellent, clean pressing coupled with *Don Juan*. The Contour cassette (not made by Decca) is less wide-ranging than the disc though quite acceptable; but the LP is an obvious bargain.

Guido Cantelli's recording, like his coupled account of the *Siegfried idyll*, was made during the 1951 season, his first with the Philharmonia. There is no lack of concentration, yet nothing is overdriven. There is fine ensemble and marvellously articulated detail (a minor lapse of chording during the opening is hardly worth mentioning) and there is total commitment and a refreshing absence of any egocentricity. The sound quality is remarkably good; few allowances have to be made on this score. There have been distinguished performances of this work in the intervening years (from Karajan, Abbado, Muti and so on) but this version still belongs among their number. The cassette transfer is smooth and well balanced.

Maazel's *Romeo and Juliet* is characteristically brilliant. It does not want passion, but there is rather more surface excitement than depth. The sound is slightly less expansive than usual in Maazel's Tchaikovsky series, and this effect seems to be emphasized in the cassette transfer.

Serenade for strings in C, Op. 48.
*** DG Dig. 2532/ *3302* 012 [id.]. Berlin PO, Karajan – DVOŘÁK: *Serenade.****

(B) **(*) RCA VICS/*VK* 2001 [AGL 1/*AGK 1* 3790]. Boston SO, Munch – BARBER: *Adagio*; ELGAR: *Introduction and allegro.***(*)
//(*) ASV Dig. DCA/*ZCDCA* 505. Orch. of St John's, Lubbock – DVOŘÁK: *Serenade.* **(*)
(M) *(*) HMV Green. ESD/*TC-ESD* 7084. Polish CO, Maksymiuk – GRIEG: *Elegiac melodies* etc.*(*)

A vigorously extrovert reading from Karajan, with taut, alert and extremely polished playing in the first movement, an elegant but slightly cool *Waltz*, a passionately intense *Elegy* and a bustling, immensely spirited finale. There is a lack of charm, but here the strikingly clear digital recording, with the strings very brightly lit above the stave, has its influence, for there is a lack of warmth in the middle range. The chrome tape, while retaining the inner clarity, is slightly richer and softer-grained on top.

A strong, full-blooded reading from Munch, with an elegant *Waltz* and an especially well-prepared finale. The conductor does not overplay his hand in the *Elegy*, and with playing from the Boston strings that is both committed and polished this is very involving. The early stereo recording sounds remarkably well, robust, yet well detailed and with plenty of colour and atmosphere. Disc and chrome cassette are virtually identical; if anything the tape has slightly more range than the disc, without loss of body. There is only a hint of the characteristic Boston ambient harshness. An excellent bargain.

Lubbock and the Orchestra of St John's, Smith Square, provided the digital début of Tchaikovsky's *Serenade*, and the sound here is if anything even more analytical than the DG recording. While one cannot complain that the timbre is untruthful, the listener is given the impression, almost, of being suspended near the first violins, with the middle resonances of violas and cellos less telling. Lubbock secures a strong, brisk first-movement allegro, but he relaxes very effectively at the end of the *Elegy* to bring a sense of repose, so that the lead into the finale is the more effective. The actual playing is of high quality, but does not quite match the Berlin Orchestra in polish. Nonetheless the performance communicates readily, and it certainly has vitality. The cassette matches the disc closely.

Maksymiuk takes the first movement of the *Serenade* very fast indeed, with remarkably crisp articulation of the secondary theme, but there is overall a lack of breadth. After a gentle and intimate *Waltz* (using mutes) comes a highly volatile *Elegy* and a very vigorous finale. The recording is balanced very close and the effect is to rob the strings of any sumptuous qualities.

Still recommended: When one turns to Marriner (Argo ZRG/*KZRC* 848) or Leppard (Philips 9500 105) one encounters a sunny quality in the music-making which is much less apparent with Karajan or Lubbock, let alone Maksymiuk. Moreover, the Philips analogue sound has a glowing resonant warmth in the lower strings to balance the brilliance, which makes an altogether more congenial effect; yet there is no sense of inner detail being clouded.

The Sleeping Beauty (complete ballet), *Op*. 66.
⊛*** BBC BBC/*ZCBBC*3001 (3) [Euro. 300575/*500575*]. BBC SO, Rozhdestvensky.
(M) *** HMV SLS 5245 (3). USSR SO, Svetlanov.
**(*) Decca D 78 D 3/*K 78 K 33* (3) [Lon. 2316/5-]. Nat. PO, Bonynge.
** Ph. 6769/*7699* 036 (3) [id.]. Concg. O., Dorati.

Rozhdestvensky's set was made as part of the BBC Symphony Orchestra's fiftieth anniversary celebrations and is fully worthy of the occasion. It is superb in every way, marvellously played and very

well recorded in an excellent acoustic that is neither too dry nor too resonant for comfort (a problem with this particular score). There is occasional minor spotlighting of wind soloists, but who would cavil when all the solo playing is so outstanding – as indeed are the contributions of the strings and brass: the trumpet and horn fanfares are splendid. Rozhdestvensky uses the original Russian score, which is absolutely complete, even including music omitted from the ballet's première. There are those who hold that this is Tchaikovsky's greatest ballet score, finer even than *Swan Lake*; and these records do much to support that view. The work could not be entrusted to more caring or sensitive direction, and the ear is continually amazed by the consistent quality of Tchaikovsky's inspiration. Rozhdestvensky's loving attention to detail and his response to the textural colouring are matched by his feeling for the narrative drama, yet he never overplays his hand, so that the big moments of spectacle – the *Rose adagio*, for instance – have ardour without becoming emotionally aggressive. Tchaikovsky's continuously fertile imagination in matters of scoring is readily demonstrated, and the lighter characteristic dances sound as fresh as the day they were written. There is atmosphere too, and the magical *Sleep entr'acte* before the happy ending of the story is given a haunting sense of anticipation and fantasy. In disc form this is an outstanding achievement in every way. Unfortunately the Dolby treatment of the cassettes has been misjudged; the treble is unacceptably muffled unless the Dolby circuitry is switched out and a treble cut substituted, with its attendant hiss problem. The rosette is for the LP box only.

Svetlanov's performance is demonstrably Russian in feeling, often fierily intense and extremely vivid in instrumental character. The quick pacing of the very opening bars is only one of many quixotic touches, with tempi sometimes faster, sometimes slower than usual, but always springing from the conductor's response to the music's dance elements. Only the *Panorama*, lovingly spacious, and rocking quite gently on its syncopated bass, suggests a moment of personal indulgence. The drama is very dramatic indeed, and there is certainly not a dull bar here. The music of the third act sums up the performance, with brilliant playing bringing characterization that is almost over-emphatic; the orchestral timbres are slightly fierce, with brassy brass, often pungent woodwind articulation and colouring, and a string sheen that is passionate rather than sensuous (the recording is without sumptuous qualities). But the directness of communication is irresistible; the recorded sound is never ugly (if not as rich as a western European balance); and this makes an exhilarating listening experience.

Bonynge secures brilliant and often elegant playing from the National Philharmonic Orchestra, and his rhythmic pointing is always characterful. As recorded, however, the upper strings lack sumptuousness. Otherwise the sound is excellent and there is much to give pleasure. Bonynge is especially good at the close of Act 2 when, after the magical *Panorama*, the Princess is awakened. There is a frisson of tension here and the atmosphere is most evocative. Rozhdestvensky finds more individuality in the various characteristic dances in Act 3, but the Decca sound has a fine sparkle here and the solo violin (Mincho Minchev) and cello (Francisco Gabarro) provide most appealing solo contributions. The tape transfer has plenty of range and detail, although the upper strings sometimes sound rather feathery and at times the bass line seems resonantly heavy.

Dorati's is a vibrant and dramatic account, supported by sumptuous recording and splendid orchestral playing (especially in the last act, which gives the orchestral wind soloists many chances to shine). Yet this is a score that – for all its melodic inspiration – can momentarily

disengage the listener's attention; and here in spite of the drama this does happen. Everything is well characterized, but at times there is a lack of magic. The low-level cassette transfer can be made to sound well but is bass-heavy and lacks the range and sparkle at the top. Moreover the layout on two tapes instead of three discs is quite arbitrary and makes no attempt to tailor the acts to fit the ends of sides.

The Sleeping Beauty: excerpts; *Swan Lake: suite.*
(M) *** Decca VIV/*KVIC* 10 [Lon. 21008/5-]. New Philh. O., Stokowski.

Stokowski secures some electrifying playing from the New Philharmonia Orchestra. The recording (made originally in Decca's Phase Four system) is somewhat artificial in balance and very brilliant, but the conductor makes the very most of the sonic possibilities to project a generous selection of music in the most vivid way. The result makes an irresistible impact, and of its kind this is a classic issue, very much worth its relatively modest price. The cassette is lively too, but has a narrower range of dynamics.

The Sleeping Beauty: suite; Swan Lake: suite.
*** DG 2531/*3301* 111 [id.]. Berlin PO, Rostropovich.
(M) **(*) Decca Jub. JB/*KJBC* 35 [Lon. 41003]. VPO, Karajan.

Rostropovich provides here a highly distinguished companion disc for his DG coupling of the *Nutcracker suite* and *Capriccio italien*. Given superb recording, the performances combine Slavonic intensity with colour. The characteristic dances balance wit with delicacy: the whimsical portrait of the cats in *The Sleeping Beauty* is matched by the sprightly fledgling swans, while the glorious *Panorama* melody is floated over its gently rocking bass with magical delicacy. The recording expands spectacularly at climaxes, and elsewhere it attractively combines bloom with detail. The cassette matches the disc closely, having only marginally less upper range.

Karajan's Jubilee reissue with the Vienna Philharmonic dates from the midsixties. The recording is brilliant and the performances have panache. This is a case where the cassette – bright and vivid – is more attractive than the disc, where the sound has rather less amplitude.

Suites (for orchestra) *Nos. 1 in D min., Op. 43; 2 in C, Op. 53; 3 in G, Op. 55; 4 in G* (*Mozartiana*), *Op. 61.*
(M) **(*) Ph. 6768 035 (3) [Mercury 77008]. New Philh. O., Dorati.

Tchaikovsky's four *Orchestral suites* are directly descended from the dance suites of the baroque era. Nos. 1 and 3 are both as long as an average symphony, although their material is slighter. The invention is slightly uneven, but each suite has its share of endearing inspiration. No. 4 draws on the music of Mozart, including the *Ave verum* and a set of piano variations which are given a tasteful orchestral dress. The weakest is No. 2, whose most striking movement is a *Scherzo burlesque* featuring the accordion as an ad lib soloist. The most famous is No. 3 with its familiar set of variations, often performed separately. Dorati's complete set first appeared at the end of the sixties, and its return to the catalogue is welcome, for there is no serious competition (except in the case of the *Third Suite*). The performances are perceptive and generally well characterized. Dorati secures first-rate playing from the New Philharmonia, but the Philips recording now sounds just a little dated. However, this is good value at medium price, and the music itself is certainly worth investigating.

Suites Nos. 2 in C, Op. 53; 4 in G (*Mozartiana*), *Op. 61.*
**(*) CBS Dig. 36702 [Col. IM/*IMT* 36702]. Philh. O., Tilson Thomas.

Michael Tilson Thomas makes a very good case for Tchaikovsky's *Mozartiana suite*, finding both sparkle and elegance in the music and effectively balancing the personalities of both the composers represented. The Philharmonia playing is first-class, but the brilliant digital recording, though admirably clear, lacks ambient bloom. The bright, clean focus of the sound tends to emphasize the unevenness of the *Second Suite*, although the *Scherzo burlesque* with its accordions is effectively bustling and Tilson Thomas finds a wistful charm in the *Rêves d'enfant*; and he directs the closing *Danse baroque* most stylishly.

Suite No. 3 in G, Op. 55.
*** CBS 76733/40- [Col. M 35124]. Los Angeles PO, Tilson Thomas.
** Decca SXL/*KSXC* 6857 [Lon. 7080/5-]. VPO, Maazel.

The performance of Tchaikovsky's *Third Suite* by Michael Tilson Thomas and the Los Angeles Philharmonic is in a class of its own; indeed it is one of the finest Tchaikovsky performances in the catalogue. So often the first three movements of this work are dwarfed by the finale, which undoubtedly contains the finest music, but here the conductor achieves a perfect balance. He opens and closes the first movement quite magically and takes its climax with just the right degree of romantic melodrama. The rhythmic character of the *Valse mélancolique* is deftly managed, and the crisp, gay scherzo is delightful, its middle section wittily and delicately pointed. At the opening of the fourth movement Tchaikovsky's fine melody is splendidly shaped, and the variations unfold with gripping spontaneity, their sheer diversity a constant joy. The closing *Polacca* is superbly prepared and Tilson Thomas ushers in the principal theme with a calculated *ritenuto* worthy of Sir Thomas Beecham. The trio has a swinging animation, and the piece closes with glorious vigour. The recording is vivid and well balanced, with fine detail. But it lacks something in bloom and warmth in the middle area of the orchestra, although it does not want brilliance. The transfer to tape is well judged, so that the final climax opens up quite impressively. However, while the performance would deserve a rosette, the recording is just not distinguished enough to deserve such an accolade.

The Decca sound for Maazel's version (not nearly so imaginative a performance) is infinitely more vivid; the reading is freshly conceived, and Maazel is supported by refined playing from the Vienna Philharmonic. The recording is beautifully clear and sparkling; woodwind detail has a pleasing individuality of colour. But the performance throughout is just that bit too literal, and any charm comes from the music itself rather than any melting quality in the music-making or any memorable shapeliness of phrasing. The cassette transfer is first-class, with plenty of weight and brilliance and a strikingly clear internal focus achieved without any loss of bloom.

Swan Lake (complete ballet), *Op. 20.*
**(*) DG 2709 099/*3371 051* (3) [id.]. Boston SO, Ozawa.

Ozawa's version omits the Act 3 *Pas de deux* but otherwise plays the complete original score as Tchaikovsky conceived it. His performance has not the irresistible vitality of Fistoulari's set (Decca 10 BB 168/70); the approach is more serious, less flexible. But the playing of the Boston orchestra is strikingly polished and sympathetic, and there are many impressive things here, with wind (and violin) solos that always give

pleasure. The end result is a little faceless, in spite of a spectacular, wide-ranging recording, as vivid as it is powerful. On cassette (with a comparatively modest transfer level) the gentler moments lack something in presence, but the climaxes open up without distortion.

While Fistoulari's set retains pride of place, in spite of its artificially balanced Phase Four recording, Ansermet's slightly abridged version on two records still sounds remarkably vivid and is now available at bargain price with an excellent equivalent double-length cassette (Decca DPA 603/4/*KDPC 7058* [Lon. 2204]).

Swan Lake: highlights.
*** HMV ASD/*TC-ASD* 3491 [Ang. S/*4XS* 37561]. LSO, Previn.
(B) *** CfP CFP/*TC-CFP* 40296. Menuhin (violin), Philh. O., Kurtz.
**(*) DG 2531/*3301* 351 [id.] (from above set cond. Ozawa).
(M) ** Ph. Fest. 6570/*7310* 187 [id.]. LSO, Monteux.
(B) ** Con. CC/*CCT* 7520. ROHCGO, Morel.

Previn's selection is both generous and felicitous. It is superbly played and shows the very best qualities of his complete set, with splendid solo wind playing and a rich-toned contribution from the violinist Ida Haendel. The recording is sumptuous and full-blooded, and considering its weight and amplitude the quality of the high-level cassette transfer is admirable.

From Classics for Pleasure a splendid bargain compilation, with Menuhin present to play the violin solos. The Philharmonia are on top form and the woodwind acquit themselves with even more style than usual in Tchaikovsky's solos. The 1960 recording, originally HMV, matches the exuberance which Kurtz brings to the music's climaxes with the widest possible dynamic range and a sound balance that underpins surface brilliance with depth and atmosphere. The elegant Philharmonia string playing is beautifully caught. Menuhin finds a surprising amount to play here; besides the famous duet with the cello in the *Danse des cygnes*, which is beautifully done, he includes a ravishing account of the *Danse russe* as a postlude to the main selection. The cassette transfer (perhaps prudently) has a slightly more limited dynamic range, but otherwise sounds well; when it is heard away from the disc there is no really striking reduction of contrast.

The DG disc offers some fifty minutes from the complete Ozawa Boston set. The sophistication of both playing and recording is impressive, and the final climax expands magnificently; but over-all this has less individuality than the Previn and Menuhin/Kurtz alternatives.

At medium price the Monteux selection might well be considered. The recording lacks the last degree of brilliance, but it is well balanced, and in the finale, which Monteux takes broadly and grandly, the weight of the sound makes a strong impact. The LSO playing is of good quality. On cassette the sound balance is rather bass-heavy.

The selection by Jean Morel and the Orchestra of the Royal Opera House, Covent Garden, was originally issued in the earliest days of stereo by RCA, although recorded by Decca. On Contour it emerges as a vivid and enjoyable disc with sound that is slightly dry but not too dated. The scale of the performance suggests the orchestral pit rather than the concert hall, but the intimacy of the *Waltz*, for instance, brings an added freshness. There is some very sensitive woodwind playing, especially by the oboe. With plenty of vitality throughout this is worth considering, though the Kurtz CfP version is even more attractive.

Symphonies Nos. 1–6.
*** DG 2740 219 (6)/*3378 084* (5) [id.]. Berlin PO, Karajan.

Symphonies Nos. 1–6; Manfred symphony.

(M) *** Ph. 6768 267 (7) [id.]. Concg. O., Haitink.
(B) **(*) Decca Jub. JBC 510/15/*K 164 K 64* (4). VPO, Maazel.

Having recorded the last three Tchaikovsky symphonies three times over in little more than ten years, Karajan finally turned to the early symphonies; and there, displaying the same superlative refined qualities, he produced performances equally illuminating. It is typical that, though the opening *Allegro tranquillo* of the first movement of No. 1 is taken fast, there is no feeling of breathlessness, as there usually is: it is genuinely *tranquillo*, though the rhythmic bite of the syncopated passages, so important in these early symphonies, could hardly be sharper. The high polish may give a hint of the ballroom to some of the dance movements, with the folk element underplayed, but no finer set of the symphonies has yet been recorded; it is commandingly consistent and vivid in sound, though (in the last three symphonies especially) it is not always richly resonant in the lower range. The tape transfers are of comparable sophistication. Because of the degree of dryness in the bass, the three later works are extremely clear and vivid. In the earlier symphonies the slight recession of the orchestral image (particularly in gentle woodwind solos) is a slight drawback. Nos. 1 and 4 are both complete on a single side each, back to back; all the others have a separate cassette. No. 5 includes the bonus of *Marche slave* (as on the separate issue), but this is not mentioned on the label or in the notes.

Haitink's complete Tchaikovsky cycle includes *Manfred* – and a very good *Manfred* it is too. Moreover the set is in the medium price-range, considerably cheaper than Karajan's. Haitink's readings are satisfyingly consistent and they have genuine symphonic strength. They are well-groomed and finely poised, and although they are only rarely incandescent and not all of them make the spine tingle, Haitink's avoidance of self-indulgence and overtly emotional responses is more than compensated for by his balance of concentration and freshness. By their side, the idiosyncrasies of Rostropovich's much more wayward interpretations – deeply felt and balancing passion and electricity with charm (sometimes at the expense of structural cohesion) – are very striking; but his LPO set has many special insights of its own (HMV SLS 5099 [Ang. SE 3487], also including *Manfred*). Haitink's special advantage (alongside the superb playing of the Concertgebouw Orchestra) is the splendid Philips recording, rich, refined in detail and bringing nobility of sound to the later works especially.

Maazel's performances from the mid-sixties have been remastered and reissued on six records or four cassettes, including *Manfred*, at bargain price. The recordings come from a vintage Decca period and are astonishingly vivid, so that the music-making seems newly minted. Indeed the performances have a gripping spontaneity throughout, helped by the freshness of the VPO playing in their first complete cycle in the recording studio and obviously relishing the experience. Maazel's readings are well-judged and clearly thought out. Sometimes they are lacking in charm (notably No. 2), while No. 5 lacks the fullest expansive qualities. But the recording balance, well lit and with excellent presence, never achieved at the expense of musical perspective, projects the performances admirably and the cycle as a whole is remarkably satisfying. The cassettes are demonstration-worthy, showing Decca's transfer technology at its most spectacular. The sound is in no way inferior to the discs and the presentation is ideal, with each of the symphonies complete on a single side, back to back, with *Manfred* offered separately on the fourth tape.

Symphony No. 1 in G min. (*Winter Daydreams*), *Op. 13.*

*** DG 2531/*3301* 284 [id.]. Berlin PO, Karajan.
*** Ph. 9500 777/*7300 851* [id.]. Concg. O., Haitink.
(M) *** Ph. Fest. 6570/*7310* 160 [id.]. LSO, Markevitch.
(M) **(*) Decca JB/*KJBC* 20. VPO, Maazel – *Hamlet.***

Symphony No. 1; Marche slave, Op. 31.
** Decca SXL/*KSXC* 6913 [Lon. 7148]. LAPO, Mehta.

Little more need be said about Karajan's marvellous performance of the *Winter Daydreams symphony*. It is not quite so richly recorded as Haitink's version, but in all other respects it is outstanding, almost certainly the finest performance of this work ever committed to disc. Karajan's approach is direct, never indulgent in the way of Rostropovich, yet his affection is obvious. The playing of the Berlin Philharmonic orchestra is little short of miraculous, and because of Karajan's warmth the refinement of detail is never clinical. The *fugato* in the last movement is given classical strength (there is never any sign that Karajan sees the first three symphonies as immature), and the peroration has regality and splendour. The sound is excellent, brilliant and with a wide dynamic range. The cassette transfer is one of DG's best: there is little appreciable difference between tape and disc.

Haitink gives a most refreshing performance of Tchaikovsky's earliest symphony. Choice of speeds – very difficult in this work – always seems apt and natural, and it is typical of Haitink's flair for balance that the big horn solo which comes at the culmination of the slow movement has nothing of vulgarity in it. At the opening of this movement he is more atmospheric than Karajan, and is helped by the warm acoustic of the Concertgebouw. He does not find all the charm inherent in the scherzo, and at the close of the finale the rhetoric of the coda is negotiated with less than ideal aplomb (Karajan is more extrovert here, to good advantage); but overall this is very satisfying, and anyone following Haitink's series will not be disappointed. The cassette is of excellent quality, matching the disc closely.

At medium price Markevitch's version remains fully competitive. He chooses a fast pace for the opening, yet skilfully retains the delicate Mendelssohnian atmosphere. The playing creates plenty of excitement but never loses the music's scale or charm. The opening of the slow movement is superbly evocative; the delightful scherzo has sylvan lightness, and the waltz at its centre is deftly pointed. The finale is no less successful, with an eloquent opening and a rousing close, before which Markevitch creates a haunting sense of desolation at the reprise of the *Andante lugubre*. The recording (from the mid-sixties) has been freshly remastered and sounds full and clear. There is no appreciable difference in quality between cassette and disc.

Maazel's version was one of the most striking performances in his cycle, and in the Jubilee reissue it is generously recoupled with the *Hamlet fantasy overture*. If the opening movement is driven hard and the Mendelssohnian quality is played down, there is also evidence of the care with which the conductor has studied the score. Much felicitous detail emerges afresh, and the delightful scherzo comes to life splendidly, showing a real feeling for the line of the waltz. The finale too is very successful; Tchaikovsky's somewhat academic *fugato* section is made to come off, with short stabbing emphases of each entry of the theme. The slow movement is not as dreamy as one might ideally ask, but the style of the playing, with strong, thrusting horn playing for the final statement of the main tune, is convincing enough in the context of the other movements. Tape and disc are closely matched, although there seems marginally less dynamic contrast on the cassette.

Mehta's account comes from a complete cycle he recorded with the Los Angeles orchestra in 1978 (Decca D 95 D 5, now withdrawn in the UK but still available in the USA on Lon. CSP 10). The performance is hard-driven and lacks charm, but it has both atmosphere and excitement. It is brilliantly recorded, but, like the complete set from which it is drawn, this is not really competitive. The *Marche slave* bonus is coarsened by the rather shrill balance of the recording.

Symphony No. 2 in C min. (Little Russian), Op. 17.
*** DG 2531/*3301* 285 [id.]. Berlin PO, Karajan.
*** HMV ASD/*TC-ASD* 3488 [Ang. S/*4XS* 37472]. Philh. O., Muti – *Romeo and Juliet.****
(M) *** Ph. Fest. 6570/*7310* 161 [id.]. LSO, Markevitch.
(M) *** RCA Gold GL/*GK* 42960. LSO, Previn – LIADOV: *8 Russian folksongs.****
(M) **(*) DG Acc. 2542/*3342* 113. New Philh. O., Abbado – *Romeo and Juliet.****
(M) **(*) HMV SXLP/*TC-SXLP* 30509. Philh. O., Giulini – *Francesca da Rimini.****
(M) ** Decca Jub. JB/*KJBC* 21. VPO, Maazel – *Romeo and Juliet.***

Symphony No. 2; The Storm, Op. 76.
*** Ph. 9500 444/*7300 650* [id.]. Concg. O., Haitink.

Karajan's performance of the *Little Russian symphony* is superbly played. Everything is in perfect scale; the tempo for the engaging *Andante* is very nicely judged, and the outer movements have plenty of drama and fire. The articulation in the finale is a joy, and the sound balance is excellent. The cassette is perhaps marginally less refined than the disc, but the difference is slight and the finale sounds especially well. However, this symphony is outstandingly well served at present, at medium as well as full price.

On HMV, Muti's version is attractive and offers a very substantial bonus, while Haitink's Philips record will be counted by many as finest of all, full of individual and imaginative touches. It offers outstandingly refined playing and recording and is altogether most refreshing. Haitink chooses tempi often slower than usual for extra expressive point – as in the solemn nobility of the opening introduction, which has nothing of pomposity about it, in the relaxed but pointed account of the *Andantino marziale*, starting most mysteriously, and above all in the finale, where the long and loud coda is given genuine joyfulness, with no blatancy. Otherwise the reading displays all the strong, thoughtful qualities that mark Haitink's Tchaikovsky. The coupling is unexpected but very worthwhile. *The Storm* is an early work (1864), not entirely convincing in construction but already showing the composer's unmistakable melodic and orchestral fingerprints. The tape transfer is not very successful; there are some problems with the bass drum, and the rich basic texture is much better defined on the LP.

Muti's account is characteristically fresh. His warmth brings an agreeable geniality to the first movement, which does not lack excitement but is not too aggressively pointed. His *Andantino* takes Tchaikovsky's *marziale* rather literally, but its precise rhythmic beat has character without heaviness. Perhaps here, as in the finale, there is less than the full degree of charm, but the scherzo is vivacious and clean. In the finale Muti's degree of relaxed affection produces much colour, and the movement has strong character, even if the performance lacks a strong forward thrust of excitement. The recording is rich and full. The cassette transfer is successful until the finale, where the bass drum gives problems and the textures are muddied. On disc, however, coupled with a quite outstanding version of *Romeo and Juliet*, this is very competitive.

At medium price Markevitch's Festivo reissue makes a clear first choice. The recording dates from 1967 but is well balanced, with plenty of body and detail. The performance is direct yet imaginative. After the finely played opening horn solo – which catches the folk quality of the melody admirably – some might feel that Markevitch's clean-cut rhythmic vigour is a little square. But the impetus of the first movement is strongly maintained, and the *Andantino marziale* is played with appealing delicacy. The scherzo is vivacious; the closing variations unfold with an attractive simplicity, and the secondary theme is nicely elegant. This is very much a performance to live with, especially as the sound is so natural. Apart from a moment of minor disturbance on the very opening chord, the cassette sound matches the disc almost exactly; it is in no way inferior.

Previn's account comes from a vintage recording period with RCA when he also recorded his outstanding set of Vaughan Williams symphonies. The reading has the freshness and eloquence of a brilliantly talented newcomer to the score. His warmth in the first movement is matched by poise and delicacy in the delightful *Andantino*, and in the finale (which is, unfortunately, slightly cut) there is plenty of energy and an attractive feeling of high spirits. The coupling too is especially valuable, a charming and much underrated set of Liadov miniatures. The tape is not recommended; its upper range is thin and unstable, with discoloration of the upper partials.

Abbado's first movement concentrates on refinement of detail and is a shade too deadpan. The *Andantino* is very nicely done and beautifully tapered off at the end, while the scherzo is admirably crisp and sparkling. The finale is quite superb, with splendid colour and thrust and a spectacular stroke on the gong before the exhilarating coda. Brilliant recording and an immaculate cassette transfer, capturing the percussive effects with aplomb.

Giulini's version is also strongly recommendable, with the single reservation that there is a clumsy cut in the coda (so arbitrary that it is quite disconcerting when it arrives). Otherwise this is an outstanding version in every way, splendidly paced – the finale is no less exhilarating than Abbado's version – and offering glowingly refined Philharmonia playing. The recording – from the early sixties – reveals its age in a certain lack of amplitude in the upper strings, but with its highly distinguished coupling this is an essential disc for Tchaikovskians.

Maazel's account, with its hard, driving *brio*, is less sympathetic than usual in his Tchaikovsky series. The reverberant recording tends to amplify his approach, and although there is plenty of colour and vitality, the music rarely smiles. The sound on cassette is rather dry, clear and bright but unexpansive.

Symphony No. 3 in D (Polish), Op. 29.
*** DG 2531/*3301* 286 [id.]. Berlin PO, Karajan.
*** Ph. 9500 776/*7300 850* [id.]. Concg. O., Haitink.
*** HMV ASD 3449 [Ang. S 37496]. Phil. O., Muti.
(M) *** Ph. Fest. 6570/*7310* 162 [id.]. LSO, Markevitch.
(M) **(*) Decca Jub. JB/*KJBC* 22. VPO, Maazel.

A clear first choice for Tchaikovsky's *Polish symphony* is difficult to determine. Karajan, Haitink and Muti each have their own virtues, and Markevitch, who is by no means to be dismissed, enjoys the advantage of economy. The playing of the Berlin orchestra is wonderfully polished and committed; Karajan's first movement is full of flair, and in the central movements he is ever conscious of the variety of Tchaikovsky's colouring. He even finds an affinity with Brahms in the second movement, and yet the climax of the *Andante* is full of Tchaikovskian fervour. In the finale the articulation of the *Polacca* is both vigorous and joyful,

and it brings a sense of symphonic strength, often lacking in other versions. The recording is bold, brilliant and clear, and the cassette transfer is strikingly successful, quite the equal of the LP.

Haitink's performance, beautifully played and warmly and resonantly recorded, has a disarmingly fresh directness of approach, bringing out the score's affinities with the ballet, which the composer saw no reason to be ashamed of. The slow movement is not as passionate as in some readings, but the delicacy of the scherzo is capped by a finale in which the rhetoric is minimized. Here the *fugato* has an attractive neoclassical feeling, and the peroration achieves remarkable dignity. Karajan is more symphonic, but throughout Haitink's version one senses that the Concertgebouw players are revelling in these consistently appealing textures. The cassette is most successful; transferred at a high level it seems almost to have greater range and brightness than the disc, an unusual occurrence for Philips.

Muti is at his finest in the three central movements, with the Philharmonia playing full of charm, the ballet associations acknowledged, and the soloists revelling in the colour and warmth of Tchaikovsky's felicitous scoring. The *Andante* is admirably volatile, and while the outer movements have not quite the forward impulse of the Maazel version, the playing is alert and sparkling. The wide dynamic range of the HMV recording brings powerful climaxes, but in the grandiose peroration at the close of the finale, Muti does not match Karajan or Haitink in minimizing the sense of rhetoric.

At medium price Markevitch continues his highly successful series with a very enjoyable account of the *Polish symphony*. The Philips recording tends to emphasize the orchestra's middle frequencies and is slightly lacking in upper range (this is most noticeable in the scherzo). In that respect the cassette is marginally brighter than the disc, although otherwise the balance is virtually identical. The rhythmic vigour of the opening movement is striking, but the strong accents emphasize the weight of the allegro's main theme rather than its incandescence, and Tchaikovsky's somewhat academic development section is left to sound rather homespun. Markevitch chooses slow tempi for both the *Alla tedesca* and the *Andante*, and his warmth is readily conveyed. The scherzo is deftly lightweight and the finale strongly full-blooded, although the recording is a little thick in the peroration. The whole performance has admirable consistency.

Maazel's approach is direct and admirably fresh. The orchestral detail emerges with glowing colours, particularly as the Decca sound is so vivid; in this respect the Jubilee issue is superior to the Markevitch Festivo version. The outer movements have a fine thrust (the main theme, on the strings, of the first is articulated with infectious vigour), and anyone collecting the Maazel series will not be disappointed here. The dynamic range is slightly narrowed on the cassette, but not seriously so, and it offers splendid quality otherwise, matching the disc closely.

Symphonies Nos. 4–6.
(M) *** DG Priv. 2726 040 (2) [2535/*3335* 235/7]. Leningrad PO, Mravinsky.
**(*) DG 2740 248 (3) [id.]. LSO, Boehm.

Symphonies Nos. 4–6; Manfred symphony.
*** Decca D 249 D 4/*K 249 K 44* (4). Philh. O., Ashkenazy.

Had Ashkenazy started making his Tchaikovsky recordings in digital sound, no doubt Decca would have got him to record a complete cycle. This collection of three outstanding versions of the last symphonies is most attractive, and the inclusion of his superb, inspirational account of *Manfred* sets the seal on his achievement. The special quality which Ashkenazy conveys is spontaneity. The freshness of his approach, his natural feeling for lyricism on the one hand and drama on the other, is consistently compelling, even if at times the ensemble is not immaculate. Digital or not, the sound is outstanding.

The classic Mravinsky performances were discussed in our last edition when they were available on three Privilege records. They have now been transferred on to four sides without any loss of quality – and a considerable gain in economy. Strongly recommended, as was the two-record set of Mravinsky's earlier recordings of the *Fifth* and *Sixth* made in mono in the mid-1950s together with Sanderling's account of the *Fourth* (DG 2700 114). These were, if anything, even more exciting and sound marvellously vivid. Unfortunately they have been withdrawn as we go to press.

It was one of the more surprising developments in Boehm's career that his close association with the LSO led him to record Tchaikovsky. His readings were often idiosyncratic, translating Tchaikovsky's Russianness into the central European tradition. One might argue that they reveal more about Boehm than they do about Tchaikovsky, but with a conductor of such stature there is value in that. The recording – digital in No. 5 – is outstanding.

Symphony No. 4 in F minor, Op. 36.
*** Ph. 9500 622/*7300 738* [id.]. Concg. O., Haitink.
*** DG 2530/*3300* 883 [id.]. Berlin PO, Karajan.
*** Decca SXL/*KSXC* 6919 [Lon. 7144/5-]. Philh. O., Ashkenazy.
*** HMV ASD/*TC-ASD* 3816 [Ang. S 37624]. Philh. O., Muti.
(M) *** Decca Jub. JB/*KJBC* 23. VPO, Maazel.
(M) *** Ph. Fest. 6570/*7310* 153 [id.]. LSO, Markevitch.
**(*) Telarc DG 10047 [id.]. Cleveland O., Maazel.

(M) **(*) DG Acc. 2542/*3342* 152. Berlin
PO, Karajan.

**(*) DG 2531/*3301* 078 [id.]. LSO,
Boehm.

(M) ** HMV SXLP/*TC-SXLP* 30433
[Ang. RL 32066]. Berlin PO, Karajan.

(B) **. CfP CFP/*TC-CFP* 40351.
Orchestre de Paris, Ozawa.

** Ph. Dig. 9500/*7300* 972 [id.]. Pittsburgh SO, Previn.

*(*) Denon Dig. OX 7137ND [id.].
Berlin SO, Sanderling.

(M) *(*) RCA Gold GL/*GK* 11328.
Boston SO, Monteux.

* RCA RL/*RK* 25050. Nat. PO, Tjeknavorian.

Karajan's newest version of Tchaikovsky's *Fourth* is outstandingly fine. Its
directness, coupled with first-class
orchestral playing and brilliant recording, will make it first choice for many.
However, Haitink's splendid Concertgebouw recording is equally distinctive
and offers wonderfully rich sound of
demonstration quality; and for some
Tchaikovskians Abbado's inspirational
account with the Vienna Philharmonic
Orchestra (DG 2530 651) is among the
most memorably compelling of all
Tchaikovsky interpretations, and it too
is very vividly recorded. Yet Haitink
steers a satisfying middle course in his
approach to this charismatic symphony,
and, supported by orchestral playing and
sound of great power and refinement, his
reading of all four movements makes an
indelible impression. Compared with an
earlier, somewhat undercharacterized
account that Haitink recorded with the
same orchestra, this one has more rhythmic flair, with the different sections of the
first movement and their often difficult
transitions beautifully drawn. Speeds are
never hectic, but particularly in the finale
the excitement of this version is second
to none, with exceptionally wide groove-
spacing allowing sound of outstanding
range and richness. The cassette too is full-
blooded, but has not quite the spectacular
range of the disc, especially in the finale.

Karajan's current version is undoubtedly more compelling than his previous
recordings (one for DG and two for
EMI). After a dramatically robust fanfare at the start of the first movement,
the theme of the *Allegro* steals in silkily,
and although its atmosphere has a tinge
of melancholy, there is a hint of suaveness
also. But any doubts are swept away by
the vitality and drive of the performance
as a whole, and the beauty of the wind
playing at the opening and close of the
slow movement can give nothing but
pleasure. The finale has tremendous force
to sweep the listener along, and the wide
dynamic range of the recording makes
the most dramatic effect. The tape transfer is extremely vivid, but there is some
slight recession of the orchestral image in
pianissimos.

Ashkenazy's opening fanfare has
plenty of edge, and while his reading of
the first movement is rhythmically
straightforward, the nervous tension is
held consistently, though the dynamic
ebb and flow of climax and repose is
handled in the most naturally spontaneous way. The two central movements
combine ardour with delicacy and wit,
and the ferociously brilliant finale confirms the Russian quality of the interpretation, projected by sound that
matches weight with brilliance and yet is
both luminous and sumptuous in Decca's
best manner. The cassette has a comparable breadth and impact, even though in
the finale there is a slightly ill-focused
moment contributed by the bass drum.

With speeds on the brisk side in all four
movements, Muti's is an urgent performance. The very opening of the symphony, with its fanfare motto, has no
pomp whatever in it, for urgency reigns
even there. With fine articulation from
the Philharmonia players the fast speeds
rarely if ever make for breathlessness,
and though charm is not a quality one
finds here, the directness is always refreshing, and the recording quality is
both forward and rich. The high-level
tape transfer is matchingly vivid and full-

blooded, with only a fractional hint of strain at climaxes. The finale, as on disc, is highly spectacular.

The very strength of Maazel's Decca reading is its basic simplicity and lack of personal mannerism. The dramatic and emotional power of the writing emerges in consequence with great effect; in the first movement the appearance of the relatively gentle second subject is not over-romanticized, and the contrast Tchaikovsky intended is underlined by this lack of emphasis. The slow movement is played most beautifully, and the scherzo is not too fast. The finale explodes just as it should and is superbly recorded. Indeed, the sound throughout belies the mid-sixties date of the original issue, although the cassette has a slightly narrowed dynamic range compared with the disc.

Markevitch's version is as exciting as any available. It has a superbly thrusting first-movement *Allegro*, and although Markevitch allows himself a lilting degree of rubato in the rocking crescendo passage it is the forward momentum of the performance that captures the listener. At the climax of the development Markevitch produces an exhilarating *stringendo* and then relaxes for the reprise of the second subject. The close of the movement, like the coda of the finale, brings the highest degree of tension and a real sense of triumph. The central movements are no less striking, with a vigorous dotted climax to the *Andantino* contrasting with the repose of the outer sections, and a fast scherzo where the duple rhythms of the woodwind trio are emphasized to bring out the peasant imagery. The recording is admirably full-blooded, and its spectacle and wide range have transferred to tape without any loss of impact and detail compared with the disc.

Maazel's Telarc Cleveland disc was one of the first digital records of any Tchaikovsky symphony and established a reputation for sound of spectacular depth and brilliance, within a natural overall balance. This is impressively borne out by the first big orchestral fortissimo chord at the end of the relatively mellow opening fanfare. The reading itself is unexpectedly low-powered, the first-movement *Allegro* lightly articulated so that the climaxes make a strong dramatic contrast, with the Cleveland brass providing a bright cutting edge. The slow movement, with a plaintive oboe solo, is distinctly appealing, but the finale seeks amplitude and breadth rather than extrovert excitement. Here the full, resonant recording makes the strongest possible impact.

Karajan's earlier DG recording from the late sixties takes rather longer to generate its full tension in the opening movement. The slow movement makes amends and the central climax really takes wing, to be followed by a beautifully shaped closing section, Karajan here at his most effective. The scherzo goes well, but the central wind interlude is rather slow and heavy. The finale is superb, taken at a fantastic pace, and tremendously exciting in a purely physical way. The orchestral playing is unbelievably accurate at this tempo. The recording still sounds remarkably well, although there is a degree of fierceness at climaxes, less noticeable on cassette, which has slightly more body than the disc and a smoother upper range.

Boehm in his first recording with the orchestra which made him president was inspired to a bluff reading of Tchaikovsky, highly personal, with one or two intrusive idiosyncrasies in the first movement that tend to underline the Viennese quality in the conductor's approach even to Russian music. Warm, easy expressiveness is the keynote; the scherzo is measured but beautifully sprung, with the middle sections full of fun. Then in the finale the main tempo, relatively relaxed, leaves one unprepared for the almost impossibly fast coda, with wit implied in the challenge. The ensemble is not always flawless, but the spirit is electrically conveyed, helped by outstanding recording.

Karajan's first recording of the *Fourth Symphony* was made for EMI in 1960. The sound is somewhat restricted in the treble but otherwise is agreeably warm and full and certainly well balanced. The reading is in many ways similar to Karajan's later DG version, but the characterization is less strong, especially in the first movement, and with no great difference in price the DG Accolade issue is a much better recommendation. In the lower-medium price-range Szell's fine Decca version with the LSO is worth remembering (SPA 206).

Ozawa's bargain-priced Classics for Pleasure version is certainly exciting; indeed the first movement has an impressively spontaneous forward sweep, the character of both principal and secondary material established with understanding and flair. The orchestral playing could do with more grip and polish. The slow movement is slightly square, although nicely shaped, and the finale lacks crispness of articulation. But within a reverberant acoustic there is considerable impact, and at bargain price this is far from negligible. As usual with CfP, disc and cassette are fairly closely matched.

Previn's view is distinctive. His preference in Tchaikovsky is for directness and no mannerism, but with unusually slow speeds for the first three movements this produces little excitement and some lack of charm. The finale makes up for that with a very fast tempo, which is a formidable challenge for the Pittsburgh orchestra, here distinguishing itself with fine playing, well recorded. The chrome cassette, however, is transferred at a modest level and is in no way strikingly spectacular, even in the finale.

Sanderling's is an early digital recording (1978) and it reflects few advantages of the new system, while the performance itself is cautious and uninspiring. Sanderling made a superb mono recording of this symphony with the Leningrad Philharmonic Orchestra a quarter of a century ago; this is not in the same league.

Monteux's early RCA performance is also disappointing. He drives the first movement hard and his accelerandos do not always convince. The *Andantino* lacks charm, and although the scherzo and finale have plenty of impetus the lack of lustre in the sound itself is a serious drawback.

Tjeknavorian's first movement is spaciously weighty, but in the last analysis it lacks something in forward momentum, and the opening of the slow movement tends to drag after the opening theme. In spite of the splendid recording (equally impressive on tape and disc) this is not really competitive.

Symphony No. 5 in E min., Op. 64.
*** Decca SXL/*KSXC* 6884 [Lon. 7107/*5*-]. Philh. O., Ashkenazy.
*** HMV ASD/*TC-ASD* 3717 [Ang. S 37625]. Philh. O., Muti.
**(*) DG Dig. 2532/*3302* 005 [id.]. LSO, Boehm.
(M) **(*) DG Acc. 2542/*3342* 108. Berlin PO, Karajan.
**(*) RCA RL/*RK* 25221. LPO, Tjeknavorian.
** Decca Dig. SXDL/*KSXDC* 7533. VPO, Chailly.
(M) ** Decca Jub. JB/*KJBC* 24. VPO, Maazel.
** DG 2530/*3300* 888 [id.]. Boston SO, Ozawa.
** Denon Dig. OX 7186ND [id.]. Berlin SO, Sanderling.
(M) *(*) Ph. Fest. 6570/*7310* 110 [id.]. LSO, Markevitch.
(B) (*) CfP CFP/*TC-CFP* 40317. LPO, Del Mar.

Ashkenazy made his major recording début on the rostrum with Tchaikovsky's *Fifth*, and at a stroke produced a richly enjoyable performance, as distinguished as any available and one which throws new light on a familiar masterpiece. The qualities of lyrical fervour and warmth that he brings to his reading have an unmistakable Russian fire. Tempi are admirably chosen throughout, and the forward flow of the music in all four movements is as natural as it is spontaneous. The second subject of the first movement blossoms with a most appealing romanticism; the slow movement too has an affecting warmth, the sense of repose in the opening and closing sections making an admirable framework for the passionate central climaxes. The *Waltz*, light and lilting, acts like an intermezzo between the second movement and the red-blooded finale with its gloriously rich string and brass tone. The recording is one of Decca's very best, brilliant and warm and with splendid detail and bloom; and on tape the sound is no less beautiful. But the sophistication of the transfer has been achieved by a very subtle reduction of the dynamic range, which means that the loudest climaxes do not expand quite so spectacularly as on the disc. For many this will be a ready first choice, but the Karajan and Haitink versions should not be forgotten. Karajan's account is undoubtedly the more physically exciting (DG 2530/*3300* 699), but Haitink's approach finds an added dimension of warmth and humanity, and the Philips recording has extra body and richness (6500 922).

Muti – like Haitink – underlines the symphonic strength of the first movement rather than immediate excitement. The approach is direct and unmannered but with no stiffness of phrasing. The *Waltz* may lack a little in charm, and certain passages perhaps let the tension relax too far, but the slow movement is beautifully controlled, with the second theme genuinely *con nobilita* when the violins first play it, and passion kept in hand for the second half of the movement. As for the finale, it presents a sharp contrast with its fast tempo and controlled excitement. The recording is warm and full in the EMI manner; the cassette matches the disc closely.

Boehm's account of the *Fifth* is distinguished from his other two late Tchai-

kovsky recordings with the LSO by its relative lack of idiosyncrasy – this reading is straighter and more direct than Boehm's accounts of Nos. 4 and 6 – and by the fine digital sound. Boehm's refusal to press the music ahead from his very steady basic pace in the slow movement may on repetition seem a little heavy, but like the others in the series this presents Tchaikovsky very much from the point of view of the central European tradition, and for that distinctive view, committedly presented, it is most welcome.

Karajan's earlier (1967) Berlin Philharmonic recording (now reissued on Accolade) is finely played and well conceived. It is more self-conscious than the later version, but the reading certainly does not lack excitement and the recording sounds remarkably fresh. There is very little difference in sound between disc and tape: the former has a slightly brighter string timbre; the cassette has greater body and richness and offers a fine account of *Marche slave* as an appreciable bonus.

An arresting performance from Tjeknavorian which would bring the house down at a concert, but which is not quite the sum of its parts. He chooses consistently fast speeds for the first three movements, and the effect is often exhilarating, with expert playing from the LPO. The tempo for the first-movement *Allegro* must be one of the fastest on record, and there is little slackening of urgency in the second subject group. Some will feel a lack of repose, both here and in the slow movement, although there is no absence of expressive feeling. The *Waltz*, however, loses some of its elegance and poise. For the finale Tjeknavorian reverts to more traditional tempi, and though there is no lack of adrenalin, this seems to unbalance the interpretation overall, even though the peroration makes a very striking impact. Excellent recording, bright and full, and a brilliant, high-level tape transfer.

Chailly's is a relatively lightweight and somewhat idiosyncratic reading which gives the impression of inexperience in this repertoire. There are some attractive things here, notably the exhilarating tempo for the finale, but the reading does not make a very convincing whole. The VPO playing is not always immaculate, and the horn solo in the slow movement is not really distinguished. Yet the lyrical momentum of the performance is certainly enjoyable, and the Decca digital recording, which has considerable richness and brilliance, is very attractive. The cassette, one of Decca's first chrome transfers, is first-rate in every way.

Maazel's Decca recording is excellent, but his is rather a cool reading. In the *Andante* he brings in the motto theme pungently enough, but the movement as a whole has no broad emotional sweep, although the horn solo is beautifully phrased. The finale too begins and closes without a great deal of conviction, although the string playing at the opening of the *Allegro vivace* is taut. The cassette sounds full and vivid. The upper strings are a little lacking in bloom, but this tape can be made to give impressive results.

Ozawa has the advantage of excellent DG sound on disc and cassette alike, and the richness of the recording is matched by the freshness of the string quality. In the finale the brass is superb; this is undoubtedly the finest movement. The music-making springs vividly to life and the listener is swept along by the impact and projection of the orchestra. But the first three movements are disappointing, and until the finale the performance is a routine one.

Sanderling's was one of the first digital recordings of Tchaikovsky's *Fifth*, but the sound is not exceptional and is hardly worth the high price. The vibrato of the horn in the slow movement will distress most western ears, and the tensions are surprisingly low from a conductor who in his Leningrad days was a most illuminating interpreter of this composer.

After a somewhat unevocative opening Markevitch applies to the first movement of the *Fifth* the forthright, highly charged approach which was so effective in the *Fourth*. He makes no concessions to the second subject group, which is presented with no let-up on the fast pace at which he takes the main *Allegro*; Tchaikovsky's romanticism evaporates, as does the intended contrast. The slow movement is undoubtedly powerful, but the *Waltz* has no charm and the finale lacks warmth: the final statement of the big tune is slow and rather stolid. A disappointing issue after the success of Markevitch's versions of the first four symphonies. The sound is full and there is little difference between tape and disc.

Del Mar's Classics for Pleasure version is undoubtedly exciting and is given a brilliant modern recording (the cassette is marginally less wide in range than the disc but still impressive). There is some splendid wind playing, and the horn solo in the slow movement (played by Nicholas Busch) is beautifully done. But the reading itself is exasperatingly wilful. In all the movements but the *Waltz* (which is graciously straightforward) there are eccentric tempo changes. At bar 108 of the first movement there is an inexplicable pulling back; later the preparation of the second subject is spoiled, and the exaggerated rubato in the presentation of the theme itself is equally difficult to take. Throughout there are unmarked accelerandos and decelerandos, and pauses too, all of which fail to convince. In the finale Del Mar does not establish his basic tempo at the beginning of the *Allegro vivace* but suddenly quickens as the secondary material arrives. Not recommended.

Symphony No. 6 in B min. (Pathétique), Op. 74.
*** Decca SXL/*KSXC* 6941 [Lon. 7170/*5*-]. Philh. O., Ashkenazy.
(M) *** DG Acc. 2542/*3342* 154. Berlin PO, Karajan.
*** HMV ASD/*TC-ASD* 3515. LPO, Rostropovich.
*** Ph. 9500 610/*7300 739* [id.]. Concg. O., Haitink.

(B) *** CfP CFP/*TC-CFP* 40220. Philh. O., Kletzki.

**(*) HMV ASD/*TC-ASD* 3901 [Ang. S 37625]. Philh. O., Muti.

(M) **(*) Ph. Fest. 6570/*7310* 047 [id.]. LSO, Markevitch.

**(*) DG 2531/*3301* 212 [id.]. LSO, Boehm.

(M) **(*) HMV SXLP/*TC-SXLP* 30534 [Ang. RL 32068]. Philh. O., Karajan.

(M) ** Decca Jub. JB/*KJBC* 25 [Lon. 41014]. VPO, Maazel.

** DG Dig. 2532/*3302* 013 [id.]. LAPO, Giulini.

** Denon Dig. OX 7183ND [id.]. Berlin SO, Sanderling.

*(*) Decca SXL/*KSXC* 6814 [Lon. 6983]. Chicago SO, Solti.

(M) * RCA Gold GL/*GK* 42920. LSO, Stokowski.

(i) *Symphony No. 6* (ii) *Marche slave;* (iii) *Eugene Onegin: Waltz.*

(M) ** HMV *TC-IDL* 503. (i) LSO, Horenstein; (ii) RPO, Sargent; (iii) RPO, Weldon.

After an arresting account of the sombre introduction, the urgency with which Ashkenazy and his Philharmonia players attack the *Allegro* of the first movement of the *Pathétique* belies the composer's *non troppo* marking. The directness and intensity of the music-making are supported by remarkably crisp articulation, producing an electrifying forward thrust. The emergence of the beautiful second subject offers the more striking contrast, with Ashkenazy's characteristic lyrical ardour bringing a natural warmth to the great melody. As in his other Tchaikovsky records this whole performance is pervaded with freshness and spontaneity, through the balletic 5/4 movement, with its essentially Russian quality of melancholy, and the vigorous march/scherzo, rhythmically buoyant and joyful rather than relentlessly high-powered, as under Karajan. The finale combines passion with tenderness, and the total absence of expressive

hysteria brings a more poignant culmination than usual. With superb Decca Kingsway Hall sound, this is among the finest *Pathétiques* ever recorded. The Philharmonia is on peak form, and although the Berlin Philharmonic playing under Karajan is even more polished, the Decca version gains by its greater amplitude, warmth and colour, with the rich cassette transfer losing only a very little of the disc's sparkle at the top.

Karajan obviously has a special affinity with Tchaikovsky's *Pathétique symphony* (and – remembering Furtwängler's famous 78 r.p.m. set – so has the Berlin Philharmonic Orchestra). He has recorded it four times in stereo. For many the most recent (1977) version (DG 2530/*3300* 774) is the finest. With a brilliant recording of the widest dynamic range (though not an especially sumptuous lower resonance) the impact of Tchaikovsky's climaxes – notably those of the first and third movements – is tremendously powerful, the articulation of the Berlin players precise and strong. The climactic peaks are created with fierce bursts of tension, and the effect on the listener is almost overwhelming. In the 5/4 movement Karajan slows the middle section to increase the elegiac feeling, against a background of remorseless but distanced drum beats, like a tolling bell. The finale has great passion and eloquence, with two gentle sforzandos at the very end to emphasize the finality of the closing phrase.

Turning back to Karajan's 1964 record (now reissued on Accolade), one finds a reading that is no less exciting but more consistent in its overall control of tension. For some ears this is the finest version of all, the steady tempo of the *Moderato mosso* in the first movement leading the ear on as the conductor builds towards the movement's climax with a steady emotional thrust. At the climactic point the deeply committed playing creates a quality of expressive fervour to send shivers down the spine, with a noble resolution from the Berlin brass. The

TCHAIKOVSKY

sound has more bloom than in the later version (especially on cassette), and this brings a lighter, elegant quality to the 5/4 movement. The march/scherzo has an exhilaratingly consistent forward momentum, and with demonic playing from the Berlin orchestra, wonderfully sharp in ensemble, the aggressive force of the climaxes communicates the greatest physical excitement. Some listeners may find the effect too brutal, but Karajan's consistency is carried through to the passionate last movement, concluded, as in the later version, with those gentle stabbing chordal emphases. It is overall an engulfing experience, with no less impact on cassette than on disc.

Of the Rostropovich readings of the three last Tchaikovsky symphonies the *Pathétique* can be recommended virtually without reservation. Like the others it is a personal view, but its eloquence is direct and its specially Russian lyric fervour is highly compelling. The outer movements have strength and nobility, and the finale balances passionate melancholy with restraint. The march/scherzo is perhaps less exhilarating than in some other versions, but it readily takes its place within the overall conception. The recording is splendidly full-blooded, and the tape transfer is first-class, with plenty of body and detail.

Whether interpretatively or in execution, it would be hard to distinguish between Haitink's later reading here and his splendid earlier account. Their confident strength, natural expressiveness allied to a degree of restraint, make them both most satisfying for repeated listening on the gramophone. Where the second version gains is in the fullness and warmth of the recorded sound, which makes this a satisfying culmination for an outstanding series. On cassette the sound balance is impressively full and wide-ranging on side one, but on side two the level drops, the climax of the march/scherzo lacks brilliance, and the bass focus is not consistently clean.

Kletzki's splendid Philharmonia per-

formance from the beginning of the sixties sounds quite different on disc and tape, and for many the cassette will be preferable. It has no lack of range and brilliance, but the strings are richer and warmer, and this gives the first-movement climax more amplitude. On LP the violins are much more brightly lit, and the bass is drier, less resonant; the brass have greater bite and the sound is slightly more open. Whichever medium is chosen this is an outstanding performance which has stood the test of time. The first movement is impetuous but convincing, Kletzki's broadening of tempo at the reprise of the march is effective because the orchestral playing has a supporting power and breadth. The deeply felt closing movement makes a powerful impact, although again the cassette produces the fullest string sound.

Muti adopts characteristically fast tempi, yet the result is fresh and youthful, not over-hectic. The lyrical second subject, flowing faster than usual, has easy expressiveness without a hint of mannerism, and the 5/4 movement, also at a speed faster than usual, is most persuasive. The march for all its urgency never sounds brutal, and though the recording does not quite match the fine fullness which marks the others in Muti's series, it hardly detracts from a most refreshing reading. The cassette matches the disc's body and wide dynamics, but is not as clearly defined at pianissimo levels. The third-movement climax expands magnificently.

Markevitch brings great intensity to his account of the first movement. He takes the *Allegro* at a fast pace and drives hard throughout, producing a *stringendo* that further tautens the climax at the reprise of the second subject. The effect is undoubtedly powerful, but with a touch of harshness to the recording some might feel that Markevitch is too aggressive, even though the performance is always under emotional control. The second movement has both warmth and elegance, and the march is treated broadly, providing suitable contrast before a deeply felt performance of the finale, where the second subject is introduced with great tenderness. The close of the symphony has an elegiac quality to complete a reading which has a wide emotional range and is gripping from first to last. The full, resonant recording is well transferred to tape.

Boehm directs a characterful and distinctive reading, easy and relaxed not just in the 5/4 second movement but even in the march, which swaggers along, with dotted rhythms delightfully lifted and no hint of aggressiveness at the end. One might count it a Viennese performance, but the close microphone balance over the string sections brings some edginess, not as ripe a sound as the reading asks for. Otherwise the recording is first-rate on disc and cassette alike. On tape the level rises on side two, which brings added brilliance and impact to the third and fourth movements.

Karajan's first stereo recording of the *Pathétique* was made for EMI in 1959, with the Philharmonia Orchestra in splendid form and the Kingsway Hall providing the most congenial balance, astonishingly full for a record made nearly a quarter of a century ago. This adds a certain character to the orchestral sound, so that the 5/4 movement is noticeably glowing, with a relaxed lyricism. Broadly speaking this reading shows itself as a chrysalis for the later versions. It is less forceful the second subject of the first movement is unmoulded and has a natural radiant freshness – and the first-movement climax has less fervour (though it is by no means uninvolving). The third movement is much more spaciously conceived, the scherzo skittishly pointed, the march climax grandiloquent rather than electrifying. The finale too is less remorseless in feeling, with surges of rubato at the first big climax and an ele-

giac close, the tension allowed to drain away without those stabbing emphases used on both the DG versions. The cassette transfer is strikingly vivid and clear, matching the disc in every way.

Maazel's is a good straightforward account, most impressive in the first and third movements, with a somewhat deadpan account of the second and a restrained finale, lacking in emotional depth. But this clean, unmannered playing offers its own rewards, and the recording is brilliant, with plenty of resonance, as in the rest of Maazel's series. The tape transfer is of outstanding quality, beautifully rich and detailed. However, this has been achieved by slightly reducing the dynamic range of the recording.

Giulini's digital *Pathétique* is curiously lightweight, the mood set with the almost *scherzando* quality of the opening *Allegro*. The 5/4 movement is relatively unlilting, and though the march is impressive, it is no match for the Karajan or Ashkenazy versions. The finale does not lack eloquence, but Giulini's Philharmonia version of two decades earlier had more individuality than this. The digital recording is impressive if slightly dry, with little difference between disc and cassette.

Horenstein's account, undoubtedly distinguished in its way, will appeal to those who look for restraint in the outer movements. His coolness is curiously compelling, although he avoids any charm in the 5/4 movement. The third movement is idiosyncratic in an old-fashioned manner, with a broadening of tempo for the emergence of the march theme in the full brass. But here the recording makes its effect, for the sound in this tape-only presentation is first-class, bold, clean and full-blooded. The layout frames the symphony in extrovert music which some may resist in the context of the main work. Yet the *Waltz* following on after the end of the symphony can be surprisingly effective; and after all, one can always stop short if required.

Though Sanderling is treated to a digital recording (at a very high price) the result is curiously small-scale. Though the directness of the reading is quite attractive, there are many finer versions at a fraction of the cost.

With dangerously fast tempi throughout the first and third movements, the element of hysteria is never far away in Solti's intense reading; and the element of nobility, so necessary to provide emotional balance, is missing. The march/scherzo loses all charm at this hectic pace; indeed the march element almost disappears altogether. The finale is more controlled in feeling but does not resolve the performance in any satisfactory way. Brilliantly clear recording to match the playing.

Stokowski's version is a non-starter. It is well played and recorded, with a satisfactory cassette equivalent, but the performance (recorded in 1974) shows too much evidence of Stokowski's desire to impose his own personality on the music. For Stokowskians only.

Symphony No. 7 in E flat (reconstructed by S. Bogatyrev).
(M) **(*) CBS 61800/40- [Col. MS 6349]. Phd. O., Ormandy.

In 1892 Tchaikovsky began a new symphony, but he was not satisfied with the way the ideas were working out, and he later reworked some of the material as the *Third Piano concerto*. He discarded the remainder, but the sketches were not destroyed. Taneiev transcribed two of the movements as the *Andante and finale* for piano and orchestra, and later the Soviet musicologist Bogatyrev used the sketches to produce this reconstruction of the originally planned symphony. As there were no sketches for a scherzo one was provided from the set of piano *Pieces*, Op. 72, written in 1893. This is so skilfully orchestrated that it might well have been done by the composer himself: the central

section, introduced by oboe and harp and then taken up by the strings, is ravishing. The finale is rumbustious, blatant, even vulgar, and the reprise of the main theme against a side-drum reminds one more of Glière than Tchaikovsky. The 1962 recording, though sounding dated now, is acceptable, and the cassette sounds quite well too, although it lacks something in transient bite.

Variations on a rococo theme for cello and orchestra, Op. 33.
(B) *** CfP CFP/*TC-CFP* 40361. Robert Cohen, LPO, Macal – DVOŘÁK: *Cello concerto.****

Variations on a rococo theme; Pezzo capriccioso, Op. 62.
*** Decca SXL/*KSXC* 6965 [Lon. 7195/5-]. Harrell, Cleveland O., Maazel – ELGAR: *Cello concerto.****

The Tchaikovsky *Variations* make a generous and apt coupling for the Dvořák in Robert Cohen's excellent bargain version. As in the *Concerto*, he tends to avoid pronounced rubato, yet the result is warmly expressive as well as strong. First-rate recording. The cassette quality matches that of the disc very closely indeed; any slight advantage of range on the LP is offset by the slightly warmer cello sound on tape.

An assured, vividly characterized set of *Variations* from Lynn Harrell, with plenty of matching colour from the Cleveland woodwind. Harrell begins a little briskly, but there is no lack of poise here. Expressive feeling and sparkle are nicely matched, as shown by the elegant account of the *Andante* (Variation 6) which acts as an interlude before the exhilarating finale. The recording is bright and colourful, the cellist given a spotlight, but there is no lack of atmosphere and resonance. Some might prefer the cassette to the disc (it is slightly smoother on top), but both are excellent.

CHAMBER MUSIC

Piano trio in A min., Op. 50.
**(*) HMV ASD 4036 [Ang. SZ 37678].
Ashkenazy, Perlman, Harrell.
** Chan. Dig. ABRD/*ABTD* 1049.
Borodin Trio.

Ashkenazy, Perlman and Harrell have been regularly joining up to play this work at a series of international recitals over the last year or two, so a recording was eagerly anticipated. Alas, the power and spontaneity of the concert hall are not consistently caught here. The dominating keyboard role of the first movement can so easily sound rhetorical rather than gripping and commanding; and this performance does not avoid that fault, though it is not without power. The *Variations* which form the second half of the work are much more successful, with engaging characterization and a good deal of electricity in the closing pages. The recording is forward, vivid and truthful, but a little more atmosphere is suitable for such an orchestrally conceived work. A very near miss.

The alternative version from Chandos is less distinguished. The clear digital recording serves to spotlight the string sounds, which are less polished and less rich than on the HMV record. The *Variations* have spontaneity and are not without charm, but the first movement is less convincing. The cassette transfer is lively, marginally less clean than the disc.

String quartets Nos. 1 in D, Op. 11; 2 in F, Op. 22; 3 in E flat min., Op. 30.
(M) *** Decca Ace SDD 524/5 [Lon. STS 15424/5]. Gabrieli Qt.

String quartet No. 1.
*** DG 2531/*3301* 283 [id.]. Amadeus Qt
– VERDI: *Quartet.****

The Gabrieli give finely conceived performances of all three quartets, producing consistently well-balanced and blended tone quality. Their ensemble is excellent,

and they are completely inside the music. The Borodin Quartet's version (now deleted) had a shade more passion in the *Third Quartet*, but there is no want of eloquence here, and the quality of the recording is splendidly clean and alive yet warm.

Though it is more expensive than the Gabrieli (and by no means superior to it), the Amadeus version of No. 1, coupled with Verdi's sole quartet, is well worth considering. It is played with genuine fervour and expertise, and beautifully recorded. The tape transfer is lively, although it benefits from a little smoothing at the top. Admirers of the Amadeus who want this coupling need not hesitate; but the Gabrieli remain first choice.

OPERA

Eugene Onegin (complete).
** HMV SLS 5191 (3) [Ang. S 4115]. Milashkina, Masurok, Atlantov, Tugarinova, Nesterenko, Kuznetsov, Bolshoi Th. Ch. and O., Ermler.

The presence in the cast of Masurok as Onegin and Nesterenko as Gremin is promising for the most recent recording of this opera from the Bolshoi, but there are precious few other compensations, and even Masurok is hardly imaginative. One unnecessary flaw is that the voices are all recorded too close – a sad shortcoming in an opera which is among the most atmospheric of all, as one registers in the opening quartet. Even Ermler's conducting – impressive when he has been heard in Britain – is hampered by poor orchestral playing. Milashkina as Tatiana is an intelligent singer, but the Slavonic unevenness is not very comfortable for western ears.

Still recommended: Solti's splendid set, with Teresa Kubiak most moving as Tatiana, Bernd Weikl as Onegin, and Stuart Burrows an excellent Lensky, remains an outstanding recommendation for this opera (Decca SET 596/8/*K 57 K 32* [Lon. 13112]).

Opera ballet music: *Eugene Onegin: Ecossaise; Polonaise; Waltz. The Maid of Orleans: Entr'acte; Danse des bohémiens; Danse des polichinelles et des histrions. The Oprichnik: Danses. The Sorceress: Introduction; Danse des histrions et scène. Oxana's Caprices: Introduction; Danse russe; Danse des cosaques.*
*** Ph. 9500 508/7300 668 [id.].
ROHCGO, Colin Davis.

An engaging collection of mostly lesser-known Tchaikovsky, revealing no new masterpieces but showing the composer's vigorous melodic resource and his brilliant use of the orchestral palette even when his melodies are less memorable. The opening items from *Eugene Onegin* tend to overshadow what follows in their tuneful inspiration, especially when they are played with such *brio* and commitment, but Tchaikovskians will not be disappointed with the rest of the programme. The lively, characterful playing is matched by richly sumptuous sound, very well balanced on LP but a little bass-heavy and lacking a degree of sparkle on cassette.

Telemann, Georg Philipp
(1681–1767)

Concerto in B flat for 2 flutes, 2 oboes and strings; Oboe concerto in E flat; Oboe d'amore concerto in D; Double concerto in E min. for recorder, flute and strings.
*** DG Arc. 2533/3310 454 [id.]. Aurèle and Christiane Nicolet, Holliger, Pellerin, Copley, Camerata Bern, Furi.

An entirely enchanting collection.

Holliger produces the most winning timbre on the oboe d'amore, and there are some delightful sounds too in the *Concerto for two flutes and two oboes.* This is a first-class production in every way, and Telemann's invention is consistently amiable and lively. The excellent recording is also available on one of Archive's rare full-priced cassettes, which offers truly splendid sound, wonderfully warm and clear.

Double recorder concerto in A min.; Double concerto in E min. for recorder, flute and strings; Suite in A min. for recorder and strings.
(M) *** Sup. 1410 2849. Stivín, Válek, Klement, Prague CO, Munclinger.

This excellent Supraphon disc duplicates two of the works on the Telefunken issue below, but offers in place of the *Overture* an agreeable four-movement *Concerto for two recorders.* The Supraphon recording is more modern than the Telefunken, and the sound is impressively full and real, the warm resonance bringing bloom without clouding detail. The soloists are naturally balanced and are all excellent players. The performance of the famous *Suite in A minor* is alert and sparkling, with brisk tempi bringing lively articulation from Jiří Stivín, the splendid solo recorder player, as well as the accompanying group. The expressive movements are gracious and elegant without being over-romanticized. The attractive finale of the *Concerto for recorder and flute* is also memorable. A first-class collection.

Double concerto in E min. for recorder, flute and strings; Overture des nations anciens et modernes in G; Suite in A min. for recorder and strings.
(M) *** Tel. AQ6/*CQ4* 41342 [641039]. Brüggen, Vester, Amsterdam CO, Rieu.

These works show Telemann as an original and often inspired craftsman. His use of contrasting timbres in the *Double concerto* has considerable charm; the *Overture* is slighter but agreeably inventive, and the *Suite in A minor*, one of his best-known works, is worthy of Handel or Bach. Frans Brüggen and Frans Vester are expert soloists, and the accompaniments are crisp and stylish. The sound is excellent, and the cassette is of demonstration quality, with splendid body and presence.

Recorder concerto in G min.; Double concerto in A min. for recorder, viola da gamba and strings; Double concerto in A for 2 violins in scordatura; Concertos for 4 violins: in C and D.
**(*) DG Arc. 2533 421 [id.]. Soloists, Col. Mus. Ant., Goebel.

These are chamber concertos rather than solo concertos such as we associate with Bach and Vivaldi. They are diverting and inventive without at any point touching great depths; like so much Telemann, they are pleasing without being memorable. They are eminently well served by these artists and nicely recorded too. Attractive but not indispensable.

Viola concerto in G; Suite in A min. for flute and strings; Tafelmusik, Production 2: Triple violin concerto in F.
(M) * Ph. 9502/*7313* 011. Ghedin, Gazzelloni, Ayo, Apostoli, Colandrea, I Musici.

The *Triple concerto* comes from the second part of Telemann's *Tafelmusik* and is also available in the Archive version (see below). The *Viola concerto* is widely recorded, and so too is the *A minor Suite*. These performances are rather heavy-going and communicate little of the freshness of the music. Charmless –

surprisingly so, considering the artists involved. Not recommended.

Suite in A min. for flute and strings.
** HMV Dig. ASD 3948 [Ang. DS/*4XS* 37330]. Wilson, LACO, Schwarz – BACH: *Suite No. 2.***
*(*) CBS 76798 [Col. M/*MT* 35133]. Rampal, Jerusalem Music Centre CO, Stern – VIVALDI: *Double violin concertos.**(*)

Suite in A min.; Flute concertos in C and G.
**(*) RCA RL/*RK* 25204 [ARL 1/*ARK* 1 3488]. Galway, Zagreb Soloists.

Charismatic and completely musical playing from Galway, his fine-spun timbre bringing much colour to all this music, even if the feeling is slightly anachronistic. The Zagreb Soloists are well balanced with the soloist, but their contribution is competent rather than adventurous. The sound is good on both disc and cassette. This is for admirers of Galway rather than Telemann specialists; Frans Brüggen's version of the *Suite* (see above), played on the recorder, for which it was intended, is from an altogether different world and gives an equally impressive display of virtuosity.

On HMV the coupling of the Telemann with the Bach *Suite in B minor* is apt, as a flautist is the star in both, but this performance is not as inspired as the best available, and the easy stylishness of the soloist is somewhat undermined by the relative sluggishness of the orchestral playing. Good recording, but not outstanding by digital standards.

Rampal is very spirited even if his performance is not authentic in style (the orchestra is distinctly big band). The quality of the recorded sound is inclined to be over-bright. Not for purists, by any means, and it is perhaps too brisk and wanting in natural, unforced dignity to enjoy the widest appeal. The solo playing is very brilliant.

Tafelmusik, Parts 1–3 (complete).

(M) *** DG Arc. 2723 064 (6) [id.]. Schola Cantorum Basiliensis, Wenzinger.

These recordings date from the mid-1960s and were recently reissued in one box to mark the tercentenary of Telemann's birth (1681). The *Tafelmusik* was published only a few years after the successful *Der getreue Music-Meister*, all three parts ('Productions') appearing in 1733. They were engraved by Telemann himself, and among the subscribers to the edition were many leading patrons of music in Germany and abroad, including such masters as Quantz, Handel and Pisandel. Each of the three parts consists of works contrasted in medium and character: an overture, concerto, quartet, trio sonata, solo sonata and a 'conclusion'. The invention is invariably fresh, always diverting and intelligent and often really distinguished. (Handel thought well enough of it to borrow ideas in the organ concertos.) The performances here are on the whole excellent and the recording is exemplary. Both surfaces and presentation are of the highest quality. At medium price these discs are mandatory purchases and can be strongly recommended.

Tafelmusik: Double concerto in A for flute and violin; Double horn concerto in E flat; Triple violin concerto in F.

(M) ** Tel. AQ6/*CQ4* 41152. Concerto Amsterdam, Brüggen.

(M) ** DG Arc. 2547/*3347* 013. Schola Cantorum Basiliensis, Wenzinger.

This collection is planned to give contrast, but the selection of works does not show Wenzinger's group at its finest. The most attractive work is the *Concerto for flute and violin*, where the textures are fresh and luminous. The *Double horn concerto*, however (a florid but attractive piece), sounds unnecessarily clumsy here, while the approach to the *Triple violin*

concerto seems a little severe. The recording sounds fresh and well balanced on disc and tape alike.

The Telefunken account of the *Double horn concerto*, with expert solo playing from Hermann Baumann and Adriaan van Woudenberg, is preferable to the version on Archive: it is no less authentic but the playing is much more polished. The performances have vitality throughout, though tonally the effect is more astringent, less elegant. The recording is fresh and bright on both disc and cassette.

Tafelmusik: Conclusions: in B flat; in D; in E min. Solo sonatas: in B min. for flute and continuo; in G min. for oboe and continuo; in A for violin and continuo.

(M) ** Tel. AQ6/*CQ4* 42257. Concerto Amsterdam, Brüggen.

This issue couples the short orchestral movements that end the three Productions of the *Tafelmusik* with the solo sonatas. There are distinguished soloists here and the playing has striking vitality, even if the music's expressive qualities are projected less strongly. The sound is bright and sharply focused in the Telefunken manner; on cassette there is an occasional hint of stridency.

CHAMBER MUSIC

Duets: in A min. and F for recorder, violin and continuo; in B flat for recorder and violino piccolo; in C, D min., F and G min. for recorder, pardessus de viole and continuo; Trio sonatas: in A min., D min. and F min. for recorder, violin and continuo.

*** Tel. EK 6.35451 (2) [id.]. Boeke, Harnoncourt, Möller, Van Asperen.

These works are cunningly selected from a great range of music of a similar nature to show Telemann at his most inventive. As can be seen, there is considerable variety of texture, and within this there is a fair variety of style. Performances are expressive and lively; in this case scholarship and authenticity do not intimidate the music-making and it communicates readily. The sound is closely balanced but fresh.

Essercizii musici: Sonatas in C and D min. Der getreue Music-Meister: Sonatas: in F; F min.; B flat and C.
*** Tel. EX 6.35359 (2). Brüggen, Bylsma, Leonhardt – HANDEL: *Recorder sonatas.****

The Telemann sonatas, like the Handel, are played with breathtaking virtuosity and a marvellous sense of style. The recording still sounds fresh. With the excellent coupling this is well worth investigating, especially for those who do not want the complete set of *Der getreue Music-Meister* (see below).

Fantasias for solo recorder: Nos. 4 in G min.; 6 in B flat; Methodical sonata in D, Op. 13/4; Partita No. 2 in G; Sonatas: in C and F; Trio sonata in B flat (all for recorder and continuo).
**(*) Ph. 9500/7300 941. Michala Petri Trio.

Michala Petri is a young Danish virtuoso who attracted attention in her teens. Her trio consists of her mother, Hanne, at the harpsichord and her brother David, cello. Her playing is breathtaking in its virtuosity and range of colour, and the programme she offers is both varied and enjoyable. At times she is open to the charge of being a shade too unyielding in her approach – she needs to allow some of this music to breathe. However, this is superb playing in every other respect and is excellently recorded. The cassette transfer is admirable, fresh and clean.

Fantasias for unaccompanied violin, Nos. 1–12.
(M) *** Ph. 9502 010. Grumiaux.

Telemann's *12 Fantasias* for solo violin are a decade later than Bach's *Partitas* and *Sonatas*, and they are less ambitious and demanding. Yet there is much that is rewarding here, particularly given such artistry as Grumiaux's; Telemann's invention is fresh, though none of these short suites can claim depth.

Partitas for guitar duo: in A; in A (Polonaise); in D; in E.
** DG 2531/3301 350 [id.]. Yepes, Monden.

Telemann's *Guitar partitas*, like the Bach *Sonatas* and *Partitas* for unaccompanied violin and cello, are essentially groups of dance movements, usually including a brief introductory 'overture'. Frankly the inspiration is not scintillating; on the whole, the most memorable ideas come in the A major work subtitled *Polonaise*, but even here the invention is ingenuous. This is essentially wallpaper music. Yepes and Monden make a good team, but their presentation is rather square; they favour the alternation of *forte* and *mezzo forte* to provide variety within the melodic phrases. Perhaps it is not entirely their fault, for there is an excessive amount of moderately paced music here, but one feels there could have been more sparkle at times. An enterprising but disappointing contribution to Telemann's tercentenary, well recorded on disc and cassette alike.

VOCAL MUSIC

Funeral cantata: Du aber, Daniel, gehe hin.
*** HM 1C 065/265 99751. Ameling, McDaniel, Aachen Domchor, Coll. Aur., Pohl – BACH: *Cantata No. 106.****

TELEMANN

Cantatas: *Du aber, Daniel, gehe hin;*
Ertrage nur das Joch der Mängel;
Hochselige Blicke voll heiliger
Wonne.
(M) *** Ph. 9502 026. Soloists, Hamburg
Monteverdi Ch., Hamburg Telemann-
Gesellschaft, Jürgens.

Telemann's *Funeral cantata* dates from
his years at Hamburg and is a work of
striking expressive intensity and imagination. The text obviously touched a
deeper vein of feeling than is often evident in this master, and both in musical
resource and invention this is a work that
can justify its presence in the company of
Bach. There are some poignant harmonic
progressions and a generous flow of
melodic inspiration. The performers on
Harmonia Mundi give an impressive
account of the piece, and though the recording is in no way outstanding, it is well
balanced in an appropriately generous
acoustic. The cassette transfer is well
managed, matching the disc closely. This
is music that should be investigated even
by readers normally resistant to Telemann's charms; it has real eloquence and
some measure of depth.

The Philips record devotes itself
entirely to Telemann cantatas, and those
who already possess the Bach cantata
offered by Harmonia Mundi will welcome this alternative which involves no
duplication, brings two other charming
Telemann works – and is also less expensive. The performance too is very fine
indeed; the soloists (Liselotte Rebmann
and William Reimer) are less celebrated
than those on the rival disc, they are
nonetheless eminently satisfactory.
Jürgen Jürgens is perhaps a little cool, but
the performance as a whole has dignity
and eloquence, and the recording is
beautifully balanced. The two cantatas
on the reverse derive from Telemann's
Der harmonische Gottesdienst (1725) and
are not otherwise available; Kurt Equiluz
is excellent in *Ertrage nur das Joch der*
Mängel. Whichever version is chosen,

Telemann's *Funeral cantata* must be
numbered among his most beautiful
compositions and should not be overlooked.

Der getreue Music-Meister (com-
plete).
*** DG Arc. 2723 073 (5). Mathis,
Töpper, Haefliger, Unger, McDaniel,
Würzburg Bach Ch., Archive Produc-
tion Soloists, Ulsamer.

Telemann's *Der getreue Music-Meister*
(*The Constant Music Master*) has been
called the first musical periodical. Telemann published twenty-five issues or
'lessons' in all, resourcefully serializing
works, so that in order to collect a complete sonata subscribers would have to
wait over three or four issues until publication was complete. Other composers
were invited to contribute (albeit at their
own expense), and the present box
includes a lute piece by Weiss, a *Gigue*
sans basse by Pisandel and an ingenious
canon by Zelenka. There is also a great
deal of refreshing instrumental music of
Telemann, and the operatic arias which
are included from *Eginhard, Belsazar* and
Sancio are of considerable interest. There
is a wealth of material here: sixty-two
pieces are recorded. Performances are
inevitably of variable quality but most of
them are excellent, and the recordings are
delightfully fresh. A very rewarding set.

Cantatas: (i) *Die Landlust;* (ii) *Der*
Schulmeister; (i) *Von geliebten Augen*
brennen.
*** HM 1C 065 99692. Coll. Aur., with
(i) Speiser, (ii) Nimsgern, Stuttgart
Hymnus Boys' Ch. (members).

Der Schulmeister is a diverting cantata
about a schoolmaster teaching his class
to sing, while its companions, *Die Land-*
lust, a lighter pastoral piece, and *Von*
geliebten Augen brennen, a darker, more
expressive work, are both inventive and
worth exploring. Committed perform-

ances from both the soloists and the Collegium Aureum (who use period instruments) and a well-judged balance from the engineers make this a useful addition to the catalogue.

St Mark Passion.

(M) **(*) Ph. 6768 027 (2). Giebel, Malaniuk, Altmeyer, Rehfuss, Günter, Lausanne Youth Ch., Mun. Pro Arte O., Redel.

Telemann was as prolific in his vocal music as in his instrumental and orchestral works, and this setting of the *St Mark Passion* is one of many. It is an expressive piece, but only in places does the writing show real individuality. The performance, however, is an outstandingly good one, with fresh, intelligent solo singing and thoroughly committed and understanding direction from Kurt Redel. The recording dates from the mid-sixties and still sounds well; but four sides of this kind of music can be recommended only to the enthusiast.

St Matthew Passion.

(M) *(*) Ph. 6768 33 (2). Jurinac, Altmeyer, Lucerne Festival Ch., Swiss Festival O., Redel.

Telemann's setting of the *St Matthew Passion* has a certain historical interest because of the interpolations in the gospel story – after the death of Christ a soprano gets up and sings a cheerful little aria – but musically the impression is one of serene competence rather than great genius. This performance under Kurt Redel does nothing to redeem the general dullness of the score, although among the soloists Sena Jurinac is outstanding.

Thomas, Ambroise
(1811–96)

Mignon (opera; complete).
*** CBS 79401 (4) [Col. M4 34590]. Horne, Welting, Vanzo, Zaccaria, Battédou, Meloni, Von Stade, Hudson, Amb. Op. Ch., Philh. O., Almeida.

It was admirably enterprising of CBS to record Thomas's once-popular adaptation of Goethe. As old record catalogues bear witness, it has many vocal plums, and here a very full account of the score is given, with virtually all the alternatives which the composer devised for productions after the first – not least one at Drury Lane in London where recitatives were used (as here) instead of spoken dialogue; an extra aria was given to the soubrette Philine, other arias were expanded and the role of Frédéric was given to a mezzo-soprano instead of a tenor. Frederica von Stade here is superb in that role, making one rather regret that she was not chosen as the heroine. Marilyn Horne sings with great character and flair, but she hardly sounds the frail figure of the ideal Mignon. Nonetheless, with Alain Vanzo a sensitive Wilhelm, Ruth Welting a charming Philine, and colourful conducting from Almeida, this is an essential set for lovers of French opera. The rest of the score may never match the plums in memorability, but it is all sweetly attractive.

Tiomkin, Dimitri
(1894–1979)

Film scores: *Duel in the Sun: suite; Giant: Prelude; High Noon: suite; Night Passage: Follow the river; Red River: suite; Rio Bravo: suite.*

** Uni. Kanchana DKP 9002. Saker, McCarthy Singers, L. Studio SO, Johnson.

The choral theme of *Red River* is truly memorable, as of course is the music for *High Noon*, although the soloist here does not match the sound-track version (Tex Ritter), and the clear digital recording suggests that the chorus is a relatively small group. The short orchestral fantasia used to heighten the tension, called by the composer *The clock and showdown*, demonstrates impressive structural skill. Good performances, but not showing quite the flair of the RCA series under Gerhardt. The recording is brilliant and makes a powerful impact, but is not sumptuous.

Film scores: (i) *Lost Horizon* (extended excerpts). *The Big Sky: suite; Friendly Persuasion: Love scene in the barn; The Fourposter: overture; The Guns of Navarone: Prelude.* (i) *Search for Paradise: choral finale.*
(M) **(*) RCA Gold GL/*GK* 43445 [ARL 1/*ARK 1* 1669]. Nat. PO, Gerhardt, (i) with John Alldis Ch.

Tiomkin's score for *Lost Horizon* may have been just what Frank Capra wanted, but it is unadulterated oriental kitsch and stands up poorly away from the visual images. The composer is heard to better effect in the brief *Prelude* for The Guns of Navarone (with a pithy theme a little like that of Walton's fugal idea for *The First of the Few*). There is plenty of atmosphere in the score for *The Big Sky*, but Tiomkin is at his most attractively lyrical in the love scene for *Friendly Persuasion*, lighthearted rather than intense like the choral finale of *Search for Paradise*. As ever in this fine series, performances and recorded sound could hardly be more persuasive. The tape sounds well but has slightly less sharpness of definition than the disc, and it omits the illustrated notes about the films.

Tippett, Michael
(born 1905)

Suite for the birthday of Prince Charles.
(M) *** Ph. Fest. 6570/*7310* 763. LSO, Colin Davis – ELGAR: *Cockaigne* etc. **(*); WALTON: *Crown Imperial.***

Sir Michael Tippett's highly engaging occasional suite is in the best tradition of British music written for the Royal Family, ensuring a ready tunefulness by quoting from national airs (including the hymn-tune *Crimond* and *Early one morning*) besides borrowing from Tippett's own works. The performance here – originally coupled with the *First Symphony* – is most felicitous and beautifully recorded on disc and cassette alike.

Symphony No. 4; Suite for the birthday of Prince Charles.
*** Decca Dig. SXDL/*KSXDC* 7564 [Lon. LDR 71046]. Chicago SO, Solti.

This is a symphony where one should not be in a hurry to form judgements, for there are unsuspected rewards that are slow to surface. Readers put off by the often bewildering density of incident and apparently athematic character of Tippett's musical thinking (not to mention the heavy breathing effects which are used) should lower their resistance and lose no time in coming to terms with this important work. Some of its quieter sonorities spring from much the same soil that one glimpses in the sudden moments of repose in Henze's symphonies, moments of a poignant melancholy that resonate long after the tumult which surrounds them has subsided. There is a keenly focused atmosphere here, and each exploration of the landscape reveals new perspectives. The symphony is brilliantly played, and though there may be depths and a tenderness in the score yet to be uncovered, no praise can be too high for the achievement of these players under Sir Georg Solti or that of the Decca engineers, who produce sound of the utmost clarity and refinement. The *Suite for the birthday of Prince Charles* makes an agreeable fill-up even though it is not as substantial. The cassette transfer is extremely brilliant but has not quite the sharpness of focus of the disc. An indispensable issue for those who are concerned with contemporary music.

Choral music: *Bonny at Morn; A Child of Our Time: 5 Negro spirituals. Dance; Clarion air; Lullaby; Magnificat and Nunc dimittis; Music; Plebs Angelica. 4 Songs from the British Isles* (*Early one morning; Lillibulero; Poortith cauld; Gwenllian*). *The Source; The Weeping Babe; The Windhover.*
*** O-L DSLO 25 [id.]. Oxford Schola Cantorum, Cleobury.

There is a wayward quality in Tippett's writing for chorus, the music rarely progressing in anything like a predictable way, which presents serious problems for any choir, and the Schola Cantorum does marvels to sound as fresh and spontaneous as it does. Always Tippett has some musical illumination for the words, whether in Edith Sitwell (*The Weeping Babe*), Yeats (*Lullaby*) or more traditional texts. The spirituals from *A Child of our Time* make an apt addition to the programme, though out of context they do not sound as effective as in the oratorio. First-rate recording.

King Priam (opera; complete).
*** Decca D 246 D 3/K 246 K 33 (3) [Lon. LDR 73006]. Bailey, Tear, Allen, Palmer, Minton, Langridge, Harper, L. Sinf. Ch., L. Sinf., Atherton.

When *King Priam* first appeared in 1962, the dry fragmentation of texture coupled with the choppy compression of the drama was disconcerting after the lyrical warmth of *The Midsummer Marriage*, particularly when a Homeric theme promised an epic approach. In this superb performance under Atherton, with an outstanding cast and vivid, immediate recording, the power of the opera, offbeat as the treatment often is, both musical and dramatic, comes over from first to last. It is a superb demonstration of Tippett's single-mindedness as an opera composer, requiring the listener to think about attitudes afresh. Norman Bailey, thanks to his long association with Wagner, sounds agedly noble to perfection, Robert Tear is a shiningly heroic Achilles and Thomas Allen a commanding Hector, vocally immaculate, illuminating every word. 'The future of any twentieth-century opera depends quite a lot on recording', says Tippett. On the showing of this recording, *King Priam* certainly deserves to succeed. The layout on three chrome cassettes matches the discs. The sound is vividly detailed but slightly less open at the top. A reduced-size booklet is provided, clearly printed but less attractive than the libretto offered with the LPs.

The Midsummer Marriage: Ritual dances.
(M) *** Ph. Seq. 6527/7311 112 [id.]. Soloists, Ch. and O. of ROHCG, Colin Davis – BRITTEN: *Peter Grimes: Sea interludes.****

The *Ritual dances* are here given not in the concert form that Tippett devised but in extracts from the complete recording of the opera, with choral contributions. This is most attractive, except that the last dance ends disconcertingly in mid-air before the final curtain. A first-rate medium-price coupling. The wide dynamic range of the recording brings a modestly levelled cassette transfer where the climaxes expand without distortion and the choral focus remains clear; however, the upper range is less refined and far-reaching than the disc.

Reminder: The complete set of *The Midsummer Marriage* from which these excerpts are taken is still available on Philips 6703 027. Sir Colin Davis's burningly committed advocacy and a cast that was inspired by live performances in the opera house are hard to resist, even for those not normally fond of modern opera. The recording is outstandingly atmospheric, and this was given a rosette in the second editon of the *Penguin Stereo Record Guide*.

Titelouze, Jehan
(1562/3–1633)

4 Verses on Veni creator.
(M) ** HM HMU 251. Chapuis (organ)
– LE JEUNE: *Mass.***

These four *versets* on *Veni creator* are worth listing, even though they are a fill-up, as Titelouze is not otherwise represented in the catalogue. Michel Chapuis produces a full-blooded sound, though as in the coupling there is insensitive editing.

Tomkins, Thomas
(1572–1656)

Musica Deo sacra (1668): Organ pieces: *Fancy; Verse of 3 parts.* (Vocal) *Blessed be the Lord God of Israel; Blessed is he; Deal with me, O Lord; Glory be to God; The heavens declare; Merciful Lord; O God, the proud are risen; O Lord, graciously*

accept; O Lord, grant the King; Put me not to rebuke; Then David mourned; Withdraw not Thou Thy mercy.
⊛ *** Argo ZRG 897. Ch. of Magdalen College, Oxford, Bernard Rose; G. Morgan (organ).

Tomkins is one of the most eloquent and appealing of English composers, and this record of music from *Musica Deo sacra* is a valuable complement to the earlier issues that Bernard Rose and the Magdalen College Choir have given us. Dr Rose, who has directed the Magdalen Choir for the best part of three decades, is an authority on Tomkins and has edited three volumes of his work in the *Early English Church Music* series. Tomkins's music is highly expressive – often poignant, as in the case of *Then David mourned* – and has a vein of mystical feeling that earns it a special place in the history of English music. Its eloquence is beautifully conveyed in these restrained yet felt performances, which are splendidly captured by the engineers. Of all the records of English seventeenth-century music to appear in the last four years, this is perhaps the most indispensable. Very strongly recommended.

Tórroba, Federico
(born 1891)

(i) *Concierto Iberico* (for 4 guitars); (ii) *Dialogos.*
**(*) Ph. 9500 749/*7300 834* [id.]. ASMF, Marriner, with (i) Los Romeros, (ii) Pepe Romero.

The *Concierto Iberico* is an amiable piece, effectively using its four guitars in concertante style. It was written in 1976, but its harmonic idiom is unadventurous. The *Dialogos* is an intimate solo concerto, also rather agreeable, written two years earlier for Segovia, who never performed it in public. Both works might be described as like Rodrigo but without the tunes. Pepe Romero is gentle and persuasive in the solo concerto, even though his material is slight, and Los Romeros give a committed and expert account of the companion piece. The recording offers beautiful sound and a natural balance on disc and tape alike.

Aires de la Mancha; Madronos; Nocturno; Piezas caracteristicas; Sonatina; Suite Castellana.
(M) ** Saga 5462. Eric Hill (guitar).

Tórroba wrote characterfully for the guitar, and these appealing pieces are likely to prove as popular as many are familiar. Eric Hill is a lively and sensitive player with a good technique. There is some uncertain tuning, but, this apart, the record can be enjoyed. The sound is clean and well focused.

Tortelier, Paul
(born 1914)

Suite in D min. for solo cello.
*** HMV ASD 3458. Composer – KODÁLY: *Sonata.****

Tortelier's own music is not unknown to the catalogue (he recorded a short cello piece on the reverse side of the Debussy *Sonata* way back in the days of 78s). Five of the movements of this *Suite* were written in 1944 and published two years later; a sixth was added in the mid-1950s. The work radiates a love of Bach's solo cello literature as well as a strong feeling for line. It has warmth and some feeling even if it does not display the strong personal creative identity that one finds in a major composer. The main attraction of the disc is the Kodály *Sonata.*

Tosti, Francesco
(1846–1916)

Songs: *L'alba separa della luce l'ombra; Aprile; 'A vucchella; Chanson de L'adieu; Goodbye; Ideale; Malia; Marechiare; Non t'amo; Segreto; La serenata; Sogno; L'ultima canzone; Vorrei morire.*
*** Ph. 9500 743/7300 828 [id.]. Carreras, ECO, Muller.

Tosti (knighted by Queen Victoria for his services to music) had a gently charming lyric gift in songs like these, and it is good to have a tenor with such musical intelligence – not to mention such a fine, pure voice – tackling once-popular trifles like *Marechiare* and *Goodbye*. The arrangements are sweetly done, and the recording is excellent. The cassette, transferred at an unbelievably low level, has very little sparkle and cannot be recommended except where no disc playing equipment is available.

Tredici, David Del
(born 1937)

Final Alice.
*** Decca Dig. SXDL 7516 [Lon. LDR 71018]. Hendricks, Chicago SO, Solti.

Improbably commissioned to celebrate the bicentennial of the United States in 1976, this instalment of Del Tredici's sequence of Lewis Carroll settings has much in it to fascinate the ear, particularly in a virtuoso performance like this. Familiar texts are neatly assembled, with the minimum of violence to the original, to present a dramatic cantata for just one voice and orchestra. Barbara Hendricks proves a characterful and urgent guide, a vibrant narrator as well as a fine singer. Solti and his superb orchestra plainly enjoy the fun from first to last: it is good to welcome an extended work which sustains its length without pomposity and with immediate warmth of communication. The recording is outstandingly brilliant.

Valls, Francisco
(1665–1747)

Mass: Scala Aretina.
*** CRD CRD 1071/*CRDC 4071.* Beattie, Hill, Long, Robson, Stafford, Fleet, Shelley, L. Oratory Ch., Thames CO, Hoban.

Valls, a contemporary of Bach and Handel, wrote this massively ceremonial setting of the Mass for use in Barcelona Cathedral, where for many years he was choirmaster. To academics in generations since then, the angularity of the writing for three choirs plus a limited orchestra (violins, cellos, trumpets and oboes with organ) may have seemed gauche, but we can now recognize an attractive earthiness. To our ears the breaking of rules merely makes the music sound modern. This fine performance, atmospherically recorded, is most welcome, restoring a totally neglected composer to his rightful place. The cassette is very well managed, although with forwardly balanced soloists there seems comparatively little dynamic contrast.

Varèse, Edgar (1885–1965)

Amériques; Arcana; Ionisation.
*** CBS 76520. NYPO, Boulez.

One might regard the block-like structures and timbres of these major works by Varèse as the equivalent of brutalistic architecture, but there is an intensity – particularly in performances as compelling as these – which makes the experiments in sound far more than pattern-making. *Amériques* is the most extended and ambitious of the three, a superb work in which sirens are given a genuinely artistic purpose. *Ionisation* for thirteen percussion players eliminates pitched sounds almost entirely, without seeming arid. An excellent issue, vividly recorded.

Vaughan Williams, Ralph
(1872–1958)

(i) *Concerto accademico for violin and orchestra in D min.;* (ii) *Tuba concerto in F min.; The England of Elizabeth: suite; The Wasps: Overture.*
(M) *** RCA Gold GL/*GK* 42953. LSO, Previn, with (i) Buswell; (ii) Fletcher.

When Previn's cycle of Vaughan Williams symphonies appeared in a collected edition, it was useful for the couplings to be issued separately. The two concertos are particularly valuable in these fine performances, and they are splendidly recorded on disc; but the cassette is not recommended. It has a shrill treble response and there is distortion too, especially in the *Tuba concerto.*

Concerto grosso for strings; (i) *Oboe concerto in A min.*
*** Argo ZRG/*KZRC* 881 [id.]. ASMF, Marriner, (i) with Nicklin – WARLOCK: *Capriol suite* etc.***

These two Vaughan Williams works, both under-appreciated, make an attractive coupling, well matched with Warlock's most popular work and the *Serenade* for his friend Delius. Celia Nicklin, first oboe of the Academy, gives a most persuasive account of the elusive *Oboe concerto*, while the rugged, easy manner of the *Concerto grosso*, written with amateurs in mind for two of the three groups of strings, is splendidly caught in this polished performance. Good wide-ranging recording and a lively, realistically balanced cassette.

(i; ii) *Oboe concerto in A min.; (iii; iv) Tuba concerto in F min.; (ii; v) The Lark Ascending.*
*** DG 2530 906 [id./*3300 906*]. (i) Black; (ii) ECO; (iii) Jacobs; (iv) Chicago SO; (v) Zukerman; cond. Barenboim.

Very good playing and recording of these three beautiful works. Zukerman's version of *The Lark Ascending* is full of pastoral rapture, and Barenboim secures sensitive pianissimo playing from the ECO. Arnold Jacobs gives a good account of himself in the *Tuba concerto*, though he is not quite as subtle as his rival John Fletcher on RCA. Neil Black's account of the *Oboe concerto*, not Vaughan Williams's strongest work, holds its own with current rivals, and the quality of sound accorded to all these performances is first-class. Though possibly not a first choice for any of the three works, it makes a very satisfying disc all the same.

English folksongs suite; Toccata marziale.
*** Telarc Dig. DG 10050 [id.]. Cleveland Symphonic Winds, Fennell – ARNAUD: *Fanfares*; GRAINGER: *Lincolnshire Posy* etc.***
*** ASV ACA/*ZCACA* 1002. L. Wind O., Wick – HOLST: *Hammersmith* etc.***

The Telarc digital disc offers essentially robust performances, marvellously played and recorded. The contrasting central movement of the *Folksongs suite* is presented gently and with attractive

delicacy of texture. Some might feel that the bass drum and cymbals are a trifle too insistent elsewhere, but the recording is so crisply spectacular (and the balance is not too forward) that it would be churlish to complain. The effect is certainly sparkling. The pressing itself is flawless.

On the analogue ASV alternative the pace is comparably zestful, and if the slow movement of the *Folksongs suite* might have been played more reflectively, the bounce of *Seventeen come Sunday* is irresistible. The *Toccata marziale*, written in 1924 for the British Empire Exhibition at Wembley, has plenty of flourish here. The sound is first-rate, if not quite so spectacular as the Telarc alternative, but the ASV cassette is a little disappointing. The relatively modest level has meant that transients (particularly the side-drum) are not ideally crisp.

Fantasia on a theme of Thomas Tallis.
🏵 (M) *** HMV mono XLP/*TC-XLP* 60002. Philh. O., Karajan – BRITTEN: *Variations.*🏵***
(M) *** Lyr. REAM 1. LPO, Boult – ELGAR: *Symphony No. 1.****

Fantasia on a theme of Thomas Tallis; The Wasps: Overture.
*** HMV ASD/*TC-ASD* 3857 [Ang. SZ/*4ZS* 37627]. LSO, Previn – ELGAR: *Enigma variations.****

Karajan's version of the *Tallis fantasia* coupled with Britten's *Variations on a theme of Frank Bridge* is one of the outstanding records of the 1950s, sounding as fresh and sonorous today as it did then. Sonically it is little short of amazing, and artistically it is no less impressive. The playing of the Philharmonia strings for Karajan is altogether superlative, and the *Tallis fantasia* sounds both idiomatic and vivid, rather like a newly cleaned painting. Recordings of this work are legion, and stereo undoubtedly brings an added dimension, but this mono version ranks among the very best, from the early Boult set of 78s through such memorable accounts as that of Mitropoulos to the more recent versions from Barbirolli, Boult and the much underrated Ormandy. The cassette of the Karajan performance is smooth and well balanced, not quite as open in sound as the spectacular coupling.

Boult's Lyrita record is generously full; the *Fantasia* is merely a bonus for his fine reading of Elgar's *First Symphony*. As in the symphony he takes a relatively cool and slightly detached view of a masterpiece equally close to his heart, and as in the symphony the degree of understatement is most affecting. First-rate recording of Lyrita's usual high standard.

Coupled with Elgar's most popular orchestral work, Previn's performances of the *Tallis fantasia* and the *Wasps overture* are warmly persuasive. The wasp-music buzzes with point and energy, while the *Fantasia*, after a restrained opening, builds up finally with great conviction into a blazing climax, with no inhibition over a stringendo. Warm, opulent recording to match; the cassette too is full-blooded and clear, although there is just a hint of roughness at the biggest climaxes.

Fantasia on a theme of Thomas Tallis; Five Variants of Dives and Lazarus; Norfolk rhapsody No. 1; (i) *Towards the Unknown Region.*
*** HMV Dig. ASD/*TCC-ASD* 4089. CBSO, Del Mar, (i) with CBSO Ch.

Norman Del Mar's strong and deeply felt account of the *Tallis fantasia* is given a splendid digital recording, with the second orchestral group creating radiant textures. The direct approach, however, lacks something in mystery, and not all of the ethereal resonance of this haunting work is conveyed. Yet this remains an attractive record with its grouping of rarities, including the early cantata *To-*

wards the Unknown Region of 1907 to words of Walt Whitman. Aptly the chorus is presented at an evocative distance. The chrome cassette matches the disc in breadth and clarity, with the big climax of the choral work splendidly caught.

Hymn-tune preludes: Nos. 1, Eventide (arr. of Monk); *2, Dominus regit me* (arr. of Dykes); *The Poisoned Kiss: overture; The Running Set; Sea Songs: Quick march.*
(M) *** Chan. CBR/*CBT* 1004. Bournemouth Sinf., Hurst – ELGAR: *Adieu* etc.***

George Hurst directs no fewer than three first recordings on the Vaughan Williams side of a delightful collection of minor pieces. The overture to the opera *The Poisoned Kiss* is merely a potpourri, but it whets the appetite for a complete recording of a piece neglected simply because of its poor libretto. *The Running Set* is an exhilarating fantasy on jig rhythms, while the *March on sea songs*, with its bounding rhythms and surging melody in the trio, would make an ideal Prom item. Ripe performances and recording.

Symphonies Nos. 1–9.
(B) *** RCA RL 43371 (7). Soloists, LSO Ch., LSO, Previn.

Previn recorded the Vaughan Williams symphonies over a five-year span from 1968 to 1972, and his achievement in this repertoire represented a peak in his recording career at that time. Here the nine symphonies minus the couplings have been neatly compressed on to seven discs. The most striking performances are those which were recorded last, Nos. 2, 3 and 5, for there Previn achieves an extra depth of understanding, an extra intensity, whether in the purity of pianissimo or the outpouring of emotional resolution. For the rest there is only one performance that can be counted at all disappointing, and that of the symphony one might have expected Previn to interpret best, the taut and dramatic *Fourth*. Even that is an impressive account, if less intense than the rest. Otherwise the great landscape of the whole cycle is presented with richness and detail in totally refreshing interpretations, brilliantly recorded.

A Sea symphony (No. 1).
(M) *** HMV Green. ESD/*TC-ESD* 7104 [(d) Ang. S 3739]. Armstrong, Carol Case, LPO Ch., LPO, Boult.
(M) *** RCA Gold GL/*GK* 43576 [AGL 1/*AGC 1* 4212]. Harper, Shirley-Quirk, LSO Ch., LSO, Previn.

Boult's is a warm, relaxed reading of Vaughan Williams's expansive symphony. If the ensemble is sometimes less perfect than one would like, the flow of the music consistently holds the listener, and this is matched by warmly atmospheric recorded sound. Boult, often thought of as a 'straight' interpreter, here demonstrates his affectionate style, drawing consistently expressive but never sentimental phrasing from his singers and players. John Carol Case's baritone does not sound well on disc with his rather plaintive tone colour, but his style is right, and Sheila Armstrong sings most beautifully. The set has been remastered and in this Greensleeve reissue it now fits comfortably on to two sides instead of three, without apparent loss of amplitude or clarity. The cassette, transformed at a high level to give the famous opening section plenty of impact, is fractionally less open than the disc but remains impressively full-bodied and clear.

Previn's is a fresh, youthful reading of a young composer's symphony. If his interpretation lacks some of the honeyed sweetness that Boult brings to music that he has known and loved for half a century and more, Previn's view provides a clearer focus. His nervous energy is obvious

from the very start. He does not always relax as Boult does, even where, as in the slow movement, he takes a more measured tempo than the older conductor. In the scherzo Boult concentrates on urgency, the emotional surge of the music, even at the expense of precision of ensemble, where Previn is lighter and cleaner, holding more in reserve. The finale similarly is built up over a longer span, with less deliberate expressiveness. The culminating climax with Previn is not allowed to be swamped with choral tone, but has the brass and timpani still prominent. The *Epilogue* may not be so deliberately expressive but it is purer in its tenderness and exact control of dynamics. Even if Vaughan Williams devotees will disagree over the relative merits of the interpretations, Previn has clear advantages in his baritone soloist and his choir. The recording too is of excellent quality, with the vivid cassette transfer very slightly less refined than the disc. It benefits from a small treble reduction, which does not rob the choral focus of its sharpness and impact. The bass is lighter and cleaner than on Boult's HMV tape.

A London symphony (No. 2).
(M) *** RCA Gold GL/*GK* 43577 (LSC 3282]. LSO, Previn.
(B) **(*) CfP CFP/*TC-CFP* 40286. LPO, Handley.

Previn underlines the greatness of this work as a symphony, not just a sequence of programmatic impressions. Though the actual sonorities are even more subtly and beautifully realized here than in rival versions, the architecture is equally convincingly presented, with the great climaxes of the first and last movements powerful and incisive. Most remarkable of all are the pianissimos, which here have new intensity, a quality of *frisson* as in a live performance. The LSO plays superbly and the recording, made in Kingsway Hall, is beautifully balanced and refined, coping perfectly with the widest possible dynamic range. The cassette transfer is most successful, full and well detailed, and any slight loss of refinement in the upper range (it is very marginal) is more than compensated for by the freedom from intrusive background noises.

Vernon Handley's performance on Classics for Pleasure is given a splendid modern recording of striking range. The subtlety of detail, especially at lower dynamic levels, means that many of the composer's orchestral effects are more telling here than in Barbirolli's 1959 version, and the brilliant scherzo gains immeasurably from the sense of spectacle and wide dynamic contrasts. The performance is straightforward and undoubtedly effective. Tempi are well chosen; the slow movement has genuine poetry and its climax, like that of the finale (before the *Epilogue*), has eloquence. The orchestral playing is sensitive throughout (notably in the closing pages of the *Lento*). The cassette has a slightly restricted upper range, compared with the disc (the muted strings in the slow movement are not absolutely clean), but still sounds fully acceptable.

(i) *A Pastoral symphony (No. 3);* (ii) *Tuba concerto in F min.*
(M) *** RCA Gold GL/*GK* 43580 [LSC 3281]. LSO, Previn, with (i) Harper; (ii) Fletcher.

Previn draws an outstandingly beautiful and refined performance of the *Pastoral* from the LSO, the bare textures sounding austere but never thin, the few climaxes emerging at full force with purity undiminished. In the third movement the final coda – the only really fast music in the whole work – brings a magic tracery of pianissimo in this performance, lighter, faster and even clearer than in Boult's version. The recording adds to the beauty in its atmospheric distancing, not least in the trumpet cadenza of the second movement and the lovely melismas for the soprano soloist in the last

movement. The high-level cassette transfer is vivid, but less refined in the upper range; this is most noticeable in the *Tuba concerto*, where the strings sound somewhat fierce.

Symphony No. 4 in F min.; (i) *Concerto accademico for violin and orchestra in D min.*
(M) **(*) RCA Gold GL/*GK* 43581. LSO, Previn, (i) with Buswell.

Symphony No. 4; (i) *The Lark Ascending.*
** HMV ASD/*TC-ASD* 3904. RPO, Berglund, (i) with Griffiths.

Previn secures a fine performance of the *F minor Symphony*; only the somewhat ponderous tempo he adopts for the first movement lets it down. But on the whole this is a powerful reading, and it is vividly recorded. A good alternative to Boult's version (HMV ASD 2375), though not superior to it. The *Concerto* makes an attractive bonus. The sound on cassette is sharply defined and benefits from a slight treble cut; but it can be made to yield first-class results.

Berglund directs a rugged, purposeful account of the *Fourth Symphony*, one which refuses to relax even in the more lyrical passages. Berglund follows the composer himself in preferring an unusually fast speed in the first movement, while the second movement is superbly sustained at a very slow tempo. The playing of the RPO may not match that of the Previn and Boult versions in polish, but Berglund's extra bite is fair compensation, not to mention his more modern recording. *The Lark Ascending* is disappointingly unatmospheric, only partly a question of close recording balances. Cassette and disc are very closely matched.

Symphony No. 5 in D; The Wasps: Overture.
⊛ (M) *** RCA Gold GL/*GK* 43578. LSO, Previn.

If anyone has ever doubted the dedication of Previn as an interpreter of Vaughan Williams, this glowing disc will provide the clearest proof. In this most characteristic – and many would say greatest – of the Vaughan Williams symphonies Previn refuses to be lured into pastoral byways. His tempi may – rather surprisingly – be consistently on the slow side, but the purity of tone he draws from the LSO, the precise shading of dynamic and phrasing, and the sustaining of tension through the longest, most hushed passages produce results that will persuade many not normally convinced of the greatness of this music. In the first movement Previn builds the great climaxes of the second subject with much warmth, but he reserves for the climax of the slow movement his culminating thrust of emotion, a moment of visionary sublimity, after which the gentle urgency of the *Passacaglia* finale and the stillness of the *Epilogue* seem a perfect happy conclusion. It is some tribute to Previn's intensity that he can draw out the diminuendi at the ends of movements with such refinement and no sense of exaggeration. This is an outstanding performance, superbly recorded. The cassette transfer is made at the highest level (especially on side two) and has striking range. The sound is less refined in the treble than the disc and needs considerable control, but there is no lack of body and with care this can be made to yield impressive results.

Symphony No. 6 in E min.; Prelude and fugue in C min.

(B) **(*) CfP CFP 40334. LPO, Handley.

Vaughan Williams's *Sixth Symphony*, written between 1944 and 1947, retains the power to shock the listener with the intensity of its triplet warning figures in the slow movement, and the bleak apocalyptic atmosphere of the finale. Yet it also offers, in the second subject of the ebullient first movement, one of the most heart-warming tunes the composer ever wrote (once famous as a TV signature tune). Handley tends slightly to underplay these strong emotional contrasts; the second movement is chill with stillness, the violence understated, and the opening of the brashly popular scherzo, though well sprung, is not as biting as it might be. Taken as a whole, however, this is a refreshing, clean-cut reading. As the composer's scoring is often so heavy with brass, it is remarkable that Handley is able to clarify textures without making them merely lightweight and without losing intensity. A beautiful performance helped by full yet refined recording, well coupled with an orchestral arrangement of an organ piece (made by the composer for the Three Choirs Festival at Hereford in 1930), never before recorded.

Symphonies Nos. 6 in E min.; 8 in D min.

(M) **(*) RCA Gold GL/GK 43579. LSO, Previn.

Previn's is a sensible and generous coupling. The *Sixth Symphony*, with its moments of darkness and brutality contrasted against the warmth of the second subject or the hushed intensity of the final other-worldly slow movement, is a work for which Previn has a natural affinity. In the first three movements his performance is superbly dramatic, clear-headed and direct, with natural understanding. His account of the mystic final movement with its endless pianissimo is not, however, on the same level, for – whether or not the fault of the recording – the playing is not quite hushed enough, and the tempo is a little too fast. In its closely wrought contrapuntal texture this is a movement which may seem difficult to interpret, but which should be allowed to flow along on its own intensity. Boult here achieves a more vital sense of mystery, even though his account is not ideal. Previn's account of the *Eighth* brings no such reservations, with finely pointed playing, the most precise control of dynamic shading, and a delightfully Stravinskian account of the bouncing scherzo for woodwind alone. Excellent recording considering the length of sides, although the string tone is not always ideally expansive. The cassette transfer, made at a high level, is extremely bright, and the upper range needs some control if it is not to sound fierce. However, the recording has plenty of body and with an adjustment can give excellent results: the strings in the *Cavatina* of the *Eighth Symphony* and in the famous lyrical melody of the first movement of the *Sixth* have impressive breadth of timbre.

Sinfonia Antartica (*No. 7*).
(M) *** RCA Gold GL/*GK* 43582. Harper, Amb. S., LSO, Previn; Ralph Richardson (narrator).

The *Antartica* may be episodic but it is still a vital and dramatic symphony, deriving as it does from the score to the film *Scott of the Antarctic*. The RCA recording, in its relatively distant balance, and Previn's interpretation concentrate on atmosphere rather than drama. The performance is sensitive and literal. Because of the recessed effect of the sound the picture of the ice fall (represented by the entry of the organ) has less impact here than in Boult's version (HMV ASD 2631 [Ang. S 36763]). But at medium price the RCA disc remains fully competitive, and the cassette transfer is highly successful, slightly sharper in focus than the disc, yet not lacking atmosphere.

Symphony No. 9 in D min.; The England of Elizabeth: suite.
(M) *** RCA Gold GL/*GK* 43583. LSO, Previn.

The *Ninth*, Vaughan Williams's last symphony, is one of his most consistently underrated works. It contains much noble and arresting invention and stimu-

lates Previn to show a freshness and sense of poetry which prove particularly thought-provoking and rewarding. He secures smooth contours in the first movement and as a result of refined string playing he produces attractively transparent textures. The RCA recording is highly successful, and the string tone is expansive, well balanced in relation to the rest of the orchestra and free from the slight hint of hardness that sometimes disturbs this cycle. Listening to this reading reinforces the view that the critics of the day were unfairly harsh to this fine score. On the whole this version is finer than Boult's HMV account. The *England of Elizabeth suite* is a film score of no great musical interest but undoubtedly pleasant to listen to; both performance and recording are first-class. The high-level cassette is vivid and clear, but slightly less refined than the disc: in the symphony the resonance brings a hint of harshness at fortissimo level. But, as in the rest of the series, with control of the treble a full and lively balance can be obtained.

The Wasps (*Aristophanic suite*).
*** HMV ASD/*TC-ASD* 3953. Bournemouth Sinf., Del Mar – HOLST: *Brook Green suite* etc.***

The *Wasps overture* – here dashingly performed – is well enough known, but the other items in the suite are delightful too. Del Mar brings out the wit of the *March of the Kitchen Utensils* with his mock pomposity, and as in the Holst items the recording is outstanding. The cassette is first-rate too; both tape and disc offer sound of demonstration quality. Highly recommended.

Violin sonata in A min.
(*) HMV ASD 3820. Y. and H. Menuhin – ELGAR: *Sonata*.(*)

The late Vaughan Williams *Sonata* is an unexpected piece for the Menuhins to record, and though in the first movement (as in the Elgar on the reverse) their tempo is controversially slow, giving the music unexpected weight, the whole performance makes a fine illumination of an elusive piece, not least from the pianist, who copes splendidly with the often awkward piano writing. The recording is first-rate.

Choral music: (i) *Bushes and briars; Down among the dead men;* (ii) *2 Elizabethan part-songs* (*Willow song; O mistress mine*); (ii; iii) *Fantasia on Christmas carols;* (iv) *Lord, Thou hast been our refuge;* (v) *5 Mystical songs: Antiphon;* (iv; vi) *O clap your hands;* (vii) *O taste and see;* (ii) *3 Shakespeare songs;* (viii; ii) *The turtle dove;* (i) *Wassail song.*

(M) *** Argo ZK 34. (i) Elizabethan Singers, Halsey; (ii) King's College Ch., Willcocks; (iii) Alan, LSO; (iv) St John's College Ch., Guest; (v) St George's Chapel, Windsor, Ch., Campbell; (vi) L. Brass Players; (vii) St Michael's College, Tenbury, Ch., Nethsingha; (viii) Lindsay Heather.

The *Fantasia on Christmas carols*, one of the highlights here, and *O clap your hands* are also available in *The world of Vaughan Williams* (see below), but this collection concentrates entirely on vocal music. The selection has been well made to provide variety as well as showing the best side of the composer in this field. Performances and recording are both excellent.

5 English folksongs; Heart's music; Prayer to the Father in Heaven; The souls of the righteous; Te Deum in C; Valiant for truth; A Vision of Aeroplanes.

*** Abbey LPB 799. BBC Northern Singers, Wilkinson; Weir (organ).

The excellent BBC Northern Singers

under their founder and conductor Stephen Wilkinson provide a most attractive programme of choral works, largely neglected. *A Vision of Aeroplanes* is improbably a setting of words from the Book of Ezekiel, an urgently imaginative piece as sung by such a choir, while the Bunyan setting, *Valiant for truth*, builds up to a superb close. Gillian Weir makes a powerful and stylish accompanist, and the recording is first-rate in its clean acoustic.

Folksong arrangements: *As I walked out; Ballade de Jésus Christ; The brewer; Bushes and briars; The captain's apprentice; Chanson de Quête; The cuckoo; Geordie; How cold the wind doth blow; Joseph and Mary; The lawyer; The maiden's lament; The morning dew; On board a 98; The ploughman; Réveillez-vous Piccarz; Rolling in the dew; The Saviour's love; Searching for lambs; She's like the swallow; The truth sent from above.*

(M) *** HMV HQS 1412. Tear, Ledger, Bean.

Robert Tear, who earlier made a delightful record of Benjamin Britten's folksong settings, here turns to the very different, more innocent settings of Vaughan Williams and conveys comparable intensity, not least in those songs where the singer has a stanza or so unaccompanied. The selection could hardly be more attractive or varied in mood and expression. Stylish accompaniments. Hugh Bean's sensitive violin obbligati in the three closing songs of the recital (*The lawyer, Searching for lambs* and *How cold the wind doth blow*) are a highlight. Excellent recording.

In Windsor Forest (cantata).
*** HMV ASD/*TC-ASD* 4061. Fields, Bournemouth SO Ch. and O., Del Mar

– ELGAR: *From the Bavarian Highlands.****

The cantata *In Windsor Forest*, which Vaughan Williams adapted from his Falstaff opera, *Sir John in Love*, makes the perfect coupling for Elgar's suite of part-songs. The movements are not always exact transcriptions from the opera, for the composer rethought and amplified certain passages. As in the Elgar, Del Mar directs warmly sympathetic performances, given excellent sound, warmly reverberant. On cassette the choral focus is not always quite clean at climaxes, though overall the sound is rich and well balanced.

On Wenlock Edge (song cycle).
*** Hyp. A 66013. Hill, Coull Qt – GURNEY: *Ludlow and Teme.****

On Wenlock Edge (orchestral version).
(*) HMV ASD/*TC-ASD* 3896. Tear, CBSO, Handley – BUTTERWORTH: *Love Blows*; ELGAR: *Songs.**
(*) Uni. Kanchana KP 8001. English, W. Australian SO, Measham – IRELAND: *The Overlanders.**

Martyn Hill's voice records very cleanly, and though he may have less beautiful colourings than some tenors, he gives a deeply understanding performance of the Vaughan Williams cycle, one which fully brings out word-meaning on the lines of German Lieder. *Is my team ploughing?* is made the more eerie when the Coull Quartet eliminates vibrato in the passages accompanying the words of the dead man. Well-recorded, with a rare and apt coupling, it is an excellent issue. However, Ian Partridge's record with the Music Group of London (coupled with settings of Blake) is outstandingly beautiful; his lovely individual tone colour is used with compelling artistry (HMV HQS 1236).

Vaughan Williams's own orchestration of the cycle, made in the early 1920s,

has been strangely neglected. It lacks something of the apt ghostly quality of the version for piano and string quartet, but some will prefer the bigger scale. Tear sings sensitively, but with the voice balanced close the tone is not always sweet. Handley draws fine playing from the Birmingham orchestra, but this has less flair and imagination than the Unicorn version conducted by David Measham.

Gerald English is no less persuasive than Robert Tear in this repertoire, and the closer recorded balance helps him to convey greater dramatic intensity and ardour. Yet the sound, though forward, is never unacceptably so. Choice will doubtless depend on individual preference as far as couplings are concerned. The Ireland suite is not among that master's finest works.

Hugh the Drover (opera; complete).
**(*) HMV SLS 5162 (2). Tear, Armstrong, Watts, Lloyd, Rippon, Amb. Op. Ch., RPO, Groves.

Hugh the Drover is the most immediately appealing of the Vaughan Williams operas, the earliest of the full-length works. Described as a ballad opera and using folk-themes in full-throated lyricism, it has – as Michael Kennedy has said – at times an almost Puccinian warmth and expansiveness. That being so, it is a pity that Robert Tear was in such dry voice when he recorded the role of Hugh. That miscasting may not have been predictable, but it seriously detracts from the work's magic, and though Sir Charles Groves's conducting is thoroughly idiomatic, the result could have more emotional thrust. Nonetheless, with a very good supporting team and beautifully recorded, it is a most welcome issue.

COLLECTION

'*The world of Vaughan Williams*': (i) *English folksongs suite*; (ii) *Fantasia*

on *Greensleeves;* (ii; iii) *The Lark*
Ascending; (iv) *Prelude· Rhosy-*
medre. (v) *Fantasia on Christmas*
carols; (vi) *O clap your hands;* (vii)
Songs: Linden Lea; Silent noon; The
vagabond.
(M) *** Decca SPA/*KCSP* 587. (i)
Boston Pops O., Fiedler; (ii) ASMF,
Marriner; (iii) Iona Brown; (iv) M.
Nicholas (organ); (v) Alan, King's
College Ch., LSO, Willcocks; (vi) St
John's College Ch., Guest; (vii) Tear,
Ledger.

Many collectors will feel that any
single-disc summation of Vaughan Williams's art without the symphonies must
include the great *Tallis fantasia.* However, this selection is undoubtedly well
made as long as there is no objection to
having songs with piano sandwiched
between *Greensleeves* and *The Lark*
Ascending, heard in Iona Brown's elysian performance. The orchestral version
of the *English folksongs suite* has less bite
than the military band original but is
brightly presented here. The lovely *Fan-*
tasia on Christmas carols is especially
welcome. The sound is excellent on disc
and cassette alike.

Verdi, Giuseppe
(1813–1901)

Overtures: Aïda (reconstructed and
arr. Spada); *Aroldo; La Forza del*
destino; Luisa Miller; Nabucco; I
Vespri siciliani.
*** RCA RL/*RK* 31378. LSO, Abbado.

Abbado directs strong and brilliant
performances of Verdi's most substantial
overtures. The recording is brilliant and
full, with resonant brass and a sparkling
upper range on disc and cassette alike.
The novelty is the introduction which

Verdi originally wrote for the first Italian
performance of *Aïda* and subsequently
rejected. It is a considerably extended
piece; in Spada's reconstruction one can
see why the composer did not want in
instrumental terms to anticipate effects
far more telling in the full operatic setting, but heard independently it is most
entertaining and deftly scored.

Overtures and *Preludes: Aïda; Un*
Ballo in maschera; Il Corsaro; La
Forza del destino; Luisa Miller;
Macbeth; Nabucco; Rigoletto; La
Traviata; I Vespri siciliani.
*** DG 2531/*3301* 145 [id.]. Berlin PO,
Karajan.

This is an excellent and generous selection from Karajan's complete set of
preludes and overtures (2707 090/*3370*
010 (2)) and can be strongly recommended. The playing has both panache
and authority, and the recording is first-
class on disc and tape; if anything the
sound is fuller, though not less vivid, than
in the original pressings.

Overtures and *Preludes: Aïda; La*
Forza del destino; Giovanna d'Arco;
Luisa Miller; La Traviata; I Vespri
siciliani. Macbeth: Ballet music.
(M) ** Ph. Seq. 6527/*7311* 078. New
Philh. O., Markevitch.

A generous medium-priced collection,
with four items to a side and strongly
dramatic performances; *Giovanna d'Arco*
and *I Vespri siciliani* are especially vivid.
The *Aïda prelude* is beautifully played,
and the *Traviata preludes* are well done
too. The only reservation is about the
recording balance. Verdi's brass writing
is powerful enough without any help
from the microphones, and here the
strings tend to be overwhelmed at times.
The middle strings in particular seem
unable always to expand their tone, although when the whole section is playing

together alone, the sound has plenty of lustre. On cassette the modest transfer level has reduced the sparkle at the top.

Overtures and *Preludes*: *La Battaglia di Legnano; La Forza del destino; Giovanna d'Arco; Luisa Miller; Nabucco; I Vespri siciliani.*
*** HMV ASD/*TC-ASD* 3366 [Ang. S/*4XS* 37407]. New Philh. O., Muti.

This must be numbered among Riccardo Muti's most successful ventures into the recording studio. The playing has great spirit and character, and the New Philharmonia responds to his direction with evident warmth. Naturally balanced orchestral sound (richer than on Karajan's DG set) makes this a highly desirable issue. On cassette the recording is immensely vivid and full-blooded; on the whole the reverberant acoustic has transferred well, although there is at times just a hint that the quality lacks the last degree of refinement.

Opera ballets from: *Aïda; Macbeth; I Vespri siciliani* (*The four seasons*).
*** HMV ASD/*TC-ASD* 4015 [Ang. SZ 37801]. Amb. Op. Ch., Philh. or New Philh. O., Muti.

Following up his highly successful disc of overtures Muti offers here a no less appealing anthology of ballet music played with scintillating brilliance and colour. The Ambrosian Opera Chorus makes a short but effective contribution to the melodramatic *Chorus of witches and Dance of the Spirits* from *Macbeth*. The *Four seasons* ballet from *I Vespri siciliani* takes a whole side, but Verdi's invention is consistently attractive. The recording is of demonstration quality; even though it has an analogue source there is an impressively sharp focus, and the ambient effect is an equal source of pleasure. The high-level cassette is also first-class, though here the transients are slightly less telling. The only drawback

to this collection is that it ends rather in mid-air because the *Aïda* excerpts are without the closing choral march.

String quartet in E min.
*** CRD CRD 1066/*CRDC 4066.* Alberni Qt – DONIZETTI: *Quartet No. 13;* PUCCINI: *Crisantemi.****
*** DG 2531/*3301* 283 [id.]. Amadeus Qt – TCHAIKOVSKY: *Quartet No. 1.****

It is odd that Verdi, having written his *String quartet* as an exercise about the time he completed *Aïda*, should then have refused to let it be heard or published for many years. To us today its skill and finesse are what strike home; it is a unique work in Verdi's output, with a distinctive tone of voice and only one excursion into a recognizably vocal style – in the Neapolitan tune of the trio in the third movement. The Alberni Quartet's performance is strong and compelling, not as polished as the Amadeus version but in many ways the more effective for that; and it is most imaginatively and attractively coupled with the Puccini and Donizetti pieces. The excellent recording on disc is matched by one of CRD's best cassette transfers; it offers demonstration sound, full and with splendid detail and presence.

The Amadeus play with total commitment, and this is among their best recordings. They bring great warmth to this piece and are admirably served by the DG engineers, although on cassette the transfer level is lower than the Tchaikovsky coupling, and while the quality remains sophisticated the sound has slightly less projection and presence.

Requiem Mass.
*** HMV SLS/*TC-SLS* 5185 (2) [Ang. SZ/*4Z2S* 3858]. Scotto, Baltsa, Luchetti, Nesterenko, Amb. Ch., Philh. O., Muti.
**(*) RCA RL/*RK* 02746 (2) [ARL 2/*ARK 2* 2746]. Price, Baker, Luchetti, Van Dam, Chicago Symphony Ch. and SO, Solti.

** DG 2707 120/*3370 032* (2) [id.]. Ricciarelli, Verrett, Domingo, Ghiaurov, Ch. and O. of La Scala, Milan, Abbado.

With spectacular sound – not always perfectly balanced but vividly wide in its tonal spectrum – the Muti performance has tremendous impact. Characteristically he prefers fast speeds, and in the *Dies irae* he rushes the singers dangerously, making the music breathless in excitement rather than grandly dramatic in its portrayal of the Day of Wrath. It is not surprising that Muti opted for a professional choir rather than the Philharmonia Chorus, and the engineers are able to give it fine impact. Unashamedly this is from first to last an operatic performance, with a passionately committed quartet of soloists, underpinned by Nesterenko in glorious voice, giving priestly authority to the *Confutatis*. Scotto is not always sweet at the top, but Baltsa is superb, and Luchetti, as on the Solti version, sings freshly. Generally speaking this Muti recording (which has a very successful tape equivalent, with a natural balance, excellent clarity and a striking absence of congestion in the spectacular *Dies irae*) must be counted first choice. By its side Giulini's set (HMV SLS 909 [Ang. S 3649]) is technically rather less satisfactory as a recording (and cannot be recommended in its cassette form). Yet Giulini's combination of refinement and elemental strength remains totally memorable. With the Philharmonia Chorus in first-class form and an array of soloists (Schwarzkopf, Ludwig, Gedda, and Ghiaurov) that could hardly be bettered, it is still a classic version.

On RCA, with an unusually sensitive and pure-toned quartet of soloists – Luchetti perhaps not as characterful as the others, Price occasionally showing strain – and with superb choral singing and orchestral playing, Solti's Chicago version has all the ingredients to make it a first choice. The pity is that the recording – so important in such a dramatic piece –

seriously undermines the impact of the performance. Certainly in sound, and in other ways too, Solti's earlier Vienna version on Decca (SET 374/5 [Lon. 1275]) has more bite. But this set is well worth having for Dame Janet Baker's deeply sensitive singing. The cassettes – although slightly fierce on top – offer vivid sound, but the climaxes in the *Dies irae* are too explosive for comfort.

Abbado's version was recorded at La Scala, Milan, when an opera project was abandoned at the last moment. So far from making the result operatic – as, for example, Muti's highly charged version is – it seems to have sapped tensions. It is a pity that so intense a Verdian did not have a more committed team of performers. The choral entry on *Te decet hymnus* gives an early indication of the slackness and lack of bite, and though the *Dies irae* is exactly in place (unlike Muti's hectic account) there is no excitement whatever, with the chorus sounding too small. The soloists too are often below their best, but, balances apart, the recording is first-rate. The cassette transfer is lively and avoids distortion in the *Dies irae*, although climaxes are rather dry and there is some recession of image at pianissimo levels.

Four Sacred pieces (Ave Maria; Stabat Mater, Laudi alla Vergine; Te Deum).
(M) *** HMV SXLP/*TC-SXLP* 30508 [Ang. S 36125]. Philh. Ch. and O., Giulini.
*** Decca SET/*KCET* 602 [Lon. 26610/5-]. Chicago Symphony Ch. and SO, Solti.
(M) *** Ph. Fest. 6570/*7310* 111. Leipzig R. Ch. and SO, Kegel.

Verdi's *Four Sacred pieces* form his very last work – or, to be precise, group of works. There are echoes of the great *Requiem*, and many of the ideas have a genuine Verdian originality, but in general they mark a falling-off after the supreme achievement of the last two Shakespeare operas, *Otello* and *Falstaff*. All the same, in a performance as polished and dramatic as the superlative one by Giulini and the Philharmonia Orchestra and Chorus, the element of greatness is magnified, and any Verdi lover should make a point of hearing this disc, even though the recording is not ideally clear. The cassette is not recommended: it lacks range and refinement at both ends of the spectrum.

Solti's brand of dedication is one of brightness and tension. Many will prefer the more spiritual, more devotional manner of Giulini in this music, but unlike Giulini Solti never runs the risk of seeming mannered in his moulding. The Chicago Symphony Chorus cannot match the finest in Europe, but Solti draws finely shaded performances from his forces and the electricity is never in doubt. The climaxes in the *Stabat Mater* and *Te Deum* are thrilling, and their effect is enhanced by the bold, brilliant recording, equally impressive on disc and the splendid cassette, one of Decca's demonstration issues. This stands effectively between Giulini and the superbly sung version by the Leipzig Choir under Herbert Kegel, which lacks something in its smaller, less spacious scale.

Yet Kegel's magnificent choir presents these very late fragments of Verdian inspiration with a directness that is intensely refreshing. There is a case for the deeply introspective view of Giulini in this music, but the sharper focus of Kegel and the fresh, bright, cleanly balanced Philips recording produce striking immediacy. This is music great enough to make its impact in maximum simplicity. The cassette has less bite than the disc; the moderate transfer level brings sound which is atmospheric rather than sharply defined, although the climaxes expand impressively. Side two has slightly more range than side one.

OPERA

Aïda (complete).

🔾 *** HMV SLS/*TC-SLS* 5205 (3) [Ang. SZ 3888]. Freni, Carreras, Baltsa, Cappuccilli, Raimondi, Van Dam, V. State Op. Ch., VPO, Karajan.

(M) (***) HMV SLS/*TC-SLS* 5108 (3). Callas, Tucker, Barbieri, Gobbi, Ch. and O. of La Scala, Milan, Serafin.

Karajan's is a performance of *Aïda* that carries splendour and pageantry to the point of exaltation. At the very end of the Triumphal Scene, when the march resumes with brass bands, there is a lift, a surge of emotion, such as is captured only rarely on record. Plainly the success of the performance – more urgent if less poised than Karajan's earlier account – owes much to its being conceived in conjunction with a Salzburg Festival production. And for all the power of the pageantry, Karajan's fundamental approach is lyrical, the moulding of phrase warmly expressive from the prelude onwards. Arias are often taken at a slow speed, taxing the singers more, yet Karajan's controversial choice of soloists is amply justified. On record at least, there can be little question of Freni lacking power in a role normally given to a larger voice, and there is ample gain (as on stage) in the tender beauty of her singing. Carreras makes a fresh, sensitive Radames, Raimondi a darkly intense Ramphis and Van Dam a cleanly focused King, his relative lightness no drawback. Cappuccilli here gives a more detailed performance than he did for Muti on HMV, while Baltsa as Amneris crowns the whole performance with her fine incisive singing. Vivid wide-ranging recording of demonstration quality, equally thrilling, sonically, on disc and cassette, with superbly believable perspectives (notably in Scene 2 of Act 1 and the first scene of Act 4).

The Nile Scene – focus of the central emotional conflict in a masterpiece which is only incidentally a pageant – has never been more powerful and characterfully performed on record as in the vintage La Scala set. Though Callas is hardly as sweet-toned as some will think essential for an Aïda, her detailed imagination is irresistible, and she is matched by Tito Gobbi at the very height of his powers. Tucker gives one of his very finest performances on record, and Barbieri is a commanding Amneris. The stereo transcription of the mono recording is outstandingly successful with the voices, which are vivid, full and immediate, and though the orchestral sound is limited, it is cleanly balanced. Discs and cassettes are closely matched.

Aïda: highlights.
*** HMV ASD/*TC-ASD* 3983 (from above set cond. Karajan).
(M) *** Decca Jub. JB/*KJBC* 81. Price, Vickers, Gorr, Merrill, Tozzi, Rome Op. Ch. and O., Solti.

The highlights disc from Karajan's superb HMV set is most intelligently compiled. In the span of a single LP it is impossible to include all the favourite items, but this one enjoyably concentrates on Karajan's most successful moments. The Triumphal Scene, for example, has been skilfully edited to include both the opening and the close. Extremely vivid recording, with little to choose between disc and cassette.

On Jubilee Decca offer a generous mid-priced reminder of the excellence of Solti's 1962 set, Leontyne Price is an outstandingly assured Aïda, and Solti's direction is superbly dramatic. First-rate sound, even by today's standards, although the high-level cassette – otherwise extremely vivid – produces moments of peaking in Vickers's vibrant *Celeste Aïda*.

Aroldo (complete).
** CBS 79328 (3) [Col. M3X 35906]. Caballé, Cecchele, Lebherz, Pons, NY Oratorio Soc., Westchester Ch. Soc., New York Op. O., Queler.

Aroldo is Verdi's radical revision of his earlier, unsuccessful opera *Stiffelio*; he translated the story of a Protestant pastor with an unfaithful wife into this tale of a crusader returning from the Holy Land. Less compact than the original, it contains some splendid new material, such as a superb aria for the heroine, here beautifully sung by Caballé. The final scene too is quite new, for the dénouement is totally different. The storm chorus – with echoes of *Rigoletto* – is most memorable, but so are the rum-ti-tum choruses common to both versions. This recording of a concert performance in New York is lively, though the tenor is depressingly coarse. The recording is more faithful than others in the series.

Un Ballo in maschera (complete).
*** DG 2740 251/*3378 111* (3) [id.]. Ricciarelli, Domingo, Bruson, Obraztsova, Gruberova, Raimondi, Ch. and O. of La Scala Milan, Abbado.
**(*) Ph. 6769 020/*7699 108* (3) [id.]. Caballé, Carreras, Wixell, Payne, Ghazarian, ROHCG Ch. and O., Colin Davis.

Abbado's is a powerful reading of *Ballo*, admirably paced and with a splendid feeling for the sparkle of comedy (so important in the rare mixture of this endlessly eventful piece), lacking just a little in the rhythmic elegance which Verdi specifically calls for in such passages as the haunting exit of the conspirators at the end of Act 2. The cast is arguably the strongest assembled for this opera on record, with Ricciarelli at her very finest, darkly intense in her two big arias (taken very slowly), with raw tone kept to a minimum. Domingo is here sweeter of tone and more deft of characterization than he is in the Muti set of five years earlier, while Bruson as the wronged husband, Renato, sings magnificently, the vocal production splendidly firm.

Obraztsova as Ulrica and Gruberova as Oscar are less consistently convincing, both a little heavy. The recording clearly separates the voices and instruments in different acoustics, which is distracting only initially and after that brings the drama closer. The DG cassette transfer is made at a rather low level and – as the opening scene demonstrates – detail at pianissimo level is less sharply defined than on disc. The voices, however, are freshly caught, and the recording's wide dynamic range is successfully encompassed without peaking.

Davis's version, based on the Covent Garden production, is particularly good in the way it brings out the ironic humour in Verdi's score. Caballé and Carreras match Davis's lightness, but the dramatic power is diminished. Despite fine recording, both the Abbado and the Muti (HMV SLS/TC-SLS 984 [Ang. SX 3762]) sets are preferable. The Philips cassettes – with an unimaginative layout – are less attractive than the discs, less open at the top.

La Battaglia di Legnano (complete).
*** Ph. 6700 120/*7699 081* (2) [id.]. Ricciarelli, Carreras, Manuguerra, Ghiuselev, Austrian R. Ch. and O., Gardelli.

First heard in January 1849, *La Battaglia di Legnano* is set against Italy's struggle in the face of Frederic Barbarossa's invasion. It is a compact, sharply conceived piece, made the more intense by the subject's obvious relationship with the situation in Verdi's own time. One weakness is that villainy is not effectively personalized, but the juxtaposition of the individual drama of supposed infidelity against a patriotic theme brings most effective musical contrasts. Gardelli directs a fine performance, helped by a strong cast of principals, with Carreras, Ricciarelli and Manuguerra all at their finest. Excellent recording; the cassette transfer is generally well managed, with good perspectives and plenty of bloom on voices and orchestra alike.

Don Carlos (complete).
*** HMV SLS/*TC-SLS* 5154 (4) [Ang. SZX 3875]. Carreras, Freni, Ghiaurov, Baltsa, Cappuccilli, German Op. Ch., Berlin PO, Karajan.

As in the Salzburg Festival production on which this recording is based, Karajan opts firmly for the later four-act version of the opera, merely opening out the cuts he adopted on stage. The result could hardly be more powerfully dramatic, one of his most involving opera performances, comparable with his vivid HMV *Aïda*. Though a recording can hardly convey the full grandeur of a stage peopled with many hundreds of singers, the Auto da fe Scene is here superb, while Karajan's characteristic choice of singers for refinement of voice rather than sheer size consistently pays off. Both Carreras and Freni are most moving, even if *Tu che le vanità* has its raw moments. Baltsa is a superlative Eboli and Cappuccilli an affecting Rodrigo, though neither Carreras nor Cappuccilli is at his finest in the famous oath duet. Raimondi and Ghiaurov as the Grand Inquisitor and Philip II provide the most powerful confrontation. Though many collectors will naturally resist the idea of the four-act rather than the five-act version on record, there is no doubt that this Karajan set is the most effective of the complete recordings, and it is very vivid as sound too, with discs and cassettes closely matched.

Reminder: Giulini, also on HMV, and Solti on Decca both opt for the full five-act text. Both have strong casts, with Caballé, Verrett, Domingo, Milnes and Raimondi on HMV (SLS 956 [Ang. S 3774]) and Tebaldi, Bumbry, Bergonzi, Fischer-Dieskau (as Rodrigo) and Ghiaurov on Decca (SET 305/8/*K 128 K 43* [Lon. 1432/5-]). The Decca cassette is strikingly vibrant.

I due Foscari (complete).

*** Philips 6700 105/7699 057 (2). Ricciarelli, Carreras, Cappuccilli, Ramey, Austrian R. Ch. and SO, Gardelli.

As in so many of Verdi's most telling dramatic situations, it is the father–daughter relationship in *I due Foscari* which prompts some of the finest music, including superb duets. It had better be explained that the precise relationship between the Doge of Venice, Francesco Foscari, and the heroine, Lucrezia, is father and daughter-in-law, but the wonder is that with a very limiting plot – based loosely on one of Byron's undramatic dramas – Verdi overcomes the shortcoming that nothing changes much in the relationships from beginning to end, and that in any case the wicked are left unpunished while the good are brought low. Even so there are Verdian high spirits in plenty, which erupt in swinging cabalettas and much writing that anticipates operas as late as *Simon Boccanegra* (obvious enough in the Doge's music) and *La Forza del destino* (particularly in the orchestral motifs which act as labels for the principal characters).

The cast is first-rate, with Ricciarelli giving one of her finest performances in the recording studio to date and with Carreras singing tastefully as well as powerfully, not least in the prison aria, which even suggests that Verdi knew his *Fidelio*. Cappuccilli as the Doge brings out the likenesses with *Boccanegra*. The crispness of discipline among the Austrian Radio forces is admirable, but there is less sense of atmosphere than in the earlier London-made recordings in the series; otherwise good clean Philips recording. The cassette transfer too is admirably clean, and the sense of perspective is excellent: where there are distanced effects the clarity of focus is retained, although Miss Ricciarelli's voice (and to a lesser extent that of Carreras) tends to harden slightly when the recording is under pressure by strongly projected top notes.

Ernani (complete).

** RCA RL 42866 (3) [LSC 6183]. Price, Bergonzi, Sereni, Flagello, RCA Italiana Op. Ch. and O., Schippers.

Ernani, based on Victor Hugo's *succès de scandale*, was Verdi's fifth opera and his first to achieve fully international success. The finest numbers, such as the aria *Ernani, involami* – with Leontyne Price here sounding a little sluggish – and the great Act 4 Trio, are among the most memorable music that Verdi had written up to that date. Though this recorded performance starts a little below par, it develops strongly, with Schippers inspiring his forces to lively singing and playing. Price is not quite at her finest, Bergonzi is strong and vivid, Sereni firm but uncharacterful, Flagello rather gritty in tone colour. The 1968 recording is fair.

Falstaff (complete).

(M) *** HMV SLS/*TC-SLS* 5211 (2) [Ang. S 3552]. Gobbi, Schwarzkopf, Alva, Panerai, Moffo, Merriman, Barbieri, Zaccaria, Philh. Ch. and O., Karajan.

**(*) Ph. Dig. 6769/7654 060 (3). Taddei, Kabaivanska, Perry, Panerai, Ludwig, Araiza, V. State Op. Ch., VPO, Karajan.

In response to the newest digital recording of *Falstaff* on Philips, EMI have reissued Karajan's 1957 HMV set, refreshing the sound, which loses nothing from its remastering on to two instead of three LPs (and cassettes). This earlier set presents not only the most pointed account orchestrally of Verdi's comic masterpiece (the Philharmonia Orchestra at its very peak) but the most sharply characterful cast ever gathered for a recording. If you relish the idea of Tito Gobbi as Falstaff (his many-coloured voice, not quite fat-sounding in humour, presents a sharper character than usual), then this is clearly the best choice, for the rest of the cast is a delight, with Schwarzkopf a tinglingly masterful Mistress Ford, Anna Moffo sweet as Nannetta and Rolando Panerai a formidable Ford. One reason why the whole performance hangs together so stylishly is the production of Walter Legge: this is a vintage example of his work. The cassette transfer is brilliantly clear and vivid and stands up remarkably well to direct comparison with the newer Philips tapes.

Karajan's second recording of Verdi's last opera, made over twenty years later than his classic Philharmonia set, has lower standards of precision, but yet conveys a relaxed and genial atmosphere. With the exception of Kabaivanska, whose voice is not steady enough for the role of Alice, it is a good cast, with Ludwig fascinating as Mistress Quickly. Most amazing of all is Taddei's performance as Falstaff himself, full and characterful and vocally astonishing from a man in his sixties. The recording is not so beautifully balanced as the Philharmonia set, but the digital sound is faithful and wide-ranging, though the level of cut is on the low side. The chrome tapes are of the highest quality: the sound has striking range, depth and atmosphere.

Reminder: The Decca set (2BB 104/6/*K 110 K 32* [Lon. 1395]) with Sir Geraint Evans, Ligabue, Merrill, Freni, Elias, Simionato and Kraus is still available at medium price (although on three discs against Karajan's two on EMI). The combination of Solti and Evans is irresistible. Their performance comes up as sparkling as ever: there is an energy, a sense of fun, that match any rival version. Evans has never sounded better in the recording studio and the rest of the cast lives up admirably to his example. The tape transfer is clean and lively.

La Forza del destino (slightly abridged).

(M) (***) HMV SLS/*TC-SLS* 5120 (3). Callas, Tucker, Rossi-Lemeni, Nicolai, Tagliabue, Capecchi, Clabassi, Ch. and O. of La Scala, Milan, Serafin.

Callas was at her very peak when she took the role of Leonora in the Scala recording. Hers is an electrifying performance, providing a focus for an opera normally regarded as diffuse. Though there are classic examples of Callas's raw tone on top notes, they are insignificant next to the wealth of phrasing which sets a totally new and individual stamp on even the most familiar passages. The pity is that the stereo transcription process has (on tape as well as LP) taken away some of the brightness and edge of the recording as originally issued in mono; but in compensation one of the major cuts (at the opening of the final scene) has now been opened out. Apart from his tendency to disturb his phrasing with sobs, Richard Tucker sings superbly; but not even he and certainly none of the others – including the baritone Carlo Tagliabue, well past his prime – begin to rival the dominance of Callas. Serafin's direction is crisp, dramatic and well paced, again drawing the threads together, and the recording has plenty of atmosphere, which is retained in the tape transfer. The detail is remarkably good.

Still recommended: In stereo, however, first choice goes to Levine's RCA set (RL/*RK* 1864 [ÁRL 4/*ARK 3* 1864]), an electrifying performance, with Leontyne Price a superb Leonora and the roles of Don Alvaro and Don Carlo ideally suited to the regular Met. team of Placido Domingo and Sherrill Milnes. The recording is not of RCA's brightest vintage, with the voices close, but it is fully acceptable. The cassette transfer is quite well managed, though here the ear is even more conscious of the lack of bite in the treble and the forward balance.

La Forza del destino, Act 3: *Solenne in quest'ora.*

(M) **(*) Decca SPA/*KCSP* 496. Di Stefano, Warren, O. of St Cecilia Ac., Rome, Previtali – PUCCINI: *Collection of duets.****(*)

This single Verdi item is included

within a collection of operatic duets by Puccini. It is a fine, dramatic performance and the voices are well projected by the recording, which only betrays its age by the quality of the string tone.

Luisa Miller (complete).
**(*) DG 2709 096 (3)/*3370 035* (2) [id.]. Ricciarelli, Obraztsova, Domingo, Bruson, ROHCG Ch. and O., Maazel.

Maazel directs a clean-cut, incisive performance based on the Covent Garden production. Its sharpness is somewhat exaggerated by the recording characteristic, which though at a relatively low level of cut gives an unpleasant edge for example to Ricciarelli in the title role. On balance the principals in the Maag set for Decca (SET 606/8/*K 2 L 25* [Lon. 13114/5-]), recorded more atmospherically with a range if anything wider, are preferable, though Domingo here and Pavarotti in the Decca set are both superb. As conductor, Maag for Decca finds more delicacy than the rather literal, if always dramatic, Maazel. The DG cassette layout (like the Decca), using two tapes against three discs, is preferable and the slightly dry recording has transferred with admirable clarity and detail. The level is modest but there seems little, if any, loss of range. However, the Decca cassettes are outstanding, vibrantly clear without loss of atmosphere.

Luisa Miller: highlights.
*** Decca SET 623. Caballé, Reynolds, Pavarotti, Milnes, Giaotti, Van Allan, L. Op. Ch. Nat. PO, Maag.

This disc offers a generous selection from the excellent Decca set, beautifully recorded.

Nabucco (complete).
*** Decca SET 298/300 (3)/*K 126 K 32* (2) [Lon. 1382/5-]. Gobbi, Suliotis,

Cava, Prevedi, V. State Op. Ch. and O., Gardelli.
**(*) HMV SLS/*TC-SLS* 5132 (3) [Ang. SX 3850]. Manuguerra, Scotto, Ghiaurov, Luchetti, Obraztsova, Amb. Op. Ch., Philh. O., Muti.

In 1966 Decca set impressive standards in this first opera to show Verdi at full stretch. True, the choral contribution was less committed than one would ideally like in a work which contains a chorus unique in Verdi's output, *Va, pensiero*, but in every other way this is a masterly performance, with dramatically intense and deeply imaginative contributions from Tito Gobbi as Nabucco and Elena Suliotis as the evil Abigaille. Gobbi was already nearing the end of his full career, but even he rarely recorded a performance so full of sharply dramatic detail, while Suliotis made this the one totally satisfying performance of an all-too-brief recording career, wild in places but no more than is dramatically necessary. Though Carlo Cava as Zaccaria is not ideally rich of tone, it is a strong performance, and Gardelli, as in his later Verdi recordings for both Decca and Philips, showed what a master he is at pointing Verdian inspiration, whether in the individual phrase or over a whole scene, simply and naturally without over forcing. The mid-sixties recording is brilliant and atmospheric, although the tape transfer (otherwise vividly detailed) needs a fair degree of control in the treble if the upper range is to sound completely natural. The layout is on two cassettes as against three discs.

When a decade later HMV attempted to rival the Decca set, the choice of Muti as conductor was promising, but in the event he failed to match Gardelli, either in detail or overall. The cast, as impressive as could be gathered at the time – with Manuguerra (an outstanding Scarpia in the Rostropovich *Tosca*) an imaginative choice as Nabucco – failed nevertheless to equal the three-dimensional characterizations of the earlier team. Renata Scotto sang well but was far less inside the role than Suliotis; Manuguerra was strong and reliable but lacked the flair of Gobbi; and although Elena Obraztsova proved stronger vocally than Dora Carral as Fenena, the casting was inappropriate. Even the recording quality, firm and warm, failed to improve on the Decca, and on tape the overall focus is less refined. The layout on two cassettes matches the Decca set.

Otello (complete).
*** RCA RL/*RK* 02951 (3) [CRL 3/*CRK 3* 2951]. Domingo, Scotto, Milnes, Amb. Op. Ch., Boys' Ch., Nat. PO, Levine.
**(*) Decca D 102 D 3 (3)/*K 102 K 32* (2) [Lon. 13130]. Cossutta, Margaret Price, Bacquier, V. Boys' Ch., V. State Op. Ch., VPO, Solti.

Levine's is the most consistently involving version of *Otello*, with on balance the best cast, and superbly conducted as well as magnificently sung. Levine combines a Toscanini-like thrust with a Karajan-like sensuousness, pointing rhythms to heighten mood, as in the Act 2 confrontation between hero and heroine over Cassio. Domingo as Otello combines glorious heroic tone with lyrical tenderness. If anyone thought he would be overstrained, here is proof to the contrary: he himself has claimed that singing Otello has helped and benefited his voice. Scotto is not always sweet-toned in the upper register, and the big ensemble at the end of Act 3 brings obvious strain, but it is a deeply felt performance which culminates in a most beautiful account of the all-important Act 4 solos, the *Willow song* and *Ave Maria*, most affecting. Milnes too is challenged by the role of Iago. His may not be a voice which readily conveys extremes of evil, but his view is far from conventional: this Iago is a handsome, virile creature beset by the biggest of chips on the shoulder. Recording could be fuller, but the balance be-

tween voices and orchestra is excellent. The cassette transfer is vivid and well balanced if without quite the range of the discs.

Although Solti recorded outstanding versions of *Aïda* and *Falstaff* in the sixties, in later years he has neglected Verdi in his recording programme, so that the warmth and tenderness of his reading of *Otello* as well as its incisive sense of drama take one freshly by surprise. The recording is bright and atmospheric to match, which leaves the vocal contributions as a third and more debatable deciding point. Of the very finest quality is the singing of Margaret Price as Desdemona, a ravishing performance with the most beautiful and varied tonal quality allied to deep imagination. Carlo Cossutta as Otello is not so characterful a singer, but more than most rivals he sings with clear, incisive tone and obvious concern for musical qualities. Gabriel Bacquier gives a thoughtful, highly intelligent performance as Iago, but his relative weakness in the upper register brings obvious disappointment. The Decca recording, however, has a sense of spectacle (notably in the opening scene) and perspective which is particularly appealing, the whole production managed with characteristic flair. The Decca cassettes too are among this company's finest issues, the sound matching brilliance with warmth and bloom. Each act is complete on one of the four cassette sides.

Otello: highlights.
*** Decca SET/*KCET* 632 (from above set cond. Solti).

A generous sampler of the Solti recording, including the *Willow song* and *Ave Maria* to show the beautifully sung and moving contribution of Margaret Price as Desdemona. Here the spectacle of the opening is less impressively contained on cassette than on the LP, but otherwise the vividly brilliant recording is common to both.

Rigoletto (complete).

(M) **(*) RCA RL 42865 (2) [LSC 7027].
Merrill, Moffo, Kraus, Flagello, RCA
Italiana Op. Ch. and O., Solti.

**(*) DG 2740 225/*3371 054* [*3*] [id.].
Cappuccilli, Cotrubas, Domingo, Ob-
raztsova, Ghiaurov, Moll, Schwarz, V.
State Op. Ch., VPO, Giulini.

(M) **(*) Ph. 6747 407/*7650 016* (2) [id.].
Capecchi, D'Angelo, Tucker, Sardi,
Ch. and O. of San Carlo Th. of Naples,
Molinari-Pradelli.

(M) (***) HMV SLS/*TC-SLS* 5018 (3).
Callas, Gobbi, Di Stefano, Zaccaria,
Ch. and O. of La Scala, Milan, Serafin
(with recital by Callas: arias from ROS-
SINI: *Il Barbiere di Siviglia*; MEYER-
BEER: *Dinorah*; DELIBES: *Lakmé*;
VERDI: *I Vespri siciliani* (***)).

*(*) HMV SLS 5193 (3) [Ang. SZX
3782]. Milnes, Sills, Kraus, Ramey,
Dunn, Amb. Op. Ch., Philh. O.,
Rudel.

Robert Merrill sang Rigoletto in a very
early RCA LP version of *Rigoletto*, but
if anything this reissued set from the mid-
sixties is even more impressive with its
rich flow of tone and clean-styled musical
strength. The Gilda of Anna Moffo is
enchanting; Joan Sutherland, on her first
Decca set (GOS 655/7), may have been
more dreamily beautiful, but helped by
the rest of the production Moffo gives a
firmer interpretation. Admittedly she is
not always helped by Solti's conducting,
for he seems determined to rush everyone
on, and his beat is often too stiff for
middle-period Verdi. But that is a comparatively small price to pay, for Solti's
briskness brings the compensation that a
complete performance, with only the
barest 'statutory' cuts, is fitted on four
sides with the breaks coming between
acts. The recording is very good for its
period, if not quite so realistic as Sutherland's newest Decca (see below), which
remains first choice; but at medium price
this can carry a strong recommendation.

Giulini, ever thoughtful for detail,
directs a distinguished performance.
Speeds tend to be slow, phrases are
beautifully shaped, and, with fine playing
from the Vienna Philharmonic, the
dynamics are subtle rather than dramatic. The conductor seems determined to
get away from any idea of *Rigoletto* as
melodrama, but in doing that he misses
the red-blooded theatricality of Verdi's
concept, the basic essential. It may be
consistent with Giulini's view but it
further reduces the dramatic impact that
Cappuccilli with his unsinister voice
makes the hunchback a noble figure from
first to last, while Domingo, ever intelligent, makes a reflective rather than an
extrovert Duke. Cotrubas is a touching
Gilda, but the close balance of her voice
is not helpful, and the topmost register is
not always comfortable. The recording,
made in the Musikverein in Vienna, has
the voices well to the fore, with much
reverberation on the instruments behind.
Although the cassette transfer level is not
high – to accommodate the recording's
wide dynamic range – the soloists are
naturally caught and have good presence.
Some orchestral detail at pianissimo
levels is not as cleanly defined as it might
be, but the sound overall is sophisticated,
and the opening, with the recessed stage
band, is given impressive perspective.

The Philips set with Capecchi, D'Angelo and Tucker dates from 1968 and was
first issued in stereo on three super-
bargain discs together costing only
slightly more than one premium-priced
LP at that time. The present reissue is at
medium price, and the recording has been
successfully retransferred on to four
sides. (It includes all the traditional cuts.)
The performance is not always polished
but it is vigorously red-blooded, with a
robust, yet not unstylish Duke from
Tucker. D'Angelo's Gilda may have a
touch of the soubrette at her first entry,
but she soon settles down, and her
beautifully sung *Caro nome* is a highlight.
The star of the set is Renato Capecchi,
whose portrayal of the name part is
rivetingly dramatic. The recording is
rather over-resonant but still fully

acceptable at budget price. The cassettes have less edge on top than the discs – the transfer level is only modest – but the sound is not muffled. However, in the medium price-range this does not match the RCA Solti issue, also on two discs.

There has never been a more compelling performance of the title role in *Rigoletto* than that of Gobbi on his classic Scala set of the fifties, originally mono, here given a generally effective stereo transcription. At every point, in almost every single phrase, Gobbi finds extra meaning in Verdi's vocal lines, with the widest range of tone-colour employed for expressive effect. Callas, though not naturally suited to the role of the wilting Gilda, is compellingly imaginative throughout, and Di Stefano gives one of his finer performances. The inclusion of some of Callas's best aria recordings of the late fifties is most welcome. The tape transfer has more presence for the solo voices and chorus than in some other EMI transfers in this vintage series, but it is not without a degree of roughness at peaks. Gobbi's voice is very well caught, however. The cassette layout is on three sides, with the recital (less smoothly transferred) on side four.

Rudel's version on HMV, well recorded, can be recommended to devotees of Beverly Sills but not really to anyone else. This was her last major opera recording before her retirement, and the voice as recorded was not beautiful, the tone shallow and often tremulous. Milnes as Rigoletto is just as strong as in the Bonynge/Sutherland set on Decca, and Kraus too effectively repeats the success of his singing on two earlier sets. But with Rudel's refreshing direction at times marred by excessive tensions, it is a set of limited value.

Still recommended: Sutherland's second Decca recording (SET 542/4/*K 2 A 3* [Lon. 13015/5-]), under Bonynge and with Milnes and Pavarotti, remains a clear first choice, fresh, dramatic and urgently enjoyable and with fine, atmospheric recording on both disc and tape.

Rigoletto: highlights.
**(*) DG 2537/*3306* 057 (from above set cond. Giulini).

The highlights from the Giulini set represent tenor and soprano rather more effectively than Rigoletto himself. The variety of expression of Domingo's performance is well caught in his three arias as well as the quartet, and though the same reservations have to be made about Cotrubas's performance as in the complete set – largely a question of recording balance – it is good to have her two big arias as well as her duets with Rigoletto. The cassette transfer is fully acceptable but rather less vivid than the disc.

Simon Boccanegra (complete).
⊛*** DG 2709 071 (3)/*3371 032* [id.]. Cappuccilli, Freni, Ghiaurov, Van Dam, Carreras, Ch. and O. of La Scala, Milan, Abbado.

Abbado's recording of *Simon Boccanegra*, directly reflecting the superb production which the Scala company brought to London, is one of the most beautiful Verdi sets ever made. From this one can appreciate not just the vigour of the composer's imagination but the finesse of the colouring, instrumental as well as vocal. Under Abbado the playing of the orchestra is brilliantly incisive as well as refined, so that the drama is underlined by extra sharpness of focus. The cursing of Paolo after the great Council Chamber Scene makes the scalp prickle, with the chorus muttering in horror and the bass clarinet adding a sinister comment, here beautifully moulded. Cappuccilli, always intelligent, gives a far more intense and illuminating performance than the one he recorded for RCA earlier in his career. He may not match Gobbi in range of colour and detail, but he too gives focus to the performance, and Ghiaurov as Fiesco sings beautifully too, though again not so characterfully as Christoff on the deleted HMV set. Freni as Amelia sings with freshness and clarity, while Van Dam is an impressive Paolo. With electrically intense choral singing too, this is a set to put alongside Abbado's superb *Macbeth* with the same company. The cassettes – because of the modest transfer level – have not quite the sharpness of detail of the discs, but solo voices are naturally caught and the distant choral perspectives are convincing.

Stiffelio (complete).
*** Ph. 6769 039/*7699 127* (2) [id.]. Carreras, Sass, Manuguerra, Ganzarolli, V. ORF Ch. and SO, Gardelli.

Coming just before the great trio of masterpieces, *Rigoletto*, *Il Trovatore* and *La Traviata*, *Stiffelio* was a total failure at its first performance in 1850. It was too much to expect either the Italian censor or the public to accept a tale involving a Protestant pastor and his unfaithful wife. To make *Aroldo* six years later the score was in effect destroyed, and only through the discovery of two copyists' scores in the 1960s was a revival made possible. Though it lacks some of the beauties of *Aroldo*, *Stiffelio* is yet a sharper, more telling work, largely because of the originality of the relationships and the superb final scene when Stiffelio reads from the pulpit the parable of the woman taken in adultery. Gardelli directs a fresh performance, at times less lively than Queler's of *Aroldo* but with more consistent singing, notably from Carreras and Manuguerra. First-rate recording, although – as is so often the case with Philips – the low-level cassette transfer has less upper range and sparkle than the discs, as can be heard immediately in the overture.

La Traviata (complete).
*** Decca Dig. D 212 D 3 (3)/*K 212 K 32* (2) [Lon. LDR 73002]. Sutherland, Pavarotti, Manuguerra, L. Op. Ch., Nat. PO, Bonynge.
**(*) HMV Dig. SLS 5240 (3)/*TCC-SLS 5240* (2) [Ang. DSX 3920]. Scotto, Kraus, Bruson, Amb. Op. Ch., Philh. O., Muti.
**(*) HMV SLS/*TC-SLS* 5097 (3) [Ang. S 3623]. Los Angeles, Del Monte, Sereni, Ch. and O. of Rome Op., Serafin.
**(*) DG 2707 103/*3370 024* (2) [id.]. Cotrubas, Domingo, Milnes, Bav. State Op. Ch. and O., Carlos Kleiber.
(***) HMV mono RLS/*TC-RLS* 757 (2). Callas, Kraus, Sereni, Ch. and O. of San Carlos Op., Lisbon, Ghione.

Sutherland's second recording of the role of Violetta has a breadth and exuberance beyond what she achieved in her earlier version of 1963 conducted by John Pritchard. This *Traviata* is dominated by the grand lady that Sutherland makes her. Some of the supremely tender moments of her earlier recording – *Ah dite alla giovine* in the Act 2 duet with Germont, for example – are more straightforward this time, but the mooning manner is dispelled, the words are clearer, and the richness and command of the singing put this among the very finest of Sutherland's later recordings. Pavarotti too, though he overemphasizes *Dei miei bollenti spiriti*, sings with splendid panache as Alfredo. Manuguerra as Germont lacks something in authority, but the firmness and clarity are splendid. Bonynge's conducting is finely sprung, the style direct, the speeds often spacious in lyrical music, generally undistracting. The digital recording is outstandingly vivid and beautifully balanced. The cassettes too offer Decca's best quality in the main, and the layout is ideal, with acts tailored to side-ends. Surprisingly, however, there is some peaking on vocal climaxes, notably in *Ah fors'è lui*; and the libretto supplied with the cassettes is below this company's highest standard, with noticeably small print, especially in the notes.

The alternative digital set from HMV is also splendidly recorded, the sound atmospheric as well as clear. With incisive conducting, full of dramatic contrasts, with exhilaratingly alert and polished singing from the Ambrosian Opera Chorus, and with finely detailed characterization from the principals, which – if flawed – is always deeply expressive, the Muti set may for many be a first choice. Sadly the evenness and beauty of Scotto's voice often disappear under pressure here, although squally moments are relatively few. Kraus makes a sensitive Alfredo and Bruson a thoughtful Germont *père*. On the chrome tapes – admirably laid out – the sound is vividly clear, with excellent detail and focus.

Even when Victoria de los Angeles made this HMV recording in the late fifties, the role of Violetta lay rather high for her voice. Nonetheless it drew from her much beautiful singing, not least in the coloratura display at the end of Act 1, which, though it may lack easily ringing top notes, has delightful sparkle and flexibility. As to the characterization, Los Angeles was a far more sympathetically tender heroine than is common, and though neither the tenor nor the baritone begins to match her in artistry, their performances are both sympathetic and feeling, thanks in part to the masterly conducting of Serafin. All the traditional cuts are made, not just the second stanzas. The sound on both tape and disc is vivid and clear and seldom betrays the age of the recording.

For some, Cotrubas makes an ideal heroine in this opera, but what is disappointing in the DG recording is that the microphone-placing exaggerates technical flaws, so that not only is her breathing too often audible, her habit of separating coloratura with intrusive aitches is underlined, and the vibrato becomes too obvious at times. Such is her magic that some will forgive the faults, for her characterization combines both strength and vulnerability. But Carlos Kleiber's direction is equally controversial, with more than a hint of Toscanini-like rigidity in the party music,

and an occasionally uncomfortable insistence on discipline. The characteristic contributions of Domingo and Milnes, both highly commendable, hardly alter the issue. The recording suggests overreliance on multi-channel techniques. However, this has the advantage that the sound on disc and cassette is very closely matched, crisp and clear if artificially balanced.

Recorded at a live performance in March 1958, Callas's Lisbon-made version is uniquely valuable in spite of very rough sound. Here far more than in her earlier Cetra recording of this opera one can appreciate the intensity which made this one of her supreme roles, with exquisite detail conveying fleeting emotions even in such an obvious passage as the *Brindisi*. Kraus is a fresh, stylish Alfredo, Sereni a positive Germont, more characterful than in the HMV set with Los Angeles. For Callas admirers – who will not object to the occasional ugliness – it is an essential set. The cassettes, like the discs, reflect the boxy quality of the basic recording; intrusive audience noises and insecure balance are a drawback to concentration.

La Traviata (complete; in English).
*** HMV SLS/*TC-SLS* 5216 (2). Masterson, Brecknock, Du Plessis, E. Nat. Op. Ch. and O., Mackerras.

The latterday economics of the gramophone have allowed few complete opera recordings in English, and this exceptional set, like the *Ring* cycle under Reginald Goodall, was recorded with the help of the Peter Moores Foundation. Unlike the *Ring* cycle, however, it is a studio performance, and it is beautifully balanced and refined in detail. Mackerras directs a vigorous, colourful reading which brings out the drama, and Valerie Masterson is at last given the chance on record she has so long deserved. The voice is beautifully – if not always very characterfully – caught, and John Brecknock makes a fine Alfredo, most effective in the final scene. Christian Du Plessis's baritone is less suitable for recording, but the conviction of the whole enterprise is infectious. Clear as most of the words are, it is a pity that no libretto is included, English or Italian, and be warned, Verdi in English has a way of sounding on record rather like Gilbert and Sullivan. The vivid cassettes match the discs closely.

La Traviata: highlights.

(M) **(*) HMV SXLP/*TC-SXLP* 30305 (from above set with Los Angeles, cond. Serafin).

**(*) DG 2537/*3306* 047 [2531/*3301* 170] (from above set with Cotrubas, cond. Kleiber).

Victoria de los Angeles' voice was not ideally suited to the role of Violetta, but on record she was a unique charmer. This medium-price selection can be recommended to anyone who wants a sample rather than the complete set, though the tenor and baritone are safe rather than imaginative. Good fifties recording, and an excellent cassette.

Though Cotrubas as Violetta is unflatteringly recorded, hers is certainly a performance, touching and intense, which deserves study, and this collection of highlights makes a convenient substitute for the complete set. It is valuable too for Carlos Kleiber's distinctive reading and the firm, musicianly contributions of Domingo and Milnes.

Il Trovatore (complete).

**(*) Ph. Dig. 6769/*7654* 063 (3) [id.]. Ricciarelli, Carreras, Mazurok, Toczyska, R O H C G Ch. and O., Colin Davis.

(M) (***) HMV SLS/*TC-SLS* 869 (3). Callas, Di Stefano, Barbieri, Panerai, Ch. and O. of La Scala, Milan, Karajan (with recital by Callas: arias from BOITO: *Mefistofele*; CATALANI: *La Wally*; CILEA: *Adriana Lecouvreur*; GIORDANO: *Andrea Chénier*(***)).

**(*) HMV SLS/*TC-SLS* 5111 (3) [Ang. SX/*4X3X* 3855]. Leontyne Price, Bonisolli, Obraztsova, Cappuccilli, Raimondi, German Op. Ch., Berlin PO, Karajan.

** Decca D 82 D 3 (3)/*K 82 K 32* (2) [Lon. 13124/5-]. Sutherland, Pavarotti, Horne, Wixell, Ghiaurov, L. Op. Ch., Nat. PO, Bonynge.

Caruso's statement that all *Il Trovatore* needs is the four greatest singers in the world is an obvious over-simplification, but this demand is still most nearly satisfied by Mehta's RCA set with Leontyne Price, Domingo, Milnes and Cossotto (an electrifying Azucena), which remains a clear first choice (SER 5586/8 [LSC 6194]).

Davis's is a refreshing and direct reading which in many ways is the antithesis of Karajan's Berlin version with its overblown sound. The refinement of the digital recording makes for wide, clean separation, but with a low level of cut and backward placing of the orchestra, the result is rather wanting in dramatic impact. Even the *Anvil chorus* sounds rather clinical, and other important numbers too lack the necessary swagger. Ricciarelli's Leonora is most moving, conveying an element of vulnerability in the character. Carreras lacks the full confidence of a natural Manrico; he is less effective in the big extrovert moments, best in such inward numbers as *Ah si ben mio*. Toczyska's voice is presented rather grittily in the role of Azucena. Mazurok similarly is not flattered by the microphones. At least with clean, refined ensemble – helped by these performers' stage experience – this emerges as the opposite of a hackneyed opera.

The combination of Karajan and Callas is formidably impressive. There is toughness and dramatic determination in Callas's singing, whether in the coloratura or in the dramatic passages, and this gives the heroine an unsuspected depth of character which culminates in

Callas's fine singing of an aria which used often to be cut entirely – *Tu vedrai che amore in terra*, here with its first stanza alone included. Barbieri is a magnificent Azucena, Panerai a strong, incisive Count, and Di Stefano at his finest as Manrico. Though the recording, originally mono, is limited, it is superbly balanced and surprisingly clear in inner detail. Unfortunately the cassette transfer is made at rather too high a level, and the sound is not always comfortable.

The new Karajan set with Leontyne Price promised much but proves disappointing, largely because of the thickness and strange balances of the recording, the product of multi-channel techniques exploited over-enthusiastically. So the introduction to Manrico's aria *Di quella pira* provides full-blooded orchestral sound, but then the orchestra fades down for the entry of the tenor, who in any case is in coarse voice. In other places he sings more sensitively, but at no point does this version match that of Mehta on RCA. If you must have Karajan, go for the stereo transcription reissue of the EMI set with Callas, which despite dated recording is clearer on detail than this modern offering.

Bonynge in most of his opera sets has been unfailingly urgent and rhythmic, but his account of *Il Trovatore* is at an altogether lower level of intensity, with elegance rather than dramatic power the dominant quality. Nor does the role of Leonora prove very apt for the present-day Sutherland; the coloratura passages are splendid, but a hint of unsteadiness is present in too much of the rest. Pavarotti for the most part sings superbly, but he falls short, for example, in the semi-quaver groups of *Di quella pira*, and, like Sutherland, Marilyn Horne as Azucena does not produce consistently firm tone. Wixell as the Count sings intelligently, but a richer tone is needed. Most recommendable in the set is the complete ballet music, more brilliantly recorded as well as better played than the rest. Discs and cassettes are closely matched.

Il Trovatore: highlights.
**(*) Decca SET/*KCET* 631 (from above set cond. Bonynge).

The selection from Bonynge's Decca set is specially valuable as a reminder of Sutherland's Leonora. The size of the voice as well as its flexibility are splendidly caught, though a latter-day beat afflicts the more sustained passages, and Bonynge does not conduct with his usual urgency. Pavarotti may be stretched by the role of Manrico, but he is nearly always magnificent. Horne is represented by her powerful *Stride la vampa*, Wixell by an undernourished *Il balen*. Excellent recording, with nothing to choose between disc and cassette versions.

Il Trovatore: highlights (in English).
(M) **(*) HMV Green. ESD/*TC-ESD* 7027. Fretwell, Johnson, Craig, Glossop, McIntyre, Hunter, Sadler's Wells Op. Ch. and O., Moores.

Anyone seeking a potted version of *Il Trovatore* in English should be well satisfied with this vividly recorded HMV Greensleeve record or cassette. The words are admirably clear and there is plenty of drama in the presentation. Away from the stage some of the singing does not stand up too well, but Elizabeth Fretwell is undoubtedly both strong and stylish, even if *Tacea la notte* is rather shaky. Charles Craig is as ringing and well-controlled a tenor as you will find anywhere. Patricia Johnson and Peter Glossop are not quite up to their stage form, but their singing has plenty of conviction, and the presence and depth of the recording are very persuasive, with excellent clarity when the chorus is in distant perspective. Indeed the ensembles, the *Miserere* and the finale to the Convent Scene, have splendid attack, while the famous *Home to our mountains* duet is beautifully sung.

COLLECTIONS

Arias: *Un Ballo in maschera: Forse la soglia . . . Ma se m'è forza perderti. I due Foscari: Ah si, ch'io sento ancora . . . Dal più remoto esiglio. Luisa Miller: Oh! fede negar potessi . . . Quando le sere. Macbeth: O figli . . . Ah, la paterna mano.*
*** Decca SXL/*KSXC* 6377 [Lon. 26087/5-]. Pavarotti, V. Op. O., Downes – DONIZETTI: *Arias.****

Like the Donizetti couplings Pavarotti's singing in this early recital shows a freshly exciting voice used without vulgarity, if sometimes with an element of reserve. The recording is excellent on disc and cassette alike.

'*Heroines*': Arias: *Don Carlos: Tu che le vanità. Ernani: Surta è la notte . . . Ernani! Ernani, involami. Macbeth: Nel dì della vittoria . . . Vieni, t'affretta; La luce langue; Una macchia è qui tuttora! (Sleepwalking Scene). Nabucco: Ben io t'invenni . . . Anch'io dischiuso un giorno.*
*** HMV ΛSD/*TC-ASD* 3817. Callas, Philh. O., Rescigno.

Much of this is Callas at her very finest. Dismiss the top-note wobbles from mind, and the rest has one enthralled by the vividness of characterization as well as the musical imagination. It is sad that Callas did not record the role of Lady Macbeth complete. Here *La luce langue* is not so intense as the Act 1 aria and the Sleepwalking Scene, which are both unforgettable. Abigaille, Elvira and Elisabetta all come out as real figures, sharply individual. Finely balanced recording. The cassette transfer is vibrantly vivid, but at vocal peaks there are hints that the level might with advantage have been just a trifle lower.

Arias: *Ernani: Surta è la notte;*

Ernani, involami. I Vespri siciliani: Mercè, dilette.
(M) *** Decca Jub. JB/*KJBC* 97 [Lon. 25111/5-]. Sutherland, Paris Conservatoire O., Santi – DONIZETTI: *Linda di Chamounix; Lucia: arias.*⊛ ***

It is primarily for the Donizetti items that this magnificent recital is famous, but these two Verdi arias show a comparable level of memorability, with superb singing throughout. The cassette transfer has been remastered and now matches the disc closely.

Choruses from (i) *Aïda;* (ii) *I Lombardi; Macbeth; Nabucco; La Traviata; Il Trovatore.*
*** HMV ASD/*TC-ASD* 3979 [Ang. SZ 37795]. Philh. or New Philh. O., Muti, with (i) ROHCG Ch.; (ii) Amb. Op. Ch.

A red-blooded selection of choruses, some extracted from Muti's complete sets. The singing is both vibrant and atmospheric; the famous *Hebrew slaves' chorus* from *Nabucco* (*Va, pensiero*) is a highlight. The selection seems to emphasize Verdi's melodramatic qualities rather than the subtleties of his choral writing as in Abbado's famous collection with the Chorus and Orchestra of La Scala, Milan (DG 2530 549/*3300 495*, awarded a rosette in the second edition of the *Penguin Stereo Record Guide*). But this programme is enjoyable for its spirit and colourful projection. The sound is appropriately ripe and brilliant; the focus on cassette is at times less sharp than on disc, but the sound has plenty of body and impact.

Choruses from *I due Foscari; Ernani; I Lombardi; Luisa Miller; Macbeth; Nabucco; Il Trovatore; I Vespri siciliani.*
**(*) HMV ASD/*TC-ASD* 3811. Welsh Nat. Op. Ch., Armstrong.

The Welsh National Opera made its initial reputation by the strength of its chorus work, and while these performances are not so refined as Abbado's (see above) they are for the most part vivid and lusty, with plenty of character and rhythmic feeling. The natural eloquence of the Welsh often surfaces in lyrical moments, but the famous *Va, pensiero* from *Nabucco*, although effective, is not as memorable as one might have expected. The witches in *Macbeth*, however, are rather quaintly characterized to provide a moment of light relief. Excellent recording, full and clear, and a good tape (especially impressive on side two, when the transfer level rises).

Victoria, Tomas Luis de
(*c.* 1548–1611)

Ascendens Christus; Ave Maria; Estote fortes in bello; Gaudent in coelis; Hic vir despiciens mundum; Iste sanctus pro lege Dei; Veni, sponsa Christi. Litaniae de Beata Virgine; Magnificat primi toni; O Magnum mysterium; O quam gloriosum (Mass and motet); *Requiem Mass* (sex vocibus).
(M) **(*) Argo ZK 70/1. St John's College Ch., Guest.

This set draws together two separate issues by the St John's College Choir under George Guest, and while there are some reservations about the style of these performances, with so little of Victoria's music available in really distinguished versions this medium-priced reissue must be accorded a warm welcome. The motets can be numbered among the finest Victoria gave us, and the rest of the music too is of the highest quality. The St John's Choir sing well in tune, but their approach is often too 'Anglican' for this passionate Spanish music. The choirboys are sometimes flabby in tone (especially in the singing of the plainchant), while the men have big vibratos, and these two elements never really mix. But the motets fare much better than the *Requiem* and here the performances are often admirable in their way. The recording throughout is clear and well-focused, and if one accepts the fact that English choirs lack the harsh lines drawn by the firmer-toned Spanish bodies, there is little to cavil at. This remains highly suitable for a collector who wants to sample the composer or his period.

Missa pro defunctis.
*** HM 1C 065 99602. Escalonia a Capella Ch., Montserrat Capella de Musica, Segarra.

This performance has plenty of atmosphere, and the fiery, untamed quality of the boy trebles is distinctive and exciting. Intonation is not always perfect, but the blend and timbre of these singers are such that few will be unmoved. The recording has greater ambience than clarity, but there is a sense of occasion here that is not often conveyed on record in this repertoire.

Vierne, Louis (1870–1937)

(Organ) *Symphony No. 1 in D min., Op. 14; Légende, Op. 31/13.*
*** Mer. E 77011. Sanger.

A pupil of Franck and Widor, Vierne was a commanding figure in the world of French organ music in his day. Since our last edition, there has been welcome evidence of greater interest in his work. David Sanger has embarked on a project to record all six organ symphonies, using as fill-ups some of the *Pièces libres*, Op. 31. Here as in the companion volumes, he appears whole-heartedly identified with this repertoire, and readers unfamiliar with Vierne will find that Sanger leaves you sharing his evident enthusiasm for this music. He has recorded all his Meridian recitals – excellently balanced they are too – on the organ of the Italian Church of St Peter in Clerkenwell, London, an instrument well suited to the demands of this music. Vierne's style is often more harmonically sophisticated than the newcomer to this repertoire would suspect, and Sanger captures its quasi-improvisational yet thoughtful quality admirably. The *D minor Symphony* dates from the turn of the century and was dedicated to Guilmant. Its sense of power and its quiet originality make it well worth seeking out.

Symphony No. 2 in E min., Op. 20; Arabesque, Op. 31/15.
*** Mer. E 77021. Sanger.

The *Second Symphony* is a finely wrought piece, perhaps more concentrated than its predecessor and played with no less sympathy by David Sanger. It receives a recording of excellent depth and range.

Symphony No. 3 in F sharp min., Op. 28; Pièces en style libre, Op. 31: Prélude; Scherzetto; Le Carillon de Longpont; Berceuse.
*** Mer. E 77024. Sanger.

Symphony No. 3; Pièces, Op. 31: Cortège; Berceuse; Divertissement; Le Carillon de Longpont.
(M) ** Saga 5456. Wills.

In the *Third Symphony*, which is demanding both technically and musically, David Sanger again proves the equal of the challenge. Though this is generally not as dark a work as the wartime *Fourth*, it is distinguished by moments of genuine depth. There is no cause to complain of the sound quality, which maintains the high standards Meridian have set themselves.

Arthur Wills also couples the *Third Symphony* with some of the Op. 31 *Pièces*, playing them on the organ of Ely Cathedral to magnificent effect. He too is an eloquent exponent of this repertoire, but he is less well served by the engineers than his rival on Meridian; the sound is less refined and detail is less transparent than is ideal.

Vieuxtemps, Henri
(1820–81)

Violin concertos Nos. 4 in D min., Op. 31; 5 in A min., Op. 37.
*** HMV ASD/*TC-ASD* 3555 [Ang. S/4*XS* 37484]. Perlman, Orchestre de Paris, Barenboim.

Vieuxtemps wrote six violin concertos, and it is surprising that so few violinists have attempted to resurrect more than the odd one. This coupling of the two best-known is not only apt; it presents superbly stylish readings, with Perlman both aristocratically pure of tone and intonation and passionate of expression. In his accompaniments Barenboim draws warmly romantic playing from the Paris Orchestra. Warm recording to match. The cassette is less refined than the disc, with a degree of fierceness on the solo image.

Villa-Lobos, Heitor
(1887–1959)

(i) *Guitar concerto. Étude in C sharp min; 5 Preludes; Suite populaire brésilienne: Schottisch-Chôro.*
*** RCA RL/*RK* 43518 [LSC 3231]. Bream, (i) with LSO, Previn.

839

A highly distinguished account of the *Guitar concerto*, a work more striking for its atmosphere than for its actual invention. The rest of the programme also shows Bream in inspirational form; several of the *Preludes* are hauntingly memorable when the concentration of the playing is so readily communicated. The cassette transfer is of excellent quality, one of RCA's best, and it matches the disc closely.

Harmonica concerto.
*** Argo ZRG 905. Reilly, L. Sinf., Atherton – ARNOLD and BENJAMIN: *Concertos.****

Villa-Lobos wrote his concerto in 1955 for the American virtuoso John Sebastian. For a long time the score was lost until it was rescued from oblivion by Tommy Reilly, who plays it here. He finds a natural affinity for its rhapsodic pastoral moods, and the beautiful orchestral playing from the London Sinfonietta under David Atherton provides an understanding backcloth for the soloist. Perhaps the music lacks something in contrast, for even the finale has not the boisterous energy of the coupled works by Malcolm Arnold and Arthur Benjamin. But the performance here is persuasive and it is superbly recorded.

12 Études for guitar; Suite populaire brésilienne.
*** RCA RL/*RK* 12499 [ARL 1/*ARK 1* 2499]. Bream.

Bream engages the listener's attention from the opening of the first study and holds it to the last. The vigour and energy of the playing are matched by its spontaneity, and there is considerable subtlety of colour. The recording is immaculate, and it has transferred cleanly and realistically to cassette. The *Suite* is no less strongly characterized, although the music is lighter in mood and less concentrated in structure. The recording here is slightly more resonant, and effectively so. The only slight criticism of this issue is that the close microphones pick up fingerboard noises, which might disturb some listeners.

Études Nos. 1, 3, 5–8, 11, 12; Gavota-Chôro; Mazurka-Chôro; 5 Preludes; Schottisch-Chôro; Suite populaire brésilienne: Valsa-Chôro.
(M) ** Saga 5453. Hill.

An ambitious recital. Eric Hill is especially good in the *Five Preludes*: these performances are first-class. He makes less of a case for the short lightweight pieces, but brings out the full character and contrasts inherent in the *Études*. The guitar is balanced very forwardly, and its closeness to the microphone reduces the range of dynamic in writing which sometimes demands strongly marked crescendos and diminuendos as part of its structure. The close balance also emphasizes odd fingerboard noises.

Vivaldi, Antonio
(1675–1741)

L'Estro armonico, Op. 3; La Stravaganza, Op. 4; The Four Seasons (from *The Trial between Harmony and Invention), Op. 8/1–4; La Cetra, Op. 9; Wind concertos, RV. 441, 443, 456, 498, 535, 539, 569, 574.*
(M) *** Argo D 101 D 10 (10) [id.]. Soloists, ASMF, Marriner or Iona Brown.

This admirable ten-disc set marks the outstanding achievement of the Academy of St Martin-in-the-Fields under Marriner and Iona Brown in the music of Vivaldi. Apart from an account of *The Four Seasons* which, after more than twelve years in the catalogue and against the most formidable competition, remains at the top of the recommended list, the box adds a marvellous miscellany of diverse wind concertos, with distinguished soloists, offering playing that is consistently alert, finely articulated and free from over-emphasis. The major collections of violin concertos, *L'Estro armonico* and *La Stravaganza* (the latter given a rosette in our second edition), are rewarding not only for the solo playing and the ever resilient accompaniments but also for the highly imaginative continuo playing, using cello and bassoon as well as harpsichord and organ. *La Cetra*, directed by Iona Brown, is well up to the standard of the rest of the series. With outstanding recording this is perhaps the most distinguished Vivaldi compilation in the catalogue.

L'Estro armonico, Op. 3; La Stravaganza, Op. 4.
(M) *** Ph. 6768 009 (5). Michelucci, Gallozzi, Ayo, Cotogni, Colandreo, I Musici.

The Vivaldi Edition, which Philips marketed in 1978 to mark the tercentenary of the composer's birth, drew on earlier performances familiar to collectors. Suffice it now to say that this is still one of the most economical and by no means the least musically satisfying ways of acquiring a basic Vivaldi collection. These are fresh and lively performances; melodies are finely drawn and there is little hint of the routine which occasionally surfaces in I Musici – and, for that matter, in Vivaldi himself. Where competition arises, this group often yields to the Academy of St Martin-in-the-Fields, who have crisper textures and convey greater enthusiasm, but here I Musici are a good choice and they are certainly thoroughly recommendable to collectors of the series.

Reminder: The outstanding ASMF recordings under Marriner are still available on Argo: *L'Estro armonico* on ZRG 733/4/*K 119 K 22* and *La Stravaganza* on ZRG 800/1.

L'Estro armonico, Op. 3 (complete).
*** O-L D 245 D 2/*K 245 K 22* (2). Holloway, Huggett, Mackintosh, Wilcock, AcAM, Hogwood.
**(*) DG 2709 100/*3371 052* (3). Brandis, Spierer, Berlin PO (members).

L'Estro armonico: Concertos Nos. 1, 3–6 and 9.
(M) ** DG Arc. 2547/*3347* 012. [id.]. Soloists, Lucerne Festival Strings, Baumgartner.

L'Estro armonico: Concertos Nos. 5–8, 10 and 12.
**(*) DG 2531/*3301* 334 [id.]. Brandis, Spierer, Berlin PO (members).

L'Estro armonico: Concerto No. 10 in B min. for 4 violins.
(M) *** HMV SXLP/*TC-SXLP* 30294 [Ang. S 36103]. Menuhin, Masters, Goren, Humphreys, Bath Festival CO – BACH and HANDEL: *Concertos for violin and oboe*.***

Even those who normally fight shy of 'authentic' performances of baroque music with their astringent timbres and purposive avoidance of romantic gestures will find it hard not to respond to the sparkling set of Vivaldi's Op. 3 from the Academy of Ancient Music directed by Christopher Hogwood. The captivating lightness of the solo playing and the crispness of articulation of the accompanying group bring music-making that combines joyful vitality with the authority of scholarship. Textures are always transparent, but there is no lack of body to the ripieno (even though there is only one instrument to each part). Hogwood's continuo is first-class, varying between harpsichord and organ, the latter used to add colour as well as substance. The balance is excellent, and the whole effect is exhilarating. While some listeners may need to adjust to the style of playing in slow movements, the underlying expressive feeling is never in doubt, and in the allegros the nimble flights of bravura from the four soloists are a constant delight. The recording is superb. Apart from the truthfulness of individual timbres there is a striking depth of acoustic, with the solo instruments given a backwards and forwards perspective as well as the expected antiphonal interplay. The overall effect is intimate yet spacious. The cassette transfer is of the Decca group's highest quality. The upper partials may be fractionally cleaner on disc, but the range, body and transparency of the sound on tape are very impressive, and with a slight reduction of treble the recording yields a demonstration standard.

As might be expected, the playing on the Berlin Philharmonic recording is superbly polished, with firm rhythms – perhaps at times a shade too firm – and the slow-movement cantilenas expressively shaped. But this is very much a German view. The continuo lacks creative importance, and there is a persistent impression that one is listening to Telemann rather than Vivaldi. The recording is first-class on both disc and cassette. Those interested in sampling the German tradition in this repertoire might do better with the single disc (or tape), which has a well-chosen selection and matches the complete set in all respects.

The Lucerne performances are well made and quite stylish (though not 'authentic', in spite of the label), with good solo playing. The impression is of sound team-work rather than extrovert manners. Good recording and generous measure at medium price. The tape is of excellent quality, clear and clean and with excellent body and range.

Menuhin's performance of the *B minor Concerto* is part of an entertaining mixed concert of baroque concertos which he shares with Leon Goossens. The performance is striking and the sound is brighter and fresher than when this compilation first appeared in the early sixties,

and the cassette matches the disc closely.

12 Concertos, Op. 7; The Trial between Harmony and Invention, Op. 8 (complete).
(M) **(*) Ph. 6768 011 (5) [id.]. Accardo, Ayo, Holliger, I Musici.

The Op. 7 set is relatively unfamiliar and by no means unrewarding; indeed much of the invention is vital and appealing. The playing of Accardo and Holliger is altogether masterly, and they have fine rapport with their fellow-musicians in I Musici. The Op. 8 set is, of course, recorded in abundance, and Ayo's version of *The Four Seasons* is more than twenty years old (presumably the later recording was not available to the planners of this compilation on contractual grounds). It is a smooth rather than imaginative account, though the sound is still more than acceptable and the playing of Ayo himself is thoroughly polished. The ensemble is at times a shade heavy-handed in the remaining concertos of Op. 8, but there is still a great deal to enjoy in these performances, and though this would not necessarily be a first choice for Op. 8, the rewards of Op. 7 make a strong claim for this box.

The Trial between Harmony and Invention (*Il Cimento dell'armonia e dell'invenzione*), *Op. 8* (complete).
*** Tel. EK6/*MH4* 35386 (2) [id.]. Alice Harnoncourt, Schaeftlein, VCM, Nikolaus Harnoncourt.
**(*) CRD CRD 1025/*CRDC 4025* (Nos. 1–4; see also below); CRD 1048/9/*CRDC 4048 and 4049*, available separately (Nos. 5–10 and 11–12 plus *Flute concerto in D, RV.429*; *Cello concerto in B min., RV.424*). Standage, Preston, Pleeth, E. Concert, Pinnock.
**(*) Chan. DBR/*DBT* 3003 (3). Thomas, Digney, Bournemouth Sinf.
** Erato STU 70680 (3). Toso, Pierlot, I Sol. Ven., Scimone.

The first four concertos of Op. 8 are a set within a set, forming what is (understandably) Vivaldi's most popular work, *The Four Seasons*. Their imaginative power and their eloquence and tunefulness tend slightly to dwarf the remaining eight concertos, but there is some splendid music throughout the complete work, well worth exploring. The Telefunken box includes one of the most impressive accounts of *The Four Seasons* to be recorded since Marriner's famous 1970 version (see below). Alice Harnoncourt's timbre is leonine, and her tone production somewhat astringent, bringing out the pithiness of timbre inherent in her baroque instrument. But the dramatic style of the solo playing is at one with the vivid pictorialism of Vivaldi's imagery. The shepherd's dog in *Spring* barks vociferously, and the dance rhythms of the finale of the same concerto are extremely invigorating. The interpretative approach throughout emphasizes this element of contrast. The languorous opening of *Summer* makes a splendid foil for the storm and the buzzing insects, yet the zephyr breezes are wistfully gentle. The continuo uses a chamber organ, to great effect, and piquant touches of colour are added to the string textures. Concertos Nos. 9 and 12 are played on the oboe by Jürg Schaeftlein, who makes a first-class contribution, and this choice of instrumentation further varies the colouring of Vivaldi's score. The recording is excellent, bright, vivid and clean in the Telefunken manner. The cassette transfer was one of the earliest made on chromium dioxide tape and the wide frequency range is very obvious: indeed there is too much brilliance in the treble, and even with the controls in use a degree of edge remains on the sound picture.

The CRD version of *The Four Seasons* is also an imaginative one and like the Telefunken set it features a baroque violin. As this first disc (and cassette) was issued separately in advance of the other two it is considered below with the other

versions. The two remaining records of the set were then issued in a double sleeve, but the three cassettes are all individually packaged. Because six concertos are fitted on the second record and tape, the third is able to include two bonus concertos, of which the *Flute concerto* is particularly attractive. The performances throughout are alert and full of character, with eloquent slow movements. As on the Telefunken set, there is a quality of astringency to the sound, which emphasizes the neat, scaled-down imagery. The acoustic is comparatively dry, and although here too a chamber organ is used in the continuo to add extra touches of colour, there is little suggestion of fantasy or Mediterranean glow. Nevertheless these are undoubtedly distinguished performances, even if they are perhaps a little lacking in charm. The cassettes match the discs closely in quality.

The Bournemouth Sinfonietta set on Chandos is beautifully recorded and has much in its favour. The use of modern instruments does not preclude a keen sense of style, and the balance is convincing, with the continuo coming through not too insistently. The later concertos are particularly successful; No. 5 (*La Tempesta di mare*) and 6 (*Il Piacere*) are excellent, and there is some delectable oboe playing from John Digney in the final group. Allegros are alert without being rigid and slow movements are expressive, with musical phrasing and a fine sense of atmosphere. The drawback for most listeners will be the account of *The Four Seasons*, which is seen as part of the whole cycle rather than as individually dramatic. Ronald Thomas's approach emphasizes the music's breadth and lyricism rather than its colourful pictorialism, so that the shepherd's dog barks gently and the winds blow amiably, certainly never reaching gale force. In its way this is pleasing, but there remains an element of disappointment in the undercharacterization. The cassette transfer is very variable in level (the second side of *The Four Seasons* registers a big drop

843

after side one), and the degree of immediacy and range varies accordingly.

I Solisti Veneti under Claudio Scimone give a thoroughly sound and reliable account of Op. 8, and they are accorded very good sound. Piero Toso is a fine player, too, but the continuo realizations are less imaginative than is ideal. The set was recorded in the early 1970s.

The Four Seasons, Op. 8/1–4.
*** HMV ASD/*TC-ASD* 3293 [Ang. S/*4XS* 37053]. Perlman, LPO.
*** DG 2531/*3301* 287 [id.]. Kremer, LSO, Abbado.
*** DG Arc. Dig. 2534/*3311* 003 [id.]. Standage, E. Concert, Pinnock.
(M) *** Decca Jub. JB/*KJBC* 63. Kulka, Stuttgart CO, Münchinger.
(M) *** Ph. Fest. 6570/*7310* 061 [id.]. Szeryng, ECO.
*** Tel. AW6/*CX4* 42500. Alice Harnoncourt, VCM, Nikolaus Harnoncourt.
*** CRD CRD 1025/*CRDC 4025*. Standage, E. Concert, Pinnock.
(B) *** Con. CC/*CCT* 7527. Ferrari, Stuttgart Soloists, Couraud.
**(*) HMV Dig. ASD/*TCC-ASD* 3964 [Ang. DS 37765]. Menuhin, Camerata Lysy Gstaad, Lysy.
(M) **(*) Ph. Seq. 6527/*7311* 088. Ayo, I Musici.
** Delos Dig. DMS 3007 [id.]. Oliveira, LACO, Schwarz.
** Ph. 9500 717/*7300 809* [id.]. Iona Brown, ASMF.
** CBS 76795/*40-* [Col. XM 35122]. Stern, Jerusalem Music Centre CO, Pianka.
(M) * Decca VIV/*KVIC* 3 [Lon. STS 15539/5-]. Bean, New Philh. O., Stokowski.

Vivaldi's *Four Seasons* is still a work much more frequently heard on records (and even in the cinema) than in the concert hall. As can be seen above, it is often recorded, yet Marriner's Academy of St Martin-in-the-Fields account with Alan

Loveday (Argo ZRG/*KZRC* 654) continues to dominate the many available versions. It has an element of fantasy that makes the music sound utterly new and is full of imaginative touches, with Simon Preston subtly varying the continuo between harpsichord and organ. The opulence of string tone may be too romantic for some, but there is no self-indulgence in the interpretation, no sentimentality, for the contrasts are made sharper and fresher, not smoothed over. The cassette is not quite as clean as the disc (especially on side two), but is still thoroughly recommendable alongside it.

For collectors seeking a second opinion there is plenty of choice. Those looking for an account of the solo role from an artist of international fame might turn to the HMV set from Itzhak Perlman. His finesse as a great violinist is evident from first to last. Though some will demand more reticence in baroque concertos, Perlman's imagination holds the sequence superbly together, and there are many passages of pure magic, as in the central *Adagio* of *Summer*. With an intimate acoustic, the sound is never inflated but in scale and sharply defined. The cassette transfer, however, is very bright, less refined than the disc.

In the DG version by Gidon Kremer with the LSO under Claudio Abbado, it is obvious from the first bar that Abbado is the dominating partner. This is an enormously vital account, with great contrasts of tempo and dynamic. The dramatization of Vivaldi's detailed pictorial effects has never been more vivid; the vigour of the dancing peasants is surpassed by the sheer fury and violence of the summer storms. Yet the delicacy of the gentle zephyrs is matched by the hazy somnolence of the beautiful *Adagio* of *Autumn*. After a freezingly evocative opening to *Winter*, Abbado creates a mandolin-like pizzicato effect in the slow movement (taken faster than the composer's marking) to simulate a rainshower. The finale opens delicately, but at the close the listener is almost blown away by the winter gales. Kremer matches Abbado's vigour with playing that combines sparkling bravura and suitably evocative expressive moments. Given the projection of a brilliantly lit recording, the impact of this version is considerable. Leslie Pearson's nimble continuo, alternating organ and harpsichord, sometimes gets buried, but drama rather than subtlety is the keynote of this arresting account. The cassette matches the disc closely, a little mellower, but the difference is marginal.

The most recent of the 'authentic' performances – the Archive version by Simon Standage with the English Concert directed from the harpsichord by Trevor Pinnock – has the advantage of using a newly discovered set of parts found in Manchester's Henry Watson Music Library, which has additionally brought the correction of minor textual errors in the Le Cène text in normal use. The Archive performance also (minimally) introduces a second soloist and is played on period instruments. The players create a relatively intimate sound, though their approach is certainly not without drama, while the solo contribution has impressive flair and bravura. The overall effect is essentially refined, treating the pictorial imagery with subtlety. The result is less voluptuous than with Marriner, less individual than with Perlman, less vibrant than the version under Abbado, but it finds a natural balance between vivid projection and atmospheric feeling. The digital recording is firts-class on disc and chrome tape alike.

At medium price on Decca's Jubilee reissue, Konstanty Kulka gives a first-class solo performance, while Münchinger and the Stuttgart Chamber Orchestra, whose early LPs did so much to reawaken interest in Vivaldi, show that their stylish and lively manner is as compelling as ever, helped by vivid recording. Though this is brighter than many versions, it stands as one of the most satisfying. The cassette, like the disc, offers first-class sound; the transfer is fresh and

transparent, the continuo and inner detail coming through clearly.

Those wanting a mellower approach will find Szeryng's Festivo reissue a good alternative, and the only reservation is that the very soft-grained tone of the harpsichord in the continuo does not come through to the listener readily. But Szeryng's performances are eloquent and beautifully played, and the alert, resilient accompaniments are stylish. The sound is atmospheric, naturally balanced (although the violin is forward) and pleasingly resonant. Perhaps there is a degree too much reverberation, but the chamber proportions of the performance are retained.

Both Alice Harnoncourt on Telefunken and Simon Standage on CRD use baroque violins, and both versions are given clear, brilliant recordings. The Telefunken version is discussed above with the complete set of Op. 8. Pinnock (at the harpsichord) and his English Concert provide a convincingly 'authentic' backing for Standage, the somewhat abrasive string textures heightening the drama. The slow movement of *Autumn*, where the harpsichord plays simple arpeggios against the sustained strings, is most beautiful. But essentially this is a dramatic performance, strongly characterized. That is well illustrated by the *Adagio* of *Summer*, where the soloist is songfully poised while the bustling strings threaten the approaching storm, which when it arrives has the fury of a tempest. This same vigour produces elsewhere tempi that verge on being too fast, but the vivacity is never in doubt and the dark colouring from the lower strings in *tutti* is another mark of the special character of this account. The cassette transfer is admirably vivid and clear, although the treble needs just a little softening.

The bargain-priced Contour reissue has a great deal to offer. Neither soloist nor orchestra plays with the last degree of polish, but there is striking commitment to the music throughout. Witness the short slow movement of *Autumn*, where the intensity is beautifully controlled, or indeed the vigour of any of the allegros, where the players' enjoyment is obvious. The music-making is helped by the excellent recording, smooth and warm yet vivid, giving Ferrari a gleaming tonal line, and enough detail for the orchestra without spotlighting any lack of precision. With such good sound and genuine stylistic sympathy this is very competitive. The cassette transfer is less wide-ranging than the disc but quite acceptable.

Menuhin's digital recording is designed as much to provide a framework for the youthful Camerata Lysy as for its illustrious soloist, whose rhythmic control is not always stable (notably in the opening movement of *Autumn*). Nevertheless this is a characterfully extrovert account, robust and exuberant rather than refined. The continuo is not significant, and while Menuhin's directness communicates readily, this cannot be given an unqualified recommendation because, in spite of the brilliant digital clarity, detail is not registered very subtly. The chrome cassette has a slightly mellower image than the disc but retains all its other qualities.

Felix Ayo's performance with I Musici dates from the beginning of the sixties, but the warm, reverberant recording still sounds well. This will be enjoyed by those for whom richness of sound is paramount, even at the cost of vitality. Felix Ayo produces lovely tone throughout and he plays as stylishly as ever.

The Delos recording by Elmar Oliveira and the excellent Los Angeles Chamber Orchestra under Gerard Schwarz made the digital début of *The Four Seasons* in 1980. The recording is extremely brilliant, the sharp spotlighting of the soloist bringing a degree of steeliness to his upper range. Tempi too are extremely brisk throughout: extrovert bravura is the keynote here rather than atmosphere. The recording balance ensures that the continuo comes through well. But – as

the opening of *Winter* demonstrates – this is not an especially imaginative version, although the alert vivacity of the playing of soloist and orchestra alike is undoubtedly exhilarating, and slow movements are expressive and sympathetic.

The Academy of St Martin's earlier Argo recording under Neville Marriner, unauthentically sumptuous, had irresistible magic; but Iona Brown's version with the same band fails to repeat that. The mannered style, with exaggerated dynamic contrasts, suggests that she may have been attempting to do so, but not even in refinement of playing is this among the Academy's finest issues. The recording is rich, the cassette less cleanly detailed than the disc.

Isaac Stern creates a novelty in the slow movement of *Spring* by his decoration of the reprise of the solo line. Otherwise this is an aggressively strong, bravura reading, with plenty of orchestral bustle to support the solo line. Stern's articulation is impressively brilliant and he provides serene contrast in slow movements. But with excessively bright sound – the harpsichord sounds metallic – this has few moments of real individuality, although the opening of *Winter* is positively icy.

Stokowski's version, originally recorded in Phase Four, with closely balanced sound, has a highly sensitive soloist, but the conductor's wilful unstylishness is endearingly wrong-headed. The mellowness of his approach – with sensuous warmth in *Spring* as well as *Summer* – irons out all Vivaldi's intended contrasts and there are curious ritenutos at the end of each allegro. The sound is over-resonant to the point of blurring most detail.

La Cetra, Op. 9 (complete).
*** Argo D 99 D 3 (3)/*K 99 K 32* (2) [id.].
Iona Brown, ASMF.

Iona Brown, for some years the leader of the St Martin's Academy, here acts as director in place of Neville Marriner. So resilient and imaginative are the results that one hardly detects any difference from the immaculate and stylish Vivaldi playing in earlier Academy issues. The recording is outstandingly vivid, even by Argo standards with the Academy, and on disc the relatively extravagant layout on six sides (against four for the earlier Erato issue with I Solisti Veneti) brings benefits in the quality of sound on wide-spaced grooves. The cassettes too offer demonstration quality; the treble is softer-grained than on some Argo issues, but the full richness and amplitude of the sound are accommodated naturally. The concertos are spaced over two cassettes.

(i) *Bassoon concertos: in A min., RV.498; in E min., RV.484; in F, RV.489; in B flat, RV.502;* (ii) *Flute concertos: Op. 10, Nos. 1 in F (La Tempesta di mare); 2 in G min. (La Notte); in A min., RV.108 and RV.440; in G, RV.436 and RV.438; in D, RV.427 and RV.429; in C min., RV.441;* (ii; iii) *Double flute concerto in C, RV.533;* (iv) *Oboe concertos: Op. 11, No. 6 in G min.; in C, RV.447 and RV.450/51; in A min., RV.461; in D, RV.453; in F, RV.455; in F (P.457), in A min. (P.463).*
(M) *** Ph. 6768 015 (5). I Musici, with (i) Thunemann, (ii) Gazzelloni, (iii) Steinberg, (iv) Holliger.

This five-record set is a cheap way of acquiring some remarkable Vivaldi. By far the most remarkable music here is to be found in the *Bassoon concertos*, which are as richly inventive as anything in Vivaldi's output. He wrote thirty-seven concertos for this instrument, as opposed to fifteen for flute and nineteen for oboe. Somewhat disproportionately, the *Bassoon concertos* occupy only one record here as opposed to two each for the flute and oboe concertos. But there are good things among them, too, and

some fine playing from all the soloists. Yet fine though such favourites as *La Notte* and *La Tempesta di mare* are, it is the *Bassoon concertos* recorded here that leave the strongest impression of originality and power. All in all, this is a most rewarding set and can be strongly recommended. The performances are all superbly accomplished and the recordings impeccable.

Cello concertos: in C, RV.398; in G, RV.413.
*** DG 2530/3300 974 [id.]. Rostropovich, Zürich Coll. Mus., Sacher – BOCCHERINI and TARTINI: *Concertos.****

Performances of great vigour and projection from Rostropovich. The playing is superbly brilliant and immensely strong in character; it may be somewhat large-scale for Vivaldi's two quite short concertos, but undoubtedly every bar of the music comes fully to life. Splendidly lively accompaniments and excellent recording, bright and clean, yet with no lack of depth. The tape transfer too is admirable.

Cello concertos: in C, RV.400; in C min., RV.401; in D min., RV.424; (i) *Double cello concerto in G min., RV.531;* (i; ii) *Triple concerto for violin and 2 cellos, RV.561 (all ed. Malipiero).*
*** HMV ASD/TC-ASD 3914. Paul Tortelier, L. Moz. Players, Ledger, with (i) Maud Tortelier, (ii) Manzone.

The performances here are strong and alive, the slow movements expressive without being over-romanticized. Philip Ledger directs the full-bodied accompanying group and provides a continuo with some flair. The playing is undoubtedly stylish, although the overall effect is not aimed at the 'authentic' lobby, rather at those who primarily seek a warmly understanding response to the composer's inspiration and readily communicated musical enjoyment. The sound is excellent and the cassette splendidly clean in focus.

Cello concerto in C min., RV.401.
(M) **(*) DG Arc. Priv. 2547/3347 046. Storck, Seiler CO, Hofmann – BOCCHERINI and TARTINI: *Concertos.***

Originally part of a Vivaldi anthology, Klaus Storck's excellent performance of the *C minor Concerto* has been recoupled with other works for the same instrument. The Vivaldi is the highlight of the collection, for it is played with assurance and flair. The recording is good, if not distinguished. The treble needs smoothing on disc; the cassette is preferable, vivid yet less strident on top.

Cello concerto in C min., RV.401; Double cello concerto in G min., RV.531; Double concertos for cello and violin: in A, RV. 546; in B flat, RV.547; Concertos for two cellos and two violins: in D, RV. 564; in G, RV.575; Harpsichord concertos: in B min., RV.168; in C, RV.112 and RV.116; in E, RV.131/2; in F, RV.137; in G min., RV.156; Violin concertos: in E (L'Amoroso), RV.271; in F, RV.542; Double violin concertos: in A (L'Eco in lontana), RV.552; in A min., RV.523; in B flat, RV.525 and RV.527; Triple violin concerto in F, RV.551; Quadruple violin concerto in B flat, RV.553; Concertos for strings: in A, RV.158; in C, RV.114; in C min., RV.119; in D, RV.126; in D min., RV.129; in E min., RV.134; in F, RV.138 and RV.141; in G min., RV.153, RV.154 and RV.157; Sinfonia in G, RV.149; Sonata a quattro in E flat (Al santo sepolcro), RV.130.

(M) *** Ph. 6768 014 (6). Various soloists, I Musici.

These performances presumably date from the early 1970s; only the first of the six records has appeared before in the UK, though they have surely been issued separately elsewhere. There is much distinguished playing, particularly in the *Violin concertos*; Pina Carmirelli's account of the *E major* (*L'Amoroso*) is beautifully warm and to be preferred to its predecessors on record (even Grumiaux's). There is a varied, well-planned sequence on most of these discs, except perhaps for the last but one, which offers instrumental concertos without soloists. The music is far from unrewarding but is best not heard all in one go. The last of the six records has some relatively unfamiliar and often unpredictable music, forward-looking and searching. The playing throughout is highly polished without being excessively bland, though in the couple of instances where direct comparison arises with the Academy of St Martin-in-the-Fields, the latter sounds fresher. Given the excellence of the recorded sound and the reasonableness of the outlay (the cost works out at rather less than medium price), the rewards of the set are clear.

Cello concertos: in G, RV.413; in G min., RV. 417 (both arr. Malipiero).
*** HMV ASD/TC-ASD 3899 [Ang. SZ 37738]. Harrell, ECO, Zukerman – C. P. E. BACH: *Concerto ***; COUPERIN: *Pièces.*(*)

Though Lynn Harrell is hardly a classicist among cellists, he gives lively, imaginative performances of two fine Vivaldi concertos (the *G major* particularly attractive), a good coupling for the C. P. E. Bach concerto, which is the most substantial work on the disc. The cassette offers lively quality, although there is a slight loss of sharpness of focus of the orchestral image.

(i) *Cello concertos: in G, RV.414; in G min., RV.417; in A min., RV.418 and 420.* (ii) *Orchestral concertos: in C, RV.556 and 558; in G min., RV.576 and 577.* (ii; iii) *Viola d'amore concertos: in F, RV.97; in D, RV.392; in D min., RV.393–5 and 540; in A, RV.396; in A min., RV.397.*

(M) *** Ph. 6768 013 (4). (i) Walevska, Netherlands CO, Redel; (ii) Dresden State O., Negri; (iii) Giuranna.

These four records contain some good things: Bruno Giuranna's accounts of six concertos for the viola d'amore, joined in the case of two other concertos by *obbligato* instruments: P.266/RV.540 is with lute, and P.286/RV.97 is also for two horns, two oboes and bassoon. The third record is taken up by concertos for miscellaneous instruments and includes the fine *Concerto per la Solennità di San Lorenzo,* all of these with the Dresden Orchestra; and the last, and in some ways most interesting of all, is the disc devoted to four cello concertos, superbly played by Christine Walevska with the Netherlands Chamber Orchestra. There is a lot of interesting music here, and the recordings are as excellent as the performances.

6 Flute concertos, Op. 10 (complete).
*** Ph. 9500/7300 942 [id.]. Petri, ASMF, Marriner.

Whereas Stephen Preston (on O-L DSLO/*KDSLC* 519) uses a baroque flute and Severino Gazzelloni (see below) a modern instrument, the young Danish virtuoso Michala Petri uses a modern recorder. At least this, like Gazzelloni's set, gives us the opportunity of hearing these concertos at present-day pitch. Michala Petri plays with breathtaking virtuosity and impeccable control, and she has the advantage of superb recording. In the slow movements – and occasionally elsewhere – there is more in the music than she finds, but the sheer vir-

tuosity of this gifted young artist is most infectious. The cassette matches the disc closely. The upper orchestral range has slightly less bite, but the solo recorder has fine naturalness and presence.

6 Flute concertos, Op. 10; Flute concertos: in A min., RV.108; in D, RV.427; in C, RV.429; in G, RV.436; in G, RV.438; in A min., RV.440; in C min., RV.441; in A min., RV.445. (i) *Double flute concerto in C, RV.533.*

(M) *** Ph. 6768 174 (3). Gazzelloni, I Musici, (i) with Steinberg.

For those who do not want the set of the Opp. 11 and 12 concertos (or who bought them separately in the mid-seventies), Philips offer Gazzelloni's 1969 recording of the Op. 10 plus a variety of other flute concertos, including a diverting *Double concerto in C.* All this is of high quality, but not for continuous listening!

(i) *6 Flute concertos, Op. 10.* (ii) *6 Violin concertos, Op. 11; 6 Violin concertos, Op. 12.*

(M) *** Ph. 6768 012 (4). I Musici, with (i) Gazzelloni, (ii) Accardo.

Severino Gazzelloni's version of the six concertos, Op. 10, has been in circulation throughout the 1970s and its merits are well established; it is probably a safer recommendation for the general collector than the authentic rivals, good though the best of these is. The Opp. 11 and 12 concertos are perhaps of uneven quality, but the best of them are very rewarding indeed, and played so superlatively by Salvatore Accardo they are likely to beguile the most unwilling listener. These were all available separately in the mid-1970s; this set is one of the most desirable of the Vivaldi Edition.

Flute concertos: in D, RV.429; in G,

RV.435; Soprano recorder concerto in C, RV.443; Treble recorder concertos: in A min., RV.108; in F, RV.434.
*** HMV ASD/*TC-ASD* 3554 [Sera. S 60362]. Linde, Prague CO.

The West German flautist Hans-Martin Linde has an attractively fresh tone both on the flute and on the two sizes of recorder he uses for three of these concertos. Two of the regular Op. 10 works are included – No. 4, expressly written for transverse flute, and No. 5, expressly written for treble recorder, as it is played here. Rhythmically lively, Linde is splendidly accompanied by the excellent strings of the Prague Chamber Orchestra. Warm, rounded recording; the cassette is marginally less rich and refined, but can be made to sound well.

Guitar concerto in C, RV.425; Double guitar concerto in G, RV.532; Concerto for 4 guitars in B min., RV.580; Concerto in A for guitar, violin, viola and cello, RV.88.
(M) **(*) Ph. Seq. 6527/*7311* 042 [Mer. 75054]. Los Romeros, San Antonio SO, Alessandro.

These are all good performances, well played and recorded. The accompaniments are alert and the balance is generally realistic. These works were all originally conceived for the mandolin, but they sound well in these formats, though not all the music is especially memorable. Vivaldi's concertos of this kind are often more effective when grouped in a miscellaneous collection with varying solo timbres. However, guitar and mandolin enthusiasts should find this satisfactory, for the recording is excellent, both on disc and on the high-level cassette.

Lute concerto in D, RV.93; Double concerto in G, RV.532.

(*) RCA RL/*RK* 11180 [ARL 1/*ARK 1* 1180]. Bream, Monteverdi O., Gardiner – HANDEL and KOHAUT: *Concertos.*(*)

The *Lute concerto* receives a first-class performance here from Julian Bream, and he is very well accompanied. The slow movement, with its delicate embroidery over a glowing texture of sustained strings, is particularly fine. In the arrangement of the *Double mandolin concerto* Bream is able by electronic means to assume both solo roles. This too is a highly effective performance, though the exaggeratedly forward recording balance makes the solo instruments sound far larger than life and negates much of the dynamic contrast with the accompanying group. Otherwise the sound is lively and full-blooded, and the high-level cassette matches the disc closely.

Oboe concertos: in C, RV. 451; in D, RV.453; in F, RV.455; in A min., RV.461; in F (P.457).
*** Ph. 9500 299 [id./*7300 568*]. Holliger, I Musici.

These five concertos, all sharply contrasted with each other, show Vivaldi at his most inspired. Holliger, with lively accompaniment from I Musici, gives delectable performances, endlessly imaginative, beautifully recorded.

Violin concertos: in C min. (Il Sospetto), RV.199; in D (L'Inquietudine), RV.234; in E (Il Riposo), RV. 270; in E (L'Amoroso), RV.271; in E min. (Il Favorito), RV.277.
(M) **(*) Ph. 6833 247. Soloists, I Musici.

Recorded originally in the late fifties, this attractive collection of five violin concertos features five different soloists, all members of I Musici. The style of Vivaldi performance has grown generally subtler since this was made, but it is still attractive, a fair medium-price issue with reasonable sound

Double violin concertos: in C min., RV.509; in D min., RV.514.
(*) CBS 76798 [Col. M/MT 35133]. Rampal (flute), Stern (violin), Jerusalem Music Centre CO – TELEMANN: Suite in A min.(*)

These arrangements of concertos written for two violins were presumably made for this occasion. The playing is very fast and brilliant and will give many of the early-music lobby a seizure. Bright recording.

MISCELLANEOUS COLLECTIONS

L'Estro armonico, Op. 3: Concertos Nos. 2 in G min.; 11 in D min. Flute concerto in G min. (La Notte), Op. 10/2; Oboe concerto in A min., RV.461; Concertos for strings: in C min., RV.120; in D min. (Madrigalesco), RV.129.
*** Chan. ABR/ABT 1008. Soloists, Cantilena, Shepherd.

Cantilena and Adrian Shepherd are fortunate in that television appearances have made them widely familiar in the UK. Their performances of baroque music in general and Vivaldi in particular are stylish without being self-consciously so. They use modern instruments and pitch, and are not afraid to express emotion, investing some of the slow movements with greater feeling than some collectors may like. However, this anthology of well-known Vivaldi is eminently well played (perhaps without the last ounce of finish sometimes), thoroughly musical and admirably recorded. It should give pleasure. The cassette transfer is clear and clean, the soloists well focused; but on tape the upper strings are rather lacking in body.

'Favourite composer': (i) L'Estro armonico: Concerto No. 10 in B min. for 4 violins. (ii) The Four Seasons, Op. 8/1–4; (iii) Flute concerto in G min. (La Notte), Op. 10/2; (iv; v) Bassoon concerto in A min., RV.498; (vi) Concerto for strings in G (Alla rustica), RV.151; (vii; v) Double trumpet concerto in C, RV.537; (viii) Gloria in D, RV.589.
(B) *** Decca DPA/KDPC 609/10. (i) Moscow CO, Barshai; (ii) Kulka, Stuttgart CO, Münchinger; (iii) Preston, AcAM, Hogwood; (iv) Gatt; (v) ASMF, Marriner; (vi) Lucerne Festival Strings, Baumgartner; (vii) Wilbraham, Philip Jones; (viii) soloists, King's College Ch., ASMF, Willcocks.

An outstandingly generous set, which can be cordially recommended on all counts. The Four Seasons is Münchinger's latest recording (1974), with Konstanty Kulka as the stylish soloist, and the other performances are all first-rate, with the bassoon and flute concertos as highlights. The recording is of consistently excellent quality, and the cassette transfer (although very bright and needing a little taming) is vivid and detailed, only slipping a little in refinement in the Concerto for two trumpets. The Gloria, however, is especially successful. This set would make a splendid basis for any Vivaldi collection, especially as the two discs (or tapes) together cost slightly less than one premium-priced LP.

L'Estro armonico: Concerto No. 10 in B min. for 4 violins. The Four Seasons; Bassoon concerto in A min., RV.498; Flute concerto in C min., RV.441; Double horn concerto in F, RV.539; Double oboe concerto in D min., RV.535; Piccolo concerto in C, RV.443; Double trumpet concerto in C, RV.537; Violin concerto in B flat, Op. 4/1; (i) Gloria in D.

(M) *** Argo D 240 D 3/*K 240 K 33* (3). Soloists, ASMF, Marriner, (i) with Vaughan, Baker, King's College Ch., Willcocks.

Those not wanting to invest in the larger ASMF Vivaldi collection (see above) might consider this instead. Very reasonably priced, it includes *The Four Seasons*, plus an attractive array of wind and brass concertos, with the invigorating *Gloria in D* as a bonus on the last side. The recording is first-class on disc and cassette alike.

L'Estro armonico: Concerto No. 10 in B min. for 4 violins. Flute concerto in C min. (La Notte), Op. 10/2; Mandolin concerto in C, RV.425; Double mandolin concerto in G, RV.532; Recorder concerto in C, RV.444; Double trumpet concerto in C, RV.537.
(B) *** CfP CFP/*TC-CFP* 40353. Soloists, Toulouse CO, Auriacombe.

A lively clutch of very agreeable concertos (those for mandolin being piquant in timbre rather than memorable in invention), and they are vividly played and very well recorded. The balance is rather forward, but this has produced an excellent cassette transfer: the disc has only fractionally more range at the top. Several of these works are available in at least one other collection, but this anthology makes a satisfying whole, diverse in colour and substance. A bargain.

Bassoon concerto in A min. RV.498; Flute concerto in C min. RV.441; Oboe concerto in F, RV.456; Concerto for 2 oboes, bassoon, 2 horns and violin, RV.369.
*** Argo ZRG/*KZRC* 839. Gatt, Bennett, Black, Nicklin, Timothy Brown, Davis, ASMF, Marriner.

This issue will give enormous pleasure.

The playing is splendidly alive and characterful, with crisp, clean articulation and well-pointed phrasing, free from over-emphasis. The work for oboes and horns is agreeably robust; the *A minor Bassoon concerto* has a delightful sense of humour, while the flute and the oboe concertos, if not showing Vivaldi at his most inventive, are still very compelling and worthwhile. The recording is a model of clarity and definition and has striking richness and atmosphere too. This is one of the very finest Vivaldi collections on disc or tape.

Cello concerto in B min., RV.424; Oboe concerto in A min., RV.461; Double concerto in C min. for oboe and violin, RV.Anh.17; Violin concerto in D, RV.208; Sinfonia in B min., RV.169; Sonata à 4 in E flat for 2 violins, viola and continuo, RV.130.
** Tel. AW6/*CX4* 42355. Soloists, Concerto Amsterdam, Schröder.

There is an element of too much rectitude here, and the forward balance seems to emphasize the somewhat stiff approach, although allegros are alert and lively. The recording readily captures the robust and somewhat pungent timbres, and those who favour Vivaldi played on baroque instruments will certainly find the sound faithful; the high-level chrome cassette also brings striking range and presence.

Double cello concerto in G min., RV.531; Double flute concerto in C, RV.533; Concertos for strings in D min. (Madrigalesco), RV.129; in G (Alla rustica), RV.151; Double trumpet concerto in C, RV.537; Concerto for 2 violins and 2 cellos in D, RV.564.
*** O-L DSLO/*KDSLC* 544. AcAM, Hogwood.

Not everything in this issue is of equal

substance: the invention in the *Double trumpet concerto*, for example, is not particularly strong, but for the most part it is a rewarding and varied programme. It is especially appealing in that authenticity is allied to musical spontancity. The best-known concertos are the *Madrigalesco* and the *Alla rustica*, but some of the others are just as captivating. The *Concerto for two flutes* has great charm and is dispatched with vigour and aplomb. The recording is first-class throughout, and readers with an interest in this often unexpectedly rewarding composer, whose unpredictability continues to astonish, should not hesitate. Performances and recording alike are first-rate; but on tape the sound is coarsened by too high a transfer level.

Flute concertos: in A min., RV.108; in G, RV.438; in C min. RV.441; (i) *Double flute concerto in C, RV.533;* (ii) *Concerto for flute, oboe, bassoon and strings in F (La Tempesta di mare), RV.570.*
(M) **(*) Ph. Fest. 6570/7310 186. Gazzelloni, I Musici, with (i) Steinberg, Schenkel, Staviček.

An impressive collection, played with considerable bravura but in good style. *La Tempesta di mare* is not the familiar version from Op. 10, but a different working of the same material for three wind instruments. It is highly effective, as is the *Concerto for two flutes*, RV.533. The *G major* and *C minor* solo concertos are less inspired, but (if not taken all at once) this recital has a good deal to offer, not least the excellent sound, equally crisp and clean on both disc and tape.

(i) *Guitar concerto in D, RV.93;* (ii; iii) *Flute concerto in G min. (La Notte), RV.439;* (ii; iv) *Piccolo concerto in C, RV.443;* (v) *Double trumpet concerto in C, RV.537;* (vi) *Double violin concerto in A (Echo), RV.552.*

(M) ** DG Priv. 2535/3335 630. (i) Behrend, I Musici; (ii) Linde; (iii) Zürich Coll. Mus., Sacher; (iv) Seiler CO, Hofman; (v) Scherbaum, Haubold, Hamburg Bar. Ens.; (vi) Soloists, Lucerne Festival Strings, Baumgartner.

Entitled *Gala concert in Venice*, this collection gathers together five contrasted concertos from diverse sources. The *Echo concerto* is particularly well managed, and Hans-Martin Linde proves a sprightly soloist in the works for flute and piccolo. The sound is variable but always good, and the tape transfer is satisfactory, although the focus slips a little in the *Concerto for two trumpets*.

Double horn concerto in F, RV.539; Double oboe concerto in D min., RV.535; Concerto in F for 2 oboes, bassoon, 2 horns and violin, RV.574; Piccolo concerto in C, RV.443.
*** Argo ZRG/KZRC 840. Soloists, ASMF, Marriner.

The musical substance may not be very weighty, but Vivaldi was rarely more engaging than when, as here, he was writing for wind instruments, particularly if he had more than one in his solo team. This delectable record makes a splendid supplement to the earlier one in the series from the Academy (ZRG KZRC 839: see above). Beautifully balanced and vivid recording, and a generally excellent equivalent cassette.

CHAMBER MUSIC

(i) *6 Cello sonatas, Op. 14;* (ii) *Il Pastor fido (6 Sonatas for recorder, harpsichord and cello);* (iii) *6 Violin sonatas (for violin and continuo), Op. 5.*
(M) *** Ph. 6768 750 (8). (i) Gendron, Sibinga, Lang; (ii) Veilham, Verlet, Lamy; (iii) Accardo, Gazeau, Canino, Saram.

Mellifluous playing from Salvatore Accardo in the Op. 5 *Sonatas* of 1716–17, four being solo sonatas with continuo, and the remainder being trio sonatas. The music is not, however, as interesting or inventive as the *Cello sonatas*, which Maurice Gendron recorded in the late 1960s (the only recordings here that have been released before). *Il Pastor fido* is given a straightforward and intelligent reading without recourse to the variety of instruments used by Hans-Martin Linde and Eduard Melkus on Archive. This is a useful and valuable set well worth the modest outlay.

12 Sonatas for 2 violins and continuo, Op.1; 12 Violin sonatas, Op. 2 (complete).
(M) *** Ph. 6768 007 (5). Accardo, Gulli, Canino, Saram.

These sonatas are not otherwise obtainable, and in any case it is unlikely that Accardo's performances, so ably supported by Bruno Canino and Rohan de Saram (and in Op. 1 by Franco Gulli) could be surpassed in terms of fluency, musicianship and sheer beauty of tone. The shadow of Corelli still hangs over the earlier set, but much of the invention is fresh, and collectors will find unexpected rewards in both sets.

VOCAL MUSIC

Choral music: *Beatus vir* (2 settings, *RV.597–8); Credidi propter quod, RV.605; Credo* (2 settings, *RV.591–2); Dixit Dominus* (2 settings, *RV.594–5*), with *Introductions, RV. 635–6; Domine ad adiuvandum me, RV.593; Gloria* (2 settings, *RV.588–9*), with *Introductions, RV.639 and 642; In exitu Israel, RV.604; Kyrie, RV.587; Laetatus sum, RV.607; Laudate Dominum, RV.606; Lauda Jerusalem, RV.609; Laudate pueri, RV.602; Magnificat* (2 settings, *RV.610–11); Sacrum, RV.586.*
(M) *** Ph. 6768 149 (7). Marshall, Lott, Burgess, Murray, Daniel, Collins, Finnilä, Finnie, Rolfe Johnson, Holl, Thomaschke, John Alldis Ch., ECO, Negri.

This is a splendid collection which, over a very wide range of works, presents lively, stylish performances, beautifully recorded. Any lover of Vivaldi is likely to be astonished that not only the well-known works but the total rarities show him writing with the keenest originality and intensity, for there is no question of routine inspiration as there can be in Vivaldi concertos. The seven discs are also available in three separate boxes (see below).

Beatus vir; Canta in prato (motet); *Dixit Dominus; Domine ad adiuvandum me; Gloria in D; In furore* (motet); *Introduction to Dixit Dominus; Juditha triumphans* (oratorio); *Kyrie; Lauda Jerusalem; Magnificat in G min.; Nulla in mundo pax; O qui coeli* (motets); *Salve Regina in C min.; Te Deum.*
(M) ** Ph. 6768 016 (8). Various soloists, choruses and orchestras, Negri.

This volume from the Vivaldi Edition devotes three of the eight records to the massive oratorio *Juditha triumphans*, and also Negri's earlier Berlin versions of the *D major Gloria*, the *C minor Salve Regina*, a spurious *Te Deum* and the double-choir version of the *Magnificat*, recorded with inferior sound in 1965. The rest duplicates the seven-record box of Vivaldi choral works (see above), which makes a far better investment if the oratorio is not a first essential. Negri is a stylish and sympathetic interpreter of Vivaldi (having obviously learnt from his 1965 Berlin recordings); he draws lively performances from his excellent English team.

Beatus vir, RV.598; Credo, RV.592; Dixit Dominus, RV.595, with Introduction, RV.635; Gloria, RV.588, with Introduction, RV.639; Laudate pueri, RV.602; Magnificat (2 settings, RV.610–11).
(M) *** Ph. 6769 046 (3) (from 6768 149, cond. Negri).

Taken from Negri's seven-disc box of choral works (see above), this three-disc selection offers superb performances of an admirable group of rare works; mostly these are less well-known versions of texts that Vivaldi set more than once, as for example the *Dixit Dominus* and *Gloria*. In the piece described as an *Introduction* to the *Gloria*, Linda Finnie sings with spectacular virtuosity; the other soloists too are splendid, and the choir captures the dark Bach-like intensity of many passages contrasted with more typical Vivaldian brilliance. First-rate recording.

Beatus vir, RV.597; Dixit Dominus, RV.594, with Introduction, RV.636; Domine ad adiuvandum me; Kyrie in G min., Lauda Jerusalem.
(M) *** Ph. 6700 116 (2) (from 6768 149, cond. Negri).

This two-disc box consists of the first two records of Negri's splendid seven-disc collection of Vivaldi choral music. Most impressive are the extended psalm settings, *Dixit Dominus* and *Beatus vir* (the better-known versions of each), and such a delightful rarity as the *Domine ad adiuvandum me* for soprano, two choirs and two orchestras. Fine singing from chorus and soloists alike, lively orchestral playing and first-rate recording.

Beatus vir, RV.597; Gloria in D, RV.589.

*(*) CBS 76596/40-. Burgess, Chamonin, Watkinson, Passaquet Vocal Ens., Gr. Écurie, Malgoire.

Malgoire has the virtue of commitment and spirit, and were the singing better and the orchestral playing a little more polished this would be recommendable. Period instruments are used, but wind intonation surely need not be as awry as this is. For all its vitality and robustness, these performances are not really satisfying enough to suffer repeated hearing, even if there are some stylish touches. Some readers may prefer this rough-and-ready but vital approach to the more bland version of the *Gloria* coupled with the *Magnificat* in Muti's version on HMV (see below). As far as recording is concerned, the CBS acoustic is not quite expansive enough for comfort and the transfer to cassette does not produce sound of adequate richness or refinement.

Dixit Dominus, RV.594; Stabat Mater, RV.621.
**(*) CBS 76682 [Col. M/MT 35847]. Hill Smith, Bernardin, Watts, Partridge, Caddy, E. Bach Festival Ch. and O., Malgoire; Tall (organ).

Malgoire's overemphatic style of baroque playing, with first beats of bars heavily underlined, is inclined to be wearing, but these fine works make an excellent coupling, and the singing is first-rate, both from the chorus and soloists in the better-known setting of *Dixit Dominus* and particularly from Helen Watts in the moving sequence of solo items that makes up the *Stabat Mater*. Reverberant, church-like acoustic.

(i) *Gloria in D, RV.588;* (ii) *Nisi Dominus in G min., RV.608.*
*** Erato STU 71200. E. Bach Festival Ch. and Bar. O., Corbóz, with (i) Jennifer Smith, Bernadin, Barham, (ii) Watts.

Vivaldi's less well-known version of the *Gloria* (shorn of the three-movement *Introduction* on a non-liturgical text) makes an attractive coupling for the *Nisi Dominus*, which is sung beautifully here by Helen Watts, arguably more apt for this music than a male alto. In the *Gloria* Corbóz may encourage his soloists to a little too much operatic expressiveness, but with fine recording and baroque orchestral playing on authentic instruments this can be recommended to those who fancy the coupling.

Gloria in D, RV.589; Kyrie in G min.
*** DG Arc. 2533 362 [id.]. Regensburg Cath. Ch., V. Capella Academica, Schneidt.

In the well-known *Gloria* and in the superb setting of the *Kyrie*, Schneidt with his fresh-toned Regensburg Choir (the celebrated *Domspatzen*, 'cathedral sparrows') brings out what may seem a surprising weight. Alongside the brilliant numbers in both these works, one can find music of Bach-like intensity. The use of semi-chorus for solo numbers is questionable, but no one hearing this will be likely to dismiss the music as trivial. Excellent recording.

(i) *Gloria in D, RV.589;* (ii) *Nulla in mundo pax.*
*** O-L DSLO/*KDSLC* 554 [id.]. Christ Church Cath. Ch., AcAM, Preston, with (i) Nelson, Watkinson, (ii) Kirkby.

The freshness and point of the Christ Church performance of the *Gloria* are irresistible; anyone who normally doubts the attractiveness of authentic string technique should sample this, for the absence of vibrato adds a tang exactly in keeping with the performance. The soloists too keep vibrato to the minimum, adding to the freshness, yet Carolyn Watkinson rivals even Dame Janet Baker in the dark intensity of the Bach-like

central aria for contralto, *Domine Deus, Agnus Dei.* The choristers of Christ Church Cathedral excel themselves, and the recording is of demonstration quality, on cassette as on disc. The solo motet provided for fill-up has Emma Kirkby as soloist coping splendidly with the bravura writing for soprano.

Gloria in D, RV.589; Magnificat, RV.611.
** HMV ASD/*TC-ASD* 3418 [Ang. S 37415]. Berganza, Valentini-Terrani, New Philh. Ch. and O., Muti.

Magnificat, RV.610.
(*) Argo ZRG/*KZRC* 854 [id. LP only]. King's College Ch., ASMF, Marriner – BACH: *Magnificat.*(*)

Although the HMV Muti record and the Argo King's coupling with Bach both list Vivaldi's *Magnificat*, these are two quite different versions of the same basic work. Muti offers the more expansive score, including extended solo arias. The Argo recording shares some material, such as the opening chorus, but here the music is on a much smaller scale. Ledger opts for boys' voices in the solos, such as the beautiful duet, *Esurientes*, and though the singers are taxed by ornamentation, the result has all the accustomed beauty of this choir's recordings, set warmly against the chapel's acoustic. This makes a fascinating and attractive coupling for the grander Bach setting of the *Magnificat*. The transfer to tape has been quite well managed but this is not one of Argo's finest cassette issues; the choral sounds are not always completely clear in focus.

Muti's approach, both in the *Magnificat* and in the *Gloria*, is altogether blander than the Argo performances. His expansiveness suits the larger-scaled *Magnificat* better than the *Gloria*, which here lacks the incisiveness and freshness of the Argo performance. The HMV cassette is not recommended; the sound is congested at peaks.

OPERA

Opera overtures: *Armida al campo d'Egitto; Arsilda regina di Ponto; Bajazet; Dorilla in Tempe; Farnace; Giustino; Griselda; L'Incoronazione di Dario; L'Olimpiade; Ottone in Villa; La Verita in cimento.*
*** Erato STU 71215. I Sol. Ven., Scimone.

Vivaldi's 'opera overtures' were conceived as mere sinfonias, scarcely related to the character of each work. These eleven make a lively and surprisingly varied collection, splendidly played and recorded. But it may be as well not to play them all in sequence.

L'Olimpiade (complete).
*(*) Hung. SLPX 110901/3. Kováts, Takács, Zempléni, Miller, Gáti, Horváth, Káplán, Budapest Madrigal Ens., Hungarian State O, Szekeres

It is delightful to find, in the first act of this long-neglected opera, a choral adaptation of an idea we know very well indeed from *The Four Seasons*. It is good too to find that Vivaldi, though very much bound by the conventions of his time not least in the complications of the plot about royal love affairs in ancient Crete – had real freshness in his arias at least. The pity is that this Hungarian performance, recorded in cleancut stereo, with sharp divisions between left and right, is rhythmically so heavy that any sprightliness of idea is undermined. The recitative – relatively little for the modern listener to swallow – is taken heavily too, with the singers adopting a nineteenth-century style. Quality of voice varies markedly, allowing only a limited recommendation.

Orlando furioso (complete).
*** Erato STU 71138 (3). Horne, Los Angeles, Valentini-Terrani, Gonzales, Kozma, Bruscantini, Zaccaria, I Sol. Ven., Scimone.

Though the greater part of this opera consists of recitative – with only fifteen arias included on the three discs, plus one for Orlando borrowed from a chamber cantata – it presents a fascinating insight into this totally neglected area of Vivaldi's work. Scimone has heavily rearranged the order of items as well as cutting many, but with stylish playing and excellent recording, it is a set well worth a Vivaldi enthusiast's attention. Outstanding in a surprisingly starstudded cast is Marilyn Horne in the title role, rich and firm of tone, articulating superbly in divisions, notably in the hero's two fiery arias. In the role of Angelica, Victoria de los Angeles has many sweetly lyrical moments, and though Lucia Valentini-Terrani is less strong as Alcina, she gives an aptly clean, precise performance.

Tito Manlio (complete).
**(*) Ph. 6769 004 (5) [id.]. Luccardi, Wagemann, Hamari, Finnilä, Marshall, Trimarchi, Lerer, Ahnsjö, Berlin R. Ch., Berlin CO, Negri.

Vivaldi claimed that he wrote this massive score in a mere five days, which sounds improbable even for him. The inspiration of the set numbers, most of them short, simple arias, is generally lively, and they are attractively spiced with obbligato solos. The very overture sets the classical scene well, with its *pomposo* trumpet-ful style, and the main snag for the modern listener is the sheer length, which achieves Wagnerian proportions. Unlike the other Vivaldi opera issued in tercentenary year, *Orlando furioso*, this one is given uncut except for some snipping of secco recitatives, which still make up a very substantial proportion of the whole. The performance is crisp and stylish, sympathetically directed by Negri and with generally excellent solo singing, though with women taking three male parts it is hard to follow the story, as the timbres are not as distinct as they might be. The recording quality has an attractive bloom on it, so that with patience the set can give pleasure. As we go to press, this set has been withdrawn in the UK, but it remains available in the USA.

Wagner, Richard
(1813–83)

Siegfried idyll.
*** DG 2707 102/*3370 023* (2) [id.]. Berlin PO, Karajan – BRUCKNER: *Symphony No. 7.****
*** Ph. 6769 028/*7699 113* (2) [id.]. Concg. O., Haitink – BRUCKNER: *Symphony No. 7.****
*** Erato STU 71333. Lausanne CO, Jordan – R. STRAUSS: *Metamorphosen* etc.**(*)
(M) (***) World mono SH/*TC-SH* 287. Philh. O., Cantelli – TCHAIKOVSKY: *Romeo and Juliet.* (***)

Karajan uses a full body of strings and secures some splendidly rich and radiant playing from the Berlin Philharmonic Orchestra. There is no finer recorded performance currently available, and the tape transfer has fine body and detail. A most successful issue.

Haitink gives a simple, unaffected reading and draws playing of great refinement from the Concertgebouw Orchestra. There is very little to choose between his account and Karajan's with the same coupling: both have a simplicity of expression and a tenderness that will leave few listeners unmoved. The Philips cassette transfer is made at quite a high level and the quality is first-class, with clear detail and plenty of bloom on the sound.

Cantelli's performance was recorded in the wake of his first London season with the Philharmonia Orchestra in 1951. It

was first issued on 78s in the following year and was highly acclaimed. Andrew Porter thought it sublime, and the late Eric Blom wrote that he could never hope on this earth to hear a more heavenly performance. They were right. It is beautifully shaped, tender and eloquent, and though there are other magnificent performances, from Furtwängler, Walter and Karajan, this eloquent reading holds its own with any of them. The recording is beautifully blended and betrays relatively few signs of its age. Of course it is not quite as expansive as recordings made a few years later, but the balance is impeccably judged. On tape the quality is full and clear, only marginally less fresh and secure than the LP.

Armin Jordan's version with the Lausanne Chamber Orchestra is very persuasive, opening and closing tenderly but with a passionately volatile climax. The central horn solo is rather thick in articulation, but otherwise the playing is beyond serious criticism, and the recording is rich and atmospheric. The Erato coupling is quite different and may suit some collectors better than the Bruckner symphony.

ORCHESTRAL COLLECTIONS

Siegfried idyll. Der fliegende Holländer (The Flying Dutchman): Overture. Die Meistersinger (The Mastersingers): Prelude to Act 3; Dance of the apprentices; Entry of the masters. Rienzi: Overture.
(B) **(*) CfP CFP/*TC-CFP* 40287. LPO, Downes.

Edward Downes was the first British conductor in the post-war period to conduct a *Ring* cycle at Covent Garden. As a Wagnerian he may lack a little in tension and excitement, but here as in the opera house he conducts fresh and direct performances; the selection is generous and well chosen, and it is all warmly and atmospherically recorded in modern stereo. The *Siegfried idyll* is especially successful, and there is some fine brass playing in the *Prelude to Act 3* of *Die Meistersinger*. In some ways the melodramatic *Rienzi* gains from Downes's slight degree of reticence, yet the opening string tune sounds gloriously ripe. The tape transfer is of outstanding quality, matching the disc closely. It has marginally less upper range, but if anything this is an advantage, smoothing the upper string timbre without robbing the sound of life.

Overtures: Die Feen; Der fliegende Holländer; Tannhäuser (with *Bacchanale*).
** Ph. Dig. 9500 746/*7300 831* [id.]. Concg. O., De Waart.

The special interest here is the rarely heard (and rarely recorded) *Die Feen overture*, written when Wagner was twenty for his first completed opera. It is agreeable music, cast in the same melodic mould as *Rienzi*, if less rumbustious in feeling. All the performances here are warmly spacious, lacking something in electricity (the *Flying Dutchman* – which uses the original ending – sounds too cultured). The digital recording faithfully reflects the acoustic of the Concertgebouw, with its richly textured strings and brass, and resonant lower range; but some listeners might feel a need for a more telling upper range.

Der fliegende Holländer: Overture. Lohengrin: Prelude to Act 3. Die Meistersinger: Overture. Tannhäuser: Overture. Tristan und Isolde: Prelude to Act 1.
(M) **(*) Ph. Fest. 6570/*7310* 030 [id.]. Dresden State O., Varviso.

A most successful medium-priced compilation of Wagnerian preludes. The Dresden orchestra produces an excellent

body of tone, and Varviso's readings are not wanting in tension and excitement. The last degree of individuality may be missing, but the music-making is vividly projected by bright, full-blooded sound. The cassette transfer is exceptionally successful; it finds plenty of amplitude for the *Meistersinger overture*, yet does not want life in the upper range.

Der fliegende Holländer: overture. Lohengrin: Preludes to Acts 1 and 3. Tristan und Isolde: Prelude and Liebestod.
*** DG 2531/*3301* 288 [id.]. VPO, Boehm.

This companion to Boehm's earlier collection of Wagner overtures and preludes (see below) follows very much the same spacious pattern, with speeds broad rather than urgent. Not all the balances seem quite natural, but sound quality is not one's first concern in one of Boehm's last records. The cassette transfer is faithful and well balanced if lacking a little in ultimate range.

Overtures: Der fliegende Holländer; Die Meistersinger; Tannhäuser (original version). *Tristan und Isolde: Prelude and Liebestod.*
*** Decca SXL/*KSXC* 6856 [Lon. 7078/*5*-]. Chicago SO, Solti.

An attractive collection of Wagner overtures superbly played and brightly recorded. Except for the *Flying Dutchman overture*, these are newly made recordings, not taken from Solti's complete opera sets. So this is the self-contained *Tannhäuser overture* from the Dresden version, and the *Liebestod* comes in the purely orchestral version. Perhaps surprisingly, comparison between Solti in Chicago and Solti in Vienna shows him warmer in America.

Overtures: Der fliegende Holländer;

Rienzi; Tannhäuser (with *Baccha-nale*).
(M) (*) Decca VIV/*KVIC* 30 [Lon. 6782].
VPO, Solti.

The Vienna Philharmonic are driven very hard by Solti, and the result sounds unnecessarily frenetic. The sound balance does not help; it is very fierce, with fizzy strings. Indeed the climax of the *Tannhäuser overture* verges on distortion.

Overtures: Der fliegende Holländer; Rienzi; Tannhäuser (original version). *Lohengrin: Prelude to Act 1.*
(M) **(*) HMV SXLP/*TC-SXLP* 30436 [Ang. RL 32039]. Philh. O., Klemperer.

It is good to have Klemperer's view of Wagner. Most of the performances here and on the two companion issues have the kind of incandescent glow found only in the interpretations of really great conductors, and the Philharmonia plays immaculately. But judged by the highest standards Klemperer falls just a degree short. The recordings have been remastered and successfully freshened, but they originally date from 1960. The cassette transfer – made at a high level – is lively, but at times the ear senses a slight constriction in the bass, which is not as clean as the upper range.

Götterdämmerung: Dawn and Siegfried's Rhine journey; Siegfried's death and funeral march. Das Rheingold: Entry of the gods into Valhalla. Siegfried: Forest murmurs. Die Walküre: Ride of the Valkyries; Wotan's farewell and Magic fire music.
*** HMV Dig. ASD/*TCC-ASD* 3985. Berlin PO, Tennstedt.

The first digital orchestral collection from *The Ring* is recorded with demonstrable brilliance. With steely metal-lic cymbal clashes in the *Ride of the Valkyries* and a splendid drum thwack at the opening of the *Entry of the gods into Valhalla*, the sense of spectacle is in no doubt. There is weight too: the climax of *Siegfried's funeral march* has massive penetration. There is also fine detail, especially in the atmospheric *Forest murmurs*. The playing itself is of the finest quality throughout and Tennstedt maintains a high level of tension. But the brass recording is rather dry and at times the ear feels some lack of amplitude and resonance in the bass. However, the grip of the playing is extremely well projected, and the degree of fierceness at the top is tameable. The chrome tape lacks some of the glittering bite of the disc (the cymbal transients less telling), but the balance overall is richer without much loss of detail. Many will prefer the quality here, and certainly this is demonstration-worthy in quite a different way. The *Magic fire music* at the end of side two is especially impressive in its cassette presentation.

Götterdämmerung: Siegfried's Rhine journey; Siegfried's death and funeral march. Das Rheingold: Entry of the gods into Valhalla. Siegfried: Forest murmurs. Die Walküre: Ride of the Valkyries.
(M) *(**) Decca SPA/*KCSP 537*. LSO, Stokowski.

This was first issued in 1966 and was not one of Decca's more successful Phase Four recordings. In *The Stereo Record Guide* we complained at the time of superficial brilliance and no real compensating weight in the bass. On this reissue the sound is slightly smoother, but hardly refined, and in some ways the balance of the cassette is preferable, often richer, with more body to the strings, although there are moments of coarseness. However, the performances are what count and this is vintage Stokowski; he is at his most electrifying in *Siegfried's funeral march.* This issue is primarily for Stokowskians, and they will not be disappointed.

Götterdämmerung: Siegfried's Rhine journey; Siegfried's funeral march; Final scene. Das Rheingold: Entry of the gods into Valhalla. Siegfried: Forest murmurs. Die Walküre: Ride of the Valkyries; Magic fire music.
(M) ** CBS 60102/40- [Col. MY 36715]. Cleveland O., Szell.

These are brilliantly played performances, and there are certainly some spectacular moments, but the recording has achieved its brilliance at the expense of weight at the bass end, which needs boosting.

Götterdämmerung: Siegfried's Rhine journey. Parsifal: Prelude to Act 1. Das Rheingold: Entry of the gods into Valhalla. Siegfried: Forest murmurs. Tannhäuser: Prelude to Act 3. Die Walküre: Ride of the Valkyries.
(M) **(*) HMV SXLP/*TC-SXLP* 30528 [Ang. RL 32058]. Philh. O., Klemperer.

The *Tannhäuser* and *Parsifal* excerpts are outstanding – characteristically spacious and superbly played. *The Ride of the Valkyries,* without the concert coda, ends rather abruptly; and in the other items the level of tension is somewhat variable. The recording has transferred well to cassette; side two (with *Parsifal* and *Tannhäuser*) sounds exceptionally full and vivid.

Götterdämmerung: Siegfried's funeral march. Siegfried: Forest murmurs. Tristan und Isolde: Prelude to Act 1. Die Walküre: Ride of the Valkyries.
**(*) Sheffield Lab. LAB 7 [id.]. LAPO, Leinsdorf.

This direct-cut disc combining four unedited performances has enjoyed a considerable vogue since it was first issued in 1977. Certainly the sound is admirably balanced and cleanly defined, yet it is without the exaggerated sharpness of outline which affects some digital issues. The performances have plenty of life and impetus (there is none of the inhibition one might have expected when there is no chance of correcting mistakes), and Leinsdorf achieves considerable passion at the climax of the *Tristan Prelude.* However, the body of tone produced by the Los Angeles strings does not match that of the Berlin Philharmonic in similar collections, and while the brass has both brilliance and sonority in *Siegfried's funeral music,* even here there are several instances where other recordings have greater weight and amplitude.

Lohengrin: Prelude to Act 3. Die Meistersinger: Overture; Dance of the apprentices; Entry of the masters. Tristan und Isolde: Prelude and Liebestod. Götterdämmerung: Siegfried's funeral march.
(M) **(*) HMV SXLP/*TC-SXLP* 30525 [Ang. RL 32057]. Philh. O., Klemperer.

After a zestful account of the *Prelude to Act 3* of *Lohengrin* the rest of the programme is given characteristically measured tempi. The plodding Mastersingers seem a bit too full of German pudding, and the *Tristan Prelude and Liebestod* does not have the sense of wonder that Toscanini brought, though the feeling of ennobled passion at its climax cannot fail to communicate. Throughout there is never any doubt that one is in the presence of a great conductor. The orchestral playing too is first-class, and though the recording lacks something in sumptuousness at the climax of *Siegfried's funeral march,* this remains well worth considering at medium price. The cassette transfer is strikingly vivid and full-bodied, quite the equal of the disc.

Overtures: Die Meistersinger; Rienzi; Tannhäuser (original version). *Parsifal: Prelude to Act 1.*
**(*) DG 2531/*3301* 214 [id.]. VPO, Boehm.

Under Boehm the Vienna Philharmonic plays beautifully in a choice of overtures spanning Wagner's full career from *Rienzi* to *Parsifal*. The performance of *Rienzi* has striking life and vigour; *Die Meistersinger* has both grandeur and detail, the *Parsifal Prelude* is superbly eloquent and spacious in feeling, and both show a compulsive inevitability in their forward flow. The recording is full, but its beauty is slightly marred by the aggressiveness of trumpet tone. On cassette, however, this is less noticeable, and the sound on tape successfully combines brilliance and weight.

CHAMBER AND INSTRUMENTAL MUSIC

Adagio for clarinet and strings.
(M) **(*) Argo ZK/*KZKC* 62. Brymer, Allegri Qt – BRAHMS: *Clarinet quintet.***(*)

There seems no doubt now that this piece, long thought to be by Wagner, is by Heinrich Baermann, a clarinet virtuoso of the early part of the nineteenth century. In any event it undoubtedly has charm, and, as in the Boskovsky version, it serves as a useful fill-up for the Brahms. Brymer and his colleagues give an eloquent and polished account, though the Boskovsky remains the preferred version (Decca SDD 249).

Piano music: *Albumblatt in C; Albumblatt in E flat; Album-Sonata in A flat; Ankunft bei den schwarzen Schwänen; Piano sonata in B flat.*

(M) *(*) Turn. TVS 34655 [id.]. Galling.
Piano sonata in A; Fantaisie in F sharp min.
(M) *(*) Turn. TVS 34654 [id.]. Galling.

Wagner's early piano music is mostly derivative, and the later pieces are pretty insubstantial. Martin Galling is an impressive player and does what he can for this music. The recordings date from the early 1960s and are acceptable rather than distinguished: the balance is somewhat synthetic. This is ideal for the occasional quiz but is unlikely to prove rewarding for repeated listening.

VOCAL MUSIC

Das Liebesmahl der Apostel (cantata).
(*) Symph. SYM/*CSYM 11* [Peters PLE 043]. Amb. Male-Voice Ch., Symph. of L., Morris – BRUCKNER: *Helgoland.**

The disappointment of Wyn Morris's account of Wagner's strange Pentecostal cantata, written originally for massed choirs in Dresden at a time when he was composing *Tannhäuser*, is that the male chorus sounds comparatively small, whereas Wagner undoubtedly envisaged a more spectacular effect. With homophonic writing the rule, the squareness and plainness of Wagner's invention are underlined, where ideally one wants a more persuasive manner. But with a fascinating Bruckner coupling, this is still a recording to cherish. The unaccompanied opening sections are splendidly vivid and immediate, helped by a recording of remarkable presence and wide dynamic range. As the work expands the chorus recedes within the orchestral framework, and the balance remains attractively spacious if lacking the monumental qualities Wagner obviously intended. The cassette and disc are closely matched.

Wesendonk Lieder. Arias: *Der flie-gende Holländer: Jo ho hoe!, Truft ihr das Schiff; Senta's ballad. Tannhäu-ser: Dich, teure Halle; Allmächt'ge Jungfrau. Tristan und Isolde: Mild und leise.*
** Hung. SLPX 11940. Sass, Hungarian State Op. Ch. and O., Kórodi.

Though the accompaniments are in-differently played and recorded, Sylvia Sass with her characterful singing makes ample amends, whether in the operatic excerpts – with each heroine sharply dis-tinguished – or in the *Wesendonk Lieder,* where the foretastes of *Tristan* come out well. As ever the vocal line is disturbed by the occasional ugliness of tone, but the command of Sass as a Wagnerian is never in doubt.

(i) *Wesedonk Lieder.* Arias: *Lohen-grin: Einsam in trüben Tagen (Elsa's dream). Parsifal: Ich sah' das Kind. Die Walküre, Act 1: Der Männer Sippe; Du bist der Lenz; (ii) Act 2: Siegmund! Sieh auf mich!*
(M) *** Decca GRV 11. Flagstad, VPO, (i) Knappertsbusch, (ii) Solti (with Svanholm).

Kirsten Flagstad's glorious voice is perfectly suited to the rich inspiration of the *Wesendonk Lieder. Im Treibhaus* is particularly beautiful. Sieglinde's solo too is magnificent, but the scale of the voice makes *Elsa's dream* sound a little unwieldy; and, fine as it is vocally, Kundry's *Herzeleide* sounds rather staid for a seductress. However, to redress the balance, for this 'Grandi voci' reissue Decca have included also Brünnhilde's aria from Solti's 1958 partial recording of Act 2 of *Die Walküre,* an outstanding reminder of one of the finest Brünnhildes of our time. The other items date from 1956, and the vintage Decca recording still sounds fresh.

OPERA

Der fliegende Holländer (complete).
(M) **(*) HMV SLS/*TC-SLS* 5226 (3) [Ang. S 3616]. Fischer-Dieskau, Schech, Wunderlich, Schock, Frick, Ch. and O. of German State Op., Berlin, Konwitschny.
(B) **(*) Decca D 97 D 3 (3) [Turn. 65095/7]. From 1955 Bay. Festival production: Varnay, Uhde, Lustig, Weber, Traxel, Bay. Festival Ch. and O., Keilberth.

The Konwitschny version was one of the first Wagner recordings which atmo-spherically attempted to use the new medium of stereo sound. Though the conductor could be more vital (he uses the single-act version) it is a warmly con-vincing reading, crowned by the superb singing of Fischer-Dieskau in the title role; his feeling for word-meaning is extraordinarily compelling, with tonal contrasts superbly controlled. Gottlob Frick makes a magnificent Daland, and Rudolf Schock has rarely sounded so well on record, though his Erik yields many points vocally to the headily beautiful singing of the young Fritz Wunderlich as the Steersman. The snag is Marianne Schech as Senta, periodically letting out sounds more apt for the Flying Scotsman than the *Flying Dutchman,* but she finds much tenderness too. The remastering of the 1960 sound is warm and agreeable. The cassette transfer is acceptable, al-though the focus is not always ideally sharp.

The live recording made by Decca at Bayreuth in 1955 – complete with the traditional fanfare from the balcony of the Festspielhaus – was recorded in stereo experimentally, and considering the date the result is amazingly fine. Above all Keilberth's urgently dramatic reading has never been surpassed since, for with chorus and orchestra steeped in the music, there is a concentration which superbly sustains the running of the three acts together. Hermann Uhde makes a strong Dutchman, Astrid Varnay was at her finest in this recording, if a little too mature for Senta, and though the rest of the singing is not so memorable, there is no serious flaw. At bargain price, complete with libretto, it makes an excellent recommendation, though the Konwitschny set with Fischer-Dieskau, costing very slightly more, has more refinement.

Still recommended: First choice remains with Solti's Chicago set (Decca D 24 D 3/*K 24 K 32* [Lon. 13119/5-]), with Norman Bailey a deeply impressive Dutchman; but the Decca sound is comparatively unatmospheric and the result is vividly immediate to the point of aggressiveness.

Der fliegende Holländer: highlights.
**(*) Decca SET/*KCET* 626. Bailey, Martin, Krenn, Talvela, Kollo, Chicago Ch. and SO, Solti.
(M) ** Ph. Fest. 6570/*7310* 081. From 1961 Bay. Festival recording: Crass, Silja, Greindl, Uhl, Bay. Festival Ch. and O., Sawallisch.

The Flying Dutchman lends itself to excerpts better than some of Wagner's late operas, but even so this Decca selection ends *Senta's ballad* without a satisfactory cadence, and the *Norwegian sailors' chorus* also finishes in mid-air. Nevertheless the excerpts show the consistency of the performance and the vibrancy of Solti's direction. The vividly forward recording sounds slightly less refined in this cassette transfer compared with the disc.

The selection from the live recording made at the 1961 Bayreuth performances has a limited appeal. Neither the conducting nor the orchestral playing is especially distinguished, and the privilege of hearing stage shufflings (and the enthusiastic stomping of the chorus in *Steuermann! Lass die Wacht!*) will not be to all tastes. Fritz Uhl is a disappointing Dutchman; Anja Silja sings in tune (sur-

prisingly rare for Sentas), but it is not a very sweet sound. However, this makes a fair sampler, and there is a certain sense of occasion. The recording is vivid, with good projection and detail on disc and cassette alike, although the drums cause an occasional hiatus in smoothness of the tape transfer.

Götterdämmerung (complete).
(M) *** DG 2740 148 (6) [2716 001]/*3378 048* [*id.*] *coupled with 'Das Rheingold'*). Dernesch, Janowitz, Brilioth, Stewart, Kelemen, Ludwig, Ridderbusch, German Op. Ch., Berlin PO, Karajan.

Karajan's DG set of *Götterdämmerung* has been reissued at medium price (though the older listing persists in the USA, according to Schwann). This version has now also been made universally available on cassette in a 'chunky' box, together with *Das Rheingold*, at what is almost bargain price; but the layout is less satisfactory than Solti's magnificent Decca set, which remains a clear first choice (SET 292/7/*K 4 W 32* [Lon. 1604/5-]).

The Twilight of the Gods (*Götterdämmerung;* complete, in English).
*** HMV SLS/*TC-SLS* 5118 (6). Hunter, Remedios, Welsby, Haugland, Hammond Stroud, Curphey, Pring, E. Nat. Op. Ch. and O., Goodall.

Goodall's account of the culminating opera in Wagner's tetralogy may not be the most powerful ever recorded, and certainly it is not the most polished, but it is one which, paradoxically, by intensifying human as opposed to superhuman emotions heightens the epic scale. The very opening may sound a little tentative (like the rest of the Goodall English *Ring*, this was recorded live at the London Coliseum), but it takes no more than a few seconds to register the body and richness of the sound. The few slight imprecisions and the occasional rawness of wind tone actually seem to enhance the earthiness of Goodall's view, with more of the primeval saga about it than the magnificent polished studio-made *Ring* cycles. Both Rita Hunter and Alberto Remedios were more considerately recorded on the earlier Unicorn version of the final scenes, with more bloom on their voices, but their performances here are magnificent in every way. In particular the golden beauty of Remedios's tenor is consistently superb, with no Heldentenor barking at all, while Aage Haugland's Hagen is giant-sounding to focus the evil, with Gunther and Gutrune mere pawns. The voices on stage are in a different, drier acoustic from that for the orchestra, but considering the problems the sound is impressive. As for Goodall, with his consistently expansive tempi he carries total concentration – except, curiously, in the scene with the Rhinemaidens, whose music (as in Goodall's *Rhinegold* too) lumbers along heavily. The cassette transfer is generally very successful and is notable for the warmth and bloom given to voices and orchestra alike.

Lohengrin (complete).
(M) ** DG 2740 141 (5) [2713 005]. Janowitz, King, Gwyneth Jones, Stewart, Ridderbusch, Bav. R. Ch. and O., Kubelik.

Like Karajan's DG *Götterdämmerung*, Kubelik's dedicated and thoughtful reading of *Lohengrin* has been reissued at medium price in the UK but not the USA. Gundula Janowitz's ravishing performance as Elsa makes this an essential set for Wagnerians to hear, and James King is an imaginative Lohengrin; but Thomas Stewart's Telramund has nothing like the dramatic intensity ideally required, and Gwyneth Jones as the wicked Ortrud makes a sad showing. First choice remains with the wonderfully rapt account directed by Kempe on

HMV (SLS 5071 [Ang. S 3641]), which has never been surpassed on record (the tapes are disappointingly unrefined). The intensity of Kempe's conducting lies even in its very restraint, and the singers too seem uplifted, with Jess Thomas, Elisabeth Grümmer and Gottlob Frick all in superb form. But it is the partnership of Christa Ludwig and Dietrich Fischer-Dieskau as Ortrud and Telramund that sets the seal on this marvellous performance.

Die Meistersinger von Nürnberg: highlights.
*** DG 2537 041 [id.]. Fischer-Dieskau, Ligendza, Ludwig, Hermann, Domingo, Laubenthal, Lagger, Ch. and O. of German Op., Berlin, Jochum.
**(*) Decca SET/*KCET* 625. Bailey, Bode, Moll, Weikl, Kollo, Dallapozza, Hamari, V. State Op. Ch., VPO, Solti.

Jochum's is a performance that more than any on record captures the light and shade of Wagner's most warmly approachable score, its humour and tenderness as well as its strength. The complete recording (DG 2740 149 (5) [2713 011]/*3378 068* (4)) was made at the same time as live opera-house performances in Berlin, and the sense of a comedy being enacted is irresistible. The balance favours the voices, which is a pity, but is otherwise wide-ranging and refined; this makes a clear first choice.

For those who opt for another complete version, these excerpts from Jochum's set are specially valuable for giving fair samples of the two most individual and memorable performances, Fischer-Dieskau as a sharply incisive Sachs, his every nuance of mood clearly interpreted, and Domingo a golden-toned if hardly idiomatic Walther. Both have three major solos, and the disc also includes such passages as the *Apprentices' chorus* in Act 2 and the entrance of the Guilds in Act 3. The recording – with voices rather close – matches the fine quality of the complete set.

865

The great glory of Solti's recording of *Die Meistersinger* (Decca D 13 D 5/*K 13 K 54* [Lon. 1512/5-]) is not the searing brilliance of the conductor but the mature and involving portrayal of Sachs by Norman Bailey. The rest of the cast is more uneven, and Solti, for all his energy, gives a surprisingly square reading of this most appealing of Wagner scores. The recording is remarkably brilliant and clear on disc and cassette alike, and tape collectors will note that the Decca sound has far more projection and detail than the DG cassettes of Jochum's set. The vividness of the sound (and its comparative lack of atmosphere) is striking on this generous set of excerpts, which effectively minimizes the principal flaws of the complete set (the contributions of Hannelore Bode and René Kollo as Eva and Walther) and rightly concentrates on Norman Bailey's noble characterization of Sachs. Kurt Moll as Pogner is also well represented. The cassette matches the disc but is slightly fiercer in the upper range.

Die Meistersinger: excerpts (*Overture; Chorale: Da zu dir der Heiland kam; Prelude to Act 3; Dance of the apprentices; Entry of the masters; Wach auf!*). *Tannhäuser: Overture and Venusberg music; Pilgrims' chorus.*
**(*) Decca SXL/*KSXC* 6860. V. State Op. Ch., VPO, Solti.

The three chunks from *Meistersinger* bleed worse than the two from *Tannhäuser*, although even here the *Pilgrims' chorus* has to be faded out at the end. But for those who want samples of both operas this is a first-rate record, with the excellent sound quality of Solti's complete sets of both operas well preserved. But the juxtaposition does bring home how much richer and warmer is Solti's reading of *Tannhäuser* than of *Meistersinger*. The cassette transfers are brilliant and clear; the sound in *Die Meistersinger* is outstanding, approaching demonstration vividness.

Parsifal (complete).
⊛ *** DG Dig. 2741/*3382* 002 (5) [id.].
Hofmann, Vejzovic, Moll, Van Dam, Nimsgern, Von Halem, German Op. Ch., Berlin PO, Karajan.

Communion, musical and spiritual, is what this intensely beautiful Karajan set provides, with pianissimos shaded in magical clarity, and the ritual of bells and offstage choruses heard as in ideal imagination. If, after the Solti recording for Decca, it seemed doubtful whether a studio recording could ever match earlier ones made on stage at Bayreuth in spiritual intensity, Karajan proves otherwise, his meditation the more intense because the digital sound allows total silences. The playing of the Berlin orchestra – preparing for performance at the Salzburg Easter Festival of 1980 – is consistently beautiful, but the clarity and refinement of sound prevent this from emerging as a lengthy serving of Karajan soup. He has rarely sounded so spontaneously involved in opera on record. Kurt Moll as Gurnemanz is the singer who more than any anchors the work vocally, projecting his voice with firmness and subtlety. José van Dam as Amfortas is also splendid: the *Lament* is one of the glories of the set, enormously wide in dynamic and expressive range. The Klingsor of Siegmund Nimsgern could be more sinister, but the singing is admirable. Dunja Vejzovic makes a vibrant, sensuous Kundry who rises superbly to the moment in Act 2 where she bemoans her laughter in the face of Christ. Only Peter Hofmann as Parsifal leaves any disappointment; at times he develops a gritty edge on the voice, but his natural tone is admirably suited to the part – no one can match him today – and he is never less than dramatically effective. He is not helped by the relative closeness of the solo voices, but otherwise the recording is near the atmospheric ideal, a superb achievement. The cassette transfer on chrome tapes is also of the very highest quality, losing little if anything in comparison with the discs. This is perhaps the finest set of cassettes DG have yet issued; the sound is very beautiful indeed.

Parsifal: highlights.
(M) **(*) Ph. Fest. 6570/*7310* 082. From 1963 Bay. Festival recording: Thomas, Dalis, Hotter, Neidlinger, Bay. Festival Ch. and O., Knappertsbusch.

With so seamlessly expansive an opera it is almost sacrilege to extract 'bleeding chunks' for a highlights disc, but those who own other complete versions, as well as those who simply want to sample a great opera and a great performance, are well served in this mid-price selection from Knappertsbusch's radiant performance recorded at Bayreuth in 1963. For its age the sound is nicely atmospheric on disc and cassette alike.

Das Rheingold (complete).
(M) *** DG 2740 145 (3) [2709 023]/*3378 048* [id.] (*coupled with 'Götterdämmerung'*). Fischer-Dieskau, Veasey, Stolze, Kelemen, Berlin PO, Karajan.
**(*) Ar. Eur. Dig. 301/*501* 137 (3). Adam, Nimsgern, Stryczek, Schreier, Bracht, Salminen, Vogel, Büchner, Minton, Popp, Priew, Schwarz, Dresden State O., Janowski.

The Eurodisc set of *Das Rheingold*, part of a promised cycle, comes from East Germany, with Marek Janowski a direct, alert conductor of the Dresden State Orchestra. This performance is treated to a digital recording totally different from Boulez's. The studio sound has the voices close and vivid (on cassette there is an element of hardness on top until the treble is cut back a little), with the orchestra rather in the background. Some Wagnerians prefer that kind of balance, but the result here rather lacks the atmospheric qualities which make the Solti

Rheingold still the most compelling in sound (Decca SET 382/4/*K 2 W 29* [Lon. 1309/5-]), thanks to the detailed production of the late John Culshaw. With Solti, Donner's hammer-blow is overwhelming; but the Eurodisc set comes up with only a very ordinary 'ping' on an anvil, and the grandeur of the moment is missing. Theo Adam as Wotan has his grittiness of tone exaggerated here, but otherwise it is a fine set, consistently well cast, including Peter Schreier, Matti Salminen, Yvonne Minton and Lucia Popp as well as East German singers of high calibre. The cassettes match the discs very closely, and the libretto with the tape box is printed in a satisfactory type-face, not too small to read comfortably.

Karajan's set has been reissued in the UK at medium price (with a companion tape box also including *Götterdämmerung* but priced very competitively). This too lacks the drama of the Solti version; Karajan is more reflective and less subtle in shaping phrases and rhythms. But on the credit side the singing cast has hardly any flaw at all, and Fischer-Dieskau's Wotan is a brilliant, memorable creation, virile, and expressive and much more agreeable in timbre than Theo Adam on Eurodisc.

Der Ring der Nibelungen (*Das Rheingold; Die Walküre; Siegfried; Götterdämmerung;* complete).
*** Ph. Dig. 6769 074 (16) [id.]. From 1979/80 Bay. Festival productions: McIntyre, Jung, Gwyneth Jones, Becht, Zednik, Salminen, Hubner, Altmeyer, Schwarz, Killibrew, Wenkel, Jerusalem, Egel, Hofmann, Mazura, Bay. Festival Ch. and O., Boulez.

It may surprise those who still think of Boulez as a cold conductor that his is the most passionate performance of *The Ring* available on disc. Speeds are fast, putting the complete cycle on fewer discs than usual (sixteen instead of nineteen), with each of the last three operas better presented for having fewer side-breaks. The four separate boxes come in a lavish package which also includes a hardback book with over a hundred pictures of Patrice Chéreau's highly controversial production at Bayreuth. Gwyneth Jones, handsome as Brünnhilde on stage, lurches between thrilling, incisive accuracy and fearsome yowls. Opposite her as Siegfried, Manfred Jung is by Heldentenor standards commendably precise and clean, but at times he sounds puny, not helped by microphone balances. But none of these obvious drawbacks can hide the fact that the recording – digital in the first three operas, analogue in *Götterdämmerung* – gives a thrilling idea of what it feels like to witness *The Ring* at Bayreuth. Boulez's concentration falters hardly once. The fast speeds convey conviction, making one ever eager to hear more rather than to contemplate. The 1980 cast was better than average. Donald McIntyre as Wotan has rarely if ever sounded so well on record, while Peter Hofmann as Siegmund is more agreeable here than he has been on other Wagner records, such as the Karajan *Parsifal*.

Among rival sets, Furtwängler – what you can hear of him in two cycles recorded live in dull mono sound – finds a greater emotional range. Goodall's English *Ring* (see below) represents the opposite view to Boulez's on tempo. Karajan on DG is richer and smoother, while Solti on Decca blazes far more brilliantly and still remains a first choice, taking everything into account. Both he and Karajan are helped by being recorded in the studio, where Boulez's live performances are beset by all kinds of stage noises, and inevitably the singing is flawed.

The Ring (The Rhinegold; The Valkyrie; Siegfried; The Twilight of the Gods; complete, in English).
(M) *** HMV SLS/*TC-SLS* 5146 (20 LPs; 15 cassettes). Soloists, Ch. and O. of E. Nat. Op., Goodall.

The recording of Goodall's *Ring* cycle during a series of live performances at the London Coliseum was an outstanding achievement. Goodall's direction, spacious yet compelling throughout, brings the music vividly to life; singing and playing maintain the highest standards; and the clarity and richness of the recording are equally remarkable, even if balances are sometimes less than ideal. This will prove a splendid investment for those who want to hear the *Ring* cycle in English. The sound on tape generally matches the discs closely.

Der Ring: excerpts: *Das Rheingold*: Scene 4: *Zur Burg führt die Brücke; Die Walküre*: Act 1: *Ein Schwert verhiess mir der Vater*; Act 3: *Ride of the Valkyries; Loge, hör; Magic fire music; Siegfried*: Act 1: *Nothung!*; *Götterdämmerung*: Act 3: *Siegfried's death and funeral march.*
(M) **(*) DG Priv. 2535/*3335* 239 (from the complete sets cond. Karajan).

The task of selecting highlights from the whole of the *Ring* cycle is an impossible one, but no one would seriously object to any of the items on this midpriced sampler from Karajan's DG cycle, all of them among the Wagnerian peaks. Good, generally refined recording, and the tape transfer is mostly of excellent quality, clear and expansive. The excerpts are nicely tailored so that one is never left unsatisfied after a clumsy fade-out.

Siegfried (complete).
(M) ** DG 2740 147 (5) [2713 003]/*3378 049* [id.] (*coupled with 'Die Walküre'*). Dernesch, Dominguez, Thomas, Stolze, Stewart, Kelemen, Berlin PO, Karajan.

Like Karajan's other *Ring* sets, his version of *Siegfried* has been reissued at medium price in the UK, and the cassettes, coupled to *Die Walküre*, are very reasonably priced. However, when Siegfried is outsung by Mime it is time to complain, and though this version has many qualities – not least the Brünnhilde of Helga Dernesch – it hardly rivals the Solti version (Decca SET 242/6/*K 3 W 31* [Lon. 1508/5-]).

Tannhäuser: highlights.
(M) **(*) Ph. Fest. 6570/*7310* 080. From 1962 Bay. Festival production: Silja, Bumbry, Windgassen, Greindl, Waechter, Stolze, Bay. Festival Ch. and O., Sawallisch.

Solti's complete set of *Tannhäuser* (Decca SET 506/9/*K 80 K 43* [Lon. 1438/5-]), by a fair margin the most compelling ever recorded, provides an electrifying experience, demonstrating beyond a shadow of doubt how much more effective the Paris revision is compared with the usual Dresden version; and there is a generally recommendable set of highlights available on Decca SET 556 [Lon. 26299]. However, at medium price this generous selection from the 1962 Bayreuth recording, incisively conducted by Wolfgang Sawallisch, is worth considering. Windgassen and Greindl both make impressive contributions, and the only drawback is the Elisabeth of Anja Silja, not very well controlled. But the recording still sounds well, and the cassette transfer too has an excellent clarity of focus: the finale is given striking breadth and impact.

Tristan und Isolde (complete).
*** Decca Dig. D 250 D 5 (5)/*K 250 K 53* (3). Mitchinson, Gray, Joll, Howell, Folwell, Harris, Wilkens, Welsh Nat. Op. Ch. and O., Goodall.
(M) **(*) DG 2740 144 [2713 001]/*3378 069* [*id.*]. From 1966 Bay. Festival production (with rehearsal sequence): Windgassen, Nilsson, Ludwig, Talvela, Waechter, Bay. Fest. Ch. and O., Bochm.

Based on the much-praised production of the Welsh National Opera company, Goodall's recording of *Tristan* was made not on stage but at Brangwyn Hall, Swansea, just when the cast was steamed up for stage performances. With long takes the result is an extremely fresh-sounding performance, vivid and immediate, more intimate than rival versions yet bitingly powerful. Typically from Goodall, it is measured and steady, but the speeds are not all exceptionally slow, and with rhythms sharply defined and textures made transparent he keeps the momentum going. So with the frenzied lovers' greetings in Act 2 Goodall's tread is inexorable at his measured speed and the result compelling. The WNO Orchestra is not sumptuous but the playing is well-tuned and responsive. Neither Linda Esther Gray nor John Mitchinson is as sweet on the ear as the finest rivals, for in both the microphone exaggerates vibrato. But Mitchinson never barks Heldentenor-style, and Gray in her first major recording provides a formidable combination of qualities, feminine vulnerability alongside commanding power. Gwynne Howell is arguably the finest King Mark on record, making his monologue at the end of Act 2, so often an anticlimax, into one of the noblest passages of all. This may not have the smoothness of the finest international sets, but with its vivid digital sound it is certainly one of the most compelling of latterday Wagner recordings. The cassette transfer is one of Decca's very finest, outstandingly rich, vivid and clear: the atmospheric horn calls in Act 2, for instance, are magically caught. The layout of three tapes against five discs is more suitable, tailoring acts to the ends of sides. The only snag is the libretto, a straightforward reduction of the LP booklet, with much smaller print.

Boehm's set, now available at medium price in the UK (with a cassette box universally available) was taken from a live performance at Bayreuth, but apart from such passages as the *Prelude* and concluding *Liebestod*, where the experience is vivid, the performance too often acquires tensions of the wrong sort, and Boehm's speeds are surprisingly fast. Nilsson is here more expressive but less bright-toned than in her Decca set, and Windgassen – in his time an incomparable Tristan – begins to show signs of wear in the voice. The recording favours the voices, suffering inevitably from live recording conditions. The cassette transfer is undoubtedly vivid.

Still recommended: Karajan's is a sensual, caressingly beautiful performance, with superbly refined playing from the Berlin Philharmonic (HMV SLS 963 [Ang. S 3777]). Helga Dernesch as Isolde is seductively feminine, and she produces glorious tone-colour through every range. Jon Vickers matches her in what is arguably his finest performance on record. The recording is warmly atmospheric, and the overall effect is radiantly compelling. Solti's performance (Decca D 41 D 5 (5)/K 41 K 53 (3) [Lon. 1502/5-]) is less flexible and sensuous than Karajan's, but he shows himself ready to relax in Wagner's more expansive periods. On the other hand, the end of Act 1 and the opening of the Love duet have a knife-edge dramatic tension. Birgit Nilsson responds superbly to Solti's direction, and Fritz Uhl makes a really musical Heldentenor partner, if dramatically he leaves the centre of the stage to Isolde. The production has the usual Decca/Culshaw imaginative touches, and the recording matches brilliance with satisfying richness. The cassettes too are outstandingly successful, with each of the three acts given a tape to itself. The libretto supplied with the cassettes is preferable to that issued with the newer Goodall set from the same company.

Tristan und Isolde: Prelude to Act 1; Isolde's narration and curse; Liebestod.
(M) **(*) Decca Jub. JB/*KJBC* 58. Nilsson, Hoffman, VPO, Knappertsbusch.

This record was made in 1960, before Nilsson recorded her first complete set under Solti, and the performance displays less overt feeling than might be expected. But the end result is in many ways made the more impressive with the emotion of the moment conveyed by reticence and controlled power. Knappertsbusch characteristically feels for the sublime lengths of Wagner rather than seeking the cutting dramatic edge of a Solti, but with spacious recording the result is persuasive. The Act 1 duet (with Grace Hoffman) goes from where Isolde sends Brangäne to fetch Tristan to the fateful moment where she selects the death potion. The recording sounds vivid in this reissue, and the cassette too is of excellent quality, with a strikingly crisp overall focus, the voice vibrant against a full-bodied orchestral sound.

Die Walküre (complete).
(M) **(*) DG 2740 146 (5) [2713 002]/*3378 049* [*id.*] (*coupled with 'Siegfried'*). Crespin, Janowitz, Veasey, Vickers, Stewart, Talvela, Berlin PO, Karajan.

The great merits of Karajan's version of *Die Walküre* – here re-issued alongside a competitively priced cassette alternative, coupled with *Siegfried* – are the refinement of the orchestral playing and the heroic strength of Jon Vickers as Siegmund. With that underlined, one cannot but note that the vocal shortcomings here are generally more marked, and the result does not add up to a compellingly dramatic experience as does the Solti version (Decca SET 312/6/*K 3 W 30* [Lon. 1509/5-]), a deliberately lyrical conception, making Act 2 the kernel of the work, perhaps even of the whole cycle. This remains first choice, with a superlative Decca recording and a first-class cassette transfer.

COLLECTION

Der fliegende Holländer: Senta's ballad. Lohengrin: Elsa's dream. Die Meistersinger: O Sachs, mein Freund. Rienzi: Gerechter Gott . . . In seiner Blüte. Tannhäuser: Elisabeth's greeting; Elisabeth's prayer. Tristan und Isolde: Liebestod. Die Walküre: Du bist der Lenz.
** Decca SXL/*KSXC* 6930 [Lon. 26612/5-]. Sutherland, Nat. PO, Bonynge.

Early in her career Sutherland resisted Covent Garden suggestions that she should develop as a Wagnerian soprano. Nonetheless it is a big as well as a flexible voice, and after her easy assumption of the role of Puccini's Turandot, it seemed natural enough for her to attempt the arias on this recital record. The results are variable. She sounds happiest in *Senta's ballad* (*Jo ho hoe* floated very sweetly) and in Elisabeth's two arias, though they lack a feeling for detail, and when it comes to Isolde's *Liebestod* and Sieglinde's *Du bist der Lenz* the generalized warmth is not really enough. It is a pity too that the *Rienzi* item (Adriano, a travesty role) comes first on the disc, for there the beat in the voice is obtrusive. Good, full-ranging recording and an admirable cassette transfer.

Waldteufel, Emil
(1837–1915)

Waltzes: Estudiantina; Je t'aime; Mon Rêve; Les Patineurs; Pluie de diamants; Les Sirènes.
(M) **(*) RCA Gold GL/*GK* 25281. Berlin SO, Stolz.

Waltzes: Les Grenadiers; Mon Rêve; Pomone; Pluie de diamants; Les Sirènes; Très Jolie.
(M) **(*) HMV Green. ESD/*TC-ESD* 7070. LPO, Boskovsky.

Robert Stolz sees these waltzes as an extension of the Viennese tradition, and his treatment of the principal melody of *Les Patineurs* is characteristic of his somewhat indulgent approach. The Berliners' playing at the opening of *Je t'aime*, attractively robust, even has something of the flavour of a beer cellar. Yet the performances have plenty of vivacity and lilt, and *Estudiantina*, with its glittering castanets and brilliant brass, has striking character. Throughout the playing is warmly committed, and with lively recording this is most enjoyable. On tape there is less body and refinement than on disc: a treble cut is needed to restore the bloom to the upper strings.

With Boskovsky too the Viennese manner is predominant. This is his second collection (the first was issued on ESD 7012 and played by the Monte Carlo Opera Orchestra), and here the playing is rather more polished. The opening of *Pomone* is deliciously pointed and the main theme is phrased very affectionately. *Les Sirènes*, appropriately, also has a seductive principal melody, and Boskovsky's treatment shows subtlety as well as affection. *Les Grenadiers*, however, seems unnecessarily brisk at its opening fanfare, and the principal tune is given a rather mannered rhythmic emphasis. *Mon Rêve* combines vivacity with warmth in a most appealing way. The recording is agreeably full and resonant on disc and cassette alike.

Walton, William
(born 1902)

Cello concerto.
** Chan. Dig. ABRD/*ABTD* 1007. Kirshbaum, SNO, Gibson – ELGAR: *Concerto.*(*)

The idea of coupling the Elgar and Walton concertos was a splendid one, but here, as in the Elgar, the reading of Kirshbaum and Gibson is disappointing, lacking the warmth, weight and expressiveness that so ripe an example of late romanticism demands. The digital recording is also disappointingly wanting in body on disc, while the cassette lacks range and sparkle at the top. First choice for this concerto rests with Tortelier (coupled with Shostakovich on HMV ASD 2924).

Violin concerto.
*** HMV ASD/*TC-ASD* 3483. Haendel, Bournemouth SO, Berglund – BRITTEN: *Concerto.****

A sunny, glowing, Mediterranean-like view of the concerto from Ida Haendel, with brilliant playing from the soloist and eloquent orchestral support from the Bournemouth orchestra under Paavo Berglund. Kyung-Wha Chung's version is wirier and in some ways more in character, but many collectors will respond equally (or even more) positively to Miss Haendel's warmth. There is an unrelieved lyricism about her tone that may not be to all tastes, but given the quality of both playing and recording (as well as the interest of the equally successful Britten coupling) this is an eminently desirable issue. The cassette is rich and has good detail (although the percussion once or twice lacks the last degree of transient crispness) and overall provides a pleasingly natural balance. This can be recommended alongside Kyung-Wha Chung's Decca version with Previn and the LSO, coupled with Stravinsky (Decca SXL/*KSXC* 6601 [Lon. 6819]).

Crown Imperial; Orb and Sceptre (coronation marches); *Façade: suite; Henry V* (incidental music): *suite; Johannesburg Festival overture; Partita for orchestra; Portsmouth Point*
overture; Richard III: Prelude; Spitfire prelude and fugue; Symphony No. 1; (i) *Belshazzar's Feast.*
(M) *** HMV mono/stereo SLS/*TC-SLS* 5246 (3/2). Philh. O., composer, (i) with D. Bell, Philh. Ch.

This box, issued to celebrate the composer's eightieth birthday, gathers together most of the recordings which Walton – for many years his own finest interpreter – made with the Philharmonia Orchestra. Only three of the six sides are in stereo, but some items such as the *Johannesburg Festival overture* (given a fizzing performance) come in stereo for the first time, and the whole compilation presents an excellent and generous conspectus of Walton's achievement. Such recordings as that of *Belshazzar's Feast* have understandably remained continuously in the catalogue, but it is good to have such an important recording as that of the *First Symphony* – less electrifying than Previn's reading, but sharply illuminating – resurrected after many years of unavailability. The booklet includes many delightful portraits and splendid notes by Gillian Widdicombe. The cassette layout too is wholly admirable, with the *Symphony* and *Belshazzar's Feast* back to back on the first of two tapes, so that each work can be heard without a break. The transfers are first-class in every way. A most desirable set.

Crown Imperial (arr. for wind).
(M) ** Ph. Fest. 6570/*7310* 763. Eastman Wind Ens., Fennell – ELGAR: *Cockaigne* etc.**(*); TIPPETT: *Birthday suite.****

Crown Imperial sounds well in its arrangement for wind, especially when the organ enters at the climax and almost doubles the recorded volume of tone. The performance is spacious rather than electrifying, with the rhythmic patterns of the main theme almost over-emphasized. The 1960 recording is still impressive on both disc and tape.

Crown Imperial; Orb and Sceptre.
*** HMV ASD/*TC-ASD* 3388 [Ang. S/
4XS 37436]. LPO, Boult – ELGAR:
Pomp and Circumstance marches
etc.***

Walton's two coronation marches make the ideal coupling for Boult's collection of Elgar marches. It was Boult who first conducted them in Westminster Abbey (in 1937 and 1953 respectively) and he brings even more flamboyance to them than to the Elgar items. The recording is immensely rich and spectacular on disc, and its wide amplitude is, on the whole, satisfactorily caught in the tape transfer, although the focus in the bass is not very clean.

Façade (an entertainment with words by Edith Sitwell; complete).
(M) **(*) Ph. Seq. 6527/*7311* 133. Laine, Ross, Ens. dir. Dankworth.

This version of *Façade* is inevitably controversial. With its distinct jazz overtones it is a performance you will enjoy very much or find slightly self-conscious. But it is certainly worth trying it in this medium-price reissue while the availability of the Pears/Sitwell record (recently on Decca Eclipse) is doubtful. The cassette, transferred at the highest level, is very vivid and immediate.

Symphony No. 1 in B flat min.
(M) *** RCA GL/*GK* 42707. LSO, Previn.
**(*) HMV Dig. ASD/*TCC ASD* 4091. Philh. O., Haitink.
(M) ** ASV ACM/*ZCACM* 2006 [Non. 71394]. Royal Liv. PO, Handley.

Previn gives a marvellously biting account of this magnificent symphony. His fast tempi may initially make one feel that he is pressing too hard, but his ability to screw the dramatic tension tighter and tighter until the final resolution is most assured, and certainly reflects the tense mood of the mid-thirties, as well as the youthful Walton's own dynamism. (The composer has since told us that the tensions express a very personal period of stress in his own emotional life.) '*Presto con malizia*' says the score for the scherzo, and malice is exactly what Previn conveys, with the hints of vulgarity and humour securely placed. In the slow movement Previn finds real warmth, giving some of the melodies an Elgarian richness, and the finale's electricity here helps to overcome any feeling that it is too facile, too easily happy a conclusion. The bright recording quality (late-sixties vintage) remains impressive on disc, but on tape, although the sound remains full and vivid, the dynamics are compressed.

The malevolent demon which inhabits the first two movements is somewhat tamed by Haitink, and in the opening movement some listeners will feel that the lack of the relentless forward thrust demonstrated by both the composer's own reading and Previn's RCA version underplays the music's character. However, this HMV account offers a legitimately spacious if less exciting view, and Haitink's directness leads to noble accounts of the slow movement and finale. The bright digital recording is lacking a little in bass in its disc format, but this is less striking in the chrome cassette, which is admirable in all respects.

Vernon Handley's interpretation of this work matured when he conducted a number of performances with the Liverpool orchestra during Walton's seventy-fifth birthday celebrations. It is essentially a broad view and tends to play down the work's cutting edge: there is very little suggestion of *malizia* in the scherzo. Indeed it must be said that the reading tends to under-characterize the music. While the first-movement climax is impressively shaped to a considerable peak of excitement, it is the orchestral brass that make the most striking effect; the string playing lacks bite and incisiveness, both here and in the finale. The recording is resonant and spacious, and the cassette transfer is first-class.

(i) *Belshazzar's Feast* (oratorio). *Coronation Te Deum.*
*** Decca SET/*KCET* 618 [Lon. 26525/5-]. LPO Ch., Choirs of Salisbury, Winchester and Chichester Cathedrals, LPO, Solti, (i) with Luxon.
(M) **(*) RCA Gold GL/*GK* 13368. SNO and Ch., Gibson, with (i) Milnes, Scottish Festival Brass Bands.

Whether or not prompted by the composer's latterday dictum that *Belshazzar's Feast* is more a choral symphony than an oratorio, Sir Georg Solti directs a sharply incisive performance which brings out the symphonic basis rather than the atmospheric story-telling. Fresh, scintillating and spiky, it is a performance that gives off electric sparks, not always quite idiomatic but very invigorating. Solti observes Walton's syncopations very literally, with little or none of the flexibility that the jazz overtones suggest, and his slow tempo for the lovely chorus *By the waters of Babylon* remains very steady, with little of the customary rubato. But with generally excellent singing from the chorus and a sympathetic contribution from Luxon (marred only slightly by vibrato) this is a big-scale reading which overall is most convincing. Moreover, from the very opening, with its dramatic trombone solo, one is aware that this is to be one of Decca's demonstration recordings, with superbly incisive and clear choral sound, slightly sparer of texture in *Belshazzar's Feast* than in the *Te Deum* written for the Queen's Coronation in 1953, a splendid occasional piece which makes the ideal coupling. The quality is equally clear and vivid on both disc and cassette.

Sir Alexander Gibson's view of Walton's brilliant oratorio tends towards brisk speeds, but is no less dramatic for that. When his version first appeared it was rather overshadowed by the more spectacular account from Solti, simultaneously issued with the same apt and attractive coupling, but at medium price it is strongly competitive, particularly with so magnificent a baritone as Sherrill Milnes as soloist. This is better sung than Loughran's Classics for Pleasure version; and it is better recorded (the cassette is well managed too; if slightly less refined than the disc) and rather cheaper than Walton's unique version on HMV Concert Classics, coupled with the *Partita for orchestra* (SXLP 30236). However, at full price Previn and the London Symphony Chorus and Orchestra offer what is arguably the richest and most spectacular account of *Belshazzar's Feast* yet recorded, with an excellent chrome cassette equivalent (HMV SAN/*TC-SAN* 324 [Ang. S 36861]).

The Bear (opera; complete).
**(*) Chan. ABR/*ABT* 1052. Harris, Yurisich, Mangin, Melbourne SO, Cavdarski.

Walton's brilliant adaptation of Chekhov's one-act farce with its array of parodies makes ideal material for LP. This Australian recording lacks some of the wit of the original cast recording (not currently available), but with first-rate sound and clean-cut, youthful-sounding singing it is well worth investigating. The tape is vivid, but there is an occasional hint of peaking.

Ward, John (1571–1638)

4 Fantasias for viols; 1st Set of English madrigals.
*** O-L D 238 D 2 (2). Cons. of Musicke, Rooley.

Ward's music speaks with a distinctive voice free from the self-conscious melancholy that afflicts some of his contemporaries. This is not to say that his output is wanting in depth of feeling or elegiac sentiment, but rather that his language is freer from artifice. He chooses poetry of high quality and his music is always finely proportioned and organic in conception. His achievement is well summed up by Richard Luckett's note about the poems: 'Together they make up an exploration of a sombre, pastoral world, a darkened Arcadia where the shepherds' eclogues are predominantly elegiac, and pain and loss in love are shaded by a sense of the pain and loss of death.' Many of the madrigals are eloquent and they are intelligently interspersed with instrumental fantasias. Anthony Rooley does not disturb the composer's own layout of the madrigals, and one can observe the growth from three-part settings which are lighter in mood to the more searching and powerful six-part madrigals. John Ward served the Honourable Henry Fanshawe as both Attorney and Musician, and his madrigals are dedicated to him. They appeared at the end of the period in which the madrigal flourished (in 1613, to be exact) but are by no means to be regarded as representing the tradition at anything less than its finest. These performances are dedicated and eminently well recorded, though the rather close balance and the vibrato-less vocal quality makes it desirable not to hear too many at one sitting.

ASMF, Marriner – VAUGHAN WILLIAMS: *Concertos.****

In an age when early and baroque music has become so popular on record, Warlock's suite based on Elizabethan dances seemed to have lost some of its popularity, but the appearance of two new recordings and one reissue confirms its vitality and appeal. Dilkes's performance with the English Sinfonia is beautifully judged, with apt tempi throughout, combining wit and warmth. It is superbly recorded (the cassette offers demonstration quality) and is part of a highly attractive anthology of English music (see the Concerts section below).

On Argo the playing of the St Martin's Academy under Marriner is characteristically polished and stylish and no less readily reveals the freshness and memorability of Warlock's inspiration. This performance is well coupled with the gentle *Serenade* written for Delius and two larger Vaughan Williams works. The recording is first-rate, and again the cassette approaches demonstration standard.

The Scottish Baroque Ensemble's forthright and lively style is quite well suited to Warlock's confection of dance movements and is well recorded. The couplings are unexpected but imaginative.

Warlock, Peter
(1894–1930)

Capriol suite.
(M) *** HMV Green. ESD/*TC-ESD* 7101. E. Sinfonia, Dilkes – *Concert.****
(*) Abbey ABY 810. Scottish Bar. Ens., Friedman – BRITTEN: *Simple symphony* **(*); ELGAR: *Serenade* **; WILLIAMSON: *English lyrics.*(*)

Capriol suite; Serenade for strings (for the sixtieth birthday of Delius).
*** Argo ZRG/*KZRC* 881 [id.].

Wassenaer, Unico
(1692–1766)

6 Concerti armonici.
**(*) DG Arc. 2533 456 [id.]. Camerata Bern, Furi.

These six concertos have been ascribed variously to Ricciotti, Birckenstock and Handel – and were originally attributed to Pergolesi. It now seems that they were the work of Count van Wassenaer and that he lent them to Ricciotti, who played the violin at their first performance. He modestly withheld them from publication, but this did not prevent Ricciotti from going ahead and engraving them, putting the name of the then popular Pergolesi on the title-page so as to facilitate their dissemination. The Swiss ensemble give performances of impeccable style and accuracy, though in the slow movements they miss something of the breadth and spaciousness inherent in the writing. The Camerata players are fewer in number than the Stuttgart Chamber Orchestra, who recorded these works together with a couple of flute concertos in the 1960s, on two as opposed to one record (that set is currently withdrawn). The DG Archive recording is excellent.

Waxman, Franz (1906–67)

Film scores: *Bride of Frankenstein: Creation of the female monster. Old Acquaintance: Elegy for strings. Philadelphia Story: Fanfare; True love. A Place in the Sun: suite. Prince Valiant: suite. Rebecca: suite. Sunset Boulevard: suite. Taras Bulba: The ride to Dubno.*
⊛ *** RCA Gold GL/*GK* 43442. Nat. PO, Gerhardt.

Of the many European musicians who crossed the Atlantic to make careers in Hollywood, Franz Waxman was, alongside Korngold, the most distinguished. Born in Upper Silesia, he had his early musical training in Germany. He was immensely gifted, and much of his music can stand on its own without the screen images it originally served to accompany. His first important score was for James Whale's *Bride of Frankenstein*, a horror movie to which many film buffs give classic status. His evocative music (a haunting Wagnerian crescendo built over a throbbing timpani beat) for *The crea-*

tion of the female monster (visually most compelling in the film sequence) was restored by the conductor, mainly from listening to the film sound-track, as the orchestral parts are lost. It builds on a memorable three-chord motif which seems instantly familiar. Readers will soon discover its associations for themselves: sufficient to say that the more familiar use of this melodic fragment comes from a score written by another composer some fourteen years later. The *Bride of Frankenstein* music dates from 1935. Waxman stayed on to write for 188 films over thirty-two years. The opening of the first item on this tape, the *Suite* from *Prince Valiant*, immediately shows the vigour of Waxman's invention and the brilliance of his Richard-Straussian orchestration, and this score includes one of those sweeping string tunes which are the very epitome of Hollywood film music. Perhaps the finest of these comes in *A Place in the Sun*, and in the *Suite* it is used to preface an imaginative rhapsodical movement for solo alto sax (brilliantly played here by Ronnie Chamberlain). The reprise of the main tune, also on the alto sax but decorated by a characteristic counter-theme in the upper strings, is a moment of the utmost magic. In this work, incidentally, there is another curious anticipation of music written by another composer: a fugal section of Waxman's score is remarkably like the end of the second movement of Shostakovich's *Eleventh Symphony* (written seven years after the film, which was not shown in the Soviet Union). To make the coincidence complete it was Waxman who conducted the West Coast première of the symphony in 1958. The collection ends with *The ride to Dubno* from *Taras Bulba*, which has thrilling impetus and energy and is scored with great flair. Some of this music is among the finest ever written for a film sound-track, and the collection nostalgically includes the famous MGM introductory title fanfare, which Waxman wrote as a backcloth for Leo the Lion. The orchestral playing is marvellously eloquent: this is undoubtedly the finest of Gerhardt's distinguished series. The recording is both brilliant and rich, and disc and cassette are quite closely matched (the disc has marginally more upper range; the cassette is slightly fuller in the middle). Only the disc, however, includes the essential illustrated leaflet giving background details of the films and Waxman's career.

Weber, Carl (1786–1826)

Clarinet concertos Nos. 1 in F min., Op. 73; 2 in E flat, Op. 74.
(B) ** RCA VICS/*VK* 2003 [AGL 1/ *AGK 1* 3788]. Goodman, Chicago SO, Martinon.

A welcome first issue in the UK of Benny Goodman's early stereo coupling of the two Weber *Clarinet concertos*. As we know from his Mozart recordings, when Goodman plays 'straight clarinet' (his term) he strictly avoids any jazz overtones, and to be honest there is an element of self-consciousness here. But there is technical wizardry too, especially in the jocular finales. The recording balance is forward, with dated orchestral sound and an edge to the clarinet timbre, but this remains a fascinating issue. There is no appreciable difference in sound between the disc and the excellent chrome cassette.

Introduction and theme and variations for clarinet and orchestra.
(M) *** Decca Ace SDD 575. Schmidl, New V. Octet (members) – BRAHMS: *Clarinet quintet.****

Peter Schmidl's creamy tone and infectiously fluent style is just right for this lightweight piece (whether or not it is by Weber). The recording is excellent.

Invitation to the Dance, Op. 65 (orch. Berlioz).
*** DG 2531/*3301* 215 [id.]. Chicago SO, Barenboim – *Concert.****

Berlioz's famous and highly successful orchestral transcription of Weber's piano piece is played here with striking warmth and elegance, and the recording is appropriately sumptuous. The rest of the concert in which this appears is also very enjoyable if not quite as memorable as this, the best stereo version available.

(i) *Invitation to the Dance* (orch. Berlioz); *Overtures: Abu Hassan;* (ii) *Der Freischütz; Euryanthe; Oberon;* (iii) *Preciosa.*
(M) ** Ph. Seq. 6527/*7311* 071. (i) LSO, Mackerras; (ii) Concg. O., Dorati; (iii) Spanish R. and TV O., Markevitch.

The two performances under Mackerras are a delight, *Abu Hassan* light and sparkling and an elegant *Invitation to the Dance.* The recording is excellent. In the three Dorati overtures the sound is brilliant but lacking warmth, and the effect is to emphasize Dorati's concentration on drama rather than atmosphere (though there is some beautiful horn playing). The Markevitch Spanish recording lies between the other two in character. The cassette offers a clean transfer of the Dorati recordings but is slightly less well focused in the two Mackerras items. A serviceable rather than outstanding mid-priced issue in an uncrowded field.

Konzertstück in F min., Op. 79.
*** Ph. 9500 677/*7300 772* [id.]. Brendel, LSO, Abbado – SCHUMANN: *Piano concerto.****

Weber's programmatic *Konzertstück* is seldom heard in the concert hall these days, and it is a rarity in the recording studio. This version is very brilliant indeed and finds the distinguished soloist in his very best form: he is wonderfully light and invariably imaginative. In every respect, including the recording quality, this is unlikely to be surpassed for a long time. The cassette has less sparkle and transparency than the disc but is well balanced.

Symphonies Nos. 1 in C; 2 in C.
*** ASV DCA/*ZCDCA* 515. ASMF, Marriner.

Weber's two symphonies were written within a period of two months between December 1806 and the end of January 1807. Curiously both are in C major, yet each has its own individuality and neither lacks vitality of invention. Marriner has their full measure, and these performances combine vigour and high spirits with the right degree of *gravitas* (not too much) in the slow movements. The orchestral playing throughout is infectiously lively and catches the music's vibrant character. The recording is first-class, and the cassette transfer is admirably bright and full.

Symphony No. 1 in C; Invitation to the dance, Op. 65 (orch. Berlioz); Overtures: Abu Hassan; Beherrscher der Geister (*Ruler of the Spirits*); Euryanthe.
*** Decca SXL 6876. VPO, Stein.

With spirited and sensitive playing of the overtures allied to first-class recording, this is a valuable issue, as it also brings a fine account of the early *First Symphony*. Played like this, and recorded in such lifelike sound, the symphony is quite captivating. This is a record to which one returns with pleasure.

Clarinet quintet in B flat, Op. 34.
*** O-L DSLO 553. Hacker, Music Party – KROMMER: *Clarinet quartet.****

If you want to hear how Weber's *Clarinet quintet* must have sounded during his lifetime, Alan Hacker and the Music Party will be your first choice. The Gerock clarinet Hacker uses is from 1804, eleven years earlier than the first complete performance of the quintet. It is not of course the smooth, mellifluous instrument that Gervase de Peyer uses in his version (HMV HQS 1395), and the strings do not sound as blended as one would expect in a modern quartet. Alan Hacker plays with his customary artistry and sensitivity, and the recording is clear and vivid. For most collectors, however, the de Peyer will remain a first choice, but there is no doubting the interest and accomplishment of this 'period-instrument' alternative.

Der Freischütz (opera; complete).
**(*) Decca D 235 D 3 (3)/*K 235 K 32* (2) [Lon. 13136/5-]. Behrens, Donath, Meven, Kollo, Moll, Brendel, Bav. R. Ch. and SO, Kubelik.

Kubelik takes a direct view of Weber's high romanticism. The result has freshness but lacks something in dramatic bite and atmosphere. There is far less tension than in the finest earlier versions, not least in the Wolf's Glen Scene, which in spite of full-ranging, brilliant recording seems rather tame. The singing is generally good – René Kollo as Max giving one of his best performances on record – but Hildegard Behrens, superbly dramatic in later German operas, here as Agathe seems clumsy in music that often requires a pure lyrical line. The cassettes offer demonstration quality, crisp, vivid and clear, and the tape layout on four sides is preferable to that on disc. However, the DG set with Janowitz, Mathis, Schreier, Adam, Vogel and Crass is much more enjoyable; Carlos Kleiber may have his extreme tempi in places, but his is an electrifying reading of an opera that must be played and sung for all it is worth (DG 2720 071/*3371 008* (3) [2709 046/ *3371 008*].

Webern, Anton

(1883–1945)

(i) *Concerto, Op. 24; 5 Movements for string quartet* (orchestral version), *Op. 5; Passacaglia, Op. 1; 6 Pieces for large orchestra, Op. 6; 5 pieces for orchestra, Op. 10; Symphony, Op. 21; Variations for orchestra, Op. 30;* Arrangements of: the *Fugue* from Bach's *Musical Offering* (1935); (ii) Schubert's *German dances* (for small orchestra), *Op. posth.* Chamber music: (iii) *6 Bagatelles for string quartet, Op. 9; 5 Movements for string quartet, Op. 5;* (iv; v) *4 Pieces for violin and piano, Op. 7;* (v; vi) *3 Small pieces for cello and piano, Op. 11;* (v;vii) *Quartet, Op. 22* (for piano, violin, clarinet, saxophone); (iii) *String quartet, Op. 28; String trio, Op. 20;* (v) *Variations for piano, Op. 27.* (Vocal) (viii; i) *Das Augenlicht, Op. 26;* (ix; x) *5 Canons on Latin texts, Op. 16;* (viii; ix; i) *Cantata No. 1, Op. 29;* (viii; ix; xi; i) *Cantata No. 2, Op. 31;* (viii) *Entflieht auf leichten Kähnen, Op. 2;* (ix; x) *5 Sacred songs, Op. 15;* (xii; v) *5 Songs, Op. 3; 5 Songs, Op. 4;* (xii; x) *2 Songs, Op. 8;* (xii; v) *4 Songs, Op. 12;* (xii; x) *4 Songs, Op. 13;* (xii; x) *6 Songs, Op. 14;* (ix; x; xiii) *3 Songs, Op. 18;* (viii; i) *2 Songs, Op. 19;* (xii; v) *3 Songs, Op. 23;* (ix; v) *3 Songs, Op. 25;* (ix; x) *3 Traditional rhymes.*

*** CBS 79402 (4) [Col. M4 35193]. (i) LSO (or members), Boulez; (ii) Frankfurt RO, composer (recorded Dec. 1932); (iii) Juilliard Qt (or members); (iv) Stern, (v) Rosen; (vi) Piatigorsky; (vii) Majeske, Marcellus, Weinstein; (viii) John Alldis Ch.; (ix) Lukomska; (x) with Ens., Boulez; (xi) McDaniel; (xii) Harper; (xiii) with John Williams. Overall musical direction: Boulez.

These four discs contain all of Webern's works with opus numbers, as well as the string orchestra arrangement of Op. 5 and the orchestration of the *Fugue* from Bach's *Musical Offering*. A rare recording of Webern himself conducting his arrangement of Schubert dances is also included. Though the recording quality varies – different items having been made over eleven years – the quality of performance remains very high, and, more important, almost all these performances convey the commitment without which such spare writing can sound merely chill. What Pierre Boulez above all demonstrates in the orchestral works (including those with chorus) is that, for all his seeming asceticism, Webern was working on human emotions. The spareness of the writing lets us appreciate how atonality can communicate tenderly, evocatively, movingly, not by any imitation of romantic models (as Schoenberg's and Berg's music often does) but by reducing the notes to the minimum. The Juilliard Quartet and the John Alldis Choir, too, convey comparable commitment, and though neither Heather Harper nor Halina Lukomska is ideally cast in this music, Boulez brings out the best in both of them in the works with orchestra. Rarely can a major composer's whole œuvre be appreciated within so compact a span. This set can be warmly recommended to anyone who wants to understand one of the key figures of the twentieth century.

Passacaglia for orchestra; 5 Pieces for orchestra; 6 Pieces for orchestra; Symphony; Variations for Orchestra. BACH: *Musical Offering: Fugue* (arr. for orchestra by Webern).
*** CBS 76911/40-. LSO, Boulez.

This excellent disc gathers together all of Webern's purely orchestral works recorded by Boulez for the integral edition. Balances are not always ideal, but hearing the whole range of Webern's mature career, from the *Passacaglia* of 1908 – written before twelve-note serialism was fully formulated – through to the *Variations* of 1940, one can appreciate his development the more sympathetically. Boulez in this music conveys expressiveness as well as clarity. The cassette is full-bodied and has quite good detail, but lacks the upper range of the LP (noticeable when the strings are muted).

Variations for piano, Op. 27.
*** DG 2530 803 [id.]. Pollini – BOULEZ: *Piano sonata No. 2.****

Webern's *Variations* of 1936 make an apt coupling for Boulez's *Second Sonata.* Pollini's account is refined yet strong, and the DG recording is outstandingly faithful. An indispensable issue for those interested in twentieth-century piano music.

Weill, Kurt (1900–1950)

Quodlibet, Op. 9.
(M) ** Turn. TVS 37124 [Can. 31091]. Westphalian SO, Landau – KORNGOLD: *Much Ado About Nothing.***

Weill's *Quodlibet*, which derives from a children's entertainment called *The Magic Night*, is a more interesting work than its companion on this record. It dates from 1924, when Weill had just finished studying with Busoni, whose influence can be detected here. There are reminders, too, of Prokofiev and Hindemith. The playing is acceptable and the recording is eminently serviceable.

The Seven Deadly Sins.
(***) CBS 73657. Lenya, Male Quartets and O., Bruckner-Ruggeberg.

Originally recorded in mono in the mid-fifties, this performance with the composer's widow as the principal singer underlines the status of this distinctive mixture of ballet and song cycle as one of Weill's most concentrated inspirations. The rhythmic verve is irresistible, and though Lenya had to have the music transposed down, her understanding of the idiom is unique. The recording is harsh by modern standards.

Widmann, Erasmus
(1572–1634)

Dances and Gagliardes Nos. 3 (Magdelena); 4 (Anna); 12 (Regina); 13 (Sophia); 15 (Agatha); 16 (Clara).
(M) *** DG Arc. 2547/*3347* 005 [198166]. Coll. Terpsichore – PRAETORIUS: *Terpsichore*; SCHEIN: *Banchetto.****

This set of dances – each charmingly titled with a lady's name – makes a good foil for the Praetorius. The music itself is less memorable but still enjoyable, and it is played most stylishly. The recording still sounds well, but the cassette transfer has a restricted upper range.

Widor, Charles-Marie
(1844–1937)

Suite latine, Op. 86; 3 Nouvelles pièces, Op. 87.
(M) *** O-L SOL 352. Parker-Smith.

The *Suite latine* (1927) has six movements, four of which are based on plainsong, although the treatment has no possible traces of medievalism. Jane Parker-Smith is an ideal exponent of this flamboyant writing, and the organ of Coventry Cathedral produces some suitably spectacular sounds. The three *New Pieces*, written in 1934, are agreeable but less adventurous. Admirers of this repertoire will find this issue of high quality, both musically and technically.

Organ symphony No. 5 in F min., Op. 42/1. (With GRISON: *Toccata in F*; JONGEN: *Sonata eroica, Op. 94.*)
(M) *** HMV HQS 1406. Parker-Smith (organ of Salisbury Cath.).

Recordings of the complete *Organ symphony No. 5* are useful, if only to show that the extraction of the famous *Toccata* finale for separate performance is entirely justified; the writing in the rest of the work is comparatively conventional and in no way equal to this famous piece. Jane Parker-Smith's account of the whole symphony is first-class, and she is very well recorded, especially in the brilliantly played *Toccata*. Her encores are also very acceptable: Jules Grison's *Toccata* is suitably flamboyant, and the Jongen *Sonata eroica* is a well-made if not distinctive piece, also with a spectacular finale, which is played with fine flair.

Wieniawski, Henryk
(1835–80)

Concert polonaise for violin and orchestra.
(M) ** Turn. TVS 34629 [id./*CT 2133*]. Rosand, R. Lux. O., Froment – ARENSKY: *Violin concerto ***; RIMSKY-KORSAKOV: *Concert fantasy.***

This is the first of Wieniawski's two *Concert polonaises* and was written at the end of the 1850s for his compatriot Carl Lipinski (1790–1861). It is a pretty insubstantial piece, but the soloist here

plays marvellously, and this is worth having for the appealing Arensky *Concerto* on the other side.

Wiklund, Adolf
(1879–1950)

(i) *Piano concerto No. 2 in B min., Op. 17. 3 Pieces for strings and harp; Sang till varen.*
** Cap. CAP 1165. Swedish RSO, Westerberg, (i) with Erikson.

Wiklund belonged to the same generation of Swedish composers as Stenhammar, whose enthusiasm for Brahms he obviously shared. But if his music speaks with much the same accents as Alfvén and Stenhammar, it has none of the latter's nobility, and it is essentially second-rate. But there are good things in it: the *Concerto*, which dates from the war years, is effective in its way and well laid out for the piano, though it lacks any powerfully individual quality. The *Three Pieces for strings and harp* are more simple and have an unaffected post-Griegian charm.

Wikmanson, Johan
(1753–1800)

String quartet in E min., Op. 1/2.
*** CRD CRD 1061/*CRDC* 4061. Chilingirian Qt – BERWALD: *Quartet.***

Wikmanson is less well-known than Berwald and never travelled outside his native Sweden. During the 1770s he studied with Johan Martin Kraus and published a Swedish translation of Tartini's *Traité des agréments de la musique.*

Three of his five string quartets survive and were published in 1801, a year after his death. They bore a dedication to Haydn, whose good offices were enlisted to assist their publication, and whose influence is all-pervasive. Indeed, at first Wikmanson's quartets seem almost too heavily indebted to his idol, but as one gets to know them better, a more distinctive profile emerges and their rewards increase. The Chilingirian Quartet give a persuasive and eloquent account of this attractive score, and with the added inducement of a valuable coupling, this issue deserves the widest circulation. Excellent recording quality; the cassette too is full and clear, although very slightly overweighted at the bass end.

Williams, Grace
(1906–77)

(i) *Carillons for oboe and orchestra.*
(ii) *Trumpet concerto. Fantasia on Welsh nursery rhymes.* (iii) *Fairest of Stars.*
*** Oriel CRM 1005. LSO, Groves, with (i) Camden, (ii) Snell, (iii) Janet Price.

It is good to find a composer who so glowingly showed that she believed in pleasing the listener's ear. The works here range attractively from the simple, well-known *Fantasia* (rather more than a colourfully orchestrated potpourri) through two crisply conceived concertante pieces to the relatively tough setting of Milton for soprano and orchestra, *Fairest of Stars*. The trumpet and oboe works – superbly played by soloists from the LSO – both show the affection and understanding of individual instrumental timbre which marked Grace Williams's work. It is a credit to the Welsh Arts Council that such a record could be produced. First-rate recording. (If difficulty is experienced in obtaining this

record, it can be ordered direct from its sponsors.)

Symphony No. 2; Ballads.
*** BBC REGL 381. BBC Welsh SO, Handley.

Grace Williams is best-known for colourful atmospheric works like the *Fantasia on Welsh nursery rhymes*, and much of her early music reflects the folk-based approach instilled in her by her principal teacher, Vaughan Williams. But in this *Second Symphony*, her most ambitious orchestral work, written in 1956 when she was fifty, she aimed at greater astringency, just as Vaughan Williams himself had done in his *Fourth Symphony*. The writing is sharp and purposeful from the start, relaxing more towards lyricism in the slow movement and the finale with its darkly Mahlerian overtones. The *Ballads* of 1968, characteristically based on Welsh ballad and *penillion* forms, also reveal the darker side of Grace Williams's writing, notably in the stark contrasts of the third ballad. Expressive, convincing performances, originally recorded for radio.

Williams, John
(born 1932)

Suites from: *Close Encounters of the Third Kind* (including new music for *Special Edition*); *The Empire Strikes Back; Star Wars; Superman.*
*** Ph. Dig. 9500 921/7300 921 [id.]. Boston Pops O., composer.

This record gathers together John Williams's four most famous film scores in an excellent digital recording under his own direction. While the music is eclectic in style and derivation, it is undoubtedly tuneful in a flamboyant way and spectacularly scored. This record tends to sweep the field in this repertoire, but the chrome tape is transferred at a low level and the quality is sumptuous and atmospheric rather than brilliant, with a lack of crispness in the transients.

Williamson, Malcolm
(born 1931)

Agnus Dei; The Morning of the Day of Days; Procession of Palms; The World at the Manger.
*** Abbey LPB 805. Holt, Thompson, Keyte, Worcester Cath. Ch., Festival Ch. Soc., Hunt; Trepte (organ).

Williamson, devout if not always orthodox in his Christian faith, has written copiously for the church. As a Roman Catholic himself his aim has been ecumenical, with immediacy of communication taking high priority. That is admirably illustrated in all the music here, including three memorable cantatas for different seasons – *Procession of Palms* for Palm Sunday, *The Morning of the Day of Days* for Easter, and *The World at the Manger* (the longest of the pieces here) for Christmas. As in its other Abbey issues, Worcester Cathedral Choir gives lively performances, helped by the rhythmic playing of Paul Trepte on the organ. Atmospheric recording.

6 English lyrics.
(*) Abbey ABY 810. Lea, Scottish Bar. Ens., Friedman – BRITTEN: *Simple symphony* **(*); ELGAR: *Serenade* **; WARLOCK: *Capriol suite.*(*)

Malcolm Williamson is president of the Scottish Baroque Ensemble, and this delightful sequence of varied settings (mostly of poems, such as *Sweet and low*, known very well in other settings) is a tribute to that. It makes an excellent foil for the three very familiar works also included on this disc. The microphone catches a disturbing vibrato in Yvonne Lea's voice, but these are warm-hearted performances, well worth investigating.

Wolf, Hugo (1860–1903)

Penthesilea (symphonic poem).
(M) **(*) DG Priv. 2726 067 (2). VSO, Gerdes – MAHLER: *Symphony No. 9.***(*)

Early in his career Hugo Wolf, much influenced by Liszt and Wagner, produced this ambitious symphonic poem, and today it makes an enjoyable curiosity, if hardly one of the composer's more important works.

The DG Privilege recording (coupled with Kubelik's version of Mahler's *Ninth*) is of a lively performance from a conductor who for many years was a recording producer for DG.

Italian serenade in G.
(M) *** Decca Ace SDD 543. Küchl Qt – KODÁLY: *String quartet No. 2*; SUK: *String quartet No. 1.****

Hugo Wolf's *Italian serenade* is so enchanting and inventive a work that it is amazing that so few ensembles have recorded it. Apart from the Guarneri (and Münchinger's version of Reger's orchestral transcription), this is the only record in the current UK catalogue. Surely it could have replaced some of the dozen or so accounts of Schubert's *Quartettsatz* as a fill-up. This disc would be worth having just for the sake of this short but always refreshing score.

Lieder

Alte Weisen (6 poems by Keller). 6 *Lieder für eine Frauenstimme. Goethe*

Lieder: Als ich auf dem Euphrat schiffte; Anakreons Grab; Die Bekehrte; Blumengrüss; Epiphanias; Frühling übers Jahr; Ganymed; Gleich und gleich; Hochbeglückt in deiner Liebe; Kennst du das Land; Mignon Lieder Nos. I–III; Philine. Nimmer will ich dich verlieren (from *Suleika Book*)*; Der Schäfer; Die Spröde; St Nepomuks Vorabend. Byron Lieder: Sonne der Schlummerlosen.*

※ (M) *** HMV SLS 5197 (2). Schwarzkopf, Moore.

These two discs contain some of the very finest singing of Wolf songs ever recorded. Walter Legge, Schwarzkopf's husband, was the force behind the first major Wolf recording project on 78 in the 1930s, but in many ways the achievement of Schwarzkopf, and certainly the vocal finesse, go even further, whether in the dark intensity of the *Mignon songs* (including *Kennst du das Land*, a culmination in every way), the lyricism of *Wiegenlied im Sommer* or the sheer fun of *Mausfallen Sprüchlein*. The recordings, made between 1956 and 1962, still sound splendid, and the glorious singing is superbly matched by Gerald Moore's inspired accompaniment.

Italienisches Liederbuch (complete).
*** DG 2707 114 (2) [id.]. Ludwig, Fischer-Dieskau, Barenboim.

Fischer-Dieskau is superb in these varied items from the *Italian Song Book*, always underlining the word-meaning with the inflections of a born actor, helped by the understanding accompaniment of Barenboim. In the women's songs Ludwig is less uninhibited, and after Schwarzkopf's accounts of such jewels as *Wer rief dich denn* these may seem under-characterized, with the voice not always perfectly steady; but Ludwig too has natural compulsion in her singing

and responds splendidly to the pointed playing of Barenboim. Excellent recording.

Das spanische Liederbuch (complete).
(M) *** DG Priv. 2726 071 (2) [id./*3372 071*]. Schwarzkopf, Fischer-Dieskau, Moore.

In this superb medium-price reissue, each of the four sides is devoted to one of Wolf's Spanish volumes, with the sacred songs providing a dark, intense prelude on side one. There Fischer-Dieskau is at his very finest, sustaining slow tempi impeccably. Schwarzkopf's dedication comes out in the three songs suitable for a woman's voice, but it is in the secular songs, particularly those which contain laughter in the music, where she is at her most memorable. Gerald Moore is backwardly balanced, but gives superb support. The voices are beautifully caught in the 1968 recording, making this a classic set.

Wood, Hugh (born 1932)

(i) *Cello concerto, Op. 12;* (ii) *Violin concerto, Op. 17.*
*** Uni. RHS 363. Royal Liv. PO, Atherton, with (i) Parikian, (ii) Welsh.

Hugh Wood has so far been represented on record only by his chamber music. This issue brings two of his most important bigger pieces: the *Cello concerto* of 1969 and the *Violin concerto*, first heard two years later. Wood is a composer of integrity who has steeped himself in the music of Schoenberg and Webern, yet emerged richer for the experience – in contrast to many post-serial composers. His music is beautifully crafted and far from inaccessible. Here it is given the benefit of good recording, and the performances are thoroughly committed. Those who like and respond to the Bartók concertos or even to Walton should try these.

Wordsworth, William
(born 1908)

String quartets Nos. 5, Op. 63; 6, Op. 75. (i) 3 Wordsworth songs, Op. 45.
*** CRD CRD 1097. Alberni Qt, (i) with Partridge.

Wordsworth, descended from the poet's brother, sets three of his namesake's most famous poems very sensitively, but the unconventionally structured quartets give a fuller idea of this neglected composer, undemanding in idiom but thoughtful and strong in argument. Excellent performances and recording.

Ysaÿe, Eugene (1858–1931)

(Unaccompanied) *Violin sonata in D min. (Ballade), Op. 27/3.*
(m) *** Ph. Fest. 6570/7310 206 [id.]. D. Oistrakh – DEBUSSY and RAVEL: *Sonatas*; PROKOFIEV: *5 Melodies*.***

All the music on this record was written within a decade, the Debussy *Sonata* in 1917, the Ravel from 1923 to 1927, the Prokofiev in 1920; and this Ysaÿe *Sonata* appeared in 1924. David Oistrakh won the first prize at the International Ysaÿe Concours in Brussels in 1937, and it would be difficult to imagine his account of the best-known of Ysaÿe's six solo sonatas being surpassed even by the composer himself.

Zelenka, Jan (1679–1745)

Capriccios Nos. 1–6; Concerto in G; Hipocondrie in A; Overture in F; Sinfonia in A min.
⚪ *** DG Arc. 2710 026 [id./3376 014].
Camerata Bern, Van Wijnkoop.

In this superb orchestral collection, as in the earlier Archive issue of Zelenka sonatas (DG 2708 027), this long-neglected composer begins to get his due some 250 years late. On this showing he stands as one of the most distinctive voices among Bach's contemporaries, and Bach himself nominated him in that role, though at the time Zelenka was serving in a relatively humble capacity. As in the sonata collection it is the artistry of Heinz Holliger that sets the seal on the performances, but the virtuosity of Barry Tuckwell on the horn is also a delight, and the music itself regularly astonishes. One of the movements in the *Capriccio No. 5* has the title *Il furibondo* (*The angry man*), and more strikingly still another piece has the significant title *Hipocondrie* and sounds amazingly like a baroque tango. Was Zelenka both a bitter man and a hypochondriac, one wonders, for in his obscurity no one even bothered to leave a portrait of him behind. What comes out from this is that in this period of high classicism, music for Zelenka was about emotion, something one recognizes clearly enough in Bach and Handel but too rarely in lesser composers. And in his bald expressiveness Zelenka comes to sound often amazingly modern, and often very beautiful, as in the slow *Aria No. 2* of the *Fourth Capriccio*. Superb recording to match Van Wijnkoop's lively and colourful performances.

Zeller, Carl (1842–98)

Der Vogelhändler (operetta; complete).
*** EMI 1C 157 30194/5. Rothenberger, Holm, Litz, Dallapozza, Berry, Unger, Forster, Donch, V. Volksoper Ch., VSO, Boskovsky.

Boskovsky's vivacious and lilting performance of Zeller's delightfully tuneful operetta is in every way recommendable. The cast is strong; Anneliese Rothenberger may be below her best form as Princess Marie, but Renate Holm is a charmer as Christel, and Adolf Dallapozza sings the title role with heady virility. There are many endearing moments, and the combination here of infectious sparkle with style tempts one to re-value the score and place it alongside *The Merry Widow* and *Die Fledermaus* among the finest and most captivating of all operettas. For English-speaking listeners some of the dialogue might have been cut, but this is an international set and it is provided with an excellent libretto translation (not always the case in this kind of repertoire). Two numbers are cut from Act 3 to fit the work on to two discs. The recording is excellent, combining atmosphere with warmth and lively projection of the principal characters.

Der Vogelhändler (abridged).
(M) **(*) Tel. AF6.21256. Gueden, Minich, Mödl, Schadle, Terkal, Kusche, Operetta Ch. and O., Breuer.

Although presented potpourri style, with no dividing bands between items, the selection here is quite generous, and the set-pieces with chorus are atmospherically recorded. The soloists, especially Peter Minich, are excellent, and the consistently tuneful score sparkles as it should. Try the Act 2 Trio, *Bescheiden mit verschämten Wangen*, to catch the flavour of the writing, very much in the spirit of the *Merry Widow* septet of Lehár.

Zemlinsky, Alexander von (1871–1942)

Lyric symphony, Op. 18.
*** DG Dig. 2532 021 [id.]. Varady, Fischer-Dieskau, Berlin PO, Maazel.

Zemlinsky's *Lyric symphony*, rather too closely based on Mahler's *Song of the Earth* for comfort, is the work which Alban Berg quoted in his *Lyric suite*. Using poems of Rabindranath Tagore (less evocative than the Chinese poems in the Mahler but very much from the same area), it provides a warm bath of music, here made relatively refreshing by a fine performance. Maazel's refined control of texture prevents the sound from cloying, and so does his incisive manner. Varady and Fischer-Dieskau make an outstanding pair of soloists, keenly responsive to the words. Excellent recording.

String quartet No. 2, Op. 15.
*** DG 2530 892 [id.]. LaSalle Qt.

Grandly rhetorical and expansive in its single movement lasting nearly forty minutes, this work gives an idea of what Schoenberg might have done had he stayed content with the idiom of *Verklaerte Nacht* and *Gurrelieder*. Zemlinsky was in fact Schoenberg's brother-in-law, but, though he remained a close friend, he refused to follow his contemporary into full atonality. This quartet written in the years leading up to the First World War represents the composer at his most dynamic, rich in texture and argument but not self-indulgently so. Much is owed to the commitment of the LaSalle Quartet, masters in this repertory, and the recording is excellent.

Collections

Concerts of Orchestral and Concertante Music

Academy of Ancient Music, Hogwood

PACHELBEL: *Canon and gigue.* VIVALDI: *Concerto in B min. for 4 violins, Op. 3/10. Double trumpet concerto in C, RV.537.* GLUCK: *Orfeo: Dance of the Furies; Dance of the Blessed Spirits.* HANDEL: *Solomon: Arrival of the Queen of Sheba. Berenice: Overture; Minuet. Water music: Air; Hornpipe.*
**(*) O·L DSLO/*KDSLC* 594.

It seems a curious idea to play popular baroque repertoire with a severe manner. Pachelbel's *Canon* here sounds rather abrasive and lacking charm; and the *Arrival of the Queen of Sheba* is altogether more seductive in Beecham's hands. But those who combine a taste for these pieces with a desire for authenticity at all costs should be satisfied. The highlight here is the pair of Gluck dances, very strongly characterized and making a splendid foil for each other. The sound is extremely vivid on both disc and tape; there is an extra degree of spikiness on side one of the cassette.

Academy of St Martin-in-the-Fields, Marriner

'*Digital concert*': WAGNER: *Siegfried idyll.* DVOŘÁK: *Nocturne in B, Op. 40.* FAURÉ: *Pavane, Op. 50.* TCHAIKOVSKY: *String quartet No.*

1 in D, Op. 11: Andante cantabile. GRIEG: *2 Elegiac melodies, Op. 34.* BOCCHERINI: *Quintet in E, Op. 13/5. Minuet.*
⊛ *** HMV Dig. ASD/*TCC-ASD* 3943 [Ang. DS/*4ZS* 37758].

This is a hi-fi demonstration record for those who have to think of their neighbours. These generally gentle pieces are given radiant performances, recorded in digital sound with ravishingly vivid results. As in his previous Argo version of the *Siegfried idyll*, Marriner uses solo strings for the gentler passages, a fuller ensemble for the climaxes, here passionately convincing. The chrome cassette also offers very high quality, although side two, transferred at a markedly higher level than side one, has strikingly more upper range, with the beautiful Tchaikovsky and Grieg items outstanding. However, the sound on the disc is quite exceptional.

'*Baroque concertos*': AVISON: *Concerto in A, Op. 9/11.* MANFREDINI: *Concerto in G min., Op. 3/10.* ALBINONI: *Concerto a 5 in A min., Op. 5/5.* HANDEL: *Concerto grosso in G, Op. 6/1.* TELEMANN: *Tafelmusik, Set 2: Concerto in F.*
(M) *** Decca Ser. SA/*KSC* 10.

This was one of two LPs that launched the Academy of St Martin-in-the-Fields as a recording group in the early sixties. This particular field of small chamber ensembles specializing in performances of baroque music had previously been cornered by Italian groups, like I Musici, often restricting themselves very much to the home product. From the beginning the St Martin's group showed themselves willing to a repertoire covering the widest possible range; furthermore the standard of playing and care for style and detail were to set and maintain a new level of excellence by any international standards. The first disc immediately showed the wide geographical range. This, the second, dating from 1963, is even more imaginative, the delightful work by Avison a most rewarding choice; and the playing is so vivacious that even the less interesting music comes fully to life.

'Scandinavian music': GRIEG: 2 Elegiac melodies, Op. 34. SIBELIUS: Kuolema: Valse triste, Op. 44. Rakastava, Op. 14. NIELSEN: Little suite, Op. 1. WIRÉN: Serenade for strings, Op. 11.
*** Argo ZRG/KZRC 877 [id.].

A splendid collection of appealing and attractive music from the north. It gives us the only domestically available version of Sibelius's magical Rakastava (there is an eloquent version by the Finnish Chamber Ensemble on BIS) as well as the perennially fresh Dag Wirén Serenade. These are good, vividly recorded performances. The cassette transfer too is of outstanding quality: the sound has striking presence and realism.

'Academy encores': HANDEL: Solomon: Arrival of the Queen of Sheba. Berenice: Minuet. Water music: Air; Hornpipe. BACH: Suite No. 3 in D, BWV 1068: Air. HAYDN: Trumpet concerto in E flat (with Stringer). MOZART: Serenade No. 13 in G (Eine kleine Nachtmusik), K.525. Divertimento No. 17 in D, K.334: Minuet.
**(*) Argo ZRG/KZRC 902 [id.].

This is much the same sort of repertoire that Decca have previously made available in two medium-priced World of the Academy selections (SPA/KCSP 101 and 163). This compilation is well made, and the sound is of good quality; but even though Eine kleine Nachtmusik is one of the finest available versions, and the Haydn Trumpet concerto is also offered complete, few collectors will feel that this should be offered at premium price. The cassette matches the disc closely, except in the Nachtmusik, where the LP offers slightly more range and freshness.

'Greensleeves' (Folksong arrangements): VAUGHAN WILLIAMS: English folksongs suite. Fantasia on Greensleeves. TRAD.: Summer is icumen in; The turtle dove; John Peel (all arr. Hazell). The keeper; The oak and the ash; Early one morning; The jolly miller; I will give my love; British Grenadiers (arr. Pearson).
** Argo ZRG/KZRC 931 [id.].

After opening with an attractively vivacious account of Vaughan Williams's English folksongs suite (in its orchestral transcription by Gordon Jacob), with Greensleeves an appropriate encore, the programme moves on to orchestrations and elaborations (mainly by Leslie Pearson, but three scored by Chris Hazell) of melodies many of which are far more effective in vocal form. The resonance of the recording creates a rather washy effect (especially on the cassette, which is less sharply focused than the disc).

Adler, Larry (harmonica)

Works for harmonica and orchestra (with (i) Morton Gould O.; (ii) RPO; cond. Gould): (i) GERSHWIN: Three-quarter blues. Merry Andrew. Lullaby Time. (ii) BENJAMIN: Harmonica concerto. VAUGHAN WILLIAMS:

Romance. ARNOLD: *Harmonica concerto, Op. 46.* MILHAUD: *Suite.*
(M) *** RCA Gold GL/*GK* 42747.

This is an indispensable collection. The four major works were all written for Larry Adler, and the Gershwin pieces make an irresistible miniature suite, as tuneful and inspired as any of the more formal concertos. Of these Malcolm Arnold's is particularly rewarding; the opening *Grazioso* is immediately appealing, and there is one of those swinging finales at which this composer is so adept. The Benjamin work is also felicitously conceived, with its haunting *Canzona* and amiable closing rondo; and Milhaud's *Suite* has a racy, extrovert inventive style which Adler captures with infectious spirit. Indeed the playing throughout is marvellous. The soloist tells us in his witty notes that he had problems learning the music (playing more readily by ear than from music), but none of that shows here. The recording is good on disc, but the tape transfer has caused problems, especially in the Gershwin, where the harmonica's upper partials are fizzy and blurred. One needs a filter or strong treble cut.

Adni, Daniel (piano)

'Music from the movies' (with Bournemouth SO, Alwyn): ADDINSELL: *Warsaw concerto.* WILLIAMS: *The Dream of Olwen.* ROZSA: *Spellbound concerto.* BATH: *Cornish rhapsody.* GERSHWIN: *Rhapsody in Blue.*
**(*) HMV ASD/*TC-ASD* 3862.

By far the finest of these film 'concertos' is Addinsell's *Warsaw concerto*, written for *Dangerous Moonlight* after Rachmaninov had failed to respond to the original commission. It is a first-class miniature romantic pastiche with an indelible main theme. The other pieces here have less distinction but are taken

seriously and presented with commitment and flair. The performance of the Gershwin *Rhapsody* (also used in a biopic of the same title) is not as distinctive as the rest of the programme. Excellent, vivid sound; the cassette is well balanced, but the transfer level is relatively low and there is not quite the sparkle of the LP.

André, Maurice (trumpet)

Trumpet concertos (with LPO, Lopez-Cobós): HAYDN: *Concerto in E flat.* TELEMANN: *Concerto in F.* ALBINONI: *Concerto in D min.* MARCELLO: *Concerto in C min.*
*** HMV ASD/*TC-ASD* 3760 [Ang. S/*4XS* 37513].

Maurice André's cultured playing gives much pleasure throughout this collection. Slow movements are elegantly phrased and communicate an appealing expressive warmth. The stylishness and easy execution ensure a welcome for the Albinoni and Marcello works, which are transcriptions but are made thoroughly convincing in this format. Excellent, lively accompaniments from the LPO under Lopez-Cobós, and good sound on disc and tape alike.

Four trumpet concertos (with Württemberg CO, Faerber): OTTO: *Concerto in E flat.* BARSANTI: *Concerto grosso in D, Op. 3/10.* ALBINONI: *Concerto a cinque in D min., Op. 9/2.* HANDEL: *Sonata in F, Op. 1/12* (originally for violin and continuo).
**(*) HMV Dig. ASD 4030.

The concerto by Luigi Otto is immensely demanding, with a fiendishly high tessitura in the first movement and the *Adagio*, yet the less spectacular rondo finale is the most attractive movement. André plays it all with aplomb, and is equally skilful in the Barsanti *Concerto grosso*. This has been rearranged with trumpet lead, but the two oboes attractively retain their concertante role in the first movement. Albinoni's work was conceived for oboe, but it transcribes well when played with such musical facility. The arrangement of the Handel *Violin sonata* is more questionable, even if it offers no technical problems here. The digital recording gives a vivid projection to the trumpet, but the resonant orchestral backing is not especially clear in detail, though effective enough.

Trumpet concertos (with (i) ECO, Mackerras; (ii) H. Bilgram; (iii) M. Sillem): (i) VIVALDI: *Double trumpet concerto in C, RV.537.* (ii) VIVIANI: *Sonata No. 1 in C for trumpet and organ.* (i) TORELLI: *Concerto in D.* STOLZEL: *Concerto in D.* (i; iii) TELE-MANN: *Concerto sonata in D.*
(M) *** DG Priv. 2535/*3335* 385.

There is a pleasing variety of textures here, and in the Vivaldi, by electronic means, André assumes a fruitful solo partnership with himself. The Viviani *Sonata* with organ obbligato is an effective piece, and the slow movement of the Stolzel concerto has genuine nobility of line. In the second movement of the Telemann André makes impressive use of a long, controlled crescendo. All in all, an entertaining compendium, with crisp, stylish accompaniments and good sound.

Trumpet concertos (with Rouen CO, Beaucamp): MOZART, Leopold: *Concerto in D.* TELEMANN: *Concerto in F min.* ALBINONI: *Concerto in D min.* (transcription of *Church sonata for organ*). VIVALDI: *Double concerto for trumpet and violin in B flat, RV.548* (with D. Artur).
(M) **(*) Ph. Seq. 6527/*7311* 082.

The Albinoni transcription is a delightful four-movement work, and the Vivaldi is hardly less enjoyable, although the violin takes a rather less than equal partnership in the outer movements and provides only an accompanying role in the eloquent *Largo*. The genuine trumpet concerto by Leopold Mozart is more demanding technically, but more conventional as music. The recording is more reverberant here and on cassette the focus (hitherto excellent) becomes slightly blurred. Accompaniments are attentive rather than especially sparkling, but this is worth trying for the Albinoni and Vivaldi items.

(i) **André, Maurice;** (ii) **Adolf Scherbaum** (trumpet)

'*Festive trumpet music*': (i) HAYDN: *Concerto in E flat.* HAYDN, Michael: *Concerto in D* (with Mun. CO, Stadlmair). (ii) MOZART, Leopold: *Concerto in D* (with Saar R. CO, Ristenpart). DELALANDE: *Symphonies pour les Soupers du Roy.* CHARPENTIER, Marc-Antoine: *Te Deum: Prelude* (with Kuentz CO).
(M) ** DG Priv. 2535/*3335* 622.

This collection is planned to show the trumpet in various roles. The two major concertos by Josef and Michael Haydn are admirably played by Maurice André (although he is rather deliberate in the famous slow movement of the popular *E flat* work). On the other side Scherbaum copes with the florid tessitura of the piece by Leopold Mozart (otherwise unmemorable) and we have some royal festive music and brass embellishments for Charpentier's *Te Deum* as an appendix. The sound is rather variable but always acceptable, and the two André recordings are excellent, on disc and cassette alike.

André, Maurice, and Brass Ens., Dart

'Royal music of King James I'.
(M) ** Decca Ser. SA/KSC 1.

As Thurston Dart points out in his sleeve-note, James I's wind band consisted·of woodwind as well as brass instruments, and it is unfortunate that it is represented here only by brass. The music, by composers such as Holborne, Farnaby and Ferrabosco II, is diverse, the playing is lively and the recording full and brilliant. But an entire record or cassette of rather similar pieces, played by a group with unvarying tone-colour, can become a little wearisome. Listened to in sections, this music is rewarding.

Ballet

'Nights at the ballet' (with (i) RPO, Weldon; (ii) Philh. O.; (iii) Kurtz; (iv) Irving; (v) RPO, Fistoulari; (vi) CBSO, Frémaux; (vii) New Philh. O., Mackerras)· excerpts from: (i) TCHAIKOVSKY: *Nutcracker; Swan Lake.* (ii; iii) PROKOFIEV: *Romeo and Juliet.* (ii; iv) ADAM: *Giselle.* (v) LUIGINI: *Ballet Egyptien* (suite). (vi) SATIE: *Gymnopédies Nos. 1 and 3.* (vii) DELIBES: *Coppélia.* GOUNOD: *Faust* (suite).
(B) *** EMI *TC2-MOM 111.*

Here (on tape only) is nearly an hour and a half of some of the most tuneful and colourful ballet music ever written. Kurtz's three excerpts from *Romeo and Juliet* are most distinguished, the inclusion of the Fistoulari recording of *Ballet Egyptien* (see under Luigini above) is most welcome, and Mackerras is at his sparkling best in the *Coppélia* and *Faust* selections. Weldon's Tchaikovsky performances lack the last degree of flair but they are alert and well played. The sound

is admirable both for home listening and in the car.

Baroque music

'The sound of baroque' (with (i) Royal Liv. PO, Groves; (ii) Scottish CO, Tortelier; (iii) LPO, Boult; (iv) Menuhin, Ferras, Bath Festival O.; (v) Bournemouth Sinf., Montgomery; (vi) Reginald Kilbey and Strings; (vii) RPO, Weldon; (viii) ASMF, Marriner): (i) ALBINONI: *Adagio for strings and organ* (arr. Giazotto). (ii) BACH: *Suite No. 3 in D, BWV 1068: Air.* (iii) *Brandenburg concerto No. 3 in G, BWV 1048.* (iv) *Double violin concerto in D, BWV 1043.* (i) GLUCK: *Orfeo: Dance of the Blessed Spirits.* (v) HANDEL: *Messiah: Pastoral symphony. Berenice overture.* (v) *Solomon: Arrival of the Queen of Sheba.* (vi) *Serse: Largo.* (vii) *Water music: suite* (arr. Harty). (viii) PACHELBEL: *Canon.*
(B) *** EMI *TC2-MOM 103.*

One of the first of EMI's *Miles of music* tapes, planned for motorway listening as well as at home, and offering about eighty minutes of favourite baroquerie, this is recommendable in every way. The sound is lively, the performances are first-class, with Bach's *Double violin concerto* and *Brandenburg No. 3* (Boult) bringing substance among the lollipops.

BBC SO

'Fiftieth anniversary concert' (cond. (i) Elgar; (ii) Boult; (iii) Fritz Busch; (iv) Toscanini; (v) Bruno Walter): (i) ELGAR: *Cockaigne overture, Op. 40.* (ii) VAUGHAN WILLIAMS: *Fantasia on a theme of Thomas Tallis.* BLISS:

Music for strings. BERLIOZ: *Overture King Lear, Op. 4.* SIBELIUS: *Night Ride and Sunrise, Op. 55.* (iii) MOZART: *Symphony No. 36 in C (Linz), K.425.* (iv) BEETHOVEN: *Symphony No. 6 in F (Pastoral).* (v) BRAHMS: *Symphony No. 4 in E min.*
(M) (***) BBC mono 4001 (4).

This was issued (alongside Rozhdestvensky's marvellous recording of Tchaikovsky's *Sleeping Beauty*) to celebrate the fiftieth anniversary of the BBC Symphony Orchestra in 1980. The recordings were chosen from the orchestra's first decade of existence, and many of them show their interpreters in their best light. Boult's performances are splendid – the Bliss *Music for strings* is especially valuable – and many will be glad to have Toscanini's famous version of the *Pastoral symphony*, recorded in the Queen's Hall in 1937. The only comparative disappointment is Bruno Walter's 1934 set of Brahms's *Fourth*, mellow to the point of lethargy in the slow movement. The transfers (apart from the Toscanini/Beethoven) are splendidly done by Keith Hardwick and Anthony Griffith; the sound is always acceptable and often surprisingly good.

Berlin PO, Karajan

'*Karajan in Paris*': BIZET: *L'Arlésienne suite No. 2.* CHABRIER: *España.* GOUNOD: *Faust: ballet music.* BERLIOZ: *La Damnation de Faust: Hungarian march.*
**(*) HMV ASD/TC-ASD 3761 [Ang. SZ/4XS 37687].

This record finds Karajan in Beecham territory, but his approach is less incandescent, and his phrasing sometimes seems heavy for a volatile French programme. His view is broad (some might say rhythmically sluggish) in the Bizet, taut in the Chabrier, though always presenting this colourful music with brilliance and flair. The *Faust ballet music*, which he has recorded before, both for EMI (with the Philharmonia) and DG, is very attractive, but the Berlioz march does not sound very French. The recording is ripely sumptuous, and the cassette is rich and full like the disc, though it does not catch the bass drum in *España* very comfortably.

'*Operatic overtures and intermezzi*': MASSENET: *Thaïs: Meditation* (with Mutter). CHERUBINI: *Anacreon: overture.* WEBER: *Der Freischütz: overture.* SCHMIDT: *Notre Dame: Intermezzo.* PUCCINI: *Suor Angelica; Manon Lescaut: Intermezzi.* MASCAGNI: *L'Amico Fritz: Intermezzo.* HUMPERDINCK: *Hänsel und Gretel: overture.*
**(*) HMV Dig. ASD/TCC-ASD 4072 [Ang. DS 37810].

A curiously planned programme, with the *Meditation* from *Thaïs* (Anne-Sophie Mutter the gentle soloist) played very romantically, immediately followed by Cherubini's *Anacreon overture*. The performances of the Weber and Humperdinck overtures are disappointing, the first lacking electricity, the second charm. Best are the intermezzi on side two, played with the utmost passion. The digital recording here is very brightly lit, and there is a fierce sheen on the violins. The chrome tape is preferable; the sound is subtly fuller and the upper range smoother, yet without loss of detail.

'*The wonder of Karajan*': *Overtures*: MENDELSSOHN: *The Hebrides (Fingal's Cave), Op. 26.* NICOLAI: *The Merry Wives of Windsor.* WEBER: *Der Freischütz.* WAGNER: *Der fliegende Holländer. Lohengrin (Prelude to Act 1).*
(M) *** HMV SXLP/TC-SXLP 30210.

This collection dating from the early

sixties is outstanding in every way. The performance of *Der Freischütz* included here is far more exciting than the more recent digital version (see above), and the *Lohengrin Prelude* moves with a compelling inevitability to its great central climax. *Fingal's Cave* too is played most beautifully, its effect enhanced by the resonantly spacious acoustic, which also prevents the recording from sounding too dated. The cassette transfer is very successful, in spite of the reverberation.

'*Karajan in concert*': DVOŘÁK: *Slavonic dance in G min., Op. 46/8*. WAGNER: *Der fliegende Holländer: overture*. BEETHOVEN. *Fidelio: overture*. SCHUBERT: *Rosamunde (Die Zauberharfe): overture, D.644*. STRAUSS, Johann, Jnr: *Die Fledermaus:* BRAHMS: *Tragic overture*.
(M) *** HMV SXLP/*TC-SXLP* 30506.

A compilation drawn from various sources and issued as a kind of visiting card for these artists. The high-voltage account of *The Flying Dutchman* originally appeared in the *Karajan conducts Wagner* issues in the mid-1970s; the dramatic account of the *Fidelio overture* comes from the complete set made in 1971. The playing is sumptuous throughout, and so too is the recorded sound. Karajan's account of the *Tragic overture* is one of the finest in the catalogue. The high-level cassette transfer has occasional hints of roughness, but with such a vibrant effect few will grumble.

'*Digital concert*': GRIEG: *Holberg suite, Op. 40*. MOZART: *Serenade No. 13 in G (Eine kleine Nachtmusik), K.525*. PROKOFIEV: *Symphony No. 1 in D (Classical), Op. 25*.
*** DG Dig. 2532/3302 031 [id.].

Some of the rustic freshness of Grieg eludes these artists: this is not unaffected speech. But how marvellous it sounds all the same! This is a great orchestral partnership 'making something' of the *Holberg suite*, perhaps, yet the music survives any over-sophistication and has never sounded more sumptuous and luxurious. Apart from a self-conscious and somewhat ponderous minuet, *Eine kleine Nachtmusik* sounds good too; the playing is beautifully cultured, with exquisitely shaped phrasing and wonderfully sprung rhythms. Only in the Prokofiev does one feel the want of charm and sparkle, except perhaps in the slow movement, which has grace and eloquence. The digital recording is excellent, though the balance in the Prokofiev is not entirely natural. Nonetheless a most desirable issue, particularly on account of the Grieg.

'*Christmas concertos*': CORELLI. *Concerto grosso in G min., Op. 6/8*. MANFREDINI: *Concerto grosso in C, Op. 3/12*. TORELLI: *Concerto a 4 in forma di pastorale per il Santissimo Natale*. LOCATELLI: *Concerto grosso in F min., Op. 1/8*.
(M) ** DG Acc. 2542/3342 123 [2530 070].

First-class playing from the Berlin Philharmonic, but Karajan's concentration on sensuous beauty of texture (the string sonorities are often quite ravishing) tends to be self-defeating when four pieces with a similar pastoral inspiration are heard together (to say nothing of the matter of stylistic accuracy). The sound is rich and atmospheric rather than lively, with disc and cassette similarly balanced.

'*Waltz dreams*': STRAUSS, Johann, Jnr: *Kaiser (Emperor) waltz*. TCHAIKOVSKY: *String serenade, Op. 48: Waltz*. STRAUSS, Josef: *Delirium waltz*. DELIBES: *Coppélia: Scene and waltz of Swanilda*. CHOPIN (arr. Douglas): *Les Sylphides: 3 Waltzes*.

BERLIOZ: *Symphonie fantastique,*
Op. 14: 2nd movt.
(M) *** DG Priv. 2535/3335 607 [id.].

A most agreeable concert with plenty
of flair. Karajan and his splendid orchestra are at their finest in the Delibes,
Chopin and Tchaikovsky waltzes; and
the Berlioz sounds well too, in spite of
being out of its usual context. The sound
is excellent and the tape transfer is first-
class.

'Meditation': BACH: *Suite No. 2 in B*
min., BWV 1067: Rondeau. Suite
No. 3 in D, BWV 1068: Air.
MOZART: *Eine kleine Nachtmusik:*
Romanze. DELIBES: *Coppélia: Bal-*
lade. MASSENET: *Thaïs: Meditation.*
CHOPIN (orch. Douglas): *Les Syl-*
phides: Prelude; Nocturne. SIBELIUS:
Legend: The Swan of Tuonela, Op.
22/2. DEBUSSY: *Prélude à l'après-*
midi d'un faune.
(M) **(*) DG Priv. 2535/3335 621.

Karajan's perfumed Bach performances are best heard as a pleasing background for the late evening, when one can
admire the superbly polished orchestral
playing (the harpsichord tinkling just
audibly in the background). The rest of
the programme is first-rate in every respect, and this anthology is most successfully compiled. The recording is resonantly atmospheric in exactly the right
way, particularly in the latter part of the
programme, where the performances are
highly distinguished. The Debussy *Pré-*
lude sounds quite ravishingly beautiful.
The cassette transfer is very successful
too.

Berlin Philharmonic Wind Ens.,
Karajan

'Radetzky march': STRAUSS: Johann,
Snr: *Radetzky march.* BEETHOVEN:

York march. ANON.: *Torgau.*
WALCH: *Entry into Paris.* WAGNER,
J. F.: *Under the Double Eagle.* FUČIK:
Florentine. PIEFKE: *Königgraetz;*
Glory of Prussia. SCHRAMMEL:
Vienna for ever. SEIFERT: *Carinthian*
songs. HENRION: *Fehrbelin.* KOM-
ZAK: *Archduke Albrecht* (etc.).
(M) ** DG Priv. 2535/3335 647.

This is taken from a two-disc collection
of Prussian and Austrian marches,
played with a certain characterful rhythmic stiffness where appropriate. The
Austrian examples are more flexible. One
does not generally hear this repertoire
played with such expertise and polish,
and the recording on disc is full-blooded
and brilliant. We have not heard the cassette.

Boston Pops O., John Williams

'Pops on the march': WAGNER, J. F.:
Under the Double Eagle. ELGAR:
Pomp and Circumstance march No.
1. TCHAIKOVSKY: *Coronation march.*
WALTON: *Orb and Sceptre.* GERSH-
WIN: *Strike up the Band.* HANDY: *St*
Louis blues. WILLIAMS: *Midway.*
WILLSON: *Music Man: 76 Trom-*
bones. HAGGART: *South Rampart*
Street parade. NEWMAN: *Conquest.*
*** Ph. Dig. 6302/7144 082.

John Williams directs exuberant performances of these highly attractive
marches. The opening piece by J. F.
Wagner (no connection with Richard)
has splendid flair, and all the American
marches are sparkling. The digital recording has plenty of weight as well as
brilliance. Surprisingly, the Tchaikovsky
march (although it has a good trio) is the
least interesting here, but the rest are very
entertaining. The cassette does not match
the disc's transients, but reproduces
agreeably if not very excitingly.

Bournemouth SO, Del Mar

'English music for strings': VAUGHAN WILLIAMS: Concerto grosso. DELIUS: Air and dance. WARLOCK: Serenade for strings (for the sixtieth birthday of Delius). ELGAR: Serenade in E min., Op. 20.
(M)**(*) HMV Green. ESD/TC-ESD 7088.

The Concerto grosso of Vaughan Williams here received its first recording. It was written for a jamboree at the Royal Albert Hall with hundreds of string players of the Rural Music Schools Association. On this record it is given as a straight work for double string orchestra. The Elgar Serenade, not quite so well played as the Vaughan Williams, makes an apt coupling, while the enchanting Delius miniatures and the hazily atmospheric Warlock tribute provide an unusual completion to a worthwhile programme, well recorded in a rich, reverberant acoustic. The cassette transfer copes with the resonance without problems and does not lack definition.

Bournemouth SO, Dunn

'British concert favourites: CLARKE: Trumpet voluntary. PURCELL: Dido and Aeneas: When I am laid in earth. SULLIVAN: The Yeomen of the Guard: overture. HANDEL: Berenice: Minuet. ELGAR: Enigma variations: Nimrod. BLISS: Things to Come: March. VAUGHAN WILLIAMS: Fantasia on Greensleeves. HOLST: The Planets: Jupiter (excerpt). QUILTER: Rosamund: Where the rainbow ends. WALTON: Crown Imperial march.
(M) ** Chan. CBR/CBT 1002.

An agreeable medium-priced collection of British popular repertoire, generally well recorded, though the Trum-

pet voluntary is not clearly focused. Sir Vivian Dunn – not surprisingly, as an ex-Musical Director of the Royal Marines – is at his best in the marches. Elsewhere the performances are somewhat routine. Dunn is especially affectionate in the Roger Quilter excerpt, but treats the central melody of Holst's Jupiter like a hymn.

Cantilena, Shepherd

'Christmas concerto': CORELLI: Concerto grosso in G min., Op. 6/8. FARINA: Pavana. WIDMANN: Canzona; Galliard; Intrada. FERRABOSCO II: Pavane No. 4. VIVALDI: Sinfonia in G, RV.149.
** Chan. ABR/ABT 1024.

An agreeable if not really distinctive programme of baroque music. The playing is alert and stylish, and the Corelli Christmas concerto sounds far more convincing here than in Karajan's scented (if more polished) version (see above). The Farina Pavana is also attractive when presented with such commitment, but the dances are lightweight and make side two less substantial. The sound is excellent on disc, marginally less refined on cassette.

Chicago SO, Barenboim

Overtures: MOZART: Le Nozze di Figaro. WEBER: Oberon. Invitation to the Dance, Op. 65 (orch. Berlioz). SCHUMANN: Manfred, Op. 115. MENDELSSOHN: A Midsummer Night's Dream, Op. 21. NICOLAI: The Merry Wives of Windsor.
*** DG 2531/3301 215 [id.].

Apart from Mozart's Marriage of Figaro, which is presented vivaciously and stylishly, these are essentially romantic performances, beautifully prepared and played with much finesse and warmth.

The *Invitation to the Dance* is brought off superbly (see under Weber in the composer index), and the sound is very good indeed, rich yet not lacking sparkle; disc and cassette are closely matched.

City of Birmingham SO, Dods

'*British music for film and TV*': AD-DISON: *A Bridge Too Far: March.* BENNETT: *Yanks: Theme. Lady Caroline Lamb: Theme.* WALTON: *Battle of Britain: Battle in the air.* BENJAMIN: *An Ideal Husband: Waltz.* BLISS: *Christopher Columbus: Suite.* FARNON: *Colditz: March.* MORLEY: *Watership Down: Kehaar's theme.* IRELAND: *The Overlanders: Romance; Intermezzo.* GOODWIN: *Frenzy: Theme.* BAX: *Malta, G.C.: Introduction and march.*
*** HMV ASD/*TC-ASD* 3797.

An excellent and imaginative anthology, ranging wide from the concert-hall style of Bliss's *Christopher Columbus* to the modern 'themes', with their concentrated romanticism, intended to catch the ear at the first whiff of melody. Walton's *Battle in the air* sequence makes a splendid little descriptive scherzo, while the amiable Benjamin *Waltz* from *An Ideal Husband* has a rather similar flavour to Constant Lambert's *Horoscope* ballet music. Farnon's *Colditz* march is both stirring and instantly memorable. The performances are well played and full of character, as is the recording balance, everything clear and vivid yet not overblown.

(i) Cleveland Sinf.; (ii) Cleveland O.; Lane

'*English music*': (i) VAUGHAN WILLIAMS: *The Lark Ascending* (with Druian). DELIUS: *Hassan: Serenade.*

WARLOCK: *Serenade for strings.* (ii) BACH (arr. Walton): *The Wise Virgins* (suite).
(M) ** CBS 61433/*40*-.

This collection dates from the mid-sixties when Louis Lane was a colleague of George Szell at Cleveland and the orchestra at the peak of its form. Rafael Druian is the highly poetic violin soloist in *The Lark Ascending*, and the orchestral playing, besides being polished, has both character and atmosphere, here and in the pieces by Delius and Warlock. The snag is the very forward balance, which tends to rob the Vaughan Williams of some of its evocative quality (although Druian triumphs over the engineers by achieving a fairly wide dynamic range). *The Wise Virgins* – not often recorded – sounds suitably vivid. The cassette is not as refined as the disc, but is acceptable with a top cut.

Concerto Amsterdam, Schröder

'*Italian solo concerti*, c. *1700*': TORELLI: *Trumpet concertos Nos. 1 and 2 in D.* VIVALDI: *Recorder concerto in F. Concerto for 2 horns and strings in F.* LOCATELLI: *Violin concerto in D.*
(M) *** Tel. AQ6/*CQ4* 41217.

With expert playing from the soloists, including Maurice André and Frans Brüggen, and clean, alert accompaniments, this collection has plenty of personality. Especially effective is Vivaldi's *Double horn concerto*, which anticipates many of the devices favoured in later eighteenth-century concertos. The distinguished soloists, Hermann Baumann and Adriaan van Woudenberg, produce some exciting bravura. Locatelli's *D major Violin concerto* is another personable work, and Jaap Schröder plays it with fine style. Altogether a first-class anthology, and the sound is fresh and clear, with disc and cassette closely matched.

Horn concertos (with Baumann):
DANZI: *Concerto in E.* HAYDN: *Concerto No. 1 in D.* ROSETTI: *Concerto in D min.*
(M) *** Tel. AQ6/*CQ4* 41288.

Hermann Baumann uses a modern valved instrument for this concert. All three works are enjoyable; the slow movement of the Haydn is especially fine. Rosetti's concerto is a highly spontaneous piece with vigorous outer movements, calling for considerable bravura, framing a brief *Romanze*. Baumann plays it splendidly. The accompaniments are crisply stylish and the recording first-rate, with little to choose between the disc and the outstanding cassette.

'Country gardens'

English music (various artists, including Bournemouth SO, Silvestri; Hallé O., Barbirolli; Royal Liv. PO, Groves; E. Sinfonia, Dilkes):
VAUGHAN WILLIAMS: *The Wasps: Overture. Rhosymedre.* WARLOCK: *Capriol suite.* DELIUS: *Summer Night on the River. A Song before Sunset.* GRAINGER: *Country Gardens. Mock Morris; Shepherd's Hey.* BRIDGE (arr.): *Cherry Ripe.* COLERIDGE TAYLOR: *Petite suite de concert* (excerpts). GERMAN: *Nell Gwyn: 3 Dances.* COATES: *Meadow to Mayfair: In the country. Summer Days: At the dance. Wood Nymphs.* ELGAR: *Chanson de matin. Salut d'amour.*
(B) *** EMI *TC2-MOM 123.*

A highly recommendable tape-only collection, essentially lightweight but never trivial. Barbirolli's Delius, and Neville Dilkes's *Capriol suite* are among the highlights; one notices in the latter that the sound is drier and sharper in focus here than in the source-cassette (*TC-ESD 7101* – see below). This gives

greater projection against motorway background noise, and certainly it makes a most entertaining concert for use on a long journey, with the lively Grainger, Coates and German pastoral dances providing an excellent foil for the lyrical music. On domestic equipment the quality is vivid, but may need a softening of the treble.

Dallas SO, Mata

'Ibéria': DEBUSSY: *Images: No. 2, Ibéria.* RIMSKY-KORSAKOV: *Capriccio espagnol, Op. 34.* TURINA: *Danzas fantásticas: Orgia.*
*(*) Telarc Dig. DG 10055 [id.].

A disappointing collection. The recording is certainly vivid, but in *Ibéria* detail registers at the expense of a panoramic view, and as an extrovert performance this does not match Stokowski's sparklingly sensuous account with the French National Radio Orchestra (deleted, alas, in the UK, but still trans-atlantically available on Seraphim S/*4XG* 60102), which is equally impressive as a recording. Here Rimsky-Korsakov's *Capriccio* has neither sumptuousness nor a compensating electricity, and one wonders why room could not have been found for all three of Turina's *Danzas fantásticas*.

Detroit SO, Dorati

'Rhapsody': LISZT: *Hungarian rhapsody No. 2 in C sharp min., G.359* (arr. Müller-Berghaus). DVOŘÁK: *Slavonic rhapsody in A flat, Op. 45/3.* ENESCO: *Rumanian rhapsody No. 1 in A, Op. 11.* RAVEL: *Rapsodie espagnole.*

*** Decca SXL/*KSXC* 6896 [Lon. 7119/5-].

One of Dorati's first records from his current association with the Detroit orchestra, this is an attractive programme, played with some flair and brightly and sumptuously recorded. The volatile Enesco piece is superbly done; the orchestra clearly enjoy themselves. The Liszt sparkles too, and the Dvořák *Slavonic rhapsody* is equally lively. Only the Ravel *Rapsodie espagnole* lacks something in subtlety; it needs more of a sense of mystery than Dorati achieves. The tape transfer is clear and vividly detailed. Indeed the Ravel is rather more sharply focused than on disc. But generally the sound has slightly less bloom and richness on cassette, although the quality remains impressive away from a direct comparison.

ECO, Barenboim

'Greensleeves' (with (i) Zukerman, violin): VAUGHAN WILLIAMS: *Fantasia on Greensleeves.* (i) *The Lark Ascending.* WALTON: *Henry V: Passacaglia (Death of Falstaff); Touch her soft lips and part.* DELIUS: *On Hearing the First Cuckoo in Spring. Summer Night on the River. Fennimore and Gerda: Intermezzo. 2 Aquarelles.*

(M) *** DG Acc. 2542/*3342* 161 [2530 505/*3300 500*].

Zukerman's account of *The Lark Ascending* is ravishing, and the spacious recording suits the music perfectly. Barenboim creates richly spun orchestral textures; some might feel they are almost too luxuriant at times, but such gorgeous sounds are hard to resist when the playing is of comparably high quality. There is a vidid cassette transfer, but the high level brings slight roughening of the focus at one or two climaxes.

ECO, Leppard

ALBINONI: *Sonates a cinque: in A; in G min., Op. 2/3 and 6.* VIVALDI: *Concertos: in D, RV.121; in G min., RV.156; Sonata in E (Al Santo Sepolcro), RV.130.* CORELLI: *Concerto grosso in F, Op. 6/9.*
(B) *** CfP CFP/*TC-CFP* 40371.

This is a charming collection of baroque concertos, played with the superb poise, sense of colour and imagination that regularly characterizes the work of Leppard with this orchestra. Other scholars may complain that Leppard goes too far in trying to re-create such works, but the result for the non-specialist listener is pure delight, particularly when recorded with such warmth as here. A bargain disc that in every way matches comparable discs at full price. The cassette too is of high quality: it has slightly less upper range, but inner detail is not lost and textures are agreeably rich.

English music

'The music of England' (with (i) Philip Jones Brass Ens.; (ii) ECO, Britten; (iii) ASMF, Marriner; (iv) LSO; (v) Collins; (vi) Tear; (vii) Vyvyan; (viii) Ferrier; (ix) Bailey; (x) NSO of L.; (xi) Nat. PO, Herrmann; (xii) RPO, Nash; (xiii) LPO, Boult; (xiv) Boston Pops O., Fiedler; (xv) Bliss): (i) BLISS: *Antiphonal fanfare for three brass choirs.* (ii) BRITTEN: *Simple symphony.* (iii) BUTTERWORTH: *The Banks of Green Willow.* (iv; v) DELIUS: *On Hearing the First Cuckoo in Spring.* (vi) VAUGHAN WILLIAMS: *Songs of Travel: The vagabond. Linden Lea.* TRAD.: (vii) *Cherry Ripe.* (viii) *Blow the Wind Southerly. The Keel Row.*

(ix) WARLOCK: *Sleep*. IRELAND: *Sea Fever*. (x; v) Balfour GARDINER: *Shepherd Fennel's dance*. (xi) WALTON: *Richard III: Prelude*. (xii) SULLIVAN: *Henry VIII* (incidental music): *March; Graceful dance*. (xiii) HOLST: *The Perfect Fool: ballet music*. (xiv) VAUGHAN WILLIAMS: *English folksongs suite*. ELGAR: (iii) *Serenade for strings, Op. 20*. (iv; xv) *Pomp and Circumstance march No. 1*.
(B) *** Decca DPA 627/8.

A most attractive anthology. Its highlights, Britten's inimitable performance of his juvenile *Simple symphony*, Marriner's fine recording of Butterworth, and the Holst ballet music from *The Perfect Fool*, have already been listed and praised in this or earlier editions. But, as can be seen above, the programme has been imaginatively chosen to include, unexpectedly, Balfour Gardiner's attractive *Shepherd Fennel's dance*, and the early and distinguished Collins/LSO version of Delius's *On Hearing the First Cuckoo in Spring*, where the sound is surprisingly good. The group of songs which comes in the middle of side two is generally successful. Jennifer Vyvyan's *Cherry Ripe* sounds too sophisticated, but the two Kathleen Ferrier items are as fresh as the day they were recorded, and Norman Bailey's account of *Sea Fever* is beautifully sung. The layout is effective; the sound is almost uniformly excellent; and it was sensible to put the inevitable *Pomp and Circumstance march* at the end.

F. Sinfonia, Dilkes

English music: BUTTERWORTH: *A Shropshire Lad* (rhapsody). *The Banks of Green Willow*. HARTY: *A John Field suite*. BRIDGE: *There Is a Willow Grows Aslant a Brook*. BAX: *Dance in the Sunlight*.

(M) *** HMV Green. ESD/TC-ESD 7100.

'English idyll': LEIGH: *Harpsichord concertino*. WARLOCK: *Capriol suite*. BUTTERWORTH: *English idylls Nos. 1–2*. MOERAN: *Lonely Waters. Whythorne's Shadow*. IRELAND: *The Holy Boy*.

(M) *** HMV Green. ESD/TC-ESD 7101.

These are collections of English music of a kind which in the age of LP has tended to be unjustly neglected by recording artists and companies. Most valuable on the first disc is the Bridge tone poem, which is given the subtlest performance. Coming after the richly evocative Butterworth pieces – with Dilkes pressing the music rather harder than usual – the Bridge piece's economy of utterance is the more telling. On the reverse the *John Field suite* and the Bax *Dance* are much lighter – charming music, persuasively played if with some slight lack of refinement of string tone. However, any reservations are set aside by the success of the collection as a whole, with its fine, ripe recording, equally impressive on disc and cassette.

The second compilation is even more imaginative than the first. Specially valuable is the *Harpsichord concertino* of Walter Leigh, a composer killed in the war who produced sadly little that is likely to last. In its way the *Concertino* is a masterpiece, with deft neoclassical outer movements framing an equally brief slow movement based on a hauntingly beautiful melody. Dilkes (his own soloist) takes the central movement a fraction too slowly but this is the only blemish on a glowing set of performances. The *Capriol suite* is a delight, and the Moeran, Butterworth and Ireland pieces all present the English pastoral tradition at its most appealing. Good rounded recording (and the cassette approaches demonstration quality), but in the Leigh the harpsichord is given too close a balance.

Galway, James (flute)

'Galway collection' (with Nat. PO, Gerhardt; Zagreb Soloists; Goldstone, piano): BACH: Suite No. 2 in B min., BWV 1067: Minuet; Badinerie. DEBUSSY: Clair de lune. Syrinx. The Little Shepherd. PAGANINI: Moto perpetuo, Op. 11. VIVALDI: The Four Seasons: Spring. GLUCK: Orfeo: Dance of the Blessed Spirits. MOZART: Flute concerto in G, K.622: Adagio. BERKELEY: Flute sonatina, Op. 13.
(B) *** Pick. CDS/CAM 1205.

Anyone wanting a sampler of the Galway charisma at bargain price need look no further. The excerpts are well chosen to show his astonishing technique and natural musicality. Spring from The Four Seasons is perhaps less sprightly than one might have expected, but the Zagreb Soloists are partly responsible for this. The inclusion of the Berkeley Sonatina is unexpected but welcome. The sound is excellent and the cassette transfer immaculate.

'Showpieces' (with Nat. PO, Gerhardt): DINICU: Hora staccato. DRIGO: Les Millions d'Arlequin: Serenade. PAGANINI: Moto perpetuo, Op. 11. BACH: Suite No. 2 in B min., BWV 1067: Minuet; Badinerie. MIYAGI: Haru no Umi. GODARD: Suite of 3 pieces, Op. 116: Waltz. RIMSKY-KORSAKOV: Tsar Saltan: Flight of the bumble bee. SAINT-SAËNS: Ascanio (ballet): Adagio and variation. CHOPIN: Waltz in D flat (Minute), Op. 64/1. GLUCK: Orfeo: Dance of the Blessed Spirits. DÖP-

PLER: Fantaisie pastorale hongroise, Op. 26.
*** RCA RCALP/RCAK 3011.

This collection of 'lollipops' shows the flair and sparkle of James Galway's playing at its most captivating, besides demonstrating a technical command to bring wonder: Paganini himself must have astonished his listeners in this way. The bravura pieces, including the Dinicu Horastaccato, Rimsky-Korsakov's Flight of the bumble bee and Godard's deliciously inconsequential little waltz, are nicely balanced by the expressive music, and there are several attractive novelties. Only Bach's famous Badinerie seems a shade too fast, and even this is infectious. Charles Gerhardt's accompaniments are characteristically adroit, and the sound is of excellent quality on both disc and cassette.

'The magic flute of James Galway' (with Nat. PO, Gerhardt): HANDEL: Solomon: Arrival of the Queen of Sheba. RACHMANINOV: Vocalise, Op. 34/14. BACH: Sonata in C min.: Allegro. MENDELSSOHN: A Midsummer Night's Dream, Op. 61: Scherzo. SCHUMANN: Kinderscenen: Träumerei. GOSSEC: Tambourin. CHOPIN: Variations on a theme from Rossini's 'La Cenerentola'. KREISLER: Schön Rosmarin. DVOŘÁK: Humoresque in G flat, Op. 101/7. BRISCIALDI: Carnival of Venice.
*** RCA RCALP/RCAK 3014 [LRL 1/ LRK 1 5131].

Galway's gift for making transcriptions sound as if the music had been originally conceived for the flute almost succeeds in the Arrival of the Queen of Sheba, and his exuberant roulades in the Chopin Variations and (especially) the Carnival of Venice are very fetching. The Midsummer Night's Dream Scherzo has an iridescent sparkle, and, among the lyrical items, Schumann's *Träumerei* is beautifully phrased. The flair and sparkle of Galway's bravura never fail to astonish, though the Bach *Allegro* is outrageously fast. The recording balances the flute well forward with an unashamed spotlight. The cassette transfer has plenty of life.

'*Songs of the Southern Cross*' (with Sydney SO, Measham): HILL: *Waiata Poi*. ROBIN: *I started a joke*. BENJAMIN: *Jamaican rumba*. GRAINER: *Robert and Elizabeth: I know how*. TRAD.: *Waltzing Matilda*. GRAINGER: *Molly on the Shore*. SPRINGFIELD: *The Carnival Is Over*. JAMES: *The Silver Stars Are in the Sky*. LEE: *Long White Cloud*. CARMICHAEL: *Thredbo suite*. DREYFUS: *Rush theme*. PACHELBEL: *Canon*.
**(*) RCA RCALP/*RCAK* 6011 [AFL 1/*AFK 1* 4063].

The very engaging *Waiata Poi* is a highlight here, the sort of delightful morsel that James Galway can make indelibly his own. Benjamin's *Jamaican rumba* is delightful too, and it is the quick, witty pieces that come off best here; the lyrical music tends to be less substantial. Nicely turned accompaniments and good recording. In the cassette transfer the rather soupy and unstylish version of Pachelbel's *Canon*, which opens the collection, has hiccoughs in the bass which most listeners will find unacceptable. Otherwise the transfer is full and clear if not as refined as the disc.

Goodman, Isador (piano)

'*World's best-loved music for piano and orchestra*' (with Melbourne SO, Thomas): ADDINSELL: *Warsaw concerto*. GERSHWIN: *Rhapsody in Blue*. LITOLFF: *Concerto symphonique, Op. 102/4: Scherzo*. RACHMANINOV:

Rhapsody on a theme of Paganini: 18th Variation. LISZT: *Hungarian fantasia for piano and orchestra, G.123*.
(M) ** Ph. Seq. 6527/*7311* 114.

In spite of the hyperbole of the title, this is a pleasant collection. The soloist is sympathetic and quite stylish (notably so in the Litolff), and the accompaniments are well balanced within a spacious acoustic. The account of the Liszt is rather lightweight, but fits well with the rest of the programme. Daniel Adni's HMV compilation (see above) is rather more distinguished, but that is at full price. The Philips cassette is transferred at rather a low level, with resultant loss of upper range. It will only sound really effective on a small portable player.

Goodwin, Ron, and his Orchestra

'*Sounds superb*': GOODWIN: *633 Squadron; The Trap; These Magnificent Men in their Flying Machines; Of Human Bondage; Operation Crossbow; Miss Marple* (film themes). *Girl with a Dream. The Headless Horseman. London serenade. Prairie serenade. India. Puppet serenade*. BINGE: *Elizabethan serenade*. RODGERS: *Song of the High Seas*. FELIX: *Under the Linden Tree*. DUNCAN: *The Girl from Corsica*. LAWRENCE: *Sunrise, Sunset*. NASCIMBENE: *Romanoff and Juliet theme*. CHAPLIN: *Limelight theme*. DEBUSSY: *Clair de lune*. WIRÉN: *Serenade for strings, Op. 11: March*. TCHAIKOVSKY: *Serenade for strings in C, Op. 48: Waltz*. MARTIN: *Elizabeth and Essex love theme. Serenade to a Double Scotch*.
(B) *** MFP MFP/*TC-MFP* 1025 (2).

Of all the double-length tapes suitable

for background listening in the car, this very generous collection is unbeatable. The quality of the transfer is slightly tart (these recordings were originally made in EMI's hi-fi-conscious Studio Two system) but it responds to the controls and is otherwise extremely vivid. Goodwin's own film music is instantly memorable, and the rest of the programme is directed with equal flair – the Dag Wirén *March* is especially pungent – and makes highly entertaining background listening. The discs are brilliant too, but for drivers with cassette players the tape is the obvious best buy. In both formats these twenty-four items come at what is virtually super-bargain price.

'Greensleeves'

English music (with (i) Sinfonia of L. or Hallé O., Barbirolli; (ii) New Philh. O., LPO or LSO, Boult; (iii) Williams, Bournemouth SO, Berglund; (iv) E. Sinfonia, Dilkes): (i) VAUGHAN WILLIAMS: *Fantasia on Greensleeves*. (ii) *The Lark Ascending* (with Hugh Bean). (iii) *Oboe concerto in A min*. (ii) *English folksongs suite*. (i) DELIUS: *A Village Romeo and Juliet: Walk to the Paradise Garden. On Hearing the First Cuckoo in Spring*. (iv) BUTTERWORTH: *The Banks of Green Willow*. (ii) ELGAR: *Serenade for strings, Op. 20*. (iii) MOERAN: *Lonely Waters*.
(B) *** EMI *TC2-MOM 104*.

Looking at the programme and artists' roster the reader will hardly need the confirmation that this is a very attractive tape anthology. Performances never disappoint, the layout is excellent, and for the car this is ideal. The sound is a little variable on domestic equipment; at times there is a degree of edge to the treble (notably in the climaxes of the Delius *Walk to the Paradise Garden*). But often

the quality is both vivid and rich, as in the title piece and the Elgar *Serenade*. Vaughan Williams's *Oboe concerto*, stylishly played by John Williams, sounds admirably fresh. With any necessary adjustments to the sound, this is excellent value.

Hallé O., Handford

'*Hallé encores*': COPLAND: *Fanfare for the Common Man*. KHACHATURIAN: *Spartacus: Adagio of Spartacus and Phrygia*. GOUNOD: *Mors et Vita: Judex*. MACCUNN: *Overture: Land of the Mountain and the Flood*. SATIE: *Gymnopédies Nos. 1 and 3* (orch. Debussy). MASSENET: *Thaïs: Meditation*. TRAD.: *Suo Gan*. BARBER: *Adagio for strings*.
(B) *** CfP CFP/*TC-CFP* 40320.

Maurice Handford and the Hallé offer an exceptionally attractive collection of miscellaneous pieces beautifully recorded. Many of the items have achieved popularity almost by accident through television and the other media (how else would the MacCunn overture have come – so rightly – to notice?), but the sharpness of the contrasts adds to the charm. The Hallé violins sound a little thin in Barber's beautiful *Adagio*, but otherwise the playing is first-rate. What is particularly attractive about this concert is the way the programme is laid out so that each piece follows on naturally after its predecessor. The cassette transfer is of excellent quality, except for a tendency to shrillness in the violins when they are above the stave in fortissimo, as in the Khachaturian and Barber items.

'*Hallé encores*', *Vol. 2* (with Hallé Ch.): ALBINONI: *Adagio for strings and organ* (arr. Giazotto). PACHELBEL: *Canon in D*. PUCCINI: *Manon*

CONCERTS OF ORCHESTRAL AND CONCERTANTE MUSIC

Lescaut: Intermezzo. FRANCK: *Panis angelicus* (arr. Sandré). HUMPERDINCK: *Overture. Hänsel und Gretel.* MASCAGNI: *Cavalleria Rusticana: Intermezzo.* FAURÉ: *Pavane, Op. 50.* TCHAIKOVSKY: *Nutcracker, Op. 71: Waltz of the snowflakes.*
(B) ** CfP CFP/*TC-CFP* 40367.

Maurice Handford's second volume of Hallé encores is rather less successful than his first. Opening with a warm but not over-lush account of the Albinoni/Giazotto *Adagio* he moves on to a rather unimaginative version of Pachelbel's *Canon*, without any sort of climax, either in the centre or at the end. The Puccini *Intermezzo* and the choral version of *Panis angelicus* are restrained, and the most memorable items are on side two, with the Fauré *Pavane* and Tchaikovsky *Waltz* again both featuring the Hallé Choir. The recording is excellent, full and clear, and there is no appreciable difference between disc and tape.

Hallé O., Loughran

'*French music*': RAVEL: *Boléro.* DUKAS: *L'Apprenti sorcier.* CHABRIER: *España. Marche joyeuse.* BERLIOZ: *La Damnation de Faust: Hungarian march; Dance of the Sylphs; Minuet of the will-o'-the wisps.*
(B) ** CfP CFP/*TC-CFP* 40312.

Although lacking something in charisma, these pieces are well played and vividly recorded. Chabrier's *España* has plenty of life, and the pictorial effects of the Dukas symphonic poem are well brought off. Ravel's *Boléro* is built steadily to its climax, but undoubtedly the highlight of the concert is the suite from *The Damnation of Faust*, with each piece very strongly characterized. The tape transfer is generally well managed, although the wide dynamic range has meant that the quiet opening side-drum

in *Boléro* is almost inaudible at normal playback level.

Heifetz, Jascha (violin)

'*Ten great violin concertos*' (with (i) New SO, Sargent; (ii) Boston SO, Munch; (iii) Chicago SO; (iv) Reiner; (v) Hendl; (vi) RCA SO): (i) BACH: *Double violin concerto in D min., BWV 1043.* MOZART: *Violin concerto No. 5 in A (Turkish), K.219* (with chamber orch.). (ii) BEETHOVEN: *Concerto in D, Op. 61.* MENDELSSOHN: *Concerto in E min., Op. 64.* (i) BRUCH: *Concerto No. 1 in G min., Op. 26.* (iii; iv) BRAHMS: *Concerto in D, Op. 77.* TCHAIKOVSKY: *Concerto in D, Op. 35.* (iii; v) SIBELIUS: *Concerto in D min., Op. 47.* (vi; v) GLAZOUNOV: *Concerto in A min., Op. 82.* (ii) PROKOFIEV: *Concerto No. 2 in G min., Op. 63.*
(M) *** RCA RL 60720 (6) [CRL 6 0720].

Here are some fabulous performances, unlikely ever to be surpassed. Heifetz was in a class of his own, and most of the performances collected in this six-record anthology show him at his best. The ten concertos were all recorded between 1955 and 1963, and were his last word on these scores. He takes a very brisk view of the Beethoven (as he had in his earlier version with Toscanini); yet it is all thoroughly convincing, and so is his warm and more spacious account of the Brahms, beautifully accompanied by Reiner and the Chicago orchestra at its prime. The Tchaikovsky has a meltingly lovely slow movement and much virtuosity elsewhere. Dazzling too is the record of the Glazounov, which will convert any doubters to this composer's cause. The Sibelius *Concerto* is if anything even finer than the version Heifetz recorded in the 1930s with Beecham (still available on

World Records) and the Prokofiev *G minor*, though not superior to the pre-war version with Koussevitzky conducting, is every bit as good and has the advantage of more modern recording. Perhaps the least impressive things here are the Mozart and the Mendelssohn, which is very fast and a shade wanting in freshness. Otherwise glories abound. This is an indispensable set, excellently transferred – and very reasonably priced.

Holliger, Heinz (oboe; cor anglais)

Concertos (with Concg. O., Zinman): DONIZETTI: *Cor anglais concerto in G.* HAYDN: *Oboe concerto in C.* REICHA: *Scene for cor anglais.* ROS-SINI: *Variations in C* (originally for clarinet).
*** Ph. 9500 564/7300 713 [id.].

Holliger's outstanding DG anthology of 1966 is still available (DG Priv. 2535/3335 417 [139152]) and is reviewed above under the composers represented, Bellini, Cimarosa, Salieri and Donizetti (the same *Cor anglais concerto*). This newer collection is given Philips' very finest recording, richer than on the earlier disc but without loss of freshness. The cassette transfer too is of demonstration quality. The performances are wholly admirable. The Haydn concerto (which has a side to itself) is played with wonderful finesse by Holliger, and the splendid orchestral contribution directed by David Zinman makes a full-bodied and stylish contrast with the soloist. In the other three works Holliger combines fabulous natural bravura with elegance. Highly recommended.

Israel PO, Mehta

ROSSINI: *William Tell: overture.* BEETHOVEN: *Overture: Leonora No. 3, Op. 72b.* TCHAIKOVSKY: *Cap-riccio italien, Op. 45.* RIMSKY-KOR-SAKOV: *Capriccio espagnol, Op. 34.*
*(*) Decca SXL/KSXC 6977.

The performances here, of which *William Tell* is the most enjoyable, are well enough played and have a fair measure of adrenalin. They are vividly recorded, although the acoustic of the recording is not especially attractive. There is in fact no real distinction here; overall this concert seldom rises much above routine. The cassette is acceptable but not one of Decca's best.

(Philip) Jones Brass Ens.

'Baroque brass': BIBER: *Sonata a 7.* ANON.: *Sonate from 'Die Bankel-sangerlieder'.* FRANCK, Melchior: *Intrata.* HASSLER: *Intrada V.* SPEER: *Sonata for trumpet and 3 trombones. Sonata for 3 trombones. Sonata for 4 trombones. Sonata for 2 trumpets and 3 trombones.* SCHEIDT: *Canzona a 10.* BACH: *Chorale: Nun danket alle Gott. Capriccio on the departure of a beloved brother, BWV 992.* (Unaccompanied) *Cello suite No. 1: Menuetto and Courante* (arr. Fletcher for solo tuba). SCARLATTI, D.: *Keyboard sonatas, Kk.380, Kk.430, Kk.443* (arr. Dodgson). BACH, C. P. E.: *March.*
*** Argo ZRG/KZRC 898 [id.].

An imaginative and highly rewarding programme, even more successful than this group's earlier anthologies, *Renaissance brass* (ZRG/KZRC 823) and *Easy winners* (ZRG/KZRC 895). The music of Daniel Speer is strikingly inventive, and the Bach and Scarlatti arrangements are highly engaging – the latter with no attempt at miniaturization. The C. P. E. Bach *March* makes a superbly vigorous coda. If you like the baroque idiom and the sound of modern brass instruments this can be recommended, though not to be taken all at once. The recording is first-class and the cassette transfer well focused.

'*Festive brass*': UHL: *Festfanfare.* JANÁČEK: *Sinfonietta: Sokol fanfare.* FRANCK: *Pièce héroïque.* BLISS: *Fanfare for the Lord Mayor of London.* CASALS: *O vos omnes* (trans. Stokowski). TOMASI: *Fanfares liturgiques: Procession de Vendredi-Saint.* COPLAND: *Fanfare for the Common Man.* BRITTEN: *Russian funeral. Fanfare: The Eagle has Two Heads.* BOURGEOIS: *Wine rhapsody.* STRAUSS, R.: *Festmusik der Stadt Wien.*
*** Argo ZRG/KZRC 912.

Another fascinating compilation, showing a remarkable background of research into usable repertoire. Franck's *Pièce héroïque* transcribes surprisingly well for brass, and there are several other works of substance here. Apart from Britten's Russian threnody, Tomasi's *Procession de Vendredi-Saint* is a powerful nine-minute piece with a hauntingly sombre atmosphere. Britten's *Eagle fanfare* reminds us of the horn variation in *The Young Person's Guide to the Orchestra.* Richard Strauss's *Festmusik* is inflated but produces a considerable variety of texture and colour. Recording well up to the standard of this excellent series, with striking depth and sonority, although the cassette has slightly less range at the top than the disc.

'*Romantic brass*': MENDELSSOHN: *Song without Words, Op. 102: Tarantella.* DVOŘÁK: *Terzetto, Op. 74: Scherzo. Humoresque, Op. 101/7.* LEONTOVICH: *2 Ukrainian folk tunes.* GLAZOUNOV: *In modo religioso, Op. 38.* RAMSOE: *Quartet No. 5, Op. 38.* EWALD: *Quintet No. 3, Op. 7.*
*** Argo ZRG/KZRC 928 [id.].

Engagingly lightweight, this is one of the most entertaining of the Philip Jones anthologies. The Mendelssohn *Song without Words* is remarkably nimble; the unforced bravura of the playing brings an agreeably relaxed atmosphere here and in the other lollipops. The Ewald *Quintet* is harmonically unadventurous but uncommonly well scored. It is obviously rewarding to play, and the performance is impeccably stylish. Excellent recording, beautifully balanced on disc and tape alike.

'*La Battaglia*': BYRD: *The Battell* (arr. Howarth). BANCHIERI: *Udite, ecco le trombe* (fantasia, arr. Jones). KUHNAU: *Biblical sonata No. 1 (The battle between David and Goliath,* arr. Hazell). JENKINS: *Newark Siege* (fantasia, arr. Reeve). HANDEL: *Royal Fireworks music: La Réjouissance* (arr. Howarth).
*** Argo ZRG/KZRC 932 [id.].

Most of these pieces are arranged, rather improbably, from keyboard works. The purists may reject the idea, but with Jones's brilliant band relishing the vigour and bite of the writing, the result is another in this Ensemble's outstanding series: a real demonstration record with vivid sound. The cassette is unsuccessful: the resonance clouds the sound picture and brings congestion.

'*Focus on PJBE*': PRAETORIUS: *Terpsichoren suite for brass* (arr. Reeve). DODGSON: *Fantasia for 6 brass.* RIMSKY-KORSAKOV: *Mlada: Procession of the Nobles* (arr. Archibald). KOETSIER: *Brass symphony, Op. 80.* JOPLIN: *Gladiolus rag.* TRAD.: *Londonderry air.* GADE: *Jealousy* (all arr. Iveson). TRAD.: *The Cuckoo* (arr. Howarth).
*** Argo Dig. ZRDL/KZRDC 1001.

For their digital début the PJBE have assembled a characteristically entertaining cocktail. There is no reason why the famous Praetorius dances should not be scored for brass alone; here piquancy is exchanged for splendour, with Stephen Dodgson's slightly sombre *Fantasia* making a good foil afterwards. The Koetsier *Symphony* with its interweaving lines in the outer movements is superbly effective played with this kind of bravura, and the lollipops are enjoyable, though the arrangement of the *Londonderry air* is a shade over-elaborate. The sound has demonstration presence and sonority on both disc and chrome cassette.

King, Thea (clarinet)

'The clarinet in concert' (with Dobrée, basset horn, Imai, viola; LSO, Alun Francis): BRUCH: *Double concerto in E min. for clarinet and viola, Op. 88.* MENDELSSOHN: *2 Concert pieces for clarinet and basset horn: in F min., Op. 113; in D min., Op. 114.* CRUSELL: *Introduction and variations on a Swedish air, Op. 12.*
*** Hyp. A 66022.

A thoroughly engaging programme of forgotten music (the Bruch is not even listed in the *New Grove*), all played with skill and real charm and excellently recorded. The Bruch is a delightful work, with genuinely memorable inspiration in its first two lyrical movements and a roistering finale making a fine contrast. Clarinet and viola are blended beautifully, with the more penetrating wind instrument dominating naturally and with melting phrasing from Thea King. The Mendelssohn duets for clarinet and basset horn are no less diverting, with their jocular finales, and they too are played with a nice blend of expressive spontaneity and high spirits. The Weberian Crusell *Variations* show Miss King's bravura at its most sparkling. This is far

from being an empty piece; its twists and turns are consistently inventive.

Leningrad PO, Mravinsky

'Mravinsky at the 1978 Vienna Festival': WEBER: *Oberon: overture.* SCHUBERT: *Symphony No. 8 in B min. (Unfinished), D.759.* BRAHMS: *Symphony No. 2 in D, Op. 73.* SHOSTAKOVICH: *Symphony No. 5 in D min., Op. 47.* TCHAIKOVSKY: *Symphony No. 5 in E min., Op. 64.*
(M) **(*) HMV SLS 5212 (4).

There is some thrilling and indeed electrifying playing here. Mravinsky appears all too rarely in the studio; these concert appearances were both recorded by Austrian Radio in 1978, and the set costs no more than a pair of tickets for one London concert, let alone two. The exceptionally wide range the Leningrad orchestra possesses obviously posed problems for the engineers, and the sound quality is distinctly subfusc – in the case of the Brahms symphony execrable. Yet what performances these are! *Oberon* opens with a magically hushed, rapt atmosphere, and the extraordinary lightness yet intensity that the strings can produce at *ppp* is heard to advantage. Every phrase means something in these performances, even if on occasion one feels that some of the nuances border on exaggeration: take the *Unfinished*, for instance, though it has all the fire and refinement for which this orchestra is famous. The Brahms is the least successful, both as performance and recording, but the Shostakovich is indispensable. Mravinsky conducted its première in 1937 and subsequently recorded it, on seven 78 rpm records. (His speed must be much faster now, since his reading takes only 42′15″, as opposed to Previn = 47′40″, Rowicki = 47′10″, Bernstein = 48′55″). This is a superb performance, though it is marred by some imperfect intonation in the slow movement. Mravinsky takes the coda of the finale at the tempo Shostakovich asked for, and the phrasing in the second group of the first movement is more imaginative than in any of its rivals. The Tchaikovsky is splendidly wild and passionate, though perhaps less controlled than on Mravinsky's earlier records, made in the studio. Despite these reservations, this is a marvellous set – and the sense of occasion is splendidly communicated.

Lloyd Webber, Julian (cello)

'Cello man' (with Nat. PO, Gerhardt): CANTELOUBE: Baïléro. FALLA: Ritual fire dance. SAINT-SAËNS: Samson et Dalila: Softly awakes my heart. BRIDGE: Scherzetto. FAURÉ: Élégie. VILLA-LOBOS: Bachianas Brasileiras No. 5. BACH: Arioso. PÖPPER: Gavotte No. 2. DELIUS: Hassan: Serenade. BRUCH: Kol Nidrei.
** RCA RL/RK 25383.

Flatteringly recorded, with the cello forward and the orchestra in a very resonant acoustic, this programme is soupily romantic and will not be to all tastes, though the playing is lushly effective. But a song like Baïléro loses its innocence with such treatment, and the arrangement of the Ritual fire dance for cello and orchestra is pointless. The Pöpper, Delius and Bruch pieces are the highlights. The chrome tape matches the disc closely.

Locke Brass Cons., Stobart

'Jubilant brass': BLISS: Fanfare for a Dignified Occasion. Fanfare for the Lord Mayor of London. Fanfare for a Coming of Age. Royal fanfares Nos. 1–6. Fanfare for Heroes. Homage to Shakespeare. BENJAMIN: Fanfare for a Festive Occasion. 3 Fanfares (For a state occasion; For a brilliant occasion; For a gala occasion). ELGAR: Civic fanfare. WALTON: Fanfare. Queen's fanfare. BRIAN: Festival fanfare. SIMPSON: Canzona. TIPPETT: Fanfare for brass. RUBBRA: Fanfare for Europe, Op. 142. JACOB: Music for a Festival: Interludes for trumpets and trombones. Arr. COE: National anthem.
(M) ** RCA Gold GL/GK 25308.

Does anyone want this many fanfares? They are played with spirit and great technical expertise, and they are brightly and sonorously recorded (although the tape is not as rich and full-blooded as the disc). There are some fine things here, and taken in small sections the music-making is impressive.

LPO (various conductors)

'Favourites of the Philharmonic': GRIEG: Peer Gynt: Morning. CHABRIER: España. LITOLFF: Concerto symphonique: Scherzo (with Katin; all cond. Pritchard). FAURÉ: Pavane (cond. Handley). BERLIOZ: Le Carnaval romain overture. SMETANA: The Bartered Bride: overture (cond. Barbier). GLINKA: Russlan and Ludmilla: overture (cond. Mackerras). WEBER: Der Freischütz: overture. NICOLAI: The Merry Wives of Windsor: overture. MENDELSSOHN: A Midsummer Night's Dream: Scherzo (cond. Lockhart). TCHAIKOVSKY: Serenade for strings: Waltz (cond. Del Mar). STRAUSS, Johann, Jnr: Tritsch-Tratsch polka; An der schönen blauen Donau (cond. Güschlbauer). STRAUSS, Johann, Snr: Radetzky march. VERDI: Aïda: Triumphal march (cond. Davison). BEETHOVEN:

Egmont: overture (cond. Andrew Davis).
(B) ** MfP MFP/*TC-MFP* 1001 (2).

No one can argue with the title: there are many favourite classical 'pops' here, but they do not make a concert, with overtures dotted all over the place and no attempt to create a prevailing mood or set up appropriate contrasts. All the performances are good; some are excellent (Fauré's *Pavane* under Handley, and Lockhart's *Merry Wives overture*, for instance). The recording is bright and clear, and as a sampler of the Classics for Pleasure range this is more than adequate, even though at least two of the discs from which the items are taken are withdrawn from the catalogue as we go to print. It is curious that a CfP collection should be issued on the 'popular' MfP label.

LPO, Herrmann

'*Clair de lune*': SATIE: *Gymnopédies Nos. 1 and 2.* DEBUSSY: *Suite bergamasque: Clair de lune. La plus que lente* (valse). RAVEL: *Five o'clock foxtrot.* FAURÉ: *Pavane.* HONEGGER: *Pastorale d'été.*
(M) * Decca SPA/*KCSP* 570.

An interesting programme is here let down by indifferent performances. The Fauré *Pavane* is very sluggish indeed, and the Debussy and Satie pieces are not much better. Indeed the music only fitfully sparks into life. The recording – originally Phase Four – is close and unnatural in balance, so that the refinement of the scoring in the Ravel and Honegger works is not seen in truthful perspective. Disc and tape are similar.

LSO, Gibson

'*Music for royal occasions*': MATH-IAS: *Investiture Anniversary fanfare.* WALTON: *Crown Imperial; Orb and Sceptre* (marches). HANDEL: *Water music suite* (arr. Harty): *Allegro; Air; Allegro deciso.* DAVIS: *Music for a Royal Wedding.* ELGAR: *Nursery suite: Aubade; The serious doll.*
(B) *** Pick. Dig. RL/*RLT* 7555.

This was the first digital record to be issued at bargain price, and it is an uncommonly good one, with a matching cassette of demonstration quality. It was released without any commensurate publicity fanfares to celebrate the occasion of the royal wedding and almost passed unnoticed. The programme is admirably chosen; Mathias's *Investiture fanfare* (written earlier for the Prince of Wales) is superbly crafted, characteristic of this unostentatious but highly musical composer, and Carl Davis's *Suite* is no less congenial. One cannot help smiling at the inclusion of the Elgar items, in the event suitably prescient. The marches have regal splendour and the recording appropriate brilliance. A real bargain.

LSO, Tausky

'*Music you have loved*': VERDI: *La Traviata: Prelude to Act 1.* GRIEG: *Norwegian dance No. 2, Op. 35.* BINGE: *Elizabethan serenade.* MENDELSSOHN: *A Midsummer Night's Dream, Op. 61: Wedding march.* MASSENET: *Thaïs: Meditation* (with Georgiadis). WALDTEUFEL: *Waltz: Les Patineurs, Op. 183.* MASCAGNI: *Cavalleria Rusticana: Intermezzo.* HUMMEL: *Trumpet concerto in E flat: finale.* DELIBES: *Sylvia: Pizzicato.* DEBUSSY: *Suite bergamasque: Clair de lune.* TCHAIKOVSKY: *Chant sans paroles, Op. 2/3.* ELGAR: *Salut d'amour.* GOUNOD: *Faust: Waltz.* STRAUSS, Johann, Snr: *Radetzky*

march. BACH (arr. Walton): *The Wise Virgins: Sheep may safely graze.* WALTON: *Façade: Popular song.* GRANADOS: *Goyescas: Intermezzo.* SIBELIUS: *Valse triste, Op. 44.* GRAINGER: *Handel in the Strand.* WOLF-FERRARI: *I Quattro Rusteghi: Intermezzo.* HANDEL: *Xerxes: Largo.* STRAUSS, Johann, Jnr, and Josef: *Pizzicato polka.* BENJAMIN: *Jamaican rumba.* MOZART: *Horn concerto No. 4 in E flat, K.495: Rondo.* THOMAS: *Mignon: Entr'acte.* REZNIČEK: *Donna Diana: overture.*
(B) *** Pick. PDA 036 (2).

This two-disc set includes twenty-six complete pieces from the same number of composers. The selection has been made with taste and discernment, and the concert is excellently laid out, which is perhaps not surprising, as the producer is Peter Gammond. The recording was made in St Giles' Church, Cripplegate, and Bob Auger, the engineer in charge, is to be congratulated on the nicely judged reverberation and orchestral bloom. The LSO is on excellent form and Vilem Tausky directs with spirit and style. The orchestra's soloists are featured in the three concertante items. The whole programme is very enjoyable, the second disc especially so; *Sheep may safely graze*, the excerpt from *Façade*, Sibelius's *Valse triste*, *Handel in the Strand*, and the Wolf-Ferrari and Rezniček items are all especially vivacious. At bargain-basement price and with clean, quiet pressings, this can be cordially recommended.

Lucerne Festival Strings, Baumgartner

'*A little night music*': MOZART: *Eine kleine Nachtmusik, K.525.* VIVALDI: *Flute concerto in G (La Notte), Op. 10/2* (with Galway). BIBER: *Serenade in C (Nightwatchman)* (with Ridderbusch). BOCCHERINI: *Quintet in G (La Musica notturna di Madrid).*
(M) **(*) RCA Gold GL/GK 25309.

Mozart's night music is reliably played, but it is the two novelties that make this collection worth considering. The Biber *Serenade*, like Boccherini's *Quintet*, has pictorial implications and is quite evocatively presented (with a short and rather gruff contribution from Karl Ridderbusch). The Boccherini is also available in a beautifully played Karajan version, but that is at full price, and certainly Baumgartner gives a good account of it. James Galway's nimble performance of Vivaldi's *La Notte concerto* is self-recommending, with a characteristically sparkling finale. The sound is full and clear, although the cassette has less body and bloom than the disc.

'*Adagio*': ALBINONI: *Adagio for strings and organ* (arr. Giazotto). PACHELBEL: *Canon and Gigue.* RAMEAU: *Tambourin.* PURCELL: *Chaconne in G min.* BACH: *Suites Nos. 2 in B min., BWV 1067: Badinerie; 3 in D, BWV 1068: Air. Fugue in E* (arr. Mozart). *Jesu, joy of man's desiring. The Musical Offering, BWV 1079: Ricercare.*
(M) ** DG Priv. 2535/3335 606.

An agreeable collection of baroque 'pops', stylishly played and recorded with full, bright sound and a style that manages to be expressive without resorting to technicolour textures. *Jesu, joy of man's desiring*, however, sounds rather dull when heard on strings alone, without the usual oboe obbligato. Disc and cassette are of matching quality.

Menuhin, Yehudi (violin)

'*Romances*' (with Philh. O., Pritchard): BEETHOVEN: *Romances for*

violin and orchestra Nos. 1 in G., Op. 40; 2 in F, Op. 50. WIENIAWSKI: *Légende, Op. 17.* CHAUSSON: *Pòeme, Op. 25.* BERLIOZ: *Romance, rêverie et caprice, Op. 8.*
(B) **(*) CfP CFP/*TC-CFP* 40365.

This is an unexpected and attractive grouping of concertante works for violin which by their very brevity tend to get neglected. It is a reissue of an HMV collection from 1965, and the performances – all of them warmly expressive – emerge freshly here, although the recording sometimes makes Menuhin's upper range sound slightly edgy. This is less noticeable on the cassette, which is smoother than the disc; otherwise the sound of both is closely matched.

Messiter, Malcolm (oboe)

'Oboe fantasia' (with Nat. PO, Mace): PASCULLI: *Concerto on themes from Donizetti's 'La Favorita'.* DEBUSSY: *Rêverie.* SCARLATTI, D.: *Sonata in C, Kk.159.* SAINT-SAËNS: *The Swan.* MUSSORGSKY: *Ballet of the unhatched chicks.* NOVAČEK: *Perpetual motion.* DE LA RUE: *Compte à rebours: Adagio.* PUCCINI: *Gianni Schicchi: O mio babbino caro.* KREISLER: *Caprice viennois.* JOSEPHS: *Enemy at the Door: Song of freedom.* POULENC: *Mouvements perpétuels No. 1.* YOUNG: *Stella by Starlight.*
**(*) RCA RL/*RK* 25367.

With a showcase issue of this kind RCA are obviously trying to promote Malcolm Messiter as a star oboist to catch the public fancy and match the achievement of James Galway's silver flute. Certainly Messiter can charm the ear, as in Debussy's *Rêverie*; he can also produce impressive bravura, as in Pasculli's reworking of tunes from Doni-

zetti's *La Favorita.* There is sparkle in Kreisler's *Caprice viennois,* and an eloquent operatic line in Puccini, but in the last result this playing has not the memorability nor quite the technical flair of Galway's. Messiter is at his best in the slighter material. The recording is faithful, the oboe well forward, the orchestral strings sometimes sounding thin, and this effect is exaggerated in the high-level cassette transfer.

Monteux, Claude (flute), LSO, Pierre Monteux

BACH: *Suite No. 2 in B min. for flute and strings, BWV 1067.* GLUCK: *Orfeo: Dance of the Blessed Spirits.* MOZART: *Flute concerto No. 2 in D, K.314.*
(B) *** Con. CC/*CCT* 7504 [Lon. STS 15493].

Claude Monteux is the son of Pierre Monteux, and the joy of family music-making shines through these charming performances. By chance the disc first appeared just after Pierre Monteux's death, and there could be no more fitting memorial for so vitally happy a musician, by turns serene and vigorous; the Mozart in particular is given the sunniest performance. The recording still sounds extremely well in this Contour reissue, although the bass is somewhat over-resonant and tends to make textures ample and rich, the very opposite of the sound one would expect from the 'authentic' original instrument school. On tape the quality is less well defined at both ends of the spectrum.

Mordkovitch, Lydia (violin)

'Hebrew melody' (with Nat. PO, Gerhardt): BRUCH: *Kol Nidrei, Op. 67* (arr. the composer). BLOCH: *Baal Shem. Abodah.* RAVEL: *Kaddisch.*

ACHRON: *Hebrew melody, Op. 35.*
Hebrew lullaby, Op. 35/2.
**(*) RCA RL/*RK* 25370.

Passionately intense performances,
warmly accompanied by Gerhardt. The
composer's own transcription of *Kol
Nidrei* from cello to violin loses some of
the work's gravitas, although here it still
communicates vividly. *Baal Shem* is a
three-movement suite (*Contrition, Improvisation* and *Rejoicing*), and Lydia
Mordkovitch's characterization is nothing if not powerful. Ravel was not
Jewish but his haunting *Kaddisch* makes
a highly effective contribution to a programme which, though perhaps not to be
listened to at a single sitting, certainly
offers some fine music, given maximum
projection. The forward balance of the
solo instrument brings a slight fierceness
of timbre at climaxes and both disc and
tape (which is a faithful transfer) benefit
from some top cut.

I Musici

Concertos for strings: CORELLI: *Concerto grosso in G min.* (*Christmas*),
Op. 6/8. MANFREDINI: *Concerto
grosso in C, Op. 3/12.* TORELLI: *Concerto in G min. Op. 8/6.* LOCATELLI.
Concerto grosso in F min., Op. 1/8.
(M) **(*) Ph. Fest. 6570/*7310* 179.

These are sunny performances in the
Italian manner, with serenely expressive
slow movements and rather sturdy allegros. There is considerable finesse in
matters of phrasing, if some lack of
rhythmic resilience. The warm acoustic,
with an organ continuo filling out the
textures, is certainly congenial. Perhaps
this is a concert to bring happy anticipations of summer on a wintry evening. The
high-level cassette transfer is first-class,
matching the disc closely.

'Baroque festival': PACHELBEL:
Canon and Gigue. VIVALDI: *Double
mandolin concerto in G, RV.532.*
ALBINONI: *Adagio for strings and
organ* (arr. Giazotto). HANDEL:
Harp concerto in B flat, Op. 4/6.
BACH: *Brandenburg concerto No. 3,
BWV 1048.* DURANTE: *Concerto for
strings in F min.* GALUPPI: *Concerto
a quattro No. 2 in G.* SCARLATTI, A.:
Concerto grosso No. 3 in F. PER-
GOLESI: *Flute concerto in G.* LOC-
ATELLI: *Concerto grosso in C min.,
Op. 1/11.*
(M) **(*) Ph. 6770 057/*7650 057* (2).

Opening with a rather delicate version
of Pachelbel's famous *Canon* and including also a perhaps over-refined view of
the Albinoni/Giazotto *Adagio*, this is an
attractively played and beautifully
recorded collection, suitable for late-
evening listening, especially in its tape-
box format which offers demonstration
quality throughout. The first half of the
programme (up to the Bach *Brandenburg
concerto*) is also available separately on
Sequenza (6527/*7311* 104), but makes a
less satisfying concert than the collection
as a whole.

Neveu, Ginette (violin)

'The early recordings': BACH (arr.
Kreisler): *Air.* CHOPIN (arr. Rodio-
nov): *Nocturne No. 20 in C sharp
min., Op. posth.* GLUCK: *Orfeo:
Melody.* PARADIES (arr. Dushkin):
Sicilienne (all with Seidler-Winkler,
piano). TARTINI (arr. Kreisler):
Variations on a theme of Corelli.
STRAUSS, R.: *Violin sonata in E flat,
Op. 18* (both with Beck, piano). SI-
BELIUS: *Violin concerto in D min.,
Op. 47* (with Philh. O., Susskind).
RAVEL: *Tzigane. Pièce en forme de
habanera.* SCARLATESCU: *Bagatelle.*
FALLA (arr. Kreisler): *La Vida breve:*

Danse espagnole. DINICU: (arr. Heifetz): *Hora staccato.* SUK: *4 Pieces, Op. 17.* DEBUSSY: *Violin sonata in G min.* (all with Jean Neveu, piano). BRAHMS: *Violin concerto in D, Op. 77.* CHAUSSON: *Poème, Op. 25* (both with Philh. O., Dobrowen).
(M) (***) HMV mono RLS 739 (4).

The brilliant career of Ginette Neveu was cut short by an air crash, in which her brother Jean also died. This compilation offers all the material that has already been issued in the UK, such as the Sibelius and Brahms concertos and the Suk *Four Pieces,* together with a number of recordings which have not. These include the Strauss *Sonata,* recorded in Berlin before the outbreak of the war. There is a vibrant intensity about Neveu's playing that is altogether remarkable; this four-record set gives the complete recorded legacy, and its quality cannot be too highly praised. The transfers are altogether excellent and have been done with great care. The *Early recordings* title applies only to the first two records.

NYPO, Bernstein

DUKAS: *L'Apprenti sorcier.* MUSSORGSKY: *Night on the Bare Mountain.* STRAUSS, R.: *Till Eulenspiegel, Op. 28.* SAINT-SAËNS: *Danse macabre, Op. 40.*
(M) *** CBS 61976/40- [Col. MS 7165].

One of Bernstein's very best records made during his regular association with the New York Philharmonic. The performances are as volatile as they are brilliant: *The Sorcerer's Apprentice* has splendid momentum; *Night on the Bare Mountain* emanates a pungent rhythmic force; *Till* is portrayed with a captivatingly mercurial projection of high spirits and *Danse macabre* has striking panache. The orchestra's bravura brings superb

ensemble throughout, matched with lively and colourful solo contributions from all departments. The CBS recording is characteristically forward, but there is atmosphere to balance the brightness. The cassette is lively but less refined than the disc: climaxes are inclined to sound explosive.

Orchestra of St John's, Lubbock

'Classical collection': VAUGHAN WILLIAMS: *Fantasia on Greensleeves. Rhosymedre.* GRIEG: *Peer Gynt: Morning.* RAVEL: *Pavane.* DELIUS: *On Hearing the First Cuckoo in Spring.* FAURÉ: *Masques et bergamasques: Overture. Berceuse, Op. 56.* SCHUBERT: *Rosamunde: Entr'acte No. 2; Ballet music No. 2.* MOZART: *Divertimento in D, K.136: Presto.*
**(*) ASV Dig. DCA/ZCDCA 503.

A pleasant collection of essentially atmospheric music for late evening. Fine playing; tempi are at times a little sleepy, notably in the Grieg, Fauré and Schubert items, but the effect is still persuasive. The digital recording is first-class, full, clear, yet not clinical in its detail. The cassette is excellent too.

Orchestre de Paris, Barenboim

French music: DUKAS: *L'Apprenti sorcier.* BERLIOZ: *Le Carnaval romain: overture. Béatrice et Bénédict: overture. La Damnation de Faust: Hungarian march.* SAINT-SAËNS: *Le Déluge: Prélude. Samson et Dalila: Bacchanale. Danse macabre, Op. 40.*
*(**) DG 2531/3301 331 [id.].

Outstanding recording here, demonstration-worthy in its sumptuousness as well as its brilliance. The finest performance is the Saint-Saëns *Bacchanale*, with a voluptuous climax of great intensity and power. *Danse macabre* comes off well too, but *The Sorcerer's Apprentice* shows Barenboim rather unsuccessfully adopting his Furtwänglerian mantle: the heavy presentation of the main theme bodes ill for a reading which produces very broad climaxes, with unconvincing use of accelerandi to reach them. The Berlioz overtures are exciting, with the orchestra on its toes, again helped by the flattering acoustic. The cassette is extremely successful, matching the disc closely.

Overtures

English overtures (with (i) LPO; (ii) LSO; (iii) New Philh. O.; (iv) Alwyn; (v) Pritchard; (vi) Braithwaite; (vii) Handley): (i; iv) ALWYN: *Derby Day*. (i; v) CHAGRIN: *Helter Skelter*. (ii; vi) ARNOLD: *Beckus the Dandipratt*. (i; v) RAWSTHORNE: *Street Corner*. (iii; vii) BUSH: *Yorick*. (iii; vi) LEIGH: *Agincourt*.
*** Lyr. SRCS 95.

Alwyn's *Derby Day* begins an anthology of extrovert English overtures, all brightly and breezily played, and emphatically not to be heard in rapid succession! Best-known are Arnold's *Beckus the Dandipratt* and Rawsthorne's *Street Corner*, which have been on record before, and perhaps Geoffrey Bush's *Yorick*, a lively piece that is frequently broadcast. But all these pieces are vividly played and recorded, and the rarities by Francis Chagrin and Walter Leigh are well worth having.

Petri, Michala (recorder)

Recorder concertos (with ASMF, Marriner): VIVALDI: *Soprano recorder concerto in C, RV.443*. SAM-

MARTINI: *Descant recorder concerto in F*. TELEMANN: *Treble recorder concerto in C*. HANDEL: *Treble recorder concerto in F* (arr. of *Organ concerto, Op. 4/5*).
*** Ph. 9500 714/7300 808 [id.].

Michala Petri plays her various recorders with enviable skill, and her nimble piping creates some delightful sounds in these four attractively inventive concertos. This is not a record to be played all at once, but taken in sections it has unfailing charm; the sound is of demonstration quality on disc and cassette alike.

Philh. O., Karajan

'Philharmonia Promenade Concert': WALDTEUFEL: *Les Patineurs waltz*. STRAUSS, Johann, Jnr: *Tritsch-Tratsch polka. Unter Donner und Blitz polka*. STRAUSS, Johann, Snr: *Radetzky march*. CHABRIER: *España. Joyeuse marche*. SUPPÉ: *Overture: Light Cavalry*. WEINBERGER: *Schwanda the Bagpiper: Polka*. OFFENBACH: *Overture: Orpheus in the Underworld*.
(B) *** CfP CFP/TC-CFP 40368.

A superb reissue from the sixties. Both Karajan and the Philharmonia Orchestra are on top form, and the whole collection has the right infectious 'fun' quality. An exhilarating experience, partly because the remarkably sumptuous recording also sparkles vividly to match the playing. Highly recommended on both disc and cassette (they sound virtually identical).

(i) **Philh. O., Krips;** (ii) **Johann Strauss O. of V., Boskovsky**

'Viennese enchantment': (i) STRAUSS:

913

Die Fledermaus: overture. Unter Donner und Blitz polka. Perpetuum mobile. Quadrille on themes from Verdi's 'Un Ballo in maschera'. Tritsch-Tratsch polka. Der Zigeunerbaron: overture. (ii) *Wein, Weib und Gesang waltz. Auf der Jagd polka.* (i) ZIEHRER: *Wiener Bürger waltz.* (i) *Die Landstreicher: overture.* (i) *Weaner Mädln waltz.* GUNGL: *Amorettentanz waltz.* LANNER: *Die Schönbrunner waltz.* LEHÁR: *Gold and silver waltz.*
(B) **(*) EMI *TC2-MOM 121.*

Henry Krips's version of the *Die Fledermaus overture* uses a degree of rubato which now seems excessive, but otherwise his performances are vivacious and the Philharmonia playing reflects the vintage period from which these recordings come. Boskovsky's contribution is also stylish. The sound, though rather reverberant, is always good and there are some attractive novelties here.

'Pomp and circumstance'

(i) Royal Liv. PO, Groves; (ii) King's College Ch., Camb. University Music Soc., New Philh. O., Ledger: (i) ELGAR: *Pomp and Circumstance marches Nos. 1 and 4. Imperial march. Coronation march. Enigma variations: Nimrod.* (ii) *Land of Hope and Glory.* (i) ARNE: *Rule, Britannia* (with Anne Collins, Liv. PO Ch.). *The British Grenadiers.* WALTON: *Spitfire prelude and fugue. Orb and Sceptre. Crown Imperial;* COATES: *Dambusters march.* (ii) PARRY: *I was glad.* (i) WALFORD DAVIES: *RAF March past.*
(B) ** EMI *TC2-MOM 105.*

Such an unrelenting stream of musical patriotism is more suitable for keeping up the spirits on the motorway than for a continuous domestic concert, although Sir Charles Groves's sturdy performances never lack character. The transfer is not too well calculated and the high level brings patches of roughness, notably at the opening of the *Spitfire prelude,* and occasionally in the choral music. This is barely noticeable in the car.

Rampal, Jean-Pierre (flute)

Flute concertos (with O. Ant. Mus., Roussel): DEVIENNE: *Concerto No. 2 in D.* NAUDOT: *Concerto in G, Op. 17/5.* LOEILLET: *Concerto in D.*
(M) **(*) Ph. Seq. 6527/7311 095.

A surprisingly enjoyable collection of concertos by lesser-known composers. The most ambitious piece – with a side to itself – is that by François Devienne (1759–1803), a work of considerable charm in the *galant* style. The rococo roulades of the outer movements are highly engaging, and there is no lack of agreeable melody. The work by Naudot (*c.* 1690–1762) looks back to Vivaldi and has plenty of vitality, like the sprightly concerto of Loeillet, his contemporary. Excellent playing from Rampal. The orchestral sound is slightly less refined but spirited, recorded in a somewhat over-resonant acoustic, which brings some slight loss of sharpness of detail in the otherwise well-managed cassette transfer.

(i) Royal Liv. PO; (ii) RPO; Groves

'Forward march'; (i) ELGAR: *Pomp and Circumstance marches Nos. 1 and 4. Coronation march. Imperial march.* COATES: *London suite: Knightsbridge march. Dambusters march.* WALFORD DAVIES: *RAF March past.* WALTON: *Crown Im-*

perial. Orb and Sceptre. HOLST: *Song without words: Marching song, Op. 22.* BLISS: *Things to Come: March.*
(M) *** HMV Green. ESD/TC-ESD 7075.

Many of the items here are also available on the *Pomp and circumstance* 'Miles of Music' tape. However, this selection seems admirably apt and the performances are vigorous without being too strenuous. The recording is consistently excellent, although there are one or two unfocused moments on the cassette.

ROHCGO

'A tribute to the Royal Ballet' (cond. Irving, Lanchbery, Fayer or Mackerras): excerpts from: PURCELL: *Comus* (arr. Lambert). BOYCE: *The Prospect before Us* (arr. Lambert). COUPERIN: *Harlequin in the Street* (orch. Jacob). MENDELSSOHN: *Lord of Burleigh* (orch. Jacob). AUBER: *Les Rendezvous* (arr. Lambert). GORDON: *The Rake's Progress.* LISZT: *Apparitions* (orch. Jacob). LAMBERT: *Horoscope.* BERNERS: *Wedding Bouquet* (with ch.). BLISS: *Adam Zero.* PROKOFIEV: *Cinderella.* ADAM: *Giselle.* LANCHBERY: *Tales of Beatrix Potter.* SATIE: *Monotones* (orch. Debussy). MESSAGER: *The Two Pigeons.* CHOPIN: *A Month in the Country* (arr. Lanchbery).
(M) *** HMV ESDW/TC-ESDW 713 (2).

Issued to celebrate the fiftieth anniversary of the Royal Ballet, this is an entertaining reminder of the music which accompanied the dance. Many of the ballets of the thirties and forties have passed into oblivion as stage productions, yet they stimulated brilliant and witty arrangements from musicians of the calibre of Gordon Jacob and Con-

stant Lambert; and Lambert's own delicious *Waltz for the Gemini* from the original score for *Horoscope* is one of the highlights of the set. The first two sides offer an exhilarating kaleidoscope of numbers from these scores, and then the selection moves on through Berners (a fascinating piece), Bliss and Prokofiev to a suite taken from Yuri Fayer's exquisitely played recording of *Giselle.* The engaging *Mouse waltz* from *Tales of Beatrix Potter* reminds us of the skills of John Lanchbery; and it is a pity that the weak and watery Chopin arrangement for *A Month in the Country* had to be chosen to end the concert instead of his arrangement of Hérold's *La Fille mal gardée.* The sound is vivid throughout (one or two of the earlier excerpts are from recordings made in the late fifties) and often outstanding, with a matching cassette transfer of high quality; the Messager, in particular, demonstrates the latter's excellence. Highly recommended.

RPO, Beecham

'Famous overtures': BEETHOVEN: *The Ruins of Athens, Op. 113.* ROSSINI: *La Gazza ladra.* MENDELSSOHN: *A Midsummer Night's Dream, Op. 21.* BERLIOZ: *Le Corsaire, Op. 21.* BRAHMS: *Academic Festival overture, Op. 80.* SUPPÉ: *Poet and Peasant.*
(B) *** CfP CFP/TC-CFP 40358.

Beecham reissues are self-recommending and hardly need our advocacy, especially when they come in the lowest price-range. The recordings here rather show their age (they are mainly from the late fifties), but Beecham is irresistible in such items as these, not just in swaggering music but in poetic moments too. An excellent bargain. (NB. The cassette was originally of unreliable technical quality, although later copies have been remastered. But it is advisable to check before purchase or make sure that a replacement is possible.)

'French lollipops' (with (i) Fr. Nat. RO): CHABRIER: *Marche joyeuse.* DEBUSSY: *L'Enfant prodigue: Cortège et Air de danse. Prélude à l'après-midi d'un faune.* SAINT-SAËNS: *Samson et Dalila: Danse; Bacchanale. Le Rouet d'Omphale, Op. 31.* GOUNOD: *Roméo et Juliette: Le sommeil.* (i) FAURÉ: *Dolly suite, Op. 56. Pavane, Op. 50.*
(M) *** HMV SXLP/TC-SXLP 30299.

This is an enchanting record, full of the imaginative and poetic phrasing that distinguished the best Beecham performances. The recording is always good and sometimes excellent, with an outstanding cassette to match the disc in vividness and detail.

'Beecham favourites': HANDEL: *Solomon: Arrival of the Queen of Sheba.* ROSSINI: *Overtures: La Cambiale di matrimonio; Semiramide.* SIBELIUS: *Kuolema: Valse triste, Op. 44.* GRIEG: *In Autumn: concert overture. Symphonic dance in A, Op. 64/2.* DVOŘÁK: *Legend in G min., Op. 59/3.* MENDELSSOHN: *Fair Melusina: overture, Op. 32.*
(M) *** HMV SXLP/TC-SXLP 30530.

Altogether delicious performances from the old magician. They come up remarkably fresh, too, after more than two decades, a tribute not only to the artistry of Beecham and the RPO but the quality of the EMI engineering. Notable are the Grieg items: the *Symphonic dance* is utterly delectable, while his little-known overture displays an unexpected degree of colour and charm. The cassette offers sound that is slightly fuller than the disc, which has more range at the top and a fresher upper string quality.

Rostropovich, Mstislav (cello)

Cello concertos (with (i) Zurich Coll. Mus., Sacher; (ii) Leningrad PO, Rozhdestvensky; (iii) Berlin PO, Karajan): (i) BOCCHERINI: *Concerto No. 2 in D.* VIVALDI: *Concerto in G, RV 143.* (ii) SCHUMANN: *Concerto in A min., Op. 129.* (iii) DVOŘÁK: *Concerto in B min., Op. 104.* TCHAIKOVSKY: *Variations on a rococo theme, Op. 33.*
(M) *** DG Acc. 2727/3374 107.

Rostropovich's performance of the Schumann concerto is the finest available in stereo and has hitherto only been available coupled to a less recommendable performance of the same composer's *Piano concerto* by Sviatoslav Richter. Here it reappears in a most attractive collection that also includes the somewhat larger-than-life but irresistible Boccherini and Vivaldi concertos and a superb collaboration with Karajan in the works of Dvořák and Tchaikovsky. With excellent sound – on disc and cassette alike – this makes an outstandingly desirable medium-priced anthology. (The cassettes are ingeniously packaged in the normal style of hinged plastic box, but twice as wide as usual across the spine.)

Russian orchestral music

'1812 overture and other Russian pops': (i) Bournemouth SO; (ii) LPO; (iii) RPO; (iv) Philh. O.; (v) Silvestri; (vi) Boult; (vii) Sargent: (i; v) TCHAIKOVSKY: *Overture 1812. Capriccio italien.* (iii; vii) *Marche slave.* (i; v) BORODIN: *In the Steppes of Central Asia.* (ii; vi) RIMSKY-KORSAKOV: *Mlada: Procession of the nobles. Capriccio espagnol.* (i; v) MUSSORGSKY (arr. Rimsky-Korsakov): *Night on the Bare mountain.*

(iv; v) GLINKA: *Overture Russlan and Ludmilla.*
(B) ** EMI *TC2-MOM 107.*

Levels have been successfully manipulated here to avoid coarseness without too much loss of dynamic range, and even at the end of *1812* (with cannon) the sound does not disintegrate as it often does in cassette versions of this piece. Silvestri's performances are good but neither especially individual nor exciting. Sargent's *Marche slave* has a lively impetus, and Boult's versions of the Rimsky-Korsakov *Capriccio* and *Procession* show plenty of character, even if there is some lack of exuberance in the closing pages of the *Capriccio.* The richly resonant recording here is well contained in this transfer, and the only real slip of refinement comes in the final climax of Silvestri's account of Tchaikovsky's *Capriccio italien,* which also has a curiously clumsy quickening of tempo in the coda.

St Louis SO, Slatkin

VAUGHAN WILLIAMS: *Fantasia on a theme of Thomas Tallis.* BARBER: *Adagio for strings.* GRAINGER: *Irish tune from County Derry.* FAURÉ: *Pavane, Op. 50.* SATIE: *Gymnopédies Nos. 1 and 3.*
**(*) Telarc Dig. DG 10059.

This was the digital début of both Vaughan Williams's *Tallis fantasia* and the Barber *Adagio.* Both are given spacious performances and are well structured with strong central climaxes. The recording too is both rich and clear though not finer than the sound given by EMI to Barbirolli in the Vaughan Williams (HMV ASD 521 [Ang. S 36101]) or Argo to Marriner and the ASMF in the Barber (ZRG/*KZRC* 845), both of which carried a rosette in our last edition. The rest of the programme here is

beautifully played, but with Slatkin favouring slow tempi the overall effect is a little lacking in vitality; this applies especially to the *Londonderry air.* The sound, however, cannot be faulted.

Sakonov, Josef (violin)

'*Meditation*' (with L. Festival O.): HUBAY: *Hejre Kati.* GODARD: *Berceuse de Jocelyn.* TCHAIKOVSKY: *Valse sentimentale. None but the Lonely Heart.* STERNHOLD: *Fêtes tzigane.* MASSENET: *Thaïs: Meditation.* HEUBERGER: *Opernball: In chambre séparée.* SARASATE: *Zigeunerweisen.* PONCE: *Estrellita.* KORNGOLD: *Garden scene.* MONTI: *Czardas.*
(M) *** Decca SPA/*KCSP* 571.

This originally had the title *Great violin encores,* more appropriate than *Meditation,* which gives a false picture of the character of this recital. Josef Sakonov is a specialist in Hungarian fireworks and Zigeuner melodies. He plays on one of a pair of Guarnerius violins dating from 1735 (Heifetz has the other) and he certainly produces a sumptuous tone from it, helped by the forward balance of the recording (originally Phase Four). Heuberger's *In chambre séparée* is used to show off the luscious effects possible on the lower strings of this superb instrument, while there are some dazzling fireworks in the bravura items (Sternhold's *Fêtes tzigane* a real highlight). There is taste as well as flamboyance here, and the opening melody and Tchaikovsky's *Valse* are very nicely done. With vivid sound on both disc and tape (the latter benefiting from a degree of top cut), this is most enjoyable.

Schaeftlein, Jürg (oboe, oboe d'amore, cor anglais), VCM, Harnoncourt

BACH: *Oboe d'amore concerto in A, BWV 1055.* HANDEL: *Oboe concerto in G min.* MOZART: *Adagio in C for cor anglais, 2 violins and cello, K.580a.* VIVALDI: *Oboe concerto in A min., RV.500.*
(M) **(*) Tel. AP6/*CR4* 42110.

The main interest of this concert lies in Jürg Schaeftlein's use of baroque instruments, which he plays skilfully, although the Mozart *Adagio* sounds rather clumsy. The music-making does not lack expressive qualities, and the robust, even fruity timbres of the oboe d'amore and cor anglais are fascinating. The recording is rather forwardly balanced but is bright and clear, emphasizing the slightly abrasive quality of the accompanying string group. The cassette matches the disc in every respect.

SNO, Gibson

'Land of the mountain and the flood': MENDELSSOHN: *The Hebrides overture (Fingal's Cave), Op. 26.* BERLIOZ: *Waverley overture, Op. 2.* ARNOLD: *Tam o'Shanter overture.* VERDI: *Macbeth: Ballet music.* MACCUNN: *Overture: Land of the Mountain and the Flood.*
**(*) Chan. Dig. ABRD/*ABTD* 1032.

The MacCunn overture, made popular by a television programme (*Sutherland's Law*), here provides an attractive foil for the Scottish National Orchestra's collection of short pieces inspired by Scotland. These performances are not as refined as the best available versions – significantly, the most dashing performance is of Arnold's difficult and rumbustious overture – but with excellent sound it makes an attractive recital. The cassette transfer is of good quality, but the comparatively unadventurous level brings a less sparkling upper range than the LP.

'Serenade for strings'

Serenades (with (i) Philh. O., Colin Davis; (ii) LSO, Barbirolli; (iii) Northern Sinfonia, Tortelier; (iv) RPO, Sargent; (v) E. Sinfonia, Dilkes; (vi) Bournemouth Sinf., Montgomery; (vii) LPO, Boult): (i) · MOZART: *Serenade No. 13 in G (Eine kleine Nachtmusik), K.525.* (ii) TCHAIKOVSKY: *String serenade, Op. 48: Waltz.* (iii) GRIEG: *Holberg suite, Op. 40. Elegiac melody: Heart's wounds, Op. 34/1.* (iv) DVOŘÁK: *String serenade, Op. 22:* 1st and 2nd movt. (v) WARLOCK: *Capriol suite.* (vi) WIRÉN: *String serenade, Op. 11: March.* (vii) ELGAR: *Introduction and allegro for strings, Op. 47.*
(B) **(*) EMI *TC2-MOM 108.*

This was the finest of EMI's first release of 'Miles of Music' tapes with an attractive programme, good and sometimes distinguished performances and fairly consistent sound quality, full and clear. Tortelier's Grieg and Boult's complete version of Elgar's *Introduction and allegro* are obvious highlights, and this certainly makes an attractive background for a car journey, yet can be sampled at home too.

'Showpieces for orchestra'

(i) LPO, Boult; (ii) RPO; (iii) Sargent; (iv) Colin Davis; (v) CBSO, Frémaux; (vi) Bournemouth SO; (vii) Silvestri; (viii) Berglund: (i) BRAHMS: *Academic Festival overture.* (ii; iii) SMETANA: *Má Vlast: Vltava.* MENDELSSOHN: *The Hebrides overture.* WAGNER: *Die Meistersinger overture.* (ii; iv) ROSSINI: *William Tell overture.* (v) DEBUSSY: *Prélude à l'après-midi d'un faune.* CHABRIER: *España.* BERLIOZ: *Le Carnaval romain overture.* (vi; vii) SAINT-SAËNS: *Danse macabre.* (vi; viii) GRIEG: *Peer Gynt suite No. 1: Morning; In the hall of the Mountain King.* (B) *(*) EMI *TC2-MOM* 109.

These are all acceptable performances, but the recording, though full, is somewhat lacking in sparkle on side one. Side two is brighter, but overall this seems an arbitrary collection that does not add up to a satisfying whole.

Smithers, Don (trumpet)

Trumpet concertos (with Berlin CO, Hauschild): HAYDN: *Concerto in E flat.* HAYDN, Michael: *Concerto in C.* MOLTER: *Concerto in D.* MOZART, Leopold: *Concert in D.*
(M) *** Ph. Fest. 6570/7310 044 [9500 109].

Don Smithers is a splendid player and his vibrant yet polished account of the Haydn *E flat Concerto* is as fine as any available; and the lesser work by Michael Haydn shows his fluency and bravura to equal effect. The other two concertos here are more conventional (the one by Leopold Mozart is recorded more often than it deserves), but they are enjoyable enough when given advocacy of this quality. Good accompaniments and recording, slightly less refined on tape than on disc (though the trumpet remains bright and vivid).

Solum, John (flute)

'A bouquet of romantic flute music' (with Philh. O., Dilkes): POPP: *Scherzo fantastique, Op. 423.* DÖPPLER: *L'Oiseau des bois (idylle), Op. 21.* KUMMER: *Divertissement.* TULOU: *L'Angélus, Op. 46.* SAINT-SAËNS: *Romance, Op. 37.* FURSTENAU: *Rondo brillante, Op. 38.*

**(*) HMV ASD/*TC-ASD* 3744 [Sera. S 60356].

What looks like an adventurous programme turns out to be music that is all very much alike in its undemanding romantic way, and it tends to cloy if taken more than one piece at a time. But John Solum plays it all engagingly, with beautiful tone, impeccable phrasing and an admirable combination of polish and style. He is flatteringly recorded (balanced well forward), and the accompaniments too are highly sympathetic.

'Stamp of greatness'

(i) RPO, Beecham; (ii) Philh. O., Sargent; (iii) L. Sinf., Allegri Qt, Barbirolli; (iv) LSO, Wood: (i) DELIUS: *Sleigh ride. On Hearing the First Cuckoo in Spring.* (ii) VAUGHAN WILLIAMS: *Fantasia on a theme of Thomas Tallis.* (iii) ELGAR: *Introduction and allegro for strings.* (iv) WOOD: *Fantasia on British sea songs.*
(M) *** HMV STAMP 1.

Prompted by the issue of commemorative stamps celebrating four great conductors, EMI compiled this anthology of delightful performances. The Henry Wood – recorded in the days of 78 – is obviously the least compelling, but it is good to have Beecham in a relative rarity of Delius as well as the *First Cuckoo*, while Barbirolli's is a classic version of Elgar's *Introduction and allegro*. Very attractive at medium price.

Stern, Isaac (violin)

'Sixtieth aniversary celebration' (with Perlman, Zukerman, NYPO, Mehta): BACH: *Double violin concerto in D min., BWV 1043.* MOZART: *Sinfonia concertante in E flat, K.364.* VIVALDI: *Triple violin concerto in F, RV.551.*

919

**(*) CBS Dig. 37244/*41-36692* [Col. IM 36692/*MT 37244*].

At a time when the pursuit of authenticity has accustomed us to pinched sound in Bach and Vivaldi it is good to have such rich performances as these, recorded live at Stern's sixtieth-birthday concert in the autumn of 1980. Stern nobly cedes first place to Perlman in the Bach *Double concerto*, and in the Vivaldi he plays third violin, though there he has the bonus of playing the melody in the lovely slow movement. With Zukerman on the viola this account of the *Sinfonia concertante* is strikingly more alive than the studio recording made ten years earlier by the same artists, heartfelt and beautifully sprung. The recording is a little thin, but digitally clear. Mehta and the New York orchestra are not ideal in this music, but the flavour of the live occasion is most compelling. The chrome cassette is extremely lively, matching the disc with its close balance and larger-than-life solo images, although it does not lack fullness.

Thompson, Robert (bassoon)

'The twentieth-century bassoon' (with ECO, Simon): DOWNEY: *The Edge of Space* (fantasy). JACOB: *Bassoon concerto*. ANDRIESSEN: *Concertino for bassoon and wind*.
*** Chan. Dig. ABRD/*ABTD* 1033.

Although these are all modern works the idiom is not in the least intimidating. John Downey's fantasy *The Edge of Space* intends to suggest 'remote distance and other-worldliness', but although there are certainly some unusual sounds here, there is nothing especially avant-garde. Indeed, with its episodic nature it sounds rather like a film score without a film. It has imaginative moments and the invention is quite attractive. Gordon Jacob's neoclassical *Concerto* dates from

1947 and is pleasant enough; the Andriessen *Concertino* is a little more adventurous. Excellent performances and a bold, forwardly balanced digital recording, with a vivid cassette to match.

'Trumpet voluntary'

(i) Philip Jones Brass Ens.; (ii) ASMF, Marriner, etc.: (i) CLARKE: *Trumpet voluntary*. (ii) BOYCE: *Symphony No. 5 in D*. (i; ii) GABRIELI, G.: *Canzon primi toni No. 1*. (ii) HANDEL: *Water music: Prelude; Hornpipe*. (i) SCHEIDT: *Battle suite Galliard battaglia*. PURCELL: *Trumpet tune and air*. (ii) *Trumpet concerto in E flat* (with Stringer). STANLEY: *Trumpet tune in D* (with Wilbraham; Pearson, organ). (i) BACH, C. P. E.: *March*.
(M) *** Decca SPA/*KCSP* 556.

A really outstanding collection for those who enjoy occasional pieces on the trumpet. Almost every item is a winner, and Alan Stringer's complete version of the Haydn *Trumpet concerto* is excellent. The florid playing by members of the Philip Jones Brass Ensemble in the pieces by Giovanni Gabrieli and Samuel Scheidt is superb, and there is a contrasting elegance in Purcell's *Trumpet tune and air*. Excellent recording throughout and vivid cassette to match the disc closely.

VCM, Harnoncourt

'Music at the court of Mannheim': BACH, J. C.: *Quintet in D, Op. 11/6* (for flute, oboe and strings). HOLZBAUER: *Quintetto for harpsichord, flute and strings*. STAMITZ: *Trio sonata in A, Op. 1/2*. RICHTER: *String quartet in B flat, Op. 5/2*.
(M) *(*) Tel. AQ6/*CQ4* 41062.

The *Quintet* by J. C. Bach is undoubtedly engaging, but the rest of this programme is of lesser interest. The performers seem rather intimidated here by the demands of authenticity: the use of period instruments brings astringent textures and minimizes the music's sunny qualities. The playing too is rather literal; charm is not its strong point. The cassette is clear but sounds rather edgy on top.

'Music in the Vienna of Maria Theresa': HAYDN: *Divertimento for 8 instruments in A.* MONN: *String quartet No. 1 in B flat.* WAGENSEIL: *Trombone concerto in E flat.* GASSMANN: *String quartet No. 3 in E min.*
(M) *(*) Tel. AQ6/CQ4 41199.

This is another collection that seems solely directed at the authentic lobby. Apart from the stimulating bravura of Wagenseil's *Trombone concerto* (Hans Pottler the accomplished soloist), this is an uninspiring concert. The playing, using baroque instruments, seems consciously to avoid expressive gestures, even in the lightweight Haydn *Divertimento.* The sound is clean, with the cassette slightly more astringent than the disc.

'Baroque concertos': HANDEL: *Organ concerto No. 7 in F* (*The Cuckoo and the Nightingale*). VIVALDI: *Flute concerto in G min.* (*La Notte*), *Op. 10/2.* TELEMANN: *Concerto in B flat for 3 oboes and 3 violins.* BIBER: *Battalia in D.* BACH: *Violin concerto No. 2 in E, BWV 1052.*
(M) *** Tel. AQ6/CQ4 42166.

An exceptionally attractive collection, making an altogether convincing case for authentic textures. All the performances here are full of life and expertly played. There are some fascinating instrumental effects in Biber's *Battle music*, and the robust combination of wind and strings in the vigorous and inventive Telemann

Concerto is an aural delight. The Handel *Organ concerto* (with Herbert Tachezi) is admirably spirited, and the Bach *E major Violin concerto* (played by Alice Harnoncourt), if not one of the most expressive recordings available, is similarly buoyant in the outer movements. The recording is first-class on disc and cassette alike.

VPO, Maazel

'New Year's concert' (1980): STRAUSS, Johann, Jnr: *Die Fledermaus: overture; Czárdás. Neue Pizzicato polka. Perpetuum mobile. Wiener Blut. Banditen Galop. Rettungs-Jubel march. Fata Morgana polka. An der schönen blauen Donau.* STRAUSS, Josef: *Eingesendet polka.* OFFENBACH: *Orpheus in the Underworld: overture.* ZIEHRER: *Loslassen.* STRAUSS, Johann, Snr: *Radetzky march.*
** DG Dig. 2532/3302 002 [id.].

This record of the 1980 Viennese New Year Concert is generously full, with applause faded quickly between items. The famous *Radetzky march* sets the pattern for the concert: the performance is crisply brilliant, with well-disciplined hand-claps from the audience. Maazel is at his best in the *Rettungs-Jubel march*, written for the Kaiser, which is infectiously volatile. The performance of *The Blue Danube* departs from the sharply rhythmic manner and is unashamedly indulgent. But charm is not a strong point here, and the brightly lit recording underlines the vigour of the playing. The sound has striking presence and detail, both on disc and the equivalent chrome tape.

'Violin favourites'

(i) Hoelscher, Mun. RO, Wallberg; (ii) Menuhin, Philh. O.; (iii) Prit-

chard; (iv) Goossens; (v) Haendel, Parsons; (vi) Ferras, Barbizet: (i) SARASATE: *Carmen fantasy. Zigeunerweisen.* (ii; iii) BEETHOVEN: *Romances Nos. 1 and 2.* (ii; iv) SAINT-SAËNS: *Introduction and rondo capriccioso. Havanaise.* (v) MENDELSSOHN: *On Wings of Song.* SARASATE: *Habañera.* SCHUBERT: *Ave Maria.* (vi) RAVEL: *Tzigane.*
(B) **(*) EMI *TC2-MOM 118.*

A reasonably attractive collection, not as enticing as some in this 'Miles of Music' series, but well recorded throughout. The highlights are Menuhin's superb Saint-Saëns performances (described in the composer index above) and the more lushly recorded Sarasate, played with panache by Ulf Hoelscher. Ida Haendel is in excellent form in her transcriptions, and Ferras gives an impressive account of Ravel's *Tzigane* (in the version for violin and piano).

Wickens, Derek (oboe)

'*The classical oboe*' (with RPO, Howarth): VIVALDI: *Oboe concerto in A min., RV.461.* MARCELLO, A.: *Oboe concerto in D min.* HAYDN: *Oboe concerto in C.*
*** ASV ACA/ZCACA 1003.

The Haydn concerto may be spurious, but it makes an attractive item in this collection, and the Vivaldi, a lively, compact piece, and the Marcello (by Alessandro, not his more famous brother Benedetto) with its lovely slow movement make a good mixture. During his years with the RPO, Wickens repeatedly demonstrated in yearningly beautiful solos

that he was one of the most characterful of London's orchestral players. Though at times he seems to be yearning for his back desk rather than his solo spot, his artistry comes out vividly on this well-recorded disc. The tape is outstandingly vivid to match the disc.

Wilbraham, John (trumpet)

Trumpet concertos (with ASMF, Marriner): TELEMANN: *Concerto in D.* ALBINONI: *Concerto in C.* HERTEL: *Concerto a cinque in D.* FASCH: *Concerto in D.* HUMMEL: *Concerto in E flat.* ALBRECHTSBERGER: *Concerto a cinque in E flat.* MOZART, Leopold: *Concerto in D.*
(M) *** Argo ZK 72/3.

Although it does not include the Haydn, this is an impressive anthology of trumpet concertos, notable not only for the outstandingly stylish and polished playing of the soloist, but also for the imaginative accompaniments from the St Martin's Academy under Marriner. The fine Telemann work and the engaging Hummel are the obvious favourites here, but there are some textural delights elsewhere: Albinoni's concerto shares the limelight between trumpet and three supporting oboes; the Hertel work, in the nature of a sinfonia concertante, is scored for trumpet, two oboes and two bassoons; and in the Fasch Wilbraham is again joined by a pair of oboes. Albrechtsberger taught Beethoven his counterpoint, and his *Concerto a cinque* features a harpsichord. As might be expected, all the solo contributions are expert, and with excellent sound this is a rewarding set, if not taken all at once.

Instrumental Recitals

(i) **Adni, Daniel;** (ii) **John Ogdon** (piano)

'Piano favourites': (i) CHOPIN: Revolutionary study in C min. Fantaisie-Impromptu. (ii) Waltz No. 6 in D flat (Minute). Polonaises Nos. 3 (Military); 6 (Heroic). RACHMANINOV: Prelude in C sharp min. (i) GRAINGER: Country Gardens; Handel in the Strand. DEBUSSY: Clair de lune. BRAHMS: Rhapsody in G min. (ii) SINDING: Rustle of Spring. LISZT: Liebestraum No. 3. La Campanella. BEETHOVEN: Für Elise. CHAMINADE: Autumn. (i) MENDELSSOHN: The Bees' Wedding. SCHUBERT: Impromptu in A flat. Moment musical in F min. GRIEG: To the Spring. Wedding Day at Troldhaugen.
(B) *(**) EMI TC2-MOM 101.

In transferring this collection to tape the EMI engineers have made electronic adjustments to produce a high level, and the sound is dry and lacking warmth. The performances are often distinguished; Daniel Adni is heard at his best in the music of Grainger, Schubert and Grieg, and Ogdon is impressive in Liszt. In the car the sound projects clearly.

'More piano favourites': (ii) BACH: Well-tempered Clavier: Prelude No. 5. Jesu, joy of man's desiring. MOZART: Fantasia in D min., K.397. BEETHOVEN: Andante favori. CHOPIN: Mazurka No. 17 in B flat min. (i) Scherzo No. 3 in C sharp min., Op. 39. Waltz No. 1 in E flat, Op. 18. Ballade No. 3 in A flat, Op. 47. (ii) SCHUMANN: Nachtstück in F, Op. 23/4. (i) DEBUSSY: L'Isle joyeuse. Reflets dans l'eau. (ii) SCOTT: Lotus Land. LISZT: Hungarian rhapsody No. 15. GRANADOS: Goyescus: The Maiden and the nightingale. ALBÉNIZ: Tango. (i) GRIEG: Lyric pieces: Album leaf; Butterfly; Shepherd's boy.
(B) *** EMI TC2-MOM 113.

With first-class sound this is an outstanding recital, easily the finest collection from these two artists in this format, with recordings taken from the beginnings of their respective careers. Both Adni and Ogdon are heard at their best, the latter especially in the music of Chopin and Debussy, the former communicating strongly in Bach and Mozart and playing Liszt with great flair.

'Piano moods': (i) CHOPIN: Scherzo No. 2, Op. 32. Waltzes in A flat and A min., Op. 34/1 and 2. Études: in A flat and G flat, Op. 25/1 and 9; in G flat, Op. 10/5. (ii) Mazurkas Nos. 5 in B flat, Op. 7/1; 23 in D, Op. 33/2. LISZT: Paganini study No. 2. Étude de concert No. 3. Valse oubliée No. 1. Mephisto waltz No. 1. (i) GRIEG: March of the Dwarfs. SCHUMANN: Arabesque, Op. 18. DEBUSSY: Poissons d'or. Arabesque No. 1. MENDELSSOHN: Songs without Words: Venetian gondola song, Op. 62/5; Spring song. RAVEL: Alborada del gracioso.
(B) ** EMI TC2-MOM 122.

There is some impressive playing again here, John Ogdon on top form in Liszt, and Daniel Adni poetic and commanding in Chopin and Debussy. But the high-level recording is dry and some of the bloom of the originals is lost.

Bate, Jennifer (Royal Albert Hall organ)

'Showpieces for organ': BACH: *Toccata and fugue in D min., BWV 565.* THALBEN-BALL: *Variations on a theme of Paganini.* MELVILLE SMITH: *Scherzo.* BATE: *Toccata on a theme of Martin Shaw.* WIDOR: *Symphony No. 5 in F: Toccata.* VIERNE: *Naïades.* DUCASSE: *Pastorale.* LANGLAIS: *Fête.*
*** Uni. Kanchana Dig. DKP 9007.

Splendid digital sound, clear and spacious and with striking depth. If anything Jennifer Bate overdoes the contrasts of volume and perspective possible with the recessional effect of this instrument. The programme, although it includes several warhorses, is imaginative, and the French repertoire (the Widor *Toccata* sounding lighter than usual but no less telling) is surprisingly well suited to this essentially Victorian instrument. The Thalben-Ball *Paganini variations* (apart from the finale) are for pedals only, and a *tour de force* in Miss Bate's impressive account.

Bonell, Carlos (guitar)

'Guitar showpieces': CHAPI: *Serenata Morisca.* ALBÉNIZ: *Asturias (Leyenda).* PAGANINI: *Grand sonata: Romance and variations.* VILLA-LOBOS: *Study No. 11; Preludes Nos. 1 and 2.* VALVERDE: *Clavelitos.* LLOBET: *Scherzo valse.* TARREGA: *Variations and fantasia on themes*

from 'La Traviata'. CHOPIN: *Prelude, Op. 28/7.* WEISS: *Ciacona in A.*
**(*) Decca SXL/KSXC 6950.

Carlos Bonell has made an outstanding digital recording of Rodrigo's *Concierto de Aranjuez* for Decca. Previously he did two solo recitals for Enigma, one of which is now available on ASV (ACM/ZCACM 2003: *Guitar music of Spain).* But his firm articulation and very positive style registers in this Decca recital with more spontaneity and atmosphere than the earlier solo records. He is especially good in the Tarrega *Variations,* and he plays the Chopin *'Les Sylphides' Prelude* very evocatively. At times his rhythms seem too precise, but his personality is strongly projected here and his expertise is in no doubt. The recording is equally impressive on disc and tape.

Brain, Dennis (horn)

'His last broadcasts' (introduced by Wilfred Parry, with Roy Plomley, Norman Del Mar, Gareth Morris, Felix Aprahamian) including: MARAIS: *La Basque.* MALIPIERO: *Dialogue No. 4.* BEETHOVEN: *Piano and wind quintet in E flat, Op. 16* (with D. Brain Wind Ens.). DUKAS: *Villanelle* (with Parry, piano).
(***) BBC mono REGL/ZCF 352.

Opening with a winning account of Marais's *La Basque* (a piece James Galway has since taken over), this is an engaging portrait of Dennis Brain the man (his gentle, slightly ingenuous charm coming over splendidly) as well as the musician: Boyd Neel was said to have described him as the finest Mozartian of his generation on *any* instrument. There is no Mozart here, but his famous set of the *Horn concertos* is still available (HMV ASD/TC-ASD 1140) and his Richard Strauss coupling is reviewed above. The musical items here offer quite good mono sound, though the Beethoven *Piano and wind quintet* lacks something in range and detail. The playing is superb and the background narrative well put together, including the priceless anecdote of Karajan rehearsing Mozart and finding only a motoring magazine on Dennis's music-stand.

Bream, Julian (lute)

'Lute music from the royal courts of Europe': LANDGRAVE OF HESSE: *Pavane.* MOLINARO: *Saltarello. Ballo detto 'Il Conte Orlando'. Saltarello. Fantasie.* PHILIPS: *Chromatic pavan and galliard.* DOWLAND: *Fantasia* (*Fancye*)*. Queen Elizabeth's galliard.* HOWETT: *Fantasia.* MUDARRA: *Fantasia.* DLUGORAJ: *Fantasia. Villanellas 1 and 2. Finales 1 and 2.* FERRABOSCO: *Pavan.* NEUSIDLER: *Mein Herz hat sich mit Lieb' verpflicht. Hie' folget ein welscher Tanz. Ich klag' den Tag. Der Juden Tanz.* BAKFARK: *Fantasia.* BESARD: *Air de Cour. Branle. Guillemette. Volte.*
(M) **(*) RCA Gold GL/*GK* 42952.

The lute has much in common with the guitar, but its slightly nasal tang gives its music-making a special colour. Julian Bream achieves miracles here in creating diversity of timbre and dynamic, to say nothing of rhythmic impulse. The quality of the music he plays for us is generally high, and his projection of musical personality strong. Having said this, one must again add that a whole LP of lute music has its limitations: a few songs would greatly enhance a concert of this kind. The recording is impeccable; the cassette transfer, made at a high level, has plenty of presence and realism, but may benefit from a slight treble reduction.

'Golden age of English lute music': JOHNSON, R.: *Two almaines. Car-*

man's whistle. JOHNSON, J.: *Fantasia.* CUTTING: *Walsingham. Almaine. Greensleeves.* DOWLAND: *Mignarda. Galliard. Batell galliard.* ROSSETER: *Galliard.* MORLEY: *Pavan.* BULMAN: *Pavan.* BATCHELOR: *Mounsiers Almaine.* HOLBORNE: *Pavan. Galliard.*
(M) **(*) RCA RL/*RK* 43514 [LSC 3196].

Bream is a marvellously sensitive artist and he conjures here a wide range of colour, matched by expressive feeling. He is naturally recorded (the excellent cassette matches the disc closely), and if this selection has slightly less electricity than its outstanding companion, *The woods so wild* (see below), its relaxed manner is still persuasive.

'The woods so wild': BYRD: *The woods so wild.* MILANO: *Fantasias Nos. 1–8.* CUTTING: *Packington's round.* DOWLAND: *Walsingham. Go from my window. Bonnie sweet Robin. Loth to depart.* HOLBORNE: *Fairy round. Heigh ho holiday. Heart's ease.* ANON.: *Greensleeves.*
(M) *** RCA RL/*RK* 43519 [LSC 3331/*RK 1309*].

This is an exceptionally vivid recital of lute music. The title piece, in Byrd's setting with variations, is immediately striking, and all the items have strong individuality; the Milano *Fantasias* are particularly distinctive, both in quality of invention and in the opportunity they afford for bravura. Try *La Compagna* (No. 4), which ends side one – most fetching and exciting. The mood of gentle melancholy which is a special feature of Elizabethan music makes effective contrasts to the virtuosity, and nowhere more touchingly than in the delightful closing piece, *Loth to depart,* appropriate for such a memorable concert. The recording projects the instrument with fine realism, and the sound on tape is of demonstration quality in this latest transfer.

Bream, Julian (guitar)

'*Classic guitar*': GIULIANI: *Grand overture, Op. 61. Guitar sonata in C, Op. 15; Allegro.* SOR: *Introduction and Allegro, Op. 14.* DIABELLI: *Guitar sonata in A.* MOZART: *Divertimento, K. Anh.229: Larghetto and Allegro.*

(M) *** RCA RL/*RK* 42761.

Extremely vivid performances, Bream's personality coming over strongly. He brings the strongest possible advocacy to these comparatively slight but inventive works, and confirms Giuliani as a composer of some substance and individuality in a repertoire over-supplied with insubstantial trifles. The RCA recording is first-rate in every way.

'*Romantic guitar*': PAGANINI: *Grand sonata in A.* MENDELSSOHN: *Song without Words, Op. 19/6: Venetian boating song. String quartet, Op. 12: Canzonetta.* SCHUBERT: *Piano sonata No. 18 in G, D.894: Menuetto.* TARREGA: *Prelude (Lágrima). 3 Mazurkas.*

(M) **(*) RCA RL/*RK* 43517 [LSC 3156].

The Paganini *Grand sonata* lasts for just over twenty minutes and is given a side to itself, which is rather short measure; but Bream's performance is highly engaging, and the other pieces are attractive too when played like this. The 'romantic' atmosphere is sustained by the intimate balance of the recording, which sounds equally well on disc or tape.

'*Baroque guitar*': SANZ: *Pavanas. Canarios.* BACH: *Prelude in D min. Fugue in A min.* SOR: *Fantasy and Minuet.* WEISS: *Passacaille. Fantasie. Tombeau sur la mort de M. Comte De Logy.* VISÉE: *Suite in D min.*

(M) *** RCA RL/*RK* 43520 [LSC 2878].

Bream is on his finest form here. He makes a very clear distinction between the world of Bach (well detailed and slightly sober) and the other music, which depends more on colour to make its effect. The pieces by Sanz are strong in personality, and the *Suite* by Robert de Visée, a French court lutenist who lived from about 1650 until 1725, has the most attractive invention. Sylvius Weiss, who played for the Dresden court in the mid-eighteenth century, also emerges with an individual voice, and his eloquent *Tombeau*, which ends the recital, inspires playing of elegiac nobility. The sound is excellent; disc and tape are equally impressive.

'*Popular classics for the Spanish guitar*': VILLA-LOBOS: *Chôros No. 1. Étude in E flat. Prelude in E min.* TÓRROBA: *Madronos.* TURINA: *Homage a Tarrega: Garrotin. Soleares. Fandanguillo.* TRAD. (arr. Llobet): *El testament d'Amelia.* ALBÉNIZ: *Suite española: Granada. Leyenda.* FALLA: *Homenaje pour le tombeau de Claude Debussy.*

(M) *** RCA RL/*RK* 43521 [LSC 2606].

This outstanding early recital, dating from 1961, places the guitar slightly back within a fairly resonant acoustic, and the effect is very like listening to a live recital in a small hall. The electricity of the music-making is consistently communicated, and all Bream's resources of colour and technical bravura are brought into play. The Villa-Lobos pieces are particularly fine, as is the Turina *Fandanguillo* (which comes at the end), and the Albéniz *Leyenda* is a *tour de force*;

here the reverberation clouds the detail a little but makes an excitingly orchestral effect. The cassette and disc are closely matched, although the focus is fractionally sharper on LP.

'Sonatas': FRESCOBALDI: *Aria detta La Frescobalda with variations.* ALBÉNIZ: *Sonata.* SCARLATTI, D.: (Keyboard) *Sonatas, Kk. 11 and Kk. 87.* CIMAROSA: *Sonatas in C sharp min. and A.* BERKELEY: *Sonatina, Op. 51.* RODRIGO: *En los trigales.* RAVEL: *Pavane pour une infante défunte.* ROUSSEL: *Segovia, Op. 29.*
(M) ** RCA RL/*RK* 43522.

An impressively wide-ranging programme. The opening *Aria* of Frescobaldi, sombre in mood and colour, is played with characteristic eloquence; but Bream is very relaxed in the classical sonatas, and there is less magnetism and sparkle here. Ravel's *Pavane*, played very slowly, is not as effective at this tempo (the guitar being a non-sustaining instrument) as it would be in an orchestral version. The recording is good in both disc and tape formats.

Bream, Julian, and John Williams (guitars)

'Together': LAWES: *Suite for 2 guitars.* CARULLI: *Duo in G, Op. 34.* SOR: *L'Encouragement, Op. 34.* ALBÉNIZ: *Cordoba.* GRANADOS: *Goyescas: Intermezzo.* FALLA: *La vida breve: Spanish dance No. 1.* RAVEL: *Pavane pour une infante défunte.*
*** RCA RCALP/*RCAK* 3003 [LSC 3257/*RK 1230*].

'Together again': CARULLI: *Serenade, Op. 96.* GRANADOS: *Danzas españolas Nos. 6 and 11.* ALBÉNIZ: *Bajo la Palmera, Op. 232. Iberia: Evocación.* GIULIANI: *Variazioni concertanti, Op. 130.*

*** RCA RCALP/*RCAK* 3006 [ARL 1/*ARK 1* 0456].

In this case two guitars are better than one; these two fine artists clearly strike sparks off each other. In the first recital Albéniz's *Cordoba* is hauntingly memorable and the concert closes with a slow, stately version of Ravel's *Pavane* which is unforgettable. Here Bream justifies a tempo which he did not bring off so effectively in his solo version (see above). On the second disc it is again music of Albéniz that one remembers for the haunting atmosphere the two artists create together. The sound of these reissues (offered at slightly less than premium price) is excellent, and the tapes have good clarity and presence.

Brüggen, Frans (recorder)

Recital on original instruments (with Bylsma, cello; Leonhardt, harpsichord): VAN EYCK: *Pavane Lachrimae figurations. Engels Nachtegaeltje. Variations on 'Doen Daphne'.* PARCHAM: *Suite in G* (with N. Harnoncourt, gamba). CARR: *Divisions upon an Italian ground.* PEPUSCH: *Sonata No. 4 in F.*
(M) **(*) Tel. AP6/*CR4* 42050.

Frans Brüggen demonstrates various period instruments here, but three of the works are unaccompanied, which perhaps restricts the interest of this recital to recorder enthusiasts, as the appeal of the music itself is relatively limited. The *Suite* by Andrew Parcham, the *Divisions* of Robert Carr and Pepusch's *Sonata* are all engaging and are played with characteristic skill and musicianship, so that only occasionally does the ear detect the limitations of the early instruments. The recording is first-class on disc, but on cassette the unaccompanied works are slightly too highly modulated, and the focus is not quite clean; otherwise the chrome tape matches the disc closely.

Bylsma, Anner (baroque cello)

BOCCHERINI: *Cello concerto in G* (with Concerto Amsterdam, Schröder). *Cello sonata No. 7 in B flat* (with Leonhardt, harpsichord; Woodrow, bass). SAMMARTINI: *Sonata No. 3 in A min. for 2 cellos.* GABRIELI, Domenico: *Canon for 2 celli* (both with Koster, cello). ANTONI: *Ricercata VIII for solo cello.*

(M) ** Tel. AP6/CR4 42653.

The main purpose of this collection is to demonstrate the sound of Anner Bylsma's baroque cello, which it does admirably, for the recording is very clear and the chrome cassette is of matching demonstration quality. The timbre is in fact rather dry and is rather more suited to the earlier music than to Boccherini's rococo elegance, where the soloist hardly seeks to charm the ear. However, the playing does not lack either musicianship or vitality, and the rest of the programme is undoubtedly stylish, if not endearing.

Byzantine, Julian (guitar)

'*Masterpieces for classical guitar*': ALBÉNIZ: *Torre bermeja. Rumores de la Caleta. Asturias* (*Leyenda*). TÓRROBA: *Madronos.* TARREGA: *Capricho arabe. La Alborada.* LAURO: *Vals venezolano No. 3.* VILLA-LOBOS: *Chôro 1. Prelude 2. Étude 1.* RODRIGO: *En los trigales.* BORGES: *Vals venezolano.* GRANADOS: *Spanish dance No. 5.* MALATS: *Serenata española.* FALLA: *The Three-cornered Hat: Miller's dance; Corregidor's dance.*

(B) **(*) CfP CFP/TC-CFP 40362.

Julian Byzantine is a thoroughly musical player; his rubato and control of light and shade are convincing. The playing

may lack the last degree of individuality and electricity, and sometimes the listener may feel that the flow is too controlled, not absolutely spontaneous, but this remains an impressive recital, generous and varied in content and very well recorded. There is no appreciable difference between tape and disc.

Clarino Cons.

'*The trumpet shall sound*': ANON.: *Hejnal Krakowski.* PURCELL: *Trumpet tune, ayre and cibell.* BLOW: *Vers. Fugue in F.* MORLEY: *La caccia. La sampogna.* HANDEL: *Concerto in B flat.* STANLEY: *Trumpet voluntary in D.* FANTINI: *Sonata a due trombe detta la guicciardini.* CAMPION: *Never weatherbeaten sail.* BULL: *Variations on the Dutch chorale 'Laet ons met herten reijne'.* BIBER: *Suite for 2 clarino trumpets.* DOWLAND: *Flow my tears.* FRESCOBALDI: *Capriccio sopra un soggetto.*

(B) ** Con. CC/CCT 7554.

The Clarino Consort consists of Don Smithers and Michael Laird (trumpets), Janet Smithers (baroque violin) and William Neil (organ). There is fine playing here, but the programme includes a fair amount of music for trumpet and organ. The most striking works are the Fantini *Sonata for two trumpets*, with its echoing fanfares, and the Biber *Suite* for a pair of (high) clarinos. Not all the other transcriptions are wholly convincing, but there is no lack of melody. The sound is good, and tape and disc are fairly closely matched, although once or twice the refinement of the upper range slips on the cassette, more noticeably on side two.

Cleobury, Stephen (organ of Westminster Abbey)

'*Wedding favourites*': MENDELS-

SOHN: *A Midsummer Night's Dream: Wedding march.* BACH: *Chorale prelude. In Dir ist Freude. Suite No. 3 in D, BWV 1068: Air. Jesu, joy of man's desiring.* WAGNER: *Lohengrin: Bridal chorus.* HANDEL: *Xerxes: Largo. Water music: Hornpipe.* CLARKE: *Trumpet voluntary.* GUILMANT: *Grand chœur in D.* WESLEY, S.: *Air and Gavotte.* BRAHMS: *Chorale prelude: Es ist ein' Ros' entsprungen, Op. 122/8.* WIDOR: *Organ Symphony No. 5 in F min., Op. 42/1: Toccata.*
(M) **(*) Decca SPA/KCSP 554.

A well-played and very well-recorded collection. In the quieter, more reflective music Stephen Cleobury's style is rather introvert, and the effect is to provide a pleasant background tapestry rather than project the music strongly. Nevertheless the playing is very musical, and in the *Grand chœur* of Guilmant and, especially, the famous Widor *Toccata* the playing springs vividly to life, using a wide dynamic range very effectively. The cassette and disc are closely matched, and although the tape has been transferred at only a modest level the spectacle of the climaxes comes over without a tremor of congestion.

Cochereau, Pierre (organ of Notre Dame, Paris)

'Organ toccatas': BACH: *Toccata and fugue in D min., BWV 565.* FRESCOBALDI: *Toccata XII.* FROBERGER: *Toccata XIX.* PACHELBEL: *Toccata.* MUFFAT: *Toccata XI.* WIDOR: *Symphony No. 5 in F min., Op. 42/1: Toccata.* GIROUD: *Toccata pour l'Élévation.* VIERNE: *Symphony No. 4, Op. 32: Toccata.* GIGOUT: *Toccata in B min.*
(M) ** Ph. Seq. 6570/7311 113.

The recording here, which dates from 1973, is spectacular but has moments of slight harshness. These are powerfully romantic performances, using a wide range of dynamic and perspective in depth to increase the feeling of contrast. The Widor is very exciting, but in the baroque music the swimmy acoustic takes much of the edge off the articulation. In spite of the title, not all this music is fast; there are lyrical interludes to balance the programme. The cassette needs reproducing at a high level; it is free from congestion but not very sharply focused.

Cole, Maggie (harpsichord)

'Seventeenth- and eighteenth-century keyboard music': ARNE: *Sonata No. 1 in F.* BACH: *Suite in B min., BWV 814.* RAMEAU: *L'entretien des muses. Le jardon. La triomphante.* SCARLATTI, D.: *Sonatas: in G, Kk.144; in A, Kk.212.* FROBERGER: *Suite in G min.* (Adler IX).
*** Hyp. A 66020.

Maggie Cole uses five different harpsichords, each matched in character and period to the repertoire. The result is unfailingly illuminating, and few recitals using original instruments are so patently self-justifying, particularly as the recording is admirably truthful and well-balanced. The music itself is all attractive, and played with such expert stylishness and communicative musicianship, it makes a most entertaining programme.

Cologne Mus. Ant.

'German chamber music before Bach': REINCKEN: *Trio sonatas: in A min.; E min.* BACH: *Sonata in A min., BWV 965.* BUXTEHUDE: *Sonatas: in G; in B flat; in C.* PACHELBEL: *Suites: in G; in E min. Aria and variations in A.*

Canon and gigue in D. ROSEN-MÜLLER: *Sonatas: in C; in E min.; in B flat.* SCHENCK: *Suite in D.* WESTOFF: *Sonata in A* (*La Guerra*).
*** DG Arc. 2723 078 (3) [id.].

This much praised collection deservedly won the *Gramophone* 1981 Award in the early music category. Here is a case where an enterprising programme of music, a good deal of it by little-known composers, is brought fully to life by expert playing – authentically stylish and accurate but never pedantic – and first-class sound, lively and very well balanced. The juxtaposition of the Reincken *Trio sonata* and Bach's keyboard transcription is characteristic of the admirable planning of the programme, which offers much to attract the ordinary music-lover as well as its specialist appeal.

Curley, Carlo (organ)

'Virtuoso French organ music' (Royal Albert Hall organ): GIGOUT: *Grand chœur dialogue.* GUILMANT: *March on a theme by Handel, Op. 15.* SAINT-SAËNS: *Fantaisie in E flat.* VIERNE: *Pièces de fantaisie: Clair de lune; Carillon de Westminster.* BOËLLMANN: *Suite gothique, Op. 25.* BONNET: *Elves.*
*** RCA RL/*RK* 25247 [ARL 1/*ARK 1* 3556].

This French repertoire is given attractively flamboyant treatment by Carlo Curley, who makes the most of the dynamic contrasts and spectacular recessional and swell effects of the Royal Albert Hall organ. The playing itself is always spirited, although at times the organ's timbre is a little bland for the music. But this is an impressive collection, and it is splendidly recorded, although on tape there is some compression; even so a

fairly wide range of dynamic remains, and there is no congestion.

'Concert curios': JOPLIN: *The Entertainer.* BACH: *Schübler chorale: Wachet auf, BWV 545.* DETHIER: *Christmas.* SCHUMANN: *Sketch in F min.* HANDEL: *Messiah: Hallelujah chorus.* SOUSA: *Washington Post.* DAWES: *Melody in A.* BEETHOVEN: *The Ruins of Athens: Turkish march.* WALFORD DAVIES: *Solemn melody.* GOTTSCHALK: *The Banjo.* ELGAR: *Pomp and Circumstance march No. 1.*
*** RCA RL/*RK* 25314.

Carlo Curley's unnamed organ has the widest range of effects, from banjo imitations to a wide panoply of fortissimo sound. The Joplin and Gottschalk pieces sound delightfully witty, and Gaston Dethier's *Christmas* (freely edited) is given the full bravura treatment. The other lighter pieces all show Mr Curley's very real charisma. Sousa's *Washington Post* has a splendid lilt, while Schumann's *Sketch*, originally written for pedal piano, sounds agreeably off-beat as presented here. The disc makes a huge impact, and the cassette is almost equally impressive.

Danby, Nicholas (organ)

St Andrew's University organ: BÖHM: *Prelude in D min.* PACHELBEL: *Ciacona in F min.* WALTHER: *Concerto of Torelli, arr. for organ.* MENDELSSOHN: *Organ sonata No. 2 in C.* HINDEMITH: *Sonata No. 1.* WEHRLE: *Fanal.*
*** Abbey LPB 806.

A well-planned and splendidly recorded recital spanning nearly three centuries of (mostly) German organ music. The fine St Andrews University instrument is admirably suited to this repertoire; its timbres are full-bodied yet clearly detailed within a perfect acoustic. Nicolas Danby invests all his programme with vitality. He is especially good in the Mendelssohn *Sonata*, and presents the baroque pieces simply and eloquently. The first of Hindemith's three sonatas also sounds highly effective in his hands, while the brilliant *Fanal* by the Swiss composer Heinz Wehrle (born in 1921) makes a colourful end-piece.

Eastman Wind Ens., Fennell

Twentieth-century wind music: GRAINGER: *Lincolnshire Posy*. ROGERS: 3 Japanese dances. MILHAUD: *Suite française*. STRAUSS, R.: *Serenade in E flat, Op. 7.*
(*) Mercury SRI 75093 [id.].

This splendidly recorded Mercury reissue from the beginning of the sixties disappoints only in the early Richard Strauss *Serenade*, where the wind instruments fail to blend homogeneously and the players seem not quite at ease. The Grainger and Milhaud works are vividly characterized, and the *Three Japanese dances* of Bernard Rogers (1893–1968) create some agreeable sounds, even if the music itself is pentatonic kitsch. An entertaining concert.

Fowke, Philip (piano)

'Virtuoso transcriptions': BACH/RACHMANINOV: *Suite from the Solo violin Partita in E min., BWV 1006*. SCHUBERT/RACHMANINOV: *Wohin.* KREISLER/RACHMANINOV: *Liebeslied; Liebesfreud.* BUSONI: *Sonatina No. 6 (Fantasy on 'Carmen')*. WEBER/TAUSIG: *Invitation to the Dance.* GLINKA/BALAKIREV: *The Lark.* STRAUSS, Johann, Jnr/SCHULZELVER: *Arabesque on themes from 'The Blue Danube'.*

* CRD CRD 1096.

Philip Fowke plays with prodigious bravura but treats these display pieces with obvious seriousness of purpose. The presentation is perhaps a little lacking in fun, yet brings freshness to every piece included here. It is amazing how pianistic Bach's violin music becomes in Rachmaninov's hands. First-rate recording.

Galway, James (flute)

'Serenade for flute' (with L. Virtuosi): BEETHOVEN: *Serenade in D for flute, violin and viola, Op. 25.* BACH: *Flute sonata in E* (for flute and continuo), *BWV 1035.* TELEMANN: *Trio sonata in E min. for flute, oboe and continuo.*
(B) ***** CfP CFP/*TC-CFP* 40318.

Since these recordings were made for Abbey Records in 1973 James Galway has become a star, and another member of the London Virtuosi, John Georgiadis (then the leader of the LSO), has taken up a successful solo career. It was a bright idea of CfP to make a recital out of these performances. Beethoven's *Serenade* is the best-known work of the three. The light and charming combination of flute, violin and viola inspired the youthful composer to write in an unexpectedly carefree and undemanding way. The sequence of tuneful, unpretentious movements reminds one of Mozart's occasional music, and this engaging performance is well projected by a bright, clean recording. The balance is a trifle close, but the sound is otherwise excellent. The other two works are hardly less attractive, and the playing in the Telemann, slightly more expressive than the Bach, achieves a distinction of style. On tape the sound quality has marginally less life and range at the top; otherwise the cassette transfer is first-class.

'Guitar favourites'

(i) Diaz; (ii) Parkening; (iii) Angel Romero; (iv) Costanto: (i) ROD-RIGO: *Concierto de Aranjuez* (with Professors of Spanish Nat. O., Früh-beck de Burgos). SOR: *Variations on a theme from 'The Magic Flute'.* (ii) BACH: *Jesu, joy of man's desiring. Sheep may safely graze. Sleepers, awake.* (iii) GRANADOS: *La maja de Goya.* RODRIGO: *Fandango.* ALBÉN-IZ: *Tango.* (iv) VILLA-LOBOS: *Pre-ludes Nos. 1–3.* TURINA: *Sevillana. Fandanguillo. Rafaga. Homenaje a Tarrega.* (i) MOMPOU: *Canción.*
(B) *** EMI *TC2-MOM 117.*

At the centre of this tape-only collection is a warmly attractive performance of Rodrigo's *Concierto de Aranjuez* from Alirio Diaz and a Spanish orchestral ensemble. Diaz is good too in the Sor and Mompou items. The contribution from Angel Romero has less electricity, but Christopher Parkening's group of Bach transcriptions is most enjoyable, especially *Sleepers, awake,* which is presented with great flair. Irma Costanto provides the most memorable playing of all, her style very free but compellingly spontaneous and full of atmosphere and colour. The sound is excellent throughout.

Holliger, Heinz (oboe) and Ursula (harp)

ROSSINI: *Andante and variations in F.* RUST: *Sonata in A.* BACH, C. P. E.: *Solo in G min. for oboe and continuo, Wq. 135; Solo for harp, Wq. 139.* BOCHSA: *Nocturne in F, Op. 50/2.*
(M) *** Ph. 6570/7310 575.

Several of these works are arrangements (both the Rossini *Variations* and the Rust *Sonata* were written for the violin), but the *Solo,* Wq. 135, by C. P. E. Bach (the most substantial piece) was conceived with the oboe in mind. All the music here is delightful when played with such point and style. Ursula Holliger holds the stage alone very successfully in her harp *Solo.* The recording is beautifully balanced and sounds wholly natural, with the cassette offering demonstration quality to match the disc.

Hollywood String Qt

BRAHMS: *Piano quintet in F min., Op. 34* (with Aller). SCHUBERT: *String quintet in C, D.956.* SMETANA: *Quartet No. 1 in E min.* (*From my life*). DVOŘÁK: *Quartet No. 12 in F* (*American*), *Op. 96.*
(M) (***) HMV mono RLS/*TC-RLS* 765 (2).

A marvellous compilation. The Hollywood Quartet were all principals in film studio orchestras, and Felix Slatkin, the leader, also led the 20th-Century Fox Orchestra. The Schubert *C major Quintet* was one of the outstanding records of its day and still ranks high. They have great technical finish and perfect ensemble, and penetrate further below the surface than so many groups do. The Brahms *F minor Piano quintet* is no less powerful and thoughtful, and much the same is true of the two Czech quartets. These are classic accounts, all dating from the early 1950s but sounding remarkably fresh all the same. The cassette transfer is of high quality, although the upper range is somewhat fierce and needs taming.

Jackson, Francis (organ of York Minster)

Nineteenth-century organ music: CAMIDGE: *Organ concerto No. 2 in G min.* STANFORD: *Fantasia and toc-cata, Op. 57.* LISZT: *Prelude and*

fugue on BACH. FRANCK: *Fantaisie in A.*
**(*) Abbey 621.

Matthew Camidge (1744–1824) was a member of a family of musicians that provided York Minster with its organists for just over a hundred years. His solo *Concerto*, which 'endeavours to imitate' the styles of Handel and Corelli, is a well-wrought piece with a rather catchy finale. Stanford's *Fantasia and toccata* make a powerful impression in the capable hands of Francis Jackson, and he gives an exciting, bravura account of the Liszt, which suits the York organ extremely well. Franck's *Fantaisie* is perhaps less responsive to the timbres of this fine instrument, but it is given an uncommonly sympathetic performance here. The recording is superb, full-bodied and weighty without clouding of detail.

Kempff, Wilhelm (piano)

'Für Elise': BEETHOVEN: *Für Elise, G.13. Rondo à capriccio in G (Rage over a lost penny), Op. 129.* MOZART: *Fantasy in D min., K.397.* SCHUBERT: *Moments musicaux, D.780, Nos. 1, 3 and 5.* BRAHMS: *3 Intermezzi, Op. 117.* SCHUMANN: *Papillons, Op. 2.*
(M) **(*) DG Priv. 2535/3335 608.

This is a well-planned recital, and although the piano tone is variable (the acoustic changes strikingly on side two) it does give a fair idea of Kempff's range. *Für Elise* is simple and totally unromantic, and the Brahms *Intermezzi* are most beautifully done; but the highlight of the collection is unquestionably the really wonderful performance of the Mozart *Fantasia*, played simply but with great art lying beneath the music's surface. The tape transfer is of excellent quality throughout, clean and clear.

Piano transcriptions (arr. Kempff): BACH: *Chorale preludes: Nun komm der Heiden Heiland, BWV 659; Befiehl du deine Wege, BWV 727; In dulci jubilo, BWV 751; Wachet auf, BWV 140; Ich ruf' zu dir, BWV 639; Jesus bleibet meine Freude, BWV 147/6. Flute sonata in E flat, BWV 1031: Siciliano. Cantata No. 29: Sinfonia. Harpsichord concerto No. 5 in F min., BWV 1056: Largo.* HANDEL: *Minuet in G min.* GLUCK: *Orfeo: Ballet music.*
(M) **(*) DG Acc. 2542/3342 158.

The Kempff magic is never entirely absent from any of this great pianist's recordings, but some may feel that it makes its presence felt rather unevenly in this recital. Several of the chorale preludes are played in a very studied way. The presentation of *Wachet auf* is very firm and clear, the background embroidery precisely articulated, and *Jesu, joy of man's desiring* is played with less delicacy, more extrovert projection than usual. The *Siciliano* from BWV 1031, however, is given an appealing lyrical flow, and the *Orfeo* excerpts, which close the recital, are very beautiful. Kempff is splendidly recorded; the piano tone is full and clear, and the tape transfer is immaculate.

King, Thea (clarinet), Clifford Benson (piano)

STANFORD: *Clarinet sonata, Op. 129.* FERGUSON: *4 Short pieces, Op. 6.* FINZI: *5 Bagatelles, Op. 23.* HURLSTONE: *4 Characteristic pieces.*
*** Hyp. A 66014.

A first-class anthology, well balanced as repertoire, excellently played and most satisfactorily recorded. Stanford's *Clarinet sonata* is clearly influenced by Brahms, but has plenty of character of

933

its own. The rest of the music is lighter in texture and content, all well crafted and worth hearing.

BLISS: *Pastorale.* COOKE, Arnold: *Clarinet sonata in B flat.* HOWELLS: *Clarinet sonata.* REIZENSTEIN: *Arabesques.*
*** Hyp. A 66044.

An admirable second anthology of twentieth-century British music for clarinet and piano, most eloquently played by both artists. The Howells *Sonata* is especially appealing, and all this repertoire rewards investigation, particularly with such persuasive playing and natural warm recording.

Klerk, Albert de (chamber organs)

Regal, table, case, positive, cabinet and secretaire organs: PALESTRINA: *Ricercare primi toni.* FRESCOBALDI: *Ave maris stella.* SANTA MARIA: *Fantasia primi toni. Fantasia terti toni. Fantasia octavi toni.* SWEELINCK: *Von der Fortuna werd' ich getrieben.* GIBBONS: *Fancy in A. The King's Juell.* ZIPOLI: *Canzona.* BUXTEHUDE: *Wie schön leuchtet der Morgenstern.* COUPERIN, L.: *Chaconne in D min.* CORRETTE: *Vous qui désirez sans fin.* CASANOVAS: *Sonata No. 5.*
(M) *** Tel. AP6/*CR4* 41036.

Albert de Klerk provides here a fascinating survey of the development of the chamber organ from about 1600 to 1790. The earliest instrument (a regal) creates the most piquant sounds in an expressive *Ricercare* of Palestrina; later in the survey De Klerk is able to show the more ambitious sounds made by cabinet organs of the last half of the eighteenth century in fine performances of Buxtehude's chorale *Wie schön leuchtet der Morgenstern*, a

sombre *Chaconne* of Louis Couperin and a set of engaging variations on *Vous qui désirez sans fin* by Michel Corrette. Albert de Klerk's mastery of articulation on these primitive instruments is astonishing, and the timbres are always attractive. The recording is close enough to catch all the mechanical clicks, but it gives each instrument great presence. The high-level chrome tape transfer is every bit the equal of the disc, offering demonstration quality throughout.

Kremer, Gidon and Elena (violin and piano)

SCHUBERT: *Fantasia in C for violin and piano, D.934.* MOZART, F. X.: *Grand violin sonata in E, Op. 19.* BEETHOVEN: *12 Variations on 'Se vuol ballare' from Mozart's 'Le Nozze di Figaro', WoO.40.*
*** Ph. 9500/*7300* 904.

The special interest of this recital is the *Sonata* by Franz Xavier Mozart, Wolfgang's younger surviving son. It is a fine work, clearly post-Mozartian and very much worth hearing, especially in this excellent performance, bold, committed and spontaneous. The Schubert *Fantasy* is also impressively played, and the engaging Beethoven *Variations* are an agreeable bonus. But it is Franz Xavier's *Sonata* that makes this worth considering. The sound is first-class on disc and cassette alike.

Kynaston, Nicolas (Royal Albert Hall organ)

'Great organ works': BACH: *Toccata and fugue in D min., BWV 565.* SCHUMANN: *Canon in B min., Op. 56/5.* MENDELSSOHN: *Athalie: War march of the priests.* SAINT-SAËNS: *Fantaisie No. 2 in E flat, Op. 101.*

GIGOUT: *Grand chœur dialogue.*
Toccata in B min. WIDOR: *Symphony
No. 1, Op. 13/1: Marche pontificale.
Symphony No. 4, Op. 13/4: Andante
cantabile. Symphony No. 5, Op. 42/1:
Toccata. Symphony No. 6, Op. 42/2:
Allegro. Symphony No. 9 (Gothique),
Op. 70: Andante sostenuto.* LISZT:
Évocation à la Chapelle Sixtine.
BONNET: *Étude de concert.* MULET:
Carillon-sortie.
(B) ** MfP MFP/*TC-MFP* 1020 (2).

This issue links together in a double-folder sleeve two excellent recitals, recorded separately in 1970 and 1972. The programme is primarily romantic and most of it sounds well on the Royal Albert Hall organ, with its wide range of dynamics. Sometimes one feels Nicolas Kynaston might have let himself go a bit more, but he is very good in the Widor items, which sound properly grandiose. The recording is bright and clear yet has plenty of weight. This set is very reasonably priced and it has very few short-comings, although some might feel at times that the dynamic range is *too* wide.

Lagoya, Alexander (guitar)

'The Spanish guitar': PUJOL: *Guajira.*
ALBÉNIZ: *Cadiz.* TÓRROBA: *Torija.*
RODRIGO: *Prelude. Nocturne. Scher-
zino.* TARREGA: *Introduction and
variations on the theme 'Carnival of
Venice'. Étude (Sueño). Gran vals.
Las dos Hermanitas. Vals.*
**(*) CBS 76946/40- [Col. M 35857].

Alexander Lagoya is an attractive player, and his style and flair bring this lightweight programme fully alive. The opening *Guajira* immediately demonstrates his technical command, which is not self-conscious, and he is especially persuasive in the three characteristic Rodrigo pieces. Perhaps Tar-

rega's *Variations* outlast their welcome, in spite of the special effects, but generally this playing communicates strongly. The recording is realistic but forward; the cassette balance is natural, if not as 'live' as the disc.

Lipatti, Dinu (piano)

Besançon Festival recital (1950):
BACH: *Partita No. 1 in B flat, BWV
825.* MOZART: *Piano sonata No. 8 in
A min., K.310.* SCHUBERT: *Im-
promptus, D.899, Nos. 2–3.* CHOPIN:
Waltzes Nos. 1–14.
(M) (***) HMV mono RLS/*TC-RLS*
761 (2).

No collector should overlook this excellent two-disc set. Most of these performances have scarcely been out of circulation since their first appearance: the haunting account of the Mozart *A minor Sonata* and the Bach *B flat Partita* have both had more than one incarnation; the collection of Chopin *Waltzes* is perhaps most famous of all, and its legendary reputation is well earned. The remastering is expertly done, and the ear notices that, among his other subtleties, Lipatti creates a different timbre for the music of each composer. The tape issue puts the recital on one double-length cassette (in a box with notes), complete with applause. The quality remains excellent, especially in the *Waltzes.*

Lloyd Webber, Julian (cello)

'The romantic cello' (with Yitkin Seow, piano): POPPER: *Elfentanz,
Op. 39.* SAINT-SAËNS: *Carnival of the
Animals: The swan Allegro appas-
sionato, Op. 43.* FAURÉ: *Après un
rêve.* MENDELSSOHN: *Song without
Words, Op. 109.* RACHMANINOV:
Cello sonata, Op. 19: slow movt.

DELIUS: *Romance*. CHOPIN: *Introduction and polonaise brillante, Op. 3*. ELGAR: *Salut d'amour, Op. 12*.
**(*) ASV ACM/*ZCACM* 2002.

Julian Lloyd Webber has gathered together a most attractive collection of showpieces for the cello, romantic as well as brilliant. Such dazzling pieces as the Popper – always a favourite with virtuoso cellists – is on record a welcome rarity. The recording, a little edgy, favours the cello; the cassette transfer is vivid, with good body and range.

Menuhin, Yehudi, and Stéphane Grappelli (violins)

'*Strictly for the birds': A Nightingale Sang in Berkeley Square. Lullaby of Birdland. When the Red, Red Robin. Skylark. Bye, bye, Blackbird. Coucou. Flamingo. Dinah. Rosetta. Sweet Sue. Once in Love with Amy. Laura. La Route du Roi. Sweet Georgia Brown*.
*** EMI Dig. EMD/*TCC-EMD* 5533 [Ang. DS/*4ZS* 37710].

An endearing continuation of a happy musical partnership that has already produced three successful collections: *Jealousy* (*Hits of the thirties*) (EMD/*TC-EMD* 5504 [Ang. S/*4XS* 36968]); *Fascinatin' Rhythm* (with music of Gershwin, Jerome Kern and Cole Porter: EMD/*TC-EMD* 5523 [Ang. S/*4XS* 37156]); and *Tea for Two* (including the delightful Max Harris items *Air on a Shoe String* and *Viva Vivaldi*: EMD/*TC-EMD* 5530 [Ang. S 60259]). The partnership of Menuhin and Grappelli started in the television studio; their brief duets (tagged on to interviews) were so successful that the idea developed of recording a whole recital. The high spirits of the collaboration are caught again here, not only in the lively numbers but also the memorable lyrical tunes like the title song and *Laura*. Superbly focused recording, with disc and chrome tape almost identical.

'*Top hat'* (with O., Riddle): BERLIN: *Puttin' on the Ritz. Isn't This a Lovely Day. The Piccolino. Change Partners. Top Hat*. KERN: *The Way You Look Tonight*. GERSHWIN: *He Loves and She Loves. They Can't Take That Away From He. They All Laughed. Funny Face*. GRAPPELLI: *Alison. Amanda*. CONRAD: *The Continental*. YOUMANS: *Carioca*.
*** EMI Dig. EMD/*TCC-EMD* 5539.

For their fifth collection, Menuhin and Grappelli are joined by a small orchestral group directed by Nelson Riddle. Aficionados might fear that this will dilute the jazz element of the playing, and perhaps it does a little at times; but Riddle's arrangements are witty and understanding and some of these tunes undeniably have an orchestral feeling. The result is just as lively and entertaining as previous collections in this series. The music itself is associated with Fred Astaire, although Grappelli contributes two numbers himself, perhaps originally intended for *Strictly for the birds*. The sound is as crisp and lively as ever, both on disc and on the excellent chrome tape.

Milan, Susan (flute)

'*The magic flute of Susan Milan'* (with Benson, piano): ROUSSEL: *Joueurs de flûte*. DEBUSSY: *Syrinx*. POULENC: *Flute sonata*. IBERT: *Pièce for solo flute*. MESSIAEN: *La Merle noire*. FAURÉ: *Fantaisie*. BOZZA: *Agrestide*.
(M) *** ASV ACM/*ZCACM* 2010.

Susan Milan is an admirable soloist in this repertoire. Her timbre seems ideally suited to French music; her phrasing is sensitive, and the control of vibrato is beautifully judged. There is bravura too, but never for its own sake (unless this is the composer's intention). The programme is imaginative and well balanced: the Roussel pieces, and the Poulenc *Sonata* are especially valuable. The recording is rather resonant, but this does not prevent clarity of focus either on disc or on the excellent equivalent cassette.

Organ music

'Great organ favourites' (with (i) Danby (organ of Blenheim Palace); (ii) Bayco (Holy Trinity, Paddington); (iii) Willcocks (King's College, Camb.); (iv) Preston (Westminster Abbey); (v) Thalben-Ball (Temple Church); (vi) Jackson (York Minster)): (i) BACH: *Toccata and fugue in D min., BWV 565.* (ii) *In dulci jubilo.* (iii) *Wachet auf.* (i) CLARKE: *Trumpet voluntary.* WIDOR: *Symphony No. 5, Op. 42/1: Toccata.* ELGAR: *Enigma variations: Nimrod.* GIGOUT: *Scherzo.* FRANCK: *Choral No. 3 in A min.* (iv) MURRILL: *Carillon.* (ii) MENDELSSOHN: *A Midsummer Night's Dream· Wedding march.* LEMARE: *Andantino.* HOLLINS: *Spring song.* WAGNER: *Lohengrin: Bridal chorus.* WOLSTENHOLME: *Allegretto.* BOËLLMANN: *Prière à Notre Dame.* HANDEL: *Water music: Air.* (v) PURCELL: *Voluntary on the Old 100th.* (vi) COCKER: *Tuba tune.*
(B) ** EMI *TC2-MOM 115.*

Obvious care has been taken with the engineering of this mixed bag of excerpts (one of the tape-only 'Miles of Music' series), but occasionally the reverberant acoustic brings moments when the focus slips a little. For the most part, however, the sound is impressive. The programme begins well with excellent versions of the Widor, Gigout, Franck's *Third Choral* and Murrill's engaging *Carillon*, but on side two Frederic Bayco, who provides the lighter fare, is sometimes unstylish: he is very mannered in the famous *Wedding march*. But how many drivers want organ music as a background for a car journey?

Parker-Smith, Jane (organ)

BACH: *Toccata and fugue in D min., BWV 565. Jesu, joy of man's desiring.* BACH–GOUNOD: *Ave Maria.* MENDELSSOHN: *A Midsummer Night's Dream, Op. 61: Wedding march.* WIDOR: *Organ symphony No. 5 in F min., Op. 42/1: Toccata. Organ symphony No. 8 in B, Op. 42/4: finale.* BOËLLMANN: *Prière à Notre Dame.* REGER: *Benedictus.*
(B) *** CfP CFP/*TC-CFP* 40324.

Jane Parker-Smith is a brilliant young organist who had already made a reputation while she was still a student at the Royal College of Music. In this début recital, which she recorded in 1973, she demonstrates an easy bravura and a strong grasp of musical essentials. The famous Bach *Toccata and fugue* is excit ing and spontaneous, but not more so than the Widor *Toccata*. This is one of the most exuberant versions on disc, notable for its lively use of the pedals, which are given a generous (and easily reproduced) bass response here. The *Wedding march* too has plenty of life, and Miss Parker-Smith shows a contrasting restraint in her approach to *Jesu, joy of man's desiring* and the Bach–Gounod *Ave Maria*, which are tastefully registered. An excellent recital on all counts, showing real star quality. The cassette, transferred at the highest level, is quite remarkably vivid, bright on top, with a full, resonant bass. Only in the Bach *Toccata* is there a hint of strain; otherwise the sound is first-rate.

937

Perlman, Itzhak (violin), **Samuel Sanders** (piano)

'*Kreisler transcriptions and arrangements*': TARTINI: *Devil's Trill sonata*. POLDINI: *Dancing Doll*. WIENIAWSKI: *Caprice in A min*. TRAD.: *Londonderry air*. MOZART: *Serenade No. 7 (Haffner), K.250: Rondo*. CORELLI: *Sarabande and Allegretto*. ALBÉNIZ: *Malagueña, Op. 165/3*. HEUBERGER: *The Midnight Bells*. MENDELSSOHN: *Song without Words, Op. 62/1*. BRAHMS: *Hungarian dance in F min*. *** HMV ASD 3346 [Ang. S/4XS 37254].

Perlman's supreme mastery has rarely been demonstrated more endearingly than in this collection of transcriptions, one of his outstanding Kreisler series, which in almost every way runs rings round any opposition today. Excellent recording.

'*Spanish album*': FALLA: *Suite populaire espagnole*. GRANADOS: *Spanish dance*. HALFFTER: *Danza de la gitana*. SARASATE: *Habañera, Op. 21/2. Playera, Op. 23. Spanish dance, Op. 26/8. Malagueña, Op. 21/1. Caprice basque, Op. 24*. *** HMV ASD/TC-ASD 3910 [Ang. SZ/4ZS 37590].

Perlman is a violinist who even on record demonstrates his delight in virtuosity in every phrase he plays. There are few more joyful records of violin firework pieces (apt for encores) than this. Excellent recording, and a first-class cassette transfer.

Pinnock, Trevor (harpsichord or virginals)

'*At the Victoria and Albert Museum*' (Queen Elizabeth's virginals; harpsichords): ANON.: *My Lady Wynkfylds rownde*. BYRD: *The Queenes alman. The Bells*. HANDEL: *Harpsichord suite No. 5 in E*. CROFT: *Suite No. 3 in C min*. ARNE: *Sonata No. 3 in G*. J. C. BACH: *Sonata in C min., Op. 5/6*. **(*) CRD CRD 1007/CRDC 4007.

Trevor Pinnock opens this recital by playing three attractive and very colourful pieces on an instrument originally belonging to Queen Elizabeth I, who was an accomplished virginal player. It is in splendid condition and has a most attractive sound. Pinnock plays it with enthusiasm, and his performance of Byrd's extraordinarily descriptive *The Bells* is a *tour de force*. For the rest of the recital he uses two different harpsichords, also part of the Victoria and Albert Museum collection. His style in the works by Handel, Croft, Arne and J. C. Bach is less flamboyant, more circumspect, but the music is strongly characterized and boldly recorded. The Handel suite is the one which has the *Harmonious Blacksmith* as its finale. Disc and cassette are closely matched.

'*A choice collection of lessons and ayres*': PLAYFORD: *From Musick's Handmaid: 3 Pieces*. LOCKE: *Melothesia: Suite No. 4 in D*. PURCELL: *Musick's Handmaid, Part 2: A new Irish tune; Ground. A Choice Collection of Lessons: Suite No. 2 in G min*. BLOW: *Musick's Handmaid, Part 2: Mortlack's Ground*. GREENE: *Overture in D*. ARNE: *Sonata No. 6 in G*. NARES: *Lesson No. 2 in D*. PARADIES: *Sonata No. 6 in A*. *** CRD CRD 1047/CRDC 4047.

An outstanding collection, splendidly played and recorded and with a very well planned programme. Pinnock uses a modern copy (by Clayson and Garrett) of a Dülcken of 1745. It is a magnificent instrument, and the three colourful opening pieces from John Playford's *Musick's Handmaid* immediately captivate the ear: *The Grange* is followed by *Lord Monck's March*, and last comes a miniature portrait of *Gerard's Mistress*. All three last for only 2′ 48″, yet demonstrate a remarkable range of colour and feeling. The music on the first side comes from important seventeenth-century collections and it is all of high quality. For side two we move on to the eighteenth century, and the programme is hardly less rewarding. All this music is splendidly alive in Trevor Pinnock's hands, and stylistically he is impeccable. The sound balance is very realistic on disc and cassette alike; indeed the tape is of demonstration quality.

'*Sixteenth-century harpsichord and virginal music*': (Harpsichord) BYRD: *Watkin's ale. La Volta* – *Lady Morley. Lord Willoughby's welcome home. The Carmans whistle.* GIBBONS: *The Woods so wild. Mask* – *The Fairest Nymph. The Lord of Salisbury his Pavin and Galiardo.* BULL: *The King's hunt. My Grief; My Self.* FARNABY: *Muscadin or Kempe's Morris. Loath to depart.* TOMKINS: *Barafostus's dream.* (Virginals) ANON.: *My Lady Carey's dompe.* TALLIS: *O ye tender babes.* RANDALL: *Dowland's Lachrimae and galliard: Can she excuse.*
*** CRD CRD 1050/*CRDC 4050*.

This programme is cleverly arranged so that on each side a central section for virginals is framed by major items on the harpsichord. On side one the two virginal pieces nearly steal the show, for the engaging *My Lady Carey's dompe* is beautifully set off by Tallis's expressively eloquent *O ye tender babes.* There is some superb bravura from Pinnock in the harpsichord music. *The King's Hunt* is splendidly vigorous, and *Lord Salisbury's*

Pavin and Galiardo have comparable poise and elegance. Indeed everything here springs vividly to life, and Pinnock's decoration is always well judged, adding piquancy and zest to the fast pieces. As on the companion recital (above) the recording is outstanding, on both disc and cassette, and the result is irresistible.

Romero, Pepe (guitar)

'*Guitar works from Renaissance to baroque*': SANZ: *Suite española.* VALDERRABANO: *Soneto 1.* PISADOR: *Pavana.* MUDARRA: *Gallarda.* NARVAEZ: *Diferencias sobre 'Guárdame las vacas'. 3 Diferencias por otra parte.* MILAN: *6 Pavanas. Fantasia No. 16 en el 5 y 6 tono.*
** Ph. 9500 351/7300 602.

Pepe Romero's playing of this repertoire for vihuela and guitar from what has been described as '*el siglo de oro*', Spain's musical golden age, is sympathetic but rather studied. There is very little flamboyance, and dynamic contrast is used sparingly. The result may be authentic, but there is not much electricity here. The recording is forward and truthful, and the excellent cassette matches the disc closely.

(Los) Romeros (guitar qt)

'*Music for four guitars*': GIMÉNEZ: *El baile de Luis Alonso* (trans. P. Romero). MOLLEDA: *Triptico.* TÓRROBA: *Estampas. Danza rapsódica.*
** Ph. 9500 296/7300 567.

By far the most attractive piece here is the opening *El baile de Luis Alonso* by the writer of *zarzuelas*, Jerónimo Giménez (who, surprisingly, studied for a while under Debussy). His *jota* is played in the popular style and sounds splendidly vigorous. Tórroba's eight *Estampas* (actually written for guitar quartet in 1973) are agreeable but instantly forgettable. The playing here has plenty of life, and the recording is excellent (the tape needs a high-level playback, then mirrors the disc closely).

Rubinstein, Artur (piano)

'*The artistry of Artur Rubinstein*': SCHUBERT: *Impromptu in G flat, D.899/3.* CHOPIN: *Mazurka in D, Op. 33/2. Berceuse in D flat, Op. 57. Waltz in D flat, Op. 64/1. Polonaise in A (Military), Op. 40/1. Fantaisie-impromptu in C sharp min., Op. 60.* POULENC: *3 Mouvements perpétuels. Intermezzo in A flat.* CHABRIER: *Scherzo-valse.* DEBUSSY: *Préludes, Book 1: La cathédrale engloutie. Images, Book 2: Poissons d'or.* LISZT: *Valse oubliée No. 1, G.215/1.* SCHUMANN: *Waldscenen, Op. 82: The prophet bird.* BRAHMS: *Ballade in D min., Op. 10/1. Capriccio in B min., Op. 76/2. Romance in F, Op. 118/5.* PROKOFIEV: *The Love of Three Oranges: March.* RAVEL: *Miroirs: La vallée des cloches.* VILLA-LOBOS: *Polichinelle.* FALLA: *El amor brujo: Ritual fire dance.*
(M) *** RCA RL 02359 (2)/*RK 02359* [ARL 2/*A RK 2* 2359].

These two records make an admirable survey of Rubinstein's art, and the French repertoire is especially welcome. Such a set is self-recommending, even if the quality of the piano sound is sometimes lacking in fullness of timbre. The cassette transfer matches the discs fairly closely.

Excerpts from live recitals: SCHUMANN: *Études symphoniques, Op. 13. Arabeske in C, Op. 18.* RAVEL: *Le Tombeau de Couperin: Forlane.* DE-
BUSSY: *La plus que lente.* ALBÉNIZ: *Navarra.*
**(*) RCA RL/*RK* 13850 [ARL 1 3850].

These varied items from different sources all convey the sparkle of Rubinstein at whatever age. As a sampler try the electrifying account of Albéniz's *Navarra*, which is full of naughty rhythmic pointing. The Debussy in quite a different way is equally compelling, and though the playing is not always flawless (maybe the reason why these items were not issued years earlier) the magnetism is irresistible. The recording is rather clangy but quite acceptable; the cassette transfer is clear, but dry.

Segovia, Andres (guitar)

'*The art of Segovia*' (the HMV recordings 1927–39): BACH: (Unaccompanied) *Violin partita No. 3, BWV 1006: Gavotte.* (Unaccompanied) *Cello suite No. 1, BWV 1007: Prelude; Cello suite No. 3, BWV 1009: Courante. Clavierbüchlein: Prelude in C min., BWV 999. Lute suite in E min., BWV 996: Allemande. Violin sonata No. 1, BWV 1001: Fugue in G min.* PONCE/WEISS: *Suite in A.* PONCE: *Sonata No. 3: 1st movt. Sonata No. 2: Canción; Postlude; Mazurka; Petite valse; Folies d'Espagne.* SOR: *Thème varié, Op. 9.* VISÉE: *Sarabande. Bourrée. Menuet.* FROBERGER: *Gigue.* TÓRROBA: *Sonatina in A: Allegretto. Suite Castellana: Fandanguillo. Preludio. Nocturno.* MALATS: *Serenata.* MENDELSSOHN: *String quartet No. 1 in E flat, Op. 12: Canzonetta.* TARREGA: *Recuerdos de la Alhambra; Study in A.* CASTELNUOVO-TEDESCO: *Sonata (Homage to Boccherini): Vivo ed energico.* ALBÉNIZ: *Suite española:*

Granada; Sevilla. TURINA: *Fandan-guillo.* GRANADOS: *Danzas españo-las, Op. 37: Nos. 5 in E min.; 10 in G.* (M) (***) HMV mono RLS/*TC-RLS* 745 (2).

It was Segovia's pioneering recitals in the thirties that re-established the guitar in the public mind as a serious solo instrument. This collection consists of his early recordings made over a span of twelve years. There are many transcriptions, including a good deal of Bach, where the style of the playing is romantic (though never showing lapses of taste). What is so striking throughout this collection is the way all the music, slight or serious, springs vividly to life. Segovia had the gift of natural spontaneity in all he played, and he was in his prime at this period, so that technically this is wonderfully assured. Guitar fans will find the set an essential purchase; others will be surprised to discover that no apologies are needed for the sound, which is natural in timbre and gives the instrument a ready projection. The cassette transfers too are of immaculate quality, and on both tape and disc there is remarkably little of the intrusive background noise associated with the 78 r.p.m. originals.

Still, Ray (oboe), **Itzhak Perlman** (violin), **Pinchas Zukerman** (viola), **Lynn Harrell** (cello)

Oboe quartets: BACH, J. C.: *Oboe quartet in B flat.* MOZART: *Oboe quartet in F, K.370.* VANHAL: *Oboe quartet, Op. 7/1;* STAMITZ: *Oboe quartet in E flat, Op. 8/4.* *** HMV ASD 3916.

Ray Still, principal oboe of the Chicago Symphony orchestra for a generation, is a superb artist, a splendid foil for the three stars of string playing who complete the ensemble. This is the finest performance available of the Mozart, gently pointed but not mannered, and the recording – close and domestic sounding – is excellent. The three companion works are no more than charming – the Stamitz clearly imitating the Mozart with a minor-key slow movement – but make an excellent coupling.

'Toccata'

Organ toccatas (with (i) Wicks: (ii) Weir; (iii) Hurford; (iv) Preston; (v) Nicholas): (i) BACH: *Toccata and fugue in D min., BWV 565.* (ii) *Toccata, adagio and fugue in C, BWV 564.* (iii) BUXTEHUDE: *Toccata and fugue in F.* (iv) WIDOR: *Symphony No. 5, Op. 42/1: Toccata.* (v) BOËLLMANN: *Suite gothique, Op. 25: Toccata.* (iv) REGER: *Toccata and fugue, Op. 59/5–6.* (ii) MULET: *Toccata: Tu es Petrus.* DUBOIS: *Toccata.* (M) **(*) Decca SPA/*KCSP* 583.

Highlights here are Gillian Weir's impressive account of Bach's *Toccata, adagio and fugue in C*, with the fugue superbly buoyant. She ends the collection with an equally exciting performance of the Dubois *Toccata*, an essentially genial piece. The famous Widor finale comes off well too, but Alan Wicks's version of Bach's most famous organ piece is a shade too relaxed, and even Simon Preston cannot make the Reger Op. 59 sound other than an academic exercise. Excellent recording throughout; the tape transfer offers no problems.

Tracey, Bradford (double virginal)

SWEELINCK: *Preludium toccata.* MORLEY: *Lachrymae pavane and galliard.* LASSUS: *Susanne un jour.* TISDALE: *Coranto.* BULL: *Lord Lumley's pavane and galliard. The Prince's galliard. Preludium and fan-*

tasia. GIBBONS: *Fantasia in A min. Ground in A min.* SCHEIDT: *Bergamasque.*
(M) **(*) Tel. AP6/*C*R4 42074.

Another of Telefunken's recital series using original instruments, this collection demonstrates the potential of the double virginal, a visually fascinating two-manual instrument nicknamed 'mother and child' because the smaller keyboard sits above its parent. The instrument here is a copy of a sixteenth-century Ruckers; it has a splendid sound and is superbly recorded – the chrome cassette and disc are alike of demonstration standard. Bradford Tracey's style is essentially robust and rhythmically strong; this suits the short dances and gives them plenty of character, but it makes the longer works seem heavy-going. One feels that more imaginative use could have been made of the contrasts of colour between the two keyboards. Nevertheless this is a thoroughly worthwhile issue.

Williams, John (guitar)

BACH: (Unaccompanied) *Cello suites Nos. 1 in G, BWV 1007; 3 in C, BWV 1009.* SCARLATTI, D.: *Sonata in E min., Kk.11.* SCARLATTI, A.: *Gavotte.*
(M) **(*) Decca SPA/*KCSP* 592.

These recordings come from the end of the fifties and were originally issued on the Delysé label. The Bach suites, arranged by John Duarte, are transcribed into keys suitable for the guitar: No. 1 is transposed up a fifth to D and No. 3 down a third to A. They are played soberly and conscientiously, and some listeners may seek more flair; yet the thoughtfulness of the music-making, with its conscious use of light and shade, is impressive both here and in the items by Alessandro and Domenico Scarlatti. The recording is of excellent quality and does not sound in the least dated.

'Recollections': ALBÉNIZ: *Sevilla. Tango.* SCARLATTI, D.: *Sonata in E, Kk.380.* RODRIGO: *Concierto de Aranjuez: Adagio* (with ECO, Barenboim). LAURO: *Vals criollo.* BACH: *Jesu, joy of man's desiring. Lute suite No. 4, BWV 1006a: Gavotte.* BARRIOS: *Maxixa.* VILLA-LOBOS: *Prelude No. 1.* GOWERS: *Stevie.* TÓRROBA: *Madronos.* GRANADOS: *Spanish dance No. 5.* THEODORAKIS: *3 Epitafios.*
**(*) CBS 10016/40-.

This collection is made up from older recitals (which are currently coming under the deletions axe). The arrangement of items is not especially felicitous, and the overall effect does not achieve the evocative nostalgia suggested by the title. Indeed the Bach chorale has an unstylish accompaniment. However, much of this playing is of high quality, and it is cleanly recorded, with the disc rather more refined than the cassette.

Yepes, Narciso (guitar)

'Spanish guitar music': ALBÉNIZ: *Suite española: Asturias. Recuerdos de viaje: Rumores de la caleta. Piezas caracteristicas: Torre Bermeja.* GRANADOS: *Danza española No. 4, Villanesca.* FALLA: *El amor brujo: El círculo mágico; Canción del fuego fatuo. The Three-cornered Hat: Miller's dance.* TURINA: *Sonata, Op. 61. Fandanguillo, Op. 36.*
(M) *** DG Acc. 2542/*3342* 157.

An extraordinarily successful recital, the playing full of electricity and immediately communicative. The opening *Asturias* immediately commands the listener's attention, and the atmospheric *Fandanguillo* of Turina and the Granados *Villanesca* are equally telling. The Falla ballet excerpts are uncannily orchestral in their colour. Highly recommended and very well recorded.

Zabaleta, Nicanor (harp)

'Spanish harp music of the sixteenth and seventeenth centuries': (Sixteenth century) CABEZÓN: *Pavana con su Glosa.* MUDARRA: *Tiento para harpa.* PALERO: *2 Romances.* ALBERTO: *Tres IV.* CABEZÓN: *Pavana Italiana. Diferencias sobre la gallarda Milanesa. Diferencias sobre el canto de caballero.* (Seventeenth century) ANON.: *Seguidillas.* RIBAYAS: *Bacas. Folias. Paredetas. Pabanas. Hachas.*

HUETE: *Canción Italiana con diferencias. Canzión Franzesa. Monsiur de la Boleta.* RODRIGUES: *Tocata II para arpa.*
(M) *** DG Arc. Priv. 2547/*3347* 049.

Although the harp was in use in Renaissance Spain, much of this music is more likely to have been heard on the vihuela or guitar, and thus textures are simple. Zabaleta plays everything on a modern harp, yet his taste is impeccable and matched by stylistic sympathy, so that nothing sounds out of period. Of its kind this is faultless, and with immaculate recording (on both disc and cassette) it can be recommended to all but those seeking the cascading roulades of nineteenth-century harp writing.

Vocal Recitals
and Choral Collections

Accademia Monteverdiana, Stevens

'Twentieth anniversary tribute': GABRIELI, G.: In excelsis. GABRIELI, A.: Ricercar. MONTEVERDI: Gloria in excelsis. FARMER: A little pretty bonny lass. MORLEY: False love. WILBYE: Adieu sweet Amaryllis. BEETHOVEN: Nei campi (2 settings). QUELDRYK: Gloria. DUNSTABLE: Veni sancte spiritus. 2 French chansons. ANON.: Sanctus. Salve sancta. LASSUS: Quand mon mari. Fuyons tous d'amour.
(M) *** HMV HQS/TC-HQS 1434.

This celebration of the twentieth anniversary of the forming of the Accademia Monteverdi under Professor Denis Stevens takes a broad musical sweep, starting with early liturgical chants and moving via the music of Lassus and Dunstable and the Renaissance spectacle of the Gabrielis through to the time of Beethoven. Any lack of polish is compensated for by the vitality of the music-making, and the recording is reliable (although on tape there are some transfer problems with the amplitude of the Gabrieli items with their resonant brass panoply).

Angeles, Victoria de los (soprano)

Songs (with Moore or Soriano, piano): SCHUBERT: An die Musik. Wohin. Der Tod und das Mädchen. BRAHMS: Dein blaues Auge. Vergebliches Ständchen. FAURÉ: Chanson d'amour. Clair de lune. HAHN: Le Rossignol des lilas. DEBUSSY: La flûte de Pan. Noël des enfants qui n'ont plus de maisons. GRANADOS: Amor y odio. El majo discreto. El majo timido. La maja de Goya. GURIDI: Cómo quieres que adivine. Arr. NIN: Granadina. TURINA: Tu pupila es azul. RODRIGO: De los álamos, vengo. MOMPOU: Damunt de tu nomes les flors. MONTSALVATGE: Canción de cuna para dormir a un negrito. VALVERDE: Clavelitos. CALLEJA: Adiós Granada.
(B) *** CfP CFP/ TC-CFP 40366.

This compilation from some of Victoria de los Angeles' vintage recordings of the fifties and sixties is one of the most delectable of all recital records. Whether in German Lieder (Schubert and Brahms radiant and sparkling) or French mélodie (Fauré rarely so tenderly affecting), or in her own Spanish repertory (taking up the whole of the second side) she gives magical performances. The recording is a little thin by today's standards, but at Classics for Pleasure bargain price this should not be missed. Disc and cassette are closely matched.

'In concert' (with Moore, piano): MONTEVERDI: Ohime! Chi'io cado, ohime!. Maledetto sia l'aspetto. HANDEL: Radamisto: Vanne! Sorella ingrata! SCHUBERT: Lachen und Weinen. Mein. BRAHMS: Liebestreu. Vergebliches Ständchen. VAUGHAN WILLIAMS: The roadside fire. TRAD.: I will walk with my love. Blow the wind southerly. RODRIGO: Canción

del grumete. Trovadoresca. De los álamos, vengo. NIN: *Paño Murciano. Asturiana.* MONTSALVATGE: *Punto de habañera.* FALLA: *7 Spanish popular songs: Jota; Polo.* VALLS: *Canciones Sefardies: Una matica de ruda.* VALVERDE: *Clavelitos.* CALLEJA: *Adiós Granada.*
**(*) HMV ASD/*TC-ASD* 3656 [Ang. SZ/*4ZS* 37546].

This delightful recital was recorded live at the Royal Festival Hall in London, and provides valuable alternative versions of many of the items which in the sixties in particular this superb artist made her own. In detail the performances may not all be so perfect as those she recorded in the studio, but the gain in atmospheric tension is obvious, not least in the final encore items which regularly marked her recitals. Good recording for the period; the tape transfer is highly modulated; the voice is given striking presence, but there is also a hint of edginess on vocal peaks.

'The art of Victoria de Los Angeles': MOZART: *Le Nozze di Figaro: Porgi amor,* ROSSINI: *Il Barbiere di Siviglia: Una voce poco fa.* VERDI: *Otello: Willow song; Ave Maria. La Traviata: Teneste la promessa . . . Addio del passato.* PUCCINI: *La Bohème: Sì, mi chiamano Mimì; Donde lieta usci. Madama Butterfly: Entrance of Butterfly; Un bel dì.* WAGNER: *Tannhäuser: Dich, teure Halle. Lohengrin: Einsam in trüben Tagen.* GOUNOD: *Faust: Jewel song.* MASSENET: *Manon: Adieu notre petite table; Obéissons. Werther: Air des lettres.* BIZET: *Carmen: Habañera; Seguidilla.* GRANADOS: *Goyescas: La maja y el ruiseñor.* FALLA: *La Vida breve: Vivan los que rien! Alli está! Riyendo!* Songs: SCHUBERT: *An*

die Musik. BRAHMS: *Dein blaues Auge. Vergebliches Ständchen.* FAURÉ: *Clair de lune.* HAHN: *Le Rossignol des lilas.* DUPARC: *L'Invitation au voyage.* Arr. CANTELOUBE: *Baïlèro.* CORNAGO: *Qué es mi vida, preguntais?* ANON.: *Ay luna que reluces.* GRANADOS: *Colección de tonadillos; La Maja dolorosa No. 3.* Arr. TARRAGÓ: *Din, dan Yolerán.* RODRIGO: *Cuatro madrigales amatorios.* CHAPI: *La Patria chica. La Chavala. Las Hijas des Zebedeo.* VALVERDE: *Clavelitos.* CALLEJA: *Adiós Granada.*
(M) (***) HMV SLS/*TC-SLS* 5233 (3).

This three-disc set contains a vintage collection of Victoria de los Angeles recordings, mostly made near the beginning of her career in mono sound. It is particularly valuable for the series of operatic portraits, not just those selected from her complete recordings (*Carmen* under Beecham, Massenet's *Manon* under Monteux, a delectable *Butterfly* in the first of the two versions she made) but the radiant portrayals given in separate items such as the *Willow Song* and *Ave Maria* from Verdi's *Otello*. The songs too provide an attractive cross-section of her work, including her incomparable recording of Granados's *La maja y el ruiseñor,* originally issued on 78. The remastering is well managed and the stereo transcriptions do not rob the sound of its clarity of focus. The cassettes too are transferred most successfully; the earlier operatic recordings sound particularly fresh, the voice radiant. As on disc, the 1960 Lieder recordings sound rather dry, but overall the quality is first-class.

Bach Ch., Philip Jones Brass Ens., Willcocks

'Family carols': O come, all ye faithful. Gabriel's message. Angelus ad

Virginem. Ding dong merrily on high. A virgin most pure. God rest ye merry, gentlemen. In dulci jubilo. Unto us a son is born. Once in Royal David's city. Hush, my dear, lie still and slumber. WILLCOCKS: *Fanfare.* RUTTER: *Shepherd's pipe carol. Star carol.* KIRKPATRICK: *Away in a manger.* GRUBER: *Stille Nacht.* Arr. VAUGHAN WILLIAMS: *Sussex carol.* MENDELSSOHN: *Hark, the herald angels sing.*
*** Decca Dig. SXDL/*KSXDC* 7514.

An admirably chosen and beautifully recorded collection of traditional carols. Fresh simplicity is the keynote here; the brass fanfares bring a touch of splendour but the music is not over-scored. *Silent night* has seldom sounded more serene, and Rutter's infectiously rhythmic *Shepherd's pipe carol* makes a refreshing contrast, the centrepiece of side two. The digital sound is in no way clinical; indeed the resonance is perfectly judged. The excellent cassette is only marginally less sharply focused, otherwise retaining all the qualities of the LP.

Baker, Janet (mezzo-soprano)

'Songs for Sunday' (with Ledger, piano): BRAHE: *Bless this house.* PARRY: *Jerusalem.* TRAD.: *Were you there.* PLUMSTEAD: *A grateful heart. Close thine eyes.* EASTHOPE MARTIN: *The holy child.* THOMPSON: *The knights of Bethlehem.* LIDDLE: *How lovely are Thy dwellings. The Lord is my shepherd. Abide with me.* VAUGHAN WILLIAMS: *The call.* FORD: *A prayer to Our Lady.* BACH–GOUNOD: *Ave Maria.* WALFORD DAVIES: *God be in my head.*
*** HMV ASD/*TC-ASD* 3981.

Dame Janet Baker's total dedication

makes this a moving experience, transforming songs that would as a rule seem merely sentimental. Sensitive accompaniment and excellent recording, which has transferred admirably to tape.

'Grandi voci': BACH: *Cantata No. 170: Vergnügte Ruh'.* PURCELL: *Dido and Aeneas: When I am laid in earth.* CAVALLI: *La Calisto: Ardo, sospiro e piango;* Duet: *Ululi, frema e strida . . . E spedito* (with Gottlieb). RAMEAU: *Hippolyte et Aricie: Quelle plainte en ces lieux m'appelle?* RAVEL: *Trois poèmes de Stéphane Mallarmé.* CHAUSSON: *Chanson perpétuelle.*
(M) *** Decca GRV 5.

This was originally a sampler disc prepared as an answer to EMI, the company with which Dame Janet Baker had then signed an exclusive contract. The choice of items may not be ideal, with nothing between the eighteenth and the twentieth centuries, but every item – especially Dame Janet's heartfelt first recording of *Dido's lament*, and Diana's aria from *La Calisto* – conveys the singer's unique intensity, and the recordings are first-rate.

'The artistry of Janet Baker': GLUCK: *Alceste: Divinités du Styx. Iphigénie en Aulide: Vous essayez en vain . . . Par la crainte; Adieu, conservez dans votre âme. Iphigénie en Tauride: Non cet affreux devoir. Orfeo; Che puro ciel; Che farò senza Euridice.* MOZART: *La Clemenza di Tito: Parto! Parto; Deh, per questo istante solo.* HANDEL: *Ariodante: Dopo notte. Atalanta: Care selve. Joshua: O had I Jubal's lyre. Serse: Ombra mai fù.*
(M) *** Ph. 6570/*7310* 829.

Compiled from several sources, this collection presents some superb examples of Dame Janet's mature artistry on record. No one interprets Gluck more compellingly than she, and the Handel items inspire singing that is not just moving but technically brilliant. Fine recording. Side one of the cassette is transferred at the highest level, the voice vibrant and full, but the level drops on the second side, which is clear and slightly more refined.

Berganza, Teresa (mezzo-soprano)

'Arias by Mozart, Gluck, Handel and Rossini'; GLUCK: Orfeo: Che farò. Paride ed Elena: O del mio dolce ardor. MOZART: La Clemenza di Tito: Parto, parto. Le Nozze di Figaro: Voi che sapete. Così fan tutte: Per pietà. HANDEL: Alcina: Sta nell'Ircana; Verdi prati. ROSSINI: Il Barbiere di Siviglia: Una voce poco fa. L'Italiana in Algeri: Cruda sorte! Amor tiranno! La Cenerentola: Nacqui all'affanno ... Non più mesta.
(M) *** Decca Jub. JB/KJBC 98.

This recital is drawn from a number of sources covering Teresa Berganza's Decca recording career from the Cenerentola aria of 1959 and the Figaro and Così items of 1963, all of which won great praise when they were first issued, to excerpts from her complete sets up to La Clemenza di Tito of 1968. Above all one notices the consistency, the rich voice controlled with the sort of vocal perfection one associates with her compatriot Victoria de los Angeles. A most satisfying collection, well recorded and with a vivid cassette transfer.

Spanish songs (with Lavilla, piano): ANCHIETA: Con amores, la mi madre. TORRE: Pámpano verde, racimo albar. ESTEVE: Alma sintamos! Ojos llorar. GRANADOS: Tonadillas: La maja dolorosa 1, Oh, muerte cruel!; 2, Ay, majo de mi vida!; 3, De aquel majo amante. El majo discreto: Dicen que mi majo es feo. El tra la lá y el punteado: Es en balde, majo mio. El majo timido: Llega a mi reja y me mira por la noche. TURINA: Saeta en forma de Salve a la Virgen de la Esperanza: Dio te salve, Macarena. Canto a Sevilla: El Fantasma (Por las calles misteriosas). Poema en forma de canciones (Cantares): Más cerca. GURIDI: Seis canciones castellanas: Llámale con el panuelo; No quiero tus avellanas; Cómo quieres que adivine. MONTSALVATGE: Canciones negras: Cuba dentro de un piano: Cuando mi madre llevaba un sorbete. Puento de Habañera: La nina criolla pasa con su mirinaque. Chévere del navajazo. Canción de cuna para dormir a un negrito: Ninghe, ninghe, ninghe. Canto negro: Yambambó, yambambó!
(M) *** DG Acc. 2542/3342 135.

A delightful collection of Spanish songs given with spirit by singer and pianist in ideal collaboration. The first of Granados's Tonadillas, La maja dolorosa, is particularly moving in its range of expressiveness. Berganza may not quite match Victoria de los Angeles in the Montsalvatge Cradle Song, but there are not many more attractive Spanish song recitals than this, and it is beautifully recorded on both disc and cassette.

Bjoerling, Jussi (tenor)

'Grandi voci': PONCHIELLI: La Gioconda: Cielo e mar. PUCCINI: La Fanciulla del West: Ch'ella mi creda. Manon Lescaut: Tra voi belle. GIORDANO: Fedora: Amor ti vieta. CILEA: L'Arlesiana: Lamento ti Federico. VERDI: Un Ballo in maschera: Di' tu

se fedele. Requiem: Ingemisco. MAS-
CAGNI: *Cavalleria Rusticana: Tu
qui, Santuzza?* (with Tebaldi); *In-
tanto, amici . . . Brindisi; Mamma,
quel vino.* LEHÁR: *Das Land des Lächelns: Dein ist mein ganzes Herz.*
(M) **(*) Decca GRV 4.

John Culshaw's autobiography has
revealed what an unhappy man Jussi
Bjoerling was at the very end of his
career, when all these recordings were
made by Decca engineers for RCA. You
would hardly guess the problems from
the flow of headily beautiful, finely
focused tenor tone. These may not be the
most characterful renderings of each aria,
but they are all among the most compellingly musical. Fine recording for its
period.

Burrows, Stuart (tenor)

'Operetta favourites' (with Nat. PO,
Stapleton): LEHÁR: *Land of Smiles:
You are my heart's delight. Frederica:
O maiden, my maiden. Frasquita:
Farewell, my love. Paganini: Girls
were made to love and kiss. Czare-
vitch: Alone, always alone. Giuditta:
Comrades, this is the life for me.*
SIECZYNSKI: *Vienna . . . city of my
dreams.* ROMBERG: *The Student
Prince: Serenade.* TAUBER: *Old
Chelsea: My heart and I.* STOLZ:
Don't ask me why. NOVELLO: *Glam-
orous Night: Shine through my
dreams.* KUNNEKE: *The Cousin from
Nowhere: I'm only a strolling vaga-
bond.*
*** O-L DSLO/*KDSLC* 16.

'The simple joys of life' (with Const-
able, piano): TOURS: *Mother o' mine.*
RAY: *The sunshine of your smile.*
FOSTER: *I dream of Jeannie.* HAYDN
WOOD: *Roses of Picardy.* MAR-
SHALL: *I hear you calling me.* BALFE:
Come into the garden, Maud.
ADAMS: *The Star of Bethlehem.
Thora.* SANDERSON: *As I sit here.*
BUTTERFIELD: *When you and I were
young, Maggie.* DANKS: *Silver
threads among the gold.* YOUNG: *I
give thanks for you.* TRAD.: *Danny
boy.* HANDEL: *Silent worship.*
*** O-L DSLO/*KDSLC* 42.

'To the land of dreams' (with Const-
able, piano): AITKEN: *Maire, my girl.*
PURCELL, Edward: *Passing by.* DE
KOVEN: *Oh, promise me.* GREEN:
Gortnamona. COATES: *I heard you
singing.* MALLOY: *The Kerry dance.*
DEL RIEGO: *O dry those tears.* PENN:
Smilin' through. RASBACH: *Trees.*
WEATHERLY: *Parted.* LATHAM
SHARP: *Dearest of all.* DESMOND:
Sitting by the window. HARRISON: *In
the gloaming.* BALL: *Mother Mach-
ree.* MURRAY: *I'll walk beside you.*
*** O-L DSLO/*KDSLC* 43.

'Life's sweet melody' (with Constable, piano): NEWTON: *Somewhere a
voice is calling.* VAUGHAN WIL-
LIAMS: *Linden Lea.* RONALD: *Down
in the forest.* HUGHES: *The stuttering
lovers.* HEAD: *Little road to Bethlehem.* SOMERVELL: *The gentle
maiden.* TRAD.: *The lark in the clear
air.* CLUTSAM: *I know of two bright
eyes.* RAY: *God keep you is my prayer.*
PATERSON: *The garden where the
praties grow.* ELGAR: *Pleading.*
GRIEG: *I love thee.* O'CONNOR: *The
old house.* BARTLETT: *A dream.* FRO-
TERE: *For your dear sake.* WESTEN-
DORF: *I'll take you home again,
Kathleen.*
*** O-L DSLO/*KDSLC* 44.

With his headily beautiful tenor voice
and simple charm, Burrows makes an
excellent interpreter of popular songs like

these, whether from operetta, musical comedy, the English school or the straight ballad repertory. The sound is excellent and each record is valuable for its particular repertory. Especially recommendable is the selection on DSLO 16 in tribute to Richard Tauber; and the ballads are sung with an eloquent simplicity that disguises their sentimental underlay. All four collections are available on tape. The transfer of *KDSLC 16* is disappointing, the voice clear but the orchestra less well focused. *KDSLC 42* and *43* are both well managed, with good balance and natural vocal projection, but *KDSLC 44* is transferred at a very high level, which brings a degree of edginess at peaks.

Caballé, Montserrat (soprano)

Spanish songs (with Zanetti, piano): FALLA: *7 Canciones populares españolas*. GRANADOS: *Cancó d'amor*. *Elegia eternal*. *La maja y el ruiseñor*. *L'Ocell profeta*. TURINA: *Anhelos*. *Cantares*. *Farruca*. *Si con mis deseos*.
*** Decca SXL/*KSXC* 6888 [Lon. 26575/5-].

This gathers together a highly attractive group of the most popular Spanish songs. As an international opera star, Caballé may have been less closely associated with this repertory than such famous compatriots as Victoria de los Angeles and Teresa Berganza, but in their way her performances are just as happily idiomatic. First-rate recording.

'More Spanish songs' (with Zanetti, piano): GRANADOS: *La maja dolorosa*. FALLA: *Tus ojillos negros*. *Oración de las madres*. ALBÉNIZ: *Besa el aura*. *Del Salon*. OBRADOES: *Del cabello mas sutil*. *El Molondron*. *El vito*. *Aquel sombrero de monte*. VIVES: *El amor y los ojos*. *El retrato*

de Isabela. *Valgame Dios*. RODRIGO: *Cuatro madrigales amatorios*.
*** Decca SXL 6935 [Lon. 26617].

With its unusual repertory this makes an attractive companion disc for Caballé's collection of popular Spanish songs (see above). The second of the two Falla items here was for long buried; it is an anti-war song written in 1914. The vocal range in every sense is formidable, the artistry commanding, the voice consistently beautiful. First-rate recording.

Opera arias: MOZART: *Così fan tutte: Come scoglio*. VERDI: *I Masnadieri: Venerabile, o padre . . . Lo sguardo; Oh! ma la pace . . . Tu del mio Carlo*. *Il Corsaro: Ne sulla terra*. PUCCINI: *Tosca: Vissi d'arte*. DONIZETTI: *Lucia di Lammermoor: Eccola! . . . Il dolce suono* (Mad scene). *Elisabetta Regina d'Inghilterra: Indegno! Fellon, la pena avrai*.
*** Ph. 9500 358/*7300 740* [id.].

This fine collection of arias is taken from the complete opera recordings Caballé has made for Philips, and very impressive it is. The characterization may not be so sharp as with a Callas, but the beauty of vocalization is a delight, and some of the less well-known items – for example the final scene from *Elisabetta* – are among the finest of all. Only the *Lucia* excerpt lacks electricity. Consistently refined recording; and the cassette transfer is clear and vivid, with excellent orchestral detail. There is just a hint of hardness on the voice at peaks.

Callas, Maria (soprano)

Operatic recital: CILEA: *Adriana Lecouvreur: Ecco, respiro appena . . . Io son l'umile; Poveri fiori*. GIORDANO: *Andrea Chénier: La mamma morta*. CATALANI: *La Wally: Ebben?*

Ne andrò lontana. ROSSINI: *Il Barbiere di Siviglia: Una voce poco fa.* MEYERBEER: *Dinorah: Shadow song.* DELIBES *Lakmé: Bell song.* VERDI: *I Vespri siciliani: Bolero.*
(***) HMV mono ALP/*TC-ALP* 3824.

This is one of the classic Callas records, ranging extraordinarily wide in its repertory and revealing in every item the uniquely intense musical imagination that set musicians of every kind listening and learning. Coloratura flexibility here goes with dramatic weight; not all the items are equally successful (the *Shadow song* from *Dinorah*, for example, lacks charm), but these are all unforgettable performances. This mono reissue is well balanced and cleanly transferred, and the cassette transfer is excellent, clear and vivid, without hardness on top.

'*Mad scenes*' (with Philh. O., Rescigno): DONIZETTI: *Anna Bolena: Piangete voi; Al dolce guidami.* THOMAS: *Hamlet: A vos jeux; Partagez-vous mes fleurs; Et maintenant écoutez ma chanson.* BELLINI: *Il Pirata: Oh! s'io potessi . . . Col sorriso d'innocenza.*
*** HMV ASD/*TC-ASD* 3801 [Ang. S. 35764].

If, as ever, the rawness of exposed top notes mars the sheer beauty of Callas's singing, few recital records ever made can match, let alone outshine, this collection of mad scenes in vocal and dramatic imagination. This is Callas at her very peak; Desmond Shawe-Taylor suggested this as the record which more than any summed up the essence of Callas's genius. Twenty years after its original issue it reappeared at full price and is still worth every penny. Excellent recording for its period, and a very good cassette, the voice vibrant without peaking, the accompaniments telling and well balanced.

Carreras, José (tenor)

Zarzuela arias (with ECO, Ros-Marba): VIVES: *Dona Francisquita: Por el humo.* SOUTULLO: *El último romantico: Noche de amor.* SERRANO: *Alma de Dios: Canción hungara. La alegría del batallón: Canción guajira. Los de Aragón: Cuantas veces solo.* GUERRERO: *El huesped del sevillano: Raquel.* CHAPI: *La Bruja: Jota.* TÓRROBA: *Luisa Fernanda: De este apacible rincón de Madrid.* LUNA: *La pícara molinera: Paxarin, ru que vuelas.* GURIDI: *El Caserio: Romanza.*
*** Ph. 9500 649/*7300 751* [id.].

The *zarzuela* genre has yet to make its mark outside Spain, but a collection like this has many charms. Carreras draws out the often rather flimsy melodies most persuasively, and the recording is excellent. The cassette transfer is acceptable, but the sound lacks sparkle at the top.

Arias (with LSO, Lopez-Cobós): PUCCINI: *Manon Lescaut: Donna non vidi mai. Turandot: Nessun dorma.* LEONCAVALLO: *Zazà: O mio piccolo tavolo. I Pagliacci: Vesti la giubba. La Bohème: Testa adorata. I Zingari: Dammi un amore.* GIORDANO: *Andrea Chénier: Un dì all'azzurro spazio.* PONCHIELLI: *La Gioconda: Cielo e mar.* MASCAGNI: *L'Amico Fritz: Ed anche Beppe amò!* GOMES: *Fosca: Intenditi con Dio!* CILEA: *L'Arlesiana: E la solita storia.*
**(*) Ph. 9500 771/*7300 846* [id.].

Including some attractive rarities, this is an impressive recital. Carreras is never less than a conscientious artist, and though one or two items stretch the lovely voice to its limits, there is none of the coarseness that most tenors of the Italian school would indulge in. Excellent recording.

'*Canciones románticas*' (with ECO, Stapleton): PADILLA: *Valencia: Princesita.* LACALLE: *Amapola.* QUINTERO: *Morucha.* FREIRE: *Ay, Ay, Ay.* ALVAREZ: *La Partida.* SORIANO: *El Guitarrico.* GREVER: *Jurame.* PONCE: *Estrellita.* LÓPEZ: *Maitechu Mia.*
*** Ph. 9500/7300 894 [id.].

These songs have much in common with the popular Neapolitan repertoire, and some of them, such as *Valencia, Amapola* and Ponce's *Estrellita*, are as familiar as any of the Italian songs. They are vigorously and quite stylishly sung here by Carreras with an operatic manner that is robust rather than seeking any subtleties. But with good recording and sparkling accompaniments this is attractive enough. The tape transfer is well managed, lacking only the last degree of brightness in the orchestra, and kind to the voice

Neapolitan songs (with ECO, Muller): DENZA: *Funiculì, funiculà; I'te vurria vasà.* CARDILLO: *Core 'ngrato.* D'ANNIBALE: *'O paese d'o sole.* FALVO: *Dicitencello vuie.* LAMA: *Silenzio cantatore.* MARIO: *Santa Lucia luntana.* DI CURTIS: *Tu, ca nun chiagne! Torna a Surriento.* DI CAPUA: *'O sole mio.* BOVIO/ TAGLIAFERRI: *Passione.* CIOFFI: *'Na sera 'e maggio.* CANNIO: *'O surdato 'nnamurato.*
**(*) Ph. Dig. 9500/7300 943 [id.].

José Carreras produces refined tone here. The performances have plenty of lyrical fervour and are entirely lacking in vulgarity. The opening *Funiculì, funiculà* is attractively lilting, but elsewhere some listeners will wish for a more gutsy style.

The recording is first-class, and the chrome cassette transfer is smooth and full and kind to the voice.

Caruso, Enrico (tenor)

'*The complete Caruso*' (recordings processed by computer): *Vol. 4* (1906–7): arias and excerpts from: VERDI: *Il Trovatore; Aïda; La Forza del destino; Rigoletto.* FLOTOW: *Martha.* GOUNOD: *Faust.* PUCCINI: *La Bohème.* DONIZETTI: *La Favorita.* MEYERBEER: *L'Africana.* GIORDANO: *Andrea Chénier.* LEONCAVALLO: *I Pagliacci.* BIZET: *The Pearl Fishers.* Songs by BARTHELEMY; TOSTI.
*** RCA RL/RK 12766 [ARM 1/ARK 1 2766].

Vol. 5 (1908–9): arias and excerpts from: DONIZETTI: *Don Sebastiano; Lucia di Lammermoor.* VERDI: *Rigoletto; Il Trovatore; Aïda.* PUCCINI: *Madama Butterfly; La Bohème; Tosca.* Songs by BARTHELEMY; PECCIA; TOSTI.
*** RCA RL/RK 12767 [ARM 1/ARK 1 2767].

Vol. 6 (1909–10): arias and excerpts from: VERDI: *La Forza del destino; Aïda; Il Trovatore.* GOLDMARK: *Queen of Sheba.* BIZET: *Carmen.* MEYERBEER: *Les Huguenots.* GOUNOD: *Faust.* RUSSO: Song: *Mamma mia.*
*** RCA RL/RK 13373 [ARM 1/ARK 1 3373].

Vol. 7 (1910): arias and excerpts from: FLOTOW: *Martha.* GOUNOD: *Faust.* FRANCHETTI: *Germania.* PONCHIELLI: *La Gioconda.* PUCCINI: *Madama Butterfly.* VERDI: *Otello.* MASCAGNI: *Cavalleria Rusticana.* LEONCAVALLO: *I Pagliacci.*
*** RCA RL/RK 13374 [ARM 1/ARK 1 3374].

These four issues, phenomenally well transferred with the help of digital techniques that seek to eliminate the unwanted resonances of an acoustic horn, are the first to appear in RCA's projected complete Caruso series. Each covers a specific year or years of Caruso's recording career, so that one can appreciate the range of his achievement, with lighter songs providing variety. The opera recordings do not offer arias alone and it is good to hear such singers as Homer and Scotto, who join Caruso in the *Rigoletto Quartet* (*Bella figlia*) in *Volume 4*, and also Melba, in the duet *O soave fanciulla* from *Bohème*. *Volume 5* includes the *Lucia di Lammermoor Sextet* (with Sembrich, Severina, Daddi, Scotti and Journet), another version of *Bella figlia* (with three of the same team), and the Act 3 *Bohème Quartet* (with Farrar, Viafora and Scotti). *Volume 6* includes excerpts from *Faust*, with Farrar, Journet, Scotti and Homer. Choice between these albums must be left to individual taste; each contains specially valuable items. The cassettes are smoothly transferred but have not quite the same freshness on top as the discs, although they still convey the improvement in the recording of the vocal timbre.

Choral music

'*Great choral classics*' (sung by various artists): excerpts from: HANDEL: *Messiah.* BERLIOZ: *L'Enfance du Christ. Requiem.* BACH: *Cantata 147. St Matthew Passion.* FAURÉ, VERDI, MOZART: *Requiems.* POULENC: *Gloria.* ORFF: *Carmina Burana.* VIVALDI: *Gloria.* GOUNOD: *St Cecilia Mass.* BRAHMS: *German Requiem.* WALTON: *Belshazzar's Feast.* MENDELSSOHN: *Elijah.* BEETHOVEN: *Missa solemnis.* PURCELL: *Rejoice in the Lord.*
(B) ** EMI *TC2-MOM 116.*

A wide-ranging programme, quite imaginatively selected as entertainment for the car. The changing acoustics and degrees of reverberation bring less variation than might be expected in clarity of focus. Even the *Dies irae* from the Berlioz *Requiem* (surely ideal for playing in a traffic jam) avoids congestion. The opening excerpts from *Messiah* sound a little dry, and it is a pity that Muti's (rather than Previn's) *O fortuna* from *Carmina Burana* was chosen, as the quieter moments lack clarity in the tape version. Also the King's acoustic in *Jesu, joy of man's desiring* brings a rather mushy choral quality. Highlights include the *Sanctus* from Muti's Verdi *Requiem*, the delightful *Shepherd's chorus* from *L'Enfance du Christ* and the vivid *Praise ye the God of Gold* from Previn's *Belshazzar's Feast.* Purcell's anthem *Rejoice in the Lord* is heard complete.

Cons. of Musicke, Rooley

'*Le Chansonnier Cordiforme*' (collection of 43 songs from the second half of the fourteenth century): includes songs by BARBINGANT, BEDYNGHAM, BINCHOIS, BUSNOIS, CARON, DUFAY, DUNSTABLE, FYRE, GHIZEGHEM, MORTON, OCKEGHEM, REGIS, VINCENET.
*** O-L D 186 D 4 (4).

'Cordiform' means 'in the shape of a heart', and that is literally what this superb collection of songs looked like in manuscript. Dufay, Dunstable and Binchois provide the core of the collection, here given with freshness in the manner which characterizes the work of this consort. The original compiler of the anthology knew what he was doing. This is a beautiful collection which, with fine balance of discreet instrumental accompaniment against stylish singing, is consistently refreshing. A superb achievement, beautifully recorded.

'The world of early music': OBRECHT: Ich dragne de Mütse Clutse. ISAAC: La la hö hö. BUSNOIS: Spinacino: Je ne fay plus. TROMBONCINO: Ostinato vo'sequire. Hor ch'el ciel e la terra. DALZA: Pavana and Piva ferrarese. TIBURTINO: La sol fa mi fa (ricercare). AZZAIOLO: Sentemi la formicula. ANON./PACOLONI: La bella Franceschina. GUAMI: La Brillantina. RONTANI: Nerinda bella. COMPERE: Virgo celesti. ANON.: Belle tenez moy. La triquoteé. Mignon allons. Christ der ist estanden. Elslein liebes Elslein. The shooting of the guns (pavan). Le rossignol. SERMISY: Las je my plains. LE JEUNE: Fière cruelle. FORSTER: Vitrum nostrum gloriosum. DE LA TORRE: La Spagna; Adoramos te, señor. FAYRFAX: I love, loved. ANON./WYATT: Blame not my lute. ANON./EDWARDES: Where grypinge griefs. ALISON: Dolorosa pavan.
(M) *** Decca SPA/KCSP 547.

This is a quite outstanding medium-priced collection for those wanting a sampler of one current view of authentic performance of early music. The selection is generous and enterprising, and it offers much that is piquant and ear-catching both vocally and instrumentally. Penguin Books have published independently a splendid and beautifully illustrated paperback which acts as a companion to this issue, but of course it can be readily enjoyed with the notes provided with the record or the cassette (which is vividly transferred and quite the equal of the disc).

Domingo, Placido (tenor)

'Portrait'; VERDI: Giovanna d'Arco: Sotto una quercia parvemi ... Pondo è letal. Un Ballo in maschera: La rivedra nell'estasi; Dì tu se fedele; Forse la sogliu ... Ma se m'è forza. Don Carlo: Fontainebleau Foresta immense ... Io la vidi. Aïda: Se quel guerrier io fossi ... Celeste Aïda. GOUNOD: Faust: Quel trouble inconnu ... Salut! demeure. BOITO: Mefistofele: Dai campi, dai prati. PUCCINI: Manon Lescaut: Tra voi belle; Donna non vidi mai; Ah, Manon, mi tradisce. Tosca: Dammi i colori ... Recondita armonia; E lucevan le stelle.
**(*) HMV ASD/TC-ASD 4031 [Ang. S/4XS 37835].

These thirteen arias from various EMI sources give a marvellous display of glorious heroic tenor tone with no coarseness. But the collection does bring home the closeness with which EMI engineers have tended to record Domingo's voice, and the result overall is a little heavy, even in an aria as slight as Des Grieux's Tra voi belle. Also some of the excerpts end a little abruptly, notably the closing E lucevan le stelle from Tosca. The cassette is just as vivid as the disc.

'Gala opera concert' (with LAPO, Giulini): DONIZETTI: L'Elisir d'amore: Una furtiva lagrima. Lucia di Lammermoor: Tomba degli avi miei ... Fra poco. VERDI: Ernani: Mercè, diletti amici ... Come rugiada; Dell'esilio nel dolore ... O tu che l'alma adora. Il Trovatore: Ah sì, ben mio; Di quella pira. Aïda: Se quel guerrier io fossi ... Celeste Aïda. HALÉVY: La Juive: Rachel, quand du Seigneur. MEYERBEER: L'Africaine: Pays merveilleux ... O Paradis. BIZET: Les Pêcheurs de perles: Je crois entendre encore. Carmen: La fleur que tu m'avais jetée (with R. Wagner Chorale).
*** DG Dig. 2532/3302 009 [id.].

Recorded in 1980 in connection with a gala in San Francisco, this is as noble and resplendent a tenor recital as you will find. Domingo improves in detail even on the fine versions of some of these arias he had recorded earlier, and the finesse of the whole gains greatly from the sensitive direction of Giulini, though the orchestra is a little backward. Otherwise excellent recording, and the chrome transfer is first-rate too, with tingling digital brass in the *Aïda* excerpt; however, the sound has a more dramatic range on side two than side one (with a rise in level).

Early Music Cons. of L., Munrow

'*Music at the Court of Maximilian I*': SENFL: *Mit Lust tritt ich an diesen Tanz. Ich stuend an einem Morgen. Das Gläut zu Speyer. Meniger Stellt nach Geld. Gottes Namen. Ach Elslein. Ich weiss nit. Entlaubet ist der Walde. Was wird es doch. Quis dabit oculis nostris.* ANON.: *Welsh dance.* KOTTER: *Kochesperger Spaniel.* ANON.: *Christ ist erstanden.* ISAAC: *Innsbruck, ich muss dich lassen. Helogierons ous. Maudit soyt. La Mora.* FINCK: *Sauff aus und machs nit lang.* KEUTZENHOFF: *Frisch und frölich wölln wir leben.*
(M) *** Decca Ser. SA/KSC 6.

Maximilian I was inordinately vain. He was also shrewd enough to realize that lavish patronage of the arts would ensure that posterity would remember him. His dedicated support meant that the decade between 1486 and 1496 became a watershed for the medieval development of the German Lied. Clearly the mid-century had been dominated by the music of Ludwig Senfl (who died about 1555) and Senfl's music is rightly given the lion's share of this excellent collection. To sample the individuality of Senfl's musical personality

try band four on side one, the piquant bell ringers' trio, *Das Gläut zu Speyer*. In variety of arrangement and sophistication of presentation this record represents the zenith of the achievement of David Munrow and his Consort. It was recorded in 1973 as part of a series of records for Argo, three of which (including this one) are also available in an outstanding boxed set, *Festival of early music* (D 40 D 3/*K 40 K 33*). There, as here, the sound is strikingly lively and vivid, with little to choose between disc and cassette.

'*The art of David Munrow*': 1, *Munrow as soloist*; 2, *Film music* (inc. SUSATO, CORELLI, PRAETORIUS); 3, *The small consort* (inc. HANDEL, PURCELL, DUFAY); 4, *The large consort* (inc. PURCELL, PRAETORIUS, DUFAY); 5, *Sacred Music* (inc. BACH, JOSQUIN DES PRÉS); 6, *Secular dance music* (HOLBORNE, SUSATO, PRAETORIUS).
(M) *** HMV SLS/*TC-SLS* 5136 (3).

The music chosen by EMI to represent the achievement of the late David Munrow is divided into six separate groups, each carefully balanced to make a diverse and enjoyable miniature concert in itself. In the first collection Munrow himself leads. The second group, music for films, includes his own compositions and arrangements. The programme for small consort is particularly attractive, ranging from Josquin's *El Grillo* and Solange's *Fumeux fume* ('He who fumes and lets off steam'), with its bizarre accompaniment for bass kortholt and bass rebec, to expressive and lively items by Purcell and Dufay. These composers are also memorably featured in the section for large consort (Dufay's Mass *Se la face ay pale* a highlight). The sacred music is balanced by the closing secular dances, with admirable invention from Holborne and Praetorius, always imaginatively and sometimes exotically scored.

The recording is of demonstration quality on disc and tape alike.

'*Music of the Gothic era*': LEONIN: *Viderunt omnes.* VITRY: *Impudenter – Virtutibus laudabilis.* ANON.: *Clap clap – Sus Robin.* MACHAUT: *Christe, qui lux es – Veni, creator spiritus. Hoquetus David. Lasse! – Se j'aime mon loyal ami – Pour quoy.* ROYLLART: *Rex Karole – Leticie.*
(M) *** DG 2547/*3347* 051 [from Arc. 2710 019].

Munrow's choice here (extracted from a three-disc survey, DG Arc. 2723 045) covers a period of two centuries, from Leonin's organum to the *Rex Karole* of Philippe Royllart, dating from the second half of the fourteenth century. Munrow projects this music with expressive liveliness. Its presentation is essentially conjectural, but to bring the music back to life is the most important thing, and Munrow certainly does that. The recording is excellent, with a good equivalent cassette.

Ely Cath. Ch., Wills

'*Service high and anthems clear*' (with le Prevost, organ): WESLEY, Samuel: *Exultate Deo.* WESLEY, S. S.: *Blessed be the God and Father.* STAINER: *Evening canticles in B flat.* ATTWOOD: *Come, Holy Ghost.* PARRY: *I was glad.* STANFORD: *Evening canticles in G.* WOOD, Charles: *O Thou, the central Orb.*
*** Hyp. Dig. A/*KA* 66012.

An outstanding demonstration of what well-balanced digital recording can offer in cathedral music. While not detracting from the natural overall blend, inner detail is remarkably clear and the choral tone has a fresh incisiveness to give all this music splendid life and vigour.

Parry's *I was glad* is superbly done, and the opening *Exultate Deo* makes an equally strong impression. The canticle settings of Stainer and Stanford are memorable and the concert closes with *O Thou, the central Orb*, showing Charles Wood at his most eloquently expressive. This is highly recommendable in every respect, and the cassette – transferred at an impressively high level – is excellent too, though there is a hint of pulsing on two fortissimo cadences.

Evans, Geraint (baritone)

'*Operatic recital*' (with SRO, Balkwill): HANDEL: *Berenice: Si, tra i ceppi. Semele: Leave me, radiant light.* MOZART: *Le Nozze di Figaro: Non più andrai. Don Giovanni: Madamina* (Catalogue aria). *Die Zauberflöte: Ein Vogelfänger. L'Oca del Cairo: Ogni momento.* BEETHOVEN: *Fidelio: Ach, welch ein Augenblick.* LEONCAVALLO: *Pagliacci: Si, puo.* DONIZETTI: *Don Pasquale: Un fuoco insolito.* VERDI: *Otello: Vanne . . . Credo in un Dio crudel. Falstaff: Ehi! paggio . . . L'onore.* BRITTEN: *A Midsummer Night's Dream: When my cue comes* (Bottom's dream). MUSSORGSKY: *Boris Godunov: Pravoslaviye.*
(M) *** Decca Jub. JB/*KJBC* 60.

This is a marvellous display of wide-ranging virtuosity, of artistic bravura such as we know from almost any performance that this ebullient and lovable singer gives. Part of Evans's mastery lies in the way he can convey the purest comedy, even draw laughs without ever endangering the musical line through excessive buffoonery. His Mozart characters are almost unmatchable – Figaro, Leporello, Papageno – while it is good to be reminded that here is a singer who can be a formidable Iago as well as the most complete Falstaff of the day. Good accompaniment and recording, and one of Decca's highest-quality cassettes, vivid vocally and with a richly atmospheric orchestral backing. Occasionally the microphone – and this is equally noticeable on ·disc and tape – catches a slightly gritty quality in the tone, but this is not serious enough to withhold the strongest recommendation for this representation of one of the greatest British singers of our generation at the peak of his form.

Ferrier, Kathleen (contralto)

MAHLER: *Das Lied von der Erde; 3 Rückert songs* (with Patzak, VPO, Walter). HANDEL: *Judas Maccabaeus: Father of Heaven. Messiah: He was despised; O thou that tellest. Samson: Return, O God of hosts.* BACH: *Mass in B min.: Agnus Dei; Qui sedes. St John Passion: All is fulfilled. St Matthew Passion: Grief for sin* (with LPO, Boult). SCHUMANN: *Frauenliebe und Leben, Op. 42.* SCHUBERT: *Die junge Nonne. Romance. Du liebst mich nicht. Der Tod und das Mädchen. Suleika. Du bist die Ruh'.* BRAHMS: *Immer leise. Der Tod das ist die Kühle Nacht. Botschaft. Von ewiger Liebe* (with Walter, piano). GLUCK: *Orfeo: What is life.* HANDEL: *Rodelinda: Art thou troubled.* MENDELSSOHN: *Elijah: O rest in the Lord.* SCHUBERT: *Gretchen am Spinnrade. An die Musik. Der Musensohn.* WOLF: *Verborgenheit. Der Gärtner. Auf ein altes Bild. Auf einer Wanderung.* TRAD.: *The Keel Row. Ma bonny lad. Blow the wind southerly. Willow, willow. Ye banks and braes. Drink to me only. Lover's curse* (with Spurr, piano). BRIDGE: *Go not, happy day.* Arr. BRITTEN: *Come you not from Newcastle.* Arr. HUGHES: *Kitty my love.* STANFORD: *The fairy lough.* VAUGHAN WILLIAMS: *Silent noon* (with Stone, piano). TRAD.: *Ca' the yowes* (with Newmark, piano).
(***) Decca *K 160 K 54* (4).

A Kathleen Ferrier anthology on tape is most welcome (there is an even more comprehensive album of seven discs, Decca AFK 1–7), and the selection here readily demonstrates not only the amazing range but the consistency with which her radiant vocal quality lit up almost everything she recorded. The transfers have been, for the most part, well done to minimize the inadequacies of the originals, although unfortunately Mahler's *Das Lied von der Erde* suffers from the restriction of high frequencies that marred the separate cassette issue; the voice is unimpaired but the orchestra is muffled. The *Rückert Lieder*, however, emerge unscathed and are among the finest treasures here. Some of the older recordings (especially those with Bruno Walter at the piano) are also restricted, but not unacceptably so. Yet even earlier records yield a fresher sound (a highlight is Schubert's *An die Musik*, recorded with Phillis Spurr). The Bach and Handel arias (also available separately – see the composer index above) have Boult's overlaid stereo orchestral accompaniments. But among the most refreshing items here are the folksongs, sung with a simple innocence that few other singers have approached.

'The singer and the person' (with Pears, Britten, Moore, Walter, Winifred Ferrier) including songs by: BRAHMS, PARRY, SCHUBERT, BERKELEY; excerpts from GLUCK: *Orfeo,* BRITTEN: *The Rape of Lucretia;* and the singer's own autobiographical and musical comments.
(***) BBC mono REGL/ZCF 368.

In every way this is an effective and moving tribute, including as it does Kathleen Ferrier's own spoken comments and contributions from Bruno Walter among others. There is a good deal of music; most of the recordings are primitive (the *Four Poems of St Teresa of Avila* by Lennox Berkeley, which ends the recital, sounds very scratchy), but the excerpt from *The Rape of Lucretia* is especially valuable.

Freni, Mirella (soprano), Luciano Pavarotti (tenor)

'*In concert*': VERDI: *La Traviata: Brindisi; Parigi o cara. I Vespri siciliani: Bolero.* PONCHIELLI: *La Gioconda: Cielo e mar.* DONIZETTI: *La Figlia del regimento: Convien partir. L'Elisir d'amore: Una parola ... chiedi all'aura.* MEYERBEER: *L'Africana: O paradiso.* BOITO: *Mefistofele: L'altra notte.* MASCAGNI: *L'Amico Fritz: Suzel, buon dì.* MASSENET: *Werther: Pourquoi me réveiller.*

(M) **(*) Decca Ace SDD/*KSDC* 578 [Lon. 41009].

Both artists come from the same small town in Italy, Modena, where they were born in 1935. The happiness of their musical partnership in these concert performances, recorded live, comes out in each of the duets, to which are added some attractive solo performances. The *Werther* and *Africana* items are both new to Pavarotti's repertory; sweet singing from Freni too, though her delivery could be more characterful. The recording is robust, forward and clear – on both disc and cassette – but not especially refined. Some might find the vociferous applause irritating.

Freni, Mirella, Renata Scotto (sopranos)

'*In duet*' (with Nat. PO, Magiera or Ansielmi): MERCADANTE: *Le due illustri rivali: Leggo già nel vostro cor.* BELLINI: *Bianca e Fernando: Ove son; Che m'avvenne ... Sorgi o padre. Norma: Dormono entrambi ... Mira, o Norma.* MOZART: *Le Nozze di Figaro: Cosa mi narri ... Sull'aria.*
**(*) Decca SXL/*KSXC* 6970.

The Mozart will win no award for style, but otherwise this is a fascinating celebration of the charms and vocal beauty of two singers who might have been thought too alike to make good duetists. Scotto by her latterday standards is in excellent voice, with the top more perfectly under control if occasionally squally. This account of the big *Norma* scene (ending with *Mira, o Norma*) is more relaxed and delicate than the one to which Scotto contributed in the complete CBS set of the opera. The other Bellini item is also most welcome, with its dreamy melody in compound time, and so is the even rarer Mercadante duet, with its traditional chains of thirds. Warm and atmospheric recording, with a matching high-level tape transfer.

'Italian opera favourites'

LEONCAVALLO: *I Pagliacci: Prologue* (Gobbi); *Vesti la giubba* (Corelli). PUCCINI: *La Bohème: Sì, mi chiamano Mimì; Una terribil tosse* (Freni, Gedda). *Madama Butterfly: Love duet; Flower duet; Humming chorus* (Bjoerling, Los Angeles, Pirazzini, Rome Op. Ch., Santini). *Manon Lescaut: Donna non vidi mai* (Fernandi); *In quelle trine morbide* (Cavalli). *Turandot: In questa reggia* (Shuard). VERDI: *Il Trovatore: Di quella pira* (Corelli); *Soldiers' chorus* (Rome Op. Ch., Schippers). *Aïda: Qui*

Radames verra! . . . O patria mia
(Cavalli); *Ritorna vincitor* (Shuard).
*Rigoletto: Questa o quella; La donna è
mobile* (Fernandi); *Caro nome*
(Grist); *Zitti zitti* (Rome Op. Ch.,
Molinari-Pradelli); *Bella figlia*
(Grist, Gedda, Di Stasio, MacNeil).
Otello: Ave Maria (Gwyneth Jones).
MASCAGNI: *Cavalleria Rusticana:
Mamma, mamma* (Fernando). BEL-
LINI: *I Puritani: A te, o cara*
(Corelli).
(B) ** EMI *TC2-MOM 120*.

Recorded loudly and vibrantly, at
times rather fiercely, for maximum impact in the car, this is a generous collection of operatic purple patches. The
finest performances come from Gobbi
(*Pagliacci*), Freni as Mimì, Gwyneth
Jones in *Otello* and the excellent excerpts
from the Los Angeles/Bjoerling set of
Madama Butterfly. Corelli makes several
appearances, and his singing is best described as lusty.

Kanawa, Kiri Te (soprano)

Recital (with Amner, piano): SCHU-
BERT: *Nacht und Träume. Gretchen
am Spinnrade. Rastlose Liebe.* SCHU-
MANN: *Du bist wie eine Blume. Stille
Tränen. Soldatenbraut.* WOLF: *Blum-
engrüss. Kennst du das Land.* FAURÉ:
Après un rêve. Nell. DUPARC: *L'invi-
tation au voyage. Le manoir. Au pays
où se fait la guerre.* WALTON:
*Daphne. Through gilded trellises. Old
Sir Faulk.*
**(*) CBS 76868/40-.

A fascinating and wide-ranging recital
reflecting Kiri Te Kanawa's live concerts. It is good to have the Walton songs,
and the rag music of *Old Sir Faulk* is delightfully characterful. For the rest the
singing is tasteful, but faced with the
microphone Kiri Te Kanawa presents her

performances with a degree less 'face'
than we know from her in the concert
hall. It is perhaps a pity that slow and
gentle songs predominate, but with the
beauty of the voice well caught, this is
still a delightful record, and one of CBS's
best cassettes, with the voice naturally
transferred and the piano timbre truthful.

King's College Ch., Ledger

'A Festival of lessons and carols'
(1979).
*** HMV ASD/*TC-ASD* 3778.

This most recent version on record of
the annual King's College ceremony has
the benefit of modern recording, even
more atmospheric than before. Under
Philip Ledger the famous choir keeps its
beauty of tone and incisive attack. The
issue of this record and cassette celebrates a golden jubilee, for these carol
services started in 1919. The opening
processional, *Once in Royal David's
city*, is as effective as ever, and this
remains a unique blend of liturgy
and music. The cassette brings the advantage of an almost silent background,
but is not quite as refined in focus as the
disc.

*'Procession with carols on Advent
Sunday'.*
*** HMV Dig. ASD/*TCC-ASD* 3907.

This makes an attractive variant to
the specifically Christmas-based service,
though the carols themselves are not
quite so memorable. Beautiful singing
and richly atmospheric recording; the
wide dynamic range is demonstrated
equally effectively by the atmospheric
opening and processional and the sumptuous closing hymn. The chrome cassette
handles this almost as impressively as the
digital disc.

King's College Ch., Ledger and Will-cocks

'Choral favourites': HANDEL: Messiah: Hallelujah chorus. BACH: Jesu, joy of man's desiring. HAYDN: The Creation: The heavens are telling. PURCELL: Rejoice in the Lord (anthem). SCHUBERT: Psalm 23. FAURÉ: Requiem: Sanctus. ELGAR: Coronation Ode: Land of hope and glory. DELIUS: To be sung of a summer night on the water. VAUGHAN WILLIAMS: O clap your hands (motet). BRITTEN: St Nicholas: Birth of Nicholas. ANON.: There is no rose. HARRIS: Faire is the heaven. WOOD: Hail, gladdening light. DYKES: Holy, holy, holy.
(M) *** HMV SXLP/TC-SXLP 30308.

This collection of choral lollipops, beautifully sung and atmospherically recorded, makes a most desirable medium-price reissue. The second side is especially attractive, with the sumptuous Elgar excerpt followed by music by Delius, Vaughan Williams and Britten, each full of character and acting as a foil to what precedes it. The sound is consistently excellent on disc, more variable in focus on cassette, though always acceptable.

King's College Ch., Willcocks

'Festival of King's': ALLEGRI: Miserere (with Goodman, treble). PALESTRINA: Stabat Mater. GIBBONS: This is the record of John. BYRD: Mass in 4 parts. CROFT: Burial service. TALLIS: O nata lux. Videte miraculum. VIVALDI: Magnificat. BACH: Jesu, priceless treasure, BWV 227. St John Passion: Rest calm, O body pure and holy; Lord Jesu, thy dear angel send. BLOW: God spake sometime in visions. PURCELL: Hear my prayer, O Lord. HANDEL: The King shall rejoice. Chandos anthem: The Lord is my light. VAUGHAN WILLIAMS: Fantasia on Christmas carols (with Hervey Allen). HOLST: Lullay my liking. ORDE: Adam lay ybounden. TRAD. (arr. Shaw): Coventry carol. HOWELLS: Collegium Regale: Te Deum; Jubilate.
(M) *** Argo D 148 D 4 (4)/K 148 K 43.

An admirable collection of vintage King's recordings, opening with the famous version of Allegri's Miserere (Roy Goodman the superb treble soloist). Other highlights include Palestrina's Stabat Mater, Vivaldi's Magnificat and Vaughan Williams's delightful Carol fantasia. The sound is first-class and generally the cassettes match the discs closely, although some slight rebalancing may be needed. (This is the record of John is very forwardly recorded, which produces some temporary loss of refinement on tape.)

'Hymns from King's' (with Preston, organ): Hark! A thrilling voice is sounding. There is a green hill far away. According to Thy gracious word. Drop, drop, slow tears. When I survey the wondrous cross. Glory be to Jesus. Up! Awake! From highest steeple (Wachet auf). Break forth, O beauteous heavenly light. On Jordan's bank the Baptist's cry. Abide with me. Holy Father, cheer our way. Glory to Thee, my God, this night. The day Thou gavest, Lord, is ended. O come, O come, Emmanuel.
(M) *** Argo SPA/KCSP 553.

The King's style in hymns is more restrained than that of some other recorded collections; it is the opposite of the 'Huddersfield Choral Society' approach. The

959

recording is admirably faithful and atmospheric, with the tape transfer lacking just a little of the upper range of the disc.

'The World of King's', Vol. 2: Once in Royal David's city. TALLIS: Salvator mundi. HANDEL: Chandos anthem: O praise the Lord. Ode for St Cecilia's Day: As from the power (finale). BYRD: Mass for 5 voices: Sanctus; Benedictus. BACH: St John Passion: Rest calm; Lord Jesu, thy dear angel send. Magnificat: Opening chorus. TAVERNER: Dum transisset sabbatum. PURCELL: Hear my prayer, O Lord. HAYDN: Mass No. 9 in D min. (Nelson): Kyrie. PALESTRINA: Hodie Beata Virgo.
(M) *** Argo SPA/KCSP 590.

An excellent follow-up to Volume 1 (Argo SPA/KCSP 245, which includes Allegri's Miserere, excerpts from Vivaldi's Gloria, and works by Bach, Byrd and Gibbons), this sampler centres on an earlier musical period than the HMV compilation (see above). The range of the King's achievement is readily demonstrated by listening to both discs side by side. The highlights here include the Byrd and Taverner items, the excerpts from the Haydn Mass and the sparkling closing chorus from Handel's Ode for St Cecilia's Day. Excellent sound on disc, but the quality of the cassette is uneven, with the focus sometimes rather blurred.

King's Singers

'Victorian collection': BRIDGE: The goslings. SUTTON: Come sweet Marguerite. PINSUTI: Goodnight beloved. HOBBS: Phyllis is my only joy. Arr. PEARSALL: Waters of Elle. CLARKE: Street music. CALKIN: Breathe soft ye winds. MARTIN: Let maids be false, so wine be true. SULLIVAN: The long day closes. MACY: Jenk's vegetable compound. BARNBY: Home they brought the warrior dead. STEVENS: All my sense thy sweetness gained. HATTON: The way to build a boat, or, Jack's opinion. He that hath a pleasant face. The letter. LESLIE: Charm me asleep. PEARSALL: Light of my soul. ROGERS: Hears not my Phyllis.
*** HMV ASD/TC-ASD 3865.

The polish and stylishness of the King's Singers are admirably employed in these period-piece items, most of them hauntingly sentimental. First-rate recording. However, those wanting a single sample of this talented group would do even better with the generous Portrait on HMV Greensleeve (below).

'A portrait': PASSEREAU: Il est bel et bon. WILLAERT: Allons. CERTON: La, la, la, je ne l'ose dire. MORLEY: Now is the month of maying. FARMER: Fair Phyllis I saw. A little pretty bonny lass. WEELKES: The nightingale. DE WERT: Valle, che de' lamenti. LASSUS: Matona, mia cara. JANNEQUIN: Au joly jeu. GRIEG: Kvaalin's Halling. MARTIN: Puppet on a string. TRAD.: The Mermaid. BYRD: Ave verum corpus. PATTERSON: Time piece. Arr. SARGENT: Mary had a baby. GLASSER: Lalela Zulu (Ilihubo; Uhambo ngesitimela). HASSLER: Tänzen und springen. MACY: Jenk's vegetable compound. SULLIVAN: The long day closes.
(M) *** HMV Green. ESD/TC-ESD 7103.

A remarkably generous medium-priced sampler of the King's style in a wide variety of music, from early madrigals, sung with superb understanding and polish, to more popular repertoire including the lively *Puppet on a string* and the delightful tale of *The Mermaid*. Patterson's *Time piece* represents the avantgarde, quite imaginative and a *tour de force* as a performance. The programme ends appropriately with a balmily sweet – but not cloying – arrangement of Sullivan's *The long day closes*. The recording is excellent; the cassette loses only a little of the upper-range sharpness.

`Kirkby, Emma (soprano), Cons. of Musicke, Rooley

'*Madrigals and wedding songs for Diana*' (with David Thomas, bass): BENNET: *All creatures now are merry-minded.* CAMPION: *Now hath Flora robbed her bowers. Move now measured sound. Woo her and win her.* LUPO: *Shows and nightly revels. Time that leads the fatal round.* GILES: *Triumph now with joy and mirth.* CAVENDISH: *Come, gentle swains.* DOWLAND: *Welcome, black night . . . Cease these false sports.* WEELKES: *Hark! all ye lovely saints. As Vesta was.* WILBYE: *Lady Oriana.* EAST: *Hence stars! too dim of light. You meaner beauties.* LANIER: *Bring away this sacred tree. The Marigold. Mark how the blushful morn.* COPERARIO: *Go, happy man. While dancing rests. Come ashore, merry mates.* GIBBONS, Ellis: *Long live fair Oriana.*
*** Hyp. A 66019.

Quite the most imaginative of all the records prompted by the royal wedding, this wholly delightful anthology celebrates earlier royal occasions, aristocratic weddings, and in its choice of Elizabethan madrigals skilfully balances praise of the Virgin Queen with a less ambivalent attitude to nuptial delights. Emma Kirkby is at her freshest and most

captivating, and David Thomas, if not quite her match, makes an admirable contribution. Accompaniments are stylish and well balanced, and the recording is altogether first-rate.

'*Amorous dialogues*' (with Hill, tenor): BARTLET: *Whither runneth my sweetheart.* FERRABOSCO: *Fayre cruell nimph. Tell me, O love.* MORLEY: *Who is it that this dark night.* FORD: *Shut not sweet breast.* LAWES: *A dialogue on a kiss: Among thy fancies. A dialogue betwixt time and a pilgrimme: Aged man that moves these fields.* GAGLIANO: *Bel pastor.* D'INDIA: *Da l'onde del mio pianto.* FERRARI: *Dialogo a due, Fileno e Lidia: Amar io ti consiglio. Amanti io vi so.* FONTEI: *Dio ti salvi, pastor.* MONTEVERDI: *Bel pastor.*
*** O-L DSLO 587.

'*Duetti da camera*' (with Nelson, soprano): NOTARI: *Intenerite voi, lagrime mie.* D'INDIA: *Alla guerra d'amore. La mia filli crudel. La virtù.* VALENTINI: *Vanne, O carta amorosa.* FRESCOBALDI: *Maddalena alla Croce.* GRANDI: *Spine care e soavi.* FONTEI: *Fortunato cantore.* ROVETTA: *Chi vuol haver felice e lieto il core. Io mi sento morir.* MONTEVERDI: *O come sei gentile.* SABBATINI: *Udite, O selve. Fulmina de la bocca.*
*** O-L DSLO 588.

These two records were issued separately but make an obvious pair, both concentrating on duets popular in the seventeenth century. For today's ears the repertoire is exceedingly rare; most of it is previously unrecorded. Almost every item is rewarding, although (obviously enough) the duo of soprano and tenor offers more dramatic contrast, as well as greater variety of timbre. Indeed DSLO 587 is the record to start with; its anticipations of Italian *opera buffa* are matched by the colourful settings of Morley and Lawes. But DSLO 588 also offers much that is effective and appealing, notably the contributions from Monteverdi, Frescobaldi and Sabbatini. Both issues are characteristically well documented and the accompaniments are stylishly authentic, as one would expect with Anthony Rooley in charge.

London Pro Cantione Antiqua, Turner

'*The flowering of Renaissance polyphony*': DUNSTABLE: *Veni sancte spiritus.* DUFAY: *Flos florum. Ave virgo quae de caelis. Alma redemptoris mater.* BINCHOIS: *Agnus Dei.* BUSNOIS: *Missa L'Homme armé.* OCKEGHEM: *Missa pro defunctis.* OBRECHT: *Salve crux.* JOSQUIN DES PRÉS: *Missa L'Homme armé super voces musicales. La Déploration sur la mort de Johan Okeghem. Huc me sydereo.* DE LA RUE: *Laudate Dominum. Pater de caelis. Salve Regina.* ISAAC: *Quis dabit capiti meo aquam. Regina caeli laetari.* BRUMEL: *O Domine Jesu Christe. Noe noe.* MOUTON: *Quaeramus cum pastoribus.* COMPERE: *Crux triumphans.* GOMBERT: *Ave Regina. Musae Jovis.* DE MORALES: *Magnificat. Emendemus in melius. Lamentabatur Jacob.* ARCADELT: *O pulcherrima mulierum.* WILLAERT: *In convertendo.* CLEMENS NON PAPA: *Pastores loquebantur.* DE RORE: *O Altitudo divitiarum.* HANDEL: *Canite tuba in Sion.* DE MONTE: *O suavitas et dulcedo.* LASSUS: *Miserere mei, Deus.* PALESTRINA: *Oratio Jeremiae Prophetae. Sicut cervus desiderat. Super flumina Babylonis. O bone Jesu.*

*** DG Arc. 2723 070 (6) [id.].

This six-record set embraces music from Dunstable and Dufay through to the late Renaissance. All of it has been issued before, and certain items (Binchois and Busnois) are still available separately. Some, however, appeared between our publications, and their catalogue life was so short that we had no opportunity to commend their contents to readers interested in this repertoire. The first record is devoted to Dufay, Dunstable and Binchois; the second to Ockeghem and Obrecht; the third to Josquin including his *Missa L'Homme armé*; the fourth to Pierre de la Rue and Isaac; the fifth to an anthology including Morales and Philippe de Monte; and the last to Lassus and Palestrina. Performances are expressive and warm, and the recordings (sometimes slightly forward in balance) are on the whole very fine.

Luxon, Benjamin (baritone)

'*Some enchanted evening*' (with Nat. PO, Hughes): RODGERS: *South Pacific: Some enchanted evening. Oklahoma: Surrey with a fringe on top. Babes in Arms: Where or when. Carousel: Soliloquy.* LOEWE: *My Fair Lady: On the street where you live.* KERN: *Showboat: Ol' man river.* BERNSTEIN: *West Side Story: Maria.* WILLSON: *Music Man: 76 trombones.* GERSHWIN: *Porgy and Bess: I got plenty o' nuttin'.* KERN: *Very Warm for May: All the things you are.* BIZET (arr. Hammerstein): *Carmen Jones: Stan' up and fight.*
*** RCA RL/*RK* 25320.

An outstanding compilation of some of the finest songs from the American musical, unsurpassed in the current catalogue (the collection by Sherrill Milnes and the Mormon Tabernacle Choir – see below – is not in the same class). Luxon is one of the most characterful of performers of this repertoire, equally effective in a full-bloodedly romantic song like *Maria* and in the lighter and charming *Surrey with a fringe on top*. His *Ol' man river* is lyrically resonant, and *76 trombones* admirably ebullient. He is given first-class accompaniments by Arwel Hughes, and only occasionally does one miss a chorus. The recording is forward but flattering, and the voice sounds warm and vibrant. The cassette matches the disc closely. Recommended.

Milnes, Sherrill (baritone)

'*A grand night for singing*' (with Mormon Tabernacle Choir, Columbia SO, Ottley): ROGERS: *State Fair: It's a grand night for singing. The Sound of Music: My favourite things. Carousel: If I loved you. Oklahoma: Oklahoma!* LOEWE: *Brigadoon: The heather on the hill; There but for you go I. On a Clear Day: On a clear day you can see forever.* WILLSON: *Music Man: 76 trombones.* YARBURG: *Finian's Rainbow: Look to the rainbow.* ROME: *Fanny; Welcome home.*
** CBS 73867/40- [Col. M/*MT* 35170].

After a vigorous opening number, the arrangements here, combined with the rather soupy style of the Mormon Choir, tend to over sentimentalize the lyrical songs. Sherrill Milnes is in vibrant form (and he has the vocal timbre and romantic virility for the repertoire), but even he at times is tempted to go slightly over the top, as in the luscious version of *Look to the rainbow*. The recording, with the soloist forward and the choir making resonantly sumptuous sounds in the background, is well integrated, with a lively orchestral backing. The cassette transfer is successful, with a bright upper range, plenty of body and no lack of focus.

Mormon Tabernacle Choir, Condie

'*The best of the Mormon Tabernacle Choir*' (with Phd. O., Ormandy): arr. WILHOUSKY: *Battle hymn of the Republic.* SIBELIUS: *Finlandia: Chorale.* BACH: *Chorales: Sleepers awake; Sheep may safely graze* (arr. Walton). MALOTTE: *Lord's prayer.* BRAHE: *Bless this house.* HANDEL: *Xerxes: Largo. Messiah: For unto us a child is born.* RIMSKY-KORSAKOV: *Glory.* DRAPER: *All creatures of our God and King.* TRAD.: *Rock of ages. Sometimes I feel like a motherless child. Guide us, O thou great Jehova. Come, come, ye saints.*
(M) **(*) CBS 61873/40-

This offers a much more generous selection than the digital record (below). These items are taken from records made over a decade from 1959 to 1969 and show the famous choir's effective range. Their natural fervour is at its most eloquent in the hymns, but they respond with appealing freshness to *For unto us a child is born*, and they are equally at home in the negro spiritual. The recording is clear and vivid, and the cassette is acceptable, if without the range of the disc.

Mormon Tabernacle Choir, Columbia SO, Ottley

'*The power and the glory*': HAYDN: *The Creation: Awake the harp.* BACH: *Chorales: Jesu, joy of man's desiring; A mighty fortress is our God.* MOZART: *Gloria, K.Anh.232.* SCHUBERT: *Ave Maria (Heavenly Father).* HANDEL: *Messiah: Hallelujah.* MENDELSSOHN: *St Paul: Rise up arise.* SULLIVAN: *Onward Christian soldiers.* MALOTTE: *Lord's prayer.* Arr. WILHOUSKY: *Battle hymn of the Republic.*

** CBS Dig. 36661/41- [Col. M/*MT* 36661].

The digital début of the Mormon Choir is in the event disappointing (the more so as there is a chrome tape which for the first time offers choral quality on cassette to match that on the LP). But the programme is not all happily chosen: the Haydn and Mozart show up the choir's technical and stylistic weaknesses, and even the *Hallelujah chorus* lacks the ultimate fervour one would expect. The last three items are by far the most effective. The sound is first-class.

Norman, Jessye (soprano)

'*Negro spirituals*' (with Amb. S.; Baldwin, piano): *Do Lawd. Ev'ry time I feel de spirit. Give me Jesus. Gospel train. Great day. Hush! Somebody's callin' my name. I couldn't hear nobody pray. Live a humble. Mary had a baby. My Lord what a morning. Soon ah will be done. There is a balm in Gilead. There's a man. Walk together. Were you there.* *** Ph. 9500 580/*7300 706* [id.].

There is a degree of restraint in Jessye Norman's singing of spirituals which may seem surprising, but the depth of feeling is never in doubt. What she has consciously done is to tilt the performances towards concert tradition, and with refined recording the result is both beautiful and moving. The cassette offers excellent quality with plenty of range, the solo voice clear and free.

'*Sacred songs*' (with Amb. S., RPO, Gibson): GOUNOD: *Messe solennelle de Sainte Cécile: Sanctus. O Divine Redeemer.* FRANCK: *Panis angelicus.* ADAMS: *The Holy City.* ANON.: *Amazing Grace. Greensleeves. Let Us Break Bread. I Wonder.* MAGGIM-

SEY: *Sweet little Jesus Boy.* YON: *Gesù Bambino.* *** Ph. Dig. 6514/*7337* 151 [id.].

Miss Norman's restraint is again telling here; she sings with fine eloquence, but her simplicity and sincerity shine through repertoire that can easily sound sentimental. The Gounod *Sanctus* is especially fine, but the simpler traditional songs are also very affecting. First-class recording and an excellent tape transfer.

Opera

'*Nights at the opera*': VERDI: *Aïda: Celeste Aïda* (Corelli); *Triumphal march. Don Carlos: O don fatale* (Verrett). *Il Trovatore: Anvil chorus; Miserere* (Tucci, Corelli). *La Traviata: Brindisi; Ah, fors' è lui* (Monte, Los Angeles). *Nabucco: Chorus of Hebrew slaves.* MASCAGNI: *Cavalleria Rusticana: Easter hymn* (Tinsley). DONIZETTI: *L'Elisir d'amore: Una furtiva lagrima* (Alva). PUCCINI: *Madama Butterfly: Un bel dì* (Scotto). *La Bohème: Che gelida manina; O soave fanciulla* (Gedda, Freni); *Musetta's waltz song* (Adani). *Turandot: Nessun dorma* (Corelli). *Gianni Schicchi: O mio babbino caro* (Los Angeles). *Tosca: Recondita armonia; E lucevan le stelle* (Bergonzi); *Vissi d'arte* (Callas). ROSSINI: *Il Barbiere di Siviglia: Largo al factotum* (Bruscantini).
(B) ** EMI *TC2-MOM 112.*

This is generally a preferable eighty minutes to the collection of *Italian opera favourites* in the same tape series (see above). Sometimes the performances are robust rather than endearing (Corelli's *Celeste Aïda* is vibrant but clumsily phrased). But there are many good things, notably the contributions of Luigi Alva, Victoria de los Angeles and Callas's *Vissi d'arte*. Vivid sound throughout, with a high transfer level, yet little roughness. However, some of the excerpts, taken from complete sets, have to be faded out quickly at the end, which tends to unsettle one's listening in an anthology of this kind.

Opera duets

'*Favourite opera duets*' (with (i) Vanzo, Sarabia; (ii) Callas, Ludwig; (iii) Bergonzi, Cappuccilli; (iv) Domingo; (v) Milnes; (vi) Freni; (vii) Pavarotti; (viii) Scotto, Allen; (ix) Caballé): (i) BIZET: *Les Pêcheurs de perles. C'était le soir . . . Au fond du temple saint*. (ii) BELLINI: *Norma: Mira, o Norma*. (iii) VERDI: *La Forza del destino: Solenne in quest'ora*. (iv; v) *Don Carlos: Dio che nell'alma infondere*. (iv; vi) GOUNOD: *Faust: Il se fait tard*. (vi; vii) MASCAGNI: *L'Amico Fritz: Suzel, buon di*. (viii) LEONCAVALLO: *I Pagliacci: E fra quest'ansie . . . Decido il mio destin*. (iv; ix) VERDI: *Aida: La fatal pietra . . . O terra addio*.
*** HMV ASD/*TC-ASD* 3908.

Taken from various EMI sources this makes an attractive and varied collection, featuring an impressive range of artists and a well-chosen programme. It is good to have, for example, the haunting *Cherry duet* from *L'Amico Fritz*. But it is a pity that the famous *Pearl Fishers* duet (which opens the recital) ends without a proper cadence, so that the following excerpt from *Norma* almost seems like a continuation. The sound is vivid on both disc and cassette.

Partridge, Ian (tenor), Stephen Roberts (baritone)

'*Songs by Finzi and his friends*' (with Benson, piano): FINZI: *To a poet; Oh fair to see, Op. 13a–b* (song collections). GURNEY: *Sleep. Down by the Salley Gardens. Hawk and buckle*. MILFORD: *If it's ever spring again. The colour. So sweet love seemed*. GILL: *In memoriam*. FERRAR: *O mistress mine*.
**(*) Hyp. A 66015.

Finzi's sensitive response to word-meanings inspires a style of setting that is often not unlike an operatic recitative. His individuality and poetic originality are not always matched by memorability, but the songs of his contemporaries and friends – even where the names are unknown – make immediate communication even on a first hearing. An imaginative collection, well sung, worth exploring by those interested in the repertoire. The recording is fair, somewhat over-resonant.

Pavarotti, Luciano (tenor)

'*Bravo Pavarotti*': excerpts from: DONIZETTI: *Lucia di Lammermoor; La Fille du régiment; L'Elisir d'amore; La Favorita*. PUCCINI: *La Bohème; Turandot; Tosca*. STRAUSS, R.: *Der Rosenkavalier*. VERDI: *Un Ballo in maschera; Luisa Miller; La Traviata; Requiem; Rigoletto; Il Trovatore*. BELLINI: *I Puritani*.
*** Decca D 129 D 2/*K 129 K 22* (2) [Lon. PAV 2001/2/5-].

Of Decca's three two-disc anthologies of Pavarotti, this is the obvious first choice. It provides an impressive survey of Pavarotti's achievement in the recording studio over a period of thirteen years. When he started recording for Decca, he was already a mature artist, and Tonio's aria from *La Fille du régiment* with its fusillade of top C's is as impressive as anything, a dazzling and infectious performance. Nowhere is there an ugly note, for as recorded Pavarotti is the Italian tenor with the most consistently beautiful tone, and the many duets and ensembles heighten his achievement in context with his finest colleagues. Taken as a whole it is a splendidly chosen and very entertaining selection. Each performance springs vividly to life, and there are only a few fades. The sound is consistently excellent on disc and cassette alike, and the order of items is perceptive.

'*Pavarotti's greatest hits*' from: PUC-CINI: *Turandot; Tosca; La Bohème.* DONIZETTI: *La Fille du régiment; La Favorita; L'Elisir d'amore.* STRAUSS, R.: *Der Rosenkavalier.* BIZET: *Carmen.* BELLINI: *I Puritani.* VERDI: *Il Trovatore; Rigoletto; Requiem.* GOUNOD: *Faust.* LEON-CAVALLO: *I Pagliacci.* PONCHIEL-LI: *La Gioconda.* Songs by LEON-CAVALLO, ROSSINI, DENZA, DE CURTIS. FRANCK: *Panis angelicus.*
*** Decca D 236 D 2/*K 236 K 22* (2) [Lon. PAV 2003/4/5-].

This collection of 'greatest hits' overlaps with the other two-disc collection, *Bravo Pavarotti,* but it can be safely recommended to all who have admired the golden beauty of the voice. Including as it does a fair proportion of earlier recordings, the four sides demonstrate the splendid consistency of his singing. Songs are included as well as excerpts from opera, including *Torna a Surriento, Funiculi, funicula,* Leoncavallo's *Mattinata* and Rossini's *La Danza.* The sound is very good on disc, always vibrant but sometimes a little fierce on cassette.

'*My own story*': arias from: PUC-CINI: *La Bohème.* DONIZETTI: *Il Duca d'Alba; La Fille du régiment; L'Elisir d'amore.* ROSSINI: *William Tell; Stabat Mater.* BOITO: *Mefisto-fele.* BELLINI: *La Sonnambula.* CILEA:

L'Arlesiana. FLOTOW: *Martha.* VERDI: *Rigoletto.* Songs by TOSTI, DONIZETTI, BIZET, DI CAPUA.
**(*) Decca D 253 D 2/*K 253 K 22* (2) [Lon. PAV 2007/5-].

Yet another variant on the Pavarotti theme, this time associated with his book of the same title (published by Sidgwick and Jackson). The leaflet with the records (and tapes) relates each item to the development of the singer's career. Opening attractively with Puccini's most famous two arias from Act 1 of *La Bohème,* the selection also includes impressive excerpts from *William Tell* and *La Fille du Régiment* and ranges into less familiar repertoire. A fair number of songs are included, which lightens the overall character of the presentation. This makes an admirable supplement to either of the first two double-albums, though it would not be a first choice among them. The recording is excellent and the cassettes are of high quality, with only a very occasional hint of peaking on one or two fortissimos.

'*Digital recital*' (with Nat. PO, Chailly or Fabritiis): GIORDANO: *Fedora: Amor ti vieta. Andrea Ché-nier: Colpito qui m'avete . . . Un dì all'azzurro spazio: Come un bel dì di maggio; Si, fui soldato.* BOITO: *Mefistofele: Dai campi, dai prati; Ogni mortal . . . Giunto sul passo estremo.* CILEA: *Adriana Lecouvreur: La dolcissima effigie; L'anima ho stanca.* MASCAGNI: *Iris: Apri la tua finestra!* MEYERBEER: *L'Africana: Mi batti il cor . . . O Paradiso.* MAS-SENET: *Werther: Pourquoi me réveil-ler.* PUCCINI: *La Fanciulla del West: Ch'ella mi creda. Manon Lescaut: Tra voi belle; Donna non vidi mai; Ah! non v'avvicinate! . . . No! No! pazzo son!* (with Howlett).
*** Decca Dig. SXDL/*KSXDC* 7504 [Lon. LDR 10020/5-].

This first digital recital record from Pavarotti has the voice more resplendent than ever. The passion with which he tackles Des Grieux's Act 3 plea from *Manon Lescaut* is devastating, and the big breast-beating numbers are all splendid, imaginative as well as heroic. But the slight pieces, Des Grieux's *Tra voi belle* and the Iris *Serenade*, could be lighter and more charming. The cassette transfer is vibrant and clear.

'Pavarotti in concert' (with O. of Teatro Comunale, Bologna, Bonynge): BONONCINI: *Griselda: Per la gloria d'adorarvi.* HANDEL: *Atalanta: Care selve.* SCARLATTI, A.: *Già il sol dal Gange.* BELLINI: *Songs: Ma rendi pur contento; Dolente immagine di fille mia; Malinconia, ninfa gentile; Bella nice, che d'amore; Vanne, o rosa fortunata.* TOSTI: *Songs: La Serenata; Luna d'estate; Malia; Non t'amo più.* RESPIGHI: *Nevicata. Poggia. Nebbie.* ROSSINI: *La Danza.*
**(*) Decca SXL/*KSXC* 6650 [Lon. 26391].

Pavarotti is more subdued than usual in the classical items here: he finds an attractive lyrical delicacy for the opening Bononcini aria, though there is a hint of strain in Handel's *Care selve*. He is in his element in Tosti, and, with evocative accompaniments from Bonynge, he makes the three Respighi songs the highlight of a recital which is nicely rounded off with a spirited but never coarse version of Rossini's *La Danza*. The Decca sound is atmospheric throughout and has transferred well to tape.

Neapolitan songs (with Ch. and O. of Teatro Comunale, Bologna, Guadagno, or Nat. PO, Chiaramello): DI CAPUA: *O sole mio. Maria, Marì.* TOSTI: *A vuchella. Marechiare.* CANNIO: *O surdato 'nnamurato.*

GAMBARDELLA: *O Marenariello.* ANON.: *Fenesta vascia.* DE CURTIS: *Torna a Surriento. Tu, ca nun chiagne.* PENNINO: *Pecchè . . .* D'ANNIBALE: *O paese d'o sole.* TAGLIAFERRI: *Piscatore 'e pusilleco.* DENZA: *Funiculi, funicula.*
*** Decca SXL/*KSXC* 6870 [Lon. 26560/5-].

Neapolitan Songs given grand treatment in passionate Italian performances, missing some of the charm but none of the red-blooded fervour. The recording is both vivid and atmospheric. The tape transfer is well managed although there is slight loss of presence in the items with chorus.

Pears, Peter (tenor), **Julian Bream** (lute)

'Sweet, stay awhile': MORLEY: *It was a lover and his lass. Absence.* ROSSETER: *What then is love but mourning. When Laura smiles.* DOWLAND: *Dear, if you change. Weep no more. Stay time. Sweet, stay awhile. Can she excuse.* FORD: *Fair, sweet, cruel.* BRITTEN: *Folksong arrangements: Master Kilbey; The shooting of his dear; Sailor-boy; I will give my love an apple; The soldier and the sailor. Songs from the Chinese (The big chariot; The old lute; The autumn wind; The herd-boy; Depression; Dance song). Gloriana: 2nd lute song of the Earl of Essex.*
(M) *** RCA Gold GL/*GK* 42752 [LSC 3131].

Any Pears–Bream recital is likely to give pleasure, and this vintage collection, recorded when Pears was at the peak of his form, is a genuine bargain with its inclusion of the Britten folksong arrangements, the lute song from *Glor-*

iana and the *Songs from the Chinese* to supplement the original Elizabethan collection. Here the Dowland songs are particularly fine, sung with Pears's usual blend of intelligence and lyrical feeling. The cassette transfer is of excellent quality, matching the disc closely.

Lute songs: DOWLAND: *Fine knacks for ladies. Sorrow stay. If my complaints. What if I never speed.* ROSSETER: *Sweet come again. What is a day. Whether men do laugh or weep.* MORLEY: *Thyrsis and Milla. I saw my lady weeping. With my love my life was nestled. What if my mistress now.* PILKINGTON: *Rest, sweet nymphs.* ANON.: *Have you seen but a white lily grow? Miserere, my Maker.* CAMPION: *Come, let us sound with melody. Fair, if you expect admiring. Shall I come sweet?*
(M) *** Decca Ser. SA/*KSC* 7.

This delightfully spontaneous recital was recorded at the beginning of the sixties and finds both artists on top form. Pears's very individual timbre readily identifies with the underlying melancholy which characterizes so many Elizabethan songs. The sound is first-rate and the balance is equally natural on disc and on the excellent cassette.

Ricciarelli, Katia (soprano), **José Carreras** (tenor)

'*Italian love duets*' (with Amb. Op. Ch., LSO, Gardelli): PUCCINI: *Madama Butterfly: Bimba, bimba, non piangere.* VERDI: *I Lombardi: Dove sola m'inoltro . . . Per dirupi e per foreste.* DONIZETTI: *Poliuto: Questo pianto favelli . . . Ah! fuggi da morte.* *Roberto Devereux: Tutto è silenzio.*
*** Ph. 9500 750/*7300 835* [id.].

The two Donizetti duets are among the finest he ever wrote, especially the one from *Poliuto*, in which the hero persuades his wife to join him in martyrdom. This has a depth unexpected in Donizetti. Both the Donizetti items receive beautiful performances here; the Puccini love duet is made to sound fresh and unhackneyed, and the *Lombardi* excerpt is given with equal tenderness. Stylish conducting and refined recording.

Sadler's Wells Opera

'*Operetta at the Wells*' (with Sadler's Wells Ch. and O., soloists, cond. (i) Tausky; (ii) Reid; (iii) Matheson; (iv) Faris): excerpts (in English) from: (i) STRAUSS, Johann, Jnr: *Die Fledermaus; The Gypsy Baron.* LEHÁR: *The Land of Smiles;* (ii) *The Merry Widow.* (iii) OFFENBACH: *La Belle Hélène;* (iv) *La Vie Parisienne; Orpheus in the Underworld.*
(M) **(*) HMV ESDW/*TC-ESDW* 712 (2).

The Sadler's Wells Company here shows its versatility in capturing both Viennese gaiety and Offenbachian high spirits. The infectious qualities of *La Belle Hélène* and the highly effective translation of *Orpheus in the Underworld*, in a production which immediately registered its wit and humour with English audiences yet retained its French poise and precision, were a remarkable achievement. *The Land of Smiles* proved less successful on stage but on disc revealed some delightful numbers, with Charles Craig outstanding in a good cast, his rich, fine tenor sounding out gloriously in *You are my heart's delight* (with different words). In Johann Strauss, individual performances are not always as memorable but the vigour of the team overall does not lack sparkle. With bright recording this is a generous sampler and makes an entertaining anthology. The cassettes have striking vividness and presence too, although the high-level transfer has brought a touch of edginess at peaks.

St John's College, Cambridge, Ch., Guest

'Hear my prayer' (with Peter White, organ): GOLDSCHMIDT: *A tender shoot* (carol). MENDELSSOHN: *Hear my prayer*. BACH: *Jesu, joy of man's desiring*. MOZART: *Ave verum, K.618*. STAINER: *I saw the Lord*. BRAHMS: *German Requiem: Ye now are sorrowful*. LIDON: *Sonata de 1. tono*. (M) *** Argo SPA/KCSP 543.

The refined style of the St John's Choir is here at its most impressive in the famous Bach chorale, the Goldschmidt carol and Mozart's *Ave verum*. In Mendelssohn's *Hear my prayer*, the treble soloist sings with striking purity but without the memorability of Master Ernest Lough's famous Temple Church version (from the early electric 78 r.p.m. era). The substitution of a treble for soprano voice in the Brahms excerpt is not wholly convincing, especially as the soloist sounds a little nervous. But the choir is on excellent form throughout, and the recording is first-class, with an outstanding cassette to match the disc. The concert ends with an attractively vigorous account of an organ sonata by the Spanish composer José Lidon, which features the *trompeta real* stop with exhilarating effect.

Schwarzkopf, Elisabeth (soprano)

'The early years' (1946–55): MOZART: operatic arias. Opera scenes with Irmgard Seefried (STRAUSS, R.: *Der Rosenkavalier;* HUMPERDINCK: *Hänsel und Gretel*). Arias by VERDI,

CHARPENTIER, PUCCINI. Lieder by BACH, GLUCK, MOZART, SCHUBERT, SCHUMANN, ARNE, R. STRAUSS, WOLF and arr. BRAHMS. Operetta excerpts by LEHÁR and JOHANN STRAUSS, Jnr.
(M) *** HMV mono RLS/TC-RLS 763 (4).

These mono recordings are well worth the stereophile's attention, for they contain performances that in their freshness and command clearly point forward to the supreme work of the mature Schwarzkopf. The Humperdinck excerpts here (with Seefried) are the ones originally on 78, not from the complete Karajan recording, and it is good to hear the young Schwarzkopf as Sophie in *Rosenkavalier*, bright-eyed and alert. Previously unpublished are a strong, incisive account of *Martern aller Arten* from *Entführung* and *Depuis le jour* from *Louise*, starting unidiomatically but developing beautifully. A whole record of Mozart, one of other opera, and a third of Lieder are rounded off with operetta favourites of Johann Strauss and Lehár. Excellent transfers on both disc and cassette. The booklet provided with the tape box is admirable in every way.

'Elisabeth Schwarzkopf Christmas album' (with Ch. and O., Mackerras): GRUBER: *Stille Nacht*. TRAD.: *O come all ye faithful. O du frölich. The first nowell. In dulci jubilo. Von Himmel hoch. I saw three ships. Maria auf dem Berge. Easter Alleluia*. Arr. BRAHMS: *Sandmännchen*. GLUCK: *In einem kühlen Grunde*. FRANCK: *Panis angelicus*. HUMPERDINCK: *Weihnachten*.
*** HMV ASD/TC-ASD 3798.

A treasurable Christmas collection from Schwarzkopf, youthfully fresh-voiced throughout and singing with great charm. In spite of the orchestral accompaniments and the inclusion of a chorus, the intimacy of her Lieder style is often conveyed here. The choral contribution is first-rate; *I saw three ships* is treated like a scherzo and taken unusually fast, to great effect. The recording is excellent and the cassette transfer of sophisticated quality.

'*Favourite scenes and arias*': WAGNER: *Tannhäuser: Elisabeth's greeting; Elisabeth's prayer. Lohengrin: Elsa's dream; Euch Luften, die mein Klagen* (with Ludwig). WEBER: *Der Freischütz: Wie nahte . . . Leise, leise; Und ob die Wolke.* PUCCINI: *Gianni Schicchi: O mio babbino caro. La Bohème: Sì, mi chiamano Mimì.* VERDI: *Otello: Willow song; Ave Maria.* SMETANA: *The Bartered Bride: Endlich allein . . . Wie Fremd.* TCHAIKOVSKY: *Eugene Onegin: Tatiana's letter scene.*
(M) *** HMV SXDW/*TC-SXDW* 3049 (2).

This two-disc folder brings together two Schwarzkopf recital records that have tended to be overlooked. The first containing Wagner and Weber is a classic, with Agathe's two arias from *Der Freischütz* given with a purity of tone and control of line never surpassed, magic performances. So too with the Wagner heroines. The second record finds Schwarzkopf keenly imaginative in less expected repertory. This was recorded eight years after the first (in 1967), and the voice has to be controlled more carefully. But Schwarzkopf's Puccini has its own individuality and she sounds radiantly fresh in the scene from *Otello*. The *Letter scene* from *Eugene Onegin* is less convincing; here the projected vocal personality seems too mature for the young Tatiana. The recording sounds splendid and has been transferred to cassette with great success.

'*To my friends*' (with Parsons, piano): WOLF: *Mörike Lieder: Storchenbotschaft; Fussreise; Elfenlied; Bei einer Trauung; Jägerlied; Selbstgeständnis; Heimweh; Nixe Binsefuss; Mausfallen Sprüchlein; Nimmersatte Liebe; Lebe Wohl; Das verlassene Mägdlein; Auf ein altes Bild.* LOEWE: *Die wandelnde Glocke.* GRIEG: *Ein Schwan.* BRAHMS: *Mädchenlied; Am jüngsten Tag; Therese; Blinde Kuh.*
*** Decca SXL/*KSXC* 6943 [Lon. 26592].

This glowing collection of Lieder was Schwarzkopf's last record and also the last recording supervised by her husband, Walter Legge. With excellent Decca sound, the charm and presence of Schwarzkopf, which in a recital conveyed extraordinary intensity right to the very end of her career, comes over vividly. Most cherishable of all are the lighter, quicker songs like *Mausfallen Sprüchlein* ('My St Trinians reading', as she says herself) and *Blinde Kuh* (*Blind Man's Buff*). Like the disc the cassette is superbly balanced, bringing the artists right into one's room.

Scotto, Renata (soprano)

'*Portrait*': ROSSINI: *Il Barbiere di Siviglia: Una voce poco fa.* BELLINI: *I Puritani: Qui la voce . . . Vien diletto.* PUCCINI: *Gianni Schicchi: O mio babbino caro. Turandot: Signore, ascolta; Tu che di gel sei cinta. Madama Butterfly: Un bel dì; Con onor muore.* DONIZETTI: *Lucia di Lammermoor: Il dolce suono.* VERDI: *La Traviata: Ah, fors'è lui.* BOITO: *Mefistofele: L'altra notte.*
**(*) HMV ASD/*TC-ASD* 4022.

Apart from the two outstanding excerpts from Scotto's complete 1967 set of

Madama Butterfly with Carlo Bergonzi, superbly conducted by Barbirolli, this recital (with the Philharmonia Orchestra under Manno Wolf-Ferrari) dates from 1959, early in her career. The widely ranging programme of arias has the voice at its freshest and most agile, giving an idea of the later dramatic developments which changed the character of the voice -and filled it out (as is shown by the *Butterfly* excerpts). The recording is faithful and clean and the cassette transfer well managed, with only a minimal hint of peaking on one or two climaxes.

Shirley-Quirk, John (baritone)

'A recital of English songs' (with Tunnard, Isepp or Parkin, piano): VAUGHAN WILLIAMS: *Songs of travel. Linden Lea. Silent noon.* BUTTERWORTH: *6 Songs from 'A Shropshire Lad'.* IRELAND: *My fair. Salley Gardens. Love and friendship. I have twelve oxen. Sea fever.* STANFORD: *Drake's drum.* KEEL: *Trade winds.* WARLOCK: *Captain Stratton's fancy.* (M) **(*) Saga 5473.

Gathered together from two earlier Saga issues, this is as attractive a record of English song as you will find. John Shirley-Quirk early in his career was at his freshest, already an intense and dedicated artist, giving magic to such a simple song as Keel's *Trade winds.* The recording is limited but acceptable.

Simpson, Glenda (mezzo-soprano), Paul Hiller (baritone)

'English ayres and duets' (with Mason, lute; Thorndycraft, viola da gamba): Ayres: CAMPION: *If thou long'st so much to learn. Shall I come, sweet love?* DOWLAND: *Fine knacks for ladies. In darkness let me dwell.*

Time's eldest son. Old age. Flow my tears. Now, O now, I needs must part. Come away, sweet love. HUME: *Tobacco.* DANYEL: *Eyes, look no more.* PILKINGTON: *My choice is made.* JONES, R.: *Now what is love?* Duets: FERRABOSCO: *Tell me, O love.* DOWLAND: *Humour, say.* Lute solos: ANON.: *Piper's galliard. The Earl of Essex's galliard.*
**(*) Hyp. A/*KA* 66003.

What makes this Elizabethan recital different from others is its use of 'authentic Elizabethan pronunciation'. The dialectal flavours seem mixed, but the words come over, especially those of Glenda Simpson, whose style is admirably fresh and whose decorative runs are as delightful as they are crisply articulated. Paul Hiller is also an accomplished singer, and his melancholy manner is certainly in accordance with many of these lyrics, although some listeners may find his expressive style rather too doleful, and he misses the intended humour of Hume's *Tobacco.* But the dialogue songs go very well, and there is a general air of spontaneity here. The mid-side lute solos are most welcome. The recording has fine realism and presence, and the cassette is of demonstration vividness in its sharpness of focus.

Sopranos

'Great sopranos of our time': (i) Scotto; (ii) Schwarzkopf; (iii) Sutherland; (iv) Nilsson; (v) Los Angeles; (vi) Freni; (vii) Callas; (viii) Cotrubas; (ix) Caballé: (i) PUCCINI: *Madama Butterfly: Un bel dì.* (vi) *La Bohème: Sì, mi chiamano Mimì.* (ii) MOZART: *Così fan tutte: Come scoglio.* (iii) *Don Giovanni: Troppo mi spiace . . . Non mi dir.* (iv) WEBER: *Oberon: Ozean du Ungeheuer.* (v) ROSSINI: *Il Barbiere di Siviglia: Una*

voce poco fa. (vii) DONIZETTI: *Lucia di Lammermoor: Sparsa è di rose . . . Il dolce suono . . . Spargi d'amaro.* (viii) BIZET: *Les Pêcheurs de Perles: Comme autrefois.* (ix) VERDI: *Aïda: Qui Radames . . . O patria mia.* *** HMV ASD/*TC-ASD* 3915.

An impressive collection drawn from a wide variety of sources. It is good to have Schwarzkopf's commanding account of *Come scoglio* and Nilsson's early recording of the Weber, not to mention the formidable contributions of Callas and the early Sutherland reading of *Non mi dir*, taken from Giulini's complete set of *Giovanni*. The cassette transfers are admirably managed throughout.

Stade, Frederica von (mezzo-soprano)

Arias (with Nat. Arts Centre O., Bernardi): MONTEVERDI: *Il Ritorno d'Ulisse in patria: Torna, torna.* ROSSINI: *Tancredi: Di tanti palpiti. Semiramide: Bel raggio lusinghier.* PAISIELLO: *Nina: Il mio ben quando verrá.* BROSCHI: *Idaspe: Ombra fedele anch'io.* LEONCAVALLO: *La Bohème: È destin.* *** CBS 76800/40- [Col. M/*MT* 35138].

The remarkable ability of Frederica von Stade to identify with each heroine in turn comes out vividly. The voice is used with endless imagination and subtlety of colour, as well as great intensity and seeming spontaneity. The only reservation is that such a programme is likely to be too wearing for the listener to take all at once. Excellent accompaniment and recording, and the cassette transfer is one of CBS's best; the voice is given presence without an artificial edge, and the orchestral backcloth is full and clear.

Opera arias: ROSSINI: *Otello: Quanto son fieri i palpiti; Che smania. Ohimè! che affano!; Assisa a piè d'un salice; Deh calma, O Ciel.* HAYDN: *La Fedeltà premiata: Per te m'accesse amore; Vanne . . . fuggi . . . traditore!; Barbaro conte . . . Dell'amor mio fedele. Il Mondo della luna: Una donna come me; Se lo commando ci venirò.* MOZART: *La Clemenza di Tito: Torna di Tito a lato; Tu tosti tradito.* *** Ph. 9500 716/*7300 807* [id.].

This attractive and varied collection is made up of excerpts from complete opera recordings. It is some tribute to Frederica von Stade's consistency that the result hangs together so impressively, each performance keenly individual and intense. Consistently good recording too, and an excellent cassette transfer; the voice sounds wholly natural and the orchestra has only marginally less life at the top than on the disc.

Stefano, Giuseppe di (tenor)

'The young Di Stefano' (with Callas and Carteri): arias and excerpts from: MASCAGNI: *L'Amico Fritz; Iris.* DONIZETTI: *L'Elisir d'amore; Lucia di Lammermoor.* MASSENET: *Manon.* THOMAS: *Mignon.* VERDI: *La Traviata; La Forza del destino.* CILEA: *L'Arlesiana.* PUCCINI: *Tosca; La Fanciulla del West; Gianni Schicchi; Turandot.* Songs.
(M) (***) HMV mono RLS/*TC-RLS* 756 (2).

Giuseppe di Stefano's recording career began in 1944 with Neapolitan songs, and they are used to open this anthology (the recording quality obviously restricted). Although the singing reveals only a conventional approach, the immediately following group of operatic arias, with piano accompaniment, already suggests an exceptional talent, the *Dream song* from *Manon* a highlight. Including as it does many unpublished items this presents a vivid portrait of one of the most characterful and gifted tenors of his time. Even early in his career Di Stefano was not entirely immune from bad stylistic habits, but the intensity and projection of this singing as well as its sheer beauty are consistently compelling. The central anthology of popular arias (especially on side three) shows the voice in its full potent freshness; then on side four the selection returns to songs of more limited appeal. The mono recordings from the fifties, although limited in range, have been effectively remastered, and the sound of the excellent cassettes matches the discs. One cannot help but reflect, however, that a very good single LP could be made from the best items here

Streich, Rita (soprano)

'Portrait' (with Berlin RIAS Ch., Berlin RO, Gabel): STRAUSS, Johann, Jnr: *Frühlingsstimmen waltz. Die Fledermaus: Mein Herr Marquis, Spiel' ich die Unschuld. Geschichten aus dem Wiener Wald waltz.* VERDI: *Lo Spazzocamino* (*The Chimneysweep*). GODARD: *Jocelyn: Berceuse.* ARDITI: *Parla-Walzer.* SAINT-SAËNS: *Le rossignol et la rose.* SUPPÉ: *Boccaccio: Hab' ich nur deine Liebe.* DVOŘÁK: *Rusalka: Song to the moon.* MEYERBEER: *Dinorah: Shadow song.*

(M) *** DG Priv. 2535/*3335* 367.

Dazzling coloratura and irresistible charm distinguish this recital of vocal lollipops recorded by Rita Streich in the earliest days of stereo, when her voice was at its freshest. In the Johann Strauss

items with which she was so much identified on stage, she is quite delightful, and her sparkling account of *Tales from the Vienna Woods* is no less captivating. She makes a purse of the finest silk out of Godard's *Berceuse* and is marvellously agile in Meyerbeer's famous *Shadow song*. No less memorable is Verdi's little-known *Chimney Sweep*, but the supreme highlight is the exquisitely delicate *Le rossignol et la rose* of Saint-Saëns, which she understandably chose to accompany her to Roy Plomley's desert island. The recording does not show its age unduly, although the tape transfer has occasional hints of peaking.

Sutherland, Joan (soprano)

'Serate musicale' (with Bonynge, piano): ROSSINI: *Serate musicale.* DALAYRAC: *Nina: Quand le bien.* Songs by LEONCAVALLO, DONIZETTI, RESPIGHI, BELLINI, ROSSINI, VERDI, CIMARA, PONCHIELLI, MASCAGNI, CAMPANA, GOUNOD, GODARD, MASSENET, LALO, THOMAS, SAINT-SAËNS, FAURÉ, BIZET, MEYERBEER, DAVID, CHAMINADE, DELIBES, HAHN, ADAM.

** Decca D 125 D 3 (3) [Lon. 13132].

Recorded in the drawing-room of their Swiss house, this set of trifles from Sutherland and Bonynge suffers a little from dry sound. With little or no ambience it is harder to register the charm of these generally unpretentious songs, even the delectable Rossini collection which provides the title for the whole box. In many ways the most successful are the French items on the last of the three records, and the six sides are not recommended for playing at one go. But the love for this music shared by Bonynge and Sutherland is never in doubt.

'Grandi voci': BONONCINI: *Griselda: Per la gloria.* PAISIELLO: *Nel cor più*

non mi sento. PICCINNI: *La Buona Figliuola: Furia di donne.* ARNE: *Love in a Village: The traveller benighted. Artaxerxes: The soldier tir'd.* SHIELD: *Rosina: When William at eve; Whilst with village maids; Light as thistledown* (all with Philomusica of L., Granville Jones). HANDEL: *Acis and Galatea: Ye verdant plains ... Hush, ye pretty warbling quire; 'Tis done ... Heart, the seat of soft delight. Alcina: Tornami a vagheggiar; Ah! Ruggiero crudel! ... Ombre pallide* (with Philomusica, Boult or Lewis).

(M) *** Decca GRV 1 [Lon. 41011].

These recordings were all made just at the time when Joan Sutherland was achieving her first international success. Though in those days the engineers found it harder to capture the full beauty of the voice, the freshness and clarity are stunning. The Handel items on side two are taken from Oiseau-Lyre recordings of that time; side one has six recordings never issued before, all most cherishable, including those like *Light as thistledown* which Sutherland went on to record again.

Sutherland, Joan (soprano), **Marilyn Horne** (mezzo-soprano), **Luciano Pavarotti** (tenor)

'Live from the Lincoln Center' (with NY City Op. O., Bonynge): excerpts from: VERDI: *Ernani; I Lombardi; I Masnadieri; Otello; Il Trovatore.* BELLINI: *Norma; Beatrice di Tenda.* PUCCINI: *La Bohème.* PONCHIELLI: *La Gioconda.* ROSSINI: *La Donna del Lago.*
*** Decca Dig. D 255 D 2/K 255 K 22 (2) [Lon. LDR 72009].

Not all gala concerts make good records, but this is an exception; almost every item here puts an important gloss on the achievements of the three principal stars, not least in the concert numbers. These include an improbable account of the *Lombardi* trio in which Marilyn Horne takes the baritone part (most effectively); and it is good to have a sample not only of Sutherland's Desdemona but of Pavarotti's Otello (so far not heard on stage) in their account of the Act 1 duet. The final scene from *Il Trovatore* is more compelling here than in the complete set made by the same soloists five years earlier, while among the solo items the one which is most cherishable is Horne's account of the brilliant coloratura aria from Rossini's *La Donna del Lago*. The microphone catches a beat in the voices of both Sutherland and Horne, but not so obtrusively as on some studio discs. Lively accompaniment under Bonynge; bright, vivid digital recording, but over-loud applause.

Temple Church Ch.; Thalben-Ball (organ)

'The Temple tradition' (with Royal College of Music O., Willcocks): STANLEY: *Organ concertos Nos. 4 in D min.; 6 in B flat.* THALBEN-BALL: *Sursum corda. Comfort ye.* WALFORD DAVIES: *Solemn melody. Tarry no longer.* WILLIAMSON: *Kerygma.* MENDELSSOHN: *Hear my prayer.*
** Abbey HMP 2280.

With royalties going to the Temple Music Trust this record celebrates a long musical tradition at London's Temple Church; and by including a new version of *Hear my prayer* it reminds us of the choir's most famous record, made in 1927 with Master Ernest Lough as treble soloist. His successor, Michael Ginn, is capable but fails to distil comparable magic, and generally the performances here (except perhaps for Malcolm Williamson's eloquent *Kerygma*) are forthright rather than inspiring. The choral recording is full but not always ideally clear. Dr Thalben-Ball is the sturdy soloist in the Stanley *Concertos* and the Orchestra of the Royal College of Music (Junior Department) provides convincingly professional support under Sir David Willcocks.

Teyte, Maggie (soprano)

'Her life and art' (with Cortot, Moore, Bowen, Muller, Alec Robertson): includes OFFENBACH: *La Périchole: Je t'adore, brigand.* PURCELL: *Dido and Aeneas: Dido's lament.* Songs by DEBUSSY, HAHN, MESSAGER, NOVELLO, PURCELL, BRAHMS, WOLF.
(***) BBC mono REGL/ZCF 369.

A vivid projection of Maggie Teyte's very strong personality. Indeed in the interview with John Bowen, Robert Muller and the late Alec Robertson she anticipates the questions and almost answers them before they are asked. Her account of her relationship with Debussy is fascinating, and although some of the vocal items are not entirely flattering and the sound is only acceptable, this has interesting documentary value.

Treorchy Male Ch., Cynan Jones

'The sound of Treorchy': THOMAS: *Fantasias on Welsh airs. Hymn tunes.* MATHIAS: *Y pren ar y bryn.* GOUNOD: *Faust: Soldiers' chorus.* TRAD.: *Steal away. Immortal invisible. All through the night. Drink to me only. Gute Nacht. Swansea town. Were you there.* GENEE: *Italian salad.* PARRY: *Jesu, lover of my soul. Myfanwy.* HUGHES: *Guide me, O thou great Redeemer.* PRITCHARD: *Alleluya.* JAMES: *Welsh national*

anthem. SULLIVAN: *The lost chord.* DAVIES: *Nant er Myreth.* Arr VAUGHAN WILLIAMS: *Loch Lomond.* VAUGHAN WILLIAMS: *Linden lea.* CAPEL: *Love, could I only tell thee.* BACH: *Jesu, joy of man's desiring.* LIDDLE: *Abide with me.*
(B) ** EMI *TC2-MOM 125.*

The opening of this collection is ill-planned, with a piano accompaniment clattering away in a resonantly 'empty' hall. But once the choir enters, the reverberation is put to good effect, although it does mean that the cassette sound is robbed of a sharply defined upper focus. All this is less noticeable in the car, where the sonorous fullness and the characteristic fervour of the Welsh voices make the strongest impact. It is the traditional material which comes off best, especially the hymns (which may tempt a lone driver to join in!). The second half of the programme – which overall runs for nearly an hour and a half – is the more attractive.

Vienna Boys' Ch.

'Serenade' (cond. Gillesberger, with Theimer, piano, and instrumentalists): SCHUBERT: *Gott meine Zuversicht. Die Nachtigall. Ständchen. La Pastorella. Widerspruch.* MOZART: *Due pupille amabile, K.439. Mi lagnerò tacendo, K.437. Luci care, luci belle, K.346. Più non si trovano, K.549.* SCHUMANN: *Zigeunerleben.* BRAHMS: *Nun stehn die Rosen in Blüte. Die Berge sind spitz. Am Wildbach die Weiden. Und gehst du über den Kirchhof.* DRECHSLER: *Brüderlein fein.*
** RCA RL/RK 19034 [PRL 1/PRK 1 9034].

The appeal of this collection is limited to those who want to hear German art songs freshly and ingenuously presented by a boys' choir. The singing is pleasing, at its most effective in the very simple items. Elsewhere the lack of the subtlety of response to word-meanings one expects from a solo performer brings a degree of monotony. The recording is good, and well transferred to tape.

Folksongs of Germany and Austria (cond. Harrer with instrumental accompaniment).
**(*) RCA RL/*RK* 30470.

This is repertoire in which the Vienna Boys excel, and they sing with a genuine spirit of innocence that is most engaging. There is a wide variety of material here, and although the planning of the layout is poor (items do not always follow each other naturally, and key changes sometimes jar on the ear) the programme itself is well chosen and of high quality. The closing hunting song (*Auf, auf zum fröhlichen Jägen*), with an appropriate accompaniment, is only one among a number of memorably vivid miniatures. The recording is excellent and the cassette transfer lively, if less refined than the LP.

'Music of the Renaissance court' (with Ch. Viennensis, VCM, Harnoncourt): ISAAC: *Imperii proceres. Carmen in fa. Fortuna in mi. An buos. La morra. Innsbruck, ich muss dich lassen. A la bataglia. J'ay pris amours. Sancti spiritus assit nobis gratia.* BRUMEL: *Tandernac. Noe noe.* JOSQUIN DES PRÉS: *Coment peult.* DE LA RUE: *Fors seulement.* SENFL: *Carmen in la. Carmen in re. Nasci, pati, mori.* FESTA: *Quis dabit oculis nostris.* HOFHAIMER: *Tandernaken.* ANON.: *Naves pont. Carmen Hercules. Si je perdu.* OBRECHT: *Vavilment.*
(M) ** DG Arc. Priv. 2547/347 029.

All this music comes from the fifteenth and sixteenth centuries, and the performances are in good style even if the overall effect is rather sombre. There is hardly a hint that the Renaissance brought a reflowering of the human spirit. The recording is good and the cassette transfer excellently managed.

White, Robert (tenor)

'When you and I were young, Maggie' (with Sanders, piano): BUTTERFIELD: *When you and I were young, Maggie.* FOSTER: *Beautiful dreamer.* FOOTE: *An Irish folk song.* TOURS: *Mother o' mine.* Arr. TAYLOR: *May day carol.* SPEAKS: *Sylvia.* NEVIN: *Little Boy Blue. The Rosary.* PENN: *Smilin' through.* ROOT: *The vacant chair.* BOND: *I love you truly.* MCGILL: *Duna.* EDWARDS: *By the bend of the river.* DANKS: *Silver threads among the gold.* WESTENDORF: *I'll take you home again, Kathleen.* BOND: *A perfect day.*
*** RCA RCALP/*RCAK* 3023 [ARL 1/*ARK 1* 1698].

Robert White is a tenor with a very individual timbre which may not appeal to every ear but certainly has a special fascination for those who – broadly generalizing – like an Irish tenor sound. White is in fact American, though clearly enough (his father was a close friend of John McCormack) he deliberately cultivates his Irish sound in such repertory as this. His manner is totally unsentimental, the style pleasingly direct and fresh, full of unforced charm. Fresh, clear recording to match, and the cassette transfer too is clean, with an excellent balance and natural piano tone.

'By the light of the silvery moon' (with O., Hyman): DONALDSON: *My blue heaven. At sundown.* HUBBELL: *Poor*

Butterfly. HENDERSON: *Bye bye blackbird.* ROMBERG: *When I grow too old to dream.* BAYES: *Shine on harvest moon.* EDWARDS: *By the light of the silvery moon.* KERN: *Look for the silver lining.* RAPEE: *Charmaine.* SHAY: *Get out and get under.* BERLIN: *All alone by the telephone. Remember.* JOLSON: *Me and my shadow.* MOLLOY: *Love's old sweet song.*
*** RCA RCALP/RCAK 6012.

Here Robert White takes a programme of twenties and thirties hits and with his keen, bright artistry and headily distinctive tenor gives them the status of art songs. He is helped by the brilliant accompaniments, yearningly sympathetic in sentimental songs like *Poor Butterfly*, adding jaunty syncopation in such charmers as *Get out and get under*. First-rate if obviously channelled recording.

'*Danny boy*' (with Nat. PO, Gerhardt): O'CONNOR: *The old house.* STANFORD: *Trottin' to the fair.* TRAD.: *The harp that once thro' Tara's halls. She moved through the fair. The bard of Armagh. Danny boy. The next market day. Believe me, if all those endearing young charms. My lagan love.* O'BRIEN: *The fairy tree.* LOUGHBOROUGH: *Ireland, Mother Ireland.* BALFE: *Killarney.* DUFFERIN: *The Irish emigrant.* CLARIBEL: *Come back to Erin.*
*** RCA RL/RK 13442 [ARL 1/ARK 1 3442].

The John McCormack repertory has become a speciality with Robert White, and here he presents a programme with an intensity of charm that the master himself surely would have applauded. Brilliant accompaniments and first-rate recording; the cassette is vivid too, and kind to the voice, although side two

seems marginally less refined than side one.

'*Songs my father taught me*' (with Nat. PO, Mace): LOHR: *Little grey home in the west.* HAWTHORNE: *Whispering hope.* DIX: *The Trumpeter.* RASBACH: *Trees.* CLAY: *I'll sing thee songs of Araby.* FOSTER: *I dream of Jeannie with the light brown hair.* BALFE: *Come into the garden, Maud.* JACOBS-BOND: *Just a-wearyin' for you.* WHITE: *Two blue eyes.* ADAMS: *Thora.* MARTINI: *Plaisir d'amour.* MURRAY: *I'll walk beside you.* FRASER-SIMPSON: *Christopher Robin is saying his prayers.*
*** RCA RL/RK 25345 [NFLI/NFKI 8005].

Here Robert White turns back to popular ballads and sings them with characteristic, artless charm. He can be dramatically vivid, as in Dix's *The Trumpeter*, or phrase a simple melody with ravishingly warm tone. In the duet *Whispering hope* (one of the gramophone's earliest million sellers in its 78 r.p.m. recording by Alma Gluck and Louise Homer) he sings with himself (by electronic means), disguising the colour of the 'second' voice so that it sounds like a light baritone, yet blends marvellously with the 'tenor'. A fascinating sleeve-note tells of White's childhood when one of an 'enormous collection' of John McCormack's records would go on the phonograph every time his mother put the kettle on for tea. This recital contains many favourites (described enthusiastically by White as 'belters') and they are sung superbly. The accompaniments under Ralph Mace are stylishly sympathetic, although the orchestral group is thin in numbers, perhaps appropriately. The cassette transfer is first-class, matching the excellent disc closely.

Winchester Cath. Ch., Neary

Evensong for Ash Wednesday.
*** ASV ALH/*ZCALH* 915.

This highly atmospheric record presents a service complete with prayers and responses. The main canticles, preces and responses are by Byrd, but the most striking item of all is the anthem, *Cast me not away* by S. S. Wesley, darkly intense. Outstanding singing by the choir under Neary. The cassette reflects the disc closely.

More About Penguins
and Pelicans

For further information about books available from
Penguins please write to Dept EP, Penguin Books Ltd,
Harmondsworth, Middlesex UB7 0DA.

In the U.S.A.: For a complete list of books available
from Penguins in the United States write to Dept CS,
Penguin Books, 625 Madison Avenue, New York,
New York 10022.

In Canada: For a complete list of books available from
Penguins in Canada write to Penguin Books Canada
Ltd, 2801 John Street, Markham, Ontario L3R 1B4.

In Australia: For a complete list of books available
from Penguins in Australia write to the Marketing
Department, Penguin Books Australia Ltd, P.O. Box
257, Ringwood, Victoria 3134.

In New Zealand: For a complete list of books available
from Penguins in New Zealand write to the Marketing
Department, Penguin Books (N.Z.) Ltd, P.O. Box
4019, Auckland 10.

THE PELICAN HISTORY OF MUSIC

1. ANCIENT FORMS TO POLYPHONY
Edited by Alec Robertson and Denis Stevens

The '1066' of our music lies somewhere in the Middle Ages, when the
Western tradition seemed to spring, fully armed with tonality,
harmony, and rhythm, from the head of medieval man. It is easy to
forget that musical languages had been evolving, both in the East and
the West, for at least five thousand years before music in Europe
began to assume the laws we are tempted to regard as perfect and
unalterable. This first volume in the Pelican History of Music traces
the story of music from the earliest known forms as far as the
beginnings of the polyphonic period in the first half of the fifteenth
century. A full section on non-Western music indicates how our
tradition is linked with or has evolved from the forms of music
prevailing in other parts of the world.

2. RENAISSANCE AND BAROQUE
Edited by Alec Robertson and Denis Stevens

This second volume of the Pelican History of Music is particularly
concerned with the social and artistic environment during the two
centuries associated with Renaissance and Baroque music. By the mid-
fifteenth century the Church's monopoly of influence was gone;
alongside its rites a wealth of courtly and civil occasions demanded
music and opened the way to every kind of experiment.

Europe knew no musical frontiers and it is possible to trace a whole
pattern of influence and counter-influence: the motet, the chanson,
and early opera are much alike in their regional forms and
adaptations.

Towards the end of the period the musician, like the artist, has
become emancipated. Composers such as Monteverdi, Vivaldi,
Purcell, and the Bachs are as individually distinct as the works that
make them famous.

THE PELICAN HISTORY OF MUSIC

3. CLASSICAL AND ROMANTIC
Edited by Alec Robertson and Denis Stevens

This volume is mainly concerned with the eighteenth and nineteenth centuries, but works by Mahler, Bloch, Bax and others are discussed in a coda.

Even in the age of enlightenment a patron's 'good taste' was something that composers had to contend with and the so-called *style galant* forms the background to the achievement of C. P. E. Bach, Mozart and Haydn. But Beethoven scorned conventional taste, and the great classical works of later eighteenth-century composers owe their boldness to the *style bourgeois*.

Nineteenth-century romantic composers, such as Wagner and Verdi, were aware of the enormous material expansion and adventure of their age. And unlike previous composers they were conscious of their kinship with writers and painters; some of their greatest musical triumphs are to be found in opera.

and, an outstanding Penguin Reference Book

THE NEW PENGUIN DICTIONARY OF MUSIC
Fourth Edition
Edited by Arthur Jacobs

The New Penguin Dictionary of Music (previously published as *A New Dictionary of Music*) compiled by Arthur Jacobs, a well-known music critic and Professor at the Royal Academy of Music, is a basic and comprehensive reference book. It covers orchestral, solo, choral and chamber music as well as opera and the ballet. Full and detailed entries deal with composers and their works, instruments of all sorts, orchestras, performers and conductors. Entries dealing with well-known authors whose work inspired musical composition are a new feature of this up-to-date dictionary which includes both information about the music of modern composers and the results of the considerable research that is going on into the music of the past.

THE NEW PELICAN GUIDE
TO ENGLISH LITERATURE

Edited by Boris Ford

Authoritative, stimulating and accessible, the original seven-volume *Pelican Guide to English Literature* has earned itself a distinguished reputation. Now enlarged to nine titles this popular series has been wholly revised and updated.

What this work sets out to offer is a guide to the history and traditions of English literature, a contour-map of the literary scene. Each volume includes these standard features:

   (i)   An account of the social context of literature in each period.

  (ii)   A general survey of the literature itself.

 (iii)   A series of critical essays on individual writers and their works – each written by an authority in the field.

 (iv)   Full appendices including short author biographies, listings of standard editions of authors' works, critical commentaries and titles for further study and reference.

The *Guide* consists of the following volumes:

Two major writers from South Africa in Penguins

A SOLDIER'S EMBRACE
Nadine Gordimer

A young white liberal embraced by two soldiers, one white and one black, in the midst of a cease-fire celebration; a married mistress long living with the secret of her third child's parentage; a lonely geologist finding solace in a forbidden love; an ancient village chief caught between black rebels and white government forces – in this superb collection of stories set in South Africa, Nadine Gordimer brings unforgettable people to life.

'Like the great nineteenth-century Russian novelists she unites vast scope with minute attention to the ordinary. Gordimer's setting is Africa ... but in her Africa we find ourselves' – *Washington Post*

WAITING FOR THE BARBARIANS
J. M. Coetzee

A novel from an extraordinary writer who belongs in the company of Nadine Gordimer, Milan Kundera and Jacobo Timerman.

For decades the Magistrate has run the affairs of a tiny frontier settlement, ignoring the impending war between the Barbarians and the Empire whose servant he is. But when interrogation experts arrive to take charge of police operations, he finds himself jolted by outrage into sympathy with their victims. A long and perversely erotic affair with one of these victims, and the barbarous treatment of prisoners of war, finally push him into a quixotic act of rebellion ...

'I have known few authors who can evoke such a wilderness in the heart of man ... Mr Coetzee evokes the elusive terror of Kafka' – *Sunday Times*